THE ATHARVAVEDA

Other Books By The Author

Samaveda, text with English translation
Yajurveda, text with English translation

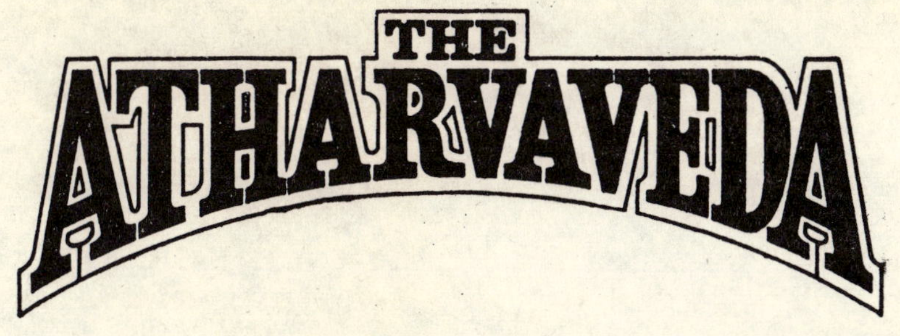

Sanskrit text with English translation

by

Devi Chand M. A.

with introductory remarks by

M. C. Joshi,

Archaeological Survey of India, New Delhi

WITH GLOSSARY AND INDEX

Munshiram Manoharlal
Publishers Pvt Ltd

ISBN 81-215-0172-5
This edition 1999

Printed and published by Munshiram Manoharlal Publishers Pvt. Ltd.,
Post Box 5715, 54 Rani Jhansi Road, New Delhi 110 055.

CONTENTS

INTRODUCTORY REMARKS

Of the Vedas, the *Atharvaveda* being the last, that is fourth in order, is sometimes regarded as of lesser importance than the other Vedas. Modern scholars with outlook conditioned by the Western learning even witnessed in it, primitive and so called non-Aryan elements especially in the hymns connected with charms and incantations. According to the tradition *Atharvaveda* is mainly a contribution of sages Atharvaṇa and Aṅgirā, but an Indian writer of modern times V.M. Apte views the fourth Veda from a different angle as would be clear from the under noted passage:

'The oldest name of the *AV* in Vedic literature is *Atharvāṅgirasaḥ*, that is, "the Atharvans and the Aṅgirasaḥ." The two words denote two different species of magic formulae: *atharvan* is "holy magic bringing happiness" and *aṅgiras* is "hostile or black magic." The former includes among others formulae for the healing of diseases, while the latter includes curses against enemies, rivals, malicious magicians, etc. These two kinds of magic formulae then form the chief contents of the *AV*, but these ancient magic songs which were originally popular poetry appear in the *Saṃhitā* in a Brahmanized form because of the priestly outlook of the compilers, which betrays itself in the similes and epithets. The gods are the same as in the *RV*, Agni, Indra, etc. But their characters have become quite colourless, all being invoked as "demon-destroyers," and their natural basis is utterly forgotten. The theosophical and cosmogonic speculations of the *AV* indicate a later stage of development than that in the *RV*. It contains more theosophic matter than any other Saṃhitā. The philosophical terminology is of an advanced type, and the pantheistic thought is practically the same as in the Upanishads. There is, of course, a magical twist given to the philosophical hymns. For example *AV*, IV, 19.6 employs the conception of *asat*, "the non-existent," as a spell to destroy enemies, demons, magicians, etc.

Above all, the principal aim of the *Atharvaveda* is to *appease* (the demons), to *bless* (friends), and to *curse* and as such it did not find much favour with the priesthood, who excluded it from the sacred triad—the threefold lore. This was, however, a later development. At their origin, magic and cult both have an identical aim—the control of the transcendental world. They have this essential unity of purpose. There soon comes a time, however, when the priest who pays homage to the gods parts company with the magician who is in league with the demons. It is remarkable fact, however, that in spite of this aversion to the Veda of magic, the ritual texts which describe the great sacrifices do incorporate exorcism-formulas and magic rites whereby the priest can destroy "the enemy whom he hates and who hates him," and the law-book of Manu (XI. 33) sanctions the use of exorcism against enemies.[1]

The statement of Apte does not appear to contain the proper assessment of *Atharvaveda*, based on objectivity, but is conditioned by over a century old European outlook and models, with an under-current of Christian ideas. Often the development of religion in Western terminology, which has now assumed a global character, is traced strictly in a unilineal succession from 'magic' which itself is regarded to be less evolved, from the stand point of the growth of civilization, and of primitive origin. Such deductions were made on the basis of anthropological studies of tribal societies which were regarded to be less advanced economically and metally, being older representatives of human species, by earlier generation of Western scholars.

Perhaps with a background of similar ideas, Winternitz[2] made his observation on *Atharvavedà :*

'Many of these magic songs, like the magic rites pertaining to them, belong to a sphere of conceptions which, spread over the whole earth, ever recur with the most surprising similarity in the most varying peoples of all countries. Among the Indians or North America, among the Negre races of Africa among Malaya and Mongols, among the ancient Greeks and Romans, and frequently still among the peasantry of the present-day Europe, we find again exactly the same views, the same strange leaps of thought in the magic songs and magic rites, as have come down to us in the *Atharvaveda* of ancient India. There are, then, numerous verses in the *Atharvaveda,* which, according to their character and often also their contents, differ just as little from the magic formulas of the American-Indian medicine-men and Tarter Shamans as from the Merseburg magic maxims, which belong to the sparse remains of the oldest German Poetry.'

The above quoted views thus clearly demonstrate the prejudices and subjectivity of approach to Atharvedic studies. Most modern scholars with occidental training have imposed their own speculated judgements on the cultural data preserved in *Atharvaveda* and other similar texts without caring to explain the internal evidence preserved in the early tradition.

If we take *Atharvaveda* itself into consideration, we find an interesting tradition relating to its compilation in *Gopathabrāhmaṇa* by Atharvana and Angirā.

तस्य हवा एतस्य भगवतोऽथर्वण ऋषेराथर्वणो वेदोऽभवत् ।.... ग्राथर्वाणानां चातुर्कृचेभ्य स्वाहा १ विंशतिः स्वाहा १७ तृचेभ्यस्वाहा १६ एकर्चेभ्य स्वाहा ब्रह्मणे स्वाहा .... दशतयानांगिरस ग्रार्षेयान्निरमिमत् । षोऽशिनोष्टादशिनो द्वादशिन एक र्चान .... सप्तर्चानिति । तस्माद्विशिनागिरस ऋषीन्निरगिमत । तेभ्योयान्मंत्रान पश्यत्स ग्रांगिरसो वेदोऽभवत् आंङ्गिरसानामाद्यैः पंचानुवाकैः स्वाहा .... ।

Further, the *Muṇḍaka Upanishad* also records an important tradition relating to the transmission of knowledge from Atharva onwards:

[1]R.C. Majumdar ed., *The Vedic Age* (Bombay, 1951), pp. 438 ff.
[2]Winternitz, *History of Indian Literature*, I. p. 128.

ॐ ब्रह्मा देवानां प्रथमः सम्बभूव विश्वस्य कर्ता भुवनस्य गोप्ता ।
स ब्रह्मविद्यां सर्वविद्या प्रतिष्ठामथर्वाय ज्येष्ठपुत्राय प्राहा ॥ १ ॥
अर्थवणे यां प्रवदेतु ब्रह्माथर्वा तां पुरोवाचाङ्गिरे ब्रह्मविद्याम् ।
स भारद्वाजाय सत्यवहाय प्राह भारद्वाजोऽङ्गिरसे परावराम ॥ २ ॥
शौनको ह वै महाशालोऽङ्गिरसं विधिवदुप्रसन्नः पप्रच्छ ।
कस्मिन्नु भगवो विज्ञाते सर्वमिदं विज्ञातं भवतीते ॥ ३ ॥
तस्मै स होवाच ।
द्वे विद्ये वेदितव्ये इति ह स्म यद्ब्रह्मविदो वदन्ति परा चैवापरा च ॥ ४ ॥
तत्तापरा ऋग्वेदो यर्जुवेदः सामवेदोऽथर्ववेदः शिक्षा कल्पो व्याकरणं
निरुक्तं छन्दो ज्योतिषमिति ।
अथ परा यया तदक्षरमधिगम्यते ॥ ५ ॥
[I-1-5]

Translations

'Brahmā' the Maker of the universe and the Preserver of the world, was the first among the devas. He told his eldest son Atharvā about the knowledge of Brahman, the foundation of all knowledge.'

* * *

'The knowledge of Brahman about which Brahma told Atharvā, Atharva, in olden times, told Angirā, Angirā taught it to Satyavāha, belonging to the clan of Bharadvāja, and the latter taught it, in succession, to Aṅgiras.'

* * *

'Śaunaka, the great householder, approached Aṅgiras in the proper manner and said: Revered Sir, what is that by the knowing of which all this becomes known?'

* * *

'To him he said: Two kinds of knowledge must be known—that is what the knowers of Brahman tell us. They are the Higher Knowledge and the lower knowledge.'

* * *

'Of these two, the lower knowledge is the *Rigveda*, the *Yajurveda*, the *Sāmaveda*, the *Atharvaveda*, sikshā (phonetics), kalpa (rituals), vyākaraṇam (grammer), nirukta (etymology), chhandas (metre), and jyotish (astronomy); and the Higher knowledge is that by which the imperishable Brahman is attained.'[1]

The *Gopathabrāhmaṇa* (II.9) gives some idea of the great volume of Vedic literature in the following words:

एवमिमे सर्वे वेदा निर्मिता सकल्पा सरहस्याः सब्राह्मणाः सोपनिषत्काः सेतिहासाः सान्वाख्यात सपुराणाः सस्वराः संस्कारा सानिरुक्ता सानुशासनाः सानुमार्जनाः सवाकोवाक्यास्तेषां यज्ञमभिपद्यमानानां छद्यते नामद्येयं यज्ञ इत्येवाचक्षते ॥ ६ ॥

The *Atharvaveda* thus has to be seen from the standpoint of its totality and

[1]The English translation of the relevent passage from *Mundaka Upanishad* is after the *Upanishads* I by Swami Nikhilananda (New York, 1949), pp. 261.

not merely in its extant form which certainly does not furnish the fuller idea of the original text. According to the tradition as recorded by grammarian Patañjali, the *Atharvaveda* had nine branches or *śākhās* नवधाऽऽथर्वणोवेद: which have been named as under:

(1) Paippalāda, (2) Tauda, (3) Muṇḍa, (4) Śaunakīya, (5) Jājala, (6) Jalada, (7) Brāhmaveda, (8) Devadarśa and (9) Chāraṇavaidya.

Now, out of these nine only two *śākhās*, viz., Śaunaka and Paippalāda are available. Therefore, any kind of inference drawn on the basis of these two branches about the *Atharvaveda* would only be partly true. It would, therefore, be utterly wrong to call lt a secondary Veda; for even in the extant form it contains remarkable references to various aspects of spiritual and temporal importance like *Brāhamavidyā*, *Prithivi* or Mother earth, kingship, marriage, treatment of ailment, poetics, etc. This Veda is also connected with subsequent development of Tantric system and mentions the significance of *japa* or chanting of *mantras* to achieve material or other benefits which forms an integral part of Indian religio-mysticism till today and which should not be taken to be something inferior in any way because accomplishment of one's desires has always been very base of almost all the religions.

So far as the authors of *Atharvaveda* or reference to associated culture in it are concerned, it may be stated that people connected with it were broadly of the same group which composed the other Vedas and were not invaders[1] at all. By the time Vedas were composed, their authors had already become Indians even if they were migrants. Besides, it has to be always kept in mind that Aryan or the people associated with Vedic cultures had much diversity amongst themselves, for their settlements were distributed over a vast area, in small geographical units. The extant Vedic literature may represent cutlures of only a section of the total population of Indo-Aryan speakers, hence attempt to search for a common culture for all the so called Indo-Aryan speakers would never be successful. Therefore, it may be impossible to find out Atharva-vedic parallels in archaeological terms.

Yet for a closer understanding of Vedic literature it may be useful to study diverse interpretations of the hymn of Vedas. From this point of view the present translation *Atharvaveda* by Devi Chand would undoubtedly prove to be of scholarly interest, for the translator's own approach is in accordance to the guidelines set up in the 19th century, by the great Hindu reformer and Vedic scholar Dayananda Sarasvati, who was mainly responsible for the revival of Vedic learning in India.

New Delhi
1 September 1982 M.C. Joshi

[1]We have already expressed our views on the subject in Devi Chand's English translation of *Sāmaveda* (New Delhi, 1981), p. i-v.

THE ATHARVAVEDA

The Atharvaveda

BOOK (Kaṇḍa) I

Chapter (Anuvāka) 1

HYMN I

१. ये त्रिषप्ताः परियन्ति विश्वा रूपाणि बिभ्रतः । वाचस्पतिर्बला तेषां तन्वो अद्य दधातु मे ॥

1. May God ever assign to me the strength and powers of those twenty one objects, which sustaining the animate and inanimate creation, are wandering round. (1)[1]

२. पुनरेहि वाचस्पते देवेन मनसा सह । वसोष्पते नि रमय मय्येवास्तु मयि श्रुतम् ।

2. O God, the Lord of speech, instruct me with Thy divine knowledge. O Lord of wealth, ever grant us delight. Let my Vedic knowledge remain under my control. (2)

३. इहैवाभि वि तनूभे आर्त्नीइव ज्यया । वाचस्पतिर्नि यच्छतु मय्येवास्तु मयि श्रुतम् ॥

3. My God, the Lord of Speech spread all around my knowledge and action like the two bow-ends strained with the cord. May He keep me under discipline. Let my Vedic knowledge remain under my control. (3)

४. उपहूतो वाचस्पतिरुपास्मान् वाचस्पतिर्ह्वयताम् ।
सं श्रुतेन गमेमहि मा श्रुतेन वि राधिषि ॥

4. Let us pray into God, the Lord of speech; may He preach nice instructions unto us. May we adhere to sacred Lore. Never may I be deprived of it. (4)

HYMN II

१. विद्मा शरस्य पितरं पर्जन्यं भूरिधायसम् । विद्मो ष्वस्य मातरं पृथिवीं भूरिवर्पसम् ॥

1. We know God, the Liberal Nourisher, like the cloud, as the Father

[1]Vāchaspati means God, the Lord of speech, the Revealer of the Vedas. Some commentators interpret the word as guru, teacher or precepter. God, being the Greatest Teacher, is aptly denoted by the word. According to Pt. Damodra Satvalekar, Vāchaspati Balā is the name of a herb, the use of which improves one's speech. The word त्रिषप्ता, (Trishapta) i.e., three times seven has been differently interpreted by different scholars. Twenty-one may refer to 12 months, five seasons, 3 lokas i.e., Earth, Atmosphere, Firmament, and Sun. It may refer to 5 Mahābhut; i.e., earth, water, light, air, space; 5 Prāṇas, i.e., Praṇa, Apāna, Vyāna, Udāna and Samāna, five organs of cognition, Gyāna Indriyas, five organs of action, Karma Indriyas, and अन्तः करण, the internal organ, the heart, the seat of thought and feeling, thinking faculty, mind, conscience. The word 'Twenty-one' means the innumerable forces of nature. In this verse God is invoked to grant a devotee all the forces of nature, that exist in the world.

(Protector) of the warrior, who wields the shaft. We know well, God, equipped with diverse objects, and vast like the Earth, as his revered Mother. (5)

२. ज्या॒के परि णो नमाश्मानं तन्वं॒ कृधि । वीडुर्वरीयोऽरातीरप द्वेषांस्या कृधि ॥

2. O King, for the sake of victory, let the Sky and the Earth bow before us. Make our body strong like a stone. Being irresistible, drive far away, malignities and feelings of hatred. (6)[1]

३. वृक्षं यद्गावः परिषस्वजाना अनुस्फुरं शरमर्चन्त्यृभुम् । शरुमस्मद् यावय दिद्युमिन्द्र ॥

3. When, closely clinging round the bow, the strings sing triumph to the learned warrior, O Commander, ward off from us the shaft, the missile. (7)[2]

४. यथा द्यां च पृथिवीं चान्तस्तिष्ठति तेजनम् । एवा रोगं चास्रावं चान्तस्तिष्ठतु मुञ्ज इत् ॥

4. Just as light hangs between Earth and Firmament, so does Munja, a healing medicine stand between fever and dysentery. (8)[3]

HYMN III

१. विद्मा शरस्य पितरं पर्जन्यं शतवृष्ण्यम् ।
तेना ते तन्वे३ शं करं पृथिव्यां ते निषेचनं बहिष्टे अस्तु बालिति ॥

1. We know God, the Master of hundred powers, like the cloud, as the father of the warrior, who wields the shaft. With that knowledge, may I bring health unto thy body. May thou prosper on the Earth, May all ills in thy body be soon removed. (9)[4]

२. विद्मा शरस्य पितरं मित्रं शतवृष्ण्यम् ।
तेना ते तन्वे३ शं करं पृथिव्यां ते निषेचनं बहिष्टे अस्तु बालिति ॥

2. We know God, the Master of hundred powers, the Friend of all like air, as the Father of the warrior, who wields the shaft. With that knowledge, may I bring health unto thy body. May thou prosper on the Earth. May all ills in thy body be soon removed. (10)

[1] 'Lord of wealth' refers to God.

[2] He refers to a devotee. Just as both ends of a bow remain strained and tightened, which enables an arrow to reach its distant goal, so should a devotee reach his goal, through knowledge and action.

[3] Dhanvantri ji writes in *Raj Nighantu* about Munja.

मुञ्जोऽतुष्णो विसर्पास्त्रमूत्रवस्त्यथिरोगनुम । बाणाह्वो मधुरः शीतं पित्तदाहतृषापहः ॥

Munja is cold in nature, cures itch, leprosy, diseases pertaining to urine and eyes. It is sweet in taste, cures bile, burns and removes thirst. This herb removes fever, diarrhoea and dysentery as well. In vernacular it is termed as दाभ Sāyana has taken 'तेजनम' in the neuter gender as तेजनः in the masculine gender, and translated it as a bamboo, which is inadmissible.

[4] Thy means the patient's body. I refers to a skilled physician. Hundred means innumerable.

३. विद्मा शरस्य पितरं वरुणं शतवृष्ण्यम ।
तेना ते तन्वे३ शं करं पृथिव्यां ते निषेचनं बहिष्टे अस्तु बालिति ।।

3. We know God, the Master of hundred powers, the Pervader of all worlds like the Space, as the Father of the warrior, who wields the shaft. With that knowledge, may I bring health unto thy body. May thou prosper on the Earth. May all ills in thy body be soon removed. (11)

४. विद्मा शरस्य पितरं चन्द्रं शतवृष्ण्यम् ।
तेना ते तन्वे३ शं करं पृथिव्यां ते निषेचनं बहिष्टे अस्तु बालिति ।।

4. We know God, the Master of hundred powers, the pleasure afforded to all like the Moon, is the Father of the warrior, who wields the shaft. With that knowledge, may I bring health unto thy body. May thou prosper on the Earth. May all ills in thy body be soon removed. (12)

५. विद्मा शरस्य पितरं सूर्यं शतवृष्ण्यम् ।
तेना ते तन्वे३ शं करं पृथिव्यां ते निषेचनं बहिष्टे अस्तु बालिति ।।

5. We know God, the Master of hundred powers, serviceable like the Sun, as the Father of the warrior, who wields the shaft. With that knowledge, may I bring health unto thy body, May thou prosper on the Earth. May all ills in thy body be soon removed. (13)

६. यदान्त्रेषु गवीन्योर्यद् वस्तावधि संश्रितम् । एवा ते मूत्रं मुच्यतां बहिर्बालिति सर्वकम् ।।

6. Whatever hath gathered, in bowels, groins or in bladder, May that urine of thine come out completely, free from check. (14)[1]

७. प्र ते भिनद्मि मेहनं वर्त्रं वेशन्त्याइव । एवा ते मूत्रं मुच्यतां बहिर्बालिति सर्वकम् ।।

7. Just as the pent-up water of a lake is let loose by cleaving its dam, so do I, O patient open thy urinary passage. May that urine of thine come out completely, free from check. (15)[2]

८. विषितं ते वस्तिबिलं समुद्रस्योदधेरिव । एवा ते मूत्रं मुच्यतां बहिर्बालिति सर्वकम् ।।

8. O patient suffering from a urinary disease, just as the water of the flooded ocean rises up, and flows into streams, so have I unclosed the orifice of thy bladder. May that urine of thine come out completely, free from check. (16)[3]

९. यथेषुका परापतदवसृष्टाधि धन्वनः । एवा ते मूत्रं मुच्यतां बहिर्बालिति सर्वकम् ।।

9. O patient suffering from a urinary disease, just as the arrow flies away

[1]If a patient is suffering from lack of free flow of the urine, he should be cured by the use of Munja or Catheter.

[2]I refers to a surgeon, who opens the urinary passage of the patient, and allows the pent-up urine flow out.

[3]I refers to a surgeon, who makes the pent-up urine of a patient flow by performing an operation or by administering medicinal herbs.

far when loosened from the archer's bow, so may that urine of thine come out completely, free from check. (17)

HYMN IV

१. अम्बयो यन्त्यध्वभिर्जामयो अध्वरीयताम् । पृञ्चन्तीर्मधुना पयः ।।

1. Streams of water, acting as mothers and sisters of non-violent performers of a yajna, glide along their paths, blending their water with mead. (18)[1]

२. अमूर्या उप सूर्ये याभिर्वा सूर्यः सह । ता नो हिन्वन्त्यध्वरम् ।।

2. These streams of water, which flow under the light of Sun or those wherewith the sun is joined, lend contentment to the yajna (sacrifice) of our life. (19)

३. अपो देवीरुप ह्वये यत्र गावः पिबन्ति नः । सिन्धुभ्यः कर्त्वं हविः ।।

3. I praise the excellent waters, where our kine drink water should be cut from those streams. (20)[2]

४. अप्स्व१न्तरमृतमप्सु भेषजम् ।
अपामुत प्रशस्तिभिरश्वा भवथ वाजिनो गावो भवथ वाजिनीः ।।

4. Nectar (Amrit) is in the waters, in the waters is healing property. By using waters of fine qualities, O horses, be ye fleet and strong, and, O ye kine, be full of strength and milk. (21)

HYMN V

१. आपो हि ष्ठा मयोभुवस्ता न ऊर्जे दधातन । महे रणाय चक्षसे ।।

1. Ye, waters, truly bring us bliss, so help ye us to strength and power, that we may succeed in big life's struggle, and look on God. (22)[3]

२. यो वः शिवतमो रसस्तस्य भाजयतेह नः । उशतीरिव मातरः ।।

2. Just as mothers in their longing love, suckle their children, so O waters, here grant to us a share of your most efficacious juice. (23)[4]

३. तस्मा अरं गमाम वो यस्य क्षयाय जिन्वथ । आपो जनयथा च नः ।।

[1]Just as mothers and sisters are serviceable to and useful for their kith and kin, so are the streams of water for the non-violent performers of a yajna. The waters are so sweet, as if honey is mixed with them.

[2]Water should be cut and brought through channels to irrigate our fields, for producing more food.

[3]See Yajur 11-50. There the interpretation is quite different. Pt. Khem Karan Das Trivedi translates आपः as noble disinterested persons.

[4]See Yajur 11-51.

3. O Waters, we fully acquire Ye, for the sake of that food, for whose abundance Ye possess strength. Give us procreant strength. (24)[1]

४. ईशाना वार्याणां क्षयन्तीश्चर्षणीनाम् । अपो याचामि भेषजम् ॥

4. I pray to God, for the medicinal waters, the controllers of remediable diseases, and the healers of the ailments of men. (25)[2]

HYMN VI

१. शं नो देवीरभिष्टय आपो भवन्तु पीतये । शं योरभि स्रवन्तु नः ॥

1. May excellent waters be helpful for our bliss and drink. May they flow all round, for curing our ailments, and preventing us from falling a prey to them. (26)

२. अप्सु मे सोमो अब्रवीदन्तर्विश्वानि भेषजा । अग्निं च विश्वशम्भुवम् ॥

2. A skilled physician tells me, that in waters lies the capacity to heal all ailments and digestive power is the bringer of all sorts of happiness. (27)[3]

३. आप: पृणीत भेषजं वरूथं तन्वे३ मम । ज्योक् च सूर्यं दृशे ॥

3. O Waters, grant me medicine to keep my body safe from harm, so that I may see the sun for long. (28)

४. शं न आपो धन्वन्या३: शमु सन्त्वनूप्या: ।
शं नः खनित्रिमा आप: शमु या: कुम्भ आभृता: शिवा नः सन्तु वार्षिकी: ॥

4. Bless us the Waters that rise in desert lands or marshy pools. Bless us the Waters dug from earth, bless us the waters brought in jars, bless us the waters of the Rains! (29)[4]

Chapter (Anuvāka) 2

HYMN VII

१. स्तुवानमग्न आ वह यातुधानं किमीदिनम् । त्वं हि देव बन्दितो हन्ता दस्योर्बभूविथ ॥

1. O learned preacher, bring hither, a eulogising person diabolic in nature, and a treacherous informer. For thou, when lauded becomest the demon's slaughterer. (30)[5]

[1]See Yajur 11-52. Rain produces food, and makes it grow abundantly. The use of food thus produced makes us strong to bear sons and grandsons.

[2]The use of pure water removes our diseases, as it acts like an efficacious medicine.

[3]Some commentators interpret Soma as God and Agni as fire, or warmth in waters.

[4]Five different kinds of water have been mentioned in the verse. Each one of them has its own healing properties for a detailed account of the efficiency of these waters, one should study Dhanvantri's *Raj Nighantu*, and other books on medicine.

[5]Bring hither means put under your control Kemīdin means a person who says 'what' is this', 'what now ',who ridicules others; and is a treacherous spy, Yatudhāna means a

२. आज्यस्य परमेष्ठिञ्जातवेदस्तनूवशिन् । अग्ने तौलस्य प्राशान यातुधानान् वि लापय ॥

2. O preacher, occupying a lofty position, master of the vedas, controller of physical organs, eat butter in a measured quantity, and make the sinners repent for their deeds through thy noble preaching. (31)[1]

३. विलपन्तु यातुधाना अत्त्रिणो ये किमीदिनः । अथेदमग्ने नो हविरिन्द्रश्च प्रति हर्यतम् ॥

3. Let tormentors, marauders and cruel persons, repent for their deeds, through the advice of a preacher. May ye both, the preacher and the king accept this offer of ours. (32)[2]

४. अग्निः पूर्व आ रभतां प्रेन्द्रो नुदतु बाहुमान् । ब्रवीतु सर्वो यातुमानयमस्मीत्येत्य ।

4. May a learned preacher first take in hand the work of reforming a sinner, may a strong-armed king then impel him to be virtuous. Let every wicked person consequently come hither and say, here am I. (33)[3]

५. पश्याम ते वीर्यं जातवेदः प्र णो ब्रूहि यातुधानान् नृचक्षः ।
त्वया सर्वे परितप्ताः पुरस्तात् त आ यन्तु प्रब्रुवाणा उपेदम् ॥

5. O learned preacher, we behold thy strength; O preacher unto mankind, instruct well the impious, who torment us. Reformed through thy noble teachings, repenting for their sins, let all approach thee here, making confession of their faults. (34)

६. आ रभस्व जातवेदोऽस्माकार्थाय जज्ञिषे । दूतो नो अग्ने भूत्वा यातुधानान् वि लापय ॥

6. O learned preacher begin thy work, thou art born for our advantage. Act as our messenger, and let ignoble souls repent for their misdeeds. (35)[4]

७. त्वमग्ने यातुधानानुपबद्धाँ इहा वह । अथैषामिन्द्रो वज्रेणापि शीर्षाणि वृश्चतु ॥

7. O learned preacher, bring hitherward to the jail, bound and chained, the terrorisers of men, who do not reform themselves in obedience to thy advice. Let the king afterward tear their heads off with his sword. (36)[5]

person who torments and teases others, being devilish in nature. Agni has been translated as a commander by Pt. Khem Karan Das Trivedi. To improve the character of a demon by sound preaching is tantamount to slaughtering and removing his evil propensities.

[1]Pt. Raja Ram differs from the generally accepted text. In place of तौलस्य, he accepts तैलस्य, and interprets it as oil.

[2]People offer money to the preacher to help him in bringing sinful persons on the path of virtue, and pay taxes to the king for preserving good administration and punishing the law-breakers.

[3]Through the moral forces of a learned preacher, and the administrative forces of a king, the sinner should be made to accept his fault, and shun it in future.

[4]Begin thy work of reforming the sinners through religious preaching.

[5]If a criminal deserves capital punishment, the king should not hesitate to inflict it.

HYMN VIII

१. इदं हविर्यातुधानान् नदी फेनमिवा वहत् । य इदं स्त्री पुमानकरिह स स्तुवतां जनः ।

1. Just as a stream carries foam from one place to the other, so should the tax paid, enable the Government to bring under control those who afflict others. Here let the doer of this misdeed, male or female praise the reformer, who has shown him the right path. (37)

२. अयं स्तुवान आगमदिमं स्म प्रति हर्यत । बृहस्पते वशे लब्ध्वाग्नीषोमा वि विध्यतम् ॥

2. This sinner has come, praising his spiritual reformer. Do ye receive him lovingly, O Brihaspati, keep him under thy guidance, O Agni and Soma, conquer his heart through moral persuasion. (38)[1]

३. यातुधानस्य सोमप जहि प्रजां नयस्व च । नि स्तुवानस्य पातय परमक्ष्युतावरम् ॥

3. O chief preacher, approach the children of a sinner, and bring them on the path of righteousness. Lower down with humility their right and left eyes, with thy moral instruction, when they sing thy praise in gratitude! (39)

४. यत्रैषामग्ने जनिमानि वेत्थ गुहा सतामत्त्रिणां जातवेदः ।
तांस्त्वं ब्रह्मणा वावृधानो जह्येषां शततर्हमग्ने ॥

4. As thou, O learned preacher, knowest the descendants of these secret greedy beings, so strengthened by the knowledge of Veda, O preacher, ameliorating them morally, destroy their sins through a hundred devices. (40)[2]

HYMN IX

१. अस्मिन् वसु वसवो धारयन्त्विन्द्रः पूषा वरुणो मित्रो अग्निः ।
इममादित्या उत विश्वे च देवा उत्तरस्मिञ्ज्योतिषि धारयन्तु ॥

1. May the forces of nature, God, Earth, Cloud, Air and Fire maintain this Brahmchari in supremacy. May learned, a heroic persons, and all practical noble souls set and support him in supremest lustre of knowledge. (41)[3]

२. अस्य देवाः प्रदिशि ज्योतिरस्तु सूर्यो अग्निरुत वा हिरण्यम् ।
सपत्ना अस्मदधरे भवन्तूत्तमं नाकमधि रोहयेमम् ॥

2. May the light of knowledge, the sun-like breaths, the digestive heat, the gold-like soul, be under his sway. May foes, like lust and anger, lie prostrate

[1]Brihaspati: a preacher who possesses the knowledge of the Vedas.
Agni: A learned person resplendent with knowledge like fire.
Soma: Chief amongst the preachers, as Soma is the chief of medicinal herbs.

[2]A hundred means various.

[3]This verse is applicable to a king as well.

beneath his feet. May he attain to the highest pitch of spiritual happiness. (42)[1]

३. येनेन्द्राय समभरः पयांस्युत्तमेन ब्रह्मणा जातवेदः ।
तेन त्वमग्न इह वर्धयेमं सजातानां श्रैष्ठ्य आ धेह्येनम् ॥

3. O God, through that mighty knowledge of the Veda, Thou hast provided an energetic soul with different sorts of knowledge. Even therewith O God, exalt this Brahmchari, and grant him highest rank among his kinsmen. (43)[2]

४. ऐषां यज्ञमुत वर्चो ददेऽहं रायस्पोषमुत चित्तान्यग्ने ।
सपत्ना अस्मदधरे भवन्तूत्तमं नाकमधि रोहयेमम् ॥

4. O God, I accept their gifts, their glory, their riches' fulness, and their hopes; May our internal foes lie prostrate beneath our feet. Grant him the highest pitch of earthly happiness. (44)[3]

HYMN X

१. अयं देवानामसुरो वि राजति वशा हि सत्या वरुणस्य राज्ञः ।
ततस्परि ब्रह्मणा शाशदान उग्रस्य मन्योरुदिमं नयामि ॥

1. This Lord, is the Ruler of divine objects, that receive sustenance from Him. Verily, the wishes of God, the Averter of sins, and the King of Kings, must be accomplished. Triumphant with the knowledge of the vedas, revealed by Him, and through the grace of the Almighty Father, I make this King occupy the throne. (45)[4]

२. नमस्ते राजन् वरुणास्तु मन्यवे विश्वं ह्यु॒ग्र निचिकेषि द्रुग्धम् ।
सहस्रमन्यान् प्र सुवामि साकं शतं जीवाति शरदस्तवायम् ।

2. Homage be paid, O God, our saviour, to thine righteous indignation, for O Dreadful God, Thou fully Knowest every malicious person. I lead a thousand others simultaneously on the path of rectitude. Let this king, thy servant, O God, live a hundred autumns. (46)[5]

३. यदुवक्थानृतं जिह्वया वृजिनं बहु । राज्ञस्त्वा सत्यधर्मणो मुञ्चामि वरुणादहम् ॥

3. O King, whatever falsehood, thou hast uttered with thy tongue, is a great sin. I liberate thee from future punishment by the Just Supreme God! (47)[6]

[1]'His' refers to the Brahmchari. This verse is applicable to a king as well.

[2]The verse is applicable to a king as well.

[3]'I' refers to the king. 'Their' refers to the subjects 'Him' refers to me, the king.

[4]I refers to the priest.

[5]I refers to the Rāj Purohit, the royal priest.

[6]One has to suffer the consequences of his sin, but he can be saved from future punishment if he ameliorates himself morally through the teachings of a spiritual Guru, 'I' refers to the royal priest.

४. मुञ्चामि त्वा वैश्वानरादर्णवान् महतस्परि । सजातानुग्रेहा वद ब्रह्म चाप चिकीहि नः ॥

4. O King, I free thee from all persons, from the great surging flood of sin, through my instructions. O King as a strict follower of religion, preach truth unto others in thy kingdom, and pay attention to our vedic teaching. (48)[1]

HYMN XI

१. वषट् ते पूषन्नस्मिन्त्सूतावर्यमा होता कृणोतु वेधाः ।
सिस्रतां नार्यृतप्रजाता वि पर्वाणि जिहतां सूतवा उ ॥

1. O God, we dedicate ourselves to Thee! May Thou, the Friend of the noble, the Creator of the universe, the Giver of all joys, help us in this child birth. Let this dame, who knows the laws of eugenics, remain cautious, and Keep her organs loose and tender. (49)

२. चतस्रो दिवः प्रदिशश्चतस्रो भूम्या उत । देवा गर्भं समैरयन् तं व्यूर्णुवन्तु सूतवे ॥

2. The forces of nature, residing in the four regions of the sky, and the four regions of the Earth, have developed the embryo, let them release the child with ease from the covering of the womb. (50)[2]

३. सूषा व्यूर्णोतु वि योनिं हापयामसि । श्रथया सूषणे त्वमव त्वं बिष्कले सृज ॥

3. O pregnant woman, keep your organs loose and soft, we expand the womb. O mother, about to deliver a child, remain happy. O brave and patient mother, give birth to the child. (51)[3]

४. नेव मांसे न पीबसि नेव मज्जस्वाहतम् ।
अवैतु पृश्नि शेवलं शुने जराय्वत्तवेऽव जरायु पद्यताम् ॥

4. Secundines do not stick to flesh, fat or the marrow of bones. Soft like the grass, they come down, fit to be eaten by a dog, Let secundines come out through the uterus. (52)[4]

५. वि ते भिनद्मि मेहनं वि योनिं वि गवीनिके ।
वि मातरं च पुत्रं च वि कुमारं जरायुणाव जरायु पद्यताम् ॥

5. I expand thy urinator, thy womb and thy groins. I separate the mother

[1]I means the royal priest. 'Our' refers to learned preceptors. This hymn has been interpreted by Sāyana as a remedy for dropsy, on the basis of the word ब्रह्म in the first verse, and अर्पण in the last. This is a far-fetched explanation which does not appeal to me.

[2]Four regions in East, West, North, South. Forces of nature: Air, water, fire, etc.

[3]'We' refers to the nurses attending upon the pregnant woman, who through their medical skill, make the delivery convenient.

Griffith has not translated the verses 3-6, remarking that they are strictly *obstetric* and not presentable in English.

[4]Secundines: जरायु the outer skin of the embryo. This word is used in the plural number. The slough must come out if a part of it remains inside it creates various sorts of diseases.

from the child, and the child from the mother. I separate the child from the secundines. Let secundines come out through the uterus. (53)[1]

६. यथा वातो यथा मनो यथा पतन्ति पक्षिणः ।
एवा त्वं दशमास्य साकं जरायुणा पताव जरायु पद्यताम् ॥

6. Just as breaths come voluntarily out of the nose, just as the mind runs spontaneously after its sensual objects, and just as birds fly freely in the atmosphere, so shouldst thou, O babe of ten months old, come easily out of the womb with slough. Let secundines come out through the uterus. (54)

Chapter (Anuvāka) 3

HYMN XII

१. जरायुजः प्रथम उस्रियो वृषा वातभ्रजा स्तनयन्नेति वृष्ट्या ।
स नो मृडाति तन्व ऋजुगो रुजन् य एकमोजस्त्रेधा विचक्रमे ॥

1. The Primordial, Refulgent, Dignity-bestowing God, happiness like a cloud, creates the world from the womb of Mother, and reigns supreme, full of strength, showering joy on humanity. He, free from crookedness, averting sins, affords ease to our body, the sole Lord, exists in Past, Present and Future. (55)[2]

२. अङ्गेअङ्गे शोचिषा शिश्रियाणं नमस्यन्तस्त्वा हविषा विधेम ।
अङ्कान्त्समङ्कान् हविषा विधेम यो अग्रभीत् पर्वास्या ग्रभीता ॥

2. Bending to Thee, O God, Who clingest to each limb with Thy refulgence, fain would we worship Thee with devotion. May we adore the individual and collective virtues of God, Who, the Encompasser, pervades each and every part of the world. (56)

३. मुञ्च शीर्षक्त्या उत कास एनं परुष्परुराविवेशा यो अस्य ।
यो अभ्रजा वातजा यश्च शुष्मो वनस्पतीन्त्सचतां पर्वतांश्च ।

3. O physician, do thou release this man from headache, free him from cough which has entered into all his limbs and joints. One should resort to forests and hills for relief from diseases resulting from excessive rains, severe wind and intense heat. (57)[3]

४. शं मे परस्मै गात्राय शमस्त्ववराय मे । शं मे चतुर्भ्यो अङ्गेभ्यः शमस्तु तन्वे३ मम ।

[1]I refers to a skilled midwife, well-versed in medical science. Pt. Jaidev Vidyalankar interprets 'I' as referring to God.

[2]Pt. Jaidev interprets the verse differently. Some commentators apply it to the Sun. I have given Pt. Khem Karan Das Trivedi's interpretation त्रेधा may also refer to three worlds, the Earth, Space and Sky.

[3]Sāyana translates the latter half of the verse, 'that diseases occurring from rain, wind and heat should go to forests and hills'. This interpretation is illogical and irrational.

4. Calm be it with my upper frame, calm be it with my lower parts. With my four limbs let there be calm. Let all my body be in health. (58)[1]

HYMN XIII

१. नमस्ते अस्तु विद्युते नमस्ते स्तनयित्नवे । नमस्ते अस्त्वश्मने येना दूडाशे अस्यसि ॥

1. Homage to Thee, O God, bright like the lightening flash. Homage to Thee, O God, powerful like the thundering cloud. Homage to Thee, O God, strong like a stone, which Thou hurlest against the undevout. (59)[2]

२. नमस्ते प्रवतो नपाद्यतस्तपः समूहसि । मृडया नस्तनूभ्यो मयस्तोकेभ्यस्कृधि ॥

2. Homage to Thee O God, who never allowest a devotee deviate from the path of righteousness, and because Thou makest our life full of penance. Be gracious to our bodies, give our children happiness and joy. (60)

३. प्रवतो नपान्नम एवास्तु तुभ्यं नमस्ते हेतये तपुषे च कृण्मः ।
विद्म ते धाम परमं गुहा यत् समुद्रे अन्तर्निहितासि नाभिः ॥

3. Yea, homage be to Thee, O God, Who never allowest a devotee deviate from the path of Righteousness. Homage we pay to Thy instrument of punishment and Thy splendour. We know full well, that the heart is Thy secret and sublimest home. Thou art the Navel of the ocean of atmosphere. (61)[3]

४. यां त्वा देवा असृजन्त विश्व इषुं कृण्वाना असनाय धृष्णुम् ।
सा नो मृड विदथे गृणाना तस्यै ते नमो अस्तु देवि ॥

4. O God, for subduing the enemy, manufacturing strong and mighty military instruments, all learned persons adore Thee. Lauded in battles, be Gracious unto us, O God. We pay our homage to Thee. (62)

HYMN XIV

१. भगमस्या वर्च आदिष्यधि वृक्षादिव स्रजम् । महाबुध्न इव पर्वतो ज्योक् पितृष्वास्ताम् ॥

1. As from the tree a wreath, have I assumed her fortune and her fame among my kinsfolk may she dwell for long, like a mountain broad-based. (63)[4]

[1]Four limbs: Two hands, two feet, or two arms and two legs. This is a prayer offered to God by an ordinary man, for health and welfare.

[2]The heavy punishment God gives to a sinner is here spoken of as a stone. Just as a person is injured by hurling a stone at him, so does God punish a sinner by inflicting severe punishment on him.

[3]Just as navel controls all the arteries in the body, so does God control all luminous bodies like the Sun, Moon and other planets in space.

[4]I refers to the bridegroom, and her refers to the bride. Sāyana interprets this verse as a misfortune, that the girl remains unmarried in the house of her parents. This is illogical. A girl is expected to remain firm and steadfast in her domestic life, after

२. एषा ते राजन् कन्या ऽवधूर्नि धूयतां यम । सा मातुर्बध्यतां गृहेऽथो भ्रातुरथो पितुः ॥

2. O bridegroom, the observer of Yamās and Niyamās, refulgent with the splendour of knowledge and Brahmcharya (celibacy), let this maiden, serving as thy wife, enjoy domestic life. May she remain bound in the ties of domestic life in the house of thy mother, brother, and father. (64)[1]

३. एषा ते कुलपा राजन् तामु ते परि दद्मसि । ज्योक् पितृष्वासाता श्रा शीर्ष्णः समोप्यात् ॥

3. O excellent bridegroom, may this girl be the guardian of thy family. We hand her over to thee. May she live long in the midst of thy kinsfolk, and through her wisdom and lofty ideas contribute to the peace and prosperity of thy family. (65)

४. असितस्य ते ब्रह्मणा कश्यपस्य गयस्य च । अन्तःकोशमिव जामयोऽपि नह्यामि ते भगम् ॥

4. Through the vedic knowledge of the unrestrained All-seeing and All-sustaining God, I preserve thy knowledge, dignity and virtues, as ladies preserve their ornaments and clothes in a box. (66)[2]

HYMN XV

१. सं सं स्रवन्तु सिन्धवः सं वाताः सं पतत्रिणः ।
इमं यज्ञं प्रदिवो मे जुषन्तां संस्राव्येण हविषा जुहोमि ॥

1. As the streams flow together, winds blow together, and birds fly together, so should learned persons serve my state devotedly and harmoniously. I welcome them with humble veneration. (67)[3]

२. इहैव हवमा यात म इह संस्रावणा उतेमं वर्धयता गिरः ।
इहैतु सर्वो यः पशुरस्मिन् तिष्ठतु या रयिः ॥

2. O learned persons, come here in my state, on my invitation. Come here, O gentle persons working in unison. O eloquent officials advance this state. May all kinds of animals come in this state, may wealth abide in this country. (68)[4]

marriage, in the house of her father-in-law, and not that of her own parents. Weber, Zimoner and Lüdwig rightly assign this verse to the bridegroom. This hymn is spoken by the bridegroom.

[1]This verse and the next two are spoken by the relatives of the bride to the bridegroom. The interpretation put by Sāyana, that when the maiden is abandoned by the husband and expelled from his house, she should remain with her mother, brother and father, does not appeal to me.

[2]Griffith wrongly considers Asita, Kashyāpa and Gayas as ancient Rishis. These words denote the qualities of God. I refers to the bridegroom. Thy refers to the bride.

[3]I refers to a king. Them refers to learned persons,

[4]My refers to the king.

३. ये नदीनां संस्रवन्त्युत्सासः सदमक्षिताः । तेभिर्मे सर्वैः संस्रावैर्धनं सं स्रावयामसि ॥

3. The inexhaustible founts of streams that flow for ever with all these confluent streams we make abundant riches flow. (69)[1]

४. ये सर्पिषः संस्रवन्ति क्षीरस्य चोदकस्य च । तेभिर्मे सर्वैः संस्रावैर्धनं सं स्रावयामसि ॥

4. All these streams of melted butter (ghee) of milk and water, which flow together with all these confluent streams of ours we make abundant riches flow. (70)[2]

HYMN XVI

१. येऽमावास्यां३ रात्रिमुदस्थुर्व्राजमत्त्रिणः । अग्निस्तुरीयो यातुहा सो अस्मभ्यमधि ब्रवत् ॥

1. May powerful king, who destroys the demons, bless and shelter us, from greedy friends who rise in troops at night-time when the moon is utterly dark. (71)

२. सीसायाध्याह वरुणः सीसायाग्निरुपावति । सीसं म इन्द्रः प्रायच्छत् तदङ्ग यातुचातनम् ॥

2. The king advises the use of lead, the Prime Minister protects the subjects through the use of lead bullets, the commander-in-chief has given me lead bullets for safety. O dear, lead verily repels the fiends. (72)[3]

३. इदं विष्कन्धं सहत इदं बाधते अत्त्रिणः । अनेन विश्वा ससहे या जातानि पिशाच्याः ॥

3. Lead overcomes the squadron of a troop, this drives the voracious fiends away by means of this have I overthrown all the diabolical brood. (73)[4]

४. यदि नो गां हंसि यद्यश्वं यदि पूरुषम् । तं त्वा सीसेन विध्यामो यथा नोऽसो अवीरहा ॥

4. If thou destroy a cow of ours, a human being, or a steed, we pierce thee with this lead bullet so that thou mayest not slay our valiant men. (74)

Chapter (Anuvāka) 4

HYMN XVII

१. अमूर्या यन्ति योषितो हिरा लोहितवाससः । अभ्रातरइव जामयस्तिष्ठन्तु हतवर्चसः ॥

1. Those veins, serviceable like maidens, which run their course clothed in blood, must now stand quiet, like sisters who are brotherless and bereft of power. (75)[5]

[1]The water of rivers should be used for agriculture, navigation and providing electricity, by means of which we can earn much money.

[2]Money can be earned through agriculture, navigation, and rearing mammals.

[3]Pt. Khem Karan Das Trivedi has translated सीसाय 'for the attainment of divine knowledge'. This knowledge averts all miseries andmis fortunes.

[4]Lead means the lead bullets. This means lead.

[5]When a surgeon performs venesection, to take out the dirty and superfluous blood he should be cautious to watch when to stop bleeding and prevent the excessive oozing of

२. तिष्ठावरे तिष्ठ पर उत त्वं तिष्ठ मध्यमे ।
कनिष्ठिका च तिष्ठति तिष्ठादिद् धमनिर्मही ॥

2. Stop bleeding, thou lower vein, stop bleeding, thou upper, stop bleeding, thou midmost one. The smallest vein of all stops bleeding, let the great vein stop bleeding. (76)[1]

३. शतस्य धमनीनां सहस्रस्य हिराणाम् । अस्थुरिन्मध्यमा इमाः साकमन्ता अरंसत ॥

3. Among hundreds of bigger veins charged with blood, among thousands of smaller veins, even these the middlemost have stopped bleeding. Let all the rest perform their function jointly. (77)

४. परि वः सिकतावती धनूर्बृहत्यक्रमीत् । तिष्ठतेलयता सु कम् ॥

4. O veins, a big bandage full of soothing sand, hath circled and encompassed you. Stop bleeding, and quietly take rest. (78)[2]

HYMN XVIII

१. निर्लक्ष्म्यं ललाम्यं निररातिं सुवामसि ।
अथ या भद्रा तानि नः प्रजाया अरातिं नयामसि ॥

1. We marry a handsome and well-behaved woman. We reject a malignant one. We welcome the good-natured girls for our progeny, but discard the miserly one. (79)[3]

२. निररणिं सविता साविषक् पदोर्निर्हस्तयोर्वरुणो मित्रो अर्यमा ।
निरस्मभ्यमनुमती रराणा प्रेमां देवा असाविषुः सौभगाय ॥

2. Let father drive away from the feet of the girl, the ill habit of loitering about vainly. Let father as chastiser, friend and benefactor drive away from the hands of the girl, stinginess and the habit of moving them uselessly. Let that women remain far away from us whose hands and feet are not well trained and disciplined. May we secure a wife, who is obedient to the husband and charitably disposed. Noble parents alone can produce such a girl, for the prosperity of the family. (80)[4]

३. यत्त आत्मनि तन्वां घोरमस्ति यद्वा केशेषु प्रतिचक्षणे वा ।
सर्वं तद् वाचाप हन्मो वयं देवस्त्वा सविता सूदयतु ॥

blood, to make the veins calm and restore health to the patient. Here veins are compared to maidens. Just as maidens are serviceable to the parents so are the veins to the body. After the performance of an operation, the veins should be made calm and quiet like brotherless sisters, to restore health to the patients.

[1]The surgeon should see that bleeding from different veins is stopped at the proper time.

[2]A bandage full of softening and soothing sand placed on a wound stops bleeding.

[3]Women of virulent and miserly nature should not be married.

[4]In some texts, in place of साविषक् we find साविषत्

3. O woman, whatever moral weakness is there in thy mind, or physical infirmity in thy body, or improve sentiment in thy head or ferocity in thy eyes; all these we drive away and banish with our speech. May thy father, thy birth-giver, lead thee on the path of virtue. (81)

४. रिश्यपदीं वृषदतीं गोषेधां विधमामुत । विलीढ्यं ललाम्यं१ ता अस्मन्नाशयामसि ॥

4. We should always refrain from marrying girls, unsteady, like the feet of an antelope, mighty-toothed like a bull, pigmy-sized like a cow, blowing hot with anger like the bellows, ever licking something, however beautiful, charming and lovely they may be. (82)[1]

HYMN XIX

१. मा नो विदन् विव्याधिनो मो अभिव्याधिनो विदन् ।
आराच्छरव्या अस्मद् विषूचीरिन्द्र पातय ॥

1. Let not the hostile archers overcome us, nor let those who attack us on all sides approach us. O Commander of the army, make the arrows flying in different directions fall far from us. (83)

२. विष्वञ्चो अस्मच्छरवः पतन्तु ये अस्ता ये चास्याः ।
दैवीर्मनुष्येषवो ममामित्रान् वि विध्यत ॥

2. Let the arrows shot, and those that will be shot, fall far from us in all directions. May the supernatural shafts shot by warriors, strike and transfix mine enemies! (84)[2]

३. यो नः स्वो यो अरणः सजात उत निष्ट्यो यो अस्माँ अभिदासति ।
रुद्रः शरव्ययैतान् ममामित्रान् वि विध्यतु ॥

3. Whoever wants to enslave us, be he our own or strange to us, a kinsman or a foreigner, may the Commander of the army with his arrows pierce and slay these enemies of mine. (85)

४. यः सपत्नो योऽसपत्नो यश्च द्विषञ्छपाति नः । देवास्तं सर्वे धूर्वन्तु ब्रह्म वर्म ममान्तरम् ॥

4. The rival and non-rival, he who in his hatred curses us, may all the learned persons injure him. My nearest, closest armour is the true teaching of the Vedas. (86)

[1]'Mighty-toothed' means voracious.

Griffith interprets रिश्यपदीं etc., as names or epithets of sorceresses, witches or female fiends of various forms. This is not so rational an interpretation. Professor Geldner argues that the subject of the hymn is some semidomesticated animal in all probability a house cat. This is a far-fetched and inappropriate explanation. The verse refers to girls who should not be accepted in marriage.

[2]Supernatural refers to Āgneya and Vāruṇeya arrows, which when let loose emit fire and water.

HYMN XX

१. अदारसृद् भवतु देव सोमास्मिन् यज्ञे मरुतो मृडता नः ।
मा नो विददभिभा मो अशस्तिर्मा नो विदद् वृजिना द्वेष्या या ।।

1. O Refulgent God, let us commit no act of disunity. O pure souls, be gracious unto us, in this noble deed of ours. Let not defeat touch us. Let not infamy approach us. Let not the sins emanating from enmity come near us. (87)

२. यो अद्य सेन्यो वधोऽघायूनामुदीरते । युवं तं मित्रावरुणावस्मद्यावयतं परि ।।

2. O Prime Minister and King, Ye twain, turn carefully away from us, the deadly massacre of the sinners, which is being conducted today by the valiant soldiers of the army! (88)[1]

३. इतश्च यदमुतश्च यद् वधं वरुण यावय । वि महच्छर्म यच्छ वरीयो यावया वधम् ।।

3. Ward off from here and from there, O God, the idea of murder. Give us Thy great protection. Turn out far away from our mind the sentiment of murder! (89)[2]

४. शास इत्था महाँ अस्यमित्रसाहो अस्तृतः । न यस्य हन्यते सखा न जीयते कदा चन ।।

4. Verily, O God, Thou art a Mighty Ruler, Unconquered, Vanquisher of foes whose friend is never slain, whose friend is never overcome. (90)

HYMN XXI

१. स्वस्तिदा विशां पतिर्वृत्रहा विमृधो वशी । वृषेन्द्रः पुर एतु नः सोमपा अभयङ्करः ।।

1. Giver of bliss, Lord of the subjects, slayer of foes, subduer of enemies, self-controlled, showerer of happiness, prosperous, learned, bestower of fearlessness, should come to rule over our cities as a king. (91)[3]

२. वि न इन्द्र मृधो जहि नीचा यच्छ पृतन्यतः । अधमं गमया तमो यो अस्माँ अभिदासति ।।

2. O King, subdue our enemies, lay low the men who fight with us! Down into nether darkness send the man who wants to enslave us! (92)

३. वि रक्षो वि मृधो जहि वि वृत्रस्य हनू रुज । वि मन्युमिन्द्र वृत्रहन्नमित्रस्याभिदासतः ।।

3. Strike down the fiend, strike down the foes, break thou asunder the

[1]We should never think of murdering wicked persons, but try to reform them through advice and instruction.

[2]We should never entertain the idea of murdering any one.

[3]The manifold qualities a king should possess are enumerated here.

enemy's jaws. O King, the dispeller of darkness, quell the wrath of the assailing foe! (93)

४. अपेन्द्र द्विषतो मनोऽप जिज्यासतो वधम् । वि महच्छर्म यच्छ वरीयो यावया वधम् ॥

4. O King, turn thou the foeman's thought away, drive away his dart who fain would conquer us. Grant us thy great protection; keep his deadly weapon far away. (94)

Chapter (Anuvāka) 5

HYMN XXII

१. अनु सूर्यमुदयतां हृद्द्योतो हरिमा च ते । गो रोहितस्य वर्णेन तेन त्वा परि दध्मसि ॥

1. As the sun rises, let thy heart disease and jaundice depart.[1]
We compass and surround thee with the red colour of the sun's rays. (95)[1]

२. परि त्वा रोहितैर्वर्णैर्दीर्घायुत्वाय दध्मसि । यथाऽयमरपा असदथो अहरितो भुवत् ॥

2. With ruddy hues we compass three that thou mayest live a lengthened life: so this patient be free from disease, and cast away his jaundice. (96)[2]

३. या रोहिणीर्देवत्या३ गावो या उत रोहिणीः । रूपंरूपं वयोवयस्ताभिष्ट्वा परि दध्मसि ॥

3. The efficacious ruddy rays of the sun and the medicinal herbs that exist with their diverse beauty and diverse power we compass thee about. (97)[3]

४. शुकेषु ते हरिमाणं रोपणाकासु दध्मसि । अथो हारिद्रवेषु ते हरिमाणं नि दध्मसि ॥

4. O patient, we control thy jaundice through the use of the seeds of shuka trees, and strong healing medicines. We cure thy jaundice through the use of efficacious mixtures. (98)[4]

[1]In this hymn the science of curing patients suffering from jaundice or heart trouble through red-coloured rays of the sun and the milk of red cows is mentioned. The naked body of the patient should be exposed to the red rays of the sun, and he should drink the milk of a red cow.

[2]The patient is surrounded with red coloured objects in order to combat the yellow which is symptomatic of the disease; should the patient see everything yellow he will not soon get well" Hindu System of Medicine, p. 248.

[3]"We" refers to the physicians, and "thee" to the patient. The physicians cure the patient by exposing him to the highly useful morning rays of the sun, and giving him red medicinal herbs, the use of which lends beauty and strength to the patient. Griffith considers the meaning of the word Devatya as uncertain. Weber translates the word as divine powers'. The St. Petersburg Dictionary leaves the word unexplained with the remark that animals of some kind must be intended. The word means 'full of good qualities.'

[4]Shuka :—A family of trees, consisting of shirish (शिरीष), sthouneyak (स्थौनेयक) Tālish (तालीश), Gandhak (गन्धक). Jambu (जम्बू), Arka (अर्क), Dādima (दाडिम) shigru (शिग्रु), kshīrī (क्षीरी). Their leaves and seeds are beneficial for a patient of jaundice for curing heart diseases see Vagbhaṭṭa's, Aṣṭaṅgasaṁgroha Chapter V.

HYMN XXIII

१. नक्तंजातास्योषधे रामे कृष्णे असिक्नि च । इदं रजनि रजय किलासं पलितं च यत् ॥

1. O Rāma, Krishnā and Asikni medicine, thou hast sprung up at night. O Rajni remove leprosy and whiteness of the body. (99)[1]

२. किलासं च पलितं च निरितो नाशया पृषत् ।
आ त्वा स्वो विशतां वर्णः परा शुक्लानि पातय ॥

2. O medicine, remove the leprosy, remove from him the whiteness of hair and skin, the festering wounds and excruciating pain. May thou regain thy healthy colour. O medicine drive far away the white specks. (100)[2]

३. असितं ते प्रलयनमास्थानमसितं तव । असिक्न्यस्योषधे निरितो नाशया पृषत् ॥

3. O medicine, thy quality of absorption in the body removes leprosy, thy quality of sticking removes whiteness of the body. O medicine, highly efficacious art thou, remove from him the painful suppuration of the wound. (101)[3]

४. अस्थिजस्य किलासस्य तनूजस्य च यत् त्वचि । दूष्या कृतस्य ब्रह्मणा लक्ष्म श्वेतमनीनशम् ॥

4. I with my knowledge have chased away the pallid sign of leprosy, caused by infection, on the skin sprung from the body or from the bones. (102)[4]

HYMN XXIV

१. सुपर्णो जातः प्रथमस्तस्य त्वं पित्तमासिथ । तदासुरी युधा जिता रूपं चक्रे वनस्पतीन् ॥

1. Most efficacious for healing this disease is the medicine known as suparna. O Rajni, thou possessest the healing power of Suparna. Āsuri named

Some commentators translate the verse thus, 'To parrots and starlings we transfer thy sickly yellowness. Now in the yellow coloured birds we lay this yellowness of thine." As nature has endawed these birds with a yellow colour, so yellowness should go to them and not remain in men, who should be free from it.

[1]Rāma, Krishnā, Asikni and Rajni are the names of medicines, which cure leprosy and whiteness of the head and body. These medicinal plants grow more at night. Rajani is the name of the Curcuma Longa, which is one of the plants used in the treatment of leprosy. The word is used here on account of its derivation from ranj, to colour.

[2]Him, thou, thy all refer to the patient.

[3]Him refers to the patient.

[4]Two varieties of the disease appear to be meant (1) communicated by contact, breathing the same air, eating with or wearing the clothes of a leper, and (2) caused by the sufferer's own sins, irregularities in eating and fasting, indigestible food, mental agitation, excessive fatigue, and lack of Brahmcharya. Brahm is the name of a medicine as well, by the use of which the physician cures the patient. Dhanvantri, the famous authority on medicines has described in detail these medicines named Mukta, Rāma Krishna, Asikni, and Brahma.

medicine, lends its colour and shape to different plants, and is made serviceable through pulverisation. (103)[1]

२. असुरी चक्रे प्रथमेदं किलासभेषजमिदं किलासनाशनम् ।
अनीनशत् किलासं सरूपामकरत् त्वचम् ॥

2. The Āsuri plant is highly curative. It is the medicine for leprosy, the banisher of leprosy. It removes leprosy and lends beautiful colour to the skin. (104)

३. सरूपा नाम ते माता सरूपो नाम ते पिता । सरूपकृत् त्वमोषधे सा सरूपमिदं कृधि ॥

3. O medicine, beautiful is thy mother, the Earth, beautiful is thy father, the sun. Beautiful art thou, make this diseased body beautiful. (105)

४. श्यामा सरूपङ्करणी पृथिव्या अध्युद्भृता । इदमू षु प्र साधय पुना रूपाणि कल्पय ॥

4. O Shyāmā named medicine, thou impartest beauty, thou hast been dug out of the earth, heal thou fully well this leprous body. Restore the colours that were his before the attack of leprosy. (106)[2]

HYMN XXV

१. यदग्निरापो अदहत् प्रविश्य यत्राकृण्वन् धर्मधृतो नमांसि ।
तत्र त आहुः परमं जनित्रं स नः संविद्वान् परि वृङ्ग्धि तक्मन् ॥

1. O fever, the wise physicians, describe thy main birth-place, as the body, through which men of character accomplish many deeds. Just as fire penetrating the waters, lends them warmth, so dost thou entering the blood and vital airs, blaze the body. O learned physician, knowing the cause of fever, expel it from our body. (107)[3]

२. यद्यर्चिर्यदि वासि शोचिः शकल्येषि यदि वा ते जनित्रम् ।
ह्रूडुर्नामासि हरितस्य देव स नः संविद्वान् परि वृङ्ग्धि तक्मन् ॥

2. O fever, if thou be fiery glow, or inflammation, or thy birthplace be each and every organ, O god of the yellow colour, rack is thy name. O learned physician, knowing the cause of fever, expel it from our body. (108)[4]

[1]This verse is rather difficult. Suparna and Āsuri are the names of medicines. This disease refers to whiteness of the skin (*Phulveri*). Suparna may also mean, the sun, whose rays lend warmth to plants. Pt. Khem Karan Das Trivedi translates suparna as God.

[2]His refers to the patient. In this Sukta (hymn) the words suparna, Āsuri, sarupā, and shyāmā are the names of medicines. Suparna kills germs and cures leprosy. Āsuri kills germs and cures wounds. Sarupā cures smellings, boils. Shyāmā denotes different medicines like Gudchi, Kasturi, Nīlpunarnvā, Nīlnī, Pippali, Rochnā, Vatpattri and Haridrā. These medicines cure leprosy, bronchitis, diabetes, boils and wounds.

[3]Thou refers to fever.

[4]'God of the yellow colour,' means fever, which makes the colour of the patient yellow Rack (ह्रूडु) means an instrument of torture ह्रूडु may also means causing shaking, trembling, because the body shivers which it is attacked by fever.

३. यदि शोको यदि वाऽभिशोको यदि वा राज्ञो वरुणस्यासि पुत्रः ।
ह्रूडुर्नामासि हरितस्य देव स नः संविद्वान् परि वृङ्ग्धि तक्मन् ॥

3. O fever, if thou tormentest our heart or all the organs of the body. Be thou the son of water, rack is thy name. O learned physician, knowing the cause of fever, expel it from our body. (109)[1]

४. नमः शीताय तक्मने नमो रूराय शोचिषे कृणोमि ।
यो अन्येद्युरुभयद्युरभ्येति तृतीयकाय नमो अस्तु तक्मने ॥

4. I bid good-bye to chilly fever, to his fierce burning glow I bid good-bye. Good-bye to the fever, that comes on alternate days, to the fever that comes after an interval of two days, and to the fever that comes after an interval of three days. (110)[2]

HYMN XXVI

१. आरे३ सावस्मदस्तु हेतिर्देवासो असत् । आरे अश्मा यमस्यथ ॥

1. Ye conquering heroes, let that destructive weapon be far from us, far be the iron weapon Ye want to hurl. (111)[3]

२. सखासावस्मभ्यमस्तु रातिः सखेन्द्रो भगः सविता चित्रराधाः ॥

2. Let God, the Giver of wealth unto all the Lord of powers, the creator of all the Master of diverse, wonderful superhuman sway, be our friend. (112)

३. यूयं नः प्रवतो नपान्मरुतः सूर्यत्वचसः । शर्म यच्छाथ सप्रथाः ॥

3. O generals, shining like the sun with the glow of your armour ; O commander of the army never allowing the falling soldiers fall, give us far-reaching protection. (113)[4]

४. सुषूदत मृडत मृडया नस्तनूभ्यो मयस्तोकेभ्यस्कृधि ॥

4. O learned persons, afford us protection, grant us happiness, grant our bodies freedom from disease. Give our children happiness ! (114)

[1]Son of water: Germs of malaria are generated in a place of stagnant, stinking water hence fever is the son of water, as non-moving water produces the germs of fever.

[2]Good-bye means may the fever remain afar, and not attack me. I protect myself through necessary precautions and the use of antidotes. Here four kinds of fever are mentioned. Some fevers begin with shivering of the body and some commence with burning heat. Some recur daily, some alternately, some after the interval of two and three days. We should be cautious against all of them.

[3]अश्मा literally means stone, but figuratively here it means an iron weapon.

[4]In some texts सप्रथाः is used, while in others it is सप्रथः

Pt. Sātvalelkar and Pt. Jaidev Vidyalankar adopt सुप्रथाः, Sāyana Pt. Raja Ram and Pt. Khem Karan Das Trivedi adopt सप्रथः

HYMN XXVII

१. अमूः पारे पृदाक्वस्त्रिषप्ता निर्जरायवः ।
तासां जरायुभिर्वयमक्ष्या३वपि व्ययामस्यघायोः परिपन्थिनः ॥

1. There on the bank are stationed in three positions, armies ferocious like serpents, having cast their armours as serpents do their slough. Attacking their discarded armours, we dazzle with them the eyes of a terrible foe. (115)[1]

२. विषूच्येतु कृन्तती पिनाकमिव बिभ्रती । विष्वक् पुनर्भुवा मनोऽसमृद्धा अघायवः ॥

2. Let the army bearing war-like instruments, cutting the enemy, advance forward in all directions. Let it confuse the mind of the re-assembled forces of the defeated foe. Ne'er are the wicked prosperous. (116)

३. न बह्वः समशकन् नार्भका अभि दाधृषुः । वेणोरद्गाइवाभितोऽसमृद्धा अघायवः ॥

3. Let not our enemy have the power to attack us in large numbers, nor the audacity to wage war against us with forces feeble like the children. Like scattered fragments of a reed, ne'er are the wicked prosperous. (117)

४. प्रेतं पादौ प्र स्फुरतं वहतं पृणतो गृहान् । इन्द्राण्येतु प्रथमाजीतामुषिता पुरः ॥

4. Go forward, feet, press quickly on, take us to the houses of our rich relatives. Let unconquered, unplundered, foremost riches lead the way. (118)[2]

HYMN XXVIII

१. उप प्रागाद् देवो अग्नी रक्षोहामीवचातनः । दहन्नप द्वयाविनो यातुधानान् किमीदिनः ॥

1. A Conquering Commander, the fiend-slayer, the chaser of disease, burning the deceitful plundering and slanderous, greedy persons, is proceeding towards us. (119)[3]

२. प्रति दह यातुधानान् प्रति देव किमीदिनः । प्रतीचीः कृष्णवर्तने सं दह यातुधान्यः ॥

2. Consume the plunderers, O Commander, meet the greedy slanderers with thy flame. Burn up the piratical adventurers as they face thee, thou whose path is black. (120)[4]

[1]Three positions: the upper, middle and lower. The word त्रिषप्ता has been translated by some commentators as three times seven, i.e., infinite. Them refers to the discarded armours of the enemy. षप्ता means स्थिताः

[2]This verse is spoken by the General of an army marching home after defeating the army of enemy.

[3]Us refers to soldiers of the army.

[4]'Piratical adventurers' refers to the army of the enemy 'whose path is black' means the path of the commander is black, as it is filled with the smoke emitted by the warlike instruments discharged by him.

३. या शशाप शपनेन याघं मूरमादधे । या रसस्य हरणाय जातमारेभे तोकमत्तु सा ॥

3. She who hath reviled us with filthy words or hath made mischief her aim, or seized our men for taking their blood, let her retard her own advancement. (121)[1]

४. पुत्रमत्तु यातुधानीः स्वसारमुत नप्त्यम् ।
अधा मिथो विकेश्यो३ वि घ्नतां यातुधान्यो३ वि तृह्यन्तामराय्यः ॥

4. Let the troublesome army of the enemy, through confusion, destroy her own son, sister and grand daughter. Let the rival forces, with their dishevelled hair, fight together and destroy themselves. Let the non tax-paying turbulent subjects be crushed down. (122)[2]

Chapter (Anuvāka) 6

HYMN XXIX

१. अभीवर्तेन मणिना येनेन्द्रो अभिवावृधे । तेनास्मान् ब्रह्मणस्पतेऽभि राष्ट्राय वर्धय ॥

1. With that victorious strength and wealth, which strengthened the power and might of a prosperous man in the past; do Thou, O God the Lord of the Vedas, increase our strength for kingly sway! (123)

२. अभिवृत्य सपत्नानभि या नो अरातयः । अभि पृतन्यन्तं तिष्ठाभि यो नो दुरस्यति ।

2. O King, subduing those who rival us, subduing all who refuse to pay taxes, withstand the man who menaces, and him who seeks to injure us! (124)

३. अभि त्वा देवः सविताभि सोमो अवीवृधत् । अभि त्वा विश्वा भूतान्यभीवर्तो यथाससि ॥

3. O God, the Sun and the Moon have glorified and exalted Thee; all elements have sung Thy greatness, as Thou art the Conqueror of all. (125)

४. अभीवर्तो अभिभवः सपत्नक्षयणो मणिः । राष्ट्राय मह्यं बध्यतां सपत्नेभ्यः पराभुवे ॥

4. Slayer of rivals, vanquisher, may that victorious kingly sway, he assumed by me for the protection of my kingdom and conquest of mine enemies. (126)[3]

५. उदसौ सूर्यो अगादुदिदं मामकं वचः । यथाहं शत्रुहोऽसान्यसपत्नः सपत्नहा ॥

5. Just as you Sun hath mounted up on high, so hath this proclamation of mine been announced, 'That I shall smite my foes and slay my rivals, and be thus rivalless.' (127)[4]

[1]She and her refer to the army of the enemy, such an army can make no progress, who curses us, is bent on mischief, or takes the blood of our soldiers.

[2]The king should subdue the non-tax-paying unruly subjects, and cause confusion in the ranks of the enemy's forces, that they destroy their own kith and kin, and annihilate themselves through mutual fight.

[3]Me, my, mine all refer to the king.

[4]I and mine refer to the king.

६. सपत्नक्षयणो वृषाभिराष्ट्रो विषासहिः । यथाहमेषां वीराणां विराजानि जनस्य च ॥

6. Destroyer of my rivals, strong, victorious, with royal sway, may I be the ruler of these men, and sovereign of the folk. (128)[1]

HYMN XXX

१. विश्वे देवा वसवा रक्षतेममुतादित्या जागृत यूयमस्मिन् ।
मेमं सनाभिरुत वान्यनाभिर्मेमं प्रापत् पौरुषेयो वधो यः ॥

1. O noble, saintly persons, guard and protect this man. Over him keep Ye watch and ward, O brilliant scholars, let not death reach him from the hands of brothers, from hands of aliens, or of human beings. (129)[2]

२. ये वो देवाः पितरो ये च पुत्राः सचेतसो मे शृणुतेदमुक्तम् ।
सर्भ्वेयो वः परि ददाम्येतं स्वस्त्येनं जरसे वहाथ ॥

2. Listen, one-minded, to the word 'I utter, the sons, O learned persons, among you, and the fathers ! I trust this man to all of you: preserve him happily, and remain under his sways till your old age. (130)[3]

३. ये देवा दिवि ष्ठ ये पृथिव्यां ये अन्तरिक्ष ओषधीषु पशुष्वप्स्व१न्तः ।
ते कृणुत जरसमायुरस्मै शतमन्यान् परि वृणक्तु मृत्यून् ॥

3. May all learned persons, well-versed in astronomy, geology, aerostatics, medicine, veterinary science, and hydropathy, grant this man life to full old age, and let him escape the hundred other ways of dying. (131)[4]

४. येषां प्रयाजा उत वानुयाजा हुतभागा अहुतादश्च देवाः ।
येषां वः पञ्च प्रदिशो विभक्तास्तान् वो अस्मै सत्रसदः कृणोमि ॥

4. Ye, learned persons, who work selflessly for the attainment of emancipation, who crave for the fruit of actions, who are the sharers of oblation, and who live on alms, diversified are your acts of sacrifice, I make you the member of the cabinet of this king. (132)[5]

HYMN XXXI

१. आशानामाशापालेभ्यश्चतुर्भ्यो अमृतेभ्यः । इदं भूतस्याध्यक्षेभ्यो विधेम हविषा वयम् ॥

1. Now do we serve with devotion the great controllers of the world, the

[1] I refers to the king.

[2] Him refers to the king. The hymn refers to the coronation of the king.

[3] I refers to the Purohit, who officiates at the coronation. 'This man' refers to the king.

[4] Him refers to the king, who should enjoy a long life, and avoid hundreds of deadly diseases.

[5] I refers to the Purohit. The king should select such learned, simple, selfless persons as his ministers.

four immortal guardians of our ambitions, in the midst of all directions. (133)[1]

२. य आशानामाशापालाश्चत्वार स्थन देवाः ।
ते नो निर्ऋत्याः पाशेभ्यो मुञ्चतांहसोअंहसः ॥

2. Ye, gods, the guardians of our ambitions, in the midst of all quarters, rescue and free us from the bonds of moral degradation, from every sort of sin ! (134)[2]

३. अस्रामस्त्वा हविषा यजाम्यश्लोणस्त्वा घृतेन जुहोमि ।
य आशानामाशापालस्तुरीयो देवः स नः सुभूतमेह वक्षत् ॥

3. Free from lassitude, I serve Thee, O God, with devotion, free from disease, I acknowledge Thee with my knowledge. Let the strong God, the Guardian of our ambitions in the universe, bring to us hither safety and well-being. (135)[3]

४. स्वस्ति मात्र उत पित्रे नो अस्तु स्वस्ति गोभ्यो जगते पुरुषेभ्यः ।
विश्वं सुभूतं सुविदत्रं नो अस्तु ज्योगेव दृशेम सूर्यम् ॥

4. Well be it with our mother and our father, well be it with our cows, and beasts, and people. Ours be all happy fortune, grace, and knowledge. Long, very long may we behold the sunlight. (136)

HYMN XXXII

१. इदं जनासो विदथ महद् ब्रह्म वदिष्यति ।
न तत् पृथिव्यां नो दिवि येन प्राणन्ति वीरुधः ॥

1. O people, know this Mighty God, of Whom a seer will speak. He is present not only on Earth, or heaven, but everywhere. The plants receive breathing from Him. (137)[4]

२. अन्तरिक्ष आसां स्थाम श्रान्तसदामिव । आस्थानमस्य भूतस्य विदुष्टद् वेधसो न वा ॥

2. The stability of all these plants lies in God, just as enlightened souls wearied of the cycle of birth and death take rest in God after salvation. The learned alone can tell, whether they know or not God to be the source of animate and inanimate creation. (138)

[1] 'In the midst of all directions' means in the universe 'Great controllers and four immortal guardians' refer to Dharma (Righteousness). Arth (worldly prosperity) Kāma (Love of God), Moksha (salvation). These are the four ends of human existence.

[2] Gods refer to Dharma, Arth, Kāma and Moksha.

[3] The word तुरीयः translated as strong God, may also mean Moksha, the fourth end of human existence.

[4] This verse clearly supports the theory that there is life in plants. This theory was put before the world by Dr. J.C. Bose. He got this idea from this verse and developed it to demonstrate its truth through scientific apparatus.

३. यद् रोदसी रेजमाने भूमिश्च निरतक्षतम् । आर्द्रं तदद्य सर्वदा समुद्रस्येव स्रोत्याः ॥

3. God, who hath produced and fashioned forth this ever moving sun and Earth, is today and ever filled with compassion, as an ocean is ever filled with water through streams that flow into it. (139)

४. विश्वमन्यामभीवार तदन्यस्यामधिश्रितम् । दिवे च विश्ववेदसे पृथिव्यै चाकरं नमः ॥

4. We know matter as the encompasser of the universe. Matter itself depends on another Power, known as God. I pay my adoration to the All-knowing, Refulgent, Diffused God. (140)

HYMN XXXIII

१. हिरण्यवर्णाः शुचयः पावका यासु जातः सविता यास्वग्निः ।
या अग्निं गर्भं दधिरे सुवर्णास्ता न आपः शं स्योना भवन्तु ॥

1. May the golden-hued, the bright, the splendid waters wherein the Sun was born and fire was born ; they, who took fire in their womb, fair-coloured, bring felicity and bless us. (141)[1]

२. यासां राजा वरुणो याति मध्ये सत्यानृते अवपश्यञ्जनानाम् ।
या अग्निं गर्भं दधिरे सुवर्णास्ता न आपः शं स्योना भवन्तु ॥

2. May the subtle primary elements, in the midst whereof the Resplendent God pervadeth, watching men's righteous and unrighteous deeds, who preserve lightning in their womb, and are beautiful in appearance, bring felicity and bless us. (142)

३. यासां देवा दिवि कृण्वन्ति भक्षं या अन्तरिक्षे बहुधा भवन्ति ।
या अग्निं गर्भं दधिरे सुवर्णास्ता न आपः शं स्योना भवन्तु ॥

3. May they, whom the beautiful objects in the sky nourish, who was manifold in air's mid-region, who preserve lightning in their womb, and are beautiful in appearance, bring felicity and bless us. (143)[2]

४. शिवेन मा चक्षुषा पश्यतापः शिवया तन्वोप स्पृशत त्वचं मे ।
घृतश्चुतः शुचयो याः पावकास्ता न आपः शं स्योना भवन्तु ॥

4. O self-abnegating souls, behold me with auspicious eye, touch Ye my skin with your auspicious hand. May they bright and pure, shedding loveliness and brilliancy, bring felicity and bless us. (144)[3]

[1]Daily we see the Sun rising from the sea, as if the water of the sea gives him birth. बड़वानल fire generally comes out of the waters of the seas hence waters are the creator of fire. Agni springs in the form of lightning from the watery clouds. Waters have been spoken of as keeping fire in their womb.

[2]'They' refers to the elements. 'Beautiful objects' mean the air, the sun, the cloud and rays.

[3]In this hymn the word आपः has been translated differently by different commenta-

HYMN XXXIV

१. इयं वीरुन्मधुजाता मधुना त्वा खनामसि । मधोरधि प्रजातासि सा नो मधुमतस्कृधि ॥

1. This divine knowledge has sprung from God. O divine knowledge, we acquire thee with exertion through the soul. Thou hast emanated from Sweet God, fill us with spiritual knowledge. (145)

२. जिह्वाया अग्रे मधु मे जिह्वामूले मधूलकम् । ममेदह क्रतावसो मम चित्तमुपायसि ॥

2. O divine knowledge may thou reside at the tip of my tongue, may the fascinating knowledge of God reside in my mind. O spiritual knowledge, stay thou without fail, in my active soul, remain steadfast in my heart. (146)

३. मधुमन्मे निक्रमणं मधुमन्मे परायणम् । वाचा वदामि मधुमद् भूयासं मधुसन्दृशः ॥

3. May my conduct be sweet, may my travels be free from travail, may I be sweet in talk, may I become the embodiment of loveliness and sweetness. (147)

४. मधोरस्मि मधुतरो मदुघान्मधुमत्तरः । मामित् किल त्वं वनाः शाखां मधुमतीमिव ॥

4. I am sweeter than honey, yet more full of sweets than licorice, so mayest thou O Knowledge love me, as birds love the branch of a tree, full of sweet fruits. (148)[1]

५. परि त्वा परितत्नुनेक्षुणागामविद्विषे । यथा मां कामिन्यसो यथा मन्नापगा असः ॥

5. O Knowledge, I have gathered thee from all sources, with a vast, ardent desire, to inspire love. Mayest thou be in love with me, never to forsake me. (149)[2]

HYMN XXXV

१. यदाबध्नन् दाक्षायणा हिरण्यं शतानीकाय सुमनस्यमानाः ।
तत् ते बध्नाम्यायुषे वर्चसे बलाय दीर्घायुत्वाय शतशारदाय ॥

1. The yogis, who live for the purity of soul, full of noble thoughts, preserve the precious semen for the body, that it may last for a hundred years, so I, thy preceptor, O pupil, advise thee to preserve it for longevity, glory, strength and a long life of a hundred autumns. (150)[3]

tors. Sāyana translates the word as water, Pt. Jaidev Vidyalankar as self-abnegating souls, i.e., आप्त पुरुष, Pt. Khem Karan Das translates it as elements. Swami Dayanand Saraswati has translated the word as subtle primary element vide his translation *Yajur*, 27-25.

[1]Licorice is sweet pudding.

[2]त्वा may refer to a wife. Husband addresses her to love him, and never to depart from him.

[3]In the opinion of Griffith, Daksha is in the Veda a creative power associated with Aditi (Infinity or Eternity) the mother of Adityas. This interpretation is illogical as there is no history in the Vedas. Dakshayanā means self-controlled yogis and noble persons, who preserve their precious semen. See *Yajur*, 34-52.

२. नैनं रक्षांसि न पिशाचा: सहन्ते देवानामोजः प्रथमजं ह्ये३तत् ।
यो बिभर्ति दाक्षायणं हिरण्यं स जीवेषु कृणुते दीर्घमायुः ॥

2. No fiends and deadly diseases, no cannibals and wasting ailments can conquer him, who preserves his semen, which is the lustre of the learned, and their primal offspring. He who preserves this invigorating semen, precious like gold, prolongs his life among the sages. (151)[1]

३. अपां तेजो ज्योतिरोजो बलं च वनस्पतीनामुत वीर्याणि ।
इन्द्रइवेन्द्रियाण्यधि धारयामो अस्मिन् तद्दक्षमाणो बिभरद्धिरण्यम् ॥

3. The light, the power, the lustre of semen, the strength of the learned, and all their forceful vigour, we lay on this Brahmchari, as powers reside in the soul ; so let him preserve this golden semen and show his valour. (152)[2]

४. समानां मासामृतुभिष्टवा वयं संवत्सरस्य पयसा पिपर्मि ।
इन्द्राग्नी विश्वे देवास्तेऽनु मन्यन्तामहृणीयमानाः ॥

4. We fill thee with the strength of friendly mouths and seasons, with the full year's sweet essence do we fill thee. May God, thy teacher and all learned persons without hesitation give thee their assent, to fulfil thy vow of celibacy. (153)[3]

BOOK (Kaṇḍa) II

Chapter (Anuvāka) 1

HYMN I

१. वेनस्तत् पश्यत् परमं गुहा यद्यत्र विश्वं भवत्येकरूपम् ।
इदं पृश्निरदुहज्जायमानाः स्वर्विदो अभ्यनूषत व्राः ॥

1. A devotee alone beholds that Highest God, Who lies hidden in the inmost recesses of the heart, in whom this whole universe remains in one form and fashion. From Him hath Matter milked life and brought into existence many objects. The learned who know God, extol Him in a nice way. (154)[4]

२. प्र तद् वोचेदमृतस्य विद्वान् गन्धर्वो धाम परमं गुहा यत् ।
त्रीणि पदानि निहिता गुहास्य यस्तानि वेद स पितुष्पितासत् ॥

[1]See *Yajur*, 34-51.

[2]See *Yajur*, 27-21. Swami Dayananda translates वनस्पति as a learned person.
Brahmchari: A person who observes the vow of celibacy.

[3]'We' refers to Achāryas, preceptors, Thee refers to the Brahmchāri. Sweet essence refers to milk, fruits and corn, the Brahmchari uses during the year.

[4]'In one form and fashion: when the universe is dissolved by God, all material objects lose their separate existence, and are resolved to a uniform atomic state, without distinction'. See *Yajur*, 32-8.

2. May the learned sage declare to us that highest station of God, who is hidden in the cave of the heart. Three steps of God lie hidden in His infinite might. He who knows them becomes the father's father. (155)[1]

३. स नः पिता जनिता स उत बन्धुर्धामानि वेद भुवनानि विश्वा ।
यो देवानां नामध एक एव तं संप्रश्नं भुवना यन्ति सर्वा ॥

3. The Almighty Creator is our kinsman, father, and begetter; He knows all beings and stages of men. He assumes all the appellations of the forces of nature: all creatures go to him to ask direction. (156)[2]

४. परि द्यावापृथिवी सद्य आयमुपातिष्ठे प्रथमजामृतस्य ।
वाचमिव वक्तरि भुवनेष्ठा धास्युरेष नन्वे३षो अग्निः ॥

4. Having renounced the Earth and Heaven, I have come towards God. I worship the First Creator of true laws, just as voice remains hidden in the speaker, so does God stand unseen in the world. He is the Sustainer and Protector of all. He, verily is Agni. (157)[3]

५. परि विश्वा भुवनान्यायमृतस्य तन्तुं विततं दृशे कम् ।
यत्र देवा अमृतमानशानाः समाने योनावध्यैरयन्त ॥

5. Having renounced the comforts of the world, I have come towards God, to behold the pleasing far extended thread of His true Law. Wherein, the Yogis, obtaining life external, have risen upward to one common Cause. (158)[4]

HYMN II

१. दिव्यो गन्धर्वो भुवनस्य यस्पतिरेक एव नमस्यो ऽ विक्ष्वीड्यः ।
तं त्वा यौमि ब्रह्मणा दिव्य देव नमस्ते अस्तु दिवि ते सधस्थम् ॥

1. The Divine God, Who is the Lord of the World, should alone be honoured and worshipped by the people. I realise Thee, O Divine God, through the knowledge of the vedas. May I enjoy Thy company in the highest stage of salvation. Homage to Thee! (159)[5]

[1]Three steps are Creation, Sustenance and Dissolution of the universe, or Past, Present, and Future, or Satva, Rajas and Tāmasa, Father's father means, he becomes wiser than, and able to instruct his elders. See *Yajur*, 32. 9.

[2]To ask direction: to learn what their several functions and duties are.

He assumes: Agni, Vayu, Indra, Āpa, etc., the forces of nature are the names of God. See *Ṛigveda*, 10-82-3, and *Yajur*, 17-27.

[3]A learned sage renounces worldly objects for the attainment of God. God is the first Revealer of the Vedas, the encyclopaedia of true laws. God is Refulgent like Agni, or just as fire is hidden in fuel, so is God hidden in all objects.

[4]'One Common Cause' refers to God, who is the primordial source of all creation. 'His true Law' refers to the Vedas, whose teachings are vast and conducive to the good of humanity.

[5]Gandharva means God, See. *Ṛgveda*, 9-83-4.

२. दिवि स्पृष्टो यजतः सूर्यत्वगवयाता हरसो दैव्यस्य ।
मृडाद् गन्धर्वो भुवनस्य यस्पतिरेक एव नमस्यः सुशेवाः ।।

2. God is our constant Companion in salvation, Adorable, Bright like the Sun, the Effacer of the lustre of luminous objects. May He, the Protector of vedic speech, the Lord of the universe, the Unequalled, Friendly and Worshippable God, bless us. (160)

३. अनवद्याभिः समु जग्म आभिरप्सरास्वपि गन्धर्व आसीत् ।
समुद्र आसां सदनं म आहुर्यतः सद्य आ च परा च यन्ति ।।

3. God is present in all the forces of Nature. He identifies Himself with these faultless, blameless forces. Their home is in God, vast like the ocean, so do the vedic scholars say unto us. They come quickly at the time of creation and vanish at the time of dissolution of the universe. (161)[1]

४. अभ्रिये दिद्युन्नक्षत्रिये या विश्वावसुं गन्धर्वं सचध्वे । ताभ्यो वो देवीर्नम इत् कृणोमि ।।

4. O beautiful forces of Nature, that reside in clouds, lightning and stars, and serve God, who pervades all worlds, I truly respect Ye! (162)[2]

५. याः क्लन्दास्तमिषीचयोऽक्षकामा मनोमुहः । ताभ्यो गन्धर्वपत्नीभ्योऽप्सराभ्योऽकरं नमः ।।

5. I pay homage to the forces of Nature, that are the creators of diverse objects, the removers of languor, the satiators of eyes, and stupefiers of mind, and remain under the protection of God. (163)

HYMN III

१. अदो यदवधावत्यवत्कमधि पर्वतात् । तत्ते कृणोमि भेषजं सुभेषजं यथाससि ।।

1. Just as that healing water runs downward from the hill, so do I make God the Pacifier like water, a medicine for thee, as He is the best medicine. (164)[3]

२. आदङ्गा कुविदङ्गा शतं या भेषजानि ते । तेषामसि त्वमुत्तममनास्रावमरोगणम् ।।

2. O dear God, O most dear God, among hundreds of medicines created by Thee; Most Excellent art Thou curing disease and morbid flow of semen. (165)[4]

[1] 'They' refers to the forces of nature.

[2] Respect Ye: Utilise the forces to the best advantage of humanity.

[3] I refers to a boy sage. Just as water heals physical ailments, so meditation and contemplation of God, remove mental ills. God is the best Healer for all spiritual weaknesses.

[4] There may be hundreds of medicines for excessive flow of semen, but the best medicine is diverting one's mind towards God, observing the laws of celibacy, as preached by Him, and meditating upon Him constantly. God's remembrance is the medicine of medicines.

३. नीचैः खनन्त्यसुरा अरुस्राणमिदं महत् । तदास्रावस्य भेषजं तदु रोगमनीनशत् ॥

3. The wise, through humility attain to this Mighty God, the ripener of vital semen. He is the medicine to stop the flow of semen. He cures all ailments physical and mental. (166)[1]

४. उपजीका उद्भरन्ति समुद्रादधि भेषजम् । तदास्रावस्य भेषजं तदु रोगमशीशमत् ॥

4. Human beings living under the shelter of God, receive remedy from God, the Ocean of power. God is the efficacious medicine for the flow of semen. He certainly eradicates this malady. (167)[2]

५. अरुस्राणमिदं महत् पृथिव्या अध्युद्भृतम् । तदास्रावस्य भेषजं तदु रोगमनीनशत् ॥

5. This Mighty God, the ripener of vital semen, is manifested through material occurrences. God is the effecacious medicine for the flow of semen. He certainly eradicates this malady. (168)

६. शं नो भवन्त्वप ओषधयः शिवाः ।
इन्द्रस्य वज्रो अप हन्तु रक्षस आराद् विसृष्टा इषवः पतन्तु रक्षसाम् ॥

6. May the Calm, Auspicious God, the source of all medicines, bless us. May the spiritual power of the soul quell diabolical sentiments. May the shafts shot by these satanic intentions fall far from us. (169)[3]

HYMN IV

१. दीर्घायुत्वाय बृहते रणायारिष्यन्तो दक्षमाणाः सदैव ।
मणिं विष्कन्धदूषणं जङ्गिडं बिभृमो वयम् ॥

1. For length of life, for success in life's struggle, uninjured, ever exerting, may we accept God, the Praiseworthy Devourer of sins, and the Averter of obstacles. (170)[4]

२. जङ्गिडो जम्भाद्विशराद्विष्कन्धादभिशोचनात् ।
मणिः सहस्रवीर्यः परि णः पातु विश्वतः ॥

[1]One can control and stop the flow of his semen through the meditation of God alone.

[2]He refers to God, Who is the most efficient physician, the curer of our ailments and the dispenser of medicines.

[3]A man should subdue baser passions through his soul-force, and allow not the carnal desires, which try to attack him, approach him. He should remain far from sinful designs.

[4]Sāyana interprets जङ्गिड as a tree found near Benaras. This explanation is illogical, as it savours of history, but the Vedas are free from history. The word means God, Who devours all sins. Griffith explains the word to mean a plant frequently mentioned in the Atharvaveda as a charm against demons and a specific for various diseases. This interpretation too is irrational. Griffith writes vishkandha is probably rheumatism, and the name of the fiend to whose malignity the diseases was attributed. This does not appeal to reason. The word means God, Who is the Averter of obstacles.

2. May the Most Excellent God, the Suppressor of sins, the Master of a thousand powers, save us, all round, from destruction, violence, obstacle and utter grief. (171)[1]

३. अयं विष्कन्धं सहतेऽयं बाधते अत्त्रिणः । अयं नो विश्वभेषजो जङ्गिडः पात्वंहसः ॥

3. May this God, the Panacea for all ills, the Devourer of sins, Who overcomes obstacles, and chases the greedy sinners away, save us from sin. (172)

४. देवैर्दत्तेन मणिना जङ्गिडेन मयोभुवा । विष्कन्धं सर्वा रक्षांसि व्यायामे सहामहे ॥

4. Through the grace of Most Excellent God, Who preached to us by the sages, grants delight, and removes physical and mental ailments may we overcome in conflict all obstacles and satanic sentiments. (173)

५. शणश्च मा जङ्गिडश्च विष्कन्धादभि रक्षताम् । अरण्यादन्य आभृतः कृष्या अन्यो रसेभ्यः ॥

5. May perseverance and God, both preserve me from obstacle. One of them is attainable through austerity and study, and the other through meditation and reflection for delights. (174)[2]

६. कृत्यादूषिरयं मणिरथो अरातिदूषिः । अथा सहस्वाञ्जङ्गिडः प्र ण आयूंषि तारिषत् ॥

6. This Excellent God prevents violence, and subdues miserliness. May the victorious God, prolong the years of our life. (175)[3]

HYMN V

१. इन्द्र जुषस्व प्र वहा याहि शूर हरिभ्याम् । पिबा सुतस्य मतेरिह मधोश्चकानश्चारुर्मदाय ॥

1. O King, remain happy, go forward, O Hero, come for attacking the foe, utilising the ever-fleeting horses of day and night. Satiated with joy, amiable in nature, enjoy here, the mature knowledge of a learned person! (176)[4]

२. इन्द्र जठरं नव्यो न पृणस्व मधोर्दिवो न । अस्य सुतस्य स्व१र्णोप त्वा मदाः सुवाचो अगुः ॥

2. O King, just as a new guest fills his belly with food, so shouldst thou fill the belly of thy treasure. Just as the Sun takes up water from the Earth with his rays, and fills the atmosphere with it, so shouldst thou enrich thyself with the collection of taxes in the state, worthy of being nourished by thee

[1]Griffith considers Jambha, Viśara, etc., as names of fiends and demons. This explanation does not appeal to reason.

[2]Perseverance is obtained through austerity and knowledge. God is realised through reflection and meditation for the attainment of joys.

[3]Pt. Jaidev Vidyalankar translates the verse thus: This wealth of celibacy extirpates baser sentiments, and uproots miserliness. Celibacy lends us courage and daring, and prolongs the days of our life. This is a plausible interpretation.

[4]Here may mean in your life, or in this world, or on the battlefield, where a king may receive instruction and guidance from experienced and learned military officers.

like a son, and treated as a paradise on Earth. If thou dost so, excellent voices from thy subjects, full of joy and praise shall reach unto thee! (177)

३. इन्द्रस्तुराषाण्मित्रो वृत्रं यो जघान यतीर्न । बिभेद वलं भृगुर्न ससहे शत्रून् मदे सोमस्य ॥

3. The Swift-conquering king is the friend of his subjects. Just as a Yogi, the observer of Yamās and Niyamās, overcomes ignorance, lust and anger, foes to his meditation, so does the king destroy the enemy of his state. Just as the Sun disperses the cloud, so does the king shatter the forces of the enemy, and quell his foes in the rapturous joy of power. (178)[1]

४. आ त्वा विशन्तु सुतास इन्द्र पृणस्व कुक्षी विड्ढि शक्र धियेह्या नः ।
श्रुधी हवं गिरो मे जुषस्वेन्द्र स्वयुग्भिर्मत्स्वेह महे रणाय ॥

4. O king, mayest thou obtain all the objects produced in thy state. Just as a person fills full both sides of the belly with food, so fill thy treasure with cash and kind. O mighty king, know all the acts of thy subjects through thy intellect come unto us. Listen to our call. Accept affectionately my supplications O King, with thy general and ministers ever remain ready for a big battle. (179)[2]

५. इन्द्रस्य नु प्र वोचं वीर्याणि यानि चकार प्रथमानि वज्री ।
अहन्नहिमन्वपस्ततर्द प्र वक्षणा अभिनत् पर्वतानाम् ॥

5. Now do I preach the manly deeds of a king, which the thunder-wielder should perform, as of first priority. Just as lightning disperses the cloud, and makes the water flow, and shatters the rocks, so should a King kill the enemy of his subjects, dig canals for them and level down the breasts (uneven spots) of the mountains for his subjects to dwell upon. (180)[3]

६. अहन्नहिं पर्वते शिश्रियाणं त्वष्टास्मै वज्रं स्वर्यं ततक्ष ।
वाश्रा इव धेनवः स्यन्दमाना अञ्जः समुद्रमव जग्मुरापः ॥

6. Just as air forcibly attacks the cloud lying on the mountain, and the Sun intensifies the thundering lightning for the air, so should the king destroy his subjects' enemy, abiding in his well-knit state. Mechanics should prepare deadly instruments for the king. Just as lowing kine yield milk in rapid flow, so should the gliding streams of water flow downward to the ocean. (181)

७. वृषायमाणो अवृणीत सोमं त्रिकद्रुकेष्वपिबत् सुतस्य ।
आ सायकं मघवादत्त वज्रमहन्नेनं प्रथमजामहीनाम् ॥

7. Just as the Sun, like a raining cloud, takes up water from the oceans, and drinks the vapoury water in its three forms, so should the king, showering

[1]Griffith describes Bhrigu as a Rishi, regarded as the ancestor of the ancient race of Bhrigus. This is unacceptable as there is no history in the Vedas.

[2]Us and our refer to the subjects. My refers to a representative of the people.

[3]I refers to God.

happiness on the subjects, assume stately power, and spend the taxes collected, on improving his army, animals and the health of subjects.

Just as lightning with its dreadful thunderbolt, attacks the first formed cloud of waters, and makes it rain, so should the king, wielding deadly instruments, kill the leader of the slaughters of his subjects. (182)[1]

Chapter (Anuvāka) 2

HYMN VI

१. समास्त्वाग्न ऋतवो वर्धयन्तु संवत्सरा ऋषयो यानि सत्या ।
सं दिव्येन दीदिहि रोचनेन विश्वा आ भाहि प्रदिशश्चतस्रः ॥

1. O learned person, may months, seasons, years, knowers of Vedic interpretation and all the verities strengthen thee. May thou shine with celestial effulgence, and illumine all the four efficacious regions! (183)[2]

२. सं चेध्यस्वाग्ने प्र च वर्धयेममुच्च तिष्ठ महते सौभगाय ।
मा ते रिषन्नुपसत्तारो अग्ने ब्रह्माणस्ते यशसः सन्तु मान्ये ॥

2. Shine thou, O learned person, advance this seeker after knowledge, rise up erect for great and happy fortune. Be those uninjured who adore thee, O learned person, let thy learned associates attain to glory, and not the ignorant, voluptuous people. (184)[3]

३. त्वामग्ने वृणते ब्राह्मणा इमे शिवो अग्ने संवरणे भवा नः ।
सपत्नहाग्ने अभिमातिजिद् भव स्वे गये जागृह्यप्रयुच्छन् ॥

3. O learned person, these masters of the Vedas elect thee as their leader. Be thou propitious unto them in this election. Be thou the slayer of rivals and the queller of foes. Free from sloth, ever remain watchful in thy house. (185)[4]

४. क्षत्रेणाग्ने स्वेन सं रभस्व मित्रेणाग्ने मित्रधा यतस्व ।
सजातानां मध्यमेष्ठा राज्ञामग्ने विहव्यो दीदिहीह ॥

4. O King, exert with thy material resources. Behave towards your friend as a friend. Act as an umpire in the midst of your co-equals. Flash forth to be invoked by kings around thee. (186)[5]

५. अति निहो अति सृधोऽत्यचित्तीरति द्विषः ।
विश्वा ह्यग्ने दुरिता तर त्वमथास्मभ्यं सहवीरं रयिं दाः ॥

[1]Three forms: Lustre, Ray, Air, i.e., ज्योति, गौ, वायु.
[2]See *Yajur*, 27-1. The verse is applicable to God as well.
[3]See *Yajur*, 27-2.
[4]See *Yajur*, 27-3.
[5]See *Yajur*, 27-5.

5. O King, suppress wicked persons, subdue lust, overcome spiritual ignorance, banish mean sentiments. Drive away all sins. Vouchsafe us opulence with heroic sons. (187)[1]

HYMN VII

१. अघद्विष्टा देवजाता वीरुच्छपथयोपनी । आपो मलमिव प्राणैक्षीत्सर्वान् मच्छपथाँ अधि ॥

1. God's might, efficacious like medicine, hates sin, is adorned by the learned, averts angry utterances. It has washed from me all ignoble words, as water washes dirt. (188)

२. यश्च सापत्नः शपथो जाम्याः शपथश्च यः । ब्रह्मा यन्मन्युतः शपात् सर्वं तन्नो अधस्पदम् ॥

2. The rebuke of a rival, each rebuke of a female relative, rebuke uttered by an angry knower of the Vedas, all these we tread beneath our feet. (189)[2]

३. दिवो मूलमवततं पृथिव्या अध्युत्ततम् । तेन सहस्रकाण्डेन परि णः पाहि विश्वतः ॥

3. As rays come down from the Sun, spread themselves on the Earth, and shed lustre, so is the knowledge of God, in the shape of the Vedas, revealed by Him, and spread all over the Earth. O God, with this Vedic knowledge of innumerable branches, fully protect us from every side. (190)

४. परि मां परि मे प्रजां परि णः पाहि यद्धनम् ।
अरातिर्नो मा तारीन्मा नस्तारिषुरभिमातयः ॥

4. O God, guard me on all sides, guard my children, and all our wealth. Let no stingy foe overpower us. Let no proud adversary conquer us. (191)

५. शप्तारमेतु शपथो यः सुहार्त तेन नः सह । चक्षुर्मन्त्रस्य दुर्हार्दः पृष्टीरपि शृणीमसि ॥

5. Let censure return to the censurer. Let us befriend him whose heart is pure. Let us split the cruel villain's ribs, who harbours evil designs with his eye. (192)

HYMN VIII

१. उदगातां भगवती विचृतौ नाम तारके । वि क्षेत्रियस्य मुञ्चतामधमं पाशमुत्तमम् ॥

1. When Prāṇa and Apāna, two auspicious elevators of mankind, begin to work with full force, they release the soul, the dweller in the body, from its lowest and uppermost bond. (193)[3]

[1] See *Yajur*, 27-6.

[2] 'Tread beneath feet': Remain indifferent to, or unmindful of. Neglect them; and don't allow them touch us. We never deserve them.

[3] 'Lowest bond' means acts of sin, that lower, the soul 'Uppermost bond' means virtuous acts. When the soul through yoga attains to salvation, it is freed from its good and bad acts.

२. अपेयं रात्र्युच्छत्वपोच्छन्त्वभिकृत्वरी: । वीरुत् क्षेत्रियनाशन्यप क्षेत्रियमुच्छतु ।।

2. Let the dark night of ignorance vanish. Let the tormenting mental attitudes depart. May the knowledge of God, end this body in which dwells the soul, and release it from the bondage of this mortal frame. (194)[1]

३. बभ्रोरर्जुनकाण्डस्य यवस्य ते पलाल्या तिलस्य तिलपिञ्ज्या ।
वीरुत् क्षेत्रियनाशन्यप क्षेत्रियमुच्छतु ।।

3. Just as the tawny-brown and silvery seed of barley is separated from the husk, and sesamum from the stalk, so may the knowledge of God, end this body in which dwells the soul, and release it from the bondage of this mortal frame. (195)

४. नमस्ते लाङ्गलेभ्यो नम ईषायुगेभ्य: । वीरुत् क्षेत्रियनाशन्यप क्षेत्रियमुच्छतु ।।

4. O Yogi, we pay homage to thy eight limbs of yoga, which are as essential for mental concentration, as ploughs are for cultivation. We revere the yogis who yoke their soul with God, just as we appreciate the pole and yoke, so essential for agriculture. May the knowledge of God, end this body in which dwells the soul, and release it from the bondage of this mortal frame. (196)[2]

५. नम: सनिस्रसाक्षेभ्यो नम: संदेश्येऽभ्यो: ।
नम: क्षेत्रस्य पतये वीरुत् क्षेत्रियनाशन्यप क्षेत्रियमुच्छतु ।।

5. Homage to the yogis, the force of whose organs has been set at rest. Homage to those who excellently impart spiritual knowledge. Homage to the soul, the master of the body, and God, the master of the world. May the knowledge of God, end this body in which dwells the soul, and release it from the bondage of this mortal frame. (197)

HYMN IX

१. दशवृक्ष मुञ्चेमं रक्षसो ग्राह्या अधि यैनं जग्राह पर्वसु ।
अथो एनं वनस्पते जीवानां लोकमुन्नय ।।

1. Free this soul, O God, from the tempting snare of the demon of destructive ignorance, that has completely taken hold of it. O God, the Lord of souls, elevate this world of sentient beings. (198)[3]

[1]The Knowledge of God grants salvation and releases the soul from the bondage of the body. It refers to the souls.

[2]Eight limbs: Yama, Niyama, Āsana, Prānayāma, Pratayahāra, Dhārmā, Dhyāna, Smādhi. These limbs are the ploughs of a yogi. With these he cultivates his soul, as a farmer cultivates the field with his plough.

[3]दशवृक्ष (Dashvriksha) means God, that cuts asunder the ten prāṇas (breaths) that bind the soul. Vriksha is spoken of as God, and वन (vana) as soul in the Vedas and Upanishads. Here vana does not refer to a tree as some commentators interpret it.

२. आगादुदगादयं जीवानां व्रातमप्यगात् । अभूदु पुत्राणां पिता नृणां च भगवत्तमः ॥

2. This God is present in the world, but is above the worldly painful shackles. He reaches all the souls through omnipresence. O God, Thou art the Father of all souls, Thy sons, Thou art the Mightiest of all men. (199)

३. अधीतीरध्यगादयमधि जीवपुरा अगन् । शतं ह्यस्य भिषजः सहस्रमुत वीरुधः ॥

3. This soul assumes different abodes, and different citadels of living beings. It has got hundreds of gurus as its spiritual physicians and thousands of sermons as its spiritual medicines. (200)[1]

४. देवास्ते चीतिमविदन् ब्रह्माण उत वीरुधः । चीतिं ते विश्वे देवा अविदन् भूम्यामधि ॥

4. O soul, the learned, the Vedic scholars and the mothers who bear children, know the science of thy bodily structure. The way in which thou developest in the body, is known to all the enlightened persons on the earth. (201)

५. यश्चकार स निष्करत् स एव सुभिषक्तमः । स एव तुभ्यं भेषजानि कृणवद् भिषजा शुचिः ॥

5. God, who makes this body, perfects it as well. He is the deftest physician for all physical and mental afflictions. O soul in bondage, He creates different sorts of aids for healing thy ailments. Attain to purity, through the help of that Great Physician. (202)[2]

HYMN X

१. क्षेत्रियात् त्वा निर्ऋत्या जामिशंसाद् द्रुहो मुञ्चामि वरुणस्य पाशात् ।
अनागसं ब्रह्मणा त्वा कृणोमि शिवे ते द्यावापृथिवी उभे स्ताम् ॥

1. From family sickness, poverty, domestic calumny, malice, and God's punishment for sin, do I free and save thee. I render thee sinless through the knowledge of the Vedas. May both, the Earth and Heaven be auspicious to thee. (203)[3]

२. शं ते अग्निः सहाद्भिरस्तु शं सोमः सहौषधीभिः ।
एवाहं त्वां क्षेत्रियान्निर्ऋत्या जामिशंसाद् द्रुहो मुञ्चामि वरुणस्य पाशात् ।
अनागसं ब्रह्मणा त्वा कृणोमि शिवे ते द्यावापृथिवी उभे स्ताम् ॥

2. O sickness-stricken person, may fire with the waters be gracious to thee. Let the Sun and the Moon, with herbs be kind to thee. From family sickness, poverty, domestic calumny, malice, and God's punishment for sin,

[1] 'Abodes' means births 'citadels' means bodies.

[2] Ailments: Physical as well as spiritual.

[3] 'I' refers to a learned physician and 'thee' to a patient in distress.

do I free and save thee. I render thee sinless through the knowledge of the Vedas. May both the Earth and Heaven be auspicious to thee! (204)

३. शं ते वातो अन्तरिक्षे वयो धाच्छं ते भवन्तु प्रदिशश्चतस्रः ।
एवाहं त्वां क्षेत्रियान्निर्ऋत्या जामिशंसाद् द्रुहो मुञ्चामि वरुणस्य पाशात् ।
अनागसं ब्रह्मणा त्वा कृणोमि शिवे ते द्यावापृथिवी उभे स्ताम् ।

3. O patient, may kind wind in the atmosphere prolong thy age. To thee may heaven's four quarters be auspicious. From family sickness, poverty, domestic calumny, malice, and God's punishment for sin, do I free and save thee. I render thee sinless through the knowledge of the Vedas. May both, Earth and Heaven be auspicious to thee! (205)[1]

४. इमा या देवीः प्रदिशश्चतस्रो वातपत्नीरभि सूर्यो विचष्टे ।
एवाहं त्वां क्षेत्रियान्निर्ऋत्या जामिशंसाद् द्रुहो मुञ्चामि वरुणस्य पाशात् ।
अनागसं ब्रह्मणा त्वा कृणोमि शिवे ते द्यावापृथिवी उभे स्ताम् ॥

4. O patient, may the lustrous four regions, full of pure fresh air, whom the Sun looks kindly, be kind to thee. From family sickness, poverty, domestic calumny, malice, and God's punishment for sin, do I free and save thee. I render thee sinless through the knowledge of the Vedas. May both, the Earth and Heaven be auspicious to thee! (206)[2]

५. तासु त्वान्तर्जरस्या दधामि प्र यक्ष्म एतु निर्ऋतिः पराचैः ।
एवाहं त्वां क्षेत्रियान्निर्ऋत्या जामिशंसाद् द्रुहो मुञ्चामि वरुणस्य पाशात् ।
अनागसं ब्रह्मणा त्वा कृणोमि शिवे ते द्यावापृथिवी उभे स्ताम् ॥

5. O patient, for long life, in the midst of these directions I set thee. May consumption and poverty pass away. From family sickness, poverty domestic calumny, malice, and God's punishment for sin, do I free and save thee. I render thee sinless through the knowledge of the Vedas. May both, the Earth and Heaven be auspicious to thee! (207)

६. अमुक्था यक्ष्माद् दुरितादवद्याद् द्रुहः पाशाद् ग्राह्याश्चोदमुक्थाः ।
एवाहं त्वां क्षेत्रियान्निर्ऋत्या जामिशंसाद् द्रुहो मुञ्चामि वरुणस्य पाशात् ।
अनागसं ब्रह्मणा त्वा कृणोमि शिवे ते द्यावापृथिवी उभे स्ताम् ॥

6. O patient, thou hast been freed from Pthisis, from sin, from ignoble deed, from the snare of malice, and from the pain that weakens the body. From family sickness, poverty, domestic calumny, malice, and God's punishment for sin, do I free and save thee. I render thee sinless through the knowledge of the vedas. May both, the Earth and Heaven be auspicious to thee! (208)

[1]Thy and thee refer to the patient.

[2]The physician advises the patient to pass his time mostly in the open, fresh air to attain to longevity, and be free from disease.

७. अहा अरातिमविदः स्योनमप्यभूर्भद्रे सुकृतस्य लोके ।
एवाहं त्वां क्षेत्रियान्निर्ऋत्या जामिशंसाद् द्रुहो मुञ्चामि वरुणस्य पाशात् ।
अनागसं ब्रह्मणा त्वा कृणोमि शिवे ते द्यावापृथिवी उभे स्ताम् ।।

7. O patient, thou hast abandoned the foe-like disease thou hast found joy, always follow the happy path of virtue. From family sickness, poverty, domestic calumny, malice, and God's punishment for sin, do I free and save thee. I render thee sinless through the knowledge of the Vedas. May both, the Earth and Heaven be auspicious to thee! (209)

८. सूर्यमृतं तमसो ग्राह्या अधि देवा मुञ्चन्तो असृजन्निरेणसः ।
एवाहं त्वां क्षेत्रियान्निर्ऋत्या जामिशंसाद् द्रुहो मुञ्चामि वरुणस्य पाशात् ।
अनागसं ब्रह्मणा त्वा कृणोमि शिवे ते द्यावापृथिवी उभे स्ताम् ।।

8. The learned, being free from sin, releasing others from the ills arising through ignorance, and the pain that results from disease and sticks to the body, describe sunlight as a true medicine for dispelling all maladies. From family sickness, poverty, domestic calumny, malice, and God's punishment for sin, do I free and save thee. I render thee sinless through the knowledge of the vedas. May both, the Earth and Heaven be auspicious to thee. (210)[1]

Chapter (Anuvāka) 3

HYMN XI

१. दूष्या दूषिरसि हेत्या हेतिरसि मेन्या मेनिरसि । आप्नुहि श्रेयांसमति समं क्राम ।।

1. O soul, thou art the averter of evil, strong like a weapon, and powerful like a missile. Attain to superiority; surpass thine equal! (211)

२. स्रक्त्योऽसि प्रतिसरोऽसि प्रत्यभिचरणोऽसि । आप्नुहि श्रेयांसमति समं क्राम ।।

2. O soul, thou art active, thou art progressive, thou art an assailant on vice. Attain to superiority; surpass thine equal. (212)[2]

३. प्रति तमभि चर योऽस्मान् द्वेष्टि यं वयं द्विष्मः । आप्नुहि श्रेयांसमति समं क्राम ।।

3. O soul, attack the man who hates us, whom we dislike. Attain to superiority; surpass thine equal ! (213)[3]

[1]In this Hymn God has instructed men to observe celibacy, lead a virtuous life, use efficacious medicines, breathe pure, fresh air, and live in well ventilated houses exposed to sunlight, for being free from various terrible diseases like consumption, epilepsy and other family maladies. Dark, dingy houses, that serve as a nidus for the propagation of germs of various diseases, should not be used for habitation.

[2]Griffith translates Sraktya as a holy tree, which is unintelligible.

[3]He, who hates godly persons, or whom virtuous persons, dislike, should be subdued.

४. सूरिरसि वर्चोधा असि तनूपानोऽसि । आप्नुहि श्रेयांसमति समं क्राम ॥

4. O soul, thou art full of knowledge, thou art the giver of splendour, thou art the defender of our bodies. Attain to superiority, surpass thine equal! (214)

५. शुक्रोऽसि भ्राजोऽसि स्वरसि ज्योतिरसि । आप्नुहि श्रेयांसमति समं क्राम ॥

5. O soul, thou art pure, thou art splendid, thou art spiritually strong, thou art lustrous. Attain to superiority; surpass thine equal! (215)

HYMN XII

१. द्यावापृथिवी उर्व१न्तरिक्षं क्षेत्रस्य पत्न्युरुगायोऽद्भुतः ।
उतान्तरिक्षमुरु वातगोपं त इह तप्यन्तां मयि तप्यमाने ॥

1. May the Earth and Heaven, the spacious Firmament, God, the Protector of the three regions, the wonderful immortal soul, praised by the learned, and the animate world dependent on air, help me in my religious austerity. (216)[1]

२. इदं देवाः शृणुत ये यज्ञिया स्थ भरद्वाजो मह्यमुक्थानि शंसति ।
पाशे स बद्धो दुरिते नि युज्यतां यो अस्माकं मन इदं हिनस्ति ॥

2. Ye learned persons, engaged in the performance of philanthropic deeds, listen to my word. God, the protector of the world, with food, strength and knowledge, preaches the vedic verses for me. May foe-like lust and anger, that degrade this soul of ours be kept strictly under control, bound in strong fetters! (217)[2]

३. इदमिन्द्र शृणुहि सोमप यत् त्वाहृदा शोचता जोहवीमि ।
वृश्चामि तं कुलिशेनेव वृक्षं यो अस्माकं मन इदं हिनस्ति ॥

3. O God, the Nourisher of the universe, listen to this prayer of mine, when I invoke Thee with pure heart. May I smite with the hatchet of knowledge, the internal spiritual foe of infatuation, as a tree is felled with a hatchet. (218)

४. अशीतिभिस्तिसृभिः सामगेभिरादित्येभिर्वसुभिरङ्गिरोभिः ।
इष्टापूर्तमवतु नः पितृणामामुं ददे हरसा दैव्येन ॥

4. May the acts of benevolence performed by many Āditya, Vasu, Rudra

[1]Three regions: Earth, Heaven, Firmament.

[2]Griffith and Sāyana translate Bhardwāja as the great Rishi of ancient times. The word means God, who sustains the universe with food, strength and knowledge, भरद्वाजः=भरत्+वाजः भरत् means पोषक sustainer, वाजः means food, power and knowledge; अन्न, बल, ज्ञान.

Brahmcharis, who know the Sāmaveda, guard us. With divine dignity I realise this noble act, performed by the Brahmcharies, fathers unto us. (219)[1]

५. द्यावापृथिवी अनु मा दीधीथां विश्वे देवासो अनु मा रभध्वम् ।
अङ्गिरस: पितर: सोम्यास: पापमार्छत्वपकामस्य कर्ता ।।

5. O Heaven and Earth, bestow favour on me. O, all forces of nature stand on my side and help me. O learned persons, O doers of noble deeds, O aged persons, the doer of a misdeed must suffer. (220)

६. अतीव यो मरुतो मन्यते नो ब्रह्म वा यो निन्दिषत् क्रियमाणम् ।
तपूंषि तस्मै वृजिनानि सन्तु ब्रह्मद्विषं द्यौरभिसंतपाति ।।

6. Whoever assumes the airs of superiority and scorns us, or blames the vedic knowledge on which we act; let his own wicked deeds be fires to burn him, let God consume the man who is the enemy of knowledge. (221)

७. सप्त प्राणानष्टौ मन्यस्तांस्ते वृश्चामि ब्रह्मणा । अया यमस्य सादनमग्निदूतो अरङ्कृत: ।।

7. O soul, I release thee from thy sevenfold vital breath, and eight marrows through the knowledge of the vedas. Depending upon the Omniscient God, adorned with thy virtuous acts, go to the final resort of God, the Governor of the universe. (222)[2]

८. आ दधामि ते पदं समिद्धे जातवेदसि । अग्नि: शरीरं वेवेष्ट्वसुं वागपि गच्छतु ।।

8. O soul, I set thy innate nature in the Refulgent Omniscient God. May yogic fire pervade this physical body, and voice be absorbed in breath. (223)[3]

HYMN XIII

१. आयुर्दा अग्ने जरसं वृणानो घृतप्रतीको घृतपृष्ठो अग्ने ।
घृतं पीत्वा मधु चारु गव्यं पितेव पुत्रानभि रक्षतादिमम् ।।

1. O Wise God, Thou art the giver of life, averting old age, O God, Refulgent like the Sun, Thou art the asylum for all lustres. Just as a father

[1]Āditya Brahmchari is he who observes celibacy for forty eight years, Vasu is he, who remains celibate for 24 years, and he who observes celibacy for 36 years is Rudra. These Brahmchari's are our fathers, grandfathers and great grandfathers by virtue of their knowledge vide *Manu*, 3-284. Sāyana interprets अशीतिभिस्तिसृभि: as reciters of 80 verses of the *Sāmaveda*, in three different metres, i.e., Gāyatri, Ushnik, and Brihati. Pt. Khem Karan Das Trivedi interprets the phrase, as three pervading powers, i.e., God, Soul and Matter. Pt. Jaidev Vidyalankar interprets the word as many, innumerable.

[2]I refers to God, Final resort means salvation. Sevenfold vital breath is drawn through two eyes, two ears, two nostrils and mouth. Eight marrows: one in each arm, hand, leg and foot.

[3]I refers to a yogi, who controls his organs, absorbs his soul in God through meditation, and attains to salvation.

nourishes his sons by making them drink savoury, nice cow's milk, so pray, protect this newly initiated Brahmchari by making him acquire the sweet, excellent spiritual knowledge! (224)[1]

२. परि धत्त धत्त नो वर्चसेमं जरामृत्युं कृणुत दीर्घमायुः ।
बृहस्पतिः प्रायच्छद् वास एतत् सोमाय राज्ञे परिधातवा उ ॥

2. O learned persons, nourish your sons nicely, by making them lead a celibate life. Make this Brahmchari of ours full of splendour; give him long life, and death after he becomes sufficiently old. God has granted this body to the lustrous soul to dwell in! (225)[2]

३. परीदं वासो अधिथाः स्वस्तयेऽभूर्गृष्टीनामभिशस्तिपा उ ।
शतं च जीव शरदः पुरूची रायश्च पोषमुपसंव्ययस्व ॥

3. O Brahmchari, thou hast clothed thyself in this garment for our welfare. Be thou the saviour of mankind from ruin. Live thou for a hundred years, nay even more and wrap thee in prosperity of riches! (226)

४. एह्यश्मानमा तिष्ठाश्मा भवतु ते तनूः । कृण्वन्तु विश्वे देवा आयुष्टे शरदः शतम् ॥

4. O Brahmchari, come near the Guru, put your foot upon the steady stone, depend upon God, fixed like a rock, and *Banisher of miseries.* Make your body strong like a stone. May all the learned persons make thy life a hundred years long. (227)

५. यस्य ते वासः प्रथमवास्यं१ हरामस्तं त्वा विश्वेऽवन्तु देवाः ।
तं त्वा भ्रातरः सुवृधा वर्धमानमनु जायन्तां बहवः सुजातम् ॥

5. O Brahmchari may all learned persons protect thee, for whom we bring raiment to be worn in the first Ashrama. May many thriving fellow-students follow thee, scion of a noble family, and ever marching on the path of advancement. (228)

HYMN XIV

१. निःसालां धृष्णुं धिषणमेकवाद्यां जिघत्स्व१म् । सर्वाश्चण्डस्य नप्त्यो१ नाशयामः सदान्वाः ॥

1. We exterminate aimless wandering, obstinacy, violence, poverty and gluttony habits which are the progeny of indignation and avarice, and conduce to mutual quarrel. (229)

२. निर्वो गोष्ठादजामसि निरक्षान्निरुपानसात् । निर्वो मगुन्द्या दुहितरो गृहेभ्यश्चातयामहे ॥

2. O evil habits, the daughters of joy-killing ill desire, we drive you out of

[1]See *Yajur*, 35-17.

[2]Just as a man puts on dress, so does soul accept the body as its dress.

our heart, organs and the body. We frighten and chase you from our homes. (230)[1]

३. असौ यो अधराद् गृहस्तत्र सन्त्वराय्यः । तत्र सेदिर्न्युच्यतु सर्वाश्च यातुधान्यः ॥

3. There, in a house situated in a low, dark place, reside calamities, dejection, despair and all sorts of diseases. (231)[2]

४. भूतपतिर्निरजत्विन्द्रश्चेतः सदान्वाः । गृहस्य बुध्न आसीनास्ता इन्द्रो वज्रेणाधि तिष्ठतु ॥

4. May God, the Lord of creatures, and soul, drive away hence these calamities. May soul control with the strength of celibacy, these maladies, that reside in the head, the pivot of the body, the home of the soul. (232)

५. यदि स्थ क्षेत्रियाणां यदि वा पुरुषेषिताः । यदि स्थ दस्युभ्यो जाता नश्यतेतः सदान्वाः ॥

5. O maladies, whether Ye result from physical or ancestral ailments, or the company of ignoble persons, or are sprung out of cherishing evil thoughts, get Ye away from here. (233)

६. परि धामान्यासामाशुर्गाष्ठामिवासरन् । अजैषं सर्वानाजीन्वो नश्यतेतः सदान्वाः ॥

6. Just as a fleet-foot horse reaches his destination, so have I discovered the real causes of these maladies. O maladies, I have conquered ye in all struggles, get ye away from here! (234)

HYMN XV

१. यथा द्यौश्च पृथिवी च न बिभीतो न रिष्यतः । एवा मे प्राण मा बिभेः ॥

1. As Heaven and Earth are not afraid, and never suffer loss or harm; even so, my spirit, fear not thou. (235)

२. यथाहश्च रात्री च न बिभीतो न रिष्यतः । एवा मे प्राण मा बिभेः ॥

2. As Day and Night are not afraid, nor ever suffer loss or harm; even so my spirit, fear not thou. (236)

३. यथा सूर्यश्च चन्द्रश्च न बिभीतो न रिष्यतः । एवा मे प्राण मा बिभेः ॥

3. As Sun and Moon are not afraid nor ever suffer harm or loss; even so my spirit, fear not thou. (237)

४. यथा ब्रह्म च क्षत्रं च न बिभीतो न रिष्यतः । एवा मे प्राण मा बिभेः ॥

[1]Magundi has been interpreted by Griffith as a female evil spirit, perhaps the wife of Chanda and mother of his progeny. This explanation is illogical as there is no history in the Vedas. The word means ill desire that destroys our happiness.

[2]Griffith translates Arāyās as female fiends and night hags. The word means calamities, mishaps.

4. As spiritual force and mundane power fear not, nor ever suffer loss or harm; even so, my spirit, fear not thou. (238)

५. यथा सत्यं चानृतं च न बिभीतो न रिष्यतः । एवा मे प्राण मा बिभेः ॥

5. As Truth and perfect frankness fear not, and never suffer loss or harm; even so, my spirit, fear not thou. (239)[1]

६. यथा भूतं च भव्यं च न बिभीतो न रिष्यतः । एवा मे प्राण मा बिभेः ॥

6. As Past and Future fear not, and never suffer loss or harm; even so, my spirit, fear not thou. (240)

HYMN XVI

१. प्राणापानौ मृत्योर्मा पातं स्वाहा ।

1. Guard me from death, Inhaling and Exhaling! This is well said. (241)

२. द्यावापृथिवी उपश्रुत्या मा पातं स्वाहा ।

2. Guard me, O Heaven and Earth, by granting me full power of hearing! This is a nice prayer. (242)

३. सूर्य चक्षुषा मा पाहि स्वाहा ।

3. O Sun, guard me by granting me the power of sight! This is a nice prayer. (243)[2]

४. अग्ने वैश्वानर विश्वैर्मा देवैः पाहि स्वाहा ।

4. O God, the Leader of all, preserve me through all learned persons! This is a nice prayer. (244)

५. विश्वम्भर विश्वेन मा भरसा पाहि स्वाहा ।

5. O All-sustainer, preserve me with Thy power of nourishing. I dedicate myself to Thee. (245)[3]

HYMN XVII

१. ओजोऽस्योजो मे दाः स्वाहा ।

1. O God, Power art Thou, give me power! This is my humble prayer. (246)

[1]The verse may also be translated thus. As love for Truth and denial of untruth fear not, and never suffer loss or harm; even so, my spirit, fear not thou See *Yajur*, 19-77.

[2]The verse can also be interpreted thus. O God, guard me by granting me the light of knowledge! May a yogi acquire power by thus addressing God.

[3]All-sustainer: God. The word svāhā in this hymn is used for prayer, supplication, dedication and nice saying.

२. सहोऽसि सहो मे दाः स्वाहा ।

2. O God, Endurance art Thou, give me endurance! This is my humble prayer. (247)

३. बलमसि बलं मे दाः स्वाहा ।

3. O God, strength art Thou, give me strength! This is my humble prayer. (248)

४. आयुरस्यायुर्मे दाः स्वाहा ।

4. O God, Life art Thou, give me life! This is my humble prayer. (249)

५. श्रोत्रमसि श्रोत्रं मे दाः स्वाहा ।

5. O God, Ear art Thou, give me hearing! This is my humble prayer. (250)[1]

६. चक्षुरसि चक्षुर्मे दाः स्वाहा ।

6. O God, Eye art Thou, give me eyes. This is my humble prayer. (251)[2]

७. परिपाणमसि परिपाणं मे दाः स्वाहा ।

7. O God, Thou art the Nourisher of the universe, give me the strength to nourish my organs and subjects! This is my humble prayer. (252)

Chapter (Anuvāka) 4

HYMN XVIII

१. भ्रातृव्यक्षयणमसि भ्रातृव्यचातनं मे दाः स्वाहा ।

1. O God, Destroyer of foes art Thou, grant me the strength to quell my internal foes! This is my humble prayer. (253)[3]

२. सपत्नक्षयणमसि सपत्नचातनं मे दाः स्वाहा ।

2. O God, the rival's is ruiner art Thou, give me the strength to drive my rivals away! This is my humble prayer. (254)

३. अरायक्षयणमस्यरायचातनं मे दाः स्वाहा ।

3. O God, Thou art the Banisher of poverty, grant me the strength to keep poverty at bay. This is my humble prayer. (255)

[1]God listens to the supplications of mankind. I should listen to the Vedas and the requests of the poor, needy persons.

[2]God is the Seer. May He grant me foresight. In the Purush Sukta Yajur 31st chapter, *Rigveda*, 10-90-1. God is spoken of as सहस्राक्षः i.e., possessing the power of a thousand eyes. God is Far-seeing may He grant me foresight.

[3]My foes: spiritual enemies like lust, anger, avarice, pride, etc.

४. पिशाचक्षयणमसि पिशाचचातनं मे दाः स्वाहा ॥

4. O God, Thou art the queller of the violent, grant me the strength to suppress violence! This is my humble prayer. (256)

५. सदान्वाक्षयणमसि सदान्वाचातनं मे दाः स्वाहा ।

5. O God, Thou art the Averter of misfortunes, grant me the strength to avert misfortunes! This is my humble request. (257)

HYMN XIX

१. अग्ने यत् ते तपस्तेन तं प्रति तप यो३स्मान् द्वेष्टि यं वयं द्विष्मः ।

1. O God, with Thy power of reforming sinners, reform him, who hates us, or whom we do not love! (258)

२. अग्ने यत् ते हरस्तेन तं प्रति हर यो३स्मान् द्वेषि यं वयं द्विष्मः ।

2. O God, with Thy strength of preventing vice, dissuade him, who hates us, or whom we do not love! (259)

३. अग्ने यत् ते ऽर्चिस्तेन तं प्रत्यर्च यो३स्मान् द्वेष्टि यं वयं द्विष्मः ।

3. O God, with Thy light of knowledge, enlighten him, who hates us, or whom we do not love! (260)

४. अग्ने यत् ते शोचिस्तेन तं प्रति शोच यो३स्मान् द्वेष्टि यं वयं द्विष्मः ॥

4. O God, with Thy purifying power, purify him, who hates us, or whom we do not love! (261)

५. अग्ने यत् ते तेजस्तेन तमतेजसं कृणु यो३स्मान् द्वेष्टि यं वयं द्विष्मः ।

5. O God, with Thy Fiery nature, make him calm, free from passion, who hates us, or whom we do not love. (262)

HYMN XX

१. वायो यत् ते तपस्तेन तं प्रति तप यो३स्मान् द्वेष्टि यं वयं द्विष्मः ।

1. O God, Omnipresent like vayu, with Thy power of penitence, let him repent for his misdeed, who hates us, or whom we do not love. (263)[1]

२. वायो यत् ते हरस्तेन तं प्रति हर यो३स्मान् द्वेष्टि यं वयं द्विष्मः ।

2. O God, with Thy Righteous indignation take him under Thy shelter and make him virtuous who hates us, or whom we do not love! (264)

[1]In hymns XX, XXI, XXII and XXIII, the words Vayu, Surya, Chandra and Āpa are used for God.

३. वायो यत् तेऽर्चिस्तेन तं प्रत्यर्च योऽ३स्मान् द्वेष्टि यं वयं द्विष्मः ।

3. O God, with Thy Lustre of wisdom, make him wise, who hates us, or whom we do not love! (265)

४. वायो यत् ते शोचिस्तेन तं प्रति शोच यो३स्मान् द्वेष्टि यं वयं द्विष्मः ।

4. O God, with Thy Refulgence, grant him, who hates us, or whom we do not love, light, so that he may abandon hatred. (266)

५. वायो यत् ते तेजस्तेन तमतेजसं कृणु यो३स्मान् द्वेष्टि यं वयं द्विष्मः ॥

5. O God, with Thy passionate power, make him, who hates us, or whom we do not love, free from violence. (267)

HYMN XXI

१. सूर्य यत् ते तपस्तेन तं प्रति तप यो३स्मान् द्वेष्टि यं वयं द्विष्मः ।

1. O God All-Creating All-Goading like the Sun, with Thy power of penitence, let him repent for his misdeed, who hates us, or whom we do not love! (268)

२. सूर्य यत् ते हरस्तेन तं प्रति हर यो३स्मान् द्वेष्टि यं वयं द्विष्मः ।

2. O God, All-Creating, All-Goading like the Sun, with Thy Righteous indignation take him under Thy shelter and make him virtuous, who hates us, or whom we do not love! (269)

३. सूर्य यत् तेऽर्चिस्तेन तं प्रत्यर्च यो३स्मान् द्वेष्टि यं वयं द्विष्मः ।

3. O God, All-Creating, All-Goading like the Sun, with Thy Lustre of wisdom, make him wise, who hates us, or whom we do not love! (270)[3]

४. सूर्य यत् ते शोचिस्तेन तं प्रति शोच यो३स्मान् द्वेष्टि यं वयं द्विष्मः ।

4. O God. All-Creating, All-Goading like the Sun, with Thy Refulgence, grant him, who hates us, or whom we do not love, light, so that we may abandon hatred! (271)

५. सूर्य यत् ते तेजस्तेन तमतेजसं कृणु यो३स्मान् द्वेष्टि यं वयं द्विष्मः ।

5. O God, All-Creating, All-Goading like the Sun with Thy Passionate power, make him, who hates us, or whom we do not love, sober and non-violent. (272)

HYMN XXII

१. चन्द्र यत् ते तपस्तेन तं प्रति तप यो३स्मान् द्वेष्टि यं वयं द्विष्मः ।

1. O God, the Gladdener of the universe like the Moon, with Thy power of penitence, let him repent for his misdeed, who hates us, or whom we do not love! (273)

२. चन्द्र यत् ते हरस्तेन तं प्रति हर योऽस्मान् द्वेष्टि यं वयं द्विष्मः ।

2. O God, the Gladdener of the universe like the Moon, with Thy Righteous indignation, take him under thy shelter and make him virtuous, who hates us, or whom we do not love. (274)

३. चन्द्र यत् तेऽर्चिस्तेन तं प्रत्यर्च योऽस्मान् द्वेष्टि यं वयं द्विष्मः ।

3. O God, the Gladdener of the universe, like the Moon, with Thy Lustre of wisdom, make him wise, who hates us, or whom we do not love! (275)

४. चन्द्र यत् ते शोचिस्तेन तं प्रति शोच योऽस्मान् द्वेष्टि यं वयं द्विष्मः ।

4. O God, the Gladdener of the universe, like the Moon, with Thy Refulgence, grant him, who hates us, or whom we do not love, light, so that he may abandon hatred. (276)

५. चन्द्र यत् ते तेजस्तेन तमतेजसं कृणु योऽस्मान् द्वेष्टि यं वयं द्विष्मः ।

5. O God, the Gladdener of the universe like the Moon, with Thy Passionate power, make him, who hates us, or whom we do not love, sober and non-violent. (277)

HYMN XXIII

१. आपो यद् वस्तपस्तेन तं प्रति तपत योऽस्मान् द्वेष्टि यं वयं द्विष्मः ।

1. O God, the Goal and shelter of all, with Thy power of penitence, let him repent for his misdeed who hates us, or whom we do not love! (278)

२. आपो यद् वो हरस्तेन तं प्रति हरत योऽस्मान् द्वेष्टि यं वयं द्विष्मः ।

2. O God, the Goal and shelter of all, with Thy Righteous indignation, take him under Thy shelter and make him virtuous, who hates us, or whom we do not love. (279)

३. आपो यद् वोऽर्चिस्तेन तं प्रत्यर्चत योऽस्मान् द्वेष्टि यं वयं द्विष्मः ।

3. O God, the Goal and Shelter of all, with Thy Lustre of wisdom, make him wise, who hates us, or whom we do not love! (280)

४. आपो यद् वः शोचिस्तेन तं प्रति शोचत योऽस्मान् द्वेष्टि यं वयं द्विष्मः ।

4. O God, the Goal and Shelter of all, with Thy Refulgence, grant him, who hates us, or whom we do not love, light, so that he may abandon hatred. (281)

५. आपो यद् वस्तेजस्तेन तमतेजसं कृणुत योऽस्मान् द्वेष्टि यं वयं द्विष्मः ।

5. O God, the Goal and Shelter of all, with Thy Passionate power, make him, who hates us, or whom we do not love, sober and non-violent! (282)

HYMN XXIV

१. शेरभक शेरभ पुनर्वो यन्तु यातवः पुनर्हेतिः किमीदिनः ।
यस्य स्थ तमत्त यो वः प्राहैत् तमत्त स्वा मांसान्यत्त ॥

1. O cruel murderer, O slaughterer, O mala-fide critics may all your distressing deeds and your weapon fall back upon you. You eat him, who befriends you. You eat him, who shows you the right path as a preacher. You eat the flesh of your own kith and kin. (283)

२. शेवृधक शेवृध पुनर्वो यन्तु यातवः पुनर्हेतिः किमीदिनः ।
यस्य स्थ तमत्त यो वः प्राहैत् तमत्त स्वा मांसान्यत्त ॥

2. O master of violence, O destroyer of peace, O mala-fide critics, may all your distressing deeds, and your weapon, fall back upon you. You eat him, who befriends you. You eat him, who shows you the right path, as a preacher. You eat the flesh of your own kith and kin! (284)

३. म्रोकानुम्रोक पुनर्वो यन्तु यातवः पुनर्हेतिः किमीदिनः ।
यस्य स्थ तमत्त यो वः प्राहैत् तमत्त स्वा मांसान्यत्त ॥

3. O thief, O friend of a thief, O mala-fide critics, may all your distressing deeds, and your weapon, fall back upon you. You eat him, who befriends you. You eat him, who shows you the right path, as a preacher. You eat the flesh of your own kith and kin! (285)

४. सर्पानुसर्प पुनर्वो यन्तु यातवः पुनर्हेतिः किमीदिनः ।
यस्य स्थ तमत्त यो वः प्राहैत् तमत्त स्वा मांसान्यत्त ॥

4. O crooked person, O friend of a crooked person, O mala-fide critics, may all your distressing deeds, and your weapon, fall back upon you, you eat him, who befriends you, eat him, who shows you the right path as a preacher. You eat the flesh of your own kith and kin. (286)

५. जूर्णि पुनर्वो यन्तु यातवः पुनर्हेतिः किमीदिनीः ।
यस्य स्थ तमत्त यो वः प्राहैत् तमत्त स्वा मांसान्यत्त ।

5. O depraved woman, the destroyer of thyself and others like a she erpent, O mala-fide critics, may all your distressing deeds, and your wea on, fall back upon you. You eat him, who befriends you. You eat him, who shows you the right path, as a preacher. You eat the flesh of your own kith and kin. (287)

६. उपब्दे पुनर्वो यन्तु यातवः पुनर्हेतिः किमीदिनीः ।
यस्य स्थ तमत्त यो वः प्राहैत् तमत्त स्वा मांसान्यत्त ॥

6. O pugnacious, adulterous woman, O mala-fide critics, may all your distressing deeds, and your weapon, fall back upon you. You eat him, who be-

friends you. You eat him, who shows you the right path, as a preacher. Ye eat the flesh of your own kith and kin! (288)

७. अर्जुनि पुनर्वो यन्तु यातवः पुनर्हेतिः किमीदिनीः ।
यस्य स्थ तमत्त यो वः प्राहैत् तमत्त स्वा मांसान्यत्त ॥

7. O revengeful woman, who earns money through immoral practices, O mala-fide critics, may all your distressing deeds, and your weapon, fall back upon you. You eat him, who befriends you. You eat him, who shows you the right path, as a preacher. Ye eat the flesh of your own kith and kin! (289)

८. भरूजि पुनर्वो यन्तु यातवः पुनर्हेतिः किमीदिनीः ।
यस्य स्थ तमत्त यो वः प्राहैत् तमत्त स्वा मांसान्यत्त ॥

8. O fraudulent woman, who pains the hearts of others with mean words, O mala-fide critics, may all your distressing deeds, and your weapon, fall back upon you. You eat him, who befriends you. You eat him, who shows you the right path, as a preacher. Ye eat the flesh of your own kith and kin! (290)[1]

HYMN XXV

१. शं नो देवी पृश्निपर्ण्यशं निर्ऋत्या अकः । उग्रा हि कण्वजम्भनी तामभक्षि सहस्वतीम् ॥

1. God's divine power, that guards the Sun and Earth, brings us joy, and woe to an epidemic. Fierce crusher of sin is she. Her have I adored. (291)[2]

२. सहमानेयं प्रथमा पृश्निपर्ण्यजायत । तयाहं दुर्णाम्नां शिरो वृश्चामि शकुनेरिव ॥

2. This is God's victorious power, the guardian of the Sun and Earth, was present in the beginning. With her aid, I cleave the head of infamous vices, as it were a bird's. (292)[3]

[1]The verses of this hymn can be interpreted spiritually, for abandoning evil motives, and ignoble tendencies. In that case, the primary words used in the verses will mean as this:

(1) शेरभक =Violence
(2) शेवृधक =Avarice
(3) अर्जुनी =Revenge
(4) भरुजी =Back-biting

[2]पृश्निपर्णी means the power of God, that guards the Sun and Earth, पृश्निः=सूर्यः, पृथिवी ।३३।६। पर्णीः पिर्त्ति पालयति.

Prishniparni is also the name of a medicine, that removes cholera and other diseases. Its leaves are like the disc of the Sun. Its use cures diseases and grants health and joy. Griffith describes Kanvyas as a class of evil spirits. There is no history in the Vedas. The interpretation is illogical. The word means sin.

[3]With the aid of the victorious power of God, 'I remove all vices as easily as is cleft the head of a tiny bird without the use of a sharp weapon. दुर्णाम्नाम् may also mean foul, loathsome diseases like piles, leprosy, etc.

३. अरायमसृक्पावानं यश्च स्फाति जिहीर्षति । गर्भादं कण्वं नाशय पृश्निपर्णि सहस्व च ।।

3. O Divine Power of God, destroy and quell the disease, that brings abortion, takes away the beauty of the body, sucks our blood and wants to retard our development. (293)[1]

४. गिरिमेनाँ आ वेशय कण्वाञ्जीवितयोपनान् । तांस्त्वं देवि पृश्निपर्ण्यग्निरिवानुदहन्निहि ।।

4. O Divine Power of God, drive and imprison in an inaccessible place, these sins, the harassers of life; follow them, consuming them like fire. (294)[2]

५. पराच एनान् प्र णुद कण्वाञ्जीवितयोपनान् ।
तमांसि यत्र गच्छन्ति तत् क्रव्यादो अजीगमम् ।।

5. O God, drive Thou away these sins, the harassers of life. Whither the shades of darkness go, thither I send the diseases that feed on flesh. (295)[3]

HYMN XXVI

१. एह यन्तु पशवो ये परेयुर्वायुर्येषां सहचारं जुजोष ।
त्वष्टा येषां रूपधेयानि वेदास्मिन् तान् गोष्ठे सविता नि यच्छतु ।।

1. Let the cattle that have wandered come back home, upon whom soft breeze has attended and delighted and refreshed them. Whose forms and figures are well known to a prudent cowherd. Let the cowherd drive these cattle within this stable. (296)[4]

२. इमं गोष्ठं पशवः सं स्रवन्तु बृहस्पतिरानयतु प्रजानन् ।
सिनीवाली नयत्वाग्रमेषामाजग्मुषो अनुमते निं यच्छ ।।

2. Let the beasts stream together to this cow-pen. Let the cow-herd, who recognises the beasts, bring them hither! Let the wife of the cowherd, who feeds the beasts, welcome them back. O intelligent cowherd's wife, enclose them, when they have come! (297)

३. सं सं स्रवन्तु पशवः समश्वाः समु पूरुषाः ।
सं धान्यऽस्य या स्फातिः संस्राव्येऽण हविषा जुहोमि ।।

3. Together stream the cattle, stream together horses and the men! Let all growth of grain be simultaneous with tender devotion. I accept the responsibility of looking after them. (298)[5]

[1]The verse may be applied to the medicine Prishniparni.

[2]In the case of Prishniparni as a medicine, कण्वान् will mean diseases.

[3]Foul diseases prevail in dark places, free from the light of the Sun. In the case of Prishniparni the medicine, कण्व will mean a disease.

[4]The cattle go out for grazing in the morning. They enjoy the pure, fresh, open air and are brought back to their stable at the time of sunset by the cowherd who knows the forms and figures of the cattle and recognises them fully well.

[5]Stream means to together. I refers to a big leader.

४. सं सिञ्चामि गवां क्षीरं समाज्येन बलं रसम् ।
संसिक्ता अस्माकं वीरा ध्रुवा गावो मयि गोपतौ ॥

4. I offer to my men the milk of kine; with butter I enhance their strength and beauty. May our valiant sons be filled with milk and butter. May cows ever remain with me, their cow-herd. (299)

५. आ हरामि गवां क्षीरमाहार्षं धान्यं१ रसम् । आहृता अस्माकं वीरा आ पत्नीरिदमस्तकम् ॥

5. From cows I obtain milk; from plants I obtain corn and their juice. May our sons be loyal to us, may wife ever accompany me, may I obtain this body as the house of my organs. (300)

Chapter (Anuvāka) 5

HYMN XXVII

१. नेच्छत्रुः प्राशं जयाति सहमानाभिभूरसि । प्राशं प्रतिप्राशो जह्यरसान् कृण्वोषधे ॥

1. Let not the enemy gain victory over me the debater, O intellect, thou art victorious and predominant. Refute the adversaries of mine, the debater. O intellect, efficacious like the medicine that removes fever, render all my opponents in the debate dull and flat! (301)

२. सुपर्णस्त्वान्वविन्दत् सूकरस्त्वाखनन्नसा । प्राशं प्रतिप्राशो जह्यरसान् कृण्वोषधे ॥

2. O intellect, thou art discovered through investigation, by a person far-seeing like an eagle, and perceived by a person sagacious and strong like a boar that unearths his food with his sprout.

O intellect, refute the adversaries of mine, the debater. O intellect efficacious like the medicine that removes fever, render all my opponents in the debate dull and flat! (302)

३. इन्द्रो ह चक्रे त्वा बाहावसुरेभ्य स्तरीतवे । प्राशं प्रतिप्राशो जह्यरसान् कृण्वोषधे ॥

3. A powerful soul, in order to suppress the demons of lust, indignation, avarice, and infatuation, utilises thee, O intellect, with his mental force, like that of arms. O intellect, refute thou the adversaries of mine, the debater. O intellect, efficacious like the medicine, that cures fever, render all my opponents in the debate, dull and flat! (303)

४. पाटामिन्द्रो व्याश्निादसुरेभ्य स्तरीतवे । प्राशं प्रतिप्राशो जह्यरसान् कृण्वोषधे ॥

4. The soul, for suppressing the ignoble sentiments, utilises his spiritual power, full of knowledge and discernment. O intellect, refute thou, thee adversaries of mine, the debater O intellect, efficacious like the medicine, that cures fever, render all my opponents in the debate, dull and flat! (304)[1]

[1]Sāyana takes पाटाम् as पाठाम् and interprets it as a medicine.

५. तयाहं शत्रून्त्साक्ष इन्द्रः सालावृकांइव । प्राशं प्रतिप्राशो जह्यरसान् कृण्वोषधे ॥

5. I, the soul, overcome my internal foes, like dogs. O intellect, refute thou, the adversaries of mine, the debater. O intellect, efficacious like the medicine, that cures fever, render all my opponents in the debate, dull and flat. (305)

६. रुद्र जलाषभेषज नीलशिखण्ड कर्मकृत् । प्राशं प्रतिप्राशो जह्यरसान् कृण्वोषधे ॥

6. O preceptor, who dilates on God, O physician, the annihilator of worldly ills, O beautiful God, the doer of infinite deeds, O intellect, refute thou, the adversaries of mine, the debater. O intellect, efficacious like the medicine, that cures fever, render all my opponents in the debate, dull and flat. (306)

७. तस्य प्राशं त्वं जहि यो न इन्द्राभिदासति । अधि नो ब्रूहि शक्तिभिः प्राशि मामुत्तरं कृधि ॥

7. O King, destroy the wealth of him, who wants to enslave us. With thy powers of knowledge, give us sound advice. Make me superior in debate. (307)

HYMN XXVIII

१. तुभ्यमेव जरिमन् वर्धतामयं मेममन्ये मृत्यवो हिंसिषुः शतं ये ।
मातेव पुत्रं प्रमना उपस्थे मित्र एनं मित्रियात् पात्वंहसः ॥

1. O old age, let this child grow to meet thee only, let not other causes of death harm him for a hundred years. Let God, the protector from death, guard him from sin caused by friends, as a kind mother guards the son she nurses. (308)

२. मित्र एनं वरुणो वा रिशादा जरामृत्युं कृणुतां संविदानौ ।
तदग्निर्होता वयुनानि विद्वान् विश्वा देवानां जनिमा विवक्ति ॥

2. May Prāṇa, our saviour from death and Apāna, the restrainer of bodily sufferings, both acting as the destroyers of the causes of death; accordant well, make this child leave his mortal coil in old age. May the Benevolent God, the Knower of all the branches of knowledge, declare unto us the source and origin of all divine objects. (309)

३. त्वमीशिषे पशूनां पार्थिवानां ये जाता उत वा ये जनित्राः ।
मेमं प्राणो हासीन्मो अपानो मेमं मित्रा वधिषुर्मो अमित्राः ॥

3. O God, Thou art the Lord of all animals and men of the Earth, who have taken birth and shall take birth. May not Prāṇa and Apāna leave this child before time. May not a friend or a foe kill this child! (310)

४. द्यौष्ट्वा पिता पृथिवी माता जरामृत्युं कृणुतां संविदाने ।
यथा जीवा अदितेरुपस्थे प्राणापानाभ्यां गुपितः शतं हिमाः ॥

4. O child, may thy father, resplendent like the Sun, and thy mother, broad-minded like the Earth, in unison, make thee leave this body in old age. May

thou resting in the lap of Nature, protected by Prāṇa and Apana, live for a hundred winters. (311)

५. इममग्न आयुषे वर्चसे नय प्रियं रेतो वरुण मित्र राजन् ।
मातेवास्मा अदिते शर्म यच्छ विश्वे देवा जरदष्टिर्यथासत् ॥

5. O fire, water, Prāṇa and king, grant this child power of procreation, and lead him on the right path, for longevity and virility. O vast Earth, grant this child mother-like shelter. O learned persons and forces of nature help the child to live long. (312)

HYMN XXIX

१. पार्थिवस्य रसे देवा भगस्य तन्वो३ बले ।
आयुष्यमिस्मा अग्निः सूर्यो वर्च आ धाद् बृहस्पतिः ॥

1. O noble souls, may this person be merry enjoying the juice derived from earthly products and the strength of his own virtue. May the All-Pervading, Refulgent Gods, the Guardian of vast worlds, grant him physical and spiritual force that conduces to longevity. (313)

२. आयुरस्मै धेहि जातवेदः प्रजां त्वष्टरधिनिधेह्यस्मै ।
रायस्पोषं सवितरा सुवास्मै शतं जीवाति शरदस्तवायम् ॥

2. O God, the Knower of all created objects, grant longevity to this Brahmchari. O Creator of the universe, grant him ample progeny, O God, the Goader of all, grant him plenty of wealth. May he, through your kindness live for a hundred winters. (314)

३. आशीर्ण ऊर्जमुत सौप्रजास्त्वं दक्षं धत्तं द्रविणं सचेतसौ ।
जयं क्षेत्राणि सहसायमिन्द्र कृण्वानो अन्यानधरान्त्सपत्नान् ॥

3. O one-minded father and mother, give us blessing, food, good progeny, wisdom and wealth. O God, may this Brahmchari, through self-help, gaining victory in diverse fields of activity, subdue till his foes. (315)

४. इन्द्रेण दत्तो वरुणेन शिष्टो मरुद्भिरुग्रः प्रहितो न आगन् ।
एष वां द्यावापृथिवी उपस्थे मा क्षुधन्मा तृषत् ॥

4. Infused with life by God, taught by his preceptor, goaded into virtuous acts by the learned, this Brahmchari has come unto us. O Heaven and Earth, resting in your lap, may he never feel hungry or thirsty. (316)[1]

५. ऊर्जमस्मा ऊर्जस्वती धत्तं पयो अस्मै पयस्वती धत्तम् ।
ऊर्जमस्मै द्यावापृथिवी अधातां विश्वे देवा मरुत ऊर्जमापः ॥

[1]Reference is made to a Brahmchari, who returns home after completing his studies.

5. O Heaven and Earth, acting as father and mother, full of food and vigour, grant this Brahmchari food and vigour Full of nourishing milk grant milk to this Brahmchari. May Heaven and Earth grant him strength and vitality. May all learned persons, merchants and saints grant him strength in finding food ! (317)

६. शिवाभिष्टे हृदयं तर्पयाम्यनमीवो मोदिषीष्ठाः सुवर्चाः ।
सवासिनौ पिबतां मन्थमेतमश्विनो रूपं परिधाय मायाम् ॥

6. O Brahmchari, I fill thy heart with ennobling instructions. Free from disease, full of loveliness, ever remain happy. O husband and wife, assuming the role and perception of father and mother, enjoy the pleasure granted by Me ! (318)[1]

७. इन्द्र एतां ससृजे विद्धो अग्र ऊर्जां स्वधामजरां सा त एषा ।
तया त्वं जीव शरदः सुवर्चा मा त आ सुस्रोद् भिषजस्ते अक्रन् ॥

7. Adorable God hath revealed in the beginning that imperishable nectar of knowledge. It is for thee, O Brahmchari. With that knowledge, full of beauty, mayest thou live long. May it never dwindle for thee. Spiritual doctors have prescribed it for thee ! (319)

HYMN XXX

१. यथेदं भूम्या अधि तृणं वातो मथायति ।
एवा मथ्नामि ते मनो यथा मां कामिन्यसो यथा मन्नापगा असः ॥

1. Just as wind moves and revolves a blade of grass on the earth, so do I move and control thy heart, so that thou mayest love me, and never leave me after marriage. (320)[2]

२. सं चेन्नयाथो अश्विना कामिना सं च वक्षथः ।
सं वां भगासो अग्मत सं चित्तानि समु व्रता ॥

2. O mutually loving young man and girl, walk together, progress together. May ye both acquire supremacy together, may your hearts work in unison, may your resolves be one and the same. (321)

३. यत् सुपर्णा विवक्षवो अनमीवा विवक्षवः । तत्र मे गच्छताद्धवं शल्य इव कुल्मलं यथा ॥

3. Where the nice-winged birds resort to chirping together; where disease-free persons go and discuss health problems, there may my fiancee accompany me on my call, just as the sharp edge of the arrow reaches its destination. (322)[3]

[1]'I' and 'Me' refer to God.

[2]Thy: the girl, a would-be wife. A young man addresses the girl he wants to marry.

[3]Marriage should be performed in a healthy, beautiful place, where birds sing, and healthy persons converse on health. Just as an arrow goes straight to its target, so should the girl to the place of marriage, on the prayer of the youngman.

४. यदन्तरं तद् बाह्यं यद् बाह्यं तदन्तरम् । कन्यानां विश्वरूपाणां मनो गृभायौषधे ॥

4. Let the love thou cherishest in the heart, be displayed outside. Let the love thou showest outside, he installed in the heart. O bridegroom, serviceable like a medicine, attract the mind of beautiful, well-built girls. (323)[1]

५. एयमगन् पतिकामा जनिकामोऽहमागमम् । अश्वः कनिक्रदद्यथा भगेनाहं सहागमम् ॥

5. This girl, longing for a husband has entered domestic life, I longing for a wife, have entered domestic life. Just as a horse neighs in pleasure at the sight of fodder, so have I entered domestic life, full of prosperity and love. (324)

HYMN XXXI

१. इन्द्रस्य या मही दृषत् क्रिमेर्विश्वस्य तर्हणी । तया पिनष्मि सं क्रिमीन् दृषदा खल्वाँ इव ॥

1. With soul's mighty millstone that which crushes worms of every sort, I bray and bruise the worms to bits like vetches on the grinding stone. (325)[2]

२. दृष्टमदृष्टमतृहमथो कुरूरुमतृहम् । अलगण्डून्त्सर्वाञ्छलुनान् क्रिमीन् वचसा जम्भयामसि ॥

2. The visible and the invisible worms, and those that utter contemptible sounds, have I crushed. Worms that produce irritation in the skin or fast enter the body, we crush all to pieces with medicine. (326)[3]

३. अलगण्डून् हन्मि महता वधेन दूना अदूना अरसा अभूवन् ।
शिष्टानशिष्टान् नि तिरामि वाचा यथा क्रिमीणां नकिरुच्छिषातै ॥

3. I kill worms, that cause irritation in the skin, with a potential medicine. The developed and the undeveloped worms have lost their vigour. I kill with medicine the foul worms that have escaped death, so that not a single worm remains alive. (327)

४. अन्वान्त्र्यं शीर्षण्य१मथो पार्ष्टेयं क्रिमीन् ।
अवस्कवं व्यध्वरं क्रिमीन् वचसा जम्भयामसि ॥

4. Worms that reside within the bowels, and cause cholera that reside in the head, and cause itch, that reside within the ribs, and cause pulmonary consumption, that enter the skin, and cause leprosy, that eat man's flesh, these we bruise to pieces with a medicine. (328)

५. ये क्रिमयः पर्वतेषु वनेष्वोषधीषु पशुष्वप्स्व१न्तः ।
ये अस्माकं तन्वमाविविशुः सर्वं तद्धन्मि जनिम क्रिमीणाम् ॥

[1]Here 'girls', the plural has been used for a girl, to show respect and regard.

[2]Millstone means power. Worms means spiritual vices, which eat into the vitals of of our souls, as worms in the belly eat our body.

[3]Vachā is the name of a medicine.

5. Worms that are found on mountains, in the forests, that live in plants, in the cattle, in the waters, those that have made their way within our bodies,—I destroy the whole generation of these worms. (329)

Chapter (Anuvāka) 6

HYMN XXXII

१. उद्यन्नादित्यः क्रिमीन् हन्तु निम्रोचन् हन्तु रश्मिभिः । ये अन्तः क्रिमयो गवि ॥

1. Let the Sun at sunrise and sunset, destroy with his beams, the worms that live on the Earth. (330)

२. विश्वरूपं चतुरक्षं क्रिमिं सारङ्गमर्जुनम् । शृणाम्यस्य पृष्टीरपि वृश्चामि यच्छिरः ॥

2. I break and crush the ribs and tear away the head of the worm, variegated in shape, four-eyed, prone to creep, and white in colour. (331)[1]

३. अत्त्रिवद् वः क्रिमयो हन्मि कण्ववज्जमदग्निवत् ।
अगस्त्यस्य ब्रह्मणा सं पिनष्म्यहं क्रिमीन् ॥

3. O disease-producing worms, I destroy ye, as a violent flesh-eaters destroys his bird of prey, as a fowl eats up all grains one by one, as kindled fire extinguishes every thing all at one stroke. I bray and bruise the worms to pieces with the Vedic knowledge of God. (332)[2]

४. हतो राजा क्रिमीणामुतैषां स्थपतिर्हतः । हतो हतमाता क्रिमिर्हतभ्राता हतस्वसा ॥

4. Slain is the sovereign of these worms, yea, their controlling lord is slain. Slain is the worm, his mother slain, brother and sister both are slain. (333)[3]

५. हतासो अस्य वेशसो हतासः परिवेशसः । अथो ये क्षुल्लकाइव सर्वे ते क्रिमयो हताः ॥

5. Slain are his ministers, and slain his followers and retinue: yea, those that seemed the tiniest things, the worms have all been put to death. (334)

६. प्र ते शृणामि शृङ्गे याभ्यां वितुदायसि । भिनद्मि ते कुषुम्भं यस्ते विषधानः ॥

6. I break both thy thorns wherewith thou bitest. I cleave and rend the bag which holds the venom which is stored in thee. (335)

[1]I refers to a physician.

[2]अग=Surya. God is Agastya, who brings into existence the Sun. Atri, Kanva, Jamadagni, and Agastya are according to Griffith, the names of celebrated Rishis or seers. This interpretation is irrational, as there is no history in the Vedas. These are yogic words, and not the names of Rishis.

[3]The whole family of the worms is slain through the use of medicine.

HYMN XXXIII

१. अक्षीभ्यां ते नासिकाभ्यां कर्णाभ्यां छुबुकादधि ।
यक्ष्मं शीर्षण्यं मस्तिष्काज्जिह्वाया वि वृहामि ते ॥

1. O patient, from both thine eyes, from both nostrils from both thine ears, and from thy chin, forth thy brain and tongue. I root consumption seated in thy head! (336)[1]

२. ग्रीवाभ्यस्त उष्णिहाभ्यः कीकसाभ्यो अनूक्यात् ।
यक्ष्मं दोषण्य१मंसाभ्यां बाहुभ्यां वि वृहामि ते ॥

2. Forth from the fourteen arteries of the neck, and from the arteries of the nape, from dorsal vertebrae and spine; from arms and shoulder-blades, I root consumption seated in thine arms. (337)

३. हृदयात् ते परि क्लोम्नो हलीक्ष्णात् पार्श्वाभ्याम् ।
यक्ष्मं मतस्नाभ्यां प्लीह्नो यक्नस्ते वि वृहामसि ॥

3. Forth from thy heart and from thy lungs, from thy gall-bladder and thy sides; from kidneys, spleen and liver thy consumption we eradicate. (338)[2]

४. आन्त्रेभ्यस्ते गुदाभ्यो वनिष्ठोरुदरादधि । यक्ष्मं कुक्षिभ्यां प्लाशेर्नाभ्या वि वृहामि ते ॥

4. From bowels and intestines, from the rectum and the belly, I extirpate thy consumption, from flanks, mesentery and navel. (339)

५. ऊरुभ्यां ते अष्ठीवद्भ्यां पार्ष्णिभ्यां प्रपदाभ्याम् ।
यक्ष्मं भसद्यं१ श्रोणिभ्यां भासदं भंससो वि वृहामि ते ॥

5. Forth from thy thighs and from thy knees, heels and the foreparts of thy feet, from thy loins and hips, from thy urinary canal and private parts, I eradicate consumption. (340)

६. अस्थिभ्यस्ते मज्जभ्यः स्नावभ्यो धमनिभ्यः ।
यक्ष्मं पाणिभ्यामङ्गुलिभ्यो नखेभ्यो वि वृहामि ते ॥

6. Forth from thy bones and thy marrows, forth from thy tendons and thy veins, I banish thy consumption, from thy hands, thy fingers, and thy nails. (341)

७. अङ्गेअङ्गे लोम्निलोम्नि यस्ते पर्वणिपर्वणि ।
यक्ष्मं त्वचस्यं ते वयं कश्यपस्य वीवर्हेण विष्वञ्चं वि वृहामसि ॥

7. In every member, every hair, in every joint wherein it lies, we under

[1] "I" refers to a skilled physician, who is expert in curing consumption. See *Rigveda*, Mandal, 10, Sukta, 163.
[2] Thy refers to a patient.

the medical advice of an experienced, able doctor, drive far away consumption settled in thy skin, and all parts of the body. (342)[1]

HYMN XXXIV

१. य ईशे पशुपतिः पशूनां चतुष्पदामुत यो द्विपदाम् ।
निष्क्रीतः स यज्ञियं भागमेतु रायस्पोषा यजमानं सचन्ताम् ॥

1. May God, Who is the Lord of souls, and is the Lord of animals, quadruped and biped, rendered favourable through prayer, and worthy of our adoration, accept our worship. May growth of wealth attend the sacrificer. (343)

२. प्रमुञ्चन्तो भुवनस्य रेतो गातुं धत्त यजमानाय देवाः ।
उपाकृतं शशमानं यदस्थात् प्रियं देवानामप्येतु पाथः ॥

2. O learned people, show the right path to this soul, who hankers after salvation, and has renounced matter, the cause of the universe. When the soul holds fast the lovely path of emancipated souls, being polished with yogic accomplishments, and eager to achieve salvation, may it reach its goal. (344)[2]

३. ये वध्यमानमनु दीध्याना अन्वैक्षन्त मनसा चक्षुषा च ।
अग्निष्ठानग्रे प्र मुमोक्तु देवो विश्वकर्मा प्रजया संरराणः ॥

3. Yogis, who in deep meditation, through mental vision and the eye of intellect visualise the soul, fettered by Matter, the first set free from the painful bondage of the body, by the Refulgent God, the Creator of the universe, who sports with Matter. (345)

४. ये ग्राम्याः पशवो विश्वरूपा विरूपाः सन्तो बहुधैकरूपाः ।
वायुष्टानग्रे प्रमुमोक्तु देवः प्रजापतिः प्रजया संरराणः ॥

4. Those, who observing the social law, keep their eye on the spiritual path, and are the cynosure of the world, being different in nature, are still alike in performing disinterested service, are first emancipated by the Refulgent God, the Guardian of His subjects, Who rejoices in His Creatures. (346)[3]

५. प्रजानन्तः प्रति गृह्णन्तु पूर्वे प्राणमङ्गेभ्यः पर्याचरन्तम् ।
दिवं गच्छ प्रति तिष्ठा शरीरैः स्वर्गं याहि पथिभिर्देवयानैः ॥

[1]Griffith describes Kashyapa to be a Rishi and father of Vivribā. This explanation is inadmissible, as there is no history in the Vedas.

How beautifully, the eradication of disease from each and every part of the body has been described in this hymn to lead a healthy life is the ideal of the vedas. We should avail of medical science to maintain health.

[2]Some commentators apply this verse to animal sacrifice, which is highly absurd. The verse refers to the emancipation of the soul.

[3]Souls, who render disinterested service are soon granted salvation. They have not to take birth again and again for long.

5. Just as ancient Rishis, knowing full well the essence of God and soul, used to control the vital breath proceeding from all parts of the body, so should the aspirants after salvation do! (347)

O man, acquire knowledge. Along with all parts of the body, make thy soul powerful. Attain to salvation through the paths trodden by the learned. (348)

HYMN XXXV

१. ये भक्षयन्तो न वसून्यानृधुर्यानिग्नयो अन्वतप्यन्त धिष्ण्या: ।
या तेषामवया दुरिष्टि: स्विऽष्टिं नस्तां कृणवद् विश्वकर्मा ।।

1. They, who enjoy worldly pleasures, and do not let their vital breaths grow strong, after sensual enjoyment, feel sorrow resulting from the sparks of their intellect. May God, the Creator of the universe, alter the evil company and vicious nature of those voluptuous persons into virtuous acts. (349)

२. यज्ञपतिमृषय एनसाहुर्निर्भक्तं प्रजा अनुतप्यमानम् ।
मथव्याऽन्त्स्तोकानप यान् रराध सं नष्टेभि: सृजतु विश्वकर्मा ।।

2. The Rishis describe the soul, full of attachment to its progeny, as immersed in infatuation. May God unite our soul with those objects, affording pleasure to the mind, which it shuns. (350)[1]

३. अदान्यान्त्सोमपान् मन्यमानो यज्ञस्य विद्वान्त्समये न धीर: ।
यदेनश्चकृवान् बद्ध एष तं विश्वकर्मन् प्र मुञ्चा स्वस्तये ।।

3. A learned person, who neither knows the science of Yajna (sacrifice) nor displays wisdom and calmness at the proper time and through arrogance considers the spiritually advanced persons as unfit for gift, thereby commits a sin, may God, the Creator of the universe release him from that sin, for the sake of his welfare. (351)[2]

४. घोरा ऋषयो नमो अस्त्वेभ्यश्चक्षुर्यदेषां मनसश्च सत्यम् ।
बृहस्पतये महिष द्युमन्नमो विश्वकर्मन् नमस्ते पाह्य१स्मान् ।।

4. Wise and calm are the vedic seers, homage to them, as their mental vision is decidedly precise. Evident homage to Thee, O Adorable God, the Lord of big worlds. O Creator of the universe, we pay homage unto Thee! Guard us. (352)

५. यज्ञस्य चक्षु: प्रभृतिर्मुखं च वाचा श्रोत्रेण मनसा जुहोमि ।
इमं यज्ञं विततं विश्वकर्मणा देवा यन्तु सुमनस्यमाना: ।।

5. Eye and Mouth are the sources for the soul, for acquiring knowledge and filling the belly. May gracious and kindly-hearted learned persons work in this world, a yajna extended by God. (353)

[1]Rishis=Learned seers. It refers to the soul.

[2]A learned person, who through pride considers himself superior to other contemplative souls commits a sin. Pride of piety and knowledge is a vice and not a virtue.

HYMN XXXVI

१. आ नो अग्ने सुमतिं संभलो गमेदिमां कुमारीं सह नो भगेन ।
जुष्टा वरेषु समनेषु वल्गुरोषं पत्या सौभगमस्त्वस्यै ॥

1. O priest, may an eloquent and wealthy suitor come unto us, and take away in wedlock this intelligent girl of ours, who is lovely to the pre-eminent, and charming to the noble-minded. May she be soon made happy with a husband. (354)

२. सोमजुष्टं ब्रह्मजुष्टमर्यम्णा संभृतं भगम् । धातुर्देवस्य सत्येन कृणोमि पतिवेदनम् ॥

2. In obedience to the upright law of God, the Creator of the universe, I prepare for accepting a husband, this lucky girl, liked by the learned, respected by the spiritually advanced, and guarded by the king. (355)[1]

३. इयमग्ने नारी पतिं विदेष्ट सोमो हि राजा सुभगां कृणोति ।
सुवाना पुत्रान् महिषी भवाति गत्वा पतिं सुभगा वि राजतु ॥

3. O God, may this woman find a husband. May the learned and prosperous husband make her happy. May she bear sons, and become queen of the household. Being blessed, may she rule beside her consort! (356)

४. यथाखरो मघवंश्चारुरेष प्रियो मृगाणां सुषदा बभूव ।
एवा भगस्य जुष्टेयमस्तु नारी सम्प्रिया पत्याविराधयन्ती ॥

4. O God, just as this beautiful lair is dear to wild beasts as a pleasant dwelling; so may this woman be her husband, darling, loved by her lord, and never separated from him. (357)

५. भगस्य नावमा रोह पूर्णामनुपदस्वतीम् । तयोपप्रतारय यो वरः प्रतिकाम्यः ॥

5. O woman, mount up, embark on thy husband's ship of domestic life, which is full and indestructible. Make him, whom thou fain wouldst wed, cross thereby the ocean of world's misery! (358)

६. आ क्रन्दय धनपते वरमामनसं कृणु । सर्वं प्रदक्षिणं कृणु यो वरः प्रतिकाम्यः ॥

6. O girl, the guardian of wealth, call thy suitor respectfully, and make him well-inclined towards thee. Let him, who is worthy of thy choice, sit on thy right hand! (359)[2]

७. इदं हिरण्यं गुल्गुल्वयमौक्षो अथो भगः । एते पतिभ्यस्त्वामदुः प्रतिकामाय वेत्तवे ॥

7. Here is the Bdellium and the gold; the cow and money are here. We

[1] "I" refers to the father or preceptor of the girl.

[2] According to the vedic ideal of marriage, a girl is herself to choose her husband. Her parents are merely to lend her a helping hand. It is a mark of respect and honour to make the bridegroom sit on the right side of the bride in marriage.

give these things in dowry to the bridegroom's party, and to thee for the welfare of thy desired husband. (360)[1]

८. आ ते नयतु सविता नयतु पतिर्यः प्रतिकाम्यः। त्वमस्यै धेह्योषधे ।

8. May God guide thee O girl. May thy desired husband take thee away in wedlock. O God, be this husband thy gift to her! (361)

BOOK (Kāṇḍa) III

Chapter (Anuvāka) 1

HYMN I

१. अग्निर्नः शत्रून् प्रत्येतु विद्वान् प्रतिदहन्नभिशस्तिमरातिम् ।
स सेनां मोहयतु परेषां निर्हस्तांश्च कृणवज्जातवेदाः ॥

1. Let the wise commander march against our foemen and burning the attacking enemy, let him bewilder our opponents army. Let the general, knowing all situations of the battlefield, smite and make them unfit to carry arms. (362)

२. यूयमुग्रा मरुत ईदृशे स्ताभि प्रेत मृणत सहध्वम् ।
अमीमृणन् वसवो नाथिता इमे अग्निर्ह्येषां दूतः प्रत्येतु विद्वान् ॥

2. Ye valiant soldiers, on the battlefield, keep your arms up, go forward, kill your foes, and win victory. These terrible, foe-tormenting citizens alone destroy their enemies. Let the wise commander, their chief, assail the foes! (363)[2]

३. अमित्रसेनां मघवन्नस्माञ्छत्रूयतीमभि । युवं तामिन्द्र वृत्रहन्नग्निश्च दहतं प्रति ॥

3. O opulent, fiend-slaying king, and wise general, ye both attack and burn the foeman's host that threatens us. (364)

४. प्रसूत इन्द्र प्रवता हरिभ्यां प्र ते वज्रः प्रमृणन्नेतु शत्रून् ।
जहि प्रतीचो अनूचः पराचो विष्वक् सत्यं कृणुहि चित्तमेषाम् ॥

4. O King, may thy bolt shot from a high place, with the swiftness of fire and lightning, go forth, destroying foes. Slay those who stand in front and follow, slay those who fly in all directions. In every way, lead the mind of these enemies on the path of virtue! (365)

[1]Bdellium: A costly fragrant gum that exudes from a plant said to be the vine palm (Borassus Flabelliformis). The Sanskrit name of the gum is gugglu.

'We' refers to Purohit, father, mother and brothers of the girl.

[2]This hymn is addressed by the general to the brave soldiers, who are Maruts i.e., ever ready to die.

५. इन्द्र सेनां मोहयामित्राणाम् । अग्नेर्वातस्य ध्राज्या तान् विषूचो वि नाशय ।।

5. O King, bewilder thou the foemen's army. With the furious rush of fiery and airy missiles drive them away to every side. (366)[1]

६. इन्द्रः सेनां मोहयतु मरुतो घ्नन्त्वोजसा । चक्षूंष्यग्निरा दत्तां पुनरेतु पराजिता ।।

6. Let the king daze their army. Let the valiant soldiers, ever ready to die, slay it with their might. Let the fiery missile take their eyes away, and let the conquered host retreat. (367)

HYMN II

१. अग्निर्नो दूतः प्रत्येतु विद्वान् प्रतिदहन्नभिशस्तिमरातिम् ।
स चित्तानि मोहयतु परेषां निर्हस्तांश्च कृणवज्जातवेदाः ।।

1. May the Commander, our wise, chief representative, tormenting our foe, who attacks us, march against him. May he bewilder our opponents, senses. May the Commander, the Knower of his subjects render them powerless. (368)[2]

२. अयमग्निरमूमुहद्यानि चित्तानि वो हृदि । वि वो धमत्वोकसः प्र वो धमतु सर्वतः ।।

2. O foes, may the Commander of the army frustrate all evil intentions you cherish in the heart. May he drive you out of your fortress; may he drive you out from all places of shelter. (369)

३. इन्द्र चित्तानि मोहयन्नर्वाङाकूत्या चर । अग्नेर्वातस्य ध्राज्या तान् विषूचो वि नाशय ।।

3. O King, bewildering their senses, come hitherward unto us with a fine determination. With the onward rush of fiery and airy missiles drive them away to every side. (370)

४. व्याकूतय एषामिताथो चित्तानि मुह्यत । अथो यदद्यैषां हृदि तदेषां परि निर्जहि ।।

4. Vanish, ye hopes and plans of theirs, be ye confounded, all their thoughts! Whatever wish is in their heart, do thou, O King, expel it utterly. (371)[3]

५. अमीषां चित्तानि प्रतिमोहयन्ती गृहाणाङ्गान्यप्वे परेहि ।
अभि प्रेहि निर्दह हृत्सु शोकैर्ग्राह्यामित्रांस्तमसा विध्य शत्रून् ।।

5. O disease, bewildering the senses of our foes, get hold of their bodies, and go afar from us. Go meet them, burn their hearts with griefs lurking

[1]Fiery missible is आग्नेयास्त्र, Airy missile is वायवास्त्र.

[2]In the text the word निर्हस्तान् literally means handless. Liberally interpreted, it means powerless.

[3]'Theirs' refers to enemies.

within. Smite thou the malignant foes with darkness and amazement. (372)[1]

६. असौ या सेना मरुतः परेषामस्मानैत्यभ्योजसा स्पर्धमाना ।
तां विध्यत तमसापव्रतेन यथैषामन्यो अन्यं न जानात् ॥

6. O valiant soldiers, ever ready to die, meet ye that army of our enemies, that comes against us with its might, defying us; and strike it with unwelcome darkness so that not one of them may know another. (373)[2]

HYMN III

१. अचिक्रदत् स्वपा इह भुवदग्ने व्यचस्व रोदसी उरूची ।
युञ्जन्तु त्वा मरुतो विश्ववेदस आमुं नय नमसा रातहव्यम् ॥

1. O Commander of the army, may this king, the nice nourisher of his subjects, proclaiming his edicts, be fit to rule over this kingdom. O leader of men, control the officials and the public, spacious like the Earth and Heaven. May learned persons, knowing all sciences, co-operate with thee. O Commander, bring back to the throne most respectfully, this king, who collects taxes from his subjects. (374)[3]

२. दूरे चित् सन्तमरुषास इन्द्रमा च्यावयन्तु सख्याय विप्रम् ।
यद् गायत्रीं बृहतीमर्कमस्मै सौत्रामण्या दधृषन्त देवाः ॥

2. Let the enterprising persons, bring the sagacious king for friendship, though he be far away. The learned then enrich through their nice statesmanship, for the king, the moral and military forces. (375)

३. अद्भ्यस्त्वा राजा वरुणो ह्वयतु सोमस्त्वा ह्वयतु पर्वतेभ्यः ।
इन्द्रस्त्वा ह्वयतु विड्भ्य आभ्यः श्येनो भूत्वा विश आ पतेमाः ॥

3. May the Emperor call thee hither O King, from watery places, and restore thee to thy kingdom. May a learned Brahman call thee hither from hills and mountains, and make the rule over the state. May the majority of thy prosperous subjects call thee hither to these people. Fly thou like a falcon, O King to these subjects. (376)[4]

४. श्येनो हव्यं नयत्वा परस्मादन्यक्षेत्रे अपरुद्धं चरन्तम् ।
अश्विना पन्थां कृणुतां सुगं त इमं सजाता अभिसंविशध्वम् ॥

[1]Apvā : according to Sāyana, a female deity who presides over sin. According to Griffith, Āpvā is a personification of colic or dysentery, likely to attack soldiers in the field.

[2]See *Yajur*, 17-47.

[3]Here is a reference to re-occupy the throne once lost. 'Leader of men' means the king.

[4]When a king is vanquished in a battle, and finds himself in distress, he flies and takes shelter in an ocean, or mountain, or with his subjects in a secret place. In this hymn, he is called back from his place of shelter or exile, and restored to his kingdom.

4. May a learned, wise, active person, bring from far away, the king, who must be summoned back, roaming secretly in an alien land. May both the spies make thy pathway easy. Come and unite yourselves with him, O kinsmen. (377)[1]

५. ह्वयन्तु त्वा प्रतिजनाः प्रति मित्रा अवृषत । इन्द्राग्नी विश्वे देवास्ते विशि क्षेममदीधरन् ॥

5. Let thy opponents call thee back. Thy friends have chosen thee again. May men active like lightning and fire, and all the learned persons, establish peace for thee, in thy subjects. (378)

६. यस्ते हवं विवदत् सजातो यश्च निष्टयः । अपाञ्चमिन्द्र तं कृत्वाथेममिहाव गमय ॥

6. He who disputes our calling thee, be he a stranger or akin, banish him, O King, far away, and proclaim his banishment. (379)

HYMN IV

१. आ त्वा गन् राष्ट्रं सह वर्चसोदिहि प्राङ् विशां पतिरेकराट् त्वं वि राज ।
सर्वास्त्वा राजन् प्रदिशो ह्वयन्तूपसद्यो नमस्योऽभवेह ॥

1. O King, to thee hath come the kingship; advance with thy splendour. As a leader, shine as the sole ruler of the people. King, let denizens of all regions invite thee. Here let men wait on thee and bow before thee! (380)[2]

२. त्वां विशो वृणतां राज्यायऽय त्वामिमाः प्रदिशः पञ्च देवीः ।
वर्ष्मन् राष्ट्रस्य ककुदि श्रयस्व ततो न उग्रो वि भजा वसूनि ॥

2. O King, the subjects shall elect thee for the kingship, these five celestial regions will accept thee as their lord. Rest on the height and top of kingly power: thence as a mighty man award us treasures! (381)[3]

३. अच्छ त्वा यन्तु हविनः सजाता अग्निर्दूतो अजिरः सं चरातै ॥
जायाः पुत्राः सुमनसो भवन्तु बहुं बलिं प्रति पश्यासा उग्रः ॥

3. Kinsmen, inviting thee, shall go to meet thee. Let your fast, fiery ambassador go about freely everywhere. Let women and their sons be friendly-minded. Thou mighty one, shalt receive abundant taxes. (382)

४. अश्विना त्वाग्रे मित्रावरुणोभा विश्वे देवा मरुतस्त्वा ह्वयन्तु ।
अधा मनो वसुदेयाय कृणुष्व ततो न उग्रो वि भजा वसूनि ॥

4. O King, first shall the Commander-in-chief, and the speaker of the Assembly, head of the Police Department and the C.I.D. head, all learned

[1]Thy, him refer to the king brought back from exile.

[2]This hymn describes the coronation of a king.

[3]Five celestial regions; the four quarters of the heavens with the addition of the Zenith or the Nadir Pt. Jaidev Vidyalankar interprets the words as five assemblies of the learned.

persons, all soldiers and businessmen accept thee as their sovereign. Then turn thy mind to giving gifts of treasure, thence, mighty one, distribute wealth among us! (383)[1]

५. आ प्र द्रव परमस्याः परावतः शिवे ते द्यावापृथिवी उभे स्ताम् ।
तदयं राजा वरुणस्तथाह स त्वायमह्वत् स उपेदमेहि ॥

5. O King, travel to distant places in your kingdom, and soon return to the capital. In this tour, may officials and subjects be propitious unto thee. Verily this king is a representative of God so does God pronounce. The same God preaches unto thee, 'Thou art a fit person for this post'! (384)

६. इन्द्रेन्द्र मनुष्या३: परेहि सं ह्यज्ञास्था वरुणैः संविदानः ।
स त्वायमह्वत् स्वे सधस्थे स देवान् यक्षत् स उ कल्पयाद् विशः ॥

6. O Emperor, control all men, consult thy ministers on all state affairs, undoubtedly arrive at definite decisions after day thought. O subjects, this king, calling ye to his palace, unifies ye. He reverently assembles the learned. He directs his subjects to fulfil their duties. (385)

७. पथ्याऽ रेवतीर्बहुधा विरूपाः सर्वाः सङ्गत्य वरीयस्ते अक्रन् ।
तास्त्वा सर्वाः संविदाना ह्वयन्तु दशमीमुग्रः सुमना वशेह ॥

7. The virtuous, wealthy subjects, though generally different in temperament have all in accord created nice kingship for thee. May all the subjects unanimously call thee to occupy the throne. May thou rule in thy state till thy tenth decade, as a strong, kind ruler. (386)[2]

HYMN V

१. आयमगन् पर्णमणिर्बली बलेन प्रमृणन्त्सपत्नान् ।
ओजोऽ देवानां पय ओषधीनां वर्चसा मा जिन्वत्वप्रयावन् ॥

1. This nice, learned king has come to rule over us. Being strong, he destroys the rivals with his power. He is the embodiment of the power of all the vital forces of the country. He removes all the weaknesses of the country, as the juice of the medicine removes all diseases. Free from sloth, he leads me, through his splendour, on the right path. (387)[3]

२. मयि क्षत्रं पर्णमणे मयि धारयताद् रयिम् । अहं राष्ट्रस्याभीवर्गे निजो भूयासमुत्तमः ॥

2. O nourishing king, in me set firmly might and opulence. Enjoying the confidence of the ruling party of the country, may I become supreme! (388)

[1]See *Rig.*, 4-15-15.

[2]The tenth decade: The last stage of thy full natural life which should extend to a hundred years.

[3]Me: he who works for the welfare of the country.

३. यं निदधुर्वनस्पतौ गुह्यं देवा: प्रियं मणिम् । तमस्मभ्यं सहायुषा देवा ददतु भर्तवे ॥

3. The dear, well-protected valuable king, whom the learned preserve for the safety of the state, like a tree; may the learned, grant that king to us, the subjects, for our nourishment, and extended life of the state. (389)[1]

४. सोमस्य पर्णः सह उग्रमागन्निन्द्रेण दत्तो वरुणेन शिष्टः ।
तं प्रियासं बहु रोचमानो दीर्घायुत्वाय शतशारदाय ॥

4. The learned guardians of the state, attain to power, in cooperation with the king. The learned acquiring supremacy from kingly power, are ruled by the king. May I, for prolonging the life of my rule for a hundred years, loving deeply my subjects and respected by them, grant protection to the learned folk. (390)

५. आ मारुक्षत् पर्णमणिर्मह्या अरिष्टतातये । यथाहमुत्तरोऽसान्यर्यम्ण उत संविदः ॥

5. God, the sustainer and Nourisher sits over me for great security from ill; so that I may be exalted above the more powerful, as well as the equally powerful king of another country. (391)[2]

६. ये धीवानो रथकाराः कर्मारा ये मनीषिणः ।
उपस्तीन् पर्ण मह्यं त्वं सर्वान् कृण्वभितो जनान् ॥

6. Sagacious builders of the war chariots, and skilful artisans and mechanics, O Minister, the guardian of the state, make all these men in my state come round near me! (392)[3]

७. ये राजानो राजकृतः सूताग्रामण्यश्च ये । उपस्तीन् पर्ण मह्यं त्वं सर्वान् कृण्वभितो जनान् ॥

7. The kings and makers of the kings, the charioteers and village leaders, O Minister, make all these men come round near me. (393)[4]

८. पर्णोऽसि तनूपानः सयोनिर्वीरो वीरेण मया । संवत्सरस्य तेजसा तेन बध्नामि त्वा मणे ॥

8. O Praiseworthy God, Thou art our Nourisher and Protector of our bodies. Thou, a Hero, are coeval with me, the heroic soul. With that splendour of God, I bind myself to Thee. (394)[5]

[1]Just as a tree preserves the fruits, the use of which prolongs life, so the king, acting as a tree of the state, preserves forces, which prolong the life of the state.

[2]पर्णमणि: has been translated as God by Pt. Khem Karan Das Trivedi, as He is the Noblest of the noble.

'I' refers to a king, who is a devotee of God.

[3]He refers to the King. It is the duty of a king to encourage intelligent, learned, skilful mechanics and artisans who can build aeroplanes, ships, motor cars and other military vehicles.

[4]The king should have friendly relations with the kings of neighbouring states, the priests and nobles who elect a king, and the charioteers in his state.

[5]A man should consider his soul eternal and co-existence with God. He should always remember Him in his heart, and maintain his connection with Him, so that he may enjoy

Chapter (Anuvāka) 2

HYMN VI

१. पुमान् पुंसः परिजातोऽश्वत्थः खदिरादधि ।
स हन्तु शत्रून् मामकान् यानहं द्वेष्मि ये च माम् ।।

1. Just as the Peepal (Ficus Religiosa) tree grows from Khadira (Acacia Catechu), so is a hero born of a hero. May he destroy my enemies, who hate me and whom I detest. (394)

२. तानश्वत्थ निः शृणीहि शत्रून् वैबाध दोधतः । इन्द्रेण वृत्रघ्ना मेदी मित्रेण वरुणेन च ।।

2. O valiant horseman, in alliance with the king, who slays the enemies and loves his subjects, the police and the C.I.D. crush down the foes of the country, who torment the people. (395)

३. यथाश्वत्थ निरभनोऽन्तर्महत्यर्णवे । एवा तान्त्सर्वान्निर्भङ्ग्धि यानहं द्वेष्मि ये च माम् ।।

3. O valiant general, unwavering like a horse on the battlefield, just as thou, entering the mighty sea like the army, thou tearest apart and rendest the enemy, so rend asunder all those men who hate me and whom I detest. (396)

४. यः सहमानश्चरसि सासहान इव ऋषभः । तेनाश्वत्थ त्वया वयं सपत्नान्त्सहिषीमहि ।।

4. O valiant general, just as thou, like a prudent person, enduring all trials and tribulations patiently, defeated thy opponents again and again, displaying thy surpassing might, so should we, with thee, overcome our enemies! (397)

५. सिनात्वेनान् निर्ऋतिर्मृत्योः पाशैरमोक्यैः ।
अश्वत्थ शत्रून् मामकान् यानहं द्वेष्मि ये च माम् ।।

5. O General, may Misfortune, with the bonds of death which may never be loosened bind those enemies of mine, who hate me and whom I detest! (398)

६. यथाश्वत्थ वानस्पत्यानारोहन् कृणुषेऽधरान् ।
एवा मे शत्रोर्मूर्धानं विष्वग् भिन्द्धि सहस्व च ।।

6. O General, just as the Peepal tree mountest on the trees and overthrowest them, so dost thou humiliate thy foes, and break my foeman's head asunder and overpower him. (399)

७. तेऽधराञ्चः प्र प्लवन्तां छिन्ना नौरिव बन्धनात् । न वैबाधप्रणुत्तानां पुनरस्ति निवर्त्तनम् ।।

7. Let the enemies drift downward like a boat torn from the rope that fastened it. There is no turning back for the enemies who have been destroyed and scattered through afflictions. (400)

happiness. संवत्सर means God. सम्यग्वसन्ति लोका यत्र, in Whom reside all worlds: निवसति लोकेषु यः: Who resides in all the worlds.

८. प्रैणान् नुदे मनसा प्र चित्तेनोत ब्रह्मणा । प्रैणान् वृक्षस्य शाखयाश्वत्थस्य नुदामहे ॥

8. I drive the enemies forth with mental power, with intellect and spiritual force. We banish and expel them with the strength of the cavalry. (401)

HYMN VII

१. हरिणस्य रघुष्यदोऽधि शीर्षणि भेषजम् । स क्षेत्रियं विषाणया विषूचीनमनीनशत् ॥

1. The fleet-foot roebuck wears upon his head a healing remedy. A learned physician, cures with the horn, pulmonary consumption, the source of various sorts of ailments. (402)[1]

२. अनु त्वा हरिणो वृषा पद्भिश्चतुर्भिरक्रमीत् । विषाणे वि ष्य गुष्पितं यदस्य क्षेत्रियं हृदि ॥

2. O horn, after thy appearance the vigorous buck begins to bound with his four feet, remove thou the chronic disease, deeply inwoven in the heart of the patient! (403)[2]

३. अदो यदवरोचते चतुष्पक्षमिवच्छदिः । तेना ते सर्वं क्षेत्रियमङ्गेभ्यो नाशयामसि ॥

3. That deer-skin which covers the body on all four sides; therewith from out thy organs we drive all the chronic malady. (404)[3]

४. अमू ये दिवि सुभगे विचृतो नाम तारके । वि क्षेत्रियस्य मुञ्चतामधमं पाशमुत्तमम् ॥

4. May these twin auspicious forces of Prāṇa and Apāna, residing in the head, and releasers of suffering, free us from the bond of chronic malady, lurking in the lowest as well as the uppermost part of the body. (405)[4]

५. आप इद् वा उ भेषजीरापो अमीवचातनीः ।
आपो विश्वस्य भेषजीस्तास्त्वा मुञ्चन्तु क्षेत्रियात् ॥

5. Water, indeed, hath power to heal. Water drives malady away. May water, the curer of all diseases, free thee from permanent disease. (406)[5]

६. यदासुतेः क्रियमाणायाः क्षेत्रियं त्वा व्यानशे । वेदाहं तस्य भेषजं क्षेत्रियं नाशयामि त्वत् ।

6. If the use of impure water or foul food, hath brought inveterate disease on thee, I know the medicine that healeth it. I release thee from the malady. (407)

[1]A healing remedy: the horn. The horn possesses the medicinal virtue of ammonia which it contains. Pt. Khem Karan Das Trivedi has translated हरिण as God, and given a spiritual interpretation to the verse.

[2]The horn of a deer possesses the property of healing cough, catarrh, cpilepsy, consumption and respiratory diseases.

[3]'Thy' refers to the patient. 'We' refers to the skilled physicians. The wearing of the deer-skin cures piles and itching.

[4]See *Atharva*, 2-8-1.

[5]Thee refers to the patient,

७. अपवासे नक्षत्राणामपवास उषसामुत । अपास्मत् सर्वं दुर्भूतमप क्षेत्रियमुच्छतु ॥

7. On the disappearance of the starlight, on the departure of the gleams of Dawn, may evil fortune pass from us, may the chronic disease disappear. (408)[1]

HYMN VIII

१. आ यातु मित्र ऋतुभिः कल्पमानः संवेशयन् पृथिवीमुस्रियाभिः ।
अथास्मभ्यं वरुणो वायुरग्निर्बृहद् राष्ट्रं संवेश्यं दधातु ॥

1. Let the Sun come equipped with seasons, lulling the Earth to rest with gleams of splendour. And so let rainy water, air and fire make our dominion tranquil and exalted. (409)[2]

२. धाता रातिः सवितेदं जुषन्तामिन्द्रस्त्वष्टा प्रति हर्यन्तु मे वचः ।
हुवे देवीमदितिं शूरपुत्रां सजातानां मध्यमेष्ठा यथासानि ॥

2. May nourishing, charitable, and goading noblemen, the Commander-in-chief and The Chief Engineer hear with favour this word of mine and accept it. I invoke divine intellect, the mother of heroes, that I may be uppermost amongst my kinsmen. (410)[3]

३. हुवे सोमं सवितारं नमोभिर्विश्वानादित्यां अहमुत्तरत्वे ।
अयमग्निर्दीदायद् दीर्घमेव सजातैरिद्धोऽप्रतिब्रुवद्भिः ॥

3. For acquiring grandeur, I invoke with homage, the aid of dignified, leading and all heroic persons. Long may this fire of national spirit, send forth its splendour, lighted by kinsmen uttering no word against me. (411)[4]

४. इहेदसाथ न परो गमाथेर्यो गोपाः पुष्टपतिर्व आजत् ।
अस्मै कामायोप कामिनीर्विश्वे वो देवा उपसंयन्तु ॥

4. O subjects, here, verily, may you stay: go ye no farther. The learned guardian of the Earth. Your nourisher is leading you on the right path. To please this man, may all the learned persons together come unto you, the subjects, the cherishers of noble desires. (412)[5]

[1]Starlight disappears, when Dawn appears, and Dawn departs, when the sun rises. The light of the sun is a healer of diseases. Sun-light gives us freshness, new life and vitality.

[2]A king should strive to improve the dignity and status of his country by the use of watery, airy and fiery instruments, i.e., Jal-Astra, Vayu Astra, and Āgneya Astra.

[3]Intellect is the source of producing heroes in a nation. 'Mine' refers to the king.

[4]I and We, refer to the king.

[5]Guardian of the Earth: King 'Nourisher' refers to the King. This man: King. 'We' refers to the officials, 'Your refers to the subjects.

५. सं वो मनांसि सं व्रता समाकूतीर्नमामसि । अमी ये विव्रता स्थन तान् वः सं नमयामसि ।।

5. We bend together all your minds, your vows and purposes. We bend together you who stand apart with hopes opposed to ours. (413)

६. अहं गृभ्णामि मनसा मनांसि मम चित्तमनु चित्तेभिरेत ।
मम वशेषु हृदयानि वः कृणोमि मम यातमनुवर्त्मान एत ।।

6. I with my spirit hold and seize your spirits. Follow with thought and wish any thoughts and wishes. I make your hearts the thralls of my dominion; on me attendant come the way I guide you. (414)[1]

HYMN IX

१. कर्शफस्य विशफस्य द्यौः पिता पृथिवी माता । यथाभिचक्र देवास्तथाप कृणुता पुनः ।।

1. Refulgent God is the sire, Expanded God is the mother of the weak and strong. Just as ye victors had conquered the foes before, so do ye again move them hence away. (415)

२. अश्रेष्माणो अधारयन् तथा तन्मनुना कृतम् । कृणोमि वध्रि विष्कन्धं मुष्काबर्हो गवामिव ।।

2. Indefatigable souls sustain the universe, as does the Omniscient God. I render important an obstacle or a foe, as one emasculateth bulls. (416)[2]

३. पिशङ्गे सूत्रे खृगलं तदा बध्नन्ति वेधसः । श्रवस्युं शुष्मं काबवं वध्रिं कृण्वन्तु बन्धुरः ।।

3. The wise bind an obstacle under strict control. Let kinsmen make impotent a strong, tormenting foe. (417)

४. येना श्रवस्यवश्चरथ देवा इवासुरमायया । शुनां कपिरिव दूषणो बन्धुरा काबवस्य च ।।

4. Ye, renowned great men, with your strength, ye behave like conquerors, in obedience to the wisdom of God. Just as the monkey on the tree scorns the dogs, so should you scorn the troublesome malady or foe. (418)

५. दुष्ट्यै हि त्वा भत्स्यामि दूषयिष्यामि काबवम् । उदाशवो रथा इव शपथेभिः सरिष्यथ ।।

5. Yea, I will chide thee for removing thy depravity, I will blame the foe. Under our rebukes, ye, like rapid cars, shall be released of thy degradation. (419)[3]

६. एकशतं विष्कन्धानि विष्ठिता पृथिवीमनु । तेषां त्वामग्र उज्जहरुर्मणिं विष्कन्धदूषणम् ।।

6. One hundred and one obstacles are there spread abroad over earth. To

[1]'I' refers to the King. 'Your' refers to the subjects.

[2]'I' refers to a learned, ceaseless worker.

[3]'I' refers to the King. 'Thee' refers to the foe. The king through his admonitions and rebuke should reform the foe.

oppose and subdue them, O Praiseworthy hero, the queller of obstacles, have sages exalted thee! (420)

HYMN X

१. प्रथमा ह व्यु_वास सा धेनुरभवद् यमे । सा नः पयस्वती दुहामुत्तरामुत्तरां समाम् ॥

1. O celibate girl, verily, thou dwellest in the house of thy husband, as an excellent, newly married wife. In the house of thy husband, thou art the diffuser of joy like a cow. In the same way, let wife in our houses, the giver of ever-increasing happiness, fill them with joy from year to year! (421)[1]

२. यां देवाः प्रतिनन्दन्ति रात्रिं धेनुमुपायतीम् ।
संवत्सरस्य या पत्नी सा नो अस्तु सुमङ्गली ॥

2. The learned feel delighted to see that newly married girl, who affords comfort to all like Night, is a source of happiness in domestic life like a cow, and goes full of love towards her husband. She is the mistress of the house of her husband, who nourishes the children with food. May she bring abundant happiness to our society. (422)

३. संवत्सरस्य प्रतिमां यां त्वा रात्र्युपास्महे । सा न आयुष्मतीं प्रजां रायस्पोषेण सं सृज ॥

3. Thou whom with reverence we approach, O wife, the afforder of solace to the household lord, and the better half of her husband, vouchsafe us children long to live, bless us with increase of our wealth. (423)

४. इयमेव सा या प्रथमा व्यौच्छदास्वितरासु चरति प्रविष्टा ।
महान्तो अस्यां महिमानो अन्तर्वधूर्जिगाय नवगज्जनित्री ॥

4. The same is this bride, who, on account of her excellent qualities, in the midst of other ladies of the house, specially displays her merits, and moves well established in their hearts. Great powers and glories are contained in this newly married girl. May she, living with her new husband, bear children, and be considered superior to all other ladies in the house. (424)

५. वानस्पत्या ग्रावाणो घोषमक्रत हविष्कृण्वन्तः परिवत्सरीणम् ।
एकाष्टके सुप्रजसः सुवीरा वयं स्याम पतयो रयीणाम् ॥

5. May the wooden mortar and pestle ring and rattle, preparing oblation for the annual yajna (sacrifice) O bride, the constant guardian of the house, may we be lords of riches, with goodly children and heroic men around us. (425)[2]

[1]'Them' refers to houses. एकाष्टका means New Year's day. The newly married girl has been compared to एकाष्टका. Just as a new year's day is a source of enjoyment, so a newly married girl is a source of happiness to the family of her husband. Pt. Khem Karan Das Trivedi has applied this hymn on Matter.

[2]In a family provisions for oblations in a yajna should always be ground with mortar

६. इडायास्पदं घृतवत् सरीसृपं जातवेदः प्रति हव्या गृभाय ।
ये ग्राम्याः पशवो विश्वरूपास्तेषां सप्तानां मयि रन्तिरस्तु ॥

6. The ever-moving nature of a cow is full of butter. O God, accept our lauds. Tame animals of varied form and colour, may all the seven abide with me contented. (426)[1]

७. आ मा पुष्टे च पोषे च रात्रि देवानां सुमतौ स्याम । पूर्णा दर्वे परा पत सुपूर्णा पुनरापत ॥
सर्वान् यज्ञान्त्संभुञ्जतीषमूर्जं न आ भर ॥

7. O Mistress of the house, comforting like Night, help me in acquiring wealth and rearing children. May we all follow the sound advice of the learned. O subduer of all afflictions, fully developed in body, devote thyself to domestic duties; with a strong physique go to thy parental house, and return to thy father-in-law's, again and again, bringing food and energy to us. Just as a ladle filled full with butter empties itself in the yajna's fire again and again. (427)[2]

८. आयमगन्त्संवत्सरः पतिरेकाष्टके तव । सा न आयुष्मतीं प्रजां रायस्पोषेण सं सृज ॥

8. O wife, the sole, constant reformer of the house, this husband of thine is an embodiment of sacrifice, who is efficient in nicely bringing up the children. Vouchsafe us children long to live, bless them with increase of wealth. (428)

९. ऋतून् यज ऋतुपतीनार्तवानुत हायनान् । समाः संवत्सरान् मासान् भूतस्य पतये यजे ॥

9. May I perform yajna in all seasons. May I render fire and water, the lords of seasons favourable to me. May I make the parts of seasons comfortable to me through yajna. May I daily perform yajna. May I perform the lunar yearly, solar yearly and monthly yajnas. May I worship God, the Lord of all existing things. (429)[3]

१०. ऋतुभ्यष्ट्वार्तवेभ्यो माद्भ्यः संवत्सरेभ्यः । धात्रे विधात्रे समृधे भूतस्य पतये यजे ॥

10. O wife, may I ever keep thee in my company, and perform all noble deeds jointly with thee, during seasons, parts of seasons, months and years, for God the Nourisher, Creator, Developer and the Lord of all existing things! (430)

---

and pestle. The verse directs the newly married girl to perform Havan daily. Pt. Jaidev Vidyalankar puts an other interpretation on the first half of the verse. 'May noble, learned preachers austere in the performance of their duty, like the Sun, the lord of rays, preach the Vedas throughout the year.'

[1]Seven animals are: Cow, goat, sheep, elephant, donkey, horse and camel. A cow that moves freely and grazes yields more butter than one who remains tied in the house.

[2]'Me' refers to the husband, subduer of afflictions: consort.

[3]One should perform daily, monthly, seasonal, lunar, and solar yearly yajnas.

११. इडया जुह्वतो वयं देवान् घृतवता यजे । गृहानलुभ्यतो वयं सं विशेमोप गोमतः ।।

11. Performing Havan with cow's milk, we adore the learned and purify the forces of nature. Free from covetousness, may we live together in homes full of kine. (432)[1]

१२. एकाष्टका तपसा तप्यमाना जजान गर्भं महिमानमिन्द्रम् ।
तेन देवा व्यसिहन्त शत्रून् हन्ता दस्यूनामभवच्छचीपतिः ।।

12. The mistress of the house, observing the laws of domestic life, and sticking to her vow, retaining the great and glorious soul in her womb, gives birth to a babe. With him the learned subdue their adversaries. The same lord of might in the prime of youth, becomes the slayer of the enemies of the state. (433)

१३. इन्द्रपुत्रे सोमपुत्रे दुहितासि प्रजापतेः । कामानस्माकं पूरय प्रति गृह्णाहि नो हविः ।।

13. O wife, the mother of illustrious and courteous sons, thou art the fulfiller of all the desires of domestic life. Satisfy thou our hearts' desires. Gladly accept our devotion. (434)

Chapter (Anuvāka) 3

HYMN XI

१. मुञ्चामि त्वा हविषा जीवनाय कमज्ञातयक्ष्मादुत राजयक्ष्मात् ।
ग्राहिर्जग्राह यद्येतदेनं तस्या इन्द्राग्नी प्र मुमुक्तमेनम् ।।

1. For peaceful long life, I set thee free by this oblation both from unmarked decline and from consumption. Or if gout has possessed, free him from it, O sunlight, and warmth of the Yajna's fire. (435)[2]

२. यदि क्षितायुर्यदि वा परेतोयदि मृत्योरन्तिकं नीत एव ।
तमा हरामि निर्ऋतेरुपस्थादस्पार्शमेनम् शतशारदाय ।।

2. Be his days ended, be his case hopeless be he brought very near to death already; I bring him back from the lap of Death, and grant him strength to live for a hundred years. (436)[3]

३. सहस्राक्षेण शतवीर्येण शतायुषा हविषाहार्षमेनम् ।
इन्द्रो यथैनं शरदो नयात्यति विश्वस्य दुरितस्य पारम् ।।

[1]Forces of nature: fire, air, water.

[2]'I' refers to a physician, 'Thee' refers to a patient. 'Unmarked decline' is some insidious disease say hypertrophy, due to over-eating, resulting in the enlargement of organs. The fresh morning air, the rays of the sun, and the warmth of the fire of Homa cure a patient, suffering from gout. See *Atharva*, 2-9-1.

[3]'I' refers to a physician, he to a patient.

3. With medicine hundred flowered and hundred powered, bringing a life of hundred years, have I rescued him from the clutches of death. May God conduct him through a hundred years, safe to the farther shore of all misfortune. (437)[1]

४. शतं जीव शरदो वर्धमानः शतं हेमन्ताञ्छतमुवसन्तान् ।
शतं त इन्द्रो अग्निः सविता बृहस्पतिः शतायुषा हविषाहार्षमेनम् ।।

4. With medicine giving a life of hundred years, have I rescued this patient from the jaws of death. May thou live waxing in thy strength the hundred autumns, live for a hundred winters, a hundred springs. May God, the omniscient, the Creator and Lord of the universe grant thee life for a hundred years. (438)[2]

५. प्र विशतं प्राणापानावनड्वाहाविव व्रजम् । व्य१न्ये यन्तु मृत्यवो यानाहुरितराञ्छतम् ।।

5. Breath, Respiration, come to the patient, as two car-oxen to their stall! Let all the other causes of death, whereof men count a hundred, pass away. (439)[3]

६. इहैव स्तं प्राणापानौ माप गातमितो युवम् । शरीरमस्याङ्गानि जरसे वहतं पुनः ।।

6. Breath, Respiration, stay Ye here. Go ye not hence away from him. Take the body and organs of this patient verily to old age. (440)[4]

७. जरायै त्वा परि ददामि जरायै नि धुवामि त्वा ।
जरा त्वा भद्रा नेष्ट व्य१न्ये यन्तु मृत्यवो यानाहुरितराञ्छतम् ।।

7. O man free from disease, I hand thee over to old age, I keep thee physically fit till old age: Let kindly old age lend thee comfort. Let all the other causes of death, whereof men count a hundred, pass away. (441)

८. अभि त्वा जरिमाहित गामुक्षणमिव रज्ज्वा । यस्त्वा मृत्युरभ्यधत्त जायमानं सुपाशया ।
तं ते सत्यस्य हस्ताभ्यामुदमुञ्चद् बृहस्पतिः ।।

8. Old age hath girt thee with its bonds even as they bind a bull or a cow with rope. The death held thee at thy birth bound with a firmly knotted noose, therefore, with both the hands of Truth, God has loosened thee. (442)[5]

HYMN XII

१. इहैव ध्रुवां नि मिनोमि शालां क्षेमे तिष्ठाति घृतमुक्षमाणा ।।
तां त्वा शाले सर्ववीराः सुवीरा अरिष्टवीरा उप सं चरेम ।।

[1]I: a physician Him: a patient.

[2]I: a physician. Thee: a patient.

[3]Other causes of death: Besides natural death through old age. 'A hundred' means many. There are innumerable causes of death.

[4]Him: a patient.

[5]Both hands of truth: the true, efficacious medicine and the true virtuous acts of a man.

1. Here, even here I build my firm-set dwelling: flowing with prosperity may it stand in safety. May we approach thee, House with all our people, unharmed and goodly men, and dwell within thee. (443)

२. इहैव ध्रुवा प्रति तिष्ठ शालेऽश्वावती गोमती सूनृतावती ।
ऊर्जस्वती घृतवती पयस्वत्युच्छ्रयस्व महते सौभगाय ॥

2. Even here, O House, stand thou on firm foundation, wealthy in horses, rich in kine and chanting of vedic verses. Full of nourishment, butter, milk and water, rise up for great felicity and fortune. (444)

३. धरुण्य꣡सि शाले बृहच्छन्दाः पूतिधान्या ।
आ त्वा वत्सो गमेदा कुमार आ धेनवः सायमास्पन्दमानाः ॥

3. A spacious store, O House, art thou, full of clean corn and lofty roofed. Let the young calf and little boy play freely in thee and milchkine come running homeward in the evening. (445)

४. इमां शालां सविता वायुरिन्द्रो बृहस्पतिर्नि मिनोतु प्रजानन् ॥
उक्षन्तूद्ना मरुतो घृतेन भगो नो राजा नि कृषिं तनोतु ॥

4. May the Sun, Air, Cloud and an intelligent, skilled artisan build this house. May traders fill it with water and wealth. May fortunate king make our ploughing fruitful. (446)

५. मानस्य पत्नि शरणा स्योना देवी देवेभिर्निमितास्यग्रे ।
तृणं वसाना सुमना असस्त्वमथास्मभ्यं सहवीरं रयिं दाः ।

5. O respect—enhancing, sheltering, comfortable, beautiful house, thou wast built by skilled engineers in former times. Clad in thy robe of grass be friendly-minded, and give us wealth with valiant sons! (447)[1]

६. ऋतेन स्थूणामधि रोह वंशोग्रो विराजन्नप वृङ्क्ष्व शत्रून् ।
मा ते रिषन्नुपसत्तारो गृहाणां शाले शतं जीवेम शरदः सर्ववीराः ॥

6. Thou Flag, in ordered fashion mount the pillar. Strong, shining forth afar, keep off our foemen. House, let not those who dwell in thy rooms suffer. May we live with all our sons, a hundred autumns. (448)[2]

७. एमां कुमारस्तरुणा आ वत्सो जगता सह । एमां परिस्रुतः कुम्भ आ दध्नः कलशैरगुः ॥

7. To this house, let the tender boy, the youngman come, to this come the calf with other domestic animals. To this come the crock of flowing honey, milk and ghee, with jars of curdled milk. (449)[3]

[1]Clad in the robe of grass: Possessing spacious grassy lawns.

[2]The Om flag should always hang in the house, and national flag should hang on certain occasions.

[3]In a good house there should be kept a store of honey, ghee, milk and curdled milk (Dahī) young boys, elderly people, and domestic animals should roam freely in the house.

८. पूर्णं नारि प्र भर कुम्भमेतं घृतस्य धारामममृतेन संभृताम् ।
इमां पात्रीममृतेना समङ्ग्धीष्टापूर्तमभि रक्षात्येनाम् ॥

8. Bring hitherward, O dame, the well-filled pitcher, and the stream of molten butter blent with nectar, and feed the guests with nice food. Yajna, vedic study and charity preserve this house. (450)[1]

९. इमा आपः प्र भराम्ययक्ष्मा यक्ष्मनाशनीः । गृहानुप प्र सीदाम्यमृतेन सहाग्निना ॥

9. Water that kills disease, and is free from disease, here I bring. May I live happily in my houses, full of food, in the company of learned persons brilliant like fire. (451)

HYMN XIII

१. यददः संप्रयतिरहावनदता हते । तस्मादा नद्यो३ नाम स्थ तावो नामानि सिन्धवः ॥

1. As ye, when the cloud was burst, flowed forth together with a roar, so are ye called the roaring ones: such like, O Ye rivers, are your names! (452)[2]

२. यत् प्रेषिता वरुणेनाच्छीभं समवल्गत । तदाप्नोदिन्द्रो वो यतीस्तस्मादापो अनु ष्ठन ॥

2. As driven forth by the Sun, ye swiftly urged your roaring waves, there the Sun reached you as you flowed: hence your name is Āpa (waters). (453)[3]

३. अपकामं स्यन्दमाना अवीवरत वो हि कम् ।
इन्द्रो वः शक्तिभिर्देवीस्तस्माद् वार्नाम वो हितम् ॥

3. The swift Sun, with his might, restrained you flowing aimlessly, hence O streams of water, your name is vāri (worthy of being restrained). (454)[4]

४. एको वो देवोऽप्यतिष्ठत् स्यन्दमाना यथावशम् । उदानिषुर्महीरिति तस्मादुदकमुच्यते ॥

4. God alone, is your Master, O waters, flowing according to your will. Mighty powers breathed upward fast, hence Water is the name they bear. (455)[5]

[1]Hitherward means towards your house. Pitchers filled with milk and ghee should always remain in the house.

[2]When it rains on the bursting of the cloud, the rivers are filled with water. The flow together with a roar, and are called roaring streams, which have got different names.

[3]In this verse both the words आप्नोत् and आपः are formed from the same root आप to obtain, attain, get. Sun sends the rain and fills the streams with waters, it again reaches or obtains them through its rays, hence waters are named आपः as they are obtained by the Sun.

[4]Both the words अवीवरत् and वार are formed from the root वृ to restrain. As the Sun restrains the aimlessly flowing streams hence they are called वार (worthy of being restrained).

[5]Water from the mighty rivers goes up to the sky through the rays of the Sun उत आनिषुः, and उदकम्, both these words are formed from the root अन to breathe. There

५. आपो भद्रा घृतमिदाप आसन्नग्नीषोमौ बिभ्रत्याप इत् ताः ।
तीव्रो रसो मधुपृचामरंगम आ मा प्राणेन सह वर्चसा गमेत् ॥

5. Water is propitious. Water verily is the enhancer of power. Hydrogen and oxygen compose water. May the satiating, strong juice of water filled with sweetness, come helpful unto me with life and vigour. (456)

६. आदित् पश्याम्युतवा शृणोम्यामा घोषो गच्छति वाङ् मासाम् ।
मन्ये भेजानो अमृतस्य तर्हि हिरण्यवर्णा अतृपं यदा वः ॥

6. Then verily, I see, yea, also bear them: their sound approaches me, their voice comes hither. O glittering waters, when I drink my fill of you I realise as if I am enjoying the elixir of life! (457)

७. इदं व आपो हृदयमयं वत्स ऋतावरीः । इहेत्थमेत शक्वरीर्यत्रेदं वेशयामि वः ॥

7. O waters, this life-infusing power of yours, is a thing valuable like the heart. This frog and other watery animalcules are your children. O invigorating waters, flow here, just here, where I use you in my machines. (458)

HYMN XIV

१. सं वो गोष्ठेन सुषदा सं रय्या सं सुभूत्या । अहर्जातस्य यन्नाम तेना वः सं सृजामसि ॥

1. O Kine, we bestow on you a comfortable pen, abundant fodder and water, prosperity, and the choicest object obtainable in the day! (459)[1]

२. सं वः सृजत्वर्यमा सं पूषा सं बृहस्पतिः । समिन्द्रो यो धनञ्जयो मयि पुष्यत यद् वसु ॥

2. May the cowherd, the domestic lord, the learned veterinary doctor and the king, the winner of wealth, rear ye. Be nourished under my care, you are a nice wealth. (460)[2]

३. संजग्माना अविभ्युषिरस्मिन् गोष्ठे करीषिणीः । बिभ्रतीः सोम्यं मध्वनमीवा उपेतन ॥

3. O Kine, moving together, free from fear, with plenteous dropping, bearing efficacious sweet milk, free from all disease, come and dwell in this pen. (461)[3]

is a pun on Ud in उदकम् and उदानिषु: The going up of waters from the rivers and oceans in the form of vapour is a kind of their breathing, hence water is called उदकम्, as it goes up.

[1]Cows should be kept in a pen, where they may sit at ease. Sufficient water and fodder should be provided for them. Full care should be taken for their welfare. The best obtainable object in a day should be given to the cows to eat.

[2]Ye: cows.

[3]Droppings: the cow dung.

४. इहैव गाव एतनेहो शकेव पुष्यत । इहैवोत प्र जायध्वं मयि संज्ञानमस्तु वः ॥

4. Come hither, to this place, O Cows: here thrive like a married woman. Even here increase and multiply; may you love me. (462)[1]

५. शिवो वो गोष्ठो भवतु शारिशाकेव पुष्यत । इहैवोत प्र जायध्वं मया वः सं सृजामसि ॥

5. Auspicious be this stall to you. Prosper like cultivated rice. Even here increase and multiply. I take you with me for roaming. (463)

६. मया गावो गोपतिना सचध्वमयं वो गोष्ठ इह पोषयिष्णुः ।
रायस्पोषेण बहुला भवन्तीर्जीवाजीवन्तीरुप वः सदेम ॥

6. Follow me, cows, as master of the cattle. Here may this cow-pen make you grow and prosper. Still while we live may we approach you living, ever increasing with the growth of fodder. (464)

HYMN XV

१. इन्द्रमहं वणिजं चोदयामि सन ऐतु पुरएता नो अस्तु ।
नुदन्न रातिं परिपन्थिनं मृगं स ईशानो धनदा अस्तु मह्यम् ॥

1. I stir and animate the wealthy merchant; may he approach us and be our guide and leader. Chasing ill-will, wild beast, and highway robber, may he who hath the power give me riches. (465)

२. ये पन्थानो बहवो देवयाना अन्तरा द्यावापृथिवी संचरन्ति ।
ते मा जुषन्तां पयसा घृतेन यथा क्रीत्वा धनमाहराणि ॥

2. The many paths which the learned traders are wont to travel, the paths which go between the earth and heaven, may they satisfy me with milk and ghee, that I may make rich profit by my purchase. (466)[2]

३. इध्मेनाग्न इच्छमानो घृतेन जुहोमि हव्यं तरसे बलाय ।
यावदीशे ब्रह्मणा वन्दमान इमां धियं शतसेयाय देवीम् ॥

3. O Agni, with fuel and butter longing for profit, mine offering I present for strength and conquest. So far as I have strength, adoring the fine intellect with vedic knowledge, may I become competent to gain a hundred treasures. (467)

४. इमामग्ने शरणिं मीमृषो नो यमध्वानमगाम दूरम् ।
शुनं नो अस्तु प्रपणो विक्रयश्च प्रतिपणः फलिनं मा कृणोतु ।
इदं हव्यं संविदानौ जुषेथां शुनं नो अस्तु चरितमुत्थितं च ॥

[1]Place: cowshed.

[2]A merchant should travel in a ship by sea, or in an aeroplane by air, to go to different countries to make his business flourish.

4. O God, pardon this mistake of ours, that we have travelled to a distant place, far from home. Propitious unto us be sale and barter, may interchange of merchandise enrich me. Accept, ye twain accordant, this sale and purchase! Prosperous be our ventures and profits. (468)

५. येन धनेन प्रपणं चरामि धनेन देवा धनमिच्छमानः ।
तन्मे भूयो भवतु मा कनीयोऽग्ने सातघ्नो देवान् हविषा नि षेध ॥

5. O experienced traders, desirous of earning wealth with wealth, the wealth wherewith I carry on my business; may this grow more for me, not less. O King, through proper device chase those who hinder profit. (469)[1]

६. येन धनेन प्रपणं चरामि धनेन देवा धनमिच्छमानः ।
तस्मिन् म इन्द्रो रुचिमा दधातु प्रजापतिः सविता सोमो अग्निः ॥

6. O experienced traders, desirous of earning wealth with wealth, the wealth wherewith I carry on my business; may Indra, Prajāpati, Savitā, Soma and Agni, develop my taste and Zest in that. (470)[2]

७. उप त्वा नमसा वयं होतर्वैश्वानर स्तुमः । स नः प्रजास्वात्मसु गोषु प्राणेषु जागृहि ॥

7. With reverence we sing Thy praise, O God, the Bestower of gifts, the Well-wisher of all. Keep Thou watch over our children, over our souls and bodies, organs and lives. (471)[3]

८. विश्वाहा ते सदमिद्भरेमाश्वायेव तिष्ठते जातवेदः ।
रायस्पोषेण समिषा मदन्तो मा ते अग्ने प्रतिवेशा रिषाम ॥

8. Still in Thy name ever will we give alms, as we give fodder to a stabled horse, O God, the knower of all created objects. Joying in food and with growth of riches may we thy servants, O God, never suffer! (472)[4]

Chapter (Anuvāka) 4

HYMN XVI

१. प्रातरग्निं प्रातरिन्द्रं हवामहे प्रातर्मित्रावरुणा प्रातरश्विना ।
प्रातर्भगं पूषणं ब्रह्मणस्पतिं प्रातः सोममुत रुद्रं हवामहे ॥

1. Agni at dawn, and Indra we invoke at dawn, and Varuṇa and Mitra,

[1]If a trader goes to a distant foreign unknown place, he is liable to commit mistake in his business. Twain: two merchants exchanging their goods.

[2]Indra is glorious God, Prajāpati is God, the Lord of all His subjects. Savitā is God, the Creator of the universe. Soma is God, tranquil like the moon. Agni is God, as He is the foremost leader of all.

[3]Griffith considers this verse to be an interpolation. He has assigned no reason for these remarks, which are wide of the mark. Traders are exhorted in this verse to carry on their business with full faith in God.

[4]Businessmen should give a part of their income for charitable purposes.

and the Asvins twain; Bhaga at dawn, Pushan and Brahmanaspati, Soma at dawn, and Rudra we invoke at dawn. (473)[1]

२. प्रातर्जितं भगमुग्रं हवामहे वयं पुत्रमदितेर्यो विधर्ता ।
आध्रश्चिद् यं मन्यमानस्तुरश्चिद् राजा चिद् यं भगं भक्षीत्याह ॥

2. We invoke God, Who is our brilliant Protector and Saviour, like the Sun, that dispels darkness at dawn. God is the sustainer of Matter. Each poor, strong man, and even a king worshipping Him, addresses thus 'May I get renown and riches.' (474)

३. भग प्रणेतर्भग सत्यराधो भगेमां धियमुदवा ददन्नः ।
भग प्र णो जनय गोभिरश्वैर्भग प्र नृभिर्नृवन्तः स्याम ॥

3. O God, our guide, O God, Whose gifts are faithful, O God, granting us steady intellect, lead us on the path of prosperity. O God, augment our store of kine and horses. O God, may we be rich in men and heroes. (475)

४. उतेदानीं भगवन्तः स्यामोत प्रपित्व उत मध्ये अह्नाम् ।
उतोदितौ मघवन्त्सूर्यस्य वयं देवानां सुमतौ स्याम ॥

4. So may felicity be ours at present, at sunset, and at moontide. May we still, O Bounteous God, be happy at sunrise in the protecting favour of the learned. (476)

५. भग एव भगवाँ अस्तु देवस्तेना वयं भगवन्तः स्याम ।
तं त्वा भग सर्व इज्जोहवीमि सनो भग पुर एता भवेह ॥

5. May Almighty God verily be Bliss-Bestower, and through Him, may happiness attend us. As such with all my might I call Thee. As such be Thou our Leader here, O God! (477)

६. समध्वरायोषसो नमन्त दधिक्रावेव शुचये पदाय ।
अर्वाचीनं वसुविदं भगं मे रथमिवाश्वा वाजिन आ वहन्तु ॥

6. The Dawns incline to our non-violent sacrifice, just as a yogi resolves to visualise God. Just as swift steeds take a chariot afar, so may wise judgements,

[1](a) Agni is Refulgent God.
(b) Indra is Powerful, Supreme God.
(c) Mitra, Varuṇa: Both the words refer to God, who is dear to all like breaths, and is omnipotent.
(d) Aswins refer to preceptor and preacher, or father and mother.
(e) Bhaga is Adorable God.
(f) Pushan is All-sustaining God.
(g) Brahmanaspati is God, the Master of the Vedas and the universe.
(h) Soma is Omnipresent God.
(i) Rudra is God, the chastiser of the sinners.
See *Rig.*, 9, 47, 1-7 and *Yajur*, chapter 34 and verses 34-50.

equipped with my yogic powers, take the soul devoted to God, directly to the Almighty Father, the Afforder of shelter. (477)[1]

७. अश्वावतीर्गोमतीर्न उषासो वीरवतीः सदमुच्छन्तु भद्राः ।
घृतं दुहाना विश्वतः प्रपीता यूयं पात स्वस्तिभिः सदा नः ॥

7. O wise judgements, brilliant like the Dawn, equipped with the soul-force, the force of organs, and the force of breaths, affording joy, enlighten my heart, strengthening the soul, streaming with abundance, do you preserve us evermore with blessings! (478)

HYMN XVII

१. सीरा युञ्जन्ति कवयो युगा वि तन्वते पृथक् । धीरा देवेषु सुम्नयौ ॥

1. The learned, contemplative yogis, individually, concentrate their mind on the arteries, for worshipping God through yoga. They perform yogic exercises. Living in the midst of the wise with ease, they attain to final beatitude. (479)[2]

२. युनक्त सीरा वि युगा तनोत कृते योनौ वपतेह बीजम् ।
विराजः श्नुष्टिः सभरा असन्नो नेदीय इत् सृण्यः पक्वमा यवन् ॥

2. O yogis, unite the soul with God and enjoy happiness. Always expand the delight of salvation. Employ your acts of devotion, and arteries full of breath, in the worship of God. Having thus purified the mind, sow the seed of knowledge in it through yoga. May we soon acquire the fruit of yogas. May we through God's grace obtain the mature fruit of pure joy. Yogic functions act like sickles in allaying sufferings. May they be endowed with peace and prosperity. Practise union with God through them. (480)[3]

३. लाङ्गलं पवीरवत् सुशीमं सोमसत्सरु ।
उदिद्वपतु गामविं प्रस्थावद्रथवाहनं पीबरीं च प्रफर्व्यम् ॥

3. The breath, full of meditation, affording joy, goes up to the aperture in the crown of the head (Brahma Raudhara). The same breath strengthens our organs of cognition, soul and the body that moves with its parts. It exalts and elevates our sense of consciousness. (481)

[1]Griffith considers Dadhikravā as a mystical being. He is described as a kind of divine horse. This interpretation is illogical, as there is no history in the Vedas. The word means a yogi.

[2]See *Rig*, 10-10-14, and *Yajur*, 12-67. This hymn is generally applied to agriculture, but Maharshi Dayananda has given it a spiritual interpretation in the *Rigveda* Ādi Bhashya Bhumika, which I have followed.

[3]See *Rig*, 10-101-3 and *Yajur*, 62-68. They and them refer to Yogi functions.

४. इन्द्रः सीतां नि गृह्णातु तां पूषाभि रक्षतु । सा नः पयस्वती दुहामुत्तरामुत्तरां समाम् ।।

4. Just as a king realises the land revenue, and the treasury officer preserves it, so should the soul determine the breath-force. The nourishing breath should sustain the soul. May God create more and more joy obtainable through yogic concentration, as agriculture produces more corn through each succeeding year. (482)[1]

५. शुनं सुफाला वि तुदन्तु भूमिं शुनं कीनाशा अनु यन्तु वाहान् ।
शुनासीरा हविषा तोशमाना सुपिप्पला ओषधीः कर्तमस्मै ।।

5. The Prāṇas alone happily remove ignorance. May the learned control their breaths. May in-going and out-going breaths, controlled through Karm Yoga, create for this soul, the nice fruitful, sin-killing knowledge. (483)[2]

६. शुनं वाहाः शुनं नरः शुनं कृषतु लाङ्गलम् । शुनं वरत्रा बध्यन्तां शुनमष्ट्रामुदिङ्गय ।।

6. May organs, breaths, souls, mental attitudes, and power of perception, create extreme felicity. (484)[3]

७. शुनासीरेह स्म मे जुषेथाम् । यद् दिवि चक्रथुः पयस्तेनेमामुप सिञ्चतम् ।।

7. O Prāṇa and Udāṇa, remain under my control in the body. Just as the sun and air, rain on the earth, the water stored in heaven, so should Ye both bedew this mind with joy derivable from deep concentration. (485)[4]

८. सीते वन्दामहे त्वार्वाची सुभगे भव । यथा नः सुमना असो यथा नः सुफला भुवः ।।

8. O auspicious mental force, we venerate thee, come thou near us. That thou mayest grant us knowledge and bring us the fruit of salvation. (486)[5]

९. घृतेन सीता मधुना समक्ता विश्वैर्देवैरनुमता मरुद्भिः ।
सा नः सीते पयसाभ्याववृत्स्वोर्जस्वती घृतवत् पिन्वमाना ।।

9. O mental faculty endowed with splendour and strength, manifest thyself through organs and breaths. May the mental faculty coupled with vigour and brilliance, come before us again and again full of knowledge. (487)

HYMN XVIII

१. इमां खनाम्योषधिं वीरुधां बलवत्तमाम् । यया सपत्नीं बाधते यया संविन्दते पतिम् ।।

1. I search for this intellect efficacious like medicine, foe to ignorance, and

[1]See *Rig*, 4-57-7, and *Atharva*, 3-10-1.

[2]Prāṇas: Breaths. See *Rig*, 4-57-8 and *Yajur*, 12-69.

[3]See *Rig*, 4-57-4.

[4]My: A Yogi.

Ye: Prāṇa and Udāṇa. Udāṇa: one of the five vital airs or life breaths which rises up the throat and enters into the head. See *Rig*, 4-57-5.

[5]See *Rig*, 4-57-6.

competent to suppress sin. Wherewith one quells nescience that overpowers the soul, and wherewith one gains God, the Lord. (488)

२. उत्तानपर्णे सुभगे देवजूते सहस्वति । सपत्नीं मे परा णुद पतिं मे केवलं कृधि ।।

2. O knowledge of God, the afforder of vast protection, Auspicious, acquired by the learned, full of power, drive away ignorance, my foe, and make the joyous God my Guardian. (489)[1]

३. नहि ते नाम जग्राह नो अस्मिन् रमसे पतौ । परामेव परावतं सपत्नीं गमयामसि ।।

3. O ignorance, I never utter thy name. Thou dalliest not with this God, the Lord. Far into distance most remote we drive the rival ignorance away! (490)[2]

४. उत्तराहमुत्तर उत्तरेदुत्तराभ्यः । अधः सपत्नी या ममाधरा साधराभ्यः ।।

4. O knowledge of God, (Brahma Vidyā) may I become stronger. I am mightier than all the mighty sciences. Beneath me be my rival ignorance. May it be lower than the lowest acts! (491)

५. अहमस्मि सहमानाथो त्वमसि सासहिः । उभे सहस्वती भूत्वा सपत्नीं मे सहावहै ।।

5. I am the conqueror of lust and indignation, thou art the conqueror of sloth; may we both, tranquil and victorious, in unison, subdue ignorance, my foe. (492)[3]

६. अभि तेऽधां सहमानामुप तेऽधां सहीयसीम् ।
मामनु प्र ते मनो वत्सं गौरिव धावतु पथा वारिव धावतु ।।

6. O ignorance, for thy removal, may I acquire the knowledge of God, and learn from preceptors the knowledge of action, (Karma Vidyā) that subdues thee. O pupil, let thy mind run after me, as a cow hastens to her calf, or water flows down on its way. (493)[4]

HYMN XIX

१. संशितं म इदं ब्रह्म संशितं वीर्यं१ बलम् ।
संशितं क्षत्रमजरमस्तु जिष्णुर्येषामस्मि पुरोहितः ।।

1. May this Vedic knowledge of mine be intensified. May the manly strength and army of my country be irresistible. May the military strength of the kings, whose conquering priest am I, ever remain free from decay. (494)[5]

[1] उत्तानपर्णे has been interpreted by some commentators as a medicine with expanded leaves. The word means Brahma Vidyā that affords vast protection.

[2] I: Brahma Vidyā.

[3] I: Brahma Vidyā.
Thou: Karma Vidya.

[4] Me: A yogi teacher.

[5] Mine: of the Purohit or priest.

२. समहमेषां राष्ट्रं स्यामि समोजो वीर्यं१ बलम् । वृश्चामि शत्रूणां बाहूननेन हविषाहम् ॥

2. I strengthen the sway, the might, the manly strength and army of these kings. I rend asunder, with a wise device the foemen's disturbances. (495)[1]

३. नीचैः पद्यन्तामधरे भवन्तु ये नः सूरिं मघवानं पृतन्यान् ।
क्षिणामि ब्रह्मणामित्रानुन्नयामि स्वानहम् ॥

3. Down fall the men, low let them lie, who fight against our learned, wealthy prince. I ruin foemen with my vedic knowledge, and raise my friends to high estate. (496)[2]

४. तीक्ष्णीयांसः परशोरग्नेस्तीक्ष्णतरा उत । इन्द्रस्य वज्रात् तीक्ष्णीयांसो येषामस्मि पुरोहितः ॥

4. Keener than the axe's edge, keener than fire, keener than Indra's bolt are the kings whose priest and leader am I. (497)[3]

५. एषामहमायुधा सं स्याम्येषां राष्ट्रं सुवीरं वर्धयामि ।
एषां क्षत्रमजरमस्तु जिष्ण्वे३षां चित्तं विश्वेऽवन्तु देवाः ॥

5. The weapons of these kings I whet and sharpen, with valiant heroes I increase their kingdom. Victorious be their power and ever ageless! May all learned persons promote their thoughts and wishes. (498)[4]

६. उद्धर्षन्तां मघवन् वाजिनान्युद् वीराणां जयतामेतु घोषः ।
पृथग् घोषा उलुलयः केतुमन्त उदीरताम् । देवा इन्द्रज्येष्ठा मरुतो यन्तु सेनया ॥

6. O King, let swift steeds, well-fed neigh, and upward go the shout of conquering heroes. Let shout, roar and shriek of banner-bearing invader, rise apart and clear. Let victory-aspiring heroes led by the king, march forth to the battlefield. (499)

७. प्रेता जयता नर उग्रा वः सन्तु बाहवः ।
तीक्ष्णेषवोऽबलधन्वनो हतोग्रायुधा अबलानुग्रबाहवः ॥

7. Advance and be victorious, men! Exceeding mighty be your arms! Smite with sharp-pointed arrows those whose bows are weak. With your strong arms and weapons smite the feeble foe. (500)[5]

८. अवसृष्टा परा पत शरव्ये ब्रह्मसंशिते ।
जयामित्रान् प्र पद्यस्व जह्येषां वरंवरं मामीषां मोचि कश्चन ॥

8. Loosed from the bowstring fly away, thou arrow, sharpened by our

[1] I: The purohit.
[2] I: The priest.
[3] I: The priest.
[4] I: The priest.
[5] See *Rig*, 10-103-13 and *Yajur*, 17-46.

vedic knowledge. Assail the foemen, vanquish them, conquer each bravest man of theirs, and let not one of them escape. (501)[1]

HYMN XX

१. अयं ते योनिर्ऋत्वियो यतो जातो अरोचथाः । तं जानन्नग्न आ रोहाधा नो वर्धया रयिम् ॥

1. O soul, this God is thy ordered place of birth, whence sprung to life thou shinest forth. O learned soul, knowing God, go forward unto Him, and cause our riches to increase! (502)

२. अग्ने अच्छा वदेह नः प्रत्यङ् नः सुमना भव । प्र णो यच्छ विशां पते धनदा असि नस्त्वम् ॥

2. O God, instruct us nicely in this world. Be friendly minded unto us. O Lord of the people, enrich us. Thou art the giver of wealth unto us. (503)[2]

३. प्र णो यच्छत्वर्यमा प्र भगः प्र बृहस्पतिः । प्र देवीः प्रोत सूनृता रयिं देवी दधातु मे ॥

3. May just God grant us wealth. May glorious God, grant us wealth, may the Lord of the Vedas, grant us the knowledge of the Vedas. May the divine powers of God, grant us divine powers. May the true vedic speech, grant us true knowledge. (504)[3]

४. सोमं राजानमवसेऽग्निं गीर्भिर्हवामहे । आदित्यं विष्णुं सूर्यं ब्रह्माणं च बृहस्पतिम् ॥

4. For our protection, with prayers, we invoke God, the Creator of the universe, the Ruler of all, the Bestower of knowledge, the Giver of light to all like the Sun, the Omnipresent, the Almighty, the Lord of the knowledge of the Vedas. (505)[4]

५. त्वं नो अग्ने अग्निभिर्ब्रह्म यज्ञं च वर्धय । त्वं नो देव दातवे रयिं दानाय चोदय ॥

5. O God, with the aid of vedic scholars, strengthen our knowledge and sacrifice (Yajna). Incite Thou us, O God, to give and send us riches to bestow! (506)

६. इन्द्रवायू उभाविह सुहवेह हवामहे ।
यथा नः सर्व इज्जनः संगत्यां सुमना असद् दानकामश्च नो भुवत् ॥

6. O Sun and Air, Ye both, in this world nicely bestow life on us. Here do we sing your attributes, that in assembly all the folk may be benevolent to us, and be inclined to give us gifts! (507)

[1]See *Rig*, 6-75-16 and *Yajur*, 17-45.
[2]See *Yajur*, 9-28, *Rig*, 10-141-1, 2, 3, 4, 5, 6, for verses 2-7 of this hymn.
[3]See *Yajur*, 9-29.
[4]See *Yajur*, 9-26.

७. अर्यमणं बृहस्पतिमिन्द्रं दानाय चोदय । वातं विष्णुं सरस्वतीं सवितारं च वाजिनम् ॥

7. O God, urge a just leader, a vedic scholar, a mighty king, the vital breath, sacrifice (Yajna) vedic speech, and the powerful Sun, to grant us strength! (508)[1]

८. वाजस्य नु प्रसवे सं बभूविमेमा च विश्वा भुवनान्यन्तः ।
उतादित्सन्तं दापयतु प्रजानन् रयिं च नः सर्ववीरं नि यच्छ ॥

8. May we be competent to acquire knowledge and power. All these worlds of life are held within God. May the All-knowing God urge even the niggard to bounty. May He give us wealth coupled with noble sons. (509)[2]

९. दुह्रां मे पञ्च प्रदिशो दुह्रामुर्वीर्यथाबलम् । प्रापेयं सर्वा आकूतीर्मनसा हृदयेन च ॥

9. May heaven's five spacious regions pour their blessings for me with all their might. May I obtain each wish and hope formed by my spirit and my heart. (510)

१०. गोसनिं वाचमुदेयं वर्चसा माभ्युदिहि । आ रुन्धां सर्वतो वायुस्त्वष्टा पोषं दधातु मे ।

10. May I utter speech full of knowledge, O God, ameliorate me through divine splendour. May God in every way save me from treading evil paths. May God grant me strength. (511)

Chapter (Anuvāka) 5

HYMN XXI

१. ये अग्नयो अप्स्व१न्तर्ये वृत्रे ये पुरुषे ये अश्मसु ।
य आविवेशोषधीर्यो वनस्पतींस्तेभ्यो अग्निभ्यो हुतमस्त्वेतत् ॥

1. All Fires that are in water and cloud, all those that man and stones contain in them, that which hath entered herbs and trees and bushes, may all these Fires be put to proper use. (512)[3]

२. यः सोमे अन्तर्यो गोष्वन्तर्य आविष्टो वयःसु यो मृगेषु ।
य आविवेश द्विपदो यश्चतुष्पदस्तेभ्यो अग्निभ्यो हुतमस्त्वेतत् ॥

2. The Fire which abides in the Moon and in cattle, that which lies deep in birds and sylvan creatures, that which hath entered quadrupeds and bipeds, may all these fires be put to proper use. (513)[4]

[1]See *Yajur*, 9-27.

[2]See *Yajur*, 9-24, 25.

[3]बड़वानल fire is found in the ocean, lightning in clouds, digestive fire is found in men, magnetic fire is found in stones, ripening fire is found in herbs and plants. All these forces should be properly utilised.

[4]In cattle: The fire is the natural heat of their bodies which maintains their strength, swiftness, ferocity and other characteristic qualities.

३. य इन्द्रेण सरथं याति देवो वैश्वानर उत विश्वदाव्यः ।
यं जोहवीमि पृतनासु सासहिं तेभ्यो अग्निभ्यो हुतमस्त्वेतत् ॥

3. The Omnipresent God, that rideth by the side of soul in this vehicle of the body, consumes the universe at the time of its dissolution. Whom, as the Victor, I remember in all souls, may my sacrifice be conducive to the good of all these souls. (514)

४. यो देवो विश्वाद्यमु काममाहुर्यं दातारं प्रतिगृह्णन्तमाहुः ।
यो धीरः शक्रः परिभूरदाभ्यस्तेभ्यो अग्निभ्यो हुतमस्त्वेतत् ॥

4. God is all-devouring. Men call Him Kāma. They call Him the Giver and Receiver. He is Wise, Mighty, All-pervading, and Invincible. May my sacrifice be offered to all these forces of God. (515)[1]

५. यं त्वा होतारं मनसाभि संविदुस्त्रयोदश भौवनाः पञ्च मानवाः ।
वर्चोधसे यशसे सूनृतावते तेभ्यो अग्निभ्यो हुतमस्त्वेतत् ॥

5. O God, Strength-Giver, Glorious, Lord of the Vedas, Whom with their reflective strength, the thirteen physical and five elemental forces, regard as Hotar—priest—may my sacrifice be offered to Thee and all Thy forces. (516)[2]

६. उक्षान्नाय वशान्नाय सोमपृष्ठाय वेधसे । वैश्वानरज्येष्ठेभ्यस्तेभ्यो अग्निभ्यो हुतमस्त्वेतत् ॥

6. May my sacrifice be offered to God, Who feeds the strong and the weak, is the Embodiment of joy, and the Creator of all material objects. May my sacrifice be offered to those wise souls, who consider the Omnipresent God as sublime. (517)

७. दिवं पृथिवीमन्वन्तरिक्षं ये विद्युतमनुसंचरन्ति ।
ये दिक्ष्व१न्तर्ये वाते अन्तस्तेभ्यो अग्निभ्यो हुतमस्त्वेतत् ॥

7. May my sacrifice be offered to learned persons, who follow spiritual and physical laws, who know the science of space and lightning, and who adhere to the knowledge of the regions and air. (518)

८. हिरण्यपाणिं सवितारमिन्द्रं बृहस्पतिं वरुणं मित्रमग्निम् ।
विश्वान् देवानङ्गिरसो हवामह इमं क्रव्यादं शमयन्त्वग्निम् ॥

[1]Kāma: The inspirer and fulfiller of our wishes. Receiver: God receives our devotion, and grants salvation to noble souls at the time of dissolution, and thereby brings them near Himself.

[2]Thirteen: Two ears, two noses, two eyes, one mouth, two hands, two feet, penis, and arms.

Five: Earth, Water, Fire, Air and Space. Some commentators interpret five as Brahmana, Kshatriya, Vaisha, Shudra and Nishāda. Sāyana interprets thirteen as months of the year including the Laund month. 'Five' has been interpreted by some commentators as seasons.

8. We invoke the wealthy, the goader of all like the Sun, the Vedic scholars, the saviours of men from sin, the protectors of people from death, learned leaders, skilled physicians, and all learned persons to appease this flesh devouring fire of Death. (519)[1]

९. शान्तो अग्निः क्रव्याच्छान्तः पुरुषरेषणः । अथा यो विश्वदाव्य१स्तं क्रव्यादमशीशमम् ॥

9. Flesh-eating fire of lust is appeased, appeased is the fire of passion which hurteth men. I have stilled the flesh-consuming fire of sexual indulgence, that burneth everything. (520)[2]

१०. ये पर्वताः सोमपृष्ठा आप उत्तानशीवरीः । वातः पर्जन्य आदग्निस्ते क्रव्यादमशीशमन् ॥

10. The mountains where the herbs grow, the waters lying calm and still exposed to the Sun and Moon, pure air that removes disease, rainy cloud, sacrificial fire that purifies homes; all these appease the flesh-consuming malady of Death. (521)[3]

HYMN XXII

१. हस्तिवर्चसं प्रथतां बृहद्यशो अदित्या यत् तन्व१ः संबभूव ।
तत् सर्वे समदुर्मह्यमेतद् विश्वे देवा अदितिः सजोषाः ॥

1. May the vast glory, born out of the body-politic, possessed by the Commander-in-Chief, strong like an elephant, spread in the whole world. All officials and subjects accordant well, give that to me. (522)[4]

२. मित्रश्च वरुणश्चेन्द्रो रुद्रश्च चेततु । देवासो विश्वधायसस्ते माञ्जन्तु वर्चसा ॥

2. May the just magistrate, the head of the Police and C.I.D. the Commander-in-Chief, the head of Law and Order, always remain alert. May the all-fostering learned persons, anoint and balm me with their strength and glory. (523)[5]

३. येन हस्ती वर्चसा संबभूव येन राजा मनुष्ये॒ष्वप्स्व१न्तः ।
येन देवा देवतामग्र आयन् तेन मामद्य वर्चसाग्ने वर्चस्विनं कृणु ॥

3. The strength wherewith the elephant becomes powerful, that decks a king among the subjects in his state, wherewith the forces in nature in the beginning of creation attained to godhead, O Resplendent God, with that strength make Thou me vigorous in this life. (524)

[1]The state should arrange to reduce mortality, and provide for the happiness and longevity of the people.

[2]I: A man possessing self-control.

[3]The medicinal herbs on the mountains, pure water, pure air, clouds, and yajna's fire 'avert' death and conduce to longevity.

[4]Body-politic: Subjects of the king. Me: King; That: Glory.

[5]Me: The King.

४. यत् ते वर्चो जातवेदो बृहद् भवत्याहुतेः । यावत् सूर्यस्य वर्च आसुरस्य च हस्तिनः ।।
तावन्मे अश्विना वर्च आ धत्तां पुष्करस्रजा ।।

4. O Omnipresent God, just as an oblation poured into the fire heightens its lustre so does the sacrifice (Yajna) of the universe enhance Thy lofty strength. What strength the sun or the cloud possesses—such strength may father and mother, my nourishers, vouchsafe to me. (525)

५. यावच्चतस्रः प्रदिशश्चक्षुर्यावत् समश्नुते । तावत् समैत्विन्द्रियं मयि तद्धस्तिवर्चसम् ।।

5. Far as the heaven's four regions spread, far as the eye's most distant ken reaches, so wide, so vast be my soulpower, like the Sun. (526)

६. हस्ती मृगाणां सुषदामतिष्ठावान् बभूव हि । तस्य भगेन वर्चसाऽभि षिञ्चामि मामहम् ।।

6. Just as the elephant is the chief of all pleasant beasts to ride, so is the sun most resplendent of all the steady planets. With his high fortune and his strength I grace and consecrate myself. (527)

HYMN XXIII

१. येन वेहद् बभूविथ नाशयामसि तत् त्वत् । इदं तदन्यत्र त्वदप दूरे नि दध्मसि ।।

1. O woman, from thee we banish and expel the cause of thy sterility. We lay this apart and far removed from thee in another place! (528)[1]

२. आ ते योनिं गर्भ एतु पुमान् बाण इवेषुधिम् । आ वीरोऽत्र जायतां पुत्रस्ते दशमास्यः ।।

2. As arrow to the quiver, so let a male embryo enter thee. Then from thy side be born a babe, a ten-month child, thy heroic son. (529)[2]

३. पुमांसं पुत्रं जनय तं पुमाननु जायताम् । भवासि पुत्राणां माता जातानां जनयाश्च यान् ।।

3. O woman, give birth to a male son. Bring forth another male after him. The mother shalt thou be of sons born and hereafter to be born! (530)

४. यानि भद्राणि बीजान्यृषभा जनयन्ति च । तैस्त्वं पुत्रं विन्दस्व सा प्रसूर्धेनुका भव ।।

4. By the use of the auspicious seeds yielded by the herbs named Rishbhak, do thou O woman, obtain thyself a son: be thou a fruitful mother—cow! (531)[3]

५. कृणोमि ते प्राजापत्यमा योनिं गर्भ एतु ते ।
विन्दस्व त्वं पुत्रं नारि यस्तुभ्यं शमसच्छमु तस्मै त्वं भव ।।

[1]This: Cause of sterility.

[2]Thee, Thy refer to the woman.

[3]In shabda kalpa Druma, a lexicon, the seeds of the herb named Rishbhak are spoken of as possessing many medicinal properties, aiding a woman to give birth to a male child.

Mother: Cow: Just as a cow rears the calf with her milk, so should a mother nourish her child with her milk.

5. I give thee power to bear a child: within thee pass the germ of life! Obtain a son, O woman, who shall be a blessing unto thee. Be thou a blessing unto him. (532)

६. यासां द्यौः पिता पृथिवी माता समुद्रो मूलं वीरुधां बभूव ।
तास्त्वा पुत्रविद्याय दैवीः प्रावन्त्वोषधयः ॥

6. May those herbs whose father is the Sun, the Earth their mother and their root the rainy cloud, may those healing plants assist thee, O woman, to obtain a son. (533)

HYMN XXIV

१. पयस्वतीरोषधयः पयस्वन्मामकं वचः । अथो पयस्वतीनामा भरेऽहं सहस्रशः ॥

1. The plants of earth are rich in milk, and rich in sweetness is this my word. So from the rich plants I bring thousand-fold profit hitherward. (534)[1]

२. वेदाहं पयस्वन्तं चकार धान्यंऽबहु ।
सम्भृत्वा नाम यो देवस्तं वयं हवामहे यो यो अयज्वनो गृहे ॥

2. I know the Beneficial God. Abundant hath He made our corn. The charitable God is our Nourisher. Him we invoke Who dwelleth even in his house who sacrifices not. (535)[2]

३. इमा याः पञ्च प्रदिशो मानवीः पञ्च कृष्टयः । वृष्टे शापं नदीरिवेह स्फातिं समावहान् ॥

3. All the five regions of the heavens, all the five races of mankind—as after rain the stream is filled with water, let them bring increase hitherward. (536)[3]

४. उदुत्सं शतधारं सहस्रधारमक्षितम् । एवास्माकेदं धान्यंऽ सहस्रधारमक्षितम् ॥

4. Just as after the rains, ponds and waterfalls are filled with hundred showers, exhaustless, with a thousand showers, so may this corn of ours be exhaustless, with a thousand varieties. (537)

५. शतहस्त समाहर सहस्रहस्त सं किर । कृतस्य कार्यस्य चेह स्फातिं समावह ॥

5. O man, earn money with a hundred hands, and give it away in charity with a thousand hands. Thus fulfil here your bounden duty. (538)

[1]Milk: here used in its figurative sense of beneficial virtue.

[2]God is kind to the virtuous as well as the sinners. He tries to uplift the degraded and the downfallen.

[3]Five regions: North, South, East, West, the Zenith or the Nadir.
Five races: Brahmanas, Kshatriyas Vaishas, Shudras, Nishadas.

६. तिस्रो मात्रा गन्धर्वाणां चतस्रो गृहपत्न्याः ।
तासां या स्फातिमत्तमा तया त्वाभि मृशामसि ॥

6. Of the corn produced, the major and best part should be handed over to the lord of the house, for use in emergency, three parts of the rest should be given to the Government for the spread of education and administration of the state, and four parts should be reserved for domestic use by the mistress of the house. (539)

७. उपोहश्च समूहश्च क्षत्तारौ ते प्रजापते । ताविहा वहतां स्फातिं बहुं भूमानमक्षितम् ॥

7. O householder, collection and preservation, these two traits of thine are thy saviours from ruin. May they bring hither increase, wealth abundant and inexhaustible. (540)[1]

HYMN XXV

१. उत्तुदस्त्वोत् तुदतु मा धृथाः शयने स्वे । इषुः कामस्य या भीमा तया विध्यामि त्वा हृदि ॥

1. O ignorance, let a learned man dispell thee. Rest not in peace in the heart, thy bed. Terrible is the shaft of the desire for knowledge, therewith I pierce thee to the heart. (541)[2]

२. आधीपर्णां कामशल्यामिषुं सङ्कल्पकुल्मलाम् । तां सुसन्नतां कृत्वा कामो विध्यतु त्वा हृदि ॥

2. That arrow of knowledge, is winged with longing thought, its stem Desire, its neck, Resolve. Let desire for knowledge, having truly aimed, shoot forth and pierce thee, ignorance, in the heart. (542)

३. या प्लीहानं शोषयति कामस्येषुः सुसंनता । प्राचीनपक्षा व्योषा तया विध्यामि त्वा हृदि ॥

3. The shaft of intellect, coupled with noble desire, winged with vedic knowledge, consumes ignorance in various ways, and withers its pace. Therewith, I pierce thee ignorance to the heart. (543)

४. शुचा विद्धा व्योषया शुष्कास्याभि सर्प मा । मृदुर्निमन्युः केवली प्रियवादिन्यनुव्रता ॥

4. O Knowledge, steal to me, just as goes to her husband, a wife, pierced through with fiercely-burning heat, with parched lips, gentle and humble, serviceable, devoted with sweet words of love. (544)

५. आजामि त्वाजन्या परि मातुरथो पितुः । यथा मम क्रतावसो मम चित्तमुपायसि ॥

5. O Knowledge, with full exertion I imbibe thee from my mother and father, that thou mayest be at my command, and yield to every wish of mine! (545)

[1] 'They' refers to two traits. A householder should grow more food, collect corn, and preserve it for use when need. In this way he will be saved from ruin or loss.

[2] I refers to a learned person.

६. व्युस्यै मित्रावरुणौ हृदश्चित्तान्यस्यतम् । अथैनामक्रतुं कृत्वा ममैव कृणुतं वशे ॥

6. O Prāna and Apāna, enhance my heart's cravings for the acquisition of this knowledge. Make it my well-wiṣher, and put it under my control! (546)

Chapter (Anuvāka) 6

HYMN XXVI

१. ये३स्यां स्थ प्राच्यां दिशि हेतयो नाम देवास्तेषां वो अग्निरिषवः ।
ते नो मृडत ते नोऽधि ब्रूत तेभ्यो वो नमस्तेभ्यो वः स्वाहा ॥

1. O learned persons, who dwell within this eastern region. Ye are the pacifiers of the turbulent. Your knowledge of annihilating the sinners constitutes your fiery arrows. Be kind and gracious unto us, and instruct us. To you be reverence, to you be welcome! (547)

२. ये३स्यां स्थ दक्षिणायां दिश्यविष्यवो नाम देवास्तेषां वः काम इषवः ।
ते नो मृडत ते नोऽधि ब्रूत तेभ्यो वो नमस्तेभ्यो वः स्वाहा ॥

2. O learned persons, who dwell within this southward region, as Ye long for the safety of mankind. Ye are known as Avishyus. Iron determination constitutes your arrows. Be kind and gracious unto us. and instruct us. To you be reverence, to you be welcome! (548)

३. ये३स्यां स्थ प्रतीच्यां दिशि वैराजा नाम देवास्तेषां व आप इषवः ॥
ते नो मृडत ते नोऽधि ब्रूत तेभ्यो वो नमस्तेभ्यो वः स्वाहा ॥

3. Ye heroes anxious for victory, who dwell in this westward region, you are known for your great supremacy. Watery instruments are your arrows. Be kind and gracious unto us, and instruct us. To you be reverence, to you be welcome! (549)[1]

४. ये३स्यां स्थोदीच्यां दिशि प्रविध्यन्तो नाम देवास्तेषां वो वात इषवः ।
ते नो मृडत ते नोऽधि ब्रूत तेभ्यो वो नमस्तेभ्यो वः स्वाहा ॥

4. Ye heroes anxious for victory, who dwell in this northern region you are the piercers of foes. Airy instruments are your arrows. Be kind and gracious unto us, and instruct us. To you be reverence, to you be welcome! (550)[2]

५. ये३स्यां स्थ ध्रुवायां दिशि निलिम्पा नाम देवास्तेषां व ओषधीरिषवः ।
ते नो मृडत ते नोऽधि ब्रूत तेभ्यो वो नमस्तेभ्यो वः स्वाहा ॥

5. Ye heroes auxious for victory, who dwell in this firm-set region, you are known as Physicians. Medicinal plants are your arrows. Be kind and

[1]The brave persons living in the west overcome their foes by the use of watery instruments.

[2]The brave persons living in the north pierce the foes with dagger and bullet, and use वायव्य airy missiles to subdue the enemy.

gracious unto us, and instruct us. To you be reverence, to you be welcome! (551)[1]

६. येऽस्यां स्थोध्र्वायां दिश्यवस्वन्तो नाम देवास्तेषां वो बृहस्पतिरिषवः ।
ते नो मृडत ते नोऽधि ब्रूत तेभ्यो वो नमस्तेभ्यो वः स्वाहा ॥

6. Ye learned persons who dwell in this upmost region, Nourishers by name, Commander-in-Chief forms your arrow. Be kind and gracious unto us and instruct us. To you be reverence, to you be welcome. (552)[2]

HYMN XXVII

१. प्राची दिगग्निरधिपतिरसितो रक्षितादित्या इषवः ।
तेभ्यो नमोऽधिपतिभ्यो नमो रक्षितृभ्यो नम इषुभ्यो नम एभ्यो अस्तु ॥
योऽस्मान् द्वेष्टि यं वयं द्विष्मस्तं वो जम्भे दध्मः ॥

1. A Commander, expert in the science of fiery instruments is regent of the East, its warder is a man of independent nature, free from shackles, men of glory, knowledge, eloquence, self-respect are its arrows. Worship to these the regents, these the warders, and to the arrows. Yea, to these all be worship. Within your jaws of justice we lay the man who hateth us and whom we dislike. (553)[3]

२. दक्षिणा दिगिन्द्रोऽधिपतिस्तिरश्चिराजी रक्षिता पितर इषवः ।
तेभ्यो नमोऽधिपतिभ्यो नमो रक्षितृभ्यो नम इषुभ्यो नम एभ्यो अस्तु ।
योऽस्मान् द्वेष्टि यं वयं द्विष्मस्तं वो जम्भे दध्मः ॥

2. A foe-conquering hero is regent of the south, he who never transgresses the moral law is its warder, powers of procreation are its arrows. Worship to these the regents, these the warders, and to the arrows, yea to these all be worship. Within your jaws of justice we lay the man who hateth us and whom we dislike. (554)[4]

[1]Dwellers in the lower region (Nadir) are known as physicians who cure the wounded soldiers.

[2]The connection of six devas with six regions is not so clear to me.

[3]One should not hate another person. None should take the law into his own hands. One who deserves punishment for his misdeeds should be handed over to the justice-loving people for punishment. East is spoken of as the abode of martial independent and learned persons. East is symbolic of progress, advancement. Sun rises in the East and advances by and by. Your refers to the regent, warders and learned, eloquent persons, who have figuratively been spoken of as arrows or instruments to be used for advancement.

[4]South is symbolic of दक्षता i.e., ability, fitness, strength of will, energy and resoluteness.

३. प्रतीची दिग् वरुणोऽधिपतिः पृदाकू रक्षितान्नमिषवः ।
तेभ्यो नमोऽधिपतिभ्यो नमो रक्षितृभ्यो नम इषुभ्यो नम एभ्यो अस्तु ।
योऽस्मान् द्वेष्टि यं वयं द्विष्मस्तं वो जम्भे दध्मः ॥

3. A noble soul is regent of the West, an energetic, enterprising person is its warder, and nourishment the arrows. Worship to these the regents, these the warders, and to the arrows, Yea to these all be worship. Within your jaws of justice, we lay the man who hateth us and whom we dislike. (555)[1]

४. उदीची दिक् सोमोऽधिपतिः स्वजो रक्षिताशनिरिषवः ।
तेभ्यो नमोऽधिपतिभ्यो नमो रक्षितृभ्यो नम इषुभ्यो नम एभ्यो अस्तु ॥
योऽस्मान् द्वेष्टि यं वयं द्विष्मस्तं वो जम्भे दध्मः ॥

4. A peace-loving person is ruler of the Northern region. An ever-active person, free from sloth is its warder, and lightning flash the arrows. Worship to these the rulers, these the warders, and to the arrows. Yea to these all be worship. Within your jaws of justice, we lay the man who hateth us and whom we dislike. (556)

५. ध्रुवा दिग् विष्णुरधिपतिः कल्माषग्रीवो रक्षिता वीरुध इषवः ।
तेभ्यो नमोऽधिपतिभ्यो नमो रक्षितृभ्यो नम इषुभ्यो नम एभ्यो अस्तु ।
योऽस्मान् द्वेष्टि यं वयं द्विष्मस्तं वो जम्भे दध्मः ॥

5. An enterprising person is ruler of the firm-set region, a man of action is its warder, plants are the arrows. Worship to these the rulers, these the warders, and to the arrows. Yea to these all be worship. Within your jaws of justice, we lay the man who hateth us and whom we dislike. (557)[2]

६. ऊर्ध्वा दिग् बृहस्पतिरधिपतिः श्वित्रो रक्षिता वर्षमिषवः ।
तेभ्यो नमोऽधिपतिभ्यो नमो रक्षितृभ्यो नम इषुभ्यो नम एभ्यो अस्तु ।
योऽस्मान् द्वेष्टि यं वयं द्विष्मस्तं वो जम्भे दध्मः ॥

6. A man of spiritual knowledge controls the topmost region, a pure-minded person is its warder, pure rainy water are the arrows. Worship to these the rulers, these the warders and to the arrows. Yea to these all be worship. Within your jaws of justice, we lay the ignorant men who hateth us and whom we dislike. (558)[3]

[1]West is symbolic of rest, relaxation. When the sun sets in the West, people go to sleep and take rest. Food or nourishment is the main source of sleep. One cannot enjoy sleep with an empty stomach. We should honour noble, enterprising souls, and take due care of our food.

[2]Firm-set region means Nadir.

[3]Topmost region means Zenith. This region refers to spiritual uplift and advancement.

HYMN XXVIII

१. एकैकयैषा सृष्टचा सं बभूव यत्र गा असृजन्त भूतकृतो विश्वरूपा: ।
यत्र विजायते यमिन्यपर्तु: सा पशून् क्षिणाति रिफती रुशती ।।

1. This world has been created by the combination of one atom with the other. Various sorts of divine forces have been set free in the universe for creating living beings. Where Divine and temporal forces go out of order, and clash with each other, that chaos degrades torments and ruins the souls. (559)

२. एषा पशून्त्सं क्षिणाति क्रव्याद् भूत्वा व्यद्वरी ।
उतैनां ब्रह्मणे दद्यात् तथा स्योना शिवा स्यात् ।।

2. That chaos, destroying each and every one, and being flesh-devourer, ruins common ignorant persons. At such a critical time, the chaos in the society should be handed over to a highly learned person, who knows the Vedas, for the restoration of peace and happiness. (560)

३. शिवा भव पुरुषेभ्यो गोभ्यो अश्वेभ्य: शिवा । शिवास्मै सर्वस्मै क्षेत्राय शिवा न इहैधि ।।

3. O royal administration, be thou auspicious to our folk, bring luck to horses and kine. Be thou auspicious unto the whole state. Bring luck and happiness to us in this world. (561)

४. इह पुष्टिरिह रस इह सहस्रसातमा भव । पशून् यमिनि पोषय ।।

4. O administrative Assembly, let there be increase in the state, let there be milk and ghee, be thou most munificent, strengthen thou the cattle and ignorant common people of the state. (562)

These six verses of this hymn XXVII can also be interpreted thus:

(1) "Wise God is Ruler of the East. He, free from shackles is its warder, the rays of the sun are like arrows." Just as arrows bring the sinner to the right path, so do the rays of the sun grant us health, vigour and freshness.

(2) Highly Refulgent God is Ruler of the South. He is our saviour from the host of the reptiles like scorpions who do not walk straight, but move away. Learned persons are like its arrows.

(3) The sublimest God is ruler of the West. He is our saviour from the attack of poisonous snakes. Food is like arrows, that protect the noble and punish the sinners

(4) "God, the Creator of the universe is ruler of the North, the unborn God is our saviour, lightning's flash acts as arrows." Just as in a dark night thc flash of lightning shows a passenger the right path, so arrows engendering fear bring a sinner to the right path of virtue.

(5) "The Omnipresent God is ruler of the Nadir, and our saviour like the green leaves of trees, plants are like arrows."

As trees with green leaves afford protection to a fatigued traveller, so God affords protection to a jaded soul. As plants give us nourishment, so arrows save good persons from marauders and free-booters.

(6) God, the Lord of the vedas and space is ruler of the Zenith. He, full of knowledge and eminence, is our saviour. The particles of rain act as arrows.

Just as drops of rain cool the scorching atmosphere, so arrows protect the noble from the hands of the wicked.

५. यत्रा सुहार्दः सुकृतो मदन्ति विहाय रोगं तन्व१ः स्वायाः ।
तं लोकं यमिन्यभिसंबभूव सा नो मा हिंसीत् पुरुषान् पशूंश्च ।।

5. Where, the noble-hearted, and the pious-minded, having left all sickness of their bodies, pass their lives in happiness, in that country the Administrative Assembly (Rajya Sabha) works nicely, and sees that our people and our cattle are not harmed. (563)

६. यत्रा सुहार्दां सुकृतामग्निहोत्रहुतां यत्र लोकः ।
तं लोकं यमिन्यभिसंबभूव सा नो मा हिंसीत् पुरुषान् पशूंश्च ।।

6. Where reside the noble-hearted, pious-minded people and performers of Agni-Hotra, there the Raj Sabha works nicely, and sees that our people and our cattle are not harmed. (564)

HYMN XXIX

१. यद् राजानो विभजन्त इष्टापूर्त्तस्य षोडशं यमस्यामी सभासदः ।
अविस्तस्मात् प्र मुञ्चति दत्तः शितिपात् स्वधा ।।

1. Whereby, prosperous great men, the subjects of God, attain to salvation, as the fruit of noble deeds like sacrifice, study of the Vedas, and acts of charity; thereby God, the same in light and darkness, retained by the soul, strengthens our soul, grants us riches and nicely releases our energetic soul. (565)

२. सर्वान् कामान् पूरयत्याभवन् प्रभवन् भवन् । आकूतिप्रोऽविर्दत्तः शितिपान्नोप दस्यति ।।

2. God, the fulfiller of resolves, worshipped by the soul, same in light and darkness, Omnipresent, Mighty and Ever-Existent, satisfies all hopes and wants and never suffers decay. (566)[1]

३. यो ददाति शितिपादमविं लोकेन संमितम् ।
स नाकमभ्यारोहति यत्र शुल्को न क्रियते अबलेन बलीयसे ।।

3. He who dedicates to God, the intelligent soul, honoured by all, ascends to the celestial height of emancipation, where tribute is not paid to one more mighty by the weak. (567)[2]

४. पञ्चापूपं शितिपादमविं लोकेन संमितम् । प्रदातोप जीवति पितॄणां लोकेऽक्षितम् ।।

4. He who dedicates to God, the conscious soul, a prey to five passions, and honoured by all, leads in the society of the learned and the aged, a life of deathless joy. (568)[3]

[1]Four Ashramas, four varnas, hearing, (श्रवण) reflecting, (मनन) meditating (निदिध्यासन), desire for the unattained, protection of the attained development of the attained, proper use of the developed. The 16th object after the fulfilment of the first fifteen is salvation.

[2]No injustice or oppression is exercised by the strong over the weak in a highly spiritualised society.

[3]Five passions: (1) Lust (2) Anger (3) Avarice (4) Infatuation (5) Pride.

५. पञ्चापूपं शितिपादमविं लोकेन संमितम् । प्रदातोप जीवति सूर्यामासयोरक्षितम् ।

5. He who dedicates to God, the conscious soul, a prey to five passions, and honoured by all, leads in the presence of the Sun and Moon, a life of deathless joy. (569)

६. इरेव नोप दस्यति समुद्रइव पयो महत् । देवौ सवासिनाविव शितिपान्नोप दस्यति ।।

6. The conscious soul faileth not like knowledge, like the ocean full of vast water, like the Sun and Moon, companions in the sky. (570)

७. क इदं कस्मा अदात् कामः कामायादात् ।
कामो दाता कामः प्रतिग्रहीता कामः समुद्रमा विवेश ।
कामेन त्वा प्रति गृह्णामि कामैतत् ते ।।

7. Who has granted this fruit of action to whom God has given it to the soul. God, is the Giver, and soul the receiver. The soul full of desires, passes into God, the ocean of felicity. All business of the world is the manifestation of desire. (571)

८. भूमिष्ट्वा प्रति गृह्णात्वन्तरिक्षमिदं महत् ।
माहं प्राणेन मात्मना मा प्रजया प्रतिगृह्य वि राधिषि ।।

8. May Earth receive thee as her own, and this great atmosphere as well. Having accepted desire, may I commit no offence with my body, mind, soul and progeny. (572)[1]

HYMN XXX

१. सहृदयं सांमनस्यमविद्वेषं कृणोमि वः । अन्यो अन्यमभि हर्यत वत्सं जातमिवाघ्न्या ।।

1. Freedom from hate I bring to you, concord and unanimity. Love one another as the cow loveth the calf that she hath borne. (573)[2]

२. अनुव्रतः पितुः पुत्रो मात्रा भवतु संमनाः । जाया पत्ये मधुमतीं वाचं वदतु शन्तिवाम् ।।

2. One-minded with his mother let the son be loyal to his sire. Let the wife speak to her husband words calm and gentle, and sweet as honey. (574)

३. मा भ्राता भ्रातरं द्विक्षन्मा स्वसारमुत स्वसा । सम्यञ्चः सव्रता भूत्वा वाचं वदत भद्रया ।।

3. Let no brother hate his brother, no sister to sister be unkind. Unanimous, with one intent, speak ye your speech in friendliness. (575)

४. येन देवा न वियन्ति नो च विद्विषते मिथः । तत् कृण्मो ब्रह्म वो गृहे संज्ञानं पुरुषेभ्यः ।।

4. That Knowledge of the Vedas, through which the sages sever not, nor

[1]Thee refers to desire.
[2]'I' refers to God.

ever bear each other hate, that unifying knowledge we spread in your house for men. (576)

५. ज्यायस्वन्तश्चित्तिनो मा वि यौष्ट संराधयन्तः सधुराश्चरन्तः ।
अन्यो अन्यस्मै वल्गु वदन्त एत सध्रीचीनान् वः संमनसस्कृणोमि ॥

5. Obedient to the elders, intelligent, rest united friendly and kind, bearing the yoke together. Come, speaking sweetly each one to the other. I make you one-intentioned and one-minded. (577)[1]

६. समानी प्रपा सह वोऽन्नभागः समाने योक्त्रे सह वो युनज्मि ।
सम्यञ्चोऽग्निं सपर्यतारा नाभिमिवाभितः ॥

6. Drink and eat together, with one common bond of love I bind you. Just as spokes are united about the chariot nave, so should you unitedly worship God. (578)[2]

७. सध्रीचीनान् वः संमनसस्कृणोम्येकश्नुष्टीन्त्संवननेन सर्वान् ।
देवाइवामृतं रक्षमाणाः सायंप्रातः सौमनसो वो अस्तु ॥

7. With binding charm I make you all united, obeying one sole leader and one-minded. Like the sages who watch and guard the eternal soul, at morn and eve may ye worship God with one mind. (579)[3]

HYMN XXXI

१. वि देवा जरसावृतन् वि त्वमग्ने अरात्या । व्य१हं सर्वेण पाप्मना वि यक्ष्मेण समायुषा ॥

1. Learned persons keep aloof old age. O learned person, keep aloof from stinginess and your foe. May I remain aloof from all sins and pulmonary disease. May I be linked with old age. (580)

२. व्यार्त्या पवमानो वि शक्रः पापकृत्यया । व्य१हं सर्वेण पाप्मना वि यक्ष्मेण समायुषा ॥

2. A pure soul remains free from physical and mental pain. An energetic and strong soul commits no sin. May I remain aloof from all sins and pulmonary disease. May I be linked with old age. (581)

३. वि ग्राम्याः पशव आरण्यैर्व्याऽपस्तृष्णयासरन् ।
व्य१हं सर्वेण पाप्मना वि यक्ष्मेण समायुषा ॥

3. Just as tame domestic beasts remain away from wild beasts of the forests, so may I remain aloof from all sins and pulmonary disease. May I be linked with old age. (582)

[1]'I' refers to God. Bearing the yoke: Men should jointly discharge the burden of their responsibility.

[2]'I' refers to God.

[3]'I' refers to God.

४. वी३मे द्यावापृथिवी इतो वि पन्थानो दिशंदिशम् ।
व्य१हं सर्वेण पाप्मना वि यक्ष्मेण समायुषा ॥

4. Just as heaven and earth are parted, and paths run separate in each direction, so may I remain aloof from all sins and pulmonary disease. May I be linked with old age. (583)

५. त्वष्टा दुहित्रे वहतुं युनक्तीतीदं विश्वं भुवनं बि याति ।
व्य१हं सर्वेण पाप्मना वि यक्ष्मेण समायुषा ॥

5. Just as a prudent father sets apart dowry for his daughter, just as planets revolve separately in the universe, so may I remain aloof from all sins and pulmonary disease. May I be linked with old age. (584)

६. अग्निः प्राणान्त्सं दधाति चन्द्रः प्राणेन संहितः ।
व्य१हं सर्वेण पाप्मना वि यक्ष्मेण समायुषा ॥

6. Just as heat of the stomach digesting food nourishes all organs, just as the moon united with breaths strengthens the soul, so may I, being free from sins and pulmonary disease be yoked with old age. (585)

७. प्राणेन विश्वतोवीर्यं देवाः सूर्यं समैरयन् । व्य१हं सर्वेण पाप्मना वि यक्ष्मेण समायुषा ॥

7. Just as the self-controlled yogis have achieved the Almighty, Omnipresent God, through the concentration of breath, so may I, being free from sins and pulmonary disease be yoked with old age. (586)

८. आयुष्मतामायुष्कृतां प्राणेन जीव मा मृथाः । व्य१हं सर्वेण पाप्मना वि यक्ष्मेण समायुषा ॥

8. O soul, don't be a prey to early death, depending upon the knowledge and strength of learned persons, who enjoy a long life, and make others live long. May I, being free from sins and pulmonary disease, be yoked with old age! (587)[1]

९. प्राणेन प्राणतां प्राणेहैव भव मा मृथाः । व्य१हं सर्वेण पाप्मना वि यक्ष्मेण समायुषा ॥

9. O soul, depart not early stay here. Breathe with the breath of those who draw the vital air. May I, being free from sins and pulmonary disease, be yoked with old age. (588)[2]

१०. उदायुषा समायुषोदोषधीनां रसेन । व्य१हं सर्वेण पाप्मना वि यक्ष्मेण समायुषा ॥

10. Let us advance enjoying a long life, and keep death away. Let us flourish in the world, acquiring a long life. Let us suppress death by the use of medicinal juices. May I, being free from sins and pulmonary disease, be yoked with old age. (589)

[1]Death means departure from the body. Soul is deathless and immortal.
[2]Here: In the body.

११. आ पर्जन्यस्य वृष्ट्योदस्थामामृता वयम् । व्य१हं सर्वेण पाप्मना वि यक्ष्मेण समायुषा ॥

11. May we acquire prosperity through rain from clouds, and be free from premature death. May I, being free from sins and pulmonary disease, be yoked with old age. (590)

BOOK (Kāṇḍa) IV

Chapter (Anuvāka) 1

HYMN I

१. ब्रह्म जज्ञानं प्रथमं पुरस्ताद् वि सीमतः सुरुचो वेन आवः ।
स बुध्न्या उपमा अस्य विष्ठाः सतश्च योनिमसतश्च वि वः ॥

1. That God alone is Adorable, Who, in the beginning of the universe created everything, is wide in expansion, Highest of all, Effulgent and worthy of worship. The Sun, Moon and other worlds in the atmosphere stationed in their orbits, testify to His knowledge. He pervades them all through His Omnipresence and comprehends the visible and the invisible in space. (591)

२. इयं पित्र्या राष्ट्र्येत्वग्रे प्रथमाय जनुषे भुवनेष्ठाः ।
तस्मा एतं सुरुचं ह्वारमह्यं घर्मं श्रीणन्तु प्रथमाय धास्यवे ॥

2. Let this royal vedic speech, prevalent in the world, emanated from God, the Father come unto us for making us lead an excellent life. Perform this pleasant Yajna, the suppressor of the ignoble, free from fault, for the acquisition of that Eternal God, the Nourisher of all. (592)

३. प्र यो जज्ञे विद्वानस्य बन्धुर्विश्वा देवानां जनिमा विवक्ति ।
ब्रह्म ब्रह्मण उज्जभार मध्यान्नीचैरुच्चैः स्वधा अभि प्र तस्थौ ॥

3. God, Who is the Controller of the universe, is the Creator and Knower of all objects. He preaches through the Vedas, the different modes of creation of all the forces of Nature like the Sun, Earth, etc. From Him comes the knowledge of the Vedas. Hence, Self-existent He pervades all places low and high. (593)

४. स हि दिवः स पृथिव्या ऋतस्था मही क्षेमं रोदसी अस्कभायत् ।
महान् मही अस्कभायद् वि जातो द्यां सद्म पार्थिवं च रजः ॥

4. Verily God is the Efficient Cause of Earth and Heaven. He established both the mighty worlds securely. The Mighty God hath propped both these mighty worlds. He through His myriad powers, supports the Heaven, the Earth, our home, and the atmosphere. (594)

५. स बुध्न्या दाष्ट्र जनुषोऽभ्यग्रं बृहस्पतिर्देवता तस्य सम्राट् ।
अहर्यच्छुक्रं ज्योतिषो जनिष्ठाथ द्युमन्तो वि वसन्तु विप्राः ॥

5. God, the Illuminator of all, is the Emperor of this world. He pervades the created universe from the bottom to the top. When the day dawns receiving light from the luminous sun, through this let sages live endowed with splendour. (595)[1]

६. नूनं तदस्य काव्यो हिनोति महो देवस्य पूर्व्यस्य धाम ।
एष जज्ञे बहुभिः साकमित्था पूर्वे अर्धे विषिते ससन् नु ॥

6. Verily, the Veda, the ocean of knowledge, sings the great glory of the Immemorial God. This Sun has been created along with many others. Before its creation it lay asleep in a state of chaos. (596)[2]

७. योऽथर्वाणं पितरं देवबन्धुं बृहस्पतिं नमसाव च गच्छात् ।
त्वं विश्वेषां जनिता यथासः कविर्देवो न दभायत् स्वधावान् ॥

7. He, who in a spirit of devotion, understands the Non-violent God, the Father, the Friend of the learned, and the Lord of mighty worlds, thus prays unto Him. O God, Thou art the Creator of all, the Sustainer of all, Wise, Omniscient and Imperishable! (597)

HYMN II

१. य आत्मदा बलदा यस्य विश्व उपासते प्रशिषं यस्य देवाः ।
योऽस्येशे द्विपदो यश्चतुष्पदः कस्मै देवाय हविषा विधेम ॥

1. God is the Bestower of spiritual force, and physical strength, His commandments, all the learned persons and the forces of Nature acknowledge. He is the Lord of the bipeds and quadrupeds. May we worship with devotion, Him, the Illuminator and Giver of happiness. (598)

२. यः प्राणतो निमिषतो महित्वैको राजा जगतो बभूव ।
यस्य च्छायामृतं यस्य मृत्युः कस्मै देवाय हविषा विधेम ॥

2. God by His grandeur is the sole Ruler of the moving world that breathes and slumbers. His support is life immortal and transgression of His Law is death. May we worship with devotion, Him, the Illuminator and Giver of happiness. (599)

३. यं क्रन्दसी अवतश्चस्कभाने भियसाने रोदसी अह्वयेथाम् ।
यस्यासौ पन्था रजसो विमानः कस्मै देवाय हविषा विधेम ॥

3. To Whom, the Earth and Heaven, standing together through mutual attraction, look for protection; Whom the Heaven and Earth invoke for aid in terror; on whose support rests this distant atmosphere. Who is the Maker of all planets; may we worship with devotion, Him, the Illuminator and Giver of happiness. (600)

[1]But for the light of the sun, the world would have been engulfed in darkness.

[2]All the forces of Nature are resolved into chaos at the time of Dissolution, and remain in that state till the next creation.

४. यस्य द्यौरुर्वी पृथिवी च मही यस्याद उर्व१न्तरिक्षम् ।
यस्यासौ सूरो विततो महित्वा कस्मै देवाय हविषा विधेम ॥

4. Through Whose power exists the spacious heaven, the mighty earth, and yonder ample firmament between them, through Whose power is yon Sun extended in His grandeur; may we worship with devotion Him, the Illuminator and Giver of happiness. (601)[1]

५. यस्य विश्वे हिमवन्तो महित्वा समुद्रे यस्य रसामिदाहुः ।
इमाश्च प्रदिशो यस्य बाहू कस्मै देवाय हविषा विधेम ॥

5. Through Whose might exist all the snowy mountains, and the streams the learned say flow into the ocean. The arms of Whom are these celestial quarters, may we worship with devotion, Him, the Illuminator and Giver of happiness. (602)

६. आपो अग्रे विश्वमावन् गर्भं दधाना अमृता ऋतज्ञाः ।
यासु देवीष्वधि देव आसीत् कस्मै देवाय हविषा विधेम ॥

6. The immortal forces of Matter, the physical cause of the animate and inanimate world, imbibing all the germs of life, before the beginning of the universe, preserve the entire world in their womb. God rules over all these divine material forces. May we worship with devotion, Him, the Illuminator and Giver of happiness. (603)[2]

७. हिरण्यगर्भः समवर्तताग्रे भूतस्य जातः पतिरेक आसीत् ।
स दाधार पृथिवीमुत द्यां कस्मै देवाय हविषा विधेम ॥

7. God, the Master of luminous planets, existed before the creation of the world. He is the One Lord of all created objects. He sustains the earth, the sun and the created world. May we worship with devotion, Him, the Illuminator, and Giver of happiness. (604)[3]

८. आपो वत्सं जनयन्तीर्गर्भमग्रे समैरयन् ।
तस्योत जायमानस्योल्ब आसीद्धिरण्ययः कस्मै देवाय हविषा विधेम ॥

8. Before the creation of the world, Matter fashioning the child of the universe retained the seed of its production. God was the outer covering of the world in the process of creation. May we worship with devotion, Him, the Illuminator and Giver of happiness. (605)[4]

[1]Whose refers to God.

[2]During the period of dissolution, and before the creation of the world, Matter remains in a nascent atomic state, preserving all the germs of life. Out of this chaos God evolves cosmos in the shape of the universe.

[3]See *Yajur*, 13-4, 25-10.

[4]Universe has been spoken of as the child, the creation of Matter. God surrounds the universe like the outer covering of the womb, before its creation.

HYMN III

१. उदितस्त्रयो अक्रमन् व्याघ्रः पुरुषो वृकः ।
हिरुग्धि यन्ति सिन्धवो हिरुग् देवो वनस्पतिर्हिरुङ् नमन्तु शत्रवः ॥

1. Let the tiger, the thief, the wolf run away from our house and path. Just as the streams flow down, just as celestial tree makes its roots grow below, so down let our foemen bend and bow. (606)[1]

२. परेणैतु पथा वृकः परमेणोत तस्करः । परेण दत्वती रज्जुः परेणाघायुरर्षतु ॥

2. Let the wolf go on a distant path. Let the thief go on a most remote pathway. Let the serpent go on a far road. Let the malicious man go away on a distant route. (607)[2]

३. अक्ष्यौ च ते मुखं च ते व्याघ्र जम्भयामसि । आत् सर्वान् विंशतिं नखान् ॥

3. We crush and rend to pieces both thine eyes, O tiger, and thy jaws, and all the twenty claws we break. (608)[3]

४. व्याघ्रं दत्वतां वयं प्रथमं जम्भयामसि । आदु ष्टेनमथो अहिं यातुधानमथो वृकम् ॥

4. We break and rend the tiger first of creatures that are armed with teeth, the robber then, and then the snake, the sorcerer, and then the wolf. (609)

५. यो अद्य स्तेन आयति स संपिष्टो अपायति । पथामपध्वंसेनैत्विन्द्रो वज्रेण हन्तु तम् ॥

5. The thief who cometh near today, departeth bruised and crushed to bits. If he goes. If he goes by a dreary, desolate, deserted path, let the king slay him with his bolt. (610)

६. मूर्णा मृगस्य दन्ता अपिशीर्णा उ पृष्टयः । निम्रुक्ते गोधा भवतु नीचायच्छशयुर्मृगः ॥

6. Let the beast's teeth be broken off, shivered and shattered be his ribs. Let lizard come down and not ascend thy house-top. Let the wild beast in ambush be subdued by thee. (611)[4]

[1]Streams should flow downward, and avoiding inundation that destroys fields, harvests and houses. Celestial tree means Pipal. Its roots should grow beneath the ground, so that it may not harm a house or a temple near which it grows.

[2]None of these i.e., wolf, thief, serpent and a malicious man should come near our house. They should remain far away from our habitation.

[3]Twenty claws: There are five claws on each foot, and hence twenty on four feet.

[4]Thieves tie a rope with the tail of a lizard, and throw that upon the roof of a house, and taking hold of the rope, themselves go up. The walls of the house should be greasy so that the lizard may fall down and not go up.

७. यत् संयमो न वि यमो वि यमो यन्न संयमः ।
इन्द्रजाः सोमजा आथर्वणमसि व्याघ्रजम्भनम् ॥

7. The law declared by God or the sages as true, cannot be untrue, and the law proclaimed by them as untrue can not be true. O man, the power thou possessest for overcoming moral foes and impediments hast come unto thee from God. (612)[1]

HYMN IV

१. यां त्वा गन्धर्वो अखनद् वरुणाय मृतभ्रजे । तां त्वा वयं खनामस्योषधिं शेपहर्षणीम् ॥

1. We dig thee from the earth, the plant which strengthens and exalts the nerves, the plant which a learned physician dug for a noble person whose power was lost. (613)[2]

२. उदुषा उदु सूर्य उदिदं मामकं वचः । उदेजतु प्रजापतिर्वृषा शुष्मेण वाजिना ॥

2. Dawn stimulates the body, the sun lends excitement to our organs, this imperative word of mine creates an urge, this semen-enhancing, man-protecting medicine named Vrisha, through its invigorating juice lends strength to the body. (614)[3]

३. यथा स्म ते विरोहतोऽभितप्तमिवानति । ततस्ते शुष्मवत्तरमियं कृणोत्वोषधिः ॥

3. O man, just as thy progressive mind through knowledge, aspires after splendour, so let this medicine lend thee greater vigour. (615)

४. उच्छुष्मौषधीनां सार ऋषभाणाम् । सं पुंसामिन्द्र वृष्ण्यमस्मिन् धेहि तनूवशिन् ॥

4. Of all excellent medicines, this is highly efficacious and potent. O learned physician, the master of human bodies, lend this man the vigour of strong men. (616)[4]

५. अपां रसः प्रथमजोऽथो वनस्पतीनाम् । उत सोमस्य भ्रातास्युतार्शमसि वृष्ण्यम् ॥

5. O medicine, thou art the most excellent essence of waters and herbs. Thou art the nourisher of semen, and the begetter of heroism and strength. (617)[5]

६. अद्याग्ने अद्य सवितरद्य देवि सरस्वति । अद्यास्य ब्रह्मणस्पते धनुरिवा तानया पसः ॥

[1]Atharvan means God who is Non-violent.

[2]The plant referred to is वृष्य which increases the semen of a weak man.

[3]In Amar Kosha 14,87-88 the following ten names of the medicine Vrisha have been enumerated. (1) Chitrā, (2) Upchitra, (3) Nyagrodha, (4) Dravanti, (5) Shambri, (6) Vrisha, (7) Pratyak shreni, (8) Sutshreni, (9) Randā, (10) Supikparni.
Mine refers to a learned physician.

[4]'This' refers to Vrisha.

[5]'Medicine' refers to Vrisha.

6. O preceptor, O father, O knowleage, O God, extend today the rule of this brave man like a bow. (618)[1]

७. आहं तनोमि ते पसो अधि ज्यामिव धन्वनि । क्रमस्वर्शइव रोहितमनवग्लायता सदा ॥

7. O man, I extend thy kingdom, like the rope in a bow. Unfatigued attack thou the foes, as a tiger attacks the deer! (619)[2]

८. अश्वस्याश्वतरस्याजस्य पेत्वस्य च । अथ ऋषभस्य ये वाजास्तानस्मिन् धेहि तनूवशिन् ॥

8. O hero, the master of thy organs, lend to this man the strength of a horse, a mule, a he-goat, a ram, and a bull ! (620)

HYMN V

१. सहस्रशृङ्गो वृषभो यः समुद्रादुदाचरत् । तेना सहस्येना वयं नि जनान्त्स्वापयामसि ॥

1. The sun with its thousand rays rises from the ocean like atmosphere. At the time of the setting of that powerful sun, we lull the folk to rest and sleep. (621)[3]

२. न भूमिं वातो अति वाति नाति पश्यति कश्चन ।
स्त्रियश्च सर्वाः स्वापय शुनश्चेन्द्रसखा चरन् ॥

2. At the time of sleep, no strong wind should blow to disturb it, none should keep the eyes open. O Prāna, friend of the soul, lull all the women, lull the dogs to sleep. (622)[4]

३. प्रोष्ठेशयास्तल्पेशया नारीर्या बह्यशीवरीः । स्त्रियो याः पुण्यगन्धयस्ताः सर्वाः स्वापयामसि ॥

3. We lull to sleep the women, wont to sleep in the court, on a couch, or in a palanquin, and the matrons of good behaviour. (623)

४. एजदेजदजग्रभं चक्षुः प्राणमजग्रभम् । अङ्गान्यजग्रभं सर्वा रात्रीणामतिशर्वरे ॥

4. I have controlled each moving part of the body. I have held the eye and breath. Each limb and member have I seized in the deep darkness of the midnight. (624)[5]

[1]The word सप : has been translated by Maharshi Dayanand as rule in *Yajur*, 23-22. In common parlance the word means penis. Many commentators have translated it as such. Through the use of medicines and observance of the laws of celibacy one should increase his semen.

[2]I refers to a statesman.

[3]In place of sun the word वृषम may mean moon as well, on whose rising men go to bed.

[4]Dogs should be kept to keep watch in the house against thieves. Dogs awake at the slight sound of thieves, begin to bark, and thus awaken the inmates of the house.

[5]'I' refers to the soul.

५. य आस्ते यश्चरति यश्च तिष्ठन् विपश्यति । तेषां सं दध्मो अक्षीणि यथेदं हर्म्यं तथा ॥

5. The man who sits, the man who walks, whoever stands and clearly sees —of these we shut the eyes, even as we closely shut this house. (625)[1]

६. स्वप्तु माता स्वप्तु पिता स्वप्तु श्वा स्वप्तु विश्पतिः ।
स्वपन्त्वस्यै ज्ञातयः स्वप्त्वयमभितो जनः ॥

6. Sleep mother, let the father sleep, sleep dog, and master of the house. Let all her kinsmen sleep, sleep all the people in the neighbourhood. (626)

७. स्वप्न स्वप्नाभिकरणेन सर्वं नि ष्वापया जनम् ।
ओत्सूर्यमन्यान्त्स्वापयाव्युषं जागृतादहमिन्द्र इवारिष्टो अक्षितः ॥

7. O sleep, with soporific charm, lull thou to slumber all the folk. Let the rest sleep till break of day. I will remain awake till dawn, like a majestic man, free from injury and harm. (627)[2]

Chapter (Anuvāka) 2

HYMN VI

१. ब्राह्मणो जज्ञे प्रथमो दशशीर्षो दशास्यः । स सोमं प्रथमः पपौ स चकाराऽरसं विषम् ॥

1. The ten-headed and ten-faced Brāhman was first brought to life. First drinker of the Soma, he made poison ineffectual. (628)[3]

२. यावती द्यावापृथिवी वरिम्णा यावत् सप्त सिन्धवो वितष्ठिरे ।
वाचं विषस्य दूषणीं तामितो निरवादिषम् ॥

2. Far as the heaven and earth are spread in compass, far as the seven rivers are extended, so far my speech, the antidote of poison, have I spoken hence. (629)[4]

[1]'Shut the eyes' means send them to sleep. Just as the houses of rich persons, are closely shut and are free from theft, so should persons build their houses in such a way, that they be strongly protected and the inmates may sleep fearlessly.

[2]'I' refers to the master of the house, who sometimes has to keep awake the whole night to guard the house against thieves and dacoits.

[3]Ten-headed: endowed with ten qualities (1) Charity, (2) Character, (3) Forgiveness, (4) Heroism, (5) Contemplation, (6) Intellect, (7) Army, (8) Expediency, (9) Secret Messengers, (10) Knowledge.
Ten-faced: possessing settled rule in ten directions. Just as a skilled physician removes the ill effect of the poison, so should we by the use of soma alleviate the sufferings of human beings.

[4]Seven rivers: The seven organs, two eyes, two ears, two nostrils and mouth. Max Müller mentions these seven rivers to be the Indus, the Saraswati, and five rivers of the Punjab. This interpretation is inadmissible as there is no history in the Vedas. My refers to a physician. Men should try to remove poison from all objects and places.

३. सुपर्णस्त्वा गरुत्मान् विष प्रथममावयत् । नामीमदो नारूरुप उतास्मा अभवः पितुः ॥

3. The strong-winged bird, first of all, O poison, fed on thee! Thou didst not make him intoxicated or unconscious, aye, thou becamest food for him. (630)[1]

४. यस्त आस्यत् पञ्चाङ्गुरिर्वक्राच्चिदधि धन्वनः । अपस्कम्भस्य शल्यान्निरवोचमहं विषम् ॥

4. O man, if a hunter with five fingers, hath filled thy body with poison from the crooked bow, I ask thee to remove the same through the leaves of the herb Apaskambh. (631)[2]

५. शल्याद् विषं निरवोचं प्राञ्जनादुत पर्णधेः । अपाष्ठाच्छृङ्गात् कुल्मलान्निरवोचमहं विषम् ॥

5. I charm away the poison with the thorn of a porcupine, with the paint of Parndhi, with Ajshringhi brought from a distant place, and by the use of Kulmal herb. (632)[3]

६. अरसस्त इषो शल्योऽथो ते अरसं विषम् । उतारसस्य वृक्षस्य धनुष्टे अरसारसम् ॥

6. Feeble, O Arrow is thy shaft, thy poison, too, hath lost its strength. Made of a worthless tree, thy bow, O feeble one, is impotent. (633)[4]

७. ये अपीषन् ये अदिहन् ये आस्यन् ये अवासृजन् । सर्वे ते वध्रयः कृता वध्रिर्विषगिरिः कृतः ॥

7. The men who bray the poison and administer it to others, smear it on their bodies, they who discharge it from a distance, and mix it with water, all these are liable to be punished by the state. All mines of poison should be administered by the state. (634)

८. वध्रयस्ते खनितारो वध्रिस्त्वमस्योषधे । वध्रिः स पर्वतो गिरिर्यतो जातमिदं विषम् ॥

8. Thy diggers, without Government's license should be punished. O poisonous plant, remain in a safe place! The rugged mountain that produces this poison, should remain under the supervision of the Government. (635)

HYMN VII

१. वारिदं वारयातै वरणावत्यामधि । तत्रामृतस्यासिक्तं तेना ते वारये विषम् ॥

1. This water mixed with the herb Varunā will remove the poison. In that water lies the secret of health. With that I ward thy poison off. (636)[5]

[1]Just as the bird, Garuda, through his capacity of digesting poison, eats the poisonous snake and builds up his body, so does a skilled physician remove poisonous diseases through medicine, and spread health in the world.

[2]Apaskambh is named as Amuk or Lodhra as well. Its leaves when rubbed on the part of the body filled with poison, serve as an antidote, and nullify the effect of the poison. 'I' refers to a physician.

[3]Parndhi, Ajshinghi and Kulmal are the names of herbs, the use of which removes the ill effect of the poison.

[4]Men should make the shafts of their arrows and bows with materials free from poison.

[5]According to Dhanvantri's Raj Nighantu varanā herb is named vrā. It is spoken of as Pāthā, Baudhya Karkotiki, Vidang, Haridra, and Kākmāchi. All these herbs remove poison. Varanā (Crataeva Roxburghii) is a plant used in medicine for the removal of poison. It is supposed to possess wondrous virtues. I refers to a physician.

२. अरसं प्राच्यं्ऽ विषमरसं यदुदीच्य्ऽम् । अथेदमधराच्यं्ऽ करम्भेण वि कल्पते ।।

2. May the poison of the East be weakened, may the poison of the North become weak, so this poison of the South is weakened through the use of flour mixed with curds. (637)

३. करम्भं कृत्वा तिर्य्ऽ पीवस्पाकमुदारथिम् । क्षुधा किल त्वा दुष्टनो जक्षिवान्त्स न रूरुपः ।।

3. O body tormenting poison, thou streamest the fat and swells up the body. If one eats thee in hunger, he will not certainly gripe, if he takes rice with curd! (638)

४. वि ते मदं मदावति शरमिव पातयामसि । प्र त्वा चरुमिव येषन्तं वचसा स्थापयामसि ।।

4. O intoxicating plant, like a shaft we make thy poison fly away, O poison, like a secret spy, we remove thee away, that spreadest in each part of the body, by using the medicine Vachā! (639)[1]

५. परि ग्राममिवाचितं वचसा स्थापयामसि । तिष्ठा वृक्षइव स्थाम्न्यभ्रिखाते न रूरुपः ।।

5. We stop thee through using the medicine vachā, as we do a host of rustic foes gathered together. Stay quiet, O poison, like a rooted tree dug up with mattocks, spread not, gripe not thou. (640)[2]

६. पवस्तैस्त्वा पर्यक्रीणन् दूर्शेभिरजिनैरुत । प्रक्रीरसि त्वमोषधेऽभ्रिखाते न रूरुपः ।।

6. For coverings, for skins of deer and woven clothes men have bartered thee. Thou art a thing of sale, O plant, dug up with mattocks, thou gripest not. (641)[3]

७. अनाप्ता ये वः प्रथमा यानि कर्माणि चक्रिरे ।
वीरान् नो अत्र मा दभन् तद् व एतत् पुरो दधे ।।

7. O men, let not the leading semi-educated persons amongst you, who perform praiseworthy deeds for you, harm our heroes here. I place before you for protection this medicinal performance. (642)[4]

HYMN VIII

१. भूतो भुतेषु पय आ दधाति स भूतानामधिपतिर्बभूव ।
तस्य मृत्युश्चरति राजसूयं स राजा राज्यमनु मन्यतामिदम् ।।

[1]Just as an arrow is thrown afar from the string of the bow, just as a secret spy in obedience to the orders of his master goes to distant places, so the use of vacha removes the poison.
'We' refers to physicians.
Vachā is an herb, which acts as an antidote to poison.

[2]'Thee' refers to poison.

[3]The plant is named Prakri as it is salable. The plant has five varieties as given in Dhanvantri's Raj Nighantu (1) Kranj (2) Udkeerya (3) Angar valli (4) Guchhkranj (5) Rithā Kranj. A patient suffering from the effect of poison is cured by its use.

[4]'Here' refers to our country. 'I' refers to a physician.

1. He who is strong and establishes his authority over others, becomes the supreme ruler of men. Death becomes subservient to his rule. Let him as king rule and allow this kingdom. (643)[1]

२. अभि प्रेहि माप वेन उग्रश्चेत्ता सपत्नहा । आ तिष्ठ मित्रवर्धन तुभ्यं देवा अधि ब्रुवन् ॥

2. O King, strong, good administrator, slayer of the foes, go forward, lower not your dignity. O augmentor of thy friends, sit on the throne. May the learned instruct you in statesmanship! (644)

३. आतिष्ठन्तं परि विश्वे अभूषञ्छ्रियं वसानश्चरति स्वरोचिः ।
महत् तद् वृष्णो असुरस्य नामा विश्वरूपो अमृतानि तस्थौ ॥

3. O King, seated on the throne, let all learned subjects serve thee all around. Thou, self-resplendent moveth in thy state, endowed with glory. That is thy lofty nature, who is the subduer of foes and the nourisher of his subjects. He, the master of manifold qualities, hath gained immortal powers! (645)

४. व्याघ्रो अधि वैयाघ्रे वि क्रमस्व दिशो महीः ।
विशस्त्वा सर्वा वाञ्छन्त्वापो दिव्याः पयस्वतीः ॥

4. Like a tiger attack a man of ferocious nature. Spread thy sway, O King in all broad regions. Let all well-fed people, philanthropic like heavenly rain long for thee! (646)[2]

५. या आपो दिव्याः पयसा मदन्त्यन्तरिक्ष उव वा पृथिव्याम् ।
तासां त्वा सर्वासामपामभि षिञ्चामि वर्चसा ॥

5 Heaven's waters joyous in their milk, the waters of middle air, and those that earth containeth. I with the gathered power and might of all these waters sprinkle thee. (647)[3]

६. अभि त्वा वर्चसासिचन्नापो दिव्याः पयस्वतीः ।
यथासो मित्रवर्धनस्तथा त्वा सविता करत् ॥

6. The heavenly waters rich in milk have sprinkled thee with power and might, to be the prosperer of thy friends, may God so fashion thee. (648)[4]

[1]In this sukta (hymn) the coronation of a king is described. Death is controlled by the king. Through his sanitary arrangements and health bureaus he lowers the rate of mortality of his subjects and makes them enjoy a long life.

[2]Long for thee: Accept thee as their Lord.

[3]'I' refers to the priest.
'Thee' refers to the king.
Milk: the blessings which they pour forth.

[4]'Thee' refers to the king.

७. एना व्याघ्रं परिषस्वजानाः सिंहं हिन्वन्ति महते सौभगाय ।
समुद्रं न सुभुवस्तस्थिवांसं मर्मृज्यन्ते द्वीपिनमप्स्व१न्तः ।।

7. These, compassing the tiger, rouse the lion to great joy and bliss. As strong floods purify the standing ocean, so men adorn the leopard in the waters. (649)[1]

HYMN IX

१. एहि जीवं त्रायमाणं पर्वतस्यास्यक्ष्यम् । विश्वेभिर्देवैर्दत्तं परिधिर्जीवनाय कम् ।।

1. Just as antimony derived from the mountain is useful to the eyes, and helpful in the protection of life, so, O all illuminating knowledge, thou, protecting the soul, emanating from the Almighty God, serves as a benefactor to the soul like light to the eye. All learned persons have preached thee to human beings. Thou art the defence that guardeth life! (650)[2]

२. परिपाणं पुरुषाणां परिपाणं गवामसि । अश्वानामर्वतां परिपाणाय तस्थिषे ।।

2. O Knowledge, thou art the protector of men, thou art the protector of kine, thou ever standest ready to protect our organs, the horses that are fleet of foot! (651)

३. उतासि परिपाणं यातुजम्भनमाञ्जन ।
उतामृतस्य त्वं वेत्थाथो असि जीवभोजनमथो हरितभेषजम् ।।

3. O God, Thou art our Protector, our Deliverer from sufferings. Thou art the Knower of the delight of salvation, the Nourisher of men, and a jaundice curing balm art Thou! (652)

४. यस्याञ्जन प्रसर्पस्यङ्गमङ्गं परुष्परुः । ततो यक्ष्मं वि बाधस उग्रो मध्यमशीरिव ।।

4. O God, whomso, Thou pervadest member by member, joint by joint, from him, like some strong arbiter in strife, Thou banishest decline! (653)[3]

५. नैनं प्राप्नोति शपथो न कृत्या नाभिशोचनम् । नैनं विष्कन्धमश्नुते यस्त्वा बिभर्त्याञ्जन ।।

5. O God, he who meditates upon Thee, remains aloof from imprecation, violence, grief and any kind of impediment! (654)

६. असन्मन्त्राद् दुष्वप्न्याद् दुष्कृताच्छमलादुत । दुर्हार्दश्चक्षुषो घोरात् तस्मान्नः पाह्याञ्जन ।।

6. From lying speech, from evil dream, from wicked deed and sinfulness, from hostile and malignant eye,—from these, O God, protect us well. (655)

[1]These: The priests who conduct the ceremony. The tiger, the lion, the leopard: the strong and valiant king. In the waters: with which he is sprinkled in the Abbeshaka or sprinkling ceremony, wherewith the king is consecrated.

[2]Knowledge is the protector of the soul, and guardian of life, as antimony is the protector of our eyes.

[3]यक्ष्म is an emaciating disease named consumption.

७. इदं विद्वानाञ्जन सत्यं वक्ष्यामि नानृतम् । सनेयमश्वं गामहमात्मानं तव पूरुष ।।

7. O God, knowing Thy supreme glory, I will speak the very truth and not a lie. May I utilise horse, cow, land and spiritual force granted by Thee! (656)[1]

८. त्रयो दासा आञ्जनस्य तक्मा बलास आदहिः । वर्षिष्ठः पर्वतानां त्रिककुन्नाम ते पिता ।।

8. Inferiority complex, pessimism, serpent-like lust are the three slaves of a man of knowledge. O Knowledge, thy protector, the strongest of all protectors is God, the grantor of spiritual, physical and elemental happiness who is present in past, present and future, and in Heaven space and Earth, who is the Revealer of Knowledge, Action and Contemplation through the Vedas! (657)

९. यदाञ्जनं त्रैककुदं जातं हिमवतस्परि । यातूंश्च सर्वाञ्जम्भयत् सर्वाश्च यातुधान्यः ।।

9. God, Who is the Giver of threefold delights, is present in past, present and future, in Heaven, Space and Earth, who is well known for non-violence, is the destroyer of all tormenting wicked persons, and all troublesome armies of the enemy. (658)[2]

१०. यदि वासि त्रैककुदं यदि यामुनमुच्यसे । उभे ते भद्रे नाम्नी ताभ्यां नः पाह्याञ्जन ।।

10. O Knowledge, if thou hast emanated from the three aspects of the Vedas, or proceeded from Yamās and Niyamās, the limbs of Yoga, both these names are auspicious by these two protect thou us! (659)[3]

HYMN X

१. वाताज्जातो अन्तरिक्षाद् विद्युतो ज्योतिषस्परि ।
स नो हिरण्यजाः शङ्खः कृशनः पात्वंहसः ।।

1. Manifested in the breath, manifested in the heart, realised through the light of yoga, may this soul of ours, the self-seeker after virtue, loved by all, the annihilator of sufferings, preserve us from sin. (660)

२. यो अग्रतो रोचनानां समुद्रादधि जज्ञिषे । शङ्खेन हत्वा रक्षांस्यत्त्रिणो वि षहामहे ।।

2. Just as a shell is born out of the sea, and a warrior achieves victory over thieves and decoits by blowing it, so does the soul, the lord of organs, receives knowledge from God, the ocean of delight. With the help of that shell of a soul, we subdue all obstacles and voluptuous organs. (661)

[1]See *Yajur* 12.78.

[2]Threefold: spiritual physical and elemental.

[3]Three aspects: Knowledge, ज्ञान, Action, कर्म, contemplation, उपासना. Yamās: (1) Non-violence (2) Truth (3) Non-stealing (4) Celibacy (5) Non-arrogance. Niyamās: (1) Purity (2) Contentment (3) Austerity (4) Study (5) Resignation to God. Griffith interprets Yamunam as obtained from the river Yamuna, त्रैककुद as three

३. शङ्खेनामीवाममतिं शङ्खेनोत सदान्वाः । शङ्खो नो विश्वभेषजः कृशनः पात्वंहसः ॥

3. Through soul's force, we subdue disease, ignorance and indigence, our soul is a panacea for all ills. May the subtlest soul preserve us from sins. (662)

४. दिवि जातः समुद्रजः सिन्धुतस्पर्याभृतः । स नो हिरण्यजाः शङ्ख आयुष्प्रतरणो मणिः ॥

4. Refulgent like the sun, recipient of happiness from God, the ocean of joy, nourished by God, the ocean of knowledge, existing on the support of Boundless God, the virtuous soul, glowing with knowledge like a pearl, prolongs the days of our life. (663)

५. समुद्राज्जातो मणिर्वृत्राज्जातो दिवाकरः । सो अस्मान्त्सर्वतः पातु हेत्या देवासुरेभ्यः ॥

5. The resplendent soul, receives knowledge and light from God, the Ocean of knowledge and light. Just as the sun released from the covering of the cloud, shines with his glowing rays, so does the soul shine, released from the covering of ignorance. May the learned soul, save us with its shaft of knowledge, from passions that degrade the sages. (664)

६. हिरण्यानामेकोऽसि सोमात् त्वमधि जज्ञिषे ।
रथे त्वमसि दर्शत इषुधौ रोचनस्त्वं प्र ण आयूंषि तारिषत् ॥

6. O soul, realizable through yoga, peerless art thou among the conscious organs. Thou gladdenest on receiving gladness from God. Thou art beautiful seated in the bodily car. Thou gleamest on controlling the cravings of the mind. May thou prolong our days of life! (665)

७. देवानामस्थि कृशनं बभूव तदात्मन्वच्चरत्यप्स्व१न्तः ।
तत् ते बध्नाम्यायुषे वर्चसे बलाय दीर्घायुत्वाय शतशारदाय कार्शनस्त्वाभि रक्षतु ॥

7. O pupil, this subtle soul, is the urger of organs. The same soul moveth in the body under its control, and performs various deeds. O pupil, I bind it on thee for life, celibacy, vigour, for long life lasting through a hundred autumns. May this subtle soul, the banisher of all sufferings guard thee safety! (666)[1]

Chapter (Anuvāka) 3

HYMN XI

१. अनड्वान् दाधार पृथिवीमुत द्यामनड्वान् दाधारोर्व१न्तरिक्षम् ।
अनड्वान् दाधार प्रदिशः षडुर्वीरनड्वान् विश्वं भुवनमा विवेश ॥

1. God supports the wide-spread earth and heaven. God supports the spacious air between them. God supports the sky's six spacious regions, the universal world hath He pervaded. (667)[2]

peaked hill. This interpretation is illogical, as it savours of history in the Vedas, which are free from it.

[1]I bind: I preach unto thee, the superiority of the soul at the time of yajnopavit ceremony. Yajnopavit means the investiture of the sacred thread.

[2]God is spoken of as Bull, as He bears the burden of the cart of the world as an ox bears the burden of the cart.
Six regions: East, West, North, South, Zenith and Nadir.

२. अनड्वानिन्द्रः स पशुभ्यो वि चष्टे त्रयां छक्रो वि मिमीते अध्वनः ।
भूतं भविष्यद्भुवना दुहानः सर्वा देवानां चरति व्रतानि ॥

2. God is Glorious, He watches over the beasts. The Mighty God measures out three several pathways. He creating all objects in the Past, Present and Future, discharges all the eternal duties of the forces of nature. (668)[1]

३. इन्द्रो जातो मनुष्येऽष्विन्तर्घर्मस्तप्तश्चरति शोशुचानः ।
सुप्रजाः सन्त्स उदारे न सर्षद्यो नाश्नीयादनडुहो विजानन् ॥

3. God appears in the hearts of the learned. He glowing and blazing like the Sun is All-pervading. He who knows God, and is free from lust, endowed with good progeny, suffers no affliction after death. (669)[2]

४. अनड्वान्दुहे सुकृतस्य लोक ऐनं प्याययति पवमानः पुरस्तात् ।
पर्जन्यो धारा मरुत ऊधो अस्य यज्ञः पयो दक्षिणा दोहो अस्य ॥

4. God fulfils all desires in the world of virtue. The All-pervading Purifying God, in earliest time develops the soul. His powers of retention are like the cloud. His power of transport is like the wind. His act of unification is like the milk. His power of charity is like the milking pot. (670)[3]

५. यस्य नेशे यज्ञपतिर्न यज्ञो नास्य दातेशे न प्रतिग्रहीता ।
यो विश्वजिद्विश्वभृद्विश्वकर्मा घर्मं नो ब्रूत यतमश्चतुष्पात् ॥

5. Neither sacrificer, nor sacrifice, neither giver nor receiver governs and rules God. He is All-winning, All-supporting, All-effecting, O sages, tell us of Him Who pervades all the four regions. (671)

६. येन देवाः स्वऽरारुरुहुर्हित्वा शरीरममृतस्य नाभिम् ।
तेन गेष्म सुकृतस्य लोकं घर्मस्य व्रतेन तपसा यशस्यवः ॥

6. Through God's contemplation, the sages, having left the body, attain to salvation, the centre of immortality. May we, seekers after God, through penance and sun-like determination reach the world of virtue. (672)[4]

७. इन्द्रो रूपेणाग्निर्वहेन प्रजापतिः परमेष्ठी विराट् ।
विश्वानरे अक्रमत वैश्वानरे अक्रमतानडुह्यक्रमत । सोऽदृंहयत सोऽधारयत ॥

[1]Three pathways: Earth, Space, Heaven.

[2]Griffith writes the hemistich is unintelligible to him. Its significance is clear.

[3]Just as cloud retains rainy water, so does God retain the knowledge of the Vedas. Just as wind sets a thing in motion, so does God make all worlds move in their orbits. Just as milk unifies and solidifies the organs of the body, so does God unify all worlds. God gives to humanity various boons out of charity, as a milking pot gives sufficient milk to a householder.

[4]World of virtue: Salvation, final beatitude.

7. God is Lustrous in appearance, Fire in setting things in motion. Nourisher of the animate and inanimate creation, the Embodiment of joy, and the Maker of the material world. He pervades all souls, fire, and beasts of burden. He firmly fortifies and holds securely the universe. (673)

८. मध्यमेतदनडुहो यत्रैष वह आहितः । एतावदस्य प्राचीनं यावान्प्रत्यङ् समाहितः ॥

8. The sustenance of the universe is the centre of God's power, the front part of creation is as big as the hind one of dissolution. (674)[1]

९. यो वेदानडुहो दोहान्सप्तानुपदस्वतः । प्रजां च लोकं चाप्नोति तथा सप्तऋषयो विदुः ॥

9. He who knows the seven exhaustless blessings of God, wins himself offspring and sovereignty of the world. The great seven Rishis know this well. (675)[2]

१०. पद्भिः सेदिमवक्रामन्निरां जङ्घाभिरुत्खिदन् ।
श्रमेणानड्वान्कीलालं कीनाशश्चाभि गच्छतः ॥

10. The soul overcoming poverty through its forces of stability, attains to salvation and the joy of God through exertion and its vital forces. Both God and soul go together in that emancipated state. (676)

११. द्वादश वा एता रात्रीर्व्रत्या आहुः प्रजापतेः ।
तत्रोप ब्रह्म यो वेद तद् वा अनडुहो व्रतम् ॥

11. Assigned are these twelve nights, they say, as holy to God. Whoever knows God and the Veda in them performs the service of God. (677)[3]

१२. दुहे सायं दुहे प्रातर्दुहे मध्यंदिनं परि । दोहा ये अस्य संयन्ति तान्विद्मानुपदस्वतः ॥

12. I worship God at evening, at early morn and at noon. We consider them as immortal, who enjoy God's streams of felicity. (678)

HYMN XII

१. रोहण्यसि रोहण्यस्थ्नश्छिन्नस्य रोहणी । रोहयेदमरुन्धति ॥

1. O Rohini named herb, thou art the healer, the healer of the broken bone. O Arundhti, wound filling medicine, fill up this wound! (679)[4]

[1]God creates, sustains and dissolves the universe. These three aspects have been spoken of as the front, middle and hind parts of God's power. Creation is the front, sustenance the middle, and dissolution the last function of God's power.

[2]Seven blessings: Sun, air, water, fire, corn, earth, rain.

Seven Rishis: Vishva Mitra and Jamdagni are two eyes. Vasishtha and Kashyap are two nostrils; Bhardwaj and Gautama are two ears Atri Rishi is speech. See Brihadaranyak Upanishad, 2-2. These are not the names of persons.

[3]Twelve nights represent twelve years, during which one should observe celibacy and study the Vedas. Twelve nights may also mean, Mind, Intellect, five organs of cognition and five organs of action.

[4]Rohini and Arundhti are two names for the plant, that possesses the medicinal property of healing a broken bone, or filling up a wound.

२. यत्ते रिष्टं यत्ते द्युत्तमस्ति पेष्ट्रं त आत्मनि ।
धाता तद्भद्रया पुनः सं दधत्परुषा परुः ॥

2. O injured person, whatever bone of thine within thy body hath been wrenched, cracked or is feeling burning pain, may a skilful physician set it properly and join together limb by limb! (680)

३. सं ते मज्जा मज्ज्ञा भवतु समु ते परुषा परुः । सं ते मांसस्य विस्रस्तं समस्थ्यपि रोहतु ॥

3. With marrow be the marrow joined, thy limb united with thy limb, let what hath fallen of thy flesh, and the bone also grow again. (681)[1]

४. मज्जा मज्ज्ञा सं धीयतां चर्मणा चर्म रोहतु । असृक्ते अस्थि रोहतु मांसं मांसेन रोहतु ॥

4. Let marrow close with marrow, let skin grow united with the skin, let blood and bone grow strong in thee, flesh grow together with the flesh. (682)[2]

५. लोम लोम्ना सं कल्पया त्वचा सं कल्पया त्वचम् ।
असृक्ते अस्थि रोहतु च्छिन्नं सं धेह्योषधे ॥

5. O physician, join thou together hair with hair, join thou together skin with skin. Let blood and bone grow strong in thee. Unite the broken part, O plant! (683)

६. स उत्तिष्ठ प्रेहि प्र द्रव रथः सुचक्रः सुपविः सुनाभिः । प्रति तिष्ठोर्ध्वः ॥

6. O patient, arise, advance, speed forth like the car having goodly wheels, naves and fellies. Stand up erect upon thy feet. (684)[3]

७. यदि कर्तं पतित्वा संशश्रे यदि वाश्मा प्रहृतो जघान ।
ऋभू रथस्येवाङ्गानि सं दधत्परुषा परुः ॥

7. If he be torn and shattered by the blow of a sword, or struck by a cast throne, let the application of the herb join limb with limb, as a skilled artisan joins the portions of a car. (685)

HYMN XIII

१. उत देवा अवहितं देवा उन्नयथा पुनः । उतागश्चक्रुषं देवा देवा जीवयथा पुनः ॥

1. O worldly wise learned persons, raise again the degraded. O charitable sages, grant again spiritual life to the sinner. (686)

२. द्वाविमौ वातौ वात आ सिन्धोरा परावतः । दक्षं ते अन्य आवातु व्य१न्यो वातु यद्रपः ॥

[1]Thy refers to the injured person.
[2]Thee: An injured person.
[3]The physician addresses this verse to the patient when he is cured.

2. Here are these two breaths. One of them (Prāna) goes down to the heart, and the other (Apāna) goes out afar. One of them (Prāna) lends thee energy, and the other (Apāna) removes thy internal impurity. (687)[1]

३. आ वात वाहि भेषजं वि वात वाहि यद्रपः । त्वं हि विश्वभेषज देवानां दूत ईयसे ॥

3. O wind, bring health, drive away disease. O wind, medicine for all ailments, thou blowest for the protection of mankind as an envoy of the forces of nature! (688)

४. त्रायन्तामिमं देवास्त्रायन्तां मरुतां गणाः । त्रायन्तां विश्वा भूतानि यथायमरपा असत् ॥

4. May all organs protect him, may the host of winds protect him, may all the elements protect him, so that he may be free from disease. (689)[2]

५. आ त्वागमं शन्तातिभिरथो अरिष्टतातिभिः । दक्षं त उग्रमाभारिषं परा यक्ष्मं सुवामि ते ॥

5. I am come nigh to thee with balms to give thee rest and keep thee safe, I bring thee mighty strength, I drive thy pulmonary consumption away. (690)[3]

६. अयं मे हस्तो भगवानयं मे भगवत्तरः । अयं मे विश्वभेषजोऽयं शिवाभिमर्शनः ॥

6. Felicitous is this my left hand, yet more felicitous is this the right one. This hand contains all healing properties, its gentle touch brings peace and welfare. (691)[4]

७. हस्ताभ्यां दशशाखाभ्यां जिह्वा वाचः पुरोगवी ।
अनामयित्नुभ्यां हस्ताभ्यां ताभ्यां त्वाभि मृशामसि ॥

7. With our tenfold fingered hands, with our tongue that leads and precedes the voice, with these two healers of disease, we stroke thee with a gentle fondling touch. (692)[5]

[1]Two breaths: Prāna and Apāna.
Thee refers to man in general. Prāna brings fresh air into our lungs, purifies the blood, and lends us energy. Apāna takes out our impurity. We breathe in Oxygen, and breathe out Carbonic acid gas.

[2]A man should keep his organs pure, practice Prānāyāma and make proper use of the five elements to rid himself of disease. Elements: Earth, Water, Air, Fire, Atmosphere.

[3]I: A physician.
Thee: A patient.

[4]My: Physician's. A skilled physician by the gentle touch of his hand can encourage and heal the patient. A doctor should never discourage a patient.

[5]We may refer to physicians or teachers. Thee may refer to the patient or pupil. A physician heals a patient by his encouraging words and soft touch of his hands. A teacher encourages a pupil by his elevating words of advice and loving touch.

HYMN XIV

१. अजो ह्य१ग्नेरजनिष्ट शोकात् सो अपश्यज्जनितारमग्रे ।
तेन देवा देवतामग्र आयन् तेन रोहान् रुरुहुर्मेध्यासः ॥

1. Verily, the unborn soul, receives knowledge from the light of God. It beholds the Primordial God. Through His grace the learned at first attain to spirituality. Through His grace the pure souls attain to exalted positions. (693)[1]

२. क्रमध्वमग्निना नाकमुख्यान् हस्तेषु बिभ्रतः । दिवस्पृष्ठं स्वर्गत्वा मिश्रा देवेभिराध्वम् ॥

2. O learned persons, taking in hands your spiritual knowledge, endowed with the lustre of God, attain to supreme happiness. Having reached the stage of final beatitude, and realising that Excellent Light, mix with the emancipated souls, and live in merriment. (694)[2]

३. पृष्ठात् पृथिव्या अहमन्तरिक्षमारुहमन्तरिक्षाद् दिवमारुहम् ॥
दिवो नाकस्य पृष्ठात् स्व१र्ज्योतिरगामहम् ॥

3. Through yoga from physical force I rise higher to mental force; from mental force I rise higher to spiritual force, from spiritual force I rise higher to God, the Blissful light. (695)[3]

४. स्व१र्यन्तो नापेक्षन्त आ द्यां रोहन्ति रोदसी । यज्ञं ये विश्वतोधारं सुविद्वांसो वितेनिरे ॥

4. Emancipated souls, in their march to salvation, the abode of happiness, care not a bit for the pleasures of this world. Transgressing both the Earth and Heaven, they continue their progress till they reach the world of light. The learned aspirants after salvation, do realise the nature of soul and God, the showerers of happiness. (696)[4]

५. अग्ने प्रेहि प्रथमो देवतानां चक्षुर्देवानामुत मानुषाणाम् ।
इयक्षमाणा भृगुभिः सजोषाः स्वर्यन्तु यजमानाः स्वस्ति ॥

5. O God, Thou art Foremost amongst the learned and all divine objects, exhibit Thyself in our heart. Thou art the Eye of man and the forces of nature. May the noble sacrificers, in the company of men of mature Knowledge, performing the yajnas, living together happily, attain to God and prosperity. (697)[5]

[1]See *Yajur*, 13-51. अज means the soul that is unborn and not the goat as translated by Griffith.

[2]See *Yajur*, 17-65.

[3]See *Yajur*, 17-61.

[4]See *Yajur*, 17-68.

[5]See *Yajur*, 17-69.

Eye: Exhibitor.

Bhrigu is not the name of a Rishi as explained by Griffith. The word means a man who has wiped out all sins and impurities and is a man of mature knowledge.

६. अजमनज्मि पयसा घृतेन दिव्यं सुपर्णं पयसं बृहन्तम् ।
तेन गेष्म सुकृतस्य लोकं स्वऽरारोहन्तो अभि नाकमुत्तमम् ।।

6. I equip with Knowledge and lustre, the divine, virtuous, enterprising, powerful unborn soul. With the help of that learned soul, keeping in view the Exalted Joyous God, may we, advancing spiritually seek for salvation, the abode of purity. (698)

७. पञ्चौदनं पञ्चभिरंगुलिभिर्दर्व्योद्धर पञ्चधैतमोदनम् ।
प्राच्यां दिशि शिरो अजस्य धेहि दक्षिणायां दिशि दक्षिणं धेहि पार्श्वम् ।

7. Elevate, through ignorance killing force, the soul, a prey to five passions, equipped with five organs of action and surrounded by five elements. After death place on the *pyre*, the head of the body of the emancipated soul to the east, and its right side to the south. (699)[1]

८. प्रतीच्यां दिशि भसदमस्य धेह्युत्तरस्यां दिश्युत्तरं धेहि पार्श्वम् ।
ऊर्ध्वायां दिश्य१जस्यानूकं धेहि दिशि ध्रुवायां धेहि पाजस्यऽमन्तरिक्षे मध्यतो मध्यमस्य ।।

8. Set the hinder part of the corpse to the West. Set the left flank to the North. Set the backbone upmost in the Zenith, and lay the belly downward in the Nadir, and the min-portion in mid-air between them. (700)[2]

९. शृतमजं शृतया प्रोणुहि त्वचा सर्वैरंगैः संभृतं विश्वरूपम् ।
स उत् तिष्ठेतो अभि नाकमुत्तमं पद्भिश्चतुर्भिः प्रति तिष्ठ दिक्षु ।।

9. O man, robe well, with thy mature, vast force, the soul, that assumes different forms in different births, feels strong with all its organs, and is equipped with mature knowledge. Advance from here to the Most Exalted God, and with thy four feet stand firmly in the world. (701)[3]

HYMN XV

१. समुत्पतन्तु प्रदिशो नभस्वतीः समभ्राणि बातजूतानि यन्तु ।
महऋषभस्य नदतो नभस्वतो वाश्रा आपः पृथिवीं तर्पयन्तु ।।

1. Let all the misty regions fly together, let all the rain-clouds, sped by wind, assemble. Let the fast streams of water flowing from the thundering and highly roaring cloud in the sky, satisfy the earth. (702)

२. समीक्षयन्तु तविषाः सुदानवोऽपां रसा ओषधीभिः सचन्ताम् ।
वर्षस्य सर्गा महयन्तु भूमिं पृथग् जायन्तामोषधयो विश्वरूपाः ।।

[1]Five passions: Lust, Anger, Avarice, Infatuation and Pride.
Five organs of action are the five fingers of the soul, with which it performs various deeds. The soul is surrounded by five elements: Earth, Water, Air, Fire, Space.

[2]The dead body should be placed on the funeral pyre in the position mentioned in the verse. The general practice is different from the directions of this verse. Belly is set towards the Zenith, and back towards the Zenith.

[3]Four feet: Dharma, Arth, Kama, Moksha.

2. Let the strong, bounteous clouds be seen by us; let plants and shrubs be hung with drops of moisture. Let floods of rain refresh the ground with gladness, and herbs spring various with each form and colour. (703)

३. समीक्षयस्व गायतो नभांस्यपां वेगासः पृथगुद् विजन्ताम् ।
वर्षस्य सर्गा महयन्तु भूमिं पृथग् जायन्तां वीरुधो विश्वरूपाः ॥

3. O winds, cause us who sing in joy to see the gathering vapours; let the rush of waters burst out in many a place. Let floods of rain refresh the ground with gladness; and herbs spring various with each form and colour! (704)

४. गणास्त्वोप गायन्तु मारुताः पर्जन्य घोषिणः पृथक् ।
सर्गा वर्षस्य वर्षतो वर्षन्तु पृथिवीमनु ॥

4. O Cloud, let troops of winds, roaring, revere thee. Let pouring torrents of the rain that raineth rain upon the earth! (705)

५. उदीरयत मरुतः समुद्रतस्त्वेषो अर्को नभ उत् पातयाथ ।
महऋषभस्य नदतो नभस्वतो वाश्रा आपः पृथिवीं तर्पयन्तु ॥

5. O winds, through warmth of the sun lift water up from the sea, and take them up. Let the fast streams of water flowing from the thundering and highly roaring cloud in the sky satisfy the earth! (706)

६. अभि क्रन्द स्तनयार्दयोदधिं भूमिं पर्जन्य पयसा समङ्धि ।
त्वया सृष्टं बहुलमैतु वर्षमाशारैषी कृशगुरेत्वस्तम् ॥

6. O Cloud, roar, thunder, set the sea in agitation, bedew the ground with thy sweet rain. Send down plenteous rainy water. Let the cultivator, desiring for rain from all sides, plough his field and come home! (707)[1]

७. सं वोऽवन्तु सुदानव उत्सा अजगरा उत । मरुद्भिः प्रच्युता मेघा वर्षन्तु पृथिवीमनु ॥

7. Let the bounteous springs and clouds tend you well. Urged by the winds let the clouds pour down their rain upon the earth. (708)

८. आशामाशां वि द्योततां वाता वान्तु दिशोदिशः ।
मरुद्भिः प्रच्युता मेघाः सं यन्तु पृथिवीमनु ॥

8. Let lightning flash from every side; from all the regions blow the winds. Urged by the winds let the clouds come down upon the earth. (709)[2]

९. आपो विद्युदभ्रं वर्षं सं वोऽवन्तु सुदानव उत्सा अजगरा उत ।
मरुद्भिः प्रच्युता मेघाः प्रावन्तु पृथिवीमनु ॥

9. May waters, lightning, cloud, and rain, big bounteous springs tend you well. Urged by the winds let the clouds drench the earth. (710)

[1]An agriculturist ploughs his field when it becomes wet through rain.
[2]अजगर is the cloud that swallows the Sun, or is long fantastic shaped like a serpent.

१०. अपामग्निस्तनूभिः संविदानो य ओषधीनामधिपा बभूव ।
स नो वर्षं वनुतां जातवेदाः प्राणं प्रजाभ्यो अमृतं दिवस्परि ॥

10. Warmth of the Sun, mingled with the particles of water is the protector of plants. May that heat bring us rain, which is life to earthly creatures, and a boon from heaven. (711)

११. प्रजापतिः सलिलादा समुद्रादाप ईरयन्नुदधिमर्दयाति ।
प्र प्यायतां वृष्णो अश्वस्य रेतोऽर्वाङेतेन स्तनयित्नुनेहि ॥

11. Sending up waters from the inundated ocean, the sun moves again the sea to agitation. May, the moisture of the fertilizing rain cloud flow forth. With this thy roar of thunder come thou hither, O cloud! (712)

१२. अपो निषिञ्चन्नसुरः पिता नः श्वसन्तु गर्गरा अपां वरुणाव नीचीरपः सृज ।
वदन्तु पृश्निबाहवो मण्डूका इरिणानु ॥

12. The sun that sends down torrents of water is our nourisher. O God, let pools and channels of water flow, let waters flow downwards; let frogs with speckled arms send out their voices in pools of water. (713)

१३. संवत्सरं शशयाना ब्राह्मणा व्रतचारिणः । वाचं पर्जन्यजिन्वितां प्र मण्डूका अवादिषुः ॥

13. Like the Brāhmans, who fulfil their vows residing in one place for a year; the frogs, have lifted up their voice, the voice inspired by the rainy cloud. (714)[1]

१४. उपप्रवद मण्डूकि वर्षमा वद तादुरि । मध्ये ह्रदस्य प्लवस्व विगृह्य चतुरः पदः ॥

14. Speak forth a welcome, female frog! Do thou O tiny frog, accost the rain. Stretch thy four feet apart, and swim in the middle of the tank! (715)[2]

१५. खण्वखा३इ खैमखा३इ मध्ये तदुरि । वर्षं वनुध्वं पितरो मरुतां मन इच्छत ॥

15. O female frog that lives in the hole, O contented female frog, O tiny female frog be jubilant in the middle of rain, O nourishers of the people, long for the reflective knowledge of the flowing winds! (716)[3]

[1]The frogs after waiting for the rainy season for a year, begin to shout. See *Rigveda*, 7-103-1.

[2]Pt. Jaidev Vidyalankar has given a spiritual interpretation also of this verse. O mind, immersed in joy, O daughter of the soul ever marching toward God, ever sing His glory, and stretching thy four feet, swim in the gladdening ocean of the heart. Four feet: Mind (मन) Perception (चित्) Intellect (बुद्धि) Ego (अहंकार) See *Nirukta*, 9-7.

[3]Khanwakhā, Khainakhā, Tādri are the names of female frogs. The spiritual interpretation of the verse, as given by Pt. Jaidev Vidyalankar is as follows. 'O Idā, Pinglā, and Sushamni at artery in the middle, give us the flow of joy. O organs, strive to acquire the intrinsic force of internal breaths.

१६. महान्तं कोशमुदचाभि षिञ्च सविद्युतं भवतु वातु वातः ।
तन्वतां यज्ञं बहुधा विसृष्टा ग्रानन्दिनीरोषधयो भवन्तु ॥

16. O God, lift up the cloud, the mighty treasure of water, and pour down rain; let the wind blow, and lightnings flash around us. Let us nobly finish this sacrifice of life. Widely scattered let herbs and plants be full of joy and gladness. (717)

Chapter (Anuvāka) 4

HYMN XVI

१. बृहन्नेषामधिष्ठाता ग्रन्तिकादिव पश्यति । य स्तायन्मन्यते चरन्त्सर्वं देवा इदं विदुः ॥

1. The mighty Ruler of these worlds beholds as though from close at hand. He protecting the whole world knows it. The learned know this trait of His. (718)

२. यस्तिष्ठति चरति यश्च वञ्चति यो निलायं चरति यः प्रतङ्कम् ।
द्वौ संनिषद्य यन्मन्त्रयेते राजा तद् वेद वरुणस्तृतीयः ॥

2. If a man stands or walks or deceives others, or acts covertly or overtly. When two men whisper as they sit together. God knows all this He is present as the third. (719)

३. उतेयं भूमिर्वरुणस्य राज्ञ उतासौ द्यौर्बृहती दूरेग्रन्ता ।
उतो समुद्रौ वरुणस्य कुक्षी उतास्मिन्नल्प उदके निलीनः ॥

3. This earth, as well as that high heaven at a vast distance is God's possession. Both the oceans are God's loins, and this small drop of water, too, contains Him. (720)[1]

४. उत यो द्यामतिसर्पात् परस्तान्न स मुच्यातै वरुणस्य राज्ञः ।
दिव स्पशः प्र चरन्तीदमस्य सहस्राक्षा ग्रति पश्यन्ति भूमिम ॥

4. If one should flee afar beyond the heaven, he cannot be free from the clutches of God. The spies of the Resplendent God are roaming in this world, who thousand-eyed look over the earth. (721)[2]

५. सर्वं तद् राजा वरुणो वि चष्टे यदन्तरा रोदसी यत् परस्तात् ।
संख्याता ग्रस्य निमिषो जनानामक्षानिव श्वघ्नी नि मिनोति तानि ॥

5. God beholdeth all between heaven and earth, and all beyond them. The twinklings of men's eyelids hath He counted. He throws down the sinners as a gambler throws dice. (722)

[1]Both oceans: the ocean of water on the Earth, and the ocean of air in the atmosphere. God is present in the grossest as well the tiniest objects, like ocean and a drop of water.

[2]Spies: Learned persons. Thousand-eyed: Who use thousand devices to catch hold of the sinners and get them punished, even though they try hard to flee afar to save themselves.

६. ये ते पाशा वरुण सप्तसप्त त्रेधा तिष्ठन्ति विषिता रुशन्तः ।
छिनन्तु सर्वे अनृतं वदन्तं यः सत्यवाद्यति तं सृजन्तु ।

6. These fatal snares of Thine which stand extended, threefold, O God, as seven lights; may they all catch the man who tells a lie, and pass unharmed the man whose words are truthful! (723)[1]

७. शतेन पाशैरभि धेहि वरुणैनं मा ते मोच्यनृतवाङ् नृचक्षः ।
आस्तां जाल्म उदरं स्रंसयित्वा कोश इवाबन्धः परिकृत्यमानः ।।

7. O God, seer of the noble and ignoble deeds of man, snare him with a hundred nooses, who tells a lie, and let him not escape Thee. Let the villain who avoids struggle sit listless, as a bud released from the flower falls to the ground and is cut to pieces. (724)

८. यः समाम्योः वरुणो यो व्याम्योः यः संदेश्योः वरुणो यो विदेश्यः ।
यो दैवो वरुणो यश्च मानुषः ।।

8. God is He, who is equally kind to each. God is He, Who specially treats each according to his deserts. God is He, Who generally pervades each place. God is He, Who is present in each place, with His special characteristics. God is He, Who loves the learned, as well as the ordinary mortals. (725)

९. तैस्त्वा सर्वैरभि ष्यामि पाशैरसावामुष्यायणामुष्याः पुत्र । तानु ते सर्वाननुसंदिशामि ।।

9. I bind and hold thee fast with all these punishments, thou son of such a man and such a mother. All these do I assign thee as thy portion. (726)[2]

HYMN XVII

१. ईशानां त्वा भेषजानामुज्जेष आ रभामहे । चक्रे सहस्रवीर्यं सर्वस्मा ओषधे त्वा ।।

1. O medicine, for eradicating all diseases, I render thee thousand-fold potent. For the healing of a malady, we prepare thee, O queen of medicines! (727)[3]

२. सत्यजितं शपथयावनीं सहमानां पुनःसराम् । सर्वाः समह्वचोषधीरितो नः पारयादिति ।।

2. O efficacious, pain-relieving malady-controlling, aperient medicine, thee, and all other medicines have I gathered, so that they may relieve us from all sorts of disease! (728)

[1]Threefold: Past, Present, Future, or low, medium and high.
Seven lights: earth, water, fire, air, physical world, atom, and matter.

[2]A man should always perform noble deeds, and shun vice, otherwise God will give him condign punishment.

[3]To make a medicine more efficacious, its potency should be enhanced, as is done by homeopaths.

३. या शशाप शपनेन् याघं मूरमादधे । या रसस्य हरणाय जातमारेभे तोकमत्तु सा ॥

3. Some disease makes a patient cry aloud and utter incoherent words, some engenders in the patient the evil of fainting. Another disease attacks a newly born child for emaciation. Such a disease devours the weak child. (729)[1]

४. यां ते चक्रुरामे पात्रे यां चक्रुर्नील लोहिते ।
आमे मांसे कृत्यां यां चक्रुस्तया कृत्याकृतो जहि ॥

4. O King, punish the druggists who use a deadly medicine, those who prepare an adverse, injurious medicine in an unbanked or fully burnt dark red earthen pot, or inject poisonous matter in raw flesh! (730)

५. दौष्वप्न्यं दौर्जीवित्यं रक्षो अभ्वऽमराय्यऽः ।
दुर्णाम्नीः सर्वा दुर्वाचस्ता अस्मन्नाशयामसि ॥

5. We drive away from us, ill dream, wretchedness of life, troublesome, emaciating, beauty-consuming diseases, piles and delirium. (731)[2]

६. क्षुधामारं तृष्णामारमगोतामनपत्यताम् । अपामार्ग त्वया वयं सर्वं तदप मृज्महे ॥

6. Death caused by famine, caused by thirst, ills of the organs and speech, sterility, with thy use, O Apāmārga, all this ill we cleanse and wipe away! (732)[3]

७. तृष्णामारं क्षुधामारमथो अक्षपराजयम् । अपामार्ग त्वया वयं सर्वं तदप मृज्महे ॥

7. O Apāmārga, we cleanse and wipe away, with thine aid, the disease caused by thirst, caused by hunger, physical debility and all other ailments! (733)

८. अपामार्ग ओषधीनां सर्वासामेक इद् वशी । तेन ते मृज्म आस्थितमथ त्वमगदश्चर ॥

8. The Apāmārga is alone the lord of all plants that grow. With this we wipe away whatever disease hath attacked thee, O patient, Get rid of it and live long! (734)

HYMN XVIII

१. समं ज्योतिः सूर्येणाह्ना रात्री समावती । कृणोमि सत्यमूतयेऽरसाः सन्तु कृत्वरीः ॥

1. Just as lustre always accompanies the sun, just as might is always connected with day, so I always reveal the Truth for the safeguard of humanity, whereby evil usages become impotent. (735)[4]

[1]This verse is the same as 1-28-3, but with a different interpretation and is therefore free from the charge of repetition. Griffith translates both the verses alike.

[2]By the use of proper medicine, we can get rid of diseases.

[3]Apāmārga is an herb, Achyranthes Aspera, a biannial plant frequently used as medicine. It is also called Parākpushpā, Pratyakpushpī, and Pratyakparṇī. This herb cures cough, piles, itch, stomach-ache and other ills. In vernacular it is called Puthkandā.

[4]I: God. Truth—the Vedas.

२. यो देवा: कृत्यां कृत्वा हरादविदुषो गृहम् । वत्सो धारुरिव मातरं तं प्रत्यगुप पद्यताम् ॥

2. O learned persons, if one take the life of an ignorant person by administering a deadly medicine to him may the same revert and cling to him, as the calf that sucks clings to the mother cow! (736)[1]

३. अमा कृत्वा पाप्मानं यस्तेनान्यं जिघांसति ।
अश्मानस्तस्यां दग्धायां बहुला: फट् करिक्रति ॥

3. If a person, in alliance with a thief or a dacoit, committing a sin, desires to kill another, let the energetic man, stony-hearted Government officials, on the failure of his plan, bring about the destruction of that evil-minded person. (737)

४. सहस्रधामन् विशिखान् विग्रीवांछायया त्वम् । प्रति स्म चक्रुषे कृत्यां प्रियां प्रियावते हर ॥

4. O highly renowned king, cut down the necks of those who use deadly medicines, and let them sleep for ever. Back to its author send the devilish deed, as a dear damsel to her friend! (738)[2]

५. अनयाहमोषध्या सर्वा: कृत्या अदूदुषम् । यां क्षेत्रे चक्रुर्या गोषु यां वा ते पुरुषेषु ॥

5. With the help of thine, O King, who assuages sufferings like medicine, I have removed all sorts of violence, they committed upon thy field, thy cattle and thy men. (739)[3]

६. यश्चकार न शशाक कर्तुं शश्रे पादमङ्गुरिम् ।
चकार भद्रमस्मभ्यमात्मने तपनं तु स: ॥

6. He who tries to commit mischief, but fails, hurts his foot, and breaks his toe. His act hath brought us happiness and pain and sorrow to himself. (740)[4]

७. अपामार्गोऽप मार्ष्टु क्षेत्रियं शपथश्च य: । अपाह यातुधानीरप सर्वा अराय्य: ॥

7. Let Apāmārga sweep away chronic disease and the evil habit of using foul language. Let it remove the disease that causes intense pain and lowers vitality. (741)

८. अपमृज्य यातुधानानप सर्वा अराय्य: । अपामार्ग त्वया वयं सर्वं तदप मृज्महे ॥

8. Curing all diseases that cause pain and lower vitality, O Apāmārga, through thy use, we purge us of every kind of painful ailment. (742)

[1]The king should punish the man, who fraudulently takes the life of an ignorant person by giving him a poisonous medicine, by making him drink the same.

[2]Devilish deed: The act of using poisonous medicines to harm others in a spirit of revenge.

[3]They: Ill-natured persons.
I: A learned person.

[4]His failure to commit mischief is a source of happiness for us.

HYMN XIX

१. उतो अस्यबन्धुकृदुतो असि नु जामिकृत् ।
उतो कृत्याकृतः प्रजां नडमिवा छिन्धि वार्षिकम् ॥

1. O King, thou art the extirpator of enemies, and the creator of friends. Uproot the violent and their followers, like a reed that grows in the rains. (743)[1]

२. ब्राह्मणेन पर्युक्तासि कण्वेन नार्षदेन ।
सेनेवैषि त्विषीमती न तत्र भयमस्ति यत्र प्राप्नोष्योषधे ॥

2. A learned Brahman, who sits in the Assembly of leaders, hath dwelt upon thy healing powers. Thou attackest a disease like a flashing army. Wherever thou art obtainable, there is no fear of any sort of disease. (744)[2]

३. अग्रमेष्योषधीनां ज्योतिषेवाभिदीपयन् । उत त्रातासि पाकस्याथो हन्तासि रक्षसः ॥

3. Illumining, as 'twere with light, O King, thou movest at the head of philanthropic persons serviceable like medicine. The saviour of the weak art thou, and slayer of the wicked! (745)

४. यददो देवा असुरांस्त्वयाग्रे निरकुर्वन् । ततस्त्वध्योषधेऽपामार्गो अजायथाः ॥

4. In earlier period, when the learned, with thy aid, expelled the fell diseases, even thence, O plant, wast thou named as Apāmārga, that wipes and sweeps away ailments! (746)

५. विभिन्दती शतशाखा विभिन्दन् नाम ते पिता ।
प्रत्यग् वि भिन्धि त्वं तं यो अस्माँ अभिदासति ॥

5. O Apāmārga, thou with hundred branches cleavest all diseases. Hence thy grower's name is Cleaver. Do thou, turn backward, cleave and rend the disease that wants to make us its prey! (747)

६. असद् भूम्याः समभवत् तद्यामेति महद् व्यचः ।
तद् वै ततो विधूपायत् प्रत्यक् कर्तारमृच्छतु ॥

6. The evil that springs from earth, mounts to heaven and spreads to vast extent. Reverted, tormenting him with pain, thence on its doer let it recoil. (748)

[1]A king has been described as a medicine. Just as medicine uproots diseases, so does the king destroy his enemies.

[2]Griffith translates Kanvā as a Rishi, son of Nrishad. This interpretation is unacceptable, as there is no history in the Vedas. Kanvā means a learned person: मेधाविना—निघ० 3825.

७. प्रत्यङ् हि सम्बभूविथ प्रतीचीनफलस्त्वम् । सर्वान् मच्छपथाँ अधि वरीयो यावया वधम् ॥

7. O King, thou art the destroyer of those who lead an ignoble life. Remove all curses of the enemy far from me. Keep most remote from me his extended weapon! (749)

८. शतेन मा परि पाहि सहस्रेणाभि रक्ष मा । इन्द्रस्ते वीरुधां पत उग्र ओज्मानमा दधत् ॥

8. Preserve me, O King with a hundred, yea, protect me with a thousand aids. O nourisher of the multi-progressing subjects, may Mighty God, give store of strength and power to thee! (750)

HYMN XX

१. आ पश्यति प्रति पश्यति परा पश्यति पश्यति ।
दिवमन्तरिक्षमाद् भूमिं सर्वं तद् देवि पश्यति ॥

1. God sees in front, He sees behind, He sees far away, He sees. The sky, the firmament, and earth, all this, He beholds. (751)

२. तिस्रो दिवस्तिस्रः पृथिवीः षट् चेमाः प्रदिशः पृथक् ।
त्वयाहं सर्वा भूतानि पश्यानि देव्योषधे ॥

2. O God, the Divine Alleviator of sufferings like medicine, through Thy aid may I behold three heavens, three earths, and these six regions one by one, and all creatures that exist. (752)[1]

३. दिव्यस्य सुपर्णस्य तस्य हासि कनीनिका । सा भूमिमा रुरोहिथ वह्यं श्रान्ता वधूरिव ॥

3. The pupil, verily, art thou of that celestial soul. On it hast thou ridden as a weary woman rides a palanquin. (753)[2]

४. तां मे सहस्राक्षो देवो दक्षिणे हस्त आ दधत् ।
तयाहं सर्वं पश्यामि यश्च शूद्र उतार्यः ॥

4. God, Who possesses the power of a thousand eyes, hath placed keenness of perception in my right hand, wherewith I look alike on a sudra or an Arya. (754)[3]

५. आविष्कृणुष्व रूपाणि मात्मानमप गूहथाः । अथो सहस्रचक्षो त्वं प्रति पश्याः किमीदिनः ॥

5. O thousand-eyed discernment, lay bare the external form of objects, hide not their intrinsic value, carefully watch the lustful organs and cravings of the mind! (755)

[1]Three: Uppermost, Middle, and Lowest. Six regions: East, South, West, North, Zenith, and Nadir.

[2]Thou: spiritual vision.

[3]In my right hand: At my disposal.
Sudra: An ignorant man.
Arya: A learned person.

६. दर्शय मा यातुधानान् दर्शय यातुधान्यः। पिशाचान्त्सर्वान् दर्शयेति त्वा रभ ओषधे ॥

6. O power of discernment, efficacious like medicine, let me have the knowledge of internal foes like anger, lust, and avarice, of tortuous mental proclivities. Let me have the knowledge of all passions that consume physical strength. For this purpose have I taken thy shelter! (756)

७. कश्यपस्य चक्षुरसि शुन्याश्च चतुरक्ष्याः। वीध्रे सूर्यमिव सर्पन्तं मा पिशाचं तिरस्करः ॥

7. O power of discernment, thou art the eye of a learned yogi, of mental power acquired through the study of the four Vedas. Conceal not from me my ignoble designs like the sun that rides in the pure sky. (757)[1]

८. उदग्रभं परिपाणाद् यातुधानं किमीदिनम्। तेनाहं सर्वं पश्याम्युत शूद्रमुतार्यम् ॥

8. For the sake of safety I have controlled the libidinous, vexatious mind, with this controlled mind, I look alike upon a Sudra or an Arya. (758)

९. यो अन्तरिक्षेण पतति दिवं यश्चातिसर्पति। भूमिं यो मन्यते नाथं तं पिशाचं प्र दर्शय ॥

9. O mental vision, make visible to me the soul, that flies in the heart, or roams in the reflective brain, or considers itself the lord of the body! (759)[2]

Chapter (Anuvāka) 5

HYMN XXI

१. आ गावो अग्मन्नुत भद्रमक्रन्त्सीदन्तु गोष्ठे रणयन्त्वस्मे।
प्रजावतीः पुरुरूपा इह स्युरिन्द्राय पूर्वीरुषसो दुहानाः ॥

1. The kine have come and brought good fortune, let them rest in the cowpen and be happy near us. Here let them stay prolific, many-coloured, and yield through many morns their milk for sacrifice in the name of God. (760)

२. इन्द्रो यज्वने गृणते च शिक्षत उपेद् ददाति न स्वं मुषायति।
भूयोभूयो रयिमिदस्य वर्धयन्नभिन्ने खिल्ये नि दधाति देवयुम् ॥

2. God grants true knowledge to him who offers sacrifice and praise. He takes not what is his, and gives him more thereto. Increasing ever more and ever more his wealth. He makes the pious dwell in a state of eternal joy, not far from Him. (761)

[1]Griffith translates Kashyapa as one of a class of semi-divine spirits or Jenü connected with or regulating the course of the sun. This explanation is not plausible. The word means a yogi who diffuses knowledge, is the seer of truth, and highly learned. He translates sumya as a bitch that has four eyes. This explanation is irrational and unacceptable. 'Four eyes' mean the four Vedas and Sumya is mental force.

[2]'Pishach' means soul, that pervades all living physical objects; or that eats our flesh and torments us. (पिशाचम) पिशिताशिनम्.

३. न ता नशन्ति न दभाति तस्करो नासामामित्रो व्यथिरा दधर्षति ।
देवांश्च याभिर्यजते ददाति च ज्योगित् ताभिः सचते गोपतिः सह ॥

3. These are ne'er lost, no robber ever injures them; no evil-minded foe attempts to harass them. The master of the kine lives a long life with these, the cows with whose milk he performs the yajna to purify the forces of nature, and whom he gives in charity. (762)[1]

४. न ता अर्वा रेणुककाटोऽश्नुते न संस्कृतत्रमुप यन्ति ता अभि ।
उरुगायमभयं तस्य ता अनु गावो मर्तस्य वि चरन्ति यज्वनः ॥

4. A violent person, or a tiger raising dust, overtakes them not, and never to the shambles do they take their way. These cows, the cattle of the pious worshipper, roam over wide-spread pasture where there is no danger. (763)

५. गावो भगो गाव इन्द्रो म इच्छाद् गावः सोमस्य प्रथमस्य भक्षः ।
इमा या गावः स जनास इन्द्र इच्छामि हृदा मनसा चिदिन्द्रम् ॥

5. Cows are wealth. God hath given me cows according to my heart's content, cows make us enjoy supreme salvation. O men these cows are my prosperity. I long for such a prosperity with my heart and spirit. (764)

६. यूयं गावो मेदयथा कृशं चिदश्रीरं चित् कृणुथा सुप्रतीकम् ।
भद्रं गृहं कृणुथ भद्रवाचो बृहद् वो वय उच्यते सभासु ॥

6. O cows your milk fattens even the worn and wasted and makes the ugly beautiful to look on. Your auspicious voices lend prosperity to my home. The efficacy of your milk and curd is highly spoken of in our assemblies. (765)

७. प्रजावतीः सूयवसे रुशन्तीः शुद्धा अपः सुप्रपाणे पिबन्तीः ।
मा व स्तेन ईशत माघशंसः परि वो रुद्रस्य हेतिर्वृणक्तु ॥

7. O Cows, may you be prolific, grazing in green meadows, and drinking, pure water at fair drinking places, may never a thief or an evil-minded tiger be your master. May God's power of destruction always protect you. (766)

HYMN XXII

१. इममिन्द्र वर्धय क्षत्रियं म इमं विशामेकवृषं कृणु त्वम् ।
निरमित्रानक्ष्णुह्यस्य सर्वास्तान् रन्धयास्मा अहमुत्तरेषु ॥

1. Exalt and strengthen this my prince, O God, Make him sole lord and leader of the people. Scatter his foes, deliver all his rivals into his hand in struggles for precedence. (767)

[1]Thes e: Cows.

२. एमं भज ग्रामे अश्वेषु गोषु निष्टं भज यो अमित्रो अस्य ।
वर्ष्म क्षत्राणामयमस्तु राजेन्द्र शत्रुं रन्धय सर्वमस्मै ॥

2. Give him a share in villages, kine and horses, and leave his enemy without a portion. Let him as king be head and chief of princes. O God, let every foeman surrender to him. (768)[1]

३. अयमस्तु धनपतिर्धनानामयं विशां विश्पतिरस्तु राजा ।
अस्मिन्निन्द्र महि वर्चांसि धेह्यवर्चसं कृणुहि शत्रुमस्य ॥

3. Let him be treasure-lord of goodly treasures, let him as king be master of the people. Grant unto him great power and might, O God, and strip his enemy of strength and vigour. (769)

४. अस्मै द्यावापृथिवी भूरि वामं दुहाथां घर्मदुघेइव धेनू ।
अयं राजा प्रिय इन्द्रस्य भूयात् प्रियो गवामोषधीनां पशूनाम ॥

4. Like two milch-kine yielding milk in incessent warm showers, grant him wealth, O Heaven and Earth. May he as king be God's well-beloved, the darling of the kine, the plants, the cattle. (770)

५. युनज्मि त उत्तरावन्तमिन्द्रं येन जयन्ति न पराजयन्ते ।
यस्त्वा करदेकवृषं जनानामुत राज्ञामुत्तमं मानवानाम् ॥

5. I make the Victorious God thy friend, with Whose support men conquer and are never defeated. He shall make thee the folk's sole lord and leader, shall make thee highest of all thoughtful rulers. (771)

६. उत्तरस्त्वमधरे ते सपत्ना ये के च राजन् प्रतिशत्रवस्ते ।
एकवृष इन्द्रसखा जिगीवाञ्छत्रूयतामा भरा भोजनानि ॥

6. Supreme art thou, beneath thee are thy rivals, and all, O King, who are thine adversaries. Thou art the sole lord and leader, the devotee of God, conqueror, bring thy foeman's goods and treasures! (772)

७. सिंहप्रतीको विशो अद्धि सर्वा व्याघ्रप्रतीकोऽव बाधस्व शत्रून् ।
एकवृष इन्द्रसखा जिगीवां छत्रूयतामा खिदा भोजनानि ॥

7. Brave like a lion, receive thy share from thy subjects, strong like a tiger, drive away thy foemen. Sole lord and leader, devoted to God, conqueror, seize thine enemies possessions. (773)[2]

[1]'Him' refers to a king.
[2]'Thou', 'thine' refer to the king.
Receive share: A king should levy taxes on the subjects, and realise money for maintaining himself, and efficiently running his administration.

HYMN XXIII

१. अग्नेर्मन्वे प्रथमस्य प्रचेतसः पाञ्चजन्यस्य बहुधा यमिन्धते ।
विशोविशः प्रविशिवांसमीमहे स नो मुञ्चत्वंहसः ॥

1. I contemplate on the Ancient, Wise God, the friend of man, created out of five elements, Whom the sages enkindle in diverse ways. We pray unto Him, Who pervades all subjects, to deliver us from sin. (774)[1]

२. यथा हव्यं वहसि जातवेदो यथा यज्ञं कल्पयसि प्रजानन् ।
एवा देवेभ्यः सुमतिं न आ वह स नो मुञ्चत्वंहसः ॥

2. O God, the knower of all created objects, just as Thou givest us edible food; O Omniscient Lord, just as Thou fashionest the Yajna of the universe, so bestow fine intellect on our learned persons. May He deliver us from sin ! (775)

३. यामन्यामन्नुपयुक्तं बहिष्ठं कर्मन्कर्मन्नाभगम् ।
अग्निमीडे रक्षोहणं यज्ञवृधं घृताहुतं स नो मुञ्चत्वंहसः ॥

3. I praise God, Helpful in each struggle, All-powerful, Adorable in each deed, the Remover of obstacles, the Goader to noble acts, and the Giver of light. May He deliver us from sin. (776)

४. सुजातं जातवेदसमग्निं वैश्वानरं विभुम् । हव्यवाहं हवामहे स नो मुञ्चत्वंहसः ॥

4. We invoke the Well-Removed God, the Knower of all created objects, the Lover of humanity, the Omnipresent, and the Bestower of nice food. May He deliver us from sin. (777)

५. येन ऋषयो बलमद्योतयन् युजा येनासुराणामयुवन्त मायाः ।
येनाग्निना पणीनिन्द्रो जिगाय स नो मुञ्चत्वंहसः ॥

5. May that God deliver us from sin, through Whose aid the sages give their power new splendour, and keep aloof the devices of devilish people, and through Whose aid the soul subdues the sinners. (778)

६. येन देवा अमृतमन्वविन्दन् येनौषधीर्मधुमतीरकृण्वन् ।
येन देवाः स्व१राभरन्त्स नो मुञ्चत्वंहसः ॥

6. May that God deliver us from sin, through Whose aid, the sages attain to salvation, and store the plants with pleasant juices, through Whose aid the learned acquire spiritual force. (779)

[1]Five elements: Fire, air, water, earth, space. The word पाञ्चजन्य has been interpreted differently, as Brahman, Kshatriya, Vaishya, Shudra and Nishad, and as five organs.

७. यस्येदं प्रदिशि यद् विरोचते यज्जातं जनितव्यं॒ च केवलम् ।
स्तौम्यग्निं नाथितो जोहवीमि स नो मुञ्चत्वंहसः ॥

7. I, suppliant, praise and ever call on God, the sole Lord of all this world, of all that shineth, of what exists and shall exist hereafter. May He deliver us from sin. (780)[1]

HYMN XXIV

१. इन्द्रस्य मन्महे शश्वदिदस्य मन्महे वृत्रघ्न स्तोमा उप मेम आगुः ।
यो दाशुषः सुकृतो हवमेति स नो मुञ्चत्वंहसः ॥

1. We worship God, We worship for ever only Him, the Extinguisher of impediments. To me His lauds appear true. He cometh for rescue on the call of a charitable and virtuous man. May He deliver us from sin. (781)

२. य उग्रीणामुग्रबाहुर्ययुर्यो दानवानां बलमारुरोज ।
येन जिताः सिन्धवो येन गावः स नो मुञ्चत्वंहसः ॥

2. May the Almighty God, Who lends strength to the warriors, Who breaks and crushes the power of the demons, Who controls the running streams and the revolving planets, deliver me from sin. (782)

३. यश्चर्षणिप्रो वृषभः स्वर्विद् यस्मै ग्रावाणः प्रवदन्ति नृम्णम् ।
यस्याध्वरः सप्तहोता मदिष्ठः स नो मुञ्चत्वंहसः ॥

3. May God, the Fulfiller of the aims of men, the showerer of joy, the Bestower of salvation, Whose valour is declared by the learned, Whose sweetest sacrifice of the universe is performed by the seven forces of Nature, deliver us from sin. (783)

४. यस्य वशास ऋषभास उक्षणो यस्मै मीयन्ते स्वरवः स्वर्विदे ।
यस्मै शुक्रः पवते ब्रह्मशुम्भितः स नो मुञ्चत्वंहसः ॥

4. May God, Who controls the noble persons, clouds and oxen, Who pervading the luminous world directs the suns revolve, Who purifying the air, guides it blow pure, fresh and fast, deliver us from sin. (784)

५. यस्य जुष्टिं सोमिनः कामयन्ते यं हवन्त इषुमन्तं गविष्टौ ।
यस्मिन्नर्कः शिश्रिये यस्मिन्नोजः स नो मुञ्चत्वंहसः ॥

5. May God, whose friendship the sages long for, Whom, the Omnipotent, the learned laud on acquiring the knowledge of the Vedas, in Whom the sun takes shelter, in Whom resides power, deliver us from sin. (785)

६. यः प्रथमः कर्मकृत्याय जज्ञे यस्य वीर्यं॒ प्रथमस्यानुबुद्धम् ।
येनोद्यतो वज्रोऽभ्यायताहिं स नो मुञ्चत्वंहसः ॥

[1]'All that shineth': the planets that shine.

6. May God, Who existed in the beginning as the Efficient Cause for creating the universe, Whose strength, as the First is known universally, Whose severe punishment falls on persons crooked like a snake, deliver us from sin. (786)

७. यः संग्रामान् नयति सं युधे वशी यः पुष्टानि संसृजति द्वयानि ।
स्तौमीन्द्रं नाथितो जोहवीमि स नो मुञ्चत्वंहसः ॥

7. Just as a general leads his army for the battle, so does God give right lead to men for the struggles of life. He grants us physical and spiritual forces. I, His devotee praise Him, and ever call on Him. May He deliver us from sin. (787)

HYMN XXV

१. वायोः सवितुर्विदथानि मन्महे यावात्मन्वद् विशथो यौ च रक्षथः ।
यौ विश्वस्य परिभू बभूवथुस्तौ नो मुञ्चतमंहसः ॥

1. O God, the Urger like the wind, and Creator like the Sun, we contemplate upon Thy characteristics. These two traits of Thine, penetrate and guard the living world. Ye twain, who pervade the whole universe, deliver us from sin! (788)[1]

२. ययोः संख्याता वरिमा पार्थिवानि याभ्यां रजो युपितमन्तरिक्षे ।
ययोः प्रायं नान्वानशे कश्चन तौ नो मुञ्चतमंहसः ॥

2. Ye, under whose shelter all important, earthly deeds are planned, through whose dual forces, watery clouds are sustained in the atmosphere, whose eminence hath ne'er been reached by any, may they both deliver us from sin. (789)[2]

३. तव व्रते नि विशन्ते जनासस्त्वय्युदिते प्रेरते चित्रभानो ।
युवं वायो सविता च भुवनानि रक्षथस्तौ नो मुञ्चतमंहसः ॥

3. O beauteously Bright God, men rest under Thy sway, and tread the path of rectitude when Thy knowledge dawns in the heart.

O Urger, O Creator, both powers of Thine, preserve all creatures. O ye both Divine powers, deliver me from sin! (790)

४. अपेतो वायो सविता च दुष्कृतमप रक्षांसि शिमिदां च सेधतम् ।
सं ह्यूर्जया सृजथः सं बलेन तौ नो मुञ्चतमंहसः ॥

[1]Ye twain: The two traits of God, i.e., Urging and Creating.
[2]They both: The two powers of God, i.e., Urging and Creating.

4. O God, the Urger and Creator, may both Thy divine powers drive away evil deeds. May they remove obstacles and privation. Ye both grant us physical and spiritual powers. May Ye both deliver us from sin. (791)[1]

५. रयिं मे पोषं सवितोत वायुस्तनू दक्षमा सुवतां सुशेवम् ।
अयक्ष्मतातिं मह इह धत्तं तौ नो मुञ्चतमंहसः ॥

5. May the two divine forces of God, acting like the sun and wind lend my body wealth, favourable strength and alacrity. May they give us here perfect freedom from consumption, and deliver us from sin. (792)[2]

६. प्र सुमतिं सवितर्वाय ऊतये महस्वन्तं मत्सरं मादयाथः ।
अर्वाग् वामस्य प्रवतो नि यच्छतं तौ नो मुञ्चतमंहसः ॥

6. Ye, Savitar and Vayu, two divine powers, grant us fine intellect for our protection, satisfy the exhilarating soul full of glow; grant directly to this progressive, beautiful soul, supreme joys. Deliver us, Ye twain, from sin. (793)

७. उप श्रेष्ठा न आशिषो देवयोर्धामन्नस्थिरन् ।
स्तौमि देवं सवितारं च वायुं तौ नो मुञ्चतमंहसः ॥

7. Our noblest prayers reach unto God, the Possessor of both the divine powers. I praise God, the Creator and the Urger. May both those divine powers deliver me from sin. (794)

Chapter (Anuvāka) 6

HYMN XXVI

१. मन्वे वां द्यावापृथिवी सुभोजसौ सचेतसौ ये अप्रथेथाममिता योजनानि ।
प्रतिष्ठे ह्यभवतं वसूनां ते नो मुञ्चतमंहसः ॥

1. O controlling and loving forces of God, Ye both are the givers of abundant gifts and full of wisdom, Ye have spread forth through measureless expanses. Ye are the supports of all living beings. May Ye twain, deliver us from sin. (795)[3]

२. प्रतिष्ठे ह्यभवतं वसूनां प्रवृद्धे देवी सुभगे उरूची ।
द्यावापृथिवी भवतं मे स्योने ते नो मुञ्चतमंहसः ॥

[1]Griffith interprets Simidā, as a female demon, or a disease attributed to her malevolence. This interpretation is illogical, as there is no history in the Vedas. The word means privation that causes mental pain.

[2]Here: In this world Two divine forces: Urging, प्रेरण, Creation, उत्पत्ति.

[3]The पितृशक्ति and मातृशक्ति of God, i.e., His powers of control and Love have been spoken of as द्यावापृथिवी.

2. Indeed, Ye are the supports of all living beings, grown strong, divine, blessed, and far-extending. To me, O divine powers of Control and Love, be Ye auspicious. May Ye twain, deliver us from sin. (796)

३. असन्तापे सुतपसौ हुवेऽहमुर्वी गम्भीरे कविभिर्नमस्ये ।
द्यावापृथिवी भवतं मे स्योने ते नो मुञ्चतमंहसः ॥

3. I call on You, who cause no sorrow, are attainable through penance, spacious, calm, and meet to be adored by sages. To me O divine powers of Control and Love, be Ye auspicious to me. May Ye twain, deliver us from sin! (797)

४. ये अमृतं बिभृथो ये हवींषि ये स्रोत्या बिभृथो ये मनुष्यान् ।
द्यावापृथिवी भवतं मे स्योने ते नो मुञ्चतमंहसः ॥

4. O divine powers, Ye twain, who grant salvation to men, produce food-stuffs, maintain blood streams in the body, and rear men, be auspicious to me. May Ye twain, deliver us from sin! (798)

५. ये उस्रिया बिभृथो ये वनस्पतीन् ययोर्वां विश्वा भुवनान्यन्तः ।
द्यावापृथिवी भवतं मे स्योने ते नो मुञ्चतमंहसः ॥

5. Ye by whom cows and forest trees are cherished, within whose range all creatures are included, to me, O divine powers, be Ye auspicious. May Ye twain, deliver us from sin. (799)

६. ये कीलालेन तर्पयथो ये घृतेन याभ्यामृते न किं चन शक्नुवन्ति ।
द्यावापृथिवी भवतं मे स्योने ते नो मुञ्चतमंहसः ॥

6. Ye who supply food, knowledge and water to the world, Ye without whom men have no strength or power, to me, O Divine powers, be Ye auspicious. May Ye twain, deliver us from sin. (800)

७. यन्मेदमभिशोचति येनयेन वा कृतं पौरुषेयान्न दैवात् ।
स्तौमि द्यावापृथिवी नाथितो जोहवीमि ते नो मुञ्चतमंहसः ॥

7. The grief that pains me here, whoever caused it, not sent by fate, hath sprung from human action. I, suppliant, praise both the Divine powers, and oft invoke them, to deliver us, Ye twain, from sin! (801)

HYMN XXVII

१. मरुतां मन्वे अधि मे ब्रुवन्तु प्रेमं वाजं वाजसाते अवन्तु ।
आशूनिव सुयमानह्व ऊतये ते नो मुञ्चन्त्वंहसः ॥

1. I know the learned persons. May they instruct me. May they preserve this knowledge at the time of imparting it. I call them like swift well-trained horses to help us. May they deliver us from sin. (802)[1]

[1]Marutas means learned persons.

२. उत्समक्षितं व्यचन्ति ये सदा य आसिञ्चन्ति रसमोषधीषु ।
पुरो दधे मरुतः पृश्निमातॄंस्ते नो मुञ्चन्त्वंहसः ॥

2. I chiefly honour the benevolent learned persons, the sons of the mother knowledge, who ever diffuse the never-failing fountain of wisdom and offer the essence of medicinal plants to men for drinking. (803)

३. पयो धेनूनां रसमोषधीनां जवमर्वतां कवयो य इन्वथ ।
शग्मा भवन्तु मरुतो नः स्योनास्ते नो मुञ्चन्त्वंहसः ॥

3. May the powerful learned persons be auspicious to us, who, the knowers of truth, invigorate the milk of milch-kine, the sap of growing plants, the speed of coursers. May they deliver us from sin. (804)

४. अपः समुद्राद् दिवमुद् वहन्ति दिवस्पृथिवीमभि ये सृजन्ति ।
ये अद्भिरीशाना मरुतश्चरन्ति ते नो मुञ्चन्त्वंहसः ॥

4. Just as winds raise water from the sea to heaven, and send it from the sky to earth in showers, and move mighty with their waters, so do the learned, deriving wisdom from the ocean of knowledge, attain to salvation, and coming back to earth from their emancipated state, roam about full of knowledge and dignity. May those souls redeemed in mortal coil, deliver us from sin. (805)

५. ये कीलालेन तर्पयन्ति ये घृतेन ये वा वयो मेदसा संसृजन्ति ।
ये अद्भिरीशाना मरुतो वर्षयन्ति ते नो मुञ्चन्त्वंहसः ॥

5. The learned persons, who satisfy us with foodstuffs and knowledge, who instruct us to acquire longevity and vigour, the highly learned persons, who through Yajnas make the clouds rain with their waters, may they deliver us from sin. (806)

६. यदीदिदं मरुतो मारुतेन यदि देवा दैव्येनेदृगार ।
यूयमीशिध्वे वसवस्तस्य निष्कृतेस्ते नो मुञ्चन्त्वंहसः ॥

6. O learned persons, whether this dreadful trouble has arisen through the violence of our breaths, or O wise persons, whether such a calamity has arisen through natural misfortune, Ye are able to drive it away. May you deliver us from sin! (807)

७. तिग्ममनीकं विदितं सहस्वन् मारुतं शर्धः पृतनासूग्रम् ।
स्तौमि मरुतो नाथितो जोहवीमि ते नो मुञ्चन्त्वंहसः ॥

7. The impetuous, conquering military force of the learned is known to all, as is known the dreadful force of the commanders in the army. I, suppliant praise and oft invoke the learned. May they deliver us from sin. (808)

HYMN XXVIII

१. भवाशर्वौ मन्वे वां तस्य वित्तं ययोर्वामिदं प्रदिशि यद् विरोचते ।
यावस्येशाथे द्विपदो यौ चतुष्पदस्तौ नो मुञ्चतमंहसः ॥

1. I revere you—mark this—O Bhava and Ṣarva, Ye under whose control is this that shineth. Lords of the world both quadruped and biped, deliver us, Ye twain, from sin! (809)[1]

२. ययोरभ्यध्व उत यद् दूरे चिद् यौ विदिताविषुभृतामसिष्ठौ ।
यावस्येशाथे द्विपदो यौ चतुष्पदस्तौ नो मुञ्चतमंहसः ॥

2. Lords of all near and distant objects, famed as the destroyers of the violent. Lords of this world both quadruped and biped, deliver us, Ye twain from sin. (810)[2]

३. सहस्राक्षौ वृत्रहणा हुवेऽहं दूरेगव्यूती स्तुवन्नेम्युग्रौ ।
यावस्येशाथे द्विपदो यौ चतुष्पदस्तौ नो मुञ्चतमंहसः ॥

3. Thousand-eyed, foe-destroyers, beyond the reach of organs, I invoke you, still praising you the strong. I reach unto God. Lords of this world both quadruped and biped, deliver us, Ye twain, from sin. (811)[3]

४. यावारेभाथे बहु साकमग्रे प्र चेदस्राष्ट्रमभिभां जनेषु ।
यावस्येशाथे द्विपदो यौ चतुष्पदस्तौ नो मुञ्चतमंहसः ॥

4. Ye who in the beginning created various objects simultaneously, and lent intellect to mankind, lords of this world, both quadruped and biped, deliver us, Ye twain from sin. (812)[4]

५. ययोर्वधान्नापपद्यते कश्चनान्तर्देवेषूत मानुषेषु ।
यावस्येशाथे द्विपदो यौ चतुष्पदस्तौ नो मुञ्चतमंहसः ॥

5. Ye from the stroke of whose destroying weapon not one among the gods or men escapeth, lords of this world both quadruped and biped, deliver us, Ye twain, from sin. (813)

६. यः कृत्याकृन्मूलकृद् यातुधानो नि तस्मिन् धत्तं वज्रमुग्रौ ।
यावस्येशाथे द्विपदो यौ चतुष्पदस्तौ नो मुञ्चतमंहसः ॥

6. Hurl your bolt, O strong Bhava and Ṣarva, on him, who is violent, tormenting, and the destroyer of our progeny. Lords of this world both quadrupeds and bipeds, deliver us, Ye twain, from sin. (814)

[1]Bhava: God power of creation.
Ṣarva: God's power of dissolution of the universe.
[2]Lords: Bhava and Ṣarva. [3]'You' refers to Bhava and Ṣarva.
Thousand-eyed: God is All-seeing. [4]'Ye' refers to Bhava and Ṣarva.

७. अधि नो ब्रूतं पृतनासूग्रौ सं वज्रेण सृजतं यः किमीदी ।
स्तौमि भवाशर्वौ नाथितो जोहवीमि तौ नो मुञ्चतमंहसः ॥

7. O strong forces of God, instruct us nicely, punish with your thunderbolt, in battles, a man of selfish and wavering nature. O Bhava and Ṣarva, I suppliant, praise and ever call on thee. Set us free from sin. (815)

HYMN XXIX

१. मन्वे वां मित्रावरुणावृतावृधौ सचेतसौ द्रुह्वणो यौ नुदेथे ।
प्र सत्यावानमवथो भरेषु तौ नो मुञ्चतमंहसः ॥

1. O Mitra and Varuṇa, I honour Ye both, advancers of truth, life-infusers, who drive away oppressors. Ye who protect the truthful in intellectual discussions, deliver us, Ye twain, from grief and trouble! (816)[1]

२. सचेतसौ द्रुह्वणो यौ नुदेथे प्र सत्यावानमवथो भरेषु ।
यौ गच्छथो नृचक्षसौ बभ्रुणा सुतं तौ नो मुञ्चतमंहसः ॥

2. Ye, who vigorously drive away internal foes, Ye, who protect the truthful in intellectual discussions; Ye, who, men's guardians, come to the subjects nourished by the king as son, deliver us, twain, from grief and trouble. (817)[2]

३. यावङ्गिरसमवथो यावगस्तिं मित्रावरुणा जमदग्निमत्रिम् ।
यौ कश्यपमवथो यौ वसिष्ठं तौ नो मुञ्चतमंहसः ॥

3. Mitra and Varuṇa, who help an energic learned person, a religious preacher, an austere householder, a sage free from the weakness of body, speech and mind, a pupil yearning for knowledge, and a great man, deliver us, Ye twain from grief and trouble! (818)[3]

४. यौ श्यावाश्वमवथो वध्र्यश्वं मित्रावरुणा पुरुमीढमत्रिम् ।
यौ विमदमवथः सप्तवध्रिं तौ नो मुञ्चतमंहसः ॥

4. Mitra and Varuṇa, who help a talented person, a man abstemious in diet, a wealthy person, a vigilant worker, a man free from pride, a man who controls the five organs of cognition, mind and intellect, deliver us, Ye twain, from grief and trouble! (819)

[1]Oppressors: Lust, Anger, Avarice, Infatuation.
Mitra and Varuna: Day and Night, or Prāna and Apāna.

[2]Ye: Prāṇa and Apāna, or Day and Night.

[3]Mitra and Varuṇa: Prāna and Apāna, or Day and Night. Griffith translates Angiras, Agastya, Jamdagni, Atri, Kashyap and Vasishta as names of mythical personages. Agastya is spoken of as the friend and counsellor of Rāma. Atri is interpreted as one of the great seven Rishis, said to have been delivered from distress by Indra and the Aświns. This interpretation is unacceptable, as there is no history in the Vedas.

५. यौ भरद्वाजमवथो यौ गविष्ठिरं विश्वामित्रं वरुण मित्र कुत्सम् ।
यौ कक्षीवन्तमवथः प्रोत कण्वं तौ नो मुञ्चतमंहसः ॥

5. Mitra and Varuṇa, who protect a man who possesses foodstuffs, strength and wisdom, a man well-versed in Vedic lore, a man who loves mankind, a man who is the vanquisher of human frailties, an enterprising administrator, a sage who lives on particles of corn, deliver us, ye twain, from grief and trouble! (820)[1]

६. यौ मेधातिथिमवथो यौ त्रिशोकं मित्रावरुणावुशनां काव्यं यौ ।
यौ गोतममवथः प्रोत मुद्गलं तौ नो मुञ्चतमंहसः ॥

6. O Prāṇa and Apāna, Night and Day, who protect a man of steady intellect, a yogi who burns with knowledge his sins of body, mind, and tongue, a wise policy of statesmen, the action of the wise, a highly spiritually advanced person, a soul emancipated in life and revelling in joy, deliver us, Ye twain, from grief and trouble! (821)

७. ययो रथः सत्यवर्त्मर्जुरश्मिर्मिथुया चरन्तमभियाति दूषयन् ।
स्तौमि मित्रावरुणौ नाथितो जोहवीमि तौ नो मुञ्चतमंहसः ॥

7. O Prāṇa and Apāna, Day and Night, who stick to the path of goodness, who are bound by the ties of straightforward demeanour, who assail and ruin him whose behaviour is untrue, I, suppliant, praise Ye with constant invocation, save us from affliction. (822)

HYMN XXX

१. अहं रुद्रेभिर्वसुभिश्चराम्यहमादित्यैरुत विश्वदेवैः ।
अहं मित्रावरुणोभा बिभर्म्यहमिन्द्राग्नी अहमश्विनोभा ॥

1. I remain in the company of all learned persons, all living objects, all luminous objects like the Sun, etc., born of matter. I support the Day and Night, the Air and Fire, the Sun and Earth. (823)[2]

२. अहं राष्ट्री सगमनी वसूनां चिकितुषी प्रथमा यज्ञियानाम् ।
तां मा देवा व्यदधुः पुरुत्रा भूरिस्थात्रां भूर्यावेशयन्तः ॥

2. I am the foremost administrative power, that bestows treasures, and knows all important topics. The learned realise, Me, existent in innumerable objects in diverse forms, by making Me rest in their soul through various devices. (824)[3]

[1]Griffith interprets Bhardwaj, Gavishthir, Vishamitra, Kutsa Kakshivant, Kanwa as names of certain Rishis. This is illogical, as there is no history in the Vedas. Proper nouns cannot occur in the Vedas.

[2]'I' refers to God.

[3]Various devices: Through contemplation, knowledge and noble deeds. 'I' refers to God.

३. अहमेव स्वयमिदं वदामि जुष्टं देवानामुत मानुषाणाम् ।
यं कामये तंतमुग्रं कृणोमि तं ब्रह्माणं तमृषिं तं सुमेधाम् ॥

3. I verily, myself announce and utter sages and men alike shall welcome. I make the man I love, exceedingly mighty, make him a Rishi, and a Brahmā. (825)[1]

४. मया सोऽन्नमत्ति यो विपश्यति यः प्राणति य ईं शृणोत्युक्तम् ।
अमन्तवो मां त उप क्षियन्ति श्रुधि श्रुत श्रद्धेयं ते वदामि ॥

4. He who eats the food, eats through My power. He who sees, sees through My power. He who breathes, breathes through My power. He who hears the word spoken, hears through My power. They who have no faith in Me, court disaster. O learned listener, listen to what I say from inside thy soul. I proclaim the Truth for thee, have faith in it! (826)[2]

५. अहं रुद्राय धनुरा तनोमि ब्रह्मद्विषे शरवे हन्तवा उ ।
अहं जनाय समदं कृणोम्यहं द्यावापृथिवी आ विवेश ॥

5. I bend the bow for striking and slaying the foe of knowledge, the violent and the tormentor. I create this pleasant, beautiful world for the people. I have penetrated Earth and Heaven. (827)

६. अहं सोममाहनसं बिभर्म्यहं त्वष्टारमुत पूषणं भगम् ।
अहं दधामि द्रविणा हविष्मते सुप्राव्या३ यजमानाय सुन्वते ॥

6. I cherish and sustain the darkness—dispelling moon, the Sun, the life-infusing air, and the prosperous person. I bestow nice, nourishing wealth, on a devotee, a distiller of the juice of knowledge, and a reverer of the sages. (828)

७. अहं सुवे पितरमस्य मूर्धन्मम योनिरप्स्व१न्तः समुद्रे ।
ततो वि तिष्ठे भुवनानि विश्वोतामूं द्यां वर्ष्मणोप स्पृशामि ॥

7. On the world's summit I bring forth the Sun, My home is in the atoms of the ocean of Matter. Thence I extend over all existing worlds, and engulf even yonder heaven with my power. (829)

८. अहमेव वातइव प्र वाम्यारभमाणा भुवनानि विश्वा ।
परो दिवा पर एना पृथिव्यैतावती महिम्ना सं बभूव ॥

8. Having created all the worlds, I feel free like the wind. Beyond this wide earth and beyond the heavens, I have become so mighty in my grandeur. (830)[3]

[1]Brahmā: Knower of the Vedas.
Rishi: A person spiritually advanced.

[2]'I, My' refer to God.

[3]Just as the wind is free in its motion, without being impelled by any one, so God is free and independent in creating the universe, without being helped by any one.

Chapter (Anuvāka) 7

HYMN XXXI

१. त्वया मन्यो सरथमारुजन्तो हर्षमाणा हृषितासो मरुत्वन् ।
तिग्मेषव आयुधा संशिशाना उप प्र यन्तु नरो अग्निरूपाः ॥

1. O perseverance of the valiant, with thy help, let our brave men, vanquishing the foe along with his conveyance, march on, like flames of fire in form, exulting, joyful, with pointed arrows, sharpening their weapons! (831)

२. अग्निरिव मन्यो त्विषितः सहस्व सेनानीर्नः सहुरे हूत एधि ।
हत्वाय शत्रून् वि भजस्व वेद ओजो मिमानो वि मृधो नुदस्व ॥

2. O persevering general, flashing like fire, subdue the foes. O victor, be thou, invoked, our army's leader. Slaying our foes, distribute their wealth, preserving thy vigour, destroy the warring foes! (832)

३. सहस्व मन्यो अभिमातिमस्मै रुजन् मृणन् प्रमृणन् प्रेहि शत्रून् ।
उग्रं ते पाजो नन्वा रुरुध्रे वशी वशं नयासा एकज त्वम् ॥

3. O persevering general, conquer the foe of this king. Go forward, breaking, slaying, crushing down the foemen. They cannot hinder thine impetuous vigour: mighty, sole born, reduce them to subjection! (833)[1]

४. एको बहूनामसि मन्य ईडिता विशंविशं युद्धाय सं शिशाधि ।
अकृत्तरुक्त्वया युजा वयं द्युमन्तं घोषं विजयाय कृण्मसि ॥

4. O persevering general, alone of many thou art worshipped, sharpen the spirit of every man for the struggle of life. With thee to aid, O thou of perfect splendour, we raise the glorious battle-shout for conquest. (834)

५. विजेषकृदिन्द्र इवानवब्रवो३स्माकं मन्यो अधिपा भवेह ।
प्रियं ते नाम सहुरे गृणीमसि विद्मा तमुत्सं यत आबभूथ ॥

5. O persevering general, never using a language of despair, bringing victory like the king, be thou here our sovran ruler. To thy dear name, O victor, we sing praises. We know the spring from which thou art come hither. (835)[2]

६. आभूत्या सहजा वज्र सायक सहो बिभर्षि सहभूत उत्तरम् ।
क्रत्वा नो मन्यो सह मेद्य१धि महाधनस्य पुरुहूत संसृजि ॥

[1]Sole born: Having none to equal thee in strength, unequalled, imparalleled.
[2]Here: In this battlefield.
Spring: The divine transcendental source i.e., God.
It may also mean, thou belongest to the same country of which we are the subjects.

6. O dreadful like the bolt of thunder, O destroyer of foes, O full of wealth, born with divine power, the highest conquering might is thine. O persevering general, be friendly to us with thy wisdom, O much invoked, in mighty shock of battle, the bringer of rich bounty. (836)

७. संसृष्टं धनमुभयं समाकृतमस्मभ्यं धत्तां वरुणश्च मन्युः ।
भियो दधाना हृदयेषु शत्रवः पराजितासो अप नि लयन्ताम् ॥

7. Let the king and persevering general, give us both kinds of wealth, acquired through battle, and collected through self-exertion. Let our enemies with stricken spirits, overwhelmed with terror, sling away defeated. (837)

HYMN XXXII

१. यस्ते मन्योऽविधद् वज्र सायक सह ओजः पुष्यति विश्वमानुषक् ।
साह्याम दासमार्यं त्वया युजा वयं सहस्कृतेन सहसा सहस्वता ॥

1. O perseverance our saviour from sins, the destroyer of foes, he who resorts to thee, develops for himself permanently every kind of physical and social force. The ignoble and noble foes will we conquer with thine aid, with the conqueror, with conquest conquest-sped. (838)

२. मन्युरिन्द्रो मन्युरेवास देवो मन्युर्होता वरुणो जातवेदाः ।
मन्युर्विश ईडते मानुषीर्याः पाहि नो मन्यो तपसा सजोषाः ॥

2. Perseverance is full of glory, divine in nature, the bestower of strength, worthy of acceptance, and the giver of wealth. The tribes of human lineage worship perseverance. Accordant with thy religious austerity, Perseverance! Guard us. (839)

३. अभीहि मन्यो तवसस्तवीयान् तपसा युजा वि जहि शत्रून् ।
अमित्रहा वृत्रहा दस्युहा च विश्वा वसून्या भरा त्वं नः ॥

3. Come hither, Perseverance! mightier than the mighty, smite, with thy fervour, for ally, our foemen. Slayer of foes, remover of impediments, slayer of violent marauders, bring thou to us all kinds of wealth and treasure. (840)

४. त्वं हि मन्यो अभिभूत्योजाः स्वयंभूर्भामो अभिमातिषाहः ।
विश्वचर्षणिः सहुरिः सहीयानस्मास्वोजः पृतनासु धेहि ॥

4. For thou art, Perseverance! of surpassing vigour, fierce, queller of the foe, and self-existent, controller of all men, victorious, subduer; vouchsafe to us superior strength in battles. (841)

५. अभागः सन्नप परेतो अस्मि तव क्रत्वा तविषस्य प्रचेतः ।
तं त्वा मन्यो अक्रतुर्जिहीडाहं स्वा तनूर्बलदावा न एहि ॥

5. O wise perseverance, deprived of thy mighty power, I have gone far away from thee. I, an unwise man, have incurred thy wrath, O perseverance! Come in thy proper form and give us vigour. (842)

६. अयं ते अस्म्युप न एह्यर्वाङ् प्रतीचीनः सहुरे विश्वदावन् ।
मन्यो वज्रिन्नभि न आ ववृत्स्व हनाव दस्यूंरुत बोध्यापेः ॥

6. I am all thine own, though invisible, come hither unto us; O victorious, all-bestowing, martial Perseverance. Come unto us, let us together destroy the foes of spiritual power, recognise me as thy friend! (843)

७. अभि प्रेहि दक्षिणतो भवा नोऽधा वृत्राणि जङ्घनाव भूरि ।
जुहोमि ते धरुणं मध्वो अग्रमुभावुपांशु प्रथमा पिबाव ॥

7. O perseverance, approach, and on our right hand hold thy station, then let us both remove a multitude of impediments. I realise thy steady, dignified pleasant nature, may, we be first to enjoy it in solitude. (844)[1]

HYMN XXXIII

१. अप नः शोशुचदघमग्ने शुशुग्ध्या रयिम् । अप नः शोशुचदघम् ॥

1. O God, destroy our sins, and let our wealth be pure. Destroy Thou our sins! (845)[2]

२. सुक्षेत्रिया सुगातुया वसूया च यजामहे । अप नः शोशुचदघम् ॥

2. O God, we worship Thee, for acquiring an excellent body, a nice course of conduct, and salvation. Destroy Thou our sins! (846)

३. प्र यद् भन्दिष्ठ एषां प्रास्माकासश्च सूरयः । अप नः शोशुचदघम् ॥

3. O God, of all our well-wishers, Thou art the best. May learned persons be our well-wishers. Keeping us in their company, destroy Thou our sins! (847)

४. प्र यत् ते अग्ने सूरयो जायेमहि प्र ते वयम् । अप नः शोशुचदघम् ॥

4. O God, learned persons have been created by Thee. May we advance receiving knowledge from Thee. Destroy Thou our sins! (848)

५. प्र यदग्नेः सहस्वतो विश्वतो यन्ति भानवः । अप नः शोशुचदघम् ॥

5. As God's ever conquering beams of splendour go to every side, may Thou, O God through Them, destroy Thou our sins! (849)

[1]Pt. Jaidev Vidyalankar interprets Manyu as God, Both soul and God should derive and enjoy happiness in solitude.

[2]Repetition here is for the sake of emphasis.

६. त्वं हि विश्वतोमुख विश्वतः परिभूरसि । अप नः शोशुचदघम् ।।

6. O All-pervading God, Thou art triumphant everywhere. Destroy Thou our sins! (850)

७. द्विषो नो विश्वतोमुखाति नावेव पारय । अप: नः शोशुचदघम् ।।

7. O All-pervading God, let us cross the ocean of internal foes like lust and anger, as an ocean is crossed through a ship. Destroy Thou our sins! (851)

८. स नः सिन्धुमिव नावाति पर्षा स्वस्तये । अप नः शोशुचदघम् ।।

8. O God, just as an ocean is crossed through a ship, so let us cross the ocean of misery in this world. Destroy Thou our sins. (852)

HYMN XXXIV

१. ब्रह्मास्य शीर्षं बृहदस्य पृष्ठं वामदेव्यमुदरमोदनस्य ।
छन्दांसि पक्षौ मुखमस्य सत्यं विष्टारी जातस्तपसोऽधि यज्ञः ।।

1. Veda is the head of this God. The vast universe is His back. The five elements created by God, are His belly. The pleasant, adorable deeds are His flanks. Truth is His face. The Vast Expanded God, through His supremacy is Most Exalted. (853)[1]

२. अनस्थाः पूताः पवनेन शुद्धाः शुचयः शुचिमपि यन्ति लोकम् ।
नैषां शिश्नं प्र दहति जातवेदाः स्वर्गे लोके बहु स्त्रैणमेषाम् ।।

2. Brahmcharis, who worship God, should be so stout and strong, that their bones be not visible. They should be pure in character, morally elevated through Prāṇāyāma (control of breath), and pure in thought. Being equipped with these qualifications, they enter the pure domestic life. The knowledge acquired by them in their stage of celibacy, does not excite their fire of lust, and they remain self-controlled, even in the midst of their female relatives. (854)

३. विष्टारिणमोदनं ये पचन्ति नैनानवर्तिः सचते कदा चन ।
आस्ते यम उप याति देवान्त्सं गन्धर्वैर्मदते सोम्येभिः ।।

3. Never doth penury or evil fortune visit those who firmly fix the Great God in their heart. A Brahmachari follows the Yamas (laws of austerity), acquires noble qualities, and enjoys supreme felicity in the company of tranquil, learned persons. (855)[2]

[1]The over-subtle, in corporeal supernatural aspect of God is spoken of in this verse, in a beautiful metaphorical language. Griffith interprets the verse for a Yajna.

[2]Yamās: Ahinsa (Non-violence), Satya (Truth), Asteya (Non-stealing), Brahmcharya (celibacy), Aprigraha (Freedom from pride).

४. विष्टारिणमोदनं ये पचन्ति नैनान् यमः परि मुष्णाति रेतः ।
रथी ह भूत्वा रथयान ईयते पक्षी ह भूत्वाति दिवः समेति ॥

4. God, the Controller of the universe, does not deprive the Brahmcharis of their strength, who fix Him firmly in their heart. A Brahmchari, being the master of his soul, attains to God, attainable through soul-force, and like a bird with two wings of cognition and action, soaring high above heaven, absorbs himself in God. (856)[1]

५. एष यज्ञानां विततो बहिष्ठो विष्टारिणं पक्त्वा दिवमा विवेश ।
आण्डीकं कुमुदं सं तनोति बिसं शालूकं शफको मुलाली ।
एतास्त्वा धारा उप यन्तु सर्वाः स्वर्गे लोके मधुमत् पिन्वमाना उप त्वा तिष्ठन्तु पुष्करिणीः समन्ताः ॥

5. This man of noble qualities, engrossed in performing fine deeds, firmly fixing the Mighty God in his heart, has realised the Refulgent Lord. He longing for peace, bettering the fruit of his actions, acquires the attainable, pleasant objects of the world, life-infusing qualities, and active habits.

May all these forces, enhancing pleasure reach thee in domestic life. May thou acquire completely these qualities strengthening the soul in diverse ways. (857)[2]

६. घृतह्रदा मधुकूलाः सुरोदकाः क्षीरेण पूर्णा उदकेन दध्ना ।
एतास्त्वा धारा उप यन्तु सर्वाः स्वर्गे लोके मधुमत् पिन्वमाना उप त्वा तिष्ठन्तु पुष्करिणीः समन्ताः ॥

6. May all these streams of butter, with their banks of honey, flowing with distilled water, and milk and curds and water reach thee in domestic life, enhancing thy pleasure. May thou acquire completely these things strengthening the soul in diverse ways. (858)[3]

७. चतुरः कुम्भांश्चतुर्धा ददामि क्षीरेण पूर्णाँ उदकेन दध्ना ।
एतास्त्वा धारा उप यन्तु सर्वाः स्वर्गे लोके मधुमत् पिन्वमाना उप त्वा तिष्ठन्तु पुष्करिणीः समन्ताः ॥

7. I bestow on thee four boons, through four diverse sources, filled with the power of supplying food, vigour and nourishment. May all these forces enhancing pleasure reach thee in domestic life. May thou acquire completely these qualities strengthening the soul in diverse ways. (859)[4]

[1]Cognition: Knowledge, Gyan, Action: Karma.

[2]This man: A Brahmchari, who has entered the domestic life.

[3]Thee: A Grihasthi, a man who has entered married life. There should be plenty of butter, honey, milk, curd and water in the house of a married person.

[4]'I' refers to God. 'Thee' refers to a married man. Four boons: Dharma, Artha, Kāma, Moksha. Four sources: Brahmcharya (celibacy) Grihastha (married life), Ban Prastha (the life of a recluse), Sanyasa (the life of complete, renunciation) or 'four sources' may mean the four Vedas.

Food: spiritual food. Vigour; mental vigour, Nourishment: intellectual nourishment

८. इममोदनं नि दधे ब्राह्मणेषु विष्टारिणं लोकजितं स्वर्गम् ।
स मे मा क्षेष्ट स्वधया पिन्वमानो विश्वरूपा धेनुः कामदुघा मे अस्तु ॥

8. I preach unto the learned, the true nature of the All-pervading, All-joyful, World-controlling God. May He, the Supplier of food to mankind, never forsake me. May this comprehensive, convincing Vedic speech fulfil all my wishes. (860)[1]

HYMN XXXV

१. यमोदनं प्रथमजा ऋतस्य प्रजापतिस्तपसा ब्रह्मणेऽपचत् ।
यो लोकानां विधृतिर्नाभिरेषात् तेनौदनेनाति तराणि मृत्युम् ॥

1. That God, Who is firmly fixed in his heart by a yogi, through austerity, for the sake of acquiring Vedic knowledge, is the First Promulgator of Laws. He is the main support of all the worlds, and beyond the reach of Death. Through Him, may I cross the ocean of death. (861)[2]

२. येनातरन् भूतकृतोऽति मृत्युं यमन्वविन्दन् तपसा श्रमेण ।
यं पपाच ब्रह्मणे ब्रह्म पूर्वं तेनौदनेनाति तराणि मृत्युम् ॥

2. Through Whose aid, the doers of noble deeds vanquished death, Whom the yogis realised through austerity, toil and trouble, Whom, the Most Exalted, the Beginningless, a Brahmchari firmly fixes in the heart through yogic exercise, may I through Him overcome death. (862)[3]

३. यो दाधार पृथिवीं विश्वभोजसं यो अन्तरिक्षमापृणाद् रसेन ।
यो अस्तभ्नाद् दिवमूर्ध्वो महिम्ना तेनौदनेनाति तराणि मृत्युम् ॥

3. Who upholds the Earth, the all-sustainer, Who hath filled air's middle realm with moisture, Who through His Exalted grandeur, established heaven, may I with the help of that God overcome death. (863)

४. यस्मान्मासा निर्मितास्त्रिंशदराः संवत्सरो यस्मान्निर्मितो द्वादशारः ।
अहोरात्रा यं परियन्तो नापुस्तेनौदनेनाति तराणि मृत्युम् ॥

4. By Whom the mouths with thirty spokes were moulded by whom the twelve-spoked year was formed and fashioned, Whom circling day and night have ne'er overtaken—may I with the help of that God overcome death. (864)[4]

५. यः प्राणदः प्राणदवान् बभूव यस्मै लोका घृतवन्तः क्षरन्ति ।
ज्योतिष्मतीः प्रदिशो यस्य सर्वास्तेनौदनेनाति तराणि मृत्युम् ॥

[1]I: A married man.

[2]God is the support of life, as food is the support of the body. Hence God is spoken of as Odam, i.e., food.

[3]'Whose,' 'Whom' 'Him' refer to God.

[4]Thirty spokes: Thirty days. Twelve spokes: Twelve months.

5. Who is breath-giver, and the Lord of life-infusing air, sun and water, under Whose control, the lustrous worlds diffuse life on Earth, under Whose sway, all the regions are full of refulgence, may I with the help of that God overcome death. (865)

६. यस्मात् पक्वादमृतं सम्बभूव यो गायत्र्या अधिपतिर्बभूव ।
यस्मिन् वेदा निहिता विश्वरूपास्तेनौदनेनाति तराणि मृत्युम् ॥

6. From Whom, Matured, sprang salvation into being Who, hath become Gayatri's Lord and Ruler, in Whom the perfect vedas have treasured—may I with the help of that God conquer death. (866)

७. अव बाधे द्विषन्तं देवपीयुं सपत्ना ये मेऽप ते भवन्तु ।
ब्रह्मौदनं विश्वजितं पचामि शृण्वन्तु मे श्रद्दधानस्य देवाः ॥

7. I drive away passions inimical to finer sentiments, and baser intentions. Far off be lust and anger, which are my foes. I firmly fix in my heart the might of God, which is the winner of all things. May all the learned persons listen to the resolve, I, a believer in Truth, make. (867)[1]

Chapter (Anuvāka) 8

HYMN XXXVI

१. तान्त्सत्यौजाः प्र दहत्वग्निर्वैश्वानरो वृषा ।
यो नो दुरस्याद् दिप्साच्चाथो यो नो अरातियात् ॥

1. Endowed with true strength, let God, the Benefactor of humanity, the Bestower of joys, burn them up; him who would consider us low in character, him who would like to injure us, him who would treat us as a foe. (868)

२. यो नो दिप्साददिप्सतो दिप्सतो यश्च दिप्सति । वैश्वानरस्य दंष्ट्रयोरग्नेरपि दधामि तम् ॥

2. Him who, unharmed, would injure us, and him who, harmed, would do us harm, I lay between the doubled fangs of the king, the well-wisher of all. (869)[2]

३. य आगरे मृगयन्ते प्रतिक्रोशेऽमावास्ये । क्रव्यादो अन्यान् दिप्सतः सर्वांस्तान्त्सहसा सहे ॥

3. Those who, at the time of a quarrel in the house, and in the darkness of midnight, hurt for others to injure them, flesh-eaters, others who would harm,—all these I overcome with might. (870)[3]

[1]Griffith translates Brahmandana as the Odana or mess of rice and milk distributed to Brahmans and especially to priests at a sacrifice. This interpretation is unacceptable. The word means, the might of God.

[2]Harmed: Punished by noble persons for misdeeds. The king should so crush the evil minded persons with his jaws of justice, as we chew food with our jaws.

[3]I: A King.

४. सहे पिशाचान्त्सहसैषां द्रविणं ददे । सर्वान् दुरस्यतो हन्मि सं म आकूतिर्ऋध्यताम् ॥

4. I conquer the blood-sucking demons with my might, and distribute their wealth amongst the deserving. All who would injure us I slay. Let mine intention be fulfilled. (871)[1]

५. ये देवास्तेन हासन्ते सूर्येण मिमते जवम् । नदीषु पर्वतेषु ये सं तैः पशुभिर्विदे ॥

5. I befriend those conquering heroes, who want to follow the path of virtue, and those wise sages, who match their rapid motion with the sun on rivers and mountains. (872)[2]

६. तपनो अस्मि पिशाचानां व्याघ्रो गोमतामिव ।
श्वानः सिंहमिव दृष्ट्वा ते न विन्दन्ते न्यञ्चनम् ॥

6. I torment the blood-sucking demons, as the tiger plaques men rich in kine. Just as dogs, seeing a lion run away in fear, so do these demons, find no hiding-place on seeing me. (873)[3]

७. न पिशाचैः सं शक्नोमि न स्तेनैर्न वनर्गुभिः । पिशाचास्तस्मान्नश्यन्ति यमहं ग्राममाविशे ॥

7. I can have no agreement with blood-sucking demons, with thieves, with plunderers who roam in woods. Demons flee and vanish from each village as I enter it. (874)[4]

८. ये ग्राममाविशत इदमुग्रं सहो मम । पिशाचास्तस्मान्नश्यन्ति न पापमुप जानते ॥

8. Into whatever village this mine aweful power penetrates, thence the demons flee away, and plot no further mischief there. (875)

९. ये मा क्रोधयन्ति लपिता हस्तिनं मशका इव । तानहं मन्ये दुर्हिताञ्जने अल्पशयूनिव ॥

9. Those who enrage me with their garrulity, as flies torment an elephant, I deem unhappy creatures, like small insects troublesome to man. (876)[5]

१०. अभि तं निर्ऋतिर्धत्तामश्वमिवाश्वाभिधान्या ।
मल्वो यो मह्यं क्रुध्यति स उ पाशान्न मुच्यते ॥

10. Destruction seize upon the man, as with a cord they hold the horse, the fool who is enraged with me! He is not rescued from the noose of misfortune. (877)

[1]I: A King.

[2]Who match: Persons who sail swiftly on rivers, and fly swiftly on mountains like the Sun.
I: A King.

[3]'I' and 'me,' refer to a king.

[4]'I' refers to a king. [5]'I', 'me' refer to a king.

HYMN XXXVII

१. त्वया पूर्वमथर्वाणो जघ्नू रक्षांस्योषधे । त्वया जघान कश्यपस्त्वया कण्वो अगस्त्यः ॥

1. O medicine, through thee, in olden time, did the steady, wise, intellectual brilliant physicians destroy the disease-germs. (878)

२. त्वया वयमप्सरसो गन्धर्वांश्चातयामहे । अजशृङ्ग्यज रक्षः सर्वान् गन्धेन नाशय ॥

2. O Ajashringi, through thee, we scare and drive away the diseases that spread in water and air. Chase the germs, cause them all to vanish with thy smell. (879)[1]

३. नदीं यन्त्वप्सरसोऽपां तारमवश्वसम् । गुल्गुलूः पीला नलद्यौ३क्षगन्धिः प्रमन्दनी ।
तत् परेताप्सरसः प्रतिबुद्धा अभूतन ॥

3. Let disease-germs spread in waters, be washed down, just as a stream, filled with water, flows fastly down.

Five medicines are helpful in dislodging them (1) Gugglu (2) Pila (3) Naladi (4) Aukshagandhi (5) Pramandni.

Ye Diseases of water, Ye have been ascertained, hence run away from our city. (880)[2]

४. यत्राश्वत्था न्यग्रोधा महावृक्षाः शिखण्डिनः । तत् परेताप्सरसः प्रतिबुद्धा अभूतन ॥

4. Where there are great trees, like Ficus Religiosa (Pipal), Ficus Indica (big tree) and peacocks, run away, thence, O diseases spread among people, as Ye have been ascertained! (881)[3]

५. यत्र वः प्रेङ्खा हरिता अर्जुना उत यत्राघाटाः कर्कर्यः संवदन्ति ।
तत् परेताप्सरसः प्रतिबुद्धा अभूतन ॥

5. There where green and white trees are swinging for you, and lutes and cymbals sound in tune, run away thence, O diseases spread among people, and be uprooted. (882)

६. एयमगन्नोषधीनां वीरुधां वीर्यावती । अजशृङ्ग्यराटकी तीक्ष्णशृङ्गी व्यृषतु ॥

[1]Ajashringi is the name of a medicinal plant, known as kakrasingi. In Latin the plant is called Odina Pinnata. It cures cough, thirst, dysentery, consumption and vomiting. Its pungent smell, when burnt drives away mosquitoes.

[2]Gugglu: Scented Bdellium.

Naladi: Smelling of spikenard.

It is called Jatā Mānsi. It has got three varieties, (1) Mānsi (2) Gandhmansi (3) Akāshmānsi. All these three cure fever, burns, poison.

Ankshagandhi is another name for Mānsi. It is known as Gandhmansi.

Pramandni: Named Pramodani, is a kind of jasmine, filled with sweet odour. It cures leprosy, tumour, Itching, burn, poison.

[3]Shikhandni means peacock, and churamani and Kālmāchi plants.

Aṣhwatha is Pipal, the holy tree.

6. We have obtained this Ajsringi, the most effectual of herbs and plants. It cures diseases, and kills the disease-germs with its pungent smell. May it drive away the deadly germs. (883)[1]

७. ग्रानृत्यतः शिखण्डिनो गन्धर्वस्याप्सरापतेः । भिनद्मि मुष्कावपि यामि शेपः ॥

7. I break the testicles and devitalise the penis of male germs, that follow smell, and dance like the dancing peacocks, wearing the tuft of hair. (884)[2]

८. भीमा इन्द्रस्य हेतयः शतमृष्टीरयस्मयीः । ताभिर्हविरदान् गन्धर्वानवकादान् व्यृषतु ॥

8. The Sun's rays are dreadful like hundreds of iron weapons. With those let it destroy the germs that feed on oblations and Blyxa Octandra. (885)[3]

९. भीमा इन्द्रस्य हेतयः शतमृष्टीर्हिरण्ययीः । ताभिर्हविरदान् गन्धर्वानवकादान् व्यृषतु ॥

9. The golden-hued rays of the Sun, are dreadful like hundreds of weapons. With those let it destroy the germs that feed on oblations and Blyxa-octandra. (886)

१०. ग्रवकादानभिशोचानप्सु ज्योतय मामकान् । पिशाचान् सर्वानोषधे प्र मृणीहि सहस्व च ॥

10. O medicine, crush and subdue the germs that reside in the waters in my body, are highly troublesome, and are blood-suckers. (887)[4]

११. श्वेवैकः कपिरिवैकः कुमारः सर्वकेशकः ।
प्रियो दृशइव भूत्वा गन्धर्वः सचते स्त्रियस्तमितो नाशयामसि ब्रह्मणा वीर्यावता ॥

11. One germ is like a dog in appearance and nature, another is like a monkey, one is a deadly killer of its victim, another is completely decked with hair. So the germ, putting on a lovely look, pursues a dame. Him with an efficacious medicine named Brahmi, we scare and cause to vanish hence. (888)

[1]Ajṣringi is known as Kākrāsingi.

[2]I: A skilled physician. A physician should take away all manhood and vitality from the male germs through medicine, so that they may be rendered unfit for procreation, and thus prevent the spread of disease through their offsprings.

[3]Those: Rays, It refers to the Sun.

Avaka: Blyxa-octandra, a water-plant, the reed (fungus) that covers water, called saivala. It is named as sivara, kahi, Bur (बूर).

[4]Medicine: Ajsringi. Pt. Khem Karan Das Trivedi and Pt. Jaidev Vidyalankar have given a spiritual interpretation of this hymn. For a detailed account consult their commentaries on Hymn XXXVII. According to this interpretation Kashyap means eye, Kanva ear, Agastya nose. Atharva means organs of senses. Ajṣringi means soul-force. Apsarsas mean organs of action and cognition. Gandharvas also mean organs of senses. Gulgulu means juice. रसना. Pila means eye. Naldi means ear. Ankshyagandhi means nose. Pramandni means skin. Testicles mean passion and ignorance. Rājas, Tāmas feelings, shapa means the feeling of virtue and goodness, satvik feeling. Havirad means, a slave of passions. Pishāch means one given to lust.

१२. जाया इद् वो अप्सरसो गन्धर्वाः पतयो यूयम् । अप धावतामर्त्या मर्त्यान् मा सचध्वम् ।।

12. Ye, male germs, shun strong smell, your wives penetrate blood and water. Without coming in contact with mortals, run ye away: forbear to interfere with men. (889)

HYMN XXXVIII

१. उद्भिन्दतीं संजयन्तीमप्सरां साधुदेविनीम् । ग्लहे कृतानि कृण्वानामप्सरां तामिह हुवे ।।

1. I invite a charming woman, the vanquisher of foes, fair in dealings, the conqueror of impediments, the performer of excellent deeds in life's struggle. (890)[1]

२. विचिन्वतीमाकिरन्तीमप्सरां साधुदेविनीम् । ग्लहे कृतानि गृह्णानामप्सरां तामिह हुवे ।।

2. I invite a charming woman, who gathers wealth, and spends it on charity, who is fair in dealings, who performs excellent deeds in life's struggle. (891)

३. यायैः परिनृत्यत्याददाना कृतं ग्लहात् । सा नः कृतानि सीषती प्रहामाप्नोतु मायया ।
सा नः पयस्वत्यैतु मा नो जैषुरिदं धनम् ।।

3. In the struggle of life she, through beautiful moral devices, performs excellent deeds and remains happy. May she, controlling and regularising our actions, advance through her fine intellect. May she, full of milk and foodstuffs come to our house, so that through her nice administration none may win this wealth of ours. (892)[2]

४. या अक्षेषु प्रमोदन्ते शुचं क्रोधं च बिभ्रती । आनन्दिनीं प्रमोदिनीमप्सरां तामिह हुवे ।।

4. Hither I invite the woman, the joyous, the delightful one, who though filled with grief and wrath, keeps her eyes filled with joy. (893)

५. सूर्यस्य रश्मीननु याः संचरन्ति मरीचीर्वा या अनुसंचरन्ति ।
यासामृषभो दूरतो वाजिनीवान्त्सद्यः सर्वान् लोकान् पर्येति रक्षन् ।
स न ऐतु होममिमं जुषाणो३ऽन्तरिक्षेण सह वाजिनावीन् ।।

5. Women who walk in the rays of the Sun, and roam in Sun's light, whose powerful protector, from afar, quickly comes from every side, guarding all

[1]Griffith has ascribed all verses of this hymn to gambling. The Vedas do not preach gambling. They condemn it; hence Griffith's interpretation is unacceptable. In this hymn the qualities a good woman in domestic life should possess are mentioned vide *Rig*, 10-34-3 अक्षैर्मा दीव्य: One should not gamble with dice.

[2]Win means take away. A skilful wife preserves the wealth of the family, and allows none to take it away and waste it.

their relatives, may that powerful man, accepting this yajna of ours, gladly come unto us. (894)[1]

६. अन्तरिक्षेण सह वाजिनीवन् कर्की वत्सामिह रक्ष वाजिन् ।
इमे ते स्तोका बहुला एह्यर्वाङियं ते कर्कीह ते मनोऽस्तु ॥

6. O strong, resolute person, guard here the handsome child with heart-felt love. These little kinds are the source of manifold pleasures for thee. Come hither. Here is the result of thy creative power. Concentrate thy mind on fostering this child. (895)

७. अन्तरिक्षेण सह वाजिनीवन् कर्की वत्सामिह रक्ष वाजिन् ।
अयं घासो अयं व्रज इह वत्सां नि बध्नीमः । यथानाम व ईश्महे स्वाहा ॥

7. O strong, mighty man, guard here the handsome calf with heart-felt love. Here is the grass, here is the stall, here do we bind the calf. Name by name, we are their masters. For them we sacrifice everything. (896)

HYMN XXXIX

१. पृथिव्यामग्नये समनमन्त्स आर्ध्नोत् ।
यथा पृथिव्यामग्नये समनमन्नेवा मह्यं संनमः सं नमन्तु ॥

1. Sages have paid homage to fire on earth, and fire has made them great. Just as they have bowed before fire on the earth, so let these persons who have come to honour me, bow before me. (897)[2]

२. पृथिवी धेनुस्तस्या अग्निर्वत्सः । सा मेऽग्निना वत्सेनेषमूर्जं कामं दुहाम् ।
आयुः प्रथमं प्रजां पोषं रयिं स्वाहा ॥

2. Earth is the Cow, her calf is Fire. May she with her calf fire yield me food, strength, my nice resolve, noble life, offspring, plenty and wealth. This is our excellent prayer. (898)[3]

३. अन्तरिक्षे वायवे समनमन्त्स आर्ध्नोत् ।
यथान्तरिक्षे वायवे समनमन्नेवा मह्यं संनमः सं नमन्तु ॥

[1]Women, who generally live inside the house, should, for the sake of health, pass some of their time in the open, and enjoy the light of the Sun. Here repetition is made for the sake of emphasis. Strong noble preachers should protect woman, and attend now and then the yajna performed by the married couple. This hymn has been ascribed by Pt. Jaidev Vidyalankar to mental faculty, and by Pt. Khem Karan Das Trivedi to God. For a detailed explanation, the reader should consult their commentaries.

[2]They refers to sages. 'Paying homage to fire' means utilising it in preparing conveyances, war-like instruments, aeroplanes, radio etc.

[3]Earth has been compared to a cow. Just as a cow yields milk, so does the proper use of fire, electricity, the child of Earth, yield us food, strength, wealth, long life and offspring.

3. Sages have paid homage to air in the atmosphere, and air has made them great. Just as they have bowed before air in the atmosphere, so let these persons who have come to honour me, bow before me. (899)

४. अन्तरिक्षं धेनुस्तस्या वायुर्वत्सः । सा मे वायुना वत्सेनेषमूर्जं कामं दुहाम् ।
आयुः प्रथमं प्रजां पोषं रयिं स्वाहा ॥

4. Atmosphere is the Cow, her calf is air. May she with her calf air yield me food, strength, my nice resolve, noble life, offspring, plenty and wealth. This is our excellent prayer, let pure air blow, and cure our ailments. (900)

५. दिव्याऽऽदित्याय समनमन्त्स आर्ध्नोत् ।
यथा दिव्याऽऽदित्याय समनमन्नेवा मह्यं संनमः सं नमन्तु ॥

5. Sages have paid homage to the Sun in heaven, and the Sun has made them great. Just as they have bowed before the Sun in heaven, so let these persons who have come to honour me, bow before me. (901)

६. द्यौर्धेनुस्तस्या आदित्यो वत्सः । सा म आदित्येन वत्सेनेषमूर्जं कामं दुहाम् ।
आयुः प्रथमं प्रजां पोषं रयिं स्वाहा ॥

6. Heaven is the Cow, her calf is the Sun. May she with her calf the Sun yield me food, strength, my nice resolve, noble life, offspring, plenty and wealth. This is our excellent prayer, that Sun should shine, remove our ailments and send rain. (902)[1]

७. दिक्षु चन्द्राय समनमन्त्स आर्ध्नोत् ।
यथा दिक्षु चन्द्राय समनमन्नेवा मह्यं संनमः सं नमन्तु ॥

7. Sages have paid homage to the Moon in the quarters, and the Moon has made them great. Just as they have bowed before the Moon in the quarters, so let these persons who have come to honour me, bow before me. (903)[2]

८. दिशो धेनवस्तासां चन्द्रो वत्सः ।
ता मे चन्द्रेण वत्सेनेषमूर्जं कामं दुहाम् । आयुः प्रथमं प्रजां पोषं रयिं स्वाहा ॥

8. The quarters are the Cows, their calf is the Moon. May they (Cows) yield with their calf the Moon, food, strength, my nice resolve, noble life, offspring, plenty and wealth. This is our excellent prayer, that Moon shines in the quarters and grants us long life, strength, and peace of mind. (904)

९. अग्नावग्निश्चरति प्रविष्ट ऋषीणां पुत्रो अभिशस्तिपा उ ।
नमस्कारेण नमसा ते जुहोमि मा देवानां मिथुया कर्म भागम् ॥

[1] She refers to heaven.
[2] Me may refer to a king or a big personage.

9. Soul moves having entered into God. It purifies the organs, and saves us from sin. O God I dedicate myself to Thee with humble homage. Let none mar the teaching of the learned! (905)

१०. हृदा पूतं मनसा जातवेदो विश्वानि देव वयुनानि विद्वान् ।
सप्तास्यानि तव जातवेदस्तेभ्यो जुहोमि स जुषस्व हव्यम् ।।

10. Knower of all objects, O Refulgent God, Thou knowest all sorts of knowledge. O wise soul thou hath got seven mouths. To them I offer the knowledge purified through heart and cleansed through yoga. Do thou accept my libation! (906)[1]

HYMN XL

१. ये पुरस्ताज्जुह्वति जातवेदः प्राच्या दिशोऽभिदासन्त्यस्मान् ।
अग्निमृत्वा ते पराञ्चो व्यथन्तां प्रत्यगेनान् प्रतिसरेण हन्मि ।।

1. O Omniscient God, may those foes, who want to destroy and attack us from the opposite eastward direction, punished by Thee, turn their back and be put to pain. I drive them back with the help of Thee, the Leader! (907)

२. ये दक्षिणतो जुह्वति जातवेदो दक्षिणाया दिशोऽभिदासन्त्यस्मान् ।
यममृत्वा ते पराञ्चो व्यथन्तां प्रत्यगेनान् प्रतिसरेण हन्मि ।।

2. O Omniscient God, may those foes, who want to destroy and attack us from the right-hand southward direction, punished by Thee, just, turn their back and be put to pain. I smite them back with the help of Thee, the Leader! (908)

३. ये पश्चाज्जुह्वति जातवेदः प्रतीच्या दिशोऽभिदासन्त्यस्मान् ।
वरुणमृत्वा ते पराञ्चो व्यथन्तां प्रत्यगेनान् प्रतिसरेण हन्मि ।।

3. O Omniscient God, may those foes, who want to destroy and attack us from behind, the westward direction, punished by Thee, the Most Exalted, turn their back and be put to pain. I smite them back, with the help of Thee, the Leader! (909)

४. ये उत्तरतो जुह्वति जातवेद उदीच्या दिशो भिदासन्त्यस्मान् ।
सोममृत्वा ते पराञ्चो व्यथन्तां प्रत्यगेनान् प्रतिसरेण हन्मि ।।

4. O Omniscient God, may those foes, who want to destroy and attack us from the left-hand northern direction, punished by Thee, the Glorious Lord, turn their back and be put to pain, I smite them back with the help of Thee the Leader! (910)

[1]Seven mouths: Two eyes, two ears, two noses and mouth. Seven mouths may also mean the seven tongues (forces) of the soul that are developed through Yoga (1) Kāli (2) Karali (3) Manojivi (4) Sulohitā (5) Sudhumnavarni (6) Suphulingni (7) Lelayamāna.

५. येऽधस्ताज्जुह्वति जातवेदो ध्रुवाया दिशोऽभिदासन्त्यस्मान् ।
भूमिमृत्वा ते पराञ्चो व्यथन्तां प्रत्यगेनान् प्रतिसरेण हन्मि ॥

5. O Omniscient God, may those foes, who want to destroy and attack us from the nether, steadfast direction, punished by Thee, the support of all, turn their back, and be put to pain. I smite them back with the help of Thee, the Leader! (911)[1]

६. येऽन्तरिक्षाज्जुह्वति जातवेदो व्यध्वाया दिशोऽभिदासन्त्यस्मान् ।
वायुमृत्वा ते पराञ्चो व्यथन्तां प्रत्यगेनान् प्रतिसरेण हन्मि ॥

6. O Omniscient God, may those foes, who want to destroy and attack us from different directions in the atmosphere, punished by Thee, the Mightiest of the mighty, turn their back and be put to pain, I smite them back with the help of Thee, the Leader! (912)

७. य उपरिष्टाज्जुह्वति जातवेद उर्ध्वाया दिशोऽभिदासन्त्यस्मान् ।
सूर्यमृत्वा ते पराञ्चो व्यथन्तां प्रत्यगेनान् प्रतिसरेण हन्मि ॥

7. O Omniscient God, may those foes, who want to destroy and attack us from the upward lofty quarter, punished by Thee, the All-Pervading, turn their back and be put to pain. I smite them back with the help of Thee, the Leader. (913)[2]

८. ये दिशामन्तर्देशेभ्यो जुह्वति जातवेदः सर्वाभ्यो दिग्भ्योऽभिदासन्त्यस्मान् ।
ब्रह्मर्त्वा ते पराञ्चो व्यथन्तां प्रत्यगेनान् प्रतिसरेण हन्मि ॥

8. O Omniscient God, may those foes, who want to destroy and attack us from all points in the intermediate regions, punished by the Mighty God, turn their back and be put to pain. I smite them back with the help of Thee, the Leader. (914)

BOOK (Kāṇḍa) V

Chapter (Anuvāka) 1

HYMN I

१. ऋधङ्मन्त्रो योनिं य आ बभूवामृतासुर्वर्धमानः सुजन्मा ।
अदब्धासुर्भ्राजमानोऽहेव त्रितो धर्ता दाधार त्रीणि ॥

1. Soul, the seeker after truth, deathless in spirit, progressing, well-born, assumes its birth. Equipped with the unyielding power of breath, shining like the day, it assumes its three stages, as their guardian and supporter. (915)[3]

[1]भूमिः God, the support of all. भवन्ति भूतानि यस्याँ सा भूमिः
Satyarth Prakash and Chapter I, steadfast direction: Nadir.

[2]Lofty quarter: Zenith.

[3]Sāyana has not translated the fifth Kāṇḍa. It looks rather queer. Pt. Raja Ram considers this hymn to be highly complex and difficult to understand. The three stages of the soul are Jāgrita, Swapan, and Sushupti. 'Trita' means guardian, protector, Griffith

२. आ यो धर्माणि प्रथमः ससाद ततो वपूंषि कृणुषे पुरूणि ।
धास्युर्योनिं प्रथम आ विवेशा यो वाचमनुदितां चिकेत ॥

2. Soul first performs virtuous deeds, and then assumes diverse beateous forms and figures. Eager for retention of its powers, it enters the womb of the mother, and understands through intuition the word yet unspoken. (916)

३. यस्ते शोकाय तन्वं रिरेच क्षरद्धिरण्यं शुचयोऽनु स्वाः ।
अत्रा दधेते अमृतानि नामास्मे वस्त्राणि विश एरयन्ताम् ॥

3. O child, for thy lustre thy father sacrifices his body, provides semen, and keeps pure his mental faculties. On thee both father and mother set glories that shall last for ever. To thee the people shall offer robes to put on, and houses to dwell in! (917)[1]

४. प्र यदेते प्रतरं पूर्व्यं गुः सदःसद आतिष्ठन्तो अजुर्यम् ।
कविः शुषस्य मातरा रिहाणे जाम्यै धुर्यं पतिमेरयेथाम् ॥

4. Ye parents of wise and strong progeny, who praise and are proud of your children, select for your daughter, a husband, fit for enduring the burden of domestic life; as all these learned persons, leading married life in their houses, have considered, their progeny, as an everlasting and excellent source for covering the journey of life. (918)

५. तदू षु ते महत् पृथुज्मन् नमः कविः काव्येना कृणोमि ।
यत् सम्यञ्चावभियन्तावभि क्षामत्रा मही रोधचक्रे वावृधेते ॥

5. O God, by holy wisdom, I, a sage, offer to Thee this lofty adoration. Both husband and wife, united together, coming towards each other full of love, heighten themselves like heaven and earth working like two wheels of a chariot. (919)

६. सप्त मर्यादाः कवयस्ततक्षुस्तासामिदेकामभ्यंहुरो गात् ।
आयोर्ह स्कम्भ उपमस्य नीडे पथां विसर्गे धरुणेषु तस्थौ ॥

6. Seven are the rules of conduct which the wise have established. He becomes a sinner who violates even one of them. He who preserves his semen, the pillar of life, resting in the refuge of God, and renouncing evil paths, acquires lofty and dignified positions. (920)[2]

considers Trita to be a mysterious ancient deity, frequently mentioned in the *Rigveda*, principally in connection with the Maruts, Vayu, and Indra. His home is in the remotest of heaven, and he is called Aptya, the Watery, that is, sprung from, or dwelling in, the sea of cloud, and vapour. This explanation is unacceptable, as there is no history in the Vedas.

[1]People offer robes and dwelling places to the sanātik (graduate) when he goes out of the Gurukula, and enters life.

[2]Seven rules of conduct vide *Nirukta*, 6-27 are:
(1) Non-theft (2) Non-adultery (3) Non-murder (4) Non-miscarriage (5) Non-drinking wine (6) Non-repetition of sin (7) Non-concealment of sin through a lie.

७. उतामृतासुर्व्रत एमि कृण्वन्नसुरात्मा तन्व१स्तत् सुमद्गुः ।
उत वा शक्रो रत्नं दधात्यूर्जया वा यत् सचते हविर्दाः ॥

7. I, a householder, enjoying a long life, acquiring knowledge, doing deeds, realise the Exalted God. Of this body, I am the life-breath and soul, equipped with gracious organs. The Almighty Father alone is the bestower of knowledge, which the self-sacrificing and devout soul enjoys through its power. (921)

८. उत पुत्रः पितरं क्षत्रमीडे ज्येष्ठं मर्यादमह्वयन्त्स्वस्तये ।
दर्शन् नु ता वरुण यास्ते विष्ठा आवर्व्रततः कृणवो वपूंषि ॥

8. I, the son, ask for riches from God, the Father. The sages have invoked for bliss, the Most Exalted God. O God, Thou fashionest the mortal frames of the souls, that roam from body to body. Let them see Thy revelations. (922)[1]

९. अर्धमर्धेन पयसा पृणक्ष्यर्धेन शुष्म वर्धसे अमुर ।
अविं वृधाम शग्मियं सखायं वरुणं पुत्रमदित्या इषिरम् ।
कविशस्तान्यस्मै वपूंष्यवोचाम रोदसी सत्यवाचा ॥

9. O Everlasting God, Thou completest this wonderous world with Thy superhuman power, and enhastest its strength.

Let us Exalt God, the Goader of the world, its Guardian, the Omnipotent, the Friend of the universe, the Saviour of the soul from the misery of sin. Betwixt the truthful Heaven and Earth, let us mention the marvels of God sung by sages. (923)

HYMN II

१. तदिदास भुवनेषु ज्येष्ठं यतो जज्ञ उग्रस्त्वेषनृम्णः ।
सद्यो जज्ञानो नि रिणाति शत्रूननु यदेनं मदन्ति विश्व ऊमाः ॥

1. In all the worlds God was the Best and Highest, whence sprung the mighty, brilliant Sun. As soon as born he overcomes his foemen, and all people rejoice, who depend upon him. (924)[2]

२. वावृधानः शवसा भूर्योजाः शत्रुर्दासाय भियसं दधाति ।
अव्यनच्च व्यनच्च सस्नि सं ते नवन्त प्रभृता मदेषु ॥

2. The Almighty God, through His power removes all obstacles, strikes terror in the heart of a sinner. He pervades the animate and inanimate world. All His subjects nourished and reared by Him, sing His praise on occasions of a festival or banquet. (925)

[1] 'Them, refers to souls. A soul assumes different bodies in different births according to the dispensation of God.

[2] Foemen: The shadows of darkness.
See *Rig*, 10-120 and *Yajur*, 33-80.

३. त्वे क्रतुमपि पृञ्चन्ति भूरि द्विर्यदेते त्रिर्भवन्त्यूमाः ।
स्वादोः स्वादीयः स्वादुना सृजा समदः सु मधु मधुनाभि योधीः ॥

3. O God, when all human beings unite their mental vigour with Thee, they become doubly and trebly strong. With Thy Exhilarative strength, grant us salvation, sweeter than the sweet, and blend that elixir with our soul! (926)

४. यदि चिन्नु त्वा धना जयन्तं रणेरणे अनुमदन्ति विप्राः ।
ओजीयः शुष्मिन्त्स्थिरमा तनुष्व मा त्वा दभन् दुरेवासः कशोकाः ॥

4. If verily in every war the sages joy and exalt in thee who winnest treasures, with mightier power, strong king, extend thy firmness: let not sinful and sorrowful persons harm thee! (927)[1]

५. त्वया वयं शाशद्महे रणेषु प्रपश्यन्तो युधेन्यानि भूरि ।
चोदयामि त आयुधा वचोभिः सं ते शिशामि ब्रह्मणा वयांसि ॥

5. O King, with thee as helper, seeing various military weapons, may we wage a severe war with the enemy.

Following thy Vedic instructions may I use my weapons. May I train and discipline my organs in obedience to thy vedic knowledge! (928)

६. नि तद् दधिषेऽवरे परे च यस्मिन्नाविथावसा दुरोणे ।
आ स्थापयत मातरं जिगत्नुमत इन्वत कर्वराणि भूरि ॥

6. O God, Thou preservest the vedic knowledge in each house (body) big or small, and nourishest us with food. O men, establish that All-pervading Mother (God) in your heart, and through His help, achieve success in various undertakings. (929)

७. स्तुष्व वर्ष्मन् पुरुवर्त्मानं समृभ्वाणमिनतममाप्तमाप्त्यानाम् ।
आ दर्शति शवसा भूर्योजाः प्र सक्षति प्रतिमानं पृथिव्याः ॥

7. O noble person, praise duly, God, Who pervades all the worlds, is Refulgent with true knowledge, Foremost of all, and the most learned of the learned. Through strength He shows Himself of ample power. Pattern of Earth, He rears us all. (930)[2]

८. इमा ब्रह्म बृहद्दिवः कृणवदिन्द्राय शूषमग्रियः स्वर्षाः ।
महो गोत्रस्य क्षयति स्वराजा तुरश्चिद् विश्वमर्णवत् तपस्वान् ॥

8. An excellent yogi, enjoying the felicity of salvation, brilliant like the great sun, in expatiating on God, displays these divine powers as his strength.

[1] 'Thee' refers to the king.

[2] Pattern of Earth: Just as Earth feeds mankind, so does God, like Earth, rear and nourish us all. Griffith interprets Aptya to be chief of deities dwelling in the waters of the sea of air. This interpretation is fantastic. The word means, a highly learned man of extreme sacrificing nature.

He, the master of self, residing in the Almighty God enjoys supremacy. Ever active, equipped with the strength of austerity, roams in the universe. (931)

९. एवा महान् बृहद्दिवो अथर्वावोचत् स्वां तन्व१मिन्द्रमेव ।
स्वसारौ मातरिभ्वरी अरिप्रे हिन्वन्ति चैने शवसा वर्धयन्ति च ॥

9. Thus does a learned, austere yogi, sporting in the lap of God, and hankering after salvation, speak of his soul as full of power. Two pure, immaulate sisters reside in God, the Creator of the universe. Yogis, with their power impel them onward and exalt them. (932)[1]

HYMN III

१. ममाग्ने वर्चो विहवेष्वस्तु वयं त्वेन्धानास्तन्वं᳘ पुषेम ।
मह्यं नमन्तां प्रदिशश्चतस्रस्त्वयाध्यक्षेण पृतना जयेम ॥

1. O God, let me acquire eminence in battles, enkindling Thee may we support our bodies and souls. May the denizens of four regions bend and bow before me: with Thee for Guardian may we win the foe's army! (933)

२. अग्ने मन्युं प्रतिनुदन् परेषां त्वं नो गोपाः परि पाहि विश्वतः ।
अपाञ्चो यन्तु निवता दुरस्यवोऽमैषां चित्तं प्रबुधां वि नेशत् ॥

2. Baffling the rage of our opponents, O God, guard us as our protector from all directions. Let troublesome, low people go far away from us, and let the knowledge of the learned among these foes be lost! (934)

३. मम देवा विहवे सन्तु सर्व इन्द्रवन्तो मरुतो विष्णुरग्निः ।
ममान्तरिक्षमुरुलोकमस्तु मह्यं वातः पवतां कामायास्मै ॥

3. May all the supreme forces of nature like the Air, Sun, Fire be on my side in battle. Mine be the middle-air's extended region and may the Wind blow favouring this wish of mine. (935)[2]

४. मह्यं यजन्तां मम यानीष्टाकूतिः सत्या मनसो मे अस्तु ।
एनो मा नि गां कतमच्चनाहं विश्वे देवा अभि रक्षन्तु मेह ॥

4. Let all my resolves be fulfilled, and let my mind's intention be accomplished. May I be guiltless of the least transgression: may all noble virtues protect me here. (936)[3]

[1]Two sisters: Perception, Reflection. God is attainable through these two pure forces free from stain.

'Them' refers to sisters. Griffith describes these sisters to be Heaven and Earth. Some commentators describe them as Day and Night. Brihad Diva and Atharva are not the names of Rishis 'Atharva' means a learned, austere yogi 'Brihad-Diva' means a Yogi hankering after salvation.

[2]'Mine' means my helper in battle. This wish: success in battle. My: General of the army.

[3]Here: In the battle.

५. मयि देवा द्रविणमा यजन्तां मय्याशीरस्तु मयि देवहूतिः ।
दैवा होतारः सनिषन् न एतदरिष्टाः स्याम तन्वाऽ सुवीराः ॥

5. May the learned grant me riches, may their blessing and invocation assist me. May the virtuous, charitable persons grant us all desired objects. May we become healthy in body and heroic in spirit. (937)

६. दैवीः षड्ुर्वीरुरु नः कृणोत विश्वे देवास इह मादयध्वम् ।
मा नो विददभिभा मो अशस्तिर्मा नो विदद् वृजिना द्वेष्या या ॥

6. Ye six divine Expanses, give us freedom. Here, ye learned persons, remain happy. Let not calamity or infamy overtake us, nor deeds of sin that merit hatred. (938)[1]

७. तिस्रो देवीर्महि नः शर्म यच्छत प्रजायै नस्तन्वे३ यच्च पुष्टम् ।
मा हास्महि प्रजया मा तनूभिर्मा रधाम द्विषते सोम राजन् ॥

7. O three Goddesses give me ample pleasure, and strength to our children and bodies Let us not lose our offspring. Let us not die before time. Let not a foe trouble us, O God, the Lord and Goader of all ! (939)[2]

८. उरुव्यचा नो महिषः शर्म यच्छत्वस्मिन् हवे पुरुहूतः पुरुक्षु ।
स नः प्रजायै हर्यश्व मृडेन्द्र मा नो रीरिषो मा परा दाः ॥

8. O All-pervading, Mighty God grant us happiness. O Much-Invoked God, grant us foodstuffs in this sacrifice (Yajna). O God, powerful like a king equipped with fleeting steeds, bless our children, harm us not, abandon us not ! (940)

९. धाता विधाता भुवनस्य यस्पतिर्देवः सविताभिमातिषाहः ।
आदित्या रुद्रा अश्विनोभा देवाः पान्तु यजमानं निर्ऋथात् ॥

9. God, the sustainer; the Dissolver, the Lord and Creator of the universe, is the queller of turbulent internal foes like lust and anger. May His forces the Adityas, the Rudras, the twin Aswins, guard the soul from destruction. (941)[3]

१०. ये नः सपत्ना अप ते भवन्त्विन्द्राग्निभ्यामव बाधामह एनान् ।
आदित्या रुद्रा उपरिस्पृशो न उग्रं चेत्तारमधिराजमक्रत ॥

10. Let those who are our foemen stay afar from us: with Indra and with Agni we will drive them off. The dignified, brilliant, benevolent persons have made the Omniscient, Powerful God as our sovereign Lord. (942)

[1]Six expanses: North, East, South, West, Nadir and Zenith. 'Here' means in my kingdom, my rule or administration.

[2]'Three Goddesses' may refer to Ida (mother tongue, Saraswati (mother civilisation) Mahi or Bharati (mother-land) or they may refer to Prāna, Apāna and Vyāna, or speech, Mind and Body.

[3]Adityas: The twelve months. Rudras: The breaths. Aswins: The Sun and Earth.

११. अर्वाञ्चमिन्द्रममुतो हवामहे यो गोजिद् धनजिदश्वजिद्यः ।
इमं नो यज्ञं विहवे शृणोत्वस्माकमभूर्हर्यश्व मेदी ॥

11. We call from a distance towards us, the king, the winner of kine, wealth and horses. May he hear this prayer of ours in battle. May thou, O powerful king, be our friend and comrade. (943)[1]

HYMN IV

१. यो गिरिष्वजायथा वीरुधां बलवत्तमः । कुष्ठेहि तक्मनाशन तक्मानं नाशयन्नितः ॥

1. O God, Thou revealest Thyself in the hearts of yogis on lofty mountains. Thou art the Mightiest of the mighty sources of quelling mental diseases. O Annihilator of the sufferings of the world, remove my worldly sufferings. Exhibit thyself in my soul. (944)[2]

२. सुपर्णसुवने गिरौ जातं हिमवतस्परि । धनैरभि श्रुत्वा यन्ति विदुर्हि तक्मनाशनम् ॥

2. God is realised in mountain solitude. Hearing His call on a snow-clad hill, His devotees sacrificing their wealth, go unto Him. They consider God alone, to be the Alleviator of their worldly sufferings. (945)

३. अश्वत्थो देवसदनस्तृतीयस्यामितो दिवि । तत्रामृतस्य चक्षणं देवाः कुष्ठमवन्वत ॥

3. Head, the home of organs, where reside the horse-like organs, is the topmost part of the body ; There God, is visualised. The yogis long there for God, Who pervades the material body. (946)[3]

४. हिरण्ययी नौरचरद्धिरण्यबन्धना दिवि । तत्रामृतस्य पुष्पं देवाः कुष्ठमवन्वत ॥

4. In the head, a yogi perceives the intellect as a boat wherewith he covers the journey of life. It is imbued with virtuous traits, and wrought with golden qualities. In that does God reveal Himself. The yogis long there for God, Who pervades the material body. (947)[4]

५. हिरण्ययाः पन्थान आसन्नरित्राणि हिरण्यया । नावो हिरण्ययीरासन् याभिः कुष्ठं निरावहन् ॥

5. Godly are the paths of a yogi. Virtuous are his accomplishments to guard him against lust and anger. Excellent are his wisdom, intellect, judgment, which he uses as paddles to cover the journey of life. The yogis attain to, through these devices, God, Who pervades the material body. (948)

[1]'Indra' may mean God as well. He bestows on us wealth, kine and horses, and is our Friend.

[2]Kushtha: A medicinal plant, Costus speciocus or Arabicus. Pt. Jaidev Vidyalankar interprets Kushtha as God. The hymn can be interpreted in favour of the healing properties of the medicinal plant, kushtha.

[3]'There' refers to the head.

[4]'It' refers to the intellect 'There': In the intellect, 'That' refers to the intellect.

६. इमं मे कुष्ठ पूरुषं तमा वह तं निष्कुरु । तमु मे अगदं कृधि ॥

6. O God, grant spiritual health to my soul that resides in the body. Free it from the ailment of anger and hatred. Release my soul from moral ill-health. (949)

७. देवेभ्यो अधि जातोऽसि सोमस्यासि सखा हितः ।
स प्राणाय व्यानाय चक्षुषे मे अस्मै मृड ॥

7. O God, Thou art the Embodiment of divine virtues. Thou art the benignant friend of a yogi. Befriend my breath and vital air. Be gracious to this mine eye. (950)

८. उदङ् जातो हिमवतः स प्राच्यां नीयसे जनम् । तत्र कुष्ठस्य नामान्युत्तमानि वि भेजिरे ॥

8. O God, Thou art realised on the lofty snowy mountain. When Thou revealest Thyself in the heart of a Yogi, Thou art spread by him in all directions. The yogis diffuse in the world the manifold, excellent names of God! (951)

९. उत्तमो नाम कुष्ठास्युत्तमो नाम ते पिता । यक्ष्मं च सर्वं नाशय तक्मानं चारसं कृधि ॥

9. Most Excellent, indeed, art Thou, O God, Most noble is thy sire, O soul, O God, destroy anger, hatred and infatuation, and render them powerless. (952)

१०. शीर्षामयमुपहत्यामक्ष्योस्तन्वो३रपः । कुष्ठस्तत् सर्वं निष्करद् दैवं समह वृष्ण्यम् ॥

10. Malady that affects the head, eye-weakness, physical frailty, violentce—all this let God heal and cure: aye, God is like an efficacious medicine. (953)[1]

HYMN V

१. रात्री माता नभः पितार्यमा ते पितामहः ।
सिलाची नाम वा असि सा देवानामसि स्वसा ॥

1. Sun is thy grandsire, Night thy mother, and the Cloud thy sire. Thy name is called Silāchī, (wax) thou, thyself, art sister of the learned. (954)[2]

[1]Malady of the head: Evil thought. Eye-weakness: Hatred. Physical frailty: Adultery, fornication.

[2]Silāchī, more usually called Arundhati, as in stanzas 5 and 9, is a medicinal climbing plant, supplied in cases of severe contusion or fracture. Night is its mother, as night fosters and nourishes like mother. It grows in the night. The frost in night time helps in its growth. Cloud helps in its growth, with rain, and is hence its father. Sun is its grandfather, being its great protector from times immemorial. Just as a sister helps and serves her brother, so this medicine cures the learned. Pt. Khem Karan Das Trivedi has applied all the verses to God. His learned interpretation is worth study.

२. यस्त्वा पिबति जीवति त्रायसे पुरुषं त्वम् । भर्त्री हि शश्वतामसि जनानां च न्यञ्चनी ।।

2. O medicine, whoever drinketh thy juice hath life; thou savest and protectest man. As nursing mother of mankind, thou art the healer of all ailments ! (955)

३. वृक्षंवृक्षमा रोहसि वृषण्यन्तीव कन्यला । जयन्ती प्रत्यातिष्ठन्ती स्परणी नाम वा असि ।।

3. Just as a girl longing for her busband, at the time of marriage resolves to seek his protection, so thou clingest close to every tree, and spreading thyself over it, coverest it, standest fast over it. Thy other name is sparni, the conqueror. (956)[1]

४. यद् दण्डेन यदिष्वा यद् वारुर्हरसा कृतम् । तस्य त्वमसि निष्कृतिः सेमं निष्कृधि पूरुषम् ।।

4. Whatever wound the arrow, or the staff, or violence inflicts, thereof thou art the remedy: as such restore this man to health. (957)

५. भद्रात् प्लक्षान्निस्तिष्ठस्यश्वत्थात् खदिराद् धवात् ।
भद्रान्न्यग्रोधात् पर्णात् सा न एह्यरुन्धति ।।

5. Thou springest from blest Plaxa, or Aṣavattha, Khadira, Dhava, blest Nyagrodha, Parṇa, so come thou to use, O medicine, the filler of wounds. (958)[2]

६. हिरण्यवर्णे सुभगे सूर्यवर्णे वपुष्टमे । रुतं गच्छासि निष्कृते निष्कृतिर्नाम वा असि ।।

6. Gold-coloured, lustrous, shining like the Sun, most lovely, O healing medicine, thou art applied on the wound or fracture. Healing is thy name ! (959)

७. हिरण्यवर्णे सुभगे शुष्मे लोमशवक्षणे । अपामसि स्वसा लाक्षे वातो ह्यात्मा बभूव ते ।।

7. Gold-coloured, lustrous, adorous, hairy-bodied one, the sister of the waters art thou, O lac, thy soul is wind! (960)[3]

[1]It is called Sparni, as it conquers old age.

[2]Plaxa: the waved lead Fig tree: Ficus Infectoria, a large and beautiful tree with small white fruit. In vernacular it is named Pilkhin. Aswatha: Ficus Religiosa, termed Pipal in the vernacular. Khadira: Khair खैर tree, Acacia Catechu Dhava: A shrub, Grislea Tomentosa, named Babul Pārṇa: Butea Frondosa, named palash or Dhāka in the vernacular. Nyagrodha: Ficus Indica, named बड़ (Bar) in vernacular. Arundhati: Laksha (lakh, lac) which fills up the wounds.

[3]Sisters of waters: It melts in waters, and leaves its juice in them. Thy soul is wind: It is solidified and strengthened by the wind.

८. सिलाची नाम कानीनोऽजबभ्रु पिता तव । अश्वो यमस्य यः श्यावस्तस्य हास्नास्युक्षिता ॥

8. Silachi is thy name, thy sire is full of lustre, and the ripener of corns. Thou hast been sprinkled by the multi-coloured horse of the Sun. (961)[1]

९. अश्वस्यास्नः सम्पतिता सा वृक्षाँ अभि सिष्यदे । सरा पतत्रिणी भूत्वा सा न एह्यरुन्धति ॥

9. O lac, pressed by the hot rays of the Sun, thou tricklest on the trees. O wound-filling medicine, oozing out of the tree, and sticking to the barks of its branches, may thou be obtained by us. (962)

Chapter (Anuvāka) 2

HYMN VI

१. ब्रह्म जज्ञानं प्रथमं पुरस्ताद् वि सीमतः सुरुचो वेन आवः ।
स बुध्न्याऽ उपमा अस्य विष्ठाः सतश्च योनिमसतश्च वि वः ॥

1. That God alone is Adorable, Who, in the beginning of the universe, created everything, is wide in expansion, Highest of all, Effulgent, and Worthy of worship. The sun, moon and other worlds in the atmosphere, stationed in their orbits, testify to His knowledge. He pervades them all through His Omnipresence and comprehends the visible and the invisible in space. (963)

२. अनाप्ता ये वः प्रथमा यानि कर्माणि चक्रिरे ।
वीरान् नो अत्र मा दभन् तद् व एतत् पुरो दधे ॥

2. O men, in order that the acts committed by those of you who are not perfect in knowledge, may not harm in this world our sons, I set before you, this Veda, is full of that knowledge, which is perfect. (964)[2]

३. सहस्रधार एव ते समस्वरन् दिवो नाके मधुजिह्वा असश्चतः ।
तस्य स्पशो न नि मिषन्ति भूर्णयः पदेपदे पाशिनः सन्ति सेतवे ॥

3. In the enjoyable realm of God, full of manifold powers, do the emancipated souls, calm and sedate, sing in a sweet voice the glory of the knowledge of the Vedas. The laws of God, acting as spies, the rearers and fosterers of humanity, watching the conduct of human beings, stand at every place, with snare and nooses in hand to bind the sinners. (965)[3]

[1]Multi-coloured horse: Rays of the sun of seven different colours. Sire: The sun.

[2]'Our' refers to mankind, i.e., the sons of all.

[3]Those who violate the laws of God, which watch as spies the conduct of all, cannot escape punishment for their misdeeds.

४. पर्यू षु प्र धन्वा वाजसातये परि वृत्राणि सक्षणि: ।
द्विषस्तदध्यर्णवेनेयसे सनिस्रसो नामासि त्रयोदशो मास इन्द्रस्य गृहः ॥

4. O God, Thou art the Remover of all impediments. Verily come unto us nicely from every side. Thou goadest us to attack the foes crossing the sea. Thou art known as the Vanquisher of foes. Thou art the thirteenth power beyond ten organs, mind and intellect. Thou art the Measurer of everything, and the refuge of the soul! (966)

५. न्वे३तेनारात्सीरसौ स्वाहा । तिग्मायुधौ तिग्महेती सुशेवौ सोमारुद्राविह सु मृडतं नः ॥

5. O God, Thou hast made, through Thy pervasion, a religious man, prosperous. Self-abnegation is the road to success. With sharpened arms and missiles, kind and friendly, be gracious unto us in this world, O King and Commander-in-chief! (967)[1]

६. अवैतेनारात्सीरसौ स्वाहा । तिग्मायुधौ तिग्महेती सुशेवौ सोमारुद्राविह सु मृडतं नः ॥

6. O God, Thou hast made, through Thy pervasion, an irreligious man, poor. Sacrifice is the road to success. With sharpened arms and missiles, kind and friendly, be gracious unto us in this world, O King and Commander-in-chief! (968)

७. अपैतेनारात्सीरसौ स्वाहा । तिग्मायुधौ तिग्महेती सुशेवौ सोमारुद्राविह सु मृडतं नः ॥

7. O God, through Thy pervasion, hast Thou declared the sinner, a criminal. Sacrifice is the root cause of success. With sharpened arms and missiles, kind and friendly, be gracious unto us, in this world, O King and Commander-in-chief! (969)

८. मुमुक्तमस्मान्दुरितादवद्याज्जुषेथां यज्ञममृतमस्मासु धत्तम् ॥

8. O King and Commander-in-chief, free us from blamable sin, accept our worship, give us knowledge and vitality! (970)[2]

९. चक्षुषो हेते मनसो हेते ब्रह्मणो हेते तपसश्च हेते ।
मेन्या मेनिरस्यमेनयस्ते सन्तु ये३स्माँ अभ्यघायन्ति ॥

9. O King, the missile of the eye, missile of mind, missile of knowledge, missile of austerity; thou art the weapon shot against the weapon. Let those be weaponless who sin against us. (971)[3]

[1]Griffith writes, the first line of this, as of each of the two following stanzas is unintelligible. The meaning is clear. Sorry Griffith has not been able to grasp it.

[2]'Us and our' refer to the subjects.

[3]The fiery eye, the strong mind, vast knowledge, and austerity of the king are his powerful weapons, wherewith thou enslavest foe.

१०. योऽस्मांश्चक्षुषा मनसा चित्त्याकूत्या च यो अघायुरभिदासात् ।
त्वं तानग्ने मेन्यामेनीन् कृणु स्वाहा ॥

10. Make with thy weapon weaponless, O King, all wicked men who want to ruin us, with eye, with thought, with spirit or intention! (972)

११. इन्द्रस्य गृहोऽसि ।
तं त्वा प्र पद्ये तं त्वा प्र विशामि सर्वगुः सर्वपूरुषः सर्वात्मा सर्वतनूः सह यन्मेऽस्ति तेन ॥

11. O God, Thou art the refuge of the soul. I betake me to Thee, I enter Thy service, with all my dynamic strength, with all my enterprising spirit, with all my spiritual force, with all my physical force, nay with mine entire possessions! (973)

१२. इन्द्रस्य शर्मासि । तं त्वा प्र पद्ये तं त्वा प्र विशामि सर्वगुः सर्वपूरुषः
सर्वात्मा सर्वतनूः सह यन्मेऽस्ति तेन ॥

12. O God, Thou art the Protector of the soul. I betake me to Thee, I enter Thy service, with all my dynamic strength, with all my enterprising spirit, with all my spiritual force, with all my physical force, nay with mine entire possessions! (974)

१३. इन्द्रस्य वर्मासि । तं त्वा प्र पद्ये तं त्वा प्र विशामि सर्वगुः सर्वपूरुषः
सर्वात्मा सर्वतनूः सह यन्मेऽस्ति तेन ॥

13. O God, Thou art the shield of the soul. I betake me to Thee, I enter Thy service, with all my dynamic strength, with all my enterprising spirit, with all my spiritual force, with all my physical force, nay with mine entire possessions! (975)

१४. इन्द्रस्य वरूथमसि । तं त्वा प्र पद्ये तं त्वा प्र विशामि सर्वगुः सर्वपूरुषः
सर्वात्मा सर्वतनूः सह यन्मेऽस्ति तेन ॥

14. O God, Thou art the shelter of the soul. I betake me to Thee. I enter Thy service, with all my dynamic strength, with all my enterprising spirit, with all my spiritual force, with all my physical force, nay with mine entire possessions! (976)

HYMN VII

१. आ नो भर मा परि ष्ठा अराते मा नो रक्षीर्दक्षिणां नीयमानाम् ।
नमो वीर्त्साया असमृद्धये नमो अस्त्वरातये ॥

1. O miser, give us our wages, detain them not, stay not the guerdon due to us. We renounce greed for wealth. We hate poverty. May thou give up miserliness. (977)[1]

[1]The wages due to a labourer should not be denied. Workmen should not be greedy, or suffer from the pangs of poverty, nor the employer should be a miser.

२. यमराते पुरोधत्से पुरुषं परिरापिणम् । नमस्ते तस्मै कृण्मो मा वनिं व्यथयीर्मम ॥

2. O miser, thou withholdest the wages of a labourer, and keepest him standing before thee, reviling thee for non-payment. We dislike thee and such a labourer of thine. Detain not my lord, my wages! (978)

३. प्र णो वनिर्देवकृता दिवा नक्तं च कल्पताम् ।
अरातिमनुप्रेमो वयं नमो अस्त्वरातये ॥

3. May our wages fixed by the learned, be paid to us day and night. We approach a miser, and say unto him, 'Down, with miserliness' (979)[1]

४. सरस्वतीमनुमतिं भगं यन्तो हवामहे । वाचं जुष्टां मधुमतीमवादिषं देवानां देवहूतिषु ॥

4. In prosperity even, we obey and revere the elders and recite Vedic verses. In the conferences of the learned, I use lovely, sweet words for them. (980)[2]

५. यं याचाम्यहं वाचा सरस्वत्या मनोयुजा ।
श्रद्धा तमद्य विन्दतु दत्ता सोमेन बभ्रुणा ॥

5. May my master from whom I claim my wages in a respectful and significant language, be filled today with desire for payment, instilled in his heart by God, the Nourisher of all. (981)

६. मा वनिं मा वाचं नो वीर्त्सीरुभाविन्द्राग्नी आ भरतां नो वसूनि ।
सर्वे नो अद्य दित्सन्तोऽरातिं प्रति हर्यत ॥

6. O master, don't detain our pay, nor reject our demand for it. May the king and learned persons bring us treasures. Ye all, ever fain to give us gifts, should condemn and oppose the miser, who refuses to pay us our wages. (982)

७. परोऽपेह्यसमृद्धे वि ते हेतिं नयामसि । वेद त्वाहं निमीवन्तीं नितुदन्तीमराते ॥

7 O Poverty! go thou far away; we turn thy harmful dart aside. I know thee well, Poverty, as the source of weakness and mental agony! (983)

८. उत नग्ना बोभुवती स्वप्नया सचसे जनम् । अराते चित्तं वीर्त्सन्त्याकूतिं पुरुषस्य च ॥

8. O Poverty, baffling the thought, and the firm intention of a man, oft coming in thy nakedness, thou makest people slothful. (984)

९. या महती महोन्माना विश्वा आशा व्यानशे । तस्यै हिरण्यकेश्यै निर्ऋत्या अकरं नमः ॥

9. I suppress the sentiment of sin, mighty, vast in size, which penetrates all points of space, and is the bringer of sufferings through greed for gold. (985)

[1]'Our' refers to labourers, workmen.

[2]In prosperity one forgets the performance of religious duties, and becomes disrespectful towards the elders. The Veda decries and condemns such an attitude. 'Them' refers to the learned.

१०. हिरण्यवर्णा सुभगा हिरण्यकशिपुर्महीे । तस्यै हिरण्यद्रापयेऽरात्या अकरं नमः ॥

10. I shun miserliness, ever greedy for gold, full of riches, pillowed on gold, mighty, and the spreader of sin for acquiring gold. (986)

HYMN VIII

१. वैकङ्कतेनेध्मेन देवेभ्य आज्यं वह । अग्ने ताँ इह मादय सर्व आ यन्तु मे हवम् ॥

1. O King, with the aid of a sharp weapon, acquire strength and valour, for the welfare of the learned. Make them all joyful in thy Kingdom, let them all come unto my call. (987)[1]

२. इन्द्रा याहि मे हवमिदं करिष्यामि तच्छृणु । इम ऐन्द्रा अतिसरा आकूतिं शं नमन्तु मे ।
तेभिः शकेम वीर्यं१ जातवेदस्तनूवशिन् ॥

2. O King, come to my battlefield, I will be victorious, so hear it thou. Let these agile soldiers of the king obey my command. O learned, self-controlled king, let us gain strength through various devices. (988)[2]

३. यदसावमुतो देवा अदेवः संश्चिकीर्षति ।
मा तस्याग्निर्हव्यं वाक्षीद्धवं देवा अस्य मोप गुर्ममैव हवमेतन ॥

3. Whatever plot from yonder, O warriors, that godless man would frame, let not the leading persons help him with provisions, let not the learned fight on his behalf, let them fight on my behalf. (989)[3]

४. अति धावतातिसरा इन्द्रस्य वचसा हत ।
अविं वृक इव मथ्नीत स वो जीवन् मा मोचि प्राणमस्यापि नह्यत ॥

4. Ye enterprising warriors, run farther on, by king's order smite and slay the foe. As a wolf worrieth a sheep, so let not him escape from you while life remains. Stop fast his breath. (990)[4]

५. यममी पुरोदधिरे ब्रह्माणमपभूतये । इन्द्र स ते अधस्पदं तं प्रत्यस्यामि मृत्यवे ॥

5. May, the learned person, whom those foes have exalted in an eminent position for our defeat, be brought beneath thy feet, O King! If you order, I will cast him to death. (991)[5]

[1]वज्रो वै विकङ्कतः : *Shatpath* 5-2-4-18.

[2]'My' refers to the Commander-in-chief. Battle is Yajna to which the king is invited by the general of the army.

[3]'My' means the king.

[4]'Him, his' refer to the foe.

[5]'I' refers to the general of the army.

६. यदि प्रेयुर्देवपुरा ब्रह्म वर्माणि चक्रिरे ।
तनूपानं परिपाणं कृण्वाना यदुपोचिरे सर्वं तदरसं कृधि ॥

6. If they have attacked the strongholds of the King, and made knowledge their shield, gaining protection for their lives, through various resources, make all their vainglorious statements powerless. (992)[1]

७. यानसावतिसरांश्चकार कृणवच्च यान् ।
त्वं तानिन्द्र वृत्रहन् प्रतीचः पुनरा कृधि यथामुं तृणहां जनम् ।

7. Let the soldiers whom that foe hath prepared or whom he is preparing for the fight, turn hostile to their master, O foe-slaying general, so that I may kill him. (993)[2]

८. यथेन्द्र उद्वाचनं लब्ध्वा चक्रे अधस्पदम् । कृत्वे३हमधरांस्तथामूंछश्वतीभ्यः समाभ्यः ॥

8. As the king hath seized and set his foot upon the bragging, boastful foe; even so for all the coming years I set those foes beneath my feet. (994)[3]

९. अत्रैनानिन्द्र वृत्रहन्नुग्रो मर्मणि विध्य । अत्रैवैनानभि तिष्ठेन्द्र मेद्य१हं तव
अनु त्वेन्द्रा रभामहे स्याम सुमतौ तव ॥

9. O foe-slaying king, with thy strength, pierce thou their vital parts on the battlefield. Here, even here, attack them, O King. Thine own dear friend am I. O King, we closely follow thee. May we be in thy favouring grace. (995)[4]

HYMN IX

१. दिवे स्वाहा ॥

1. I invoke God for help. (996)

२. पृथिव्यै स्वाहा ॥

2. I crave for wise statesmanship. (997)

३. अन्तरिक्षाय स्वाहा ॥

3. I pray for the purity of heart. (998)

४. अन्तरिक्षाय स्वाहा ॥

4. I pray for the knowledge of space. (999)

[1]The king addresses this verse to the general of the army.

[2]'I' refers to the king, and 'him' to the foe.

[3]'I' refers to the general of the army. Griffith considers Udvāchana to be the name of a demon. This is wrong. There is no history in the Vedas. The word means boastful, bragging.

[4]'Their' refers to the foes. Here' refers to the battlefield. 'I' refers to the general of the army. 'We' refers to the officials and soldiers of the army.

५. दिवे स्वाहा ॥

5. I pray for success in business. (1000)

६. पृथिव्यै स्वाहा ॥

6. I long for rule over the Earth. (1001)

७. सूर्यो मे चक्षुर्वातः प्राणोऽन्तरिक्षमात्मा पृथिवी शरीरम् ।
अस्तृतो नामाहमयमस्मि स आत्मानं नि दधे द्यावापृथिवीभ्यां गोपीथाय ॥

7. My eye is brilliant like the Sun. My breath is ever moving like the air. My soul resides in the body as sky in space. My body is full of endurance like the Earth. I am immortal. I hand over myself to my father and mother for safety. (1002)[1]

८. उदायुरुद् बलमुत् कृतमुत्कृत्यामुन्मनीषामुदिन्द्रियम् ।
आयुष्कृदायुष्पत्नी स्वधावन्तौ गोपा मे स्तं गोपायतं मा ।
आत्मसदौ मे स्तं मा मा हिंसिष्टम् ॥

8. O father the creator of life, O mother the mistress of life, exalt my life, my strength, my deed and action, increase my understanding and my vigour. Be Ye my powerful keepers, watch and guard me. Dwell Ye in my soul, and forbear to harm me. (1003)

HYMN X

१. अश्मवर्म मेऽसि यो मा प्राच्या दिशोऽघायुरभिदासात् । एतत् स ऋच्छात् ॥

1. O mind, thou art my armour of stone against the sinner who fights against me from the eastern quarter. May the enemy knock his head against that armour ! (1004)

२. अश्मवर्म मेऽसि यो मा दक्षिणाया दिशोऽघायुरभिदासात् । एतत् स ऋच्छात् ॥

2. O mind, thou art my armour of stone against the sinner who fights against me from the southern quarter. May the enemy knock his head against that armour! (1005)

३. अश्मवर्म मेऽसि यो मा प्रतीच्या दिशोऽघायुरभिदासात् । एतत् स ऋच्छात् ॥

3. O mind, thou art my armour of stone against the sinner who fights against me from the western quarter. May the enemy knock his head against that armour ! (1006)

[1] 'I' means the soul.

४. अश्मवर्म मेऽसि यो मोदीच्या दिशोऽघायुरभिदासात् । एतत् स ऋच्छात् ॥

4. O mind, thou art my armour of stone against the sinner who fights against me from the northern quarter. May the enemy knock his head against that armour! (1007)

५. अश्मवर्म मेऽसि यो मा ध्रुवाया दिशोऽघायुरभिदासात् । एतत् स ऋच्छात् ॥

5. O mind, thou art my armour of stone against the sinner who fights against me from the stedfast region. May the enemy knock his head against that armour! (1008)[1]

६. अश्मवर्म मेऽसि यो मोर्ध्वाया दिशोऽघायुरभिदासात् । एतत् स ऋच्छात् ॥

6. O mind, thou art my armour of stone against the sinner who fights against me from the lofty region. May the enemy knock his head against that armour! (1009)[2]

७. अश्मवर्म मेऽसि यो मा दिशामन्तर्देशेभ्योऽघायुरभिदासात् । एतत् स ऋच्छात् ॥

7. O mind, thou art my armour of stone against the sinner who from points intermediate fights against me. May the enemy knock his head against that armour! (1010)

८. बृहता मन उप ह्वये मातरिश्वना प्राणापानौ ।
सूर्याच्चक्षुरन्तरिक्षाच्छ्रोत्रं पृथिव्याः शरीरम् ।
सरस्वत्या वाचमुप ह्वयामहे मनोयुजा ॥

8. I strengthen my intellect through, the contemplation of God, my in-going, out-going breaths through the control of air, my eye through the light of the sun, my ear through vibrations in space, my body through food-stuffs grown in the Earth. We strengthen our speech through Vedic verses which suit the mind. (1011)

Chapter (Anuvāka) 3

HYMN XI

१. कथं महे असुरायाब्रवीरिह कथं पित्रे हरये त्वेषनृम्णः ।
पृश्नि वरुण दक्षिणां ददावान् पुनर्मघ त्वं मनसाचिकित्सीः ॥

1. How hast thou spoken here of the great God, how hast thou, full of majesty and wealth, spoken of the Almighty Father, the Averter of afflictions. O King, thou hast given food and land in charity. O master of various kinds of riches, how dost thou feel in thy mind. (1012)[3]

[1]Stedfast region: The nadir.

[2]Lofty region: the Zenith.

[3]'Thou' refers to the king. God is spoken of as Asura, as He grants breath to all living beings. The king sings the glories of God, grants food, land to his subjects, and always feels for their welfare. This hymn is a dialogue between a learned person and God.

२. न कामेन पुनर्मघो भवामि सं चक्षे कं पृश्निमेतामुपाजे ।
केन नु त्वमथर्वन् काव्येन केन जातेनासि जातवेदाः ॥

2. Not through desire alone have I become the lord of riches. I carefully look after this cow, the Earth, I always serve and rear her. O Brahman, the knower of divine knowledge, by what lore, by what inherent nature, knowest thou all things that exist! (1013)[1]

३. सत्यमहं गभीरः काव्येन सत्यं जातेनास्मि जातवेदाः ।
न मे दासो नार्यो महित्वा व्रतं मीमाय यदहं धरिष्ये ॥

3. Truly I am profound in wisdom through Vedic lore, truly I know by nature all existing things. Neither a low nor a noble person can Violate the law that I establish through my spiritual power. (1014)[2]

४. न त्वदन्यः कवितरो न मेधया धीरतरो वरुण स्वधावन् ।
त्वं ता विश्वा भुवनानि वेत्थ स चिन्नु त्वज्जनो मायी बिभाय ॥

4. None, O God, the Master of Matter, existeth wiser than thou or sager by his wisdom. Thou knowest well all these created beings: even the man of wondrous powers fears Thee! (1015)[3]

५. त्वं ह्य१ङ्ग वरुण स्वधावन् विश्वा वेत्थ जनिमा सुप्रणीते ।
किं रजस एना परो अन्यदस्त्येना किं परेणावरममुर ॥

5. O dear God, the Master of souls and Matter, Wise Director, Thou knowest verily all generations. What is, Unerring One, beyond this material world! What is more remote than that which is most distant? (1016)

६. एकं रजस एना परो अन्यदस्त्येना पर एकेन दुर्णशं चिदर्वाक् ।
तत् ते विद्वान् वरुण प्र ब्रवीम्यधोवचसः पणयो भवन्तु नीचैर्दासा उप सर्पन्तु भूमिम् ॥

6. One thing, God, there is beyond this universe. Besides Him, but next to Him is Matter, which is indestructible. O God, I, the Knower of Thy true nature, do declare, that churls fail to depict Thee fully. Unwise, ignorant people, grope in the dark on Earth, in their degraded position. (1017)

७. त्वं ह्य१ङ्ग वरुण ब्रवीषि पुनर्मघेष्ववद्यानि भूरि ।
मो षु पणीँरभ्ये३तावतो भून्मा त्वा वोचन्नराधसं जनासः ॥

7. O dear King, thou preachest, that greedy misers who amass wealth are full of faults worthy of reproach. Be not thou added to that crowd of niggards: so that men may not call thee an illiberal giver. (1018)[4]

[1]'I' refers to Varuna, the king. In the second half of the verse, the learned ask the Atharvan, the knower of divine knowledge, how he has become the knower of all things. Atharvan is not a proper Noun. One who knows the *Atharvaveda* is called an Atharvan.

[2]Atharvan, the learned person, replies to Varuna, the rich king or God.

[3]'Varuna' means God or King.

[4]Atharvan, the learned person speaks to Varuna, the wealthy king.

८. मा मा वोचन्नराधसं जनासः पुनस्ते पृश्निं जरितर्ददामि ।
स्तोत्रं मे विश्वमा याहि शचीभिरन्तर्विश्वासु मानुषीषु दिक्षु ॥

8. Let not men call Me an illiberal Giver, O worshipper, I give thee Vedic Knowledge! Preach, in every place where men inhabit, with all thy powers, my Vedic song. (1019)[1]

९. आ ते स्तोत्राण्युद्यतानि यन्त्वन्तर्विश्वासु मानुषीषु दिक्षु ।
देहि नु मे यन्मे अदत्तो असि युज्यो मे सप्तपदः सखासि ॥

9. O God, let Thy lofty Vedic hymns be preached in every place of human habitation. Give me now the gift Thou hast not given. Thou art my Friend for ever firm and faithful. (1020)[2]

१०. समा नौ बन्धुर्वरुण समा जा वेदाहं तद्यन्नावेषा समा जा ।
ददामि तद् यत् ते अदत्तो अस्मि युज्यस्ते सप्तपदः सखास्मि ॥

10. One origin, O God, one bond unites us. I know the nature of that common kinship. I give thee the gift that I retracted. I am thy friend for ever firm and faithful. (1021)[3]

११. देवो देवाय गृणते वयोधा विप्रो विप्राय स्तुवते सुमेधाः ।
अजीजनो हि वरुण स्वधावन्नथर्वाणं पितरं देवबन्धुम् ॥
तस्मा उ राधः कृणुहि सुप्रशस्तं सखा नो असि परमं च बन्धुः ॥

11. O God, Thou art the Giver of food, to the learned man who lauds Thee, the Excellent Bestower of intellect to the sage who sings Thy praise. O Powerful God, Thou makest an extremely learned person, the nourisher of all, and the friend of the learned. On him bestow most highly lauded riches. Thou art our friend, high over all, our kinsman! (1022)

HYMN XII

१. समिद्धो अद्य मनुषो दुरोणे देवो देवान् यजसि जातवेदः ।
आ च वह मित्रमहश्चिकित्वान् त्वं दूतः कविरसि प्रचेताः ॥

1. O wise person, respecter of friends, thou, this day, kindled like the illuminated fire, walkest in their company, as a reflective, literary person. Rich in intellect, tormentor of the wicked, highly conscious, possessing unobstructed knowledge of all subjects, cultivate fully noble virtue in the house! (1023)

[1]In this hymn 'Varuna' means God.

[2]Saptapada: literally means 'having taken seven steps by which an alliance or a marriage is confirmed' Atharvan speaks this stanza and the first hemistich of the 10th verse.

[3]Varuna speaks the second hemistich. Both God and soul are immortal, the same in this aspect. They are related to each other. God is infinite, the soul isfi nite. God is All-pervading, the soul resides in one place. God is Omniscient, soul's knowledge is limited.

२. तनूनपात् पथ ऋतस्य यानान् मध्वा समञ्जन्त्स्वदया सुजिह्व ।
मन्मानि धीभिरुत यज्ञमृन्धन् देवत्रा च कृणुह्यध्वरं नः ॥

2. O fair-tongued preserver of various objects, make pleasant for all, the commendable paths of rectitude, with thy sweet sermon and excellent exposition. Develop the society and philosophical subjects with thy holy thoughts, and strengthen our innocuous worship through learned persons! (1024)

३. आजुह्वान ईड्यो वन्द्यश्चा याह्यग्ने वसुभिः सजोषाः ।
त्वं देवानामसि यह्व होता स एनान् यक्षीषितो यजीयान् ॥

3. O learned person, full of noble qualities, amongst scholars, thou art charitable and companionable. Walk in the company of these prompt scholars. Being lovely towards the learned, deserving praise and adoration, go near them! (1025)

४. प्राचीनं बर्हिः प्रदिशा पृथिव्या वस्तोरस्या वृज्यते अग्रे अह्नाम् ।
व्यु प्रथते वितरं वरीयो देवेभ्यो अदितये स्योनम् ॥

4. O men, in this world, the Immortal God, All-pervading like space, beyond the light of day, early in the morning before dawn, grants to the learned and immortal soul happiness that removes miseries and is most excellent. Know and realise Him following the instructions of the Vedas! (1026)[1]

५. व्यचस्वतीरुर्विया वि श्रयन्तां पतिभ्यो न जनयः शुम्भमानाः ।
देवीर्द्वारो बृहतीर्विश्वमिन्वा देवेभ्यो भवत सुप्रायणाः ॥

5. O men, learn all sciences, just as wives, highly cultured and virtuous, well experienced in all domestic dealings, dwellers in nice houses, decorated with ornaments, tall like doors, deck their beauty for their noble husbands, and serve them! (1027)

६. आ सुष्वयन्ती यजते उपाके उषासानक्ता सदतां नि योनौ ।
दिव्ये योषणे बृहती सुरुक्मे अधि श्रियं शुक्रपिशं दधाने ॥

6. O learned person, acquire prosperity by properly using day and night, that move continuously in the wheel of time, each close to each, seated at their stations, assuming light and darkness, lofty, fair and radiant beauty like two women! (1028)

७. दैव्या होतारा प्रथमा सुवाचा मिमाना यज्ञं मनुषो यजध्यै ।
प्रचोदयन्ता विदथेषु कारू प्राचीनं ज्योतिः प्रदिशा दिशन्ता ॥

7. O men, learn fine arts from two skilled persons, who are competent amongst the learned, charitably disposed, well known, sweet voiced, executors of projects, inducers of men to scientific knowledge, and acts of sacrifice,

[1]Those who say their prayer and remember God early in the morning before sunrise, attain to happiness and get freedom from misery.

preachers of the doctrines of the Vedas, and expounders of mechanical knowledge. (1029)[1]

८. आ नो यज्ञं भारती तूयमेत्विडा मनुष्वदिह चेतयन्ती ।
तिस्रो देवीर्बर्हिरेदं स्योनं सरस्वती: स्वपस: सदन्ताम् ॥

8. May Bharti, Ida, Saraswati, in this mechanical work, comes unto us from all sides, speedily expounding the secrets of mechanical science, like a thoughtful person. May these three intellectual forces, guide us, the performers of nice enterprises, in this mighty project, the source of comfort. (1030)[2]

९. य इमे द्यावापृथिवी जनित्री रूपैरपिंशद् भुवनानि विश्वा ।
तमद्य होतरिषितो यजीयान् देवं त्वष्टारमिह यक्षि विद्वान् ॥

9. O seeker after knowledge, extremely fond of companionship, urged, receiving education from everywhere, thou deservest homage, as thou always rememberest that God, Who, in this world, creates different spheres, these Earth and Sun, the progenitors of various actions and brings about the creation and dissolution of the universe! (1031)

१०. उपावसृज त्मन्या समञ्जन् देवानां पाथ ऋतुथा हवींषि ।
वनस्पति: शमिता देवो अग्नि: स्वदन्तु हव्यं मधुना घृतेन ॥

10. O learned person, put into fire, at different seasons with devotion, in the form of oblations, eatables mixed with honey and butter, fit to be taken by the learned. May the sun, cloud, and fire receive thy oblations. (1032)[3]

११. सद्यो जातो व्यऽमिमीत यज्ञमग्निर्देवानामभवत् पुरोगा: ।
अस्य होतु: प्रशिष्यृतस्य वाचि स्वाहाकृतं हविरदन्तु देवा: ॥

11. The enlightened person, who speedily attains to fame and manages different transactions, with truth-imbued words of a learned fellow, and precedes scholars, and the remnants of whose properly performed Homa are eaten by the learned, deserves all-round veneration. (1033)

HYMN XIII

१. ददिर्हि मह्यं वरुणो दिव: कविर्वचोभिरुग्रैर्नि रिणामि ते विषम् ।
खातमखातमुत सक्तमग्रभमिरेव धन्वन्नि जजास ते विषम् ॥

1. I have been instructed by a learned person, the knower of the essence of wonderful objects: with his words of mighty power I draw thy poison out. Dug up, not dug, adherent, I have ceased it fast: I make it disappear like water in the sands. (1034)[4]

[1]The word कारू in the verse means two persons, one of whom is skilled in teaching fine arts, and the other is expert in handicrafts.

[2]Bharti: The knowledge of fine arts. Ida: Beautiful, trained, sweet voice. Saraswati: Wisdom full of knowledge.

[3]Articles put into the fire in the performance of Havan, being rarefied reach the sun and cloud.

[4]'I' refers to a physician 'Thy' refers to a snake. 'It' refers to the poison.

२. यत् ते अपोदकं विषं तत् त एतास्वग्रभम् ।
गृह्णामि ते मध्यममुत्तमं रसमुतावमं भियसा नेशदादु ते ॥

2. O snake, I stop thy blood-sucking venom in the veins, and prevent it from spreading further in the body. I control thy poison of extreme, medium and ordinary intensity. Even when there is no trace of poison in the body, sometimes the victim dies out of thy fear alone. (1035)

३. वृषा मे रवो नभसा न तन्यतुरुग्रेण ते वचसा बाध आदु ते ।
अहं तमस्य नृभिरग्रभं रसं तमस इव ज्योतिरुदेतु सूर्यः ॥

3. Strong is my word-like thunder with the rainy cloud: with powerful words I remove thee and thy venom. With the aid of efficacious medicines, I remove that venom of thine, just as light removes the gloom, and lets the sun rise. (1036)[1]

४. चक्षुषा ते चक्षुर्हन्मि विषेण हन्मि ते विषम् ।
अहे म्रियस्व मा जीवीः प्रत्यगभ्येतु त्वा विषम् ॥

4. With the power of my eye, I destroy thine eye, and with this poison conquer thine. Live not, O snake, but die the death: back go thy venom on thyself. (1037)[2]

५. कैरात पृश्न उपतृण्य बभ्र आ मे शृणुतासिता अलीकाः ।
मा मे सख्युः स्तामानमपि ष्ठाताश्रावयन्तो नि विषे रमध्वम् ॥

5. Listen to me, O snakes, dwellers in forests, spotty, lurkers in grass, brown, dark, hateful creatures. Approach not near the house of my friend, give this warning to others, and rest quiet with your poison. (1038)[3]

६. असितस्य तैमातस्य बभ्रोरपोदकस्य च ।
सात्रासाहस्याहं मन्योरव ज्यामिव धन्वनो वि मुञ्चामि रथाँ इव ॥

6. I slacken the venom of a serpent, that is dark, dwells in a wet place, or resides in a dry place far from water, or is full of all conquering wrath, just as the string is loosened from the bow, or the horses of a cart are unyoked in a desert. (1039)

[1]As light removes darkness and the sun sets in, so the removal of vemon restores the light of life to the victim. 'Thee' 'thy' refer to a snake. 'I', 'my' refer to a physician. The physician through his powerful words of assurance encouragement, convinces the patient to be cured soon. If a patient loses heart, he cannot be cured. Doctor's words go a long way to cure a patient.

[2]The physician should overpower the spirit with his skill and spiritual force, and destroy his venom through some poisonous drug and kill him with it.

[3]I refers to a physician, or a snake controller.

७. आलिगी च विलिगी च पिता च माता च ।
विद्म वः सर्वतो बन्ध्वरसाः किं करिष्यथ ॥

7. O serpents, your father and mother are movers in all directions, and are movers awry. We know all your kinsfolk; deprived of venom, what will ye do! (1040)

८. उरुगूलाया दुहिता जाता दास्यसिक्न्या । प्रतङ्कं दद्रुषीणां सर्वासामरसं विषम् ॥

8. The daughter of a venomous female serpent, is equally venomous, born of a black she-serpent. May the deadly poison of all venomous she-serpents be rendered impotent. (1041)

९. कर्णा श्वावित् तदब्रवीद् गिरेरवचरन्तिका ।
याः काश्चेमाः खनित्रिमास्तासामरसतमं विषम् ॥

9. Dwelling beside the mountain's slope, the quick-eared porcupine exclaimed: Of all these she-snakes homed in earth the poison is most powerless. (1042)[1]

१०. ताबुवं न ताबुवं न घेत् त्वमसि ताबुवम् । ताबुवेनारसं विषम् ॥

10. A developing object is not the source of pain. O serpent thou art verily not an object free from pain. May thy poison be removed through the medicine named Tabuva. (1043)

११. तस्तुवं न तस्तुवं न घेत् त्वमसि तस्तुवम् । तस्तुवेनारसं विषम् ॥

11. A censurable object is not like an object free from censure. Thou, O serpent art verily a censurable object. May thy poison be removed through the medicine Tastuva. (1044)[2]

HYMN XIV

१. सुपर्णस्त्वान्वविन्दत् सूकरस्त्वाखनन्नसा ।
दिप्सौषधे त्वं दिप्सन्तमव कृत्याकृतं जहि ॥

1. O medicine, a person far-sighted like an eagle has discovered thee, a quick-witted and strong person, has dug thee, like a boar with his snout! O King, the remover of calamity like medicine, harm thou, him who wants to harm us, and drive the violent away. (1045)

[1]The quills of the porcupine protect her from the attacks of snakes.

[2]Tabuva and Tastuva (Mantra 10 and 11) are supposed antidotes that render snakes' poison ineffectual. Snake-charmers at the present day exhibit stones which they say have the power of drawing the poison out of a wound inflicted by a snake. The exact significance of the antidotes Tabuva and Trastuva is not known.

२. अव जहि यातुधानानव कृत्याकृतं जहि ।
अथो यो अस्मान् दिप्सति तमु त्वं जह्योषधे ॥

2. O King, the remover of calamity like medicine, harm thou the tormenting souls, destroy the violent people. Chase afar, the man who fain would do us injury. (1046)

३. रिश्यस्येव परीशासं परिकृत्य परि त्वचः ।
कृत्यां कृत्याकृते देवा निष्कमिव प्रति मुञ्चत ॥

3. O learned persons, just as a violent animal is controlled by piercing his skin all round with daggers, so should a man-eating cannibal, being put to distress from all sides, be overpowered and left to his fate! (1047)

४. पुनः कृत्यां कृत्याकृते हस्तगृह्य परा णय । समक्षमस्मा आ धेहि यथा कृत्याकृतं हनत् ॥

4. O King, catch hold again and again red-handed, of a violent person, committing mischief and put him in solitary confinement. Tell him clearly in his face, how mischief-mongers, who take the life of others are liable to be given capital punishment! (1048)[1]

५. कृत्याः सन्तु कृत्याकृते शपथः शपथीयते । सुखो रथ इव वर्ततां कृत्या कृत्याकृतं पुनः ॥

5. Let him, who behaves violently, be punished adequately. Let the public revile him, who reviles others. Just as a car rolls peacefully in an open space, so let the criminal, through fear behave, properly. Let him be punished, if he again commits mischief. (1049)

६. यदि स्त्री यदि वा पुमान् कृत्यां चकार पाप्मने ।
तामु तस्मै नयामस्यश्वमिवाश्वाभिधान्या ॥

6. When a woman or a man commits violence with an intention of sin, we overpower him with a similar violence, just as we control a horse with a rope. (1050)

७. यदि वासि देवकृता यदि वा पुरुषैः कृता । तां त्वा पुनर्णयामसीन्द्रेण सयुजा वयम् ॥

7. O violence, whether thou hast been committed by the forces of nature or by men, with the aid of our friend, the king, we ward thee off. (1051)

८. अग्ने पृतनाषाट् पृतनाः सहस्व । पुनः कृत्यां कृत्याकृते प्रतिहरणेन हरामसि ॥

8. O King, victorious in fight, subdues the armies of our foes! Back on the violent person we cast his violence, and beat it home! (1052)

९. कृतव्यधनि विध्य तं यश्चकार तमिज्जहि । न त्वामचक्रुषे वयं वधाय सं शिशीमहि ॥

[1]A king should strike terror in the heart of a miscreant by threatening him to be put to death, if he does not give up his violence.

9. Thou who hast piercing weapons, pierce him who hath wrought violence; conquer him. O king, we do not excite thee to slay the man who hath not practised violence! (1053)

१०. पुत्र इव पितरं गच्छ स्वज इवाभिष्ठितो दश । बन्धमिवावक्रामी गच्छ कृत्ये कृत्याकृतं पुनः ।।

10. O violence, go to the miscreant who uses thee against others, as a son goes to his sire, bite him as a trampled viper bites. As one who flies from bonds, go back, O violence, go back to him, who commits violence. (1054)

११. उदेणीव वारण्य्]भिस्कन्दं मृगीव । कृत्या कर्तारमृच्छतु ।।

11. Just as a female antelope, or a female elephant or a female deer jumps at her assailant, so should violence overtake him who resorts to violence. (1055)

१२. इष्वा ऋजीयः पततु द्यावापृथिवी तं प्रति । सा तं मृगमिव गृह्णातु कृत्या कृत्याकृतं पुनः ।।

12. O King and subjects, straighter than any arrow let it fly against him, let violence seize against the violent person like a beast of prey. (1056)[1]

१३. अग्निरिवैतु प्रतिकूलमनुकूलमिवोदकम् । सुखो रथ इव वर्ततां कृत्या कृत्याकृतं पुनः ।।

13. Let it go against the foe, contrary like flame, like water following its course. Let it roll back upon the violent person, as a car rolls freely in an open space. (1057)[2]

HYMN XV

१. एका च मे दश च मेऽपवक्तार ओषधे । ऋतजात ऋतावरि मधु मे मधुला करः ।।

1. O God, the Companion and Embodiment of Truth, the Bestower of knowledge and sweetness, grant me knowledge and sweetness, though my revilers be one and ten! (1058)[3]

२. द्वे च मे विंशतिश्च मेऽपवक्तार ओषधे । ऋतजात ऋतावरि मधु मे मधुला करः ।।

2. O God, the Companion and Embodiment of Truth, the Bestower of knowledge and sweetness, grant me knowledge and sweetness, though my revilers be two and twenty! (1059)

[1]'It' refers to the foe-destroying army.
'Him' refers to the man who resorts to violence.

[2]'It' refers to the foe-destroying army.

[3]In this hymn a learned person is instructed to have implicit, unflinching, and absolute faith in God, never to renounce his sweetness of speech or be ever prey to ignorance, however great be the number of his adversaries, detractors andr evilers. This sentiment has beautifully been expressed in the eleven verses, where the number of revilers is enumerated in Arithmetical and Geometrical Progressions.

३. तिस्रश्च मे त्रिंशच्च मेऽपवक्तार ओषधे । ऋतजात ऋतावरि मधु मे मधुला करः ।।

3. O God, the Companion and Embodiment of Truth, the Bestower of knowledge and sweetness, grant me knowledge and sweetness, though my revilers be three and thirty! (1060)

४. चतस्रश्च मे चत्वारिंशच्च मेऽपवक्तार ओषधे । ऋतजात ऋतावरि मधु मे मधुला करः ।।

4. O God, the Companion, and Embodiment of Truth, the Bestower of knowledge and sweetness, grant me knowledge and sweetness, though my revilers be four and forty! (1061)

५. पञ्च च मे पञ्चाशच्च मेऽपवक्तार ओषधे । ऋतजात ऋतावरि मधु मे मधुला करः ।।

5. O God, the Companion, and Embodiment of Truth, the Bestower of knowledge and sweetness, grant me knowledge and sweetness, though my revilers be five and fifty! (1062)

६. षट् च मे षष्टिश्च मेऽपवक्तार ओषधे । ऋतजात ऋतावरि मधु मे मधुला करः ।।

6. O God, the Companion and Embodiment of Truth, the Bestower of knowledge and sweetness, grant me knowledge and sweetness, though my revilers be six and sixty! (1063)

७. सप्त च मे सप्ततिश्च मेऽपवक्तार ओषधे । ऋतजात ऋतावरि मधु मे मधुला करः ।।

7. O God, the Companion and Embodiment of Truth, the Bestower of knowledge and sweetness, grant me knowledge and sweetness, though my revilers be seven and seventy! (1064)

८. अष्ट च मेऽशीतिश्च मेऽपवक्तार ओषधे । ऋतजात ऋतावरि मधु मे मधुला करः ।।

8. O God, the Companion and Embodiment of Knowledge, the Bestower of knowledge and sweetness, grant me knowledge and sweetness, though my revilers be eight and eighty! (1065)

९. नव च मे नवतिश्च मेऽपवक्तार ओषधे । ऋतजात ऋतावरि मधु मे मधुला करः ।।

9. O God, the Companion and Embodiment of Truth, the Bestower of knowledge and sweetness, grant me knowledge and sweetness, though my revilers be nine and ninety! (1066)

१०. दश च मे शतं च मेऽपवक्तार ओषधे । ऋतजात ऋतावरि मधु मे मधुला करः ।।

10. O God, the Companion and Embodiment of Truth, the Bestower of knowledge and sweetness, grant me knowledge and sweetness, though my revilers be ten and hundred! (1067)

११. शतं च मे सहस्रं चापवक्तार ओषधे । ऋतजात ऋतावरि मधु मे मधुला करः ।।

11. O God, the Companion and Embodiment of Truth, the Bestower of knowledge and sweetness, grant me knowledge and sweetness, though my revilers be a hundred and a thousand! (1068)

HYMN XVI

१. यद्येकवृषोऽसि सृजारसोऽसि ॥

1. O man, if thou art powerful in unison with God alone, enhance thy pleasure, otherwise thou art powerless! (1069)

२. यदि द्विवृषोऽसि सृजारसोऽसि ॥

2. O man, if thou art powerful through the realisation of God and soul, enhance thy pleasure, otherwise thou art powerless! (1070)

३. यदि त्रिवृषोऽसि सृजारसोऽसि ॥

3. O man, if thou art powerful, through properly understanding the nature of Satva, Rajas and Tamas, enhance thy pleasure, otherwise thou art powerless! (1071)[1]

४. यदि चतुर्वृषोऽसि सृजारसोऽसि ॥

4. O man, if thou art powerful through observing Dharam, Arth, Kama, Moksha, enhance thy pleasure, otherwise thou art powerless. (1072)

५. यदि पञ्चवृषोऽसि सृजारसोऽसि ॥

5. O man, if thou art powerful through the knowledge of five elements, enhance thy pleasure, otherwise thou art powerless. (1073)

६. यदि षड्वृषोऽसि सृजारसोऽसि ॥

6. O man, if thou hast controlled lust, anger, avarice, infatuation, pride and egotism, enhance thy pleasure, otherwise thou art powerless. (1074)

७. यदि सप्तवृषोऽसि सृजारसोऽसि ॥

7. O man, if thou hast mastery over five organs of cognition, mind and intellect, enhance thy pleasure, otherwise thou art powerless. (1075)[2]

८. यद्यष्टवृषोऽसि सृजारसोऽसि ॥

8. O man, if thou possessest the knowledge of eight limbs of yoga, enhance thy pleasure, otherwise thou art powerless. (1076)[3]

[1]Satva: Godly disposition.
Rajas: Active life.
Tamas: Ignorance, darkness.

[2]Five organs of cognition: Jñan Indriyas.

[3]Eight limbs of yoga: Yama, Niyama, Āsan, Prāṇāyāma, Pratyahār, Dhārnā, Dhyāna, Smādhi.

९. यदि नववृषोऽसि सृजारसोऽसि ॥

9. O man, if thou fully understandest thy body, having nine gates, enhance thy pleasure, otherwise thou art powerless. (1077)[1]

१०. यदि दशवृषोऽसि सृजारसोऽसि ॥

10. O man, if thou possessest the ten characteristics of charity, character, forgiveness, heroism, contemplation, intellect, army, expediency, messengers and knowledge, enhance thy pleasure, otherwise thou art powerless. (1078)

११. यद्येकादशोऽसि सोऽपोदकोऽसि ॥

11. O man, if thou art the eleventh, devoid of enterprise, thou art powerless. (1079)[2]

HYMN XVII

१. तेऽवदन् प्रथमा ब्रह्मकिल्बिषेऽकूपारः सलिलो मातरिश्वा ।
वीडुहरास्तप उग्रं मयोभूरापो देवीः प्रथमजा ऋतस्य ॥

1. These chief forces of nature, the boundless sea, wind, fierce glowing fire, the strong sun, the bliss-bestowing moon, the tranquil waters, first created by God, stand as witnesses against the onslaught on a Brahman. (1080)

२. सोमो राजा प्रथमो ब्रह्मजायां पुनः प्रायच्छदहृणीयमानः ।
अन्वर्तिता वरुणो मित्र आसीदग्निर्होता हस्तगृह्या निनाय ॥

2. Without reluctance has the Almighty God, verily bestowed the vedic knowledge. A highly gifted philanthropic and learned person willingly accepts it, and takes in hand its propagation. (1081)[3]

३. हस्तेनैव ग्राह्य आधिरस्या ब्रह्मजायेति चेदवोचत् ।
न दूताय प्रहेया तस्थ एषा तथा राष्ट्रं गुपितं क्षत्रियस्य ॥

3. He has declared it to be vedic knowledge. The right of its propagation rests with a learned person. An ignoble person can't preach it. Thus is the kingdom of a ruler guarded. (1082)[4]

४. यामाहुस्तारकैषा विकेशीति दुच्छुनां ग्राममवपद्यमानाम् ।
सा ब्रह्मजाया वि दुनोति राष्ट्रं यत्र प्रापादि शश उल्कुषीमान् ॥

[1]Nine gates: Two eyes, two ears, two nostrils, mouth, anus, penis, नवद्वारेपुरे देही *Gita*, 5-13.

[2]If a man does not possess any of the qualifications mentioned in the first ten verses, he is verily a powerless man without enterprise.

[3]Griffith interprets ब्रह्मजाया as the wife of a Brahmin. The word means the knowledge of the Vedas, revealed by God.

[4]'He' refers to the learned person in the previous verse. 'Thus' means the proper propagation of the Vedas.

4. Ignorance that overtakes a village, is spoken of as a star with contradictory light. Lack of Vedic knowledge disturbs the kingdom, where fall a lot of meteors and shooting stars. (1083)[1]

५. ब्रह्मचारी चरति वेविषद् विषः स देवानां भवत्येकमङ्गम् ।
तेन जायामन्वविन्दद् बृहस्पतिः सोमेन नीतां जुह्वं१ न देवाः ॥

5. Performing noble deeds, a Brahmchari roams about observing, Vedic laws. He becomes a member of the assembly of the learned. That is why, O learned people, that Brahmchari, the guardian of major sciences, has now acquired the gracious knowledge of the Vedas, revealed by God! (1084)[2]

६. देवा वा एतस्यामवदन्त पूर्वे सप्तऋषयस्तपसा ये निषेदुः ।
भीमा जाया ब्राह्मणस्यापनीता दुर्धां दधाति परमे व्योऽमिन् ॥

6. In ancient times the sages who practised penance through seven vital forces, verily thus declared about this divine Vedic knowledge. 'Dreadful is the result of neglecting divine knowledge, which causes confusion and calamity, where its teachings are violated. (1085)

७. ये गर्भा अवपद्यन्ते जगद् यच्चापलुप्यते । वीरा ये तृह्यन्ते मिथो ब्रह्मजाया हिनस्ति तान् ॥

7. When infants die, untimely born, when herds of cattle waste away, when heroes strike each other dead, the neglect of Vedic knowledge destroyeth them. (1086)[3]

८. उत यत् पतयो दश स्त्रियाः पूर्वे अब्राह्मणाः । ब्रह्मा चेद्धस्तमग्रहीत् स एव पतिरेकधा ॥

8. Even if ten former guardians, none of whom is a Brahmin, espouse the cause of Vedic knowledge, they are no match for a Brahman, who takes into his hand the task of propagating her. He alone is her true guardian. (1087)[4]

९. ब्राह्मण एव पतिर्न राजन्योः न वैश्यः । तत् सूर्यः प्रब्रुवन्नेति पञ्चभ्यो मानवेभ्यः ॥

9. Not Vaiśya, not Rajanya, nor the Brahman alone is indeed her guardian. God, in His dispensation proclaims this to the five races of mankind. (1088)[5]

[1]Just as meteors and shooting stars falling on a place damage it seriously, so a country is ruined where prevails ignorance and lack of Vedic knowledge.

[2]Sāyana has quoted a legend in connection with this verse, that Juhu the wife of Brihaspati, who is identified with Brahmā, had been deserted by her husband. The Gods then consulted together as to the means of expiating his sin, and restored her to him. Juhu is not the name of a woman, It means gracious, charitable दानशील. There is no history in the Vedas. The legend is the result of misunderstanding the verse.

[3]Where Vedic laws and instructions are not followed, there occur cases of abortion, there the cattle die through starvation, and there the heroes fight and kill each other.

[4]'Her' refers to Vedic knowledge.

[5]Five races: Brahman, Kshatriya, Vaiśya, Shudra, Nishāda. 'Rajanya' means Kshatriya. Brahman: One who is well versed in the knowledge of the Vedas. 'Her' refers to Vedic knowledge.

१०. पुनर्वै देवा अददुः पुनर्मनुष्या॒ अददुः । राजानः सत्यं गृह्णाना ब्रह्मजायां पुनर्ददुः ॥

10. The sages, mortals, and the kings, the lovers of truth, have verily given the knowledge of the Vedas to others. (1089)

११. पुनर्दाय ब्रह्मजायां कृत्वा देवैर्निकिल्बिषम् । ऊर्जं पृथिव्या भक्त्वोरुगायमुपासते ॥

11. Having propagated the Vedic knowledge and freed themselves from sin, through fine traits; and having shared the invigorating food of the earth, the learned worship the Most Glorious God. (1090)

१२. नास्य जाया शतवाही कल्याणी तल्पमा शये । यस्मिन् राष्ट्रे निरुध्यते ब्रह्मजायाचित्त्या ॥

12. In a country where the spread of Vedic knowledge is prohibited through lack of sense, knowledge, the implementer of hundreds of deeds, and the bestower of virtue, can never attain to stability. (1091)

१३. न विकर्णः पृथुशिरास्तस्मिन् वेश्मनि जायते । यस्मिन् राष्ट्रे निरुध्यते ब्रह्मजायाचित्त्या ॥

13. In a country where the spread of Vedic knowledge is prohibited through lack of sense, no precocious and intelligent son is ever born in a house. (1092)

१४. नास्य क्षत्ता निष्कग्रीवः सूनानामेत्यग्रतः । यस्मिन् राष्ट्रे निरुध्यते ब्रह्मजायाचित्त्या ॥

14. In a country where the spread of Vedic knowledge is prohibited through lack of sense, no steward, golden-necklaced, goes before eminent persons. (1093)[1]

१५. नास्य श्वेतः कृष्णकर्णो धुरि युक्तो महीयते । यस्मिन् राष्ट्रे निरुध्यते ब्रह्मजायाचित्त्या ॥

15. In a country where the spread of Vedic knowledge is prohibited through lack of sense, no black-eared courser, white of hue, moves proudly, harnessed to his car. (1094)[2]

१६. नास्य क्षेत्रे पुष्करिणी नाण्डीकं जायते बिसम् । यस्मिन् राष्ट्रे निरुध्यते ब्रह्मजायाचित्त्या ॥

16. In a country where the spread of Vedic knowledge is prohibitedt hrough lack of sense, no lily grows with oval bulbs, no lotus pool is found in its field. (1095)

१७. नास्मै पृश्निं वि दुहन्ति ये॒ऽस्या दोहमुपासते । यस्मिन् राष्ट्रे निरुध्यते ब्रह्मजायाचित्त्या ॥

17. In a country where the spread of Vedic knowledge is prohibited through lack of sense, the men whose task it is to till the land, do not cultivate it for the king. (1096)

[1]On account of poverty well-paid servants cannot be employed. A country that neglects the teachings of the Vedas become poor, its employees are low paid, and cannot afford to wear a golden necklace.

[2]A country which does not follow the instructions of the Vedas, does not produce excellent horses.

१८. नास्य धेनुः कल्याणी नानड्वान्त्सहते धुरम् । विजानिर्यत्र ब्राह्मणो रात्रिं वसति पापया ॥

18. In a country where a Brahmin devoid of knowledge, passes his sinful life in the night of ignorance, milch-cow doth not profit one, his ox endures not the yoke. (1097)[1]

HYMN XVIII

१. नैतां ते देवा अददुस्तुभ्यं नृपते अत्तवे । मा ब्राह्मणस्य राजन्य गां जिघत्सो अनाद्याम् ॥

1. The sages, O King, have not bestowed this knowledge on thee for abuse! Seek not, O King, to destroy the Brahman's Vedic knowledge, which is unworthy of destruction. (1098)[2]

२. अक्षद्रुग्धो राजन्यः पाप आत्मपराजितः । स ब्राह्मणस्य गामद्यादद्य जीवानि मा श्वः ॥

2. A voluptuous, sinful, spiritually degraded king, who destroys the Vedic knowledge of a learned person, may live for today, but not tomorrow. (1099)[3]

३. आविष्टिताघविषा पृदाकूरिव चर्मणा । सा ब्राह्मणस्य राजन्य तृष्टैषा गौरनाद्या ॥

3. The Brahmin's Vedic knowledge is like a snake, charged with dire poison, clothed with skin. O King, terrible is she, none may destroy her. (1100)[4]

४. निर्वै क्षत्रं नयति हन्ति वर्चोऽग्निरिवारब्धो वि दुनोति सर्वम् ।
यो ब्राह्मणं मन्यते अन्नमेव स विषस्य पिबति तैमातस्य ॥

4. He, who counts the Brahman's property as mere food to feed him, drinks poison of the deadly serpent, loses his strength, mars his splendour, and ruins everything like fire enkindled. (1101)

५. य एनं हन्ति मृदुं मन्यमानो देवपीयुर्धनकामो न चित्तात् ।
सं तस्येन्द्रो हृदयेऽग्निमिन्ध उभे एनं द्विष्टो नभसी चरन्तम् ॥

5. Whoever, inimical to the learned, coveting wealth, foolishly smites a Brahman, deeming him a weakling-God sets fire alight within his bosom. He who acts thus is loathed by the denizens of both Earth and Sun. (1102)[5]

६. न ब्राह्मणो हिंसितव्योऽग्निः प्रियतनोरिव ।
सोमो ह्यस्य दायाद इन्द्रो अस्याभिशस्तिपाः ॥

[1]In a country where there is paucity of learned persons, milch-kine and strong bulls become extinct.

[2]Brahman: A learned person who knows the Vedas.

[3]A king who is opposed to the spread of Vedic knowledge cannot enjoy a long life.

[4]She and her, refer to Vedic knowledge.

[5]The inhabitants of the Earth and Sun hate such a man, just as there are living beings on the Earth, so are they on the Sun.

6. A Brahmin, dear as fire to the body, must not be injured, for God is his Friend, and He guards him from infamy. (1103)

७. शतापाष्ठां नि गिरति तां न शक्नोति निःखिदन् ।
अन्नं यो ब्रह्मणां मल्वः स्वाद्व१द्मीति मन्यते ॥

7. A mean fellow, who snatches the Brahman's food and thinks it pleasant to the taste, falls a prey to manifold calamities, and cannot overcome them in spite of his best efforts. (1104)

८. जिह्वा ज्या भवति कुल्मलं वाङ्नाडीका दन्तास्तपसाभिदिग्धाः ।
तेभिर्ब्रह्मा विध्यति देवपीयून् हृद्बलैर्धनुर्भिर्देवजूतैः ॥

8. His tongue acts as a bow-string, his voice an arrow's neck, his teeth sharpened through penance act as heads of arrows. With these the Brahman pierces through blasphemers, with god-sped bows that quell the hearts. (1105)

९. तीक्ष्णेषवो ब्राह्मणा हेतिमन्तो यामस्यन्ति शरव्यां३ न सा मृषा ।
अनुहाय तपसा मन्युना चोत दूरादव भिन्दन्त्येनम् ॥

9. The Brahmans equipped with sharp arrows, armed with missiles, discharge the round of shafts, which never faileth. Pursuing the enemy with fiery zeal and righteous indignation, they pierce him even from a distance. (1106)

१०. ये सहस्रमराजन्नासन् दशशता उत । ते ब्राह्मणस्य गां जग्ध्वा वैतहव्याः पराभवन् ॥

10. They who, robbed the sages of their foodstuffs, and were the rulers of a thousand men, themselves numbering ten hundred, were finally vanquished as they destroyed the knowledge of a Vedic scholar. (1107)[1]

११. गौरेव तान् हन्यमाना वैतहव्याँ अवातिरत् । ये केसरप्राबन्धायाश्चरमाजामपेचिरन् ॥

11. The knowledge of a Vedic scholar, being destroyed, overthrows the wicked persons, who rob the sages of their foodstuffs and harm God's universal knowledge of the Vedas. (1108)[2]

१२. एकशतं ता जनता या भूमिर्व्यधूनुत । प्रजां हिंसित्वा ब्राह्मणीमसंभव्यं पराभवन् ॥

12. One and a hundred stains of the state are the persons, whom the Mother Earth shakes off from her. They, harming the progeny of the Brahman, perish in conceivably. (1109)

१३. देवपीयुश्चरति मर्त्येषु गरगीर्णो भवत्यस्थिभूयान् ।
यो ब्राह्मणं देवबन्धुं हिनस्ति न स पितृयाणमप्येति लोकम् ॥

[1]Griffith considers Vaitahavyas as a tribe or people in the north; literally, descendants of Vītahavya, a Rishi. This explanation is unacceptable, as there is no history in the Vedas. The word means, the persons who rob the sages of their foodstuffs.

They who destroy, burn the library of a Vedic scholar are finally ruined.

[2]Griffith considers Kesaraprābandhā to be a woman. The word means God, Who resides in the soul and full of the joy of salvation.

13. The despiser of the learned moveth among mankind: he hath drunk poison, naught but bone is left him, who wrongs the Brahman, the lover of God, gains not the sphere attained by the ancestors. (1110)[1]

१४. अग्निर्वै नः पदवायः सोमो दायाद उच्यते । हन्ताभिशस्तेन्द्रस्तथा तद् वेधसो विदुः ॥

14. God, in sooth, is our Guide. God is known as the Bestower of all riches, God quells him who curses us. Sages know well that this is so. (1111)

१५. इषुरिव दिग्धा नृपते पृदाकूरिव गोपते । सा ब्राह्मणस्येषुर्घोरा तया विध्यति पीयतः ॥

15. O King, like a poisoned arrow, like a deadly snake, O lord of land! Dire is the Brahman's arrow-like strong determination, wherewith he pierces his enemies. (1112)

HYMN XIX

१. अतिमात्रमवर्धन्त नोदिव दिवमस्पृशन् । भृगुं हिंसित्वा सृञ्जया वैतहव्याः पराभवन् ॥

1. Vanquishers of foes, robbers of the foodstuffs of sages, not only wax exceeding strong, but even having attained to great eminence are finally overthrown, when they wrong a learned scholar. (1113)[2]

२. ये बृहत्सामानमाङ्गिरसमार्पयन् ब्राह्मणं जनाः । पेत्वस्तेषामुभयादमविस्तोकान्यावयत् ॥

2. Those persons, who torment a highly learned and celibate Brahman, get their progeny crushed with the teeth between the jaws of God, Who is the Guardian and Protector. (1114)[3]

३. ये ब्राह्मणं प्रत्यष्ठीवन् ये वास्मिन्छुल्कमीषिरे ।
अस्नस्ते मध्ये कुल्यायाः केशान् खादन्त आसते ॥

3. They, who dishonour a Brahmin, or snatch his money, ever fall a prey to afflictions, in the middle of a stream running with blood. (1115)[4]

४. ब्रह्मगवी पच्यमाना यावत् साभि विजङ्गहे ।
तेजो राष्ट्रस्य निर्हन्ति न वीरो जायते वृषा ॥

4. Where the knowledge of the Vedas is suppressed and kept in suspense for long, there it mars the kingdom's splendour, there no vigorous hero springs to life. (1116)

[1]Sphere: The eminent spiritual height.

[2]Bhrigu, Srinjayas, Vitahavya are not Proper Nouns, as Griffith considers. 'Bhrigu' means, a learned scholar. 'Srinjayas' means the vanquishers of foes. 'Vitahavyas' means persons who rob the sages of their foodstuffs.

[3]Earth and Heaven are figuratively spoken of as the jaws of God. He punishes all ignoble persons living between the Earth and Heaven.

[4]Persons who show disrespect to a Brahmin or rob him of his money, suffer calamity through bloodshed.

५. क्रूरमस्या आशसनं तृष्टं पिशितमस्यते। क्षीरं यदस्याः पीयते तद् वै पितृषु किल्बिषम् ॥

5. Suppression of Vedic knowledge is a sinful act, its refutation is painful like thirst. Violation of its didactic teachings is counted sin for the rulers of a state. (1117)

६. उग्रो राजा मन्यमानो ब्राह्मणं यो जिघत्सति। परा तत् सिच्यते राष्ट्रं ब्राह्मणो यत्र जीयते ॥

6. Rent and disrupted is that realm, where a king deeming himself mighty wants to harm a Vedic scholar or where a knower of the Vedas is suppressed. (1118)

७. अष्टापदी चतुरक्षी चतुःश्रोत्रा चतुर्हनुः।
द्व्यास्या द्विजिह्वा भूत्वा सा राष्ट्रमव धूनुते ब्रह्मज्यस्य ॥

7. Vedic knowledge grows eight-footed, and four-eyed, four-eared, four-jawed, two-faced, two-tongued, and shatters down the kingdom of the man, who doth wrong to a Vedic scholar. (1119)[1]

८. तद् वै राष्ट्रमा स्रवति नावं भिन्नामिवोदकम्।
ब्रह्माणं यत्र हिंसन्ति तद् राष्ट्रं हन्ति दुच्छुना ॥

8. Misfortune smites the realm wherein a learned person suffers harm and dishonour. As water swamps a leaky boat so ruin overflows that realm. (1120)

९. तं वृक्षा अप सेधन्ति छायां नो मोपगा इति। यो ब्राह्मणस्य सद्धनमभि नारद मन्यते ॥

9. The very trees repel the man, and drive him from their sheltering shade, whoever claims. O King, the treasure that a learned person owns. (1121)[2]

१०. विषमेतद् देवकृतं राजा वरुणोऽब्रवीत्। न ब्राह्मणस्य गां जग्ध्वा राष्ट्रे जागार कश्चन ॥

10. Venerable God hath declared in the Vedas, the property of a Vedic scholar is a kind of poison, prepared by the sages. He who usurps that cannot remain alive in the state. (1122)[3]

११. नवैव ता नवतयो या भूमिर्व्यधूनुत। प्रजां हिंसित्वा ब्राह्मणीमसंभव्यं पराभवन् ॥

[1]Eight feet: (1) Simplicity (2) Brevity (3) Attainment (4) Independence (5) Grandeur (6) Superiority (7) Self-control (8) True determination. Four eyes: Brahman, Kshatriya, Vaisha, Shudra. Four ears: Brahmcharya, Grihastha, Bānprastha, Sanyāsa. Four jaws: Dharma, Artha, Kāma, Moksha. Two faces: God, soul. Two tongues: Worldly and spiritual joy.

[2]Nārada is mentioned by Griffith as a saint of the celestial class who often comes down to earth to report what is going on in heaven and return with his account of what is being done on earth. This explanation is unacceptable, as it savours of history in the Vedas. The word means a king, the leader of men.

[3]The property of a Vedic scholar is sacred, and should not be touched by any one. Just as poison, if taken kills a man, so the man who usurps the property of a scholar is liable to be punished with death by a king.

11. Innumerable are the sinners whom Earth destroys. When they wrong the progeny of a Vedic scholar, they are ruined inconceivably. (1123)[1]

१२. यां मृतायानुबध्नन्ति कूद्यं पदयोपनीम् । तद् वै ब्रह्मज्य ते देवा उपस्तरणमब्रुवन् ॥

12. O Oppressor of Vedic scholars, the thorny fetter, painful to the feet, fastened to punish a culprit to death has been declared by the sages as thy couch. (1124)[2]

१३. अश्रूणि कृपमाणस्य यानि जीतस्य वावृतुः । तं वै ब्रह्मज्य ते देवा अपां भागमधारयन् ॥

13. O Oppressor of learned personsl tears shed by the man who suffers wrong and defeat, these are the share of water which the sages have destined to be thine. (1125)[3]

१४. येन मृतं स्नपयन्ति श्मश्रूणि येनोन्दते । तं वै ब्रह्मज्य ते देवा अपां भागमधारयन् ॥

14. O Oppressor of the learned the share of water which the sages have destined to be thine, is that, wherewith men lave the corpse and wet his beard. (1126)[4]

१५. न वर्षं मैत्रावरुणं ब्रह्मज्यमभि वर्षति । नास्मै समितिः कल्पते न मित्रं नयते वशम् ॥

15. In a country where learned persons are oppressed, the rain produced by the air and sun does not fall. In his country the Assembly does not function successfully, he wins no friend to do his will. (1127)[5]

HYMN XX

१. उच्चैर्घोषो दुन्दुभिः सत्वनायन् वानस्पत्यः संभृत उस्रियाभिः ।
वाचं क्षुणुवानो दमयन्त्सपत्नान्त्सिंह इव जेष्यन्नभि तंस्तनीहि ॥

1. May the loud War-drum, playing the part of a hero, bequeathed by the commanders, preserved by the armies, whetting its voice and vanquishing opponents, roar at them like a lion fain to conquer. (1128)

२. सिंह इवास्तानीद् द्रुवयो विबद्धोऽभिक्रन्दन्नृषभो वासितामिव ।
वृषा त्वं वध्रयस्ते सपत्ना ऐन्द्रस्ते शुष्मो अभिमातिषाहः ॥

2. Thou, made of wood, tightly fastened, roarest as it were a lion like a bull bellowing to meet the heifer. Thou art powerful, thine enemies are weaklings thine is the foe-subduing mighty strength! (1129)[6]

[1]नव नवतिः (9+90) or (9+90) i.e., innumerable.

[2]An oppressor of learned persons should be punished to lie on thorny fetters.

[3]An oppressor of learned persons deserves to be given for drinking the water derived from the tears of a distressed by way of punishment.

[4]An oppressor deserves to be given for drinking the water, wherewith the corpse is bathed or his beard is washed.

[5]'He, his' refer to an oppressor.

[6]'Thou' refers to the war-drum. In these verses a king is spoken of as a war-drum, as he roars loudly like the war-drum.

३. वृषेव यूथे सहसा विदानो गव्यन्नभि रुव संधनाजित् ।
शुचा विध्य हृदयं परेषां हित्वा ग्रामान् प्रच्युता यन्तु शत्रवः ॥

3. Just as a bull seeking kine, is suddenly recognised among the herd of cattle, so roar thou, O War-drum (king) willing to win wealth, pierce through our adversaries hearts with sorrow, and let our routed foes desert their hamlets. (1130)

४. संजयन् पृतना ऊर्ध्वमायुर्गृह्या गृह्णानो बहुधा वि चक्ष्व ।
दैवीं वाचं दुन्दुभ आ गुरस्व वेधाः शत्रूणामुप भरस्व वेदः ॥

4. Victorious in the battle, loudly roaring, seizing what may be seized, keep watch all around thee. Utter, O King, thy divine voice with triumph. Bring, as a master-mind, our enemies possessions. (1131)

५. दुन्दुभेर्वाचं प्रयतां वदन्तीमाशृण्वती नाथिता घोषबुद्धा ।
नारी पुत्रं धावतु हस्तगृह्यामित्री भीता समरे वधानाम् ॥

5. Hearing the Drum's far-reaching, resounding voice, let the foe's dame, waked by the roar, afflicted grasping her son, run forward, being afraid of the murders in the battle. (1132)

६. पूर्वो दुन्दुभे प्र वदासि वाचं भूम्याः पृष्ठे वद रोचमानः ।
अमित्रसेनामभिजञ्जभानो द्युमद् वद दुन्दुभे सूनृतावत् ॥

6. O Drum, thou art sounded before the commencement of the battle. O king, thou proclaimest thy orders in the world, speak forth exultantly. Crunching with might the army of the foemen, declare thy message pleasantly and clearly. (1133)

७. अन्तरेमे नभसी घोषो अस्तु पृथक् ते ध्वनयो यन्तु शीभम् ।
अभि क्रन्द स्तनयोत्पिपानः श्लोककृन्मित्रतूर्याय स्वर्धी ॥

7. Loud be thy roar between the earth and heaven swift let thy sounds go forth in all directions. Ye, full of significance; singing praises, roar and thunder, and act as a good ally for the conquest of friends. (1134)[1]

८. धीभिः कृतः प्र वदाति वाचमुद्धर्षय सत्वनामायुधानि ।
इन्द्रमेदी सत्वनो नि ह्वयस्व मित्रैरमित्राँ अव जङ्घनीहि ॥

8. The drum fashioned by skilled artisans sends forth its voice. O drum, make thou the weapons of our warriors bristle. With the Commander-in-chief as thy ally, call out our heroes to the battlefield, and with thy friends scatter and chase the foemen! (1135)

[1]'Thy, ye' refer to the war-drum.

९. संक्रन्दनः प्रवदो धृष्णुषेणः प्रवेदकृद् बहुधा ग्रामघोषी ।
श्रेयो वन्वानो वयुनानि विद्वान् कीर्तिं बहुभ्यो वि हर द्विराजे ।।

9. O King, roaring, issuing important orders, possessing a powerful army, acquiring knowledge and wealth, sending thy message to the army in diverse ways, knowing the rules of warfare, winning advantage, bring fame to many warriors where two kings are fighting! (1136)

१०. श्रेयःकेतो वसुजित् सहीयान्त्संग्रामजित् संशितो ब्रह्मणासि ।
अंशूनिव ग्रावाधिषवणे अद्रिर्गव्यन् दुन्दुभेऽधि नृत्य वेदः ।।

10. O drum or King bent on advantage, mightier, gaining treasures, victor in war, knowledge hath made thee keener. Just as determined, far-seeing learned person, masters the finer aspects of things in his search after truth, so shouldst thou, hankering after victory, possess the foes' property! (1137)

११. शत्रूषाण्नीषाडभिमातिषाहो गवेषणः सहमान उद्भित् ।
वाग्वीव मन्त्रं प्र भरस्व वाचं सांग्रामजित्यायेषमुद् वदेह ।।

11. O King, foe-conqueror, ever-victor, vanquishing opponents, seeker after knowledge and land, mastering, destroying the foes, utter nice words, as a skilled speaker does in the Assembly. In this war, announce thy order, so that we may win the battle! (1138)

१२. अच्युतच्युत् समदो गमिष्ठो मृधो जेता पुरएतायोध्यः ।
इन्द्रेण गुप्तो विदथा निचिक्यद्धृद्द्योतनो द्विषतां याहि शीभम् ।।

12. O King, the shaker of the unshaken foes, readiest comer to battles, conqueror of foes, resistless leader, guarded by the Commander-in-chief, knower of the secrets of warfare, breaker of the hearts of those who hate us, go quickly to the war-front. (1139)

HYMN XXI

१. विहृदयं वैमनस्यं वदामित्रेषु दुन्दुभे ।
विद्वेषं कश्मशं भयममित्रेषु नि दध्मस्यवैनान् दुन्दुभे जहि ।।

1. Preach to our enemies, O King, discouragement and wild dismay. We bring upon our foemen fear, discord and discomfiture. O King, drive these enemies away! (1140)

२. उद्वेपमाना मनसा चक्षुषा हृदयेन च । धावन्तु बिभ्यतोऽमित्राः प्रत्रासेनाज्ये हुते ।।

2. When once the furious fire of battle has flared up, let our foemen flee, through consternation, terrified, trembling in mind and eye and heart. (1141)[1]

[1]When once the oblation of butter is put into the fire, it blazes up, so when once the first shot of gun is fired, the battle-fire flares up, तेजो वा आज्यम् । तै० 3-9-4-6. The fervour of a king is आज्य butter in a battle.

३. वानस्पत्यः संभृत उस्रियाभिर्विश्वगोत्र्यः । प्रत्रासममित्रेभ्यो वदाज्येनाभिघारितः ।।

3. O King, full of power like the sun, fortified with forces, dear to all clans, blazing with dignity and arms, preach terror to our armies. (1142)

४. यथा मृगाः संविजन्त आरण्याः पुरुषादधि ।
एवा त्वं दुन्दुभेऽमित्रानभि क्रन्द प्र त्रासयाथो चित्तानि मोहय ।।

4. As the wild creatures of the wood flee in their terror from a huntsman, even so do thou, O king, roar out against our foes to frighten them, and then bewilder thou their thoughts. (1143)

५. यथा वृकादजावयो धावन्ति बहु बिभ्यतीः ।
एवा त्वं दुन्दुभेऽमित्रानभि क्रन्द प्र त्रासयाथो चित्तानि मोहय ।।

5. As when the wolf approaches goats and sheep run away terrified, even so do thou, O Drum or King, roar out against our foes to frighten them, and then bewilder thou their thoughts. (1144)

६. यथा श्येनात् पतत्रिणः संविजन्ते अहर्दिवि सिंहस्य स्तनथोर्यथा ।
एवा त्वं दुन्दुभेऽमित्रानभि क्रन्द प्र त्रासयाथो चित्तानि मोहय ।।

6. As birds of air, day after day, fly in a wild terror from the hawk, as from a roaring lion's voice, even so do thou, O Drum or a hero, roar out against our foes to frighten them, and then bewilder thou their thoughts. (1145)

७. परामित्रान् दुन्दुभिना हरिणस्याजिनेन च । सर्वे देवा अतित्रसन् ये संग्रामस्येशते ।।

7. May all the learned persons who are experts in the art of warfare, defeat and frighten away our enemies with Drum made of the skin of an antelope. (1146)

८. यैरिन्द्रः प्रक्रीडते पद्घोषैश्छायया सह । तैरमित्रास्त्रसन्तु नोऽमी ये यन्त्यनीकशः ।।

8. Let those our enemies who go yonder in battalions shake in fear at shadows and the sounds of feet which the Commander-in-chief sporteth with. (1147)[1]

९. ज्याघोषा दुन्दुभयोऽभि क्रोशन्तु या दिशः । सेनाः पराजिता यतीरमित्राणामनीकशः ।।

9. To all the quarters of the sky let clang of bow-strings and our Drums, cry out to hosts of foes, that go discomfited in serried ranks. (1148)

१०. आदित्य चक्षुरा दत्स्व मरीचयोऽनु धावत । पत्सङ्गिनीरा सजन्तु विगते बाहुवीर्ये ।।

10. O Commander-in-chief blazing like the sun, take their sight away! O soldiers fast like rays, follow them close! When their strength of arms hath faded, let their feet be fastened with fetters. (1149)

[1]The enemy is likely to be terrified hearing the sounds of feet and seeing the shadow of innumerable warriors marching against him.

११. यूयमुग्रा मरुतः पृश्निमातर इन्द्रेण युजा प्र मृणीत शत्रून् ।
सोमो राजा वरुणो राजा महादेव उत मृत्युरिन्द्रः ॥

11. O mighty warriors, who measure heaven in aerial flights, crush down our foemen, with Commander-in-chief as your supporter! The dignified Commander, is the solver of all intricate military problems, full of splendour, an excellent ruler, and a terrible lord like Death. (1150)

१२. एता देवसेनाः सूर्यकेतवः सचेतसः । अमित्रान् नो जयन्तु स्वाहा ॥

12. May these forces of the victorious commander, brilliant like the rays of the sun, one-minded, conquer our foes. This is our resolve for conquest. (1151)

HYMN XXII

१. अग्निस्तक्मानमप बाधतामितः सोमो ग्रावा वरुणः पूतदक्षाः ।
वेदिर्बर्हिः समिधः शोशुचाना अप द्वेषांस्यमुया भवन्तु ॥

1. Hence, let a learned, discriminating, far-seeing, venerable physician, possessing healing power, brilliant like the glowing fuel, banish fever. Let all hateful things stay at a distance yonder. (1152)

२. अयं यो विश्वान् हरितान् कृणोष्युच्छोचयन्नग्निरिवाभिदुन्वन् ।
अधा हि तक्मन्नरसो हि भूया अधा न्यङ्ङधराङ् व परेहि ॥

2. And thou thyself which makest all men pale, consuming them with burning heat like fire, thou, Fever! then be weak and ineffective. Pass hence into the places below or vanish. (1153)

३. यः परुषः पारुषेयोऽवध्वंस इवारुणः । तक्मानं विश्वधावीर्याधराञ्चं परा सुव ॥

3. O all powerful physician! send downward, far away, the fever, which is virulent, born out of violation of the laws of nature, and consumes the body like fire. (1154)

४. अधराञ्चं प्र हिणोमि नमः कृत्वा तक्मने । शकम्भरस्य मुष्टिहा पुनरेतु महावृषान् ॥

4. I lower the fever through medicine and drive it away. It is suppressed by vegetarians, and visits the marshy places again and again. (1155)[1]

५. ओको अस्य मूजवन्त ओको अस्य महावृषाः ।
यावज्जातस्तक्मंस्तावानसि बल्हिकेषु न्योचरः ॥

5. Grassy places are its home. Marshy places are its home. O fever, since thy birth, thou gradually overtakest the able-bodied persons. (1156)[2]

[1]'I' refers to a physician.

[2]Griffith interprets Mājavans a hill tribe in the north-west of India, Mahāvishas, as a people in the same region. He interprets Bahlikas: as a Bactrian race, the people of Balkh. This interpretation is wrong, as it savours of history. 'Majāvans' means grassy places. 'Mahavrishas' means marshy places. 'Bahlikas' means able-bodied persons. Fever resides in grassy and marshy places, due to the multiplicity of mosquitoes.

६. तक्मन् व्याल वि गद व्यङ्ग भूरि यावय । दासीं निष्टक्वरीमिच्छ तां वज्रेण समर्पय ॥

6. O Fever, poisonous like a snake, virulent in nature, deformer of the body, keep thyself far away from us. Thou longest for the fever-spreading and biting race of mosquitoes, and strengthenest it with thy deadly venom. (1157)

७. तक्मन् मूजवतो गच्छ बल्हिकान् वा परस्तराम् ।
शूद्रामिच्छ प्रफर्व्यं तां तक्मन् वीव धूनुहि ॥

7. O Fever, thou attackest first the weak, and then the strong, even stronger persons. Long for the young biting race of mosquitoes, and make it ever restless. (1158)[1]

८. महावृषान् मूजवतो बन्ध्वद्धि परेत्य । प्रैतानि तक्मने ब्रूमो अन्यक्षेत्राणि वा इमा ॥

8. Go hence and eat thy kinsmen in grassy and marshy places. These and those foreign regions we proclaim to Fever for its home. (1159)

९. अन्यक्षेत्रे न रमसे वशी सन् मृडयासि नः । अभूदु प्रार्थस्तक्मा स गमिष्यति बल्हिकान् ॥

9. Fever, thou joyest not in a body, other than that of a human being, subdued, thou wilt be kind to us. When thou becomest powerful, thou attackest even the able-bodied persons! (1160)

१०. यत् त्वं शीतोऽथो रूरः सह कासावेपयः ।
भीमास्ते तक्मन् हेतयस्ताभिः स्म परि वृङ्ग्धि नः ॥

10. Since thou now cold, now burning hot, with cough besides, hast made us shake, terrible, Fever are thy darts: forbear to injure us with these. (1161)

११. मा स्मैतान्त्सखीन् कुरुथा बलासं कासमुद्युगम् ।
मा स्मातोऽर्वाङैः पुनस्तत् त्वा तक्मन्नुप ब्रुवे ॥

11. Take none of these to be thy friends, cough, or consumption, or a wasting disease: never come thence again to us, O Fever, thus I counsel thee. (1162)

१२. तक्मन् भ्रात्रा बलासेन स्वस्रा कासिकया सह । पाप्मा भ्रातृव्येण सह गच्छामुमरणं जनम् ॥

12. Go, Fever, with consumption, thy brother, and with thy sister, cough, and with thy nephew Herpes, go away unto that despicable person. (1163)[2]

१३. तृतीयकं वितृतीयं सदन्दिमुत शारदम् । तक्मानं शीतं रूरं ग्रैष्मं नाशय वार्षिकम् ॥

13. O physician, chase Fever whether cold or hot, brought by the summer or the rains, tertian, intermittent, or autumnal, or continual! (1164)

[1]Mosquitoes being restless fly and bite the people injecting poison in them.
[2]Fever and other diseases attack a dirty, mean fellow.

१४. गन्धारिभ्यो मूजवद्भ्योऽङ्गेभ्यो मगधेभ्यः । प्रैष्यन् जनमिव शेवधिं तक्मानं परि दद्मसि ॥

14. Just as a person is sent from one country to another, or treasurer is transferred from one person to another, so we hand over Fever to the dirty, physically weak, inabstemious and servile persons. (1165)[1]

HYMN XXIII

१. ओते मे द्यावापृथिवी ओता देवी सरस्वती ।
ओतौ म इन्द्रश्चाग्निश्च क्रिमिं जम्भयतामिति ॥

1. Sun and Earth are interwoven for me, divine knowledge is meant for me, electricity and fire are intermingled for me. May these destroy the worms. This is my prayer. (1166)[2]

२. अस्येन्द्र कुमारस्य क्रिमीन् धनपते जहि । हता विश्वा अरातय उग्रेण वचसा मम ॥

2. O opulent physician, kill the worms that prey upon this boy. All the malignant worms have been smitten by my potent Vedic word. (1167)

३. यो अक्ष्यौ परिसर्पति यो नासे परिसर्पति । दतां यो मध्यं गच्छति तं क्रिमिं जम्भयामसि ॥

3. We utterly destroy the worm that creeps around the eyes, the worm that crawls about the nose, the worm that gets between the teeth. (1168)

४. सरूपौ द्वौ विरूपौ द्वौ कृष्णौ द्वौ रोहितौ द्वौ । बभ्रुश्च बभ्रुकर्णश्च गृध्रः कोकश्च ते हताः ॥

4. Two worms of like colour, two unlike, two coloured black, two coloured red; the tawny and the tawny-eared worm, vulture and wolf all have been killed. (1169)[3]

५. ये क्रिमयः शितिकक्षा ये कृष्णाः शितिबाहवः ।
ये के च विश्वरूपास्तान् क्रिमीन् जम्भयामसि ॥

5. Worms that are white-flanked, those that are black, and those with white-hued arms, all that show various tints and hues, these worms we utterly destroy. (1170)

६. उत् पुरस्तात् सूर्य एति विश्वदृष्टो अदृष्टहा ।
दृष्टांश्चघ्नन्नदृष्टांश्च सर्वांश्च प्रमृणन् क्रिमीन् ॥

6. Eastward the Sun is rising, seen of all, destroying worms unseen, crushing and killing all the worms visible and invisible. (1171)

[1]Fever attacks persons, who are dirty, physically weak, irregular in life, and dependent for their livelihood on their masters. Griffith considers Gandharis to be the inhabitants of Ghandāra, a country to the west of the Indus and to the south of Kabul river. At present it is named Kandhāra. Angas and Maghadas are mentioned by Griffith as tribes living in south Bihar and the country bordering it on the west. This explanation is unacceptable, as it says about history, from which the Vedas are free.

[2]The rays of the sun, fire, electricity, knowledge, destroy the worms.

[3]Vulture and wolf: Worms ferocious in nature like the vulture and wolf.

७. येवाषासः कष्कषास एजत्काः शिपवित्नुकाः । दृष्टश्च हन्यतां क्रिमिरुतादृष्टश्च हन्यताम् ।।

7. Let the fast-moving, highly painful, shining, trembling, and injurious worms, let both the worm that we can see, and that we see not, be destroyed. (1172)

८. हतो येवाषः क्रिमीणां हतो नदनिमोत । सर्वान् नि मष्मषाकरं दृषदा खल्वाँ इव ।।

8. Slain the fast-moving of the worms, slain too is the crying worm. I have reduced them all to dust like vetches with the pounding-stone. (1173)[1]

९. त्रिशीर्षाणं त्रिककुदं क्रिमिं सारङ्गमर्जुनम् । शृणाम्यस्य पृष्टीरपि वृश्चामि यच्छिरः ।।

9. The spotted worm, white of hue, three-headed, with a triple hump, I split and tear his ribs away, I wrench off every head he has. (1174)[2]

१०. अत्रिवद् वः क्रिमयो हन्मि कण्ववज्जमदग्निवत् । अगस्त्यस्य ब्रह्मणा सं पिनष्म्यहं क्रिमीन् ।।

10. I kill you worms, like fire, air and sun. I crush the worms to pieces with the Vedic knowledge of God. (1175)[3]

११. हतो राजा क्रिमीणामुतैषां स्थपतिर्हतः । हतो हतमाता क्रिमिर्हतभ्राता हतस्वसा ।।

11. The king of worms hath been destroyed, he who was lord of these is slain. Slain is the worm whose mother, whose brother and sister have been slain. (1176)

१२. हतासो अस्य वेशसो हतासः परिवेशसः । अथो ये क्षुल्लका इव सर्वे ते क्रिमयो हताः ।।

12. Destroyed are his dependants, those who dwell around him are destroyed. All the worms, that seem to be the little ones are done to death. (1177)

१३. सर्वेषां च क्रिमीणां सर्वासां च क्रिमीणाम् । भिनद्म्यश्मना शिरो दहाम्यग्निना मुखम् ।।

13. Of every worm and insect, of the female and the male alike, I crush the head to pieces with a stone and burn the face with fire. (1178)

HYMN XXIV

१. सविता प्रसवानामधिपतिः स मावतु । अस्मिन् ब्रह्मण्यस्मिन् कर्मण्यस्यां पुरोधायामस्यां
प्रतिष्ठायामस्यां चित्त्यामस्यामाकूत्यामस्यामाशिष्यस्यां देवहूत्यां स्वाहा ।।

[1] 'I' refers to the physician.

[2] 'I' refers to the physician.

[3] Atri, Kanva and Jamadagni and Agastya, are not proper nouns. They are not the names of Rishis. Atri means fire, Kanya means air, Jamadagni means the sun. Agastya means God. Just as fire, air and sun kill worms, so does a physician with his Vedic knowledge.

1. God is the Lord of all created objects. May He protect me, in this my study of the Vedas, in this duty of mine, in this my sacerdotal charge, in this noble performance, in this meditation, in this my resolve and determination, in this administration, in this assembly of the learned. May this noble prayer of mine be fulfilled. (1179)

२. अग्निर्वनस्पतीनामधिपतिः स मावतु । अस्मिन् ब्रह्मण्यस्मिन् कर्मण्यस्यां पुरोधायामस्यां प्रतिष्ठायामस्यां चित्त्यामस्यामाकूत्यामस्यामाशिष्यस्यां देवहूत्यां स्वाहा ॥

2. Just as fire is the Lord of forest trees, so is God, the Lord of souls. May He protect me, in this my study of the Vedas, in this duty of mine, in this my sacerdotal charge, in this noble-performance, in this meditation, in this my resolve and determination, in this administration, in this assembly of the learned. May this noble prayer of mine be fulfilled. (1180)

३. द्यावापृथिवी दातॄणामधिपत्नी ते मावताम् । अस्मिन् ब्रह्मण्यस्मिन् कर्मण्यस्यां पुरोधायामस्यां प्रतिष्ठायामस्यां चित्त्यामस्यामाकूत्यामस्यामाशिष्यस्यां देवहूत्यां स्वाहा ॥

3. May Heaven and Earth, the queens of bounties protect me, in this my study of the Vedas, in this duty of mine, in this my sacerdotal charge, in this noble performance, in this meditation, in this my resolve and determination, in this administration, in this assembly of the learned. May this noble prayer of mine be fulfilled. (1181)

४. वरुणोऽपामधिपतिः स मावतु । अस्मिन् ब्रह्मण्यस्मिन् कर्मण्यस्यां पुरोधायामस्यां प्रतिष्ठायामस्यां चित्त्यामस्यामाकूत्यामस्यामाशिष्यस्यां देवहूत्यां स्वाहा ॥

4. Just as Ocean is the lord of waters, so is God the Lord of worlds and His subjects. May He protect me, in this my study of the Vedas, in this duty of mine, in this my sacerdotal charge, in this noble performance, in this meditation, in this my resolve and determination, in this administration, in this assembly of the learned. May this noble prayer of mine be fulfilled. (1182)

५. मित्रावरुणौ वृष्ट्या अधिपती तौ मावताम् । अस्मिन् ब्रह्मण्यस्मिन् कर्मण्यस्यां पुरोधायामस्यां प्रतिष्ठायामस्यां चित्त्यामस्यामाकूत्यामस्यामाशिष्यस्यां देवहूत्यां स्वाहा ॥

5. May Sun and Ocean, lords of rain, preserve me, in this my study of the Vedas, in this duty of mine, in this my sacerdotal charge, in this noble performance, in this meditation, in this my resolve and determination, in this administration, in this assembly of the learned. May this noble prayer of mine be fulfilled. (1183)

६. मरुतः पर्वतानामधिपतयस्ते मावन्तु । अस्मिन् ब्रह्मण्यस्मिन् कर्मण्यस्यां पुरोधायामस्यां प्रतिष्ठायामस्यां चित्त्यामस्यामाकूत्यामस्यामाशिष्यस्यां देवहूत्यां स्वाहा ॥

6. Lords of the mountains, may the airs preserve me, in this my study of the Vedas, in this duty of mine, in this my sacerdotal charge, in this noble

performance, in this meditation, in this my resolve and determination, in this administration, in this assembly of the learned. May this noble prayer of mine be fulfilled. (1184)[1]

७. सोमो वीरुधामधिपतिः स मावतु । अस्मिन् ब्रह्मण्यस्मिन् कर्मण्यस्यां पुरोधायामस्यां प्रतिष्ठायामस्यां चित्त्यामस्यामाकूत्यामस्यामाशिष्यस्यां देवहूत्यां स्वाहा ॥

7. Just as Soma is the lord of medicinal plants, so is God, the Lord of His subjects, may He preserve me, in this my study of the Vedas, in this duty of mine, in this my sacerdotal charge, in this noble performance, in this meditation, in this my resolve and determination, in this administration, in this assembly of the learned. May this noble prayer of mine be fulfilled. (1185)

८. वायुरन्तरिक्षस्याधिपतिः स मावतु । अस्मिन् ब्रह्मण्यस्मिन् कर्मण्यस्यां पुरोधायामस्यां प्रतिष्ठायामस्यां चित्त्यामस्यामाकूत्यामस्यामाशिष्यस्यां देवहूत्यां स्वाहा ॥

8. May air, the lord of atmosphere, protect me, in this my study of the Vedas, in the duty of mine, in this my sacerdotal charge, in this noble performance, in this meditation, in this my resolve and determination, in this administration, in this assembly of the learned. May this noble prayer of mine be fulfilled. (1186)

९. सूर्यश्चक्षुषामधिपतिः स मावतु । अस्मिन् ब्रह्मण्यस्मिन् कर्मण्यस्यां पुरोधायामस्यां प्रतिष्ठायामस्यां चित्त्यामस्यामाकूत्यामस्यामाशिष्यस्यां देवहूत्यां स्वाहा ॥

9. Just as the Sun is the lord of eyes, so God is the Lord of our spiritual eyes. May he preserve me, in this my study of the Vedas, in this duty of mine, in this my sacerdotal charge, in this noble performance, in this meditation, in this my resolve and determination, in this administration, in this assembly of the learned. May this noble prayer of mine be fulfilled. (1187)

१०. चन्द्रमा नक्षत्राणामधिपतिः स मावतु । अस्मिन् ब्रह्मण्यस्मिन् कर्मण्यस्यां पुरोधायामस्यां प्रतिष्ठायामस्यां चित्त्यामस्यामाकूत्यामस्यामाशिष्यस्यां देवहूत्यां स्वाहा ॥

10. Just as the Moon is the lord of constellation, so God is the Lord of His subjects. May He preserve me, in this my study of the Vedas, in this duty of mine, in this my sacerdotal charge, in this noble performance, in this meditation, in this my resolve and determination, in this administration, in this assembly of the learned. (1188)

११. इन्द्रो दिवोऽधिपतिः स मावतु । अस्मिन् ब्रह्मण्यस्मिन् कर्मण्यस्यां पुरोधायामस्यां प्रतिष्ठायामस्यां चित्त्यामस्यामाकूत्यामस्यामाशिष्यस्यां देवहूत्यां स्वाहा ॥

11. Just as the sun is the lord of heaven, so is God the Lord of luminous suns. May He preserve me, in this my study of the Vedas, in this duty of mine, in this my sacerdotal charge, in this noble performance, in this meditation, in this my resolve and determination, in this administration, in this assembly of the learned. May this noble prayer of mine be fulfilled. (1189)

[1]Air is the lord of mountains as it takes rain to their top with its strength and velocity.

१२. मरुतां पिता पशूनामधिपतिः स मावतु । अस्मिन् ब्रह्मण्यस्मिन् कर्मण्यस्यां पुरोधायामस्यां
प्रतिष्ठायामस्यां चित्त्यामस्यामाकूत्यामस्यामाशिष्यस्यां देवहूत्यां स्वाहा ॥

12. The Guardian of gold is the preserver of souls. May He preserve me, in this my study of the Vedas, in this duty of mine, in this my sacerdotal charge, in this noble performance, in this meditation, in this my resolve and determination, in this administration, in this assembly of the learned. May this noble prayer of mine be fulfilled. (1190)[1]

१३. मृत्युः प्रजानामधिपतिः स मावतु । अस्मिन् ब्रह्मण्यस्मिन् कर्मण्यस्यां पुरोधायामस्यां
प्रतिष्ठायामस्यां चित्त्यामस्यामाकूत्यामस्यामाशिष्यस्यां देवहूत्यां स्वाहा ॥

13. Just as Death is the lord of all living creatures, so God is the Lord of all mortals. May He preserve me, in this my study of the Vedas, in this duty of mine, in this my sacerdotal charge, in this noble performance, in this meditation, in this my resolve and determination, in this assembly of the learned. May this noble prayer of mine be fulfilled. (1191)

१४. यमः पितॄणामधिपतिः स मावतु । अस्मिन् ब्रह्मण्यस्मिन् कर्मण्यस्यां पुरोधायामस्यां
प्रतिष्ठायामस्यां चित्त्यामस्यामाकूत्यामस्यामाशिष्यस्यां देवहूत्यां स्वाहा ॥

14. Just as a Brahmchari is the lord of breaths, or a king, the lord of officials, or soul, the lord of organs, or Sun, the lord of rays, so God is the Guardian of all guardians. May He preserve me, in this my study of the Vedas, in this duty of mine, in this my sacerdotal charge, in this noble performance, in this meditation, in this my resolve and determination, in this administration, in this assembly of the learned. May this noble prayer of mine be fulfilled. (1192)

१५. पितरः परे ते मावन्तु । अस्मिन् ब्रह्मण्यस्मिन् कर्मण्यस्यां पुरोधायामस्यां
प्रतिष्ठायामस्यां चित्त्यामस्यामाकूत्यामस्यामाशिष्यस्यां देवहूत्यां स्वाहा ॥

15. May my illustrious parents preserve me, in this my study of the Vedas, in this duty of mine, in this my sacerdotal charge, in this noble performance, in this meditation, in this my resolve and determination, in this administration, in this assembly of the learned. May this noble prayer of mine be fulfilled. (1193)

१६. तता अवरे ते मावन्तु । अस्मिन् ब्रह्मण्यस्मिन् कर्मण्यस्यां पुरोधायामस्यां
प्रतिष्ठायामस्यां चित्त्यामस्यामाकूत्यामस्यामाशिष्यस्यां देवहूत्यां स्वाहा ॥

16. May my venerable forefathers preserve me, in this my study of the Vedas, in this duty of mine, in this my sacerdotal charge, in this noble performance, in this meditation, in this my resolve and determination, in this administration, in this assembly of the learned. May this noble prayer of mine be fulfilled. (1194)

[1] 'Guardian of gold' means God.

१७. ततस्ततामहास्ते मावन्तु । अस्मिन् ब्रह्मण्यस्मिन् कर्मण्यस्यां पुरोधायामस्यां प्रतिष्ठायामस्यां चित्त्यामस्यामाकूत्यामस्यामाशिष्यस्यां देवहूत्यां स्वाहा ॥

17. May the venerable of venerable persons preserve me, in this my study of the Vedas, in this duty of mine, in this my sacerdotal charge, in this noble performance, in this meditation, in this my resolve and determination, in this administration, in this assembly of the learned. May this noble prayer of mine be fulfilled. (1195)[1]

HYMN XXV

१. पर्वताद् दिवो योनेरङ्गादङ्गात् समाभृतम् । शेपो गर्भस्य रेतोधाः सरौ पर्णमिवा दधत् ॥

1. Let an able-bodied man, use for producing laudable progeny, his power of procreation, culled from mountainous medicines, from the cloud, air and light of the atmosphere, and from each of his limbs, like a feather in the flowing water. (1196)[2]

२. यथेयं पृथिवी मही भूतानां गर्भमादधे । एवा दधामि ते गर्भं तस्मै त्वामवसे हुवे ॥

2. Just as this broad Earth receives the germ of all the things that be, thus within thee I lay the germ, and instruct thee to protect it. (1197)[3]

३. गर्भं धेहि सिनीवालि गर्भं धेहि सरस्वति । गर्भं ते अश्विनोभा धत्तां पुष्करस्रजा ॥

3. Conceive, O abstemious wife, conceive, O learned wife. May both the invigorating Day and Night, fully develop the child in thy womb! (1198)[4]

४. गर्भं ते मित्रावरुणौ गर्भं देवो बृहस्पतिः । गर्भं त इन्द्रश्चाग्निश्च गर्भं धाता दधातु ते ॥

4. Let Prāna and Apāna, let the luminous Sun, let air and fire, let the Nourishing God, develop the child in thy womb. (1199)

५. विष्णुर्योनिं कल्पयतु त्वष्टा रूपाणि पिंशतु । आ सिञ्चतु प्रजापतिर्धाता गर्भं दधातु ते ॥

5. May the All-pervading God, strengthen thy womb, may the All-powerful God duly shape the joints, may God, the Protector of His subjects protect thy womb, may the Nourishing God, develop the child in the womb. (1200)[5]

[1] Pt. Jaidev Vidyalankara translated ततामहाः ते as sons and grandsons.

[2] Just as a feather flows peacefully and calmly in a rivulet, so should the semen of a strong person establish itself peacefully and calmly in the womb to ensure conception.

[3] I: husband. Thee: wife.

[4] Griffith considers Siniwali to be the Goddess of the day of new moon and also of fecundity and easy birth. This explanation is unacceptable, as there is no history in the Vedas. The word means a woman who is careful and regular in her diet. The verse has been translated by Swami Dayanand in the Sanskara Vidhi: See *Rigveda*, 10-184-2.

[5] Swami Dayananda has translated this verse in the Sanskara Vidhi: See *Rigveda*, 10-184-1.

६. यद् वेद राजा वरुणो यद् वा देवी सरस्वती । यदिन्द्रो वृत्रहा वेद तद् गर्भकरणं पिब ॥

6. Drink thou the procreative draught, well-known to thy venerable husband, to thee, the learned wife, and to the physician, the remover of diseases. (1201)

७. गर्भो अस्योषधीनां गर्भो वनस्पतीनाम् । गर्भो विश्वस्य भूतस्य सो अग्ने गर्भमेह धाः ॥

7. O God, Thou art the stay of plants and herbs, Thou art the support of forest trees, Thou art the Refuge of all existing things. Develop the child in my womb! (1202)

८. अधि स्कन्द वीरयस्व गर्भमा धेहि योन्याम् । वृषासि वृष्ण्यावन् प्रजायै त्वा नयामसि ॥

8. Rise up, put forth thy manly strength, and lay the semen within the womb. Powerful art thou with vigorous strength: for progeny we bring thee near. (1203)[1]

९. वि जिहीष्व बार्हत्सामे गर्भस्ते योनिमा शयाम् । अदुष्टे देवाः पुत्रं सोमपा उभयाविनम् ॥

9. Exert, O Woman, the singer of Brihat Sāma, so that semen be laid within thy womb. The learned preservers of semen, have given a son to thee, who guards me and thee. (1204)[2]

१०. धातः श्रेष्ठेन रूपेणास्या नार्या गवीन्योः । पुमांसं पुत्रमा धेहि दशमे मासि सूतवे ॥

10. O Nourishing God, develop in a noble way, in the body of this dame, the male child, to be born in the tenth month. (1205)

११. त्वष्टः श्रेष्ठेन रूपेणास्या नार्या गवीन्योः । पुमांसं पुत्रमा धेहि दशमे मासि सूतवे ॥

11. O All-powerful God, develop in a noble way, in the body of this dame, the male child, to be born in the tenth month. (1206)

१२. सवितः श्रेष्ठेन रूपेणास्या नार्या गवीन्योः । पुमांसं पुत्रमा धेहि दशमे मासि सूतवे ॥

12. O All-creating God, develop in a noble way, in the body of this dame, the male child, to be born in the tenth month. (1207)

१३. प्रजापते श्रेष्ठेन रूपेणास्या नार्या गवीन्योः । पुमांसं पुत्रमा धेहि दशमे मासि सूतवे ॥

13. O God, the Protector of the universe, develop in a noble way, in the body of this dame, the male child, to be born in the tenth month. (1208)

HYMN XXVI

१. यजूंषि यज्ञे समिधः स्वाहाग्निः प्रविद्वानिह वो युनक्तु ॥

[1]We refers to learned persons who arrange for the marriage of a young, healthy person with a girl.

[2]Me: husband. Thee: wife.

1. An enlightened yogi, full of knowledge, should offer sacrificial breaths as an oblation in God. O breaths, may he concentrate ye on God through samadhi! (1209)[1]

२. युनक्तु देवः सविता प्रजानन्नस्मिन् यज्ञे महिषः स्वाहा ॥

2. May the strong, goading soul, full of knowledge, concentrate breaths on the most Glorious God. This is the best oblation. (1210)

३. इन्द्र उक्थामदान्यस्मिन् यज्ञे प्रविद्वान् युनक्तु सुयुजः स्वाहा ॥

3. An able, highly learned, venerable person, should offer to the sacrificing God, joyous recitations of His praise. This is the best oblation. (1211)

४. प्रैषा यज्ञे निविदः स्वाहा शिष्टाः पत्नीभिर्वहतेह युक्ताः ॥

4. Dedicate your mental cravings to God, this is the Vedic instruction. This is the best oblation. O learned persons, controlling your mind and organs, with full concentration in samadhi, with your nourishing powers reach unto this God! (1212)

५. छन्दांसि यज्ञे मरुतः स्वाहा मातेव पुत्रं पिपृतेह युक्ताः ॥

5. Just as a mother nourishes her son, so should you, full of love, concentrated on God, nourish the breaths. Breaths concentrated on God, are the vital airs or life winds. This is the best oblation. (1213)

६. एयमगन् बर्हिषा प्रोक्षणीभिर्यज्ञं तन्वानादितिः स्वाहा ॥

6. This power of discernment, appears, making us visualise God, through divine knowledge and flow of joy. This sort of concentration is the best oblation. (1214)

७. विष्णुर्युनक्तु बहुधा तपांस्यस्मिन् यज्ञे सुयुजः स्वाहा ॥

7. O learned, nice practisers of yoga, may God furnish Ye with various sorts of austerity, in this spiritual yoga-yajna. This is the best oblation. (1215)

८. त्वष्टा युनक्तु बहुधा नु रूपा अस्मिन् यज्ञे सुयुजः स्वाहा ॥

8. O excellent yogis, may the All-creating God, yoke your various organs, in this spiritual yoga-yajna. This is the best oblation. (1216)

९. भगो युनक्त्वाशिषोन्व१स्मा अस्मिन् यज्ञे प्रविद्वान् युनक्तु सुयुजः स्वाहा ॥

9. O excellent yogis, may the Omnipotent God, fulfil all the desires of this soul. May a learned person concentrate on God in this spiritual yoga-yajna. This is the best oblation. (1217)

[1]He refers to the yogi, samadhi means deep concentration.

१०. सोमो युनक्तु बहुधा पयांस्यस्मिन् यज्ञे सुयुजः स्वाहा ॥

10. O excellent yogis, may the All-Goading God, endow our heart, with all sorts of joy, in this spiritual yoga yajna. This is the best oblation. (1218)

११. इन्द्रो युनक्तु बहुधा वीर्याण्यस्मिन् यज्ञे सुयुजः स्वाहा ॥

11. O excellent yogis, may the Refulgent God, endow this sacrificing soul with innumerable powers. This is the best oblation. (1219)

१२. अश्विना ब्रह्मणा यातमर्वाञ्चौ वषट्कारेण यज्ञं वर्धयन्तौ ।
बृहस्पते ब्रह्मणा याह्यर्वाङ् यज्ञो अयं स्वरिदं यजमानाय स्वाहा ॥

12. O man and woman doers of noble acts exalting the soul, through Vedic knowledge and charity, come hitherward. O God, the Protector of vast worlds, came unto us with Vedic knowledge. May this soul be a source of joy and dignity for this learned person. This is a nice saying. (1220)

HYMN XXVII

१. ऊर्ध्वा अस्य समिधो भवन्त्यूर्ध्वा शुक्रा शोचींष्यग्नेः ।
द्युमत्तमा सुप्रतीकः ससूनुस्तनूनपादसुरो भूरिपाणिः ॥

1. Lofty are the worlds like Sun, Moon, of this Refulgent God. Uplifted are His brilliant, shining lights. God is beautiful, coupled with all his offspring, the protector of all heavenly bodies, the possessor of the strength of myriad hands. (1221)

२. देवो देवेषु देवः पथो अनक्ति मध्वा घृतेन ॥

2. God is the Illuminator of all luminous bodies. He sheds joy and knowledge on all walks of life. (1222)

३. मध्वा यज्ञं नक्षति प्रैणानो नराशंसो अग्निः सुकृद् देवः सविता विश्ववारः ॥

3. Refulgent God, praised by mankind, the Doer of nice deeds, the Creator, Acceptable to all, pervades the universe exalting the soul with knowledge. (1223)[1]

४. अच्छायमेति शवसा घृता चिदीडानो वह्निर्नमसा ॥

4. This yogi, the performer of the Yajna of life, nicely attains to the Refulgent. God, praising Him with knowledge and devotion. (1224)[2]

५. अग्निः स्रुचो अध्वरेषु प्रयक्षु न यक्षदस्य महिमानमग्नेः ॥

5. A learned person, should in non-violent yajnas, worship the greatness of the wisdom of this God. (1225)[3]

[1]See *Yajur*, 27-13.
[2]See *Yajur*, 27-14, and *Rig*, 1-142-5.
[3]Yajnas: Deeds, enterprises: See *Yajur*, 27-15.

६. तरी मन्द्रासु प्रयक्षु वसवश्चातिष्ठन् वसुधातरश्च ॥

6. In gladdening yogic exercises, God alone rescues us from griefs. In Him do all worlds and wise yogis reside. (1226)

७. द्वारो देवीरन्वस्य विश्वे व्रतं रक्षन्ति विश्वहा ॥

7. Intelligent organs obey the behest of this soul. All learned persons, in diverse ways, fulfil the duties preached by the soul. (1227)

८. उरुव्यचसाऽग्नेर्धाम्ना पत्यमाने ।
आ सुष्वयन्ती यजते उपाके उषासानक्तेमं यज्ञमवतामध्वरं नः ॥

8. May Dawn and Night, exalted by the vast lustre of God, united together, abiding near each other, coming joyfully, protect this immortal soul of ours. (1228)[1]

९. दैवा होतार ऊर्ध्वमध्वरं नोऽग्नेर्जिह्वयाभि गृणत गृणता नः स्विष्टये ।
तिस्रो देवीर्बर्हिरेदं सदन्तामिडा सरस्वती मही भारती गृणाना ॥

9. O noble learned persons, exalt this immortal soul of ours. Praise God with His Vedic verses. Give us instructions for the acquisition of God. May the three highly qualified and instructive forces of statesmanship, intellect and knowledge adorn this soul! (1229)[2]

१०. तन्नस्तुरीपमद्भुतं पुरुक्षु । देव त्वष्टा रायस्पोषं वि ष्य नाभिमस्य ॥

10. That mind of ours, fast in motion, wonderful in nature, resides in the organs. O Refulgent God, release this soul from the bondage of the body, nourished through knowledge and breaths. (1230)[3]

११. वनस्पतेऽव सृजा रराणः । त्मना देवेभ्यो अग्निर्हव्यं शमिता स्वदयतु ॥

11. O soul, the lord of organs, rejoicing, with thy spiritual force, go unto God. May the peace bestowing God, make all learned persons, enjoy the bliss of salvation! (1231)[4]

१२. अग्ने स्वाहा कृणुहि जातवेदः । इन्द्राय यज्ञं विश्वे देवा हविरिदं जुषन्ताम् ॥

12. O Lustrous God, the knower of all created objects, we humbly pray unto Thee, to create the world for the soul to work in. May all the learned persons reap in this world the fruit of their actions! (1232)

HYMN XXVIII

१. नव प्राणान्नवभिः सं मिमीते दीर्घायुत्वाय शतशारदाय ।
हरिते त्रीणि रजते त्रीण्ययसि त्रीणि तपसाविष्ठितानि ॥

[1]See *Yajur*, 27-17; *Rig*, 1-142-7; *Atharva*, 5-12-6.
[2]See *Yajur*, 27-18, 19; *Rig*, 1-142-10; *Atharva*, 5-12-8.
[3]Release: Grant salvation: See *Yajur*, 27-20.
[4]See *Yajur*, 27-21; *Rig*, 1-142-11.

1. For lengthened life, to last through hundred autumns, God has nicely united nine vital airs with nine organs. Three of them, through their power, are stationed in their virtuous nature, three are stationed in their passionate nature, and three are stationed in their dark nature (1233)[1]

२. अग्निः सूर्यश्चन्द्रमा भूमिरापो द्यौरन्तरिक्षं प्रदिशो दिशश्च ।
आर्त्तवा ऋतुभिः संविदाना अनेन मा त्रिवृता पारयन्तु ॥

2. May Fire, Sun, Moon, Earth, Waters, Sky, Air, the quarters, and sub-quarters, and parts of years accordant with the seasons, by this three-threaded yajnopavit preserve me. (1234)[2]

३. त्रयः पोषास्त्रिवृति श्रयन्तामनक्तु पूषा पयसा घृतेन ।
अन्नस्य भूमा पुरुषस्य भूमा भूमा पशूनां त इह श्रयन्ताम् ॥

3. In the three-threaded yajnopavit rest three kinds of fulness. May God fill us with milk and butter. O man, for thee, in this world, rest abundant store of food, plenty of people, and ample store of cattle. (1235)

४. इममादित्या वसुना समुक्षतेममग्ने वर्धय वावृधानः ।
इममिन्द्र सं सृज वीर्ये्णास्मिन् त्रिवृच्छ्रयतां पोषयिष्णु ॥

4. O noble persons fill this child with wealth. O magnificent God, magnify this child. O Mighty God, endow him with heroic strength. May this three-threaded yajnopavit, the releaser of griefs and miseries rest on him. (1236)

५. भूमिष्ट्वा पातु हरितेन विश्वभृदग्निः पिपर्त्वयसा सजोषाः ।
वीरुद्भिष्टे अर्जुनं संविदानं दक्षं दधातु सुमनस्यमानम् ॥

5. Let al'-sustaining Earth protect thee with poverty-eradicating enterprise. Let the lovely fire protect thee with its glow and lustre. Let thy accumulated wealth, derived from the people, grant thee vigour, fit to arouse noble resolves in the mind. (1237)

६. त्रेधा जातं जन्मनेदं हिरण्यमग्नेरेकं प्रियतमं बभूव सोमस्यैकं हिंसितस्य परापतत् ।
अपामेकं वेधसां रेत आहुस्तत् ते हिरण्यं त्रिवृदस्त्वायुषे ॥

[1]There are three parts of the body (1) Neck, which includes eye, ear, nostril, which are golden, virtuous or satvik in nature (2) From the mouth to the navel is the second part, which includes mouth, tongue and hand which are silvery passionate, rajsak in nature (3) From the navel to foot is the third part, which includes the anus, penis and foot, which are iron, dark, ignorant, tāmas in nature. Some commentators consider nine organs to be two eyes, two ears, two nostrils, mouth, anus and penis, the nine gates of the body. Nine vital airs are (1) Prāna (2) Apāna (3) Vyāna (4) Udāna (5) Samāna (6) Nāga (7) Kurma (8) Kriklu (9) Deva Dutta.

[2]All the forces of nature are supposed to be contained in the Yajnopavit, and are invoked to preserve the wearer of the Yajnopavit. Yajnopavit is three-threaded, and not six-threaded as is usually worn in these days.

Yajnopavit: the sacred thread with which a pupil was invested at the time of the commencement of his studies. Three threads are symbolic of his three debts, i.e., debt due to the parents, the sages and the forces of nature, spoken of as Pitri, Rishi, Deva debts.

6. This lovely God manifests Himself by nature in three aspects. His first aspect became the most charming fire. His second aspect is the Moon, that is covered with darkness, and receives light from the sun. His third aspect is called the procreative semen of human beings. May God, in His three aspects prolong our life. (1238)[1]

७. त्र्यायुषं जमदग्नेः कश्यपस्य त्र्यायुषम् । त्रेधामृतस्य चक्षणं त्रीण्यायूंषि तेऽकरम् ॥

7. A healthy person with a good digestion lives for three hundred years. A Brahmchari who possesses knowledge and control over his passions lives for three hundred years. Salvation is obtainable through three things. I grant thee, the worshipper and devotee, a life of three hundred years. (1239)[2]

८. त्रयः सुपर्णास्त्रिवृता यदायन्नेकाक्षरमभिसंभूय शक्राः ।
प्रत्यौहन्मृत्युममृतेन साकमन्तर्दधाना दुरितानि विश्वा ॥

8. When three kinds of powerful, learned souls, with the help of threefold breaths, realising the One God, symbolised by Om, attain to salvation, then, they, with the power of divine soul, simultaneously suppressing all sins, gain full mastery over death. (1240)[3]

९. दिवस्त्वा पातु हरितं मध्यात् त्वा पात्वर्जुनम् ।
भूम्या अयस्मयं पातु प्रागाद् देवपुरा अयम् ॥

9. Soul enters the body, endowed with different faculties of enjoyment. May thy virtuous (sātvik) nature protect thee from the wrath of Sun, may thy passionate (Rājsik) nature protect thee from the onslaught of mid-air. May thy Tāmas (dark) nature protect thee from calamities on the Earth. (1241)

१०. इमास्तिस्रो देवपुरास्तास्त्वा रक्षन्तु सर्वतः । तास्त्वं बिभ्रद् वर्चस्व्युत्तरो द्विषतां भव ॥

10. May these three kinds of thy nature, keep thee secure on every side. Endowed with strength, possessing these, be thou the master of thy foes like lust, anger, etc. (1242)[4]

११. पुरं देवानाममृतं हिरण्यं य आबेधे प्रथमो देवो अग्रे ।
तस्मै नमो दश प्राचीः कृणोम्यनु मन्यतां त्रिवृदाबधे मे ॥

11. I salute in ten vast directions the Illustrious God, who established in times immemorial for the guidance of the learned, the immortal light of the Vedas. May the three-threaded yajnopavit be blest, which I bind upon myself. (1243)[5]

[1]Man should lengthen his life by observing celibacy, preserving his semen, by being ever energetic and active like fire, and by being calm and peaceful like the moon.

[2]I: God. Three things:—(1) Knowledge (2) Training (3) Self-abnegation.

[3]'Three kinds of souls' refer to Vasu, Rudra and Aditya Brahmcharis.
Three breaths: Prāna, Apāna, Vyāna.

[4]Three kinds: Sātvik, Rājas and Tāmsik. All these three tendencies of the soul, are useful, if properly used.

[5]'Bind' means wear त्रिवृत may also mean Om, which consists of three letters, अ, उ, म्. I ever remember Om in my heart; may this grand name of God ever bless me with good fortune.

१२. आ त्वा चृतत्वर्यमा पूषा बृहस्पतिः । अहर्जातस्य यन्नाम तेन त्वाति चृतामसि ॥

12. God, the Suppressor of internal foes like lust and anger, the Nourisher of all, the Lord of vast worlds and Vedic speech, binds thee O soul. With the lustre of the Sun, born in day time, we invest thee with yajnopavit! (1244)[1]

१३. ऋतुभिष्ट्वार्तवैरायुषे वर्चसे त्वा । संवत्सरस्य तेजसा तेन संहनु कृण्मसि ॥

13. O Brahmchari, we firmly unite thee, for vigour and extended life, with seasons, months, and all the splendour of the sun! (1245)

१४. घृतादुल्लुप्तं मधुना समक्तं भूमिदृंहमच्युतं पारयिष्णु ।
भिन्दत् सपत्नानधरांश्च कृण्वदा मा रोह महते सौभगाय ॥

14. O soul, thou art, full of knowledge, replete with the pleasure of yogic practices, firm like the earth, unshakable and triumphant, breaking down thy foes and casting them below, take shelter under me for exalted fortune. (1246)[2]

HYMN XXIX

१. पुरस्ताद् युक्तो वह जातवेदोऽग्ने विद्धि क्रियमाणं यथेदम् ।
त्वं भिषग् भेषजस्यासि कर्ता त्वया गामश्वं पुरुषं सनेम ॥

1. O learned person, take upon thy shoulders the responsibility of performing effectively all tasks, before they are undertaken. Know well how this task is to be performed. Thou bringest medicine and healest diseases. Through thy help, may we get healthy kine, horses and people! (1247)

२. तथा तदग्ने कृणु जातवेदो विश्वेभिर्देवैः सह संविदानः ।
यो नो दिदेव यतमो जघास यथा सो अस्य परिधिष्पताति ॥

2. O learned person, in consultation with other physicians, arrange in such a way, that the fort of this disease may fall, which hath caused us pain, whichever hath consumed our flesh! (1248)

३. यथा सो अस्य परिधिष्पताति तथा तदग्ने कृणु जातवेदः ।
विश्वेभिर्देवैः सह संविदानः ॥

3. O learned person, in consultation with other physicians, arrange so, that the stronghold of the germs of this disease may fall and fail! (1249)

४. अक्ष्यौ३ नि विध्य हृदयं नि विध्य जिह्वां नि तृन्द्धि प्र दतो मृणीहि ।
पिशाचो अस्य यतमो जघासाग्ने यविष्ठ प्रति तं शृणीहि ॥

[1]We: The preceptors, Acharyas.
Thee: The child initiated in Brahmcharya Ashram, and invested with Yajnopavit. The child is bound with the sacred thread, possessing the triple characteristics of the sin-annihilating body-nourishing, knowledge-augmenting God.
[2]Me refers to God or the Preceptor.

4. Pierce thou his eyes, pierce thou his heart, crush thou his teeth, and cleave his tongue asunder, destroy thou, most youthful physician, the flesh-consuming germ, whoso eats the flesh of this man. (1250)

५. यदस्य हृतं विहृतं यत् पराभृतमात्मनो जग्धं यतमत् पिशाचैः ।
तदग्ने विद्वान् पुनरा भर त्वं शरीरे मांसमसुमेरयामः ॥

5. Whatever of the body of this sick man hath been taken, plundered, borne off, or eaten by the flesh-consuming germs, that, O learned physician restore to him again through medicine. We give back flesh and spirit to his body. (1251)[1]

६. आमे सुपक्वे शबले विपक्वे यो मा पिशाचो अशने ददम्भ ।
तदात्मना प्रजया पिशाचा वि यातयन्तामगदो३यमस्तु ॥

6. If some flesh-consuming germ, entering my raw, cooked, half cooked, thoroughly cooked food, hath injured me, let the germs with their lives and offspring be destroyed, so that this man be free from disease. (1252)

७. क्षीरे मा मन्थे यतमो ददम्भाकृष्टपच्ये अशने धान्ये३ यः ।
तदात्मना प्रजया पिशाचा वि यातयन्तामगदो३यमस्तु ॥

7. If some flesh-consuming germ, entering milk, curd, food, and corn of spontaneous growth, hath injured me, let the germs with their lives and offspring be destroyed, so that this man be free from disease. (1253)

८. अपां मा पाने यतमो ददम्भ क्रव्याद् यातूनां शयने शयानम् ।
तदात्मना प्रजया पिशाचा वि यातयन्तामगदो३यमस्तु ॥

8. If some flesh-consuming germ, entering the drinking water, or my bed while sleeping on the ground with travellers, hath injured me, let the germs with their lives and offspring be destroyed, so that this man be free from disease. (1254)

९. दिवो मा नक्तं यतमो ददम्भ क्रव्याद् यातूनां शयने शयानम् ।
तदात्मना प्रजया पिशाचा वि यातयन्तामगदो३यमस्तु ॥

9. If some flesh consuming germ, like mosquito or flea hath injured me in day or night time while sleeping in the bed on the ground with travellers, let the germs with their lives and offspring be destroyed, so that this man be free from disease. (1255)

१०. क्रव्यादमग्ने रुधिरं पिशाचं मनोहनं जहि जातवेदः ।
तमिन्द्रो वाजी वज्रेण हन्तु च्छिनत्तु सोमः शिरो अस्य धृष्णुः ॥

10. O learned physician, slay the bloody germ, flesh-devourer, mind-destroyer. Let an able doctor strike him with his healing power, let an efficacious medicine cut his head to pieces! (1256)

[1] 'We' may refer to physicians, or learned relatives.

११. सनादग्ने मृणसि यातुधानान् न त्वा रक्षांसि पृतनासु जिग्युः ।
सहमूराननु दह क्रव्यादो मा ते हेत्या मुक्षत दैव्यायाः ॥

11. O fire, thou ever slayest the troublesome germs of diseases, these fiends have never conquered thee in struggles. Consume thou from the root the flesh-devourers, let none of them escape thy divine weapon! (1257)

१२. समाहर जातवेदो यद्धृतं यत् पराभृतम् । गात्राण्यस्य वर्धन्तामंशुरिवा प्यायतामयम् ॥

12. Restore, O learned physician, what hath been removed and borne. away. Let this sick man's organs grow, let him wax like moon! (1258)[1]

१३. सोमस्येव जातवेदो अंशुरा प्यायतामयम् । अग्ने विरप्शिनं मेध्यमयक्ष्मं कृणु जीवतु ॥

13. O learned physician, let this sick man grow like a digit of the moon. Make him free from fault, impurity and disease, so that he may live long! (1259)

१४. एतास्ते अग्ने समिधः पिशाचजम्भनीः । तास्त्वं जुषस्व प्रति चैना गृहाण जातवेदः ॥

14. O learned person, these thy manifest performances of knowledge, are the annihilators of flesh-devouring diseases. Be pleased with them, and willingly accept them, O learned fellow! (1260)[2]

१५. तार्ष्टाघीरग्ने समिधः प्रति गृह्णाह्यर्चिषा । जहातु क्रव्याद्रूपं यो अस्य मांसं जिहीर्षति ॥

15. O learned person, reverentially, certainly, accept the wise instructions condemning greed. Let the flesh-devouring disease, which would take the flesh of this patient lose its form. (1261)[3]

HYMN XXX

१. आवतस्त आवतः परावतस्त आवतः ।
इहैव भव मा नु गा मा पूर्वाननु गाः पितृनसुं बध्नामि ते दृढम् ॥

1. From thy vicinity, I call, from near at hand, from far, from nigh at hand, stay here with me, depart not; follow not the fathers of the olden time. I bind thy soul fast. (1262)[4]

२. यत् त्वाभिचेरुः पुरुषः स्वो यदरणो जनः । उन्मोचनप्रमोचने उभे वाचा वदामि ते ॥

2. If any man, a stranger or akin, wants to do a sinful act unto thee, I with my voice to thee declare, how to get rid of his snare, and how to remain away from it. (1263)[5]

[1]What hath been removed: All the flesh that the sick man has lost.

[2]'Them' refers to performances.

[3]Lose its form: be annihilated. A learned person should shun greed, and destroy the greedy germs of a disease, that feed upon the flesh of a patient.

[4]Thy: A Brahmchari 'I, me' refer to the Acharya, preceptor. A pupil is instructed not to die early and go in the wake of his dead ancestors but to live with his teacher and carry on his study.

[5]Thee: The pupil. I: Preceptor, Acharya.

३. यद् दुद्रोहिथ शेपिषे स्त्रियै पुंसे अचित्त्या । उन्मोचनप्रमोचने उभे वाचा वदामि ते ॥

3. O pupil, if in thy folly thou hast lied or spoken ill to a woman or a man, I instruct thee how to get rid of this sin and shun it. (1264)

४. यदेनसो मातृकृताच्छेषे पितृकृताच्च यत् । उन्मोचनप्रमोचने उभे वाचा वदामि ते ॥

4. If thou art lying on the sick bed because of mother's or of father's sin, I through vedic speech instruct thee how to get free from, and remain aloof from it. (1265)

५. यत् ते माता यत् ते पिता जामिर्भ्राता च सर्जतः ।
प्रत्यक् सेवस्व भेषजं जरदष्टिं कृणोमि त्वा ॥

5. Accept the healing medicine, thy mother, thy father, thy sister and thy brother bring. I make thee live for long years. (1266)[1]

६. इहैधि पुरुष सर्वेण मनसा सह । दूतौ यमस्य मानु गा अधि जीवपुरा इहि ॥

6. O pupil, stay here in my house with full devotion and attention. Care not for hunger and thirst, the messengers of Death, control thy body, the citadel wherein dwells the soul ! (1267)[2]

७. अनुहूतः पुनरेहि विद्वानुदयनं पथः । आरोहणमाक्रमणं जीवतोजीवतोऽयनम् ॥

7. O pupil, taught by the learned, full of knowledge, try again and again to reach the paths of salvation. To rise up and go forward, is the behaviour of each living soul! (1268)

८. मा बिभेर्न मरिष्यसि जरदष्टिं कृणोमि त्वा । निरवोचमहं यक्ष्ममङ्गेभ्यो अङ्गज्वरं तव ॥

8. O pupil, be not alarmed, thou wilt not die, I give thee lengthened years of life. Forth from thy members I drive consumption that caused the fever there! (1269)

९. अङ्गभेदो अङ्गज्वरो यश्च ते हृदयामयः । यक्ष्मः श्येन इव प्रापप्तद् वाचा साढः परस्तराम् ॥

9. O pupil, gone is the pain that racked thee, gone thy fever, gone thy heart's disease. Consumption, overcome by my Vedic instructions, hath, like a hawk, fled far away! (1270)

१०. ऋषी बोधप्रतीबोधावस्वप्नो यश्च जागृविः ।
तौ ते प्राणस्य गोप्तारौ दिवा नक्तं च जागृताम् ॥

10. O pupil, two sages, sense and vigilance, the sleepless and the watchful one, may these, the protectors of thy life, remain awake both day and night! (1271)

११. अयमग्निरुपसद्य इह सूर्यं उदेतु ते । उदेहि मृत्योर्गम्भीरात् कृष्णाच्चित् तमसस्परि ॥

[1] I refers to the preceptor.

[2] My house: the family of the preceptor.

11. This All-pervading God is serviceable. In His contemplation, let thy soul, brilliant like the sun rise high. O soul, getting free from the fear of deep, dark, dismal death, rise thou up! (1272)

१२. नमो यमाय नमो अस्तु मृत्यवे नमः पितृभ्य उत ये नयन्ति ।
उत्पारणस्य यो वेद तमग्निं पुरो दधेऽस्मा अरिष्टतातये ।।

12. Homage be paid to the Just God, to Him who frees us from the fear of death, from fathers who guide us. I always honour, for the welfare of this soul, that God, who well knowest how to save it. (1273)[1]

१३. ऐतु प्राण ऐतु मन ऐतु चक्षुरथो बलम् । शरीरमस्य सं विदां तत् पद्भ्यां प्रति तिष्ठतु ।।

13. Let breath and mind return to it, let sight and vigour come again, let intellect be restored to its body, so that it may firmly stand upon its feet. (1274)[2]

१४. प्राणेनाग्ने चक्षुषा सं सृजेमं समीरय तन्वा३ सं बलेन ।
वेत्थामृतस्य मा नु गान्मा नु भूमिगृहो भुवत् ।।

14. O God, provide this soul with breath and sight, unite it with body and strength. Thou art the knower of immortality. Let not the soul go hence, nor dwell in house of clay. (1275)[3]

१५. मा ते प्राण उप दसन्मो अपानोऽपि धायि ते । सूर्यस्त्वाधिपतिर्मृत्योरुदायच्छतु रश्मिभिः ।।

15. Let not thine in-going breath fail, let not thy out-going breath be lost. Let God Who is Lord supreme raise thee from death with His beams of light. (1276)[4]

१६. इयमन्तर्वदति जिह्वा बद्धा पनिष्पदा । त्वया यक्ष्मं निरवोचं शतं रोपीश्च तक्मनः ।।

16. Tied, tumultuously moving, this tongue speaks in the mouth. O speech, with thy strength, I drive away consumption and fever's hundred agonies! (1277)[5]

१७. अयं लोकः प्रियतमो देवानामपराजितः । यस्मै त्वमिह मृत्यवे दिष्टः पुरुष जज्ञिषे ।
स च त्वानु ह्वयामसि मा पुरा जरसो मृथाः ।।

17. This unconquerable world is most beloved of all learned persons. To whatsoever death thou wast destined when thou wast born, O man, This death and we call after thee, 'Do not die before extreme age'! (1278)[6]

[1]Fathers: Father, mother, Achārya, i.e., preceptor. 'It' refers to the soul.

[2]'It' refers to the soul.

[3]Let not the soul: The soul should not leave the body at an early age. After enjoying full age, let it enjoy salvation, and not assume earthly body through birth again and again.

[4]'Thine, thee' refer to the patient.

[5]'I' refers to a physician, who instructs the patient as how to get rid of diseases.

[6]Life is sweet, one must not die before time.

HYMN XXXI

१. यां ते चक्रुरामे पात्रे यां चक्रुर्मिश्रधान्ये ।
आमे मांसे कृत्यां यां चक्रुः पुनः प्रति हरामि ताम् ॥

1. The deadly poison, the enemies mix in food, thy drinkable water, mingled meal, or administer it in the marrow of raw fruits the same do I remove. (1279)[1]

२. यां ते चक्रुः कृकवाकावजे वा यां कुरीरिणि ।
अव्यां ते कृत्यां यां चक्रुः पुनः प्रति हरामि ताम् ॥

2. The mischief the enemies commit upon thy forest cock, goat, horned ram, and thy ewe, the same do I remove. (1280)

३. यां ते चक्रुरेकशफे पशूनामुभयादति ।
गर्दभे कृत्यां यां चक्रुः पुनः प्रति हरामि ताम् ॥

3. The mischief the enemies have committed upon thy beast that hath uncloven hooves, the ass with teeth in both his jaws, the same do I remove. (1281)

४. यां ते चक्रुरमूलायां वलगं वा नराच्याम् ।
क्षेत्रे ते कृत्यां यां चक्रुः पुनः प्रति हरामि ताम् ॥

4. The mischief and the secret sin, they commit upon the medicinal plants Anula or Narachi, to render them ineffective, or upon thy field, the same do I remove. (1282)[2]

५. यां ते चक्रुर्गार्हपत्ये पूर्वाग्नावुत दुश्चितः ।
शालायां कृत्यां यां चक्रुः पुनः प्रति हरामि ताम् ॥

5. The mischief that wicked men have committed upon thy Gārhpatya and Abvniya fire, and on thy sacrificial hall, the same do I remove. (1283)[3]

६. यां ते चक्रुः सभायां यां चक्रुरधिदेवने ।
अक्षेषु कृत्यां यां चक्रुः पुनः प्रति हरामि ताम् ॥

6. The mischief that evil-minded persons have committed upon the Assembly, the gambling-board, and upon the dice, the same do I remove. (1284)

[1]Thy refers to the king. Enemies are liable to mix poison in the food, water and meals of a king and his subjects. They mix the seeds of poisonous drugs in corn and fruits, and export them for consumption to another country. Such mischief-mongers should be punished. 'I' may refer to a physician or king.

[2]Amūlā: the Methonica superba; a species of lily. Narāchī: an unidentified plant.

[3]Gārhpatya: The original household-fire in the west, that is ever kept ablaze. Abvniya: fire established in the East.

७. यां ते चक्रुः सेनायां यां चक्रुरिष्वायुधे ।।
दुन्दुभौ कृत्यां यां चक्रुः पुनः प्रति हरामि ताम् ।।

7. The mischief that they have committed upon the army, shafts and weapons, and upon the drum, the same do I remove. (1285)[1]

८. यां ते कृत्यां कूपेऽवदधुः श्मशाने वा निचख्नुः ।
सद्मनि कृत्यां यां चक्रुः पुनः प्रति हरामि ताम् ।।

8. The mischief that they have committed in the well by poisoning it, or in the cemetery by throwing obnoxious objects into the burning pyre or in the home by throwing filth into it, the same do I remove. (1286)

९. यां ते चक्रुः पुरुषास्थे अग्नौ संकसुके च याम् ।
म्रोकं निर्दाहं क्रव्यादं पुनः प्रति हरामि ताम् ।।

9. I remove the mischief they committed in human bones and blazing fire of the pyre. I punish the sinners who are dreadful like a thief, burn the houses of the people, and eat raw flesh through violence. (1287)[2]

१०. अपथेना जभारैणां तां पथेतः प्र हिण्मसि ।
अधीरो मर्याधीरेभ्यः सं जभाराचित्त्या ।।

10. A wicked person has brought this mischief in the country through unfair means, we drive it back through fair means. A foolish person in folly brings it to those who observe established laws. (1288)

११. यश्चकार न शशाक कर्तुं शश्रे पादमङ्गुरिम् ।
चकार भद्रमस्मभ्यमभगो भगवद्भ्यः ।।

11. He who tries to commit mischief but has no power to do it, hurts his own foot and hand before hurting others. The unlucky fellow does good in disguise to us, the virtuous. (1289)[3]

१२. कृत्याकृतं वलगिनं मूलिनं शपथेय्यम् ।
इन्द्रस्तं हन्तु महता वधेनाग्निर्विध्यत्वस्तया ।।

12. May the king slay with mighty bolt, may the Commander-in-chief with his missile pierce the mischief-monger, who is low-bred, deep rooted, and slanderous. (1290)

[1]In army they spread disloyalty in shafts they commit the mischief of using poisoned arrows. On drums they sprinkle poison and thus harm those who play on them.

[2]'I' refers to the king.

[3]By his failure in achieving success in his evil act, he warns us to be on the alert, and thus does good in disguise unto us.

BOOK (Kāṇḍa) VI

HYMN I

१. दोषो गाय बृहद् गाय द्युमद्धेहि । आथर्वण स्तुहि देवं सवितारम् ॥

1. O worshipper of God, sing His glory day and night, sing loudly, contemplate upon the Refulgent God. Praise the All-creating God! (1291)[1]

२. तमु ष्टुहि यो अन्तः सिन्धौ सूनुः । सत्यस्य युवानम् अद्रोघवाचं सुशेवम् ॥

2. Yea, praise Him Whose home is in the inmost recesses of the heart, Who is the Preacher of Truth, Whose Word is guileless, Who is a Gracious Friend. (1292)

३. स घा नो देवः सविता साविषदमृतानि भूरि । उभे सुष्टुती सुगातवे ॥

3. The same All-creating God grants us various means of acquiring salvation. Both morning and evening eulogies are meant to sing His glory. (1293)[2]

HYMN II

१. इन्द्राय सोममृत्विजः सुनोता च धावत । स्तोतुर्यो वचः शृणवद्धवं च मे ॥

1. O Yogis who control the breath in samadhi, creates for the soul the joy of God, and make it pure. The soul listens to the praiser's word and my call. (1294)[3]

२. आ यं विशन्तीन्दवो वयो न वृक्षमन्धसः । विरप्शिन्वि मृधो जहि रक्षस्विनीः ॥

2. O mighty soul, spoken of in diverse ways, in whom reside the vivacious hankerers after salvation, as birds in a tree, drive away evil propensities full of obstacles. (1295)

३. सुनोता सोमपाव्ने सोममिन्द्राय वज्रिणे । युवा जेतेशानः स पुरुष्टुतः ॥

3. For the soul, that enjoys the pleasure of yoga, wields the armour of knowledge to cut asunder the shackles of the world, acquire immortal felicity. The soul youthful, conqueror, and lord, is praised by all. (1296)

HYMN III

१. पातं न इन्द्रापूषणादितिः पान्तु मरुतः ।
अपां नपात् सिन्धवः सप्त पातन पातु नो विष्णुरुत द्यौः ॥

[1]Day and night: Morning and evening. 'Atharvan' does not mean the son of Atharva Rishi. The word means a worshipper of God, or the knower of the Atharvaveda.

[2]Both eulogies may also refer to Brihat Rathantra Sama songs.

[3]'It' refers to joy.

1. May lightning and air guard us. May Matter and the learned guard us. May physical strength that lets not the souls decay, guard us. May the seven ever active forces guard us. May God and intellect guard us. (1297)[1]

२. पातां नो द्यावापृथिवी अभिष्टये पातु ग्रावा पातु सोमो नो अंहसः ।
पातु नो देवी सुभगा सरस्वती पात्वग्निः शिवा ये अस्य पायवः ॥

2. May Sun and Earth protect us for reaping the desired fruit. May a learned fellow and God save us from sin. May the auspicious Vedic speech, the giver of joy protect us. May God and His Kind protecting powers preserve us. (1298)

३. पातां नो देवाश्विना शुभस्पती उषासानक्तोत न उरुष्यताम् ।
अपां नपादभिह्रुती गयस्य चिद् देव त्वष्टर्वर्धय सर्वतातये ॥

3. May both father and mother, the doers of noble deeds preserve us. Let Day and Night protect us. O God, the saviour of souls, protect our house from every harm. O God, the Maker of all worlds, make us strong for health and wealth. (1299)

HYMN IV

१. त्वष्टा मे दैव्यं वचः पर्जन्यो ब्रह्मणस्पतिः ।
पुत्रैर्भ्रातृभिरदितिर्नु पातु नो दुष्टरं त्रायमाणं सहः ॥

1. May God, the Creator of all, the showerer of joy on all, the Lord of the vedas hear my holy prayer. May the Immortal God, guard our invincible protecting power, along with our sons and brothers. (1300)

२. अंशो भगो वरुणो मित्रो अर्यमादितिः पान्तु मरुतः ।
अप तस्य द्वेषो गमेदभिह्रुतो यावयच्छत्रुमन्तितम् ॥

2. May God, the Definer of the duties of men, Glorious, Most Eminent, the Saviour from death, the Subduer of foes, Omnipotent, and learned persons, preserve us. May we be freed from that oppressor's hatred. May the foeman who is near us be kept far away. (1301)

३. धिये समश्विना प्रावतं न उरुष्या ण उरुज्मन्नप्रयुच्छन् । द्यौ३ष्पितर्यावय दुच्छुना या ॥

3. O father and mother, preserve us well for good conduct. O All-pervading God, with ceaseless care protect us. O Nourisher of mankind, O Refulgent God, keep away from us avarice, the bringer of evil fruits. (1302)

[1]Seven forces: skin, eye, ear, tongue, nose, mind, knowledge.

HYMN V

१. उदेनमुत्तरं नयाग्ने घृतेनाहुत । समेनं वर्चसा सृज प्रजया च बहुं कृधि ॥

1. O fire, ablaze with the butter oblation, lift up this man to a high position, endow him with full store of strength, and make him rich in progeny. (1303)[1]

२. इन्द्रेमं प्रतरं कृधि सजातानामसद् वशी । रायस्पोषेण सं सृज जीवातवे जरसे नय ॥

2. Advance him, O God. Let him be ruler of all his relatives. Grant him sufficiency of wealth, guide him for life to old age. (1304)[2]

३. यस्य कृण्मो हविर्गृहे तमग्ने वर्धया त्वम् । तस्मै सोमो अधि ब्रवदयं च ब्रह्मणस्पति ॥

3. Prosper this man, O Agni, in whose house we perform Havan. May a learned fellow and this guardian of the Vedas bless him! (1305)

HYMN VI

१. योऽस्मान् ब्रह्मणस्पतेऽदेवो अभिमन्यते । सर्वं तं रन्धयासि मे यजमानाय सुन्वते ॥

1. O Lord of the universe, place the man who disgraces us, under my control, who performs the yajna with Soma juice! (1306)

२. यो नः सोम सुशंसिनो दुःशंस आदिदेशति । वज्रेणास्य मुखे जहि स संपिष्टो अपायति ॥

2. O King, if any spiteful man tries to enslave us, the noble-minded; smite with thy bolt upon his face, so that he, crushed to pieces and runs away! (1307)

३. यो नः सोमाभिदासति सनाभिर्यश्च निष्टचः । अप तस्य बलं तिर महीव द्यौर्वधत्मना ॥

3. O King, whoever troubleth us, be he a stranger or akin, deprive him of the strength he hath, slay him with thy deadly missile as Sun does remove darkness! (1308)

HYMN VII

१. येन सोमादितिः पथा मित्रा वा यन्त्यद्रुहः । तेना नोवसा गहि ॥

1. O King, what pathway, the Earth and Sun, like companions free from guile use, come thou thereby to us, with thy power of protection. (1309)[3]

२. येन सोम साहन्त्यासुरान् रन्धयासि नः । तेना नो अधि वोचत ॥

2. O conquering King, with whatever power, thou subduest the evil-minded persons, bless us with the same power. (1310)

[1] He who daily performs Havan, rises in the world, gets health, wealth, longevity, and good progeny. Agni may mean God as well.

[2] 'Him' refers to the man, who daily performs Havan.

[3] A king should be friendly to his subjects, as the Sun and Earth are to each other.

३. येन देवा असुराणामोजांस्यवृणीध्वम् । तेना नः शर्म यच्छत ॥

3. Whereby Ye learned persons have repelled and stayed the powers of the ignoble persons, thereby give shelter unto us. (1311)

HYMN VIII

१. यथा वृक्षं लिबुजा समन्तं परिषस्वजे ।
एवा परि ष्वजस्व मां यथा मां कामिन्यसो यथा मन्नापगा असः ॥

1. Just as the creeper throws her arms on every side around the tree, so shouldst thou, O knowledge hold me in thine embrace, that thou mayst be in love with me, my darling, never to depart! (1312)[1]

२. यथा सुपर्णः प्रपतन् पक्षौ निहन्ति भूम्याम् ।
एवा नि हन्मि ते मनो यथा मां कामिन्यसो यथा मन्नापगा असः ॥

2. As, when he mounts, the eagle strikes his pinions downward on the earth, so do I, O knowledge, concentrate my mind on thee, that thou mayst be in love with me, my darling, never to depart. (1313)

३. यथेमे द्यावापृथिवी सद्यः पर्येति सूर्यः ।
एवा पर्येमि ते मनो यथा मां कामिन्यसो यथा मन्नापगा असः ॥

3. Just as the sun at dawn rapidly encompasses the Heaven and Earth with its light, so do I fix, O knowledge, my mind on thee, that thou mayst be in love with me, O darling, never to depart! (1314)

HYMN IX

१. वाञ्छ मे तन्वं१ पादौ वाञ्छाक्ष्यौ३ वाञ्छ सक्थ्यौ॒ ।
अक्ष्यौ॒ वृषण्यन्त्याः केशा मां ते कामेन शुष्यन्तु ॥

1. Desire my body, love my feet, love thou mine eyes, and love my legs. Let both thine eyes and hair, fond girl! be dried and parched through love of me. (1315)

२. मम त्वा दोषणिश्रिषं कृणोमि हृदयश्रिषम् । यथा मम क्रतावसो मम चित्तमुपायसि ॥

2. I make thee seek support of my arm. I make thee live in my heart, so that thou acceptest my wish, that thou mayst act according to my will. (1316)

३. यासां नाभिरारेहणं हृदि संवननं कृतम् । गावो घृतस्य मातरोऽमूं सं वानयन्तु मे ॥

3. May the cows, mothers of butter, incline that maid to love of me, whose heart is filled with love, praise and devotion. (1317)[2]

[1]See *Atharva*, 1-34-5 and 2-30-1.
[2]'Whose' refers to the maid.

HYMN X

१. पृथिव्यै श्रोत्राय वनस्पतिभ्योऽग्नयेऽधिपतये स्वाहा ॥

1. Offer butter oblation for the good of the vast Earth, for directions, the ears of the Earth, for the plants, for fire the lord of Earth! (1318)[1]

२. प्राणायान्तरिक्षाय वयोभ्यो वायवेऽधिपतये स्वाहा ॥

2. Offer butter oblation for the good of breath, for atmosphere, for the birds residing in the atmosphere, for air the Lord of atmosphere. (1319)

३. दिवे चक्षुषे नक्षत्रेभ्यः सूर्यायाधिपतये स्वाहा ॥

3. Offer butter oblation for the sake of producing light, for the eye, the recipient of light, for the stars that shine with light, for the Sun, the Lord of light. (1320)

HYMN XI

१. शमीमश्वत्थ आरूढस्तत्र पुंसवनं कृतम् । तद् वै पुत्रस्य वेदनं तत् स्त्रीष्वा भरामसि ॥

1. An able-bodied husband should cohabit with a calm, tranquil wife. This ceremony of producing a son, will certainly produce a son. Let us men instil semen in women. (1321)

२. पुंसि वै रेतो भवति तत् स्त्रियामनु षिच्यते ।
तद् वै पुत्रस्य वेदनं तद् प्रजापतिरब्रवीत् ॥

2. Man possesses the semen, he discharges it in the womb of a woman. That is the source of getting a son. God, the Lord of humanity has thus ordained. (1322)

३. प्रजापतिरनुमतिः सिनीवाल्यचीक्लृपत् । स्त्रैषूयमन्यत्र दधत् पुमांसमु दधदिह ॥

3. Father and agreeable mother are competent to tend and foster the child in the womb. In certain circumstance a girl is conceived, but under other conditions a boy is conceived. (1323)[2]

HYMN XII

१. परि द्यामिव सूर्योऽहीनां जनिमागमम् । रात्री जगदिवान्यद्धंसात् तेना ते वारये विषम् ॥

[1]Havan should be performed for purifying the earth and all its directions, for the rapid and abundant growth of plants, and for preventing the pollution of air, through purified smoke arising out of fire.

[2]In another circumstance: Where the menstrual discharge of a woman is abundant. In this condition: Where the semen of man is abundant. Griffith considers Anumati and Siniwāli as deities presiding over different phases of the moon and associated with conception and child birth. This explanation is unacceptable, as there is no history in the Vedas.

1. Just as the sun knows the Heaven, so have I know the birth of sins deadly like serpents. Just as Night separates the world from the light of the sun, so do I separate thee from sin. (1324)[1]

२. यद् ब्रह्मभिर्यदृषिभिर्यद् देवैर्विदितं पुरा । यद् भूतं भव्यमासन्वत् तेना ते वारये विषम् ॥

2. The knowledge possessed in the past by the knowers of the Vedas, the Rishis (Seers) and the sages, is everlasting in the Past, Present and Future. With that knowledge I remove thy moral frailty. (1325)[2]

३. मध्वा पृञ्चे नद्य१: पर्वता गिरयो मधु। मधु परुष्णी शीपाला शमास्ने अस्तु शं हृदे ॥

3. With efficacious medicine do I rub the body of the patient. Streams, mountains, hillocks contain useful medicines. May the nourishing, sleep-inducing medicine be effective. May it bring peace to thy mouth, peace to thy heart. (1326)[3]

HYMN XIII

१. नमो देववधेभ्यो नमो राजवधेभ्य: । अथो ये विश्यानां वधास्तेभ्यो मृत्यो नमोऽस्तु ते ॥

1. O Death, we pay homage to thee, for saving us from the scientific weapons of the learned, from the instruments and arms of the kings, and from the economic troubles created by business men! (1327)

२. नमस्ते अधिवाकाय परावाकाय ते नम: । सुमत्यै मृत्यो ते नमो दुर्मत्यै त इदं नम: ॥

2. O Death, we fully consider all that is said for thee, we know what is said against thee. We respect thy good will, and subdue thy malevolence! (1328)

३. नमस्ते यातुधानेभ्यो नमस्ते भेषजेभ्य: । नमस्ते मृत्यो मूलेभ्यो ब्राह्मणेभ्य इदं नम: ॥

3. O Death, we subdue the diseases painful like thee. We use medicines to keep thee away. We investigate thy causes, and revere the Vedic scholars who know them. (1329)[4]

HYMN XIV

१. अस्थिस्रंसं परुस्रंसमास्थितं हृदयामयम् । बलासं सर्वं नाशयाङ्गेष्ठा यश्च पर्वसु ॥

[1]I refers to a yogi. Just as the sun knows all the objects in the atmosphere, so does a yogi know the birth of sins in men. Just as night removes the world from the sun, so does a yogi remove the moral weaknesses of a sinner. Thee: a degraded, morally low sinful person.

[2]I refers to a yogi.

[3]Griffith explains Purushni as one of the rivers of the Punjab, now called Ravi. Sīpālā, is described by Griffith as a stream full of the aquatic plant Sīpālā. This explanation is irrational, as there is no history in the Vedas. The words are the names of medicines.

[4]Them: the causes of death.

1. O medicine, remove thou the breaking of the bones and the joints, the firmly-settled heart-disease, the strength decaying bronchitis that racks the bones and rends the limbs. (1330)

२. निर्बलासं बलासिनः क्षिणोमि मुष्करं यथा । छिनद्म्यस्य बन्धनं मूलमुर्वार्वाइव ॥

2. I remove cough from the consumptive man, as a lotus is removed with its root from the tank. I cut the bond of the disease that fetters him, like a root of the cucumber. (1331)[1]

३. निर्बलासेतः प्र पताशुङ्गः शिशुको यथा । अथो इट इव हायनोऽप द्राह्यवीरहा ॥

3. Begone, Consumption, from this body away, like a young foal that runs at speed. Then, not pernicious to our offspring, flee, like yearly visitant grass! (1332)[2]

HYMN XV

१. उत्तमो अस्योषधीनां तव वृक्षा उपस्तयः । उपस्तिरस्तु सोऽस्माकं यो अस्माँ अभिदासति ॥

1. O God, Thou art the most Excellent of all healing medicines. Embodied souls are Thy worshippers. Let him, who wants to injure us, become our friend. (1333)

२. सबन्धुश्चासबन्धुश्च यो अस्माँ अभिदासति । तेषां सा वृक्षाणामिवाहं भूयासमुत्तमः ॥

2. Whoever seeks to injure us, be he our relative or not; may I be uppermost of all of them, just as this plant is the queen of trees. (1334)

३. यथा सोम ओषधीनामुत्तमो हविषां कृतः । तलाशा वृक्षाणामिवाहं भूयासमुत्तमः ॥

3. Just as Soma has been made the best of all oblations amid the medicinal plants, so, as wealth is the best of worldly supports may I be chief of all. (1335)

HYMN XVI

१. आबयो अनाबयो रसस्त उग्र आबयो । आ ते करम्भमद्मसि ॥

1. O All-pervading, O Motionless, O Refulgent God, excellent is Thy joy. We nicely eat the food bestowed by Thee! (1336)

२. विहल्हो नाम ते पिता मदावती नाम ते माता ।
स हिन त्वमसि यस्त्वमात्मानमावयः ॥

2. O God, wonderful is Thy well-known characteristic of protection. Joyful is Thy famous power of creation. Thou art He, Who hast well protected our soul! (1337)

[1]'I' refers to a physician.

[2]Just as the grass that grows in the rainy season is removed, so should the disease be removed.

३. तौविलिकेऽवेलयावायमैलब ऐलयीत् । बभ्रुश्च बभ्रुकर्णश्चापेहि निराल ॥

3. O Matter, this Lord of full power, is goading the whole universe. Through His strength, O Matter, thou art running the universe. O soul, hankering after salvation, the nourisher of all, equipped with the sources of breaths release thyself from the bondage of matter! (1338)[1]

४. अलसालासि पूर्वा सिलाञ्जालास्युत्तरा । नीलागलसाला ॥

4. O God, Thy mighty power prevents people from becoming lazy. Thy excellent power creates all objects, and pervades the universe! (1339)[2]

HYMN XVII

१. यथेयं पृथिवी मही भूतानां गर्भमादधे । एवा ते ध्रियतां गर्भो अनु सूतुं सवितवे ॥

1. Just as this mighty Earth conceives the germs of all the things that be, so may the germ of life be laid in thee that thou mayst bear a son. (1340)[3]

२. यथेयं पृथिवी मही दाधारेमान् वनस्पतीन् । एवा ते ध्रियतां गर्भो अनु सूतुं सवितवे ॥

2. Just as this mighty Earth bears the stately forest trees, so may the germ of life be borne in thee that thou mayst bear a son. (1341)

३. यथेयं पृथिवी मही दाधार पर्वतान् गिरीन् । एवा ते ध्रियतां गर्भो अनु सूतुं सवितवे ॥

3. Even as this mighty Earth bears the mountains and the hills, so may the germ of life be borne in thee that thou mayst bear a son. (1342)

४. यथेयं पृथिवी मही दाधार विष्ठितं जगत् । एवा ते ध्रियतां गर्भो अनु सूतुं सवितवे ॥

4. Just as this mighty Earth supports the animate and inanimate world that dwells thereon, so may the germ of life be borne in thee that thou mayst bear a son. (1343)

HYMN XVIII

१. ईर्ष्याया ध्राजिं प्रथमां प्रथमस्या उतापराम् । अग्निं हृदय्यं१ शोकं तं ते निर्वापयामसि ॥

1. The first approach of jealousy, and that which followeth the first, the anguish, the fire of anger that burns within thy heart, we quench and drive away. (1344)[4]

[1]Lord means God.
[2]Griffith writes, the verse is untranslatable. He has not translated it.
[3]'Thee' refers to wife.
[4]Thy: a jealous person.

२. यथा भूमिर्मृतमना मृतान्मृतमनस्तरा । यथोत मम्रुषो मन एवेर्ष्योर्मृतं मनः ।।

2. Just as the earth is dead to sense, Yea, more unconscious than the dead, so like a corpse's spirit is the spirit of the jealous man. (1345)

३. अदो यत् ते हृदि श्रितं मनस्कं पतयिष्णुकम् । ततस्त ईर्ष्यां मुञ्चामि निरूष्माणं दृतेरिव ।।

3. O jealous person, the petty mind that harbours in thy heart, leads thee to degradation. I drive jealousy out of thy mind, just as a blacksmith drives hot air out of a pair of bellows. (1346)

HYMN XIX

१. पुनन्तु मा देवजनाः पुनन्तु मनवो धिया । पुनन्तु विश्वा भूतानि पवमानः पुनातु मा ।।

1. Let the sages purify me. Let thoughtful men purify me through their wisdom. Let all the creatures that exist cleanse me. Let God make me pure. (1347)

२. पवमानः पुनातु मा क्रत्वे दक्षाय जीवसे । अथो अरिष्टतातये ।।

2. May God make me pure for wisdom and for power and life, and unassailed security. (1348)

३. उभाभ्यां देव सवितः पवित्रेण सवेन च । अस्मान् पुनीहि चक्षसे ।।

3. O God, the Creator, through both of Thy knowledge and goading, purify us that we may visualise Thee. (1349)

HYMN XX

१. अग्नेरिवास्य दहत एति शुष्मिण उतेव मत्तो विलपन्नपायति ।
अन्यमस्मदिच्छतु कं चिदव्रतस्तपुर्वधाय नमो अस्तु तक्मने ।।

1. Fever comes like this fierce burning fire, and makes the patient run lamenting and inebriated. Let fever seek another intemperate person and not us. We assuage the fever armed with fiery heat. (1350)[1]

२. नमो रुद्राय नमो अस्तु तक्मने नमो राज्ञे वरुणाय त्विषीमते ।
नमो दिवे नमः पृथिव्यै नम ओषधीभ्यः ।।

2. Pay homage to the healing physician. Eradicate fever. Worship the Refulgent God, the Lord of all. Take full advantage of the sun, the Earth and the medicinal plants. (1351)

३. अयं यो अभिशोचयिष्णुर्विश्वा रूपाणि हरिता कृणोषि ।
तस्मै तेऽरुणाय बभ्रवे नमः कृणोमि वन्याय तक्मने ।।

3. O fever, thou, causing excruciating pain, makest all bodies pale. Thee, red, brown, prevalent in densely wooded places, I eradicate! (1352)[2]

[1]Those who are temperate in habits and observe the laws of hygiene remain free from fever. It attacks those who are intemperate and violate the laws of health.

[2]I: physician.

HYMN XXI

१. इमा यास्तिस्रः पृथिवीस्तासां ह भूमिरुत्तमा । तासामधि त्वचो अहं भेषजं समु जग्रभम् ।।

1. In all the three terrestrial regions God is verily the Best. I have truly realised the fear-banishing God, Who far transcends the vastness of these regions. (1353)[1]

२. श्रेष्ठमसि भेषजानां वसिष्ठं वीरुधानाम् । सोमो भग इव यामेषु देवेषु वरुणो यथा ।।

2. O God, Thou art the Best of all fear-banishing objects, Most Excellent of progressing subjects art Thou, just as Moon is best 'mid the wandering stars, and the sun is most excellent amongst the lustrous objects! (1354)

३. रेवतीरनाधृषः सिषासवः सिषासथ । उत स्थ केशदृंहणीरथो ह केशवर्धनीः ।।

3. O wealthy, non-violent, charitable subjects, long to give your gifts freely. Thou art the strengthener and augmentor of glory and renown. (1355)

HYMN XXII

१. कृष्णं नियानं हरयः सुपर्णा अपो वसाना दिवमुत् पतन्ति ।
त आववृत्रन्त्सदनादृतस्यादिद् घृतेन पृथिवीं व्यू्दुः ।।

1. The fast flying rays of the Sun, attracting water from the earth, passing through the atmosphere enrobed in waters, go aloft to heaven. Then from the Sun, the seat of water, they come down and inundate the earth with water. (1356)[2]

२. पयस्वतीः कृणुथाप ओषधीः शिवा यदेजथा मरुतो रुक्मवक्षसः ।
ऊर्जं च तत्र सुमतिं च पिन्वत यत्रा नरो मरुतः सिञ्चथा मधु ।।

2. O gold-breasted airs, when ye stir, ye make the waters invigorating and the plants propitious. O cloud-bearing airs, where ye sprinkle water, there ye produce strengthening food, and develop the intellect of the people. (1357)[3]

३. उदप्रुतो मरुतस्तां इयर्त वृष्टिर्या विश्वा निवतस्पृणाति ।
एजाति ग्लहा कन्येव तुन्नैरुं तुन्दाना पत्येव जाया ।।

3. O monsoon, the bringer of water, send down rain which fills all low-lying places and streams moving down. This agreeable rain goes to the running ocean, just as a distressed girl goes to her father, or an afflicted wife to her husband. (1358)

[1]God is Bhumi भवन्ति सर्वे लोका यस्यां सा भूमि, परमेश्वरः Bhumi is God, as all worlds reside in Him. Three:—Sun, Earth, Atmosphere.

[2]They: the rays of the sun.

[3]Gold-breasted: Lustrous.

HYMN XXIII

१. ससुषीस्तदपसो दिवा नक्तं च ससुषीः । वरेण्यक्रतुरहमपो देवी रुप ह्वये ॥

1. Most excellently wise and energetic I, invoke day and night, the extremely active and brilliant powers of the All-pervading Vast God. (1359)

२. ओता आपः कर्मण्या मुञ्चन्त्वितः प्रणीतये । सद्यः कृण्वन्त्वेतवे ॥

2. May the well-ordered powers of God, useful in actions, release us from this affliction, for adopting a better line of action. May they equip me for advancement. (1360)

३. देवस्य सवितुः सवे कर्म कृण्वन्तु मानुषाः । शं नो भवन्त्वप ओषधीः शिवाः ॥

3. Let all people perform their religious duties as ordained by God the Creator. Let waters be consoling unto us, and plants propitious. (1361)

HYMN XXIV

१. हिमवतः प्रस्रवन्ति सिन्धौ समह संगमः ।
आपो ह मह्यं तद् देवीर्ददन् हृद्योत-भेषजम् ॥

1. Waters flow from the snowy mountains, and simultaneously meet in in the ocean. May these efficacious waters serve me as a medicine that heals the heart's disease. (1362)[1]

२. यन्मे अक्ष्योरादिद्योत पार्ष्ण्योः प्रपदोश्च यत् ।
आपस्तत् सर्वं निष्करन् भिषजां सुभिषक्तमाः ॥

2. Whatever disease I have had, that causes pain in the eyes, heels or toes, all this the waters; the best of medicines, shall cure. (1363)

३. सिन्धुपत्नीः सिन्धुराज्ञीः सर्वा या नद्य१ स्थन । दत्त नस्तस्य भेषजं तेना वो भुनजामहै ॥

3. All the big streams feed the ocean and add to its glory. May they give us the balm that heals this ill. May we enjoy this boon from you. (1364)[2]

HYMN XXV

१. पञ्च च या पञ्चाशच्च संयन्ति मन्या अभि ।
इतस्ताः सर्वा नश्यन्तु वाका अपचितामिव ॥

1. May all the fifty-five tumours that appear on the neck, depart and vanish hence away, like the words of the weak. (1365)[3]

[1]Waters that flow from snowy mountains are pure, and having passed through various regions are mixed with minerals, and thus serve as a medicine for the heart's disease.

[2]They and you refer to streams, whose water possesses medicinal properties.

[3]Fifty-five: various. Just as the words of the weak vanish, as none cares for them, so may the diseases of the neck depart.

२. सप्त च याः सप्ततिश्च संयन्ति ग्रैव्या अभि ।
इतस्ताः सर्वा नश्यन्तु वाका अपचितामिव ॥

2. May all the seventy-seven afflictions that appear in the throat, depart and vanish hence away, like the words of the weak. (1366)[1]

३. नव च या नवतिश्च संयन्ति स्कन्ध्या अभि ।
इतस्ताः सर्वा नश्यन्तु वाका अपचितामिव ॥

3. May all the ninety-nine ills that attack the shoulder, depart and vanish hence away, like the words of the weak. (1367)[2]

HYMN XXVI

१. अव मा पाप्मन्त्सृज वशी सन् मृडयासि नः ।
आ मा भद्रस्य लोके पाप्मन् धेह्यविह्रुतम् ॥

1. Get away from me, O sin, do thou, the mighty, pity us. Set me uninjured in the world of happiness, O sin! (1368)

२. यो नः पाप्मन् न जहासि तमु त्वा जहिमो वयम् ।
पथामनु व्यावर्तनेऽन्यं पाप्मानु पद्यताम् ॥

2. O sin, if thou leavest us not, we leave thee. Thou at the turning of the paths, let sin fall on someone else! (1369)

३. अन्यत्रास्मन्न्युच्यतु सहस्राक्षो अमर्त्यः । यं द्वेषाम तमृच्छतु यमु द्विष्मस्तमिज्जहि ॥

3. O sin, unworthy of man, the annihilator of thousands, go thou for away from us. Dwell thou in the course of action we dislike. Demolish thou the line of conduct we shun! (1370)

HYMN XXVII

१. देवाः कपोत इषितो यदिच्छन् दूतो निर्ऋत्या इदमाजगाम ।
तस्मा अर्चाम कृणवाम निष्कृतिं शं नो अस्तु द्विपदे शं चतुष्पदे ॥

1. O learned persons, let us honour the man, who is suitable, the banisher of poverty, far-sighted and talented like a pigeon, and comes to our house as a seeker after venerable God. Let us seek relief from misery, and well-being for our bipeds and quadrupeds through him. (1371)

२. शिवः कपोत इषितो नो अस्त्वनागा देवाः शकुनो गृहं नः ।
अग्निर्हि विप्रो जुषतां हविर्नः परि हेतिः पक्षिणी नो वृणक्तु ॥

[1]Seventy-seven: Manifold.
[2]Ninety-nine: Innumerable.

2. O learned persons, let an agreeable, sinless, powerful person, far-sighted like a pigeon, who visits us, be auspicious for us and our dwelling. May that talented, wise person, gladly accept the food offered by us. May the thirst for partiality avoid us! (1372)

३. हेतिः पक्षिणी न दभात्यस्मानाष्ट्री पदं कृणुते अग्निधाने ।
शिवो गोभ्य उत पुरुषेभ्यो नो अस्तु मा । नो देवा इह हिंसीत् कपोतः ।।

3. Let not the thirst for partiality distract us. Let this learned person who visits us establish his authority in the famous assembly full of learned persons. O godly persons, let this person far-sighted like a pigeon bring welfare to our men and cattle. Let him forbear to harm us in this assembly. (1373)

HYMN XXVIII

१. ऋचा कपोतं नुदत प्रणोदमिषं मदन्तः परि गां नयामः ।
सं लोभयन्तो दुरिता पदानि हित्वा न ऊर्जं प्र पदात् पथिष्ठः ।।

1. O learned persons, advance through Vedic knowledge, this venerable, far-sighted leader. Rejoicing, obliterating traces of misfortune, we spread foodstuffs and knowledge all round. May this active learned person advance, giving us vigour. (1374)

२. परीमेऽग्निमर्षत परीमे गामनेषत । देवेष्वक्रत श्रवः क इमाँ आ दधर्षति ।।

2. They have secured a learned person, and diffused knowledge all around. They have established their prestige amongst the learned. Who is the man that conquers them? (1375)[1]

३. यः प्रथमः प्रवतमाससाद बहुभ्यः पन्थामनुपस्पशानः ।
योऽस्येशे द्विपदो यश्चतुष्पदस्तस्मै यमाय नमो अस्तु मृत्यवे ।।

3. He, while exploring the path for many, is Foremost and Exalted. May reverence be paid to Him, the Lord of the world of quadrupeds and bipeds, the Just, the Saviour of souls from spiritual death. (1376)[2]

HYMN XXIX

१. अमून् हेतिः पतत्रिणीन्येतु यदुलूको वदति मोघमेतत् ।
यद् वा कपोतः पदमग्नौ कृणोति ।।

[1]They: seekers after knowledge.
[2]He: God.

1. May the onrushing, cruel army fall on the yonder foes. Whatever, a foolish person full of darkness like an owl says, is ineffective. A person far-sighted and intelligent like a pigeon, establishes his authority in an assembly of the learned. (1377)

२. यौ ते दूतौ निर्ऋत इदमेतोऽप्रहितौ प्रहितौ वा गृहं नः । कपोतोलूकाभ्यामपदं तदस्तु ।।

2. O ever-gladdening God, Thy powers of punishment and reward, visit this dwelling of ours, May the Vast God throw away our unsavoury affliction, through His praiseworthy knowledge and power of preservation from ignorance! (1378)

३. अवैरहत्यायेदमा पपत्यात् सुवीरताया इदमा ससद्यात् ।
पराङेव परा वद पराचीमनु संवतम्
यथा यमस्य त्वा गृहेऽरसं प्रतिचाकशानाभूकं प्रतिचाकशान् ।।

3. O venerable person far-sighted like a pigeon, come here to save our heroes from slaughter, sit here for the well-being of our excellent heroes. O owl-like foolish foe, speak, standing at a distance far away, so that people may see thee in the house of a justice-loving man bereft of all thy power, and see thee impotent! (1379)

HYMN XXX

१. देवा इमं मधुना संयुतं यवं सरस्वत्यामधि मणावचर्कृषुः ।
इन्द्र आसीत् सीरपतिः शतक्रतुः कीनाशा आसन् मरुतः सुदानवः ।।

1. Learned persons have again and again acquired through the force of Vedic knowledge and superiority, salvation, replete with sweet pleasure. An Acharya, the master of hundreds of noble deeds, and intellect is the main cultivator, and the charitably disposed learned persons are the laborious workers after salvation. (1380)[1]

२. यस्ते मदोऽवकेशो विकेशो येनाभिहस्यं पुरुषं कृणोषि ।
आरात् त्वदन्या वनानि वृक्षि त्वं शमि शतवल्शा वि रोह ।।

2. O solace-bestowing Vedic knowledge, thy joy is explicit and manifold in lustre, wherewith thou fillest a man with laughter and pleasure I keep away far from thee suppliant acts of unwisdom. May thou, O Vedic knowledge, grow up with a hundred branches! (1381)[2]

३. बृहत् पलाशे सुभगे वर्षवृद्ध ऋतावरि । मातेव पुत्रेभ्यो मृड केशेभ्यः शमि ।।

[1]Acharya: Preceptor, Guru, Cultivator: An Acharya is an ardent seeker after salvation. Just as a peasant tills the land, sows the seed, and reaps the harvest of barley, so do the learned acquire through Vedic wisdom emancipation full of joy.

[2]Hundred branches: Different sorts of sciences and branches of knowledge. Yogis attain happiness by spreading knowledge and dispelling ignorance.

3. O solace-bestowing Vedic knowledge, thou art equipped with immense power of protection, thou art auspicious, exalted through laudable merits, thou, the embodiment of truth, be gracious to the manifestation of knowledge, like a mother to her sons! (1382)

HYMN XXXI

१. आयं गौः पृश्निरक्रमीदसदन्मातरं पुरः । पितरं च प्रयन्त्स्वः ॥

1. This Earth revolves in the space, it revolves with its mother water in its orbit. It moves round its father, the sun. (1383)[1]

२. अन्तश्चरति रोचना अस्य प्राणादपानतः । व्यख्यन्महिषः स्वः ॥

2. The radiance and warmth of this sun penetrate all human beings who inhale and exhale. The great sun illumines the atmosphere and sky. (1384)[2]

३. त्रिंशद् धामा वि राजति वाक् पतङ्गो अशिश्रियत् । प्रति वस्तोरहर्द्युभिः ॥

3. Thirty divisions of the day and night are illumined by the rays of the sun. Sun alone is the shelter and support of our speech. (1385)[3]

HYMN XXXII

१. अन्तर्दावे जुहुता स्वे३तद् यातुधानक्षयणं घृतेन ।
आराद् रक्षांसि प्रति दह त्वमग्ने न नो गृहाणामुप तीतपासि ॥

1. O learned persons, put into blazing fire, with butter, this oblation, full of substances which cure painful diseases. Remove from afar demons, O God, afflict not the inmates of our houses. (1386)

२. रुद्रो वो ग्रीवा अशरैत् पिशाचाः पृष्टीर्वोऽपि शृणातु यातुधानाः ।
वीरुत् वो विश्वतोवीर्या यमेन समजीगमत् ॥

2. O flesh-eating diseases or cannibals, may a physician or a king break your necks. O painful diseases or violent persons, may he split your ribs asunder! The Omnipotent God hath proclaimed His law for the actions of you all. (1387)[4]

३. अभयं मित्रावरुणाविहास्तु नोऽर्चिषात्त्रिणो नुदतं प्रतीचः ।
मा ज्ञातारं मा प्रतिष्ठां विदन्त मिथो विघ्नाना उप यन्तु मृत्युम् ॥

[1]Water is the mother of Earth as Earth is produced by the mixture of the particles of water with its own particles, and remains pregnant with water. Sun is the father of the Earth, as from the sun, it derives all light and sustenance. See *Yajur*, 3-6. See *Sāma*, 630, and *Rig*, 10-186-1.

[2]See *Yajur*, 3-7.

[3]Voice is carried from one place to the other by the rays of Sun, hence the Sun is spoken of as the shelter and support of our speech.

[4]He: A physician or a king.

3. O King and Commander-in-chief, may we dwell in this country free from fear. With your glittering weapon drive the greedy demons backward. Let them not find a wise leader or a refuge, but fighting together let them go down to Death. (1388)

HYMN XXXIII

१. यस्येदमा रजो युजस्तुजे जना वनं स्वः। इन्द्रस्य रन्त्यं बृहत् ॥

1. Mighty is the beautiful power of God, under Whose control lie, the solar system, all human beings, the Earth and Sun. (1389)

२. नाधृष आ दधृषते धृषाणो धृषितः शवः। पुरा यथा व्यथिः श्रव इन्द्रस्य नाधृषे शवः ॥

2. God is Unconquerable. His overpowering strength conquers even the unconquerable. As erst still, God is aweinspiring. Unassailable is God's fame and force. (1390)

३. स नो ददातु तां रयिमुरुं पिशङ्गसंदृशम्। इन्द्रः पतिस्तुविष्टमो जनेष्वा ॥

3. May God bestow on us that wealth, far-spreading, bright with yellow hue like gold. God is mightiest Lord among the folk. (1391)

HYMN XXXIV

१. प्राग्नये वाचमीरय वृषभाय क्षितीनाम्। स नः पर्षदति द्विषः ॥

1. O learned person, sing the praise of God, Most Powerful of all men. May He bear us past our foes! (1392)[1]

२. यो रक्षांसि निजूर्वत्यग्निस्तिग्मेन शोचिषा। स नः पर्षदति द्विषः ॥

2. May that God, Who consumes our devilish sentiments with His sharp splendour, bear us past our foes. (1393)

३. यः परस्याः परावतस्तिरो धन्वातिरोचते। स नः पर्षदति द्विषः ॥

3. May God, Who from distance far remote shineth across the atmosphere and sky, transport us past our foes. (1394)

४. यो विश्वाभि विपश्यति भुवना सं च पश्यति। स नः पर्षदति द्विषः ॥

4. May God, Who beholds all creatures, Who beholds them with a careful eye, transport us past our foes. (1395)

५. यो अस्य पारे रजसः शुक्रो अग्निरजायत। स नः पर्षदति द्विषः ॥

5. May that Refulgent God, Who exists even beyond this region of the air transport us past our foes. (1396)

[1]Foes: Internal foes like lust, avarice, anger, pride etc,

HYMN XXXV

१. वैश्वानरो न ऊतय आ प्र यातु परावतः । अग्निर्नः सुष्टुतीरुप ॥

1. Forth from the distance far away, may God, the Benefactor of humanity, come to succour us. May God accept our eulogies. (1397)

२. वैश्वानरो न आगमदिमं यज्ञं सजूरुप । अग्निरुक्थेष्वंहसु ॥

2. May God, the Lover of all souls, come as a Friend to this our noble deed. May God be our companion in our desirable, praiseworthy acts. (1398)

३. वैश्वानरोऽङ्गिरसां स्तोममुक्थं च चाक्लृपत् । ऐषु द्युम्नं स्वर्यमत् ॥

3. God, the Benefactor of all souls, makes the lauds and Vedic recitations of the sages fruitful. The same Refulgent God bestows wisdom and wealth on those sages. (1399)

HYMN XXXVI

१. ऋतावानं वैश्वानरमृतस्य ज्योतिषस्पतिम् । अजस्रं घर्ममीमहे ॥

1. We incessantly pray to God, the Embodiment of truth, the Benefactor of humanity, the Lord of wealth and light, the Master of refulgence. (1400)

२. स विश्वा प्रति चाक्लृप ऋतूंरुत् सृजते वशी । यज्ञस्य वय उत्तिरन् ॥

2. God lends sustenance to all men, He, the Controller, creates different seasons. He produces nice corn for the yajña. (1401)

३. अग्निः परेषु धामसु कामो भूतस्य भव्यस्य । सम्राडेको वि राजति ॥

3. God is the Fulfiller of the desires of men created in the past and yet to be created in future. He like a sole Imperial Lord rules over distant worlds. (1402)

HYMN XXXVII

१. उप प्रागात् सहस्राक्षो युक्त्वा शपथो रथम् । शप्तारमन्विच्छन् मम वृक इवाविमतो गृहम् ॥

1. A far-sighted king, the shower of the path of peace, yoking his steeds, hath come seeking for my reviler, to punish him, as a wolf seeks for the house of the owner of sheep to destroy them. (1403)[1]

२. परि णो वृङ्धि शपथ ह्रदमग्निरिवा दहन् । शप्तारमत्र नो जहि दिवो वृक्षमिवाशनिः ॥

2. O King, the exhibitor of the path of peace, avoid us, as consuming fire avoids the lake. Smite thou the man who curses us, as lightning from the sky strikes the tree. (1404)

३. यो नः शपादशपतः शपतो यश्च नः शपात् । शुने पेष्ट्रमिवावक्षामं तं प्रत्यस्यामि मृत्यवे ॥

[1]A king should punish the revilers and cursers of noble persons.

3. Who curses us, without being cursed, or, cursed, who curses us again, I cast him, a poor fellow, to Death, as to a dog one throws a piece of bread. (1405)

HYMN XXXVIII

१. सिंहे व्याघ्र उत या पृदाकौ त्विषिरग्नौ ब्राह्मणे सूर्ये या ।
इन्द्रं या देवी सुभगा जजान सा न ऐतु वर्चसा संविदाना ।।

1. Whatever energy a lion, tiger, adder, burning fire, Brahman, or the sun hath, and the blessed, spiritual force, that makes a man a king, may that come unto us conjoined with strength and vigour. (1406)

२. या हस्तिनि द्वीपिनि या हिरण्ये त्विषिरप्सु गोषु या पुरुषेषु ।
इन्द्रं या देवी सुभगा जजान सा न ऐतु वर्चसा संविदाना ।।

2. All energy of elephant and panther, all halo and lustre of gold, men, kine, and waters, and the blessed spiritual force that makes a man a king, may that come unto us conjoined with strength and vigour. (1407)

३. रथे अक्षेष्वृषभस्य वाजे वाते पर्जन्ये वरुणस्य शुष्मे ।
इन्द्रं या देवी सुभगा जजान सा न ऐतु वर्चसा संविदाना ।।

3. Whatever might that exists in car, axles, in the strong bull's courage, in wind, in cloud, and in the warmth of the Sun, and the blessed spiritual force, that makes a man a king, may that come unto us conjoined with strength and vigour. (1408)

४. राजन्ये दुन्दुभावायतायामश्वस्य वाजे पुरुषस्य मायौ ।
इन्द्रं या देवी सुभगा जजान सा न ऐतु वर्चसा संविदाना ।।

4. Whatever energy that is found in the warrior, in the war-drum stretched for battle, in the horse's speed, and in the man's roar, and the blessed spiritual force that makes a man a king, may that come unto us conjoined with strength and vigour. (1409)

HYMN XXXIX

१. यशो हविर्वर्धतामिन्द्रजूतं सहस्रवीर्यं सुभृतं सहस्कृतम् ।
प्रसर्स्राणमनु दीर्घाय चक्षसे हविष्मन्तं मा वर्धय ज्येष्ठतातये ।।

1. May my fame and strength, bestowed by God, possessing a thousand powers, well-ordered, augmenting might, thrive, spreading far and wide. O God, to a life of long duration and highest rank raise me, full of devotion. (1410)

२. अच्छा न इन्द्रं यशसं यशोभिर्यशस्विनं नमसाना विधेम ।
स नो रास्व राष्ट्रमिन्द्रजूतं तस्य ते रातौ यशसः स्याम ।।

2. May we, bowing, nicely worship our glorious God, famous for His glories, May He grant us a kingdom well-administered by a king. May we be prosperous in this boon of Thine. (1411)

३. यशा इन्द्रो यशा अग्निर्यशाः सोमो अजायत ।
यशा विश्वस्य भूतस्याहमस्मि यशस्तमः ॥

3. Glorious is the sun, glorious is fire, and glorious is the Moon. I, longing for glory, am the most glorious of all human beings. (1412)

HYMN XL

१. अभयं द्यावापृथिवी इहास्तु नोऽभयं सोमः सविता नः कृणोतु ।
अभयं नोऽस्तूर्व१न्तरिक्षं सप्तऋषीणां च हविषाभयं नो अस्तु ॥

1. O Heaven and Earth make us free from fear. May the Moon and Sun grant us freedom from fear. May the vast space make us fearless. May we be free from fear through the sacrifice of the Seven Rishis. (1413)[1]

२. अस्मै ग्रामाय प्रदिशश्चतस्र ऊर्जं सुभूतं स्वस्ति सविता नः कृणोतु ।
अशत्र्विन्द्रो अभयं नः कृणोत्वन्यत्र राज्ञामभि यातु मन्युः ॥

2. May God grant prosperity, wealth and bliss, in all the four quarters of this village of ours. May God make us free from foes and danger; may wrath of kings be turned to other places. (1414)

३. अनमित्रं नो अधरादनमित्रं न उत्तरात् । इन्द्रानमित्रं नः पश्चादनमित्रं पुरस्कृधि ॥

3. O God, make Thou us free from enemies from the South, from the North, from the West and from the East. (1415)

HYMN XLI

१. मनसे चेतसे धिय आकूतय उत चित्तये । मत्यै श्रुताय चक्षसे विधेम हविषा वयम् ॥

1. For acquiring the strength of mind, thought, intellect, purpose, intelligence, discernment, hearing, and sight, let us adore God with devotion. (1416)[2]

२. अपानाय व्यानाय प्राणाय भूरिधायसे । सरस्वत्या उरुव्यचे विधेम हविषा वयम् ॥

2. For expiration, vital air, and breath that amply nourishes, and for acquiring vast knowledge, let us adore God with devotion. (1417)

३. मा नो हासिषुर्ऋषयो दैव्या ये तनूपा ये नस्तन्व१स्तनूजाः ।
अमर्त्या मर्त्यां अभि नः सचध्वमायुर्धत्त प्रतरं जीवसे नः ॥

[1]Seven Rishis: Two eyes, two ears, two nostrils, and the mouth, or skin, eye, ear, tongue, nose, mind and intellect.

[2]Rishis: Seven Rishis referred to in verse 1, Hymn XL. They are immortal, deathless.

3. Let not the Rishis, the divine, forsake us, our own, our very selves, our lives' protectors. Do ye immortal, still attend us mortals, and give us noble life to live long. (1418)

HYMN XLII

१. अव ज्यामिव धन्वनो मन्युं तनोमि ते हृदः ।
यथा संमनसौ भूत्वा सखायाविव सचावहै ॥

1. O Comrade, I loose the anger from thy heart as 'twere the bow-string from a bow, that we, one-minded now, may walk together as familiar friends! (1419)

२. सखायाविव सचावहा अव मन्युं तनोमि ते ।
अधस्ते अश्मनो मन्युमुपास्यामसि यो गुरुः ॥

2. Together let us walk as friends: thy wrathful feeling I remove. Beneath a heavy stone we cast thy wrath away and bury it. (1420)[1]

३. अभि तिष्ठामि ते मन्युं पार्ष्ण्या प्रपदेन च । यथावशो न वादिषो मम चित्तमुपायसि ॥

3. O angry person, I trample on thine anger, I tread it down with heel and toe. So dost thou yield thee to my will, so that being subdued thou utterest no more angry words. (1421)

HYMN XLIII

१. अयं दर्भो विमन्युकः स्वाय चारणाय च । मन्योर्विमन्युकस्यायं मन्युशमन उच्यते ॥

1. Just as a blade of grass is free from wrath for a friend or foe, is free from thorn and bends with the draft of wind, but fastens many strung in a string, similarly, a man who is free from wrath for his kin or enemy, consolidates the society like a string, and is called the appeaser of the wrath of an angry person or one free from anger. (1422)

२. अयं यो भूरिमूलः समुद्रमवतिष्ठति । दर्भः पृथिव्या उत्थितो मन्युशमन उच्यते ॥

2. Just as grass, abundant in roots, sprung out of Earth, remains calm below the space, so this man, competent to organise the society, born in his motherland, remains under the protection of God the Almighty, and is called the appeaser of wraths and the assuager of all strifes. (1423)

३. वि ते हनव्यां शरणिं वि ते मुख्यां नयामसि । यथावशो न वादिषो मम चित्तमुपायसि ॥

3. O man, we control thy tongue, which creates the feeling of violence and anger in thy chin or mouth, so that being helpless thou utterest not angry words, and becomest subservient to my will. (1424)

[1]Anything put under a heavy weight cannot move or rise up, so wrath thrown under a heavy stone is symbolic of appeasement.

HYMN XLIV

१. अस्थाद् द्यौरस्थात् पृथिव्यस्थाद् विश्वमिदं जगत् ।
अस्थुर्वृक्षा ऊर्ध्वस्वप्नास्तिष्ठाद् रोगो अयं तव ॥

1. Just as the heaven stands firm, the earth stands firm, this universal world stands firm, and the trees that sleep erect stand firm, so let this thy malady, O patient, be still! (1425)[1]

२. शतं या भेषजानि ते सहस्रं संगतानि च । श्रेष्ठमास्रावभेषजं वसिष्ठं रोगनाशनम् ॥

2. O patient, of all thy hundred remedies, a thousand remedies combined, this is surest cure for flux, most excellent to heal disease! (1426)

३. रुद्रस्य मूत्रमस्यमृतस्य नाभिः ।
विषाणका नाम वा असि पितॄणां मूलादुत्थिता वातीकृतनाशनी ॥

3. Rainy water from the thundering cloud is the source of prolonged life. O medicine thy name is Vishāṇaka. Thou removest illness caused by wind, and uproots the disease inherited from father and mother. (1427)[2]

HYMN XLV

१. परोऽपेहि मनस्पाप किमशस्तानि शंससि ।
परेहि न त्वा कामये वृक्षां वनानि सं चर गृहेषु गोषु मे मनः ॥

1. Sin of the Mind, avaunt, get away! Why sayest thou what none should say. Go hence away, I love thee not, go to the forests and the trees. My heart is in our homes and cows. (1428)

२. अवशसा निःशसा यत् पराशसोपारिम जाग्रतो यत् स्वपन्तः ।
अग्निर्विश्वान्यप दुष्कृतान्यजुष्टान्यारे अस्मद् दधातु ॥

2. Whatever wrong we have committed, sleeping or waking, by ill-will, dislike, or slander, all these offences, which deserve displeasure, may God take from us and keep them distant. (1429)

३. यदिन्द्र ब्रह्मणस्पतेऽपि मृषा चरामसि । प्रचेता न आङ्गिरसो दुरितात् पात्वंहसः ॥

3. O Glorious God, the Lord of the universe, whatever foolish deed we plan, may Thou, the Wise God, the Lover of the learned, preserve us from that woeful sin. (1430)

[1]Be still: Advance no further and stay away from us. The sleeping and waking of the trees show that the trees have life and soul.

[2]Water is the urine of thundering. Rain water is considered to be the purest, and most healing and efficacious in nature. Vishāṇaka medicine denotes the family of medicinal plants named as Ajshringhi, Avartaki shringhi, virishchkali, Sātalā and Rohini.

Vishāṇaka (Asclepias Germinata)=*karkaṭa*=*śṛiṅgī* and sātalā., *Sanskrit-English Dictionary* of Monier Monier Williams.

HYMN XLVI

१. यो न जीवोसि न मृतो देवानाममृतगर्भोऽसि स्वप्न ।
वरुणानी ते माता यमः पितारुर्नामासि ॥

1. O dream, thou art neither living nor dead. Thou art the source of solace to the organs. Night, the queen of darkness, is thy mother, and the Sun, the regulator, is thy father. Thou art the enemy of longevity. (1431)

२. विद्म ते स्वप्न जनित्रं देवजामीनां पुत्रोऽसि यमस्य करणः ।
अन्तकोऽसि मृत्युरसि । तं त्वा स्वप्न तथा सं विद्म स नः स्वप्न दुष्वप्न्यात् पाहि ॥

2. O dream, we know thy birth. Thou art the son of the forces of organs, and product of the soul. Thou art the Finisher. Thou art Death. So well we know thee who thou art. O dream guard us from evil thoughts. (1432)[1]

३. यथा कलां यथा शफं यथर्णं संनयन्ति । एवा दुष्वप्न्यं सर्वं द्विषते सं नयामसि ॥

3. As men discharge a debt, by paying one sixteenth or one eighth of their income, so all the evil thoughts of the dream do we pay and assign unto our foe. (1433)

HYMN XLVII

१. अग्निः प्रातःसवने पात्वस्मान् वैश्वानरो विश्वकृद् विश्वशंभूः ।
स नः पावको द्रविणे दधात्वायुष्मन्तः सहभक्षाः स्याम ॥

1. May God, the Lover of mankind, the Creator of the universe, the Bringer of peace and prosperity unto all, guard us in the first stage of our life. May He, the purifier of all, give us riches: may we have long life enjoying food together. (1434)[2]

२. विश्वे देवा मरुत इन्द्रो अस्मानस्मिन् द्वितीये सवने न जह्युः ।
आयुष्मन्तः प्रियमेषां वदन्तो वयं देवानां सुमतौ स्याम ॥

2. May all noble qualities, learned persons and God, forsake us not during the second stage of our life. Enjoying a long life and speaking words that please them, may we act according to the sound advice of the learned. (1435)[3]

३. इदं तृतीयं सवनं कवीनामृतेन ये चमसमैरयन्त ।
ते सौधन्वनाः स्वऽरानशानाः स्विऽष्टिं नो अभि वस्यो नयन्तु ॥

[1]Dream does not exist in the waking (Jagrit) state, nor in (sushupti) profound sleep. Day is the father of dreams, as what we see and think in the day time, appears in the shape of dreams at night. Dream is spoken of as Arru, i.e., the enemy of long life. Dreams decrease age.

[2]First stage: The early period of Vasu Brahmcharya.

Together: With our relatives and friends.

[3]Second stage: The period of Rudra Brahmcharya.

3. The third stage of life is meant for those learned persons, who exert their knowledge and penance to fulfil their vow. They wielding the bow of Om like skilled archers, attaining to salvation and the felicity of God, lend fruition to our nice vow of celibacy. (1436)[1]

HYMN XLVIII

१. श्येनोऽसि गायत्रच्छन्दा अनु त्वा रभे । स्वस्ति मा सं वहास्य यज्ञस्योदृचि स्वाहा ॥

1. O first kind of Vasu Brahmcharya, thou art the imparter of knowledge and spiritual glow, like the twenty-four syllables of the Gayatri, thou extendest over the first twenty-four years of life. I stick fast unto thee. Happily bear me to the last goal of this my sacrifice of celibacy. This is my grim determination! (1437)

२. ऋभुरसि जगच्छन्दा अनु त्वा रभे । स्वस्ति मा सं वहास्य यज्ञस्योदृचि स्वाहा ॥

2. O Aditya Brahmcharya, thou art coupled with spiritual knowledge, truth and glory. Like the forty-eight syllables of the Jagti metre, thou extendest over the first forty eight years of life. I stick, fast unto thee. Happily bear me to the last goal of my sacrifice of celibacy. This is my grim determination! (1438)

३. वृषासि त्रिष्टुप्छन्दा अनु त्वा रभे । स्वस्ति मा सं वहास्य यज्ञस्योदृचि स्वाहा ॥

3. O medium Rudra Brahmcharya, thou art powerful. Like the forty-four syllables of the Trishtup metre, thou extendest over the first forty-four years of life. I stick fast unto thee. Happily bear me to the last goal of this my sacrifice of celibacy. This is my grim determination! (1439)

HYMN XLIX

१. नहि ते अग्ने तन्वः क्रूरमानंश मर्त्यः । कपिर्बभस्ति तेजनं स्वं जरायु गौरिव ॥

1. O God, mortal man cannot comprehend the immensity and virility of Thy power. Thou makest every one tremble with Thy fear. Thou destroyest sin, as a cow eats her secundines. (1440)[2]

२. मेष इव वै सं च वि चोर्वच्यसे यदुत्तरद्रावुपरश्च खादतः ।
शीर्ष्णा शिरोऽप्ससाप्सो अर्दयन्नंशून् बभस्ति हरितेभिरासभिः ॥

[1]Griffith has translated Sudhanvanā as three sons of Sudhanvan, who is said to have been a descendant of Angiras. They were named separately Ribhu, Vibhvan, and Vāja, and styled collectively Ribhus. Through their assiduous performance of good works they obtained divinity, and became entitled to receive praise and adoration. This explanation is unacceptable as it savours of history in the Vedas, which are absolutely free from it.

Third stage: The period of Aditya Brahmcharya extending upto 48 years.

[2]God is subtle in contemplation, and grand, expanded in nature to the naked eye, just as the sun contracts in the morning and evening when it sets, and expands and grows warmer in the day time. Just as the jaws of a man press and chew the food, so the destructive powers of God devour the universe at the time of dissolution.

2. O God, Thou art subtle and gross like the Sun. Just as the upper and lower jaws of a man taking food chew it, so dost Thou devour the universe between the Earth and Heaven. Closely compressing the beautiful world with Thy All-pervading power, and the lofty parts of the world with Thy grandeur, with Thy destructive powers, Thou dissolvest all these worlds. (1441)

३. सुपर्णा वाचमक्रतोप द्यव्याखरे कृष्णा इषिरा अनर्तिषुः ।
नि यन्नियन्त्युपरस्य निष्कृतिं पुरू रेतो दधिरे सूर्यश्रितः ॥

3. Rays, the dwellers with the Sun, send forth their voice in the empty ether. They dance, as it were drawing water and moving fast. They are filled with huge water, when they determine to come down as rain from the cloud. (1442)

HYMN L

१. हतं तर्दं समङ्कमाखुमश्विना छिन्तं शिरो अपि पृष्टीः शृणीतम् ।
यवान्नेददानपि नह्यतं मुखमथाभयं कृणुतं धान्याय्रिय ॥

1. Ye husband and wife, the growers and protectors of corn, destroy the crow, the swine, the rat, cut off their heads and crush their ribs. Bind fast their mouths; let them not eat our barley; so guard, Ye twain, the growing corn from danger. (1443)

२. तर्द है पतङ्ग है जभ्य हा उपक्वस ।
ब्रह्मेवासंस्थितं हविरनदन्त इमान् यवानहिंसन्तो अपोदित ॥

2. Ho! crow, ho! thou locust, ho! obnoxious grass-hopper. As a priest rejects the not well-prepared oblation, so go hence devouring not, injuring not this corn. (1444)

३. तर्दापते वघापते तृष्टजम्भा आ शृणोत मे ।
य आरण्या व्यद्वरा ये के च स्थ व्यद्वरास्तान्त्सर्वाञ्जम्भयामसि ॥

3. Hearken to me, lord of the violent birds, lord of the locusts, ye sharp-toothed vermins! whatever ye be, dwelling in woods or villages, devourers of my harvest, we crush and mangle all those. (1445)

HYMN LI

१. वायोः पूतः पवित्रेण प्रत्यङ् सोमो अति द्रुतः । इन्द्रस्य युज्यः सखा ॥

1. The pure internal soul, cleansed through the ennobling contemplation of God, soon attains to salvation, and becomes His friend through yogic samadhi. (1446)[1]

२. आपो अस्मान् मातरः सूदयन्तु घृतेन नो घृतप्वः पुनन्तु ।
विश्वं हि रिप्रं प्रवहन्ति देवीरुदिदाभ्यः शुचिरा पूत एमि ॥

[1]Samadhi: Deep concentration.

2. May all the world-building forces strengthen me. May glittering objects like the Sun, purify me with their brilliance. Divine forces alone bear off each blot and sin. Bathing in them may I become cleansed and stainless, and attain to God. (1447)

३. यत् किं चेदं वरुण दैव्ये जनेऽभिद्रोहं मनुष्या३श्चरन्ति ।
अचित्त्या चेत् तव धर्मा युयोपिम मा नस्तस्मादेनसो देव रीरिषः ॥

3. O God, whatever offence men commit against noble persons, or when through want of thought we violate thy laws, punish us not, O God, for that iniquity! (1448)

HYMN LII

१. उत् सूर्यो दिव एति पुरो रक्षांसि निजूर्वन् । आदित्यः पर्वतेभ्यो विश्वदृष्टो अदृष्टहा ॥

1 The Sun, removing all sorts of darkness, seen of all, destroying unseen maladies, mounts upward in the front of heaven, from the mountains. (1449)

२. नि गावो गोष्ठे असदन् नि मृगासो अविक्षत । न्यू३र्मयो नदीनां न्य१दृष्टा अलिप्सत ॥

2. At the time of sun-set, the kine had settled in their pen, wild animals had sought their lairs; the wavelets of the brooks had passed away, and being unseen were longed for to be seen. (1450)

३. आयुर्ददं विपश्चितं श्रुतां कण्वस्य वीरुधम् ।
आभारिषं विश्वभेषजीमस्यादृष्टान् नि शमयत् ॥

3. May I obtain Vedic wisdom, the giver of longevity, full of knowledge, illustrious, the bestower of spiritual knowledge to a learned person, and the averter of all calamities. May it suppress the evil sentiments of the soul. (1451)

HYMN LIII

१. द्यौश्च म इदं पृथिवी च प्रचेतसौ शुक्रो बृहन् दक्षिणया पिपर्तु ।
अनु स्वधा चिकितां सोमो अग्निर्वायुर्नः पातु सविता भगश्च ॥

1. May father and mother, like Heaven and Earth, wise pair, protect this body of mine. May lofty God, nourish me with His power of knowledge and action. May my mental faculty accept the knowledge granted by God and act according to it. May God, the Creator, Omniscient, All-pervading, the Urger, Dignified always rear us. (1452)

२. पुनः प्राणः पुनरात्मा न ऐतु पुनश्चक्षुः पुनरसुर्न ऐतु ।
वैश्वानरो नो अदब्धस्तनूपा अन्तस्तिष्ठाति दुरितानि विश्वा ॥

2. Again return to us our breath and spirit, again come back to us our vision and intellect. The immortal soul, the lord of organs, our bodies' guardian, knowing our sins, being undismayed rests patiently in us. (1453)[1]

३. सं वर्चसा पयसा सं तनूभिरगन्महि मनसा सं शिवेन ।
त्वष्टा नो अत्र वरीयः कृणोत्वनु नो मार्ष्टु तन्वो३ यद् विरिष्टम् ॥

3. May we be united with splendour, strength, nice bodies, and happy mind. May God grant us excellent riches, knowledge and fame, and remove each deformity from our body. (1454)

HYMN LIV

१. इदं तद् युज उत्तरमिन्द्रं शुम्भाम्यष्टये । अस्य क्षत्रं श्रियं महीं वृष्टिरिव वर्धया तृणम् ॥

1. Just as rain increases the grass, so shouldst thou, O king, increase the military strength and immense wealth of this country. For this purpose, I appoint the exalted king in this office, and adorn him so that he may carry out the administration efficiently. (1455)[2]

२. अस्मै क्षत्रमग्नीषोमावस्मै धारयतं रयिम् । इमं राष्ट्रस्याभीवर्गे कृणुतं युज उत्तरम् ॥

2. O Commander-in-chief and priest, confirm the princely power in him, grant him wealth, Make him competent for protecting his dominion. For the same purpose, I set him on this exalted position! (1456)[3]

३. सबन्धुश्चासबन्धुश्च यो अस्माँ अभिदासति । सर्वं तं रन्धयासि मे यजमानाय सुन्वते ॥

3. O priest, the man who wants to subjugate us, whether a stranger or kin, hand him over to me, who administers the state and controls the subjects. (1457)

HYMN LV

१. ये पन्थानो बहवो देवयाना अन्तरा द्यावापृथिवी संचरन्ति ।
तेषामज्यानिं यतमो वहाति तस्मै मा देवाः परि धत्तेह सर्वे ॥

1. Of all the many pathways frequented by the learned, that traverse realms between God and Matter, consign me, all Ye sages, to that which leadeth to perfect and inviolable safety in the world. (1458)

२. ग्रीष्मो हेमन्तः शिशिरो वसन्तः शरद् वर्षाः स्विते नो दधात ।
आ नो गोषु भजता प्रजायां निवात इद् वः शरणे स्याम ॥

2. Maintain us in well-being Summer, Winter, Dew-time, Spring, Autumn, and Rainy season. Grant us happiness in cattle and children. May we enjoy your unassailed protection. (1459)

[1] The first part of the hymn preaches the doctrine of the transmigration of soul.

[2] I: Priest.

[3] 'Him' refers to the ring, and 'I' to the priest.

३. इदावत्सराय परिवत्सराय संवत्सराय कृणुता बृहन्नमः ।
तेषां वयं सुमतौ यज्ञियानामपि भद्रे सौमनसे स्याम ॥

3. Pay lofty adoration to the teacher who makes us dwell in knowledge, to the father who affords us shelter, to the king who grants us residence. May we abide in the auspicious favour and gracious love of these who claim our worship. (1460)

HYMN LVI

१. मा नो देवा अहिर्वधीत् सतोकान्त्सहपूरुषान् ।
संयतं न वि ष्परद् व्यात्तं न सं यमन्नमो देवजनेभ्यः ॥

1. O learned persons, let not vice like the serpent attack us, with our children and our folk. Let it not close the opened mouth nor close that which now is opened. We adore the learned persons! (1461)[1]

२. नमोऽस्त्वसिताय नमस्तिरश्चिराजये । स्वजाय बभ्रवे नमो नमो देवजनेभ्यः ॥

2. Use thunderbolt for the black serpent, for that with stripes across, for the brown viper that twists and clings round. Let us pay reverence to the learned who know the art of controlling these snakes. (1462)[2]

३. सं ते हन्मि दता दतः समु ते हन्वा हनू । सं ते जिह्वाया जिह्वां सम्वास्नाह आस्य१म् ॥

3. O serpent, I crush thy teeth, striking the upper against the lower ones. I break thy jaws, making the one collide with the other. I injure thy tongues, making them both hit against each other. I break thy face, making it strike against the other, and thus bring thee under my control. (1463)[3]

HYMN LVII

१. इदमिद् वा उ भेषजमिदं रुद्रस्य भेषजम् । येनेषुमेकतेजनां शतशल्यामपब्रवत् ॥

1. This Vedic knowledge alone is verily the dispeller of fear. This is a sovereign remedy prescribed by God. With its help a man can ward off the shaft of a hundred maladies in this single body. (1464)[4]

२. जालाषेणाभि षिञ्चत जालाषेणोप सिञ्चत । जालाषमुग्रं भेषजं तेन नो मृड जीवसे ॥

2. O physician besprinkle the wound with anodyne, bedew it with relieving balm. Vedic knowledge is a strong, soothing medicine, O God, bless us therewith, that we may live. (1465)[5]

[1]'It' refers to the serpent-like vice. If the mouth of the serpent is opened, it should not close, if it is closed, it should not open to bite us. We should shun vice and make it ineffective to attack us.

[2]नमः—मयति शत्रुन् । वज्रनाम—निघ० 2-20. Just as serpents are controlled by serpent charmers, so should we control our vices by coming in contact with learned persons.

[3]I: snake charmer.

[4]Men should remove their sins with the knowledge of the Vedas and become happy, as they feel comfortable by extricating the arrow from the wound.

[5]Just as a physician cures diseases through medicine, so should a man remove his moral weaknesses through the knowledge of the Vedas, and try to live long.

३. शं च नो मयश्च नो मा च नः किं चनाममत् ।
क्षमा रपो विश्वं नो अस्तु भेषजं सर्वं नो अस्तु भेषजम् ॥

3. Let us get peace and joy. Let no disease vex us. Down with the sin! Let all things relieve us from affliction. Let all substances release us from disease, (1466)

HYMN LVIII

१. यशसं मेन्द्रो मघवान् कृणोतु यशसं द्यावापृथिवी उभे इमे ।
यशसं मा देवः सविता कृणोतु प्रियो दातुर्दक्षिणाया इह स्याम् ॥

1. May the Opulent God give me name and glory, May Heaven and Earth this couple, make me famous. May my teacher, the giver of knowledge, make me honoured. Here may the king who gives the guerdon love me. (1467)

२. यथेन्द्रो द्यावापृथिव्योर्यशस्वान् यथाप ओषधीषु यशस्वतीः ।
एवा विश्वेषु देवेषु वयं सर्वेषु यशसः स्याम ॥

2. Just as God is Glorious between the Heaven and Earth, just as waters have their glory among the plants by contributing to their growth and sustenance; even so may we be glorious amid all the sages and all the ordinary mortals. (1468)

३. यशा इन्द्रो यशा अग्निर्यशाः सोमो अजायत । यशा विश्वस्य भूतस्याहमस्मि यशस्तमः ॥

3. Glorious is God, glorious is a fiery soul, glorious is a calm yogi. May I, longing for glory, am the most glorious of all human beings. (1469)[1]

HYMN LIX

१. अनडुद्भ्यस्त्वं प्रथमं धेनुभ्यस्त्वमरुन्धति । अधेनवे वयसे शर्म यच्छ चतुष्पदे ॥

1. O pleasant mistress of the house, protect our oxen and milch-kine. Give protection to young oxen less than five years old, besides kine, and other quadrupeds. (1470)[2]

२. शर्म यच्छत्वोषधिः सह देवीररुन्धती । करत् पयस्वन्तं गोष्ठमयक्ष्माँ उत् पूरुषान् ॥

2. Let the mistress of the house, along with other ladies afford us joy. May she avert consumption from our men, andm ake our cow-pen rich in milk. (1471)

३. विश्वरूपां सुभगामच्छावदामि जीवलाम् । सा नो रुद्रस्यास्तां हेतिं दूरं नयतु गोभ्यः ॥

3. I extol the auspicious, life-giving, mistress of the house, who nicely examines all household objects. Far from our cattle may she turn the deadly dart of disease. (1472)

[1]See 6-39-3.

[2]Give protection: Construct separate sheds for the oxen, kine and other quadrupeds. Pt. Khem Karan Das Trivedi interprets Arundhati as God, Sayāna, Satyavalekar Damodar interpret as a medicinal plant. See 4-12-1, 5-5-5.

HYMN LX

१. अयमा यात्यर्यमा पुरस्ताद् विषितस्तुपः । अस्या इच्छन्नग्रुवै पतिमुत जायामजानये ॥

1. Here comes the illustrious father of the bride, seeking a husband for this bride, a wife for this unmarried man. (1473)

२. अश्रमदियमर्यमन्नन्यासां समनं यती । अङ्गो न्वर्यमन्नस्या अन्याः समनमायति ॥

2. O relatives of the girl, she has toiled hard, in going to others' marriages. Now in her wedding, O relatives, her other female companions should come! (1474)

३. धाता दाधार पृथिवीं धाता द्यामुत सूर्यम् । धातास्या अग्रुवै पतिं दधातु प्रतिकाम्यम् ॥

3. God upholds the spacious earth, upholds the sky, upholds the sun. O God, bestow upon this maid, a husband suited to her wish. (1475)

HYMN LXI

१. मह्यमापो मधुमदेरयन्तां मह्यं सूरो अभरज्ज्योतिषे कम् ।
मह्यं देवा उत विश्वे तपोजा मह्यं देवः सविता व्यचो धात् ॥

1. In obedience to My order, the sweet waters flow. In obedience to My order, the sun has filled all directions with rays. In obedience to My order, all austere learned persons and a brilliant teacher expand their knowledge. (1476)[1]

२. अहं विवेच पृथिवीमुत द्यामहमृतूंरजनयं सप्त साकम् ।
अहं सत्यमनृतं यद् वदाम्यहं दैवीं परि वाचं विशश्च ॥

2. I have set the Earth and Heaven asunder. I have created together the seven Rishis. My word is truth, what I deny is falsehood. I preach to all people the divine Vedic knowledge. (1477)[2]

३. अहं जजान पृथिवीमुत द्यामहमृतूंरजनयं सप्त सिन्धून् ।
अहं सत्यमनृतं यद् वदामि यो अग्नीषोमावजुषे सखाया ॥

3. I give existence to the Earth and Heaven. I create the seven organs and their attributive powers. I declare what is Truth and what is Falsehood. I use fire and water, mutual friends, in the creation of the universe. (1478)[3]

HYMN LXII

१. वैश्वानरो रश्मिभिर्नः पुनातु वातः प्राणेनेषिरो नभोभिः ।
द्यावापृथिवी पयसा पयस्वती ऋतावरी यज्ञिये नः पुनीताम् ॥

[1]My: God.
[2]I: God. Seven Rishis: skin, eye, tongue, ear, nose, mind and intellect.
[3]I; God.

1. Let Sun purify us with its rays of splendour. Let quickening air cleanse us with breath and clouds. Let Earth and Heaven, rich in milky rain, worshipful, holy, purify us with their water. (1479)

२. वैश्वानरीं सूनृतामा रभध्वं यस्या आशास्तन्वो वीतपृष्ठाः ।
तया गृणन्तः सधमादेषु वयं स्याम पतयो रयीणाम् ॥

2. O learned persons, study daily the Vedas, the Word of God, Whose bodies are resplendent regions. Through hers may we in sacrificial banquets singing her glory, be the lords of riches! (1480)[1]

३. वैश्वानरीं वर्चस आ रभध्वं शुद्धा भवन्तः शुचयः पावकाः ।
इहेडया सधमादं मदन्तो ज्योक् पश्येम सूर्यमुच्चरन्तम् ॥

3. O learned persons, for splendour, study the Vedic speech, the benefactor of humanity, being pure and brilliant yourselves, and purifying others. In this world, through our prayer, rejoicing in the banquet, long may we look upon the ascending Sun! (1481)

HYMN LXIII

१. यत् ते देवी निर्ऋतिराबबन्ध दाम ग्रीवास्वविमोक्यं यत् ।
तत् ते वि ष्याम्यायुषे वर्चसे बलायादोमदमन्नमद्धि प्रसूतः ॥

1. O man, that collar round the veins of thy neck, not to be loosened, which captivating poverty has fastened, I loose for thy long life and strength and prosperity. Eat, thus goaded, food that brings no sorrow! (1482)

२. नमोऽस्तु ते निर्ऋते तिग्मतेजोऽयस्मयान् वि चृता बन्धपाशान् ।
यमो मह्यं पुनरित् त्वां ददाति तस्मै यमाय नमो अस्तु मृत्यवे ॥

2. O poverty, thunderbolt to thee. O Glorious God, loose Thou the binding fetters wrought of iron. To me, verily, again doth God give thee. To God, the Deliverer from death be homage. (1483)

३. अयस्मये द्रुपदे बेधिष इहाभिहितो मृत्युभिर्ये सहस्रम् ।
यमेन त्वं पितृभिः संविदान उत्तमं नाकमधि रोहयेमम् ॥

3. Compassed by death which comes through various causes, in this world, O man, art thou fastened to the iron pillar. In conformity with the laws of God, and the teachings of the learned preceptors, make thyself rise and reach the summit of human felicity! (1484)[2]

[1] 'Whose' refers to the Vedas. Whose bodies—regions:—whose knowledge is spread every where. Her: Vedic speech. See *Yajur*, 19-44.

[2] Iron pillar: hard, tough, firm body.

४. संसमिद्युवसे वृषन्नग्ने विश्वान्यर्य आ । इडस्पदे समिध्यसे स नो वसून्या भर ॥

4. O Powerful God, the Lord of all, Thou nicely gatherest up all precious things. Bring us all treasures, Thou art enkindled in the heart and soul! (1485)[1]

HYMN LXIV

१. सं जानीध्वं सं पृच्यध्वं सं वो मनांसि जानताम् ।
देवा भागं यथा पूर्वो संजानाना उपासते ॥

1. Agree and be united: let your minds be all of one accord, even as the learned sages of ancient days, unanimously worship God. (1486)

२. समानो मन्त्रः समितिः समानी समानं व्रतं सह चित्तमेषाम् ।
समानेन वो हविषा जुहोमि समानं चेतो अभिसंविशध्वम् ॥

2. Common the rede, Common the Assembly, Common the religious law, so be their minds united. I urge ye to follow the same line of conduct. May ye, one-minded live in the city. (1487)[2]

३. समानी व आकूतीः समाना हृदयानि वः । समानमस्तु वो मनो यथा वः सुसहासति ॥

3. One and the same be your resolve, be all your hearts in harmony: one and the same be all your minds, so that all your enterprises may succeed happily. (1488)

HYMN LXV

१. अव मन्युरवायताव बाहू मनोयुजा ।
पराशर त्वं तेषां पराञ्चं शुष्ममर्दयाधा नो रयिमा कृधि ॥

1. O foe-killing Commander of the army, appease thy indignation, lower thy uplifted instruments, hold down thy arms that act with mind. Do thou overcome and drive these foemen's might away, and then bring opulence to us! (1489)

२. निर्हस्तेभ्यो नैर्हस्तं यं देवाः शरुमस्यथ । वृश्चामि शत्रूणां बाहूननेन हविषाहम् ॥

2. O warriors, hankering after conquest, the snaft ye cast for the protection of weak subjects on the weak foes, with the same instrument I rend the arms of enemies! (1490)[3]

३. इन्द्रश्चकार प्रथमं नैर्हस्तमसुरेभ्यः । जयन्तु सत्वानो मम स्थिरेणेन्द्रेण मेदिना ॥

[1]इडा वै श्रद्धा । श० 11-2-7-20 इडस्पदे means in the heart, the seat of devotion.
[2]The same line of conduct: the teachings of the Vedas.
[3]'I' refers to the king.

3. The Commander of the army first made the foes bereft of the strength of hand. Victorious shall my heroes be with the help of the Commander as their constant friend. (1491)

HYMN LXVI

१. निर्हस्तः शत्रुरभिदासन्नस्तु ये सेनाभिर्युधमायन्त्यस्मान् ।
समर्पयेन्द्र महता वधेन द्रात्वेषामघहारो विविद्धः ॥

1. Deprived of the strength of hand be every foeman who assaileth us. Dash them together with great slaughter, O Commander of the army, who with armies come to fight against us, and let their robber chief run pierced with arrows. (1492)

२. आतन्वाना आयच्छन्तोऽस्यन्तो ये च धावथ ।
निर्हस्ताः शत्रवः स्थनेन्द्रो वोद्य पराशरीत् ॥

2. Ye who run hither bending bows, brandishing swords, and casting darts, deprived of the strength of hand be Ye, O enemies! Let Commander of the army mangle you today. (1493)

३. निर्हस्ताः सन्तु शत्रवोऽङ्गैषां म्लापयामसि । अथैषामिन्द्र वेदांसि शतशो वि भजामहै ॥

3. Powerless be these our enemies! We enervate their languid limbs. So let us divide among ourselves, in hundreds, O Commander! all their wealth. (1494)

HYMN LXVII

१. परि वर्त्मानि सर्वत इन्द्रः पूषा च सस्रतुः । मुह्यन्त्वद्यामूः सेना अमित्राणां परस्तराम् ॥

1. Let the king and his minister go about along all paths on every side, so that those hosts of enemies be completely bewildered today. (1495)

२. मूढा अमित्राश्चरताशीर्षाण इवाहयः । तेषां वो अग्निमूढानामिन्द्रो हन्तु वरंवरम् ॥

2. Ye foes, wander dismayed, on the battlefield not knowing how to win victory like headless blind serpents. Let the Commander-in-chief slay each bravest one of you whom a fiery missile has confused. (1496)

३. ऐषु नह्य वृषाजिनं हरिणस्या भियं कृधि । पराङमित्र एषत्वर्वाची गौरुपेषतु ॥

3. O King, the showerer of joys, gird on these soldiers the deer's hide to act as an armour. Let our soldiers strike terror in the hearts of the soldiers of the enemy. Let the foe flee away, and his land come under our possession. (1497)

HYMN LXVIII

१. आयमगन्त्सविता क्षुरेणोष्णेन वाय उदकेनेहि ।
आदित्या रुद्रा वसव उन्दन्तु सचेतसः सोमस्य राज्ञो वपत प्रचेतसः ॥

1. This intelligent barber has come hither with the razor. O active person, come thou, with the heated water. One-minded let dignified wise, noble learned persons moisten the hair of the child. O learned persons, get the calm, brilliant child shaved! (1498)[1]

२. अदितिः श्मश्रु वपत्वाप उन्दन्तु वर्चसा । चिकित्सतु प्रजापतिर्दीर्घायुत्वाय चक्षसे ॥

2. Let sharp-edged razor shave the hair and let the waters moisten them with their strength. Let father restore his health for sight and days of lengthened life. (1499)

३. येनावपत् सविता क्षुरेण सोमस्य राज्ञो वरुणस्य विद्वान् ।
तेन ब्रह्माणो वपतेदमस्य गोमानश्ववानयमस्तु प्रजावान् ॥

3. The way in which the skilled barber hath shaven with the razor, this calm, brilliant and good-natured child, in the same way, O Brahmans get the head of this child shaved. Let him be rich in kine, horses, and children. (1500)

HYMN LXIX

१. गिरावरगराटेषु हिरण्ये गोषु यद् यशः । सुरायां सिच्यमानायां कीलाले मधु तन्मयि ॥

1. Mine be the glory, that is found in the ascetics living on mountains, in the celebates (Brahmcharis) residing in the midst of the preachers of knowledge, in gold, and in cattle. Mine be the sweetness, that is found in flowing water and in food. (1501)[2]

२. अश्विना सारघेण मा मधुनाङ्क्तं शुभस्पती । यथा भर्गस्वतीं वाचमावदानि जनाँ अनु ॥

2. O parents, the doers of noble deeds, fill me with the knowledge, that brings strength and wealth! May the voice I utter to humanity be vigorous and clear. (1502)

३. मयि वर्चो अथो यशोथो यज्ञस्य यत् पयः । तन्मयि प्रजापतिर्दिवि द्यामिव दृंहतु ॥

3. May God, the Nourisher of His subjects establish in me strength, fame, and soul force, as He has established the sun in heaven. (1503)

HYMN LXX

१. यथा मांसं यथा सुरा यथाक्षा अधिदेवने । यथा पूंसो वृषण्यत स्त्रियां निहन्यते मनः ।
एवा ते अघ्न्ये मनोधि वत्से निहन्यताम् ॥

[1]The verse refers to the Mundan Sanskar, the tonsure ceremony.

[2]Sayāna has translated Argrāta as a shout of victory by the warriors, or as a king who travels in conveyances. Griffith has translated the word as a vale. Some commentators translate the word as a water-mill घराट, and some as an electrical weapon.

1. Just as knowledge, prosperity, various dealings are associated with kingship, just as a strong man's desire is firmly set upon a dame, so let thy heart and soul, O unassailable subjects be firmly set upon the All-pervading God! (1504)

२. यथा हस्ती हस्तिन्याः पदेन पदमुद्युजे । यथा पुंसो वृषण्यत स्त्रियां निहन्यते मनः ।
एवा ते अघ्न्ये मनोधि वत्से नि हन्यताम् ॥

2. As the male elephant pursues with eager step his female's track, just as a strong man's desire is firmly set upon a dame, so let thy heart and soul, O unassailable subjects be firmly set upon the All-pervading God. (1505)

३. यथा प्रधिर्यथोपधिर्यथा नभ्यं प्रधावधि । यथा पूंसो वृषण्यत स्त्रियां निहन्यते मनः ।
एवा ते अघ्न्ये मनोधि वत्से नि हन्यताम् ॥

3. Just as iron felly is firmly attached to the wooden wheel, and the wheel rim is attached to the nave through spokes, just as a strong man's desire is firmly set upon a dame, so let thy heart and soul, O unassailable subjects be firmly set upon the All-pervading God! (1506)

HYMN LXXI

१. यदन्नमद्मि बहुधा विरूपं हिरण्यमश्वमुत गामजामविम् ।
यदेव किं च प्रतिजग्रहाहमग्निष्टद्धोता सुहुतं कृणोतु ॥

1. Whatever food of varied form and nature, I generally eat due to hunger, without caring to ascertain whether it is good or bad; whatever gift of gold, horse, cow, goat or sheep, I receive on account of poverty, may God, the Giver, make it worthy of acceptance. (1507)

२. यन्मा हुतमहुतमाजगाम दत्तं पितृभिरनुमतं मनुष्यैः ।
यस्मान्मे मन उदिव रारजीत्यग्निष्टद्धोता सुहुतं कृणोतु ॥

2. Whatever wealth hath been given to me by my parents, or acquired through self-exertion, or given by the sages, or presented by friends, whereby my heart leaps up through pleasure, may God, the Giver make it worthy of acceptance. (1508)

३. यदन्नमद्म्यनृतेन देवा दास्यन्नदास्यन्नुत संगृणामि ।
वैश्वानरस्य महतो महिम्ना शिवं मह्यं मधुमदस्त्वन्नम् ॥

3. O learned persons, whatever food I eat unjustly, or store it for bestowing or preserving, may the Almighty God, through His greatness, make that food sweet and blessed for me. (1509)

HYMN LXXII

१. यथासितः प्रथयते वशाँ अनु वपूंषि कृण्वन्नसुरस्य मायया ।
एवा ते शेपः सहसायमर्कोङ्गेनाङ्गं संसमकं कृणोतु ॥

1. Just as the Unfettered God, for the sake of living beings under Him, with the intellect of an intellectual, creating innumerable bodies, expands the universe, so does this Vedic discernment add to thy strength and unite limb with limb. (1510)[1]

२. यथा पसस्तायादरं वातेन स्थूलभं कृतम् । यावत् परस्वतः पसस्तावत् ते वर्धतां पसः ॥

2. Just as government is made worthy of respect through nice administration, and is rendered enlightened in the eyes of the people through exertion, just as the sway of a strong man extends far and wide, so should thy rule be extended. (1511)[2]

३. यावदङ्गीनं पारस्वतं हास्तीनं गार्दभं च यत् । यावदश्वस्य वाजिनस्तावत् ते वर्धतां पसः ॥

3. Just as a good government should be endowed with necessary accoutrements, able administrators, elephants, asses, and swift horses, so should thy rule be extended. (1512)[3]

HYMN LXXIII

१. एह यातु वरुणः सोमो अग्निर्बृहस्पतिर्वसुभिरेह यातु ।
अस्य श्रियमुपसंयात सर्व उग्रस्य चेत्तुः संमनसः सजाताः ॥

1. Let a person shining like the Sun, calm like the Moon come hither. Let a person blazing like fire, a Vedic scholar equipped with noble traits come hither. Unanimous, ye kinsmen, come united, and enjoy the wealth of this dignified learned person. (1513)[4]

२. यो वः शुष्मो हृदयेष्वन्तराकूतिर्या वो मनसि प्रविष्टा ।
तान्त्सीवयामि हविषा घृतेन मयि सजाता रमतिर्वो अस्तु ॥

2. O ministers, the fervour which your hearts have harboured, the resolve which hath occupied your mind, these I cement with my love and grant of livelihood. O Kinsmen, may ye be kind and loving unto me! (1514)[5]

३. इहैव स्त माप याताध्यस्मत् पूषा परस्तादपथं वः कृणोतु ।
वास्तोष्पतिरनु वो जोहवीतु मयि सजाता रमतिर्वो अस्तु ॥

[1]Just as God has rendered unique service to humanity by creating the universe through His wisdom, so should men through Vedic knowledge enhance their strength and develop their bodies.

[2]Just as the government of a wise, enterprising, subjects-nourishing king makes progress, so should men improve their government through noble virtues.

[3]Accoutrements: (1) King (2) Minister (3) Treasury (4) Army (5) Forts (6) Friends (7) Administration vide *Amarkosh* 18-17-18.

[4]A householder should often come in contact with learned persons, and make advancement in life.

[5]The king addresses his ministers.

3. O ministers, remain here forsake me not, otherwise I, the king shall make your path unfit to travel. May God incessantly recall you for my service. O Kinsmen, may ye be kind and loving unto me! (1515)[1]

HYMN LXXIV

१. सं वः पृच्यन्तां तन्व१ः सं मनांसि समु व्रता ।
सं वोयं ब्रह्मणस्पतिर्भगः सं वो अजीगमत् ॥

1. O learned persons, close together be your vast knowledge of different sciences, your minds and vows in unison. The Glorious God, the Lord of the universe hath rightly united you, for your welfare. (1516)

२. संज्ञपनं वो मनसोथो संज्ञपनं हृदः । अथो भगस्य यच्छ्रान्तं तेन संज्ञपयामि वः ॥

2. Let there be union of your minds, let there be union of your hearts. I admire you for your penance for the attainment of God. (1517)

३. यथादित्या वसुभिः संबभूवुर्मरुद्भिरुग्रा अहृणीयमानाः ।
एवा त्रिणामन्नहृणीयमान इमान् जनान्त्संमनसस्कृधीह ॥

3. As strong learned persons, free from anger, with noble qualities and foe-killing heroes, have become valorous, sc O God, the Lord of Past, Present and Future, cause thou these people here to be one-minded! (1518)[2]

HYMN LXXV

१. निरमुं नुद ओकसः सपत्नो यः पृतन्यति । नैर्बाध्येऽन हविषेन्द्र एनं पराशरीत् ॥

1. O heroic person, drive out of our country, the enemy who assaileth us. O king, kill him with your prompt order and expedient! (1519)

२. परमां तं परावतमिन्द्रो नुदतु वृत्रहा । यतो न पुनरायति शश्वतीभ्यः समाभ्यः ॥

2. May king, the Foe-slayer, drive him forth into the most remote place, whence never more shall he return in all the years that are to come. (1520)

३. एतु तिस्रः परावत एतु पञ्च जनाँ अति । एतु तिस्रोऽति रोचना यतो न पुनरायति ।
शश्वतीभ्यः समाभ्यो यावत् सूर्यो असद् दिवि ॥

3. Beyond the three distances, beyond mankind's five races, let the enemy go. Beyond the three lights let him go, whence he shall never come again, in all the years that are to be, long as the sun is in heaven. (1521)[3]

[1] Vāstospati: Lord of habitations, i.e., God.

[2] God is त्रिनामन्: Lord of three titles; i.e., Lord of three worlds, i.e., Earth, Space and Heaven or Lord of Past, Present and Future. Pt. Jaidev Vidyalankar interprets the word as a king, who keeps the subjects under his control through three forces, i.e., Wisdom, Perseverance, strength, or Ministers, Treasure and Army.

[3] Three distances: Beyond earth, firmament and heaven. Five races: Brahman, Kshatriya, Vaisha, Shudra, Nishada or animals, birds, trees of low birth. Three lights: Sun, Moon, Fire. The enemy be deprived of any kind of light, to pass his days in darkness, hidden in his cell.

HYMN LXXVI

१. य एनं परिषीदन्ति समादधति चक्षसे । संप्रेद्धो अग्निर्जिह्वाभिरुदेतु हृदयादधि ॥

1. Those persons who sit round this austere Brahmin and get instructions from him, look upon him with respect. Just as fire is kindled with its flames, so this austere Brahmin kindled with his excellent knowledge should preach to all wisdom that proceeds from his pure heart in the form of words full of learning. (1522)

२. अग्नेः सांतपनस्याहमायुषे पदमा रभे । अद्धातिर्यस्य पश्यति धूममुद्यन्तमास्यतः ॥

2. For length of life, I accept the knowledge of this learned Brahmin, practising penance, whose learning, the sage who knows the truth, beholds proceeding from his mouth like smoke. (1523)[1]

३. यो अस्य समिधं वेद क्षत्रियेण समाहिताम् । नाभिह्वारे पदं नि दधाति स मृत्यवे ॥

3. He who knows the life and property of the austere Brahmin are protected by the king, does not set his foot upon showing disrespect to him for fear of being heavily punished by the king. (1524)

४. नैनं घ्नन्ति पर्यायिणो न सन्नाँ अव गच्छति । अग्नेर्यः क्षत्रियो विद्वान्नाम गृह्णात्यायुषे ॥

4. Those who encompass the penetential Brahman slay him not, as he does not disturb those sitting near. A learned kshatriya takes the name of the austere Brahman for length of life. (1525)[2]

HYMN LXXVII

१. अस्थाद् द्यौरस्थात् पृथिव्यस्थाद् विश्वमिदं जगत् ।
आस्थाने पर्वता अस्थु स्थाम्न्यश्वाँ अतिष्ठिपम् ॥

1. As ordered by God, firm stands the heaven, firm stands the earth, firm stands this universal world, firm stands the mountains in their place, so do I make the breaths stand firmly in the body. (1526)

२. य उदानट् परायणं य उदानण्न्यायनम् । आवर्तनं निवर्तनं यो गोपा अपि तं हुवे ॥

2. I invoke God, the Lord of the worlds, Who resides in exalted final beatitude, and elevates the low dark worlds, Who controls the soul in its march to salvation, and its return. (1527)[3]

३. जातवेदो नि वर्तय शतं ते सन्त्वावृतः । सहस्रं त उपावृतस्ताभिर्नः पुनरा कृधि ॥

[1]Just as smoke rises out of fire. so does knowledge come out of the mouth of an austere Brahman.

[2]Takes the name: seeks the shelter.

[3]Final beatitude: Salvation Elevates the low dark worlds: Morally and spiritually uplifts the mortals residing in the universe through His Vedic teachings.

3. O Omniscient, Omnipresent God, hundreds are the mortal frames created by Thee, release us from all of them by granting us salvation. Thousands are the shackles imposed by Thee on our deeds, grant us strength to visualise Thee, again, in spite of them. (1528)[1]

HYMN LXXVIII

१. तेन भूतेन हविषायमा प्यायतां पुनः । जायां यामस्मा आवाक्षुस्तां रसेनाभि वर्धताम् ॥

1. Let this husband be endowed with sufficient food again and again. Let him strengthen the woman with whom his parents have married him, with curd, honey and butter. (1529)

२. अभि वर्धतां पयसाभि राष्ट्रेण वर्धताम् । रय्या सहस्रवर्चसेमौ स्तामनुपक्षितौ ॥

2. Let him feed her with milk, and raise her high with princely sway. With wealth that hath a thousand powers, let this pair be free from penury. (1530)

३. त्वष्टा जायामजनयत् त्वष्टास्यै त्वां पतिम् । त्वष्टा सहस्रमायूंषि दीर्घमायुष्कृणोतु वाम् ॥

3. God hath created the wife. God hath created thee to be her husband. May God grant you a long life lasting for a thousand years. (1531)

HYMN LXXIX

१. अयं नो नभसस्पतिः संस्फानो अभि रक्षतु । असमातिं गृहेषु नः ॥

1. May God, the Invigorating Lord of the sun protect us. May there be unusually immense riches in our homes. (1532)

२. त्वं नो नभसस्पत ऊर्जं गृहेषु धारय । आ पुष्टमेत्वा वसु ॥

2. O God, the Lord of the Sun, fill our abodes with nutritious food stuffs. Let prosperity and wealth come to us. (1533)

३. देव संस्फान सहस्रापोषस्येशिषे ।
तस्य नो रास्व तस्य नो धेहि तस्य ते भक्तिवांसः स्याम ॥

3. O Prosperous God, Thou art the Lord of infinite prosperity, grant us thereof, give us thereof, may we share that with Thee, through thy indulgence. (1534)[2]

HYMN LXXX

१. अन्तरिक्षेण पतति विश्वा भूतावचाकशत् । शुनो दिव्यस्य यन्महस्तेना ते हविषा विधेम ॥

1. God, pervading like the firmament, keenly observing all souls, is the supreme Lord. Whatever greatness belongs to the Omnipresent, Refulgent God, urged with the same, we worship Thee with devotion, O God! (1535)

[1]Hundreds and thousands mean countless.
[2]That: Prosperity.

२. ये त्रयः कालकाञ्जा दिवि देवा इव श्रिताः । तान्त्सर्वानह्व ऊतयेऽस्मा अरिष्टतातये ॥

2. The lustres of God, the Enumerator of all substances, are present in the firmament like three gods. I invoke all of them for the security and betterment of this soul. (1536)[1]

३. अप्सु ते जन्म दिवि ते सधस्थं समुद्रे अन्तर्महिमा ते पृथिव्याम् ।
शुनो दिव्यस्य यन्महस्तेना ते हविषा विधेम ॥

3. O God, Thou art present in the breaths, stationed in heaven, seen in the space and on earth. Whatever greatness belongs to the Omnipresent, Refulgent God, urged with the same, we worship Thee with devotion, O God! (1537)

HYMN LXXXI

१. यन्तासि यच्छसे हस्तावप रक्षांसि सेधसि । प्रजां धनं च गृह्णानः परिहस्तो अभूदयम् ॥

1. O husband, thou art, the observer of laws, thou supportest me with both thy hands. May this husband of mine, my supporter with his hand, be the holder of progeny and riches. (1538)

२. परिहस्त वि धारय योनिं गर्भाय धातवे । मर्यादे पुत्रमा धेहि तं त्वमा गमयागमे ॥

2. O husband, the holder of my hand in marriage, feed well, me, the progenitor of progeny, that I may develop the embryo. O abstemious wife, conceive the child, and give birth to the infant at the proper time. (1539)[2]

३. यं परिहस्तमबिभरदितिः पुत्रकाम्या । त्वष्टा तमस्या आ बध्नाद् यथा पुत्रं जनादिदि ॥

3. A celibate woman, desirous of a son, accepts whomsoever as her husband, God binds him with that wife, for this purpose that she may give birth to a son. (1540)

HYMN LXXXII

१. आगच्छत आगतस्य नाम गृह्णाम्यायतः । इन्द्रस्य वृत्रघ्नो वन्वे वासवस्य शतक्रतोः ॥

1. I call the name of him who comes, hath come, and still draws nigh to us. I select as husband for my daughter—him, who is imposing like a king, slayer of foes, master of riches and a hundred powers. (1541)[3]

[1]I: A learned person.

Three gods: fire, air, sun, vide *Nirukta*, 7-5. Sayāna interprets Kālkānjas as demons. This interpretation savours of history, and is hence inadmissible, as the Vedas are free from history. Pt. Damodar Sātavalekar interprets the word as three seasons, Summer, Rainy, Winter.

[2]At the proper time: child should be born in due time, not premature.

[3]I call—him: I, the father of the girl name my future son-in-law, so that every one knows how strong and wealthy he is!

२. येन सूर्यां सावित्रीमश्विनोहतुः पथा । तेन मामब्रवीद् भगो जायामा वहतादिति ॥

2. The way in which Day and Night have accepted the light of the sun, in the same way God hath ordered thus to me, to ceremoniously accept this wife. (1542)[1]

३. यस्तेऽङ्कुशो वसुदानो बृहन्निन्द्र हिरण्ययः । तेना जनीयते जायां मह्यं धेहि शचीपते ॥

3. Great, O God, is that administration of Thine, bestowing treasure, excellent like gold therewith. O Lord of Might, bestow a wife on me who long to wed. (1543)

HYMN LXXXIII

१. अपचितः प्र पतत सुपर्णो वसतेरिव । सूर्यः कृणोतु भेषजं चन्द्रमा वोपोच्छतु ॥

1. Hence Sores and Pustules, fly away as the eagle from his nest. Let a goading physician bring a remedy, the pleasant physician banish you. (1544)[2]

२. एन्येका श्येन्येका कृष्णैका रोहिणी द्वे । सर्वासामग्रभं नामावीरघ्नीरपेतन ॥

2. One of them is bright with variegated tints, one pure white, one black, a couple red—the names of all sores have I declared. Begone, and injure not our men. (1545)[3]

३. असूतिका रामायण्यऽपचित् प्र पतिष्यति । ग्लौरितः प्र पतिष्यति स गलुन्तो नशिष्यति ॥

3. The pustule that does not emit puss, and remains hidden in blood veins shall be removed. The boil shall be removed from this part of the body, and shall vanish on maturity. (1546)

४. वीहि स्वामाहुतिं जुषाणो मनसा स्वाहा मनसा यदिदं जुहोमि ॥

4. O patient, with a happy mind, eat thy prescribed food. Accept gladly the efficacious, pungent medicine I give you to eradicate the disease. (1547)[4]

HYMN LXXXIV

१. यस्यास्त आसनि घोरे जुहोम्येषां बद्धानामवसर्जनाय कम् ।
भूमिरिति त्वाभिप्रमन्वते जना निर्ऋतिरिति त्वाहं परि वेद सर्वतः ॥

1. O sinful idleness, in thy dreadful mouth, I sacrifice my joy, that these organs, thy bound victims, may obtain their freedom. Ignorant, ease-loving people deem that thou art their shelter and support: I know thee thoroughly and I say thou art Destruction, calamity and dissolution! (1548)[5]

[1]Pt. Damodar Sātavalekar interprets Bhaga as father of the girl.

[2]The words Surya and Chandrama may mean the rays of the Sun and the light of Moon which cure the disease.

[3]There are five kinds of pustules. 'Them' refers to sores and pustules.

[4]The verse can be translated thus also. Gladly take your food. Accept reflectively whatever I (God) bestow on you. Don't use or eat anything without discrimination and thorough examination.

[5]Ignorant persons engaged in sensual pleasures consider idleness their support and stay, but a learned person considers it an evil and calamity. I: A learned person see *Yajur*, 12-64.

२. भूते हविष्मती भवैष ते भागो यो अस्मासु । मुञ्चेमानमूनेनसः स्वाहा ॥

2. O sorrowful poverty, be enriched with food-stuffs, here, among us is thy allotted portion. Free us from sin in this life as well as in future life! This is our pious prayer. (1549)

३. एवो ष्व१स्मन्निर्ऋ्‌ते तेनेहा त्वमयस्मयान् वि चृता बन्धपाशान् ।
यमो मह्यं पुनरित् त्वां ददाति तस्मै यमाय नमो अस्तु मृत्यवे ॥

3. O poverty, trouble us not, release us from the iron bonds of sin that bind us. To me doth God verily restore thee. Homage be to that God, who releases the body from the soul, and the soul from the fetters of birth and rebirth. (1550)

४. अयस्मये द्रुपदे बेधिष इहाभिहितो मृत्युभिर्ये सहस्रम् ।
यमेन त्वं पितृभिः संविदान उत्तमं नाकमधि रोहयेमम् ॥

4. O man, thou hast been fastened to an iron pillar of the body, surrounded in this world by various forms of death around thee. In full accord with the direction of God and the advice of the learned, lift thyself to the highest heaven of prosperity, (1551)[1]

HYMN LXXXV

१. वरणो वारयाता अयं देवो वनस्पतिः । यक्ष्मो यो अस्मिन्नाविष्टस्तमु देवा अवीवरन् ॥

1. May this qualified, experienced, capable physician keep disease away. The learned persons have driven off consumption that entered and possessed this man. (1552)[2]

२. इन्द्रस्य वचसा वयं मित्रस्य वरुणस्य च । देवानां सर्वेषां वाचा यक्ष्मं ते वारयामहे ॥

2. O patient, we drive away consumption from thee, according to the instructions of glorious, sympathetic, respectable, and all learned persons! (1553)

३. यथा वृत्र इमा आपस्तस्तम्भ विश्वधा यतीः । एवा ते अग्निना यक्ष्मं वैश्वानरेण वारये ॥

3. Just as a cloud retains in itself these waters flowing everywhere, so, with the aid of fire, the benefactor of mankind, I check and banish thy consumption. (1554)

[1]See *Atharva*, 6-63-3.

[2]Varaṇa is the name of a tree as well, Crataeva Roxburghii, found in all parts of India, used in medicine to cure consumption. Varana is named also as Varuna and Jīrak. Jīrak is of three kinds, white, dark and Brihatpāli, which cures fever. All three kinds of Jīrak are the killers of the bacilli of consumption. Varana, through its intense fragrance helps curing consumption. Varana is the name of a medicine also, which is called Varuna, Varanā and Urna. This medicine is pungent, hot in nature, purifies blood and removes wind, vide *Shabdakalpadrum a*; Monier-Williams, *Sanskrit-English Dictionary*.

I: Physician.

Thy:—Patient's.

HYMN LXXXVI

१. वृषेन्द्रस्य वृषा दिवो वृषा पृथिव्या श्रयम् । वृषा विश्वस्य भूतस्य त्वमेकवृषो भव ॥

1. This God is the Lord of the Sun, the Lord of Heaven, the Lord of Earth, the Lord of all creatures. O man, be thou the one and only lord! (1555)

२. समुद्र ईशे स्रवतामग्निः पृथिव्या वशी । चन्द्रमा नक्षत्राणामीशे त्वमेकवृषो भव ॥

2. The sea is regent of the floods, the Sun is ruler of the earth, the Moon is regent of the stars, be thou, O man, the one and only lord! (1556)

३. सम्राडस्यसुराणां ककुन्मनुष्याणाम् । देवानामर्धभागसि त्वमेकवृषो भव ।

3. Thou art the king of the intellectuals, the crown and summit of mankind, the head of scientists, be thou, O man, the one and only lord. (1557)

HYMN LXXXVII

१. श्रा त्वाहार्षमन्तरभूर्ध्रुवस्तिष्ठाविचाचलत् ।
विशस्त्वा सर्वा वाञ्छन्तु मा त्वद्राष्ट्रमधि भ्रशत् ॥

1. O King, I bring thee here to the Assembly. Stay in our midst as a ruler. Stand steadfast and immovable. Let all thy subjects desire thee. Let not thy kingdom slip away from thy control! (1558)[1]

२. इहैवैधि माप च्योष्ठाः पर्वत इवाविचाचलत् । इन्द्र इवेह ध्रुवस्तिष्ठेह राष्ट्रमु धारय ॥

2. O King, stick to thy seat of royalty, forsake not thy duty, remove immovable like a mountain, stand steadfast in thy state like the sun, and hold the kingship in thy grasp. (1559)

३. इन्द्र एतमदीधरद् ध्रुवं ध्रुवेण हविषा । तस्मै सोमो श्रधि ब्रवदयं च ब्रह्मणस्पतिः ॥

3. God has firmly established this man as king, through his constant bounty. May God, the Creator of all and the Guardian of the Vedas, amply instruct him. (1560)[2]

HYMN LXXXVIII

१. ध्रुवा द्यौर्ध्रुवा पृथिवी ध्रुवं विश्वमिदं जगत् । ध्रुवासः पर्वता इमे ध्रुवो राजा विशामयम् ।

1. Firm is the sky, firm is the earth, and firm is all this living world; firm are these mountains on their base, so steadfast like them is this king of men. (1561)

[1] I: Priest, who anoints the king. See *Yajur*, 12-11, *Rig*, 10-173-1.

[2] Him : King.

२. ध्रुवं ते राजा वरुणो ध्रुवं देवो बृहस्पतिः। ध्रुवं त इन्द्रश्चाग्निश्च राष्ट्रं धारयतां ध्रुवम् ॥

2. O King, may the Most Exalted God, the Protector of all vast worlds, the Glorious, Omniscient God, preserve thy steadfast reign! (1562)[1]

३. ध्रुवोऽच्युतः प्र मृणीहि शत्रूञ्छत्रूयतोऽधरान् पादयस्व।
सर्वा दिशः संमनसः सध्रीचीर्ध्रुवाय ते समितिः कल्पतामिह ॥

3. O King remain firm, never abandon thy duty, crush thy foemen, lay those under thy feet who behave like enemies towards thee. One-minded, true to thee be the residents of all regions; faithful to thee, the firm, be this Parliament! (1563)

HYMN LXXXIX

१. इदं यत् प्रेण्यः शिरो दत्तं सोमेन वृष्ण्यम्। ततः परि प्रजातेन हार्दि ते शोचयामसि ॥

1. O man, God hath placed in thy hands the mighty honour of this loving wife. We animate the feelings of thy heart, arising out of thy performing the duty of preserving her honour. (1564)[2]

२. शोचयामसि ते हार्दि शोचयामसि ते मनः। वातं धूम इव सध्र्य१ङ् मामेवान्वेतु ते मनः ॥

2. We enkindle the feelings of thy heart, we animate thy mind with love. O wife, as smoke accompanies the wind, so let thy fancy follow me! (1565)[3]

३. मह्यं त्वा मित्रावरुणौ मह्यं देवी सरस्वती। मह्यं त्वा मध्यं भूम्या उभावन्तौ समस्यताम् ॥

3. O wife, may Prāna and Upāna, may divine learning, may the denizens of the earth, and both her limits unite thee with me! (1566)[4]

[1]Varuna, Brihaspati, Indra, Agni are the names of officials of the state, who work for its safety and advancement.

(1) Varuna: Head of the Police Department.
(2) Brihaspati: Prime Minister.
(3) Indra: Commander-in-chief.
(4) Agni: Speaker of the Assembly.

[2]Men should consider it their duty to protect the honour of women. They should never tolerate their disgrace, and be full of indignation at the man who shows disrespect to women. Women should also protect the honour of their men.

[3]We: the relatives.

Thy: Husband or wife. Husband and wife should mutually say to each other, to live in amity and accord and hold mutual counsel. Husband should follow the advice of the wife and vice versa.

[4]Husband and wife should always remain together bound by the ties of love. If they go to the extreme, distant parts of the earth, they should go together. In fact they should never be separated.

HYMN XC

१. यां ते रुद्र इषुमास्यदङ्गेभ्यो हृदयाय च । इदं तामद्य त्वद् वयं विषूचीं वि वृहामसि ॥

1. O man, whatever pain, God, the Chastiser of the sinners creates in thy organs or the heart, the same do we draw from thee today, and turn it hence to every side! (1567)[1]

२. यास्ते शतं धमनयोऽङ्गान्यनु विष्ठिताः । तासां ते सर्वासां वयं निर्विषाणि ह्वयामसि ॥

2. O patient, from all the hundred nerves spread throughout the organs of thy body, from all those vessels and canals, we, the physicians, through medicine, drive out the poisonous matter! (1568)

३. नमस्ते रुद्रास्यते नमः प्रतिहितायै । नमो विसृज्यमानायै नमो निपतितायै ॥

3. O painful disease, let us root out thy cause, failing that, let us suppress thy appearance, failing that, let us stop thy development, failing that, let us eradicate thee when thou hast actually overpowered us. (1569)

HYMN XCI

१. इमं यवमष्टायोगैः षड्योगेभिरचर्कृषुः । तेना ते तन्वो३ रपोऽपाचीनमप व्यये ॥

1. We purify this soul with eight limbs of yoga, and six accomplishments of tranquillity, self-restraint, abstention from sexual enjoyment, forbearance faith, and desire for salvation. With the practice of yoga, I drive far away the sin of thy soul, and the disease of thy body. (1570)[2]

२. न्य१ग्वातो वाति न्यक् तपति सूर्यः । नीचीनमघ्न्या दुहे न्यग् भवतु ते रपः ॥

2. Just as air breathes downward from above, and downward the sun sends his heat; downward is drawn the milch-cow's milk, so downward go thy malady, O patient! (1571)

३. आप इद् वा उ भेषजीरापो अमीवचातनीः ।
आपो विश्वस्य भेषजीस्तास्ते कृण्वन्तु भेषजम् ॥

[1]We: Noble persons. By doing good deeds and listening to the instructions of virtuous, learned persons can a man be relieved of physical and mental anguish, which he falls a prey to, through his misdeeds. A painful disease has been spoken of as a shaft.

[2]Intelligent persons should first try to uproot the causes of the disease, secondly they should try to stop its appearance, thirdly they should stop its development, fourthly they should remove it through the proper use of medicine. Disease should be checked in all its four stages.

Eight: (1) Yamas (2) Niyamas (3) Āsana (4) Prānāyāma (5) Pratyahār (6) Dharma (7) Dhyāna (8) Smādhi. Pt. Khem Karan Das Trivedi interprets yava as God and six accomplishments as six duties of a Brahman, i.e., to learn, to teach, to perform Yajña, to officiate at a Yajña, to give alms, to receive alms. Griffith translates Ashta Yoga, as ploughed by eight oxen, and Shata Yoga, as ploughed by six oxen.

3. The waters verily bring health, the Waters drive disease away. The waters cure all malady: may they serve as medicine for thee. (1572)[1]

HYMN XCII

१. वातरंहा भव वाजिन् युज्यमान इन्द्रस्य याहि प्रसवे मनोजवाः ।
युञ्जन्तु त्वा मरुतो विश्ववेदस आ ते त्वष्टा पत्सु जवं दधातु ॥

1. O powerful king, with full consciousness, be fast as wind. Go forth as swift as thought at God's behest. May wealthy, ennobling learned persons yoke thee to royal administration. May God lay swiftness in thy foot. (1573)[2]

२. जवस्ते अर्वन् निहितो गुहा यः श्येने वात उत योऽचरत् परीत्तः ।
तेन त्वं वाजिन् बलवान् बलेनाजिं जय समने पारयिष्णुः ॥

2. O learned King, the speed that lies concealed in thy heart, speed granted to the hawk or wind that wanders—with that speed, strong king, saving in shock of battle, endowed with might, by might win thou the contest! (1574)[3]

३. तनूष्टे वाजिन् तन्वं नयन्ती वाममस्मभ्यं धावतु शर्म तुभ्यम् ।
अह्रुतो महो धरुणाय देवो दिवीव ज्योतिः स्वमा मिमीयात् ॥

3. O powerful king, may thy body urging our body bring useful wealth and joy for thee and us. Free from crookedness, desirous of victory, nicely establish thy lustre for our support, as does the Sun in heaven. (1575)

HYMN XCIII

१. यमो मृत्युरघमारो निर्ऋथो बभ्रुः शर्वोऽस्ता नीलशिखण्डः ।
देवजनाः सेनयोत्तस्थिवांसस्ते अस्माकं परि वृञ्जन्तु वीरान् ॥

1. God is Just, the Banisher of sin, the Bringer of Death, the Chastiser of the wicked, the Nourisher of the virtuous, the Alleviator of misery, Adorable, and the Bestower of treasures and dwellings. May these persons desirous of victory, uprisen with their army avoid our heroes on every side. (1576)

२. मनसा होमैर्हरसा घृतेन शर्वायास्त्र उत राज्ञे भवाय ।
नमस्येभ्यो नम एभ्यः कृणोम्यन्यत्रास्मदघविषा नयन्तु ॥

[1]Pastor Kusipp the famous Bavarian water-doctor, maintains that what cannot be cured by water is altogether incurable. Water is the panacea. Hydropathy is the one saving principle which can be applied in every case.

[2]The verse has been applied to Prāna by Pt. Jaidev Vidyalankar and to horse by Sāyana and Griffith. Pt. Jaidev Vidyalankar and to horse by Sāyana and Griffith. Pt. Jaidev has translated Vājin as breath, and Sāyana as horse. For detailed rendering, consult their translations. Pt. Khem Karan Das Trivedi has translated Vājin as a strong king.

[3]In this verse Arvana has been translated as horse by Sāyana, Prāna by Pt. Jaideva, and King by Pt. Khem Karan Das Trivedi.

2. With mind, stores of wealth, courage and strength of character, let us help the foe-killer, the thrower of arrows on the enemy, and the joy-bestowing king. To these the worshipful I pay my homage: may they keep away from us the low, ignoble persons full of sin. (1577)

३. त्रायध्वं नो अघविषाभ्यो वधाद् विश्वे देवा मरुतो विश्ववेदसः ।
अग्नीषोमा वरुणः पूतदक्षा वातापर्जन्ययोः सुमतौ स्याम ॥

3. May all learned persons highly intelligent leaders of the army, the general, the king, and the emperor, whose might is pure, save us from the murderous stroke of sinful persons. May air and cloud bless us with their favour. (1578)

HYMN XCIV

१. सं वो मनांसि सं व्रता समाकूतीर्नमामसि । अमी ये विव्रता स्थन तान् वः सं नमयामसि ।।

1. We bend your minds in unison, bend in harmony your acts and resolves. You there, who think and act differently, we bend and bow in unison. (1579)[1]

२. अहं गृभ्णामि मनसा मनांसि मम चित्तमनु चित्तेभिरेत ।
मम वशेषु हृदयानि वः कृणोमि मम यातमनुवर्त्मान एत ॥

2. I with my mind make your minds captive: with your thoughts follow my thought and wishes. I make your hearts subservient to mine order. Come after me on the path I tread. (1580)[2]

३. ओते मे द्यावापृथिवी ओता देवी सरस्वती । ओतौ म इन्द्रश्चाग्निश्चर्ध्यास्मेदं सरस्वति ॥

3. Just as Heaven and Earth are in my view, interunited, so should we be united together. Just as Vedic speech is inextricably united with God, so should we be united together. Just as soul and spiritual knowledge, are in my estimation inalienably mingled together, so should we be united together. O Vedic speech show us the path, so that observing the principle of unification, we may thrive. (1581)[3]

HYMN XCV

१. अश्वत्थो देवसदनस्तृतीयस्यामितो दिवि । तत्रामृतस्य चक्षणं देवाः कुष्ठमवन्वत ॥

1. Head, the home of organs, where reside the horse-like organs, is the topmost part of the body: There, God is visualised. The yogis long there for God, Who pervades the material body. (1582)[4]

[1]We: Learned person. You: Common persons. See *Atharva*, 3-8-5.

[2]See *Atharva*, 3-8-6. I may refer to the teacher or the king. You may refer to the pupils or the subjects.

[3]See *Atharva*, 5-23-1.

[4]See *Atharva*, 5-4-3. Organs: Two eyes, two ears, two nostrils and mouth, called seven Rishis, on account of their usefulness and serviceableness.

२. हिरण्ययी नौरचरद्धिरण्यबन्धना दिवि । तत्रामृतस्य पुष्पं देवाः कुष्ठमवन्वत ॥

2. In the head, a yogi perceives the intellect as a boat wherewith he crosses the journey of life. It is imbued with virtuous traits, and wrought with golden qualities. In that does God reveal Himself. The yogis long there for God, Who pervades the material body. (1583)[1]

३. गर्भो अस्योषधीनां गर्भो हिमवतामुत । गर्भो विश्वस्य भूतस्येमं मे अगदं कृधि ॥

3. O God, Thou art the Creator of the plants, the Maker of the snowy hills: the Bringer to life of everything that exists. Free this my soul from sin and the pangs of birth and death. (1584)[2]

HYMN XCVI

१. या ओषधयः सोमराज्ञीर्बह्वीः शतविचक्षणाः । बृहस्पति प्रसूतास्ता नो मुञ्चन्त्वंहसः ॥

1. The many plants of hundred uses, that Soma rules as King, administered by a learned physician, possessing Vedic knowledge, deliver us from grief and sorrow. (1585)

२. मुञ्चन्तु मा शपथ्या३दथो वरुण्या॒दुत ।
अथो यमस्य पड्वीशाद् विश्वस्माद् देवकिल्बिषात् ॥

2. O learned persons, just as medicines relieve me from sickness, so should ye, relieve me from the curse's evil, the offence committed towards the virtuous, violation of the orders of the ruler, and the entire sin against the sages. (1586)

३. यच्चक्षुषा मनसा यच्च वाचोपारिम जाग्रतो यत् स्वपन्तः ।
सोमस्तानि स्वधया नः पुनातु ॥

3. From every sin, we have committed, awake or sleeping, with our eye, mind or tongue, may God, with his pure nature, cleanse us. (1587)

HYMN XCVII

१. अभिभूर्यज्ञो अभिभूरग्निरभिभूः सोमो अभिभूरिन्द्रः ।
अभ्य१हं विश्वाः पृतना यथासान्येवा विधेमाग्निहोत्रा इदं हविः ॥

1. Concerted action conquers everything. A learned military leader brings victory and removes obstacles. A learned statesman subdues all foes. A powerful king conquers the enemies. O brave persons, let us unitedly with mutual consent, thu, perform all deeds so that I, the king, may defeat all armies, and bring all men under my control. (1588)

[1]'It', 'that', 'there' refer to the intellect. See *Atharva*, 5-4-4.

[2]See *Atharva*, 5-25-7.

२. स्वधास्तु मित्रावरुणा विपश्चिता प्रजावत् क्षत्रं मधुनेह पिन्वतम् ।
बाधेथां दूरं निर्ऋतिं पराचैः कृतं चिदेनः प्र मुमुक्तमस्मत् ॥

2. Praise to you, O wise father and mother! Here swell with God's knowledge, dominion blest with children. Far into distant regions drive adversity, and even from committed sin absolve us. (1589)[1]

३. इमं वीरमनु हर्षध्वमुग्रमिन्द्रं सखायो अनु सं रभध्वम् ।
ग्रामजितं गोजितं वज्रबाहुं जयन्तमज्म प्रमृणन्तमोजसा ॥

3. O friendly countrymen, encourage the Commander of the army, and begin the battle in obedience to the orders of him, who conquers the enemies villages, usurps their land, is armed with weapons, subdues the enemy in the battle, and conquers him with his might. (1590)[2]

HYMN XCVIII

१. इन्द्रो जयाति न परा जयाता अधिराजो राजसु राजयातै ।
चर्कृत्य ईड्यो वन्द्यश्चोपसद्यो नमस्यो॒ भवेह ॥

1. Let the king be victor, never to be vanquished. Let him reign among the kings as sovran ruler. Here be thou meet for praise and supplication, to be revered and waited on and worshipped. (1591)[3]

२. त्वमिन्द्राधिराजः श्रवस्युस्त्वं भूरभिभूतिर्जनानाम् ।
त्वं दैवीर्विश इमा वि राजायुष्मत् क्षत्रमजरं ते अस्तु ॥

2. Thou fain for glory, an imperial ruler, has won dominion over men, O King, of these learned subjects be thou the sovran: long lasting and undecaying be thy sway! (1592)

३. प्राच्या दिशस्त्वमिन्द्रासि राजोतोदीच्या दिशो वृत्रहञ्छत्रुहो॒सि ।
यत्र यन्ति स्रोत्यास्तज्जितं ते दक्षिणतो वृषभ एषि हव्यः ॥

3. Thou governest the north and eastern regions, O King! fiend—slayer! thou destroyest foemen. Thou hast won all the places, far as the rivers wander. O King, the showerer of joys on thy subjects, the realiser of taxes from them, come to our right hand for help! (1593)

HYMN XCIX

१. अभि त्वेन्द्र वरिमतः पुरा त्वांहूरणाद्धुवे । ह्वयाम्युग्रं चेत्तारं पुरुणामानमेकजम् ।

1. O God, before affliction comes, I call Thee, on account of Thy greatness. I invoke Thee, the Mighty, the Knower of Truth and Untruth, the Bearer of many names, and the Peerless! (1594)

[1]Here: In the state, country.

[2]See *Yajur*, 17-38, and *Rigveda*, Adi Bhashya Bhumika, where this verse has been translated by Swami Dayanand on page 224, in the chapter on the king and his subjects.

[3]Here means in the battle, or in the state. The verse is applicable to God as well.

२. यो अद्य सेन्यो वधो जिघांसन् न उदीरते । इन्द्रस्य तत्र बाहू समन्तं परि दद्मः ॥

2. Whatever deadly missile of the enemy launched today flieth forth to slaughter us, we accept both arms of God to encompass us on every side for protection. (1595)[1]

३. परि दद्म इन्द्रस्य बाहू समन्तं त्रातुस्त्रायतां नः ।
देव सवितः सोम राजन्त्सुमनसं मा कृणु स्वस्तये ॥

3. We draw about us both the arms of God, our Deliverer. May they protect us thoroughly. O Refulgent, All-Goading, Prosperous God, make Thou me pious-minded for my welfare. (1596)[2]

HYMN C

१. देवा अदुः सूर्यो अदाद् द्यौरदात् पृथिव्यदात् । तिस्रः सरस्वतीरदुः सचित्ता विषदूषणम् ॥

1. The learned, with full accord, give us the antidote to poison. The sun sheds his lustre and kills poisonous germs. Heaven gives pure air which kills poison, Earth lends its power to eradicate poison. The three kinds of Vedic knowledge instruct us how to undo the effect of poison. (1597)[3]

२. यद् वो देवा उपजीका आसिञ्चन् धन्वन्युदकम् । तेन देवप्रसूतेनेदं दूषयता विषम् ॥

2. O men dependent upon God, that water which the learned have poured for you on thirsty soil, with that same water sent by the learned, drive ye away this poison! (1598)[4]

३. असुराणां दुहितासि सा देवानामसि स्वसा । दिवस्पृथिव्याः संभूता सा चकर्थारसं विषम् ॥

3. O medicine, thou art the fulfiller of the desires of the noble, wise men, the displayer of fine qualities. Thou which hast sprung from the warmth of the Sun, and the Earth, hast robbed the poison of its power. (1599)

HYMN CI

१. आ वृषायस्व श्वसिहि वर्धस्व प्रथयस्व च । यथाङ्गं वर्धतां शेपस्तेन योषितमिज्जहि ॥

1. O King, behave nicely like a great man, be strong, make progress, advance thy subjects. Let thy strength develop in each organ, and may thou follow wise statesmanship. (1600).

२. येन कृशं वाजयन्ति येन हिन्वन्त्यातुरम् । तेनास्य ब्रह्मणस्पते धनुरिवा तानया पसः ॥

[1]Both arms: The might, strength.

[2]Both arms: Power, potency.

[3]The dust besmeared on the body nullifies the effect of the poison. Three kinds: The physical, moral and spiritual teachings of the Vedas.

[4]The water of a thirsty land possesses the quality of mitigating the ill effects of poison.

2. Wherewith a weak man is made strong, and a restless person pacified, in the same way, O God, the Guardian of corn, wealth, the Brahman and the Vedas, extend Thou nicely the sway of this king like a bow. (1601)[1]

३. आहं तनोमि ते पसो अधि ज्यामिव धन्वनि । क्रमस्वर्श इव रोहितमनवग्लायता सदा ।।

3. I, nicely, extend thy rule, as the string is strung on the bow. Attack the foes without exhaustion, as a bear attacks the deer. (1602)[2]

HYMN CII

१. यथायं वाहो अश्विना समैति सं च वर्तते । एवा मामभि ते मनः समैतु सं च वर्त्तताम् ।।

1. O husband and wife, just as this horse constantly goes with the rider, and remains under his control, so should, O beloved, come thou near me, and be united with me. (1603)[3]

२. आहं खिदामि ते मनो राजाश्वः पृष्ट्यामिव । रेष्मच्छिन्नं यथा तृणं मयि ते वेष्टतां मनः ।।

2. I draw thee to myself as a good horse draws the conveyance fastened to his back. Like grass that storm hath rent so be thy mind attached to me. (1604)[4]

३. आञ्जनस्य मदुघस्य कुष्ठस्य नलदस्य च । तुरो भगस्य हस्ताभ्यामनुरोधनमुद्भरे ।।

3. For acquiring strength in both the hands, I nicely resort to the contemplation of God, the Maker of the universe, the Embodiment of joy, the Scrutinizer of virtues, the Annihilator of fetters, Agile and Prosperous. (1605)

HYMN CIII

१. संदानं वो बृहस्पतिः संदानं सविता करत् । संदानं मित्रो अर्यमा संदानं भगो अश्विना ।।

1. O foemen, may the Commander of big forces, capture ye. May the General urging his soldiers to attack, capture ye. May the justice-loving head of the army, the friend of all capture ye. May the prosperous king, law-abiding like the Sun and Moon capture ye! (1606)[5]

[1]The word: पसः is translated by many commentators as penis. Swami Dayanand translates it as sway, rule, vide *Yajur*, 23-22.

[2]I: God.

[3]The husband should thus address his wife and vice versa.

[4]Just as the blade of grass rent by the storm remains stuck to it, and does not leave it, just as a horse is attached to the conveyance so should husband be attached to his wife and vice versa. I may refer to husband or wife. 'Thy' 'me' also refer to husband or wife.

[5]Capture ye: Take the enemies as prisoners of war. Some commentators interpret Brihaspati, Savita, Mitra, Aryamā, Bhaga and Ashwins as different officials of the state. Griffith interprets them as different deities.

२. सं परमान्त्समवमानथो सं द्यामि मध्यमान् । इन्द्रस्तान् पर्यहार्दाम्ना तानग्ने सं द्या त्वम् ॥

2. I bind together all the enemies of the first, the low or the middle rank. The powerful king has routed them all from every side. O Commander of the army, capture them all as prisoners of war, with fetters on! (1607)[1]

३. ग्रमी ये युधमायन्ति केतून् कृत्वानीकशः । इन्द्रस्तान् पर्यहार्दाम्ना तानग्ने सं द्या त्वम् ॥

3. The king has routed from every side, those yonder foemen, approaching to fight, with hammers raised along their ranks. O Commander of the army, capture them all as prisoners of war, with fetters on. (1608)

HYMN CIV

१. ग्रादानेन संदानेनामित्राना द्यामसि । ग्रपाना ये चैषां प्राणा ग्रसुनासून्त्समच्छिदन् ॥

1. We bind our foemen by capturing and subduing them. I dissever their breath and respiration. I cut to pieces their organs with my wisdom. (1609)

२. इदमादानमकरं तपसेन्द्रेण संशितम् । अमित्रा येऽत्र नः सन्ति तानग्न आ द्या त्वम् ॥

2. This bond, made keen by the Acharya, I have formed with heat of holy zeal. Securely bind our enemies, O Commander of the army, who are standing here on the battlefield! (1610)[2]

३. ऐनान् द्यतामिन्द्राग्नी सोमो राजा च मेदिनौ । इन्द्रो मरुत्वानादानममित्रेभ्यः कृणोतु नः ॥

3. May the Defence Minister and the Lord of Justice, friendly, and active like wind and fire bind them fast. May the king, equipped with warriors arrange for the capture of our enemies. (1611)

HYMN CV

१. यथा मनो मनस्केतैः परापतत्याशुमत् । एवा त्वं कासे प्र पत मनसोऽनु प्रवाय्यम् ॥

1. Rapidly as the fancy flies forth with conceptions of the mind, so following the fancy's flight, O mental vigour, flee rapidly away! (1612)

२. यथा बाणः सुसंशितः परापतत्याशुमत् । एवा त्वं कासे प्र पत पृथिव्या ग्रनु संवतम् ॥

2. Rapidly as an arrow flies away with keenly sharpened point, so swiftly flee away, so, O mental vigour over the region of the earth! (1613)[3]

३. यथा सूर्यस्य रश्मयः परापतन्त्याशुमत् । एवा त्वं कासे प्र पत समुद्रस्यानु विक्षरम् ॥

3. Rapidly as the beams of light, the rays of the Sun, fly away, so, O mental vigour fly rapidly away over the current of the mighty soul, vast like the ocean. (1614)

[1] I refers to the General of the army.

[2] Acharya: Guru, teacher, preceptor. I: A veteran warrior.

[3] Griffith translates कास as cough, Pt. Jaidev Vidyalankar as mental vigour, Pt. Khem Karan Das Trivedi as knowledge or device.

HYMN CVI

१. आयने ते परायणे दूर्वा रोहन्तु पुष्पिणीः ; उत्सो वा तत्र जायतां ह्रदो वा पुण्डरीकवान् ॥

1. In front and behind thy house, let flowery Dūrvā grass grow. There let a spring of water rise, or a tank with blooming lotuses. (1615)[1]

२. अपामिदं न्ययनं समुद्रस्य निवेशनम् । मध्ये ह्रदस्य नो गृहाः पराचीना मुखा कृधि ॥

2. May this dwelling place of men be the abode of abundant water. May our house be built amid the tank, O king, turn thou the faces of the enemy away from it! (1616)[2]

३. हिमस्य त्वा जरायुणा शाले परि व्ययामसि । शीतह्रदा हि नो भुवोऽग्निष्कृणोतु भेषजम् ॥

3. O House, we compass thee about with coolness to envelop thee. Cool as a tank be thou to us. Let there be fire in our house to remedy our diseases! (1617)

HYMN CVII

१. विश्वजित् त्रायमाणायै मा परि देहि ।
त्रायमाणे द्विपाच्च सर्वं नो रक्ष चतुष्पाद् यच्च नः स्वम् ॥

1. O All-conquering God, entrust me to Thy protecting power. O protecting power of God, guard all our men, guard all our quadrupeds, and our wealth! (1618)[3]

२. त्रायमाणे विश्वजिते मा परि देहि ।
विश्वजिद् द्विपाच्च सर्वं नो रक्ष चतुष्पाद् यच्च नः स्वम् ॥

2. O protecting power, entrust me to the All-conquering God. O All-conquering God, guard all our men, guard all our quadrupeds, and our wealth! (1619)

३. विश्वजित् कल्याण्यै मा परि देहि ।
कल्याणि द्विपाच्च सर्वं नो रक्ष चतुष्पाद् यच्च नः स्वम् ॥

3. O All-conquering God, entrust me to Thy benevolent power. O benevolent power of God, guard all our men, guard all our quadrupeds, and our wealth! (1620)[4]

[1]Dūrvā grass Panicum Dactyion, a creeping grass with flower—bearing branches erect. By far the most common and useful grass in India. It grows everywhere abundantly, and flowers all the year round. In Hindustani it is called dūb.

[2]'It' refers to the house. Fort should have a ditch of water round it, so that the enemy may not easily attack it. See *Yajur*, 17-7.

[3]त्रायमाणा is also the name of a medicine. Its other names are त्रायन्ती, and बलभद्रिका.

[4]कल्याणी is also the name of a medicine, which is called मासपर्णी.

४. कल्याणि सर्वविदे मा परि देहि ।
सर्वविद् द्विपाच्च सर्वं नो रक्ष चतुष्पाद् यच्च नः स्वम् ॥

4. O benevolent power of God, entrust me to the All-knowing God. O All-knowing God, guard al! our men, guard all our quadrupeds, and our wealth! (1621)

HYMN CVIII

१. त्वं नो मेधे प्रथमा गोभिरश्वेभिरा गहि । त्वं सूर्यस्य रश्मिभिस्त्वं नो असि यज्ञिया ॥

1. Intelligence, thou art foremost, worshipped by men and sages. Come unto us with the organs of cognition and action. Come with God's rays of knowledge. Thou art the accomplisher of the Yajna (sacrifice) of life! (1622)[1]

२. मेधामहं प्रथमां ब्रह्मण्वतीं ब्रह्मजूतामृषिष्टुताम् । प्रपीतां ब्रह्मचारिभिर्देवानामवसे हुवे ॥

2. I invoke for the protection of organs, Intelligence, possessed by highly learned Vedic scholars, loved by the sages. lauded by the seers, and welcomed by the celibates. (1623)

३. यां मेधामृभवो विदुर्यां मेधामसुरा विदुः । ऋषयो भद्रां मेधां यां विदुस्तां मय्या वेशयामसि ॥

3. That excellent intelligence, which the learned know, and the yogis know, intelligence which the sages, we cause to enter our soul. (1524)[2]

४. यामृषयो भूतकृतो मेधां मेधाविनो विदुः । तया मामद्य मेधयाग्ने मेधाविनं कृणु ॥

4. Do Thou, O God, make me wise this day with that intellect, which the creative Rishis which the men endowed with wisdom know. (1625)

५. मेधां सायं मेधां प्रातर्मेधां मध्यन्दिनं परि । मेधां सूर्यस्य रश्मिभिर्वचसा वेशयामहे ॥

5. We plant in our soul, with Vedic words, wisdom, at eve, at morn, wisdom at noon of day, and at the time of the rising of the Sun's beams. (1626)[3]

HYMN CIX

१. पिप्पली क्षिप्तभेषज्यू३तातिविद्धभेषजी । तां देवाः समकल्पयन्नियं जीवितवा अलम् ॥

1. Pippali heals insanity, it heals the deeply-piercing wound. The physicians prepared and fashioned it. This hath sufficient power for longevity. (1627)[4]

[1]Organs of cognition and action: Gyana Indriyas and Karama Indriyas.

[2]Asurā: Controllers of breath, The yogis who practise Prāṇāyama: असु vital breaths.

[3]At no time should we be bereft of wisdom. It should be our constant companion.

[4]Pippali मघ heals fever, urinary diseases, spleen, piles, constipation and excruciating pain, vide Shabd Kalp Druma. In Raj Nighantu, the following names have been given to this medicine, Ashwathi, Laghuputri, Sayat, Patrikā, Harasva Patrikā, Pippalikā, Vanasthā, Ashwatha, Sannibha, Kshudrā, It is sweet in taste, removes bile, purifies blood, cures poison, and heals wounds.

२. पिप्पल्य१: समवदन्तायतीर्जननादधि । यं जीवमश्नवामहै न स रिष्याति पूरुषः ।

2. Coming from their birth, the different kinds of Pippali spoke among themselves, he who shall use us as medicine, shall never suffer injury. (1628)

३. असुरास्त्वा न्य१ खनन् देवास्त्वोदवपन् पुनः । वातीकृतस्य भेषजीमथो क्षिप्तस्य भेषजीम् ॥

3. Learned physicians buried thee in earth, the sages again uprooted thee, healer of sickness caused by wind and healer of insanity. (1629)[1]

HYMN CX

१. प्रत्नो हि कमीड्यो अध्वरेषु सनाच्च होता नव्यश्च सत्सि ।
स्वां चाग्ने तन्वं१ पिप्रायस्वास्मभ्यं च सौभगमा यजस्व ॥

1. Ancient, verily Meet for praise at sacrifices, Primordial Benefactor, Ever young, Ageless, art Thou present in our hearts, O God. O Lord, Thou pervadest the entire universe, Thy body; grant us felicity. (1630)

२. ज्येष्ठघ्न्यां जातो विचृतोर्यमस्य मूलबर्हणात् परि पाह्येनम् ।
अत्येनं नेषद् दुरितानि विश्वा दीर्घायुत्वाय शतशारदाय ॥

2. This child is born to a woman, whose first child has died. Preserve him from the uprooting effect of extremely terrible Death. He shall conduct him safe past all misfortunes to lengthened life that lasts a hundred autumns. (1631)[2]

३. व्याघ्रेऽह्न्यजनिष्ट वीरो नक्षत्रजा जायमानः सुवीरः ।
स मा वधीत् पितरं वर्धमानो मा मातरं प्र मिनीज्जनित्रीम् ॥

3. A son born on a day when warriors display their tiger-like valour, is a hero indeed. He is born of celebate parents and hence becomes brave and courageous. Let him not wound, when grown in strength, his father, nor disregard his mother, who gave him birth. (1632)

HYMN CXI

१. इमं मे अग्ने पुरुषं मुमुग्ध्ययं यो बद्धः सुयतो लालपीति ।
अतोऽधि ते कृणवद् भागधेयं यदानुन्मदितोऽसति ॥

1. Unbind and loose for me this soul, O God, who bound and well-restrained, is chattering foolishly. Afterward he will worship Thee more eagerly, when he hath been delivered from his ignorance through salvation. (1633)

[1] Thee: Pippali. In *Raj Nighantu,*, *Bhāvaprakasha* and *Charak*, *Samhita* the uses of Pippali are mentioned in details. It is spoken of as the healer of fever, bronchitis, cough. It develops intellect and sharpens the appetite. It should be taken with honey or treacle in the ratio of 1 to 2.

[2] He may refer to father.

२. अग्निष्टे नि शमयतु यदि ते मन उद्युतम् । कृणोमि विद्वान् भेषजं यथानुन्मदितोऽससि ॥

2. Let a learned man greatly soothe thy mind when great excitement troubles it. Well-skilled I make a medicine that thou mayest be free from mental unrest. (1634)[1]

३. देवैनसादुन्मदितमुन्मत्तं रक्षसस्परि । कृणोमि विद्वान् भेषजं यदानुन्मदितोऽसति ॥

3. Insane through sin against the learned, or maddened by a fell disease—well-skilled I make a medicine that thou mayest be free from mental unrest. (1635)[2]

४. पुनस्त्वा दुरप्सरसः पुनरिन्द्रः पुनर्भगः । पुनस्त्वा दुर्विश्वे देवा यथानुन्मदितोऽससि ॥

4. May showers of water again restore thee to consciousness. May the Sun again restore thee to consciousness. May the Moon again restore thee to consciousness. May all the forces of nature again restore thee to consciousness, that thou mayest be free from mental unrest. (1636)

HYMN CXII

१. मा ज्येष्ठं वधीदयमग्न एषां मूलबर्हणात् पाह्येनम् ।
स ग्राह्याः पाशान् वि चृत प्रजानन् तुभ्यं देवा अनु जानन्तु विश्वे ॥

1. Let not this man kill his elder brother. O King, preserve him from their utter ruin. Knowing the way, do thou untie the nooses of captivity, as advised by all learned persons. (1637)[3]

२. उन्मुञ्च पाशांस्त्वमग्न एषां त्रयस्त्रिभिरुत्सिता येभिरासन् ।
सं ग्राह्याः पाशान् वि चृत प्रजानन् पितापत्रौ मातरं मुञ्च सर्वान् ॥

2. Rend thou the bonds of these asunder, O King! the threefold noose whereby the three were fastened. Knowing the way, do thou untie the noose of captivity free all, the son, the father, and the mother. (1638)[4]

३. येभिः पाशैः परिवित्तो विबद्धोऽङ्गेअङ्ग आर्पित उत्सितश्च ।
वि ते मुच्यन्तां विमुचो हि सन्ति भ्रूणघ्नि पूषन् दुरितानि मृक्ष्व ॥

3. The bonds with which the usurper of the rights of his elder brother is tied, fettered in every limb, and bound securely, should be loosened, if they are fit to be unloosened. O King, turn away woes upon the murderer of a Vedic scholar. (1639)[5]

[1]I refers to a learned person.

[2]I refers to a learned person.

[3]The king should keep a man imprisoned unless advised by learned persons to release him.

[4]If the rights of the elder brother are violated, the king should arrest the father, mother and the younger son, and release them only if they are innocent, not otherwise.

[5]भ्रूण generally means the child in the womb, but in the opinion of Bodhāyana, it means a Vedic scholar, who studies the Vedas with their branches. कल्पप्रवचनाध्यायि भ्रूणः 'They' refers to bonds. A younger brother who usurps the rights of his elder brother should be punished. He should be released only, if he is found guiltless.

HYMN CXIII

१. त्रिते देवा अमृजतैतदेनस्त्रित एनन्मनुष्येषु ममृजे ।
ततो यदि त्वा ग्राहिरानशे तां ते देवा ब्रह्मणा नाशयन्तु ॥

1. Through the grace of God, the sages have wiped off this sin, and God has wiped off this sin from amongst human beings. Even then, O man if thou art awarded imprisonment for this sin, the learned through Vedic knowledge shall remove it and free thee! (1640)[1]

२. मरीचीर्धूमान् प्र विशानु पाप्मन्नुदारान् गच्छोत वा नीहारान् ।
नदीनां फेनाँ अनु तान् वि नश्य भ्रूणघ्नि पूषन् दुरितानि मृक्ष्व ॥

2. O sinner, expose thyself to the burning rays of the Sun, or put thyself in the midst of strangulating smoke, or go to the pure, noble souls for instruction, or be deprived for ever of serviceable things, or vanish like those evanescent foams of rivers. O King, turn away woes upon the murderer of a Vedic scholar. (1641)[2]

३. द्वादशधा निहितं त्रितस्यापमृष्टं मनुष्यैनसानि ।
ततो यदि त्वा ग्राहिरानशे तां ते देवा ब्रह्मणा नाशयन्तु ॥

3. The sins of human beings, which God hath washed away, lie stored in twelve different places. Even then if, O soul, nescience has caught thee in its grip, the learned through Vedic knowledge shall remove it and free thee! (1642)[3]

HYMN CXIV

१. यद् देवा देवहेडनं देवासश्चकृमा वयम् । आदित्यास्तस्मान्नो यूयमृतस्यर्तेन मुञ्चत ॥

1. O learned persons, whatever wrong, we learned people have committed to disgrace the learned and provoke their wrath; may ye O persons brilliant like the Sun, deliver us from that sin, through the knowledge of the Vedas, the word of God! (1643)

२. ऋतस्यर्तेनादित्या यजत्रा मुञ्चतेह नः । यज्ञं यद् यज्ञवाहसः शिक्षन्तो नोपशेकिम ॥

2. O learned persons, worthy of worship, release us, in this world, from the fetters of sin, through the true Vedic knowledge of God. O preservers of God in your heart, when we in our attempt to realise God, fail to visualise Him, show us the path of salvation, preaching unto us, the true Vedic knowledge of God. (1644)

[1]This sin: Usurpation of the rights of the elder brother. Trita means God, Who is present in Past, Present and Future, and in the three regions, Earth, Heaven and Space. Sages and God condemn this sin. If one is caught in it and punished he should seek the advice of the learned for future guidance or release from captivity if he is innocent.

[2]Griffith translates भ्रूणाघ्न as babe-destroyer.

[3]Twelve different places: five karama Indriyas, five jñān Indriyas, mind, and intellect.

३. मेदस्वता यजमानाः स्रुचाज्यानि जुह्वतः । अकामा विश्वे वो देवाः शिक्षन्तो नोपशेकिम ॥

3. Worshipping God, sustaining together the soul and body through diet, absorbing our organs in the soul through breath-control, being selfless and disinterested, exerting for the attainment of God, if we have failed to get release from the fetters of sin, O learned persons, free us through preaching unto us the true Vedic knowledge of God! (1645)[1]

HYMN CXV

१. यद् विद्वांसो यदविद्वांस एनांसि चकृमा वयम् ।
यूयं नस्तस्मान्मुञ्चत विश्वे देवाः सजोषसः ॥

1. Whatever sin we wittingly or in our ignorance have done, do ye deliver us therefrom. O all ye learned persons, of one accord. (1646)

२. यदि जाग्रद् यदि स्वपन्नेन एनस्योऽकरम् । भूतं मा तस्माद् भव्यं द्रुपदादिव मुञ्चताम् ॥

2. If I, a sinner, when awake or sleeping, have committed sin, free me therefrom, as an animal from a stake, from past and from future guilt. (1647)

३. द्रुपदादिव मुमुचानः स्विन्नः स्नात्वा मलादिव । पूतं पवित्रेणेवाज्यं विश्वे शुम्भन्तु मैनसः ॥

3. As one unfastened from a stake, or cleansed by bathing after toil, as butter which the sieve hath cleansed, so all shall purge me from the sin. (1648)

HYMN CXVI

१. यद् यामं चक्रुर्निखनन्तो अग्रे कार्षीवणा अन्नविदो न विद्यया ।
वैवस्वते राजनि तज्जुहोम्यथ यज्ञियं मधुमदस्तु नोऽन्नम् ॥

1. Whatever law, the peasants, like experts in agriculture have wisely fixed before digging the earth; according to that rule, I, the landlord, pay revenue to the opulent king. Sweet be our food, conducive to the development of the state. (1649)[2]

२. वैवस्वतः कृणवद् भागधेयं मधुभागो मधुना सं सृजाति ।
मातुर्यदेन इषितं न आगन् यद् वा पितापराद्धो जिहीडे ॥

2. The head of the state fixes the portion of tax to be paid by each. King, the recipient of taxes, arranges for the supply of food to all. May our sin in hasty mood against our mother, or guilt whereby a sire is wronged and angered be appeased. (1650)

[1]Sayaṇa makes a reference to animal sacrifice in the verse, which is inappropriate. मेदो वै मेधः *Shatapatha* 3-8-4-6. मेधाय अन्नाय इत्येतत *Shatapatha* 7-5-2-33. The word means here diet and not the fat of an animal.

[2]The peasants should pay to the Govt., the revenue fixed by law. They should feel no hesitation in its payment, and should try to grow more food for the development of the state.

३. यदीदं मातुर्यदि वा पितुर्नः परि भ्रातुः पुत्राच्चेतस एन आगन् ।
यावन्तो अस्मान् पितरः सचन्ते तेषां सर्वेषां शिवो अस्तु मन्युः ॥

3. Whether this sin into our heart hath entered regarding mother, father, son or brother, may the wrath of all our elders related to us be appeased. (1651)

HYMN CXVII

१. अपमित्यमप्रतीत्तं यदस्मि यमस्य येन बलिना चरामि ।
इदं तदग्ने अनृणो भवामि त्वं पाशान् विचृतं वेत्थ सर्वान् ॥

1. I am a debtor as I have not paid the debt which I ought to have paid, and have fallen into the clutches of the creditor, due to heavy debt. May I now be free from that debt by its payment. O learned person, thou knowest how to rend all bonds asunder. (1652)

२. इहैव सन्तः प्रति दद्म एनज्जीवा जीवेभ्यो नि हराम एनत् ।
अपमित्य धान्यं१ यज्जघसाहमिदं तदग्ने अनृणो भवामि ॥

2. In our life-time we should pay back the debt. The debtors while living should pay the debt to their creditors in their life-time. The corn I have eaten as a loan, O learned person, I pay back and become free from debt. (1653)[1]

३. अनृणा अस्मिन्ननृणाः परस्मिन् तृतीये लोके अनृणाः स्याम ।
ये देवयानाः पितृयाणाश्च लोकाः सर्वान् पथो अनृणा आ क्षियेम ॥

3. May we be free from debt in the first stage of boyhood, in the second stage of youth, and in the third stage of old age. May we, debt-free, abide in all the pathways in all the places, which the learned and the wise visit. (1654)

HYMN CXVIII

१. यद्धस्ताभ्यां चकृम किल्बिषाण्यक्षाणां गत्नुमुप लिप्समानाः ।
उग्रंपश्ये उग्रजितौ तदद्याप्सरसावनु दत्तामृणं नः ॥

1. Whatever sin, we, anxious to go to the gambling den, have committed with our hands, let the vigilant criminal Investigation Department, and the Controlling Police Department, serving as two spies make us pay off our debt. (1655)[2]

२. उग्रंपश्ये राष्ट्रभृत् किल्बिषाणि यदक्षवृत्तमनु दत्तं न एतत् ।
ऋणान्नो नर्णमेर्त्समानो यमस्य लोके अधिरज्जुरायत् ॥

[1]A father should discharge his debt in his life time and not leave it for his children to pay..

[2]There are three kinds of debt, which each human being has to discharge in life. They are Rishi, Deva, Pitri debts. The first is discharged by observing celibacy and acquiring knowledge, the second by performing Yajnas, and the third by producing progeny.

2. May the vigilant C.I.D. and the Police, the protector of the state from the guilty, punish us for the crime of gambling and other crimes, and save us from running into debt through gambling. The creditor failing to realise the debt, will get fetters put on the debtor and take him to a court of law. (1656)

३. यस्मा ऋणं यस्य जायामुपैमि यं याचमानो अभ्यैमि देवाः ।
ते वाचं वादिषुर्मोत्तरां मद्देवपत्नी अप्सरसावधीतम् ॥

3. My creditor, the man whose wife 'I visit for a loan, he, O wise persons! whom I approach with supplication,—let not these men speak harshly unto me. Mind this, ye two departments of C.I.D. and Police, the nourishers and protectors of the learned. (1657)

HYMN CXIX

१. यददीव्यन्नृणमहं कृणोम्यदास्यन्नग्न उत संगृणामि ।
वैश्वानरो नो अधिपा वसिष्ठ उदिन्नयाति सुकृतस्य लोकम् ॥

1. The debt which I incur, not for gambling, and being unable to repay, acknowledge its payment, O King, the benefactor of all, the best, our sovereign, lift us into the realm of virtue. (1658)[1]

२. वैश्वानराय प्रति वेदयामि यद्यृणं संगरो देवतासु ।
स एतान् पाशान् विचृतं वेद सर्वानथ पक्वेन सह सं भवेम ॥

2. I will acknowledge unto God, the Leader of humanity, the debt I have incurred, and the promises made to the sages. He knows how to tear asunder all these nooses, so that we may dwell with Him, the resolute-minded. (1659)[2]

३. वैश्वानरः पविता मा पुनातु यत् संगरमभिधावाम्याशाम् ।
अनाजानन् मनसा याचमानो यत् तत्रैनो अप तत् सुवामि ॥

3. O God, the Benefactor of humanity, the Purifier purge me when I oppose their hope and break my promise. Unknowing in my heart, hankering after worldly pleasure, whatever guilt there is in that, I banish. (1660)[3]

HYMN CXX

१. यदन्तरिक्षं पृथिवीमुत द्यां यन्मातरं पितरं वा जिहिंसिम ।
अयं तस्माद् गार्हपत्यो नो अग्निरुदिन्नयाति सुकृतस्य लोकम् ॥

[1]If a debtor is imprisoned for non-payment of debt, but promises, to repay it, the king should set him free believing in his word as a gentleman. Vaishwanar may refer to God as well.

[2]Nooses: The bonds of debt.

[3]Their hope: The hope of the creditors for payment.

1. If we have injured the denizens of Air, Earth, or Heaven, if we have wronged our Mother or our Father, May God, the Lord of the universe, absolve us from this sin, and bear us up into the world of virtue. (1661)

२. भूमिर्मातादितिर्नो जनित्रं भ्रातान्तरिक्षमभिशस्त्या नः ।
द्यौर्नः पिता पित्र्याच्छं भवाति जामिमृत्वा माव पत्सि लोकात् ॥

2. Earth is our Mother, Matter is our birth-place, Air is our brother, Sun is our Father. May all these save us from afflictions and conduce to our welfare. Approaching our relatives, may we never forsake the company of the Almighty Father. (1662)[1]

३. यत्रा सुहार्दः सुकृतो मदन्ति विहाय रोगं तन्व१ः स्वायाः ।
अश्लोणा अङ्गैरह्रुताः स्वर्गे तत्र पश्येम पितरौ च पुत्रान् ॥

3. In that house where virtuous, noble-minded persons, leaving behind their bodily infirmities, reside happily, there in that paradise of a happy home, may we behold our sons and parents from distortion of the limbs and lameness. (1663)

HYMN CXXI

१. विषाणा पाशान् विष्याध्यस्मद् य उत्तमा अधमा वारुणा ये ।
दुष्वप्न्यं दुरितं नि ष्वास्मदथ गच्छेम सुकृतस्य लोकम् ॥

1. O heroic person, with full devotion, untie from the upper, lower snares imposed by God for our faults. Drive from us evil dream, drive off sin, then let us go into the world of virtue. (1664)[2]

२. यद् दारुणि बध्यसे यच्च रज्ज्वां यद् भूम्यां बध्यसे यच्च वाचा ।
अयं तस्माद् गार्हपत्यो नो अग्निरुदिन्नयाति सुकृतस्य लोकम् ॥

2. O soul, if thou art bound by body, matter, birth or Vedic word, may God, the Lord of the universe absolve us from this bondage and lift us up into the world of virtue. (1665)[3]

३. उदगातां भगवती विचृतौ नाम तारके । प्रेहामृतस्य यच्छतां प्रैतु बद्धकमोचनम् ॥

3. When two auspicious, releasing forces named Prānā and Apāna are in full play and grant immortality to the soul, then the soul imprisoned in the body attains to emancipation. (1666)

[1]Air is our brother as it is our constant companion like a brother. Sun is our father, as it nourishes us like a father through rain and its rays.

[2]Upper: intense, or located in the upper part of the body. Lower: mild in nature, or located in the lower part of the body. World: state, condition, assembly.

[3]Vedic word: The laws laid down in the Vedas about virtue and vice. We should try to be free from evil and accept virtue.

४. वि जिहीष्व लोकं कृणु बन्धान्मुञ्चासि बद्धकम् ।
योन्या इव प्रच्युतो गर्भः पथः सर्वाँ अनु क्षिय ॥

4. O soul, roam in different bodies. Make room for thy advancement. Release thy imprisoned self from bodily fetters. Freed, like an infant newly born, dwell in all pathways where thou wilt! (1667)[1]

HYMN CXXII

१. एतं भागं परि ददामि विद्वान् विश्वकर्मन् प्रथमजा ऋतस्य ।
अस्माभिर्दत्तं जरसः परस्तादच्छिन्नं तन्तुमनु सं तरेम ॥

1. O God, the Maker of the universe, Thou art the Primordial Cause of true knowledge. Knowing this, I, am aspirant after salvation deliver this body unto Thee. In our search beyond old age, let us fully realise the true nature of this immortal soul dedicated unto Thee by us, the devotees! (1668)

२. ततं तन्तुमन्वेके तरन्ति येषां दत्तं पित्र्यमायनेन ।
अबन्ध्वेके ददतः प्रयच्छन्तो दातुं चेच्छिक्षान्त्स स्वर्ग एव ॥

2. Those, why have discharged their debt to the parents through begetting progeny, fulfil their duty through producing children. Others, who are childless, attain to a happy state of mind, if, like their elders competent to give, they dedicate their wealth and knowledge to God. (1669)

३. अन्वारंभेथामनुसंरभेथामेतं लोकं श्रद्दधानाः सचन्ते ।
यद् वां पक्वं परिविष्टमग्नौ तस्य गुप्तये दम्पती सं श्रयेथाम् ॥

3. O husband and wife, begin performing noble deeds, begin them unitedly. The faithful enjoy this domestic life. Help each other in safeguarding the son, the excellent result of your domestic life! (1670)

४. यज्ञं यन्तं मनसा बृहन्तमन्वारोहामि तपसा सयोनिः ।
उपहूता अग्ने जरसः परस्तात् तृतीये नाके सधमादं मदेम ॥

4. Through austerity and mental vigour, depending upon His sole support, I attain to the Almighty F..ther, Worthy of attainment O Refulgent God, after reaching old age, as if invited by Thee, may we feast and enjoy with Thee, in Thy third stage higher than Matter and soul! (1671)

५. शुद्धाः पूता योषितो यज्ञिया इमा ब्रह्मणां हस्तेषु प्रपृथक् सादयामि ।
यत्काम इदमभिषिञ्चामि वोहमिन्द्रो मरुत्वान्त्स ददातु तन्मे ॥

5. These sinless, pure, holy women, I place singly in the hands of learned vedic scholars. May the Omnipotent God, grant me the blessing. I long for, as I pour this libation on you, the couple. (1672).[2]

[1]Pathways: Worlds. An emancipated soul is free to roam in any place he likes, say the Sun, Moon, Venus, Mercury, etc.

[2]I: The father of the girl.

HYMN CXXIII

१. एतं सधस्थाः परि वो ददामि यं शेवधिमावहाज्जातवेदाः ।
अन्वागन्ता यजमानः स्वस्ति तं स्म जानीत परमे व्योऽमिन् ।।

1. Ye Comrades, I offer unto you this treasure, which God reveals for you again and again. Know the worshipper who will happily follow this treasure, as having certainly attained to final beatitude. (1673)[1]

२. जानीत स्मैनं परमे व्योऽमिन् देवाः सधस्था विद लोकमत्र ।
अन्वागन्ता यजमानः स्वस्तीऽष्टापूर्तं स्म कृणुताविरस्मै ।।

2. Ye learned Comrades, know this sacrificer as having attained to final beatitude. Know that state of emancipation as his place. A devotee of God alone can happily reach that stage. O learned persons preach unto him the contemplation of God and the performance of noble actions. (1674).

३. देवाः पितरः पितरो देवाः । यो अस्मि सो अस्मि ।।

3. The learned are my protecting fathers. They reveal intricate truths, I, your pupil, am, what I am. Pray duly instruct me. (1675)[2]

४. स पचामि स ददामि स यजे स दत्तान्मा यूषम् ।।

4. I cook the fruit of my actions, I give in charity, I worship God. May I be never separated from my acts of charity. (1676)

५. नाके राजन् प्रति तिष्ठ तत्रैतत् प्रति तिष्ठतु । विद्धि पूर्तस्य नो राजन्त्स देव सुमना भव ।।

5. O strong soul reside in God, free from grief. Dedicate this noble act of thine to Him. O Glorious God, know Thou the means for the edification of our soul. Be Gracious unto us! (1677)

HYMN CXXIV

१. दिवो नु मां बृहतो अन्तरिक्षादपां स्तोको अभ्यऽपप्तद् रसेन ।
समिन्द्रियेण पयसाहमग्ने छन्दोभिर्यज्ञैः सुकृतां कृतेन ।।

1. Just as from the high firmament, Yea, out of heaven, a water drop with dew falls on the earth, and lends life, vigour and joy to mankind, so does the drop of knowledge and action full of joy fall on me from the Refulgent, Almighty God, Thereby, I, am emancipated soul, O God, am equipped with soul-force, knowledge, Vedic verses, noble deeds, and the fruit of virtuous deeds! (1678)

[1] I: A learned scholar of the Vedas. Treasure: Vedas, the store-house of spiritual knowledge. He who follows the teachings of the Vedas attains to salvation.

[2] A teacher knows the mental capacity of his pupil, and should instruct him accordingly.

२. यदि वृक्षादभ्यपप्तत् फलं तद् यद्यन्तरिक्षात् स उ वायुरेव ।
यत्रास्पृक्षत् तन्वो३ यच्च वासस आपो नुदन्तु निर्ऋतिं पराचैः ॥

2. It is a fruit if any tree hath dropped it, a breath, if from the sky it hath descended. Where it hath touched my body or my garment, thence may the waters drive dirt away. (1679)[1]

३. अभ्यञ्जनं सुरभि सा समृद्धिर्हिरण्यं वर्चस्तदु पूत्रिममेव ।
सर्वा पवित्रा वितताध्यस्मत् तन्मा तारीन्निर्ऋतिर्मो अरातिः ॥

3. It is a fragrant ointment, happy fortune, sheen all of gold, yea, purified from blemish. Spread over us are all purifications. May not poverty and parsimony subdue us. (1680)[2]

HYMN CXXV

१. वनस्पते वीड्वङ्गो हि भूया अस्मत्सखा प्रतरणः सुवीरः ।
गोभिः संनद्धो असि वीडयस्वास्थाता ते जयतु जेत्वानि ॥

1. O King, powerful like the Sun, be our friend, conqueror of foes, yoked with brave, victorious heroes, firm and strong in body. Thou art the possessor of various parts of Earth, make us strong. May thy Commander-in-chief win foes deserving defeat! (1681)

२. दिवस्पृथिव्याः पर्योज उद्भृतं वनस्पतिभ्यः पर्याभृतं सहः ।
अपामोज्मानं परि गोभिरावृतमिन्द्रस्य वज्रं हविषा रथं यज ॥

2. O learned person, give us the vitality possessed by the Sun and Earth, the strength of trees, the vitalising juice of waters. Fill thy car with warlike weapons shining like the rays of the Sun! (1682)

३. इन्द्रस्यौजो मरुतामनीकं मित्रस्य गर्भो वरुणस्य नाभिः ।
स इमां नो हव्यदातिं जुषाणो देव रथ प्रति हव्या गृभाय ॥

3. O beautiful, highly educated person, accepting gifts we offer, know the significance of the fall of lightning, realise the force of the army of men, the inner feelings of friends, the promptings of the soul of the virtuous, and enjoy our company, and all acceptable gifts. (1683)

HYMN CXXVI

१. उप श्वासय पृथिवीमुत द्यां पुरुत्रा ते वन्वतां विष्ठितं जगत् ।
स दुन्दुभे सजूरिन्द्रेण देवैर्दूराद् दवीयो अप सेध शत्रून् ॥

[1]It means water. Water purifies our clothes, fruit purifies our body. We reap fruit from the tree of our actions. Omnipresent God grants us life, which removes the dirt of the soul and body.

[2]It means water.

1. O Commander, thundering aloud like the drum, being full of supremacy, with the help of the learned, drive thou afar, yea, very far, our foemen. Grant life to the denizens of the Earth, and persons exalted like Heaven. May the world existing in its various aspects seek thy shelter! (1684)

२. श्रा क्रन्दय बलमोजो न श्रा धा श्रभि ष्टन दुरिता बाधमानः ।
अप सेध दुन्दुभे दुच्छुनामित इन्द्रस्य मुष्टिरसि वीडयस्व ।।

2. O Commander, whose army thunders like the war drum, drive away all dangers, fill us full of vigour, gain supremacy, expand the army, drive away those who behave like depraved dogs, let thy administration be well knit like the fist, make efficient arrangements for electricity in the army, and enjoy all comforts! (1685)

३. प्रामूं जयाभी३मे जयन्तु केतुमद् दुन्दुभिर्वावदीतु ।
समश्वपर्णाः पतन्तु नो नरोऽस्माकमिन्द्र रथिनो जयन्तु ।।

3. O Commander, conquer the yonder troops of the enemy. May our heroes be victorious. Let the war drum beat loudly with the furling of the flag. Let our cavalry march forth. Let our car-warriors be triumphant! (1686)

HYMN CXXVII

१. विद्रधस्य बलासस्य लोहितस्य वनस्पते । विसल्पकस्योषधे मोच्छिषः पिशितं चन ।।

1. Of abscess, of consumption of inflammation of the eyes, O Plant, of painful itch, thou Herb, let not a particle remain. (1687)

२. यो ते बलास तिष्ठतः कक्षे मुष्कावपश्रितौ । वेदाहं तस्य भेषजं चीपुद्रुरभिचक्षणम् ।।

Those two eruptions, Consumption! which stand closely hidden in thy groin—I know the medicine for them, Chipudru is their magic cure. (1688)[1]

३. यो श्रङ्ग्यो यः कर्ण्यो यो अक्ष्योर्विसल्पकः । वि वृहामो विसल्पकं विद्रधं हृदयामयम् ।
परा तमज्ञातं यक्ष्ममधराञ्चं सुवामसि ।।

3. We draw from thee piercing pain that penetrates and racks thy limbs, that pierces ears, that pierces eyes, the abscess, and the heart's disease. Downward and far away from thee we banish that unknown consumption. (1689)

HYMN CXXVIII

१. शकधूमं नक्षत्राणि यद् राजानमकुर्वत । भद्राहमस्मै प्रायच्छन्निदं राष्ट्रमसादिति ।।

[1]Thy: A patient. I: A physician. Chipudru is an unknown plant or tree. The word does not occur elsewhere. Physicians should make a search after the nature and efficacy of this medicine. No mention of this medicine is found in books on medicine.

1. Just as heavenly bodies select the Moon as their king, so do the powerless subjects elect as their king a person, who makes all quake with his might. They bring him the auspicious day of coronation, on which they declare that domain to be his. (1690)[1]

२. भद्राहं नो मध्यंदिने भद्राहं सायमस्तु नः । भद्राहं नो अह्नां प्राता रात्री भद्राहमस्तु नः ।।

2. May we have weather fair at noon. May we have weather fair at eve. May we have fair weather when the morning breaks. May we have fair weather when the night is come. (1691)

३. अहोरात्राभ्यां नक्षत्रेभ्यः सूर्याचन्द्रमसाभ्याम् । भद्राहमस्मभ्यं राजञ्छकधूम त्वं कृधि ।।

3. Fair weather to the day and night, and to the stars and sun and moon, give favourable weather unto us, thou king, who makes all quake with his might. (1692)

४. यो नो भद्राहमकरः सायं नक्तमथो दिवा । तस्मै ते नक्षत्रराज शकधूमं सदा नमः ।।

4. Be worship ever paid to thee, O King of the weak subjects, who makest all quake with thy might, who hast given us good weather in the evening and by night and day! (1693)

HYMN CXXIX

१. भगेन मा शांशपेन साकमिन्द्रेण मेदिना । कृणोमि भगिनं माप द्रान्त्वरातयः ।।

1. With thee fortune of the Friendly God, yoked with peace, I verily make myself fortunate. May all our habits of niggardliness fly and begone. (1694)[2]

२. येन वृक्षाँ अभ्यभवो भगेन वर्चसा सह । तेन मा भगिनं कृण्वप द्रान्त्वरातयः ।।

2. That splendour and felicity, O God, wherewith Thou hast excelled all desirable objects—give me therewith a happy fate. May all our habits of niggardliness fly and begone. (1695)

३. यो अन्धो यः पुनःसरो भगो वृक्षेष्वाहितः । तेन मा भगिनं कृण्वप द्रान्त्वरातयः ।।

3. O God, make me fortunate with the vitality, support of life and ever-developing force, Thou hast planted in all desirable objects. May all our habits of niggardliness fly and begone. (1696)

[1]Griffith considers Sakadhama to be an old Brahmin, who, as supposed to have the power of foretelling the weather, was naturally regarded as its controller. This interpretation is inacceptable as it favours of history of which the Vedas are free. The word means a person who makes all quake with his might. Pt. Khem Karan Das Trivedi interprets Sakadhama as God, Who makes powerful planets like the Sun tremble with His might.

[2]Shanshapa is interpreted by some commentators as a timber tree, known for its rapid growth, beauty and usefulness. Pt. Khem Karan Das Trivedi interprets the word as 'equipped, yoked with peace.'

HYMN CXXX

१. रथजितां राथजितेयीनामप्सरसामयं स्मरः । देवाः प्र हिणुत स्मरमसौ मामनु शोचतु ॥

1. This power of recollection is the conqueror of delightful, enjoyable objects, the companion of valiant persons who conquer charming, lovely objects, and the associate of sentient beings, O learned persons, fully develop this power of remembrance. May this memory ever remain fresh and pure in me. (1697)[1]

२. असौ मे स्मरतादिति प्रियो मे स्मरतादिति । देवाः प्र हिणुत स्मरमसौ मामनु शोचतु ॥

2. May that power of recollection keep my knowledge in memory, may that lovely memory retain what I have learnt. O learned persons fully develop this power of remembrance. May this memory ever remain fresh and pure in me! (1698)

३. यथा मम स्मरादसौ नामुष्याहं कदा चन । देवाः प्र हिणुत स्मरमसौ मामनु शोचतु ॥

3. May memory reflect over my attainments in knowledge. May I never neglect that power of remembrance. O learned persons fully develop this power of recollection. May this memory ever remain fresh and pure in me! (1699)

४. उन्मादयत मरुत उदन्तरिक्ष मादय । अग्न उन्मादया त्वमसौ मामनु शोचतु ॥

4. O learned persons give me pleasure. O soul give me happiness. O God give me joy. May this power of recollection ever remain fresh and pure in me. (1700)

HYMN CXXXI

१. नि शीर्षतो नि पत्तत आध्यो३ नि तिरामि ते । देवा. प्र हिणुत स्मरमसौ मामनु शोचतु ॥

1. O man with the force of my brain and the strength of my feet, I verily remove thy mental anguish. O learned persons, fully develop this power of recollection. May this memory ever remain fresh and pure in me. (1701)

२. अनुमतेन्विदं मन्यस्वाकूते समिदं नमः । देवाः प्र हिणुत स्मरमसौ मामनु शोचतु ॥

2. Assent to this noble deed, O agreeable intellect, O Determination may this food be conducive to our growth. O learned persons fully develop this power of recollection. May this memory ever remain fresh and pure in me. (1702)[2]

[1]Memory helps men in acquiring lovable objects, and achieving success in life. स्मर: means memory and love. The verse has been interpreted by some commentators; as instructing man and woman to develop love mutually. Purify me: keep my knowledge fresh and ever ready for use.

[2]Through determination and resolution can we have control over our diet and resist the cravings of the palate.

३. यद् धावसि त्रियोजनं पञ्चयोजनमाश्विनम् । ततस्त्वं पुनरायसि पुत्राणां नो असः पिता ॥

3. If thou goest to a place twelve or twenty miles distant or if thou goest to a far-off place on horseback, thence thou shouldst come back, and be the father of us sons. (1703)[1]

HYMN CXXXII

१. यं देवाः स्मरमसिञ्चन्नप्स्व१न्तः शोशुचानं सहाध्या । तं ते तपामि वरुणस्य धर्मणा ॥

1. I develop in thee through God's law, the brilliant power of recollection, which the learned have developed in the people through concentration. (1704)[2]

२. यं विश्वे देवाः स्मरमसिञ्चन्नप्स्व१न्तः शोशुचानं सहाध्या । तं ते तपामि वरुणस्य धर्मणा ॥

2. I develop in thee through God's law, the brilliant power of recollection, which all the sages have developed in the people, through concentration. (1705)

३. यमिन्द्राणी स्मरमसिञ्चदप्स्व१न्तः शोशुचानं सहाध्या । तं ते तपामि वरुणस्य धर्मणा ॥

3. I develop in thee through God's law, the brilliant power of recollection, which statesmanship has developed in the people through concentration. (1706)

४. यमिन्द्राग्नी स्मरमसिञ्चतामप्स्व१न्तः शोशुचानं सहाध्या । तं ते तपामि वरुणस्य धर्मणा ॥

4. I develop in thee through God's law, the brilliant power of recollection, which electricity and fire have developed in the people through their proper application. (1707)

५. यं मित्रावरुणौ स्मरमसिञ्चतामप्स्व१न्तः शोशुचानं सहाध्या । तं ते तपामि वरुणस्य धर्मणा ॥

5. I develop in thee through God's law, the brilliant power of recollection, which Prāna and Apāna have developed in the people through concentration. (1708)

HYMN CXXXIII

१. य इमां देवो मेखलामाबबन्ध यः संननाह य उ नो युयोज ।
यस्य देवस्य प्रशिषा चरामः स पारमिच्छात् स उ नो वि मुञ्चात् ॥

1. The learned preceptor, who fastens this girdle on the body of the Brahmchari, who prepares us for observing celibacy, who yokes us to fulfil our vow, under whose sway we prosecute our studies, longs for the completion of our pledge. May he free us from all impediments in our studies. (1709)

[1] A man should go to distant to acquire learning and amass wealth, but he should not permanently remain absent from home. He should return home to look after his children.

[2] 'I' refers to the teacher, 'thee' refers to the pupil.

२. श्राहूतास्यभिहुत ऋषीणामस्यायुधम् । पूर्वा व्रतस्य प्राश्नती वीरघ्नी भव मेखले ।।

2. O Zone, worthy of adoration and praise, thou art the armour of the sages against lust. Thou engirdlest the body of the Brahmchari in the beginning of his vow of celibacy. Remain firm in the company of heroic souls. (1710)

३. मृत्योरहं ब्रह्मचारी यदस्मि निर्याचन् भूतात् पुरुषं यमाय ।
तमहं ब्रह्मणा तपसा श्रमेणानयैनं मेखलया सिनामि ।।

3. As I am the Brahmchari of my learned preceptor, my releaser from ignorance, I am making an effort to free my soul from this body for the acquisition of God. O preceptor, I, thy pupil, bind this soul with prayer, austerity, fervour and this girdle. (1711)[1]

४. श्रद्धाया दुहिता तपसोधि जाता स्वस ऋषीणां भूतकृतां बभूव ।
सा नो मेखले मतिमा धेहि मेधामथो नो धेहि तप इन्द्रियं च ।।

4. She hath become Faith's daughter, sprung from Yoga, the sister of sages, the preachers of Truth. As such, O Girdle, give us thought and wisdom, give us religious zeal and mental vigour. (1712)[2]

५. यां त्वा पूर्वे भूतकृत ऋषयः परिबेधिरे । सा त्वं परि ष्वजस्व मां दीर्घायुत्वाय मेखले ।।

5. Thou whom primeval Rishis (sages) girt about them, they who preached the Truth, as such do thou encircle me, O Girdle, for long days of life! (1713)

HYMN CXXXIV

१. अयं वज्रस्तर्पयतामृतस्यावास्य राष्ट्रमप हन्तु जीवितम् ।
शृणातु ग्रीवाः प्र श्रृणातूष्णिहा वृत्रस्येव शचीपतिः ।।

1. Let this administration the averter of crimes, establish Law and Order. Let it scare life away and overthrow the kingdom of the enemy. Let it tear necks of the enemies to pieces, rend their napes asunder, just as the Sun, the Lord of Might rends asunder the neck of the cloud. (1714)

२. अधरोऽधर उत्तरेभ्यो गूढः पृथिव्या मोत्सृपत् । वज्रेणावहतः शयाम् ।।

2. Down, down beneath the conquerors, let him not rise, concealed in earth, but lie down-smitten with the bolt. (1715)[3]

[1]Brahmchari: Pupil Binding the soul means making it fit and efficient to fulfil the vow of celibacy.

[2]Daughter: lovely, dear like daughter. Sister: Well-wisher like the sister. She refers to girdle.

[3]Him: The wicked person.

३. यो जिनाति तमन्विच्छ यो जिनाति तमिज्जहि ।
जिनतो वज्र त्वं सीमन्तमन्वञ्चमनु पातय ॥

3. Seek out the fierce oppressor, yea, strike only the oppressor dead. Down on the fierce oppressor's head strike at full length, O ruler. (1716)

HYMN CXXXV

१. यदश्नामि बलं कुर्व इत्थं वज्रमा ददे । स्कन्धानमुष्य शातयन् वृत्रस्येव शचीपतिः ॥

1. Whatever I eat I turn to strength, and thus I grasp the reins of administration. I rend the shoulders of that foe, as the Sun shatters the cloud. (1717)[1]

२. यत् पिबामि सं पिबामि समुद्र इव संपिबः । प्राणानमुष्य संपाय सं पिबामो अमुं वयम् ॥

2. I drink well what I drink, just as the sea swallows the water of the streams. Drinking the life-breath of that man, we drink that foe and swallow him. (1718)[2]

३. यद् गिरामि सं गिरामि समुद्र इव संगिरः । प्राणानमुष्य संगीर्य सं गिरामो अमुं वयम् ॥

3. Whatever I devour, I devour well, just as the sea swallows completely the water of the streams. Swallowing that foe's vital breath, we swallow him completely up. (1719)

HYMN CXXXVI

१. देवी देव्यामधि जाता पृथिव्यामस्योषधे । तां त्वा नितत्नि केशेभ्यो दृंहणाय खनामसि ॥

1. Born from the bosom of wide Earth, the Goddess, godlike plant, art thou, So we Nitatni ! dig thee up to strengthen and fix fast the hair. (1720)[3]

२. दृंह प्रत्नाञ्जनयाजाताञ्जातानु वर्षीयसस्कृधि ।

2. Make the old hair firm, O Nitatni! make new hair spring, lengthen the hair already grown. (1721)

३. यस्ते केशोऽवपद्यते समूलो यश्च वृश्चते । इदं तं विश्वभेषज्याभि षिञ्चामि वीरुधा ॥

[1] 'I' refers to a king or ruler.

[2] Drink and swallow: Destroy and kill.

[3] Nitatni: an unidentified plant with deep roots and therefore supposed to strengthen the roots of the hair. Kāchmāchi, Jivanti, Bharingrāj and Bhangra are other plants, whose juice, rubbed on the hair strengthens them and helps in their growth. The exact nature of Nitatni is not known. Medical men should make research to find out the full particulars of the medicine. Godlike: Efficacious, healing. According to Raj Nighantu, देवी plant denotes six hair medicines, named (1) Moorchā (2) Spreekka (3) Sehdevi (4) Devdroni (5) Kesar (6) Āditya Bhaktā (137-1) Griffith and Sāyana consider Jamadagni, Veethavya and Asita to be the names of Rishis. This explanation is unacceptable as there is no history in the Vedas. Jamadagni and Veethavya mean learned, experienced physicians. Asita means God free from bondage.

3. Thy hair where it is falling off, and with the roots is torn away, I wet and sprinkle with the juice of the plant Nitatni, the sovereign remedy for all hair diseases. (1722)

HYMN CXXXVII

१. यां जमदग्निरखनद् दुहित्रे केशवर्धनीम् । तां वीतहव्य आभरदसितस्य गृहेभ्यः ॥

1. The medicine which a learned physician digs and prepares to make the locks of girls grow long, the same another scholar of the science of medicine, brings from different places created by God, free from bondage. (1723)

२. अभीशुना मेया आसन् व्यामेनानुमेयाः । केशा नडा इव वर्धन्तां शीर्ष्णस्ते असिताः परि ॥

2. Locks which could be measured with fingers, become measurable with extended hands after the use of medicine. Let the black locks spring thick and strong and grow like reeds upon thy head. (1724)

३. दृंह मूलमाग्रं यच्छ वि मध्यं यामयौषधे । केशा नडा इव वर्धन्तां शीर्ष्णस्ते असिताः परि ॥

3. O medicine, strengthen the roots of locks, prolong the points, and lengthen the middle part. Let the black locks spring thick and strong and grow like reeds upon thy head! (1725)

HYMN CXXXVIII

१. त्वं वीरुधां श्रेष्ठतमाभिश्रुतास्योषधे । इमं मे अद्य पूरुषं क्लीबमोपशिनं कृधि ॥

1. O medicine, thy fame is spread abroad as best of all the herbs that grow. Make for me this imbecile person fit for work! (1726)

२. क्लीबं कृध्योपशिनमथो कुरीरिणं कृधि । अथास्येन्द्रो ग्रावभ्यामुभे भिनत्त्वाण्ड्यौ ॥

2. O medicine make an imbecile person serviceable and fit for work. O famous physician, remove the defect of both the testicles of this patient with stone like strong instruments. (1727)[1]

३. क्लीब क्लीबं त्वाकरं वध्रे वध्रिं त्वाकरमरसारसं त्वाकरम् ।
कुरीरमस्य शीर्षणि कुम्बं चाधिनिदध्मसि ॥

3. O strength consuming disease, I make thee devoid of strength. O power wasting disease I make thee powerless. O vigour exhausting disease, I deprive thee of vigour. We adorn the head of this healthy person with strength to work, and lustre of an ornament! (1728)[2]

[1] The doctor should operate upon the testicles of the patient with strong instruments and cure him of his disease.

[2] I: A skilled doctor.

४. ये ते नाड्यौ देवकृते ययोस्तिष्ठति वृष्ण्यम् । ते ते भिनद्मि शम्ययामुष्या अधि मुष्कयोः ॥

4. O patient, thy two veins cause pain through insanity, and are full of slackness. Leaving aside the healthy vein, I operate upon them, above the testicles, with the aid of a healing instrument! (1729)

५. यथा नडं कशिपुने स्त्रियो भिन्दन्त्यश्मना । एवा भिनद्मि ते शेपोऽमुष्या अधि मुष्कयोः ॥

5. Just as women split the reeds with stone for making a mat, so do I, leaving aside the healthy vein, remove the ferocity of disease in the penis above the testicles. (1730)

HYMN CXXXIX

१. न्यस्तिका रुरोहिथ सुभगंकरणी मम । शतं तव प्रतानास्त्रयस्त्रिंशन्नितानाः ।
तया सहस्रपर्ण्या हृदयं शोषयामि ते ॥

1. O Knowledge, full of lustre, thou hast manifested thyself to bless me with prosperity. A hundred (innumerable) are thy branches. Thy orderly expansion betokens of thirty-three gods. O celibate woman, with the thousand fold powers of knowledge I fill thy heart with love. (1731)[1]

२. शुष्यतु मयि ते हृदयमथो शुष्यत्वास्यम् । अथो नि शुष्य यां कामेनाथो शुष्कास्या चर ॥

2. Let thy heart wither for my love, and let thy mouth be dry for me. Parch and dry up with longing for me, go with lips that love of me hath dried. (1732)[2]

३. संवननी समुष्पला बभ्रु कल्याणि सं नुद । अमूं च मां चं सं नुद समानं हृदयं कृधि ॥

3. O fostering, auspicious, adorable knowledge, the guardian of domestic life, draw us together, her and me, and give us both one mind. (1733)

४. यथोदकमपपुषोऽपशुष्यत्यास्यम् । एवा नि शुष्य मां कामेनाथो शुष्कास्या चर ॥

4. Just as his mouth is parched who finds no water for his burning thirst, so parch and burn with longing, go with lips that love of me hath dried. (1734)[3]

५. यथा नकुलो विच्छिद्य संदधात्यहिं पुनः । एवा कामस्य विच्छिन्नं सं धेहि वीर्यावति ॥

5. Just as the mungoose, after biting and rending the snake, preserves the calmness and tranquillity of mind, so do thou, O powerful wife, restore the fracture of our severed love. (1735)

[1]Thirty-three gods are (1) Eight vasues (2) Eleven Rudras (Breaths) (3) Twelve Adityas months (4) Indra, Electricity (5) Prajapati (Yajna).

[2]The learned bridegroom and the bride, full of mutual love should enter domestic life.

[3]Husband and wife should live together with mutual affection.

HYMN CXL

१. यौ व्याघ्राववरूढौ जिघत्सतः पितरं मातरं च । तौ दन्तौ ब्रह्मणस्पते शिवौ कृणु जातवेदः ॥

1. Two tiger-like strong teeth of the child have grown up which long to tease the mother and the sire. O learned householder, the lord of food, soothe both these teeth! (1736)[1]

२. व्रीहिमत्तं यवमत्तमथो माषमथो तिलम् ।
एष वां भागो निहितो रत्नधेयाय दन्तौ मा हिंसिष्टं पितरं मातरं च ॥

2. Let rice and barley be your food, and also beans and sesamum. This is the share allotted you, to make you shine like jewels, ye two teeth, harm not your mother and your sire. (1737)

३. उपहूतौ सयुजौ स्योनौ दन्तौ सुमङ्गलौ ।
अन्यत्र वां घोरं तन्व१: परैतु दन्तौ मा हिंसिष्टं पितरं मातरं च ॥

3. Praiseworthy are both fellow teeth, gentle and bringers of happiness. Else whither let the fierceness of your nature turn away. O Teeth! harm not your mother or your sire. (1738)[2]

HYMN CXLI

१. वायुरेनाः समाकरत् त्वष्टा पोषाय ध्रियताम् ।
इन्द्र आभ्यो अधि ब्रवद् रुद्रो भूम्ने चिकित्सतु ॥

1. An active teacher should collect the pupils. Let the far-sighted teacher exert for their mental and physical development. Let the dignified preceptor give them sound moral advice. Let the knowledge imparting master control their progress. (1739)

२. लोहितेन स्वधितिना मिथुनं कर्णयोः कृधि । अकर्तामश्विना लक्ष्म तदस्तु प्रजया बहु ॥

2. O preceptor, with the lustre of thy knowledge and spiritual force fill our ears with knowledge. Our parents have imbued us with a noble quality, that will multiply our progeny! (1740)

३. यथा चक्रुर्देवासुरा यथा मनुष्या उत । एवा सहस्रपोषाय कृणुतं लक्ष्माश्विना ॥

3. Just as learned, strong, thoughtful persons have worked for our development, so should ye, O parents imbue us with noble quality for multifarious progress! (1741)

[1]When teeth grow up in a child, he bites the teats of the mother when he drinks milk from them, or cuts the finger of the father if it is placed in his mouth. At that time the child should be weaned from milking, and his अन्न प्राशन ceremony should be performed.
[2]Fierceness: the habit of biting the mother's teats.

HYMN CXLII

१. उच्छ्रयस्व बहुर्भव स्वेन महसा यव । मृणी हि विश्वा पात्राणि मा त्वा दिव्याशनिर्वधीत् ॥

1. Spring high, O Barley, grow in abundance, through thine own magnificence. Fill all the bins; let the bolt from heaven forbear to strike thee down! (1742)[1]

२. आशृण्वन्तं यवं देवं यत्र त्वाच्छावदामसि । तदुच्छ्रयस्व द्यौरिव समुद्र इवैध्यक्षितः ॥

2. As we invite and call to thee, O nutritious barley, that heareth us, so raise thyself up like heaven on high, and be exhaustless like the sea! (1743)

३. अक्षितास्त उपसदोक्षिताः सन्तु राशयः । पृणन्तो अक्षिताः सन्त्वत्तारः सन्त्वक्षिताः ॥

3. Exhaustless be thine out-turns, O barley, exhaustless be thy gathered heaps, exhaustless be thy givers, and exhaustless be thy eaters. (1744)

BOOK (Kāṇḍa) VII

HYMN I

१. धीती वा ये अनयन् वाचो अग्रं मनसा वा येऽवदन्नृतानि ।
तृतीयेन ब्रह्मणा वावृधानास्तुरीयेणामन्वत नाम धेनोः ॥

1. They, who through action have realised the excellence of Vedic thought, who through knowledge, have preached the words of truth, who have gained strength with the strength of God, higher than action and knowledge, know the true nature of God, in the fourth and final stage of emancipation. (1745)[2]

२. स वेद पुत्रः पितरं स मातरं स सूनुर्भुवत् स भुवत् पुनर्मघः ।
स द्यामौर्णोदन्तरिक्षं स्व१ः स इदं विश्वमभवत् स आभवत् ॥

2. This soul being the son of God, knows Him as his father and mother. The soul takes birth in the body, and reaps the fruit of its actions again and again. God hath encompassed heaven, and air's mid-realm, and sky. He creates the universe, and is All-pervading. (1746)

HYMN II

१. अथर्वाणं पितरं देवबन्धुं मातुर्गर्भं पितुरसुं युवानम् ।
य इमं यज्ञं मनसा चिकेत प्र णो वोचस्तमिहेह ब्रवः ॥

1. A learned person, who, through mental concentration knows the adorable soul, as eternal lord of all the organs, friend of God, dweller in the mother's womb, recipient of life-breath from the father, ever young, ageless, and deathless, should explain to us the attributes of the soul, and proclaim them in each and every place. (1747)

[1]Pt. Jaidev Vidyalankar has interpreted यव as progeny, whom the teacher gives instructions for moral elevation.

[2]The first three stages are (1) Dharama (2) Arth (3) Kāma.

HYMN III

१. अया विष्ठा जनयन् कर्वराणि स हि घृणिरुरुर्वराय गातुः ।
स प्रत्युदैद् धरुणं मध्वो अग्रं स्वया तन्वाऽऽतन्वऽऽमैरयत ॥

1. This soul, in its various aspects, with the aid of matter, performs various deeds in the world. This is the lustrous, grand path for the adorable soul. Hence the soul marches on to God, the Resplendent, and sustainer of the whole universe. With its subtle force it draws the true nature of God towards itself. (1748)[1]

HYMN IV

१. एकया च दशभिश्चा सुहुते द्वाभ्यामिष्टये विंशत्या च ।
तिसृभिश्च वहसे त्रिंशता च वियुग्भिर्वाय इह ता वि मुञ्च ॥

1. O soul, devoted to God through yoga, thou preservest this body with mental faculty, and ten breaths. Ye are the fulfilment of thy wish, thou preservest the body through two vital breaths, Prāna and Apāna and twenty other forces. Thou preservest this body with thirty-three well-yoked divine forces. Cast aside all these binding forces in this world, and achieve final beatitude (1749)[2]

HYMN V

१. यज्ञेन यज्ञमयजन्त देवास्तानि धर्माणि प्रथमान्यासन् ।
ते ह नाकं महिमानः सचन्त यत्र पूर्वे साध्याः सन्ति देवाः ॥

1. The learned worship God through yoga. Their body ordinances for the worship of God are immemorial, such noble souls in particular enjoy the happiness of salvation, in which dwell the ancient sages and learned devotees. (1750)[3]

२. यज्ञो बभूव स आ बभूव स प्र जज्ञे स उ वावृधे पुनः ।
स देवानामधिपतिर्बभूव सो अस्मासु द्रविणमा दधातु ॥

2. God is worthy of worship. He is All-pervading. He creates the whole universe. He dissolves it again and again. He is the Lord of all divine objects. May He bestow on us wisdom and spiritual strength. (1751)

३. यद् देवा देवान् हविषायजन्तामर्त्यान् मनसामर्त्येन ।
मदेम तत्र परमे व्योऽऽमन् पश्येम तदुदितौ सूर्यस्य ॥

[1]Draws: Realises.

[2]Final beatitude: Śalvation. Ten breaths: Prāna, Apāna, Vyāna, Udāna, Samāna, Nāga, Kurma, Krikla, Deva Dutt, Dhananjya. Twenty: five subtle and five gross elements, five organs of cognition and five organs of action. Thirty-three: Eight vasus, Eleven Rudras, Twelve Ādityas, Indra (Electricity), Prajapati (Yajna).

[3]Holy ordinances: The teachings of the Vedas.

3. Seekers after God have worshipped the immortal characteristics of God with devotion and immortal spirit. May we feel happiness in that Mighty Protector, and visualise Him at the rising of the Sun. (1752)

४. यत् पुरुषेण हविषा यज्ञं देवा अतन्वत । अस्ति नु तस्मादोजीयो यद् विहव्येनेजिरे ॥

4. When the learned perform, meditating upon the Adorable God, the sacrifice of mental worship, and when they hold communion with Him through yoga alone, that sacrifice (yajna) of theirs is therefore certainly superior to all other forms of sacrifice. (1753)[1]

५. मुग्धा देवा उत शुनायजन्तोत गोरङ्गैः पुरुधायजन्त ।
य इमं यज्ञं मनसा चिकेत प्र णो वोचस्तमिहेह ब्रवः ॥

5. Sages, bewildered at the immensity of God, worship Him in various ways through knowledge, Vedic verses and yogic practices. Let the sage, who, through mental concentration, realises this Adorable God, expatiate to us upon God, and preach unto each and every man the sublimity of God. (1754)[2]

HYMN VI

१. अदितिर्द्यौरदितिरन्तरिक्षमदितिर्माता स पिता स पुत्रः ।
विश्वे देवा अदितिः पञ्च जना अदितिर्जातमदितिर्जनित्वम् ॥

1. Immortal is the heaven. Immortal is the atmosphere. Matter the mother of all is immortal. Immortal is Father God. Immortal is the soul that nourishes the body. All divine objects are immortal. Five vital breaths are immortal. All that is born and shall be born is immortal because of its immortal cause. (1755)[3]

२. महीमू षु मातरं सुव्रतानामृतस्य पत्नीमवसे हवामहे ।
तुविक्षत्रामजरन्तीमुरूचीं सुशर्माणमदितिं सुप्रणीतिम् ॥

2. We call to protect us, the unimpaired, true Vedic speech, the venerable mother of those who stick steadfastly to their vow, the rearer of truth, full of wealth and strength, free from decay, pervaded in the Almighty God, the bestower of joy, and the guide of mankind on the right path. (1756)

३. सुत्रामाणं पृथिवीं द्यामनेहसं सुशर्माणमदितिं सुप्रणीतिम् ।
दैवीं नावं स्वरित्रामनागसो अस्रवन्तीमा रुहेमा स्वस्तये ॥

[1]The Yajna performed through the sacrifice of soul and mind is superior to the Yajna performed through fuel, butter and oblations of corn.

[2]Sayana and Griffith have interpreted शुना and गोरङ्गैः as meat containing parts of dog, and limb of cow. The devta, i.e., subject-matter of this verse is soul, so a reference to the performance of Yajna with the meat of a dog or cow is out of place.

[3]God, soul, matter are by nature eternal and immortal. Other created things are as they are created again and again, and their cause is also immortal. Panch Jana may also mean, Brahmans, Kshatriyas, Vaishas, Shudras, and Nishadas, the barbarians. Panch Jana may also mean the five elements air, water, fire, earth and space.

3. May we, free from sin, for weal ascend the boat of knowledge, affording protection, vast in size, well renowned, flawless, bestower of peace and shelter to all souls, guide of mankind on the right path, revealed by God, equipped with the rudders of virtuous deeds, free from blemish, and never likely to sink. (1757)[1]

४. वाजस्य नु प्रसवे मातरं महीमदितिं नाम वचसा करामहे ।
यस्या उपस्थ उर्व१न्तरिक्षं सा नः शर्म त्रिवरूथं नि यच्छात् ॥

4. We acknowledge through Vedic verses, the organising immense, unassailable strength of God, for developing spiritual force in Whose lap lies the vast space. May He grant us the bliss of salvation that frees us from elemental, mental and physical pains. (1758)

HYMN VII

१. दितेः पुत्राणामदितेरकारिषमव देवानां बृहतामनर्मणाम् ।
तेषां हि धाम गभिषक् समुद्रियं नैनान् नमसा परो अस्ति कश्चन ॥

1. I have subordinated the inanimate objects, the sons of lifeless Matter, to non-violent, virtuous, dignified living beings, whose splendour is mighty, due to their soul-force. None excelleth them in strength. (1759)[2]

HYMN VIII

१. भद्रादधि श्रेयः प्रेहि बृहस्पतिः पुरएता ते अस्तु ।
अथेममस्या वर आ पृथिव्या आरेशत्रुं कृणुहि सर्ववीरम् ॥

1. O man, go forward on thy way from good to better. May God, the Lord of all vast worlds, precede thy steps and guide thee. O God, place this man within the earth's enclosure, afar from foes and valiant amongst all. (1760)

HYMN IX

१. प्रपथे पथामजनिष्ट पूषा प्रपथे दिवः प्रपथे पृथिव्याः ।
उभे अभि प्रियतमे सधस्थे आ च परा च चरति प्रजानन् ॥

1. God, the Nourisher of the world, is present in the pathways of the atmosphere, sun and earth. The Omniscient Lord is near us and far from us, in both the lovely and mutually attracted Sun and Earth. (1761)[3]

२. पूषेमा आशा अनु वेद सर्वाः सो अस्माँ अभयतमेन नेषत् ।
स्वस्तिदा आघृणिः सर्ववीरोऽप्रयुच्छन् पुर एतु प्रजानन् ॥

[1]Ascend: Resort to act upon. Boat of knowledge: The Vedas.

[2]I: God. Sons: Material objects, the creation of Matter.

[3](1-4) In these verses Pusha has been translated as God. Pusha may also mean, the king Octroi officer, Treasurer, Householder, Tax collector, vide *Shatpath*, 3-4-1-14, 11-4-3-15, 2-5-1-11, 11-1-2-17.

2. God fully knows all these realms: may He conduct us by ways that are free from fear and danger. Giver of blessings, glowing, all heroic, may He the Wise and Watchful lead us. (1762)

३. पूषन् तव व्रते वयं न रिष्येम कदा चन । स्तोतारस्त इह स्मसि ॥

3. We are Thy praisers, O God; never let us be injured under thy protection. (1763)

४. परि पूषा परस्ताद्धस्तं दधातु दक्षिणम् । पुनर्नो नष्टमाजतु सं नष्टेन गमेमहि ॥

4. From out the distance, far and wide, may God stretch His right hand support to us. Let Him restore our lost strength. Let us regain our lost strength. (1764)

HYMN X

१. यस्ते स्तनः शशयुर्यो मयोभूर्यः सुम्नयुः सुहवो यः सुदत्रः ।
येन विश्वा पुष्यसि वीर्याणि सरस्वति तमिह धातवे कः ॥

1. O Vedic knowledge, that sweet sermon of thine is the bestower of peace, the source of joy, the supplier of mental satisfaction, worthy of remembrance, and the giver of wisdom. Wherewith thou feedest all sorts of choice sciences. O Vedic knowledge, deliver that sermon unto us in this house of the Guru (preceptor) to derive knowledge. (1765)

HYMN XI

१. यस्ते पृथु स्तनयित्नुर्य ऋष्वो दैवः केतुर्विश्वमाभूषतीदम् ।
मा नो वधीर्विद्युता देव सस्यं मोत वधी रश्मिभिः सूर्यस्य ॥

1. O watery cloud, that high celestial signal [sent by thee in the shape of far-spread thunder pervades all this world. Strike not, our growing corn with lightning, nor destroy it with the burning rays of the Sun! (1766)[1]

HYMN XII

१. सभा च मा समितिश्चावतां प्रजापतेर्दुहितरौ संविदाने ।
येना संगच्छा उप मा स शिक्षाच्चारु वदानि पितरः संगतेषु ॥

1. In concord may the king's two daughters, the House of Commons and the House of Lords, both protect me. May every member I meet respect and aid me. Fair be my words, O learned persons at your meetings. (1767)[2]

[1]Agriculturists should protect their crops from abundance or lack of rain. Intense heat and intense rains are both harmful to the crops.

[2]A king should treat and protect both the houses of the Parliament like his daughters. 'Me' refers to the King, 'My' also refers to the King. All the members of the Parliament should be free to see the king and discuss state affairs and help the king in administration with their sound advice. The king should now and then address both the Houses jointly. Some commentators interpret सभा (sabha) as Village Panchayat.

२. विद्म ते सभे नाम नरिष्टा नाम वा असि । ये ते के च सभासदस्ते मे सन्तु सवाचसः ॥

2. We know thy name, O Assembly; thy name is Narishta. Let all the members who join the Assembly agree with me. (1768)[1]

३. एषामहं समासीनानां वर्चो विज्ञानमा ददे । अस्याः सर्वस्याः संसदो मामिन्द्र भगिनं कृणु ॥

3. I take full advantage of the splendour and learning of the members seated here. O God, make me conspicuous in all this gathered assembly! (1769)[2]

४. यद् वो मनः परागतं यद् बद्धमिह वेह वा । तद् व आ वर्तयामसि मयि वो रमतां मनः ॥

4. Whether your thoughts are turned away, or bound or fastened here and there, we draw them hitherward again: let your mind firmly rest on me. (1770)[3]

HYMN XIII

१. यथा सूर्यो नक्षत्राणामुद्यंस्तेजांस्याददे । एवा स्त्रीणां च पुंसां च द्विषतां वर्च आ ददे ॥

1. As the Sun, rising, eclipses the brightness of the stars, so I assume the glory of women and men my enemies. (1771)

२. यावन्तो मा सपत्नानामायन्तं प्रतिपश्यथ । उद्यन्त्सूर्यइव सुप्तानां द्विषतां वर्च आ ददे ॥

2. All Ye among my rivals who behold me as I come to you, I seize the glory of my foes as the Sun, rising, theirs who sleep. (1772)

HYMN XIV

१. अभि त्यं देवं सवितारमोण्योः कविक्रतुम् । अर्चामि सत्यसवं रत्नधामभि प्रियं मतिम् ॥

1. I always praise this God, the creator of heaven and earth, the source of all knowledge, the Embodiment of splendour, the Giver of knowledge and treasure, the Centre of Love, and Adorable by all. (1773)

२. ऊर्ध्वा यस्यामतिर्भा अदिद्युतत् सवीमनि । हिरण्यपाणिरमिमीत सुक्रतुः कृपात् स्वः ॥

2. I adore God, Whose lofty effulgent Self is divulged in the created world, Who has fixed the bright Sun and Moon in their orbits, Who is the Wisest Actor, Whose mercy grants us salvation. (1774)

[1]Narishta has got double significance नरैः इष्ट, liked by leaders. Leading persons like the Legislature, as it protects the rights of the people, and through them their grievances are ventilated and conveyed to the king. The second meaning of the word is (न-रिष्टा) not violent. The Legislature does not violate the fundamental human rights. It gives them full protection. Griffith translates the word as 'interchange of talk.'

[2]I and me refer to the king.

[3]The members of the Legislature should stick to the subject under discussion and not waste their time or fritter away their energy in irrelevant talk. They should listen attentively to the Speaker of the House. 'Me' means the Speaker.

३. सावीर्हि देव प्रथमाय पित्रे वर्ष्माणमस्मै वरिमाणमस्मै ।
अथास्मभ्यं सवितर्वार्याणि दिवोदिव आ सुवा भूरि पश्वः ॥

3. O God, as thou createst all objects for the grand soul, the guardian of vital life-breaths, and endowest it with body and sublimity, so unto us, O God, send treasures and abundant cattle day by day! (1775)

४. दमूना देवः सविता वरेण्यो दधद् रत्नं दक्षं पितृभ्य आयूंषि ।
पिबात् सोमं ममददेनमिष्टे परिज्मा चित् क्रमते अस्य धर्मणि ॥

4. The Refulgent, Urging, Friendly God, grants to all the objects desired by them. He bestows wealth, knowledge, long life on souls, the guardians of their bodies, organs, minds and people. Under His law, the soul enjoys extreme felicity, which makes the soul self absorbed. The active soul then realises its goal, the Venerable God. (1776)

HYMN XV

१. तां सवितः सत्यसवां सुचित्रामाहं वृणे सुमतिं विश्ववाराम् ।
यामस्य कण्वो अदुहत् प्रपीनां सहस्रधारां महिषो भगाय ॥

1. O God, I crave for the fine intellect, that urges one to Truth, is wonderful, acceptable to all, highly developed, and master of a thousand subjects. A mighty learned person acquires such an intellect for his welfare! (1777)[1]

HYMN XVI

१. बृहस्पते सवितर्वर्धयैनं ज्योतयैनं महते सौभगाय ।
संशितं चित् संतरं सं शिशाधि विश्व एनमनु मदन्तु देवाः ॥

1. O God, the Lord of the Vedas and vast worlds, the Creator, develop the soul of this Brahmchari, illume his soul with knowledge for high and happy fortune. Instruct thoroughly this austere Brahmchari, so that all the learned persons may be glad at his success! (1778)[2]

HYMN XVII

१. धाता दधातु नो रयिमीशानो जगतस्पतिः । स नः पूर्णेन यच्छतु ॥

1. May God, the Guardian, the Lord of the universe, give us wealth. May He give us strength in full. (1779)

२. धाता दधातु दाशुषे प्राचीं जीवातुमक्षिताम् । वयं देवस्य धीमहि सुमतिं विश्वराधसः ॥

2. May God grant honourable, imperishable life to a sacrificing soul. May we obtain the favour of God, the Lord of wealth. (1780)[3]

[1]See *Yajur*, 17-74.

[2]See *Yajur*, 27-8. Brihaspati, Savita may also refer to the Acharya, the teacher. Brahmchari: He who has taken the vow of celibacy.

[3]Imperishable: Not to be finished earlier, long, full span of life.

३. धाता विश्वा वार्या दधातु प्रजाकामाय दाशुषे दुरोणे ।
तस्मै देवा अमृतं सं व्ययन्तु विश्वे देवा अदितिः सजोषाः ।।

3. May God grant all the necessaries of life in the house of a charitable householder, craving for children. May all the learned persons, the harmonious forces of nature, and wise persons grant him complete happiness. (1781)

४. धाता रातिः सवितेदं जुषन्तां प्रजापतिर्निधिपतिर्नो अग्निः ।
त्वष्टा विष्णुः प्रजया संरराणो यजमानाय द्रविणं दधातु ।।

4. O priest, thou art the source of happiness to all, the begetter of prosperity, the bringer-up of children, the guardian of the treasure of knowledge, the controller of vices, the enlarger of pleasure, the pervader in all noble qualities and acts, being charitably disposed towards thy offspring, fulfil thou rightly the duties of married life, and grant stores of riches to the sacrificer! (1782)

HYMN XVIII

१. प्र नभस्व पृथिवि भिन्द्धी३दं दिव्यं नभः ।
उन्दो दिव्यस्य नो धातरीशानो वि ष्या दृतिम् ।।

1. O Earth, mayest thou be ploughed thoroughly. O powerful Sun, cleave asunder the celestial cloud, and untie the cloud filled with pure water. (1783)[1]

२. न घ्रंस्तताप न हिमो जघान प्र नभतां पृथिवी जीरदानुः ।
आपश्चिदस्मै घृतमित् क्षरन्ति यत्र सोमः सदमित् तत्र भद्रम् ।।

2. Let not the Sun's heat burn, nor cold destroy the Earth. Let Earth, the producer of life-giving food be well cultivated. Drops of rain water, say, bring for the farmer food invigorating like butter. Where cloud is even there is bliss for ever. (1784)

HYMN XIX

१. प्रजापतिर्जनयति प्रजा इमा धाता दधातु सुमनस्यमानः ।
संजानानाः संमनसः सयोनयो मयि पुष्टं पुष्टपतिर्दधातु ।।

1. God engenders these earthly creatures: may the Benevolent Sustainer nourish them. Let them have one common source, and mind, and spirit. May He Who is Lord of plenty give me plenty! (1785)[2]

HYMN XX

१. अन्वद्य नोऽनुमतिर्यज्ञं देवेषु मन्यताम् । अग्निश्च हव्यवाहनो भवतां दाशुषे मम ।।

[1]Earth should be tilled thoroughly. Filled with the rain water, it should produce bumper crop.

[2]'Them' refers to creatures. 'Me' refers to the worshipper.

1. May the man of favourable knowledge approve friendly this day our sacrifice (Yajna) among the learned. May prowess bring all desired objects for me, a charitably disposed person. (1786)

२. अन्विदमनुमते त्वं मंससे शं च नस्कृधि । जुषस्व हव्यमाहुतं प्रजां देवि ररास्व नः ।।

2. O learned king of favourable disposition, thou verily always acceptest our prayer. Grant us health and happiness. Accept the wealth we offer. O King give us progeny. (1787)

३. अनु मन्यतामनुमन्यमानः प्रजावन्तं रयिमक्षीयमाणम् ।
तस्य वयं हेडसि मापि भूम सुमृडीके अस्य सुमतौ स्याम ।।

3. May the Omniscient God, accord us wealth inexhaustible with store of children. Never may we be subject to His anger, but rest in His benevolence and mercy. (1788)[1]

४. यत् ते नाम सुहवं सुप्रणीतेऽनुमते अनुमतं सुदानु ।
तेना नो यज्ञं पिपृहि विश्ववारे रयिं नो धेहि सुभगे सुवीरम् ।।

4. O woman, nicely devoted to the performance of domestic duty, obedient to thy husband, thy nature is praiseworthy, well-known, and charitable, O embodiment of various virtues, with thy nice nature, make our domestic life successful. O Blessed one, grant us wealth and heroic children! (1789)

५. एमं यज्ञमनुमतिर्जगाम सुक्षेत्रतायै सुवीरतायै सुजातम् ।
भद्रा ह्यऽस्याः प्रमतिर्बभूव सेमं यज्ञमवतु देवगोपा ।।

5. May a well-disposed woman enter this domestic life to fulfil her desired aim and bless us with valiant sons. Thus does this domestic life succeed. Her noble thought certainly blesses us. God-protected, may she assist this domestic Yajna. (1790)

६. अनुमतिः सर्वमिदं बभूव यत् तिष्ठति चरति यदु च विश्वमेजति ।
तस्यास्ते देवि सुमतौ स्यामानुमते अनु हि मंससे नः ।।

6. Whatever standeth, or walketh everything that moveth in the world, all is in obedience to the Law of God. O Mighty power of God, may we enjoy Thy gracious love. O All-controlling power of God, regard us with favour! (1791)

HYMN XXI

१. समेत विश्वे वचसा पतिं दिव एको विभूरतिथिर्जनानाम् ।
स पूर्व्यो नूतनमाविवासत् तं वर्तनिरनु वावृत एकमित् पुरु ।।

[1]Griffith considers Anumati to be a deity connected with procreation. The hymn according to Griffith is used in charms to remove sterility in cows. This explanation is unacceptable. Anumati means the All-knowing God.

1. Ye men, with prayer come all together to God, the Lord of Heaven: He is the Peerless One, Omnipresent, Venerable like guest of men. He, the Most Ancient, pervades the universe created anew by Him; to Him alone is turned the path which all must tread. (1792)[1]

HYMN XXII

१. अयं सहस्रमा नो दृशे कवीनां मतिर्ज्योतिर्विधर्मणि ।।

1. This Omnipotent, Omniscient God, appearing as Light in the soul, the performer of special duties, grants knowledge to us, the learned sages. (1793)

२. ब्रध्नः समीचीरुषसः समैरयन् । अरेपसः सचेतसः स्वसरे मन्युमत्तमाश्चिते गोः ।।

2. God, Resplendent like the Sun, hath sent forth the Dawns, a closely gathered band, immaculate, unanimous, brightly refulgent, for exhibiting the earth in the day time. (1794)

HYMN XXIII

१. दौष्वप्न्यं दौर्जीवित्यं रक्षो अभ्वऽमराय्यऽः । दुर्णाम्नीः सर्वा दुर्वाचस्ता अस्मन्नाशयामसि ।।

1. We drive away from us, the fearful dream, miserable life, misfortune of the violent, poverty, suffering of distress, abusive language, and every kind of evil utterance. (1795)

HYMN XXIV

१. यन्न इन्द्रो अखनद् यदग्निर्विश्वे देवा मरुतो यत् स्वर्काः ।
तदस्मभ्यं सविता सत्यधर्मा प्रजापतिरनुमतिर्नि यच्छात् ।।

1. Whatever supremacy the King, the Achārya, all the learned ministers of the state, valiant persons, and scientists bestow on us, that is really granted us by God, the Embodiment of Truth, the Nourisher of mankind, the Creator of all, and the Commander of all. (1796)[2]

HYMN XXV

१. ययोरोजसा स्कभिता रजांसि यौ वीर्यैऽर्वीरतमा शविष्ठा ।
यौ पत्येते अप्रतीतौ सहोभिर्विष्णुमगन् वरुणं पूर्वहूतिः ।।

1. May the morning prayer realise God's two powers of Pervasion and Excellence, which govern the universe unrestricted through might. Through these two powers, different planets are established, which are strongest and most heroic in their vigour. (1797)[3]

[1]God creates the world again and again. After each dissolution, he creates the world anew, which lasts for a period of 4320000000 years.

[2]Achārya means the preceptor, the instructor.

[3]Which refers to powers.

२. यस्येदं प्रदिशि यद् विरोचते प्र चानति वि च चष्टे शचीभिः ।
पुरा देवस्य धर्मणा सहोभिर्विष्णुमगन् वरुणं पूर्वहूतिः ॥

2. In Whose control is all this world that shineth, all that hath powers to see and all that breatheth. Through God's law and high power this world shove in the previous cycle of creation. May the early morning prayer reach that All-pervading Excellent God. (1798)

HYMN XXVI

१. विष्णोर्नु कं प्रा वोचं वीर्याणि यः पार्थिवानि विममे रजांसि ।
यो अस्कभायदुत्तरं सधस्थं विचक्रमाणस्त्रेधोरुगायः ॥

1. I will declare the mighty deeds of God, of Him Who hath measured out the earthly regions, Who propped the highest Heaven full of stars, Who pervades the Earth, Atmosphere and Sky, and is sung by sages. (1799)[1]

२. प्र तद् विष्णुः स्तवते वीर्याणि मृगो न भीमः कुचरो गिरिष्ठाः ।
परावत आ जगम्यात् परस्याः ॥

2. God speaks in the Vedas of His supernatural, manifold powers. He is Awe-inspiring like a tiger. He is Omnipresent, and sung in Vedic verses. He approaches our heart from the farthest distance. (1800)[2]

३. यस्योरुषु त्रिषु विक्रमणेष्वधिक्षियन्ति भुवनानि विश्वा ।
उरु विष्णो वि क्रमस्वोरु क्षयाय नस्कृधि । घृतं घृतयोने पिब प्रप्र यज्ञपतिं तिर ॥

3. O God, Thou within whose three-fold vast creation all worlds and creatures have their habitation, pervadest them in extenso. Thou createst for our dwelling all these worlds. O support of luminous bodies like the Sun, Thou devourest the resplendest world at the time of dissolution. Promote this active soul more and more. (1801)[3]

४. इदं विष्णुर्वि चक्रमे त्रेधा नि दधे पदा । समूढमस्य पांसुरे ॥

4. The All-pervading God has created this world, and has established His dignity in three ways. His invisible form is hidden in space. (1802)[4]

[1]See *Yajur*, 5-18; *Rig*, 1-154-1.

[2]See *Yajur*, 5-20; *Rig*, 1-154-2.

[3]See *Yajur*, 5-19. Threefold creation: Earth, Space, Sky. It may also mean Creation, Sustenance and Dissolution. At the time of Dissolution God engulfs the whole universe, by resolving Matter into atoms.

[4]See *Yajur*, 5-15, *Rig*, 1-22-17. त्रेधा may refer to Satva, Rajas and Tamas. It may also refer to a earth, air and sky. It may also refer to sun full of brightness to earth devoid of light, and minute atoms.

५. त्रीणि पदा वि चक्रमे विष्णुर्गोपा अदाभ्यः । इतो धर्माणि धारयन् ।।

5. The Unconquerable, Protecting, All-pervading God, establishing His sacred laws, is thenceforth the Creator of the three steps of the causal, subtle and gross forms. (1803)[1]

६. विष्णोः कर्माणि पश्यत यतो व्रतानि पस्पशे । इन्द्रस्य युज्यः सखा ।।

6. O man, study God's works of Creation, Sustenance and Dissolution of the universe, whereby He determines His laws. He is the close-allied friend of the soul. (1804)[2]

७. तद् विष्णोः परमं पदं सदा पश्यन्ति सूरयः । दिवीऽव चक्षुराततम् ।

7. Learned persons realise the lofty attributes of God, as the extended eye gazes at the Sun! (1805)[3]

८. दिवो विष्ण उत वा पृथिव्या महो विष्ण उरोरन्तरिक्षात् ।
हस्तौ पृणस्व बहुभिर्वसव्यैराप्रयच्छ दक्षिणादोत सव्यात् ।।

8. O Omnipresent God, fill both of our hands with riches derived from all sources like electricity, earth, and vast wide air's mid-region. Grant us pleasures from the right and the left. (1806)

HYMN XXVII

१. इडैवास्माँ अनु वस्तां व्रतेन यस्याः पदे पुनते देवयन्तः ।
घृतपदी शक्वरी सोमपृष्ठोप यज्ञमस्थित वैश्वदेवी ।।

1. May intellect with her knowledge dwell beside us, under whose influence the pious purge and cleanse themselves. She, brilliant, mighty, the bestower of the knowledge of God and soul, the lover of all the learned, is fixed in God. (1807)

HYMN XXVIII

१. वेदः स्वस्तिर्द्रुघणः स्वस्तिः परशुर्वेदिः परशुर्नः स्वस्ति ।
हविष्कृतो यज्ञिया यज्ञकामास्ते देवासो यज्ञमिमं जुषन्ताम् ।।

1. Blest be the Veda May the mace bring a blessing, and may the altar and the hatchet bless us. May the adorable learned persons, lovers of sacrifice, and sacrificers accept this sacrifice (Yajna)! (1808)[4]

[1]Three steps may also mean, Earth, Atmosphere and Sun, or the three conditions of the soul, waking (Jagrit) sleeping (swapna) (sushupti) profound sleep. These words may also mean, creation, sustenance and dissolution of the universe. See *Yajur*, 34-43.

[2]See *Yajur*, 6-4, 13-33.

[3]See *Yajur*, 6-5; *Rig*, 1-22-20; *Sāma-Uttra*, 8.2.5.

[4]The Vedic verses recited at the time of the performance of Havan, the altar in which oblations are put, and the hatchet with which sticks to be put in the altar are cut, should all help the sacrificer at the time of Havan in its successful performance.

HYMN XXIX

१. अग्नाविष्णू महि तद् वां महित्वं पाथो घृतस्य गुह्यस्य नाम ।
दमेदमे सप्त रत्ना दधानौ प्रति वां जिह्वा घृतमा चरण्यात् ।।

1. This is your glorious might, O soul and God! Ye indeed drink the essence of devotion reposed in the inmost recesses of the heart. Placing in everybody the seven costly treasures, let your conquering strength establish explicitly that essence. (1809)[1]

२. अग्नाविष्णू महि धाम प्रियं वां वीथो घृतस्य गुह्या जुषाणौ ।
दमेदमे सुष्टुत्या वावृधानौ प्रति वां जिह्वा घृतमुच्चरण्यात् ।।

2. O householder and priest, ye love the great law, joying Ye feast on the soul's essences of knowledge and action. Exalted in each house with fair laudation, let your strength of assimilation establish explicitly that essence of knowledge! (1810)[2]

HYMN XXX

१. स्वाक्तं मे द्यावापृथिवी स्वाक्तं मित्रो अकरयम् ।
स्वाक्तं मे ब्रह्मणस्पतिः स्वाक्तं सविता करत् ।।

1. May mother and father tell me all things plainly. Let this friend fill my eyes with the collyrium of knowledge and explain all things to me. May my preceptor, the master of the Vedas, instruct me in all branches of knowledge, May God, the Creator make my heart prudent and far-seeing. (1811)

HYMN XXXI

१. इन्द्रोतिभिर्बहुलभिर्नो अद्य यावच्छ्रेष्ठाभिर्मघवञ्छूर जिन्व ।
यो नो द्वेष्टयधरः सस्पदीष्ट यमु द्विष्मस्तमु प्राणो जहातु ।।

1. Rouse us today, O wealthy valiant king, with thy best possible and varied succours. May he who hateth us fall low beneath us, and him whom we detest let life abandon. (1812)

HYMN XXXII

१. उप प्रियं पनिप्नतं युवानमाहुतीवृधम् । अगन्म बिभ्रतो नमो दीर्घमायुः कृणोतु मे ।।

1. May we put food in our digestive fire, friendly, active, young and strengthener of the sacrifice. May it bestow long life on me. (1813)[3]

[1]Seven costly treasures: five organs of cognition, mind and intellect. or रस (juice), रुधिर (blood), माँस (flesh), मेद (fat), अस्थि (bone), मज्जा (marrow), वीर्य (semen).

[2]अग्नि विष्णु may also mean king and Minister, or King and Commander-in-chief, or fire and Sun.

[3]Sacrifice: Food, which is put as an oblation in the stomach. Those whose digestion is strong attain to longevity.

HYMN XXXIII

१. सं मा सिञ्चन्तु मरुतः सं पूषा सं बृहस्पतिः ।
सं मायमग्निः सिञ्चतु प्रजया च धनेन च दीर्घमायुः कृणोतु मे ॥

1. Let fresh, pure breezes, strong mind, soul or God, and this digestive fire bestow on me long life, with children and riches. (1814)

HYMN XXXIV

१. अग्ने जातान् प्र णुदा मे सपत्नान् प्रत्यजाताञ्जातवेदो नुदस्व ।
अधस्पदं कृणुष्व ये पृतन्यवोऽनागसस्ते वयमदितये स्याम ॥

1. O King, drive off my rivals born and living, repel those yet unborn, O learned person! Cast down beneath my feet mine adversaries. May we be sinless for thee the supreme ruling king. (1815)[1]

HYMN XXXV

१. प्रान्यान्त्सपत्नान्त्सहसा सहस्व प्रत्यजाताञ्जातवेदो नुदस्व ।
इदं राष्ट्रं पिपृहि सौभगाय विश्व एनमनु मदन्तु देवाः ॥

1. O King, who knows the friend and foe, subdue with conquering might other rivals, and repel those yet unborn. For great felicity protect this kingdom and in this king let all learned persons be joyful. (1816)

२. इमा यास्ते शतं हिराः सहस्रं धमनीरुत । तासां ते सर्वासामहमश्मना बिलमप्यधाम् ॥

2. O King thou hast got hundreds of subtle and thousands of gross veins. I stop the defects of all of thy veins, with measures strong like a stone. (1817)[2]

३. परं योनेरवरं ते कृणोमि मा त्वा प्रजाभि भून्मोत सूनुः ।
अस्वं१ त्वाप्रजसं कृणोम्यश्मानं ते अपिधानं कृणोमि ॥

3. I lower thy exalted position. Let not thy subjects or thy son be disrespectful to thee O King. I make thee wise and strong. I make thy armour hard like a stone! (1818)[3]

[1]See *Yajur*, 15-1 (Hymn 34).

[2]The king has got various sources of acquiring power and sucking the blood of the subjects, which the people should stop. I: the leader of the public.

[3]Griffith has not translated the second and third verses, taking them to be vulgar and obscene. Sāyana has interpreted these verses for a spiteful woman to deprive her of the power of procreation and make her barren. The interpretation given by me is clear. I refers to the Purohit whose position is higher than that of the King.

HYMN XXXVI

१. अक्ष्यौ॑ नौ मधुसंकाशे अनीकं नौ समञ्जनम् । अन्तः कृणुष्व मां हृदि मन इन्नौ सहासति ।।

1. Sweet like honey be the lovely glances of the husband and wife, may our faces look equally beautiful. Within thy bosom harbour me; may one spirit dwell in both of us. (1819)

HYMN XXXVII

१. अभि त्वा मनुजातेन दधामि मम वाससा । यथासो मम केवलो नान्यासां कीर्तयाश्चन ।।

1. With this my robe, woven dexterously, I envelop thee, so that thou mayst be all mine own and give no thought to other dames. (1820)

HYMN XXXVIII

१. इदं खनामि भेषजं मांपश्यमभिरोरुदम् । परायतो निवर्तनमायतः प्रतिनन्दनम् ।।

1. I take this propitious vow that makes my husband look on me, that deters him from going afar from me, that bids the parting friend return and kindly greets him as he returns. (1821)[1]

२. येना निचक्र आसुरीन्द्रं देवेभ्यस्परि । तेना नि कुर्वे त्वामहं यथा तेऽसानि सुप्रिया ।।

2. Just as intellectual perception establishes the authority of the soul over the organs, so do I accept thee as my lord, that I may be most dear to thee. (1822)[2]

३. प्रतीची सोममसि प्रतीच्युत सूर्यम् । प्रतीची विश्वान् देवान् तां त्वाच्छावदामसि ।।

3. O Woman, with definite knowledge, thou art calm like the Moon, with positive vow, thou art radiant like the Sun, full of fame, thou art endowed with all noble virtues. We respectfully greet thee. (1823)

४. अहं वदामि नेत् त्वं सभायामह त्वं वद । ममेदसस्त्वं केवलो नान्यासां कीर्तयाश्चन ।।

4. I am the speaker before the assembly, not thou: speak thou after me to denote your intention. Thou shalt be mine and only mine, and never think of other dames. (1824)[3]

५. यदि वासि तिरोजनं यदि वा नद्य॑स्तिरः । इयं ह मह्यं त्वामोषधिर्बद्ध्वेव न्यानयत् ।।

[1]Just as skilled physicians dig herbs and derive advantage from them, so husband and wife should enhance their happiness and worldly prosperity through the vow of marriage.

[2]Griffith interprets Asuri as a female fiend, named Vilistengā. This interpretation is unacceptable, as there is no history in the Vedas. The word means intellectual perception.

[3]At the time of taking the vow of marriage before learned persons, the woman speaks first expressing her desire to wed the bridegroom, who shall speak afterwards giving his consent to accept her as his wife.

5. O husband, if thou are far away beyond the rivers, far away from men, this nuptial vow will seem to bind thee fast and bring thee back to me. (1825)

HYMN XXXIX

१. दिव्यं सुपर्णं पयसं बृहन्तमपां गर्भं वृषभमोषधीनाम् ।
अभीपतो वृष्टचा तर्पयन्तमा नो गोष्ठे रयिष्ठां स्थापयाति ॥

1. May we remember God, realizable in salvation, nicely endowed with knowledge and nourishment, full of spiritual strength, the Almighty, the Recipient of all deeds, the source of the growth of plants through rain, the satisfier with happiness of the souls who seek His shelter, Who establishes life and vigour in our body, the home of organs. (1826)

HYMN XL

१. यस्य व्रतं पशवो यन्ति सर्वे यस्य व्रत उपतिष्ठन्त आपः ।
यस्य व्रते पुष्टपतिर्निविष्टस्तं सरस्वन्तमवसे हवामहे ॥

1. We invoke God, under Whose Law all men reside, to preserve and aid us. Him under, Whose ordinance abide the waters, whose Command, the Sun, the lord of plenty, obeys. (1827)

२. आ प्रत्यञ्चं दाशुषे दाश्वंसं सरस्वन्तं पुष्टपतिं रयिष्ठाम् ।
रायस्पोषं श्रवस्युं वसाना इह हुवेम सदनं रयीणाम् ॥

2. Abiding here, let us invoke God, the Ocean of knowledge and strength, All-pervading, the Giver of knowledge and wealth to the worshipper, the Rich Possessor, the Lord of Fulness, Wealth-Increaser, the Giver of food, and the seat of riches. (1828)

HYMN XLI

१. अति धन्वान्यत्यपस्ततर्द श्येनो नृचक्षा अवसानदर्शः ।
तरन् विश्वान्यवरा रजांसीन्द्रेण सख्या शिव आ जगम्यात् ॥

1. Just as the Sun pours water over arid places, and is useful everywhere in the form of a cloud, so does God, the Observer of men, the Seer of the fruit of action at the time of dissolution, suppressing our carnal pleasures, showers knowledge, and traversing all air's lower realms, with soul as a friend appear before us as highly auspicious in salvation. (1829)

२. श्येनो नृचक्षा दिव्यः सुपर्णः सहस्रपाच्छतयोनिर्वयोधाः ।
स नो नि यच्छाद् वसु यत् पराभृतमस्माकमस्तु पितृषु स्वधावत् ॥

2. May God, the Observer of men, Refulgent, the Nourisher of all, All-pervading, the Home of innumerable worlds, the Bestower of food, give us wealth, fit to be preserved through endeavour, and giver of spiritual force to our p arents. (1830)[1]

[1]Soma and Rudra may also mean water and fire, or Sun and Cloud.

HYMN XLII

१. सोमारुद्रा वि वृहतं विषूचीममीवा या नो गयमाविवेश ।
बाधेथां दूरं निर्ऋतिं पराचैः कृतं चिदेनः प्र मुमुक्तमस्मत् ।।

1. O King and physician, scatter and drive away the sickness that hath appeared in our body. Afar into the distance chase all sorts of afflictions and sufferings, and release us from the sin committed by us! (1831)

२. सोमारुद्रा युवमेतान्यस्मद् विश्वा तनूषु भेषजानि धत्तम् ।
अव स्यतं मुञ्चतं यन्नो असत् तनूषु बद्धं कृतमेनो अस्मत् ।।

2. O King and physician, ye twain, use on our bodies all those medicines that heal diseases. Set free and draw away the sin committed, which we have still inherent in our bodies. (1832)

HYMN XLIII

१. शिवास्त एका अशिवास्त एकाः सर्वा बिभर्षि सुमनस्यमानः ।
तिस्रो वाचो निहिता अन्तरस्मिन् तासामेका वि पपातानु घोषम् ।।

1. O man, some words uttered for thee are full of praise, and some of calumny. Listen to them all with an unperturbed mind. In this soul are laid three speeches, one of them comes out in various ways, in the form of words. (1833)[1]

HYMN XLIV

१. उभा जिग्यथुर्न परा जयेथे न परा जिग्ये कतरश्चनैनयोः ।
इन्द्रश्च विष्णो यदपस्पृधेथां त्रेधा सहस्रं वि तदैरयेथाम् ।।

1. Ye twain have conquered, and have not been vanquished not either of the pair hath been defeated, ye, Indra, Vishnu, when ye fight your battle, ye control this entire universe in three ways. (1834)[2]

HYMN XLV

१. जनाद् विश्वजनीनात् सिन्धुतस्पर्याभृतम् ।
दूरात् त्वा मन्य उद्भृतमीर्ष्याया नाम भेषजम् ।।

[1]One should gladly listen to praise and abuse, without losing his balance of mind. Three speeches: (1) परा (Parā) which remains nascent in the soul. (2) पश्यन्ती (Pashyanti) which comes in the mind of a speaker in the form of resolve (3) मध्यमा (Madhyamā) which remains hidden in a man's resolves and gives him pain and pleasure. The fourth kind of speech is वैखरी (Vaikheri) which comes out of the mouth in the form of utterances. The first three remain hidden. Some commentators are of the view that परा resides in the navel, पश्यन्ती in the heart मध्यमा in the upper part of the chest.

[2]Indra means soul. Vishnu means God. Both soul and God fight against sin and vice and establish their sovereignty over the universe. Three ways: High, medium, low places, or heaven, firmament and earth. Pt. Khem Karan Das Trivedi interprets Indra as Commander-in-chief and Vishnu as King.

1. O Knowledge, the averter of fear, brought from a distant person, calm and deep like the ocean, well-wisher of humanity, I deem thee, nicely nourished, a balm that cureth jealousy. (1835)

२. अग्नेरिवास्य दहतो दावस्य दहतः पृथक् । एतामेतस्येर्ष्यामुद्नाग्निमिव शमय ॥

2. As one with water quencheth fire, so O Knowledge calm this person's jealousy, that burneth like heat of fire, or like flame that rageth through the wood. (1836)

HYMN XLVI

१. सिनीवालि पृथुष्टुके या देवानामसि स्वसा । जुषस्व हव्यमाहुतं प्रजां देवि दिदिड्ढि नः ॥

1. O lovely, famous, educated virgin, possessor of noble traits, accept the desired husband, and grant us progeny. (1837)

२. या सुबाहुः स्वङ्गुरिः सुषूमा बहुसूवरी । तस्यै विश्पत्न्यै हविः सिनीवाल्यै जुहोतन ॥

2. Always supply food to the lovely wife, the nourisher of children, lovely armed, beautiful-fingured, prolific, bearing many a child. (1838)

३. या विश्पत्नीन्द्रमसि प्रतीची सहस्रस्तुकाभियन्ती देवी ।
विष्णोः पत्नि तुभ्यं राता हवींषि पतिं देवि राधसे चोदयस्व ॥

3. O woman, who nourishes children, possesses definite, positive knowledge, is praised in manifold ways, and travels in different directions, attains to supremacy. O consort of a hero, thou art offered all nice objects. O woman urge thy husband to bounty. (1839)

HYMN XLVII

१. कुहूं देवीं सुकृतं विद्मनापसमस्मिन् यज्ञे सुहवा जोहवीमि ।
सा नो रयिं विश्ववारं नि यच्छाद् ददातु वीरं शतदायमुक्थ्यम् ॥

1. In this sacrifice (Yajna) with favoured cry I call the woman, the doer of noble deeds, the knower of duties, the master of fine traits, and the possessor of extraordinary nature. May she always vouchsafe us highly serviceable wealth, and a charitable praiseworthy heroic son. (1840)

२. कुहूर्देवानाममृतस्य पत्नी हव्या नो अस्य हविषो जुषेत ।
शृणोतु यज्ञमुशती नो अद्य रायस्पोषं चिकितुषी दधातु ॥

2. May the wife of an energetic person, worthy of being invoked, from amongst the learned, enjoy this sacrifice of ours. Let her, desirous of religious assembly, hear us today. May she, intelligent, lend increase to our wealth. (1841)

HYMN XLVIII

१. राकामहं सुहवा सुष्टुती हुवे शृणोतु नः सुभगा बोधतु त्मना ।
सीव्यत्वपः सूच्याच्छिद्यमानया ददातु वीरं शतदायमुक्थ्यम् ॥

1. With fair laud and reverent cry I call my pleasure-giving wife, brilliant like the full moon. May she, auspicious, hear us and herself observe, with never-breaking needle may she sew her work of bearing children. May she give us a charitable, praiseworthy heroic son. (1842)[1]

२. यास्ते राके सुमतयः सुपेशसो याभिर्ददासि दाशुषे वसूनि ।
ताभिर्नो अद्य सुमना उपागहि सहस्रापोषं सुभगे रराणा ॥

2. O pleasure-giving wife, brilliant like the full moon all thy precious counsels, wherewith thou grantest treasures to thy charitable husband, with these come thou to us this day, benevolent, O blessed one, bestowing wealth of thousand sorts! (1843)

HYMN XLIX

१. देवानां पत्नीरुशतीरवन्तु नः प्रावन्तु नस्तुजये वाजसातये ।
याः पार्थिवासो या अपामपि व्रते ता नो देवीः सुहवाः शर्म यच्छन्तु ॥

1. May the learned consorts of kings, aid us of their own free will. May they come unto us for protecting our offspring, and spreading knowledge. May the queens of royal family, who are devoted to the moral elevation of the subjects, learned as they are, expert in nice preaching, shower happiness and peace on the subjects. (1844)

२. उत ग्ना व्यन्तु देवपत्नीरिन्द्राण्य१ग्नाय्यश्विनी राट् ।
आ रोदसी वरुणानी शृणोतु व्यन्तु देवीर्य ऋतुर्जनीनाम् ॥

2. May the dignified wives of learned persons, the royal queen, the wife of the Commander-in-chief, the wife of a skilled artisan study the Vedas with full versification. May the wife of a scholar, the wife of the chief justice bear our complaints. May these learned women call the lady complainants for administering justice at the appointed time. (1845)[2]

HYMN L

१. यथा वृक्षमशनिर्विश्वाहा हन्त्यप्रति । एवाहमद्य कितवानक्षैर्वध्यासमप्रति ॥

1. Just as the lightning flash always irresistibly burns the tree, so, irresistibly, may I ever suppress the brute passions with my mental powers. (1846)[3]

[1](1-2) Rāka has been translated by Pt. Jaideva Vidyalankara as Lok Sabha or Parliament.

[2]The Vedas preach that females should be appointed as magistrates and judges for hearing the complaints of women, who cannot frankly lay their complaints before the male magistrates. Female judges should be highly learned.

[3]'I' means the soul.

२. तुराणामतुराणां विशामवर्जुषीणाम् । समैतु विश्वतो भगो अन्तर्हस्तं कृतं मम ॥

2. May the fortune of the quick, show subjects, who cannot cast away their weaknesses, pass into my hands. My action is the creation of my hand. (1847)[1]

३. ईडे अग्नि स्वावसुं नमोभिरिह प्रसक्तो वि चयत् कृतं नः ।
रथैरिव प्र भरे वाजयद्भिः प्रदक्षिणं मरुतां स्तोममृध्याम् ॥

3. I praise with reverence the Resplendent God, Who resides within the soul. He, pervading in the universe watches our actions. Just as I with swift conveyances visit distant places and control them, so may I, the master of the soul, subdue the powerful organs. (1848)[2]

४. वयं जयेम त्वया युजा वृतमस्माकमंशमुदवा भरेभरे ।
अस्मभ्यमिन्द्र वरीयः सुगं कृधि प्र शत्रूणां मघवन् वृष्ण्या रुज ॥

4. O God, with Thy help, may we subdue evil propensities. O God, in each struggle of life, elevate our soul. O God, make salvation the highest stage of spiritual advancement easily attainable by us. O opulent God, break down the forces of lust, and anger, etc. the enemies of the soul. (1849)[3]

५. अजैषं त्वा संलिखितमजैषमुत संरुधम् । अविं वृको यथा मथदेवा मथ्नामि ते कृतम् ॥

5. O dark, base tendency, I have subdued the evil designs inscribed on the tablet of my heart, like an inscription engraved on a marble slab. I have conquered all the impediments that stand in the way of my moral progress. As a wolf tears and rends a sheep, so do I avert the fruit of thy evil intention. (1850)

६. उत प्रहामतिदीवा जयति कृतमिव श्वघ्नी वि चिनोति काले ।
यो देवकामो न धनं रुणद्धि समित् तं रायः सृजति स्वधाभिः ॥

6. An energetic, sagacious, jubilant soul conquers the assailant. A gambler who wastes his money realises his wrong act when he suffers loss. A devotee who keeps not back his riches for himself, but spends them for the good of humanity, is overwhelmed with wealth's inherent powers. (1851)

७. गोभिष्टरेमामतिं दुरेवां यवेन वा क्षुधं पुरुहूत विश्वे ।
वयं राजसु प्रथमा धनान्यरिष्टासो वृजनीभिर्जयेम ॥

7. O much-invoked king, may we all remove with knowledge poverty that brings sin, repel hunger with store of barley. May we observing non-violence, first among the princes, obtain riches by our own exertions. (1852)

[1]The king should collect money from his strong and weak subjects, and spend it for their amelioration.

[2]Sayāna has applied the verses of this hymn on gambling, which is unfair.

[3]Sayāna has applied this verse on gambling. This is irrational. There is no reference to gambling in the verse.

८. कृतं मे दक्षिणे हस्ते जयो मे सव्य आहितः ।
गोजिद् भूयासमश्वजिद् धनंजयो हिरण्यजित् ।।

8. When there is enterprise in my right hand, victory will certainly lie in my left, I would that I were winner of cattle and horses, wealth and gold. (1853)

९. अक्षाः फलवतीं द्युवं दत्त गां क्षीरिणीमिव । सं मा कृतस्य धारया धनुः स्नाव्नेव नह्यत ।।

9. O men of practical wisdom, just as a rich man gives a milch cow in charity, so grant me fruitful knowledge. Just as the bowstring binds the bow, so unite me with the tradition of noble deeds. (1854)

HYMN LI

१. बृहस्पतिर्नः परि पातु पश्चादुतोत्तरस्मादधरादघायोः ।
इन्द्रः पुरस्तादुत मध्यतो नः सखा सखिभ्यो वरीयः कृणोतु ।।

1. May God, the Master of Knowledge protect us from the sinner, from rearward, from above, and from below us! May God, from the front, and from the centre, vouchsafe us room and freedom, as friend to friends. (1855)

HYMN LII

१. संज्ञानं नः स्वेभिः संज्ञानमरणेभिः । संज्ञानमश्विना युवमिहास्मासु नि यच्छतम् ।।

1. O father and mother, give us agreement with our own, with strangers give us unity. Do Ye, in this world join us in sympathy and love. (1856)

२. सं जानामहै मनसा सं चिकित्वा मा युष्महि मनसा दैव्येन ।
मा घोषा उत्स्थुर्बहुले विनिर्हते मेषुः पप्तदिन्द्रस्याहन्यागते ।।

2. May we agree in mind, agree in purpose, let us not fight against the spirit of the learned. Around us rise no din of frequent slaughter in battle. Let not the king's arrow fly on the eve of the day of battle. (1857)

HYMN LIII

१. अमुत्रभूयादधि यद्यमस्य बृहस्पते अभिशस्तेरमुञ्चः ।
प्रत्यौहतामश्विना मृत्युमस्मद् देवानामग्ने भिषजा शचीभिः ।।

1. O learned fellow, the guardian of big persons, be free from the fruit of sins in the next birth.

Chase death far from him who follows the instructions of the religious and law-abiding persons. O skilled physician, just as the teacher and preacher achieve their aim by dint of deeds and wisdom, so shouldst thou skilfully prepare efficacious medicines, whereby thou preservest the health of the people! (1858)[1]

[1]See *Yajur*. 27-9

२. सं क्रामतं मा जहीतं शरीरं प्राणापानौ ते सयुजाविह स्ताम् ।
शतं जीव शरदो वर्धमानोऽग्निष्टे गोपा अधिपा वसिष्ठः ।।

2. O inspiration (Apāna) and expiration (Prāṇa) move both together; do not leave the body. Let both the breathings stay united for thee, O man. Waxing in strength live thou a hundred autumns, God is thy noblest Guardian and thy Lord! (1859)

३. आयुर्यत् ते अतिहितं पराचैरपानः प्राणः पुनरा ताविताम् ।
अग्निष्टदाहार्निॠतेरुपस्थात् तदात्मनि पुनरा वेशयामि ते ।।

3. Let Prāṇa and Apāna bring back thy life, that hath vanished through misdeeds. A physician has snatched it from the bosom of Death: Into thyself again I introduce it. (1860)[1]

४. मेमं प्राणो हासीन्मो अपानोऽवहाय परा गात् ।
सप्तर्षिभ्य एनं परि ददामि त एनं स्वस्ति जरसे वहन्तु ।।

4. Let not the vital breath he draws forsake him, let not his expiration part and leave him. I give him over to the Seven Rishis: let them conduct him to old age in safety. (1861)[2]

५. प्र विशतं प्राणापानावनड्वाहाविव व्रजम् । अहं जरिम्णः शेवधिररिष्ट इह वर्धताम् ।।

5. Enter the body, both ye breaths, like two draught-oxen entering their stall. Let this soul, the treasure of old age, still wax in strength, free from violence, in the world. (1862)

६. आ ते प्राणं सुवामसि परा यक्ष्मं सुवामि ते । आयुर्नो विश्वतो दधदयमग्निर्वरेण्यः ।।

6. I send thee back thy vital breath; I drive consumption far from thee. May digestive fire, most excellent, sustain our life to full length. (1863)[3]

७. उद् वयं तमसस्परि रोहन्तो नाकमुत्तमम् । देवं देवत्रा सूर्यमगन्म ज्योतिरुत्तमम् ।।

7. May we, looking mentally upon God, free from darkness, highest of all, noblest among the noble, the light that is most excellent, nicely attain to happiness on all sides. (1864)[4]

HYMN LIV

१. ऋचं साम यजामहे याभ्यां कर्माणि कुर्वते । एते सदसि राजतो यज्ञं देवेषु यच्छतः ।।

[1] 'It' refers to life, 'I' refers to a learned physician.

[2] 'He' refers to the child, 'I' refers to the father or teacher. Griffith mentions seven rishis to be, Bhardwaja, Kasyapa, Gotama, Atri, Vasishtha, Visvamitra and Jamadagni. This explanation is unacceptable, as there is no history in the Vedas. Seven Rishis refer to, Touch, Sight, Hearing, Taste, Smell, Mind and Intellect as mentioned in *Yajur*, 34-55.

[3] Full length: Hundred years.

[4] See *Yajur*, 20-21, 27-10, 35-14, 38-24.

1. We preach to our pupils, the Rigveda and Sāmaveda. Men perform their worldly and philanthropic acts through both of them. These twain shine in the world, and preach to the learned, the true nature of God. (1865)

२. ऋचं साम यदप्राक्षं हविरोजो यजुर्बलम् । एष मा तस्मान्मा हिंसीद् वेदः पृष्टः शचीपते ॥

2. May I acquire knowledge by the study of the Rigveda, spiritual strength from the Sāma and physical power by the study of the Yajurveda. O Preceptor, the lord of speech, deed and intellect, may not this Atharvaveda, full of scientific knowledge, I have studied, do me harm. (1866)

HYMN LV

१. ये ते पन्थानोऽव दिवो येभिर्विश्वमैरयः । तेभिः सुम्नया धेहि नो वसो ॥

1. O God, the Creator of the universe, Thy urging powers have controlled the entire solar system, wherewith Thou administerest the whole world; Keep us in safety through them. (1867)[1]

HYMN LVI

१. तिरश्चिराजेरसितात् पृदाकोः परि संभृतम् । तत् कङ्कपर्वणो विषमियं वीरुदनीनशत् ॥

1. This herb renders powerless the poison, that comes from a snake with transverse stripes, from a black snake, from a viper, or a flying snake with joints of a crow. (1868)

२. इयं वीरुन्मधुजाता मधुश्चुन्मधुला मधूः । सा विह्रुतस्य भेषज्यथो मशकजम्भनी ॥

2. This herb, born of earth, honey-dropping, rich in sweetness, is honey itself. It is an efficacious remedy for the poison instilled by a crooked serpent. It kills the gnat that bites and stings. (1869)

३. यतो दष्टं यतो धीतं ततस्ते निर्ह्वयामसि । अर्भस्य तृप्रदंशिनो मशकस्यारसं विषम् ॥

3. O patient, in whatever part of the body, thou hast been bitten by the snake, or from where thy blood hath been sucked, thence we drive the poison out. We render ineffectual the poison of the little sharply-stinging gnat. (1870)

४. अयं यो वक्रो विपरुर्व्यङ्गो मुखानि वक्रा वृजिना कृणोषि ।
तानि त्वं ब्रह्मणस्पत इषीकामिव सं नमः ॥

4. This snake-bitten patient, has a crooked body, deformed joints, loose limbs like hands and feet, who twists and makes awry the parts of the face like teeth, nose and eyes O skilled physician set right and bend together these jaws like a reed. (1871)

[1]Them: Urging powers.

५. अरसस्य शर्कोटस्य नीचीनस्योपसर्पतः । विषं ह्य१स्यादिष्यथो एनमजीजभम् ॥

5. I have removed the poison of this scorpion or snake and then utterly demolished him, that creeps along, low on the earth and is poisonless. (1872)[1]

६. न ते बाह्वोर्बलमस्ति न शीर्षे नोत मध्यतः । अथ किं पापयामुया पुच्छे बिभर्ष्यर्भकम् ॥

6. O scorpion, no strength in thy two arms hast thou, nor in thy head, nor in thy waist. Then what is the good of that poison thou so viciously bearest in thy tail! (1873)[2]

७. अदन्ति त्वा पिपीलिका वि वृश्चन्ति मयूर्यः । सर्वे भल ब्रवाथ शार्कोटमरसं विषम् ॥

7. O snake, the emmets devour thee, and peahens tear and mangle thee! All ye are crying out, in sooth the snake's poison hath no strength. (1874)[3]

८. य उभाभ्यां प्रहरसि पुच्छेन चास्ये॒न च । आस्ये३ न ते विषं किमु ते पुच्छधावसत् ॥

8. Thou scorpion, who inflictest both with thy mouth and with thy tail! no poison in thy mouth hast thou; what at thy tail's root will there be. (1875)

HYMN LVII

१. यदाशसा वदतो मे विचुक्षुभे यद् याचमानस्य चरतो जनाँ अनु ।
यदात्मनि तन्वो मे विरिष्टं सरस्वती तदा पृणद् घृतेन ॥

1. Whatever mental trouble I feel from the violence of the people conversing with them for their welfare, whatever mental agony I sustain by going to the people again and again and imploring them for their betterment; whatever imperfection I find in my body, mind or soul, may God remove that with His wisdom and love. (1876)

२. सप्त क्षरन्ति शिशवे मरुत्वते पित्रे पुत्रासो अप्यवीवृतन्नृतानि ।
उभे इदस्योभे अस्य राजत उभे यतेते उभे अस्य पुष्यतः ॥

2. Seven faculties work for the soul, full of Prānās (breaths). Just as sons perform various deeds for their father, so do the Prānās, the sons of the soul, spread truth and knowledge for the soul, their father, nourisher and generator. Two ears contribute to the strength of the soul. Two eyes derive light from the soul. Two nostrils work for the soul, Mouth and tongue strengthen the soul. (1877)[4]

[1] 'I' refers to a snake-charmer.

[2] Men should be straightforward in their behaviour, and give up the crooked nature of a scorpion, that is outwardly gentle, but carries poison in his tail.

[3] All ye: Emmets and peahens, or medicines that remove poison.

[4] Seven faculties: Mind, intellect, five organs of cognition. Sāyana interprets सप्त as seven rivers, which is unacceptable, as there is no history in the Vedas.

HYMN LVIII

१. इन्द्रावरुणा सुतपाविमं सुतं सोमं पिबतं मद्यं धृतव्रतौ ।
युवो रथो अध्वरो देववीतये प्रति स्वसरमुप यातु पीतये ॥

1. O valiant, calm, noble persons, you are the enjoyers of knowledge and mental joy. Enjoy knowledge and felicity, acquired through effort, the givers of joy and satisfaction, being unwavering and energetic. (1878)

२. इन्द्रावरुणा मधुमत्तमस्य वृष्णः सोमस्य वृषणा वृषेथाम् ।
इदं वामन्धः परिषिक्तमासद्यास्मिन् बर्हिषि मादयेथाम् ॥

2. In ye both, may the charming, non-violent, immortal soul, for enjoying knowledge derived through organs, and realising the joy resulting from reflection, pervade each moving organ of the body. (1879)

HYMN LIX

१. यो नः शपादशपतः शपतो यश्च नः शपात् । वृक्ष इव विद्युता हत आ मूलादनु शुष्यतु ॥

1. Like a tree struck by lightning may the man be withered from the root, who curses us who curse him not, or, when we curse him, curseth us. (1880)

HYMN LX

१. ऊर्जं बिभ्रद् वसुवनिः सुमेधा अघोरेण चक्षुषा मित्रियेण ।
गृहानैमि सुमना वन्दमानो रमध्वं मा बिभीत मत् ॥

1. When I come from a distant place to the inmates of my house, I bring nutritious foodstuffs for them, distribute money amongst them, prudently look upon them with amicable eye that strikes no terror. Full of glee I salute them all, and say "O inmates of the house, be glad and joyful, be not afraid of me"! (1881)

२. इमे गृहा मयोभुव ऊर्जस्वन्तः पयस्वन्तः । पूर्णा वामेन तिष्ठन्तस्ते नो जानन्त्वायतः ॥

2. Let these delightful houses, that are rich in foodstuffs and store of milk, replete with wealth and standing firm, become aware of our approach. (1882)

३. येषामध्येति प्रवसन् येषु सौमनसो बहुः । गृहानुप ह्वयामहे ते नो जानन्त्वायतः ॥

3. A man in exile remembers his relatives and entertains good intentions about them. May we always remember the members of our family, and invoke them on our return, so that they be aware of our approach. (1883)

४. उपहूता भूरिधनाः सखायः स्वादुसंमुदः । अक्षुध्या अतृष्या स्त गृहा मास्मद् बिभीतन ॥

4. Thus greeted, ye of ample wealth, friends who enjoy delightful sweets, be ever free from hunger, free from thirst! Ye inmates of the house, fear us not. (1884)[1]

[1]Us: Relatives who have returned from foreign lands.

५. उपहूता इह गाव उपहूता अजावयः । अथो अन्नस्य कीलाल उपहूतो गृहेषु नः ॥

5. May we in this world get cows, goats, sheep and abundant food in our houses. (1885)

६. सूनृतावन्तः सुभगा इरावन्तो हसामुदाः । अतृष्या अक्षुध्या स्त गृहा मास्मद् बिभीतन ॥

6. Ye, members of the family, always speak the truth, ever attain to prosperity, ever remain full of foodstuffs, be full of laughter and felicity. Be ever free from hunger, free from thirst, and be not afraid of us. (1886)

७. इहैव स्त मानु गात विश्वा रूपाणि पुष्यत । ऐष्यामि भद्रेणा सह भूयांसो भवता मया ॥

7. Ye relatives, stay here in the house, follow me not, when I go abroad. Nourish all beautiful children! With happy fortune will I come back. On my return grow more abundant through my help. (1887)

HYMN LXI

१. यदग्ने तपसा तप उपतप्यामहे तपः । प्रियाः श्रुतस्य भूयास्मायुष्मन्तः सुमेधसः ॥

1. O God, we want to undergo austerity, which is observed through divine knowledge. May we be the lovers of the Sacred Lore, may we be wise and live long! (1888)[1]

२. अग्ने तपस्तप्यामह उप तप्यामहे तपः । श्रुतानि शृण्वन्तो वयमायुष्मन्तः सुमेधसः ॥

2. O God, we practise acts austere, we undergo austerity. Listening to Holy Lore, may we grow wise and live long! (1889)

HYMN LXII

१. अयमग्निः सत्पतिर्वृद्धवृष्णो रथीव पत्तीनजयत् पुरोहितः ।
नाभा पृथिव्यां निहितो दविद्युतदधस्पदं कृणुतां ये पृतन्यवः ॥

1. This Omniscient God, the Guardian of the virtuous. Almighty, Foremost of all, conquers all passions, the spiritual foes, just as a car-warrior conquers footmen. Just as the sun laid in the centre of the world lends light to all, so does God illumine the universe. May He lay our enemies below our feet. (1890)[2]

HYMN LXIII

१. पृतनाजितं सहमानमग्निमुक्थैर्हवामहे परमात् सधस्थात् ।
स नः पर्षदति दुर्गाणि विश्वा क्षामद् देवोऽति दुरितान्यग्निः ॥

[1]Sacred Lore: The Vedas.

[2]Enemies: Foes like lust, anger and those who attack us with an army (64-1) Griffith following Sayāna has translated Āpa as waters, and कृष्ण शकुनि as black raven, which is not so logical and rational. Āpā means internal moral forces in man granted by God. कृष्ण means fascinating, शकुनि means overpowering sin.

1. We call with lauds from his most lofty position, victorious King, conqueror in battles. May he convey us over all distresses, may the fiery king destroy all our vices. (1891)

HYMN LXIV

१. इदं यत् कृष्णः शकुनिरभिनिष्पतन्नपीपतत् ।
आपो मा तस्मात् सर्वस्माद् दुरितात् पान्त्वंहसः ॥

1. This fascinating overpowering sin, attacking our soul with great vehemence from all sides, pushes us into the paths of vice. May the inherent forces granted me by God, save and rescue me from all that woe and vice. (1892)

२. इदं यत् कृष्णः शकुनिरवामृक्षन्निर्ऋते ते मुखेन ।
अग्निर्मा तस्मादेनसो गार्हपत्यः प्र मुञ्चतु ॥

2. O sentiment of sin that degrades the soul, this fascinating and overpowering vice, similar to theo in nature debases me morally. May the fervour of my soul save and set me free from all that guilt! (1893)

HYMN LXV

१. प्रतीचीनफलो हि त्वमपामार्ग रुरोहिथ । सर्वान् मच्छपथाँ अधि वरीयो यावया इतः ॥

1. O soul, the purifier of deeds, being the direct reaper of the fruit of actions, thou growest more powerful. Remove completely far from this body all sentiments of sin! (1894)

२. यद् दुष्कृतं यच्छमलं यद् वा चेरिम पापया । त्वया तद् विश्वतोमुखापामार्गाप मृज्महे ॥

2. Whatever evil or whatever vile or sinful act we have done, with thy help, O Prāna, the remover of sin and pervader in the body, we wipe it off. (1895)

३. श्यावदता कुनखिना बण्डेन यत्सहासिम । अपामार्ग त्वया वयं सर्वं तदप मृज्महे ॥

3. If we have dined with the cripple, whose teeth are black and nails deformed, with thee, O Apāmārga, we wipe all that ill away from us. (1896)[1]

HYMN LXVI

१. यद्यन्तरिक्षे यदि वात आस यदि वृक्षेषु यदि वोलपेषु ।
यदस्रवन् पशव उद्यमानं तद् ब्राह्मणं पुनरस्मानुपैतु ॥

1. God is present in the atmosphere, in the wind, in the trees and in the bushes. He pervades all living beings. We realise that Visible God again and again. (1897)[2]

[1]Apāmarga: A medicine that cures contagious diseases. Cripple: Lame and hideous personage, the embodiment of disease.

[2]Again and again: In this life as well as the next one.

HYMN LXVII

१. पुनर्मैत्विन्द्रियं पुनरात्मा द्रविणं ब्राह्मणं च ।
पुनरग्नयो धिष्ण्या यथास्थाम कल्पयन्तामिहैव ॥

1. May I, after rebirth, acquire prosperity, spiritual force, riches and Vedic knowledge. May eloquent learned persons, according to the fruit of my actions make me successful in my next life in this world. (1898)[1]

HYMN LXVIII

१. सरस्वति व्रतेषु ते दिव्येषु देवि धामसु । जुषस्व हव्यमाहुतं प्रजां देवि ररास्व नः ॥

1. O Vedic knowledge, in thy celestial laws and decrees, accept our offered contribution, and grant us intellect! (1899)[2]

२. इदं ते हव्यं घृतवत् सरस्वतीदं पितृणां हविरास्यं१ यत् ।
इमानि त उदिता शंतमानि तेभिर्वयं मधुमन्तः स्याम ॥

2. O Vedic knowledge, this is thy brilliant, acceptable beauty, which even the preceptors acquire, and which is worthy of being imparted to the pupils. May all these utterances of thine be auspicious, and may we acquire knowledge and joy through them! (1900)

३. शिवा नः शंतमा भव सुमृडीका सरस्वति । मा ते युयोम संदृशः ॥

3. O Vedic knowledge, be kind and most auspicious, be gracious to us. May we never lose thy sight. (1901)

HYMN LXIX

१. शं नो वातो वातु शं नस्तपतु सूर्यः ।
अहानि शं भवन्तु नः शं रात्री प्रति धीयतां शमुषा नो व्युच्छतु ॥

1. May the wind kindly blow on us, may the Sun pleasantly warm us. May days pass happily for us, may night draw near delightfully, may dawn break joyfully for us. (1902)

HYMN LXX

१. यत् किं चासौ मनसा यच्च वाचा यज्ञैर्जुहोति हविषा यजुषा ।
तन्मृत्युना निर्ऋतिः संविदाना पुरा सत्यादाहुतिं हन्त्वस्य ॥

1. Whatever sacrifice that man performeth with mind, voice, verses of the Yajurveda, and oblations of corn, may his sinful conduct, in accord with Death, ruin his offering before it gain fulfilment. (1903)[3]

[1]This verse preaches the doctrine of the transmigration of soul.

[2]Man should try to contribute his share to the vast ocean of Vedic knowledge, by its study and propagation.

[3]That man: A man of debased character and sinful nature.

२. यातुधाना निर्ऋतिराद् रक्षस्ते अस्य घ्नन्त्वनृतेन सत्यम् ।
इन्द्रेषिता देवा आज्यमस्य मथ्नन्तु मा तत् सं पादि यदसौ जुहोति ।।

2. Distressing events, chill penury, troublesome obstacle render ineffective the success of a sinner through his unrighteous conduct. Physical calamities sent by God destroy the strength of a sinner, with the result that his sacrifice never fructifies. (1904)

३. अजिराधिराजौ श्येनौ संपातिनाविव । आज्यं पृतन्यतो हतां यो नः कश्चाभ्यघायति ।।

3. Let Death and Poverty, like two falcons swooping on their prey, destroy the strength of the foe who attacks us with an army, or entertains evil designs against us. (1905)[1]

४. अपाञ्चौ त उभौ बाहू अपि नह्याम्यास्य॒म् । अग्नेर्देवस्य मन्युना तेन तेऽवधिषं हविः ।।

4. O foe, behind thy back I tie thine arms, I bind a bandage on thy mouth, I with the anger of a conquering king have destroyed all thy strength and vitality! (1906)[2]

५. अपि नह्यामि ते बाहू अपि नह्याम्यास्य॒म् । अग्नेर्घोरस्य मन्युना तेन तेऽवधिषं हविः ।।

5. O foe, behind thy back I tie thine arms, I bind a bandage on thy mouth. I with the anger of an awe-inspiring king have destroyed all thy strength and vitality! (1907)

HYMN LXXI

१. परि त्वाग्ने पुरं वयं विप्रं सहस्य धीमहि । धृषद्वर्णं दिवेदिवे हन्तारं भङ्गुरावतः ।।

1. O powerful King, we, thy subjects, establish as our lord, thee, the fulfiller of all desires, a sage, renowned for suppressing all foes, and the destroyer of deceitful persons who disintegrate the state! (1908)[3]

HYMN LXXII

१. उत् तिष्ठताव पश्यतेन्द्रस्य भागमृत्वियम् । यदि श्रातं जुहोतन यद्यश्रातं ममत्तन ।।

1. O worshippers arise, visualise salvation attainable by soul. If the soul is fully developed for it, let it achieve salvation, if not, make it fit for salvation through penance! (1909)[4]

[1]Sayāna interprets अजिर and अधिराज as two messengers of death.

[2]I: A powerful General. Bind a bandage: so that thou may not utter nonsensical disrespectful words.

[3]See *Rigveda*, 10-87-22.

[4]See *Rigveda*, 10-179-1.

२. श्रातं हविरो ष्विन्द्र प्र याहि जगाम सूरो अध्वनो वि मध्यम् ।
परि त्वासते निधिभिः सखायः कुलपा न व्राजपतिं चरन्तम् ।।

2. O God, deep concentration (Samadhi) has been achieved, Show Thyself unto us. The urging soul, with its full splendour is seated in the centre of the heart. O soul, breaths (Prānās) thy friends, adore thee on all sides, with their spiritual forces, as sons, the protectors of the family, sit round their father at the time of dining. (1910)[1]

३. श्रातं मन्य ऊधनि श्रातमग्नौ सुशृतं मन्ये तदृतं नवीयः ।
माध्यन्दिनस्य सवनस्य दध्नः पिबेन्द्र वज्रिन् पुरुकृज्जुषाणः ।।

3. O soul, I fully well realise the supernatural Laudable, Wise God in the state of salvation. I have pondered over Him in the company of my learned preceptor. Now I completely visualise Him in deep concentration (Samadhi). O soul, contemplate upon Him at the time of mid-day, O powerful soul, full of pleasure, controlling all the organs, enjoy the company of God through contemplation. (1911)[2]

HYMN LXXIII

१. समिद्धो अग्निर्वृषणा रथी दिवस्तप्तो घर्मो दुह्यते वामिषे मधु ।
वयं हि वां पुरुदमासो अश्विना हवामहे सधमादेषु कारवः ।।

1. O heroic man and woman, Sun, the charioteer of heaven has arisen, sweet milk has been milked and is being boiled to be your food. We, the masters of organs, experts in doing deeds, invite ye to be present at our festivals. (1912)[3]

२. समिद्धो अग्निरश्विना तप्तो वां घर्म आ गतम् ।
दुह्यन्ते नूनं वृषणेह धेनवो दस्रा मदन्ति वेधसः ।।

2. O wise, heroic man and woman, the yajna-fire is all aglow, milk is being boiled for you; Come to this house, where Vedic verses are being recited, and the sages rejoice! (1913)

३. स्वाहाकृतः शुचिर्देवेषु यज्ञो यो अश्विनोश्चमसो देवपानः ।
तमु विश्वे अमृतासो जुषाणा गन्धर्वस्य प्रत्यास्ना रिहन्ति ।।

3. The soul, being pure, released from the coverings of darkness, pervades the learned with its inherent strength. The soul is the source of lending strength to the Prāṇa and Apāna, and guards all organs of sense. All immortal souls serving Him alone, achieve Him, following the commands of God. (1914)[4]

[1]See *Rig*, 10-179-2.

[2]See *Rig*, 10-179-3.

[3]Learned men and women should be invited on occasion of festivals and banquets.

[4]Griffith and Sayāna have translated Gandharva as fire. The word means God, Who is the Master of Vedic speech.

४. यदुस्रियास्वाहुतं घृतं पयोऽयं स वामश्विना भाग श्रा गतम् ।
माध्वी धर्तारा विदथस्य सत्पती तप्तं घर्मं पिबतं रोचने दिवः ।:

4. O wise man and woman, the molten butter and milk given to the cows, is your portion. Come ye hitherward. Ye, masters of the sweet knowledge of the Vedas occupants of the conscious Yajna of life, guardians of the noble, drink ye the warm milk in the light of the Sun! (1915)

५. तप्तो वां घर्मो नक्षतु स्वहोता प्र वामध्वर्युश्चरतु पयस्वान् ।
मधोर्दुग्धस्याश्विना तनाया वीतं पातं पयस उस्रियायाः ॥

5. O learned man and woman, may ye get warm milk. May the learned, non-violent sacrificer serve ye. May ye obtain and drink the sweet milk yielded by a stout cow. (1916)

६. उप द्रव पयसा गोधुगोषमा घर्मे सिञ्च पय उस्रियायाः ।
वि नाकमख्यत् सविता वरेण्योऽनुप्रयाणमुषसो वि राजति ।

6. Come hither, quickly come, thou milker of the Kine; into the caldron pour milk of the cow. The precious Sun illumines the Earth, a paradise, and sends forth his light after Dawn's going forth. (1917)

७. उप ह्वये सुदुघां धेनुमेतां सुहस्तो गोधुगुत दोहदेनाम् ।
श्रेष्ठं सवं सविता साविषन्नोऽभीद्धो घर्मस्तदु षु प्र वोचत् ॥

7. I acknowledge this Vedic knowledge, the nice fulfiller of desires. May an expert learned person imbibe it. May God grant us excellent supremacy. The Refulgent, Almighty God, hath fully instructed us in this Vedic knowledge. (1918)[1]

८. हिङ्कृण्वती वसुपत्नी वसूनां वत्समिच्छन्ती मनसा न्यागन् ।
दुहामश्विभ्यां पयो अघ्न्येयं सा वर्धतां महते सौभगाय ॥

8. Vedic knowledge, ever-elevating, the guardian of wealth, hankering after a missionary amongst noble persons, hath reached us, with all its wisdom. May this indestructible knowledge impart scientific knowledge to wise man and woman. May Vedic knowledge prosper to our great advantage. (1919)[2]

९. जुष्टो दमूना अतिथिर्दुरोण इमं नो यज्ञमुप याहि विद्वान् ।
विश्वा अग्ने अभियुजो विहत्य शत्रूयतामा भरा भोजनानि ॥

9. O noble, well-served, self-controlled, ever-energetic, learned king, having destroyed all assailants, take hold of the possessions of our foes! (1920)[3]

[1]See *Rig*, 1-164-26.
[2]See *Rig*, 1-164-27.
[3]See *Rig*, 5-4-5.

१०. अग्ने शर्ध महते सौभगाय तव द्युम्नान्युत्तमानि सन्तु ।
सं जास्पत्यं सुयममा कृणुष्व शत्रूयतामभि तिष्ठा महांसि ॥

10. O brave King, may thy excellent effulgent splendours be for our bliss. Strengthen through Brahmcharya the well-knit bond of wife and husband, and trample down the might of our foes! (1921)[1]

११. सूयवसाद् भगवती हि भूया अधा वयं भगवन्तः स्याम ।
अद्धि तृणमघ्न्ये विश्वदानीं पिब शुद्धमुदकमाचरन्ती ॥

11. Fortunate mayest thou be with goodly pasture, and may we also be exceedingly wealthy. Feed on the grass, O Cow at every season and, coming hither, drink the limpid water. (1922)

HYMN LXXIV

१. अपचितां लोहिनीनां कृष्णा मातेति शुश्रुम । मुनेर्देवस्य मूलेन सर्वा विध्यामि ता अहम् ॥

1. Black vein is the mother, we have heard of red hued pustules. I pierce and penetrate them, with the aid of an original masterpiece on medicine written by a learned physician. (1923)[2]

२. विध्याम्यासां प्रथमां विध्याम्युत मध्यमाम् । इदं जघन्यामासामा च्छिनद्मि स्तुकामिव ॥

2. I pierce the foremost one of these pustules. I perforate one of medium intensity. Here I cut asunder the pustule of little intensity like a lock of hair. (1924)

३. त्वाष्ट्रेणाहं वचसा वि त ईर्ष्याममीमदम् । अथो यो मन्युस्ते पते तमु ते शमयामसि ॥

3. O wife, I dispel thy jealousy with the Word of God, O husband, we mitigate and pacify the anger that thou feelest! (1925)[3]

४. व्रतेन त्वं व्रतपते समक्तो विश्वाहा सुमना दीदिहीह ।
तं त्वा वयं जातवेदः समिद्धं प्रजावन्त उप सदेम सर्वे ॥

4. O God, the Fulfiller of vows, sticking to Thy Law, shine Thou forth in the world for ever friendly-minded. May we all with children, O God, the Knower of all created objects, worship, Thee Enkindled. (1926)

HYMN LXXV

१. प्रजावतीः सूयवसे रुशन्तीः शुद्धा अपः सुप्रपाणे पिबन्तीः ।
मा व स्तेन ईशत माघशंसः परि वो रुद्रस्य हेतिर्वृणक्तु ॥

[1] See *Rig*, 5-28-3, *Yajur*, 33-12.

[2] Pustules: Apachitas. Scrofulous or inflammatory swellings affecting the glands of the neck. Apachitas mean gandamālās or King's evil. According to Damodar Satyavalekar, Muni (मुनि) is the name of an herb, the root of which is efficacious in curing the pustule.

[3] Word of God: As ordained in the Vedas.

1. O cows, prolific, grazing in the goodly pasture, drinking at pleasant pools the pure water, let not a thief or wicked man possess ye: let not the dart of a ferocious king come near ye! (1927)[1]

२. पदज्ञा स्थ रमतयः संहिता विश्वनाम्नीः ।
उप मा देवीर्देवेभिरेत । इमं गोष्ठमिदं सदो घृतेनास्मान्त्समुक्षत ॥

2. O cows, ye know your dwelling place, ye rest content, ye live together, ye are called by many a name. Come to me, O cows, with calves. Reside in this cattle-pen, this is your house, remain here. Give us milk and butter in abundance. (1928)[2]

HYMN LXXVI

१. आ सुस्रसः सुस्रसो असतीभ्यो असत्तराः । सेहोररसतरा लवणाद् विक्लेदीयसीः ॥

1. Even the worst pimples of pustules freely festering, can be easily cured. If they are more sapless than a dried up bone, the sprinkling of salt makes them suppurate. (1929)

२. या ग्रैव्या अपचितोऽथो या उपपक्ष्याः । विजाम्नि या अपचितः स्वयंस्रसः ॥

2. Pustules that rise upon the neck, pustules upon the shoulder-joints, pustules that spring upon the abdomen begin to fester by the use of medicine. (1930)

३. यः कीकसाः प्रशृणाति तलीद्यमवतिष्ठति ।
निर्हास्तं सर्वं जायान्यं यः कश्च ककुदि श्रितः ॥

3. Expel and banish consumption, that breaks the ribs, that settles in the lungs, that harbours in the back, and that springs from excessive sexual intercourse. (1931)[3]

४. पक्षी जायान्यः पतति स आ विशति पूरुषम् । तदक्षितस्य भेषजमुभयोः सुक्षतस्य च ॥

4. The germ of consumption, arising from excessive cohabitation, flies like a bird from one place to the other, and enters the body of a man. There is remedy for both kinds, the chronic and the transient. (1932)

५. विद्म वै ते जायान्य जानं यतो जायान्य जायसे ।
कथं ह तत्र त्वं हनो यस्य कृण्मो हविर्गृहे ॥

5. We know thine origin, consumption, know whence thou, consumption art born. How can'st thou strike this man here, in whose house we perform Homa (sacrifice). (1933)[4]

[1]See *Atharva*, 4-21-7.

[2]In *Satapatha Brahmana*, 4-5-8-10, a cow is named as (1) इडे (2) रन्ते (3) हव्ये (4) काम्ये (5) चन्द्रे (6) ज्योते (7) अदिति (8) सरस्वति (9) महि. In *Apasthamba*, 4-10-4, a cow is named as (1) चित (2) मना (3) धीर (4) रन्तोरमतिः (5) सूनुः (6) सूवरी.

[3]Consumption should be removed by the use of medicine, after consulting a physician.

[4]Consumption cannot attack the inmates of a house, where Havan is daily performed as the germ-killing ingredients of the provisions of Havan, keep the disease away.

६. धृषत् पिब कलशे सोममिन्द्र वृत्रहा शूर समरे वसूनाम् ।
माध्यन्दिने सवन आ वृषस्व रयिष्ठानो रयिमस्मासु धेहि ॥

6. O powerful soul, equipped with the power of avoiding diseases in the body from the neck to the navel, drink thou the pure air, the destroyer of disease that shortens life, in the battle of breaths that reside in the body. O disease-killing soul at the time of entertaining guests in mid-day, eat nice food and grow strong. Thyself possessing the riches of breath, grant us the same riches! (1934)[1]

HYMN LXXVII

१. सांतपना इदं हविर्मरुतस्तज्जुजुष्टन । अस्माकोती रिशादसः ॥

1. O austere, sacrificing learned persons here is this food in abundance for you. Accept this offering gladly. Ye, slayers of foe, stay here for our protection! (1935)[2]

२. यो नो मर्तो मरुतो दुर्हृणायुस्तिरश्चित्तानि वसवो जिघांसति ।
द्रुहः पाशान् प्रति मुञ्चतां सस्तपिष्ठेन तपसा हन्तना तम् ॥

2. O charitable, brave fellows, the man who filled with rage against us would like to defeat our aims through crookedness may he be caught in the noose of treachery: smite ye him down with your most flaming weapon! (1936)[3]

३. संवत्सरीणा मरुतः स्वर्का उरुक्षयाः सगणा मानुषासः ।
ते अस्मत् पाशान् प्र मुञ्चन्त्वेनसः सांतपना मत्सरा मादयिष्णवः ॥

3. May the annual visitors, revered, dwellers in spacious mansions, accompanied by their companions, thoughtful learned persons, exhilarating, gladdening, chastisers of foes, deliver us from the binding bonds of sin. (1937)

HYMN LXXVIII

१. वि ते मुञ्चामि रशनां वि योक्त्रं वि नियोजनम् । इहैव त्वमजस्र एध्यग्ने ॥

1. I free thee from the cord, I loose the bond, I loose the fastening. Even here in Me, O immortal soul, wax thou strong. (1938)[4]

२. अस्मै क्षत्राणि धारयन्तमग्ने युनज्मि त्वा ब्रह्मणा दैव्येन ।
दीदिह्य१स्मभ्यं द्रविणेह भद्रं प्रेमं वोचो हविर्दां देवतासु ॥

[1]Us: organs.
[2]See *Rig*, 7-59-9.
[3]See *Rig*, 7-59-8.
[4]God delivers the soul kinds of bonds, physical elemental, mental, spiritual and grants it salvation where the immortal soul resides in perfect glee. 'I' refers to God. 'Me' also refers to God.

2. O soul, I unite thee with Vedic knowledge, revealed by God, for maintaining this man in manifold powers. In this world grant us wealth and joy. Declare thou to the learned, this man, as the giver of charity! (1939)[1]

HYMN LXXIX

१. यत् ते देवा अकृण्वन् भागधेयममावास्ये संवसन्तो महित्वा ।
तेना नो यज्ञं पिपृहि विश्ववारे रयिं नो धेहि सुभगे सुवीरम् ॥

1. O sociable woman, whatever right, out of reverence for thee, the learned living together in a place have assigned thee, therewith fulfil our domestic Yajna (sacrifice) all-bounteous! blessed one, grant us wealth with manly offspring. (1940)[2]

२. अहमेवास्म्यमावास्या३ मामा वसन्ति सुकृतो मयीमे ।
मयि देवा उभये साध्याश्चेन्द्रज्येष्ठाः समगच्छन्त सर्वे ॥

2. I alone am Amāvasya, as all these good and pious, with me as their ideal, depend upon me. Both men of knowledge and action, with full faith on God, the Most Auspicious, work together under my authority. (1941)[3]

३. आगन् रात्री संगमनी वसूनामूर्जं पुष्टं वस्वावेशयन्ती ।
अमावास्यायै हविषा विधेमोर्जं दुहाना पयसा न आगन् ॥

3. The woman has come, the gatherer of treasures, bestowing strength, prosperity, and riches. Let us honour the woman with devotion. She has come, giving us strength coupled with knowledge. (1942)

४. अमावास्ये न त्वदेतान्यन्यो विश्वा रूपाणि परिभूर्जजान ।
यत्कामास्ते जुहुमस्तन्नो अस्तु वयं स्याम पतयो रयीणाम् ॥

4. O woman, none besides thee, has the strength to give birth to these children. Give us our heart's desire when we approach thee. May we be the lords of riches! (1943)[4]

HYMN LXXX

१. पूर्णा पश्चादुत पूर्णा पुरस्तादुन्मध्यतः पौर्णमासी जिगाय ।
तस्यां देवैः संवसन्तो महित्वा नाकस्य पृष्ठे समिषा मदेम ॥

[1]'I' refers to God.

[2]A woman is spoken of as Amāvasya, as she lives together with her husband and relatives. Amāvasya is also translated as God, Who lives with all animate and inanimate creation.

[3]'I' refers to woman.

[4]Heart's desire: A nice son. The verse can be interpreted thus also, if we understand 'Amāvasya' to mean God. O God, none besides Thee, comprehends all these created worlds. Give us our heart's desire when we invoke Thee. May we be the lords of riches. See *Rig*, 10-121-10 and *Yajur*, 23-65.

1. God was perfect after, and perfect before the creation of the universe. His power of creation is perfect in the middle as well. May we, residing in the company of emancipated souls, through our strength and His grace, derive full joy in a state of final beatitude. (1944)[1]

२. वृषभं वाजिनं वयं पौर्णमासं यजामहे । स नो ददात्वक्षितां रयिमनुपदस्वतीम् ।।

2. We worship the Most Exalted, Omnipotent God, the Creator of the universe. May He bestow upon us wealth unwasting, inexhaustible. (1945)

३. प्रजापते न त्वदेतान्यन्यो विश्वा रूपाणि परिभूर्जजान ।
यत्कामास्ते जुहुमस्तन्नो अस्तु वयं स्याम पतयो रयीणाम् ।।

3. O God, the Protector of His subjects, All-pervading, none besides Thee, can give birth to all these worlds. Give us our heart's desire when we invoke Thee. May we be the lords of riches. (1946)

४. पौर्णमासी प्रथमा यज्ञियासीदह्नां रात्रीणामतिशर्वरेषु ।
ये त्वां यज्ञैर्यज्ञिये अर्धयन्त्यमी ते नाके सुकृतः प्रविष्टाः ।।

4. The All-pervading, All-creating power of God is first of all worthy of adoration among] the days and in the night's deep darkness. O Venerable God, those pious souls, who honour Thee with worship, enter into Thy blissful abode! (1947)

HYMN LXXXI

१. पूर्वापरं चरतो माययैतौ शिशू क्रीडन्तौ परि यातोऽर्णवम् ।
विश्वान्यो भुवना विचष्ट ऋतूँरन्यो विदधज्जायसे नवः ।।

1. Forward and backward by the wondrous law of God, move these two youths, disporting, round the space. One illumines all worlds, and the other arranging seasons, is born again. (1948)[2]

२. नवोनवो भवसि जायमानोऽह्नां केतुरुषसामेप्यग्रम् ।
भागं देवेभ्यो वि दधास्यायन् प्र चन्द्रमस्तिरसे दीर्घमायुः ।।

2. Thou art reborn for ever new: thou marchest, ensign of days, in forefront of the Dawns, marching thou dealest to the gods their portion. Thou lengthenest, Moon! the days of man's existence. (1949)[3]

३. सोमस्यांशो युधां पतेऽनूनो नाम वा असि । अनूनं दर्श मा कृधि प्रजया च धनेन च ।।

[1]Final beatitude: Salvation.

[2]These two youths: Sun and Moon. One refers to the Sun. Other refers to the Moon.

[3]Dealest to the gods their portion: Lustre lent to the Earth, Water, Ocean, Air, Moon nourishes the herbs with frost. Ensign of days: Days are counted according to the waxing and waning of the Moon.

3. O God, the Nourisher of the yogis, O Treasure of delightful strength, All-perfect verily art Thou. Make me perfect, O Beautiful God, in riches and in progeny! (1950)[1]

४. दर्शो ऽसि दर्शतो ऽसि समग्रोऽसि समन्तः ।
समग्रः समन्तो भूयासं गोभिरश्वैः प्रजया पशुभिर्गृहैर्धनेन ।।

4. O Beautiful God, Thou art Worthy of being discerned through devotion and Yoga (concentration). Thou art the Leader of all. Thou art the Absorber in self of all at the time of dissolution. May I be foremost of all, and fully blest in every way in kine, horses, children, cattle, houses, wealth. (1951)

५. योऽस्मान् द्वेष्टि यं वयं द्विष्मस्तस्य त्वं प्राणेना प्यायस्व ।
आ वयं प्याशिषीमहि गोभिरश्वैः प्रजया पशुभिर्गृहैर्धनेन ।।

5. O God, place at our disposal the resources of the life of the man, who dislikes us and whom we do not like. May we grow rich in kine, horses, children, cattle, houses, wealth. (1952)[2]

६. यं देवा अंशुमाप्याययन्ति यमक्षितमक्षिता भक्षयन्ति ।
तेनास्मानिन्द्रो वरुणो बृहस्पतिरा प्याययन्तु भुवनस्य गोपाः ।।

6. Whose glory of the All-pervading God, the learned magnify, the immortal souls resort to and enjoy Whom, the Immortal God, through His divine Knowledge, may the learned preceptor, the kings, the averters of sins, and the protectors of Vedic speech, all the guardians of the world, increases us. (1953)

HYMN LXXXII

१. अभ्य र्चत सुष्टुतिं गव्यमाजिमस्मासु भद्रा द्रविणानि धत्त ।
इमं यज्ञं नयत देवता नो घृतस्य धारा मधुमत् पवन्ताम् ।।

1. O learned persons, sing the praise of God, the Friend of souls, bestow on us excellent possessions, equip this soul of ours with divinity, let sweet streams of knowledge flow everywhere! (1954)

२. मय्यग्रे अग्निं गृह्णामि सह क्षत्रेण वर्चसा बलेन ।
मयि प्रजां मय्यायुर्दधामि स्वाहा मय्यग्निम् ।।

2. I first appropriate God, with power, with splendour, and with might. Through Vedic knowledge, I preserve in myself children, longevity, physical and spiritual strength. (1955)

[1]Yogis have been spoken of as warriors who constantly wage war against sin and immorality.

[2]The man who hates us should be brought under our control, so that we may reform him and remove his feeling of hatred.

३. इहैवाग्ने अधि धारया रयिं मा त्वा नि क्रन् पूर्वचित्ता निकारिणः ।
क्षत्रेणाग्ने सुयममस्तु तुभ्यमुपसत्ता वर्धतां ते अनिष्टृतः ॥

3. O King, amass wealth in this world. Let not the old, exalted, learned persons, ever devoted to action, tolerate thy moral degradation. O ruler, let thy administration be run by just laws. May thy adorers, following non-violence make thee strong. (1956)

४. अन्वग्निरुषसामग्रमख्यदन्वहानि प्रथमो जातवेदाः ।
अनु सूर्यं उषसो अनु रश्मीनन् द्यावापृथिवी आ विवेश ॥

4. God illumines the fore-part of Dawns. The Immemorial Omniscient God then brings to light the days. He creates the Sun, the Mornings and the stars. He pervades the Heaven and Earth. (1957)

५. प्रत्यग्निरुषसामग्रमख्यत् प्रत्यहानि प्रथमो जातवेदाः ।
प्रति सूर्यस्य पुरुधा च रश्मीन् प्रति द्यावापृथिवी आ ततान ॥

5. The same God explicitly illumines the fore-part of Dawns. The Primordial Omniscient God clearly brings to light the days. He sends the rays of the Sun in countless places. He extends the Heaven and Earth. (1958)[1]

६. घृतं ते अग्ने दिव्ये सधस्थे घृतेन त्वां मनुरद्या समिन्धे ।
घृतं ते देवीर्नप्त्य१ आ वहन्तु घृतं तुभ्यं दुह्रतां गावो अग्ने ।

6. O soul, thy lustre is present in this beautiful body. A reflective sage always illumines thee with knowledge. May the excellent organs of cognition acquire knowledge for thee. O soul, let organs of action lend thee knowledge. (1959)

HYMN LXXXIII

१. अप्सु ते राजन् वरुण गृहो हिरण्ययो मिथः । ततो धृतव्रतो राजा सर्वा धामानि मुञ्चतु ॥

1. O God, the Averter of sins, thy controlling sway over souls is known, glittering like gold. O All-pervading God, the Master of Knowledge and action, release us from all shackles! (1960)

२. धाम्नोधाम्नो राजन्नितो वरुण मुञ्च नः ।
यदापो अघ्न्या इति वरुणेति यदूचिम ततो वरुण मुञ्च नः ॥

2. O Resplendent, Most Exalted God, free us in this world, from all fetters. When we invoke Thee as All-pervading, Immortal, Most Dignified, free us, O God, from restraints! (1961)

३. उदुत्तमं वरुण पाशमस्मदवाधमं वि मध्यमं श्रथाय ।
अधा वयमादित्य व्रते तवानागसो अदितये स्याम ॥

[1]Fifth verse is almost a repetition of the 4th for the sake of emphasis.

3. O Most Exalted God, release us from the upmost bond, let down the lowest and remove the midmost so may we, O Resplendent God, for acquiring Thy undecaying joy, be sinless in the observance of Thy true and just laws. (1962)

४. प्रास्मत् पाशान् वरुण मुञ्च सर्वान् य उत्तमा अधमा वारुणा ये ।
दुःष्वप्न्यं दुरितं नि ष्वास्मदथ गच्छेम सुकृतस्य लोकम् ॥

4. O God, the Averter of sins, free us from all snares that bind us, natural bonds, the upper and the lower. Drive from us evil dream, drive off misfortune then let us pass into the world of virtue. (1963)

HYMN LXXXIV

१. अनाधृष्यो जातवेदा अमर्त्यो विराडग्ने क्षत्रभृद् दीदिहीह ।
विश्वा अमीवाः प्रमुञ्चन् मानुषीभिः शिवाभिरद्य परि पाहि नो गयम् ॥

1. O King, invincible, full of knowledge, free from misery, refulgent, and an able administrator, shine here. Chase human ills with the help of philanthropic persons. Ever guard our house. (1964)

२. इन्द्र क्षत्रमभि वाममोजोऽजायथा वृषभ चर्षणीनाम् ।
अपानुदो जनममित्रायन्तमुरुं देवेभ्यो अकृणोरु लोकम् ॥

2. Thou, O King, lord and leader of the people, hast been born for lovely strength, and high dominion. Drive off the unfriendly folk, and make for the virtuous, wide room and freedom. (1965)

३. मृगो न भीमः कुचरो गिरिष्ठाः परावत आ जगम्यात् परस्याः ।
सृकं संशाय पविमिन्द्र तिग्मं वि शत्रून् ताढि वि मृधो नुदस्व ॥

3. O King, like a dreadful, wild tiger roaming in the mountains with a crooked pace, thou attackest the foe from the farthest distance. Whetting thy bolt and thy sharp arrow, O King, crush down our foes, and destroy those who want to attack us. (1966)[1]

HYMN LXXXV

१. त्यमू षु वाजिनं देवजूतं सहोवानं तरुतारं रथानाम् ।
अरिष्टनेमिं पृतनाजिमाशुं स्वस्तये तार्क्ष्यमिहा हुवेम ॥

1. We invoke for our welfare, the Powerful God, Master of Knowledge, Adored by the sages, Almighty, Pervader of diverse worlds wherein roam the souls, Inciter of all on the path of virtue, Controller of His subjects and Omnipresent. (1967)

[1]See *Yajur*, 18-71.

HYMN LXXXVI

१. त्रातारमिन्द्रमवितारमिन्द्रं हवेहवे सुहवं शूरमिन्द्रम् ।
हुवे नु शक्रं पुरुहूतमिन्द्रं स्वस्ति न इन्द्रो मघवान् कृणोतु ।।

1. God, the Rescuer, God, the Helper, God, the Brave, Who hears each invocation, God, the Almighty, Invoked of many, I call. May the Opulent God, prosper and bless us. (1968)[1]

HYMN LXXXVII

१. यो अग्नौ रुद्रो यो अप्स्व१न्तर्य ओषधीर्वीरुध आविवेश ।
य इमा विश्वा भुवनानि चाक्लृपे तस्मै रुद्राय नमो अस्त्वग्नये ।।

1. To the Wise God in the fire, to Him Who dwells in floods, to Him Who hath entered into herbs and plants, to Him Who formed and fashioned all these worlds, to Him the sin-subduing God, the All-pervading, reverence be paid! (1969)

HYMN LXXXVIII

१. अपेह्यरिरस्यरिर्वा असि । विषे विषमपृक्था विषमिद् वा अपृक्थाः ।
अहिमेवाभ्यपेहि तं जहि ।।

1. O poison, depart, thou art a foe, verily a foe art thou. Mix thyself with a poisonous snake. Mix thyself with the poison of the snake. Go to the serpent strike him dead. (1970)[2]

HYMN LXXXIX

१. अपो दिव्या अचायिषं रसेन समपृक्ष्महि । पयस्वानग्न आगमं तं मा सं सृज वर्चसा ।।

1. May I glean divine knowledge and action, and equip myself with their essence. O Wise God, thus have I become a man of knowledge and action; endow me with divine halo. (1971)[3]

२. सं माग्ने वर्चसा सृज सं प्रजया समायुषा ।
विद्युर्मे अस्य देवा इन्द्रो विद्यात् सह ऋषिभिः ।।

2. O preceptor, endow me with glory, with children and a lengthened life. May the learned persons understand me, mav God with Vedic scholars know me as such. (1972)[4]

[1]The verse can apply to the King or Commander-in-chief as well.

[2]Physicians are of the opinion, that a snake-bitten patient is cured by injecting the poison of the snake, which acts as an antidote.

[3]'I' refers to a Brahmchari, a celebate pupil.

[4]Such: A pupil, an aspirer after knowledge, a Brahmchari.

३. इदमापः प्र वहतावद्यं च मलं च यत् । यच्चाभिदुद्रोहानृतं यच्च शेपे अभीरुणम् ॥

3. O Masters of Knowledge, just as waters purify us, so do ye wash away this indescribable sin and ignorance of mine. O learned persons keep me away from malice and falsehood, and accusation of the innocent. (1973)[1]

४. एधोऽस्येधिषीय समिदसि समेधिषीय । तेजोऽसि तेजो मयि धेहि ॥

4. O God, Thou art Great, may I be great, Thou art Glorious, may I achieve glory. Thou art splendid, give splendour unto me. (1974)[2]

HYMN XC

१. अपि वृश्च पुराणवद् व्रततेरिव गुष्पितम् । ओजो दासस्य दम्भय ॥

1. O King, just as a gardener lops off the tangles of a creeping plant, so do thou tear asunder and demolish the might of a violent person! (1975)

२. वयं तदस्य संभृतं वस्विन्द्रेण वि भजामहै । म्लापयामि भ्रजः शिभ्रं वरुणस्य व्रतेन ते ॥

2. May we divide the gathered treasure of the foe with the help of the king. I bring down thy pride and wantonness according to the administrative law of the king. (1976)[3]

३. यथा शेपो अपायातै स्त्रीषु चासदनावयाः ।
अवस्थस्य क्नदीवतः शाङ्कुरस्य नितोदिनः । यदाततमव तत्तनु यदत्ततं नि तत्तनु ॥

3. O King, diminish the multiplying strength and wealth, lower down the exalted position of a violent reviler, mental torturer and physical tormentor, whereby his carnal lust be extinguished and he be disabled to approach and molest women! (1977)[4]

HYMN XCI

१. इन्द्रः सुत्रामा स्ववाँ अवोभिः सुमृडीको भवतु विश्ववेदाः ।
बाधतां द्वेषो अभयं नः कृणोतु सुवीर्यस्य पतयः स्याम ॥

1. A King, the nice protector of his subjects, wins the sympathy of the people, through his diverse sources of protection. May he, the lord of treasures be the giver of joy and happiness to us. May he drive off our foes and give us peace and safety. May we be the lords of goodly strength. (1978)[5]

[1]See *Yajur*, 6-17.

[2]See *Yajur*, 38-25.

[3]The confiscated wealth of the enemy should go to the state treasury, to be spent for the social, moral and physical uplift of the subjects.

[4]Griffith has not translated this verse, taking it to be obscene. Sayāna, following the application of Kaushika sutras has applied this verse to an immoral person. Kaushika has written that a debauchee should be stoned to death and pierced with arrows. These remarks are wide of the mark, as there is no mention of obscenity in the verse.

[5]See *Rig*, 6-47-12, 10-131-6, *Yajur*, 20-51. The verse is applicable to God as well.

HYMN XCII

१. स सुत्रामा स्ववाँ इन्द्रो अस्मदाराच्चिद् द्वेषः सनुतर्युयोतु ।
तस्य वयं सुमतौ यज्ञियस्यापि भद्रे सौमनसे स्याम ॥

1. May the ruler, our good preserver, with his noble family members, drive away far from us, through various devices, our foemen. May we dwell in the auspicious favour of and obey the orders of ruler, who is fit for adoration. (1979)[1]

HYMN XCIII

१. इन्द्रेण मन्युना वयमभि ष्याम पृतन्यतः । घ्नन्तो वृत्राण्यप्रति ॥

1. With the aid of the king, filled with righteous indignation, may we subdue our enemies, willing to attack us, and resistlessly remove all impediments. (1980)

HYMN XCIV

१. ध्रुवं ध्रुवेण हविषाव सोमं नयामसि । यथा न इन्द्रः केवलीर्विशः संमनसस्करत् ॥

1. With steadfast devotion, we accept the man of determination as our ruler. May he render for us his subjects self-reliant and one-minded. (1981)[2]

HYMN XCV

१. उदस्य श्यावौ विथुरौ गृध्रौ द्यामिव पेततुः । उच्छोचनप्रशोचनावस्योच्छोचनौ हृदः ॥

1. Lust and anger, are the two energetic and distressing passions of the soul, that lurk in it, like two vultures flying in the sky. These grief-developer and drier-up passions parch the heart. (1982)

२. अहमेनावुदतिष्ठिपं गावौ श्रान्तसदाविव । कुर्कुराविव कूजन्तावुदवन्तौ वृकाविव ॥

2. I banish lust and anger, as a peasant makes the exhausted, resting oxen stand up by pulling their tail, just as two loud-snarling curs are stoned to run away, or as a cowherd drives away the two wolves that attack his cows. (1983)[3]

३. आतोदिनौ नितोदिनावथो संतोदिनावुत ।
अपि नह्याम्यस्य मेढ्रं य इतः स्त्री पुमाञ्जभार ॥

3. I control lust and anger, that thrust, that pierce, that strike with mutual blows. I make the man or dame who shelters them lose all vitality and vigour. (1984)

[1]See *Rig*, 6-47-13, 10-131-7, *Yajur*, 20-52.

[2]That country alone progresses whose inhabitants are self-reliant and undivided. See *Rig*, 10-173-6, *Yajur*, 7-25.

[3]'I' refers to a learned person.

HYMN XCVI

१. असदन् गाव: सदनेऽपप्तद् वसतिं वय: ।
आस्थाने पर्वता अस्थु: स्थाम्नि वृक्कावतिष्ठिपम् ।।

1. Just as the kine are resting in the stall, and the bird hath flown to its nest, and the hills are firmly rooted, so have I controlled lust and anger, and put them in their proper place. (1985)

HYMN XCVII

१. यदद्य त्वा प्रयति यज्ञे अस्मिन् होतश्चिकित्वन्नवृणीमहीह ।
ध्रुवमयो ध्रुवमुता शविष्ठ प्रविद्वान् यज्ञमुप याहि सोमम् ।।

1. O learned person, we have today, in this world, accepted thee as Hota in this Yajna which is performed through ceaseless effort. O knower of the details of sacrifice, come certainly to this firm Yajna, and attain to prosperity. (1986)[1]

२. समिन्द्र नो मनसा नेष गोभि: सं सूरिभिर्हरिवन्त्सं स्वस्त्या ।
सं ब्रह्मणा देवहितं यदस्ति सं देवानां सुमतौ यज्ञियानाम् ।।

2. O Refulgent God, equip us with a reflective mind, Vedic teachings, learned persons, virtue, knowledge beneficent to the scholars, and lead us on the path of righteousness. Let us follow the good-will of the sages who merit adoration (1987)

३. यानावह उशतो देव देवांस्तान् प्रेरय स्वे अग्ने सधस्थे ।
जक्षिवांस: पपिवांसो मधून्यस्मै धत्त वसवो वसूनि ।।

3. O good-natured teacher, persuade them to be religious-minded, who have gathered round thee to acquire knowledge. O learned persons, taking nutritious diet, drinking pure, sweet milk, impart all sorts of knowledge to this disciple. (1988)

४. सुगा वो देवा: सदना अकर्म य आजग्म सवने मा जुषाणा: ।
वहमाना भरमाणा: स्वा वसूनि वसुं घर्मं दिवमा रोहतानु ।।

4. O learned persons, for ye, have we erected these comfortable houses. Full of love, ye have come to my kingdom. Accepting deserving salary for your livelihood, strengthening your splendid knowledge and technical skill, spread them for the benefit of, and according to the needs of my state. (1989)[2]

[1] 'We' refers to married people.

[2] A king addresses these words to learned persons, whom he has invited from outside to work in his country as his employees.

५. यज्ञ यज्ञं गच्छ यज्ञपतिं गच्छ । स्वां योनिं गच्छ स्वाहा ॥

5. O soul, go to God, the Venerable. O soul, realise God, the Nourisher of all souls. O soul, understand God, thy last Resort! What a nice instruction is this? (1990)[1]

६. एष ते यज्ञो यज्ञपते सहसूक्तवाकः । सुवीर्यः स्वाहा ॥

6. O God, the Lord of all sacrifices, this soul, the master of organs, mind and breaths, and Thy visualiser in Samādhi, is Thine. It is spoken of in beautiful words and verses and is the bestower of nice strength. It merges itself in Thee. O God! (1991)

७. वषड्ढुतेभ्यो वषडहुतेभ्यः । देवा गातुविदो गातुं वित्त्वा गातुमित ॥

7. Dedication of soul is the only way for utilizing the gifts of God, and self-acquired objects. O learned yogis, ye know the highest station, knowing that, attain to the highest bliss of salvation. (1992)

८. मनसस्पत इमं नो दिवि देवेषु यज्ञम् ।
स्वाहा दिवि स्वाहा पृथिव्यां स्वाहान्तरिक्षे स्वाहा वाते धां स्वाहा ॥

8. O All-pervading God, the Lord of Mind, I have set the ideal of salvation before this soul, that pervades the organs. May it merge itself in the Refulgent God. May it merge itself in the All-Sustaining Mighty God. May it merge itself in the Omnipresent God. May it merge itself in the Omnipotent God! (1993)[2]

HYMN XCVIII

१. सं बर्हिरक्तं हविषा घृतेन समिन्द्रेण वसुना सं मरुद्भिः ।
सं देवैर्विश्वदेवेभिरक्तमिन्द्रं गच्छतु हविः स्वाहा ॥

1. This soul has been endowed with knowledge and dignity. It has been endowed with Prāna, the chief vital breath and other subsidiary breaths. Endowed with all divine powers and noble ambitions, developing itself through tranquillity and self-control, let it go to God, as an oblation goes to fire. (1994)

HYMN XCIX

१. परि स्तृणीहि परि धेहि वेदिं मा जामिं मोषीरमुया शयानाम् ।
होतृषदनं हरितं हिरण्ययं निष्का एते यजमानस्य लोके ॥

1. O learned person, spread knowledge all round, and perfect it in every way. Rob not its current flow and scope. The house of a charitable person is ever flourishing and filled with gold. Golden ornaments are found in the house of a sacrificer, who hospitably entertains the learned. (1995)

[1]See *Yajur*, 8-22.
[2]Lord of Mind: Lord of the mental powers.

HYMN C

१. पर्यावर्ते दुष्वप्न्यात् पापात् स्वप्न्यादभूत्याः । ब्रह्माहमन्तरं कृण्वे परा स्वप्नमुखाः शुचः ॥

1. I turn away from evil dream, from dream of sin, from indigence. I make the prayer mine inmost friend, and thus suppress dreamy phantasies. (1996)

HYMN CI

१. यत् स्वप्ने अन्नमश्नामि न प्रातरधिगम्यते । सर्वं तदस्तु मे शिवं नहि तद् दृश्यते दिवा ॥

1. The food that I eat in a dream is not perceived at early morn. May all that I see or do in a dream be blest to me because it is not seen by day. (1997)

HYMN CII

१. नमस्कृत्य द्यावापृथिवीभ्यामन्तरिक्षाय मृत्यवे । मेक्षाम्यूर्ध्वस्तिष्ठन् मा मा हिंसिषुरीश्वराः ॥

1. Having worshipped father, mother, the Omnipresent, All-Destroying God, I lead a life of high character. Let not these lords of mine harm me. (1998)

HYMN CIII

१. को अस्या नो द्रुहोऽवद्यवत्या उन्नेष्यति क्षत्रियो वस्य इच्छन् ।
को यज्ञकामः क उ पूर्तिकामः को देवेषु वनुते दीर्घमायुः ॥

1. Who, besides the God Almighty, the Giver of the nice fruit of our actions, will free us from this censurable malice. Who, but God, wills to control the Yajña of the world in which millions of souls work together. Who else than God desires to perfect this Yajña of the world. Who, besides God, grants longevity to the sages. (1999)[1]

HYMN CIV

१. कः पृश्नि धेनुं वरुणेन दत्तामथर्वणे सुदुघां नित्यवत्साम् ।
बृहस्पतिना सख्यं जुषाणो यथावशं तन्वः कल्पयाति ॥

1. A learned person, willingly enjoying the alliance of his soul with God, should strengthen Vedic speech, the solver of the subtle questionings of the soul, granted by God to a determined Yogi, spiritual developer of man, and constant preacher of nice moral truths. (2000)

HYMN CV

१. अपक्रामन् पौरुषेयाद् वृणानो दैव्यं वचः । प्रणीतीरभ्यावर्तस्व विश्वेभिः सखिभिः सह ॥

1. O learned yogi, unmindful of the praise or censure of humanity, choose the Word of God. Follow the instructions of the Veda, with all your associates. (2001)

[1]None but God controls the universe. He grants us the fruit of actions, and long life.

HYMN CVI

१. यदस्मृति चकृम किं चिदग्न उपारिम चरणे जातवेदः ।
ततः पाहि त्वं नः प्रचेतः शुभे सखिभ्यो अमृतत्वमस्तु नः ॥

1. Each thoughtless ill that we have done, O God, all error in our conduct, O Omniscient God!, therefrom do thou, O sapient God, preserve us. May we thy friends, for bliss, have life eternal. (2002)

HYMN CVII

१. अव दिवस्तारयन्ति सप्त सूर्यस्य रश्मयः । आपः समुद्रिया धारास्तास्ते शल्यमसिस्रसन् ॥

1. The seven bright beams of the Sun bring the streams of water downward from the sky, these streams remove thy misery. (2003)[1]

HYMN CVIII

१. यो नस्तायद् दिप्सति यो न आविः स्वो विद्वानरणो वा नो अग्ने ।
प्रतीच्येत्वरणी दत्वती तान् मैषामग्ने वास्तु भून्मो अपत्यम् ॥

1. Whoso by stealth or openly would harm us, be he a friend who knows us, or a stranger, O King! May the terrible excruciating pain attack them, O King, theirs be neither home nor children! (2004)

२. यो नः सुप्ताञ्जाग्रतो वाभिदासात् तिष्ठतो वा चरतो जातवेदः ।
वैश्वानरेण सयुजा सजोषास्तान् प्रतीचो निर्दह जातवेदः ॥

2. Whoso oppresseth us, O King, asleep or waking, standing still or moving; accordant with God, (the Lover of all) thy comrade, O King meet those foes and consume them. (2005)

HYMN CIX

१. इदमुग्राय बभ्रवे नमो यो अक्षेषु तनूवशी । घृतेन कलिं शिक्षामि स नो मृडातीदृशे ॥

1. My homage to the strong, nourishing Brahmchari, who controls the organs of his body. With lustrous knowledge I train my mind, that lends me pleasure in the performance of such a noble deed. (2006)[2]

२. घृतमप्सराभ्यो वह त्वमग्ने पांसूनक्षेभ्यः सिकता अपश्च ।
यथाभागं हव्यदातिं जुषाणा मदन्ति देवा उभयानि हव्या ॥

2. O Brahmchari blazing like fire, bestow knowledge to the organs of cognition, and space, sand and water to the organs of action. The organs delight in both kinds of food, joying in receiving their share of food apportioned duly. (2007)[3]

[1] Sun sends down rain through its rays, wherewith crops ripen, more food is produced, which feeds men and keeps them free from disease.

[2] 'I' refers to the Brahmchari.

[3] Organs of cognition require knowledge, but organs of action stand in need of water, sand, earth and material objects to work upon. Both oblations: the butter produced from the milk of cattle, and the juices of herbs. Each organ gets due share of the food we eat.

३. अप्सरसः सधमादं मदन्ति हविर्धानमन्तरा सूर्यं च ।
ता मे हस्तौ सं सृजन्तु घृतेन सपत्नं मे कितवं रन्धयन्तु ॥

3. The organs lend pleasure to the soul between the Earth and the Sun. Let them fill my hands with knowledge; and kill my lust and anger, the destroyers of wisdom, and the foes of soul. (2008)[1]

४. आदिनवं प्रतिदीव्ने घृतेनास्माँ अभि क्षर । वृक्षमिवाशन्या जहि यो अस्मान् प्रतिदीव्यति ॥

4. I fight against my opponent. O God, shower wealth on us. Smite mine adversary in the battle, as lightning flash burns a tree. (2009)[2]

५. यो नो द्युवे धनमिदं चकार यो अक्षाणां ग्लहनं शेषणं च ।
स नो देवो हविरिदं जुषाणो गन्धर्वेभिः सधमादं मदेम ॥

5. A celibate amongst us, by observing the vow of celibacy, develops this undecaying physical and spiritual strength. A self-controlled learned person amongst us, who grasps and controls the senses acquires, this desirable joy, knowledge and food. Let us pass our life happily in the company of such a person who is the master of the Vedas and controls his organs. (2010)

६. संवसव इति वो नामधेयमुग्रंपश्या राष्ट्रभृतो ह्य१क्षाः ।
तेभ्यो व इन्दवो हविषा विधेम वयं स्याम पतयो रयीणाम् ॥

6. O learned person, your name is 'Containers of wealth, as you are far-sighted, dominion supporters, and men of practical wisdom. O exalted persons, may we worship you with devotion, and become lords of wealth. (2011)[3]

७. देवान् यन्नाथितो हुवे ब्रह्मचर्यं यदूषिम । अक्षान् यद् बभ्रूनालभे ते नो मृडन्त्वीदृशे ॥

7. As I serve the learned with humility, as I have led a life of chastity, may these turbulent organs, when I have controlled them, grant me bliss in salvation. (2012)[4]

HYMN CX

१. अग्न इन्द्रश्च दाशुषे हतो वृत्राण्यप्रति । उभा हि वृत्रहन्तमा ॥

1. O King and Commander of the army, smite resistlessly the foes of your subjects; for best foe-slayers are ye both. (2013)

२. याभ्यामजयन्त्स्व१रग्र एव यावातस्थतुर्भुवनानि विश्वा ।
प्रचर्षणी वृषणा वज्रबाहू अग्निमिन्द्रं वृत्रहणा हुवेऽहम् ॥

2. I invoke the king and the Commander, foe-destroyers, carriers of arms in hand, powerful, adored by many, through whom the subjects secured peace and safety in the beginning, these who have controlled all parts of their kingdom. (2014)

[1]'Them' refers to the organs. First 'My' refers to the.

[2]'Us' refers to warriors, soldiers.

[3]संवसव: may also mean 'Fellow-inhabitants.'

[4]'I' refers to a Brahmchari, a celibate.

३. उप त्वा देवो अग्रभीच्चमसेन बृहस्पतिः । इन्द्र गीर्भिर्न आ विश यजमानाय सुन्वते ॥

3. O King, the Refulgent God, hath supported thee with food. Full of eulogies by us, come unto us for a discriminating worshipper! (2015)[1]

HYMN CXI

१. इन्द्रस्य कुक्षिरसि सोमधान आत्मा देवानामुत मानुषाणाम् ।
इह प्रजा जनय यास्त आसु या अन्यत्रेह तास्ते रमन्ताम् ॥

1. O youngman, thou art God's treasure for procreation. Thou art the custodian of semen. Thou art the soul of sages and ordinary mortals. Staying in domestic life create children, who, living amongst thy relatives, or in foreign countries, all thy subjects, should lead a happy life. (2016)

HYMN CXII

१. शुम्भनी द्यावापृथिवी अन्तिसुम्ने महिव्रते । आपः सप्त सुस्रुवुर्देवीस्ता नो मुञ्चन्त्वंहसः ॥

1. Radiant with beauty are Heaven and Earth, who give us mental joy, whose sway is vast. We have been endowed with seven godly organs. May they deliver us from sin. (2017)[2]

२. मुञ्चन्तु मा शपथ्या३दथो वरुण्या३दुत ।
अथो यमस्य पड्बीशाद् विश्वस्माद् देवकिल्बिषात् ॥

2. May these organs save me from the sin arising from slandering others, or entertaining evil thoughts for God. May they free me from the fetters of Death, and from every sin committed towards the learned. (2018)

HYMN CXIII

१. तृष्टिके तृष्टवन्दन उदमूं छिन्धि तृष्टिके । यथा कृतद्विष्टासोऽमुष्मै शेप्यावते ॥

1. O contemptible greed, O parasite of avarice, O covetousness thou art destroying that man, who is thy prey. Thou art the enemy of that strong man. (2019)

२. तृष्टासि तृष्टिका विषा विषातक्य३सि । परिवृक्ता यथासस्यृषभस्य वशेव ॥

2. O greed, thou art the embodiment of desire. Thou art poisonous and deadly. Thou art worthy of being abandoned, like a barren cow by a bull. (2020)

HYMN CXIV

१. आ ते ददे वक्षणाभ्य आ तेऽहं हृदयाद् ददे । आ ते मुखस्य संकाशात् सर्वं ते वर्च आ ददे ॥

1. O foe, I have extracted from thy sides, I have extracted from thy heart. I have extracted from thy face the strength and splendour that were thine. (2021)

[1] 'Us' refers to the subjects.
[2] Seven organs: Two eyes, two ears, two nostrils and mouth.

२. प्रेतो यन्तु व्याऽध्यः प्रानुध्याः प्रो अशस्तयः । अग्नी रक्षस्विनीर्हन्तु सोमो हन्तु दुरस्यतीः ॥

2. Let diseases and sufferings pass away, let cares and calumnies vanish hence. Let a powerful king destroy fiendish armies, let a dignified king destroy the disloyal subjects. (2022)

HYMN CXV

१. प्र पतेतः पापि लक्ष्मि नश्येतः प्रामुतः पत । अयस्मयेनाङ्केन द्विषते त्वा सजामसि ॥

1. Hence, Evil Fortune! fly away, vanish from this place and from the distant one. We fix thee with an iron hook unto the man who hateth us. (2023)

२. या मा लक्ष्मीः पतयालूरजुष्टाभिचस्कन्द वन्दनेव वृक्षम् ।
अन्यत्रास्मत् सवितस्तामितो धा हिरण्यहस्तो वसु नो रराणः ॥

2. Granting us riches, O God, the Creator, and Lord of wealth!, send thou away from us to other regions, the degrading and abominable Fortune which hath assailed me and is exhausting my vigour, as a creeper climbs a tree and dries it up. (2024)

३. एकशतं लक्ष्म्यो३ मर्त्यस्य साकं तन्वाऽ जनुषोऽधि जाताः ।
तासां पापिष्ठा निरितः प्र हिण्मः शिवा अस्मभ्यं जातवेदो नि यच्छ ॥

3. One hundred and one characteristics all together are at his birth born with a mortal's body. Of these we send away the most unlucky; Keep lucky ones for us, O God, the knower of all created objects. (2025)

४. एता एना व्याकरं खिले गा विष्ठिताइव । रमन्तां पुण्या लक्ष्मीर्याः पापीस्ता अनीनशम् ॥

4. I have separated the good and bad characteristics, as a cowherd distinguishes cows who stray on common lands. Here let auspicious characteristics stay, hence have I banished evil ones. (2026)

HYMN CXVI

१. नमो रूराय च्यवनाय नोदनाय धृष्णवे । नमः शीताय पूर्वकामकृत्वने ॥

1. Use different remedies for the removal of fever, that torments the patient, saps his physical vigour, makes him delirious, disappoints him, causes shivering, and kills all his previous desires. (2027)

२. यो अन्येद्युरुभयद्युरभ्येतीमं मण्डूकमभ्येऽत्वव्रतः ॥

2. May the lawless fever, that comes on every third or fourth day, pass over and possess the man who sings his praise like a frog. (2028)[1]

[1]A self-praiser is censured and condemned in the verse. Just as a frog cries and utters his praise, so a man who sings his praise deserves to be attacked by fever. Nine kinds of fever are mentioned in this hymn.

HYMN CXVII

१. आ मन्द्रैरिन्द्र हरिभिर्याहि मयूररोमभिः ।
मा त्वा के चिद् वि यमन् विं न पाशिनोऽति धन्वेव ताँ इहि ॥

1. O King, go forth, with excellent steeds having tails like peacock plumes. Let none check thy onward march, as fowlers capture the bird. Just as a thirsty person crosses the waterless desert, so come unto us conquering the foes. (2029)

HYMN CXVIII

१. मर्माणि ते वर्मणा छादयामि सोमस्त्वा राजामृतेनानु वस्ताम् ।
उरोर्वरीयो वरुणस्ते कृणोतु जयन्तं त्वानु देवा मदन्तु ॥

1. O valiant warrior, thy vital parts I cover with armour. May this calm, considerate king protect thee with invincible strength. May the Exalted God give thee a very long life. May the learned enjoy thy triumph over the wicked. (2030)[1]

BOOK (Kāṇḍa) VIII

Chapter (Anuvāka) 1

HYMN I

१. अन्तकाय मृत्यवे नमः प्राणा अपाना इह ते रमन्ताम् ।
इहायमस्तु पुरुषः सहासुना सूर्यस्य भागे अमृतस्य लोके ॥

1. Homage to God, the Ender of all through Death. May thy breathings, inward and outward still remain within Him. May this man, united with his intellect stay in this world, in the realm of God, and then in the world of life eternal. (2031)[2]

२. उदेनं भगो अग्रभीदुदेनं सोमो अंशुमान् । उदेनं मरुतो देवा उदिन्द्राग्नी स्वस्तये ॥

2. Savoury food hath lifted up this man, and delicious water, fast vital breaths, mental vigour, digestive strength have raised him up to health. (2032)[3]

३. इह तेऽसुरिह प्राण इहायुरिह ते मनः ।
उत् त्वा निर्ऋत्याः पाशेभ्यो दैव्या वाचा भरामसि ॥

3. O man, dedicate thy intellect, thy breath, thy life, thy soul to God. Through divine utterance of the Vedas we raise thee from the bonds of ignorance. (2033)[4]

[1]'I' refers to the Commander-in-chief.

[2]World of life eternal: Salvation. Surya means God, vide *Yajur*, 7-42.

[3]Vital breaths: Prāna, Apāna, Vyāna, Udāna, Samāna, Nāga, Kurma, Krikala, Dev Dutt, Dhananjya, the eleven breaths that conduce to health and longevity.

[4]'We' refers to learned persons.

४. उत् क्रामातः पुरुष माव पत्था मृत्योः पड्बीशमवमुञ्चमानः ।
मा च्छित्था अस्माल्लोकादग्नेः सूर्यस्य संदृशः ।।

4. Up from thy present position, O soul, rise! sink not downward, casting away the fetters of ignorance and poverty that hold thee. Be not parted from this world, enjoy long the sight of your preceptor (Guru) and God. (2034)

५. तुभ्यं वातः पवतां मातरिश्वा तुभ्यं वर्षन्त्वमृतान्यापः ।
सूर्यस्ते तन्वे३ शं तपाति त्वां मृत्युर्दयतां मा प्र मेष्ठाः ।।

5. O soul, may the wind moving in the atmosphere blow purely for thee, and let waters rain on thee their nectar. The Sun shall shine with efficacy on thy body; Death shall have mercy on thee: don't die early! (2035)

६. उद्यानं ते पुरुष नावयानं जीवातुं ते दक्षतातिं कृणोमि ।
आ हि रोहेममृतं सुखं रथमथ जिर्विर्विदथमा वदासि ।।

6. Upward must be thy way, O soul, not downward: with life and mental vigour I endow thee. Ascend this bodily car, the giver of deathless joy; then preach knowledge to humanity in old age! (2036)[1]

७. मा ते मनस्तत्र गान्मा तिरो भून्मा जीवेभ्यः प्र मदो मानु गाः पितॄन् ।
विश्वे देवा अभि रक्षन्तु त्वेह ।।

7. Let not thy soul follow sin, nor be absorbed in it. Slacken not your efforts to serve humanity. Follow not your aged parents to death. Let all the organs retain thee here in safety. (2037)[2]

८. मा गतानामा दीधीथा ये नयन्ति परावतम् ।
आ रोह तमसो ज्योतिरेह्या ते हस्तौ रभामहे ।।

8. Yearn not for the departed ones, for they lead your thoughts to the other world. Rise up from the darkness of sin, come into the light of virtue. We clasp both thy hands to help thee. (2038)[3]

९. श्यामश्च त्वा मा शबलश्च प्रेषितौ यमस्य यौ पथिरक्षी श्वानौ ।
अर्वाङेहि मा वि दीध्यो मात्र तिष्ठः पराङ्मनाः ।।

9. Let not the black night and the bright day seize thee, two ever moving warders of thy path of life sent forth by God. Go forward, grieve not. Don't sit in this world brooding over the past. (2039)

१०. मैतं पन्थामनु गा भीम एष येन पूर्वं नेयथ तं ब्रवीमि ।
तम एतत् पुरुष मा प्र पत्था भयं परस्तादभयं ते अर्वाक् ।।

[1] 'I' refers to God.
[2] 'Here' refers to body.
[3] 'We' refers to learned persons, through whose help a man can rise from darkness to light.

10. Forbear to tread this path of sin, for it is aweful: that path I speak of, which thou hast not travelled before. Enter it not, O man; this way is darkness: forward is danger, hitherward is safety. (2040)

११. रक्षन्तु त्वाग्नयो ये अप्स्व१न्ता रक्षतु त्वा मनुष्या३ यमिन्धते ।
वैश्वानरो रक्षतु जातवेदा दिव्यस्त्वा मा प्र धाग् विद्युता सह ॥

11. Thy guardians be the learned persons amongst the subjects. Thy guardian be the fire which men enkindle. Thy guardian be the All-knowing God, the Well-wisher of all: let not celestial fire with lightning burn thee. (2041)

१२. मा त्वा क्रव्यादभि मंस्तारात् संकसुकाच्चर ।
रक्षतु त्वा द्यौ रक्षतु पृथिवी सूर्यश्च त्वा रक्षतां चन्द्रमाश्च । अन्तरिक्षं रक्षतु देवहेत्याः ॥

12. Let not a flesh-consuming animal or disease attack thee. Keep far away from an avaricious, violent person. Be Heaven and Earth and Sun and Moon thy protectors. May Air protect thee from the attack of Nature's forces. (2042)

१३. बोधश्च त्वा प्रतीबोधश्च रक्षतामस्वप्नश्च त्वानवद्राणश्च रक्षताम् ।
गोपायंश्च त्वा जागृविश्च रक्षताम् ॥

13. May the teacher, the imparter of knowledge, and the preacher, the propagator of learning protect thee. May sleepless watchman and the high charactered Acharya, who never resorts to low and mean devices, protect thee. May thy guardian and wakeful sentry protect thee. (2043)

१४. ते त्वा रक्षन्तु ते त्वा गोपायन्तु तेभ्यो नमस्तेभ्यः स्वाहा ॥

14. Let these be thy preservers, these thy keepers. Honour them, and converse respectfully with them. (2044)[1]

१५. जीवेभ्यस्त्वा समुद्रे वायुरिन्द्रो धाता दधातु सविता त्रायमाणः ।
मा त्वा प्राणो बलं हासीदसुं तेनु ह्वयामसि ॥

15. May the All-pervading, Most Exalted, Nourishing, Protecting God, the Creator, rear thee for lending joy and shelter to others. May not thy vigour or thy breath forsake thee. We invoke intellect for thee. (2045)

१६. मा त्वा जम्भः संहनुर्मा तमो विदन्मा जिह्वा बर्हिः प्रमयुः कथा स्याः ।
उत् त्वादित्या वसवो भरन्तूदिन्द्राग्नी स्वस्तये ॥

16. Let not a nerve-breaking disease attack thee. Let not lockjaw attack thee. Let not dimness of eyes attack thee. May thou not suffer from a tongue-disease. Ever maintaining good health, how canst thou fall a prey to death. May the Āditya learned Brahmcharis, the Vasu Brahmcharis, the king and Ācharya save thee from death and lead thee to prosperity. (2046)[2]

[1] 'These' refers to teacher, preacher, watchman, etc. mentioned in the previous verse.

[2] Aditya Brahmcharies: Learned persons who observe celibacy for 48 years. Vasu Brahmcharies: Persons who study the Vedas and observe celibacy for 24 years.

१७. उत् त्वा द्यौरुत् पृथिव्युत् प्रजापतिरग्रभीत् । उत् त्वा मृत्योरोषधयः सोमराज्ञीरपीपरन् ॥

17. May the Sun, the Earth and God save thee from death. May the plants and herbs with Moon as their King rescue thee from death. (2047)

१८. अयं देवा इहैवास्त्वयं मामुत्र गादितः । इमं सहस्रवीर्येण मृत्योरुत् पारयामसि ॥

18. O learned persons, let this man remain here in this world, let him not go to yonder world. We rescue him from death with a thousand devices! (2048)

१९. उत् त्वा मृत्योरपीपरं सं धमन्तु वयोधसः । मा त्वा व्यस्तकेश्यो३ मा त्वाघरुदो रुदन् ॥

19. O men, I have delivered thee from death. May thou get life-infusing objects. Let not the females with wild loose locks, and thy relatives deeply mourn over thy death. (2049)[1]

२०. आहार्षमविदं त्वा पुनरागाः पुनर्णवः । सर्वाङ्ग सर्वं ते चक्षुः सर्वमायुश्च तेऽविदम् ॥

20. O soul, I bring thee unto this body. I look after thee. Thou assumest body again and again, and art born anew. Perfect in body: so have I restored all thy sight, and all thy life. (2050)[2]

२१. व्यवात् ते ज्योतिरभूदप त्वत् तमो अक्रमीत् ।
अप त्वन्मृत्युं निर्ऋतिमप यक्ष्मं नि दध्मसि ॥

21. Life hath breathed on thee; light hath come: darkness hath past away from thee. Far from thee we have removed poverty, death and consumption. (2051)

HYMN II

१. आ रभस्वेमाममृतस्य श्नुष्टिमच्छिद्यमाना जरदष्टिरस्तु ते ।
असुं त आयुः पुनरा भरामि रजस्तमो मोप गा मा प्र मेष्ठाः ॥

1. O man, try to secure the enjoyment of this full life of a hundred years. Thine be longevity which nothing shortens. Thy spirit and thy life again I bring thee die not, shun luxury and ignorance! (2052)[3]

२. जीवतां ज्योतिरभ्येह्यर्वाङां त्वा हरामि शतशारदाय ।
अवमुञ्चन् मृत्युपाशानशस्तिं द्राघीय आयुः प्रतरं ते दधामि ॥

2. O man, come hither to the light of living men. I have brought thee to this world for enjoying a life of hundred autumns. Loosing the bonds of death and disgrace, I give thee age of very long duration! (2053)[4]

[1]'I' refers to God, or a learned person. A man should not die before the attainment of full age of hundred years, so that his relatives may not weep over his premature death.

[2]'I' refers to God. All thy sight: All thy organs. All thy life: Full life of one hundred years.

[3]The verse is addressed to a sick person at the point of death. 'I' refers to a learned physician, or God.

[4]'I' refers to God.

३. वातात् ते प्राणमविदं सूर्याच्चक्षुरहं तव ।
यत् ते मनस्त्वयि तद् धारयामि सं वित्स्वाङ्गैर्वद जिह्वयालपन् ॥

3. For thee, I create breathe from the wind, and vision from the Sun. Thy mind I establish and secure within thee. Acquire knowledge with thy organs, speak clearly with thy tongue. (2054)[1]

४. प्राणेन त्वा द्विपदां चतुष्पदामग्निमिव जातमभि सं धमामि ।
नमस्ते मृत्यो चक्षुषे नमः प्राणाय तेऽकरम् ॥

4. O soul, just as fire is kindled with the blow of breath or a fan, so do I enliven thee with the breath of bipeds and quadrupeds. O God, the Severer of men from the mortal, I feed the eye granted by Thee with beautiful scenery, and the breath granted by thee with food. (2055)[2]

५. अयं जीवतु मा मृतेमं समीरयामसि । कृणोम्यस्मै भेषजं मृत्यो मा पुरुषं वधीः ॥

5. Let this man live, let him not die, we make him conscious. I make for him a healing balm. O Death, forbear to slay this man. (2056)[3]

६. जीवलां नघारिषां जीवन्तीमोषधीमहम् ।
त्रायमाणां सहमानां सहस्वतीमिह हुवेऽस्मा अरिष्टतातये ॥

6. For the health of this man, I grant a living animating medicine, life-infusing, injuring, preserving, efficacious, and invigorating. (2057)[4]

७. अधि ब्रूहि मा रभथाः सृजेमं तवैव सन्त्सर्वहाया इहास्तु ।
भवाशर्वौ मृडतं शर्म यच्छतमपसिध्य दुरितं धत्तमायुः ॥

7. O God, the Dissolver of the universe tell this soul how to live long. Harm it not, let it develop. Let this person, being thine, live in this world for full hundred years. O Creation and Dissolution lend joy to this soul, give it full life and drive away misfortunes! (2058)

८. अस्मै मृत्यो अधि ब्रूहीमं दयस्वोदितोऽयमेतु ।
अरिष्टः सर्वाङ्गः सुश्रुज्जरसा शतहायन आत्मना भुजमश्नुताम् ॥

8. O God, instruct this soul, nourish this person. Rising above afflictions let him tread the right path of life. Harmless with intellect and all organs in tact, let him enjoy full old age of hundred years, and attain to prosperity through self effort! (2059)

[1] 'I' refers to God.

[2] In the first part God addresses the soul, and in the second, the soul addresses God.

[3] The verse refers to a sick person. 'We' refers to learned persons. 'I' refers to a skilled physician.

[4] 'I' refers to God. Jivanti is the name of a plant, which has got manifold medicinal and curative properties.

९. देवानां हेतिः परि त्वा वृणक्तु पारयामि त्वा रजस उत् त्वा मृत्योरपीपरम् ।
आरादग्निं क्रव्यादं निरूहं जीवातवे ते परिधिं दधामि ॥

9. May the missile of the forces of nature pass by thee. I save thee from the attack of passions. I have preserved thee from death. Far have I banished flesh-consuming fire: I define a proper code of conduct for thy life's protection. (2060)[1]

१०. यत् ते नियानं रजसं मृत्यो अनवधर्ष्यम् ।
पथ इमं तस्माद् रक्षन्तो ब्रह्मास्मै वर्म कृण्मसि ॥

10. O Death, invincible is thy misty path. Saving him from that path, we make Vedic knowledge an armour for him! (2061)[2]

११. कृणोमि ते प्राणापानौ जरां मृत्युं दीर्घमायुः स्वस्ति ।
वैवस्वतेन प्रहितान् यमदूतांश्चरतोऽप सेधामि सर्वान् ॥

11. I firmly establish Prāna and Apāna (both the breaths) in thee. I keep away from thee, old age and death. I give thee long life, which may prove propitious to thee. I chase away the messengers of death, which roam about. (2062)[3]

१२. आरादरातिं निर्ऋतिं परो ग्राहिं क्रव्यादः पिशाचान् ।
रक्षो यत् सर्वं दुर्भूतं तत् तम इवाप हन्मसि ॥

12. Far off we drive stinginess, poverty, avarice, and demons who feast on flesh. All the devil kind the brood of sin, like darkness, we dispel. (2063)

१३. अग्नेष्टे प्राणममृतादायुष्मतो वन्वे जातवेदसः ।
यथा न रिष्या अमृतः सजूरसस्तत् ते कृणोमि तदु ते समृध्यताम् ॥

13. I win thy life from the Refulgent, Immortal, Everlasting, Omniscient God. This I procure for thee, that thou mayst not suffer harm, and befriending Him, become free from the fear of death, and all be well with thee. (2064)

१४. शिवे ते स्तां द्यावापृथिवी असंतापे अभिश्रियौ ।
शं ते सूर्य आ तपतु शं वातो वातु ते हृदे ।
शिवा अभि क्षरन्तु त्वापो दिव्याः पयस्वतीः ॥

14. Gracious to thee be Heaven and Earth, bringing no grief, and bestowing wealth! Pleasantly shine the sun for thee, the Wind blow sweetly to thy heart! Let the celestial Waters full of sweetness like milk flow happily for thee. (2065)

[1] 'I' refers to God. Missile of nature: Affliction caused by excessive rain, flood, and heat.

[2] 'We' refers to learned persons.

[3] 'I' refers to God. Messengers: Seconds minute, hour, day, month, year, which shorten our life.

१५. शिवास्ते सन्त्वोषधय उत् त्वाहार्षमधरस्या उत्तरां पृथिवीमभि ।
तत्र त्वादित्यौ रक्षतां सूर्याचन्द्रमसावुभा ॥

15. Auspicious be the Plants to thee! I have upraised thee from the lower to the upper part of the earth. Let the lustrous Sun and Moon prolong thy life there. (2066)[1]

१६. यत् ते वासः परिधानं यां नीविं कृणुषे त्वम् ।
शिवं ते तन्वे३ तत् कृण्मः संस्पर्शेऽद्रूक्ष्णमस्तु ते ॥

16. Whatever robe to cover thee or zone thou makest for thyself, we make it pleasant to thy frame; may it be soft and smooth to touch. (2067)

१७. यत् क्षुरेण मर्चयता सुतेजसा वप्ता वपसि केशश्मश्रु । शुभं मुखं मा न आयुः प्र मोषीः ॥

17. O barber, when, with a very sharp and cleansing razor, our hair and beards thou shavest, beautifying our face, harm not our body! (2068)[2]

१८. शिवौ ते स्तां व्रीहियवावबलासावदोमधौ । एतौ यक्ष्मं वि बाधेते एतौ मुञ्चतो अंहसः ॥

18. Auspicious unto thee be rice and barley, nutritious and sweet in taste. They cure consumption and free us from physical suffering. (2069)

१९. यदश्नासि यत्पिबसि धान्यं कृष्याः पयः । यदाद्यं१ यदनाद्यं सर्वं ते अन्नमविषं कृणोमि ॥

19. Whatever corn grown by cultivation thou eatest, or whatever milk thou drinkest, food eatable and drinkable, I make all poisonless for thee. (2070)[3]

२०. अह्ने च त्वा रात्रये चोभाभ्यां परि दद्मसि । अरायेभ्यो जिघत्सुभ्य इमं मे परि रक्षत ॥

20. O man, we grant thee freedom to pass both day and night according to your pleasure. O learned administrators, save my property and body from indigent dacoits, and violent cannibals! (2071)

२१. शतं तेऽयुतं हायनान् द्वे युगे त्रीणि चत्वारि कृण्मः ।
इन्द्राग्नी विश्वे देवास्तेऽनु मन्यन्तामहृणीयमानाः ॥

[1]Upper part: Mountain. A patient for recovery and men for improvement of health should resort to hills, where the air is purer, and the light of the Sun and Moon pleasanter than in a low level place.

'Thee refers to a patient.

[2]Harm not our body: Don't injure our body through inexperience or carelessness, or by the use of a bad non-disinfected razor, which may bruise a part of the face or produce a skin disease like eczema. Swami Dayananda has used this verse for Mundan Sanskar in the Sanskar Vidhi.

[3]आद्यम्, अनाद्यम् may also mean eatable, uneatable according to Sayāna, or stale and fresh food according to Pt. Khem Karan Das Trivedi. Pt. Jaidev Vidyalankar translates अनाद्यम् as uneatable i.e. drinkable.

21. O man, thine is the age of a hundred years, with two intervals of day and night and three seasons of summer, winter and rains, and four stages of childhood, youth, middle age, and old age. We render your age unbroken and complete. May the King, Commander-in-chief and all the learned persons willingly admire you for this age! (2072)[1]

२२. शरदे त्वा हेमन्ताय वसन्ताय ग्रीष्माय परि दद्मसि ।
वर्षाणि तुभ्यं स्योनानि येषु वर्धन्त ओषधीः ॥

22. O man, to Autumn we deliver thee, to Winter, Spring and Summer's care. May the rainy season wherein the plants and herbs grow up, be auspicious for thee. (2073)

२३. मृत्युरीशे द्विपदां मृत्युरीशे चतुष्पदाम् । तस्मात् त्वां मृत्योर्गोपतेरुद्भरामि स मा बिभेः ॥

23. Death is the lord of bipeds. Death is the supreme lord of Quadrupeds. O ruler, away from that Death I bear thee, be not thou afraid. (2074)[2]

२४. सोऽरिष्ट न मरिष्यसि न मरिष्यसि मा बिभेः । न वै तत्र म्रियन्ते नो यन्त्यधमं तमः ॥

24. O non-violent immortal soul, thou shalt not die: be not afraid; thou shalt not die. Learned emancipated persons do not die after the attainment of salvation, nor go to the lowest depths of darkness! (2075)

२५. सर्वो वै तत्र जीवति गौरश्वः पुरुषः पशुः । यत्रेदं ब्रह्म क्रियते परिधिर्जीवनाय कम् ॥

25. Here verily all creatures live, the cow, the horse, the men, the beast, here where this Vedic knowledge is used as a rampart that protects life. (2076)

२६. परि त्वा पातु समानेभ्योऽभिचारात् सबन्धुभ्यः ।
अमम्रिर्भवामृतोऽतिजीवो मा ते हासिषुरसवः शरीरम् ॥

26. Let this Vedic knowledge preserve thee from thy friends, from evil deeds, from thy relatives. Thou art deathless, immortal soul. Live long in the body. Let not the vital breath forsake thy body. (2077)

२७. ये मृत्यव एकशतं या नाष्ट्रा अतितार्याः । मुञ्चन्तु तस्मात् त्वां देवा अग्नेर्वैश्वानरादधि ॥

27. There are one and a hundred modes of death, and many destructive fetters of ignorance that may be overcome; may learned persons deliver thee from this when the All-pervading Refulgent God bids. (2078)[3]

[1]This verse has been translated by some scholars as denoting the time for which the universe lasts, which is called the Brahma Day, and the period for which Matter in its nascent, atomic stage lasts after dissolution, before the world is re-created. This period is termed the Brahma Night. Multiply 100 (शत) by 10,000 (अयुत) and put 2, 3, 4 respectively to the left, we get 4,320000000 years which is the age of the world.

[2]'I' refers to God.

[3]'This' refers to Death, ignorance.

२८. अग्नेः शरीरमसि पारयिष्णु रक्षोहासि सपत्नहा । अथो अमीवचातनः पूतुद्रुर्नाम भेषजम् ॥

28. O man, thou art the body of this wise soul, saviour from worldly sufferings, slayer of fiends and foes art thou, yea, banisher of maladies, Thou art the purifier of the tree of this body, and healing balm for spiritual ailments! (2079)

Chapter (Anuvāka) 2

HYMN III

१. रक्षोहणं वाजिनमा जिघर्मि मित्रं प्रथिष्ठमुप यामि शर्म ।
शिशानो अग्निः क्रतुभिः समिद्धः स नो दिवा स रिषः पातु नक्तम् ॥

1. I make the mighty demon-slayer still more powerful, to the most famous friend, the king, I come for shelter. May the zealous king, renowned through his deeds, protect us in the day and night from evil. (2080)

२. अयोदंष्ट्रो अर्चिषा यातुधानानुप स्पृश जातवेदः समिद्धः ।
आ जिह्वया मूरदेवान् रभस्व क्रव्यादो वृष्ट्वापि धत्स्वासन् ॥

2. O King, the knower of thy subjects, armed with thy military instruments, enkindled with thy dignity, trample the demons under thy feet. Control the ignorant, voluptuous gamblers with thy advice. With thy heroism, send to jail the raw flesh-eaters! (2081)

३. उभोभयाविन्नुप धेहि दंष्ट्री हिंस्रः शिशानोऽवरं परं च ।
उतान्तरिक्षे परि याह्यग्ने जम्भैः सं धेह्यभि यातुधानान् ॥

3. O King, the protector of the good and bad, high and low, as slayer of the ignoble, keen in nature, keep under thy control the weak and strong foes. Fly on all sides in the air, and assail the wicked spirits with thy sharp instruments. (2082)

४. अग्ने त्वचं यातुधानस्य भिन्धि हिंस्राशनिर्हरसा हन्त्वेनम् ।
प्र पर्वाणि जातवेदः शृणीहि क्रव्यात् क्रविष्णुर्वि चिनोत्वेनम् ॥

4. O King, pierce through the wicked person's skin; let the destroying dart with fire consume him. Rend his joints, O King, let the eater of raw flesh, anxious for flesh, tear and destroy him! (2083)[1]

५. यत्रेदानीं पश्यसि जातवेदस्तिष्ठन्तमग्न उत वा चरन्तम् ।
उतान्तरिक्षे पतन्तं यातुधानं तमस्ता विध्य शर्वा शिशानः ॥

5. O wise king, where now thou seest, a wicked person, standing still or roaming, or flying through the air's mid-region, kindled to fury as an archer pierce him with an arrow! (2084)

[1]Eater of flesh: A tiger or wolf.

६. यज्ञैरिषू: संनममानो अग्ने वाचा शल्याँ अशनिभिर्दिहानः ।
ताभिर्विध्य हृदये यातुधानान् प्रतीचो बाहून् प्रति भङ्ग्ध्येषाम् ॥

6. O King, throwing the shafts through soldiers, ordering the sharpening of the arrows through electrification, pierce to the heart therewith the wicked persons, and break their arms uplifted to attack thee! (2085)

७. उतारब्धान्त्स्पृणुहि जातवेद उतारेमाणाँ ऋष्टिभिर्यातुधानान् ।
अग्ने पूर्वो नि जहि शोशुचान आमादः क्ष्विङ्कास्तमदन्त्वेनीः ॥

7. O King, protect the captives. O King, foremost of all, blazing with thy lustre, kill with double-edged swords, the terrible foes, who want to capture us. Let spotted carrion-eating vultures devour that violent person! (2086)

८. इह प्र ब्रूहि यतमः सो अग्ने यातुधानो य इदं कृणोति ।
तमा रभस्व समिधा यविष्ठ नृचक्षसश्चक्षुषे रन्धयैनम् ॥

8. O King, declare here, who the demon is, that commits the evil deed. Grasp him, O thou most youthful, with thy prestige; and punish him, keeping in view the welfare of the people! (2087)

९. तीक्ष्णेनाग्ने चक्षुषा रक्ष यज्ञं प्राञ्चं वसुभ्यः प्र णय प्रचेतः ।
हिंस्रं रक्षांस्यभि शोशुचानं मा त्वा दभन् यातुधाना नृचक्षः ॥

9. O King, with a vigilant eye, guard the Yajna of thy administration make it, O prudent King, excellent for thy subjects. Let not the fiends, O Man-Beholder harm thee burning against the demons to slay them. (2088)[1]

१०. नृचक्षा रक्षः परि पश्य विक्षु तस्य त्रीणि प्रति शृणीह्यग्रा ।
तस्याग्ने पृष्टीर्हरसा शृणीहि त्रेधा मूलं यातुधानस्य वृश्च ॥

10. O King, the Man-Beholder, look on the fiend, 'mid men, rend thou his three extremities in pieces. Demolish with thy strength his ribs. O King, destroy thou triply the lower part of the fiend! (2089)[2]

११. त्रिर्यातुधानः प्रसितिं त एत्वृतं यो अग्ने अनृतेन हन्ति ।
तमर्चिषा स्फूर्जयञ्जातवेदः समक्षमेनं गृणते नि युङ्ग्धि ॥

11. Thrice, O King, let thy noose surround the demon who with his falsehood injures truth. Roaring loud with thy strength. O King, fetter him in the presence of all, for the good of him who praises God. (2090)[3]

[1]Man-Beholder: The King who watches keenly the welfare and interests of his subjects.

[2]Extremities: Head, and two shoulders; or strength, wealth and men, the three agencies of a wicked person. Triply: Both the legs and waist.

[3]'Thrice' means three times, again and again, or in three parts of the body, the lower, middle and upper, i.e., feet, legs, hands.

१२. यदग्ने अद्य मिथुना शपातो यद् वाचस्तृष्टं जनयन्त रेभाः ।
मन्योर्मनसः शरव्या३ जायते या तया विध्य हृदये यातुधानान् ॥

12. O King, whenever the pair utters curse against a fiend, or learned persons use rude, rough words for him, the flame of wrath is kindled in thy indignant mind; pierce thou to the heart therewith the fiends! (2091)[1]

१३. परा शृणीहि तपसा यातुधानान् पराग्ने रक्षो हरसा शृणीहि ।
परार्चिषा मूरदेवाञ्छृणीहि परासुतृपः शोशुचतः शृणीहि ॥

13. O King, with thy deadly strength exterminate the demons, destroy the fiends with thy destructive power. Destroy with the flame of fire the foolish pleasure-hunters. Destroy the murderous dacoits weeping with grief! (2092)

१४. पराद्य देवा वृजिनं शृणन्तु प्रत्यगेनं शपथा यन्तु सृष्टाः ।
वाचास्तेनं शरव ऋच्छन्तु मर्मन् विश्वस्यैतु प्रसितिं यातुधानः ॥

14. May the learned ever destroy the evil-doer: may uttered curses turn back and attack him. Let arrows pierce the liar in his vitals, and the fetters of the all-controlling king fasten the criminal. (2093)

१५. यः पौरुषेयेण क्रविषा समङ्क्ते यो अश्व्येन पशुना यातुधानः ।
यो अघ्न्याया भरति क्षीरमग्ने तेषां शीर्षाणि हरसापि वृश्च ॥

15. The fiend who feeds on the flesh of cattle, the flesh of horses and of human bodies, who steals the milch-cow's milk away, O King,—tear off the heads of such with fiery fury! (2094)

१६. विषं गवां यातुधाना भरन्तामा वृश्चन्तामदितये दुरेवाः ।
परैणान् देवः सविता ददातु परा भागमोषधीनां जयन्ताम् ॥

16. The fiends who poison the cows, the evil-doers who cut the cow into pieces, let the king, the urger of all, banish them from his state, and their share of herbs and plants be denied them. (2095)[2]

१७. संवत्सरीणं पय उस्रियायास्तस्य माशीद् यातुधानो नृचक्षः ।
पीयूषमग्ने यतमस्तितृप्सात् तं प्रत्यञ्चमर्चिषा विध्य मर्मणि ॥

17. O King, the Man-Beholder, let not the fiend ever taste the milk, the cow yields in a year. O King, if any one of ignoble persons would like to glut himself with milk, pierce with thy flame his vitals as he meets thee! (2096)[3]

[1]When a pair, i.e., husband and wife cry against the atrocity of a wicked person, or learned persons condemn in strong language the misdeeds of a satanic person, the king feels enraged after hearing them, and should give condign punishment to such devils.

[2]This verse is a clear condemnation of flesh eating. Verse 15th also condemns the eating of flesh.

[3]Flame: Fire of anger or strength.

१८. सनादग्ने मृणसि यातुधानान् न त्वा रक्षांसि पृतनासु जिग्युः ।
सहमूराननु दह क्रव्यादो मा ते हेत्या मुक्षत दैव्यायाः ॥

18. O King, from days of old thou slayest demons: never have they overcome thee in battles. Burn up the flesh-devourers, along with their foolish companions: let none of them escape thy wonderful instrument! (2097)

१९. त्वं नो अग्ने अधरादुदक्तस्त्वं पश्चादुत रक्षा पुरस्तात् ।
प्रति त्ये ते अजरासस्तपिष्ठा अघशंसं शोशुचतो दहन्तु ॥

19. Guard us, O King, from below and above, protect us from behind and from front. May thy instruments most fierce and never wasting, glowing with fervent heat, consume the sinner! (2098)[1]

२०. पश्चात् पुरस्तादधरादुतोत्तरात् कविः काव्येन परि पाह्यग्ने ।
सखा सखायमजरो जरिम्णे अग्ने मर्तां अमर्त्यस्त्वं नः ॥

20. From rear, from front, from under, from above us, O King, protect us a sage with wisdom. Guard to old age thy friend as friend eternal: O King, as immortal, guard us mortals! (2099)

२१. तदग्ने चक्षुः प्रति धेहि रेभे शफारुजो येन पश्यसि यातुधानान् ।
अथर्ववज्ज्योतिषा दैव्येन सत्यं धूर्वन्तमचितं न्योऽष ॥

21. Lend thou the garrulous prattler that eye, O King, wherewith thou lookest on the demons, who revile and defame others. Like a non-violent sage, with wise light of the learned, burn up the fool who ruins truth with falsehood! (2100)

२२. परि त्वाग्ने पुरं वयं विप्रं सहस्य धीमहि । धृषद्वर्णं दिवेदिवे हन्तारं भङ्गुरावतः ॥

22. O foe-suppressing, powerful king, may we daily seek thy shelter, as thou art the nourisher of all, wise, the controller of powerful foes, and the destroyer of the tormentors of the subjects! (2101)

२३. विषेण भङ्गुरावतः प्रति स्म रक्षसो जहि । अग्ने तिग्मेन शोचिषा तपुरग्राभिरर्चिभिः ॥

23. O King, with thy sharpened glow, with rays that flash with points of flame, strike thou back the treacherous brood of evil-minded persons who kill others with poison. (2102)

२४. वि ज्योतिषा बृहता भात्यग्निराविर्विश्वानि कृणुते महित्वा ।
प्रादेवीर्मायाः सहते दुरेवाः शिशीते शृङ्गे रक्षोभ्यो विनिक्ष्वे ॥

24. The King shines far and wide with lofty splendour, and by his greatness performs all acts conducive to the welfare of his subjects. He conquers godless and malign illusions, and sharpens both his horns (weapons) to gore the ogres. (2103)[2]

[1]Below: South. Above: North. Behind: West. Front: East.
[2]Horns: Protection of the subjects, and annihilation of the foes.

२५. ये ते शृङ्गे अजरे जातवेदस्तिग्महेती ब्रह्मसंशिते ।
ताभ्यां दुर्हार्दमभिदासन्तं किमीदिनं प्रत्यञ्चमर्चिषा जातवेदो वि निक्ष्व ॥

25. O learned King, thy two unwasting horns are keen-pointed weapons, sharpened by Vedic knowledge. With these transfix the wicked-souled person, who cares not an iota for the life and property of others, and is aggressive in nature, with fierce flame of wrath, O King, when he meets thee! (2104)

२६. अग्नी रक्षांसि सेधति शुक्रशोचिरमर्त्यः । शुचिः पावक ईड्यः ॥

26. Pure, purifier, adorable, energetic with refulgent glow, the king drives demons away. (2105)

HYMN IV

१. इन्द्रासोमा तपतं रक्ष उब्जतं न्यर्पयतं वृषणा तमोवृधः ।
परा शृणीतमचितो न्योषतं हतं नुदेथां नि शिशीतमत्त्रिणः ॥

1. O King and the Commander-in-chief, burn, destroy the demon foe. Send downward, O ye powerful both, the protagonists of ignorance. Annihilate the fools, slay them and burn them up: chase them away from us, pierce the voracious fiends! (2106)[1]

२. इन्द्रासोमा समघशंसमस्यघं तपुर्ययस्तु चरुरग्निमाँ इव ।
ब्रह्मद्विषे क्रव्यादे घोरचक्षसे द्वेषो धत्तमनवायं किमीदिने ॥

2. O King and the Commander-in-chief, boldly face the sinful preacher of vice. May sin be burnt like an oblation put into fire. Keep perpetual dislike for the enemy of the Vedas, eater of flesh, the fearful-eyed Cormorant! (2107)

३. इन्द्रासोमा दुष्कृतो वव्रे अन्तरनारम्भणे तमसि प्र विध्यतम् ।
यतो नैषां पुनरेकश्चनोदयत् तद् वामस्तु सहसे मन्युमच्छवः ॥

3. O King and the Commander-in-chief, plunge the wicked in the depth, yea, cast them into deep darkness, so that not one of them may ever thence return: so may your wrathful might prevail and conquer them! (2108)

४. इन्द्रासोमा वर्तयतं दिवो वधं सं पृथिव्या अघशंसाय तर्हणम् ।
उत् तक्षतं स्वर्यं पर्वतेभ्यो येन रक्षो वावृधानं निजूर्वथः ॥

4. O King and the Commander-in-chief, hurl your deadly crushing bolt down on the wicked fiend frcm heaven and from the earth. Yea, fashion from the lofty mountains your roaring fiery instruments, wherewith you burn to death the waxing demons! (2109)

[1]Voracious fiends: Low-minded persons who feed on the flesh and property of others.

५. इन्द्रासोमा वर्तयतं दिवस्पर्यग्नितप्तेभिर्युवमश्महन्मभिः ।
तपुर्वधेभिरजरेभिरत्त्रिणो नि पर्शाने विध्यतं यन्तु निस्वरम् ।।

5. O King and Commander-in-chief, cast ye downward from the sky your deadly weapons of steel burning with fiery flame, unfailing, scorching darts. Shoot the voracious fiends in the ribs, and let them die without a sound! (2110)

६. इन्द्रासोमा परि वां भूतु विश्वत इयं मतिः कक्ष्याश्वेव वाजिना ।
यां वां होत्रां परिहिनोमि मेधयेमा ब्रह्माणि नृपती इव जिन्वतम् ।।

6. O King and Commander-in-chief, just as the girth beautifies two vigorous steeds, so should this intellect adorn you to carry on the administration efficiently. I offer you with wisdom this Vedic song of praise. May these Vedic verses animate you, as do the eulogies of prisoners please the kings! (2111)

७. प्रति स्मरेथां तुजयद्भिरेवैर्हतं द्रुहो रक्षसो भङ्गुरावतः ।
इन्द्रासोमा दुष्कृते मा सुगं भूद्यो मा कदा चिदभिदासति द्रुहः ।।

7. O King and Commander-in-chief oppose the foes in fast conveyances, kill the disloyal, treacherous evil-minded subjects. Let the wicked have no rest whoso at any time attacks and injures us. (2112)

८. यो मा पाकेन मनसा चरन्तमभिचष्टे अनृतेभिर्वचोभिः ।
आप इव काशिना संगृभीता असन्नस्त्वासत इन्द्र वक्ता ।।

8. Whoso accuses me with words of falsehood when I pursue my way with guileless spirit, may he, the speaker of untruth, be non-existent, O King, like water which the hollowed hand compresses. (2113)

९. ये पाकशंसं विहरन्त एवैर्ये वा भद्रं दूषयन्ति स्वधाभिः ।
अहये वा तान् प्रददातु सोम आ वा दधातु निर्ऋतेरुपस्थे ।।

9. Those who destroy, as is their wont, the pure-minded, and with their evil natures harm the righteous, may the King, hand them over to the executioner awful like a serpent, or consign them to the lap of poverty. (2114)

१०. यो नो रसं दिप्सति पित्वो अग्ने अश्वानां गवां यस्तनूनाम् ।
रिपु स्तेन स्तेयकृद् दभ्रमेतु नि ष हीयतां तन्वा३ तना च ।।

10. O King, whosoever seeks to injure the essence of our food, steeds, kine, or bodies. May be, the adversary, thief, and robber, sink to destruction, both himself and his offsprings. (2115)

११. परः सो अस्तु तन्वा३ तना च तिस्रः पृथिवीरधो अस्तु विश्वाः ।
प्रति शुष्यतु यशो अस्य देवा यो मा दिवा दिप्सति यश्च नक्तम् ।।

11. May he be deprived of his body and children; may all the three earths press him down beneath them. May his fair glory, O ye learned persons, be blighted, who in the day or night would fain destroy us. (2116)[1]

१२. सुविज्ञानं चिकितुषे जनाय सच्चासच्च वचसी पस्पृधाते ।
तयोर्यत् सत्यं यतरदृजीयस्तदित् सोमोऽवति हन्त्यासत् ॥

12. A prudent person finds it easy to distinguish the true and false, and know that these words oppose each other. Of these two that which is the true and honest God protects, and brings the false to nothing. (2117)[2]

१३. न वा उ सोमो वृजिनं हिनोति न क्षत्रियं मिथुया धारयन्तम् ।
हन्ति रक्षो हन्त्यासद् वदन्तमुभाविन्द्रस्य प्रसितौ शयाते ॥

13. God never tolerates sin, or a Kshatriya, who espouses untruth. He destroys the ignoble, and him who tells a lie: both lie entangled in the grip of God. (2118)[3]

१४. यदि वाहमनृतदेवो अस्मि मोघं वा देवाँ अप्यूहे अग्ने ।
किमस्मभ्यं जातवेदो हृणीषे द्रोघवाचस्ते निर्ऋथं सचन्ताम् ॥

14. As if I am a worshipper of falsehood, or think vain thoughts about the sages; O King, why art thou angry with us, O King. May destruction fall on those who lie against thee! (2119)[4]

१५. अद्या मुरीय यदि यातुधानो अस्मि यदि वायुस्ततप पूरुषस्य ।
अधा स वीरैर्दशभिर्वि यूया यो मा मोघं यातुधानेत्याह ॥

15. May I die this day if I have harassed any man's life, or if I be a demon. Yea, may he lose all his ten breaths or sons, who with false tongue hath called me Yatudhana, a tormentor of others. (2120)

१६. यो मायातुं यातुधानेत्याह यो वा रक्षाः शुचिरस्मीत्याह ।
इन्द्रस्तं हन्तु महता वधेन विश्वस्य जन्तोरधमस्पदीष्ट ॥

16. He who calls me a demon though devoid of demon nature, and being a fiend says that he is pure, may the king slay him with a mighty weapon, and let him perish as the vilest of all creatures. (2121)

१७. प्र या जिगाति खर्गलेव नक्तमप द्रुहुस्तन्वं१ गूहमाना ।
वव्रमनन्तमव सा पदीष्ट ग्रावाणो घ्नन्तु रक्षस उपब्दैः ॥

[1]Three earths: Three stages, physical, social spiritual; or three castes, Brahmanas, Kshatriyas, Vaishas, i.e., he shall always remain a Shudra.

[2]Soma may mean a just Judge or King.

[3]Soma refers to God or a justice-loving King.

[4]A king should not be angry with us, as we are not the votaries of falsehood or revilers of sages. We should not be mistaken as such, and considered worthy of indignation by the king.

17. A woman who wanders like an owl at night-time hiding her body in her guile and malice, should be thrown into long imprisonment. If the culprit is a male, such demons should be punished by the learned with their rebukes. (2122)

१८. वि तिष्ठध्वं मरुतो विक्ष्वी३च्छत गृभायत रक्षसः सं पिनष्टन ।
वयो ये भूत्वा पतयन्ति नक्तभिर्ये वा रिपो दधिरे देवे अध्वरे ।

18. O state employees, spread out among the people, perform your duty willingly, seize ye, and grind to pieces, the mischievous persons who roam about quickly like birds at night time, and put obstacles in the way of fair administration by a King. (2123)

१९. प्र वर्तय दिवोऽश्मानमिन्द्र सोमशितं मघवन्त्सं शिशाधि ।
प्राक्तो अपाक्तो अधरादुदक्तो३भि जहि रक्षसः पर्वतेन ॥

19. O King, hurl down from heaven thy steel weapon. Give condign punishment to the guilty who deserves it, O powerful ruler. Smite down the demons with thy heavy weapon from the East, West, North and South! (2124)

२०. एत उ त्ये पतयन्ति श्वयातव इन्द्रं दिप्सन्ति दिप्सवोऽदाभ्यम् ।
शिशीते शक्रः पिशुनेभ्यो वधं नूनं सृजदशनिं यातुमद्भ्यः ॥

20. The demon dogs roam about, and, bent on mischief, fain would they harm the indomitable king, who sharpens his weapon for slaying the wicked, and certainly casts his bolt at violent fiends. (2125)[1]

२१. इन्द्रो यातूनामभवत् पराशरो हविर्मथीनामभ्या३विवासताम् ।
अभीदु शक्रः परशुर्यथा वनं पात्रेव भिन्दन्त्सत एतु रक्षसः ॥

21. A King is ever the destroyer of fiends who openly oppose him on the battlefield and disobey his orders. Just as an axe splits the timber and a stone breaks the earthen vessels, so should the powerful king assail and smash men devilish in nature, who come to fight against him. (2126)

२२. उलूकयातुं शुशुलूकयातुं जहि श्वयातुमुत कोकयातुम् ।
सुपर्णयातुमुत गृध्रयातुं दृषदेव प्र मृण रक्ष इन्द्र ॥

22. O learned person, suppress with iron determination the six enemies of the soul, as birds are killed with stone, (1) the unwisdom of an owl, (2) the violence of a wolf (3) the jealousy of a dog (4) the lust of a sparrow, (5) the pride of a garuda (6) the avarice of a vulture. (2127)[2]

२३. मा नो रक्षो अभि नड्यातुमावदपोच्छन्तु मिथुना ये किमीदिनः ।
पृथिवी नः पार्थिवात् पात्वंहसोऽन्तरिक्षं दिव्यात् पात्वस्मान् ॥

[1]Demon dogs: Violent persons who attack and injure others like dogs.

[2]A wise man should subdue with an iron hand, (1) folly (2) violence (3) jealousy (4) lust (5) pride (6) avarice.

23. Let not a troublesome ignoble person approach us, may the slanderous couple remain away from us. May Earth keep us safe from earthly woe and trouble. May the Mid-air preserve us from heavenly harm! (2128)

२४. इन्द्र जहि पुमांसं यातुधानमुत स्त्रियं मायया शाशदानाम् ।
विग्रीवासो मूरदेवा ऋदन्तु मा ते दृशन्त्सूर्यमुच्चरन्तम् ।।

24. O King, destroy the troublesome person, destroy the woman, joying and triumphing in deceit. Let the worshippers of fools, with bent necks fall and perish, and see no more the Sun when he rises! (2129)[1]

२५. प्रति चक्ष्व वि चक्ष्वेन्द्रश्च सोम जागृतम् । रक्षोभ्यो वधमस्यतमशनिं यातुमद्भ्यः ।।

25. O King, take care of your enemies. O Commander-in-chief watch their movements. Ye, both should remain alert. Cast forth your weapon at the fiends: against the troublesome persons hurl your bolt. (2130)

Chapter (Anuvāka) 3

HYMN V

१. अयं प्रतिसरो मणिर्वीरो वीराय बध्यते ।
वीर्यऽवान्त्सपत्नहा शूरवीरः परिपाणः सुमङ्गलः ।।

1. This precious Vedic Law, giver of right lead, potent, strong, foe-slayer, valiant, good protector happy and fortunate is meant for the strong. (2131)[2]

२. अयं मणिः सपत्नहा सुवीरः सहस्वान् वाजी सहमान उग्रः । प्रत्यक् कृत्या दूषयन्नेति वीरः ।।

2. This Vedic Law, foe-slayer, giver of valiant sons, strong, powerful, victorious and mighty, goes bravely forth crushing all impediments. (2132)

३. अनेनेन्द्रो मणिना वृत्रमहन्ननेनासुरान् पराभावयन्मनीषी ।
अनेनाजयद् द्यावापृथिवी उभे इमे अनेनाजयत् प्रदिशश्चतस्रः ।।

3. A wise king, following Vedic teachings has removed ignorance, slaughtered the foes. With this Vedic Law, he has conquered the Heaven and Earth, and mastered all the four directions. (2133)

४. अयं स्राक्त्यो मणिः प्रतीवर्तः प्रतिसरः ।
ओजस्वान् विमृधो वशी सो अस्मान् पातु सर्वतः ।।

4. May this valuable Vedic teaching energising, universal, giver of right lead, mighty, subduing the violent, keep us secure on every side. (2134)

५. तदग्निराह तदु सोम आह बृहस्पतिः सविता तदिन्द्रः ।
ते मे देवाः पुरोहिताः प्रतीचीः कृत्याः प्रतिसरैरजन्तु ।।

[1]Deceitful, troublesome, foolish persons should be destroyed and made to lose their life before the rising of the Sun.

[2]A weak man cannot follow the Vedic law मणि has been translated by Griffith as an amulet. The word means precious Vedic law.

5. The Commander-in-chief hath declared the Lord of justice declared it, the Vedic scholar and King, the urger of all, hath declared it, that all learned military officials under my command, should render ineffective, with the help of valiant soldiers, the evil designs of the enemy. (2135)[1]

६. अन्तर्दधे द्यावापृथिवी उताहरुत सूर्यम् ।
ते मे देवाः पुरोहिताः प्रतीचीः कृत्याः प्रतिसरैरजन्तु ॥

6. If the enemy of his attack observes even the heaven and earth, the daylight and Sun, let all learned officials under my command, render ineffective, with the help of valiant soldiers, the evil designs of the enemy. (2136)

७. ये स्राक्त्यं मणिं जना वर्माणि कृण्वते । सूर्य इव दिवमारुह्य वि कृत्या बाधते वशी ॥

7. He, who uses the excellent principle of hard work as his armour, like the Sun risen up to heaven, controlling his state, quells the evil designs of the enemy. (2137)

८. स्राक्त्येन मणिन ऋषिणेव मनीषिणा । अजैषं सर्वाः पृतना वि मृधो हन्मि रक्षसः ॥

8. As following the excellent principle of hard work, with the aid of a thoughtful sage, I vanquish the enemy's forces, so do I smite the violent demons. (2138)

९. याः कृत्या आङ्गिरसीर्याः कृत्या आसुरीर्याः कृत्याः स्वयंकृता या उ चान्येभिराभृताः ।
उभयीस्ताः परा यन्तु परावतो नवतिं नाव्या३ अति ॥

9. All violent deeds, mentioned by the learned scholars of the Atharva Veda, or committed by powerful persons, or self-created, or perpetrated by other foemen; may these depart completely to a distant place crossing ninety streams. (2139)[2]

१०. अस्मै मणिं वर्म बध्नन्तु देवा इन्द्रो विष्णुः सविता रुद्रो अग्निः ।
प्रजापतिः परमेष्ठी विराड् वैश्वानर ऋषयश्च सर्वे ॥

10. May venerable persons, dignified king, prudent minister, benevolent general, imparter of knowledge, precocious preceptor, nourisher of the people, seeker after salvation, sublime Refulgent God, and all the sages, determine an excellent principle as an armour for this heroic person. (2140)

११. उत्तमो अस्योषधीनामनड्वाञ्जगतामिव व्याघ्रः श्वपदामिव ।
यमैच्छामाविदाम तं प्रतिस्पाशनमन्तितम् ॥

11. O Vedic law, thou art most efficacious like medicine, just as a bull is chief among the cattle, and a tiger among the beasts of prey. We sought for thee, and have found thee, universal in nature and highly potent. (2141)[3]

[1] My: Ruler.
[2] Crossing ninety streams: Going far away.
[3] Thee: Vedic law.

१२. स इद् व्याघ्रो भवत्यथो सिंहो अथो वृषा । अथो सपत्नकर्शनो यो बिभर्तीमं मणिम् ॥

12. Powerful like a tiger is he, he is a lion and a bull in strength, subduer of his foes is he, who follows the excellent Vedic teachings. (2142)

१३. नैनं घ्नन्त्यप्सरसो न गन्धर्वा न मर्त्याः । सर्वा दिशो वि राजति यो बिभर्तीमं मणिम् ॥

13. Neither women with their allurements, nor kings with their crooked policy, nor mortal beings can harm him, who follows the excellent Vedic teachings. (2143)

१४. कश्यपस्त्वामसृजत कश्यपस्त्वा समैरयत् ।
अबिभस्त्वेन्द्रो मानुषे बिभ्रत् संश्रेषिणेऽजयत् । मणिं सहस्रवीर्यं वर्म देवा अकृण्वत ॥

14. O excellent Vedic law, God formed and fashioned thee. An intelligent person has followed thee in this world, and acting upon thy behests has overcome the struggles of life. The sages have made the Vedic law of boundless might, a coat of mail! (2144)

१५. यस्त्वा कृत्याभिर्यस्त्वा दीक्षाभिर्यज्ञैर्यस्त्वा जिघांसति ।
प्रत्यक् त्वमिन्द्र तं जहि वज्रेण शतपर्वणा ॥

15. Whoever would destroy thee through evil machinations, self-styled devices, organised forces, meet him and smite him, O King, with thy army of hundred weapons (2145)

१६. अयमिद्वै प्रतीवर्त ओजस्वान्त्संजयो मणिः । प्रजां धनं च रक्षतु परिपाणः सुमङ्गलः ॥

16. Verily, may this follower of Vedic teachings, foe-opposer, powerful, conqueror, protector, and fortunate, preserve our children and wealth. (2146)

१७. असपत्नं नो अधरादसपत्नं न उत्तरात् । इन्द्रासपत्नं नः पश्चाज्ज्योतिः शूर पुरस्कृधि ॥

17. O brave king, set light before us, peace and security from below, peace and security from above, peace and security from behind. (2147)[1]

१८. वर्म मे द्यावापृथिवी वर्माहर्वर्म सूर्यः । वर्म म इन्द्रश्चाग्निश्च वर्म धाता दधातु मे ॥

18. May Heaven and Earth serve as my armour against calamities, may Day and Sun be my coat of mail against diseases, may Air and Fire protect me, may God preserve me from misfortunes. (2148)

१९. ऐन्द्राग्नं वर्म बहुलं यदुग्रं विश्वे देवा नाति विध्यन्ति सर्वे ।
तन्मे तन्वं त्रायतां सर्वतो बृहदायुष्माञ्जरदष्टिर्यथासानि ॥

19. Not all the organs, all leagued together, may pierce the vast strong protection which Air and Fire give. May that shield on all sides guard my body, that to full old age my life may be extended. (2149)[2]

[1]Let there be peace and security for us from South, North, West, and light in the East before us.

[2]Shield: The protection given by Air and Fire, which serves as a shield or armour.

२०. आ मारुक्षद् देवमणिर्मह्या ग्ररिष्टतातये ।
इमं मेथिमभिसंविशध्वं तनूपानं त्रिवरूथमोजसे ॥

20. Excellent Vedic law has been taught to me to keep me safe from every ill. O learned persons, come ye and accept for strength this law, the averter of moral foes, the guardian of the body, the triple protector! (2150)[1]

२१. अस्मिन्निन्द्रो नि दधातु नृम्णमिमं देवासो ग्रभिसंविशध्वम् ।
दीर्घायुत्वाय शतशारदायायुष्मान्जरदष्टिर्यथासत् ॥

21. In this person, may God lay a store of wealth and strength. O learned persons, come and accept the Vedic law. May this person lead a long life of a hundred years, may his days be extended to full age! (2151)[2]

२२. स्वस्तिदा विशां पतिर्वृत्रहा विमृधो वशी ।
इन्द्रो वध्नातु ते मणिं जिगीवाँ अपराजितः सोमपा अभयंकरो वृषा ।
स त्वा रक्षतु सर्वतो दिवा नक्तं च विश्वतः ॥

22. May God, the Bestower of bliss, Lord of the subjects, Dispeller of ignorance, Controller of foes, conqueror, unconquered, Preserver of kingdom, Granter of fearlessness, Omnipotent, instruct thee in Vedic teaching, and protect thee round about, by night and day on every side. (2152)

HYMN VI

१. यौ ते मातोन्ममार्ज जातायाः पतिवेदनौ । दुर्णामा तत्र मा गृधदलिश उत वत्सपः ॥

1. O girl, fit for marriage, thy mother rejects as thy husband, him who suffers from skin disease of leprosy, and him who is far advanced in age. They should never long to marry thee. (2153)

२. पलालानुपलालौ शर्कुं कोकं मलिम्लुचं पलीजकम् । ग्राश्रेषं वव्रिवाससमृक्षग्रीवं प्रमीलिनम् ॥

2. The mother should reject as her daughter's husband, the meat-eater, the companion of meat-eaters, a man violent in nature, one cruel like a wolf, a thief, a grey-haired person, one who suffers from gonorrhoea, a dandy, one stiff-necked like a bear, one suffering from photophobia. (2154)[3]

३. मा सं वृतो मोप सृप ऊरू माव सृपोऽन्तरा । कृणोम्यस्यै भेषजं बजं दुर्णामचातनम् ॥

3. O leper, don't try to be married, if married through mistake, cohabit not with this girl. Don't live in her house. For this girl I select a beautiful husband as remedy for one suffering from leprosy. (2155)[4]

[1]Triple protector: That protects us from spiritual (आध्यात्मिक) physical (आधिभौतिक) and elemental (ग्राधिदैविक) afflictions.

[2]This person: The man who follows the teachings of the Vedas.

[3]Mr. Griffith interprets all the words in this verse as names of different demons, This explanation does not appeal to me.

[4]'I' refers to mother or father.

४. दुर्णामा च सुनामा चोभा संवृतमिच्छतः । अरायानप हन्मः सुनामा स्त्रैणमिच्छताम् ॥

4. A miserable person suffering from a fell disease, and a beautiful virtuous man, both long for marriage. We drive away the characterless, low man, and let the beautiful, noble one woo the girl. (2156)

५. यः कृष्णः केश्यसुर स्तम्बज उत तुण्डिकः । अरायानस्या मुष्काभ्यां भंससोप हन्मसि ॥

5. We keep away from the generative organ, and haunches of this girl, to preserve her chastity, a doer of dark deeds, a long-haired uncultured person, a glutton, a savage, a man ugly faced like a monkey, and all such ill-mannered, low-bred people. (2157)[1]

६. अनुजिघ्रं प्रमृशन्तं क्रव्यादमुत रेरिहम् । अरायाञ्छ्वकिष्किणो बजः पिङ्गो अनीनशत् ॥

6. A powerful, wealthy, eloquent person eclipses one who resorts to fragrant substances in overpowering a girl, or captivates her through his magic touch, is a meat-eater, a greedy fellow, or subservient to others like a dog, and all other ill-mannered and low-bred people. (2158)[2]

७. यस्त्वा स्वप्ने निपद्यते भ्राता भूत्वा पितेव च । बजस्तान्त्सहतामितः क्लीबरूपांस्तिरीटिनः ॥

7. O woman, whoever in thy brother's shape or father's comes to thee in sleep,—let thy excellent, noble husband rout and chase them, who are eunuchs and sinful persons! (2159)

८. यस्त्वा स्वपन्तीं त्सरति यस्त्वा दिप्सति जाग्रतीम् ।
छायामिव प्र तान्त्सूर्यः परिक्रामन्ननीनशत् ॥

8. Whoever steals to thee asleep or thinks to harm thee when awake, let the vigilant king, ever awake, remove them, as the sun drives darkness away. (2160)[3]

९. यः कृणोति मृतवत्सामवतोकामिमां स्त्रियम् । तमोषधे त्वं नाशयास्याः कमलमञ्जिवम् ॥

9. Whoever causeth her bear a dead child, or brings about her abortion, O thou terrible king, destroy him, the lustful paramour of hers. (2161)[4]

१०. ये शालाः परिनृत्यन्ति सायं गर्दभनादिनः ।
कुसूला ये च कुक्षिलाः ककुभाः करुमाः स्रिमाः ।
तानोषधे त्वं गन्धेन विषूचीनान् वि नाशय ॥

[1]'We' refers to parents and relatives. They should protect the chastity of the girl, and save her from falling into the clutches of debauchees.

[2]A strong, virtuous, wealthy person should be selected as bridegroom and not others who are greedy, flattering, meat-eaters and resorters to cruel and objectionable devices.

[3]'Thee' refers to the woman.

[4]A king like medicine is a panacea for all ills and misdeeds in his state.

10. The wanderers, who at evening, like the bray of asses, dance about, those who are unnecessary intruders, corpulent, ill-clad, slanderers, and vagabonds, O King, the punisher of sinners, destroy these depraved people with thy chastising might, as medicine with its pungent smell destroys the germs! (2162)

११. ये कुकुन्धाः कुकूरभाः कृत्तीर्दूर्शानि बिभ्रति ।
क्लीबा इव प्रनृत्यन्तो वने ये कुर्वते घोषं तानितो नाशयामसि ॥

11. Eaters of flesh and bones, users of foul language, who dress themselves in hides and skins, who dance about like eunuchs, who raise a wild clamour in the wood, all these we banish far away. (2163)

१२. ये सूर्यं न तितिक्षन्त आतपन्तममुं दिवः ।
अरायान् बस्तवासिनो दुर्गन्धील्लोहितास्यान् मककान् नाशयामसि ॥

12. All those who cannot bear the Sun who warms us yonder from the sky, and hide themselves at night, penniless, wretched people, who dress themselves in goat's skin, maladorous, with bloody mouths, such characterless persons, we drive away. (2164)

१३. य आत्मानमतिमात्रमंस आधाय बिभ्रति । स्त्रीणां श्रोणिप्रतोदिन इन्द्र रक्षांसि नाशय ॥

13. All those who on their shoulders bear a head of monstrous magnitude, who pierce the women's loins with pain,—those demons, O king, drive away! (2165)[1]

१४. ये पूर्वे वध्वो३ यन्ति हस्ते शृङ्गाणि बिभ्रतः ।
आपाकेष्ठाः प्रहासिन स्तम्बे ये कुर्वते ज्योतिस्तानितो नाशयामसि ॥

14. Those, who bearing arms in their hands approach the ladies, or standing in lonely, dreary, dilapidated places cut jokes with them, those who in bushes flash forth light to frighten people, all these we banish hence away. (2166)

१५. येषां पश्चात् प्रपदानि पुरः पार्ष्णीः पुरो मुखा ।
खलजाः शकधूमजा उरुण्डा ये च मट्मटाः कुम्भमुष्का अयाशवः ।
तानस्या ब्रह्मणस्पते प्रतीबोधेन नाशय ॥

15. Those who have retroverted toes, and heels and faces in the front, sons of rascals; powerful, ignorant prattlers, copartners in mischief, highly vexacious people, those who possess pitcher-like big scrotum, and are impotent, these O Vedic scholar, drive thou, far from this girl with vigilance. (2167)[2]

[1]All those: Persons who are hypocrites, try to pass as rich, intellectual persons.
Pierce the women's loins: Misbehave towards women.

[2]Learned persons should protect innocent girls from falling into the clutches of men of bad character.

१६. पर्यस्ताक्षा अप्रचङ्कशा अस्त्रैणाः सन्तु पण्डगाः ।
अव भेषज पादय य इमां संविवृत्सत्यपतिः स्वपतिं स्त्रियम् ॥

16. Squint-eyed, lame, sightless, impotent persons should remain womanless. O king, cast away him, who, not being her husband, would approach this woman wedded to her lord. (2168)[1]

१७. उद्धर्षिणं मुनिकेशं जम्भयन्तं मरीमृशम् । उपेषन्तमुदुम्बलं तुण्डेलमुत शालुडम् ।
पदा प्र विध्य पार्ष्ण्या स्थालीं गौरिव स्पन्दना ॥

17. Just as a hasty cow kicks over with foot and heel the milk-pan, so do thou O woman trample under thy foot and heel, a lascivious person, an impostor who wears long hair like a sage, a violent man, one who touches his private parts again and again, a frequent visitor, a debauchee, a snouty fellow, and a rascal. (2169)

१८. यस्ते गर्भं प्रतिमृशाज्जातं वा मारयाति ते । पिङ्गस्तमुग्रधन्वा कृणोतु हृदयाविधम् ॥

18. If one should injure the babe in thy womb, or kill thine infant newly born, the king with mighty bow shall pierce him even to the heart. (2170)

१९. ये अम्नो जातान् मारयन्ति सूतिका अनुशेरते ।
स्त्रीभागान् पिङ्गो गन्धर्वान् वातो अभ्रमिवाजतु ॥

19. Those who kill infants unawares, and cohabit the new-made mothers, let the powerful king chase the amorous debauchees as wind chases cloud. (2171)

२०. परिसृष्टं धारयतु यद्धितं माव पादि तत् । गर्भं त उग्रौ रक्षतां भेषजौ नीविभार्यौ ॥

20. Let the woman preserve the genial seed: let the laid embryo rest secure. Let both strong king and husband, the guardians of the wealth and conception of the woman, protect the babe (2172).

२१. पवीनसात् तङ्गल्वा३च्छायकादुत नग्नकात् ।
प्रजायै पत्ये त्वा पिङ्गः परि पातु किमीदिनः ॥

21. O woman, for thy children and husband, may the king shield thee well, from foul-nosed, swollen cheeked, ugly, naked, stupid uncivilised vagabonds! (2173)

२२. द्व्यास्याच्चतुरक्षात् पञ्चपादादनङ्गुरेः । वृन्तादभि प्रसर्पतः परि पाहि वरीवृतात् ॥

22. O physician, guard the woman from the birth of a double-faced, four-eyed, five-footed, fingerless, round-bodied, child, descending from the uterus! (2174)

[1]Physically deformed and impotent persons should not be allowed to marry.

२३. य आमं मांसमदन्ति पौरुषेयं च ये क्रविः । गर्भान् खादन्ति केशवास्तानितो नाशयामसि ॥

23. Those who eat flesh uncooked, and those who eat the bleeding flesh of man, feeders on babes unborn, long-haired impostors, far from this place we banish them. (2175)

२४. ये सूर्यात् परिसर्पन्ति स्नुषेव श्वशुरादधि ।
बजश्च तेषां पिङ्गश्च हृदयेऽधि नि विध्यताम् ॥

24. Thieves and dacoits shun the light of the Sun, as a woman through modesty shuns her husband's father. Deep down into the heart of these let an energetic and powerful person pierce. (2176)

२५. पिङ्ग रक्ष जायमानं मा पुमांसं स्त्रियं क्रन् ।
आण्डादो गर्भान्मा दभन् बाधस्वेतः किमीदिनः ॥

25. O physician, preserve the babe at birth, let not the male or female child be put to trouble. Let not the germ that devours the unborn babe, destroy the embryos. Drive far away such mean, hungry worms. (2177)

२६. अप्रजास्त्वं मार्तवत्समाद् रोदमघमावयम् । वृक्षादिव स्रजं कृत्वाप्रिये प्रति मुञ्च तत् ॥

26. Sterility, and infants' death, and weeping that announceth woe,—O man, lay them on the enemy, as thou wouldst lay a garland made from the flowers of a tree on one dear and near to thee. (2178)

Chapter (Anuvāka) 4

HYMN VII

१. या बभ्रवो याश्च शुक्रा रोहिणीरुत पृश्नयः ।
असिक्नीः कृष्णा ओषधीः सर्वा अच्छावदामसि ॥

1. All invigorating, semen, augmenting, health-infusing, highly brittle, highly efficacious, attractive medicines, we use for curing ailments. (2179)[1]

२. त्रायन्तामिमं पुरुषं यक्ष्माद् देवेषितादधि ।
यासां द्यौष्पिता पृथिवी माता समुद्रो मूलं वीरुधां बभूव ॥

2. May the herbs, whose father is the Sun, their mother Earth, the water their root, deliver this man from consumption, born of lust. (2180)[2]

[1]These medicines are distinguished by their colours as well. The verse can then mean, the tawny-coloured, the pale, the variegated, the red, the dusky tinted and the black medicines.

[2]Father: The heat of the Sun nourishes the herbs.

Mother: Herbs derive their juice and sustenance from Earth.

Root: In rainy season, water makes the herbs grow. Excessive sexual indulgence results in consumption.

३. आपो अग्रं दिव्या ओषधयः । तास्ते यक्ष्ममेनस्य१मङ्गादङ्गादनीनशन् ॥

3. The waters are the sovereign remedy, herbs possess divine efficacy, from every limb of thine, O patient, have they removed Consumption caused by sin. (2181)[1]

४. प्रस्तृणती स्तम्बिनीरेकशुङ्गाः प्रतन्वतीरोषधीरा वदामि ।
अंशुमतीः काण्डिनीर्या विशाखा ह्वयामि ते वीरुधो वैश्वदेवीरुग्राः पुरुषजीवनीः ॥

4. I instruct thee in the use of leafy, bushy, single sprouted, wide spreading herbs. I inform thee, of fibrous, bunchy, multi-branched, highly efficacious, powerful herbs, giving life to men. (2182)[2]

५. यद् वः सहः सहमाना वीर्यं१ यच्च वो बलम् ।
तेनेममस्माद् यक्ष्मात् पुरुषं मुञ्चतौषधीरथो कृणोमि भेषजम् ॥

5. Ye, healing plants, the conquering strength, the power and might, which ye possess, therewith deliver this man from this consumption: for this I prepare the remedy. (2183)[3]

६. जीवलां नघारिषां जीवन्तीमोषधीमहम् ।
अरुन्धतीमुन्नयन्तीं पुष्पां मधुमतीमिह हुवेऽस्मा अरिष्टतातये ॥

6. For restoring this patient to health, I use the strength-infusing harmless, life-prolonging health-maintaining, healing, flowery, sweet medicine. (2184)[4]

७. इहा यन्तु प्रचेतसो मेदिनीवर्चसो मम । यथेमं पारयामसि पुरुषं दुरितादधि ॥

7. Hitherward let the efficacious medicines come, as directed by me, a skilled physician, that we may give this man relief and raise him from his miserable plight. (2185)

८. अग्नेर्घासो अपां गर्भो या रोहन्ति पुनर्णवाः । ध्रुवाः सहस्रनाम्नीर्भेषजीः सन्त्वाभृताः ॥

8. Plants, increasing physical strength, full of juice, ever growing fresh and new, sure, healing, bearing thousand names, let them be all collected here. (2186)

९. अवकोल्बा उदकात्मान ओषधयः । व्यृषन्तु दुरितं तीक्ष्णशृङ्ग्यः ॥

[1]The science of hydropathy cures ailments through the proper use of water.

[2]I: God. Thee: the patient.

[3]I: A skilled physician.

[4]Some commentators consider Jivanti and Arundhati as names of medicines. Jivanti means life-prolonging. Arundhati means a medicine that prevents the body from decaying.

I: A learned physician.

9. Let plants that banish pain, whose soul is water, piercing with their sharp horns expel the malady. (2187)[1]

१०. उन्मुञ्चन्तीर्विवरुणा उग्रा या विषदूषणीः ।
अथो बलासनाशनीः कृत्यादूषणीश्च यास्ता इहा यन्त्वोषधीः ॥

10. Medicines that free us from disease, cure dropsy, are strong in action, are antidotes of poison, remove cough and pneumonia, alleviate pain; let all of them be collected in this medical hall. (2188)

११. अपक्रीताः सहीयसीर्वीरुधो या अभिष्टुताः । त्रायन्तामस्मिन् ग्रामे गामश्वं पुरुषं पशुम् ॥

11. Let purchased herbs of great potency, herbs that are praised for excellence, here in this village preserve cow, horse, man and beast. (2189)

१२. मधुमन्मूलं मधुमदग्रमासां मधुमन्मध्यं वीरुधां बभूव । मधुमत् पर्णं मधुमत्
पुष्पमासां मधोः संभक्ता अमृतस्य भक्षो घृतमन्नं दुह्रतां गोपुरोगवम् ॥

12. Sweet is their root, sweet are these plants, top branches, sweet also is their intermediate portion; sweet is their foliage, and sweet their blossom. All these plants are combined with sweetness. They conduce to longevity. They bestow butter and food, of which all the cow's milk is the best. (2190)

१३. यावतीः कियतीश्चेमाः पृथिव्यामध्योषधीः । ता मा सहस्रपर्ण्यो मृत्योर्मुञ्चन्त्वंहसः ॥

13. These plants that grow upon the earth, whate'er their number and their size,—let these with all their thousand leaves free me from the pangs of death. (2191)

१४. वैयाघ्रो मणिर्वीरुधां त्रायमाणोऽभिशस्तिपाः ।
अमीवाः सर्वा रक्षांस्यप हन्त्वधि दूरमस्मत् ॥

14. May the plants' excellent efficacy, protective, guardian from pain, drive all maladies afar from us, and beat off the brood of their germs. (2192)[2]

१५. सिंहस्येव स्तनथोः सं विजन्तेऽग्नेरिव विजन्त आभृताभ्याः ।
गवां यक्ष्मः पुरुषाणां वीरुद्भिरतिनुत्तो नाव्या एतु स्रोत्याः ॥

15. As cattle are afraid of a lion's roar or fire, so are diseases afraid of medicinal herbs. Expelled by herbs, let men's and kine's consumption go away from our organs, as streams are crossed through boats. (2193)

१६. मुमुचाना ओषधयोऽग्नेर्वैश्वानरादधि । भूमिं संतन्वतीरित यासां राजा वनस्पतिः ॥

16. O medicinal herbs, whose ruler is Soma, ye, emancipators from all ailments, depending upon God, the Benefactor of humanity, go and spread yourselves on the earth! (2194)

[1]Whose soul is water: which cannot live and grow without water.

[2]मणि has been translated by Griffith as amulet. The word means efficacy, potency.

१७. या रोहन्त्याङ्गिरसीः पर्वतेषु समेषु च । ता नः पयस्वतीः शिवा ओषधीः सन्तु शं हृदे ॥

17. May these be pleasant to our heart, auspicious, rich in store of milk, these plants tested by the learned physicians, which grow on mountains and on plains. (2195)

१८. याश्चाहं वेद वीरुधो याश्च पश्यामि चक्षुषा ।
अज्ञाता जानीमश्च या यासु विद्म च संभृतम् ॥

18. The plants I know myself, the plants that with mine eye I look upon, plants yet unknown, and those we know, wherein we find that healing power is stored. (2196)

१९. सर्वाः समग्रा ओषधीर्बोधन्तु वचसो मम । यथेमं पारयामसि पुरुषं दुरितादधि ॥

19. Let all the aggregated plants attend and mark mine utterance, that we may rescue this man and save him from distressing disease. (2197)[1]

२०. अश्वत्थो दर्भो वीरुधां सोमो राजामृतं हविः । व्रीहिर्यवश्च भेषजौ दिवस्पुत्रावमर्त्यौ ॥

20. The holy fig tree, sacrificial grass, Soma, the King of plants, water, corn, possesses medicinal properties. Rice, barley are highly healing balms, which nourish us from heaven like sons. (2198)[2]

२१. उज्जिहीध्वे स्तनयत्यभिक्रन्दत्योषधीः । यदा वः पृश्निमातरः पर्जन्यो रेतसावति ॥

21. O healing plants, ye children of Earth, ye lift yourselves up, when the cloud thunders, roars, and blesseth you with full flow of water. (2199)

२२. तस्यामृतस्येमं बलं पुरुषं पाययामसि । अथो कृणोमि भेषजं यथासच्छतहायनः ॥

22. We give the essence of that stream of nectar to this man to drink so I prepare a remedy that he may live a hundred years. (2200)

२३. वराहो वेद वीरुधं नकुलो वेद भेषजीम् । सर्पा गन्धर्वा या विदुस्ता अस्मा अवसे हुवे ॥

23. I call, to aid this ailing man, the plants which the wild boar, the mungoose, the serpents, the kine, cowherds and learned persons know. (2201)[3]

२४. याः सुपर्णा आङ्गिरसीर्दिव्या या रघटो विदुः ।
वयांसि हंसा या विदुर्याश्च सर्वे पतत्रिणः । मृगा या विदुरोषधीस्ता अस्मा अवसे हुवे ॥

[1]Mine: Of a learned physician.

[2]Holy fig tree: Pipal.
Sacrificial grass: Durbh, Kushā, Rice and barley grow through rain, and nourish us, as sons do their parents. Fig tree is called Ficus Religiosa. Its shelter, use of drinking of the boiled water of its leaves are the cure for consumption.

[3]Wild pigs are quick at discovering and unearthing potatoes and all sorts of edible roots (Griffith) Mungoose, serpents, cows also know some medicines by their smell.
I: A skilled physician.

24. Plants described by learned sages, which hawks know, healing plants which eagles know, plants known to crows and swans, plants known to all the birds that fly, plants that are known to sylvan beasts,—I call them all to aid this ailing man. (2202)

२५. यावतीनामोषधीनां गावः प्राश्नन्त्यघ्न्या यावतीनामजावयः ।
तावतीस्तुभ्यमोषधीः शर्म यच्छन्त्वाभृताः ॥

25. The multitude of herbs whereon the cows whom none may slaughter feed, all that are food for goats and sheep, so many plants, brought hitherward, give health and happiness to thee! (2203)

२६. यावतीषु मनुष्या भेषजं भिषजो विदुः । तावतीर्विश्वभेषजीरा भरामि त्वामभि ॥

26. Hitherward unto thee I bring the plants that cure all maladies, all plants wherein physicians have discovered health-bestowing power. (2204)

२७. पुष्पवतीः प्रसूमतीः फलिनीरफला उत । संमातर इव दुह्रामस्मा अरिष्टतातये ॥

27. Let plants with flower and plants with bud, the fruitful and the fruitless, all, like nice mothers, yield their stores for this man's perfect health. (2205)

२८. उत् त्वाहार्षं पञ्चशलादथो दशशलादुत ।
अथो यमस्य पड्वीशाद् विश्वस्माद् देवकिल्बिषात् ॥

28. I have delivered thee from the sufferings of five breaths (Pranas), from the sufferings of ten organs. I have freed thee from Death's fetter and from all offence against the behest of God. (2206)[1]

HYMN VIII

१. इन्द्रो मन्थतु मन्थिता शक्रः शूरः पुरंदरः । यथा हनाम सेना अमित्राणां सहस्रशः ॥

1. May King, the fort-demolisher, brave, powerful, shaker of foes, shake them up, so that we may kill thousands of soldiers of our enemies! (2207)

२. पूतिरज्जुरुपध्मानी पूतिं सेनां कृणोत्वमूम् । धूममग्निं परादृश्यामित्रा हृत्स्वा दधतां भयम् ॥

2. Just as a decayed string easily catches fire, so should the king shatter this army of the enemy. O King let terror smite our foemen's hearts when fire and smoke are seen afar. (2208)[2]

३. अमूनश्वत्थ निः शृणीहि खादामून खदिराजिरम् ।
ताजद्भङ्ग इव भज्यन्तां हन्त्वेनान् वधको वधैः ॥

3. O horsemen, destroy these foes. O warriors, attack these enemies quickly. Let the enemies be broken through like a dry castor-oil plant. Let armed soldiers kill the enemies with different deadly war-like instruments. (2209)[3]

[1]Thee: The patient.

[2]Fire and smoke: The smoke that arises when fiery instruments are exploded.

[3]Ashwath, Khadira and Badhaka are three kinds of soldiers, who fight in a battle. Pt. Khem Karan Trivedi interprets Khadira as general of the army.

४. परुषानमून् परुषाह्वः कृणोतु हन्त्वेनान् वधको वधैः ।
क्षिप्रं शर इव भज्यन्तां बृहज्जालेन संदिताः ॥

4. Let the hard-hearted general make his soldiers strong-minded. Let armed soldiers kill these enemies with deadly weapons. Bound in a mighty net let them break quickly like a blade of grass. (2210)

५. अन्तरिक्षं जालमासीज्जालदण्डा दिशो महीः । तेनाभिधाय दस्यूनां शक्रः सेनामपावपत् ॥

5. Atmosphere is the net, the poles thereof are the great quarters of the sky. A powerful general therewith makes the army of dacoits run hither and thither. (2211)

६ बृहद्धि जालं बृहतः शक्रस्य वाजिनीवतः ।
तेन शत्रूनभि सर्वान् न्युब्ज यथा न मुच्यातै कतमश्चनैषाम् ॥

6. Verily mighty is the net of the mighty general, rich in military equipment. O general subjugate all the foemen so that not one of them may escape! (2212)[1]

७. बृहत् ते जालं बृहत इन्द्र शूर सहस्रार्घस्य शतवीर्यस्य ।
तेन शतं सहस्रमयुतं न्यर्बुदं जघान शक्रो दस्यूनामभिधाय सेनया ॥

7. O brave Commander, match for a thousand, lord of hundred powers, great and mighty is thy net; therewith, holding with thy army, O powerful general, the dacoits thou can slaughter a hundred, thousand, myriad, hundred millions of them! (2213)

८. अयं लोको जालमासीच्छक्रस्य महतो महान् ।
तेनाहमिन्द्रजालेनामूंस्तमसाभि दधामि सर्वान् ॥

8. This mighty world is the net of the Almighty Father. With this, the net of God, I envelop all those foes with gloom. (2214)[2]

९. सेदिरुग्रा व्यृद्धिरार्तिश्चानपवाचना । श्रमस्तन्द्रीश्च मोहश्च तैरमूनभि दधामि सर्वान् ॥

9. Great weakness and misfortune, pain which words can never charm away, langour, fatique, bewilderment with these I compass, all the foes. (2215)[3]

१०. मृत्यवेऽमून् प्र यच्छामि मृत्युपाशैरमी सिताः ।
मृत्योर्ये अघला दूतास्तेभ्य एनान् प्रति नयामि बद्ध्वा ॥

[1]Net: Binding force.

[2]'I' refers to the King or commander-in-chief Indarjal is, in the Mahabharata, the name of a wonderful weapon wielded by the hero Arjuna. A king envelopes the enemies in this world with the smoke of fiery weapons and kills them.

[3]'I' refers to the Commander-in-Chief.

10. I give these foemen up to Death: bound in the bonds of Death are they. I bind and carry them away to meet Death's wicked messengers. (2216)[1]

११. नयतामून् मृत्युदूता यमदूता अपोम्भत । परःसहस्रा हन्यन्तां तृणेढ्वेनान् मत्यं भवस्य ॥

11. Bear them away, ye executioners, Death's messengers! envoys of Death! finish them. May they be slain in thousands. May the king's thunderbolt crush them to pieces. (2217)

१२. साध्या एकं जालदण्डमुद्यत्य यन्त्योजसा । रुद्रा एकं वसव एकमादित्यैरेक उद्यतः ॥

12. Forth go the Sadhyas in their might bearing one pillar of administration raised aloft. One pillar the Rudras carry, one the vasus, and the Adityas one. (2218)[2]

१३. विश्वे देवा उपरिष्टादुब्जन्तो यन्त्वोजसा । मध्येन घ्नन्तो यन्तु सेनामङ्गिरसो महीम् ॥

13. All warriors anxious for victory should attack from above, depressing the foe with might. Learned soldiers well versed in the use of special weapons should go in the midst, slaying the mighty army of the enemy. (2219)

१४. वनस्पतीन् वानस्पत्यानोषधीरुत वीरुधः । द्विपाच्चतुष्पादिष्णामि यथा सेनाममूं हनन् ॥

14. God-fearing soldiers with their equipment, trappings and outfit, herbs and plants, biped, and quadruped, send I forth that they may strike the army of the enemy dead. (2220)[3]

१५. गन्धर्वाप्सरसः सर्पान् देवान् पुण्यजनान् पितॄन् ।
दृष्टानदृष्टानिष्णामि यथा सेनाममूं हनन् ॥

15. Patriots, aeronauts soldiers keen-sighted like serpents, victory-minded noble, learned, seen and unseen warriors, I send them forth that they may strike the army of the enemy dead. (2221)[4]

१६. इम उप्ता मृत्युपाशा यानाक्रम्य न मुच्यसे । अमुष्या हन्तु सेनाया इदं कूटं सहस्रशः ॥

16. Here spread are snares of Death, wherefrom thou, once within them, ne'er art freed, full many a thousand of the host yonder this horn shall smite and slay. (2222)

[1]Wicked messengers: Executioners, slaughters appointed by the king to kill the captured foes.

[2]Sadhyas: Men full of philanthrophy and public spirit, resourceful in nature.

Rudra: Rudra Brahmcharies or powerful persons who kill the foes.

Wasus: Wasu Brahmcharies or noble, intellectual persons.

Adityas: Fully learned persons, having full control over their senses.

These four kinds of persons, successfully carry on the administration of the state.

[3]Herbs and plants: Medicines required for the wounded soldiers.

Quadruped: Horses, mules, elephants, etc., required for transport.

'I' refers to the Commander-in-Chief.

[4]Seen and unseen: A king is not expected to know each and every soldier of his army. He knows some of them and some he has not seen.

१७. धर्मः समिद्धो अग्निनायं होमः सहस्रहः । भवश्च पृश्निबाहुश्च शर्व सेनाममूं हतम् ॥

17. The blazing Yajna of battle, wherein thousands are killed, has been kindled by the king. O powerful King, O stout-armed general, O foe-destroying warrior strike dead that army of the enemy. (2223)[1]

१८. मृत्योराषमा पद्यन्तां क्षुधं सेदिं वधं भयम् । इन्द्रश्चाक्षुजालाभ्यां शर्व सेनाममूं हतम् ॥

18. Let the enemy deserve the pang of death, hunger, exhaustion, slaughter, fear. With your entangling snares and nets, O King and foe-destroying warrior, slay that army of the enemy. (2224)

१९. पराजिताः प्र त्रसतामित्रा नुत्ता धावत ब्रह्मणा ।
बृहस्पतिप्रणुत्तानां मामीषां मोचि कश्चन ॥

19. Fly, conquered, in alarm, ye foes, run driven away by the learned general. Let not one man escape of those when routed by a Vedic scholar. (2225)

२०. अव पद्यन्तामेषामायुधानि मा शकन् प्रतिधामिषुम् ।
अथैषां बहु बिभ्यतामिषवो घ्नन्तु मर्मणि ॥

20. Down fall their weapons on the ground; no strength be theirs to shoot a shaft: then in their dreadful terror let arrows wound their vital parts. (2226)

२१. सं क्रोशतामेनान् द्यावापृथिवी समन्तरिक्षं सह देवताभिः ।
मा ज्ञातारं मा प्रतिष्ठां विदन्त मिथो विघ्नाना उप यन्तु मृत्युम् ॥

21. Let Heaven and Earth, and Air with all the forces of Nature censure them. Let them not find a learned man for assistance nor a shelter, but fighting mutually let them go down to Death together. (2227)[2]

२२. दिशश्चतस्रोऽश्वतर्यो देवरथस्य पुरोडाशाः शफा अन्तरिक्षमुद्धिः ।
द्यावापृथिवी पक्षसी ऋतवोऽभीशवोऽन्तर्देशाः किंकरा वाक् परिरथ्यम् ॥

22. The mules of this world-like car of God are heaven's four quarters; their hooves are the materials of the Yajña, the air its body, its sides are Heaven and Earth, its reins the seasons, voice is its hood, its grooms are sky's mid-regions. (2228)[3]

२३. संवत्सरो रथः परिवत्सरो रथोपस्थो विराडीषाग्नी रथमुखम् ।
इन्द्रः सव्यष्ठाश्चन्द्रमाः सारथिः ॥

[1]Griffith translates Prisnibahu as a mythical being, having speckled arms. This explanation is unacceptable as there is no history in the Vedas. The word means a stout-armed general.

[2]Them: Foes.

[3]The language is figurative, and not so clear to me. It is strange no commentator has given its full explanation, neither Pt. Raja Ram, nor Pt. Jaidev Vidyalankar, nor Pt. Khem Karan Das Trivedi nor Damodar Satvalekar nor Sayāna nor Griffith.

23. Year is the car, full year the seat for driving, Created world the pole, the chariot, front is fire, the sun is the warrior, and the Moon the driver. (2229)[1]

२४. इतो जयेतो वि जय सं जय जय स्वाहा ।
इमे जयन्तु परामी जयन्तां स्वाहैभ्यो दुराहामीभ्यः । नीललोहितेनामूनभ्यवतनोमि ॥

24. O King, conquer, conquer well, be thou the full victor, gain victory, get fame and renown in the world. Let these our men be conquerors, and those of the foe be conquered. Let these court reputation and they disgrace. With the help of dark-blue and red dressed soldiers I subdue the foes. (2230)

Chapter (Anuvāka) 5

HYMN IX

१. कुतस्तौ जातौ कतमः सो अर्धः कस्माल्लोकात् कतमस्याः पृथिव्याः ।
वत्सौ विराजः सलिलादुदैतां तौ त्वा पृच्छामि कतरेण दुग्धा ॥

1. Whence were these two (God and soul) manifested. Out of many that God possesses supernatural powers. From which world, from which earth have they, the expositors of minute Matter come into being from an ocean-like unfathomable state! I ask thee of these twain, who out of them has perfected Matter. (2231)[2]

२. यो अक्रन्दयत् सलिलं महित्वा योनिं कृत्वा त्रिभुजं शयानः ।
वत्सः कामदुघो विराजः स गुहा चक्रे तन्वः पराचैः ॥

2. God agitates Matter. Preparing a threefold home through His greatness, He pervades all objects. God, the Fulfiller of all wishes, the Enveloper of Matter, creates in the atmosphere, vast distant worlds. (2232)

३. यानि त्रीणि बृहन्ति येषां चतुर्थं वियुनक्ति वाचम् ।
ब्रह्मैनद् विद्यात् तपसा विपश्चिद् यस्मिन्नेकं युज्यते यस्मिन्नेकम् ॥

3. These are the three mighty forces. The fourth of them is God Who reveals the Vedas. A learned Vedic scholar can realise him through penance. Wherein He alone is discerned through deep concentration Wherein God alone is seen. (2233)[3]

४. बृहतः परि सामानि षष्ठात् पञ्चाधि निर्मिता ।
बृहद् बृहत्या निर्मितं कुतोऽधि बृहती मिता ॥

[1]My remarks about the previous verse apply to this also. Mr. Griffith considers Virät to be a mythical being, created by speculation. This explanation does not appeal to me.

[2]They: God and soul.

Thee: A learned person God and soul, out of their power, exist in all worlds and at all times. Through them are brought into existence all the material forms of matter. God possesses supernatural powers. He creates and dissolves the material universe.

[3]Threefold: Heaven, Firmament, Earth, or high, middle, low places.

4. Five elements were fashioned forth by the sixth Mighty God. From Matter was this vast universe formed whence was the Matter composed. (2234)[1]

५. बृहती परि मात्राया मातुर्मात्राधि निर्मिता ।
माया ह जज्ञे मायाया मायाया मातली परि ॥

5. This material world evolves out of the subtle primary Matter. God changes the subtle matter into material objects. Intellect is born of God the Embodiment of intellect. God lords over the soul. (2235)[2]

६. वैश्वानरस्य प्रतिमोपरि द्यौर्यावद् रोदसी विबबाधे अग्निः ।
ततः षष्ठादामुतो यन्ति स्तोमा उदितो यन्त्यभि षष्ठमह्नः ॥

6. God's extent is as vast as the sky above us. The Refulgent God pervades the Heaven and Earth. From that Omnipresent God come the souls, and go back from here to the same All-pervading Deity. (2236)

७. षट् त्वा पृच्छाम ऋषयः कश्यपेमे त्वं हि युक्तं युयुक्षे योग्यं च ।
विराजमाहुर्ब्रह्मणः पितरं तां नो वि धेहि यतिधा सखिभ्यः ॥

7. O learned soul, we six Rishis ask thee for thou unites a yogi in samadhi, with God, realizable through concentration. God is called the Father of the vast universe. Tell us thy friends, of Him in all His aspects. (2237)[3]

८. यां प्रच्युतामनु यज्ञाः प्रच्यवन्त उपतिष्ठन्त उपतिष्ठमानाम् ।
यस्या व्रते प्रसवे यक्षमेजति सा विराडृषयः परमे व्योऽमन् ॥

8. With the dissolution of Matter into its nascent atomic state. The world, disappear. With its reappearance the worlds reappear. Under whose law and behest this universe comes into existence, that God is Supreme, and Protector of the world. (2238)[4]

९. अप्राणैति प्राणेन प्राणतीनां विराट् स्वराजमभ्येऽति पश्चात् ।
विश्वं मृशन्तीमभिरूपां विराजं पश्यन्ति त्वे न त्वे पश्यन्त्येनाम् ॥

9. Breathless Matter moves by breath of living creatures. Lifeless Matter goes closely after the self-luminous Supreme Being. Some wise persons behold and some ignorant persons do not behold the matter when it assumes different forms by the touch of the All-pervading God. (2239)

[1]Five elements: Panch Bhut, Air, Water, Fire, Earth, Atmosphere, i.e., Vayu, Jal, Agni, Prithivi and Akash.

[2]Mr. Griffith interprets Mātali as the name of a divine being. This is wrong, as there is no history in the Vedas. The word means the soul.

[3]Six Rishis: Skin, Eye, Ear, Tongue, Nose, Mind. सप्त ऋषयः षडिन्द्रियाणि विधा सप्तमी निरुता १२-३७.

[4]God creates the universe out of Matter. It lasts for 4320000000 years. God dissolves it and recreates it. This process is going on since eternity. This is Vedic doctrine.

१०. को विराजो मिथुनत्वं प्र वेद क ऋतून् क उ कल्पमस्याः ।
क्रमान् को अस्याः कतिधा विदुग्धान् को अस्या धाम कतिधा व्युऽष्टीः ॥

10. Who knows exactly the relation of Matter with God? Who knows her timings of creating the universe? Who knows her creative power? Who knows her rules? Who knows how often it has been resolved into material creation? Who knows its retentive power? Who knows its manifold captivating powers? (2240)[1]

११. इयमेव सा या प्रथमा व्यौच्छदास्वितरासु चरति प्रविष्टा ।
महान्तो अस्यां महिमानो अन्तर्वधूर्जिगाय नवगज्जनित्री ॥

11. This Matter first of all sent forth her lustre. She moves on assuming the shape of these and other worlds. Exalted power and might are stored within her. Just as a girl newly made mother wins the heart of her husband, so does Matter captivate all. (2241)

१२. छन्दःपक्षे उषसा पेपिशाने समानं योनिमनु सं चरेते ।
सूर्यपत्नी सं चरतः प्रजानती केतुमती अजरे भूरिरेतसा ॥

12. Both morning and evening rich in beauty, independently move on together to their common dwelling. Day and Night, two wives of the sun knowing their path, rich in light, unwasting, most prolific move together. (2242)[1]

१३. ऋतस्य पन्थामनु तिस्र आगुस्त्रयो घर्मा अनु रेत आगुः ।
प्रजामेका जिन्वत्यूर्जमेका राष्ट्रमेका रक्षति देवयूनाम् ॥

13. He who follows the teachings of the Vedas, develops his three physical, mental and spiritual forces. The duties of the Brahmchari Grihastha and Banprastha orders can be fully discharged through heroism alone. Out of these three forces, one quickens progeny, one strengthens vigour and one protects the kingdom of the pious. (2243)[3]

१४. अग्नीषोमावदधुर्या तुरीयासीद्यज्ञस्य पक्षावृषयः कल्पयन्तः ।
गायत्रीं त्रिष्टुभं जगतीमनुष्टुभं बृहदर्की यजमानाय स्वऽराभरन्तीम् ॥

[1]Who knows: None knows. God alone knows the different aspects and powers of Matter.

[2]Wives of the Sun: Sustained and nourished by the Sun, as wives are by the husband.
Common dwelling: The Sun.
Most prolific: Day and Night give birth to thousands of creatures.

[3]The word three has been interpreted differently by different commentators. Pt. Jaidev interprets it as Ādhiatmic, Ādhibhautik and Ādhidevik forces. Pt. Khem Karn Das Trivedi interprets it as Ida, Saraswati and Bharti, i.e., statemanship, Intellect and knowledge. Mr. Griffith interprets it as Dawn, Sunlight and Night.
Sayāna interprets it as Fire, Sun and Moon.
I have accepted the interpretation of Pt. Damodar Satvalekar.

14. The sages consider God and soul as two flanks of the Yajña of life. They realise the fourth highest power of God, which guards our vital breaths is worshipped through action, contemplation and knowledge, is ever active and wise, ever worthy of veneration, highly adorable, and the bestower of salvation to the worshipper. (2244)[1]

१५. पञ्च व्युष्टीरनु पञ्च दोहा गां पञ्चनाम्नीमृतवोऽनु पञ्च ।
पञ्च दिशः पञ्चदशेन क्लृप्तास्ता एकमूर्ध्नीरभि लोकमेकम् ॥

15. Five senses are linked with five elements. Five seasons are like the five breaths of the mind. Five directions are the five organs of cognition, controlled by the soul. These organs are located in the head and connected with the soul. (2245)[1]

१६. षड् जाता भूता प्रथमजर्तस्य षडु सामानि षडहं वहन्ति ।
षड्योगं सीरमनु सामसाम षडाहुर्द्यावापृथिवीः षडुर्वीः ॥

16. Six entities were created in the beginning through the power of God. Those six with their united strength sustain the universe. Breath alone helps the body yoked with six breaths. Hence the learned the learned call the Earth and Heaven sixfold, and the vast Earth sixfold. (2246)[2]

१७. षडाहुः शीतान् षडु मास उष्णानृतुं नो ब्रूत यतमोऽतिरिक्तः ।
सप्त सुपर्णाः कवयो नि षेदुः सप्त च्छन्दांस्यनु सप्त दीक्षाः ॥

17. They call the cold months six, and six the hot ones, which tell us, is there a season besides these? Seven sharp-witted sages are seated in the head. Seven breaths are yoked with seven forces of knowledge. (2247)[3]

१८. सप्त होमाः समिधो ह सप्त मधूनि सप्त ऋतवो ह सप्त ।
सप्ताज्यानि परि भूतमायन् ताः सप्तगृध्रा इति शुश्रुमा वयम् ॥

[1]Fourth: Beyond.

Satva, Rajas, Tamas or beyond the stages of Jagrit (wakeful) Swapana (sleep) Sushupti (Deep slumber). For detailed explanation consult Mandukya Upanishad.

[2]Five senses: Hearing, Touch, Sight, Taste, Smell. Five elements: Earth, Water, Fire, Air, Atmosphere. Five breaths: Prāna, Apāna, Vyāṇa, Udāna, Samāna. Here mind is spoken as a cow. Five organs of cognition: Five Jnāna Indriya i.e., Eye, Ear, Nose, Tongue, Skin. Five directions: North, South, East, West, Zenith. Soul is spoken of as Panchdash possessing the fifteenfold qualities of Prāna, Apāna, Vyāna, Udāna, Samāna, hearing, touch, sight, taste, smell, earth, water, fire, air and atmosphere.

[3]Six entities: Eye, Ear, Tongue, Nose, Skin, Mind. Six breaths: Prāna, Apāna, Vyāna, Udāna, Samāna, Nāga.

[4]There are six cold and six hot months. All seasons are included in these months. Six sages: Two eyes, two ears, two nostrils and mouth.

18. We, the learned, have heard, the soul is equipped with seven rough senses which excite passions, seven subtle senses which imbibe knowledge, seven kinds of knowledge, seven tendencies, seven sources of lust, and seven desires emanating from the organs. (2248)[1]

१९. सप्त च्छन्दांसि चतुरुत्तराण्यन्यो अन्यस्मिन्नध्यार्पितानि ।
कथं स्तोमाः प्रति तिष्ठन्ति तेषु तानि स्तोमेषु कथमार्पितानि ॥

19. Seven apertures in the head are interlinked with the four higher sentiments. How do these seven depend upon the four, and how the four depend upon the seven. (2249)[2]

२०. कथं गायत्री त्रिवृतं व्याप कथं त्रिष्टुप् पञ्चदशेन कल्पते ।
त्रयस्त्रिंशेन जगती कथमनुष्टुप् कथमेकविंशः ॥

20. How does splendour surround the soul, possessing the threefold qualities of Satva, Rajas, Tamas. How is salvation, attainable through action, contemplation, knowledge acquired by the soul, full of fifteen traits. How is the world created by God, the Master of thirty-three forces. How does soul possessing twenty-one forces acquire the knowledge of the Vedas (2250)[3]

२१. अष्ट जाता भूता प्रथमजर्तस्याष्टेन्द्रर्त्विजो दैव्या ये ।
अष्टयोनिरदितिरष्टपुत्राष्टमीं रात्रिमभि हव्यमेति ॥

21. Eight elements sprang up, first born of Matter. O soul, these are the eight divine forces, which contribute to the creation, sustenance and dissolution of the world. Eight are the stages for the acquisition of God, and eight His protecting powers. His infinite power takes man to salvation the giver of tranquility. (2251)[4]

[1]Seven rough senses: Skin, Eye, Ear, Nose, Tongue, Mind, Intellect. Seven subtle senses: Sound, Touch, Sight, Taste, smell, Thought, Meditation.

Seven kinds of knowledge: Knowledge of God, Soul, Matter, Military science, Medicine, Music, Economics. Seven tendencies: Lust, Anger, Avarice, Infatuation, Pride, Hatred, Self-praise. Seven desires: Fame, Wealth, Progeny, Happiness, Worldly position, Health, Salvation.

[2]Seven apertures: Two eyes, two nostrils, two ears, mouth. Four sentiments: Dharma, Arth, Kama, Moksha. These forces are linked with each other. Through the right use of the seven apertures, one attains to these higher sentiments.

[3]Fifteen qualities: See footnote to verse 15. Thirty three forces: Eight vasus, Eleven Rudras, Twelve Adityās, Indra, Prajapati. Vasus: Fire, Earth, Air, Atmosphere, Sun, Moon, Heaven, A star. Rudras: Prāna, Apāna, Vyāna, Udāna, Samāna, Nāga, Kurma, Krikla, Deva Dutta, Dhananjya and Jiv Atma (soul). Adityas: Twelve months. Indra: Lightning, and Prajāpati, i.e., Yajna. Twenty one forces: Five Bhutas, Earth, Water, Fire, Air, Atmosphere, Five Prānas, Five Jnāna Indriyas, Five Karma Indriyas, and Mind.

[4]Eight elements: Intellect, Ego, Earth, Water, Fire, Air, Atmosphere, Mind. Eight stages: Yama, Niyama, Āsana, Prānāyāma, Pratahār, Dhārma, Dhyāna, Smadhi. Protecting powers: Minuteness, (अणिमा) Lightness (लघुमा) Acquisition (प्राप्ति) Freedom of will (पराकाम्य) Greatness, Glory, (महिमा) Supremacy (ईशित्व), Power (वशित्व).

२२. इत्थं श्रेयो मन्यमानेदमागमं युष्माकं सख्ये अहमस्मि शेवा ।
समानजन्मा क्रतुरस्ति वः शिवः स वः सर्वाः सं चरति प्रजानन् ।।

22. So planning bliss for you have I come hither to win your friendship. Kind am I, and gracious. Your companion, God is your well-wisher. He is All-pervading, knowing all your acts and ambitious. (2252)[1]

२३. अष्टेन्द्रस्य षड् यमस्य ऋषीणां सप्त सप्तधा ।
अपो मनुष्या३नोषधीस्ताँ उ पञ्चानु सेचिरे ।।

23. Eight directions and mid-directions, six seasons, organs with their sevenfold inherent powers are the benefactors of a self-controlled soul. Five elements lend vigour to all deeds, men and herbs. (2253)[2]

२४. केवलीन्द्राय दुदुहे हि गृष्टिर्वशं पीयूषं प्रथमं दुहाना ।
अथातर्पयच्चतुरश्चतुर्धा देवान् मनुष्याँ३ असुरानुत ऋषीन् ।।

24. Just as a cow on her first delivery, yields her sweet milk for her first born calf, so does Matter, first yield beautiful immortal pleasure to the emancipated soul, and then satisfies, in four ways. The four categories of victory-minded, reflective, intellectual, religious-minded persons. (2254)[3]

२५. को नु गौः क एकऋषिः किमु धाम का आशिषः ।
यक्षं पृथिव्यामेकवृदेकऋतुः कतमो नु सः ।।

25. Who makes the planets revolve ? Who is the Revealer of the path of righteousness? Who is the sustainer of the universe? Who is the Controller of all objects? Who on the earth, exists alone, and who is beyond the shackles of time? Who is worthy of adoration? (2255)

२६. एको गौरेक एक ऋषिरेकं धामैकधाशिषः । यक्षं पृथिव्यामेकवृदेकऋतुर्नाति रिच्यते ।।

26. God alone is the Revolver of planets. God alone reveals the path of righteousness. He alone sustains the universe. He controls all objects. On this earth He alone is Adorable, Existent and Timeless. He is Unconquerable. (2256)

[1]God is as eternal as the soul. He is therefore the friend of the soul. God is named क्रतु as He is the doer of infinite deeds.

[2]Eight directions: North, East, South, West and four mid-directions. Sevenfold powers: Touch, Sight, Smell, Hearing, Thought, Perception. Five elements: Earth, Water, Fire, Air and Atmosphere.

[3]Four ways: Dharma, Arth, Kāma, Moksha. भोगापवर्गार्थं दृश्यम् ! Sankhya Sutra. Matter is the source of worldly enjoyment as well as of salvation Mr. Griffith considers this Hymn to be unintelligible. He has not been to grasp the real sense of this hymn, which beautifully describes the powers of God and Matter. It is regrettable that the western scholars generally fail to understand the Vedic verses correctly.

HYMN X

Paryaya 1

१. विराड् वा इदमग्र आसीत्तस्या जाताया: सर्वमबिभेदियमेवेदं भविष्यतीति ।

1. In the beginning existed Matter in its primordeal, subtle form. On its change from the invisible to the visible state, all were struck with terror, thinking that this matter in its visible shape, will become the universe. (2257a)

२. सोदक्रामत् सा गार्हपत्ये न्यक्रामत् ॥

2. Matter manifested itself in different physical forms, but was still under the control of God. (2257b)[1]

३. गृहमेधी गृहपतिर्भवति य एवं वेद ॥

3. A householder who knows this secret, becomes the guardian of his wife. (2257c)

४. सोदक्रामत् साहवनीये न्यक्रामत् ॥

4. When matter manifested itself in different physical forms, it assumed the shape of sky, lightning, Yajna and breaths. (2258a)[2]

५. यन्त्यस्य देवा देवहूतिं प्रियो देवानां भवति य एवं वेद ॥

5. He who knows this secret of Matter or the glory of God, becomes dear to the learned, and noble persons listen to his call. (2258b)[3]

६. सोदक्रामत् सा दक्षिणाग्नौ न्यक्रामत् ॥

6. That glory of God manifested itself, and appeared in the shape of the blazing fire of the Sun. (2259a)

७. यज्ञर्तो दक्षिणीयो वासतेयो भवति य एवं वेद ॥

7. Whoso knows this secret becomes a nice performer of Yajnas, worthy of veneration, and the bestower of dwelling place to others. (2259b)

८. सोदक्रामत् सा सभायां न्यक्रामत् ॥

8. The glory of God arose and appeared in the form of the Assembly of of the learned. (2260a)[4]

[1]प्रजापतिर्हं गार्हपत्य: कौ० 29-9 गार्यपत्य is God.

[2]द्यौरा हवनीय: श० 8-6-3-11 Sky is आहवनीय ! इन्द्रो ह्याहवनीय: श० 2-7-1-38 Lightning is Ahvniya यज्ञस्य शिर आहवनीय: श० 6-5-2-1 प्राणोदानायेवाहवनीचश्र गार्हपत्य: श० 2-2-2-18 Prāna and Udāna are Ahvniya.

[3]Virat means glory of God, as well as Matter.

[4]Learned people alone realise the glory of God.

९. यन्त्यस्य सभां सभ्यो भवति य एवं वेद ॥

9. He who knows this secret, is honoured in the Assembly and learned persons resort to his assembly. (2260b)

१०. सोदक्रामत् सा समितौ न्यक्रामत् ॥

10. The glory of God arose, and appeared in the form of battle. (2261a)[1]

११. यन्त्यस्य समितिं सामित्यो भवति य एवं वेद ॥

11. He who knows this secret, becomes a hero on the battlefield, and soldiers accompany him to the battlefield. (2261b)

१२. सोदक्रामत् सामन्त्रणे न्यक्रामत् ॥

12. The glory of God arose, and appeared in the form of mutual love and respectful invitation. (2262a)

१३. यन्त्यस्यामन्त्रणमामन्त्रणीयो भवति य एवं वेद ॥

13. He who knows this secret of the glory of God, receives respectful invitation from others and people respond to his invitation. (2262b)

Paryaya 2

१. सोदक्रामत् सान्तरिक्षे चतुर्धा विक्रान्तातिष्ठत् ॥

1. The glory of God arose and dividing herself in four directions took her seat in the atmosphere. (2263a)

२. तां देवमनुष्या अब्रुवन्नियमेव तद् वेद यदुभय उपजीवेमेमामुप ह्वयामहा इति ॥

2. Of her the sages and men said, she knoweth the truth, wherewith we both may have life. Let us invite her. (2263b)

३. तामुपाह्वयन्त ॥

3. Thus did they cry to her. (2264a)[2]

४. ऊर्जं एहि स्वध एहि सूनृत एहीरावत्येहीति ॥

4. Come, Strength! Come, Wealth! Come, true, lovely Speech! Come, Food! (2264b)[3]

५. तस्या इन्द्रो वत्स आसीद् गायत्र्य भिधान्यभ्रमूधः ॥

5. Soul is the darling of God; praiseworthy Vedic knowledge is His speech, Cloud is His power of benefaction. (2265a)

[1]Battle is won through the grace of God. (समितौ) संग्रामे । *Nighantu*, 2-17.

[2]All men invoke God to alleviate their sufferings.

[3]God is the Giver of strength, wealth, true instruction and food.

६. बृहच्च रथन्तरं च द्वौ स्तनावास्तां यज्ञायज्ञियं च वामदेव्यं च द्वौ ॥

6. Sky and world are the two powers of God, Vedic knowledge, and five elements are the other two powers of God. (2265b)[1]

७. ओषधीरेव रथन्तरेण देवा अदुह्रन् व्यचो बृहता ॥

7. The learned derived eatables from the Earth and the idea of vastness from the sky. (2266a)

८. अपो वामदेव्येन यज्ञं यज्ञायज्ञियेन ॥

8. They drew men from the five elements, and learnt the art of performing Yajña from Vedic knowledge. (2266b)[2]

९. ओषधीरेवास्मै रथन्तरं दुहे व्यचो बृहत् ॥

9. For him, who knows the secret of the glory of God, the Earth produces eatables, and sky gives space. (2267a)

१०. अपो वामदेव्यं यज्ञं यज्ञायज्ञियं य एवं वेद ॥

10. For him, who knows the secret of the glory of God, the five elements grant progeny, and Vedic knowledge inculcates the right course of conduct. (2267b)

Paryaya 3

१. सोदक्रामत् सा वनस्पतीनागच्छत्तां वनस्पतयोऽघ्नत सा संवत्सरे समभवत् ॥

1. The glory of God manifested itself, and appeared in the shape of trees. They enjoyed her. She lived with them for a year. (2268a)

२. तस्माद् वनस्पतीनां संवत्सरे वृक्णमपि रोहति वृश्चतेऽस्याप्रियो भ्रातृव्यो य एवं वेद ॥

2. Hence in a year the trimmed twigs of trees grow again. He who knows this secret gets his mental frailty cured. (2268b)

३. सोदक्रामत् सा पितॄनागच्छत्तां पितरोऽघ्नत सा मासि समभवत् ॥

3. The glory of God arose. She approached the Fathers. They lived with her. She lived with them for a month, (2269a)

४. तस्मात् पितृभ्यो मास्युपमास्यं ददति प्र पितृयाणं पन्थां जानाति य एवं वेद ॥

4. Hence the Fathers are given every month their monthly salary. He who knows this, knows the way the elders have trodden. (2269b)[3]

[1]Just as a cow has four teats, so God has fourfold powers. Five elements: Earth, water, Air, Fire, Atmosphere. For detailed explanation see Pt. Khem Karan Das Trivedi's commentary.

[2]अपः—प्रजा दयानन्दभाषये *Yajur*, 6-27.

[3]Fathers: The able elderly administrators of the state, who rear the subjects like parents. He who performs his duty conscientiously knows the path of truth, wisdom and virtue the elders have set before us.

५. सोदक्रामत् सा देवानागच्छत्तां देवा अघ्नत सार्धमासे समभवत् ॥

5. The glory of God arose. She approached the sages. They welcomed her. She lived with them for half a month. (2270a)

६. तस्माद् देवेभ्योऽर्धमासे वषट् कुर्वन्ति प्र देवयानं पन्थां जानाति य एवं वेद ॥

6. Hence the sages are respectfully offered food every half month. He who knows this, knows the path the sages have trodden (2270b)[1]

७. सोदक्रामत् सा मनुष्या३नागच्छत्तां मनुष्याऽ अघ्नत सा सद्यः समभवत् ॥

7. The glory of God arose, she approached contemplative persons. They received her. She remained with them for only one day. (2271a)[2]

८. तस्मान्मनुष्येऽभ्य उभयद्युरुप हरन्त्युपास्य गृहे हरन्ति य एवं वेद ॥

8. Hence men are daily offered food. People take necessary provisions to his house, who knows this secret. (2271b)[3]

Paryaya 4

१. सोदक्रामत् सासुरानागच्छत्तामसुरा उपाह्वयन्त माय एहीति ॥

1. The glory of God arose. She approached the wise. They called her. O intellect, come thou hither! (2272a)[4]

२. तस्या विरोचनः प्राह्लादिर्वत्स आसीदयस्पात्रं पात्रम् ॥

2. The world created by God was her dwelling place. God, the Mainstay of all luminous planets was her Guardian. (2272b)[5]

३. तां द्विमूर्धार्त्व्योऽधोक्तां मायामेवाधोक् ॥

3. The wise and active soul, doubly fettered has realised her. It has cultivated intellect. (2273a)[6]

४. तां मायामसुरा उप जीवन्त्युपजीवनीयो भवति य एवं वेद ॥

4. The wise depend for life on intellect. He who knows this secret, becomes the supporter of others. (2273b)

[1]Every half month: On occasion of Amavasya (full darkness) Purnmasi, (full moon).
[2]Men of contemplative nature soon realise the glory of God.
[3]Labourers are daily given wages.
[4]माया=प्रज्ञा *Nighantu*, 3-9. असुर=प्रज्ञावान् वा प्राणवान् *Nirukta*, 10-34. All wise persons contemplate on the power of God.
[5]Her: Virāta, the glory of God Virochna: Luminous objects like the Sun, Moon, Fire, i.e., world Praharadi: Created by God, the Embodiment of Joy. Vatsa=Dwelling place. वस निवासे (अयस्पात्रम्) God. अयो हिरण्यम् *Nighantu*, 1-2.
[6]Doubly fettered: Bound by the deeds of past life and those of the present.

५. सोदक्रामत् सा पितृनागच्छत्तां पितर उपाह्वयन्त स्वध एहीति ॥

5. The glory of God arose, she approached the Sun and other planets. They called her, O soul-preserving strength, come hither! (2274a)

६. तस्या यमो राजा वत्स आसीद् रजतपात्रं पात्रम् ॥

6. The self-controlled soul is her preacher from her. The loving, wise, and venerable God is her Guardian. (2274b)

७. तामन्तको मार्त्यवोऽधोक्तां स्वधामेवाधोक् ॥

7. The fascinating soul, conscious of the nature of Death has realised that glory. It has realised the soul-preserving strength. (2275a)

८. तां स्वधां पितर उप जीवन्त्युपजीवनीयो भवति य एवं वेद ॥

8. The Sun and other planets live on the glory of God. He who knows this secret becomes the supporter of others. (2275b)

९. सोदक्रामत् सा मनुष्या३नागच्छत्तां मनुष्या३ उपाह्वयन्तेरावत्येहीति ॥

9. The glory of God arose, She approached men. They called her, O Food-Giver come hither! (2276a)

१०. तस्या मनुर्वैवस्वतो वत्स आसीत् पृथिवी पात्रम् ॥

10. The thoughtful person, the knower of the nature of men was her preacher and the vast God, her Guardian. (2276b)

११. तां पृथी वैन्यो ऽधोक्तां कृषिं च सस्यं चाधोक् ॥

11. The highly intellectual person, the friend of the wise realised her. He understood the use of husbandry and grain for sowing. (2277a)

१२. पिं च सस्यं च मनुष्या३ उप जीवन्ति कृष्टराधिरुपजीवनीयो भवति य एवं वेद ॥

12. These men depend for life on corn and tillage. He who knows this secret, becomes successful in the culture of his corn-land, and a supporter of others. (2277b)

१३. सोदक्रामत् सा सप्तऋषीनागच्छत्तां सप्तऋषय उपाह्वयन्त ब्रह्मण्वत्येहीति ॥

13. The glory of God arose. She approached the seven Rishis. They called her, O rich in knowledge, come hither! (2278a)[1]

१४. तस्याः सोमो राजा वत्स आसीच्छन्दः पात्रम् ॥

14. The beautiful soul was her preacher, and Independent God, the Guardian. (2278b)

[1]Seven Rishis: Skin, Eye, Nose, Ear, Tongue, Mind, Intellect. Griffith interprets these Rishis as Bhardwaj, Kasyapa, Gotama, Atri, Vasishtha, Visvamitra and Jamadagni. This interpretation is unacceptable as there is no history in the Vedas.

१५. तां बृहस्पतिराङ्गिरसोऽधोक् तां ब्रह्म च तपश्चाधोक् ॥

15. The highly qualified knower of God realised her, and drew from her Vedic knowledge and holy fervour. (2279a)

१६. पिं च तपश्च सप्तऋषय उप जीवन्ति ब्रह्मवर्चस्युऽपजीवनीयो भवति य एवं वेद ॥

16. The seven Rishis depend on Vedic knowledge and holy fervour. He who knows this secret, becomes the master of the Vedas, and the supporter of others. (2279b)

Paryaya 5

१. सोदक्रामत् सा देवानागच्छत्तां देवा उपाह्वयन्तोर्ज एहीति ॥

1. The glory of God arose. She came unto the aspirants for victory. They called her, crying, O Vigour, come hither. (2280a)

२. तस्या इन्द्रो वत्स आसीच्चमसः पात्रम् ॥

2. The glorious soul was her preacher, and God, the Guardian. (2280b)

३. तां देवः सविताधोक् तामूर्जामेवाधोक् ॥

3. The wise, all-urging person has realised, he has certainly realised the glory of God. (2281a)

४. तामूर्जां देवा उप जीवन्त्युपजीवनीयो भवति य एवं वेद ॥

4. The aspirants for victory depend for life upon that Vigour. He who knows this secret becomes the supporter of others. (2281b)

५. सोदक्रामत् सा गन्धर्वाप्सरस आगच्छत्तां गन्धर्वाप्सरस उपाह्वयन्त पुण्यगन्ध एहीति ॥

5. The glory of God arose. She approached the Gandharvas and Apsaras. They called her, Come to us, O pure knowledge. (2282a)[1]

६. तस्याश्चित्ररथः सौर्यवर्चसो वत्स आसीत् पुष्करपर्णं पात्रम् ॥

6. The multi-merited soul who knows the brilliance of the Sun was her preacher, and All-invigorating God, the Guardian. (2282b)

७. तां वसुरुचिः सौर्यवर्चसोऽधोक् तां पुण्यमेव गन्धमधोक् ॥

7. The soul, that loves the All-pervading God, and appreciates the beauty of the Sun has realised her. It has verily mastered that pure knowledge. (2283a)

८. तं पुण्यं गन्धं गन्धर्वाप्सरस उप जीवन्ति पुण्यगन्धिरुपजीवनीयो भवति य एवं वेद ॥

8. Gandharvas and Apsaras depend for their life upon that pure knowledge. He who knows this secret, becomes the possessor of pure knowledge and the supporter of others. (2283b)

[1]Gandharvas: Those who possess organs. Apsaras: Those who move through Pranas.

९. सोदक्रामत् सेतरजनानागच्छत् तामितरजना उपाह्वयन्त तिरोध एहीति ॥

9. The glory of God arose. She approached the ignorant. They called her, crying, Come, Mysterious Power, come hither! (2284a)[1]

१०. तस्याः कुबेरो वैश्रवणो वत्स आसीदामपात्रं पात्रम् ॥

10. A highly wise, learned person is her preacher, and God, the Mainstay of all actions, her Guardian. (2284b)

११. तां रजतनाभिः काबेरकोऽधोक् तां तिरोधामेवाधोक् ॥

11. A highly qualified intellectual Kshatriya has realised her. He has verily realised the mysterious Power. (2285a)

१२. तां तिरोधामितरजना उप जीवन्ति तिरो धत्ते सर्वं पाप्मानमुपजीवनीयो भवति
य एवं वेद ॥

12. The ignorant depend for their life on that Mysterious Power. He who knows this secret, makes all evil disappear and vanish, and becomes the supporter of others. (2285b)

१३. सोदक्रामत् सा सर्पानागच्छत्तां सर्पा उपाह्वयन्त विषवत्येहीति ॥

13. The glory of God arose. She approached the serpents. The serpents called her, venomous, come hither! (2286a)[2]

१४. तस्यास्तक्षको वैशालेयो वत्स आसीदलाबुपात्रं पात्रम् ॥

14. An intuitive recogniser and knower of the knowledge of God is her preacher, and Unfailing God, her Guardian. (2286b)[3]

१५. तां धृतराष्ट्र ऐरावतोऽधोक् तां विषमेवाधोक् ॥

15. A good ruler of the State, who knows the requirements of his peasants comprehended her, and drew forth poison. (2287a)[4]

१६. तद् विषं सर्पा उप जीवन्त्युपजीवनीयो भवति य एवं वेद ॥

16. That poison quickens and supports the serpents. He who knows this secret becomes the supporter of others. (2287b)[5]

[1]God is the benefactor of the ignorant, and instructs them to rise mentally intellectually and spiritually.

[2]One of the aspects of virat, the glory of God in Poison.

[3]Takshaka means the knower of the knowledge of God. Vaishalaya means a man of intuition, सूक्ष्मदर्शी. See Pt. Khem Karan Das Ji's commentary.

[4]Airavata: Who knows the requirements of the pleasants, इरावतां भूमिवतां स्वभाववेता. Dhritrashtra: A nice ruler of the State. (धृतराष्ट्रः) धृतं राष्ट्रं येन । राज्य धारकः For detailed explanation see Pt. Khem Karan Das Trivedi's commentary on this hymn.

[5]God infuses poison in the serpents through his magic power.

Paryaya 6

१. तद्यस्मा एवं विदुषेऽलाबुनाभिषिञ्चेत् प्रत्याहन्यात् ॥

1. An educated person, whom the Vast God, thus promotes through His unfailing might removes all his vices. (2288a)

२. न च प्रत्याहन्यान्मनसा त्वा प्रत्याहन्मीति प्रत्याहन्यात् ॥

2. He should now drive out his weakness. O vice, I remove thee, through my will power. He should thus wipe out his vice. (2288b)[1]

३. यत् प्रत्याहन्ति विषमेव तत् प्रत्याहन्ति ॥

3. The Guiding God thus removes, the Vast God removes the weakness of the soul. (2289a)[2]

४. विषमेवास्याप्रियं भ्रातृव्यमनुविषिच्यते य एवं वेद ॥

4. He who knows this secret sees, that Vice thus destroys his unfriendly foe and the reviler of God. (2289b)

BOOK (Kāṇḍa) IX

Chapter (Anuvāka) 1

HYMN I

१. दिवस्पृथिव्या अन्तरिक्षात् समुद्रादग्नेर्वातान्मधुकशा हि जज्ञे ।
तां चायित्वामृतं वसानां हृद्भिः प्रजाः प्रति नन्दन्ति सर्वाः ॥

1. The glory of Vedic knowledge is obvious from heaven, earth, middle air, ocean, fire and wind. Adoring that knowledge fraught with immortality, all living creatures derive joy in their hearts (2290)[3]

२. महत् पयो विश्वरूपमस्याः समुद्रस्य त्वोत रेत आहुः ।
यत ऐति मधुकशा रराणा तत् प्राणस्तदमृतं निविष्टम् ॥

2. The learned call thee earth's great strength in every form, they call the lustre, beauty of God. Whence comes the Vedic knowledge bestowing bounty, in Him is treasured life, in Him, salvation's joy. (2291)[4]

३. पश्यन्त्यस्याश्चरितं पृथिव्यां पृथङ् नरो बहुधा मीमांसमानाः ।
अग्नेर्वातान्मधुकशा हि जज्ञे मरुतामुग्रा नप्तिः ॥

3. In sundry ways, reflecting from different points of view, the learned view upon the earth her course and action. Unfailing Vedic knowledge the mighty resort of the valiant, is realised in the shape of fire and wind. (2292)[5]

[1] न does not mean no. It means now. (न) सम्प्रति—निरु० 7-31.

[2] (यत्) यमयतीति, नियन्तृ ब्रह्म (तत्) तनोतीति तत् । तनु विस्तारे । विस्तारकं ब्रह्म ।

[3] The Vedas expatiate on the beauty of heaven, earth, fire, wind and water etc.

[4] Whence: From God.

[5] Her: The knowledge of God. All objects of nature sing, denote and remind us of the glory of God.

४. मातादित्यानां दुहिता वसूनां प्राणः प्रजानाममृतस्य नाभिः ।
हिरण्यवर्णा मधुकशा घृताची महान् भर्गश्चरति मर्त्येषु ॥

4. Vedic knowledge is the nourisher of Aditya Brahmcharies, the fulfiller of the ambitions of men, life of living creatures, the bestower of salvation, full of splendour, the infuser of strength. It moves amid mortals like a mighty lighthouse. (2293)

५. मधोः कशामजनयन्त देवास्तस्या गर्भो अभवद् विश्वरूपः ।
तं जातं तरुणं पिपर्ति माता स जातो विश्वा भुवना वि चष्टे ॥

5. The learned have spread Vedic knowledge. God was her source. That Vedic knowledge exists in full in that Illustrious, Almighty God. That Renowned God watches all worlds. (2294)[1]

६. कस्तं प्र वेद क उ तं चिकेत यो अस्या हृदः कलशः सोमधानो अक्षितः ।
ब्रह्मा सुमेधाः सो अस्मिन् मदेत ॥

6. Who knows God fully well? Who has perceived Him? Who is the inexhaustible reservoir of knowledge stored in the heart of the Veda. Let the wise Vedic scholar derive joy in God's contemplation. (2295)

७. स तौ प्र वेद स उ तौ चिकेत यावस्याः स्तनौ सहस्रधारावक्षितौ ।
ऊर्जं दुहाते अनपस्फुरन्तौ ॥

7. A learned man alone knows and fully understands the two inexhaustible powers of Vedic knowledge, which nourish thousands of souls, Those immortal powers yield strength and vigour. (2296)[2]

८. हिङ्करिक्रती बृहती वयोधा उच्चैर्घोषाभ्येति या व्रतम् ।
त्रीन् घर्मानभि वावशाना मिमाति मायुं पयते पयोभिः ॥

8. Ever progressing, grand, life-infusing, preaching lofty principles, Vedic knowledge is acquired by a disciplined learned person. Controlling the three forces, it reveals its teachings to a learned person, and satisfies him with the showers of knowledge. (2297)[3]

९. यामापीनामुपसीदन्त्यापः शाक्वरा वृषभा ये स्वराजः ।
ते वर्षन्ति ते वर्षयन्ति तद्विदे काममूर्जमापः ॥

[1]Her: Vedic knowledge. The learned know the Vedas are in God, and God in Vedas.

[2]Two powers: Retention and Attraction. These powers have been spoken of as teats. Just as the teats of a cow yield milk, so do these yield strength. Pt. Jaidev interprets these two teats as Prakriti and Vikrati. The Vedas retain knowledge, and attract scholars and sages to study and spread them. (Prakriti and Vikrati).

[3]Three forces: Spiritual, physical, social.

9. They, who know the mighty Vedic knowledge, are energetic, self-controlled and highly learned, revere the fully developed knowledge of God. Those learned persons acquire knowledge, and equip him with ambition and strength who knows the Vedas. (2298)[1]

१०. स्तनयित्नुस्ते वाक् प्रजापते वृषा शुष्मं क्षिपसि भूम्यामधि ।
अग्नेर्वातान्मधुकशा हि जज्ञे मरुतामुग्रा नप्तिः ॥

10. O Lord of creatures, Thy Vedic speech assuages the hearts of men, as a thundering cloud moistens the earth with rain. Through Thy supremacy, Thou castest vigour on the earth. Unfailing Vedic knowledge, the mighty resort of the valiant is realised in the shape of fire and wind. (2299)[2]

११. यथा सोमः प्रातःसवने अश्विनोर्भवति प्रियः । एवा मे अश्विना वर्च आत्मनि ध्रियताम् ॥

11. Just as a child in early age is dear to father and mother, so may both the Aswins lay splendour and strength within my soul. (2300)[3]

१२. यथा सोमो द्वितीये सवन इन्द्राग्न्योर्भवति प्रियः ।
एवा म इन्द्राग्नी वर्च आत्मनि ध्रियताम् ॥

12. Just as a child in youth is dear to father and mother, so may both father and mother lay splendour and strength in my soul. (2301)[4]

१३. यथा सोमस्तृतीये सवन ऋभूणां भवति प्रियः । एवा म ऋभवो वर्च आत्मनि ध्रियताम् ॥

13. Just as an old person, is honoured and loved by the wise in old stage, the third stage of life, even so may they the learned persons store splendour and strength within my soul. (2302)[5]

१४. मधु जनिषीय मधु वंशिषीय । पयस्वानग्न आगमं तं मा सं सृज वर्चसा ॥

14. May I advance knowledge. May I pray for knowledge. O preceptor, I, an energetic pupil, have come! Bestow splendour and strength on me. (2303)

१५. सं माग्ने वर्चसा सृज सं प्रजया समायुषा ।
विद्युर्मे अस्य देवा इन्द्रो विद्यात् सह ऋषिभिः ॥

[1]Knowledge of God: The Vedas.

[2]See the second part of verse 3 of this hymn.

[3]Both the Aswins: Acharya (preceptor) and God. Acharya is Guru and so God is the Guru of Gurus.

[4]Father and mother have been compared to the Sun and fire. Just as the Sun warms and protects us, so does a father protect his son. Just as fire lends warmth to us, so does the mother lend the warmth of her love to the child.

[5]Griffith interprets Ribhus the three renowned artists who by their excellent work obtained divinity, exercised superhuman powers, and became entitled to worship. As there is no history in the Vedas, this interpretation is unacceptable. ऋभूणाम=मेधाविनाम् *Nighantu*, 3—14.

15. Grant me, O Guru, splendid strength and progeny and lengthened life. May the learned know me as I am. May God with the sages know me. (2304)[1]

१६. यथा मधु मधुकृतः संभरन्ति मधावधि । एवा मे अश्विना वर्चं आत्मनि ध्रियताम् ।।

16. As honey-bees collect honey in spring; even so may both the Gurus God and teacher lay splendour of knowledge and spiritual strength within my soul. (2305)

१७. यथा मक्षा इदं मधु न्यञ्जन्ति मधावधि ।
एवा मे अश्विना वर्चस्तेजो वलमोजश्च ध्रियताम् ।।

17. As honey-bees collect honey in spring, so may God and teacher, my Gurus, enhance my splendour, strength, power and might. (2306)[2]

१८. यद् गिरिषु पर्वतेषु गोष्वश्वेषु यन्मधु । सुरायां सिच्यमानायां यत् तत्र मधु तन्मयि ।।

18. May I possess the majesty of mountains, the splendour of hills, the sweetness of the milk of kine, the swiftness of horses, and beauty of flowing waters. (2307)

१९. अश्विना सारघेण मा मधुनाङ्क्तं शुभस्पती । यथा वर्चस्वतीं वाचमावदानि जनाँ अनु ।।

19. O God and teacher, Lords of light, equip me with knowledge, the bestower of wealth and strength, that I may speak among the folk words full of splendour and strength. (2308)

२०. स्तनयित्नुस्ते वाक् प्रजापते वृषा शुष्मं क्षिपसि भूम्यां दिवि ।
तां पशव उप जीवन्ति सर्वे तेनो सेषमूर्जं पिपर्ति ।।

20. O God, the Lord of Creatures, Thy Vedic speech is imposing like the thunder of a cloud. Thou art the Bestower of joys and comfort. Thou castest strength on earth and heaven. To that Vedic knowledge all sentient souls look for their existence that is why she nourishes men with food, force and vigour. (2309)[3]

२१. पृथिवी दण्डोऽन्तरिक्षं गर्भो द्यौः कशा विद्युत् प्रकशो हिरण्ययो बिन्दुः ।।

21. Earth is God's court of justice, where men are punished and rewarded for their acts. Space is His womb, in which revolve innumerable planets. The Sun is His hunter, which gives light to men and keeps them under his control. Lightning is His whip. Luminous nebula are a particle of His power of productivity. (2310)[4]

[1]In the presence of the learned, sages and God, a pupil takes this vow to receive knowledge from his Guru, by remaining obedient and loyal to him.

[2]Aswins may mean mother and father as well.

[3]She: Vedic knowledge.

[4]Whip: Just as erring persons are punished with a whip, so does God punish the si nners with lightning.

२२. यो वै कशायाः सप्त मधूनि वेद मधुमान् भवति ।
ब्राह्मणश्च राजा च धेनुश्चानड्वांश्च व्रीहिश्च यवश्च मधु सप्तमम् ॥

22. Whoever knows the seven kinds of Veda's learning, becomes himself a man endowed with wisdom. They are, (1) Brahman, the knower of the Vedas (2) King, (3) Milch cow (4) Ox the giver of corn (5) Rice (6) Barley (7) Knowledge. (2311)[1]

२३. मधुमान् भवति मधुमदस्याहार्यं̐ भवति । मधुमतो लोकाञ्जयति य एवं वेद ॥

23. Who knows the secret of God's power, becomes wise. His food becomes sweet and delicious. He masters comfortable places and lives conveniently in them. (2312)

२४. यद् वीध्रे स्तनयति प्रजापतिरेव तत् प्रजाभ्यः प्रादुर्भवति ।
तस्मात् प्राचीनोपवीतस्तिष्ठे प्रजापतेऽनु मा बुध्यस्वेति ।
अन्वेनं प्रजा अनु प्रजापतिर्बुध्यते य एवं वेद ॥

24. When clouds thunder in the sky, it is verily a manifestation of God to living creatures. Just as a pupil, with the Yajnopavit on the right, stands before his teacher, and prays for instructions, so I stand with the sacred thread on the right side, and pray, O God, be gracious unto me! He who knows this secret, is honoured by living beings and loved by God. (2313)

HYMN II

१. सपत्नहनमृषभं घृतेन कामं शिक्षामि हविषाज्येन ।
नीचैः सपत्नान् मम पादय त्वमभिष्टुतो महता वीर्ये̐ण ॥

1. I worship God, the slayer of my moral foes, with affection, devotion and vigour. O God, cast down my spiritual foes with Thy great manly power, when I have adored Thee. (2314)

२. यन्मे मनसो न प्रियं न चक्षुषो यन्मे बभस्ति नाभिनन्दति ।
तद् दुःष्वप्न्यं प्रति मुञ्चामि सपत्ने कामं स्तुत्वोदहं भिदेयम् ॥

2. That which is hateful to mine eye and mind, that harasses and robs me of enjoyment and causes uneasiness, I loose upon my foemen. May I advance spiritually, with iron determination and praise of God. (2315)

३. दुःष्वप्न्यं काम दुरितं च कामाप्रजस्तामस्वगतामवर्तिम् ।
उग्र ईशानः प्रति मुञ्च तस्मिन् यो अस्मभ्यमंहूरणा चिकित्सात् ॥

3. O God, do Thou a mighty Lord and Ruler, let loose evil design, misfortune, lack of progeny, utter destitution unemployment, upon the sinner who designs our ruin. (2316)

[1]Madhu means honey in common parlance. Here the word means knowledge.

४. नुदस्व काम प्र णुदस्व कामावर्तिं यन्तु मम ये सपत्नाः ।
तेषां नुत्तानामधमा तमांस्यग्ने वास्तूनि निर्दह त्वम् ॥

4. O true determination, O fire of knowledge, drive away, drive afar, my internal moral foes. May they refrain from degrading me. When they have been cast down to utter darkness, consume their dwellings with thy fire, O knowledge! (2317)

५. सा ते काम दुहिता धेनुरुच्यते यामाहुर्वाचं कवयो विराजम् ॥
तया सपत्नान् परि वृङ्ग्धि ये मम पर्येनान् प्राणः पशवो जीवनं वृणक्तु ॥

5. O God, Thy Vedic speech is spoken of as the Fulfiller of all desires. The sages name it as the Revealer of true ideas. Through her, drive away my internal foes, O God! May vital breath, cattle and life forsake them. (2318)

६. कामस्येन्द्रस्य वरुणस्य राज्ञो विष्णोर्बलेन सवितुः सवेन ॥
अग्नेर्होत्रेण प्र णुदे सपत्नाञ्छम्बीव नावमुदकेषु धीरः ॥

6. Through the might and exhortation of the Refulgent, Glorious, Adorable, Royal, All-pervading, All-impelling God, and through the performance of Agni Hotar, I chase my internal moral foes, as a deft steersman drives his boat through deep waters. (2319)

७. अध्यक्षो वाजी मम काम उग्रः कृणोतु मह्यमसपत्नमेव ।
विश्वे देवा मम नाथं भवन्तु सर्वे देवा हवमा यन्तु म इमम् ॥

7. May God, Mighty One, my Potent Warder, give me full freedom from my moral adversaries. May all noble traits be my protectors. May all learned persons come nigh to this Yajña of mine. (2320)

८. इदमाज्यं घृतवज्जुषाणाः कामज्येष्ठा इह मादयध्वम् । कृण्वन्तो मह्यमसपत्नमेव ॥

8. O learned persons, enjoying brilliant activity, and acknowledging God, as the sublimest of all, freeing me from my internal foes, lend me joy in this life! (2321)

९. इन्द्राग्नी काम सरथं हि भूत्वा नीचैः सपत्नान् मम पादयाथः ।
तेषां पन्नानामधमा तमांस्यग्ने वास्तून्यनुनिर्दह त्वम् ॥

9. O my soul force, wisdom and determination riding together in the chariot of my body, cast my moral foes down beneath me. O fire of my knowledge, consume the low, dark dwellings of these defeated moral foes. (2322)

१०. जहि त्वं काम मम ये सपत्ना अन्धा तमांस्यव पादयैनान् ॥
निरिन्द्रिया अरसाः सन्तु सर्वे मा ते जीविषुः कतमच्चनाहः ॥

10. Remove my internal moral foes, O true determination! Headlong to depth of blinding darkness hurl them. Bereft be they all of manly strength and vigour. Let them not have a single day's existence. (2323)

११. अवधीत् कामो मम ये सपत्ना उरुं लोकमकरन्मह्यमेधतुम् ।
मह्यं नमन्तां प्रदिशश्चतस्रो मह्यं षडुर्वीर्घृतमा वहन्तु ॥

11. True determination hath slain my internal moral opponents, and afforded me ample room to grow and prosper. Let the four regions bow them down before me, and let the six expenses bring me invigorating substances. (2324)[1]

१२. तेऽधराञ्चः प्र प्लवन्तां छिन्ना नौरिव बन्धनात् ।
न सायकप्रणुत्तानां पुनरस्ति निवर्त्तनम् ॥

12. Just as a boat torn from the rope that holds it fast, drifts in the stream; so may my internal moral foes drift away from my body. There is no turning back for those whom keen arrows have repelled. (2325)

१३. अग्निर्यव इन्द्रो यवः सोमो यवः । यवयावानो देवा यावयन्त्वेनम् ॥

13. Wise God is the Averter of sin. Glorious God is Annihilator of evil deeds. Blissful God is the Bestower of joy. May the learned, who dislike the detractors of religion, attain to God. (2326)

१४. असर्ववीरश्चरतु प्रणुत्तो द्वेष्यो मित्राणां परिवर्ग्यः स्वानाम् ।
उत पृथिव्यामव स्यन्ति विद्युत उग्रो वो देवः प्र मृणत् सपत्नान् ॥

14. May moral foe, expelled, be deprived of all its forces. May those who loved it, begin to detest it. May their associates abandon it. O men, may knowledge, determination, soul-force destroy all your internal moral enemies in the world. May the Almighty Father nullify them. (2327)

१५. च्युता चेयं बृहत्यच्युता च विद्युद् बिभर्ति स्तनयित्नूंश्च सर्वान् ।
उद्यन्नादित्यो द्रविणेन तेजसा नीचैः सपत्नान् नुदतां मे सहस्वान् ॥

15. This Potent, Refulgent God nourishes all perishable and imperishable objects and the thundering clouds. May the Majestic, Lustrous God, with strength and splendour, in His victorious might, drive downward my moral foes. (2328)

१६. यत् ते काम शर्म त्रिवरूथमुद्भु ब्रह्म वर्म विततमनतिव्याध्यं कृतम् ।
तेन सपत्नान् परि वृङ्ग्धि ये मम पर्येनान् प्राणः पशवो जीवनं वृणक्तु ॥

16. O God, Thou hast made the powerful Vedic knowledge a three-barred protection, and an extended invulnerable armour. With that drive Thou my internal moral foes to a distance. May vital breath, cattle and life forsake them. (2329)[2]

[1]Four regions: North, East, South, West. Six expenses: Four mid-regions, Āgneya, Nairiti, Vāyavi, Aishāni, and the upper and lower spaces, or Heaven, Earth, Day, Night, Water and Plants.

[2]Three-barred protection: Vedic knowledge affords physical, spiritual, social protection. Vedas are a kind of armour for the soul of a man.

१७. येन देवा असुरान् प्राणुदन्त येनेन्द्रो दस्यूनधमं तमो निनाय ।
तेन त्वं काम मम ये सपत्नास्तानस्माल्लोकात् प्र णुदस्व दूरम् ॥

17. Far from this body of mine, O iron determination, drive thou my moral foes with that selfsame weapon of Vedic knowledge, wherewith the learned repelled vices, and a spiritually advanced soul cast down immoral tendencies into deepest darkness! (2330)

१८. यथा देवा असुरान् प्राणुदन्त यथेन्द्रो दस्यूनधमं तमो वबाधे ।
तथा त्वं काम मम ये सपत्नास्तानस्माल्लोकात् प्र णुदस्व दूरम् ॥

18. As the learned conquered, moral weaknesses, and a spiritually developed soul overcame satanic leanings, so, O firm resolve, from this world, to distant places, drive thou my internal moral adversaries! (2331)

१९. कामो जज्ञे प्रथमो नैनं देवा आपुः पितरो न मर्त्याः ।
ततस्त्वमसि ज्यायान् विश्वहा महांस्तस्मै ते काम नम इत् कृणोमि ॥

19. God existed before the creation of the universe. Sages, Nature's forces, Fathers and mortal men have never matched Him, Stronger than these art Thou, and great for ever, O God, to Thee, to Thee I offer worship! (2332)

२०. यावती द्यावापृथिवी वरिम्णा यावदापः सिष्यदुर्यावदग्निः ।
ततस्त्वमसि ज्यायान् विश्वहा महांस्तस्मै ते काम नम इत् कृणोमि ॥

20. Wide is the space which heaven and earth encompass, far do the waters flow, far does the fire spread. Stronger than these art Thou, and great for ever, O God, to Thee, to Thee I offer worship. (2333)[1]

२१. यावतीर्दिशः प्रदिशो विषूचीर्यावतीराशा अभिचक्षणा दिवः ।
ततस्त्वमसि ज्यायान् विश्वहा महांस्तस्मै ते काम नम इत् कृणोमि ॥

21. Vast as the quarters of the sky and regions that lie between them spread in all directions, vast as are celestial tracts and views of heaven; stronger than these art Thou, and great for ever, O God, to Thee, to Thee I offer worship! (2334)

२२. यावतीर्भृङ्गा जत्वऽः कुरूरवो यावतीर्वघा वृक्षसर्प्योऽ बभूवुः ।
ततस्त्वमसि ज्यायान् विश्वहा महांस्तस्मै ते काम नम इत् कृणोमि ॥

22. Many as are the bees, bats, vultures, locusts, and reptiles that creep on the trees; stronger than these all art Thou, and great for ever, O God, to Thee I offer worship! (2335)

२३. ज्यायान् निमिषतोऽसि तिष्ठतो ज्यायान्त्समुद्रादसि काम मन्यो ।
ततस्त्वमसि ज्यायान् विश्वहा महांस्तस्म ते काम नम इत् कृणोमि ॥

[1]आपः (Āpa) may also mean the subtle atoms of Matter.

23. Stronger art Thou than aught that stands or twinkles stronger art Thou than ocean, O Beautiful, worshipful God! Stronger than these art Thou, and great for ever, O God, to Thee, to Thee I offer worship! (2336)[1]

२४. न वै वातश्चन काममाप्नोति नाग्निः सूर्यो नोत चन्द्रमाः ।
ततस्त्वमसि ज्यायान् विश्वहा महांस्तस्मै ते काम नम इत् कृणोमि ।।

24. Not even Air, nor Fire, nor Moon, nor Sun is the peer of God. Stronger than these art Thou, and great for ever, O God, to Thee, to Thee I offer worship! (2337)

२५. यास्ते शिवास्तन्वः काम भद्रा याभिः सत्यं भवति यद् वृणीषे ।
ताभिष्ट्वमस्माँ अभिसंविशस्वान्यत्र पापीरप वेशया धियः ।।

25. Lovely and auspicious are Thy forces, O God, whereby Thou createst the universe and nourishest it. With these come Thou and make Thy home among us, and make malignant thoughts inhabit elsewhere. (2338)

Chapter (Anuvāka) 2

HYMN III

१. उपमितां प्रतिमितामथो परिमितामुत । शालाया विश्ववाराया नद्धानि वि चृतामसि ।।

1. Let us construct a beautiful, well-designed, commodious house. Let us strengthen the ties and fastenings of the house that has doors on all sides and holds all precious things. (2339)

२. यत् ते नद्धं विश्ववारे पाशो ग्रन्थिश्च यः कृतः ।
बृहस्पतिरिवाहं बलं वाचा वि स्रंसयामि तत् ।।

2. O house, the holder of all precious objects, I untie each knot and band, each cord that is attached to thee, as a scholar of the Vedas wards off all evil propensities with his Vedic knowledge! (2340)[2]

३. आ ययाम सं बबर्ह ग्रन्थींश्चकार ते दृढान् । परूंषि विद्वाञ्छस्तेवेन्द्रेण वि चृतामसि ।।

3. An artizan draws close, presses fast, makes secure thy knotted bands. Just as a skilful surgeon operates upon the diseased joints, so we strengthen all thy parts, O house. (2341)[3]

[1]Stands or twinkles: Inanimate and animate nature. All that stands without the power of moving away, as trees and plants, and mountains; and all creatures that open and shut their eyelids, as many beasts and birds.

[2]I: A householder.

[3]Thy: House Griffith interprets शस्ता as a slaughterer who cuts up the victim whose joints are to be carefully apportioned to several Gods to whom the offering is made. The word means a surgeon. Knotted bands; Doors, windows, skylights, rafters of the roof of a house.

४. वंशानां ते नहनानां प्राणाहस्य तृणस्य च । पक्षाणां विश्ववारे ते नद्धानि वि चृतामसि ॥

4. We strengthen the bands of thy bamboos, of bolts, of fastening, of thatch; we strengthen the ties of thy side posts, O House, that holds all precious things. (2342)

५. संदंशानां पलदानां परिष्वञ्जल्यस्य च । इदं मानस्य पत्न्या नद्धानि वि चृतामसि ॥

5. We strengthen the ties and bands of straw in bundles, and of clamps of this house which is the preserver of our honour. (2343)

६. यानि तेऽन्तः शिक्यान्याबेधू रण्याय कम् ।
प्र ते तानि चृतामसि शिवा मानस्य पत्नी न उद्धिता तन्वे भव ॥

6. We strenhgten the loops which artisans have bound within thee for beauty and comfort. O house, the preserver of our honour, be gracious to our bodies, with thy majestic height. (2344)

७. हविर्धानमग्निशालं पत्नीनां सदनं सदः । सदो देवानामसि देवि शाले ॥

7. O beautiful house, thou art equipped with a pantry, a Yajna shala, a kitchen a ladies, bower, a guest-room, and an Assembly hall for the learned. (2345)[1]

८. अक्षुमोपशं विततं सहस्राक्षं विषूवति । अवनद्धमभिहितं ब्रह्मणा वि चृतामसि ॥

8. We construct an elevated thousand-eyed, commodious, serviceable, vast, securely tied and well-designed house. (2346)[2]

९. यस्त्वा शाले प्रतिगृह्णाति येन चासि मितां त्वम् ।
उभौ मानस्य पत्नि तौ जीवतां जरदष्टी ॥

9. The man who takes thee as his own, and he who has built thee, House! both these, O preserver of honour, shall live to long-extended years. (2347)

१०. अमुत्रैनमा गच्छताद् दृढा नद्धा परिष्कृता । यस्यास्ते विचृतामस्यङ्गमङ्गं परुष्परुः ॥

10. Welcome this man to live in thee for future, O house, firm, strongly built and well decorated art thou whose several limbs and joints we strengthen one by one. (2348)[3]

११. यस्त्वा शाले निमिमाय संजभार वनस्पतीन् ।
प्रजायै चक्रे त्वा शाले परमेष्ठी प्रजापतिः ॥

11. He, the protector of his offspring, the supreme lord of the house, who collected timber and built thee up, O House, has made thee for coming progeny! (2349)

[1]Yajña-shala: A room where Agnihotra is daily performed. A good house must have rooms for storing provisions, performing havan, entertaining guests, ladies to sit and rest, and the learned persons to talk and discuss religious topics.

[2]Thousand-eyed: Having several skylights.

[3]This man: The owner of the house.

१२. नमस्तस्मै नमो दात्रे शालापतये च कृण्मः । नमोऽग्नये प्रचरते पुरुषाय च ते नमः ।।

12. We pay homage to the man who has chiselled stones, carved wood. We bow to the mansion's lord. We revere the learned person who performs ceremonies with fire in the house. We honour the inmates of the house. (2350)

१३. गोभ्यो अश्वेभ्यो नमो यच्छालायां विजायते ।
विजावति प्रजावति वि ते पाशांश्चृतामसि ।।

13. Food to kine and steeds! to all that shall be born within the house! We strengthen the bonds that fasten thee, O house, full of variety of articles and children! (2351)

१४. अग्निमन्तश्छादयसि पुरुषान् पशुभिः सह । विजावति प्रजावति वि ते पाशांश्चृतामसि ।।

14. O house, thou shelterest within thee, fire, and people with domestic beasts. We strengthen the bonds that fasten thee, full of variety of articles and children. (2352)[1]

१५. अन्तरा द्यां च पृथिवीं च यद् व्यचस्तेन शालां प्रति गृह्णामि त इमाम् ।
यदन्तरिक्षं रजसो विमानं तत् कृण्वेऽहमुदरं शेवधिभ्यः ।
तेन शालां प्रति गृह्णामि तस्मै ।।

15. All open space that lies between the earth and heaven, therein I erect this house for thy possession. The middle part of the house I erect wide like the belly to contain thy treasures. For this purpose I erect the house for his possession. (2353)[2]

१६. ऊर्जस्वती पयस्वती पृथिव्यां निमिता मिता ।
विश्वान्नं बिभ्रती शाले मा हिंसीः प्रतिगृह्णतः ।।

16. Rich in prosperity, rich in milk and water, founded and built upon a nice plot, injure not thy inmates, House, that holdest food of every kind! (2354)

१७. तृणैरावृता पलदान् वसाना रात्रीव शाला जगतो निवेशनी ।
मिता पृथिव्यां तिष्ठसि हस्तिनीव पद्वती ।।

17. Grass-covered, clad with straw, the house like Night, gives rest to man and beast. Built upon a beautiful plot, thou standest upon the massive pillars as a she-elephant does upon her firm, heavy feet. (2355)

१८. इटस्य ते बि चृताम्यपि नद्धमपोर्णुवन् । वरुणेन समुब्जितां मित्रः प्रातर्व्युब्जतु ।।

18. O house, opening the bolt of thy door, I fasten it well! What the darkness of night hath firmly closed, the sun shall ope at early morn. (2356)

[1]Fire that is used for cooking food and performing Agnihotar. Garhpatya and Ahvniya fire.

[2]Thy and his refer to the householder.

१६. ब्रह्मणा शालां निमितां कविभिर्निमितां मिताम् ।
इन्द्राग्नी रक्षतां शालाममृतौ सौम्यं सदः ॥

19. May ~~air,~~ fire, deathless forces of nature, protect the house, which affords us ease and comfort, house that was planned intelligently, built and erected by skilled, expert engineers. (2357)

२०. कुलायेऽधि कुलायं कोशे कोशः समुब्जितः ।
तत्र मर्तो वि जायते यस्माद् विश्वं प्रजायते ॥

20. In the nest of the house, lies the nest of the body. In the sheaf of the body, lies the embryo in the womb. There mortal man shall propagate his kind, and there shall everything be born. (2358)

२१. या द्विपक्षा चतुष्पक्षा षट्पक्षा या निमीयते ।
अष्टापक्षां दशपक्षां शालां मानस्य पत्नीमग्निर्गर्भइवा शये ॥

21. Within the house built with two, four, six, eight or ten rooms, I, its owner rest like a babe in the womb. (2359)[1]

२२. प्रतीचीं त्वा प्रतीचीनः शाले प्रैम्यहिंसतीम् । अग्निर्ह्य१न्तरापश्चर्तस्य प्रथमा द्वाः ॥

22. O house, standing in the west, afforder of comfort, I come unto thee with my face towards the west. Within thee are fire and water, the main doors of life. (2360)[2]

२३. इमा आपः प्र भराम्ययक्ष्मा यक्ष्मनाशनीः । गृहानुप प्र सीदाम्यमृतेन सहाग्निना ॥

23. Water that kills consumption, free from all consumption, here I bring. With food, butter, milk, saviours from death and fire, I enter and possess the house. (2361)[3]

२४. मा नः पाशं प्रति मुचो गुरुर्भारो लघुर्भव । वधूमिव त्वा शाले यत्र कामं भरामसि ॥

24. Lay thou O house no noose or impediment on us: a weighty burden, still be light! Wheresoever be our will, we carry thee, decorating thee like a bride. (2362)[4]

२५. प्राच्या दिशः शालाया नमो महिम्ने स्वाहा देवेभ्यः स्वाह्ये१भ्यः ॥

[1]These two verses have been translated by Swami Dayanand in the Samskar Vidhi.

[2]The verse may also mean; within thee reside learned persons, and men who have renounced worldly desires and attachments, the main sources of knowledge.

[3]See *Atharvaveda*, 3-12-9. A householder must always keep milk, butter, corn, water and fire in the house.

[4]Swami Dayanand has translated this verse in the Sanskar Vidhi. The house should be constructed in a way, that it be light and portable houses can be made from one place to the other. Such of timber and straw.

25. Now from the east side of the house to the Almighty God be homage paid. Reverence to the learned whom reverence is due. (2363)[1]

२६. दक्षिणाया दिशः शालाया नमो महिम्ने स्वाहा देवेभ्यः स्वाह्येऽभ्यः ॥

26. Now from the south side of the house to the Almighty God be homage paid. Reverence to the learned whom reverence is due. (2364)

२७. प्रतीच्या दिशः शालाया नमो महिम्ने स्वाहा देवेभ्यः स्वाह्येऽभ्यः ॥

27. Now from the west side of the house to the Almighty God be homage paid. Reverence to the learned whom reverence is due. (2365)

२८. उदीच्या दिशः शालाया नमो महिम्ने स्वाहा देवेभ्यः स्वाह्येऽभ्यः ॥

28. Now from the north side of the house to the Almighty God be homage paid. Reverence to the learned whom reverence is due. (2366)

२९. ध्रुवाया दिशः शालाया नमो महिम्ने स्वाहा देवेभ्यः स्वाह्येऽभ्यः ॥

29. Now from the nadir of the house to the Almighty God be homage paid. Reverence to the learned whom reverence is due. (2367)

३०. ऊर्ध्वाया दिशः शालाया नमो महिम्ने स्वाहा देवेभ्यः स्वाह्येऽभ्यः ॥

30. Now from the Zenith of the house to the Almighty God be homage paid. Reverence to the learned whom reverence is due. (2368)

३१. दिशोदिशः शालाया नमो महिम्ने स्वाहा देवेभ्यः स्वाह्येऽभ्यः ॥

31. So from the mansion's every side to the Almighty God be homage paid. Reverence to the learned whom reverence is due. (2369)

HYMN IV

१. साहस्रस्त्वेष ऋषभः पयस्वान् विश्वा रूपाणि वक्षणासु बिभ्रत् ।
भद्रं दात्रे यजमानाय शिक्षन् बार्हस्पत्य उस्रियस्तन्तुमातान् ॥

1. God, the Master of innumerable powers, full of refulgence, vigour, bearing within His flanks all luminous worlds, the Lord of mighty planets, All-pervading, granting a blissful body to the magnanimous soul, has stretched the thread of this vast universe. (2370)

२. अपां यो अग्रे प्रतिमा बभूव प्रभूः सर्वस्मै पृथिवीव देवी ।
पिता वत्सानां पतिरघ्न्यानां साहस्रे पोषे अपि नः कृणोतु ॥

2. May God, Who in the beginning of Creation pervaded the atoms of subtle matter, is the Creator and Lord of the universe, the Afforder of shelter to all like Earth the goddess, the Guardian of emancipated souls, the sovereign of immortal elements of Matter, secure us thousandfold abundance. (2371)

[1](25-31) These verses have been translated by Swami dayanand in the *Sanskarvidhi* in the Grihastha Ashram Chapter.

३. पुमानन्तर्वान्त्स्थविरः पयस्वान् वसोः कबन्धमृषभो बिभर्ति ।
तमिन्द्राय पथिभिर्देवयानैर्हुतमग्निर्वहतु जातवेदाः ॥

3. God, the Motivator of the world, Foremost of all, the Engulfer of all planets, steadfast, full of vigour, sustain the entire structure of the universe, fit to live in. May a learned Yogi, attain to that All-pervading God, for supremacy through pathways traversed by the sages. (2372)

४. पिता वत्सानां पतिरघ्न्यानामथो पिता महतां गर्गराणाम् ।
वत्सो जरायुः प्रतिधुक् पीयूष आमिक्षा घृतं तद् वस्य रेतः ॥

4. God is the Guardian of emancipated souls, the Lord of immortal forces, and the Father of enterprising preachers of Vedic knowledge. Residence secundines, newly drawn fresh milk, curds, butter, all these testify to the power of God. (2373)

५. देवानां भाग उपनाह एषा३पां रस ओषधीनां घृतस्य ।
सोमस्य भक्षमवृणीत शक्रो बृहन्नद्रिरभवद् यच्छरीरम् ॥

5. This God is the last resort of the learned in their contemplation. He, due to proximity unifies and keeps them under His control. He sustains the subtle atoms of Matter, divine forces, and luminous objects. The Omnipotent God, controls the life of souls in the world, and affording shelter to all, being Most Mighty, Indivisible, brings about their dissolution. (2374)

६. सोमेन पूर्णं कलशं बिभर्षि त्वष्टा रूपाणां जनिता पशूनाम् ।
शिवास्ते सन्तु प्रजन्व॒ इह या इमा न्य१स्मभ्यं स्वधिते यच्छ या अमूः ॥

6. O God, Thou fully nourishest this universe with Thy strength of procreation. Thou art the Framer of all forms, the Begetter of all beings. O Controller of the universe, may these powers of thine apparent on the earth be propitious unto us. Use thy yonder latent powers for our good. (2375)

७. आज्यं बिभर्ति घृतमस्य रेतः साहस्रः पोषस्तमु यज्ञमाहुः ।
इन्द्रस्य रूपमृषभो वसानः सो अस्मान् देवाः शिव एतु दत्तः ॥

7. The blazing strength of God sustains divine objects. He is the Nourisher of innumerable worlds. The wise call Him The Great Soul. O learned persons, may He, the Great Seer, assuming the rank of God, the Bestower of all objects, Full of bliss, come unto us. (2376)

८. इन्द्रस्यौजो वरुणस्य बाहू अश्विनोरंसौ मरुतामियं ककुत् ।
बृहस्पतिं संभृतमेतमाहुर्ये धीरासः कवयो ये मनीषिणः ॥

8. God possesses the vigour of the Sun, both the arms of water, the shoulders of day and night, and the joy infusing power of the vital breaths, Prāna and Apāna. They who are sages, wise and learned Rishis, call Him the Lord of mighty worlds, and power. (2377)[1]

[1]Arms of water: Sweetness, coolness. Shoulders of day and night: Brilliance and heat of the day, and calmness of night.

९. दैवीर्विशः पयस्वाना तनोषि त्वामिन्द्रं त्वां सरस्वन्तमाहुः ।
सहस्रं स एकमुखा ददाति यो ब्राह्मण ऋषभमाजुहोति ॥

9. O God, being vigorous, Thou stretchest noble subjects on all sides. The learned call Thee highly Powerful, and a vast ocean of knowledge. He who bestows the knowledge of God on a learned person, preaches thousands of Vedic verses pertaining to One God. (2378)

१०. बृहस्पतिः सविता ते वयो दधौ त्वष्टुर्वायोः पर्यात्मा त आभृतः ।
अन्तरिक्षे मनसा त्वा जुहोमि बर्हिष्टे द्यावापृथिवी उभे स्ताम् ॥

10. O man, the All-urging God, the Lord of all the worlds has given thee vital vigour. The All-pervading, All-Creating God has fully strengthened thy soul. With wisdom do I accept thee in the presence of God. May Heaven and Earth contribute to thy progress. (2379)[1]

११. य इन्द्र इव देवेषु गोष्वेति विवावदत् । तस्य ऋषभस्याङ्गानि ब्रह्मा सं स्तौतु भद्रया ॥

11. Just as the soul moves in vital breaths, so does God, preaching moral laws to humanity, manifest Himself in Vedic verses. A Brahma should joyfully extol the merits and virtues of that God. (2380)

१२. पार्श्वे आस्तामनुमत्या भगस्यास्तामनूवृजौ ।
अष्ठीवन्तावब्रवीन्मित्रो ममैतौ केवलाविति ॥

12. Both the sides of God represent intellect, both the rib-pieces represent supremacy. Air said, both the knee-bones are mine and mine alone. (2381)[2]

१३. भसदासीदादित्यानां श्रोणी आस्तां बृहस्पतेः । पुच्छं वातस्य देवस्य तेन धूनोत्योषधीः ॥

13. Myriad Suns represent His hinder part. His loins represent the fervour of fire. Air represents His tail, wherewith He stirs the plants and herbs. (2382)[3]

१४. गुदा आसन्त्सिनीवाल्याः सूर्यायास्त्वचमब्रुवन् । उत्थातुरब्रुवन् पद ऋषभं यदकल्पयन् ॥

14. His arteries of the anus are likened to Night. To dawn the learned assigned the skin. His feet were described as those of an energetic person, when they thought of God, in their imagination. (2383)[4]

[1]I: A learned person.

[2]The language of this verse is figurative, metaphorical not literal God is Incorporeal. His qualities have been mentioned through bodily parts. Just as air is active and moves from one place to the other, so does man move through the strength of knee-joints. The strength of knee joints is compared to that of air.

[3]The language is metaphorical. God has virtually got no physical parts.

[4]They: Learned persons. Sinivali: The night preceding that of new moon, or that night on which the moon rises with a scarcely visible crescent. The connection between the supposed physical parts of God, and worldly objects is not clear.

१५. क्रोड आसीज्जामिशंसस्य सोमस्य कलशो धृतः । देवाः संगत्य यत् सर्व ऋषभं व्यकल्पयन् ॥

15. God is like the lap of a mother, for the devotee who consider Him as a Mother, Who creates the universe. God is known as the store-house of joy. All the learned persons do think of God in various aspects. (2384)

१६. ते कुष्ठिकाः सरमायै कूर्मेभ्यो अदधुः शफान् । ऊबध्यमस्य कीटेभ्यः श्ववर्तेभ्यो अधारयन् ॥

16. The sages assigned thievish tendencies to the bitch, violent propensities to the tortoises. His undigested food, they assigned to worms that creep, crawl and feed on dead bodies. (2385)[1]

१७. शृङ्गाभ्यां रक्ष ऋषत्यवर्ति हन्ति चक्षुषा । शृणोति भद्रं कर्णाभ्यां गवां यः पतिरघ्न्यः ॥

17. Immortal God, Who is the Lord of the Vedas and innumerable worlds, removes obstacles with His two presiding forces, banishes poverty with His benign eye, and bears good tidings with His ears. (2386)[2]

१८. शतयाजं स यजते नैनं दुन्वन्त्यग्नयः ।
जिन्वन्ति विश्वे तं देवा यो ब्राह्मण ऋषभमाजुहोति ॥

18. The Brahmana who propitiates God, performs an act of hundred sacrifices (Yajñas) spiritual, elemental, physical privations torment him not. All the learned persons and the forces of nature satisfy him. (2387)[3]

१९. ब्राह्मणेभ्य ऋषभं दत्त्वा वरीयः कृणुते मनः । पुष्टिं सो अघ्न्यानां स्वे गोष्ठेऽव पश्यते ॥

19. An Acharya, imparting the knowledge of God to the seekers after God, enlarges and cheers his soul. He witnesses the growth of immortal virtues in his body. (2388)

२०. गावः सन्तु प्रजाः सन्त्वथो अस्तु तनूबलम् । तत् सर्वमनु मन्यन्तां देवा ऋषभदायिने ॥

20. Let there be learning, let there be progeny and bodily strength: all this may the learned grant to him who spreads true knowledge about God. (2389)

२१. अयं पिपान इन्द्र इद् रयिं दधातु चेतनीम् ।
अयं धेनुं सुदुघां नित्यवत्सां वशं दुहां विपश्चितं परो दिवः ॥

21. May this Mighty God verily grant us mental wealth. May this God grant to a wise man, free from violence and pride, supremacy, and a speech that fulfils all desires, and ever affords shelter. (2390)

[1]The sages believe that bitches, dogs, tortoises, worms, who are violent in nature, are the fruits, according to God's dispensation of thievish tendencies of human souls.

[2]God has no Physical eye, but possesses the power of a thousand eyes. He is All-seeing. He has no physical ear, but hears all suppliants. Hs is All-hearing. Two presiding forces: The powers of protecting the virtuous and punishing the wicked.

[3]Brahmana: He knows God and the Vedas.

२२. पिशङ्गरूपो नभसो वयोधा ऐन्द्रः शुष्मो विश्वरूपो न आगन् ।
आयुरस्मभ्यं दधत् प्रजां च रायश्च पोषैरभि नः सचताम् ॥

22. We have realised God, Lustrous like fire, the sustainer of Suns, clouds in the atmosphere, full of dignity, Almighty, All-pervading. Granting us longevity, progeny, riches, may he shower on us from all sides strength-giving objects. (2391)

२३. उपेहोपपर्चनास्मिन् गोष्ठ उप पृञ्च नः । उप ऋषभस्य यद् रेत उपेन्द्र तव वीर्यम् ॥

23. O God, our constant companion, Thou residest here in the mind. May we ever realise Thee in our heart. O God, the strength of creation, that lies in Thee, the Almighty, is verily Thy strength! (2392)

२४. एतं वो युवानं प्रति दध्मो अत्र तेन क्रीडन्तीश्चरत वशाँ अनु ।
मा नो हासिष्ट जनुषा सुभागा रायश्च पोषैरभि नः सचध्वम् ॥

24. O men we dedicate ye to this ever young, active God. In this world, controlling your organs, sporting with Him, remain in His Company. O fortunate persons, never forsake us by your nature, and approach us with riches, invigorating milk and food! (2393)[1]

Chapter (Anuvāka) 3

HYMN V

१. आ नयैतमा रभस्व सुकृतां लोकमपि गच्छतु प्रजानन् ।
तीर्त्वा तमांसि बहुधा महान्त्यजो नाकमा क्रमतां तृतीयम् ॥

1. O man, control the soul, and take it on the right path. Be energetic. May thy soul, full of wisdom, attain to the dignity of pious greatmen. The soul, overcoming many mighty moral frailties, like grief, infatuation, avarice, lust and anger, and being unborn and immortal, should attain to the third blissful God. (2394)[2]

२. इन्द्राय भागं परि त्वा नयाम्यस्मिन् यज्ञे यजमानाय सूरिम् ।
ये नो द्विषन्त्यनु तान् रभस्वानागसो यजमानस्य वीराः ॥

2. O soul, in this yajña of life, I take thee the sacrificer; for supremacy towards the Wise God. Overcome the vices that torment us; as all the valiant sons of God are sinless. (2395)

३. प्र पदोऽव नेनिग्धि दुश्चरितं यच्चचार शुद्धैः शफैरा क्रमतां प्रजानन् ।
तीर्त्वा तमांसि बहुधा विपश्यन्नजो नाकमा क्रमतां तृतीयम् ॥

[1]We, Us: Learned persons. Sporting: Deriving joy in God's company.

[2]Third: Higher than Matter and Soul. Transcending the two stages of Matter and Soul. Swami Dayanand has translated this verse in the Sanskar Vidhi. See *Atharva*, Kāṇḍa IV, Hymn XIV.

3. O God, wash from the jurisdiction of the soul all trace of evil-doing; May it, full of knowledge, go upward with noble sentiments. Overcoming manifold sins, let the far-sighted, unborn, immortal soul attain to the Blissful God, higher than Matter and Soul. (2396)

४. अनु च्छ्य श्यामेन त्वचमेतां विशस्तर्यथापर्व१सिना माभि मंस्थाः ।
माभि द्रुहः परुशः कल्पयैनं तृतीये नाके अधि वि श्रयैनम् ॥

4. O preceptor, the dispeller of nescience, cut asunder completely, with knowledge and exertion, this covering of ignorance overshadowing the mind. Don't be proud. O thinker for sustenance, entertain malice for none. Strengthen this soul, and establish it in the Blissful God, higher than Matter and Soul. (2397)[1]

५. ऋचा कुम्भीमध्यग्नौ श्रयाम्या सिञ्चोदकमव धेह्येनम् ।
पर्याधत्ताग्निना शमितारः शृतो गच्छतु सुकृतां यत्र लोकः ॥

5. Just as a cauldron is heated being placed on fire, so do I, an aspirant after salvation, through the fire of knowledge, depending upon the guru blazing with learning, strengthen myself. O Guru, just aswater is put in a heated cauldron, so preach unto me, a seeker after truth, the knowledge of God, whereby I may obtain bliss. O disciple, "understand the true nature of this soul." O self-controlled preceptors, "Unite me with that Wise God." Perfected through penance, let the disciple go to a place where dwell the righteous. (2398)

६. उत्क्रामातः परि चेदतप्तस्तप्ताच्चरोरधि नाकं तृतीयम् ।
अग्नेरग्निरधि सं बभूविथ ज्योतिष्मन्तमभि लोकं जयैतम् ॥

6. O aspirant after salvation, thus acquiring knowledge, rise to a position higher than the present. If thou hast not practised sufficient austerity, then just as boiling water rises from the hot cauldron in the shape of steam, so shouldst thou by practising penance, rise to God, higher than Matter and Soul. Become wise, acquiring wisdom from God, the great Teacher, conquer and win this lucid world of splendour. (2399)

७. अजो अग्निरजमु ज्योतिराहुरजं जीवता ब्रह्मणे देयमाहुः ।
अजस्तमांस्यप हन्ति दूरमस्मिंल्लोके श्रद्दधानेन दत्तः ॥

7. The immortal soul is full of lustre like fire. The sages name the soul as Light, and say that living man must dedicate the soul to God. Dedicated in this world by a devout believer, the soul dispels and drives away sins. (2400)

[1]God occupies the third stage of spiritual elevation. Matter is the first, Soul the second, and God the third highest stage. Thinker for sustenance: The teacher thinks for the welfare and sustenance of the pupil.

८. पञ्चौदनः पञ्चधा वि क्रमतामाक्रंस्यमानस्त्रीणि ज्योतींषि ।
ईजानानां सुकृतां प्रेहि मध्यं तृतीये नाके अधि वि श्रयस्व ।

8. Let the soul, protected by five elements, willing to acquire three lights through five channels, advance further. Let the soul go amidst the pious who have performed their worship, and dwell in God, third in superiority to Matter and Soul. (2401)[1]

९. अजा रोह सुकृतां यत्र लोकः शरभो न चत्तोऽति दुर्गाण्येषः ।
पञ्चौदनो ब्रह्मणे दीयमानः स दातारं तृप्त्या तर्पयाति ॥

9. O unborn soul, rise to that position where dwell the righteous. This soul, when solicited, overcomes all obstacles like a lion. The soul, dedicated to God, satisfies the dedicator with all fulness! (2402)

१०. अजस्त्रिनाके त्रिदिवे त्रिपृष्ठे नाकस्य पृष्ठे ददिवांसं दधाति ।
पञ्चौदनो ब्रह्मणे दीयमानो विश्वरूपा धेनुः कामदुघास्येका ॥

10. The Unborn God, sets an aspirant after salvation on the pitch of heavenly felicity, free from spiritual elemental, and physical woes, full of three lights, and equipped with three joys. The soul is fit to be dedicated to God. This convincing Vedic speech is the unique bestower of all joys, and the fulfiller of all desires. (2403)

११. एतद् वो ज्योतिः पितरस्तृतीयं पञ्चौदनं ब्रह्मणेऽजं ददाति ।
अजस्तमांस्यप हन्ति दूरमस्मिंल्लोके श्रद्दधानेन दत्तः ॥

11. Ye Fathers, God is the third Light that is yours. He dedicates the unborn soul, protected by five elements, for the spread of Vedic knowledge. Dedicated in this world by the devout believer, the soul dispels and drives away sins. (2404)[2]

१२. ईजानानां सुकृतां लोकमीप्सन् पञ्चौदनं ब्रह्मणेऽजं ददाति ।
स व्याप्तिमभि लोकं जयैतं शिवो३स्मभ्यं प्रतिगृहीतो अस्तु ॥

12. He, who, being desirous to seek the company of pious persons who perform spiritual sacrifice, (Yajña) dedicates to God, his unborn soul, protected by five elements, can attain to the high rank of pious persons for the acquisition of mental peace. May he, accepted by God, be auspicious unto us. (2405)

१३. अजो ह्य१ग्नेरजनिष्ट शोकाद् विप्रो विप्रस्य सहसो विपश्चित् ।
इष्टं पूर्तमभिपूर्तं वषट्कृतं तद् देवा ऋतुशः कल्पयन्तु ॥

[1]Five elements: Earth, Water, Fire, Air, Ether (Ākāsha). Three lights: Fire, Lightning, Sun, or Prāna, Apāna, Vyāna, or Sun, Moon, Fire. Five channels: Nose, Tongue, Eye, Skin, Ear.

[2]Fathers: Learned persons. Third light: The first two being Matter and soul. Five elements: Earth, Water, Fire, Air, Ether (Ākāsha).

13. The unborn soul springs from the glow of God. The wise soul understands the strength of the Wise God. Hence the learned should arrange at proper seasons, the study of the Vedas, and performance of noble deeds of charity, with full devotion. (2406)[1]

१४. अमोतं वासो दद्याद्धिरण्यमपि दक्षिणाम् ।
तथा लोकान्त्समाप्नोति ये दिव्या ये च पार्थिवाः ।।

14. Let a learned pupil give home-woven raiment, and gold as guerdon to his preceptor. So he obtains completely all celestial and terrestrial positions of dignity. (2407)

१५. एतास्त्वाजोप यन्तु धाराः सोम्या देवीर्घृतपृष्ठा मधुश्चुतः ।
स्तभान पृथिवीमुत द्यां नाकस्य पृष्ठे अधि सप्तरश्मौ ।।

15. O soul, may these beautiful, lustrous, pleasure-promulgating powers of God, reach thee. God, in His divine, supreme state, reigning high above the seven-rayed Sun, is supporting Heaven and Earth. (2408)

१६. अजो३स्यज स्वर्गोऽसि त्वया लोकमङ्गिरसः प्राजानन् । तं लोकं पुण्यं प्र ज्ञेषम् ।।

16. O soul, thou art unborn, and full of joy. Through thee, the sages realise God. May I know that Holy God. (2409)

१७. येना सहस्रं वहसि येनाग्ने सर्ववेदसम् । तेनेमं यज्ञं नो वह स्वर्देवेषु गन्तवे ।।

17. O God, with whatever strength Thou sustainest the entire universe, and retainest all knowledge, with that, take our sacrificing soul to learned emancipated persons, for the acquisition of salvation. (2410)[2]

१८. अजः पक्वः स्वर्गे लोके दधाति पञ्चौदनो निर्ऋतिं बाधमानः ।
तेन लोकान्त्सूर्यवतो जयेम ।।

18. The mature, unborn soul protected by five elements, dispelling ignorance, establishes itself in Blissful God. With the help of that soul, let us acquire positions aglow with knowledge. (2411)

१९. यं ब्राह्मणे निदधे यं च विक्षु या विप्रुष ओदनानामजस्य ।
सर्वं तदग्ने सुकृतस्य लोके जानीतान्नः संगमने पथीनाम् ।।

19. The unborn soul, which has been placed by God in the body of a Vedic scholar, or those of ordinary mortals, possesses manifold powers of breaths. O God, let us know that all these powers are the pathways for reaching the pure state of emancipation. (2412)

[1]Springs: Assumes bodily form.
[2]See *Yajur*, 14-55. This verse has been explained by Swami Dayanand in *Sanskār vidhi* in the chapter on Sanyāsa.

२०. अजो वा इदमग्रे व्यक्रमत तस्योर इयमभवद् द्यौः पृष्ठम् ।।
अन्तरिक्षं मध्यं दिशः पार्श्वे समुद्रौ कुक्षी ।।

20. The Eternal God, in the beginning, created this world. The Earth became His breast. Heaven was His back. The regions were His sides. Both oceans formed the hollow of His body. (2413)[1]

२१. सत्यं चर्तं च चक्षुषी विश्वं सत्यं श्रद्धा प्राणो विराट् शिरः ।
एष वा अपरिमितो यज्ञो यदजः पञ्चौदनः ।।

21. Laws of Nature and the Vedas are His eyes. Complete truth and faith are His breaths. Highly lustrous Matter is His head. Eternal God, the Absorber of five elements at the time of Dissolution, is indeed, the unlimited sacrifice. (2414)[2]

२२. अपरिमितमेव यज्ञमाप्नोत्यपरिमितं लोकमव रुन्धे ।
यो३जं पञ्चौदनं दक्षिणाज्योतिषं ददाति ।।

22. He, who dedicates himself to the Eternal God, the Absorber of five elements, Illumined with charity, attains to the unlimited God, and realises in his heart, the unlimited, beautiful God. (2415)

२३. नास्यास्थीनि भिन्द्यान्न मज्ज्ञो निर्धयेत् । सर्वमेनं समादायेदमिदं प्र वेशयेत् ।।

23. A wise man, taking God to be Omnipresent, should not break the bones of any living being, nor suck out his marrow. Realizing God truly and fully, let him know Him present in each and every sentient being. (2416)

२४. इदमिदमेवास्य रूपं भवति तेनैनं सं गमयति ।
इषं मह ऊर्जमस्मै दुहे यो३जं पञ्चौदनं दक्षिणाज्योतिषं ददाति ।।

24. The grandeur of God is visible in each and every object. His All-pervading nature unites this soul with God. He, who dedicates himself to the Unborn God, the Absorber of five elements, Illumined with charity, receives from Him, food, greatness and strength. (2417)

२५. पञ्च रुक्मा पञ्च नवानि वस्त्रा पञ्चास्मै धेनवः कामदुघा भवन्ति ।
यो३जं पञ्चौदनं दक्षिणाज्योतिषं ददाति ।।

25. He, who dedicates himself to the Unborn God, the Absorber of five elements, Illumined with charity, gets various precious articles like gold, many new garments, and many Vedic verses, which fulfil all his wishes. (2418)[3]

[1]Both oceans: The earthly ocean full of water, and atmosphere, the ocean full of air and vapours. God has no body. He is incorporeal. The language is metaphorical.

[2]Sacrifice: The giver of the fruit of our actions.

[3]Pt. Jaidev Vidyalankar has translated पंच वस्त्राः as five sheaths (Koshās), पंच धेनवः as five organs of cognition.

२६. पञ्च रुक्मा ज्योतिरस्मै भवन्ति वर्म वासांसि तन्वे॒ भवन्ति ।
स्वर्गं लोकमश्नुते यो३जं पञ्चौदनं दक्षिणाज्योतिषं ददाति ॥

26. He, who dedicates himself to the Unborn God, the Absorber of five elements. Illumined with charity, achieves blissful salvation. Robes become armour to defend his body; various attractive, glittering substances like gold serve him as a beacon-light. (2419)[1]

२७. या पूर्वं पतिं वित्त्वाथान्यं विन्दतेऽपरम् । पञ्चौदनं च तावजं ददातो न वि योषतः ॥

27. A woman, who having realised God, the Primordial Lord of the universe, accepts another worldly man as husband, is never separated from God, along with her husband, if they respectively dedicate to God, their unborn soul, protected by five elements. (2420)

२८. समानलोको भवति पुनर्भुवापरः पतिः । यो३जं पञ्चौदनं दक्षिणाज्योतिषं ददाति ॥

28. He, who dedicates himself to the Unborn God, the Absorber of five elements, Illumined with charity, being the second husband of the re-married woman, attains to the Beautiful God, as does his wife. (2421)

२९. अनुपूर्ववत्सां धेनुमनड्वाहमुपबर्हणम् । वासो हिरण्यं दत्त्वा ते यन्ति दिवमुत्तमाम् ॥

29. They, who selflessly dedicate their heart-inspired words, their life breaths, their food, their bodies and souls to the service of mankind attain to the highest state of salvation. (2422)[2]

३०. आत्मानं पितरं पुत्रं पौत्रं पितामहम् । जायां जनित्रीं मातरं ये प्रियास्तानुप ह्वये ॥

30. I call my soul, father, son, grandson, grandfather, wife, mother who bore me, and give them advice. (2423)[3]

३१. यो वै नैदाघं नाम ऋतुं वेद । एष वै नैदाघो नाम ऋतुर्यदजः पञ्चौदनः ।
निरेवाप्रियस्य भ्रातृव्यस्य श्रियं दहति भवत्यात्मना ।
यो३जं पञ्चौदनं दक्षिणाज्योतिषं ददाति ॥

[1]Beacon-light: As light from the light-house shows the right path to the ships travelling in the ocean at night, so for the devotees of God, wealth is meant not for luxury, but for the service of suffering humanity, the poor, the sick, the ignorant, and the blind.

[2]अनुपूर्ववत्सां धेनु : A cow that yields a calf each year. Figuratively it means a speech that comes out of the depth of the heart. अनड्वाह: An of Figuratively the word means life-breath. उपबर्हणम् : A coverlet Figuratively it means food. वासः A robe, Figuratively it means body. हिरण्यम् : Gold, Figuratively soul.

[3]A pious, highly, spiritually advanced person.

31. God, Who verily knows the scorching season, being Unborn and the Absorber of five elements, is worthy of worship like the sultry season. He, who dedicates himself to the Unborn God, the Absorber of five elements at the time of Dissolution, illumined with charity, rests on the strength of his soul, and eclipses the force of his unfriendly foes, like lust, anger and avarice. (2424)[1]

३२. यो वै कुर्वन्तं नाम ऋतुं वेद । कुर्वतींकुर्वतीमेवाप्रियस्य भ्रातृव्यस्य श्रियमा दत्ते ।
एष वै कुर्वन्नाम ऋतुर्यदजः पञ्चौदनः ।
निरेवाप्रियस्य भ्रातृव्यस्य श्रियं दहति भवत्यात्मना ।
योऽजं पञ्चौदनं दक्षिणाज्योतिषं ददाति ॥

32. This powerful rainy season is another beauty of the Unborn God. He, who knows the nature of the rainy season, and knows God, its Creator, overcomes the active force of passion, the unfriendly foe. He who dedicates himself to the Unborn God, the Absorber of five elements at the time of Dissolution, Illumined with charity, rests on the strength of his soul, and eclipses the force of his unfriendly foes like lust, anger and avarice. (2425)

३३. यो वै संयन्तं नाम ऋतुं वेद । संयतींसंयतीमेवाप्रियस्य भ्रातृव्यस्य श्रियमा दत्ते ।
एष वै संयन्नाम ऋतुर्यदजः पञ्चौदनः ।
निरेवाप्रियस्य भ्रातृव्यस्य श्रियं दहति भवत्यात्मना ।
योऽजं पञ्चौदनं दक्षिणाज्योतिषं ददाति ॥

33. He, who knows the cold weather, fit for self-restraint, overcomes the binding and restricting force of his unfriendly foes like lust and anger. This cold weather is another beauty of the Unborn God. He who dedicates himself to the Unborn God, the Absorber of five elements at the time of Dissolution, Illumined with charity, rests on the strength of his soul, and eclipses the force of his unfriendly foes like lust, anger and avarice. (2426)[2]

३४. यो वै पिन्वन्तं नाम ऋतुं वेद । पिन्वतीपिन्वतीमेवाप्रियस्य भ्रातृव्यस्य श्रियमा दत्ते ।
एषं वै पिन्वन्नाम ऋतुर्यदजः पञ्चौदनः ।
निरेवाप्रियस्य भ्रातृव्यस्य श्रियं दहति भवत्यात्मना ।
योऽजं पञ्चौदनं दक्षिणाज्योतिषं ददाति ॥

34. He, who knows the invigorating winter season, overcomes the developed advanced force of his unfriendly foes like lust and anger. This winter season is another beauty of the Unborn God. He who dedicates himself to the Unborn God, the Absorber of five elements at the time of Dissolution, Illumined with charity, rests on the strength of his soul, and eclipses the force of his unfriendly foes like lust, anger and avarice. (2427)

[1]Scorching season: Summer. Just as summer is worthy of respect, as without its heat there can be no rainy season, and no cultivation of crops, so God is worthy of worship, without whose mercy there can be no spiritual advancement.

[2]Winter is the best season for meditation and contemplation.

३५. यो वा उद्यन्तं नाम ऋतुं वेद । उद्यतीमुद्यतीमेवाप्रियस्य भ्रातृव्यस्य श्रियमा दत्ते ।
एष वा उद्यन्नाम ऋतुर्यदजः पञ्चौदनः ।
निरेवाप्रियस्य भ्रातृव्यस्य श्रियं दहति भवत्यात्मना ।
योऽजं पञ्चौदनं दक्षिणाज्योतिषं ददाति ॥

35. He, who knows the Dewy season, when the Sun begins to progress towards the North, overcomes the rising force of his unfriendly foes like lust and anger. This dewy season is another beauty of the Unborn God. He who dedicates himself to the Unborn God, the Absorber of five elements at the time of Dissolution, Illumined with charity, rests on the strength of his soul, and eclipses the force of his unfriendly-foes like lust, anger and avarice. (2428)

३६. यो वा अभिभुवं नाम ऋतुं वेद ।
अभिभवन्तीमभिभवन्तीमेवाप्रियस्य भ्रातृव्यस्य श्रियमा दत्ते ।
एष वा अभिभूर्नाम ऋतुर्यदजः पञ्चौदनः ।
निरेवाप्रियस्य भ्रातृव्यस्य श्रियं दहति भवत्यात्मना ।
योऽजं पञ्चौदनं दक्षिणाज्योतिषं ददाति ॥

36. He, who knows the spring season, that lowers the intensity of winter, overcomes the surpassing force of his unfriendly foes like lust and anger. This spring season is another beauty of the Unborn God. He who dedicates himself to the Unborn God, the Absorber of five elements at the time of Dissolution, Illumined with charity, rests on the strength of his soul, and eclipses the force of his unfriendly foes like lust, anger and avarice. (2429)

३७. अजं च पचत पञ्च चौदनान् ।
सर्वा दिशः संमनसः सध्रीचीः सान्तर्देशाः प्रति गृह्णन्तु त एतम् ॥

37. O learned persons fully meditate on the Eternal God, strengthen the five breaths that build our body. O man may the denizens of all quarters and sub-quarters accept this resolve of thine. (2430)[1]

३८. तास्ते रक्षन्तु तव तुभ्यमेतं ताभ्य आज्यं हविरिदं जुहोमि ॥

38. O man, may all persons preserve this resolve of thine. May they obey thy behest. May they be thy well-wishers, I, a spiritually advanced person, offer to them the knowledge of God, like an oblation of molten butter. (2431)

HYMN VI

Paryāya 1

१. यो विद्याद् ब्रह्म प्रत्यक्षं परूंषि यस्य संभारा ऋचो यस्यानूक्यम् ॥

[1]May all persons be as determined in meditating on God and controlling the breaths as thou art.

1. A learned person is worthy of honour, who verily knows God, Whose nourishing strength is manifold, Whose Vedic verses are friendly, favourable words. (2432)[1]

२. सामानि यस्य लोमानि यजुर्हृदयमुच्यते परिस्तरणमिद्धविः ॥

2. Whose hairs are Sāma verses, Whose heart is the Yajurveda, Whose vastness is verily oblation. (2433)

३. यद् वा अतिथिपतिरतिथीन् प्रतिपश्यति देवयजनं प्रेक्षते ॥

3. When a householder waits for learned guests, verily he means to honour the holy persons. (2434)

४. यदभिवदति दीक्षामुपैति यदुदकं याचत्यपः प्र णयति ॥

4. When he salutes them reverently he undergoes preparation for a religious ceremony: when he calls for water, he solemnly brings sacrificial water. (2435)[2]

५. या एव यज्ञ आपः प्रणीयन्ते ता एव ताः ॥

5. The water that is solemnly brought at a sacrifice (Yajña) is the same water as is offered to an honourable guest. (2436)

६. यत् तर्पणमाहरन्ति य एवाग्नीषोमीयः पशुर्बध्यते स एव सः ॥

6. Milk, honey, invigorating articles are brought for the honourable guest. He is an ideal guest, who is a recluse, bound by the ties of love, and full of knowledge and superhuman power. (2437)

७. यदावसथान् कल्पयन्ति सदोहविर्धानान्येव तत् कल्पयन्ति ॥

7. Whereas the householders arrange dwelling rooms for the guests, they look for places fit for Brahmins to sit upon, and where provisions for a Yajña (sacrifice) are stored. (2438)

८. यदुपस्तृणन्ति बर्हिरेव तत् ॥

8. The couch spread by a householder for a hermit, is for him a seat of grass. (2439)

९. यदुपरिशयनमाहरन्ति स्वर्गमेव तेन लोकमवरुन्द्धे ॥

9. Just as a householder feels joy in lying on a well-spread couch, so does a hermit verily enjoy the attainment of the Beautiful God, the Embodiment of happiness. (2440)

[1]Verses 1-4 and 6th verse have been explained by Maharshi Dayananda in the *Sanskar Vidhi*, in the chapter on Sanyāsa Ashrama.

[2]First 'he' refers to the householder, second 'he' to the guest and third 'he' also to the householder. Religious ceremony: Honouring the guest.

१०. यत् कशिपूपबर्हणमाहरन्ति परिधय एव ते ॥

10. The vast, manifest powers of God are to a hermit, what coverings and pillows are to a householder. (2441)

११. यदाञ्जनाभ्यञ्जनमाहरन्त्याज्यमेव तत् ॥

11. Just as householders use ointment for the eyes, and oil for the body, so does a Sanyasi realise God, the Creator of the universe. (2442)[1]

१२. यत् पुरा परिवेषात् खादमाहरन्ति पुरोडाशावेव तौ ॥

12. Whereas the householders eat nice food served beforehand, a Sanyasi is contented with two cakes of rice meal. (2443)

१३. यदशनकृतं ह्वयन्ति हविष्कृतमेव तद्ध्वयन्ति ॥

13. Whereas the householders call the man who prepares food, the hermits invoke God, the Giver of gifts and Receiver of homage. (2444)

१४. ये व्रीहयो यवा निरुप्यन्तेऽशव एव ते ॥

14. Just as rice and barley well served are food for the householders, so subtle deliberations are the mental food for the hermits. (2445)

१५. यान्युलूखलमुसलानि ग्रावाण एव ते ॥

15. Just as the pestle and mortar are for the householders to prepare food for the learned guests, so are religious sermons for the hermits. (2446)[2]

१६. शूर्पं पवित्रं तुषा ऋजीषाभिषवणीरापः ॥
१७. स्रुग् दर्विर्नेक्षणमायवनं द्रोणकलशाः कुम्भ्यो॒ वायव्या॒नि पात्राणीयमेव कृष्णाजिनम् ॥

16,17. Just as the winnowing-basket, the filter, the chaff, the Soma dregs, the bathing basins the sacrificial water, the spoon, the ladle. the fork, the stirring prong, the Soma tubs, the cooking pots and the vessels are useful for the householders, so does this earth serve for the hermits, the purpose of the black-antelope's skin to lie on. (2447)

Paryāya 2

१. यजमानब्राह्मणं वा एतदतिथिपतिः कुरुते यदाहार्या॒णि प्रेक्षत इदं भूया३ इदा३मिति ॥

1. When a householder looks at the eatables prepared for the guest, he says, More here! Yet more here, and behaves towards him, as a sacrificer (Yajña) does towards a learned Ritvij. (2448)[3]

[1]Sanyasi: A recluse, hermit or anchorite.
[2]Learned guests: Atithis just as the householders by grinding eatables with pestle and mortar prepare food, so do the hermits through penance preach religious sermons.
[3]Ritwij: The priest who officiates at the Yajña, or a ceremony.

२. यदाह भूय उद्धरेति प्राणमेव तेन वर्षीयांसं कुरुते ॥

2. When a householder requests the guest to take more, he brings more invigorating food for him. (2449)[1]

३. उप हरति हवींष्या सादयति ॥

3. When a householder brings materials near the guest, he brings them for oblations. (2450)

४. तेषामासन्नानामतिथिरात्मञ्जुहोति ॥

4. Of the materials brought, the guest (hermit) makes an oblation in his mouth. (2451)[2]

५. स्रुचा हस्तेन प्राणे यूपे स्रुक्कारेण वषट्कारेण ॥

5. With hand as a ladle, with breath strong like a post, with the use of ladle, with the exclamation of Swāhā, the anchoretic guest puts the eatables into his mouth as an oblation. (2452)

६. एते वै प्रियाश्चाप्रियाश्चर्त्विजः स्वर्गं लोकं गमयन्ति यदतिथयः ॥

6. These guests (hermits) as priests beloved or not beloved, take the householder to a happy mental attitude. (2453)[3]

७. स य एवं विद्वान् न द्विषन्नश्नीयान्न द्विषतोऽन्नमश्नीयान्न मीमांसितस्य न मीमांसमानस्य ॥

7. A hermit who hath this knowledge should not eat the food of one whom he dislikes, should not eat the food of one who hates him, nor of one who is doubtful, nor of one who is undecided. (2454)

८. सर्वो वा एष जग्धपाप्मा यस्यान्नमश्नन्ति ॥

8. This man whose food they eat hath all his vice blotted out. (2455)[4]

९. सर्वो वा एषोऽजग्धपाप्मा यस्यान्नं नाश्नन्ति ॥

9. All that man's sin whose food they do not eat remains unblotted out. (2456)[5]

१०. सर्वदा वा एष युक्तग्रावार्द्रपवित्रो वितताध्वर आहृतयज्ञक्रतुर्य उपहरति ॥

[1]Him: The guest.

[2]Makes an oblation: Eats.

[3](4,5,6) These three verses are explained by Maharshi Dayananda in the *Sanskarvidhi* in the chapter on the Sanyāsa Ashrama.

[4]They: The hermits who visit the householders as guests. Blotted out: Literally burnt up.

[5]Unblotted: Unburnt unremoved literally.

10. The man who supplies food to the hermits hath always pressing stones adjusted to crush Soma, a wet Soma filter, well prepared sacrifice (Yajña) to be performed, and mental power to complete the arranged sacrifice and reap the fruit thereof. (2457)

११. प्राजापत्यो वा एतस्य यज्ञो विततो य उपहरति ॥

11. The man who makes a valuable offering of food and water to a hermit, verily performs a sacrifice for the acquisition of God, and the welfare of domestic life. (2458)[1]

१२. प्रजापतेर्वा एष विक्रमाननुविक्रमते य उपहरति ॥

12. The man who offers food to a learned guest, follows the footsteps of God. (2459)[2]

१३. योऽतिथीनां स आहवनीयो यो वेश्मनि स गार्हपत्यो यस्मिन् पचन्ति स दक्षिणाग्निः ॥

13. The company of learned hermits is like Ahvniya fire for them. Their stay in the Ashrama is like Garhpatya fire. The fire whereon they cook food is like Dakshina fire. (2460)[3]

Paryāya 3

१. इष्टं च वा एष पूर्तं च गृहाणामश्नाति यः पूर्वोऽतिथेरश्नाति ॥

1. The man who eats before the guest eats up the fruit of Vedic study and deeds of charity by his kinsmen. (2461)

२. पयश्च वा एष रसं च गृहाणामश्नाति यः पूर्वोऽतिथेरश्नाति ॥

2. The man who eats before the guest devours the milk and sap of the house. (2462)[4]

३. ऊर्जां च वा एष स्फातिं च गृहाणामश्नाति यः पूर्वोऽतिथेरश्नाति ॥

3. The man who eats before the guest destroys the vigour and prosperity of the house. (2463)

४. प्रजां च वा एष पशूंश्च गृहाणामश्नाति यः पूर्वोऽतिथेरश्नाति ॥

[1]Prajāpati means God, and the welfare of domestic life.

[2]Follows: Obeys the behest of God, to honour the learned hermits who visit his house. 11, 12, 13 These three verses have been explained by Maharshi Dayananda ji in the *Sanskāravidhi* in the chapter on the Sanyāsa Ashrama.

[3]Them, their, they refer to learned hermits. Ahvniya fire: The eastern sacrificial fire, in which the Bramcharis perform homa. Gārhpatya fire: The western sacred fire in which householders perform Yajña. Dakshina: The southern sacrificial fire in which Vanprasthis perform havan.

[4]Devours: Destroys.

4. The man who eats before the guest destroys the progeny and the cattle of the house. (2464)

५. कीर्ति च वा एष यशश्च गृहाणामश्नाति यः पूर्वोऽतिथेरश्नाति ।।

5. The man who eats before the guest destroys the fame and reputation of the house. (2465)

६. श्रियं च वा एष संविदं च गृहाणामश्नाति यः पूर्वोऽतिथेरश्नाति ।।

6. The man who eats before the guest destroys the glory and unity of the house. (2466)

७. एष वा अतिथिर्यच्छ्रोत्रियस्तस्मात् पूर्वो नाश्नीयात् ।।

7. The householder should not eat before the guest who is a Brahmin versed in Vedic lore. (2467)

८. अशितावत्यतिथावश्नीयाद् यज्ञस्य सात्मत्वाय यज्ञस्याविच्छेदाय तद् व्रतम् ।।

8. A householder should eat when the guest hath eaten. This is the rule a householder should follow for the animation of the sacrifice and the preservation of its continuity. (2468)

९. एतद् वा उ स्वादीयो यदधिगवं क्षीरं वा मांसं वा तदेव नाश्नीयात् ।।

9. A householder should not eat before the guest, delicious corn produced from the earth, milk, and intellect-developing articles like milk-products and fruits. (2469)[1]

Paryāya 4

१. स य एवं विद्वान् क्षीरमुपसिच्योपहरति ।।
२. यावदग्निष्टोमेनेष्ट्वा सुसमृद्धेनावरुन्द्धे तावदेनेनाव रुन्द्धे ।।

1,2. The man, who having this knowledge of honouring a guest, pouring milk in a basin offers it to the hermit (guest) wins for himself as much fruit thereby as he gains by the performance of a very successful Agnishtoma sacrifice. (2470)[2]

[1]गो means earth: अधिगवम् means eatables produced from the earth. The word मांस does not mean meat, मांस माननं वा मानसं वा मनोऽस्मिन्तसीदतीति वा—निरु० ४/३ मननसाधकं बुद्धिवर्धकं वस्तु । The word means an article that develops intellect and is pleasant to the mind. As meat-eating has been condemned by the Vedas in various verses, it cannot be supposed to be encouraged here, for fear of self-contradiction. Shri Apte the famous lexicographer interprets मांस as roughage of a fruit.

[2]Agnishtoma is a Yajña performed in praise of God in the spring season.

३. स य एवं विद्वान्त्सर्पिरुपसिच्योपहरति ॥
४. यावदतिरात्रेणेष्ट्वा सुसमृद्धेनावरुन्द्धे तावदेनेनाव रुन्द्धे ॥

3,4. The man, who having this knowledge of honouring a guest, pouring clarified butter in a basin offers it to the hermit, wins for himself as much fruit as he gains by the performance of a very successful Atirātra sacrifice. (2471)[1]

५. स य एवं विद्वान् मधूपसिच्योपहरति ॥
६. यावत् सत्रसद्येनेष्ट्वा सुसमृद्धेनावरुन्द्धे तावदेनेनाव रुन्द्धे ॥

5,6. The man, who having this knowledge of honouring a guest, pouring honey in a basin offers it to the hermit, wins for himself as much fruit as he gains by the performance of Sattrasadya sacrifice. (2472)[2]

७. स य एवं विद्वान् मांसमुपसिच्योपहरति ॥
८. यावद् द्वादशाहेनेष्ट्वा सुसमृद्धेनावरुन्द्धे तावदेनेनाव रुन्द्धे ॥

7,8. The man, who having this knowledge of honouring a guest, putting intellect-developing, and pleasant to the mind articles in a basin, like fruits, milk, butter offers them to the hermit, wins for himself as much fruit as he gains by the performance of a very successful twelve-day sacrifice. (2473)

९. स य एवं विद्वानुदकमुपसिच्योपहरति ॥
१०. प्रजानां प्रजननाय गच्छति प्रतिष्ठां प्रियः प्रजानां भवति य एवं
विद्वानुदकमुपसिच्योपहरति ॥

9,10. The man, who having this knowledge of honouring a guest, takes water in a basin and offers it to the learned guest, obtains a support for the procreation of progeny, and becomes dear to the progeny, even the man who having this knowledge of honouring a guest takes water in a basin and offers it to the guest. (2474)[3]

Paryāya 5

१. तस्मा उषा हिङ्कृणोति सविता प्र स्तौति ॥
२. बृहस्पतिरूर्जयोद् गायति त्वष्टा पुष्टया प्रति हरति विश्वे देवा निधनम् ॥
३. निधनं भूत्याः प्रजायाः पशूनां भवति य एवं वेद ॥

[1]Atirātra: A sacrifice that is performed throughout the night, like that of Holi and Dipāwali. An optional part of the Jyotishtoma sacrifice.

[2]Sattrasadya: A long sacrifice, conducted by many officiating priests, and lasting, according to some authorities, from thirteen to a hundred days.

[3]Repetition in the verse is for the sake of emphasis. A householder must honour and respect a Sanyasi who comes to his house as a guest.

1,2,3. For the householder, who knows how to honour a guest, Dawn brings the message of joy, the Sun sings praise, Air with full vigour chants his virtues, God grants nourishment, all the forces of nature grant shelter. He becomes the abiding place of welfare, of progeny, and of cattle. (2475)[1]

४. तस्मा उद्यन्त्सूर्यो हिङ्कृणोति संगवः प्र स्तौति ॥

५. मध्यंदिन उद्गायत्यपराह्णः प्रति हरत्यस्तंयन् निधनम् ।
निधनं भूत्याः प्रजायाः पशूनां भवति य एवं वेद ॥

4,5. For the householder, who knows how to honour a guest, the rising Sun brings the message of joy, the early morning Sun filled with rays sings praise, the mid-day Sun chants his virtues, the afternoon Sun grants nourishment, the setting Sun grants shelter. He becomes the abiding place of welfare, of progeny, and of cattle. (2476)

६. तस्मा अभ्रो भवन् हिङ्कृणोति स्तनयन् प्र स्तौति ॥

७. विद्योतमानः प्रति हरति वर्षन्नुद्गायत्युद्गृह्णन् निधनम् ॥
निधनं भूत्याः प्रजायाः पशूनां भवति य एवं वेद ॥

6,7. For the householder who knows how to honour a guest, the would-be-cloud brings the message of joy, the thundering cloud sings praise, the lightening cloud grants nourishment, the raining cloud chants his virtues, the cloud grants shelter when it stays the downpour. He becomes the abiding place of welfare, of progeny, and of cattle. (2477)

८. अतिथीन् प्रति पश्यति हिङ्कृणोत्यभि वदति प्र स्तौत्युदकं याचत्युद् गायति ॥

९. उप हरति प्रति हरत्युच्छिष्टं निधनम् ॥

१०. निधनं भूत्याः प्रजायाः पशूनां भवति य एवं वेद ॥

8,9,10. When a householder looks at the guests, he verily utters a sound of joy. When he salutes the guests, he verily praises them. When he requests the guests to accept water, he verily acts an Udgātā. When he offers food to the guests, he verily acts as a Pratihartā. The residue of food prepared for the guests is the last free gift of the sacrifice. The householder who knows how to honour a guest becomes the abiding place of welfare, of progeny and of cattle. (2478)[2]

Paryāya 6

१. यत् क्षत्तारं ह्वयत्या श्रावयत्येव तत् ॥

1. When the guest summons the householder, the fulfiller of his wants, he verily gives Vedic instruction. (2479)

[1]Hinkāra, Prastāva, Udgitha, Pratihāra and Nidhana are the five parts of Sāma recitation. This verse describes the fruit of honouring a learned sage as a guest.

[2]Udgātā: A reciter of the Vedas. Pratiharta: An assistant of the Udgātā.

२. यत् प्रतिशृणोति प्रत्याश्रावयत्येव तत् ॥

2. When the householder listens attentively, the guest (hermit) preaches unto him Vedic truth with full meditation. (2480)

३. यत् परिवेष्टारः पात्रहस्ताः पूर्वे चापरे च प्रपद्यन्ते चमसाध्वर्यव एव ते ॥

3. When the attendants with food vessels in their hands, foremost and hindmost, come in, they just wish for the non-violent usage of corn. (2481)

४. तेषां न कश्चनाहोता ॥

4. Not one of them is incompetent to perform sacrifice (Yajña). (2482)[1]

५. यद् वा अतिथिपतिरतिथीन् परिविष्य गृहानुपोदैत्यवभृथमेव तदुपावैति ॥

5. When the householder, having offered food to his guests, goes to his kinsmen, he virtually performs the bath of purification. (2483)[2]

६. यत् सभागयति दक्षिणाः सभागयति यदनुतिष्ठत उदवस्यत्येव तत् ॥

6. When the householder offers some money to the guests, he virtually distributes Dakshina (fee) to the priests in a Yajña (sacrifice). When he accompanies them for some distance to bid them parting farewell, he virtually performs Udavsāna, i.e., returning home from the place of sacrifice in an orderly manner. (2484)

७. स उपहूतः पृथिव्यां भक्षयत्युपहूतस्तस्मिन् यत् पृथिव्यां विश्वरूपम् ॥

7. A guest respectfully invited in any part of the earth, eats all the nice articles of the earth, as an invitee. (2485)

८. स उपहूतोऽन्तरिक्षे भक्षयत्युपहूतस्तस्मिन् यदन्तरिक्षे विश्वरूपम् ॥

8. A guest respectfully invited in space, enjoys all the nice articles of space, as an invitee. (2486)[3]

९. स उपहूतो दिवि भक्षयत्युपहूतस्तस्मिन् यद् दिवि विश्वरूपम् ॥

9. A guest respectfully invited in the Sun, enjoys all the nice articles of the Sun as an invitee. (2487)[4]

[1]Them: The attendants who serve the food.

[2]Having served food to his guests, when the host goes home to his relatives, he virtually is deemed to have performed the Avbrith bath, a purificatory bath taken at the end of the sacrifice.

[3]All the articles: Air, fruits, etc. Flying in the air and examining all the occurrences in space is like enjoying the nice articles of space. This verse indicates aviation was current in Vedic time.

[4]This verse indicates that there was communication between the Earth and Sun in Vedic times.

१०. स उपहूतो देवेषु भक्षयत्युपहूतस्तस्मिन् यद् देवेषु विश्वरूपम् ॥

10. A guest respectfully invited by the learned, enjoys as an invitee all the nice articles found in the learned. (2488)[1]

११. स उपहूतो लोकेषु भक्षयत्युपहूतस्तस्मिन् यल्लोकेषु विश्वरूपम् ॥

11. A guest respectfully invited in the worlds, enjoys all the nice articles of these worlds, as an invitee. (2489)[2]

१२. स उपहूत उपहूतः ॥

12. A learned guest is respectfully invited in this world as well as the next. (2490)

१३. आप्नोतीमं लोकमाप्नोत्यमुम् ॥

13. A householder who honours a learned guest gains this world and the world yonder. (2491)

१४. ज्योतिष्मतो लोकाञ्जयति य एवं वेद ॥

14. He who knows the importance of honouring a learned guest finds a place in the hearts of learned persons. (2492)

HYMN VII

१. प्रजापतिश्च परमेष्ठी च शृङ्गे इन्द्रः शिरो अग्निर्ललाटं यमः कृकाटम् ॥

1. Protection of the world, and Omnipotence, the two forces of God, are the two horns of the cow of universe; the Sun is the head, Fire the forehead, Air the joint of the neck. (2493)[3]

२. सोमो राजा मस्तिष्को द्यौरुत्तरहनुः पृथिव्यधरहनुः ॥

2. Soma, the king of herbs, is the brain, Sky is the upper jaw, Earth is the lower jaw. (2494)

३. विद्युज्जिह्वा मरुतो दन्ता रेवतीर्ग्रीवाः कृत्तिका स्कन्धा घर्मो वहः ॥

3. Lightning is the tongue, the Winds are the teeth, Revati is the neck, the Krittikās are the shoulders, the Summer is the shoulder-bar. (2495)[4]

[1]Nice articles: Celibacy, study and profound meditation in God.

[2]Worlds: Sun, Moon, Mars, Mercury, Uranus, Neptune, etc. In Vedic times all the worlds were connected with the Earth through aviation. Pt. Jaidev Vidyalankar interprets Loka as common, ordinary folk. A guest is invited and honoured by the learned and ordinary people.

[3]In this hymn, the universe has been compared to a cow. Different forces of nature are spoken of as her parts. Language is highly figurative.

[4]Revati: A star, a lunar mansion. Krittika: The third of the lunar mansions.

४. विश्वं वायुः स्वर्गो लोकः कृष्णद्रं विधरणी निवेष्यः ॥

4. The whole universe is life-breath. The throat is heavenly region. The earth is seating place. (2496)

५. श्येनः क्रोडो३न्तरिक्षं पाजस्यं१ बृहस्पतिः ककुद् बृहतीः कीकसाः ॥

5. The revolving Sun is the breast. Atmosphere is the belly. Jupiter is the hump. Vast quarters are the breast-bone and cartilages of the ribs. (2497)

६. देवानां पत्नीः पृष्टय उपसदः पर्शवः ॥

6. The rearing forces of fire and air are the back-bones, the subtle elements of fire and air are the ribs. (2498)

७. मित्रश्च वरुणश्चांसौ त्वष्टा चार्यमा च दोषणी महादेवो बाहू ॥

7. Prāna and Apāna breaths are the shoulders, the cloud and the Sun are the back-legs, desire for victory and praise efficacy are the fore-legs. (2499)

८. इन्द्राणी भसद् वायुः पुच्छं पवमानो बालाः ॥

8. Lightning is the hinder parts, Air the tail, the purifying substances like fire and air the hair. (2500)

९. ब्रह्म च क्षत्रं च श्रोणी बलमूरू ॥

9. Priestly rank and princely power are the hips, and military strength is the thighs. (2501)

१०. धाता च सविता चाष्ठीवन्तौ जङ्घा गन्धर्वा अप्सरसः कुष्ठिका अदितिः शफाः ॥

10. Retention and prosperity are the two knee-bones, males and the legs, females are bits of the feet, Earth is the hooves. (2502)

११. चेतो हृदयं यकृन्मेधा व्रतं पुरीतत् ॥

11. Thought is the heart, intelligence is the liver, law the pericardium. (2503)

१२. क्षुत् कुक्षिरिरा वनिष्ठुः पर्वताः प्लाशयः ॥

12. Hunger is the belly, corn is the rectum, clouds are the inward parts. (2504)

१३. क्रोधो वृक्कौ मन्युराण्डौ प्रजा शेपः ॥

13. Wrath is the kidneys, enthusiasm the testicles, offspring the generative organ. (2505)

१४. नदी सूत्री वर्षस्य पतय स्तना स्तनयित्नुरूधः ॥

14. The river is the womb, the clouds, the lords of rain are the breasts, the thunder is the udder. (2506)

१५. विश्वव्यचास्चर्मौषधयो लोमानि नक्षत्राणि रूपम् ॥

15. The all-embracing sky is the hide, the herbs are her hair, and the stars her variegated spots on the body. (2507)

१६. देवजना गुदा मनुष्या आन्त्राण्यत्रा उदरम् ॥

16. Godly persons are her entrails, ordinary men are her bowels, and learned guests her abdomen. (2508)

१७. रक्षांसि लोहितमितरजना ऊवध्यम् ॥

17. Devils are the blood, low, wicked, stupid persons are the undigested contents of the stomach. (2509)

१८. अभ्रं पीवो मज्जा निधनम् ॥

18. The rain-cloud is her fat, her resting place her marrow. (2510)

१९. अग्निरासीन उत्थितोऽश्विना ॥

19. Sitting He is fire, when He hath stood up He is day and night. (2511)[1]

२०. इन्द्रः प्राङ् तिष्ठन् दक्षिणा तिष्ठन् यमः ॥

20. Standing eastwards God is full of glory, standing southwards He is full of justice. (2512)

२१. प्रत्यङ् तिष्ठन् धातोदङ् तिष्ठन्त्सविता ॥

21. Standing westwards, He is the Supporter, standing northwards He is the Creator. (2513)[2]

२२. तृणानि प्राप्तः सोमो राजा ॥

22. Pervading in all objects of the universe, He is the Creator and Ruler of all. (2514)

२३. मित्र ईक्षमाण आवृत्त आनन्दः ॥

23. God is Friend when He looks upon mankind with an eye of mercy. He is full of joy when He pervades all objects. (2515)

२४. युज्यमानो वैश्वदेवो युक्तः प्रजापतिर्विमुक्तः सर्वम् ॥

24. In meditation He is the Friend of the learned. In concentration (Smādhi) He is the Protector of mankind, Free from all bonds He is Omnipotent. (2516)

[1]Ashvina may also mean Sun and Moon.

[2]God is present in all directions, as Creator, Supporter, Glorious and Just.

२५. एतद् वै विश्वरूपं सर्वरूपं गोरूपम् ॥

25. God fashions the whole universe. He gives shape to animate and inanimate creation. He bestows joy on all. (2517)

२६. उपैनं विश्वरूपाः सर्वरूपाः पशवस्तिष्ठन्ति य एवं वेद ॥

26. He, who knows this Omnipresent God, is worshipped by men of all grades, ranks, speaking and non-speaking souls. (2518)[1]

HYMN VIII

१. शीर्षक्तिं शीर्षामयं कर्णशूलं विलोहितम् । सर्वं शीर्षण्यं ते रोगं बहिर्निर्मन्त्रयामहे ॥

1. Each pain and ache that racks the head, earache, and erysipelas, all malady that wrings thy brow we charm away. through exertion. (2519)[2]

२. कर्णाभ्यां ते कङ्कूषेभ्यः कर्णशूलं विसल्पकम् । सर्वं शीर्षण्यं ते रोगं बहिर्निर्मन्त्रयामहे ॥

2. From both thine ears, from parts thereof, thine earache, and the throbbing pain, all malady that wrings thy brow we charm away with exertion. (2520)[3]

३. यस्य हेतोः प्रच्यवते यक्ष्मः कर्णत आस्यतः । सर्वं शीर्षण्यं ते रोगं बहिर्निर्मन्त्रयामहे ॥

3. So that consumption may depart forth from thine ears and from thy mouth, all malady that wrings thy brow we charm away with exertion. (2521)

४. यः कृणोति प्रमोतमन्धं कृणोति पूरुषम् । सर्वं शीर्षण्यं ते रोगं बहिर्निर्मन्त्रयामहे ॥

4. The disease that makes one deaf or dumb, and that makes one blind, all malady that wrings thy brow we charm away with exertion. (2522)

५. अङ्गभेदमङ्गज्वरं विश्वाङ्ग्यं विसल्पकम् । सर्वं शीर्षण्यं ते रोगं बहिर्निर्मन्त्रयामहे ॥

5. The throbbing pain in all thy limbs that rends thy frame with fever-throes, and all malady that wrings thy brow we charm away with exertion. (2523)

६. यस्य भीमः प्रतीकाश उद्वेपयति पूरुषम् । तक्मानं विश्वशारदं बहिर्निर्मन्त्रयामहे ॥

6. The malady whose awful look makes a man quiver with alarm, fever that prevails in each season, we charm away with exertion. (2524)

[1]Non-speaking: Animals. I have not been able to understand the connection between the parts of the body of the cow or bull, and the forces of nature. No commentator has thrown light on this relation.

[2]'We' refers to learned experienced physicians.

[3]Thine: Patient's.

७. य ऊरू अनुसर्पत्यथो एति गवीनिके । यक्ष्मं ते अन्तरङ्गेभ्यो बहिर्निर्मन्त्रयामहे ॥

7. Disease that creeps about the thighs and, afterwards, reaches both the groins, consumption from thine inward parts we charm away with exertion. (2525)

८. यदि कामादपकामाद्धृदयाज्जायते परि । हृदो बलासमङ्गेभ्यो बहिर्निर्मन्त्रयामहे ॥

8. If the disease originates from the heart, through our own wrong act, or through an unknown cause, forth from the heart and from the limbs we drive out the wasting malady. (2526)

९. हरिमाणं ते अङ्गेभ्योऽप्वामन्तरोदरात् । यक्ष्मोधामन्तरात्मनो बहिर्निर्मन्त्रयामहे ॥

9. The yellow jaundice from thy limbs, and colic from the parts within, and phthisis from thy inward lungs we drive out with exertion. (2527)

१०. आसो बलासो भवतु मूत्रं भवत्वामयत् । यक्ष्माणां सर्वेषां विषं निरवोचमहं त्वत् ॥

10. Let wasting malady be driven out. Let disease-producing elements come out in the shape of urine. I have evoked the poison of all diseases out of thee. (2528)

११. बहिर्बिलं निर्द्रवतु काहाबाहं तवोदरात् । यक्ष्माणां सर्वेषां विषं निरवोचमहं त्वत् ॥

11. Let cough-producing malady run out of thy belly. I have evoked the poison of all wasting diseases out of thee. (2529)

१२. उदरात् ते क्लोम्नो नाभ्या हृदयादधि । यक्ष्माणां सर्वेषां विषं निरवोचमहं त्वत् ॥

12. Forth from thy belly and thy lungs, forth from thy belly and thy heart, I have evoked the poison of all wasting diseases out of thee. (2530)

१३. याः सीमानं विरुजन्ति मूर्धानं प्रत्यर्षणीः । अहिंसन्तीरनामया निर्द्रवन्तु बहिर्बिलम् ॥

13. The penetrating stabs of pain which rend asunder the skull and head, let them depart and pass out of the body, free from disease and harming not. (2531)

१४. या हृदयमुपर्षन्त्यनुतन्वन्ति कीकसाः । अहिंसन्तीरनामया निर्द्रवन्तु बहिर्बिलम् ॥

14. The pangs that stab the heart and reach the breast-bone and connected parts, let them depart and pass out of the body, free from disease and harming not. (2532)

१५. याः पार्श्वे उपर्षन्त्यनुनिक्षन्ति पृष्टीः । अहिंसन्तीरनामया निर्द्रवन्तु बहिर्बिलम् ॥

15. The pangs that penetrate the sides and pierce their way along the ribs, let them depart and pass out of the body, free from disease and harming not. (2533)

१६. यास्तिरश्चीरुपर्षन्त्यर्षणीर्वक्षणासु ते । अहिंसन्तीरनामया निर्द्रवन्तु बहिर्बिलम् ॥

16. The penetrating pangs that pierce the parts of thy breast as they shoot across, let them depart and pass out of the body, free from disease and harming not. (2534)

१७. या गुदा अनुसर्पन्त्यान्त्राणि मोहयन्ति च । अहिंसन्तीरनामया निर्द्रवन्तु बहिर्बिलम् ॥

17. The pains that through the bowels creep, disordering the inward parts, let them depart and pass out of the body, free from disease and harming not. (2535)

१८. या मज्ज्ञो निर्धयन्ति परूंषि विरुजन्ति च । अहिंसन्तीरनामया निर्द्रवन्तु बहिर्बिलम् ॥

18. The pains that suck the marrow out, and rend and tear the bones apart, may they speed forth and pass out of the body, free from disease and harming not. (2536)

१९. ये अङ्गानि मदयन्ति यक्ष्मासो रोपणास्तव । यक्ष्माणां सर्वेषां विषं निरवोचमहं त्वत् ॥

19. The perplexing, wasting maladies which make thy limbs insensible, I have evoked the poison of all such maladies out of thee. (2537)

२०. विसल्पस्य विद्रधस्य वातीकारस्य वालजे: । यक्ष्माणां सर्वेषां विषं निरवोचमहं त्वत् ॥

20. Of piercing pain, of abscesses, rheumatic ache, opthalmia—I have evoked the poison of all diseases out of thee. (2538)[1]

२१. पादाभ्यां ते जानुभ्यां श्रोणिभ्यां परि भंससः ।
अनूकादर्षणीरुष्णिहाभ्यः शीर्ष्णो रोगमनीनशम् ॥

21. I have dispelled the piercing pains from thy feet, knees, hips, and hinder parts, and spine, and from the arteries of the neck, the malady that racked the head. (2539)

२२. सं ते शीर्ष्णः कपालानि हृदयस्य च यो विधुः ।
उद्यन्नादित्य रश्मिभिः शीर्ष्णो रोगमनीनशोऽङ्गभेदमशीशमः ॥

22. O patient, sound are the skull-bones of thy head and thy heart's beat is regular, Thou, Sun, arising with thy beams hath chased away the head's disease, hath stilled the pain that racked the limbs. (2540)[2]

Chapter (Anuvāka) 5

HYMN IX

१. अस्य वामस्य पलितस्य होतुस्तस्य भ्राता मध्यमो अस्त्यश्नः ।
तृतीयो भ्राता घृतपृष्ठो अस्यात्रापश्यं विश्पतिं सप्तपुत्रम् ॥

[1]Alaji: Disease of the eye attended with the appearance of small red pimples at the juncture of the cornea and sclerotica.

[2]The beams of the Sun cure headache and many other diseases.

1. The second brother of this lovely, sustaining, satisfying Sun is the voracious lightning. The third brother is the fire whose back is balmed with butter. Here have I seen God, the Lord of His subjects and the Purifier of seven organs. (2541)[1]

२. सप्त युञ्जन्ति रथमेकचक्रमेको अश्वो वहति सप्तनामा ।
त्रिनाभि चक्रमजरमनर्वं यत्रेमा विश्वा भुवनाधि तस्थुः ॥

2. The seven organs yoke the chariot of the body with the soul. The solitary soul, immortal, undecaying, bound by three virtues of Satva, Rajas, Tamas takes itself to God, on Whom these worlds of life are all dependent. (2542)

३. इमं रथमधि ये सप्त तस्थुः सप्तचक्रं सप्त वहन्त्यश्वाः ।
सप्त स्वसारो अभि सं नवन्त यत्र गवां निहिता सप्त नामा ॥

3. These seven organs are mounted on the body. They draw the body like seven horses. They act together in unison like seven sisters. The seven qualities of these organs are held and treasured in the heart. (2543)[2]

४. को ददर्श प्रथमं जायमानमस्थन्वन्तं यदनस्था बिभर्ति ।
भूम्या असुरसृगात्मा क्व स्वित् को विद्वांसमुप गात् प्रष्टुमेतत् ॥

4. Who hath beheld the Primal Being (soul), that being boneless supports the bony body? Where do the breath, blood, and soul live in the body? Who hath approached the man who knows, to ask it? (2544)[3]

५. इह ब्रवीतु य ईमङ्ग वेदास्य वामस्य निहितं पदं वेः ।
शीर्ष्णः क्षीरं दुह्रते गावो अस्य वव्रिं वसाना उदकं पदापुः ॥

5. O learned person, let him who knoweth declare here, this lovely Bird's securely founded station. Forth from his head the rays pour water, which they have drunk with their foot wearing the brilliance of the Sun. (2545)[4]

६. पाकः पृच्छामि मनसाविजानन् देवानामेना निहिता पदानि ।
वत्से बष्कयेऽधि सप्त तन्तून् वि तत्निरे कवय ओतवा उ ॥

[1]Seven organs: Skin, Eye, Ear, Tongue, Nose, Mind, Intellect. The verses in this hymn occur also in the *Rigveda*, Mandal 1, Sukta 164.

[2]Seven qualities: Touch, sight, sound, taste, smell, thought, intellect.

[3]Boneless: Matter may also be interpreted for अनस्था. Both soul and matter in nascent state are boneless.

[4]The verse is a kind of riddle. Who is the bird, whose cows (rays, organs) drink water with their feet, and pour it in the form of rain or knowledge from above. There are two answers to the riddle. The birds are the Sun and Soul गावः i.e., cows are the rays of the Sun and organs of the body. Just as rays take away water from the earth and pour it in the form of rain from the sky, so do the organs receive knowledge by their contact with external objects and spread them out through the soul for the happiness of mankind.

6. Unripe in intellect, in spirit undiscerning, I ask of my mind, where are these established places of the Sun and other luminous planets? How have the sages, depending upon the Truthful, All-pervading, Adorable God, woven their own seven threads for their progress in the world? (2546)[1]

७. अचिकित्वांश्चिकितुषश्चिदत्र कवीन् पृच्छामि विद्मनो न विद्वान् ।
वि यस्तस्तम्भ षडिमा रजांस्यजस्य रूपे किमपि स्विदेकम् ॥

7. In this connection, I, ignorant, as one who knows not, ask the wise sages who know it, for the sake of knowledge, what is that One God, Who in the Unborn's image hath established and fixed firm this world's six regions. (2547)[2]

८. माता पितरमृत आ बभाज धीत्यग्रे मनसा सं हि जग्मे ।
सा बिभत्सुर्गर्भरसा निविद्धा नमस्वन्त इदुपवाकमीयुः ॥

8. The mother Matter, serves the Father God, controlled by Him. Before the creation of the world, the Matter through self-dynamic force and the wisdom of God united itself with Him. Matter, desirous of contact with God, through His dignity, creates the universe, highly endowed with energy. The learned alone realise this real truth. (2548)

९. युक्ता मातासीद्धुरि दक्षिणाया अतिष्ठद् गर्भो वृजनीष्वन्तः ।
अमीमेद् वत्सो अनु गामपश्यद् विश्वरूप्यं त्रिषु योजनेषु ॥

9. The mother Matter was yoked to God, the Centre of mighty power. In the midst of the atoms of subtle matter, existed the controlling and creative power of God. Just as a calf lows on seeing the cow, so does the soul on seeing the All-pervading God, invoke Him, and realise in three worlds, Him, the shaper of the universe and the creator of the world. (2549)[3]

१०. तिस्रो मातृस्त्रीन् पितॄन् बिभ्रदेक ऊर्ध्वस्तस्थौ नेमव ग्लापयन्त ।
मन्त्रयन्ते दिवो अमुष्य पृष्ठे विश्वविदो वाचमविश्वविन्नाम् ॥

10. The Almighty God alone, bearing three mothers and three fathers, the forces that work for the creation of the world, exists higher above them. These three are undecaying in strength. Sages who know the secret of the universe, meditate on the nature of that Refulgent God, in words not known to all. (2550)[4]

११. पञ्चारे चक्रे परिवर्तमाने यस्मिन्नातस्थुर्भुवनानि विश्वा ।
तस्य नाक्षस्तप्यते भूरिभारः सनादेव न च्छिद्यते सनाभिः ॥

[1]Seven threads: Seven organs i.e., Skin, Eye, Ear, Tongue, Nose, Mind and intellect. This verse is also a kind of riddle. It tells that in soul are placed all stationed all forces of Nature; and on God does this world depend for its sustenance.

[2]Six regions: North, East, South, West, Nadir, Zenith.

[3]Three worlds: Earth, Mid-air, Sky.

[4]Three mothers: Satva, Rajas, Tāmas, i.e., Truth, Energy, Darkness. Three fathers: Past, Present and Future. These three: God, Mothers, Fathers.

11. Upon the ever-revolving five-spoked wheel of five elements rest and are dependent all worlds and regions. God, its axle, though heavily laden, is not heated. The Immemorial God, the Nave of the universe, is never extirpated. (2551)[1]

१२. पञ्चपादं पितरं द्वादशाकृतिं दिव आहुः परे अर्धे पुरीषिणम् ।
अथेमे अन्य उपरे विचक्षणे सप्तचक्रे षडर आहुरर्पितम् ॥

12. The learned sages speak of the mighty nature of the Refulgent God, Who resides in the universe, as Father, five-footed, and twelve shaped. Other learned persons speak of the All-pervading and All-seeing God, existing as seven-wheeled and six-spoked. (2552)[2]

१३. द्वादशारं नहि तज्जराय वर्वर्ति चक्रं परि द्यामृतस्य ।
आ पुत्रा अग्ने मिथुनासो अत्र सप्त शतानि विंशतिश्च तस्थुः ॥

13. O God, thy twelve spoked wheel of the visible world is revolving in the atmosphere, and is indestructible. Herein, joined in pairs together are established seven hundred and twenty days and nights for alleviating the misery of mankind. (2553)[3]

१४. सनेमि चक्रमजरं वि वावृत उत्तानायां दश युक्ता वहन्ति ।
सूर्यस्य चक्षू रजसैत्यावृतं यस्मिन्नातस्थुर्भुवनानि विश्वा ॥

14. The All-controlling, Immortal wheel of the universe is revolving spaciously: Ten, yoked together draw it in this wide world. The wisdom of God, united with Energy, manages the whole universe. On this Energy rest and depend all regions and planets. (2554)[4]

१५. स्त्रियः सतीस्ताँ उ मे पुंस आहुः पश्यदक्षण्वान्न वि चेतदन्धः ।
कविर्यः पुत्रः स ईमा चिकेत यस्ता विजानात् स पितुष्पितासत् ॥

15. My mighty powers that create firmness in matter's atoms are spoken of by the learned as masculine forces. He who hath eyes sees this secret, the ignorant person discerns it not. A child who is a sage comprehends it. Who knows these powers rightly is his father's father. (2555)[5]

[1]Five spoked: Five elements, Earth, Water, Air, Fire and Atmosphere constitute the ever-revolving five spoked wheel on which rest all worlds. The axle of a wheel, if laden is soon heated and the nave is broken through overwork, but God, the Axle and Nave of the wheel of the universe, though overladen with the task of controlling mighty Matter since the beginning of the universe is never disturbed or extirpated.

[2]Five-footed: Residing in five elements: Earth, Water, Air, Fire, Atmosphere. Twelve-formed: Five organs of action, i.e., Ear, Eye, Nose, Tongue and Skin, and five organs of action, Hands, Feet, Mouth, Anus, Penis, Mind and intellect. Seven wheeled: Two eyes, two ears, two noses, mouth. Six-spoked: Four directions, North, South, East, West, Nadir, Zenith.

[3]Twelve spoked: Twelve months of the year. Seven hundred and twenty: 360 days and 360 nights.

[4]Ten: The ten regions of space, the four cardinal and the four intermediate points, with the Zenith and the Nadir, or ten vital breaths.

[5]My; God's. His father's father: Is more advanced in knowledge than his father.

१६. साकंजानां सप्तथमाहुरेकजं षडिद्यमा ऋषयो देवजा इति ।
तेषामिष्टानि विहितानि धामश स्थात्रे रेजन्ते विकृतानि रूपशः ॥

16. Of the co-born the learned call the seventh single-born. The six organs, the regulators of the body, the bestowers of knowledge are born with the soul. Their duties are ordained by God in due order, and they work in various forms for the good of the soul. (2556)[1]

१७. अवः परेण पर एनावरेण पदा वत्सं बिभ्रती गौरुदस्थात् ।
सा कद्रीची कं स्विदर्धं परागात् क्वऽ स्वित् सूते नहि यूथे अस्मिन् ॥

17. Beneath the upper realm above, this lower one, this power of God sustaining the universe is visible everywhere. None knows whence it comes and whither it goes, and to what Gracious God it returns. How it creates innumerable creatures is not known God Himself belongs not to the world of Matter. (2557)

१८. अवः परेण पितरं यो अस्य वेदावः परेण पर एनावरेण ।
कवीयमानः क इह प्र वोचद् देवं मनः कुतो अधि प्रजातम् ॥

18. He, who knows the soul, the father of this mind, as second to God, and the mind as second to soul, but higher than the organs, considering himself a sage, can alone declare in this world, whence hath this godly mind had its rising. (2558)

१९. ये अर्वाञ्चस्ताँ उ पराच आहुर्ये पराञ्चस्ताँ उ अर्वाच आहुः ।
इन्द्रश्च या चक्रथुः सोम तानि धुरा न युक्ता रजसो वहन्ति ॥

19. Souls, that are devoted to luxury in this world, are spoken of as far removed from God. Those who have shunned luxury are spoken of as close to God. Ye God and soul, whatever laws ye frame, they draw this world, as yoked horses draw a chariot. (2559)[2]

२०. द्वा सुपर्णा सयुजा सखाया समानं वृक्षं परि षस्वजाते ।
तयोरन्यः पिप्पलं स्वाद्वत्त्यनश्नन्नन्यो अभि चाकशीति ॥

20. Living together, knit with bonds of friendship, possessing fine knowledge and power are God and soul like two birds, dwell on the same tree of Matter. One of the twain, the soul eats the sweet fruit of its actions, the other, God, eating not, acts as a seer. (2560)[3]

[1]Seventh: The soul. Six organs: Eye, Ear, Nose, Tongue, Skin, Mind.

[2]Indra: God. Soma: Soul.

[3]God and soul dwelling in the world are spoken of as two birds who reside together and are mutual friends. Soul reaps the fruit of its action, God is the Seer and Awarder to the soul the fruit of its good and bad acts. Matter is the tree. This verse preaches the eternity of God, Soul and Matter. Soul and Matter are eternal and not created by God. For detailed explanation consult the Muṇḍak, Katha and Shwetashwatra Upanishadas.

२१. यस्मिन् वृक्षे मध्वदः सुपर्णा निविशन्ते सुवते चाधि विश्वे ।
तस्य यदाहुः पिप्पलं स्वाद्वग्रे तन्नोन्नशद्यः पितरं न वेद ।।

21. Souls, that revel in spiritual advancement, and possessing the knowledge of God, rest on Him, a tree, return to this world from the state of salvation. They speak of the supreme sweet fruit of joy in God. He who knows not the Almighty Father, gains it not. (2561)[1]

२२. यत्रा सुपर्णा अमृतस्य भक्षमनिमेषं विदथाभिस्वरन्ति ।
एना विश्वस्य भुवनस्य गोपाः स मा धीरः पाकमत्रा विवेश ।।

22. The emancipated souls, residing in God, through their knowledge ceaselessly enjoy eternal happiness. The Wise God, the keeper of the universe hath entered into me, an aspirant after salvation. (2562)[2]

HYMN X

१. यद् गायत्रे अधि गायत्रमाहितं त्रैष्टुभं वा त्रैष्टुभान्निरतक्षत ।
यद्वा जगज्जगत्याहितं पदं य इत् तद् विदुस्ते अमृतत्वमानशुः ।।

1. Soul is dependent on God. The organs rest on the soul. The strength of 48 years celibacy resides in Aditya Brahmcharis. They who know this secret enjoy the immortal life of salvation. (2563)[3]

२. गायत्रेण प्रति मिमीते अर्कमर्केण साम त्रैष्टुभेन वाकम् ।
वाकेन वाकं द्विपदा चतुष्पदाक्षरेण मिमते सप्त वाणीः ।।

2. The learned realize God through soul. Through food are formed breath and mind. Sound is produced through air. The Vedas are preached through speech. The seven metres sing the praise of soul and Eternal God. (2564)

३. जगता सिन्धुं दिव्यस्कभायद् रथन्तरे सूर्यं पर्यपश्यत् ।
गायत्रस्य समिधस्तिस्र आहुस्ततो मह्ना प्र रिरिचे महित्वा ।।

3. God, through His mobility hath established the Sun in heaven. A yogi visualises in God, the Refulgent Light. The universe has got three blazing lights. God excels all in majesty and vigour. (2565)[4]

४. उप ह्वये सुदुघां धेनुमेतां सुहस्तो गोधुगुत दोहदेनाम् ।
श्रेष्ठं सवं सविता साविषन्नोऽभीद्धो घर्मस्तदु षु प्र वोचत् ।।

[1]It: The joy in residing with God in Moksha (emancipated state). God is spoken of as a tree, on which the emancipated souls dwell.

[2]Just as yogis have acquired salvation so should each devotee aspire for salvation with determination.

[3]Aditya Brahmcharis: They who observe celibacy for 48 years. The first eight verses of this hymn are found with some variation in *Rigveda*, 1-164-23-3011.

[4]Three lights: Fire, Sun, Lightning.

4. I remember God, the Bestower of joys, and the Fulfiller of desires. One expert in the knowledge of soul, alone can realise Him. God grants us excellent knowledge, and is perceived as full of joy and refulgence. The sages nicely speak of Him to their pupils. (2566)[1]

५. हिङ्कृण्वती वसुपत्नी वसूनां वत्समिच्छन्ती मनसाभ्यागात् ।
दुहामश्विभ्यां पयो अघ्न्येयं सा वर्धतां महते सौभगाय ॥

5. Just as a cow longing for the calf, lowing approaches her child, so does mental power, through its strength approach its children the breaths. Just as this indestructible cow yields milk for the males and females of the family, so does the thinking faculty give life-infusing knowledge to the soul and mind. May she prosper to our high advantage. (2567)[2]

६. गौरमीमेदभि वत्सं मिषन्तं मूर्धानं हिङ्ङकृणोन्मातवा उ ।
सृक्वाणं घर्ममभि वावशाना मिमाति मायुं पयते पयोभिः ॥

6. The All-pervading power of God bestows knowledge on the anxious soul. The soul also expresses restlessness in itself for God, a Lover like mother. The God-given fine intellect, longing for the Refulgent God, acquires excellent knowledge, and satisfies us with everlasting pleasures. (2568)

७. अयं स शिङ्क्ते येन गौरभीवृता मिमाति मायुं ध्वसनावधि श्रिता ।
सा चित्तिभिर्नि हि चकार मर्त्यान् विद्युद्भवन्ती प्रति वव्रिमौहत ॥

7. This same God preaches the knowledge of the Vedas. He, who possesses full knowledge, reveals the Vedic speech. The Vedic speech resides in God, the Dissolver of the universe. The Vedic speech, through its teachings prepares all mortals to perform their duties. The same Vedic speech, competent to throw light on all topics, is replete with all sorts of knowledge. (2569)

८. अनच्छये तुरगातु जीवमेजद् ध्रुवं मध्य आ पस्त्यानाम् ।
जीवो मृतस्य चरति स्वधाभिरमर्त्यो मर्त्येना सयोनिः ॥

8. In the midst of all houses, worlds and men, the Everlasting God, putting all in motion, highly Conscious. Pervading everything swiftly, giving life and breath to all, invisibly exists everywhere. The soul, according to the dispensation of God, reaping the fruits of the deeds of past life, assumes different births. The immortal soul is the brother of the mortal body. (2570)[3]

९. विधुं दद्राणं सलिलस्य पृष्ठे युवानं सन्तं पलितो जगार ।
देवस्य पश्य काव्यं महित्वाद्या ममार स ह्यः समान ॥

[1]See *Atharva*, 7-73-7.
[2]See *Atharva*, 7-73-8. 'She' refers to the thinking faculty.
[3]Soul is the brother of the body as it dwells in, and exists with the body.

9. The All-pervading God absorbs in Himself the powerful soul, that moves and breathes on the support of the Ocean-like Vast God. O soul, in that state, behold the wisdom of God, through Whose greatness, he who was living yesterday is dead today. (2571)[1]

१०. य ईं चकार न सो अस्य वेद य ईं ददर्श हिरुगिन्नु तस्मात् ।
स मातुर्योना परिवीतो अन्तर्बहुप्रजा निर्ऋतिरा विवेश ॥

10. He, who performs little deeds in this world, does not behold God. He Who visualises the world and controls it, is hidden from the soul. God enveloping the womb of the Mother Matter, creating innumerable worlds, pervades this unconscious, senseless Matter. (2572)[2]

११. अपश्यं गोपामनिपद्यमानमा च परा च पथिभिश्चरन्तम् ।
स सध्रीचीः स विषूचीर्वसान आ वरीवर्ति भुवनेष्वन्तः ॥

11. I, a yogi, have visualised God, the Guardian of the universe, Who pervades the near and distant worlds and is Immortal. He, engulfing all the quarters and innumerable subjects is present within the worlds. (2573)[3]

१२. द्यौर्नः पिता जनिता नाभिरत्र बन्धुर्नो माता पृथिवी महीयम् ।
उत्तानयोश्चम्बो३र्योनिरन्तरत्रा पिता दुहितुर्गर्भमाधात् ॥

12. Like the refulgent Sun, God is our father, begetter, and most efficient cause of creation. Like the vast-expanded Earth, He is our Kin and Mother. Between the wide-spread heaven and earth, He is the main support of all. God infuses in Matter the power of creating myriad objects. (2574)[4]

१३. पृच्छामि त्वा परमन्तं पृथिव्याः पृच्छामि वृष्णो अश्वस्य रेतः ।
पृच्छामि विश्वस्य भुवनस्य नाभिं पृच्छामि वाचः परमं व्योम ॥

13. O learned preceptor, I ask thee of Earth's extremest limit. I ask thee of the infinite power of the Almighty, All-pervading God. What is the efficient cause of the whole universe, I ask thee. I ask of the highest abode of Vedic knowledge. (2575)[5]

१४. इयं वेदिः परो अन्तः पृथिव्या अयं सोमो वृष्णो अश्वस्य रेतः ।
अयं यज्ञो विश्वस्य भुवनस्य नाभिर्ब्रह्मायं वाचः परमं व्योम ॥

[1]See *Rig*, 10-55-5. He who lived yesterday dies today. He who dies today is reborn tomorrow. This is the wisdom of God, which a contemplative soul alone can realise.

[2]See *Rig*, 1-164-32. Matter is spoken of as mother, as it is the source of the creation of infinite objects in the world.

[3]See *Rig*, 1-164-31, 10-177-3; *Yajur*, 37-17.

[4]See *Rig*, 1-164-33.

[5]See *Rig*, 1-164-34; *Yajur*, 23-61.

14. This power of God is the ultimate support of the universe. This Sun is the light of the Almighty, All-pervading God. This sacrificing God is the support of the whole universe. This Great God is the highest Guardian of Vedic knowledge. (2576)[1]

१५. न वि जानामि यदिवेदमस्मि निण्यः संनद्धो मनसा चरामि ।
यदा मागन् प्रथमजा ऋतस्यादिद् वाचो अश्नुवे भागमस्याः ॥

15. What thing I truly am I know not clearly: mysterious, fettered in resolve and doubt. I pass the days of my life, reaping the fruit of my actions. When the first-born perceptions of the truth dawn on me, then I obtain a portion of this Vedic speech. (2577)[2]

१६. अपाङ् प्राङेति स्वधया गृभीतोऽमर्त्यो मर्त्येना सयोनिः ।
ता शश्वन्ता विषूचीना वियन्ता न्य१न्यं चिक्युर्न नि चिक्युरन्यम् ॥

16. The immortal soul, living together with the mortal body, bound by the fruit of its actions, degrades and elevates itself. Ceaselessly they move in all directions, and go to different places. Men mark the one and fail to mark the other. (2578)[3]

१७. सप्तार्धगर्भा भुवनस्य रेतो विष्णोस्तिष्ठन्ति प्रदिशा विधर्मणि ।
ते धीतिभिर्मनसा ते विपश्चितः परिभुवः परि भवन्ति विश्वतः ॥

17. The seven fully developed forces are the prolific seed of the universe: their functions they maintain by God's ordinance. Present on every side they compass us about. (2579)[4]

१८. ऋचो अक्षरे परमे व्यो॒मन् यस्मिन् देवा अधि विश्वे निषेदुः ।
यस्तन्न वेद किमृचा करिष्यति य इत् तद् विदुस्ते अमी समासते ॥

18. All the Vedas remain under the highest protection of the Immortal God; under Whose sway reside all learned persons and the forces of nature. What benefit will he derive from the Vedas, who knows not Him? They who know Him can alone attain to salvation. (2580)[5]

१९. ऋचः पदं मात्रया कल्पयन्तोऽर्धर्चेन चाक्लृपुर्विश्वमेजत् ।
त्रिपाद् ब्रह्म पुरुरूपं वि तष्ठे तेन जीवन्ति प्रदिशश्चतस्रः ॥

[1]See *Rig*, 1-164-34; *Yajur*, 23-62. The questions put in the 13th verse have been replied in the 14th.

[2]See *Rig*, 1-164-37.

[3]They: The soul and body. One: Body. Other: The soul. See *Rig*, 1-164-38.

[4]Seven forces: (1) Mahat-tatva, Intellect (2) Ahankāra, ego (3) Prithvi, Earth (4) Water (5) Fire (6) Air (7) Ākasha, Atmosphere. Professor Ludwig remarks, this verse is one of the most unintelligible in the whole Veda. I fail to understand this view. The significance is clear. See *Rig*, 1-164-36.

[5]See *Rig*, 1-164-39.

19. The Rishis minutely contemplating on God, Attainable through Vedic speech, thought through vast Vedic knowledge of Him, the Mobiliser of the world. In fact, the most Beautiful God, working in Past, Present and Future, stands in His various forms. Through His power, the denizens of the world's four regions have their being. (2581)

२०. सूयवसाद् भगवती हि भूया अधा वयं भगवन्तः स्याम ।
अद्धि तृणमघ्न्ये विश्वदानीं पिब शुद्धमुदकमाचरन्ती ॥

20. Fortunate mayst thou be with goodly pasture, and may we also be exceeding wealthy, Feed on the grass, O indestructible cow, through all the seasons, and roaming everywhere drink limpid water. (2582)[1]

२१. गौरिन्मिमाय सलिलानि तक्षत्येकपदी द्विपदी सा चतुष्पदी ।
अष्टापदी नवपदी बभूवुषी सहस्राक्षरा भुवनस्य पङ्क्तिस्तस्याः समुद्रा अधि वि क्षरन्ति ॥

21. The Vedic speech has spoken of various forms of knowledge and preached multifarious duties. It deals with one God. It gives us the knowledge of the past and future. It tells us of religion, worldly prosperity, desirable objects, and salvation. It grants us eight boons. It is attainable through nine organs. Dealing with various topics it is a vast force in the world. Through Divine force inexhaustible stores of Matter are flowing in various forms. (2583)[2]

२२. कृष्णं नियानं हरयः सुपर्णा अपो वसाना दिवमुत्पतन्ति ।
तं आववृत्रन्त्सदनादृतस्यादिद् घृतेन पृथिवीं व्यूदुः ॥

22. The lustrous, learned souls, equipped with knowledge and virtuous deeds go to God, their highest shelter, and attain to salvation. After enjoying the pleasure of emancipation, they return from God, the House of truth, and satisfy the inhabitants of Earth with resplendent knowledge. (2584)[3]

२३. अपादेति प्रथमा पद्वतीनां कस्तद् वां मित्रावरुणा चिकेत ।
गर्भो भारं भरत्या चिदस्या ऋतं पिपर्त्यनृतं नि पाति ॥

23. The incorporeal soul is superior to material objects. O teacher and disciple, who of you both knows the soul! The mobile soul endures all the burden of Matter. It guards Truth and destroys Falsehood. (2585)[4]

[1]See *Atharva*, 7-73-11.

[2]Chatushpadi: Dharma, Artha, Kāma, Moksha. Ashtpadi: (1) Smallness (Animā) (2) Lightness (Laghima) (3) Acquisition (Prāpti) (4) Freedom (Prākāmayam) (5) Greatness (Mahimā) (6) Superiority (Īshitvam) (7) Control over senses (Jitendryata) (8) True resolve (Kāma Ansāyita). Navpadi: Mind, Intellect (बुद्धि) two ears, two eyes, two noses, mouth.

[3]See *Rig*, 1-164-47; *Atharva*, 6-22-1.

[4]See *Rig*, 1-152-3.

२४. विराड् वाग् विराट् पृथिवी विराडन्तरिक्षं विराट् प्रजापतिः ।
विराण्मृत्युः साध्यानामधिराजो बभूव तस्य भूतं भव्यं वशे स मे भूतं भव्यं वशे कृणोतु ॥

24. God is the Encyclopaedia of knowledge. God is vast like the Earth. God is All-pervading like space. God is the Nourisher of mankind. God is the Destroyer of the wicked, and the Protector of the self-sacrificing persons. He rules over the Past and Future. May he make me lord of my past and future. (2586)

२५. शकमयं धूममारादपश्यं विषूवता पर एनावरेण ।
उक्षाणं पृश्निमपचन्त वीरास्तानि धर्माणि प्रथमान्यासन् ॥

25. I have directly seen the Almighty God, Who is higher than this world below, full of various sorts of creation. The celibate, learned persons, through yoga and penance, fully perceive God, the Controller of the universe, and full of lustre and joy. These are the primary laws of celibacy and austerity through which God is realised. (2587)[1]

२६. त्रयः केशिन ऋतुथा वि चक्षते संवत्सरे वपत एक एषाम् ।
विश्वमन्यो अभिचष्टे शचीभिर्ध्राजिरेकस्य ददृशे न रूपम् ॥

26. Three resplendent forces work at different times. One of them creates animate and inanimate objects during the year. The other sustains the universe through its resources. The third dissolves the universe. Its impulse is seen but not the form. (2588)[2]

२७. चत्वारि वाक् परिमिता पदानि तानि विदुर्ब्राह्मणा ये मनीषिणः ।
गुहा त्रीणि निहिता नेङ्गयन्ति तुरीयं वाचो मनुष्या३ वदन्ति ॥

27. Speech hath been measured out in four divisions: the Brahmans who have wisdom comprehend them. Three, kept in close concealment, cause no motion. Of speech men speak the fourth division only. (2589)[3]

२८. इन्द्रं मित्रं वरुणमग्निमाहुरथो दिव्यः स सुपर्णो गरुत्मान् ।
एकं सद् विप्रा बहुधा वदन्त्यग्निं यमं मातरिश्वानमाहुः ॥

[1]See *Rig*, 1-164-43.

[2]God creates, sustains, and dissolves the universe. In this verse these three sorts of the power of God are mentioned. That power being immaterial is not seen. It is only felt. Three forces may also refer to fire, Sun and Air, as interpreted by some commentator. See *Rig*, 1-164-44.

[3]See *Rig*, 1-164-45. Four divisions have been interpreted differently by scholars. Some interpret them as Bhur, Bhuva, Suva, and Om. Niruktists interpret them as *Rig*, *Yajur*, *Sāma* and worldly speech. The first three reside in God. Some interpret them as (1) परा that rises from the navel (2) पश्यन्ती that rises from the heart (3) मध्यमा that rises from mind (4) वैखरी, that comes out of the mouth. The yogis alone understand the first three divisions. Some interpret them as (1) Fire in the Earth (2) Air in space (3) Sun in Heaven (4) Analysed speech.

28. The All-pervading God is spoken by the sages as Indra (Highly Glorious), Mitra (Friendly, loving) Varuna (Excellent). They call him as Divya (Refulgent) Suparna (Great Nourisher) Garutmāna (Adorable, Wise, Great soul). The bards call the Everlasting: One by many a title; they call Him Agni (Refulgent) Yama (Controller) Mātrishwānam (Pervaded in space or Matter). (2590)

BOOK (Kāṇḍa) X

Chapter (Anuvāka) 1

HYMN I

१. यां कल्पयन्ति वहतौ वधूमिव विश्वरूपां हस्तकृतां चिकित्सवः ।
सारादेत्वप नुदाम एनाम् ॥

1. After let her depart; away we drive her, whom skilled men prepare and fashion, violent in nature, but beautiful in appearance like a bride at the time of marriage. (2591)[1]

२. शीर्षण्वती नस्वती कर्णिनी कृत्याकृता संभृता विश्वरूपा । सारादेत्वप नुदाम एनाम् ॥

2. Complete, with head and nose and ears, all beauteous, wrought with skill, afar let her depart: away we drive her. (2592)[2]

३. शूद्रकृता राजकृता स्त्रीकृता ब्रह्मभिः कृता । जाया पत्या नुत्तेव कर्तारं बन्ध्वृच्छतु ॥

3. Just as a profligate woman banished by her husband goes to her father or a relative so does a violent deed committed by a Sudra or a Prince, by priests or women, go back to the doer as a kinsman. (2593)

४. अनयाहमोषध्या सर्वाः कृत्या अदूदुषम् । यां क्षेत्रे चक्रुर्यां गोषु यां वा ते पुरुषेषु ॥

4. I with this salutary herb destroy the violent deeds, which they have committed upon the field, cattle, or thy men. (2594)[3]

५. अघमस्त्वघकृते शपथः शपथीयते । प्रत्यक् प्रतिप्रहिण्मो यथा कृत्याकृतं हनत् ॥

5. May ill fall on him who doeth ill, on him who curseth may the curse fall. We drive the evil deed back that it may slay the man who commits the evil deed. (2595)

६. प्रतीचीन आङ्गिरसोऽध्यक्षो नः पुरोहितः । प्रतीचीः कृत्या आकृत्याऽमून् कृत्याकृतो जहि ॥

6. A Vedic scholar opposes the wrong action of a violent person. He is our guardian and leader. Let him turning back all evil deeds slay those who practise them. (2596)[4]

[1]Her: Destructive contrivance violent device or artifice.

[2]Her: A destructive image having head, nose, ears.

[3]Salutary herb: Apamārga or deserving punishment which serves as healing machine. They: The evil-doers. See *Atharva*, 4-18-4.

[4]अङ्गि रसः—अङ्गिरसा वेदानां ज्ञातः i.e. he who knows the Vedas. Griffith and western scholars wrongly translate the word as a Rishi named Angirasa. There is no history in the Vedas, hence this interpretation is illogical.

७. यस्त्वोवाच परेहीति प्रतिकूलमुदाय्य१म् । तं कृत्येऽभिनिवर्तस्व माऽस्मानिच्छो अनागसः ॥

7. Whoever said to thee, "Go forth against the advancing foeman." To him O violent deed, go thou back. Pursue not us, the sinless ones. (2597)

८. यस्ते परूंषि संदधौ रथस्येवर्भुर्धिया । तं गच्छ तत्र तेऽयनमज्ञातस्तेऽयं जनः ॥

8. O violent deed, he who composed thy limbs, as a deft artisan builds a car with skill, go to him: thither lies thy way! This man is quite unknown to thee. (2598)

९. ये त्वा कृत्वाऽऽलेभिरे विद्वला अभिचारिणः ।
शंभ्वी३दं कृत्यादूषणं प्रतिवर्त्म पुनःसरं तेन त्वा स्नपयामसि ॥

9. O violent deed, the cunning persons of violent nature, fashioned thee and held thee fast! The best way to cure and mar the effect of their evil is to drive it back the way it came. With this device we ward off violence. (2599)

१०. यद् दुर्भगां प्रस्नपितां मृतवत्सामुपेयिम । अपैतु सर्वं मत् पापं द्रविणं मोप तिष्ठतु ॥

10. When I have approached a hapless woman of noble character, whose son hath died, at the sight of her miserable plight, let all my evil depart and let abundant riches come to me. (2600)

११. यत् ते पितृभ्यो ददतो यज्ञे वा नाम जगृहुः ।
संदेश्या३त् सर्वस्मात् पापादिमा मुञ्चन्तु त्वौषधीः ॥

11. If in the performance of a noble deed, or in giving financial aid to your parents or teacher, they have falsely accused or slandered thee, let learned persons after investigation release thee from all false accusation levelled against thee. (2601)[1]

१२. देवैनसात् पित्र्यान्नामग्राहात् संदेश्या१दभिनिष्कृतात् ।
मुञ्चन्तु त्वा वीरुधो वी१र्येण ब्रह्मण ऋग्भिः पयस ऋषीणाम् ॥

12. O man, from sin against the learned and the parents from the sin of slander abusive oratory, and the disgrace of others, these self-sacrificing people shall release thee by their spiritual power, Vedic teachings and the knowledge of the sages. (2602)

१३. यथा वातश्च्यावयति भूम्या रेणुमन्तरिक्षाच्चाभ्रम् ।
एवा मत् सर्वं दुर्भूतं ब्रह्मनुत्तमपायति ॥

13. As the wind stirs the dust from earth and drives the rain-cloud from the sky, so dispelled by Vedic knowledge, all my sin departs from me. (2603)

[1]They: Evil minded persons. Just as herbs free a man from a disease, so do learned persons deliver a man from false accusation.

१४. अप क्राम नानदती विनद्धा गर्दभीव । कर्तॄन् नक्षस्वेतो नुत्ता ब्रह्मणा वीर्या॒वता ॥

14. O evil deed! go with a resonant cry, depart, like a she-ass whose cords are loosened. Go away to thy makers from this place, ostracised by a powerful learned person. (2604)

१५. अयं पन्थाः कृत्येति त्वा नयामोऽभिप्रहितां प्रति त्वा प्र हिण्मः ।
तेनाभि याहि भञ्जत्यनस्वतीव वाहिनी विश्वरूपा कुरूटिनी ॥

15. O violent army, this is thy path, we guide thee on this path. If thou hast been sent against us, we drive thee back. Go by this pathway, breaking the forts of the enemy, as does an army equipped with cars and horses, assuming different arrangements and formations and making dreadful noise. (2605)

१६. पराक् ते ज्योतिरपथं ते अर्वागन्यत्रास्मदयना कृणुष्व ।
परेणेहि नवतिं नाव्या३ अति दुर्गाः स्रोत्या मा क्षणिष्ठाः परेहि ॥

16. O violent army, no path leads hitherward for thee to travel. Turn thee from us: far off, thy light is yonder. Fly hence across the ninety floods, the rivers most hard to pass through boats. Begone, wound us not. (2606)

१७. वात इव वृक्षान् नि मृणीहि पादय मा गामश्वं पुरुषमुच्छिष एषाम् ।
कर्तॄन् निवृत्येतः कृत्येऽप्रजास्त्वाय बोधय ॥

17. O violent army, as wind the trees, so smite and overthrow the mischievous foes: leave not cow, horse, or man of them surviving. Returning from this place wake them from sleep to find that they are childless. (2607)

१८. यां ते बर्हिषि यां श्मशाने क्षेत्रे कृत्यां वलगं वा निचख्नुः ।
अग्नौ वा त्वा गार्हपत्येऽभिचेरुः पाकं सन्तं धीरतरा अनागसम् ॥

18. O man! the violent deed or secret mischief which they have wrought for thee in cattle, field or cemetery, or evil which men more cunning have designed in household fire against thee, pure, noble, innocent, try to undo their vexatious conduct. (2608)[1]

१९. उपाहृतमनुबुद्धं निखातं वैरं त्सार्यन्वविदाम कर्त्रम् ।
तदेतु यत आभृतं तत्राश्व इव वि वर्ततां हन्तु कृत्याकृतः प्रजाम् ॥

19. We have discovered the destructive, crooked, deep-rooted, well understood, nicely planned hatred. Let that go back to whence it came, turn thither like a horse and kill the children of its perpetrator. (2609)

२०. स्वायसा असयः सन्ति नो गृहे विद्मा ते कृत्ये यतिधा परूंषि ।
उत्तिष्ठैव परेहीतोऽज्ञाते किमिहेच्छसि ॥

[1](18, 19) A wise general should adequately punish the enemies who dig trenches or use other open and secret devices to harm the people.

20. Within our house are swords of goodly iron. O destructive army we know all thy component parts! Arise this instant and begone! What, stranger[1] art thou seeking here. (2610)[1]

२१. ग्रीवास्ते कृत्ये पादौ चापि कर्त्स्यामि निर्द्रव ।
इन्द्राग्नी अस्मान् रक्षतां यौ प्रजानां प्रजापती ॥

21. O destructive army, I will cut thy throat and hew thy feet off, run, begone! May the king and Commander shield us. These two protect the subjects like a prolific mother. (2611)

२२. सोमो राजाधिपा मृडिता च भूतस्य नः पतयो मृडयन्तु ॥

22. A tranquil king is the guardian of his subjects, and the giver of joy. May the world's masters look on us with favour. (2612)

२३. भवाशर्वावस्यतां पापकृते कृत्याकृते । दुष्कृते विद्युतं देवहेतिम् ॥

23. May the king and the chief minister cast electrical missile, the weapon of the learned, against the sinner, who is violent and satanic. (2613)

२४. यद्येयथ द्विपदी चतुष्पदी कृत्याकृता संभृता विश्वरूपा ।
सेतोऽष्टापदी भूत्वा पुनः परेहि दुच्छुने ॥

24. If thou hast come two-footed or four-footed made by a violent person, assuming different shapes, become eight-footed and go hence. Speed back again, thou evil design! (2614)[2]

२५. अभ्य१क्ताक्ता स्व१रंकृता सर्वं भरन्ती दुरितं परेहि ।
जानीहि कृत्ये कर्तारं दुहितेव पितरं स्वम् ॥

25. Anointed, balmed, and well adorned, bearing all trouble with thee, go. Even as a daughter knows her sire, so know thy maker, O violence, thou! (2615)

२६. परेहि कृत्ये मा तिष्ठो विद्धस्येव पदं नय । मृगः स मृगयुस्त्वं न त्वा निकर्तुमर्हति ॥

26. O violent army! begone, stay not. Just as a wounded animal is traced by his feet, so tracing the feet, reach thy foe. He is the chase, the hunter thou: he may not slight or humble thee. (2616)

२७. उत हन्ति पूर्वासिनं प्रत्यादायापर इष्वा । उत पूर्वस्य निघ्नतो नि हन्त्यपरः प्रति ॥

27. There are two ways of fighting. Either a man aiming with his shaft smites him who is sitting unawares, or when the foeman deals a blow on him, he smites him down in self-defence. (2617)

[1]Stranger: Unfamiliar foreign army.

[2]Two-footed: Working in men and women. Four-footed: Working amidst cattle, or in Brahmcharya, Grihastha, Banprastha, Sanyāsa Ashramās. Eight-footed: working in four quarters and four sub-quarters.

२८. एतद्धि शृणु मे वचोऽथेहि यत एयथ । यस्त्वा चकार तं प्रति ॥

28. O violent deed! hearken to this my word; then go thither away whence thou hast come, to him who designed thee go thou back. (2618)

२९. अनागोहत्या वै भीमा कृत्ये मा नो गामश्वं पुरुषं वधीः ।
यत्रयत्रासि निहिता ततस्त्वोत्थापयामसि पर्णाल्लघीयसी भव ॥

29. O violent army! the slaughter of an innocent is an awful deed. Slay not cow, horse, or man of ours. In whatsoever place thou art concealed we rouse thee up therefrom become thou lighter than a leaf. (2619)

३०. यदि स्थ तमसाऽऽवृता जालेनाभिहिता इव । सर्वाः संलुप्येतः कृत्याः पुनः कर्त्रे प्र हिण्मसि ॥

30. O soldiers! if ye be girt about with death, bound as with a net; we remove all terrible armies hence, and to their maker send them back for his destruction. (2620)

३१. कृत्याकृतो वलगिनोऽभिनिष्कारिणः प्रजाम् ।
मृणीहि कृत्ये मोच्छिषोऽमून् कृत्याकृतो जहि ॥

31. O destructive army!, crush thou the brood of the violent, the wicked, and the doer of evil deed, spare them not, kill those practisers of violence. (2621)

३२. यथा सूर्यो मुच्यते तमसस्परि रात्रिं जहात्युषसश्च केतून् ।
एवाहं सर्वं दुर्भूतं कर्त्रं कृत्याकृता कृतं हस्तीव रजो दुरितं जहामि ॥

32. As the Sun frees himself from depth of darkness, and casts away the night and rays of morning, so I repel each hateful device a violent person hath prepared. Just as an elephant shakes off the dust, I cast the sin aside. (2622)

HYMN II

१. केन पार्ष्णी आभृते पूरुषस्य केन मांसं संभृतं केन गुल्फौ ।
केनाङ्गुलीः पेशनीः केन खानि केनोच्छ्लङ्खौ मध्यतः कः प्रतिष्ठाम् ॥

1. Who framed the heels of man! Who fashioned the flesh of him! Who formed and fixed his ankles! Who made the beautiful fingers! Who made the organs! Who gave him foot-soles! Who made the central haunches to sit upon! (2623)

२. कस्मान्नु गुल्फावधरावकृण्वन्नष्ठीवन्तावुत्तरौ पूरुषस्य ।
जङ्घे निर्ऋत्य न्यदधुः क्वस्विज्जानुनोः सन्धी क उ तच्चिकेत ॥

2. Who made the ankles that are under, and the knee-bones of man above them! Why have the legs been constructed apart! How have the knees' articulations been planned and formed! Who knows this secret! (2624)

३. चतुष्टयं युज्यते संहितान्तं जानुभ्यामूर्ध्वं शिथिरं कबन्धम् ।
श्रोणी यदूरू क उ तज्जजान याभ्यां कुसिन्धं सुदृढं बभूव ॥

3. A fourfold frame is fixed with ends connected, and up above the knees a loose belly. The hips and thighs, who was their generator, those props whereby the trunk grew firmly stablished! (2625)

४. कति देवा: कतमे त आसन् य उरो ग्रीवाश्चिक्युः पूरुषस्य ।
कति स्तनौ व्यदधुः कः कफोडौ कति स्कन्धान् कति पृष्टीरचिन्वन् ॥

4. Which and how many were those supernatural forces which fastened the chest of man and neck together! How many fixed his breasts! Who formed his cheeks. How many joined together ribs and shoulders. (2626)

५. को अस्य बाहू समभरद् वीर्यं करवादिति । अंसौ को अस्य तद्देवः कुसिन्धे अध्या दधौ ॥

5. God, the Creator, has put together both his arms, so that he may show manly strength. Hence the Refulgent God has set the shoulder-blades upon the trunk. (2627)[1]

६. कः सप्त खानि वि ततर्द शीर्षणि कर्णाविमौ नासिके चक्षणी मुखम् ।
येषां पुरुत्रा विजयस्य मह्मनि चतुष्पादो द्विपदो यन्ति यामम् ॥

6. God pierced the seven openings in the head. He made these ears, these nostrils, eyes and mouth, through whose surpassing might in various forms, bipeds and quadrupeds complete their journey of life. (2628)

७. हन्वोर्हि जिह्वामदधात् पुरूचीमधा महीमधि शिश्राय वाचम् ।
स आ वरीवर्ति भुवनेष्वन्तरपो वसानः क उ तच्चिकेत ॥

7. God set within the jaws the tongue that moves fast, and thereon placed the mighty power of speech. He pervades all the worlds, Matter and souls. Who hath understood it? (2629)

८. मस्तिष्कमस्य यतमो ललाटं ककाटिकां प्रथमो यः कपालम् ।
चित्वा चित्यं हन्वोः पूरुषस्य दिवं रुरोह कतमः स देवः ॥

8. God, Who first of all fashioned his brain, forehead, occiput and skull, exists supporting the pile of man's two jaws. Who is that Adorable God Who has risen to the pinnacle of splendour. (2630)

९. प्रियाऽप्रियाणि बहुला स्वप्नं संबाधतन्द्र्यः । आनन्दानुग्रो नन्दांश्च कस्माद् वहति पूरुषः ॥

9. How does a strong person acquire pleasant and unpleasant deeds, of varied sort, sleep, and alarm, fatigue, enjoyments and delights? (2631)

[1] कः—कर्ता=Creator, Prajapati देवः प्रकाशमानः, Refulgent. This verse gives a reply to the questions raised in the previous ones.

१०. आर्तिरवर्तिर्निर्ऋतिः कुतो नु पुरुषेऽमतिः । राद्धिः समृद्धिरव्यृद्धिर्मतिरुदितयः कुतः ॥

10. Whence is there found in man suffering, poverty, disease and stupidity. Whence come success, prosperity, opulence, wisdom, and tendencies for advancement. (2632)

११. को अस्मिन्नापो व्यदधाद् विषूवृतः पुरूवृतः सिन्धुसृत्याय जाताः ।
तीव्रा अरुणा लोहिनीस्ताम्रधूम्रा ऊर्ध्वा अवाचीः पुरुषे तिरश्चीः ॥

11. God hath stored in man floods of blood, which turn in all directions, move in diverse organs, and flow in arteries. They are hasty, red, purple, and copper-hued, running all ways, upward, downward and oblique. (2633)

१२. को अस्मिन् रूपमदधात् को मह्मानं च नाम च ।
गातुं को अस्मिन् कः केतुं कश्चरित्राणि पूरुषे ॥

12. God gave man visible form and shape. God gave him majesty and renown. God gave him knowledge and different modes of conduct. (2634)

१३. को अस्मिन् प्राणमवयत् को अपानं व्यानमु । समानमस्मिन् को देवोऽधि शिश्राय पूरुषे ॥

13. God wove the Prāna, Apāna, and Vyāna in man, Adorable God bestowed Samāna to man. (2635)[1]

१४. को अस्मिन् यज्ञमदधादेको देवोऽधि पूरुषे ।
को अस्मिन्त्सत्यं कोऽनृतं कुतो मृत्युः कुतोऽमृतम् ॥

14. What God, what only Deity placed sacrificing soul in man? Who gave him truth and falsehood? Whence came Death and Immortality. (2636)[2]

१५. को अस्मै वासः पर्यदधात् को अस्यायुरकल्पयत् ।
बलं को अस्मै प्रायच्छत् को अस्याकल्पयज्जवम् ॥

15. God wrapped the garment of body round him. God has determined the duration of man's life. God granted him strength. God gave fleetness to his feet. (2637)

१६. केनापो अन्वतनुत केनाहरकरोद् रुचे । उषसं केनान्वैन्द्ध केन सायंभवं ददे ॥

16. Who has spread the waters out? Who has made the day to shine? Who has enkindled the Dawn? Who has given the gift of even-tide? (2638)

१७. को अस्मिन् रेतो न्यदधात् तन्तुरा तायतामिति ।
मेधां को अस्मिन्नध्यौहत् को बाणं को नृतो दधौ ॥

[1]Prāna: The ingoing breath. Apāna: The outgoing vital air Vyāna: The breath that roams throughout the body. Samāna: The breath that resides in the heart. Just as a weaver weaves the threads into cloth, so does God equip our body with vital breaths and make it fit for work.

[2]Truth and falsehood: The knowledge of right and wrong.

17. God hath set the seed in man, so that the thread of life be spun out. God gave him intellect besides. God gave him voice and gestic power. (2639)

१८. केनेमां भूमिमौर्णोत् केन पर्यभवद् दिवम् । केनाभि मह्ना पर्वतान् केन कर्माणि पूरुषः ॥

18. Who has bedecked the Earth? Who has encompassed Heaven? Who through His might has covered the mountains? Through Whose help does man perform deeds? (2640)

१९. केन पर्जन्यमन्वेति केन सोमं विचक्षणम् । केन यज्ञं च श्रद्धां च केनास्मिन् निहितं मनः ॥

19. Through God does man utilize the cloud, and receive beautiful water and food. Through God does man acquire sacrifice and faith in truth. God hath laid mind in man. (2641)

२०. केन श्रोत्रियमाप्नोति केनेमं परमेष्ठिनम् । केनेममग्निं पूरुषः केन संवत्सरं ममे ॥

20. What leads man to a preceptor learned in Vedic lore? What leads him to this Lord Supreme? How doth he realise this soul? How doth he gain the knowledge of God, the Controller of Time. (2642)

२१. ब्रह्म श्रोत्रियमाप्नोति ब्रह्मेमं परमेष्ठिनम् । ब्रह्मेममग्निं पूरुषो ब्रह्म संवत्सरं ममे ॥

21. For Vedic knowledge does man go near a learned preceptor. Through Vedic knowledge does he gain this Lord Supreme. Through Vedic study does he visualise soul. Through the Vedas does he acquire the knowledge of God, the Controller of Time. (2643)

२२. केन देवाँ अनु क्षियति केन दैवजनीर्विशः । केनेदमन्यन्नक्षत्रं केन सत् क्षत्रमुच्यते ॥

22. Through what power doth man control the forces of Nature? Through what power does he make cattle, birds, insects created by God subservient to him? Bereft of what power is man powerless? Equipped with what power is he called full of strength and consciousness? (2644)

२३. ब्रह्म देवाँ अनु क्षियति ब्रह्म दैवजनीर्विशः । ब्रह्मेदमन्यन्नक्षत्रं ब्रह्म सत् क्षत्रमुच्यते ॥

23. Through God's grace doth man control the forces of Nature. Through God's grace doth man make animate and inanimate creation subservient to him. Bereft of His grace man is powerless. Equipped with it, he is called full of strength and consciousness. (2645)[1]

२४. केनेयं भूमिर्विहिता केन द्यौरुत्तरा हिता । केनेदमूर्ध्वं तिर्यक् चान्तरिक्षं व्यचो हितम् ॥

24. By whom was this Earth disposed? By whom was Heaven placed over it? By whom was this expanse of air raised up on high and stretched across? (2646)

२५. ब्रह्मणा भूमिर्विहिता ब्रह्म द्यौरुत्तरा हिता । ब्रह्मेदमूर्ध्वं तिर्यक् चान्तरिक्षं व्यचो हितम् ॥

[1]It refers to God's glory.

25. By God was this Earth disposed. By God is sky arranged above. By God is this expanse of air lifted on high and stretched across. (2647)

२६. मूर्धानमस्य संसीव्याथर्वा हृदयं च यत् । मस्तिष्कादूर्ध्वः प्रैरयत् पवमानोऽधि शीर्षतः ।।

26. A steady yogi uniting together his head and heart, impels the breath in the head above the brain. (2648)

२७. तद्वा अथर्वणः शिरो देवकोशः समुब्जितः ।
तत् प्राणो अभि रक्षति शिरो अन्नमथो मनः ।।

27. The head of the yogi is verily the well-guarded treasure of the organs. Vital air, food and noble thoughts protect that head. (2649)

२८. ऊर्ध्वो नु सृष्टा३स्तिर्यङ् नु सृष्टा३ः सर्वा दिशः पुरुष आ बभूवाँ३ ।
पुरं यो ब्रह्मणो वेद यस्याः पुरुष उच्यते ।।

28. Was man created in Heaven, or the atmosphere or in all directions is a question worth consideration. He who knows the Creation of God, can best answer this question. The soul is called Purusha as it lives in the world created by God. (2650)

२९. यो वै तां ब्रह्मणा वेदामृतेनावृतां पुरम् । तस्मै ब्रह्म च ब्राह्माश्च चक्षुः प्राणं प्रजां ददुः ।।

29. God and His worshippers have bestowed sight, progeny and life on him, who knows this world created by God, as full of extreme joy and felicity. (2651)

३०. न वै तं चक्षुर्जहाति न प्राणो जरसः पुरा । पुरं यो ब्रह्मणो वेद यस्याः पुरुष उच्यते ।।

30. Sight leaves him not, breath quits not him before old age, who knows the mighty strength of God, whereby He is named as Purusha. (2652)

३१. अष्टाचक्रा नवद्वारा देवानां पूरयोध्या । तस्यां हिरण्ययः कोशः स्वर्गो ज्योतिषाऽऽवृतः ।।

31. This citadel of the body, unconquerable by the ignorant, equipped with circles eight and portals nine, contains the soul full of myriad powers, ever marching on to Joyful God, surrounded by the Refulgent Supreme Being. (2653)[1]

३२. तस्मिन् हिरण्यये कोशे त्र्यरे त्रिप्रतिष्ठिते ।
तस्मिन् यद् यक्षमात्मन्वत् तद्वै ब्रह्मविदो विदुः ।।

32. Men deep in lore of Brahma know that Adorable God, Who dwells in the multi-powered soul that hath three spokes and three supports. (2654)[2]

[1]Eight circles: Eight parts of yoga. Yama, Niyama, Āsana, Prānāyama, Pratyahāra, Dharnā, Dhyana, Smadhi. Nine portals: The orifices of the human body. Two eyes, two ears, two nostrils, mouth, anus and penis.

[2]Three spokes: स्थान (capacity) नाम (Token, sign) जन्म (Existence). Three supports: कर्म (Action) उपासना (Contemplation) ज्ञान (Knowledge).

३३. प्रभ्राजमानां हरिणीं यशसा संपरीवृताम् । पुरं हिरण्ययीं ब्रह्मा विवेशापराजिताम् ।।

33. God resides in the soul, bright with exceeding brilliancy, beautiful, compassed with glory round about, multi-powered ne'er subdued. (2655)

Chapter (Anuvāka) 2

HYMN III

१. अयं मे वरणो मणिः सपत्नक्षयणो वृषा । तेना रभस्व त्वं शत्रून् प्र मृणीहि दुरस्यतः ।।

1. Here is my laudable Vedic knowledge, slayer of rivals, strong in action. O man, with this grasp thou thine enemies, crush those who fain would injure thee. (2656)[1]

२. प्रैणाञ्छृणीहि प्र मृणा रभस्व मणिस्ते अस्तु पुरएता पुरस्तात् ।
अवारयन्त वरणेन देवा अभ्याचारमसुराणां श्वःश्वः ।।

2. O King break them to pieces, grasp them and destroy them. Let Vedic knowledge go before and lead thee. With Vedic knowledge have the sages warded off the daily misdeeds of the wicked. (2657)

३. अयं मणिर्वरणो विश्वभेषजः सहस्राक्षो हरितो हिरण्ययः ।
स ते शत्रूनधरान् पादयाति पूर्वस्तान् दभ्नुहि ये त्वा द्विषन्ति ।।

3. This beautiful Vedic knowledge is a panacea for all physical and spiritual ills, throws light on a thousand topics, is the destroyer of all calamities, and is full of precious moral gems. This knowledge shall conquer and cast down thy foemen. Be thou the first to slay the men who hate thee. (2658)

४. अयं ते कृत्यां विततां पौरुषेयादयं भयात् । अयं त्वा सर्वस्मात् पापाद् वरणो वारयिष्यते ।।

4. This will stay the violence wrought for thee, will guard thee from the fear of man: from all sin this Vedic knowledge will shield thee well. (2659)

५. वरणो वारयाता अयं देवो वनस्पतिः । यक्ष्मो यो अस्मिन्नाविष्टस्तमु देवा अवीवरन् ।।

5. Guard against ill of varied kind is this divine Vedic knowledge, that affords shelter like a tree. The learned take shelter under the Adorable, Mighty soul, that exists in man. (2660)[2]

६. स्वप्नं सुप्त्वा यदि पश्यासि पापं मृगः सृतिं यति धावादजुष्टाम् ।
परिक्षवाच्छकुनेः पापवादादयं मणिर्वरणो वारयिष्यते ।।

6. I in thy sleep thou feel an evil dream; or see the deer running in unpleasant paths, this excellent Vedic knowledge will guard thee from the sneeze and the bird's ill-omened words. (2661)[3]

[1]Varna is also the name of a medicine, vide Bhāva Prakasha Purvakhanda, Vatātiverga Shalok 56, 57. Pt. Khem Karan Das Trivedi has translated it as Vedic knowledge. Pt. Jaidev Vidyalankar translates it as general of the army. Griffith translates this as charm, amulet.

[2]See *Atharva*, 6-85-1.

[3]Man should develop his physical and spiritual force to be free from bad dreams and the violence of cattle and birds. Bird: Vulture.

७. अरात्यास्त्वा निर्ऋत्या अभिचारादथो भयात् । मृत्योरोजीयसो वधाद् वरणो वारयिष्यते ॥

7. From miserliness, from decay, from wrongful conduct, from alarm, from death, from stronger foeman's stroke, the Vedic knowledge will guard thee well. (2662)[1]

८. यन्मे माता यन्मे पिता भ्रातरो यच्च मे स्वा यदेनश्चकृमा वयम् ।
ततो नो वारयिष्यतेऽयं देवो वनस्पतिः ॥

8. Each sinful act that my mother, my father, my kinsmen and we have done, from all that guilt this divine Vedic knowledge, that affords shelter to all, will be our guard and sure defence. (2663)

९. वरणेन प्रव्यथिता भ्रातृव्या मे सबन्धवः । असूर्तं रजो अप्यगुस्ते यन्त्वधमं तमः ॥

9. Eclipsed by Vedic knowledge, let my rivals along with their relatives, pass to the low sentiment of anger devoid of light, to deepest darkness let them go. (2664)

१०. अरिष्टोऽहमरिष्टगुरायुष्मान्त्सर्वपूरुषः । तं मायं वरणो मणिः परि पातु दिशोदिशः ॥

10. I have become free from violence. I have secured peace of mind. May I live long with my descendants and employees. May this Vedic knowledge guard me well on every side. (2665)

११. अयं मे वरण उरसि राजा देवो वनस्पतिः ।
स मे शत्रून् वि बाधतामिन्द्रो दस्यूनिवासुरान् ॥

11. This supreme, divine Vedic knowledge, affording shelter like a tree, resides in my breast. Let it afflict my foeman as a king quells fiends and profligates. (2666)

१२. इमं बिभर्मि वरणमायुष्मान्छतशारदः । स मे राष्ट्रं च क्षत्रं च पशूनोजश्च मे दधत् ॥

12. I accept the Vedic knowledge, so that it may help me in living a long life of hundred years. May it bestow on me royalty, power, cattle and vitality. (2667)

१३. यथा वातो वनस्पतीन् वृक्षान् भनक्त्योजसा ।
एवा सपत्नान् मे भङ्ग्धि पूर्वान्जातां उतापरान् वरणस्त्वाभि रक्षतु ॥

13. As with its might the wind uproots the trees the lords of the wood, even so rend my rivals, O king, born before me and born after! Let the Vedic knowledge protect thee well. (2668)

१४. यथा वातश्चाग्निश्च वृक्षान् प्सातो वनस्पतीन् ।
एवा सपत्नान् मे प्साहि पूर्वान्जातां उतापरान् वरणस्त्वाभि रक्षतु ॥

[1]Death: Early death

14. As fire and the wind devour the trees, the lords of the wood; even so devour my rivals, O king, born before me and born after. Let the Vedic knowledge protect thee well. (2669)

१५. यथा वातेन प्रक्षीणा वृक्षाः शेरे न्यर्पिताः ।
एवा सपत्नांस्त्वं मम प्र क्षिणीहि न्यर्पय पूर्वाञ्जातां उतापरान् वरणस्त्वाभि रक्षतु ॥

15. As, shattered by the tempest trees lie withering ruined on the ground; thus overthrow my rivals thou, so crush them down and ruin them, those born before and after me. Let the Vedic knowledge protect thee well. (2670)[1]

१६. तांस्त्वं प्र च्छिन्धि वरण पुरा दिष्टात् पुरायुषः ।
य एनं पशुषु दिप्सन्ति ये चास्य राष्ट्रदिप्सवः ॥

16. Cut them to pieces, O Vedic knowledge! before their destined term of life, those who would hurt his cattle, those who fain would harm the realm he rules. (2671)

१७. यथा सूर्यो अतिभाति यथाऽस्मिन् तेज आहितम् ।
एवा मे वरणो मणिः कीर्तिं भूतिं नि यच्छतु तेजसा मा समुक्षतु यशसा समनक्तु मा ॥

17. As the Sun shines with brightest sheen, as splendour hath been stored in him, so may the excellent Vedic knowledge give me fame and prosperity. With lustre let it sprinkle me, and balm me with magnificence. (2672)

१८. यथा यशश्चन्द्रमस्यादित्ये च नृचक्षसि ।
एवा मे वरणो मणिः कीर्तिं भूतिं नि यच्छतु तेजसा मा समुक्षतु यशसा समनक्तु मा ॥

18. As glory dwelleth in the Moon and in the sun who vieweth men, so may the excellent Vedic knowledge give me fame and prosperity. With lustre let it sprinkle me and balm me with magnificence. (2673)

१९. यथा यशः पृथिव्यां यथास्मिञ्जातवेदसि ।
एवा मे वरणो मणिः कीर्तिं भूतिं नि यच्छतु तेजसा मा समुक्षतु यशसा समनक्तु मा ॥

19. As glory dwelleth in the Earth and in this Fire, so may the excellent Vedic knowledge give me fame and prosperity. With lustre let it sprinkle me, and balm me with significance. (2674)

२०. यथा यशः कन्यायां यथाऽस्मिन्त्संभृते रथे ।
एवा मे वरणो मणिः कीर्तिं भूतिं नि यच्छतु तेजसा मा समुक्षतु यशसा समनक्तु मा ॥

20. As glory dwelleth in a noble girl, and in this car well constructed for the battle, so may the excellent Vedic knowledge give me fame and prosperity. With lustre let it sprinkle me, and balm me with magnificence. (2675)

[1]Thou, thee refer to the king.

२१. यथा यशः सोमपीथे मधुपर्के यथा यशः ।
एवा मे वरणो मणिः कीर्तिं भूतिं नि यच्छतु तेजसा मा समुक्षतु यशसा समनक्तु मा ।।

21. As glory dwelleth in the draught of Soma and the honeyed drink, so may the excellent Vedic knowledge give me fame and prosperity. With lustre let it sprinkle me, and balm me with magnificence. (2676)[1]

२२. यथा यशोऽग्निहोत्रे वषट्कारे यथा यशः ।
एवा मे वरणो मणिः कीर्तिं भूतिं नि यच्छतु तेजसा मा समुक्षतु यशसा समनक्तु मा ।।

22. As glory dwelleth in the performance of Havan and the application of fire for scientific works, and liberal charity, so may the excellent Vedic knowledge give me fame and prosperity. With lustre let it sprinkle me, and balm me with magnificence. (2677)

२३. यथा यशो यजमाने यथाऽस्मिन् यज्ञ आहितम् ।
एवा मे वरणो मणिः कीर्तिं भूतिं नि यच्छतु तेजसा मा समुक्षतु यशसा समनक्तु मा ।।

23. As glory is bestowed upon the patron and this sacrifice (Yajña) so may the Vedic knowledge give me fame and prosperity. With lustre let it sprinkle me, and balm me with magnificence. (2678)

२४. यथा यशः प्रजापतौ यथाऽस्मिन् परमेष्ठिनि ।
एवा मे वरणो मणिः कीर्तिं भूतिं नि यच्छतु तेजसा मा समुक्षतु यशसा समनक्तु मा ।।

24. As glory dwelleth in the king, the Lord of his subjects, and in this God supreme, so may the Vedic knowledge give me fame and prosperity. With lustre let it sprinkle me, and balm me with magnificence. (2679)

२५. यथा देवेष्वमृतं यथैषु सत्यमाहितम् ।
एवा मे वरणो मणिः कीर्तिं भूतिं नि यच्छतु तेजसा मा समुक्षतु यशसा समनक्तु मा ।।

25. As enterprise and true resolve have been established in heroic persons desirous for victory, so may the Vedic knowledge give me fame and prosperity. With lustre let it sprinkle me, and balm me with magnificence. (2680)

HYMN IV

१. इन्द्रस्य प्रथमो रथो देवानामपरो रथो वरुणस्य तृतीय इत् ।
अहीनामपमा रथ स्थाणुमारदथार्षत् ।।

1. The first of all is soul's strength, next is the strength of the organs, the third is that of breaths. The last is the strength of the serpents, poison, that enters the body and deprives it of life. (2681)

[1]Honeyed drink Madhuparka: A drink offered at the time of marriage, consisting of honey, curd, clarified butter, water and sugar.

२. दर्भः शोचिस्तरूणकमश्वस्य वारः परुषस्य वारः । रथस्य बन्धुरम् ॥

2. The Durbha grass, fire, the grass sprout, Ashvaivāra, Parushawāra act as antidotes against the serpents' poison. (2682)[1]

३. अव श्वेत पदा जहि पूर्वेण चापरेण च । उदप्लुतमिव दार्वहीनामरसं विषं वारुग्रम् ॥

3. O shweta medicine, just as water weakens the piece of wood that floats on it, so do thou stay the dire poison of the snakes, and make it weak. (2683)[2]

४. अरंघुषो निमज्योन्मज्य पुनरब्रवीत् । उदप्लुतमिव दार्वहीनामरसं विषं वारुग्रम् ॥

4. A gourd diving below in water and rising up, declares that through its power, the deadly poison of the snakes can be removed and rendered ineffective, just as water weakens the piece of wood that floats on it. (2684)[3]

५. पैद्वो हन्ति कसर्णीलं पैद्वः श्वित्रमुतासितम् । पैद्वो रथर्व्याः शिरः सं बिभेद पृदाक्वाः ॥

5. Paidva kills Kasarnila serpent, kills both the white serpent and the black. Paidva cleaves in twain Ratharvi's and the viper's head. (2685)[4]

६. पैद्व प्रेहि प्रथमोऽनु त्वा वयमेमसि । अहीन् व्यस्यतात् पथो येन स्मा वयमेमसि ॥

6. Go onward, Paidva! go thou first: we follow after thee. Cast thou aside the serpents from the pathway whereupon we tread. (2686)

७. इदं पैद्वो अजायतेदमस्य परायणम् । इमान्यर्वतः पदाहिघ्न्यो वाजिनीवतः ॥

7. Here is this Paidva medicine. It is an excellent thing. It is a nice remedy for the snake-bite. These are the special traits of Paidva, the mighty slayer of the snakes. (2687)

८. संयतं न वि ष्परद् व्यात्तं न सं यमत् ।
अस्मिन् क्षेत्रे द्वावही स्त्री च पुमांश्च तावुभावरसा ॥

8. Let not the snake open his closed mouth to bite us, nor close the opened mouth. Through this expedient both male and female serpents become venomless. (2688)

[1]Ashvawāra and Parushawāra are medicines that remove the poison of the serpents. Their details are given in Raj Nighantu. In Ayurveda Ashvawāra is named as Ashvamara and Hayamāra.

[2]श्वेत is the name of a medicine.

[3]Aranghushā is also named Ikshwaku. It possesses the power of eradicating the poison of the serpents.

[4]Paidva is the name of a medicine. It is also called Ashvagandhā, Ashvakshuraka or Girkarnik. Kasarnila: An unidentified venomous serpent. Ratharvi: Another species of serpent, so-called on account of its rapid motion.

६. अरसास इहाहयो ये अन्ति ये च दूरके । घनेन हन्मि वृश्चिकमहिं दण्डेनागतम् ॥

9. Powerless be the serpents here, those that are near and those afar. I kill the scorpion with a club, with a staff the coming snake. (2689)

१०. अघाश्वस्येदं भेषजमुभयोः स्वजस्य च । इन्द्रो मेऽहिमघायन्तमहिं पैद्वो अरन्धयत् ॥

10. This is the remedy against Aghāṣva and Svaja both. Indra subdues the snake that attacks me, just as Paidva tames the serpent. (2690)[1]

११. पैद्वस्य मन्महे वयं स्थिरस्य स्थिरधाम्नः । इमे पश्चा पृदाकवः प्रदीध्यत आसते ॥

11. We fix our thoughts on Paidva, steady in nature, and strong in lustre, seeing which these serpents crouch behind. (2691)

१२. नष्टासवो नष्टविषा हता इन्द्रेण वज्रिणा । जघानेन्द्रो जघ्निमा वयम् ॥

12. Bereft of life and poison they lie slain by the powerful medicine Indra. Indra and we have slaughtered them. (2692)

१३. हतास्तिरश्चिराजयो निपिष्टासः पृदाकवः । दर्विं करिक्रतं श्वित्रं दर्भेष्वसितं जहि ॥

13. Serpents with transverse streaks have been slain, and vipers crushed and brayed to bits. Slay Darvi, Karikrata, white and black serpents in the Durbha grass. (2693)[2]

१४. कैरातिका कुमारिका सका खनति भेषजम् । हिरण्ययीभिरभ्रिभिर्गिरीणामुप सानुषु ॥

14. Kairatika or Kumarika drug is dug on the high ridges of the hills with lustrous shovels, (2694)[3]

१५. आयमगन् युवा भिषक् पृश्निहापराजितः । स वै स्वजस्य जम्भन उभयोर्वृश्चिकस्य च ॥

15. Hither hath come the young unconquered physician, who slays the speckled snake. He verily demolishes adder and scorpion; both of them. (2695)

१६. इन्द्रो मेऽहिमरन्धयन्मित्रश्च वरुणश्च । वातापर्जन्योऽभा ॥

16. A majestic physician, urging like the Sun, serviceable like water, and both water and cloud has slain the serpent approaching me. (2696)

१७. इन्द्रो मेऽहिमरन्धयत् पृदाकुं च पृदाक्वम् । स्वजं तिरश्चिराजिं कसर्णीलं दशोनसिम् ॥

[1]Aghāsva is the name of a serpent that jumps up like a horse and makes an attack. Swaja is the name of a serpent that coils and twists round the body and bites. Indra is the name of a medicine that assuages the pain caused by the snake-bite and removes the deadly effect of its poison.

[2]Darvi and Karikrata are species of serpents.

[3]Kairatika: A special drug, known in the vernacular as. चिरायता. Kumarika: A special drug, known in the vernacular as कुवारपाठा.

17. An expert physician hath killed for my safety, the female viper and the male, the adder, him with stripes athwart, Kasarpīla, Daṣonasi. (2697)[1]

१८. इन्द्रो जघान प्रथमं जनितारमहे तव । तेषामु तृह्यमाणानां कः स्वित्तेषामसद्रसः ॥

18. O serpent, a skilled physician hath destroyed the sire who first engendered thee: and whenth ese snakes are pierced and bored what poison and sap will be theirs! (2698)

१९. सं हि शीर्षाण्यग्रभं पौञ्जिष्ठ इव कर्वरम् । सिन्धोर्मध्यं परेत्य व्यनिजमहेर्विषम् ॥

19. Their heads have I seized firmly as a fisherman grasps the spotted prey. Wading half through the stream have I washed off the poison of the serpents. (2699)[2]

२०. अहीनां सर्वेषां विषं परा वहन्तु सिन्धवः । हतास्तिरश्चिराजयो निपिष्टासः पृदाकवः ॥

20. Let the floods hurry on and bear the poison of all snakes afar. Tiraschirajis have been slain and vipers crushed and brayed to pieces. (2700)

२१. ओषधीनामहं वृण उर्वरीरिव साधुया । नयाम्यर्वतीरिवाहे निरैतु ते विषम् ॥

21. As from the salutary plants I deftly pick out the efficacious ones, and guide them like intelligent girls, so let thy venom, Snake! depart. (2701)[3]

२२. यदग्नौ सूर्ये विषं पृथिव्यामोषधीषु यत् । कान्दाविषं कनक्नकं निरैत्वैतु ते विषम् ॥

22. All poison that the Sun and fire, all that the earth and plants contain, the poison the herbs receive through the cloud, the paralysing poison, may they all mix with thine, O snake, and turn out thy venom! (2702)[4]

२३. ये अग्निजा ओषधिजा अहीनां ये अप्सुजा विद्युत आबभूवुः ।
येषां जातानि बहुधा महान्ति तेभ्यः सर्पेभ्यो नमसा विधेम ॥

23. Serpents which fire or plants have generated, those which have sprung from waters or the lightning, whose mighty broods are found in many places, these serpents we control with a destructive weapon. (2703)

२४. तौदी नामासि कन्या घृताची नाम वा असि । अधस्पदेन ते पदमा ददे विषदूषणम् ॥

[1]Kasarpīla and Dasonasi are species of serpents. Indra is the name of a drug as well. This medicine kills all kinds of serpents.

[2]Their: Serpents. I: A skilled snake-charmer.

[3]Just as intellectual girls are honoured by learned persons, so should physicians collect good herbs and utilize them. The word अर्वती has been translated by Griffith as a mare. Rishi Dayananda translates it thus, अर्वतीः प्रशस्तबुद्धिमत्याः कन्याः *Rigveda* translation 1-145-3, i.e. intelligent girls.

[4]Poison acts as an antidote against poison.

24. O plant, thou art named as Taudi, Kauyā, or Ghritāchi. I take from underneath thy root, the part that is poison-killing. (2704)[1]

२५. अङ्गादङ्गात् प्र च्यावय हृदयं परि वर्जय । अधा विषस्य यत् तेजोऽवाचीनं तदेतु ते ॥

25. O medicine! from every member drive away the venom, and free the heart from it. Thus let the poison's burning heat pass downward and away from thee. (2705)

२६. आरे अभूद्विषमरौद्विषे विषमप्रागपि ।
अग्निर्विषमहेर्निरधात् सोमो निरणयीत् । दंष्टारमन्वगाद् विषमहिरमृत ॥

26. For removing the effect of poison, let a strong bandage be fastened on the affected part, let poison be added to counteract the effect of poison. Let fire eradicate the poison. Let assuaging Soma plant neutralise the poison. Let poison return to the biting snake, so that it be killed. (2706)[2]

Chapter (Anuvāka) 3

HYMN V

१. इन्द्रस्यौज स्थेन्द्रस्य सह स्थेन्द्रस्य बलं स्थेन्द्रस्य वीर्यं१ स्थेन्द्रस्य नृम्णं स्थ ।
जिष्णवे योगाय ब्रह्मयोगैर्वो युनज्मि ॥

1. O subjects, ye are the power of the King, ye the force and strength of the King, ye his manliness and wealth. I join you through the wise teachings of the Vedas to the victorious King! (2707)[3]

२. इन्द्रस्यौज स्थेन्द्रस्य सह स्थेन्द्रस्य बलं स्थेन्द्रस्य वीर्यं१ स्थेन्द्रस्य नृम्णं स्थ ।
जिष्णवे योगाय क्षत्रयोगैर्वो युनज्मि ॥

2. O subjects, ye are the power of the King, ye the force and strength of the King, ye his manliness and wealth. I join you through royal power with the victorious King! (2708)

३. इन्द्रस्यौज स्थेन्द्रस्य सह स्थेन्द्रस्य बलं स्थेन्द्रस्य वीर्यं१ स्थेन्द्रस्य नृम्णं स्थ ।
जिष्णवे योगायेन्द्रयोगैर्वो युनज्मि ॥

3. O subjects, ye are the power of the King, ye the force and strength of the Kings, ye his manliness and wealth. I join you through spiritual forces with the victorious King! (2709)

[1]Taudi: That develops the intellect Ghritāchi: Shining like butter. Kanyā: Beautiful. Griffith has translated Kanyā as a maid. This is the name of a medicinal herb.

[2]In this verse various methods of nullifying the effect of snake's poison are mentioned (1) Fastening a strong bandage on the affected part, to prevent the poison from spreading. (2) Injection of poison to neutralise the poison. (3) Putting hot bandage on the affected part (4) Applying the plaster of Soma, a medicinal herb.

[3]I: Purohit, priest.

४. इन्द्रस्यौज स्थेन्द्रस्य सह स्थेन्द्रस्य बलं स्थेन्द्रस्य वीर्यं१ स्थेन्द्रस्य नृम्णं स्थ ।
जिष्णवे योगाय सोमयोगैर्वो युनज्मि ॥

4. O subjects, ye are the power of the King, ye the force and strength of the King, ye his manliness and wealth. I join you through peaceful means with the victorious King! (2710)

५. इन्द्रस्यौज स्थेन्द्रस्य सह स्थेन्द्रस्य बलं स्थेन्द्रस्य वीर्यं१ स्थेन्द्रस्य नृम्णं स्थ ।
जिष्णवे योगायाप्सुयोगैर्वो युनज्मि ॥

5. O subjects, ye are the power of the King, ye the force and strength of the King, ye his manliness and wealth. I join you through concentration in and control of breaths, with the victorious King! (2711)[1]

६. इन्द्रस्यौज स्थेन्द्रस्य सह स्थेन्द्रस्य बलं स्थेन्द्रस्य वीर्यं१ स्थेन्द्रस्य नृम्णं स्थ ।
जिष्णवे योगाय विश्वानि मा भूतान्युप तिष्ठन्तु युक्ता म आप स्थ ॥

6. O subjects, ye are the power of the King, ye the force and strength of the King, ye his manliness and wealth. Let all creation stand by me for the victorious enterprise. May all highly learned persons be interested in the performance of Yoga as instructed by me! (2712)[2]

७. अग्नेर्भाग स्थ । अपां शुक्रमापो देवीर्वर्चो अस्मासु धत्त ।
प्रजापतेर्वो धाम्नास्मै लोकाय सादये ॥

7. O learned persons, ye are the subjects of the fiery King. O divine noblemen, grant us the energy and brilliance of noble deeds. According to the law of God, I set you down for the welfare of this world! (2713)[3]

८. इन्द्रस्य भाग स्थ । अपां शुक्रमापो देवीर्वर्चो अस्मासु धत्त ।
प्रजापतेर्वो धाम्नास्मै लोकाय सादये ॥

8. O learned persons, ye are the subjects of the mighty King. O divine noblemen, grant us the energy and brilliance of noble deeds. According to the law of God, I set you down for the welfare of the world! (2714)

९. सोमस्य भाग स्थ । अपां शुक्रमापो देवीर्वर्चो अस्मासु धत्त ।
प्रजापतेर्वो धाम्नास्मै लोकाय सादये ॥

9. O learned persons, ye are the subjects of the peace-loving King. O divine noblemen, grant us the energy and brilliance of noble deeds. According to the law of God, I set you down for the welfare of the world! (2715)

१०. वरुणस्य भाग स्थ । अपां शुक्रमापो देवीर्वर्चो अस्मासु धत्त ।
प्रजापतेर्वो धाम्नास्मै लोकाय सादये ॥

[1]अप्सु प्राणेषु—दयानन्द भाष्ये यजु 8-25; प्राणेषु ध्यानैः सहः ।
[2]आपः—हे सर्वविद्याव्यापिणो विपश्चितः यथा दयानन्द भाष्ये यजु 6-17. ।
[3]I:Priest.

10. O learned persons, ye are the subjects of the King, who is the alleviator of all miseries. O divine noblemen, grant us the energy and brilliance of noble deeds. According to the law of God, I set you down for the welfare of the world! (2716)

११. मित्रावरुणयोर्भाग स्थ । अपां शुक्रमापो देवीर्वर्चो अस्मासु धत्त ।
प्रजापतेर्वो धाम्नास्मै लोकाय सादये ॥

11. O learned persons, ye are the subjects of the King, who is your saviour from death and calamities. O divine noblemen, grant us the energy and brilliance of noble deeds. According to the law of God, I set you down for the welfare of the world! (2717)

१२. यमस्य भाग स्थ । अपां शुक्रमापो देवीर्वर्चो अस्मासु धत्त ।
प्रजापतेर्वो धाम्नास्मै लोकाय सादये ॥

12. O learned persons, ye are the subjects of a just, impartial King. O divine noblemen, grant us the energy and brilliance of noble deeds. According to the law of God, I set you down for the welfare of the world! (2718)

१३. पितृणां भाग स्थ । अपां शुक्रमापो देवीर्वर्चो अस्मासु धत्त ।
प्रजापतेर्वो धाम्नास्मै लोकाय सादये ॥

13. O learned persons, ye are the subjects of administrators who are the protectors of the State. O divine noblemen, grant us the energy and brilliance of noble deeds. According to the law of God, I set you down for the welfare of the world! (2719)

१४. देवस्य सवितुर्भाग स्थ । अपां शुक्रमापो देवीर्वर्चो अस्मासु धत्त ।
प्रजापतेर्वो धाम्नास्मै लोकाय सादये ॥

14. O learned persons, ye are the subjects of an all-impelling King. O divine noblemen, grant us the energy and brilliance of noble deeds. According to the law of God, I set you down for the welfare of the world! (2720)

१५. यो व आपोऽपां भागो३प्स्व१न्तर्यजुष्यो॒ देवयजनः ।
इदं तमति सृजामि तं माभ्यवनिक्षि ।
तेन तमभ्यतिसृजामो यो३स्मान् द्वेष्टि यं वयं द्विष्मः ।
तं वधेयं तं स्तृषीयानेन ब्रह्मणानेन कर्मणानया मेन्या ॥

15. O learned persons, the King of ye subjects, living amongst you, is worthy of reverence and worship by godly persons. I hand over the administration of this State to him. May I never show him disrespect. With his help we invade the enemy who hates us and whom we abhor. Him would I fain overthrow and slay with this Vedic knowledge, with this heroic deed, and with this army! (2721)[1]

[1]I: A Purohit, priest.

१६. यो व आपोऽपामूर्मिरप्स्व१न्तर्यजुष्यो॒ देवयजनः । इदं तमति सृजामि तं माभ्यवनिक्षि ।
तेन तमभ्यतिसृजामो यो३स्मान् द्वेष्टि यं वयं द्विष्मः ।
तं वधेयं तं स्तृषीयानेन ब्रह्मणानेन कर्मणानया मेन्या ॥

16. O learned persons, the King powerful like the current of waters, controlling your actions, living among you, is worthy of reverence and worship by godly persons. I hand over the administration of this State to him. May I never show him disrespect. With his help we invade the enemy who hates us and whom we abhor. Him would I fain overthrow and slay with this Vedic knowledge, with this heroic deed, and with this army! (2722)

१७. यो व आपोऽपां वत्सो३प्स्व१न्तर्यजुष्यो॒ देवयजनः ।
इदं तमति सृजामि तं माभ्यवनिक्षि ।
तेन तमभ्यतिसृजामो यो३स्मान् द्वेष्टि यं वयं द्विष्मः ।
तं वधेयं तं स्तृषीयानेन ब्रह्मणानेन कर्मणानया मेन्या ॥

17. O learned persons, the King, who grants habitation to Ye subjects, living amongst you, is worthy of reverence and worship by godly persons. I hand over the administration of this State to him. May I never show him disrespect. With his help we invade the enemy who hates us and whom we abhor. Him would I fain overthrow and slay with this Vedic knowledge, with this heroic deed, and with this army! (2723)

१८. यो व आपोऽपां वृषभो३ऽप्स्व१न्तर्यजुष्यो॒ देवयजनः ।
इदं तमति सृजामि तं माभ्यवनिक्षि ।
तेन तमभ्यतिसृजामो यो३स्मान् द्वेष्टि यं वयं द्विष्मः ।
तं वधेयं तं स्तृषीयानेन ब्रह्मणानेन कर्मणानया मेन्या ॥

18. O learned persons, the King who bestows upon ye subjects all sorts of happiness like the cloud, living amongst you, is worthy of reverence and worship by godly persons. I hand over the administration of this State to him. May I never show him disrespect. With his help we invade the enemy who hates us and whom we abhor. Him would I fain overthrow and slay with this Vedic knowledge, with this heroic deed, and with this army! (2724)

१९. यो व आपोऽपां हिरण्यगर्भो३ऽप्स्व१न्तर्यजुष्यो॒ देवयजनः ।
इदं तमति सृजामि तं माभ्यवनिक्षि ।
तेन तमभ्यतिसृजामो यो३स्मान् द्वेष्टि यं वयं द्विष्मः ।
तं वधेयं तं स्तृषीयानेन ब्रह्मणानेन कर्मणानया मेन्या ॥

19. O learned persons, the King, who is the support of ye subjects for the achievement of desirable splendour, living amongst you, is worthy of reverence and worship by godly persons. I hand over the administration of this State to him. May I never show him disrespect. With his help we invade the enemy who hates us and whom we abhor. Him would I fain overthrow and slay with this Vedic knowledge, with this heroic deed, and with this army! (2725)

२०. यो व आपोऽपामश्मा पृश्निर्दिव्यो३ऽप्स्व१न्तर्यजुष्यो्ऽ देवयजनः ।
इदं तमति सृजामि तं माभ्यवनिक्षि ।
तेन तमभ्यतिसृजामो यो३स्मान् द्वेष्टि यं वयं द्विष्मः ।
तं वधेयं तं स्तृषीयानेन ब्रह्मणानेन कर्मणानया मेन्या ॥

20. O learned persons, the King, the ruler of ye subjects, endowed with fine qualities, the master of all sorts of elegance and beauty like the Sun, living amongst you, is worthy of reverence and worship by godly persons. I hand over the administration of this State to him. May I never show him disrespect. With his help we invade the enemy who hates us and whom we abhor. Him would I fain overthrow and slay with this Vedic knowledge, with this heroic deed, and with this army. (2726)

२१. ये व आपोऽपामग्नयोऽप्स्व१न्र्यजुष्याऽ देवयजनाः ।
इदं तानति सृजामि तान् माभ्यवनिक्षि ।
तैस्तमभ्यतिसृजामो यो३स्मान् द्वेष्टि यं वयं द्विष्मः ।
तं बधेयं तं स्तृषीयानेन ब्रह्मणानेन कर्मणानया मेन्या ॥

21. O learned persons, the foe-slaying heroes, from amongst ye subjects, living amidst you, are worthy of reverence and worship by godly persons. I hand over the administration of this State to them. May I never show them disrespect. With their help we invade the enemy who hates us and whom we abhor. Him would I fain overthrow and slay with this Vedic knowledge, with this heroic deed, and with this army. (2727)

२२. यदर्वाचीनं त्रैहायणादनृतं किं चोदिम ।
आपो मा तस्मात् सर्वस्माद् दुरितात्पान्त्वंहसः ॥

22. Whatever evil I have done within the last triennium, from all that woe and sin let the learned shield and guard me. (2728)

२३. समुद्रं वः प्र हिणोमि स्वां योनिमपीतन ।
अरिष्टाः सर्वहायसो मा च नः किं चनाममत् ॥

23. O learned persons just as ocean is the final resort of waters and they all flow into it, so I urge you all on towards God, the Treasure of virtues like ocean of gems. Enter your own Most Efficient Cause. Free from violence may we enjoy the full span of life for a hundred years. Let nothing produce disease in us. (2729)

२४. अरिप्रा आपो अप रिप्रमस्मत् । प्रास्मदेनो दुरितं सुप्रतीकाः प्र दुष्वप्न्यं प्र मलं वहन्तु ॥

24. Immaculate are learned persons. May they cleanse us from defilement. O beautiful learned persons remove our sin and trouble, and bear away ill-dream and all mental pollution! (2730)

२५. विष्णोः क्रमोऽसि सपत्नहा पृथिवीसंशितोऽग्नितेजाः ।
पृथिवीमनु वि क्रमेऽहं पृथिव्यास्तं निर्भजामो यो३स्मान् द्वेष्टि यं वयं द्विष्मः ।
स मा जीवीत् तं प्राणो जहातु ॥

25. O King, thou followest the dictate of God, and are the protector of the people like Him. Thou art foe-slayer. Thou rulest over Earth and are vigorous like fire! I, as king consider it my duty to make huge efforts to control the Earth. We, the subjects, banish him from the state, who hates us and whom we dislike. Let him not live, let vital breath desert him. (2731)

२६. विष्णोः क्रमोऽसि सपत्नहान्तरिक्षसंशितो वायुतेजाः ।
अन्तरिक्षमनु वि क्रमेऽहमन्तरिक्षात् तं निर्भजामो यो३स्मान् द्वेष्टि यं वयं द्विष्मः ।
स मा जीवीत् तं प्राणो जहातु ॥

26. O King, thou followest the dictate of God, and art the protector of the people like Him. Thou art foe-slayer. Thou art mighty in space. Thou art forceful like air! I, as king consider it my duty to make huge effort to control the space. We, the subjects, banish him from the space, who hates us and whom we dislike. Let him not live, let vital breath desert him. (2732)

२७. विष्णोः क्रमोऽसि सपत्नहा द्यौसंशितः सूर्यतेजाः ।
दिवमनु वि क्रमेऽहं दिवस्तं निर्भजामो यो३स्मान् द्वेष्टि यं वयं द्विष्मः ।
स मा जीवीत् तं प्राणो जहातु ॥

27. O King, thou followest the dictate of God, and art the protector of the people like Him. Thou art foe-slayer. Thou art the Lord of the Atmosphere. Thou art lustrous like the Sun. I, as King, consider it my duty to exert to make enterprise in the atmosphere. We, the subjects, deprive from the joys of atmosphere, him who hates us and whom we dislike. Let him not live, let vital breath desert him. (2733)

२८. विष्णोः क्रमोऽसि सपत्नहा दिक्संशितो मनस्तेजाः ।
दिशोऽनु वि क्रमेऽहं दिग्भ्यस्तं निर्भजामो यो३स्मान् द्वेष्टि यं वयं द्विष्मः ।
स मा जीवीत् तं प्राणो जहातु ॥

28. O King, thou followest the dictate of God and art the protector of the people like Him. Thou art foe-slayer. Thou art the master of all quarters. Thou art full of beauty like the mind. I, as king, consider it my duty to perform heroic deeds in all quarters. We, the subjects, expell from all quarters, him who hates us and whom we dislike. Let him not live, let vital breath desert him. (2734)

२९. विष्णोः क्रमोऽसि सपत्नहाशासंशितो वाततेजाः ।
आशा अनु वि क्रमेऽहमाशाभ्यस्तं निर्भजामो यो३स्मान् द्वेष्टि यं वयं द्विष्मः ।
स मा जीवीत् तं प्राणो जहातु ॥

29. O King, thou followest the dictate of God, and art the protector of the people like Him. Thou art foe-slayer. Thou art splendid in sub-quarters. Thou art virulent like the wind! I, as king, consider it my duty to be enterprising in sub-quarters. We, the subjects, expel from sub-quarters, him who hates us and whom we dislike. Let him not live, let vital breath desert him. (2735)

३०. विष्णोः क्रमोऽसि सपत्नह ऋक्संशितः सामतेजाः ।
ऋचोऽनु वि क्रमेऽहमृग्भ्यस्तं निर्भजामो योऽस्मान् द्वेष्टि यं वयं द्विष्मः ।
स मा जीवीत् तं प्राणो जहातु ॥

30. O King, thou followest the dictate of God, and art the protector of the people like Him. Thou art foe-slayer. Thy Intellect has been developed through the study of the Rigveda. Thou art brilliant through the knowledge of the Sāmaveda, that leads to salvation! I, as king, consider it my duty, to make research in the knowledge of the Rigveda. We, the subjects, deprive of the knowledge of the Rigveda, him who hates us and whom we dislike. Let him not live, let vital breath desert him. (2736)

३१. विष्णोः क्रमोऽसि सपत्नहा यज्ञसंशितो ब्रह्मतेजाः ।
यज्ञमनु वि क्रमेऽहं यज्ञात् तं निर्भजामो योऽस्मान् द्वेष्टि यं वयं द्विष्मः ।
स मा जीवीत् तं प्राणो जहातु ॥

31. O King, thou followest the dictate of God, and art the protector of the people like Him. Thou art foe-slayer. Thou hast advanced spiritually through the performance of virtuous deeds. Knowledge has made you lustrous! I, as king, consider it my duty to perform noble deeds. We, the subjects, help not in the performance of Yajña, him who hates us and whom we dislike. Let him not live, let vital breath desert him. (2737)

३२. विष्णोः क्रमोऽसि सपत्नहौषधीसंशितः सोमतेजाः ।
ओषधीरनु वि क्रमेऽहमोषधीभ्यस्तं निर्भजामो योऽस्मान् द्वेष्टि यं वयं द्विष्मः ।
स मा जीवीत् तं प्राणो जहातु ॥

32. O King, thou followest the behest of God, and art the protector of the people like Him. Thou art foe-slayer. Thou art strengthened through the use of medicines, and possess the glow and vigour of Soma, the king of medicinal plants! I, as king, consider it my duty to get research made in medical science. We, the subjects, prevent from the abuse of medicinal herbs, him who hates us and whom we dislike. Let him not live, let vital breath desert him. (2738)

३३. विष्णोः क्रमोऽसि सपत्नहाऽप्सुसंशितो वरुणतेजाः ।
अपोऽनु वि क्रमेऽहमद्भ्यस्तं निर्भजामो योऽस्मान् द्वेष्टि यं वयं द्विष्मः ।
स मा जीवीत् तं प्राणो जहातु ॥

33. O King, thou followest the behest of God and art the protector of the people like Him. Thou art foe-slayer. Thou shinest midst thy subjects. Through art brilliant through thy kingly glow! I, as king, consider it my duty to lead expeditions on the strength of my subjects We, the subjects, prevent from polluting water, him who hates us and whom we dislike. Let him not live, let vital breath desert him. (2739)

३४. विष्णोः क्रमोऽसि सपत्नहा कृषिसंशितोऽन्नतेजाः ।
कृषिमनु वि क्रमेऽहं कृष्यास्तं निर्भजामो यो३स्मान् द्वेष्टि यं वयं द्विष्मः ।
स मा जीवीत् तं प्राणो जहातु ॥

34. O King, thou followest the behest of God, and art the protector of the people like Him. Thou art foe-slayer. Thou art expert in the science of agriculture. Thou art full of vigour through proper diet! I, as king, consider it my duty to improve Agriculture. We, the subjects, prevent from abusing agricultural products, him who hates us and whom we dislike. Let him not live, let vital breath desert him. (2740)

३५. विष्णोः क्रमोऽसि सपत्नहा प्राणसंशितः पुरुषतेजाः ।
प्राणमनु वि क्रमेऽहं प्राणात् तं निर्भजामो यो३स्मान् द्वेष्टि यं वयं द्विष्मः ।
स मा जीवीत् तं प्राणो जहातु ॥

35. O King, thou followest the behest of God and art the protector of the people like Him. Thou art foe-slayer. Thou attainest strength through Prāṇāyāma. Thou art glorious through soul-force! I, asking, consider it my duty to exert to control my breaths. We, the subjects, prevent from the abuse of breaths, him who hates us and whom we dislike. Let him not live, let vital breath desert him. (2741)

३६. जितमस्माकमुद्भिन्नमस्माकमभ्यष्ठां विश्वाः पृतना अरातीः । इदमहमामुष्यायण-
स्यामुष्याः पुत्रस्य वर्चस्तेजः प्राणमायुर्नि वेष्टयामीदमेनमधराञ्चं पादयामि ॥

36. Whatever is obtained through conquest belongs to us. Whatever is gained through war is ours. May I conquer all the forces of the enemy. I seize the power and splendour, the life and vital breathing of the son of such a sire and such a mother. Here do I overthrow and cast him downward. (2742)[1]

३७. सूर्यस्यावृतमन्वावर्ते दक्षिणामन्वावृतम् । सा मे द्रविणं यच्छतु सा मे ब्राह्मणवर्चसम् ॥

37. I follow the course of the Sun. Just as the Sun is intense in heat in the South, so should I be equipped with glory and fervour. May that behaviour bestow upon me wealth and glory of knowledge. (2743)[2]

[1]Us: The subjects. I: The King. Him: The enemy.

[2]I: The king. Follow the course: Just as the Sun illumines the world with his light, so should I rule over my subjects with zeal and strength.

३८. दिशो ज्योतिष्मतीरभ्यावर्ते । ता मे द्रविणं यच्छन्तु ता मे ब्राह्मणवर्चसम् ॥

38. I go to the regions bright with splendour. May they bestow upon me wealth and glory of knowledge. (2744)

३९. सप्तऋषीनभ्यावर्ते । ते मे द्रविणं यच्छन्तु ते मे ब्राह्मणवर्चसम् ॥

39. I make proper use of the seven Rishis; may they bestow upon me wealth and glory of knowledge. (2745)[1]

४०. ब्रह्माभ्यावर्ते । तन्मे द्रविणं यच्छन्तु तन्मे ब्राह्मणवर्चसम् ॥

40. I follow the behest of the Veda. May it bestow upon me wealth and glory of knowledge. (2746)

४१. ब्राह्मणाँ अभ्यावर्ते । ते मे द्रविणं यच्छन्तु ते मे ब्राह्मणवर्चसम् ॥

41. I seek the protection of pious learned persons. May they bestow upon me wealth and glory of knowledge. (2747)

४२. यं वयं मृगयामहे तं वधै स्तृणवामहै । व्यात्ते परमेष्ठिनो ब्रह्मणापीपदाम तम् ॥

42. We chase the enemy, and destroy him with instruments, or hand him over to the control of the king for condign punishment according to Vedic law. (2748)

४३. वैश्वानरस्य दंष्ट्राभ्यां हेतिस्तं समधादभि । इयं तं प्सात्वाहुतिः समिद् देवी सहीयसी ॥

43. Let the shot missile hand over the foe to the King's two mighty fangs. May the powerful, shining, noble king destroy him, as an offering with blazing, strong fuel destroys foul smell. (2749)[2]

४४. राज्ञो वरुणस्य बन्धोऽसि । सोऽमुमामुष्यायणममुष्याः पुत्रमन्ने प्राणे बधान ॥

44. O jail, thou art the prison-house of the king, the averter of sins. Bind that prisoner, the son of such a man and such a woman, and feed him with food for maintaining his life-breath. (2750)[3]

४५. यत् ते अन्नं भुवस्पत आक्षियति पृथिवीमनु । तस्य नस्त्वं भुवस्पते संप्रयच्छ प्रजापते ॥

45. O King, the Lord of Earth, all food of thine that lies upon the face of earth, thereof bestow thou upon us, O Lord of Earth, O Lord of subjects! (2751)

४६. अपो दिव्या अचायिषं रसेन समपृक्ष्महि । पयस्वानग्न आगमं तं मा सं सृज वर्चसा ॥

[1]Seven Rishis: Two eyes, two ears, two nostrils and mouth, or touch, sight, Hearing, Taste, Smell, Mind, Intellect.

[2]The king is spoken of as Vaishwānara as he is the protector of all his subjects.

[3]Prisoners should be well-treated and properly fed, so that they may remain healthy and active, and die not of starvation.

46. I have worshipped the noble learned persons, purifiers like water. We have been equipped with prowess. O learned person, I, a hero, have come. Bestow upon me splendid strength. (2752)

४७. सं माग्ने वर्चसा सृज सं प्रजया समायुषा ।
विद्युर्मे अस्य देवा इन्द्रो विद्यात् सह ऋषिभिः ॥

47. Give me the boon of splendid strength, O learned person, give progeny and life! May the learned know this prayer of mine, may the preceptor with the sages know. (2753)

४८. यदग्ने अद्य मिथुना शपातो यद्वाचस्तृष्टं जनयन्त रेभाः ।
मन्योर्मनसः शरव्या३ जायते या तया विध्य हृदये यातुधानान् ॥

48. O King, whatever ill-words the two violent persons use against the godly persons, whatever bitter speech the chatterers utter, with righteous indignation's arrow, offspring of the mind, transfix thou to the heart the evil tormentors. (2754)

४९. परा शृणीहि तपसा यातुधानान् पराऽग्ने रक्षो हरसा शृणीहि ।
परार्चिषा मूरदेवाञ्छृणीहि परासुतृपः शोशुचतः शृणीहि ॥

49. O King crush the tormentors with thy fervour, consume the demons with thy wrath, destroy the fools with thy fiery splendour, destroy the blazing ones, the insatiable cannibals! (2755)

५०. अपामस्मै वज्रं प्र हरामि चतुर्भृष्टिं शीर्षभिद्याय विद्वान् ।
सो अस्याङ्गानि प्र शृणातु सर्वा तन्मे देवा अनु जानन्तु विश्वे ॥

50. Well skilled, I hurl against this foe, the all round destructive bolt designed by the learned, to cleave his head asunder. May it destroy all members of his body. Let all the learned persons sanction my purpose. (2756)

HYMN VI

१. अरातीयोर्भ्रातृव्यस्य दुर्हार्दो द्विषतः शिरः । अपि वृश्चाम्योजसा ॥

1. With power I cut away the head of my miserly unfriendly, evil-hearted enemy. (2757)

२. वर्म मह्यमयं मणिः फालाज्जातः करिष्यति । पूर्णो मन्थेन मागमद्रसेन सह वर्चसा ॥

2. This laudable Vedic Law devised by God shall prove an armour for me. Filled with minute deliberation, this Vedic Law, with strength and majesty hath come unto me. (2758)

३. यत् त्वा शिक्वः पराऽवधीत् तक्षा हस्तेन वास्या ।
आपस्त्वा तस्माज्जीवलाः पुनन्तु शुचयः शुचिम् ॥

3. If a strong-armed, overpowering foe has cleft thee with his hand and axe, the noble learned persons shall relieve thee, pure in nature, of that injury. (2759)

४. हिरण्यस्रगयं मणिः श्रद्धां यज्ञं महो दधत् । गृहे वसतु नोऽतिथिः ॥

4. May this Vedic Law, the bestower of splendour, granting us faith, sacrifice, power, dwell in our house honoured like a guest. (2760)

५. तस्मै घृतं सुरां मध्वन्नमन्नं क्षदामहे ।
स नः पितेव पुत्रेभ्यः श्रेयः श्रेयश्चिकित्सतु भूयोभूयः श्वःश्वो देवेभ्यो मणिरेत्य ॥

5. For the acquisition of Vedic Law we utilise correct knowledge, sovereignty, brain, and all sorts of good food. May it, be preached by the learned, provide each boon for us as doth a father for his sons, again and again, from morn to morn. (2761)[1]

६. यमबध्नाद् बृहस्पतिर्मणिं फालं घृतश्चुतमुग्रं खदिरमोजसे ।
तमग्निः प्रत्यमुञ्चत सो अस्मै दुह आज्यं भूयोभूयः श्वःश्वस्तेन त्वं द्विषतो जहि ॥

6. God, the Lord of mighty worlds, hath created for strength, this laudable Vedic Law, the giver of reward, the rainer of lustre, mighty, full of eternal truths. A heroic person hath accepted it. It grants him all desired objects again and again, from morn to morn. With this subdue thine enemies. (2762)[2]

७. यमबध्नाद् बृहस्पतिर्मणिं फालं घृतश्चुतमुग्रं खदिरमोजसे ।
तमिन्द्रः प्रत्यमुञ्चतौजसे वीर्या्य कम् ।
सो अस्मै बलमिद् दुहे भूयोभूयः श्वःश्वस्तेन त्वं द्विषतो जहि ॥

7. God, the Lord of mighty worlds hath created for strength, this laudable Vedic Law, the giver of reward, the rainer of lustre, mighty, full of eternal truths. A philanthropist hath gladly accepted it for power and manly puissance. It grants him strength again and again, from morn to morn. With this subdue thine enemies. (2763)

८. यमबध्नाद् बृहस्पतिर्मणिं फालं घृतश्चुतमुग्रं खदिरमोजसे ।
तं सोमः प्रत्यमुञ्चत महे श्रोत्राय चक्षसे ।
सो अस्मै वर्च इद् दुहे भूयोभूयः श्वःश्वस्तेन त्वं द्विषतो जहि ॥

[1]It: Vedic Law. Madhu: Correct knowledge, Surāma: Sovereignty, superhuman power, Gharitam: Brain, तेज.

[2]It, this: Vedic Law. Him: Heroic person, full of energy and zeal like fire. Brihaspati: God. Phālama: The giver of reward, Garitashchutam: The rainer of lustre. Ugrama: Mighty. Khadirama: Full of eternal truths. Manima: Vedic law.

8. God, the Lord of mighty worlds hath created for strength, this laudable Vedic Law, the giver of reward, the rainer of lustre, mighty, full of eternal truths. A peace-loving man, the benefactor of humanity hath accepted it for might, for hearing, and for sight. It yields him energy indeed, again and again, from morn to morn. With this subdue thine enemies. (2764)

९. यमबध्नाद् बृहस्पतिर्मणिं फालं घृतश्चुतमुग्रं खदिरमोजसे ।
तं सूर्यः प्रत्यमुञ्चत तेनेमा अजयद् दिशः ।
सो अस्मै भूतिमिद् दुहे भूयोभूयः श्वःश्वस्तेन त्वं द्विषतो जहि ॥

9. God, the Lord of mighty worlds hath created for strength, this laudable Vedic Law, the giver of reward, the rainer of lustre, mighty, full of eternal truths. A king with nice administrative capacity hath accepted it. With its help he hath conquered all the regions. This yields him majesty again and again, from morn to morn. With this subdue thine enemies. (2765)

१०. यमबध्नाद् बृहस्पतिर्मणिं फालं घृतश्चुतमुग्रं खदिरमोजसे ।
तं बिभ्रच्चन्द्रमा मणिमसुराणां पुरोऽजयद् दानवानां हिरण्ययीः ।
सो अस्मै श्रियमिद् दुहे भूयोभूयः श्वःश्वस्तेन त्वं द्विषतो जहि ॥

10. God, the Lord of mighty worlds, hath created for strength, this laudable Vedic Law, the giver of reward, the rainer of lustre, mighty, full of eternal truths. A King calm like the Moon, who accepts it, conquers with its help the forts of demons and the golden citadels of evil persons. This yields him glory and renown, again and again, from morn to morn. With this subdue thine enemies. (2766)

११. यमबध्नाद् बृहस्पतिर्वाताय मणिमाशवे ।
सो अस्मै वाजिनं दुहे भूयोभूयः श्वःश्वस्तेन त्वं द्विषतो जहि ॥

11. The laudable Vedic Law, which God, the Lord of mighty worlds hath created for an enterprising person, grants him prowess again and again, from morn to morn. With this subdue thine enemies. (2767)

१२. यमबध्नाद् बृहस्पतिर्वाताय मणिमाशवे । तेनेमां मणिना कृषिमश्विनावभि रक्षतः ।
स भिषग्भ्यां महो दुहे भूयोभूयः श्वःश्वस्तेन त्वं द्विषतो जहि ॥

12. With the help of Vedic Law, which God, the Lord of mighty worlds hath created for an enterprising person, men and women protect this vast field of the world. This law grants power to the physician and surgeon again and again, from morn to morn. With this subdue thine enemies. (2768)

१३. यमबध्नाद् बृहस्पतिर्वाताय मणिमाशवे । तं बिभ्रत् सविता मणिं तेनेदमजयत् स्वः ।
सो अस्मै सूनृतां दुहे भूयोभूयः श्वःश्वस्तेन त्वं द्विषतो जहि ॥

13. The laudable Vedic Law, which God, the Lord of mighty worlds, hath created for an enterprising person, is accepted by a prosperous King, with whose help he acquires this worldly pleasure. This law grants him truthful speech again and again from morn to morn. With this subdue thine enemies. (2769)

१४. यमबध्नाद् बृहस्पतिर्वाताय मणिमाशवे । तमापो बिभ्रतीर्मणिं सदा धावन्त्यक्षिताः ।
स आभ्योऽमृतमिद् दुहे भूयोभूयः श्वःश्वस्तेन त्वं द्विषतो जहि ॥

14. God, the Lord of mighty worlds hath created for strength, this laudable Vedic Law, the giver of reward, the rainer of lustre, mighty, full of eternal truths. The subjects observing this law ever remain energetic, being undecayed. This law gives them long life, again and again, from morn to morn. With this subdue thine enemies. (2770)

१५. यमबध्नाद् बृहस्पतिर्वाताय मणिमाशवे । तं राजा वरुणो मणिं प्रत्यमुञ्चत शंभुवम् ।
सो अस्मै सत्यमिद् दुहे भूयोभूयः श्वःश्वस्तेन त्वं द्विषतो जहि ॥

15. The laudable Vedic Law, which God, the Lord of mighty worlds hath created for an enterprising person, is accepted by a prosperous king as the giver of tranquillity. This law develops in him the sense of true justice, again and again, from morn to morn. With this subdue thine enemies. (2771)

१६. यमबध्नाद् बृहस्पतिर्वाताय मणिमाशवे । तं देवा बिभ्रतो मणिं सर्वांल्लोकान् युधाऽजयन् ।
स एभ्यो जितिमिद् दुहे भूयोभूयः श्वःश्वस्तेन त्वं द्विषतो जहि ॥

16. The laudable Vedic Law, which God, the Lord of mighty worlds hath created for an enterprising person, is accepted by victory-loving people, wherewith they conquer in battle all the worlds. This law grants victory for them again and again, from morn to morn. With this subdue thine enemies. (2772)

१७. यमबध्नाद् बृहस्पतिर्वाताय मणिमाशवे । तमिमं देवता मणिं प्रत्यमुञ्चन्त शंभुवम् ।
स आभ्यो विश्वमिद् दुहे भूयोभूयः श्वःश्वस्तेन त्वं द्विषतो जहि ॥

17. The laudable Vedic Law, which God, the Lord of mighty worlds hath created for an enterprising person, has been accepted by the learned as giver of tranquillity. This law yieldeth all kinds of joys for the learned, again and again, from morn to morn. With this subdue thine enemies. (2773)

१८. ऋतवस्तमबध्नतार्तवास्तमबध्नत । संवत्सरस्तं बद्ध्वा सर्वं भूतं वि रक्षति ॥

18. Government officials observe this Vedic Law. The valiant soldiers follow it. The king obeying this law protects mankind. (2774)[1]

[1]See Pt. Jaidev Vidyalankar's commentary for the detailed significance of Ritva, Ārtvā, and Samvatsara.

१९. अन्तर्देशा अबध्नत प्रदिशस्तमबध्नत । प्रजापतिसृष्टो मणिर्द्विषतो मेऽधरां अकः ॥

19. This Vedic Law prevails in all quarters and sub-quarters. May the Vedic Law created by God, cast my foemen down. (2775)

२०. अथर्वाणो अबध्नताथर्वणा अबध्नत ।
तैर्मेदिनो अङ्गिरसो दस्यूनां बिभिदुः पुरस्तेन त्वं द्विषतो जहि ॥

20. Calm, steadfast sages have observed this Vedic Law. The judicious knowers of stable God have followed this law. With their help the wise Rishis have demolished the citadels of dacoits. O King, with the help of Vedic Law, subdue thine enemies! (2776)[1]

२१. तं धाता प्रत्यमुञ्चत स भूतं व्यकल्पयत् । तेन त्वं द्विषतो जहि ॥

21. God created this Vedic Law. He hath controlled the universe. O King, with the help of this Vedic Law, do thou subdue thy foes. (2777)

२२. यमबध्नाद् बृहस्पतिर्देवेभ्यो असुरक्षितिम् । स मायं मणिरागमद् रसेन सह वर्चसा ॥

22. The demon-destroying Vedic Law, which God, the Lord of mighty worlds created for the victorious hath descended to me with prowess and glory. (2778)[2]

२३. यमबध्नाद् बृहस्पतिर्देवेभ्यो असुरक्षितिम् ।
स मायं मणिरागमत् सह गोभिरजाविभिरन्नेन प्रजया सह ॥

23. The demon-destroying Vedic Law, which God the Lord of mighty worlds created for the victorious, hath come to me for giving me cows, goats, sheep, food and progeny. (2779)[3]

२४. यमबध्नाद् बृहस्पतिर्देवेभ्यो असुरक्षितिम् ।
स मायं मणिरागमत् सह व्रीहियवाभ्यां महसा भूत्या सह ॥

24. The demon-destroying Vedic Law, which God, the Lord of mighty worlds created for the victorious hath come to me for giving me store of barley and of rice, greatness and prosperity. (2780)

२५. यमबध्नाद् बृहस्पतिर्देवेभ्यो असुरक्षितिम् ।
स मायं मणिरागमन्मधोर्घृतस्य धारया कीलालेन मणिः सह ॥

25. The demon-destroying Vedic Law, which God, the Lord of mighty worlds created for the victorious, hath come to me with streams of butter and of meath, with sweet delicious beverage. (2781)

[1]Their: The philosophic.
[2]Me: The king.
[3]Me: The king.

२६. यमबध्नाद् बृहस्पतिर्देवेभ्यो असुरक्षितिम् ।
स मायं मणिरागमदूर्जया पयसा सह द्रविणेन श्रिया सह ॥

26. The demon-destroying Vedic Law, which God, the Lord of mighty worlds created for the victorious hath come to me with power and knowledge, with wealth and majesty. (2782)

२७. यमबध्नाद् बृहस्पतिर्देवेभ्यो असुरक्षितिम् ।
स मायं मणिरागमत् तेजसा त्विष्या सह यशसा कीर्त्या सह ॥

27. The demon-destroying Vedic Law, which God, the Lord of mighty worlds created for the victorious, hath come to me with splendour and a blaze of light, with honour and illustrious fame. (2783)

२८. यमबध्नाद् बृहस्पतिर्देवेभ्यो असुरक्षितिम् । स मायं मणिरागमत् सर्वाभिर्भूतिभिः सह ॥

28. The demon-destroying Vedic Law, which God, the Lord of mighty worlds created for the victorious hath come to me, combined with all prosperities. (2784)

२९. तमिमं देवता मणिं मह्यं ददतु पुष्टये । अभिभुं क्षत्रवर्धनं सपत्नदम्भनं मणिम् ॥

29. May the learned bestow on me to win success, the Vedic Law, which is conquering, strength-increasing and the suppressor of enemies. (2785)

३०. ब्रह्मणा तेजसा सह प्रति मुञ्चामि मे शिवम् ।
असपत्नः सपत्नहा सपत्नान् मेऽधराँ अकः ॥

30. With Vedic Light, I acknowledge for myself God as my Well-wisher, Who is foeless, destroyer of the foe, and has brought my enemies under me. (2786)

३१. उत्तरं द्विषतो मामयं मणिःकृणोतु देवजाः । यस्य लोका इमे त्रयः पयो दुग्धमुपासते ।
स मायमधि रोहतु मणिः श्रैष्ठ्याय मूर्धतः ॥

31. May this Vedic Law, the revelation of God, make me superior to my foe. The three stages of Creation, Sustenance, Dissolution testify to its perfect knowledge. May this Vedic Law lift me to a lofty sovereign position. (2787)[1]

३२. यं देवाः पितरो मनुष्या उपजीवन्ति सर्वदा ।
स मायमधि रोहतु मणिः श्रैष्ठ्याय मूर्धतः ॥

32. May the Vedic Law, on which the sages, protecting parents and ordinary mortals always depend, lift to a lofty sovereign position. (2788)

३३. यथा बीजमुर्वरायां कृष्टे फालेन रोहति । एवा मयि प्रजा पशवोऽन्नमन्नं वि रोहतु ॥

[1]Me: The king.

33. As, when the plough hath tilled the soil, the seed springs up in fertile soil, so may I get progeny, cattle and food of every kind by observing this Vedic Law. (2789)

३४. यस्मै त्वा यज्ञवर्धन मणे प्रत्यमुञ्चं शिवम् ।
तं त्वं शतदक्षिण मणे श्रैष्ठ्याय जिन्वतात् ॥

34. O Vedic Law, the developer of noble acts, speed to pre-eminence the king for whom I have accepted thee, the Well-wisher, O Vedic Law, full of manifold powers! (2790)

३५. एतमिध्मं समाहितं जुषाणो अग्ने प्रति हर्य होमैः ।
तस्मिन् विदेम सुमतिं स्वस्ति प्रजां चक्षुः पशून्त्समिद्धे जातवेदसि ब्रह्मणा ॥

35. O king, blazing like fire, love this well-contemplated God, with fondness and acts of charity and self-sacrifice. In Him kindled with Vedic knowledge, we find right understanding, welfare, progeny, knowledge and cattle. (2791)

Chapter (Anuvāka) 4

HYMN VII

१. कस्मिन्नङ्गे तपो अस्याधि तिष्ठति कस्मिन्नङ्ग ऋतमस्याध्याहितम् ।
क्व व्रतं क्व श्रद्धाऽस्य तिष्ठति कस्मिन्नङ्गे सत्यमस्य प्रतिष्ठितम् ॥

1. In what part of Him does austerity reside? What part is the base of Vedic knowledge? Where in Him standeth Holy Duty? Where Faith? Where in what part of Him is Truth implanted? (2792)

२. कस्मादङ्गाद् दीप्यते अग्निरस्य कस्मादङ्गात् पवते मातरिश्वा ।
कस्मादङ्गाद् वि मिमीतेऽधि चन्द्रमा मह स्कम्भस्य मिमानो अङ्गम् ॥

2. Out of which part glows the light of fire? From which blows air? From which doth Moon shine, exhibiting the nature of Mighty God? (2793)

३. कस्मिन्नङ्गे तिष्ठति भूमिरस्य कस्मिन्नङ्गे तिष्ठत्यन्तरिक्षम् ।
कस्मिन्नङ्गे तिष्ठत्याहिता द्यौः कस्मिन्नङ्गे तिष्ठत्युत्तरं दिवः ॥

3. Which of His members is the Earth's upholder? Which gives the middle air a base to rest on? Where, in which member is the sky established? Where hath the space above the sky its dwelling? (2794)

४. क्व१ प्रेप्सन् दीप्यत ऊर्ध्वो अग्निः क्व१ प्रेप्सन् पवते मातरिश्वा ।
यत्र प्रेप्सन्तीरभियन्त्यावृतः स्कम्भं तं ब्रूहि कतमः स्विदेव सः ॥

4. Whitherward Yearning blazeth the lofty Sun? Whitherward Yearning bloweth wind? Who out of many, tell me, O learned person, is that All-pervading God, to Whom with longing flow the streams of water? (2795)

५. क्वार्धमासाः क्व यन्ति मासाः संवत्सरेण सह संविदानाः ।
यत्र यन्त्यृतवो यत्रार्तवाः स्कम्भं तं ब्रूहि कतमः स्विदेव सः ॥

5. Whitherward go the half-months and the months, accordant with the full year? Who out of many, tell me, O learned person, is the All-pervading God, to Whom go seasons and parts of seasons? (2796)

६. क्व१ प्रेप्सन्ती युवती विरूपे अहोरात्रे द्रवतः संविदाने ।
यत्र प्रेप्सन्तीरभियन्त्यापः स्कम्भं तं ब्रूहि कतमः स्विदेव सः ॥

6. Whitherward yearning speed the two Damsels, accordant Day and Night of different colour? Who out of many, tell me, O learned person, is the All-pervading God, to whom the people take way with longing? (2797)

७. यस्मिन्त्स्तब्ध्वा प्रजापतिर्लोकान्त्सर्वाँ अधारयत् । स्कम्भं तं ब्रूहि कतमः स्विदेव सः ॥

7. Who out of many, tell me, O learned person, is that All-pervading God, on Whose support Prajapati set up and firmly established all the worlds? (2798)[1]

८. यत् परममवमं यच्च मध्यमं प्रजापतिः ससृजे विश्वरूपम् ।
कियता स्कम्भः प्र विवेश तत्र यन्न प्राविशत् कियत् तद् बभूव ॥

8. That universe which the All-pervading God created, wearing all forms, the highest midmost, lowest, how far did God penetrate within it? What portion did he leave unpenetrated? (2799)[2]

९. कियता स्कम्भः प्र विवेश भूतं कियद् भविष्यदन्वाशयेऽस्य ।
एकं यदङ्गमकृणोत् सहस्रधा कियता स्कम्भः प्र विवेश तत्र ॥

9. How far within the past hath God entered? How much of Him hath entered into the future? That one part which He set in thousand places in the present,—how far did God penetrate within it. (2800)[3]

१०. यत्र लोकांश्च कोशांश्चापो ब्रह्म जना विदुः ।
असच्च यत्र सच्चान्त स्कम्भं तं ब्रूहि कतमः स्विदेव सः ॥

10. Who out of many, tell me, is that All-pervading God, in Whom learned persons know reside the worlds, all riches, the knowledge of the Vedas, the non-permanent created world and the permanent Matter, the cause of the universe? (2801)

११. यत्र तपः पराक्रम्य व्रतं धारयत्युत्तरम् ।
ऋतं च यत्र श्रद्धा चापो ब्रह्म समाहिताः स्कम्भं तं ब्रूहि कतमः स्विदेव सः ॥

[1]Prajāpati: The Sun or Atmosphere.

[2]God is vaster than the universe, which is but a part of Him. 'All created worlds are only a part of God' *Yajur*, chapter 31.

[3]None knows the beginning or end of God. He pervades the universe in entirety.

11. Declare that All-pervading God, Who is he of many, in Whom, exerting full power, Fervour maintains her loftiest vow? In Whom are comprehended Law, Faith, all souls and Vedic knowledge. (2802)

१२. यस्मिन् भूमिरन्तरिक्षं द्यौर्यस्मिन्नध्याहिता ।
यत्राग्निश्चन्द्रमाः सूर्यो वातस्तिष्ठन्त्यार्पिताः स्कम्भं तं ब्रूहि कतमः स्विदेव सः ॥

12. Who out of many, tell me, is that All-pervading God, on Whom as their foundation Earth, and Atmosphere and Sky are set, in Whom as their appointed place rest Fire and Moon, and Sun and Wind? (2803)

१३. यस्य त्रयस्त्रिंशद् देवा अङ्गे सर्वे समाहिताः । स्कम्भं तं ब्रूहि कतमः स्विदेव सः ॥

13. Who out of many, tell me, is that All-pervading God, in Whom are contained all three and thirty forces of Nature. (2804)[1]

१४. यत्र ऋषयः प्रथमजा ऋचः साम यजुर्मही ।
एकर्षिर्यस्मिन्नार्पितः स्कम्भं तं ब्रूहि कतमः स्विदेव सः ॥

14. Who out of many, tell me, is that All-pervading God, in Whom the sages earliest born, the Rigveda, the Sāmaveda, the Yajurveda and the Atharvaveda, and impartiality abide. (2805)[2]

१५. यत्रामृतं च मृत्युश्च पुरुषेऽधि समाहिते ।
समुद्रो यस्य नाड्य१ः पुरुषेऽधि समाहिताः स्कम्भं तं ब्रूहि कतमः स्विदेव सः ॥

15. Who out of many, tell me, is that All-pervading God, Who comprehendeth, for mankind, both immortality and death, Who containeth for mankind the vast space as His veins? (2806)

१६. यस्य चतस्रः प्रदिशो नाड्य१स्तिष्ठन्ति प्रथमाः ।
यज्ञो यत्र पराक्रान्तः स्कम्भं त ब्रूहि कतमः स्विदेव सः ॥

16. Who out of many is that All-pervading God, He Whose chief arteries are the sky's four regions, He in Whom Sacrifice putteth forth its might? (2807)[3]

१७. ये पुरुषे ब्रह्म विदुस्ते विदुः परमेष्ठिनम् । यो वेद परमेष्ठिनं यश्च वेद प्रजापतिम् ।
ज्येष्ठं ये ब्राह्मणं विदुस्ते स्कम्भमनुसंविदुः ॥

17. They who in man understand Brahma, the divine essence, know Him Who is Supreme? He who knows Him Who is Supreme, and he who knows the Lord of life, these know the loftiest Power Divine, and thence know the All-pervading God thoroughly. (2808)

[1]Thirtythree deities: Eight vasus i.e., Fire, Earth, Air, Atmosphere (अन्तरिक्ष), Sky, Sun, Moon, Star. (नक्षत्र). Eleven Rudras: Prāna. Apāna, Vyāna, Udāna, Samāna, Nāga, Kurma, Krikal, Dev Dutt, Dhananjya and Soul. Twelve Ādityas: Twelve months. Indra: Lighting, Prajāpati: Yajna. See Brihadāranyak Upnishada for a detailed account.

[2]Mahi has been translated by Pt. Jaidev Vidyalankar, Pt. Khem Karan Das Trivedi, and Pt. Dāmodar Satvalekar as *Atharvaveda*, which deals with the high knowledge of God and salvation.

[3]Four regions: North, East, South, West.

१८. यस्य शिरो वैश्वानरश्चक्षुरङ्गिरसोऽभवन् ।
अङ्गानि यस्य यातवः स्कम्भं तं ब्रूहि कतमः स्विदेव सः ॥

18. Who out of many tell me is that All-pervading God, of Whom the Sun became the head, the planets His eye, and all revolving worlds His corporeal parts? (2809)[1]

१९. यस्य ब्रह्म मुखमाहुर्जिह्वां मधुकशामुत ।
विराजमूधो यस्याहुः स्कम्भं तं ब्रूहि कतमः स्विदेव सः ॥

19. Who out of many, tell me is that All-pervading God, Whose Mouth the sages say is this world, Whose tongue is the Vedic lore, and multi-powered Matter is Whose source of enjoyment for mankind. (2810)[2]

२०. यस्मादृचो अपातक्षन् यजुर्यस्मादपाकषन् ।
सामानि यस्य लोमान्यथर्वाङ्गिरसो मुखं स्कम्भं तं ब्रूहि कतमः स्विदेव सः ॥

20. Who out of many, tell me, is that All-pervading God, Who revealed the Rigveda, the Yajurveda, Whose hairs are Sāma-verses, and mouth the hymns of the Atharvaveda. (2811)[3]

२१. असच्छाखां प्रतिष्ठन्तीं परममिव जना विदुः । उतो सन्मन्यन्तेऽवरे ये ते शाखामुपासते ॥

21. The ignorant count the conspicuous, impermanent created world as a thing supreme. The wise, in the created world, search for the All-pervading God, as the Efficient cause of the universe. (2812)[4]

२२. यत्रादित्याश्च रुद्राश्च वसवश्च समाहिताः ।
भूतं च यत्र भव्यं च सर्वे लोकाः प्रतिष्ठिताः स्कम्भं तं ब्रूहि कतमः स्विदेव सः ॥

22. Who out of many, tell me, is that All-pervading God, in Whom Adityas dwell, in Whom Rudras and vasus are contained, in Whom, the past and the future and all the worlds are firmly set. (2813)

२३. यस्य त्रयस्त्रिंशद् देवा निधिं रक्षन्ति सर्वदा । निधिं तमद्य को वेद यं देवा अभिरक्षथ ॥

23. Whose secret treasure evermore the three and thirty forces protect? Who knoweth now the treasure which, O gods ye watch and guard? (2814)

[1]The language is metaphorical. God is Incorporeal. To show the vastness and grandeur of God, the Sun is described as His head, the planets as eye, and all moving worlds as limbs.

[2]Just as udder yields milk which strengthens the body, so Nature is God's udder ऊधस which yields enjoyment to mankind.

[3]The knowledge of the Vedas is co-eternal with God. Never was there a time when God existed, not the Vedas. Just as hairs form the part and parcel of the body, and mouth is its part, they co-exist with the body, so the Vedas co-existed with God. God and His knowledge, the Vedas exist together. God out of his infinite knowledge, reveals a part of it in the shape of the Vedas in the beginning of each cycle of creation, which was quite adequate for the complete development of the soul.

[4]Secret treasure: Primordial Veda. Thirty-three forces: See verse 13th. Who knoweth: Very few know.

२४. यत्र देवा ब्रह्मविदो ब्रह्म ज्येष्ठमुपासते ।
यो वै तान् विद्यात् प्रत्यक्षं स ब्रह्मा वेदिता स्यात् ॥

24. Where the sages, versed in sacred lore, worship, the loftiest Power Divine—the man who knows them face to face becomes in their company a learned person, who knows the truth. (2815)

२५. बृहन्तो नाम ते देवा येऽसतः परि जज्ञिरे । एकं तदङ्गं स्कम्भस्यासदाहुः परो जनाः ॥

25. Great, verily, are those forces of Nature which sprang from Matter. The wise say that the impermanent created world is a part of the All-pervading God. (2816)

२६. यत्र स्कम्भः प्रजनयन् पुराणं व्यवर्तयत् । एकं तदङ्गं स्कम्भस्य पुराणमनुसंविदुः ॥

26. Where God creating the universe gave the ancient matter its diverse shape and form, the wise recognise that ancient Matter as a part of God. (2817)[1]

२७. यस्य त्रयस्त्रिंशद् देवा अङ्गे गात्रा विभेजिरे ।
तान् वै त्रयस्त्रिंशद् देवानेके ब्रह्मविदो विदुः ॥

27. The three and thirty forces of Nature constitute a part of Him, disposed as limbs. Only those deeply versed in Holy Lore know these three and thirty forces. (2818)[2]

२८. हिरण्यगर्भं परममनत्युद्यं जना विदुः । स्कम्भस्तदग्रे प्रासिञ्चद्धिरण्यं लोके अन्तरा ॥

28. Men know God as Supreme and Inexpressible. In the beginning, in the midst of the world, God poured the brilliant power of creation in Matter. (2819)

२९. स्कम्भे लोकाः स्कम्भे तपः स्कम्भेऽध्यृतमाहितम् ।
स्कम्भं त्वा वेद प्रत्यक्षमिन्द्रे सर्वं समाहितम् ॥

29. On God the worlds and penance rest. Vedic knowledge reposes on Him. O God I clearly know Thee, on Thee, Indra rests the whole universe. (2820)[3]

३०. इन्द्रे लोका इन्द्रे तप इन्द्रेऽध्यृतमाहितम् ।
इन्द्रं त्वा वेद प्रत्यक्षं स्कम्भे सर्वं प्रतिष्ठितम् ॥

30. On Indra the worlds and penance rest. Vedic knowledge reclines on Indra. O Indra I clearly know Thee, on Thee, skambh rests the whole universe. (2821)[4]

[1]Where: In the beginning of creation God is higher and vaster than Matter. God is indivisible, and has no material part. Metaphorically Matter has been spoken of as a part of God, smaller than Him in all aspects.

[2]Thirty-three forces: Eight Vasus. Eleven Rudras, Twelve Adityas, Indra and Yajna. For detailed explanation see verse 13.

[3]Indra and Skambh are both synonyms for God.

[4]Indra, Skambh: God.

३१. नाम नाम्ना जोहवीति पुरा सूर्यात् पुरोषसः ।
यदजः प्रथमं संबभूव स ह तत् स्वराज्यमियाय यस्मान्नान्यत् परमस्ति भूतम् ॥

31. Ere sun and dawn a devotee worships God with different names. When the unborn soul first comes in contact with God, it enjoys sovereign felicity, than which aught higher never hath arisen. (2822)

३२. यस्य भूमिः प्रमाऽन्तरिक्षमुतोदरम् । दिवं यश्चक्रे मूर्धानं तस्मै ज्येष्ठाय ब्रह्मणे नमः ॥

32. Be reverence paid to Him, that Highest God, Whose base is Earth, His belly atmosphere, Who made the sky to be His head. (2823)[1]

३३. यस्य सूर्यश्चक्षुश्चन्द्रमाश्च पुनर्णवः । अग्निं यश्चक्र आस्यं१ तस्मै ज्येष्ठाय ब्रह्मणे नमः ॥

33. Homage to Him, that Highest God, Whose eye is the Sun and the Moon who groweth young and new again, Him Who made fire for His mouth. (2824)

३४. यस्य वातः प्राणापानौ चक्षुरङ्गिरसोऽभवन् ।
दिशो यश्चक्रे प्रज्ञानीस्तस्मै ज्येष्ठाय ब्रह्मणे नमः ॥

34. Homage to Him, that Highest God, Whose two breaths were the Wind, the learned His sight. Who made the regions as His ears. (2825)[2]

३५. स्कम्भो दाधार द्यावापृथिवी उभे इमे स्कम्भो दाधारोर्व१न्तरिक्षम् ।
स्कम्भो दाधार प्रदिशः षडुर्वीः स्कम्भ इदं विश्वं भुवनमा विवेश ॥

35. God set fast these two, the earth and heaven, God maintained the ample air between them. God established the six spacious regions: this whole world God entered and pervaded. (2826)[3]

३६. यः श्रमात् तपसो जातो लोकान्त्सर्वान्त्समानशे ।
सोमं यश्चक्रे केवलं तस्मै ज्येष्ठाय ब्रह्मणे नमः ॥

36. Homage to Him, that Highest God, Who through His Fervour and Power, pervaded all the worlds completely, and granted salvation to the soul alone. (2827)[4]

३७. कथं वातो नेलयति कथं न रमते मनः । किमापः सत्यं प्रेप्सन्तीर्नेलयन्ति कदा चन ॥

37. Why doth the wind move ceaselessly? Why doth the mind take no rest? Why do the waters following the natural law of their being, never at any time repose? (2828)[5]

[1](32, 33) The language is metaphorical.
[2]Two breaths: Prāna and Apāna. Ears: Means of sense.
[3]Six regions: North, East, South, West, Nadir, Zenith.
[4]Salvation: His proximity.
[5]Air, mind, waters perform their tasks, as ordained by God.

३८. महद् यक्षं भुवनस्य मध्ये तपसि क्रान्तं सलिलस्य पृष्ठे ।
तस्मिञ्छ्रयन्ते य उ के च देवा वृक्षस्य स्कन्धः परित इव शाखाः ॥

38. Attainable through austerity, in the world's centre, is the Adorable God, pervading the atmosphere's surface. In Him reside all divine objects, as branches stand round the tree-trunk. (2829)

३९. यस्मै हस्ताभ्यां पादाभ्यां वाचा श्रोत्रेण चक्षुषा ।
यस्मै देवाः सदा बलिं प्रयच्छन्ति विमितेऽमितं स्कम्भं तं ब्रूहि कतमः स्विदेव सः ॥

39. Who out of many, tell me, is that All-pervading God, To Whom the learned with hands, with feet, and voice, and ear, and eye present tribute. Who is Infinite in the finite universe? (2830)

४०. अप तस्य हतं तमो व्यावृत्तः स पाप्मना ।
सर्वाणि तस्मिञ्ज्योतींषि यानि त्रीणि प्रजापतौ ॥

40. He who knows God remains away from ignorance, and becomes free from sin. In him are all the lights, the three abiding in God. (2831)[1]

४१. यो वेतसं हिरण्ययं तिष्ठन्तं सलिले वेद । स वै गुह्यः प्रजापतिः ॥

41. He verily Who knows the shining world that stands in the atmosphere is the mysterious God, the Lord of life. (2832)

४२. तन्त्रमेके युवती विरूपे अभ्याक्रामं वयतः षण्मयूखम् ।
प्रान्या तन्तूंस्तिरते धत्ते अन्या नाप वृञ्जाते न गमातो अन्तम् ॥

42. Singly the two young Maids (Day and Night) of different colours (bright and dark) approach the six seasoned warp of the year in turns and weave it. The one (day) draws out the threads, the other (night) lays them: they never take rest, they reach no end of labour. (2833)

४३. तयोरहं परिनृत्यन्त्योरिव न वि जानामि यतरा परस्तात् ।
पुमानेनद् वयत्युद् गृणत्ति पुमानेनद्वि जभाराधि नाके ॥

43. Of these two (Day and Night) dancing round as 'twere, I cannot distinguish which precedes the other. God inweaves this web of creation. He dissolves it. He hath stretched this world to the cope of heaven. (2834)

४४. इमे मयूखा उप तस्तभुर्दिवं सामानि चक्रुस्तसराणि वातवे ॥

44. These rays have buttressed up the Sun. The Sāmans serve as threads for weaving this world. (2835)[2]

[1]Three lights: Sun, lightning, fire, or Sanyog, creation, viyog dissolution, sathiti, sustenance. Some commentators interpret them as Satva, Rajasa, Tamasa.

[2]Sāmans: Cloud, Air, Speech, Mind, Ear.

HYMN VIII

१. यो भूतं च भव्यं च सर्वं यश्चाधितिष्ठति ।
स्व१र्यस्य च केवलं तस्मै ज्येष्ठाय ब्रह्मणे नमः ॥

1. Worship to loftiest God, Lord of the Past and Future. To Him Who rules over the universe, and is the embodiment of joy. (2836)

२. स्कम्भेनेमे विष्टभिते द्यौश्च भूमिश्च तिष्ठतः ।
स्कम्भ इदं सर्वमात्मन्वद्यत् प्राणन्निमिषच्च यत् ॥

2. Upheld by God's power these two, the heaven and the earth, stand fast. All this world of life, whatever breathes or shuts an eye, rests in God. (2837)

३. तिस्रो ह प्रजा अत्यायमायन् न्य१न्या अर्कमभितोऽविशन्त ॥
बृहन् ह तस्थौ रजसो विमानो हरितो हरिणीरा विवेश ॥

3. Three kinds of men are subject to transmigration, but the emancipated souls attain to the Most Worshipful God. The Almighty God, creating different worlds, is All-pervading. God, Most Refulgent like the Sun is present in all regions. (2838)[1]

४. द्वादश प्रधयश्चक्रमेकं त्रीणि नभ्यानि क उ तच्चिकेत ।
तत्राहतास्त्रीणि शतानि शङ्कवः षष्टिश्च खीला अविचाचला ये ॥

4. One is the wheel, the tires are twelve in number, the naves are three. What man hath understood it? Three hundred and sixty spokes and three hundred and sixty pins have been hammered thereupon, which are firmly set in their places. (2839)[2]

५. इदं सवितर्वि जानीहि षड्यमा एक एकजः ।
तस्मिन् हापित्वमिच्छन्ते य एषामेक एकजः ॥

5. Discern thou this, O learned man, six are the law—abiding forces, and one singly born. They claim relationship in that among them which is born alone. (2840)[3]

६. आविः सन्निहितं गुहा जरन्नाम महत् पदम् । तत्रेदं सर्वमार्पितमेजत् प्राणत् प्रतिष्ठितम् ॥

[1]Three kinds: Imbued with Satva, Rajasa, Tamasa i.e., ordinary mortals.

[2]Soul has been compared to the year, one wheel. Twelve tires: Twelve months. Three naves: Three seasons, Summer, Rains, and Winter. 360 spokes are 360 days. 360 pins are 360 nights in the year. Similarly, the solitary soul is equipped with twelve breaths, three attributes of Satva, Rajsa, Tamsa. 720 spokes and pins are the 720 arteries of the body.

[3]Six law-abiding forces: Five organs of cognition and mind. One singly born: The soul. They: Six law-abiding forces, soul is unborn in nature. Its assuming the body is spoken of as its birth.

6. God is Manifest, Eternal, concealed in the heart, Adorable, Famous, Worshipful and Attainable. Therein is firmly stationed all the moving breathing universe. (2841)

७. एकचक्रं वर्तत एकनेमि सहस्राक्षरं प्र पुरो नि पश्चा ।
अर्धेन विश्वं भुवनं जजान यदस्यार्धं क्व१ तद् बभूव ।।

7. With unchanging refulgence, with unalterable Law, with thousand powers, God exists before the creation and after the dissolution of the universe. With a part of His strength, He has begotten all creation. Where hath the other half become unnoticed? (2842)

८. पञ्चवाही वहत्यग्रमेषां प्रष्टयो युक्ता अनुसंवहन्ति ।
अयातमस्य ददृशे न यातं परं नेदीयोऽवरं दवीयः ।।

8. God, the Controller of five elements, exists before all these created worlds. All knowable objects follow Him. His near visible strength is known to the learned, but not His invisible vast distant power. Most Exalted, Supreme God is nearest to the learned and farthest from the ignorant. (2843)

९. तिर्यग्बिलश्चमस ऊर्ध्वबुध्नस्तस्मिन् यशो निहितं विश्वरूपम् ।
तदासत ऋषयः सप्त साकं ये अस्य गोपा महतो बभूवुः ।।

9. Head is a receptacle, inclined in shape and closed at the top. Full knowledge resides in it. Seven Rishis united together dwell in it, and act as protectors of this mighty body. (2844)[1]

१०. या पुरस्ताद्युज्यते या च पश्चाद्या विश्वतो युज्यते या च सर्वतः ।
यया यज्ञः प्राङ् तायते तां त्वा पृच्छामि कतमा सर्चाम् ।।

10. Who exists before the Creation and after the dissolution of the universe, Who is present everywhere, and at all times. Through Whom sacrifice proceedeth onward, I ask thee Who is that Adorable Power of all the powers. (2845)

११. यदेजति पतति यच्च तिष्ठति प्राणदप्राणन्निमिषच्च यद् भुवत् ।
तद् दाधार पृथिवीं विश्वरूपं तत् संभूय भवत्येकमेव ।।

11. God, the Fashioner of the universe upholds the earth, and everything in the world, which has power of motion, that which flies, or stands which breathes or breathes not, which existing, shuts the eye. God, Full of Power remains only one. (2846)

[1]Seven Rishis: Two ears known as Gautama and Bhardwāja, two eyes known as Vishwāmitra and Jamdagni, two nostrils known as Vasishta and Kashyapa, and mouth known as Attri.

१२. अनन्तं विततं पुरुत्रानन्तमन्तवच्चा समन्ते ।
ते नाकपालश्चरति विचिन्वन् विद्वान् भूतमुत भव्यमस्य ॥

12. The Endless God is extended in every direction. God, the Lord of the joy of salvation, distinguishing the Infinite Cause from the finite effect, the world, which both are inter-related, and knowing the Past, Present and Future of the universe, controls both the Cause and the Effect. (2847)

१३. प्रजापतिश्चरति गर्भे अन्तरदृश्यमानो बहुधा वि जायते ।
अर्धेन विश्वं भुवनं जजान यदस्यार्धं कतमः स केतुः ॥

13. God resides within the soul, Though Unseen, he exhibits Himself in various shapes like the Sun, Moon and Planets. He with one half engendered all creation. What sign is there to tell us of the other? (2848)

१४. ऊर्ध्वं भरन्तमुदकं कुम्भेनेवोदहार्यम् । पश्यन्ति सर्वे चक्षुषा न सर्वे मनसा विदुः ॥

14. Just as all men behold with eye, the water-bearer who holds aloft the water in the jar, but know him not with the mind, so men observe the material visible strength of God, but not His subtle power. (2849)

१५. दूरे पूर्णेन वसति दूर ऊनेन हीयते ।
महद्यक्षं भुवनस्य मध्ये तस्मै बलिं राष्ट्रभृतो भरन्ति ॥

15. God remains away from him who suffers from superiority complex, and him who is prey to inferiority complex. A Mighty Being exists in creation's centre: to Him the rulers of the realms pay tribute. (2850)

१६. यतः सूर्य उदेत्यस्तं यत्र च गच्छति । तदेव मन्येऽहं ज्येष्ठं तदु नात्येति किं चन ॥

16. That, whence the Sun arises, that whither he goes to take his rest, that God verily I hold supreme: naught in the world surpasses Him. (2851)

१७. ये अर्वाङ् मध्य उत वा पुराणं वेदं विद्वांसमभितो वदन्ति ।
आदित्यमेव ते परि वदन्ति सर्वे अग्निं द्वितीयं त्रिवृतं च हंसम् ॥

17. Those who in recent, mediaeval, or ancient times, on all sides greet God, the knower of the Veda, one and all, verily, discuss God, the Absorber of the universe. Next to Him they discuss the learned emancipated soul. Thirdly they discuss the ordinary soul subject to transmigration, bound by tri-attributed Matter. (2852)[1]

१८. सहस्राह्ण्यं वियतावस्य पक्षौ हरेर्हंसस्य पततः स्वर्गम् ।
स देवान्त्सर्वानुरस्युपदद्य संपश्यन् याति भुवनानि विश्वा ॥

[1]Tri-attributed: Possessing the attributes of Satva, Rajasa, Tamasa.

18. Both the wings of this Omnipresent God, the Embodiment of perfect joy, the Alleviator of misery, All-pervading, are spread over endless time and place. Retaining all divine virtues in His bosom, beholding all the created worlds, He controls the universe. (2853)[1]

१९. सत्येनोर्ध्वस्तपति ब्रह्मणाऽर्वाङ् वि पश्यति ।
प्राणेन तिर्यङ् प्राणति यस्मिन्ज्येष्ठमधि श्रितम् ।।

19. The man, who realises the Highest God residing in him, blazes up aloft through truth looks at the created world in different ways through Vedic knowledge, and lives happily through soul-force, moving hither and thither. (2854)

२०. यो वै ते विद्यादरणी याभ्यां निर्मथ्यते वसु ।
स विद्वान्ज्येष्ठं मन्येत स विद्याद् ब्राह्मणं महत् ।।

20. The sage who knows the kindling-sticks of Om and the body, whence by attrition God, the All-Pervader is realised, will comprehend what is Most High, will know the Mighty God. (2855)[2]

२१. अपादग्रे समभवत् सो अग्रे स्व१राभरत् । चतुष्पाद् भूत्वा भोग्यः सर्वमादत्त भोजनम् ।।

21. God, the Indivisible, existed before the creation of the world. He realised perfect joy before creation, as soul does in salvation. Being Four-footed, and Ruler of the world, He absorbed the whole universe in Himself as food at the time of its dissolution. (2856)[3]

२२. भोग्यो भवदथो अन्नमदद् बहु । यो देवमुत्तरावन्तमुपासातै सनातनम् ।।

22. The man who humbly worshippeth the Eternal and Victorious God, prospers in life and gives great store of food in charity. (2857)

२३. सनातनमेनमाहुरुताद्य स्यात् पुनर्णवः । अहोरात्रे प्र जायेते अन्यो अन्यस्य रूपयोः ।।

23. The sages call God immemorial, but He is ever fresh and new. Day and Night reproduce themselves anew, each from the form the other wears. (2858)[4]

[1]Both wings: Cause and Effect, कारण, कार्य ।

[2]Just as by rubbing together two sticks we get fire, the great giver of riches, so by rubbing together the body and Om we realise God. See Shwetashwatara Upanishad.

[3]Four-footed: प्रकाशवान्, अनन्तवान्, ज्योतिष्मान् and आयतनवान्. These are the four feet of God metaphorically, i.e., Lustre, Infinity, Intelligence, Immensity. God engulfs the whole world at the time of its dissolution. Scherman considers speech, Breath, Eye and Ear to be the four feet. Pt. Khem Karn Das Trivedi considers four directions to be four feet.

[4]God, though old and immemorial is ever new and fresh, just as Day and Night, though ancient come fresh and new daily. Day comes out of Night, and Night out of Day.

२४. शतं सहस्रमयुतं न्यर्बुदमसंख्येयं स्वमस्मिन् निविष्टम् ।
तदस्य घ्नन्त्यभिपश्यत एव तस्माद् देवो रोचत एष एतत् ।।

24. A hundred, thousand, myriad, Yea a hundred million stores of wealth are laid in God. This wealth the men obtains as He looks on, and that is why He is loved by all. (2859)

२५. बालादेकमणीयस्कमुतैकं नेव दृश्यते । ततः परिष्वजीयसी देवता सा मम प्रिया ।।

25. One is yet finer than a hair, One is not even visible. Hence God, Who embraces the soul with firmer hold, is dear to me. (2860)[1]

२६. इयं कल्याण्य१जरा मर्त्यस्यामृता गृहे । यस्मै कृता शये स यश्चकार जजार सः ।।

26. This lovely Matter is untouched by age, being immortal it resides in the body of the mortal man. God, for Whose obedience it was made lies hidden in Matter. God, Who converted Matter from the invisible into the visible shape, is worthy of adoration. (2861)

२७. त्वं स्त्री त्वं पुमानसि त्वं कुमार उत वा कुमारी ।
त्वं जीर्णो दण्डेन वञ्चसि त्वं जातो भवसि विश्वतोमुखः ।।

27. O soul, thou art a woman, and a man, thou art a boy, and a damsel. Grown old thou totterest with a staff. Assuming the physical body, thou appearest in different forms. (2862)

२८. उतैषां पितोत वा पुत्र एषामुतैषां ज्येष्ठ उत वा कनिष्ठः ।
एको ह देवो मनसि प्रविष्टः प्रथमो जातः स उ गर्भे अन्तः ।।

28. Soul is the father of these children, the son of these parent, the eldest or the youngest child God alone dwells in the mind. He existed before all created objects, and is present in the heart. (2863)

२९. पूर्णात् पूर्णमुदचति पूर्णं पूर्णेन सिच्यते । उतो तदद्य विद्याम यतस्तत् परिषिच्यते ।।

29. From God, the Complete proceedeth this complete world. God, the Full, creates this entire world. Now also may we know the source from which this world progresses all round. (2864)[2]

३०. एषा सनत्नी सनमेव जातैषा पुराणी परि सर्वं बभूव ।
मही देव्यु१षसो विभाती सैकेनैकेन मिषता वि चष्टे ।।

30. God, from times immemorial, is known as the Leader of the devotees. This Primordial God pervades the entire universe. The Mighty God illumines all the Dawns, and looks all in the twinkling of an eye. (2865)

[1]The first 'one' refers to the soul. The second 'one' refers to God.
[2]Source: God.

३१. अविर्वै नाम देवतर्तेनास्ते परीवृता । तस्या रूपेणेमे वृक्षा हरिता हरितस्रजः ॥

31. Known by the name of Protector God rests girt by Eternal Truth. Through His grace, the green-garlanded trees have taken their robe of green. (2866)[1]

३२. अन्ति सन्तं न जहात्यन्ति सन्तं न पश्यति । देवस्य पश्य काव्यं न ममार न जीर्यति ॥

32. God abandons not the soul that goes nearest to Him. The soul sees not God, nearest to it. Look at the Vedic poetry of God, which is deathless and ageless. (2867)[2]

३३. अपूर्वेणेषिता वाचस्ता वदन्ति यथायथम् । वदन्तीर्यत्र गच्छन्ति तदाहुर्ब्राह्मणं महत् ॥

33. The Vedic verses revealed by God, preceded by none, speak nothing but Truth. Whither they go and speak, they say 'God is great.' (2868)

३४. यत्र देवाश्च मनुष्याश्चारा नाभाविव श्रिताः ।
अपां त्वा पुष्पं पृच्छामि यत्र तन्मायया हितम् ॥

34. In Whom the sages and ordinary mortals reside, as spokes are fastened in the nave, of thee, O learned person, I ask of God, the most efficient Cause of the universe, where He dwells in subtle Matter. (2869)

३५. येभिर्वात इषितः प्रवाति ये ददन्ते पञ्च दिशः सध्रीचीः ।
य आहुतिमत्यमन्यन्त देवा अपां नेतारः कतमे त आसन् ॥

35. What are the divine forces of Nature, which give command unto the wind that blowest, which control the five united heavenly regions, which care not for the entreaty of the populace, which are the guides of the subtle atoms of Matter? (2870)[3]

३६. इमामेषां पृथिवीं वस्त एकोऽन्तरिक्षं पर्येको बभूव ।
दिवमेषां ददते यो विधर्ता विश्वा आशाः प्रति रक्षन्त्येके ॥

36. One of these, forces, the fire, inhabiteth the earth, another, i.e., air hath encompassed the atmosphere. One, the Sun, the supporter in diverse ways gives light. Some keeping watch guard all the quarters safely. (2871)[4]

३७. यो विद्यात् सूत्रं विततं यस्मिन्नोताः प्रजा इमाः ।
सूत्रं सूत्रस्य यो विद्यात् स विद्याद् ब्राह्मणं महत् ॥

[1]Green-garlanded: Having green leaves.

[2]The truths of the Vedas are never exploded. They are eternal and ever fresh. The Vedic knowledge can never be destroyed, as it always remains with God, Who is beyond the reach of death.

[3]Care not—populace: Being devoid of life and consciousness they know not the requirements and requests of the people.

[4]Some refer to Moon and other planets.

37. The man who knows the Vast Matter, on which all these creatures are strung, the man who knows the cause of Matter, knows the Mighty God. (2872)[1]

३८. वेदाहं सूत्रं विततं यस्मिन्नोताः प्रजा इमाः । सूत्रं सूत्रस्याहं वेदाथो यद् ब्राह्मणं महत् ॥

38. I know the Vast Matter, on which all these creatures are strung. I know the Efficient Cause of Matter, Who is God the Almighty. (2873)

३९. यदन्तरा द्यावापृथिवी अग्निरैत् प्रदहन् विश्वदाव्यः ।
यत्रातिष्ठन्नेकपत्नीः परस्तात् क्वेवासीन्मातरिश्वा तदानीम् ॥

39. When the blazing, all-consuming fire pervades between the earth and heaven when dwelt afar the spouses of one husband, where at that moment was Air? (2874)[2]

४०. अप्स्वासीन्मातरिश्वा प्रविष्टः प्रविष्टा देवाः सलिलान्यासन् ।
बृहन् ह तस्थौ रजसो विमानः पवमानो हरित आ विवेश ॥

40. At the time of dissolution the air enters the subtle atoms of Matter, other forces of Nature resolve themselves into subtle Matter. At that time God alone, the Purifier, and Creator of different worlds, exists pervading all regions. (2875)

४१. उत्तरेणेव गायत्रीममृतेऽधि वि चक्रमे । साम्ना ये साम संविदुरजस्तद् ददृशे क्व ॥

41. A yogi goes beyond his mental faculty that preserves the vital breaths, and realises the immortal soul. The yogis, who through soul visualise God, know, what the true nature of the unborn soul is. (2876)

४२. निवेशनः संगमनो वसूनां देव इव सविता सत्यधर्मा । इन्द्रो न तस्थौ समरे धनानाम् ॥

42. God, the Seer, Whose laws are constant like the all-illuminating Sun is the supporter and Motivator of planets like the Earth. He stands firm like a king in the war for riches. (2877)[3]

४३. पुण्डरीकं नवद्वारं त्रिभिर्गुणेभिरावृतम् ।
तस्मिन् यद्यक्षमात्मन्वत् तद् वै ब्रह्मविदो विदुः ॥

43. Men versed in sacred knowledge know that Venerable God, the Lord of soul, in the nine-portalled Lotus Flower, enclosed with three bonds. (2878)[4]

[1]Cause of Matter: Most efficient cause.

[2]Spouses: All the four directions, North, East, South, West. One husband: The Sun. At that moment: At the time of dissolution.

[3]Men seek the support of God in their attempt to amass wealth, just as subjects pray to the king for their livelihood.

[4]Nine portalled: Having nine gates, two eyes, two ears, two nostrils, mouth, anus, and penis. Lotus Flower: The body.
Three bonds: Satva, Rajas, Tamas.

४४. अकामो धीरो अमृतः स्वयंभू रसेन तृप्तो न कुतश्चनोनः ।
तमेव विद्वान् न बिभाय मृत्योरात्मानं धीरमजरं युवानम् ॥

44. Free from the fear of Death is he, who knoweth the Desireless, Firm, Immortal, Self-existent, Joyful, Lacking nothing, Courageous, Undecaying, and Powerful God. (2879)

Chapter (Anuvāka) 5

HYMN IX

१. अघायतामपि नह्या मुखानि सपत्नेषु वज्रमर्पयैतम् ।
इन्द्रेण दत्ता प्रथमा शतौदना भ्रातृव्यघ्नी यजमानस्य गातुः ॥

1. O Vedic speech, bind the mouths of the sinners, cast this bolt of thunder against my rivals. God revealed in the beginning of creation, the foe-destroying Veda, the guide of the worshippers. (2880)[1]

२. वेदिष्टे चर्म भवतु बर्हिर्लोमानि यानि ते । एषा त्वा रशनाग्रभीद् ग्रावा त्वैषोऽधि नृत्यतु ॥

2. O Vedic speech, let my body be thy altar, my hair thy seat in the sacrifice. This tongue of mine hath grasped thee. Let this learned person, the preacher of the scriptures, master thee and be up and doing in life. (2881)

३. बालास्ते प्रोक्षणीः सन्तु जिह्वा सं माष्ट्वर्घ्न्ये ।
शुद्धा त्वं यज्ञिया भूत्वा दिवं प्रेहि शतौदने ॥

3. O unviolate Vedic speech, may thy purifying forces be a brush for me. May my tongue be pure. O Vedic speech, being sincere and adorable, attain to renown and glory. (2882)

४. यः शतौदनां पचति कामप्रेण स कल्पते । प्रीता ह्यऽस्यर्त्विजः सर्वे यन्ति यथायथम् ॥

4. He, who strictly follows the Vedic Law, fulfils all his desires. Hence all his ministering priests, contented, achieve their purpose. (2883)

५. स स्वर्गमा रोहति यत्रादस्त्रिदिवं दिवः । अपूपनाभिं कृत्वा यो ददाति शतौदनाम् ॥

5. He, who makes the Vedic speech his inseparable companion and preaches its truths to mankind attains to extreme felicity, the centre of threefold victory. (2884)[2]

६. स तांल्लोकान्त्समाप्नोति ये दिव्या ये च पार्थिवाः ।
हिरण्यज्योतिषं कृत्वा यो ददाति शतौदनाम् ॥

6. He, who preaches Vedic speech to mankind, making it aglow with the strength of its golden principles, comes in contact with persons who possess practical wisdom and are the rulers of the world. (2885)

[1]Veda is spoken of as Sataudnā as it fulfils hundreds of requirements of mankind.
[2]Threefold: Income, Expenditure and Advancement.

७. ये ते देवि शमितारः पक्तारो ये च ते जनाः ।
ते त्वा सर्वे गोप्स्यन्ति मैभ्यो भैषीः शतौदने ॥

7. O Vedic speech, be not afraid of thy foes, as all those who study thee, and strengthen their faith in thy infallibility will guard thee. (2886)

८. वसवस्त्वा दक्षिणत उत्तरान्मरुतस्त्वा ।
आदित्याः पश्चाद् गोप्स्यन्ति साग्निष्टोममति द्रव ॥

8. O Vedic speech, the sages will guard thee from the right, the valiant from the left, the celibates will guard thee from behind, so sing thou quickly in full the praise of God. (2887)

९. देवाः पितरो मनुष्या गन्धर्वाप्सरसश्च ये । ते त्वा सर्वे गोप्स्यन्ति सातिरात्रमति द्रव ॥

9. O Vedic speech, aspirants after victory, sacrificing persons, reflective souls, rulers of the earth, and judicious cosmonauts, all will be thy guards, Infuse soon in them the spirit of charity. (2888)

१०. अन्तरिक्षं दिवं भूमिमादित्यान् मरुतो दिशः ।
लोकान्त्स सर्वानाप्नोति यो ददाति शतौदनाम् ॥

10. He, who imparts the knowledge of the Vedas to others, becomes the master of the atmosphere, heaven and earth, and the friend of the celibates, the heroes, the rulers, and all noble persons. (2889)

११. घृतं प्रोक्षन्ती सुभगा देवी देवान् गमिष्यति । पक्तारमघ्न्ये मा हिंसीर्दिवं प्रेहि शतौदने ॥

11. The progressive, valorous Vedic speech, spreading knowledge will go to the learned. O Vedic Speech, harm not thy firm believer, and attain to glory and celebrity. (2890)

१२. ये देवा दिविषदो अन्तरिक्षसदश्च ये ये चेमे भूम्यामधि ।
तेभ्यस्त्वं धुक्ष्व सर्वदा क्षीरं सर्पिरथो मधु ॥

12. For the learned, who reside in the Sun, roam in the atmosphere or dwell on the Earth, grant thou, O Vedic speech, milk, butter and knowledge of God. (2891)

१३. यत्ते शिरो यत्ते मुखं यौ कर्णौ ये च ते हनू ।
आमिक्षां दुह्रतां दात्रे क्षीरं सर्पिरथो मधु ॥

13. Let thy head, let thy mouth, let both thine ears, and let those two jaws of thine, grant for a charitably disposed person, curd, milk, butter and knowledge of God. (2892)[1]

[1]From the 13th to the 24th verse Vedic speech has been compared to a cow. The parts of the body of the cow are the different forces of the Vedic speech. What significance each part conveys with reference to Vedic knowledge is not clear.

१४. यौ त ओष्ठौ ये नासिके ये शृङ्गे ये च तेऽक्षिणी ।
आमिक्षां दुह्रतां दात्रे क्षीरं सर्पिरथो मधु ॥

14. Let both thy lips, thy nostrils, both thy horns, and these two eyes of thine, grant for a charitably disposed person, curd, milk, butter and the knowledge of God. (2893)

१५. यत्ते क्लोमा यद्धृदयं पुरीतत् सहकण्ठिका । आमिक्षां दुह्रतां दात्रे क्षीरं सर्पिरथो मधु ॥

15. Let thy lungs, thy heart, and thy throat with all the bronchial tubes, grant for a charitably disposed person, curd, milk, butter and the knowledge of God. (2894)

१६. यत्ते यकृद्ये मतस्ने यदान्त्रं याश्च ते गुदाः ।
आमिक्षां दुह्रतां दात्रे क्षीरं सर्पिरथो मधु ॥

16. Let liver, and let kidneys, let thine entrails, and let anus-arteries, grant for a charitably disposed person, curd, milk, butter and the knowledge of God. (2895)

१७. यस्ते प्लाशिर्यो वनिष्ठुर्यौ कुक्षी यच्च चर्म ते ।
आमिक्षां दुह्रतां दात्रे क्षीरं सर्पिरथो मधु ॥

17. Let thy spleen, rectum, thy belly's bellows; and thy skin, grant for a charitably disposed person, curd, milk, butter and the knowledge of God. (2896)

१८. यत्ते मज्जा यदस्थि यन्मांसं यच्च लोहितम् ।
आमिक्षां दुह्रतां दात्रे क्षीरं सर्पिरथो मधु ॥

18. Let all thy marrow, every bone, let all thy flesh, and all thy blood, grant for a charitably disposed person, curd, milk, butter and the knowledge of God. (2897)

१९. यौ ते बाहू ये दोषणी यावंसौ या च ते ककुत् ।
आमिक्षां दुह्रतां दात्रे क्षीरं सर्पिरथो मधु ॥

19. Let both thy forelegs, hind legs, both thy shoulders and thy hump grant for a charitably disposed person, curd, milk, butter and the knowledge of God. (2898)

२०. यास्ते ग्रीवा ये स्कन्धा याः पृष्टीर्याश्च पर्शवः ।
आमिक्षां दुह्रतां दात्रे क्षीरं सर्पिरथो मधु ॥

20. Let thy neck-bones, thy shoulder-bones, thy back-joints and ribs grant for a charitably disposed person, curd, milk, butter and the knowledge of God. (2899)

२१. यौ त ऊरू अष्ठीवन्तौ ये श्रोणी या च ते भसत् ।
आमिक्षां दुह्रतां दात्रे क्षीरं सर्पिरथो मधु ॥

21. Let thy thighs, and thy knee-bones, thy buttocks, and thy urinary organ, grant for a charitably disposed person, curd, milk, butter and the knowledge of God. (2900)

२२. यत्ते पुच्छं ये ते बाला यदूधो ये च ते स्तनाः ।
आमिक्षां दुह्रतां दात्रे क्षीरं सर्पिरथो मधु ॥

22. Let thy tail and all the hairs thereof, thine udder and thy teats, grant for a charitable person, curd, milk, butter and the knowledge of God. (2901)

२३. यास्ते जङ्घा याः कुष्ठिका ऋच्छरा ये च ते शफाः ।
आमिक्षां दुह्रतां दात्रे क्षीरं सर्पिरथो मधु ॥

23. Let all thy legs, the nails of thy feet, the upper parts of thy hooves and thy hooves, grant for a charitable person, curd, milk, butter and the knowledge of God. (2902)

२४. यत्ते चर्म शतौदने यानि लोमान्यघ्न्ये । आमिक्षां दुह्रतां दात्रे क्षीरं सर्पिरथो मधु ॥

24. O Non-violent Vedic Speech, Imparter of Hundred-fold knowledge, let thy principles and teachings grant for a charitably disposed person, curd, milk, butter and the knowledge of God. (2903)[1]

२५. क्रोडौ ते स्तां पुरोडाशावाज्येनाभिघारितौ । तौ पक्षौ देवि कृत्वा सा पक्तारं दिवं वह ॥

25. O victorious Vedic Speech, Heaven and Earth are two laps of thine, filled with lustre. Make them thy wings, and take the man who has perfect faith in thy infallibility to the high pedestal of salvation. (2904)

२६. उलूखले मुसले यश्च चर्मणि यो वा शूर्पे तण्डुलः कणः ।
यं वा वातो मातरिश्वा पवमानो ममाथाग्निष्टद्धोता सुहुतं कृणोतु ॥

26. Each grain of rice in mortar or on pestle, all on the skin or in the winnowing basket, whatever purifying, powerful wind, hath sifted; let the Gracious God make of it acceptable oblation. (2905)[2]

२७. अपो देवीर्मधुमतीर्घृतश्चुतो ब्रह्मणां हस्तेषु प्रपृथक् सादयामि ।
यत्काम इदमभिषिञ्चामि वोऽहं तन्मे सर्वं सं पद्यतां वयं स्याम पतयो रयीणाम् ॥

27. In the hands of a scholar of the Vedas, I lay in separate order the Vedic verses, divine, full of the knowledge of God, and the showerers of truth. O learned persons, as here I initiate Ye in Vedic mysteries, may all my wishes be granted unto me in perfect fulness. May we have ample wealth of different sorts of knowledge. (2906)

[1]चर्म: Skin, principles, लोमानि: Hair, teachings.
[2]Sifted: Separated the husk from the corn.

HYMN X

१. नमस्ते जायमानायै जाताया उत ते नमः । बालेभ्यः शफेभ्यो रूपायाघ्न्ये ते नमः ।।

1. O Immortal power of God, worship to thee springing to life, and worship unto thee as manifested in the world? Worship to thee, for thy manifold forces, for thy rules of peaceful conduct and for thy immensity. (2907)

२. यो विद्यात् सप्त प्रवतः सप्त विद्यात् परावतः ।
शिरो यज्ञस्य यो विद्यात् स वशां प्रति गृह्णीयात् ।।

2. He, who understands the right use of seven lower, active organs of the body, who knows the true significance of the far-reaching upper seven organs of the body who realises the soul, the head of all noble acts, can grasp the beautiful, wonderful power of God. (2908)[1]

३. वेदाहं सप्त प्रवतः सप्त वेद परावतः । शिरो यज्ञस्याहं वेद सोमं चास्यां विचक्षणम् ।।

3. I know the seven lower active organs of the body. I know the far-reaching upper seven organs of the body, I know the soul, the head of all noble acts. I know God Who resides within His beautiful, wonderful power. (2909)[2]

४. यया द्यौर्यया पृथिवी ययापो गुपिता इमाः । वशां सहस्रधारां ब्रह्मणाच्छावदामसि ।।

4. We invoke with reverence, through Vedic verses, the beautiful power of God, the sustainer of a thousand objects, by whom the heaven, by whom the earth, by whom these subjects are preserved. (2910)

५. शतं कंसाः शतं दोग्धारः शतं गोप्तारो अधि पृष्ठे अस्याः ।
ये देवास्तस्यां प्राणन्ति ते वशां विदुरेकधा ।।

5. Hundreds of aspirants and hundreds of seekers after God, and hundreds of benefactors of humanity depend upon the support of God's power. Learned persons alone who pass their lives with full faith in God, truly know His strength. (2911)

६. यज्ञपदीराक्षीरा स्वधाप्राणा महीलुका । वशा पर्जन्यपत्नी देवाँ अप्येति ब्रह्मणा ।।

6. The beautiful power of God, the source of noble deeds, the bestower of food and water, self-existent, full of lustre, the protector of clouds, is realised by the learned through the study of the Vedas. (2912)

७. अनु त्वाग्निः प्राविशदनु सोमो वशे त्वा । ऊधस्ते भद्रे पर्जन्यो विद्युतस्ते स्तना वशे ।।

[1]Lower organs: Two hands, two feet, anus, penis, belly. Upper organs: Two eyes, two nostrils, two ears and mouth. Griffith interprets सप्त प्रवतः as Seven Floods, the Celestial Rivers, corresponding to the Seven rivers of the country occupied by the Aryan immigrants. This interpretation is not so plausible.

[2]I: A learned person.

7. O beautiful power of God, fire pervades objects in obedience to thee, soul enters the body in obedience to thee. O auspicious power, cloud is thy udder, and lightnings thy teats! (2913)[1]

८. अपस्त्वं धुक्षे प्रथमा उर्वरा अपरा वशे । तृतीयं राष्ट्रं धुक्षेऽन्नं क्षीरं वशे त्वम् ॥

8. O beautiful power of God, thou grantest fertile lands to big and small people. Thou grantest excellent princely sway, pure food and milk! (2914)

९. यदादित्यैर्हूयमानोपातिष्ठ ऋतावरि । इन्द्रः सहस्रं पात्रान्त्सोमं त्वापाययद्वशे ॥

9. O beautiful power of God, thou, the embodiment of truth, when thou comest nigh invited by Aditya celibates, God grants through thee salvation to thousands of noble persons! (2915)

१०. यदनूचीन्द्रमैरात् त्व ऋषभोऽह्वयत् । तस्मात्ते वृत्रहा पयः क्षीरं क्रुद्धोऽहरद्वशे ॥

10. O beautiful power of God, when the soul claims its supremacy over thee, the Subtle God calls thee back and in righteous indignation, God, the dispeller of darkness takes away from the soul its vigour and vitality lent by thee! (2916)[2]

११. यत्ते क्रुद्धो धनपतिरा क्षीरमहरद्वशे । इदं तदद्य नाकस्त्रिषु पात्रेषु रक्षति ॥

11. O beautiful power of God, the Lord of Riches full of righteous indignation deprives an ignoble soul of all resources of life, and He, free from suffering and full of joy, preserveth them in three regions! (2917)[3]

१२. त्रिषु पात्रेषु तं सोममा देव्यहरद्वशा । अथर्वा यत्र दीक्षितो बर्हिष्यास्त हिरण्यये ॥

12. The victorious, beautiful, power of God, is the constant companion of God Who pervades the three regions, Where the Unwavering God, according to His Law resides in His beautiful prosperity. (2918)

१३. सं हि सोमेनागत समु सर्वेण पद्वता । वशा समुद्रमध्यष्ठाद् गन्धर्वैः कलिभिः सह ॥

13. The beautiful power of God, in its majesty is linked with each enterprising person, and with its qualities of sustaining the Earth and measuring its extent controls the atmosphere. (2919)

१४. सं हि वातेनागत समु सर्वैः पतत्रिभिः । वशा समुद्रे प्रानृत्यदृचः सामानि बिभ्रती ॥

14. The beautiful power of God, equipped with the Rigveda and Sāmaveda rules supreme in the atmosphere, linked with air and all sorts of birds. (2920)[4]

[1]Through the dispensation of God fire, soul, clouds and lightnings perform their duties.

[2]When the soul denies the All-pervading power of God and claims its usurpation it is punished by God, and is put to grief.

[3]Regions: Higher, middle, and lower. God deprives an atheist of all resources of life, and preserveth them for godly people in the three regions.

[4]The power of God sustains the air and birds in the atmosphere.

१५. सं हि सूर्येणागत समु सर्वेण चक्षुषा । वशा समुद्रमत्यख्यद् भद्रा ज्योतींषि बिभ्रती ॥

15. The beautiful power of God, controlling the auspicious brilliant planets, contacting the Sun and every creature that hath eyes, hath intensely illumined the atmosphere. (2921)

१६. अभीवृता हिरण्येन यदतिष्ठ ऋतावरि । अश्वः समुद्रो भूत्वाध्यस्कन्दद्वशे त्वा ॥

16. O righteous, beautiful power of God, when thou covered around with lustre standest in thy majesty, God, the support of mankind, being All-pervading authoritatively manifests thy strength. (2922)

१७. तद् भद्राः समगच्छन्त वशा देष्ट्र्यथो स्वधा । अथर्वा यत्र दीक्षितो बर्हिष्यास्त हिरण्यये ॥

17. Where the Unwavering God, according to His Law, resides in His beautiful Majesty, there gather noble persons, and the beautiful power of God, the distributor of food to mankind, acts like a preacher. (2923)

१८. वशा माता राजन्यस्य वशा माता स्वधे तव । वशाया यज्ञ आयुधं ततश्चित्तमजायत ॥

18. The beautiful power of God is the maker of princely sway. O food, it is thy creator also! The power of God is the main support in a noble deed. Knowledge has arisen out of that power. (2924)

१९. ऊर्ध्वो बिन्दुरुदचरद् ब्रह्मणः ककुदादधि । ततस्त्वं जज्ञिषे वशे ततो होताजायत ॥

19. From God's eminence there went forth a drop that mounted up on high: from that wast thou produced, O beautiful power of God, from that the soul sprang to life. (2925)[1]

२०. आस्नस्ते गाथा अभवन्नुष्णिहाभ्यो बलं वशे । पाजस्याज्जज्ञे यज्ञ स्तनेभ्यो रश्मयस्तव ॥

20. Forth from thy mouth came the Vedic verses fit to be sung, from thy neck's nape sprang strength, O beautiful power of God! Sacrifice from thy flanks was born, and rays of sunlight from thy teats. (2926)

२१. ईर्माभ्यामयनं जातं सक्थिभ्यां च वशे तव । आन्त्रेभ्यो जज्ञिरे अत्रा उदरादधि वीरुधः ॥

21. From thy fore-legs and thy thighs motion was generated, O beautiful power of God! Food from thine entrails was produced, and from thy belly came the plants. (2927)

२२. यदुदरं वरुणस्यानुप्राविशथा वशे । ततस्त्वा ब्रह्मोदह्वयत् स हि नेत्रमवेत्तव ॥

22. When into God's belly, O beautiful power of God, at the time of dissolution found a passage for thyself! God called thee thence at the time of creation of the universe, for He knew how to guide and lead thee forth. (2928)[2]

[1]Sprang to life: Assumed bodily form.

[2]At the time of the dissolution of the universe God hides His strength within Himself and brings it forth at the time of the creation of the universe.

२३. सर्वे गर्भादवेपन्त जायमानादसूस्वऽ: ।
ससूव हि तामाहुर्वशेति ब्रह्मभिः क्लृप्तः स ह्यऽस्या बन्धुः ॥

23. All the sages trembled at the sight of the world, created through the power of God, that brings objects into existence. They say the beautiful power of God hath created this world and God, Powerful with His Knowledge of the Vedas is its companion. (2929)[1]

२४. युध एकः सं सृजति यो अस्या एक इद्वशी ।
तरांसि यज्ञा अभवन् तरसां चक्षुरभवद्वशा ॥

24. God alone is the fittest Creator of objects opposite in character. He is the One Lord of this power of Creation. Noble deeds are the ignorance—dispelling instruments of God, and the beautiful power of God is their eye. (2930)[2]

२५. वशा यज्ञं प्रत्यगृह्णाद्वशा सूर्यमधारयत् । वशायामन्तरविशदोदनो ब्रह्मणा सह ॥

25. The beautiful power of God hath welcomed sacrifice. It hath held the Sun in its orbit. The cloud along with the food it produces is subservient to it. (2931)[3]

२६. वशामेवामृतमाहुर्वशां मृत्युमुपासते ।
वशेदं सर्वमभवद् देवा मनुष्या३ असुराः पितर ऋषयः ॥

26. The learned call this beautiful power of God as the bestower of salvation. They pay homage to it as the bringer of Death. It has pervaded the universe victors, philosophers, intellectuals, guardian-fathers and sages all realise its potency. (2932)

२७. य एवं विद्यात् स वशां प्रति गृह्णीयात् । तथा हि यज्ञः सर्वपाद् दुहे दात्रेऽनपस्फुरन् ॥

27. The man who hath this knowledge realises the beautiful power of God. A perfect noble act willingly yields nice fruit for the giver. (2933)

२८. तिस्रो जिह्वा वरुणस्यान्तर्दीद्यत्यासनि । तासां या मध्ये राजति सा वशा दुःप्रतिग्रहा ॥

28. In this universe the mouth of God three tongues are glittering with light. That which shines midmost of them is the beautiful power of God, which is most difficult to understand. (2934)

२९. चतुर्धा रेतो अभवद्वशायाः । आपस्तुरीयममृतं तुरीयं यज्ञस्तुरीयं पशवस्तुरीयम् ॥

29. Fourfold is the progeny of the beautiful power of God. One-fourth is water one-fourth life eternal, one-fourth is sacrifice (Yajña), one-fourth are cattle. (2935)

[1]They: The sages. Its: The beautiful power of God. The sages wonder at the mighty power of God, Who created the universe.

[2]Opposite in character: Pain and pleasure, fire and water, lion and goat. Eye: Giver of light, for removing the darkness of ignorance.

[3]It: The power of God.

३०. वशा द्यौर्वशा पृथिवी वशा विष्णुः प्रजापतिः । वशाया दुग्धमपिबन्त्साध्या वसवश्च ये ॥

30. The beautiful power of God, is present in Heaven, in Earth, in the Sun, the Lord of Life. Self-abnegating souls, and morally high persons realise the fulness of God's power. (2936)

३१. वशाया दुग्धं पीत्वा साध्या वसवश्च ये । ते वै ब्रध्नस्य विष्टपि पयो अस्या उपासते ॥

31. Self-abnegating souls, and morally high persons realising the fulness of the beautiful power of God, supported by Him, acquire the knowledge of God's power. (2937)

३२. सोममेनामेके दुह्रे घृतमेक उपासते । ये एवं विदुषे वशां ददुस्ते गतास्त्रिदिवं दिवः ॥

32. Some sages acquire prosperity from this, some enjoy its essence. Those who inculcate to such a learned person the beautiful power of God, have gone up to the threefold conduct of victory. (2938)[1]

३३. ब्राह्मणेभ्यो वशां दत्त्वा सर्वांल्लोकान्त्समश्नुते । ऋतं ह्यऽस्यामार्पितमपि ब्रह्माथो तपः ॥

33. He who imparts the knowledge of the beautiful power of God to the Brahmans acquires all desirable positions of honour, for in it are firmly set Truth, knowledge of the Vedas, and religious Zeal. (2939)[2]

३४. वशां देवा उप जीवन्ति वशां मनुष्याऽ उत । वशेदं सर्वमभवद्यावत् सूर्यो विपश्यति ॥

34. Both sages and ordinary mortal men depend for life and being upon the beautiful power of God. This power pervades the universe, say all that God surveys. (2940-41)

BOOK (Kāṇḍa) XI

Chapter (Anuvāka) 1

HYMN I

१. अग्ने जायस्वादितिर्नाथितेयं ब्रह्मौदनं पचति पुत्रकामा ।
सप्तऋषयो भूतकृतस्ते त्वा मन्थन्तु प्रजया सहेह ॥

1. O noble learned person, attain to fame! Just as a married, high spirited woman, yearning for children, firmly fixes in her mind God, the Bestower of Vedic knowledge, food, and riches, so should the seven Rishis, the doers of noble deeds, in domestic life, kindle thee with offspring. (2942)[3]

[1]Threefold: आय (Acquisition) व्यय (Expenditure) वृद्धि (Prosperity).

[2]In this hymn वशा has been translated as the beautiful power of God by Pt. Khem Karan Das Trivedi. Pt. Jaidev Vidyalankar has interpreted it as Earth. Griffith and Sayana interpret it as Cow.

[3]Seven Rishis: Skin, Eye, Ear, Tongue, Nostril, Mind and Intellect.

२. कृणुत धूमं वृषणः सखायोऽद्रोघाविता वाचमच्छ ।
अयमग्निः पृतनाषाट् सुवीरो येन देवा असहन्त दस्यून् ॥

2. O strong companions, exert hard! Utter words that protect the lovers of freedom from deceit and malice. Here is this hero, victor in fights, equipped with valiant soldier by whom the sages subdue the hostile demons. (2943)

३. अग्नेऽजनिष्ठा महते वीर्याय ब्रह्मौदनाय पक्तवे जातवेदः ।
सप्तऋषयो भूतकृतस्ते त्वाजीजनन्नस्यै रयिं सर्ववीरं नि यच्छ ॥

3. O noble, learned hero, thou art born for mighty valour, and firmly fixing in the mind, God, the Bestower of Vedic knowledge, food, and riches. These seven Rishis, the doers of noble deeds, have made thee renowned. Grant to this Earth wealth with store of heroes! (2944)

४. समिद्धो अग्ने समिधा समिध्यस्व विद्वान् देवान् यज्ञियाँ एह वक्षः ।
तेभ्यो हविः श्रपयञ्जातवेद उत्तमं नाकमधि रोहयेमम् ॥

4. O King, just as fire is kindled with sticks of wood, so shouldst thou shine, blazing with lustre! Learned as thou art, appoint scholarly, civilized officials, fit to rule over the state. I prepare nice objects fit to be offered to them. O learned king, take thy subjects to the highest summit of joy! (2945)

५. त्रेधा भागो निहितो यः पुरा वो देवानां पितॄणां मर्त्यानाम् ।
अंशाञ्जानीध्वं वि भजामि तान् वो यो देवानां स इमां पारयाति ॥

5. Your portion from eternity is triply parted, portion of Devas, of Fathers and of mortals. Know all, your shares. I deal them out among you. The portion of the Devas shall save this land. (2946)

६. अग्ने सहस्वानभिभूरभीदसि नीचो न्युब्ज द्विषतः सपत्नान् ।
इयं मात्रा मीयमाना मिता च सजातांस्ते बलिहृतः कृणोतु ॥

6. Strong art thou, O King! Conquering, all-surpassing. Crush down our foes, ruin those who hate us. Let this administrative machinery, well-designed, efficiently worked, make all our kin thy tributary vassals. (2947)[1]

७. साकं सजातैः पयसा सहैध्युदुब्जैनां महते वीर्याय ।
ऊर्ध्वो नाकस्याधि रोह विष्टपं स्वर्गो लोक इति यं वदन्ति ॥

7. O King, with military strength, advance with thy fellow princes, and lift up thy country and subjects to mighty strength and power! In a stately manner ascend the throne free from suffering which men call paradise. (2948)

८. इयं मही प्रति गृह्णातु चर्म पृथिवी देवी सुमनस्यमाना । अथ गच्छेम सुकृतस्य लोकम् ॥

[1]Tributary vassals: Who will pay taxes to the king.

8. May this great, noble, well-pleased subjects on the earth acquire knowledge. Then may we go unto the world of virtue. (2949)[1]

९. एतौ ग्रावाणौ सयुजा युङ्ग्धि चर्मणि निर्भिन्ध्यंशून् यजमानाय साधु ।
अवघ्नती नि जहि य इमां पृतन्यव ऊर्ध्वं प्रजामुद्धरन्त्युदूह ॥

9. O priest, unite through knowledge, both the king and the subjects who constantly live together, and acquire through thy strength, for the king, nice invigorating eatables! O army, attacking the foe, strike down and slay those who assail the subjects elevating, raise the subjects on high! (2950)[2]

१०. गृहाण ग्रावाणौ सकृतौ वीर हस्त आ ते देवा यज्ञिया यज्ञमगुः
त्रयो वरा यतमांस्त्वं वृणीषे तास्ते समृद्धीरिह राधयामि ॥

10. O King, grasp in thy hand the Kshatriya and Vaisha, the doers of noble deeds. The venerable learned persons have come unto thy sacrifice. Three wishes of thy heart which thou askest for, these happy gains for thee I here make ready. (2951)[3]

११. इयं ते धीतिरिदमु ते जनित्रं गृह्णातु त्वामदितिः शूरपुत्रा ।
परा पुनीहि य इमां पृतन्यवोस्यै रयिं सर्ववीरं नि यच्छ ॥

11. O King, thy subjects are like children who depend upon thee as mother. They are thy birth place. May Earth, the mother of brave sons, accept thee. Wipe away those who fight against this country of thine. Endow it wealth and noble sons. (2952)

१२. उपश्वसे द्रुवये सीदता यूयं वि विच्यध्वं यज्ञियासस्तुषैः ।
श्रिया समानानति सर्वान्त्स्यामाधस्पदं द्विषतस्पादयामि ॥

12. O subjects, remain steady for the journey of life! O venerable persons remain away from the low and degraded. May we surpass in glory all our rivals. I cast beneath my feet the men who hate us. (2953)[4]

१३. परेहि नारि पुनरेहि क्षिप्रमपां त्वा गोष्ठोऽध्यरुक्षद् भराय ।
तासां गृह्णीताद् यतमा यज्ञिया असन् विभाज्य धीरीतरा जहीतात् ॥

[1]Griffith translates चर्म as skin on which the pressure of the Soma and the bruising and husking of the rice used in oblations are performed. Maharshi Dayanand translates the word as knowledge in his commentary, *Yajur*, 30-15.

[2]ग्रावाणौ may mean the king and subjects or the Kshatriya and Vaisha.

[3]Grasp in thy hand: Control the military personnel and the businessmen. I: The priest. Three wishes: स्थान stability; नाम Fame, जन्म Human life, or success in action, success in this world, success in the next world.

[4]I: King.

13. Just as a water-woman goes afar to bring water, and soon comes back with a pitcher of water on her head. She keeps the pure and throws away the impure waters, so should the members of the House of Lords go to distant countries and come back to the Parliament. O House of Representatives. knowledge, action, a host of public spirited persons, in order to strengthen thee, are ever vigilant. Select thou of the subjects such as are fit for service, skilfully separating leaves the others! (2954)[1]

१४. एमा अगुर्योषितः शुम्भमाना उत्तिष्ठ नारि तवसं रभस्व ।
सुपत्नी पत्या प्रजया प्रजावत्या त्वाऽऽगन् यज्ञः प्रति कुम्भं गृभाय ।।

14. These subjects are attained in their radiant beauty. O House of Lords, be active, elect a strong man as thy head! As a good wife, thou art the nice administrator of the State of thy Lord, the King. Thou art fortunate with good people as thy subjects. Nice administration of justice is thy rule of conduct. Accept the administration of this big State. (2955)

१५. ऊर्जो भागो निहितो यः पुरा व ऋषिप्रशिष्टाप आ भरैताः ।
अयं यज्ञो गातुविन्नाथवित् प्रजाविदुग्रः पशुविद् वीरविद् वो अस्तु ।।

15. O learned subjects, pure like water, thy share of strength and food has of old been assigned you! O House of Representatives, controlled by saintly, Vedic scholars, foster these subjects. This highly sacrificing king knows all the rules of government, is the Bestower of prosperity, offspring, cattle and heroic persons. (2956)

१६. अग्ने चरुर्यज्ञियस्त्वाऽध्यरुक्षच्छुचिस्तपिष्ठस्तपसा तपैनम् ।
आर्षेया दैवा अभिसङ्गत्य भागमिमं तपिष्ठा ऋतुभिस्तपन्तु ।।

16. O learned person, adorable knowledge has conduced to thy advancement. Thou, pure in character, highly austere, with thy vow of celibacy, shouldst make its best use. Persons renowned amongst the sages, virtuous, abstemious, in unison with the help of scholars, should take full advantage of this knowledge. (2957)[2]

१७. शुद्धाः पूता योषितो यज्ञिया इमा आपश्चरुमव सर्पन्तु शुभ्राः ।
अदुः प्रजां बहुलान् पशून् नः पक्तौदनस्य सुकृतामेतु लोकम् ।।

17. May these immaculate, pure, adorable, serviceable, well-behaved, learned women, verily acquire knowledge. May these learned ladies give us cattle and many children. May he who intensely worships God acquire salvation (2958)[3]

१८. ब्रह्मणा शुद्धा उत पूता घृतेन सोमस्यांशवस्तण्डुला यज्ञिया इमे ।
अपः प्र विशत प्रति गृह्णातु वश्चरुरिमं पक्त्वा सुकृतामेत लोकम् ।।

[1]Thou: The Parliament.

[2]Its: That of knowledge. चरुज्ञानलायं—दयानन्द भाष्ये.

Rig, 1-7-6. Charu means knowledge as interpreted by Maharshi Dayananda ऋत्वो वै देवाः श० 7-2-4-29 ऋतुभि : With the help of scholars.

[3]Odana: God, Who showers joy like a cloud.

18. Ye, purified through the vedas cleansed through the light of knowledge, distributors of power, adorable, chastisers of the wicked, come in contact with the people. May you acquire knowledge. Making its best use attain to final beatitude. (2959)

१९. उरुः प्रथस्व महता महिम्ना सहस्रपृष्ठः सुकृतस्य लोके ।
पितामहाः पितरः प्रजोपजाहं पक्ता पञ्चदशस्ते अस्मि ॥

19. O God, worthy of a thousand eulogies, expand thyself abroad in all Thy greatness, in the world of virtue. Grandfathers, fathers, children, descendants depend upon thee. I, the soul, the master of fifteen forces, deeply worship Thee in the heart! (2960)[1]

२०. सहस्रपृष्ठः शतधारो अक्षितो ब्रह्मौदनो देवयानः स्वर्गः ।
अमूंस्त आ दधामि प्रजया रेषयैनान् बलिहाराय मृडतान्मह्यमेव ॥

20. O God, Thou art worthy of a thousand eulogies, sustainest the universe in a hundred ways, Undecaying, Attainable by the learned, Bestower of joy, and Giver of Vedic knowledge, riches and food! I hand over these foes to Thee. Punish them with their children. Be gracious unto me for service. (2961)

२१. उदेहि वेदि प्रजया वर्धयैनां नुदस्व रक्षः प्रतरं धेह्येनाम् ।
श्रिया समानानति सर्वान्त्स्यामाधस्पदं द्विषतस्पादयामि ॥

21. O God, rise in the altar of my heart, bless me with offspring, remove all obstacles, grant special promotion to me. May we surpass in glory all our rivals, I cast beneath my feet the men who hate us. (2962)

२२. अभ्यावर्तस्व पशुभिः सहैनां प्रत्यङेनां देवताभिः सहैधि ।
मा त्वा प्रापच्छपथो माभिचारः स्वे क्षेत्रे अनमीवा वि राज ॥

22. O King, rear this earth with cattle. Acquire it with learned, godly persons. Let not people's calumny and the enemy's hidden attack reach thee. In thine own country shine forth free from sickness. (2963)

२३. ऋतेन तष्टा मनसा हितैषा ब्रह्मौदनस्य विहिता वेदिरग्रे ।
अंसद्रीं शुद्धामुप धेहि नारि तत्रौदनं सादय दैवानाम् ॥

23. This heart, the altar of God, the Bestower of Vedic knowledge, riches and food, was at first fashioned after truth and equipped with knowledge. O people, develop the cauldron of pure intellect, and seat in it God, the-showerer of joy for the sages. (2964)[2]

२४. अदितेर्हस्तां स्रुचमेतां द्वितीयां सप्तऋषयो भूतकृतो यामकृण्वन् ।
सा गात्राणि विदुष्योदनस्य दर्विर्वेद्यामध्येनं चिनोतु ॥

[1]पृष्ठं स्तोत्रं वा । सहस्राणि स्तोत्राणि यस्य सः परमेश्वरः Fifteen forces: Prāna, Apāna, Vyāna, Udāna, Smāna, Ear, Skin, Eye, Tongue, Nostril, Earth, Water, Fire, Air, Atmosphere.

[2]A yogi should place, the cauldron of intellect on the mind and carefully seat God in it.

24. Seven Rishis, the performers of worthy acts, have fashioned this beautiful second mental faculty of the people. This mental faculty knowing the attributes of God, the Bestower of joy, should fix Him in the heart. (2965)[1]

२५. शृतं त्वा हव्यमुप सीदन्तु दैवा निःसृप्याग्नेः पुनरेनान् प्र सीद ।
सोमेन पूतो जठरे सीद ब्रह्मणामार्षेयास्ते मा रिषन् प्राशितारः ॥

25. O God, may noble persons sit near Thee, Perfect, Adorable Resplendent with lustre lend them joy. Pure in Thy Immortal elegance, reside in the bosom of seekers after Thee. May not Thy worshippers, renowned amongst the sages, be injured! (2966)

२६. सोम राजन्त्संज्ञानमा वपैभ्यः सुब्राह्मणा यतमे त्वोपसीदान् ।
ऋषीनार्षेयांस्तपसोऽधि जातान् ब्रह्मौदने सुहवा जोहवीमि ॥

26. O All-goading God, grant knowledge to the learned who approach Thee! To expatiate on God, I duly call again and again, the Rishis, their sons, and the ascetics. (2967)

२७. शुद्धाः पूता योषितो यज्ञिया इमा ब्रह्मणां हस्तेषु प्रपृथक् सादयामि ।
यत्काम इदमभिषिञ्चामि वोऽहमिन्द्रो मरुत्वान्त्स ददादिदं मे ॥

27. I place in the hands of spiritually advanced persons, in diverse ways, these good-natured well-behaved, venerable, serviceable subjects. May God, the Averter of sin, grant me the blessing which as I anoint you, my heart desireth. (2968)[2]

२८. इदं मे ज्योतिरमृतं हिरण्यं पक्वं क्षेत्रात् कामदुघा म एषा ।
इदं धनं नि दधे ब्राह्मणेषु कृण्वे पन्थां पितृषु यः स्वर्गः ॥

28. This ripened grain from the field is my immortal, brilliant wealth. This Earth is the fulfiller of all my ambitions. I spend this wealth for propagating the Vedas, and thus prepare the path that lends joy to the learned. (2969)

२९. अग्नौ तुषाना वप जातवेदसि परः कम्बूकाँ अप मृड्ढि दूरम् ।
एतं शुश्रुम गृहराजस्य भागमथो विद्म निर्ऋतेर्भागधेयम् ॥

29. Lay thou the chaff in fire, that is present in all created objects, remove the husks and drive them to a distance. We have heard, this purified grain is the portion of the master of the house; We know chaff and husks are the share of destruction. (2970)[3]

[1]Darvi: Mental faculty. Vedi: Heart. Gātrāni: The attributes. Second: Besides the external physical faculties. A yogi should concentrate his mental faculties on the attributes of God, and seat Him in his heart, just as a good cook puts the cauldron on the fire, and cautiously shakes its contents with the spoon, to cook it.

[2]Sprinkle you: Initiate you as my subjects.

[3]Just as a householder burns the chaff, throws away the husks and keeps the pure kernel for use, so should the king drive out the sinners and preserve the noble.

३०. श्राम्यतः पचतो विद्धि सुन्वतः पन्थां स्वर्गमधि रोहयैनम् ।
येन रोहात् परमापद्य यद् वय उत्तमं नाकं परमं व्योऽऽम ॥

30. O King, know the austere, highly learned preceptor, who imparts knowledge to the pupils! O God, make this man climb the path that leads to godliness. May he, enjoying the full life of a hundred years, reach the highest stage of salvation, entirely free from suffering. (2971)

३१. बभ्रेरध्वर्यो मुखमेतद् वि मृड्ढ्याज्याय लोकं कृणुहि प्रविद्वान् ।
घृतेन गात्रानु सर्वा वि मृड्ढि कृण्वे पन्थां पितृषु यः स्वर्गः ॥

31. O non-violent persons, purify this king, the nourisher of the subjects. Being highly, learned prepare thou ground for enjoying military strength. Duly decorate all thy limbs with lustre! On the support of Fathers I prepare the path that leads to felicity. (2972)[1]

३२. बभ्रे रक्षः समदमा वपैभ्योऽब्राह्मणा यतमे त्वोपसीदान् ।
पुरीषिणः प्रथमानाः पुरस्तादार्षेयास्ते मा रिषन् प्राशितारः ॥

32. O King, the nourisher of the subjects, destroy the troublesome fiends for the highly spiritually advanced persons who sit near thee. Let not thy dependents, the citizens, with their great possessions, the famous, and foremost Rishis, children be injured! (2973)[2]

३३. आर्षेयेषु नि दध ओदन त्वा नानार्षेयाणामप्यस्त्यत्र ।
अग्निर्मे गोप्तां मरुतश्च सर्वे विश्वे देवा अभि रक्षन्तु पक्वम् ॥

33. O King, I set thee in the midst of Rishis' sons and pupils. Ordinary people, who are Non-rishis also have a part in thy state! The king is my guardian. May all ferocious soldiers active like air, and all learned persons, guard the mature, experienced king. (2974)[3]

३४. यज्ञं दुहानं सदमित् प्रपीनं पुमांसं धेनुं सदनं रयीणाम् ।
प्रजामृतत्वमुत दीर्घमायू रायश्च पोषैरुप त्वा सदेम ॥

34. O King, having won thee, the fulfiller of sacrifice, ever prosperous, the home of treasures, powerful like a bull, the best among men! We, the subjects acquire, besides invigorating cereals, the immortality of our dynasty, long life, and riches. (2975)

३५. वृषभोऽसि स्वर्ग ऋषीनार्षेयान् गच्छ । सुकृतां लोके सीद तत्र नौ संस्कृतम् ॥

[1]Fathers: Mother, father, preceptor, king, Govt. officials, the protectors of the people. I: A learned person.

[2]Sayāna's rendering is अब्रह्मणाः instead of ब्रह्मणाः meaning thereby Non-Brahmanas. There is no justification for this interpretation.

[3]My: Country's.

35. O King, thou art the showerer of all blessings on the state, thou art the bestower of happiness. Befriend the Rishis and their offspring. Rest in the world of pious men: there is the place prepared for us both! (2976)[1]

३६. समाचीनुष्वानुसंप्रयाह्यग्ने पथः कल्पय देवयानान् ।
एतैः सुकृतैरनु गच्छेम यज्ञं नाके तिष्ठन्तमधि सप्तरश्मौ ॥

36. O King, organise the soldiers, and then attack those who deserve to be attacked. Define the code of conduct for the learned and the officials! With these noble deeds, let us follow the king, seated in a comfortable place in the midst of seven ministers of his. (2977)[2]

३७. येन देवा ज्योतिषा द्यामुदायन् ब्रह्मौदनं पक्त्वा सुकृतस्य लोकम् ।
तेन गेष्म सुकृतस्य लोकं स्वरारोहन्तो अभि नाकमुत्तमम् ॥

37. May we invested with that light go upward, ascending to the most lofty summit of joy, wherewith, the seers, after developing and strengthening Vedic knowledge, mounted to the lustrous world of virtue. (2978)

HYMN II

१. भवाशर्वौ मृडतं माऽभि यातं भूतपती पशुपती नमो वाम् ।
प्रतिहितामायतां मा वि स्राष्टं मा नो हिंसिष्टं द्विपदो मा चतुष्पदः ॥

1. O Bhava, and Sarva, gladden us, don't attack us. Homage to you, twin Lords of all living beings, beasts and emancipated souls! Shoot not the arrow aimed and drawn against us: forbear to harm our bipeds and quadrupeds. (2979)[3]

२. शुने क्रोष्ट्रे मा शरीराणि कर्तमलिक्लवेभ्यो गृध्रेभ्यो ये च कृष्णा अविष्यवः ।
मक्षिकास्ते पशुपते वयांसि ते विघसे मा विदन्त ॥

2. Cast not our bodies to the dog or jackal, nor, Lord of all living beings! to carrion kites or vultures, or violent, black germs. Let not Thy flies, let not thy birds approach us at the time of meals. (2980)[4]

३. क्रन्दाय ते प्राणाय याश्च ते भव रोपयः । नमस्ते रुद्र कृण्मः सहस्राक्षायामर्त्य ॥

3. O Bhava, the Creator, O Rudra, the Chastiser, O Immortal God, we pay homage to Thee, the thousand-eyed Seer, for allaying our lamentations, for prolonging our life and for alleviating our miseries! (2981)

४. पुरस्तात् ते नमः कृण्म उत्तरादधरादुत । अभीवर्गाद् दिवस्पर्यन्तरिक्षाय ते नमः ॥

[1]Both: The king and the subjects.

[2]Just as a Yogi controlling the seven breaths realises the soul, so the king rightly directing his ministers should efficiently administer his state.

[3]Bhava: God's power of creation. Sarva: God's power of dissolution and destruction.

[4]Let no bird or beast eat our dead body. It should be preserved and duly cremated. When we dine, flies or birds should not be allowed to come near us.

4. O God, we offer reverence to Thee from eastward, and from north and south, to thee, the All-pervading, beyond the sky and All-encompassing atmosphere! (2982)

५. मुखाय ते पशुपते यानि चक्षूंषि ते भव । त्वचे रूपाय संदृशे प्रतीचीनाय ते नमः ॥

5. O Lord of souls, homage to Thee, for the protection of our mouth. O All-creating God, homage to Thee, for all the resources of our sight. Homage to Thee, the All-pervading God, for preserving our skin, beauty and complexion! (2983)

६. अङ्गेभ्यस्त उदराय जिह्वाया आस्याय ते । दद्भ्यो गन्धाय ते नमः ॥

6. O God, we offer homage to Thee, for the good of our limbs, belly, tongue, mouth, teeth, and smelling power. (2984)

७. अस्त्रा नीलशिखण्डेन सहस्राक्षेण वाजिना । रुद्रेणार्धकघातिना तेन मा समरामहि ॥

7. Never may we contend with God, the spreader of light, the Bestower of treasures, the watcher of hundreds of our acts, the Lord of power, the Averter of suffering, and the Destroyer of the violent. (2985)[1]

८. स नो भवः परि वृणक्तु विश्वत आप इवाग्निः परि वृणक्तु नो भवः ।
मा नोऽभि मांस्त नमो अस्त्वस्मै ॥

8. May God, the Creator of the universe, avoid us from ignoble acts. Avoid us even as fire avoids the waters. Let Him not harm us. To Him be homage! (2986)

९. चतुर्नमो अष्टकृत्वो भवाय दशकृत्वः पशुपते नमस्ते ।
तवेमे पञ्च पशवो विभक्ता गावो अश्वाः पुरुषा अजावयः ॥

9. Four times, eight times be homage paid to God the Creator of the universe, Yea, Lord of sentient beings, ten times be reverence paid thee! Thou hast divided these animals into five classes, kine, horses, men, goats, sheep, lend them protection. (2987)[2]

१०. तव चतस्रः प्रदिशस्तव द्यौस्तव पृथिवी तवेदमुग्रोर्व१न्तरिक्षम् ।
तवेदं सर्वमात्मन्वद् यत् प्राणत् पृथिवीमनु ॥

10. Thine the four regions, Thine are earth and heaven, Thine Omnipotent God, this vast firmament between them; Thine is everything with soul and breath here on the surface of the earth. (2988)

[1]Griffith interprets Ardhak as a demon. This explanation is illogical, as there is no history in the Vedas. The word means a violent person, अर्द हिंसायाम्.

[2]Four times: Taking into consideration the four Ashramas. Eight times: Taking into consideration the eight limbs of Yoga, Yama, Niyama, Āsana, Prāṇāyāma, Pratyahāra, Dhārna, Dhyāna, Smādhi. Ten times: Taking into consideration the five organs of cognition and five of action.

११. उरुः कोशो वसुधानस्तवायं यस्मिन्निमा विश्वा भुवनान्यन्तः ।
स नो मृड पशुपते नमस्ते परः क्रोष्टारो अभिभाः श्वानः परो यन्त्वघरुदो विकेश्यः ॥

11. Thine is this ample wealth-containing storehouse of the world that holds within it all these living creatures. Favour us, Lord of sentient beings, to Thee be homage! Far from us go miseries, dogs and jackals and wild haired women with their horrid shrieking due to their sin. (2989)

१२. धनुर्बिभर्षि हरितं हिरण्ययं सहस्रघ्नि शतवधं शिखण्डिनम् ।
रुद्रस्येषुश्चरति देवहेतिस्तस्यै नमो यतमस्यां दिशीऽतः ॥

12. O most active God, thou wieldest the instrument of destruction, that destroys foes, is full of power, the killer of thousands of enemies and the annihilator of hundreds of adversaries! God's shaft, His marvellous weapon is ever in action. Wherever it may be, we pay it homage. (2990)

१३. योऽऽभियातो निलयते त्वां रुद्र निचिकीर्षति । पश्चादनुप्रयुङ्क्षे तं विद्धस्य पदनीरिव ॥

13. O King, the chastiser of the wicked, a defeated foe, flies and hides himself, and wants to conquer thee, attack him from behind, like a hunter who pursues the footsteps of the wounded game. (2991)

१४. भवारुद्रौ सयुजा संविदानावुभावुग्रौ चरतो वीर्याय । ताभ्यां नमो यतमस्यां दिशीऽतः ॥

14. Both God's powers of Creation and Dissolution, accordant and allies, with mighty strength exhibit deeds of valour. Wherever they may be, we pay them homage. (2992)

१५. नमस्तेऽस्त्वायते नमो अस्तु परायते । नमस्ते रुद्र तिष्ठत आसीनायोत ते नमः ॥

15. O King, the chastiser of the wicked, be homage, unto thee approaching, and departing hence! Homage to thee when standing still, to thee when seated and at rest! (2993)

१६. नमः सायं नमः प्रातर्नमो रात्र्या नमो दिवा । भवाय च शर्वाय चोभाभ्यामकरं नमः ॥

16. Homage to God at evening and at morn, homage at night, homage by day. To God's powers of Creation and Dissolution, both, have I paid lowly reverence. (2994)

१७. सहस्राक्षमतिपश्यं पुरस्ताद् रुद्रमस्यन्तं बहुधा विपश्चितम् । मोपाराम जिह्वयेयमानम् ॥

17. Let us not contend with God, the Seer of thousands of acts, Far-seeing, the Thrower of sins far away, Erudite All-pervading with His Death-like tongue. (2995)[1]

१८. श्वावाश्वं कृष्णमसितं मृणन्तं भीमं रथं केशिनः पादयन्तम् ।
पूर्वे प्रतीमो नमो अस्त्वस्मै ॥

[1]Death is metaphorically spoken of as the tongue of God, with which He punishes the wicked and devours the sinner.

18. First of all, we realise God, Full of knowledge, Attractive, Free from fetters, the Dissolver of the universe, Terrible, and the Revolver of the chariot of the Sun, full of rays. Let reverence be paid to him. (2996)

१९. या नोऽभि स्रा मत्यं॒ देवहेतिं मा नः क्रुधः पशुपते नमस्ते ।
अन्यत्रास्मद् दिव्यां शाखां वि धूनु ॥

19. O King, the guardian of his subjects, cast not thy club at us, thy divine weapon. Be not wrath with us, Let reverence be paid to thee. Shake thy royal arm above some others elsewhere, not o'er us! (2997)[1]

२०. मा नो हिंसीरधि नो ब्रूहि परि णो वृङ्ग्धि मा क्रुधः । मा त्वया समरामहि ॥

20. O God, do us no harm, instruct us, keep sin away from us, be not angry! Never let us contend with Thee. (2998)[2]

२१. मा नो गोषु पुरुषेषु मा गृधो नो अजाविषु । अन्यत्रोग्र वि वर्तय पियारूणां प्रजां जहि ॥

21. Covet not thou our kine or men, covet not thou our goats or sheep. Elsewhere, O strong general! turn thine aim. Destroy the family of the violent. (2999)

२२. यस्य तक्मा कासिका हेतिरेकमश्वस्येव वृषणः क्रन्द एति ।
अभिपूर्वं निर्णयते नमो अस्त्वस्मै ॥

22. Homage to God Whose weapon, Cough or Fever, assails one like the neighing of a powerful stallion, Who grants us the fruit of our past acts. (3000)

२३. योऽ३न्तरिक्षे तिष्ठति विष्टभितोऽयज्वनः प्रमृणन् देवपीयून् ।
तस्मै नमो दशभिः शक्वरीभिः ॥

23. Homage be paid to Him, with ten fingers, Who stands established in the air's mid-region, slaying non-sacrificing sage-despisers. (3001)[3]

२४. तुभ्यमारण्याः पशवो मृगा वने हिता हंसाः सुपर्णाः शकुना वयांसि ।
तव यक्षं पशुपते अप्स्व१न्तस्तुभ्यं क्षरन्ति दिव्या आपो वृधे ॥

24. O King, the lord of people! for thee were forest beasts and sylvan creatures placed in the wood, and small birds, swans, eagles, and garudas. Thy venerable soul works amongst the subjects; to swell thy strength flow waters from the sky. (3002)[4]

[1]शाखाम्: बाहम् see Shabda Kalpa Dram Kosha.

[2]The verse is applicable to the king as well.

[3]Ten fingers: With folded hands.

[4]God placed these beasts and birds in the forest to be protected by the king. These Sylvan birds should be preserved from destruction by the king.

२५. शिशुमारा अजगराः पुरीकया जषा मत्स्या रजसा येभ्यो अस्यसि ।
न ते दूरं न परिष्ठास्ति ते भव सद्यः सर्वान् परि पश्यसि भूमिं
पूर्वस्माद्धंस्युत्तरस्मिन्त्समुद्रे ॥

25. O Jubilant God, porpoises, serpents, strange acquatic birds, fishes, testify to Thy glory! Nothing is far from Thee, naught checks Thee, Thou surveyest everything in a moment. Thou pervadest the Earth from the eastern sea to the northern. (3003)

२६. मा नो रुद्र तक्मना मा विषेण मा नः सं स्रा दिव्येनाग्निना ।
अन्यत्रास्मद् विद्युतं पातयैताम् ॥

26. O God, overwhelm us not with fever or with poison, nor, with the fire from the Sun. Elsewhere and not on us, cast down this lightning. (3004)

२७. भवो दिवो भव ईशे पृथिव्या भव आ पप्र उर्वऽन्तरिक्षम् ।
तस्मै नमो यतमस्यां दिशीऽतः ॥

27. Ruler of heaven and Lord of Earth is God. He pervades the spacious air's mid-region. Wherever He be, to Him be paid our homage. (3005)

२८. भव राजन् यजमानाय मृड पशूनां हि पशुपतिर्बभूथ ।
यः श्रद्दधाति सन्ति देवा इति चतुष्पदे द्विपदेऽस्य मृड ॥

28. O Joy-bestowing God, be kind to the virtuous. Thou art the Guardian of all living creatures. Be gracious to the quadruped and biped of the believer in the myriad merits of God. (3006)

२९. मा नो महान्तमुत मा नो अर्भकं मा नो वहन्तमुत मा नो वक्ष्यतः ।
मा नो हिंसीः पितरं मातरं च स्वां तन्वं रुद्र मा रीरिषो नः ॥

29. O God, harm Thou not our elders nor our children, not one who bears us, not our future bearers. Injure no sire among us, harm no mother. Forbear to injure our own bodies! (3007)

३०. रुद्रस्यैलबकारेभ्योऽसंसूक्तगिलेभ्यः । इदं महास्येभ्यः श्वभ्यो अकरं नमः ॥

30. This lowly reverence have I paid to God, for keeping away dogs with mighty mouths, hounds who bark and howl terribly, who utter incoherent words. (3008)

३१. नमस्ते घोषिणीभ्यो नमस्ते केशिनीभ्यः । नमो नमस्कृताभ्यो नमः सम्भुञ्जतीभ्यः ।
नमस्ते देव सेनाभ्यः स्वस्ति नो अभयं च नः ॥

31. O King, homage to thy loud-shouting hosts and thy long-haired followers. Homage to hosts that are adored, homage to armies that protect the state. Homage to all thy troops. May bliss and fearlessness be ours! (3009)

Chapter (Anuvāka) 2

HYMN III

Paryāya 1

१. तस्यौदनस्य बृहस्पतिः शिरो ब्रह्म मुखम् ॥

1. Cloud is the head, and Vedic knowledge, the mouth of God, the Bestowerer of joy. (3010)[1]

२. द्यावापृथिवी श्रोत्रे सूर्याचन्द्रमसावक्षिणी सप्तऋषयः प्राणापानाः ॥

2. Heaven and Earth are the ears of God, the Sun and Moon are the eyes, the seven Rishis are the vital airs inhaled and exhaled. (3011)[2]

३. चक्षुर्मुसलं काम उलूखलम् ॥

3. Vision is the pestle, Desire the mortar. (3012)[3]

४. दितिः शूर्पमदितिः शूर्पग्राही वातोऽपाविनक् ॥

4. The destructive power of God, is like the winnowing basket. Earth is the recipient of unclean material of the winnowing basket, air separates the pure from the impure substance. (3013)[4]

५. अश्वाः कणा गावस्तण्डुला मशकास्तुषाः ॥

5. Horses are the grains, kine the winnowed rice, gnats the husks. (3014)[5]

६. कब्रु फलीकरणाः शरोऽभ्रम् ॥

6. This multi-coloured wonderful world is the husk, the rain-cloud is the reed. (3015)[6]

७. श्याममयोऽस्य मांसानि लोहितमस्य लोहितम् ॥

7. Black iron is His flesh, copper His blood. (3016)[7]

[1]The language is metaphorical.

[2]Seven Rishis: Five organs of cognition, skin, eye, ear, tongue, nose, mind and intellect.

[3]Just as pestle reduces the rough objects to fine ones, so does God casting His vision on the sinners purify them. Just as in a mortar, rough objects are pulverised and made intensely fine, so as desired by God, the physical, rough matter is resolved into a beautiful, fine world.

[4]Just as people, separate the pure from the impure substance by means of the winnowing basket through air, so does God create the world through His power by uniting and separating the atoms. Similarly do discerning people, through knowledge give up sins and acquire virtues.

[5]Horses, oxen, gnats are the minor parts of the glory of God.

[6]This beautiful world and cloud testify to a part of God's glory.

[7]Iron and copper have been created by God.

८. त्रपु भस्म हरितं वर्णः पुष्करमस्य गन्धः ॥

8. Tin is His ashes, gold His colour, the blue lotus flower His scent. (3017)[1]

९. खलः पात्रं स्फयावंसावीषे अनूक्ये ॥

9. The threshing floor is His dish, the wooden sticks of the cart His shoulders, the shafts of the plough His backbones. (3018)[2]

१०. आन्त्राणि जत्रवो गुदा वरत्राः ॥

10. Strings to yoke the oxen in the cart are His entrails, the straps to yoke the oxen in the plough His intestines. (3019)

११. इयमेव पृथिवी कुम्भी भवति राध्यमानस्यौदनस्य द्यौरपिधानम् ॥

11. This vast Earth is the cauldron of God, the Bestower of pleasure-giving well-cooked food. Heaven is its lid. (3020)[3]

१२. सीताः पर्शवः सिकता ऊबध्यम् ॥

12. Furrows are His ribs, sandy soils the undigested contents of His stomach. (3021)

१३. ऋतं हस्तावनेजनं कुल्योऽपसेचनम् ॥

13. Truth is His water for washing the hands, and family usage His aspersion. (3022)

१४. ऋचा कुम्भ्यधिहितार्त्विज्येन प्रेषिता ॥

14. The cauldron has been placed on fire through the Rigveda, and heated through the Yajurveda. (3023)[4]

१५. ब्रह्मणा परिगृहीता साम्ना पर्यूढा ॥

15. The cauldron is protected by the Atharvaveda, and solemnly directed by the Sāmaveda. (3024)[5]

१६. बृहदायवनं रथन्तरं दर्विः ॥

16. The vast atmosphere is His stirring spoon, the universe the ladle. (3025)[6]

[1]Tin, gold and lotus have been created by God.

[2]The sense is not clear to me. The connections mentioned by way of simile are not comprehensible.

[3]Its: Cauldron's. In this vast cauldron of the earth, God makes cereals grow to serve as food to mankind.

[4]Just as the cauldron cooks food for men, so the teachings of the *Rigveda* and *Yajurveda* elevate our souls.

[5]The teachings of the *Atharvaveda* and *Sāmaveda* conduce to the good of humanity.

[6]For God the atmosphere and the universe are so tiny things, as spoon and ladle are for a householder.

१७. ऋतवः पक्तार आर्तवाः समिन्धते ॥

17. The seasons are the dressers, the days and nights kindle the fire. (3026)

१८. चरुं पञ्चबिलमुखं घर्मो३ऽभीन्धे ॥

18. The Sun flames the cauldron, the cooking vessel which has got five openings. (3027)[1]

१९. ओदनेन यज्ञवचः सर्वे लोकाः समाप्याः ॥

19. Through the grace of God are attainable all eminent positions, that result from noble deeds. (3028)

२०. यस्मिन्त्समुद्रो द्यौर्भूमिस्त्रयोऽवरपरं श्रिताः ॥

20. In God rest in order the three regions, the atmosphere, heaven and earth. (3029)

२१. यस्य देवा अकल्पन्तोच्छिष्टे षडशीतयः ॥

21. Under the control of God, lie all the luminous planets, and the six vast pervading directions. (3030)[2]

२२. तं त्वौदनस्य पृच्छामि यो अस्य महिमा महान् ॥

22. O preceptor, I ask thee of the glory of God, which is mighty! (3031)

२३. स य ओदनस्य महिमानं विद्यात् ॥

23. A yogi who knows the glory of God. (3032)

२४. नाल्प इति ब्रूयान्नानुपसेचन इति नेदं च किं चेति ॥

24. Would say, God is not small. He is great. He is not devoid of grandeur. He is not a Non-entity. (3033)

२५. यावद् दाताभिमनस्येत तन्नाति वदेत् ॥

25, A preacher or teacher should not exaggerate the knowledge he conceives to impart. (3034)[3]

२६. ब्रह्मवादिनो वदन्ति पराञ्चमोदनं प्राशी३ः प्रत्यञ्चा३मिति ॥

26. The theologians say, O man, hast thou realised the distant or proximate God. (3035)[4]

[1]Five openings: Earth, Water, Fire, Air, Space. The grotesquely fantastic character of the hymn precludes attempts at serious explanation.

[2]Six directions: North, East, South, West, Zenith, Nadir.

[3]A teacher or preacher should tell the truth, as it is, without putting a gloss on it.

[4]God is near the learned, who seek Him in their heart, and away from the ignorant, who seek Him in material objects. He is everywhere, neither near nor far.

२७. त्वमोदनं प्राशी३स्त्वामोदना३ इति ।।

27. O man, hast thou realised God, or will He devour thee at the time of dissolution. (3036)[1]

२८. पराञ्चं चैनं प्राशीः प्राणास्त्वा हास्यन्तीत्येनमाह ।।

28. If thou believest God to be distant, the preceptor will say, 'The Prānās will abandon thee.' (3037)[2]

२९. प्रत्यञ्चं चैनं प्राशीरपानास्त्वा हास्यन्तीत्येनमाह ।।

29. If thou believest God to be near at hand, the preceptor will say, 'The Apānās will abandon thee.' (3038)

३०. नैवाहमोदनं न मामोदनः ।।

30. Neither I, the soul can harm God, nor God harms the soul. (3039)[3]

३१. ओदन एवौदनं प्राशीत् ।।

31. God has devoured this created universe. (3040)[4]

Paryāya 2

३२. ततश्चैनमन्येन शीर्ष्णा प्राशीर्येन चैतं पूर्व ऋषयः प्राश्नन् ।
ज्येष्ठतस्ते प्रजा मरिष्यतीत्येनमाह । तं वा अहं नार्वाञ्चं न पराञ्चं न प्रत्यञ्चम् ।
बृहस्पतिना शीर्ष्णा । तेनैनं प्राशिषं तेनैनमजीगमम् ।
एष वा ओदनः सर्वाङ्गः सर्वपरुः सर्वतनूः ।
सर्वाङ्ग एव सर्वपरुः सर्वतनूः सं भवति य एवं वेद ।।

32. The preceptor should say to the seeker after truth, 'If thou wilt try to realise God, with a mental vision different from that adopted by the ancient sages, thy offspring, reckoning from the eldest, will die.' Verily have I now realised God, who exists after the dissolution of the universe, is far from the ignorant, and near the learned. Like the ancient sages, with a brain full of knowledge, have I visualised God, and acquired Him. Verily, this God is Resourceful, Nourishing, serviceable. He, who thus knows God, becomes resourceful, nourishing, and serviceable. (3041)[5]

[1]Those who realize God get salvation, all others are destroyed by God at the time of the dissolution of the universe.

[2](28, 29) Those who think of God as bound by the limits of place or distance are mistaken. Such persons lose the strength of their breaths and become weak.

[3]Both soul and God are beginningless, endless and deathless.

[4]God, through His infinite power creates the world in the beginning and then dissolves it at the end. The process of creation and dissolution is eternal.

[5]I: A seeker after truth, who thus replies.

३३. ततश्चैनमन्याभ्यां श्रोत्राभ्यां प्राशीर्याभ्यां चैतं पूर्व ऋषयः प्राश्नन् ।
बधिरो भविष्यसीत्येनमाह । तं वा ग्रहं नार्वाञ्चं न पराञ्चं न प्रत्यञ्चम् ।
द्यावापृथिवीभ्यां श्रोत्राभ्याम् । ताभ्यामेनं प्राशिषं ताभ्यामेनमजीगमम् ।
एष वा ओदनः सर्वाङ्गः सर्वपरुः सर्वतनूः ।
सर्वाङ्ग एव सर्वपरुः सर्वतनूः सं भवति य एवं वेद ॥

33. The preceptor should say to the seeker after truth, 'If thou wilt try to realise God with ears different from those of the ancient sages, thou wilt be deaf.' Verily have I now realised God, Who exists after the Dissolution, of the universe, is far from the ignorant, and near the learned. Like the ancient sages with divine ears of Heaven and Earth, have I visualised God and acquired Him. Verily this God is Resourceful, Nourishing, Serviceable. He who thus knows God, becomes resourceful, nourishing, and serviceable. (3042)[1]

३४. ततश्चैनमन्याभ्यामक्षीभ्यां प्राशीर्याभ्यां चैतं पूर्व ऋषयः प्राश्नन् ।
अन्धो भविष्यसीत्येनमाह । तं वा ग्रहं नार्वाञ्चं न पराञ्चं न प्रत्यञ्चम् ।
सूर्याचन्द्रमसाभ्यामक्षीभ्याम् । ताभ्यामेनं प्राशिषं ताभ्यामेनमजीगमम् ।
एष वा ओदनः सर्वाङ्गः सर्वपरुः सर्वतनूः ।
सर्वाङ्ग एव सर्वपरुः सर्वतनूः सं भवति य एवं वेद ॥

34. The preceptor should say to the seeker after truth, 'If thou wilt try to realise God with eyes different from those of the ancient sages, thou wilt be blind' verily have I now realised God, Who exists after the dissolution of the universe, is far from the ignorant, and near the learned. Like the ancient sages with divine eyes of the Sun and Moon, have I perceived God and acquired Him. Verily this God is Resourceful, Nourishing, Serviceable. He who thus knows God becomes resourceful, nourishing, and serviceable. (3043)[2]

३५. ततश्चैनमन्येन मुखेन प्राशीर्येन चैतं पूर्व ऋषयः प्राश्नन् ।
मुखतस्ते प्रजा मरिष्यतीत्येनमाह । तं वा ग्रहं नार्वाञ्चं न पराञ्चं न प्रत्यञ्चम् ।
ब्रह्मणा मुखेन । तेनैनं प्राशिषं तेनैनमजीगमम् ।
एष वा ओदनः सर्वाङ्गः सर्वपरुः सर्वतनूः ।
सर्वाङ्ग एव सर्वपरुः सर्वतनूः सं भवति य एवं वेद ॥

35. The preceptor should say to the seeker after truth, 'If thou wilt try to realise God with a mouth different from that of the ancient sages, thy offspring will die in thy presence.' Verily have I now realised God, Who exists after the dissolution of the universe, is far from the ignorant, and near the learned. Like the ancient sages, with the mouth of Vedic knowledge, have I realised God and acquired Him. Verily this God is Resourceful, Nourishing, Serviceable. He who thus knows God becomes resourceful, nourishing. and serviceable. (3044)[3]

[1]I: A seeker after truth, who thus replies. Divine ears of heaven and earth: Knowledge and meditation.

[2]I: A seeker after truth, who thus replies. Divine eyes of the Sun and Moon: Acting like them according to law.

[3]One should try to realise God through the Vedas, His word. They are the best exponents of God.

३६. ततश्चैनमन्यया जिह्वया प्राशीर्यया चैतं पूर्व ऋषयः प्राश्नन् ।
जिह्वा ते मरिष्यतीत्येनमाह । तं वा अहं नार्वाञ्चं न पराञ्चं न प्रत्यञ्चम् ।
अग्नेर्जिह्वया । तयैनं प्राशिषं तयैनमजीगमम् । एष वा ओदनः सर्वाङ्‌गः सर्वपरुः सर्वतनूः ।
सर्वाङ्ग एव सर्वपरुः सर्वतनूः सं भवति य एवं वेद ॥

36. The preceptor should say to the seeker after truth, 'If thou wilt try to realise God with a tongue different from that of the ancient sages, thy tongue will become dry and lifeless.' Verily have I now realised God, Who exists after the dissolution of the universe, is far from the ignorant, and near the learned. Like the ancient sages with a tongue full of fervour and brilliance like fire, have I realised God and acquired Him. Verily this God is Resourceful, Nourishing, Serviceable. He who thus knows God becomes resourceful, Nourishing and serviceable. (3045)[1]

३७. ततश्चैनमन्यैर्दन्तैः प्राशीर्यैश्चैतं पूर्व ऋषयः प्राश्नन् ।
दन्तास्ते शत्स्यन्तीत्येनमाह । तं वा अहं नार्वाञ्चं न पराञ्चं न प्रत्यञ्चम् ।
ऋतुभिर्दन्तैः । तैरेनं प्राशिषं तैरेनमजीगमम् ।
एष वा ओदनः सर्वाङ्‌गः सर्वपरुः सर्वतनूः ।
सर्वाङ्ग एव सर्वपरुः सर्वतनूः सं भवति य एवं वेद ॥

37. The preceptor should say to the seeker after truth, 'If thou wilt try to realise God with teeth different from those of the ancient sages, thy teeth will fall out.' Verily have I now realised God, Who exists after the dissolution of the universe, is far from the ignorant and near the learned. Like the ancient sages, with teeth united together like the seasons, have I realised God and acquired Him. Verily this God is Resourceful, Nourishing and Serviceable. He who thus knows God becomes resourceful, nourishing, and serviceable. (3046)

३८. ततश्चैनमन्यैः प्राणापानैः प्राशीर्यैश्चैतं पूर्व ऋषयः प्राश्नन् ।
प्राणापानास्त्वा हास्यन्तीत्येनमाह । तं वा अहं नार्वाञ्चं न पराञ्चं न प्रत्यञ्चम् ।
सप्तर्षिभिः प्राणापानैः । तैरेनं प्राशिषं तैरेनमजीगमम् ।
एष वा ओदनः सर्वाङ्‌गः सर्वपरुः सर्वतनूः ।
सर्वाङ्ग एव सर्वपरुः सर्वतनूः सं भवति य एवं वेद ॥

38. The preceptor should say to the seeker after truth, 'If thou wilt try to realise God with vital airs different from those of the ancient sages, thy vital airs will leave thee.' Verily have I now realised God, Who exists after the dissolution of the universe, is far from the ignorant, and near the learned. Like the ancient sages with seven vital airs, efficacious like seven rishis, have I realised God and acquired Him. Verily this God is Resourceful, Nourishing and Serviceable. He who thus knows God becomes resourceful, nourishing, and serviceable. (3047)[2]

[1]One should sing the praise of God with a tongue full of fervour and lustre like fire.
[2]Seven Rishis: Touch, Sight, Speech, Smell, Hearing, Mind, Intellect.

३९. ततश्चैनमन्येन व्यचसा प्राशीर्येन चैतं पूर्व ऋषयः प्राश्नन् ।
राजयक्ष्मस्त्वा हनिष्यतीत्येनमाह । तं वा अहं नार्वाञ्चं न पराञ्चं न प्रत्यञ्चम् ॥
अन्तरिक्षेण व्यचसा । तेनैनं प्राशिषं तेनैनमजीगमम् ।
एष वा ओदनः सर्वाङ्गः सर्वपरुः सर्वतनूः ।
सर्वाङ्ग एव सर्वपरुः सर्वतनूः सं भवति य एवं वेद ॥

39. The preceptor should say to the seeker after truth, 'If thou wilt try to realise God with broad-mindedness not equal to that of the ancient sages, consumption will destroy thee.' Verily have I now realised God, Who exists after the dissolution of the universe, is far from the ignorant, and near the learned. Like the ancient sages, with broad-mindedness vast like the atmosphere, have I realised God and acquired him. Verily this God is Resourceful, Nourishing and Serviceable. He who thus knows God becomes resourceful, nourishing and serviceable. (3048)

४०. ततश्चैनमन्येन पृष्ठेन प्राशीर्येन चैतं पूर्व ऋषयः प्राश्नन् ।
विद्युत् त्वा हनिष्यतीत्येनमाह । तं वा अहं नार्वाञ्चं न पराञ्चं न प्रत्यञ्चम् ।
दिवा पृष्ठेन । तेनैनं प्राशिषं तेनैनमजीगमम् ।
एष वा ओदनः सर्वाङ्गः सर्वपरुः सर्वतनूः ।
सर्वाङ्ग एव सर्वपरुः सर्वतनूः सं भवति य एवं वेद ॥

40. The preceptor should say to the seeker after truth, 'If thou wilt try to realise God, in a manner different from that of the ancient sages, without yogic practices of Sashumna artery in the back, lightning will kill thee.' Verily have I now realised God, Who exists after the dissolution of the universe, is far from the ignorant and near the learned. Like the ancient sages, with divine yogic power of arteries in the back, have I realised God and acquired Him. Verily this God is Resourceful, Nourishing and Serviceable. He who thus knows God becomes resourceful, nourishing, and serviceable. (3049)

४१. ततश्चैनमन्येनोरसा प्राशीर्येन चैतं पूर्व ऋषयः प्राश्नन् ।
कृष्या न रात्स्यसीत्येनमाह । तं वा अहं नार्वाञ्चं न पराञ्चं न प्रत्यञ्चम् ।
पृथिव्योरसा । तेनैनं प्राशिषं तेनैनमजीगमम् ।
एष वा ओदनः सर्वाङ्गः सर्वपरुः सर्वतनूः ।
सर्वाङ्ग एव सर्वपरुः सर्वतनूः सं भवति य एवं वेद ॥

41. The preceptor should say to the seeker after truth, 'If thou wilt try to realise God, with a bosom different from that of the ancient sages, devoid of devotion, agriculture will fail thee.' Verily have I now realised God, Who exists after the dissolution of the universe, is far from the ignorant and near the learned. Like the ancient sages, with bosom calm and composed like the Earth, have I realised God and acquired Him. Verily this God is Resourceful, Nourishing and Serviceable. He who thus knows God becomes resourceful, nourishing, and serviceable. (3050)

४२. ततश्चैनमन्येनोदरेण प्राशीर्येन चैतं पूर्व ऋषयः प्राश्नन् ।
उदरदारस्त्वा हनिष्यतीत्येनमाह । तं वा अहं नार्वाञ्चं न पराञ्चं न प्रत्यञ्चम् ।
सत्येनोदरेण । तेनैनं प्राशिषं तेनैनमजीगमम् ।
एष वा ओदनः सर्वाङ्गः सर्वपरुः सर्वतनूः ।
सर्वाङ्ग एव सर्वपरुः सर्वतनूः सं भवति य एवं वेद ॥

42. The preceptor should say to the seeker after truth, 'If thou wilt try to realise God with a belly different from that of the ancient sages, dysentery will destroy thee.' Verily have I now realised God, Who exists after the dissolution of the universe, is far from the ignorant and near the learned. Like the ancient sages with a faithful, sincere belly have I realised God and acquired Him. Verily this God is Resourceful, Nourishing and Serviceable. He who thus knows God becomes resourceful, nourishing and serviceable. (3051)[1]

४३. ततश्चैनमन्येन वस्तिना प्राशीर्येन चैतं पूर्व ऋषयः प्राश्नन् ।
अप्सु मरिष्यसीत्येनमाह । तं वा अहं नार्वाञ्चं न पराञ्चं न प्रत्यञ्चम् ।
समुद्रेण वस्तिना । तेनैनं प्राशिषं तेनैनमजीगमम् ।
एष वा ओदनः सर्वाङ्गः सर्वपरुः सर्वतनूः ।
सर्वाङ्ग एव सर्वपरुः सर्वतनूः सं भवति य एवं वेद ॥

43. The preceptor should say to the seeker after truth, 'If thou wilt try to realise God with abdomen other than that of the ancient sages, thou wilt die in the water, Verily have I now realised God, Who exists after the dissolution of the universe, is far from the ignorant and near the learned. Like the ancient sages, with the sea as abdomen, have I realised God and acquired Him. Verily this God is Resourceful, Nourishing and Serviceable. He who thus knows God becomes resourceful, nourishing, and serviceable. (3052)[2]

४४. ततश्चैनमन्याभ्यामूरुभ्यां प्राशीर्याभ्यां चैतं पूर्व ऋषयः प्राश्नन् ।
ऊरू ते मरिष्यत इत्येनमाह । तं वा अहं नार्वाञ्चं न पराञ्चं न प्रत्यञ्चम् ।
मित्रावरुणयोरूरुभ्याम् । ताभ्यामेनं प्राशिषं ताभ्यामेनमजीगमम् ।
एष वा ओदनः सर्वाङ्गः सर्वपरुः सर्वतनूः ।
सर्वाङ्ग एव सर्वपरुः सर्वतनूः सं भवति य एवं वेद ॥

44. The preceptor should say to the seeker after truth, 'If thou wilt try to realise God with thighs not strong like those of the ancient sages, thy thigh will perish.' Verily have I now realised God, Who exists after the dissolution of the universe, is far from the ignorant, and near the learned. Like the ancient sages, with thighs cooperating like Mitra and Varuna, have I realised God and acquired Him. Verily this God is Resourceful, Nourishing, and Serviceable. He who thus knows God becomes resourceful, nourishing and serviceable. (3053)[3]

[1]One should realize God with sincerity and faithfulness possessed by the belly, which duly digests the food and distributes its essence among all the organs.

[2]Connection between the sea and abdomen is not clear.

[3]Mitra and Varuna: The teacher and pupil. Just as they cooperate with each other and work together, so should the thighs of a seeker working together take him to Yogis from whom he can learn about God.

४५. ततश्चैनमन्याभ्यामष्ठीवद्भ्यां प्राशीर्याभ्यां चैतं पूर्व ऋषयः प्राश्नन् ।
स्रामो भविष्यसीत्येनमाह । तं वा अहं नार्वाञ्चं न पराञ्चं न प्रत्यञ्चम् ।
त्वष्टुरष्ठीवद्भ्याम् । ताभ्यामेनं प्राशिषं ताभ्यामेनमजीगमम् ।
एष वा ओदनः सर्वाङ्गः सर्वपरुः सर्वतनूः ।
सर्वाङ्ग एव सर्वपरुः सर्वतनूः सं भवति य एवं वेद ॥

45. The preceptor should say to the seeker after truth, 'If thou wilt try to realise God with knees other than those of the ancient sages, thou wilt become lame.' Verily have I now realised God, Who exists after the dissolution of the universe, is far from the ignorant, and near the learned. Like the ancient sages, with the knees of a wise person, have I realised God and acquired Him. Verily this God is Resourceful, Nourishing and Serviceable. He who thus knows God becomes resourceful, nourishing, and serviceable. (3054)

४६. ततश्चैनमन्याभ्यां पादाभ्यां प्राशीर्याभ्यां चैतं पूर्व ऋषयः प्राश्नन् ।
बहुचारी भविष्यसीत्येनमाह । तं वा अहं नार्वाञ्चं न पराञ्चं न प्रत्यञ्चम् ।
अश्विनोः पादाभ्याम् । ताभ्यामेनं प्राशिषं ताभ्यामेनमजीगमम् ।
एष वा ओदनः सर्वाङ्गः सर्वपरुः सर्वतनूः ।
सर्वाङ्ग एव सर्वपरुः सर्वतनूः सं भवति य एवं वेद ॥

46. The preceptor should say to the seeker after truth, 'If thou wilt try to realise God with feet other than those of the ancient sages, thou wilt become a wanderer.' Verily have I now realised God, Who exists after the dissolution of the universe, is far from the ignorant, and near the learned. Like the ancient sages with the feet of father and mother, have I realised God and acquired Him. Verily this God is Resourceful, Nourishing and Serviceable. He who thus knows God becomes resourceful, nourishing, and serviceable. (3055)

४७. ततश्चैनमन्याभ्यां प्रपदाभ्यां प्राशीर्याभ्यां चैतं पूर्व ऋषयः प्राश्नन् ।
सर्पस्त्वा हनिष्यतीत्येनमाह । तं वा अहं नार्वाञ्चं न पराञ्चं न प्रत्यञ्चम् ।
सवितुः प्रपदाभ्याम् । ताभ्यामेनं प्राशिषं ताभ्यामेनमजीगमम् ।
एष वा ओदनः सर्वाङ्गः सर्वपरुः सर्वतनूः ।
सर्वाङ्ग एव सर्वपरुः सर्वतनूः सं भवति य एवं वेद ॥

47. The preceptor should say to the seeker after truth, 'If thou wilt try to realise God with fore-parts of the feet other than those of the ancient sages, a serpent will kill thee.' Verily have I now realised God, Who exists after the dissolution of the universe, is far from the ignorant, and near the learned. Like the ancient sages with the fore-parts of the feet of a prosperous person, have I realised God and acquired Him. Verily this God is Resourceful, Nourishing, and Serviceable. He who thus knows God becomes resourceful, nourishing and serviceable. (3056)

४८. ततश्चैनमन्याभ्यां हस्ताभ्यां प्राशीर्याभ्यां चैतं पूर्व ऋषयः प्राश्नन् ।
ब्राह्मणं हनिष्यसीत्येनमाह । तं वा अहं नार्वाञ्चं न पराञ्चं न प्रत्यञ्चम् ।
ऋतस्य हस्ताभ्याम् । ताभ्यामेनं प्राशिषं ताभ्यामेनमजीगमम् ।
एष वा ओदनः सर्वाङ्गः सर्वपरुः सर्वतनूः ।
सर्वाङ्ग एव सर्वपरुः सर्वतनूः सं भवति य एवं वेद ॥

48. The preceptor should preach to the seeker after truth, 'If thou wilt try to realise God with hands other than those of the ancient sages, thou wilt kill a Vedic scholar.' Verily have I now realised God, Who exists after the dissolution of the universe, is far from the ignorant and near the learned. Like the ancient sages with the hands of true knowledge, have I realised God and acquired Him. Verily this God is Resourceful, Nourishing and Serviceable. He who thus knows God becomes resourceful, nourishing and serviceable. (3057)

४९. ततश्चैनमन्यया प्रतिष्ठया प्राशीर्यया चैतं पूर्व ऋषयः प्राश्नन् ।
अप्रतिष्ठानोऽनायतनो मरिष्यसीत्येनमाह ।
तं वा अहं नार्वाञ्चं न पराञ्चं न प्रत्यञ्चम् । सत्ये प्रतिष्ठाय ।
तयैनं प्राशिषं तयैनमजीगमम् । एष वा ओदनः सर्वाङ्गः सर्वपरुः सर्वतनूः ।
सर्वाङ्ग एव सर्वपरुः सर्वतनूः सं भवति य एवं वेद ॥

49. The preceptor should preach to the seeker after truth, 'If thou wilt try to realise God with a basis other than that of the ancient sages, shelterless and homeless wilt thou die.' Verily have I now realised God, Who exists after the dissolution of the universe, is far from the ignorant, and near the learned. Like the ancient sages, having taken my stand on truth, with this have I realised God and acquired Him. Verily this God is Resourceful, Nourishing and Serviceable. He who thus knows God becomes resourceful, nourishing and serviceable. (3058)

Paryāya 3

५०. एतद् वै ब्रध्नस्य विष्टपं यदोदनः ॥

50. This Adorable God is the support of the mighty Sun. (3059)

५१. ब्रध्नलोको भवति ब्रध्नस्य विष्टपि श्रयते य एवं वेद ॥

51. He who thus knows God, resides in the Almighty, and takes shelter under Him. (3060)

५२. एतस्माद् वा ओदनात् त्रयस्त्रिंशतं लोकान् निरमिमीत प्रजापतिः ॥

52. With His power of bestowing happiness, God, the Protector of mankind, created thirty-three forces of nature. (3061)[1]

५३. तेषां प्रज्ञानाय यज्ञमसृजत ॥

53. For the excellent knowledge of these forces, God created the universe. (3062)

[1]Thirty-three: Eight vasus. Eleven Rudras, Twelve months, Lightning and Yajna.

५४. स य एवं विदुष उपद्रष्टा भवति प्राणं रुणद्धि ।।

54. He who reviles him who knows the true nature of God, soon ends his vital breaths. (3063)

५५. न च प्राणं रुणद्धि सर्वज्यानिं जीयते ।।

55. Not only does he end his vital breaths, but suffers entire ruination. (3064)[1]

५६. न च सर्वज्यानिं जीयते पुरैनं जरसः प्राणो जहाति ।।

56. Not only does he suffer entire ruination, but vital breaths leave him before old age. (3065)[2]

HYMN IV

१. प्राणाय नमो यस्य सर्वमिदं वशे । वो भूतः सर्वस्येश्वरो यस्मिन्त्सर्वं प्रतिष्ठितम् ।।

1. Homage to God, Him Who hath dominion over the universe, Who, Self-Existent is the Sovereign Lord of all, on Whom the whole world depends! (3066)

२. नमस्ते प्राण क्रन्दाय नमस्ते स्तनयित्नवे । नमस्ते प्राण विद्युते नमस्ते प्राण वर्षते ।।

2. Homage unto Thee, O God, the Embodiment of joy. Homage unto Thee, O God, the Bestower of corns, waters and life on humanity. Homage unto Thee, O God, Lustrous like the lightning. Homage unto Thee, O God, the showerer of the streams of joy! (3067)

३. यत् प्राण स्तनयित्नुनाभिक्रन्दत्योषधीः । प्र वीयन्ते गर्भान् दधतेऽथो बह्वीर्वि जायन्ते ।।

3. When God shouts His loud message to the plants through the thunderous cloud, they straightway impregnate, they conceive, and bear abundantly. (3068)[3]

४. यत् प्राण ऋतावागतेऽभिक्रन्दत्योषधीः । सर्वं तदा प्र मोदते यत् किं च भूम्यामधि ।।

4. When the due season, and God shouteth to herbs through the crowd, then the whole animate world is joyful, yea, each thing upon the surface of the earth. (3069)

५. यदा प्राणो अभ्यवर्षीद् वर्षेण पृथिवीं महीम् ।
पशवस्तत् प्र मोदन्ते महो वै नो भविष्यति ।।

5. When God waters the mighty land with flood of rain; cattle and beasts rejoice thereat: now great will be the production of corn for us, they cry. (3070)

[1]Entire ruination: Complete downfall in all respects.
[2]Vital breaths: Dies a premature death.
[3]They: Plants. Rainy season is the time when plants grow abundantly.

६. अभिवृष्टा ओषधयः प्राणेन समवादिरन् । आयुर्वै नः प्रातीतरः सर्वा नः सुरभीरकः ॥

6. Watered by the rain sent by God, the plants raise their voice in accord: and say "Thou hast prolonged our life, and given fragrance to us all"! (3071)

७. नमस्ते अस्त्वायते नमो अस्तु परायते । नमस्ते प्राण तिष्ठत आसीनायोत ते नमः ॥

7. O God, homage to Thee for the good of the man coming, homage to Thee, for the good of the man departing, homage to Thee for the good of the man standing, homage to Thee for the good of the man sitting! (3072)

८. नमस्ते प्राण प्राणते नमो अस्त्वपानते ।
पराचीनाय ते नमः प्रतीचीनाय ते नमः सर्वस्मै त इदं नमः ॥

8. O God, homage to Thee, for the good of the man inhaling, homage to Thee, for the good of the man exhaling, homage to Thee for the good of the man going out, homage to thee for the good of the man in front of us! (3073)

९. या ते प्राण प्रिया तनूर्यो ते प्राण प्रेयसी । अथो यद् भेषजं तव तस्य नो धेहि जीवसे ॥

9. O God, communicate to us. Thy dear, Thy dearest form. Whatever Immortal Nature Thou hast to console our soul, and avert afflictions, give us thereof that we may live! (3074)

१०. प्राणः प्रजा अनु वस्ते पिता पुत्रमिव प्रियम् ।
प्राणो ह सर्वस्येश्वरो यच्च प्राणति यच्च न ॥

10. God nourishes living creatures as a father his beloved son. God is sovereign Lord of all, of all that breathes, all that breathes not. (3075)

११. प्राणो मृत्युः प्राणस्तक्मा प्राणं देवा उपासते ।
प्राणो ह सत्यवादिनमुत्तमे लोक आ दधत् ॥

11. God causes death when we disobey His laws. He is the source of life. God is worshipped by the sages. God sets in the loftiest sphere the man who speaks the words of truth. (3076)

१२. प्राणो विराद् प्राणो देष्ट्री प्राणं सर्वे उपासते ।
प्राणो ह सूर्यश्चन्द्रमाः प्राणमाहुः प्रजापतिम् ॥

12. God is highly Luminous, He shows the path of duty, He is reverenced by all. He is the Goader like the Sun, and the Bestower of joy like the Moon. The wise call Him the Protector of the world. (3077)

१३. प्राणापानौ व्रीहियवावनड्वान् प्राण उच्यते । यवे ह प्राण आहितोऽपानो व्रीहिरुच्यते ।।

13. Both breaths are strength infusing like rice and barley. God draws the chariot of our life as a bullock the cart. The power of God, that keeps in tact the five elements is hidden beneath them. It is the power of God that develops and strengthens them. (3078)[1]

१४. अपानती प्राणति पुरुषो गर्भे अन्तरा । यदा त्वं प्राण जिन्वस्यथ स जायते पुनः ।।

14. The soul inhales and exhales in the womb. When thou, O God, develops the babe it springs anew to life! (3079)

१५. प्राणमाहुर्मातरिश्वानं वातो ह प्राण उच्यते ।
प्राणे ह भूतं भव्यं च प्राणे सर्वं प्रतिष्ठितम् ।।

15. The sages speak of God as Pervader in the atmosphere, God, the Bestower of life is spoken of as Active like the wind. On God, Past and Future, yea, on God depends everything. (3080)

१६. आथर्वणीराङ्गिरसीर्दैवीर्मनुष्यजा उत । ओषधयः प्र जायन्ते यदा त्वं प्राण जिन्वसि ।।

16. All herbs and plants spring forth and grow when Thou, O God, developest them, plants that advance our spiritual force, develop our physical strength, strengthen our organs, and are grown by men. (3081)[2]

१७. यदा प्राणो अभ्यवर्षीद् वर्षेण पृथिवीं महीम् ।
ओषधयः प्र जायन्तेऽथो याः काश्च वीरुधः ।।

17. When God hath poured down His flood of rain on upon the mighty earth, the plants are wakened into life, and every herb that grows on ground. (3082)

१८. यस्ते प्राणेदं वेद यस्मिश्चासि प्रतिष्ठितः । सर्वे तस्मै बलिं हरानमुष्मिंल्लोक उत्तमे ।।

18. The man who knows this grandeur of Thee, O God, in which Thou abidest, to him will all present their gift of tribute in that excellent world! (3083)

१९. यथा प्राण बलिहृतस्तुभ्यं सर्वाः प्रजा इमाः ।
एवा तस्मै बलिं हरान् यस्त्वा शृणवत् सुश्रवः ।।

19. As all these living creatures are thy worshippers, O God, so shall they bring tribute unto him who hears Thee with attentive ears! (3084)

[1]Yava: The power of God that keeps in tact the five elements. Brihi: The power of God that develops and strengthens them. Five elements: Air, Water, Fire, Earth, Space.

[2]Sayana interprets herbs produced by Atharva Rishi as Ātharvāni, those produced by Angira Rishis as Āngirsi. This interpretation is illogical, as it snacks of history in the Vedas, which are entirely free from it.

२०. अन्तर्गर्भश्चरति देवतास्वाभूतो भूतः स उ जायते पुनः ।
स भूतो भव्यं भविष्यत् पिता पुत्रं प्र विवेशा शचीभिः ॥

20. The All-pervading, Eternal God abidest in the midst of all the forces of nature, and exhibits Himself, when He creates again the universe. The Eternal God has pervaded with His powers the beautiful future world, as a father-his son by giving him sound education. (3085)[1]

२१. एकं पादं नोत्खिदति सलिलाद्धंस उच्चरन् ।
यदङ्ग स तमुत्खिदेन्नैवाद्य न श्वः स्यान्न रात्री नाहः स्यान्न व्युच्छेत् कदाचन ॥

21. The Omniscient God arising out of His power unfathomable like the ocean, never renounces His one law of Truth. O learned person, if He renounced it, there would be no more tomorrow or today, never would there be night, no more would daylight shine, or morning flush. (3086)

२२. अष्टाचक्रं वर्तत एकनेमि सहस्राक्षरं प्र पुरो नि पश्चा ।
अर्धेन विश्वं भुवनं जजान यदस्यार्धं कतमः स केतुः ॥

22. God, Who pervades the eight directions, observes One Law, possesses the power of a thousand eyes, exists before the creation and after the dissolution of the universe. With a part of His power, He hath created the whole world. What sign is there to tell us of the other? (3087)

२३. यो अस्य विश्वजन्मन ईशे विश्वस्य चेष्टतः । अन्येषु क्षिप्रधन्वने तस्मै प्राण नमोऽस्तु ते ॥

23. Homage to Thee, O God, Who rules over all living beings, and the world that stirs and works, and quickly pervades all atoms. (3(88)[2]

२४. यो अस्य सर्वजन्मन ईशे सर्वस्य चेष्टतः । अतन्द्रो ब्रह्मणा धीरः प्राणो माऽनु तिष्ठतु ॥

24. May God, Who rules over all living beings and the world that stirs and works, Who is Alert and Wise assist me through Vedic knowledge. (3089)

२५. ऊर्ध्वः सुप्तेषु जागार ननु तिर्यङ् नि पद्यते । न सुप्तमस्य सुप्तेष्वनु शुश्राव कश्चन ॥

25. Elevated among the sleepers He wakes, and is never laid at length. No one hath ever heard that He hath been asleep while others slept. (3090)

२६. प्राण मा मत् पर्यावृतो न मदन्यो भविष्यसि ।
अपां गर्भमिव जीवसे प्राण बध्नामि त्वा मयि ॥

26. Thou, O God, never shalt be away, never shalt be estranged from me. I bind Thee on myself for life, O God, Powerful to perform all deeds and possess all sorts of knowledge. (3091)

[1]God creates the universe, dissolves it, and recreates it through His wonderful powers. This process of creation, and dissolution is eternal.

[2]God is the Lord of Matter, out of which the world is created and this created world.

Chapter (Anuvāka) 3

HYMN V

१. ब्रह्मचारीष्णंश्चरति रोदसी उभे तस्मिन् देवा: संमनसो भवन्ति ।
स दाधार पृथिवीं दिवं च स आचार्यं१ तपसा पिपर्ति ॥

1. The Brahmchari moveth loving both his father and mother. The learned are kind unto him. He nourishes his father and mother, and satisfies his preceptor with his religious austerity. (3092)[1]

२. ब्रह्मचारिणं पितरो देवजना: पृथग् देवा अनुसंयन्ति सर्वे ।
गन्धर्वा एनमन्वायन् त्रयस्त्रिंशत् त्रिशता: षट्सहस्रा: सर्वान्त्स देवांस्तपसा पिपर्ति ॥

2. Sons devoted to their parents, virtuous people, scholars of metaphysics separately obey the behest of the Brahmchari. Enterprising persons, who sustain the earth follow him. He satisfies with his fervent devotion the thirty-three, three hundred and six thousand forces of nature. (3093)[2]

३. आचार्य॒ उपनयमानो ब्रह्मचारिणं कृणुते गर्भमन्त: ।
तं रात्रीस्तिस्र उदरे बिभर्ति तं जातं द्रष्टुमभिसंयन्ति देवा: ॥

3. The Ācharya, welcoming his new disciple, into his Ashram takes the Brahmchari. Three nights he holds him under his supervision. On being invested with the sacred thread the learned assemble to see him. (3094)

४. इयं समित् पृथिवि द्यौर्द्वितीयोतान्तरिक्षं समिधा पृणाति ।
ब्रह्मचारी समिधा मेखलया श्रमेण लोकांस्तपसा पिपर्ति ॥

4. This Earth is the first sacrificial stick, Sun the second, and mid-region the third stick of the Brahmchari, who preserves all these three with his learned soul, kindled by the fervour of the preceptor. A Brahmchari initiated in Vedic knowledge, nourishes all men, with the performance of Yajna, with sacrificial girdle, with his toil and penance. (3095)[3]

५. पूर्वो जातो ब्रह्मणो ब्रह्मचारी धर्मं वसानस्तपसोदतिष्ठत् ।
तस्माज्जातं ब्राह्मणं ब्रह्म ज्येष्ठं देवाश्च सर्वे अमृतेन साकम् ॥

5. A Brahmchari, through Vedic study, attains to foremost renown, and acquiring dignity, rises high through his vow of celibacy. Through him is displayed the most excellent knowledge of God, through his sermons do all the learned persons attain to salvation. (3096)

[1]Brahmchari: A celebate student who studies the Vedas.

[2]The words, thirty-three, three hundred, and six thousand mean innumerable.

[3]Just as Earth, Sun and Space rear and nourish human beings, so does the Brahmchari nourish them. Fire in the Earth, Lightning in the Space and Sun in the firmament are three fuels compared to the three sacrificial sticks with which the Brahmchari burns fire while he performs homa.

६. ब्रह्मचार्येति समिधा समिद्धः कार्ष्णं वसानो दीक्षितो दीर्घश्मश्रुः ।
स सद्य एति पूर्वस्मादुत्तरं समुद्रं लोकान्त्संगृभ्य मुहुराचरिक्रत् ।।

6. A Brahmchari, illuminated through the light of knowledge, clad in black buck skin, fulfilling the vow of celibacy, long-bearded, leaves the house of his preceptor, and soon leaving the Brahmcharya Ashrama enters the Grihastha Ashrama, and preaches truth again and again to all men assembled together. (3097)[1]

७. ब्रह्मचारी जनयन् ब्रह्मापो लोकं प्रजापतिं परमेष्ठिनं विराजम् ।
गर्भो भूत्वाऽमृतस्य योनाविन्द्रो ह भूत्वाऽसुरांस्ततर्ह ।।

7. A Brahmchari, seated in the womb of immortal knowledge, with his preceptor, expatiating on the Veda, Karma, common-folk, the Highest, Refulgent God, the Lord of His subjects, being verily resplendent like the Sun, destroys the ignoble. (3098)

८. आचार्यस्ततक्ष नभसी उभे इमे उर्वी गम्भीरे पृथिवीं दिवं च ।
ते रक्षति तपसा ब्रह्मचारी तस्मिन् देवाः संमनसो भवन्ति ।।

8. Just as God fashions these profound and spacious regions, the Earth and Heaven, so does the preceptor make the father and mother of the Brahmchari, glorious and prosperous. The Brahmchari guards them with his penance. On him all learned persons bestow kindness with one mind. (3099)

९. इमां भूमिं पृथिवीं ब्रह्मचारी भिक्षामा जभार प्रथमो दिवं च ।
ते कृत्वा समिधावुपास्ते तयोरार्पिता भुवनानि विश्वा ।।

9. A Brahmchari, first of all accepts this vast earth and heaven as alms. He makes these twain two fuel logs, and worships God. All living creatures reside between them. (3100)[2]

१०. अर्वागन्यः परो अन्यो दिवस्पृष्ठाद् गुहा निधी निहितौ ब्राह्मणस्य ।
तौ रक्षति तपसा ब्रह्मचारी तत् केवलं कृणुते ब्रह्म विद्वान् ।।

10. In the intellect of a learned person lie hidden both treasures one of them is near, the other far above the heaven's region. The Brahmchari guards them both with his austerity, and through knowledge, attains to God, the Bestower of salvation. (3101)[3]

[1]Brahmcharya Ashrama: the life of celibacy. Grihastha Ashrama: the domestic life of a married person.

[2]Them: Earth and Heaven, Mother and father are the earth and heaven received as gifts from God. With the help of his parents he worships God.

[3]Both treasures: Veda and God.

११. अर्वागन्य इतो अन्यः पृथिव्या अग्नी समेतो नभसी अन्तरेमे ।
तयोः श्रयन्ते रश्मयोधि दृढास्ताना तिष्ठति तपसा ब्रह्मचारी ॥

11. Two fires, one below the earth and the other terrestrial meet between the Earth and Heaven. Close to these two fires are clinging firm rays of light. The Brahmchari masters them through his Yogic power. (3102)[1]

१२. अभिक्रन्दन् स्तनयन्नरुणः शितिङ्गो बृहच्छेपोऽनु भूमौ जभार ।
ब्रह्मचारी सिञ्चति सानौ रेतः पृथिव्यां तेन जीवन्ति प्रदिशश्चतस्रः ॥

12. Thundering, shouting, ruddy-hued, and pallid, the powerful cloud filled with water, duly rears the earth. It rains water over mountains and earth, and thus gives life to heaven's four regions. (3103)[2]

१३. अग्नौ सूर्ये चन्द्रमसि मातरिश्वन् ब्रह्मचार्य१प्सु समिधमा दधाति ।
तासामर्चींषि पृथगभ्रे चरन्ति तासामाज्यं पुरुषो वर्षमापः ॥

13. A Brahmchari establishes his spiritual force in fire, sun, moon, air, waters. Their respective lustres are manifest in the space. Butter, progeny, timely rain, and learned persons proceed from them. (3104)[3]

१४. आचार्यो᳚ मृत्युर्वरुणः सोम ओषधयः पयः । जीमूता आसन्त्सत्वानस्तैरिदं स्व१राभृतम् ॥

14. A teacher punishes the student for his faults, as death punishes men, he consoles the pupil like water, assuages him like Moon, acts as his benefactor like herbs, and stimulator of his spiritual force like butter. The noble qualities of the teacher work like clouds, through which this resplendent world is sustained. (3105)[4]

१५. अमा घृतं कृणुते केवलमाचार्यो᳚ भूत्वा वरुणो यद्यदैच्छत् प्रजापतौ ।
तद् ब्रह्मचारी प्रायच्छत् स्वान्मित्रो अध्यात्मनः ॥

15. A noble man acting as a teacher displays his vast knowledge and immense dignity. Whatever he wants from his pupil as Dakshina, the same, being his friend, the pupil gives unto his teacher, according to his financial resources. (3106)[5]

[1]Below the earth: The fire that causes earthquakes. Terrestrial: The fire that burns forests. A Brahmchari possessing the strength of both the fires destroy the evil-doers, and masters the rays of light through his yogic practices.

[2]Cloud has been mentioned in the verse as Brahmchari. Just as a Brahmchari is full of semen so cloud is full of water. Just as a Brahmchari preserves his semen and wastes it not, so does cloud preserve its water and rains at the proper time.

[3]Butter: Butter-giving cows.

[4]Just as clouds satisfy the thirsty ground with water, so does the teacher satisfy the craving of the pupil for knowledge with his learning.

[5]Dakshina: It is a common practice that a student at the completion of his studies, and the time of departure from his teacher's Ashrama, offers something to his guru, according to his resources. This offering is called Guru Dakshina.

१६. आचार्यो ब्रह्मचारी ब्रह्मचारी प्रजापतिः । प्रजापतिर्वि राजति विराडिन्द्रोऽभवद् वशी ॥

16. A teacher should be a Brahmchari, a state official who protects the subjects must also be a Brahmchari. Such an official shines eminently. A self-controlled person, refulgent with his knowledge becomes an ideal teacher. (3107)

१७. ब्रह्मचर्येण तपसा राजा राष्ट्रं वि रक्षति । आचार्यो ब्रह्मचर्येण ब्रह्मचारिणमिच्छते ॥

17. Through austerity and self-restraint, the king protects the realm he rules. Through self-restraint the teacher seeks a celibate pupil to instruct. (3108)

१८. ब्रह्मचर्येण कन्या३ युवानं विन्दते पतिम् । अनड्वान् ब्रह्मचर्येणाश्वो घासं जिगीर्षति ॥

18. Through self-restraint a maiden finds a youth to be her husband. Through self-restraint the ox and horse seek to get and digest fodder for themselves. (3109)[1]

१९. ब्रह्मचर्येण तपसा देवा मृत्युमपाघ्नत । इन्द्रो ह ब्रह्मचर्येण देवेभ्यः स्व१राभरत् ॥

19. By self-restraint and fervour, the learned have conquered the fear of death. Through self-restraint the king bestows felicity on his subjects. (3110)

२०. ओषधयो भूतभव्यमहोरात्रे वनस्पतिः । संवत्सरः सहर्तुभिस्ते जाता ब्रह्मचारिणः ॥

20. The plants, Past and Future, day and night, the tall tree of the forest, the year with its seasons, all spring from the self-controlled Sun. (3111)

२१. पार्थिवा दिव्याः पशव आरण्या ग्राम्याश्च ये ।
अपक्षाः पक्षिणश्च ये ते जाता ब्रह्मचारिणः ॥

21. All creatures of the earth and heaven, tame domestic animals and sylvan beasts, winged and wingless creatures have sprung to life as Brahmcharis. (3112)[2]

२२. पृथक् सर्वे प्राजापत्याः प्राणानात्मसु बिभ्रति ।
तान्त्सर्वान् ब्रह्म रक्षति ब्रह्मचारिण्याभृतम् ॥

22. All sons of God have breath distinctly in their bodies. The knowledge that is stored within the Brahmchari guards them all. (3113)

२३. देवानामेतत् परिषूतमनभ्यारूढं चरति रोचमानम् ।
तस्माज्जातं ब्राह्मणं ब्रह्म ज्येष्ठं देवाश्च सर्वे अमृतेन साकम् ॥

[1]In the texts published by the Vedic Yantralya, Ajmer, and Govt. Book Depot, Bombay, जिगीर्षति is given, but in *Rigveda, adi bhashya bhumika* by Rishi Dayanand, and in the text published by Sevak Lal, Krishan Das the word is जिगीषति which means willing to conquer.

[2]Animals and birds also follow the law of self-restraint.

23. God, the Goader of all luminous worlds, Unconquerable, exists, shining brightly. From Him springs the Vedic knowledge about God, and come into existence all learned persons enjoying salvation. (3114)

२४. ब्रह्मचारी ब्रह्म भ्राजद् बिभर्ति तस्मिन् देवा अधि विश्वे समोताः ।
प्राणापानौ जनयन्नाद् व्यानं वाचं मनो हृदयं ब्रह्म मेधाम् ॥

24. A Brahmchari wields the radiant Vedic knowledge. All noble traits reside in him. He creates and imbibes in himself, Prāna, Apāna, Vyāna, elocution, mental force, heart, knowledge and wisdom. (3115)

२५. चक्षुः श्रोत्रं यशो अस्मासु धेह्यन्नं रेतो लोहितमुदरम् ॥

25. O Brahmchari bestow on us the power of sight and hearing, glory and food, seed for progeny, pure blood and strong belly. (3116)

२६. तानि कल्पद् ब्रह्मचारी सलिलस्य पृष्ठे तपोऽतिष्ठत् तप्यमानः समुद्रे ।
स स्नातो बभ्रुः पिङ्गलः पृथिव्यां बहु रोचते ॥

26. Having mastered the above mentioned forces, the Brahmchari, exercising austerity in the Brahmcharya Ashrama, deep like the ocean, exerts to bathe in the water of knowledge. After graduation, being glorious and vigorous, he shines exceedingly on earth. (3117)[1]

HYMN VI

१. अग्निं ब्रूमो वनस्पतीनोषधीरुत वीरुधः । इन्द्रं बृहस्पतिं सूर्यं ते नो मुञ्चन्त्वंहसः ॥

1. We call on God, on the trees lords of the forest, herbs and plants, on the learned teacher, a Vedic scholar and the Sun: may they deliver us from sin. (3118)

२. ब्रूमो राजानं वरुणं मित्रं विष्णुमथो भगम् । अंशं विवस्वन्तं ब्रूमस्ते नो मुञ्चन्त्वंहसः ॥

2. We call on the noble king, on a comrade, on a person devoted to deeds, on a dignified person, on the All-pervading God, Who dwells in the hearts of all in diverse forms: may they deliver us from sin. (3119)

३. ब्रूमो देवं सवितारं धातारमुत पूषणम् । त्वष्टारमग्रियं ब्रूमस्ते नो मुञ्चन्त्वंहसः ॥

3. We call on God, the Bestower, the sustainer, the nourisher, the Creator, the Primordial, Efficient Cause: may these attributes of God deliver us from sin. (3120)

४. गन्धर्वाप्सरसो ब्रूमो अश्विना ब्रह्मणस्पतिम् । अर्यमा नाम यो देवस्ते नो मुञ्चन्त्वंहसः ॥

4. We call on the lords of earth, on the fliers in air, on father and mother, on the Acharya, the Custodian of Vedic knowledge, on the justice-loving king: may they deliver us from sin. (3121)

[1]After graduation: When he finishes his studies and becomes a Sanātaka.

५. अहोरात्रे इदं ब्रूमः सूर्याचन्द्रमसावुभा । विश्वानादित्यान् ब्रूमस्ते नो मुञ्चन्त्वंहसः ॥

5. This word of ours we speak to Day and Night, and to the Sun and Moon, all the learned persons we address: may they deliver us from sin. (3122)

६. वातं ब्रूमः पर्जन्यमन्तरिक्षमथो दिशः । आशाश्च सर्वा ब्रूमस्ते नो मुञ्चन्त्वंहसः ॥

6. We invoke the air, cloud, firmament, quarters and all the regions of the sky: may they deliver us from sin. (3123)

७. मुञ्चन्तु मा शपथ्याऽदहोरात्रे अथो उषाः । सोमो मा देवो मुञ्चन्तु यमाहुश्चन्द्रमा इति ॥

7. May Day and Night and Dawn deliver me from the evil of imprecation. May the pleasant, serviceable Moon, called so by the learned, free me. (3124)

८. पार्थिवा दिव्याः पशव आरण्या उत ये मृगाः ।
शकुन्तान् पक्षिणो ब्रूमस्ते नो मुञ्चन्त्वंहसः ॥

8. All creatures both of heaven and earth, wild beasts and sylvan animals and winged birds of air we call: may they deliver us from sin. (3125)[1]

९. भवाशर्वाविदं ब्रूमो रुद्रं पशुपतिश्च यः । इषूर्या एषां संविद्म ता नः सन्तु सदा शिवाः ॥

9. May we praise the different aspects of God, as Bhava, Sharva, Rudra, and sustainer of souls. May we know the forces of these aspects. May they be ever kind to us. (3126)[2]

१०. दिवं ब्रूमो नक्षत्राणि भूमिं यक्षाणि पर्वतान् ।
समुद्रा नद्योऽ वेशन्तास्ते नो मुञ्चन्त्वंहसः ॥

10. We speak to Heaven, constellations, to Earth, to Holy places, and to Hills, to Seas, to Rivers and to Lakes: may they deliver us from sin. (3127)

११. सप्तर्षीन् वा इदं ब्रूमोऽपो देवीः प्रजापतिम् ।
पितॄन् यमश्रेष्ठान् ब्रूमस्ते नो मुञ्चन्त्वंहसः ॥

11. We address the Seven Rishis, their divine powers, soul, the guardian of the people, noble Fathers who follow Yamas and Niyamas: may they deliver us from sin. (3128)[3]

१२. ये देवा दिविषदो अन्तरिक्षसदश्च ये । पृथिव्यां शक्रा ये श्रितास्ते नो मुञ्चन्त्वंहसः ॥

[1]Creatures of heaven: Sun, Moon, Planets. Creatures of earth: mountains, rivers. Sylvan animals: Tiger, Elephant, Deer.

[2]Bhava, Shava, Rudra, Pashupati are the names of God. See *Atharva*, Kāṇḍa 11, verse 2.

[3]Seven Rishis: Touch, Sight, Smell, Taste, Hearing, Mind and Intellect. See *Yajur*, 34-55.

12. All the divine forces in the shape of Sun in Heaven, and air, cloud in the atmosphere, and great men, and mighty kings living on the earth: may they deliver us from sin. (3129)

१३. आदित्या रुद्रा वसवो दिवि देवा अथर्वाणः । अङ्गिरसो मनीषिणस्ते नो मुञ्चन्त्वंहसः ॥

13. Aditya, Rudra, Vasu Brahmcharis, noble persons, steadfast learned people, and wise, reflective persons: may they deliver us from sin. (3130)[1]

१४. यज्ञं ब्रूमो यजमानमृचः सामानि भेषजा । यजूंषि होत्रा ब्रूमस्ते नो मुञ्चन्त्वंहसः ॥

14. To sacrifice, to worshipper, Rigvedic hymns, pure songs of the Sāmaveda, healing expendients of the Atharvaveda, we speak, to ceremonial verses of the Yajurveda and priestly acts: may they deliver us from sin. (3131)

१५. पञ्च राज्यानि वीरुधां सोमश्रेष्ठानि ब्रूमः । दर्भो भङ्गो यवः सहस्ते नो मुञ्चन्त्वंहसः ॥

15. To the five kingdoms of the plants which Soma rules as Lord we speak: Darbha, hemp, barley, saha: may these deliver us from disease. (3132)[2]

१६. अरायान् ब्रूमो रक्षांसि सर्पान् पुण्यजनान् पितॄन् ।
मृत्यूनेकशतं ब्रूमस्ते नो मुञ्चन्त्वंहसः ॥

16. To misers, and fierce fiends we speak, to holy persons, Fathers, and persons deadly like serpents and to the hundred and one causes of death: may they deliver us from sin. (3133)

१७. ऋतून् ब्रूम ऋतुपतीनार्तवानुत हायनान् । समाः संवत्सरान् मासांस्ते नो मुञ्चन्त्वंहसः ॥

17. We speak to Seasons, Season-Lords, trees that grow in different seasons, Winters, summers, years and months: may they deliver us from sin. (3134)[3]

१८. एत देवा दक्षिणतः पश्चात् प्राञ्च उदेत ।
पुरस्तादुत्तराच्छक्रा विश्वे देवाः समेत्य ते नो मुञ्चन्त्वंहसः ॥

18. Come hither from the south, ye learned persons, rise and come forward from the west. Gathered together, all ye noble persons, ye mighty ones, come from east and north: may they deliver us from sin setting example by their virtuous lives. (3135)

१९. विश्वान् देवानिदं ब्रूमः सत्यसंधानृतावृधः ।
विश्वाभिः पत्नीभिः सह ते नो मुञ्चन्त्वंहसः ॥

[1]Adityas: Who observe celibacy for 48 years. Rudras: Who remain celebate for 36 years. Vasus: Who observe celibacy for 24 years.

[2]Darbha: Kusa grass (Poa cynosuroides) used in sacred ceremonies. Hemp: Bhanga (Cannabis Sativa). Saha: A powerful drug.

[3]Season-lords: Sun, Moon, Earth, Air.

19. This we address to all the learned persons true to their resolve, advancers of knowledge, with all their consorts by their side: may they deliver us from sin. (3136)

२०. सर्वान् देवानिदं ब्रूमः सत्यसंधानृतावृधः । सर्वाभिः पत्नीभिः सह ते नो मुञ्चन्त्वंहसः ॥

20. We speak to all practical persons, seekers after truth, true in their dealings and conduct, with all their protecting forces: may they deliver us from sin. (3137)

२१. भूतं ब्रूमो भूतपतिं भूतानामुत यो वशी । भूतानि सर्वा संगत्य ते नो मुञ्चन्त्वंहसः ॥

21. We speak to a contemplative yogi, to God, the Lord of mankind, to king, the ruler of men. Together let all men meet: may they deliver us from sin. (3138)

२२. या देवीः पञ्च प्रदिशो ये देवा द्वादशर्तवः ।
संवत्सरस्य ये दंष्ट्रास्ते नः सन्तु सदा शिवाः ॥

22. May the excellent five regions, nice twelve months, the jaws of the completed year, be gracious unto us. (3139)[1]

२३. यन्मातली रथक्रीतममृतं वेद भेषजम् । तदिन्द्रो अप्सु प्रावेशयत् तदापो दत्त भेषजम् ॥

23. Mind, the charioteer of the soul, realises the joy of salvation, the dispeller of fear, secured through the exertion of body, the chariot of the soul. God equips learned persons with an exalted soul. O learned persons, grant me spiritual knowledge. (3140)

Chapter (Anuvāka) 4

HYMN VII

१. उच्छिष्टे नाम रूपं चोच्छिष्टे लोक आहितः ।
उच्छिष्ट इन्द्रश्चाग्निश्च विश्वमन्तः समाहितम् ॥

1. God containeth name and form, and world. Cloud and Sun and the whole universe are comprised within Him. (3141)[2]

२. उच्छिष्टे द्यावापृथिवी विश्वं भूतं समाहितम् ।
आपः समुद्र उच्छिष्टे चन्द्रमा वात आहितः ॥

2. God holdeth Earth, Heaven, and all living substances. He holdeth waters, sea, Moon and Wind. (3142)

[1]Five regions: North, East, South, West, Nadir or Zenith.

[2]God is spoke of as Uchchishta or Residue, as He alone exists when everything else in the world ceases to exist after dissolution. Every thing in the universe besides God is mortal. He alone is immortal who remains behind all objects.

३. सन्नुच्छिष्टे असंश्चोभौ मृत्युर्वाजः प्रजापतिः ।
लौक्या उच्छिष्ट आयत्ता व्रश्च द्रश्चापि श्रीर्मयि ॥

3. The physical world, and Matter in its atomic state both exist in God. Death, strength and cloud all are subservient to Him. All human beings, atmosphere, Time and the spiritual force of my soul are under His control. (3143)[1]

४. दृढो दृंहस्थिरो न्यो ब्रह्म विश्वसृजो दश । नाभिमिव सर्वतश्चक्रमुच्छिष्टे देवताः श्रिताः ॥

4. The powerful world that stands through its innate strength, the motivating force of the Ved, the All-creating Ten, and the forces of Nature like the Sun, Moon etc., are fixed round God, like a wheel about the nave. (3144)[2]

५. ऋक् साम यजुरुच्छिष्ट उद्गीथः प्रस्तुतं स्तुतम् ।
हिङ्कार उच्छिष्टे स्वरः साम्नो मेडिश्च तन्मयि ॥

5. Rig, Sāma, Yajur, three kinds of verses, chanting of the Sāmaveda by Udgāta priest, the Sāma sung by Prastota (a praiser) in the beginning, and the Sāma texts lauded, the hum, the tone, the murmur of the psalm, all rest in God. May He reside in me, the soul. (3145)[3]

६. ऐन्द्राग्नं पावमानं महानाम्नीर्महाव्रतम् । उच्छिष्टे यज्ञस्याङ्गान्यन्तर्गर्भ इव मातरि ॥

6. Āgneya, Aindraya, Pāvamanya Kāṇḍas (parts) of the Sāmaveda, the Mahānāmni verses, and Mahāvrat part of the Sāmaveda, the parts of sacrifice, reside in God, as the unborn babe does in the womb of the mother. (3146)[4]

७. राजसूयं वाजपेयमग्निष्टोमस्तदध्वरः । अर्काश्वमेधावुच्छिष्टे जीवबर्हिर्मदिन्तमः ॥

[1]Griffith remarks, Dra and Vra: these words are absolutely meaningless, and probably corrupt. It is extremely regrettable that Griffith failing to understand the true significance of these words, passes unpleasant, unscholarly strictures. Vra means atmosphere (आकाश) in which move men and birds, वज्र गतौ ! Dra means Time, which sets in motion all objects, द्रु गतौ !

[2]Muir suggests, ten refers to the ten Maharshis or Great Rishis mentioned by Manu 1.34. This explanation is quite unacceptable, as it refers to history in the Vedas which are absolutely free from it. Ten refers to (1) Atmosphere (2) Air (3) Fire (4) Water (5) Earth (6) Hearing (7) Touch (8) Sight (9) Taste (10) Smell. Ten may also refer to ten breaths: Prāna, Apāna, Vyāna, Udāna, Samāna, Nāga, Kurma, Krikal, Dev Dutt, Dhananjaya.

[3]Udgitha: The portion of the *Sāmaveda*, sung by Udgātā. Prastut: The portion sung by Prastota in the beginning. Hinkāra: The sound, hum or hiṅ in the chanting, sung by Udgātā in the beginning. Tone (स्वर): Krushta, Prathma, Dwitiya, Tritiya, Chaturtha, Mandra, Ati mandra. Meḍi: the praise song, which unites the syllables of a verse.

[4]Agni, Indra, Pāvmāna Kāṇḍas occur in the first half of the *Sāmaveda*. Mahānāmni verses, ten in number occur in between the first and second parts of the *Sāmaveda*. Mahāvrata: verses which are given in the second half of the *Sāmaveda*, with which a long sacrifice (homa) is performed. This verse has thus been interpreted by Pt. Khem Karan Das Triveda: The knowledge of clouds, Sun, purifying air, grand, vedic verses, mighty resolves, all the parts of sacrifice, rest in God, as the unborn babe does in the womb of the mother.

7. Rājsu Yajna, Vājpeya Yajna, Agnishtoma Yajna, and other non-violent Yajnas, Arka and Ashvamedhya Yajnas, Jīvbarhī and Madintama Yajnas all reside in God, and sung His glory. (3147)[1]

८. अग्न्याधेयमथो दीक्षा कामप्रश्छन्दसा सह । उत्सन्ना यज्ञाः सत्राण्युच्छिष्टेऽधि समाहिताः ॥

8. The ceremony of setting the fire on the sacrificial fire-place, the initiatory rite, the Yajna which fulfils the wish of the sacrificer when performed with Vedic verses, the Yajnas which lead the soul to salvation, Yajnas with long sessions: all these rest in God. (3148)

९. अग्निहोत्रं च श्रद्धा च वषट्कारो व्रतं तपः । दक्षिणेष्टं पूर्तं चोच्छिष्टेऽधि समाहिताः ॥

9. Fire-oblation, faith, charitable acts, vow, austerity, priestly guerdon, Vedic study, entertainment of guests, philanthropic acts of public utility depend on God. (3149)

१०. एकरात्रो द्विरात्रः सद्यः क्रीः प्रक्रीरुक्थ्यः । ओतं निहितमुच्छिष्टे यज्ञस्याणूनि विद्यया ॥

10. Sacrifice of one day, or two, Sadyakri, Prakri, Ukthya, reside interwoven in God, and so are all the fine modes of the contemplation of God through knowledge. (3150)[2]

११. चतूरात्रः पञ्चरात्रः षड्रात्रश्चोभयः सह ।
षोडशी सप्तरात्रश्चोच्छिष्टाज्जज्ञिरे सर्वे ये यज्ञा अमृते हिताः ॥

11. Sacrifice of four days, of five, of six days, or of eight, ten, twelve days, sixteen days or seven days: all these sprang from God, and are contained in the Immortal soul. (3151)

१२. प्रतीहारो निधनं विश्वजिच्चाभिजिच्च यः ।
साह्नातिरात्रावुच्छिष्टे द्वादशाहोऽपि तन्मयि ॥

12. Pratihāra and Nidhnam, the Visvajit, the Abhijit, the two Sāhnātiratrās and the Twelve day rite reside in God. May He reside in my soul and strengthen it. (3152)

१३. सूनृता संनतिः क्षेमः स्वधोर्जामृतं सहः । उच्छिष्टे सर्वे प्रत्यञ्चः कामाः कामेन तातृपुः ॥

13. Pleasant, truthful speech, humility, protection, food, valour, enterprise strength, and all the desires that arise in the soul, rest in God. They satisfy the man with their desired fruit. (3153)

[1]Rājsu Yajna: Coronation ceremony. Vājpeya: An important Sāma Yajna. Agnishtoma: A Yajna in which the praise of God, learned persons and electricity is sung. Arka: A Yajna in which philosophical topics are discussed. Ashwamedhya: A Yajna in which prayer is offered for a stable government. It does not mean horse-sacrifice as interpreted by Sayāna and Griffith. Jīvbarhī: A Yajna through which spiritual force is advanced. Madintama: A Yajna that gives extreme joy.

[2]Sadyahkri: The name of a certain one-day sacrifice. Prakri: A sacrifice similar to Sadyahkri. Uktha: A sacrifice supplementary to, or a modification of, the Agnishtoma.

१४. नवभूमीः समुद्रा उच्छिष्टेऽधि श्रिता दिवः ।
आ सूर्यो भात्युच्छिष्टेऽहोरात्रे अपि तन्मयि ।।

14. Nine material forces, heavenly bodies, luminous planets take shelter in God. Bright shines the Sun in Him. Day and Night also rest in God, May He reside in my soul. (3154)[1]

१५. उपहव्यं विषूवन्तं ये च यज्ञा गुहा हिताः ।
बिभर्ति भर्ता विश्वस्योच्छिष्टो जनितुः पिता ।।

15, God, the Father's sire, Who bears this universe, supports Uphavya, Vishuvāna, and all worship offered secretly. (3155)[2]

१६. पिता जनितुरुच्छिष्टोऽसोः पौत्रः पिता महः ।
स क्षियति विश्वस्येशानो वृषा भूम्यामतिघ्न्यः ।।

16. God is our Father's sire, the grandson and grandfather of our life. Lord of the universe, the Powerful God dwells on the earth unconquerable. (3156)[3]

१७. ऋतं सत्यं तपो राष्ट्रं श्रमो धर्मश्च कर्म च ।
भूतं भविष्यदुच्छिष्टे वीर्यं लक्ष्मीर्बलं बले ।।

17. Scriptures, truth, self-control, dominion, exertion, justice and true conduct, charitable deeds, past, future, valour, prosperity, and strength dwell in the Almighty God. (3157)

१८. समृद्धिरोज आकूतिः क्षत्रं राष्ट्रं षडुर्व्यः । संवत्सरोऽध्युच्छिष्ट इडा प्रैषा ग्रहा हविः ।।

18. Welfare, energy, resolve, martial spirit, kingship, the six expanses, the year, prayer, direction, planets, oblation: all rest in God. (3158)[4]

१९. चतुर्होतार आप्रियश्चातुर्मास्यानि नीविदः । उच्छिष्टे यज्ञा होत्राः पशुबन्धास्तदिष्टयः ।।

19. The duties of Brahman, Kshatriya, Vaish, Sudra, acts of comradeship, four-monthly rites, exact sciences, sacrifices, Vedic verses worth preaching and observing, the literary compositions of scholars, noble desires: all rest in God. (3159)

२०. अर्धमासाश्च मासाश्चार्तवा ऋतुभिः सह । उच्छिष्टे घोषिणीराप: स्तनयित्नुः श्रुतिर्मही ।।

[1]Nine forces: Two eyes, two ears, two nostrils, mouth, anus, penis.

[2]Uphavya and Vishuvāna are two Yajnas.

[3]God is the grandfather of our life as He exists before us like our grandfather. He is the grandson of our soul, as He exists after our death, as our grandson does.

[4]Six expanses: North, East, South, West, Nadir and Zenith. They may also mean, (1) Heaven (2) Earth (3) Day (4) Night (5) Waters (6) Herbs, as stated in Āshvalayan shrout Sutra 1-2-1. Direction: A liturgical order given during the performance of a sacrifice.

20. Half-months, months, seasons along with their products, resonant waters, thundering clouds, Vedic speech and Earth all testify to the glory of God. (3160)

२१. शर्कराः सिकता अश्मान ओषधयो वीरुधस्तृणा ।
अभ्राणि विद्युतो वर्षमुच्छिष्टे संश्रिता श्रिता ॥

21. Pebbles, sand, stones, and herbs, and plants, and grass rest in God. Closely embraced and laid therein are lightnings and the clouds and rain. (3161)

२२. राद्धिः प्राप्तिः समाप्तिर्व्याप्तिर्मह एधतुः ।
अत्याप्तिरुच्छिष्टे भूतिश्चाहिता निहिता हिता ॥

22. Gain, acquisition, success, fulness, complete prosperity, great gain and wealth are laid, concealed and treasured, in God. (3162)

२३. यच्च प्राणति प्राणेन यच्च पश्यति चक्षुषा ।
उच्छिष्टाज्जज्ञिरे सर्वे दिवि देवा दिविश्रितः ॥

23. All things that breathe the breath of life, all creatures that have eyes to see, all the luminous objects in heaven, and all emancipated souls spring from God. (3163)

२४. ऋचः सामानि छन्दांसि पुराणं यजुषा सह ।
उच्छिष्टाज्जज्ञिरे सर्वे दिवि देवा दिविश्रितः ॥

24. The verses of the Rigveda, the Sāmaveda, the Atharvaveda, and the Yajurveda, along with the verses pertaining to the creation and dissolution of the universe, all the luminous objects in heaven, and all emancipated souls spring from God. (3164)

२५. प्राणापानौ चक्षुः श्रोत्रमक्षितिश्च क्षितिश्च या ।
उच्छिष्टाज्जज्ञिरे सर्वे दिवि देवा दिविश्रितः ॥

25. Inbreath and outbreath, eye and ear, decay and freedom from decay, all the luminous objects in heaven, and all emancipated souls spring from God. (3165)[1]

२६. आनन्दा मोदाः प्रमुदोऽभीमोदमुदश्च ये। उच्छिष्टाज्जज्ञिरे सर्वे दिवि देवा दिविश्रितः ॥

26. All pleasures and enjoyments, all delights and rapturous ecstasies, all luminous objects in heaven, and all emancipated souls spring from God. (3166)

[1]Decay: objects that are mortal and liable to decay e.g., bodies. Freedom from decay: Deathless objects like Time, Space etc. God grants salvation to the souls.

२७. देवाः पितरो मनुष्याऽ गन्धर्वाप्सरसश्च ये ।
उच्छिष्टाज्जज्ञिरे सर्वे दिवि देवा दिविश्रितः ॥

27. The sages, the Father's men, rulers of the earth, those who fly in air, all luminous objects in heaven, and all emancipated souls spring from God. (3167)[1]

HYMN VIII

१. यन्मन्युर्जायामावहत् संकल्पस्य गृहादधि ।
क आसं जन्याः के वराः क उ ज्येष्ठवरोऽभवत् ॥

1. When God, through the force of His resolve, created the universe with His authority, what were the objects with which it was created? What was the aim or purpose in its creation? Who was its chief creator? (3168)[2]

२. तपश्चैवास्तां कर्म चान्तर्महत्यर्णवे । त आसं जन्यास्ते वरा ब्रह्म ज्येष्ठवरोऽभवत् ॥

2. The strength of God, and the fruit of the actions of men, were under the control of Mighty God. These two were the causes of the creation of the universe. They were the aim of its creation. God was the chief Bestower of the fruit of actions. (3169)[3]

३. दश साकमजायन्त देवा देवेभ्यः पुरा ।
यो वै तान् विद्यात् प्रत्यक्षं स वा अद्य महद् वदेत् ॥

3. Ten forces were created simultaneously as the fruit of our actions in the past. He who knows them distinctly is competent to speak of God. (3170)[4]

४. प्राणापानौ चक्षुः श्रोत्रमक्षितिश्च क्षितिश्च या ।
व्यानोदानौ वाङ्मनस्ते वा आकूतिमावहन् ॥

4. Inbreath and outbreath, eye and ear, deathless knowledge, evanescent action, Vyāna, Udāna, voice, mind contribute to our resolve. (3171)[5]

[1]This verse has been translated by Maharshi Dayananda in the *Rigveda*, Adi Bhashya Bhumika pp. 135, 136. गन्धर्वः गां पृथिवीं भरन्ति चे ते गन्धर्वाः । अप्सु आकाशे सरन्ति ये ते अप्सरसः ।

[2]Just as a bridegroom marries the bride from the house of his father-in-law, so does God create the universe out of His resolve.

[3]तप (strength of God) and कर्म (fruit of the actions of men) were the two sources of the creation of the universe. God creates the universe to award the souls the fruit of their actions in past lives, and establish His strength of creating it. The aim of creating of the world was to award or punish the souls according to their deeds. The questions raised in the first verse have been answered in the second.

[4]Ten forces: Five organs of cognition (jnān) i.e., (1) Ear (hearing) (2) Skin (touch) (3) Eye (sight) (4) Tongue (taste) (5) Nose (smell) and five organs of action (1) Speech (2) Hand (3) Foot (4) Anus (5) Penis.

[5]Vyāna: The breath that is diffused throughout the body. Udāna: The breath that goes upward for eructation.

५. अजाता आसन्नृतवोऽथो धाता बृहस्पतिः । इन्द्राग्नी अश्विना तर्हि कं ते ज्येष्ठमुपासत ॥

5. In the beginning of the universe, when the seasons, atmosphere, air, cloud, sun, day and night were yet unborn, whom then did they worship as supreme? (3172)

६. तपश्चैवास्तां कर्म चान्तर्महत्यर्णवे । तपो ह जज्ञे कर्मणस्तत् ते ज्येष्ठमुपासत ॥

6. Fervour and action both were under the control of Mighty God. Fervour sprang up from Action. They served and worshipped this God as supreme. (3173)[1]

७. येत आसीद् भूमिः पूर्वा यामद्धातय इद् विदुः ।
यो वै तां विद्यान्नामथा स मन्येत पुराणवित् ॥

7. He may account himself well versed in ancient history, who knows exactly the earth that was before this visible earth, which only wise sages know. (3174)

८. कुत इन्द्रः कुतः सोमः कुतो अग्निरजायत । कुतस्त्वष्टा समभवत् कुतो धाताऽजायत ॥

8. From whom did cloud spring? From whom sprang air? Whence was sun born? From whom did lightning spring to life? Whence is atmosphere's origin? (3175)[2]

९. इन्द्रादिन्द्रः सोमात् सोमो अग्नेरग्निरजायत । त्वष्टा ह जज्ञे त्वष्टुर्धातुर्धाताजायत ॥

9. Cloud from cloud, air from air, Sun from Sun sprang. Lightning from lightning was produced, Atmosphere was Atmosphere's origin. (3176)[3]

१०. ये त आसन् दश जाता देवा देवेभ्यः पुरा । पुत्रेभ्यो लोकं दत्त्वा कस्मिंस्ते लोक आसते ॥

10. Ten forces were born as the fruit of actions in the past. What world did they inhabit after giving their own seats to their sons, the organs? (3177)[4]

११. यदा केशानस्थि स्नाव मांसं मज्जानमाभरत् ।
शरीरं कृत्वा पादवत् कं लोकमनु प्राविशत् ॥

[1]They: Seasons etc., mentioned in the previous, when they were still in their nascent state in the beginning of the universe when God brings Cosmos out of chaos.

[2]The earth that was: The earth in the previous cycle of creation.

[3]God created all these objects in this cycle in the same shape as they existed in the previous cycle of creation. See *Rigveda*, 10. 190.3. "सूर्याचन्द्रमसौ धाता यथापूर्वम् अकल्पयत्", God has created the Sun and Moon in this cycle as He did in the last cycle of creation.

[4]See *Atharva*, 11.8.3. Ten forces: Five subtle forces of cognition and five of action. Just as parents give their homes to their sons, and themselves go to the Vanprastha Ashram, so do these forces lend their strength to the organs. The question is answered in verse 13th.

11. When God in the beginning brought together hair, bone, sinew, flesh, and marrow, and to the body added feet, hands etc., then to what world did he depart? (3178)[1]

१२. कुतः केशान् कुतः स्नाव कुतो अस्थीन्याभरत् ।
अङ्गा पर्वाणि मज्जानं को मांसं कुत आभरत् ॥

12. Whence, from what region did the creator bring the hair, the sinews, and the bones, limbs, joints, marrow and flesh? Who was the bringer, and from whence? (3179)[2]

१३. संसिचो नाम ते देवा ये संभारान्त्समभरन् । सर्वं संसिच्य मर्त्यं देवाः पुरुषमाविशन् ॥

13. Impregnators, those gods were called, who brought together all the elements. When they had fused the mortal man complete, they entered the soul in the body. (3180)[3]

१४. ऊरू पादावष्ठीवन्तौ शिरो हस्तावथो मुखम् ।
पृष्ठीर्बर्जह्ये पार्श्वे कस्तत् समदधादृषिः ॥

14. Who is the wise sage who hath constructed the thighs, the feet, the knee-bones, the head, both the hands, the face, the ribs, the nipples, and both the sides? (3181)[4]

१५. शिरो हस्तावथो मुखं जिह्वां ग्रीवाश्च कीकसाः ।
त्वचा प्रावृत्य सर्वं तत् संधा समदधान्मही ॥

15. The mighty uniting force of God, hath conjoined together, head, both the hands, face, tongue, neck, and intercostal parts, investing them all with skin. (3182)

१६. यत्तच्छरीरमशयत् संधया संहितं महत् । येनेदमद्य रोचते को अस्मिन् वर्णमाभरत् ॥

16. When the mighty body lay firmly compact through the uniting force of God, who gave its colour to the body, the hue wherewith it shines today. (3183)[5]

१७. सर्वे देवा उपाशिक्षन् तदजानाद् वधूः सती ।
ईशा वशस्य या जाया सास्मिन् वर्णमाभरत् ॥

[1]For answer see *Atharva*, 11.8.13.

[2]These questions raised in 10, 11, 12 are answered in the next verse.

[3]Gods: Earth, Water, Air, Fire and Space. Through the dispensation of God, the five divine forces, i.e., earth, water, air, fire, space uniting together make up all the organs of the body, themselves enter the embodied soul.

[4]Answer to this question is given in the next verse.

[5]The question is answered in the next verse. Who made the body white, black or yellow, after its completion?

17. All the forces of nature wanted to assist in the completion of the body. The true power of God knew it. The divine creative power of God lent colour to the body. (3184)[1]

१८. यदा त्वष्टा व्यतृणत् पिता त्वष्टुर्य उत्तरः । गृहं कृत्वा मर्त्यं देवाः पुरुषमाविशन् ॥

18. When God, the Loftier sire of the soul, bored and hollowed the body, organs and breaths made the mortal body their abode, and entered and possessed it. (3185)[2]

१९. स्वप्नो वै तन्द्रीर्निर्ऋतिः पाप्मानो नाम देवताः ।
जरा खालत्यं पालित्यं शरीरमनु प्राविशन् ॥

19. Sleep, sloth, poverty, distressing desires arising out of sinful mind, old age, baldness, and hoary hairs then found their way within the body. (3186)

२०. स्तेयं दुष्कृतं वृजिनं सत्यं यज्ञो यशो बृहत् । बलं च क्षत्रमोजश्च शरीरमनु प्राविशन् ॥

20. Theft, evil-doing, deceit, truth, sacrifice exalted fame, strength, martial spirit, and energy then entered the body as a home. (3187)

२१. भूतिश्च वा अभूतिश्च रातयोऽरातयश्च याः ।
क्षुधश्च सर्वास्तृष्णाश्च शरीरमनु प्राविशन् ॥

21. Prosperity and poverty, kindnesses and malignities, hunger and thirst of every kind then entered the body as a home. (3188)

२२. निन्दाश्च वा अनिन्दाश्च यच्च हन्तेति नेति च ।
शरीरं श्रद्धा दक्षिणाश्रद्धा चानु प्राविशन् ॥

22. Censures, praises, all blamable, all blameless deeds, bounty, belief, and disbelief then entered the body as a home. (3189)

२३. विद्याश्च वा अविद्याश्च यच्चान्यदुपदेश्यम् । शरीरं ब्रह्म प्राविशदृचः सामाथो यजुः ॥

23. All knowledge and all ignorance, each other thing that one may learn, the Rigveda, the Sāmaveda, the Yajurveda, and the Brahm (Atharva) Veda then entered the body. (3190)

२४. आनन्दा मोदाः प्रमुदोऽभीमोदमुदश्च ये । हसो नरिष्टा नृत्तानि शरीरमनु प्राविशन् ॥

24. Enjoyments, pleasures, and delights, gladness and rapturous ecstasies, laughter and merriment and dance then entered the body. (3191)

२५. आलापाश्च प्रलापाश्चाभीलापलपश्च ये । शरीरं सर्वे प्राविशन्नायुजः प्रयुजो युजः ॥

25. Useful, useless discourse, mutual questions and answers, motives and purposes, and yogic practices all then entered the body. (3192)

[1]God made the body white, black, yellow etc.

[2]Bored, hollowed: Made eyes, ears, nostrils, as openings in the body.

२६. प्राणापानौ चक्षुः श्रोत्रमक्षितिश्च क्षितिश्च या ।
व्यानोदानौ वाङ्मनः शरीरेण त ईयन्ते ॥

26. Inbreath and outbreath, ear and eye, decay and strength of the body, breath upward and diffused, voice, mind, these quickly move with the body. (3193)

२७. आशिषश्च प्रशिषश्च संशिषो विशिषश्च याः ।
चित्तानि सर्वे संकल्पाः शरीरमनु प्राविशन् ॥

27. All earnest wishes, all commands, directions, and admonishments, reflections, all deliberate plans entered the body as a home. (3194)

२८. आस्तेयीश्च वास्तेयीश्च त्वरणाः कृपणाश्च याः ।
गुह्याः शुक्रा स्थूल अपस्ता बीभत्सावसादयन् ॥

28. Waters in the blood, urine, fast and slow moving waters in the body, waters in the bowels and semen, waters taken in the shape of food, are all laid in this well-constructed body. (3195)

२९. अस्थि कृत्वा समिधं तदष्टापो असादयन् । रेतः कृत्वाज्यं देवाः पुरुषमाविशन् ॥

29. The All-pervading, divine law of God, making bones the fuel, and semen the molten butter, equipped the body with eight agents, and entered into it. (3196)[1]

३०. या आपो याश्च देवता या विराड् ब्रह्मणा सह ।
शरीरं ब्रह्म प्राविशच्छरीरेऽधि प्रजापतिः ॥

30. All innate forces of the organs, their globes, Matter, with God by its side, and food passed into the body. Soul is Lord thereof. (3197)[2]

३१. सूर्यश्चक्षुर्वातः प्राणं पुरुषस्य वि भेजिरे । अथास्येतरमात्मानं देवाः प्रायच्छन्नग्नये ॥

31. The Sun and Wind formed, separate, the eye and vital breath of man. His other person have the organs bestowed on Agni as a gift. (3198)[3]

३२. तस्माद् वै विद्वान् पुरुषमिदं ब्रह्मेति मन्यते ।
सर्वा ह्यस्मिन् देवता गावो गोष्ठ इवासते ॥

32. Therefore whoever verily knoweth the structure of the body, regardeth God as supreme. For all the Luminous planets abide in Him as cattle in their pen. (3199)

[1]Just as molten butter (Ghee) is invigorating, so is the semen. Just as fuel is used for cooking and preparing meals, so bones are used to strengthen the body. Eight agents: (1) (रस) Essence of food (2) (रक्त) Blood (3) (मांस) Flesh (4) (मेदा) Fat (5) (अस्थि) Bone (6) (मज्जा) Marrow (7) (वीर्य) Semen (8) (मन) Mind.

[2]ब्रह्म—अन्नम—नि० घ० 217.

[3]Other persons: Other parts of the body. Just as light of the Sun predominantly influences the eye, and wind the Pran, so does fire prevail in all other parts of the body.

३३. प्रथमेन प्रमारेण त्रेधा विष्वङ् वि गच्छति ।
अद एकेन गच्छत्यद एकेन गच्छतीहैकेन नि षेवते ॥

33. On the release of first vital breath at the time of death, the soul goeth hence, asunder, to three different regions. It attains to salvation through virtue, goeth to low, dark life of insects through sin, and is born again in the world through mixed deeds of virtue and vice. (3200)

३४. अप्सु स्तीमासु वृद्धासु शरीरमन्तरा हितम् ।
तस्मिञ्छवोऽध्यन्तरा तस्माच्छवोऽध्युच्यते ॥

34. In the moist, unruffled, vast space the body is placed. In the body is the active, progressive soul. Higher than the soul is the Powerful, Advanced God. (3201)[1]

Chapter (Anuvāka) 5

HYMN IX

१. ये बाहवो या इषवो धन्वनां वीर्याणि च । असीन् परशूनायुधं चित्ताकूतं च यद्धृदि ।
सर्वं तदर्बुदे त्वममित्रेभ्यो दृशे कुरूदारांश्च प्र दर्शय ॥

1. O heroic Commander-in-chief, make thou visible to frighten the enemies, all arms and every arrow, all the power and might that soldiers possess, swords, axes, warlike weapons, plan and purpose in the heart. Prepare thou deadly weapons and show them to the enemies. (3202)[2]

२. उत्तिष्ठत सं नह्यध्वं मित्रा देवजना यूयम् । संदृष्टा गुप्ता वः सन्तु या नो मित्राण्यर्बुदे ॥

2. Arise, prepare for war, ye friendly, victorious soldiers. O Commander-in-chief let our friends be well looked after and protected by thee. (3203)

३. उत्तिष्ठतमा रभेथामादानसंदानाभ्याम् । अमित्राणां सेना अभि धत्तमर्बुदे ॥

3. Rise both of you: begin the battle with fettering and binding fast. Assail, both of you, Arbudi, the armies of our enemies. (3204)[3]

४. अर्बुदिर्नाम यो देव ईशानश्च न्यर्बुदिः ।
याभ्यामन्तरिक्षमावृतमियं च पृथिवी मही । ताभ्यामिन्द्रमेदिभ्यामहं जितमन्वेमि सेनया ॥

4. The general whose name is Arbudi, and Nyarbudi the mighty general, the two by whom the air and this great earth are compassed and possessed, with these two friends of the king. I go forth with the army to control the conquered territory. (3205)[4]

[1]In space reside objects like cloud, air etc. In different regions of the space reside all the bodies.

[2]Griffith writes in the wake of Sāyana that Arbuda was a serpent-like demon of the air. Sāyana says that Arbudi and Nyarbudi were the sons of Kadru. This interpretation is unacceptable, as there is no history in the Vedas. The word means the Commander-in-chief of the army.

[3]Both of You: Arbudi, the Commander of a lakh of soldiers. Nyarbudi, the Commander of a million soldiers.

[4]I: King.

५. उत्तिष्ठ त्वं देवजनार्बुदे सेनया सह । भञ्जन्नमित्राणां सेनां भोगेभिः परि वारय ।।

5. Rise, stand up with the army, thou victory-loving general. Breaking the hosts of enemies, surround them with thy winding coils. (3206)[1]

६. सप्त जातान् न्यर्बुद उदाराणां समीक्षयन् । तेभिष्ट्वमाज्ये हुते सर्वैरुत्तिष्ठ सेनया ।।

6. O ever-enterprising general, exhibiting to the enemy, the seven well-known sources of strength of the state, rise with all of them and with thy army, as fire rises when butter is poured into it! (3207)[2]

७. प्रतिघ्नानाश्रुमुखी कृधुकर्णी च क्रोशतु । विकेशी पुरुषे हते रदिते अर्बुदे तव ।।

7. Beating her breast, with tearful face, let the short-eared, the wild-haired wife shriek loudly when her husband is slain, pierced through by thee, O valiant general ! (3208)[3]

८. संकर्षन्ती करूकरं मनसा पुत्रमिच्छन्ती । पतिं भ्रातरमात् स्वान् रदिते अर्बुदे तव ।।

8. Snatching away the vertebra, with her mind she seeks her son, her husband, brother, kinsmen, and weeps when her relative, O valiant general has been pierced by thee! (3209)

९. अलिक्लवा जाष्कमदा गृध्राः श्येनाः पतत्रिणः ।
ध्वाङ्क्षाः शकुनयस्तृप्यन्त्वमित्रेषु समीक्षयन् रदिते अर्बुदे तव ।।

9. Let vultures, ravens, kites, hawks, crows and every carrion-eating bird, feast on our foes, seeing them dead, pierced by thee, O valiant general. (3210)

१०. अथो सर्वं श्वापदं मक्षिका तृप्यतु क्रिमिः । पौरुषेयेऽधि कुणपे रदिते अर्बुदे तव ।।

10. Then let each greedy beast of prey, and fly and worm regale itself upon the human corpse, when a foe hath been piereed by thee, O valiant general. (3211)

११. आ गृह्णीतं सं बृहतं प्राणापानान् न्यर्बुदे ।
निवाशा घोषाः सं यन्त्वमित्रेषु समीक्षयन् रदिते अर्बुदे तव ।।

11. Attack them, both of you; bear off their vital breaths, O Nyarbudi and Arbudi! Let mingled shouts and echoing cries of woe come out of our foemen, seeing where thou hast pierced them, O Arbudi ! (3212)

[1]Winding coils: Arrangements of the army in the shape of योगव्यूह, चक्रव्यूह, दण्डव्यूह, शकटव्यूह ।

[2]The seven pillars of the state have been mentioned in the Shabd Kalpa Druma as (1) King (2) Minister (3) Grandeur of the capital (4) Citadel (5) Treasury (6) Military strength (7) Friendly nations.

[3]Short-eared: Light-eared, wearing no ornaments. Wife, or mother, or sister i.e., a female relative weeps over the death of the male relative.

१२. उद् वेपय सं विजन्तां भियामित्रान्त्सं सृज । उरुग्राहैर्बाह्वङ्कैर्विध्यामित्रान् न्यर्बुदे ॥

12. Shake them, and let them run through fear, overwhelm our enemies with dread. With widely grasping bends of arm, O valiant general, crush down our foes! (3213)

१३. मुह्यन्त्वेषां बाहवश्चित्ताकूतं च यद्धृदि । मैषामुच्छेषि किं चन रदिते अर्बुदे तव ॥

13. Let these men's arms grow faint and weak, dull be the purpose of their heart; and let not aught of them be left when thou, O valiant general hast pierced them. (3214)

१४. प्रतिघ्नानाः सं धावन्तूरः पटूरावाघ्नानाः ।
अघारिणीर्विकेश्यो रुदत्यः पुरुषे हते रदिते अर्बुदे तव ॥

14. Self-smiting, beating breast and thighs, careless of unguent, with their hair dishevelled, weeping, the women shall run together, when their relative is slain, when thou, O valiant general hast pierced him! (3215)

१५. श्वन्वतीरप्सरसो रूपका उतार्बुदे । अन्तःपात्रे रेरिहतीं रिशां दुर्णिहितैषिणीम् ।
सर्वास्ता अर्बुदे त्वममित्रेभ्यो दृशे कुरूदारांश्च प्र दर्शय ॥

15. O valiant general, reserve for friends, acts, magnanimous in nature, connected with the subjects, and displaying beauty and excellence. Exhibit to the enemies, the affliction, struggling hard in the mind, searching for evil aims, and all similar afflictions. Show us all thy stratagems! (3216)[1]

१६. खडूरेऽधिचङ्क्रमां खर्विकां खर्ववासिनीम् ।
य उदारा अन्तर्हिता गन्धर्वाप्सरसश्च ये । सर्पा इतरजना रक्षांसि ॥

16. Show to the enemy to frighten and defeat him, the army that can fearlessly tread on the sword, is full of pride, and millions in number, show to him the rulers of the earth who are charitable and benevolent in nature, and learned persons who know the science of flying in the air. Shake those who are violent like a serpent, low in mentality, and diabolic in nature. (3217)[2]

१७. चतुर्दंष्ट्राञ्छ्यावदतः कुम्भमुष्कां असृङ्मुखान् । स्वभ्यसा ये चोद्भयसाः ॥

17. Shake the animals armed with four fangs and yellow teeth, with scrotum big like a pitcher, bloody mouthed lions, and persons terrible in nature and awe-inspiring in appearance. (3218)

१८. उद् वेपय त्वमर्बुदेऽमित्राणाममूः सिचः । जयांश्च जिष्णुश्चामित्राञ्जयतामिन्द्रमेदिनौ ॥

[1]Stratagems: Means of success against the enemy. Searching aims: Tending to create disease and physical torture.

[2](16, 17) वेपय in both these verses is taken from the 18th verse.

18. Make thou, O valiant general, those wings of hostile armies quake with dread. Let Conqueror and victor friends of Indra, overcome our foes. (3219)[1]

१९. प्रब्लीनो मृदितः शयां हतोऽमित्रो न्यर्बुदे । अग्निजिह्वा धूमशिखा जयन्तीर्यन्तु सेनया ॥

19. O ever-enterprising general, let the surrounded, crushed, smitten foeman lie low. Let fiery warlike instruments and weapons emitting smoke go conquering with our host! (3220)

२०. तयार्बुदे प्रणुत्तानामिन्द्रो हन्तु वरंवरम् । अमित्राणां शचीपतिर्मामीषां मोचि कश्चन ॥

20. May the king, Lord of Might, strike down each bravest warrior of the foes; whom this army of ours has put to flight: let not, O valiant general, one man of these escape! (3221)

२१. उत्कसन्तु हृदयान्यूर्ध्वः प्राण उदीषतु । शौष्कास्यमनु वर्ततामममित्रान् मोत मित्रिणः ॥

21. Let their hearts burst asunder, let their breath fly up and pass out of the body. Let dryness of the mouth overtake our foes, but not the friendly ones. (3222)

२२. ये च धीरा ये चाधीराः पराञ्चो बधिराश्च ये ।
तमसा ये च तूपरा अथो बस्ताभिवासिनः ।
सर्वांस्ताँ अर्बुदे त्वममित्रेभ्यो दृशे कुरूदारांश्च प्रदर्शय ॥

22. The calm and restless soldiers, those who shun the battlefield, and are deaf to advice, rogues engulfed in darkness, violent persons, those fond of enterprise: all these, O valiant general, do thou make visible to our enemies, and show them thy deadly military devices! (3223)

२३. अर्बुदिश्च त्रिषन्धिश्चामित्रान् नो वि विध्यताम् ।
यथैषामिन्द्र वृत्रहन् हनाम शचीपतेऽमित्राणां सहस्रशः ॥

23. O valiant general, and a learned commander full of action, contemplation and knowledge, fall upon our foes and scatter them, so that, O king, Lord of Might, Dispeller of darkness, we may kill thousands of these our enemies! (3224)

२४. वनस्पतीन् वानस्पत्यानोषधीरुत वीरुधः ।
गन्धर्वाप्सरसः सर्पान् देवान् पुण्यजनान् पितॄन् ॥
सर्वास्ताँ अर्बुदे त्वममित्रेभ्यो दृशे कुरूदारांश्च प्र दर्शय ॥

24. Tall trees, and weapons made out of them, the herbs and creeping plants of Earth, rulers of the earth, and those who fly in the air, persons violent like serpents, victory-loving, noble, learned persons: all these do thou, O valiant general, make visible to our enemies to frighten them, and show them thy deadly military devices! (3225)

[1]Conqueror and Victor: Arbudi, Nyarbudi. Indra: King.

२५. ईशां वो मरुतो देव आदित्यो ब्रह्मणस्पतिः ।
ईशां व इन्द्रश्चाग्निश्च धाता मित्रः प्रजापतिः ।
ईशां व ऋषयश्चक्रुरमित्रेषु समीक्षयन् रदिते अर्बुदे तव ॥

25. High sway have heroes, victors, celibates, a Vedic savant, high sway have dignified the king, a tormentor of the foe-like fire, a protector of the people, a goader, a nourisher of the subjects, high sway have sages given you upon our enemies. O valiant look at them and destroy them! (3226)

२६. तेषां सर्वेषामीशाना उत्तिष्ठत सं नह्यध्वं मित्रा देवजना यूयम् ।
इमं संग्रामं संजित्य यथालोकं वि तिष्ठध्वम् ॥

26. Ye friendly kings and learned warriors with full dominion over these, rise, stand ye up, prepare yourselves for battle. Winning this battle, go each to your respective post of duty! (3227)

HYMN X

१. उत्तिष्ठत सं नह्यध्वमुदाराः केतुभिः सह । सर्पा इतरजना रक्षांस्यमित्राननु धावत ॥

1. O munificent soldiers, rise up with your banners, put on the armour for battle! Ye violent, wicked, fiendish persons charge and pursue our enemies! (3228)

२. ईशां वो वेद राज्यं त्रिषन्धे अरुणैः केतुभिः सह ।
ये अन्तरिक्षे ये दिवि पृथिव्यां ये च मानवाः । त्रिषन्धेस्ते चेतसि दुर्णामान उपासताम् ॥

2. O general, devoted to duty, devotion and knowledge, I acknowledge thy power and sway with ruddy flags. May all men in air, heaven and on earth, and all evil-minded persons remain under thy control O general! (3229)[1]

३. अयोमुखाः सूचीमुखा अथो विकङ्कतीमुखाः ।
क्रव्यादो वातरंहस आ सजन्त्वमित्रान् वज्रेण त्रिषन्धिना ॥

3. Let birds with faces dreadful like iron, with hills sharp like needles, and hard like combs, flesh-eaters, rapid as the wind, cling closely to the corpses of our foemen killed by the thunderbolt of the general. (3230)

४. अन्तर्धेहि जातवेद आदित्य कुणपं बहु । त्रिषन्धेरियं सेना सुहितास्तु मे वशे ॥

4. O learned, brilliant general cast down many a corpse during the battle. Let the devoted army of Trishandhi be in my control. (3231)[2]

५. उत्तिष्ठ त्वं देवजनार्बुदे सेनया सह । अयं बलिर्व आहुतस्त्रिषन्धेराहुतिः प्रिया ॥

[1]Remain under: Work according to thy will. I: one of the subjects. The colour of the flag should be red, to strike terror in the heart of the foe.

[2]Trishandhi: A general devoted to duty, devotion, and knowledge. My: Another Commander of the army, who with the assistance of Trishandhi wins the foe.

5. Rise up, O victorious enterprising general, with thine army. This tribute of righteous war is offered thee, as a learned general welcomes war to espouse the cause of truth. (3232)

६. शितिपदी सं द्यतु शरव्ये३यं चतुष्पदी । कृत्येऽमित्रेभ्यो भव त्रिषन्धेः सह सेनया ॥

6. May this army, that marches in day-time and night, is entitled to four-fold progress, and knows the science of archery, destroy the enemy. O destructive army, be ready to kill the foe, with the host of the general devoted to duty, devotion and knowledge. (3233)[1]

७. धूमाक्षी सं पततु कृधुकर्णी च क्रोशतु । त्रिषन्धेः सेनया जिते अरुणाः सन्तु केतवः ।

7. Let the army of the enemy fall down blinded by the smoke of warlike instruments. Let it shriek deafened by the noise of military drums. Let red banners be raised when the host of a learned general hath won the day. (3234)

८. अवायन्तां पक्षिणो ये वयांस्यन्तरिक्षे दिवि ये चरन्ति ।
श्वापदो मक्षिकाः सं रभन्तामामादो गृध्राः कुणपे रदन्ताम् ॥

8. Let all the birds that move on wings, all fowls that roam the heaven and air's mid-regions, come downward upon the carcase. Let beasts of prey and flies attack, and vultures that eat raw flesh mangle and gnaw the corpse. (3235)

९. यामिन्द्रेण संधां समधत्था ब्रह्मणा च बृहस्पते ।
तयाहमिन्द्रसंधया सर्वान् देवानिह हुव इतो जयत मामुतः ॥

9. O King! by the same vow which thou hast made with man and with God, by man's pledge I bid the conquest-loving warriors come hither, and ask them to fight for conquest on this side, not on the yonder side of the enemy. (3236)[2]

१०. बृहस्पतिराङ्गिरस ऋषयो ब्रह्मसंशिताः । असुरक्षयणं वधं त्रिषन्धि दिव्याश्रयन् ॥

10. The learned king, and the sages made strong and keen through Vedic knowledge, for the sake of conquest, have used the brave general as a dire weapon that destroys the fiends. (3237)

११. येनासौ गुप्त आदित्य उभाविन्द्रश्च तिष्ठतः । त्रिषन्धि देवा अभजन्तौजसे च बलाय च ॥

11. Lovers of conquest have utilised the expert general for spiritual strength and physical force, under whose protection stand both the prosperous person and you Aditya Brahmchari. (3238)[3]

[1]Four-fold: Dharma (Religion) Artha (Wealth) Kama (Fulfilment of ambition) Moksha (Emancipation).

[2]The king makes a vow with God and with each of his subjects to protect and advance his country. I: A general.

[3]Āditya Brahmchari: A person who observes celibacy for 48 years.

१२. सर्वांल्लोकान्त्समजयन् देवा आहुत्यानया ।
बृहस्पतिराङ्गिरसो वज्रं यमसिञ्चतासुरक्षयणं वधम् ।।

12. Lovers of conquest win for themselves all desirable objects through the help of this general, whom a learned king prepares, as a very thunderbolt, a weapon to destroy the fiends. (3239)

१३. बृहस्पतिराङ्गिरसो वज्रं यमसिञ्चतासुरक्षयणं वधम् ।
तेनाहममूं सेनां नि लिम्पामि बृहस्पतेऽमित्रान् हन्म्योजसा ।।

13. That fiend-destroying general whom the learned king has prepared as a weapon and a thunderbolt, with his aid, O King! I destroy that enemy, and strike the foemen down with my might. (3240)[1]

१४. सर्वे देवा अत्यायन्ति ये अश्नन्ति वषट् कृतम् । इमां जुषध्वमाहुतिमितो जयत मामुतः ।।

14. Over to us come all the learned persons who eat the hallowed remnants of the sacrifice trampling down the foe. With this offering of ours, be ye pleased; fight for victory on this side, not on the yonder side of the enemy. (3241)[2]

१५. सर्वे देवा अत्यायन्तु त्रिषन्धेराहुतिः प्रिया । संधां महतीं रक्षत ययाग्रे असुरा जिताः ।।

15. Over to us let all learned persons come trampling down the foe. A brave general loves enterprise. O heroes, keep the great pledge through which of old, the evil-minded persons were overthrown. (3242)[3]

१६. वायुरमित्राणामिष्वग्राण्याञ्चतु । इन्द्र एषां बाहून् प्रति भनक्तु मा शकन् प्रतिधामिषुम् ।
आदित्य एषामस्त्रं वि नाशयतु चन्द्रमा युतामगतस्य पन्थाम् ।।

16. Let a King fast like the air bend the arrow-points of those who are our enemies. Let a brave general break their arms away, and render them powerless to lift a shaft. Let a commander blazing like the Sun utterly destroy their missile. Let a general calm and cool like the Moon bar the path of the foe who follows not the right course of conduct. (3243)

१७. यदि प्रेयुर्देवपुरा ब्रह्म वर्माणि चक्रिरे ।
तनूपानं परिपाणं कृण्वाना यदुपोचिरे सर्वं तदरसं कृधि ।।

17. If they have attacked the citadels of kings, prepared their armours through knowledge, gained protection for their bodies, and everything else, and are organising and consolidating themselves, O King! make all their designs powerless. (3244)[4]

१८. क्रव्यादानुवर्तयन् मृत्युना च पुरोहितम् । त्रिषन्धे प्रेहि सेनया जयामित्रान् प्र पद्यस्व ।।

[1]I: A brave man.
[2]This side: Our side.
[3]Pledge: Resolve to defeat the enemy.
[4]They: The enemies. See *Atharva*, 5-8-6.

18. O brave general, surround the raw flesh-eating foes, face them with death, attack them with thy army, conquer and subjugate them! (3245)

१९. त्रिषन्धे तमसा त्वममित्रान् परि वारय । पृषदाज्यप्रणुत्तानां मामीषां मोचि कश्चन ॥

19. O valiant general, do thou with the gloom of military weapons compass round the foes; let none escape of them conquered with great heroism. (3246)

२०. शितिपदी सं पतत्वमित्राणाममूः सिचः । मुह्यन्त्वद्यामूः सेना अमित्राणां न्यर्बुदे ॥

20. May this army that marches in day-time and during night, fall upon those wings of our opponents' army. Amazed and bewildered be those bands of foes this day, O ever-enterprising king! (3247)

२१. मूढा अमित्रा न्यर्बुदे जह्येषां वरंवरम् । अनया जहि सेनया ॥

21. Amazed are the foemen, O ever-enterprising king! Slay thou each bravest man of them: with this our army slaughter them. (3248)

२२. यश्च कवची यश्चाकवचोऽमित्रो यश्चाज्मनि ।
ज्यापाशैः कवचपाशैरज्मनाभिहतः शयाम् ॥

22. Low lie the warrior, mailed, unmailed, each foeman in the rush of war, down-smitten with the strings of bows, the fastenings of mail, the charge! (3249)

२३. ये वर्मिणो येऽवर्माणो अमित्रा ये च वर्मिणः ।
सर्वांस्ताँ अर्बुदे हतांञ्छ्वानोऽदन्तु भूम्याम् ॥

23. The armour-clad, the armourless enemies clothed with coats of mail, all these struck down, O enterprising Commander! Let dogs devour on the battlefield. (3250)

२४. ये रथिनो ये अरथा असादा ये च सादिनः ।
सर्वानदन्तु तान् हतान् गृध्राः श्येनाः पतत्रिणः ॥

24. Car-borne and carless fighting men, riders and those who go on foot, all these killed, O enterprising general ! let vultures, kites, and all the birds of air devour. (3251)

२५. सहस्रकुणपा शेतामामित्री सेना समरे वधानाम् । विविद्धा ककजाकृता ॥

25. Low let the hostile army lie, thousands of corpses, on the ground, pierced through and rent to pieces where the deadly weapons clash in fight. (3252)[1]

२६. मर्माविधं रोरुवतं सुपर्णैरदन्तु दुश्चितं मृदितं शयानम् ॥

[1]Kakjākrita has been translated by Pt. Khem Karan Das Trivedi as 'tormented by thirst.' Sāyana translates the word as 'reduced to a miserable plight.'

26. Let eagles eat the evil-hearted, pierced in the vitals, lying crushed and howling, the foe whoe'er will fight against this our war strategy. (3253)

२७. यां देवा अनुतिष्ठन्ति यस्या नास्ति विराधनम् । तयेन्द्रो हन्तु वृत्रहा वज्रेण त्रिषन्धिना ॥

27. With this war strategy which the learned observe, with this which never fails to gain its end, let the foe-slaying king smite the enemy, using as a bolt the general devoted to duty, devotion and knowledge. (3254)

BOOK (Kāṇḍa) XII

Chapter (Anuvāka) 1

Prithvi Suktā

HYMN 1

१. सत्यं बृहदृतमुग्रं दीक्षा तपो ब्रह्म यज्ञः पृथिवीं धारयन्ति ।
सा नो भूतस्य भव्यस्य पत्न्युरुं लोकं पृथिवी नः कृणोतु ॥

1. Truth, Material prosperity, Justice, Military strength, Efficiency, Hard work, Knowledge, Mutual regard, Unity and Charity sustain a state. May this motherland of ours grant us ample scope for advancement. (3255)

२. असंबाधं मध्यतो मानवानां यस्या उद्वतः प्रवतः समं बहु ।
नानावीर्या ओषधीर्या बिभर्ति पृथिवी नः प्रथतां राध्यतां नः ॥

2. Amongst the wise persons of our motherland, though worldly high and low, there reigns intense feeling of equality and comradeship. May our motherland which bears plants endowed with many healing powers, expand and grow more food for us. (3256)

३. यस्यां समुद्र उत सिन्धुरापो यस्यामन्नं कृष्टयः संबभूवुः ।
यस्यामिदं जिन्वति प्राणदेजत् सा नो भूमिः पूर्वपेये दधातु ॥

3. In whom the sea, canals, lakes, wells, tanks, in whom our food and corn-fields had their being, in whom this all that breathes and moves is active, may this motherland of ours grant us all excellent eatable and drinkable objects like milk, fruits, water and cereals. (3257)[1]

४. यस्याश्चतस्रः प्रदिशः पृथिव्या यस्यामन्नं कृष्टयः संबभूवुः ।
या बिभर्ति बहुधा प्राणदेजत् सा नो भूमिर्गोष्वप्यन्ने दधातु ॥

4. She who has got four vast regions, in whom cultivators produce food through agriculture. She who protects the breathing and moving creatures, may this motherland vouchsafe us kine and food. (3258)

५. यस्यां पूर्वे पूर्वजना विचक्रिरे यस्यां देवा असुरानभ्यवर्तयन् ।
गवामश्वानां वयसश्च विष्ठा भगं वर्चः पृथिवी नो दधातु ॥

[1]पूर्वपेये may also mean foremost rank and station.

5. On whom in ancient times our ancestors performed heroic deeds, on whom the sages subdued the violent demons, which is the varied home of kine, horses and birds, may that motherland vouchsafe us prosperity and splendour! (3259)

६. विश्वंभरा वसुधानी प्रतिष्ठा हिरण्यवक्षा जगतो निवेशनी ।
वैश्वानरं बिभ्रती भूमिरग्निमिन्द्रऋषभा द्रविणे नो दधातु ॥

6. All-bearing, store of treasures, advancer of glory, gold-breasted, barbourer of all that moveth, the sustainer of mankind, and their well-wisher the king, ferocious like fire, the establisher over it of the rule of a sovereign, may this motherland give us great possessions. (3260)

७. यां रक्षन्त्यस्वप्ना विश्वदानीं देवा भूमिं पृथिवीमप्रमादम् ।
सा नो मधु प्रियं दुहामथो उक्षतु वर्चसा ॥

7. May our vast motherland, always protected with ceaseless care by the learned kings who are free from idleness, may she pour out for us full, lovely knowledge, may she bedew us with a flood of splendour. (3261)

८. यार्णवेऽधि सलिलमग्र आसीद् यां मायाभिरन्वचरन् मनीषिणः ।
यस्या हृदयं परमे व्योमन्त्सत्येनावृतममृतं पृथिव्याः ।
सा नो भूमिस्त्विषिं बलं राष्ट्रे दधातूत्तमे ॥

8. She who at first was water in the ocean, upon whom the learned labour hard with their wondrous intellectual powers. Whose motive force, the everlasting sun is in the highest heaven, compassed about with lustre. May she, this motherland, bestow upon us lustre, and grant us power in loftiest kingdom. (3262)[1]

९. यस्यामापः परिचराः समानीरहोरात्रे अप्रमादं क्षरन्ति ।
सा नो भूमिर्भूरिधारा पयो दुहामथो उक्षतु वर्चसा ॥

9. On whom the sacrificing truthful hermits, calm like water, imbued with the spirit of service, with one mind work ceaselessly day and night. May she, our motherland with many streams pour milk to feed us, may she bedew us with a flood of splendour. (3263)[2]

१०. यामश्विनावमिमातां विष्णुर्यस्यां विचक्रमे । इन्द्रो यां चक्र आत्मनेऽनमित्रां शचीपतिः ।
सा नो भूमिर्वि सृजतां माता पुत्राय मे पयः ॥

[1]At first: In the beginning of the creation. In the beginning waters alone formed the universe (*Shatpathbrahman*, XIV 6.8.1), and the earth was without form.

[2](आपः) आप्ताः प्रजाः—दयानन्द भाष्ये यजु० 6-27. Āpa has been translated by Maharshi Dayanand as sacrificing truthful persons in the *Yajurveda*, chapter six, verse twenty-seven.

10. She whom the learned scientists measured out, upon whom the All-pervading God creates different kinds of creation, whom the glorious king, Lord of speech, action, and intellect, freed from all foemen for himself, may that motherland of ours pour out her milk for me, as a mother does unto her son. (3264)

११. गिरयस्ते पर्वता हिमवन्तोऽरण्यं ते पृथिवि स्योनमस्तु ।
बभ्रुं कृष्णां रोहिणीं विश्वरूपां ध्रुवां भूमिं पृथिवीमिन्द्रगुप्ताम् ।
अजीतोऽहतो अक्षतोऽध्यष्ठां पृथिवीमहम् ॥

11. O motherland, auspicious be thy woodlands, auspicious be thy hills and snow-clad mountains. Unslain, unwounded, unsubdued, I rule over the Earth, on earth, the nourisher of all, cultivated by the peasants, full of various kinds of cereals and plants, inhabited by men of different complexions, on the firm, vast earth, well-guarded by the king against danger. (3265)[1]

१२. यत् ते मध्यं पृथिवि यच्च नभ्यं यास्त ऊर्जस्तन्वः संबभूवुः ।
तासु नो धेह्यभि नः पवस्व माता भूमिः पुत्रो अहं पृथिव्याः ।
पर्जन्यः पिता स उ नः पिपर्तु ॥

12. O motherland, whatever act of justice is thine, whatever act of welfare for the military men is thine, whatever invigorating articles thou growest out of thy body, set us in their midst. Purify us. I am the son of Earth, Earth is my Mother. Cloud is my father, may it nourish us. (3266)[2]

१३. यस्यां वेदिं परिगृह्णन्ति भूम्यां यस्यां यज्ञं तन्वते विश्वकर्माणः ।
यस्यां मीयन्ते स्वरवः पृथिव्यामूर्ध्वाः शुक्रा आहुत्याः पुरस्तात् ।
सा नो भूमिर्वर्धयद् वर्धमाना ॥

13. Earth on whose surface people prepare the altar for performing the Yajna, in which all enterprising persons perform philanthropic deeds. In whom the stakes of sacrifice, resplendent, are fixed and raised on high before pouring the oblation, where encouraging sermons are delivered, may she, this motherland, prospering, make us prosper. (3267)

१४. यो नो द्वेषत् पृथिवि यः पृतन्याद् योऽभिदासान्मनसा यो वधेन ।
तं नो भूमे रन्धय पूर्वकृत्वरि ॥

14. The man who hates us, O motherland! Who fights against us, who wants to subjugate us, or kill us with a deadly weapon, make him our thrall as thou hast done before. (3268)

१५. त्वज्जातास्त्वयि चरन्ति मर्त्यास्त्वं बिभर्षि द्विपदस्त्वं चतुष्पदः ।
तवेमे पृथिवि पञ्च मानवा येभ्यो ज्योतिरमृतं मर्त्येभ्य उद्यन्त्सूर्यो रश्मिभिरातनोति ॥

[1]I: A brave general.

[2]Cloud is spoken of as the sire of man, as it produces for him, by timely rain, fruits, cereals and all articles that sustain his life.

15. Produced from thee, on thee move mortal creatures: thou bearest them, both quadruped and biped. Thine, O motherland! are these five human beings, for whom, the Sun as he rises spreads with his rays the light that is immortal. (3269)[1]

१६. ता नः प्रजाः सं दुह्रतां समग्रा वाचो मधु पृथिवि धेहि मह्यम् ॥

16. In concert may these men of ours advance themselves. O motherland! endow me with the sweetness of tongue. (3270)

१७. विश्वस्वं मातरमोषधीनां ध्रुवां भूमिं पृथिवीं धर्मणा धृताम् ।
शिवां स्योनामनु चरेम विश्वहा ॥

17. Sacrificing our all, for all the days of our life, we will serve our motherland, the producer of plants and herbs, steadfast, vast in extent, sustained through truth, knowledge and valour, gracious, and the giver of joy. (3271)

१८. महत् सधस्थं महती बभूविथ महान् वेग एजथुर्वेपथुष्टे महांस्त्वेन्द्रो रक्षत्यप्रमादम् ।
सा नो भूमे प्र रोचय हिरण्यस्येव संदृशि मा नो द्विक्षत कश्चन ॥

18. A vast dwelling place art thou for us. Thou art mighty. Great are thy speed, trembling and shaking. Great God guards thee with unceasing care. So make us shine, O motherland with the splendour of gold. Let no man hate us. (3272)[2]

१९. अग्निर्भूम्यामोषधीष्वग्निमापो बिभ्रत्यग्निरश्मसु । अग्निरन्तः पुरुषेषु गोष्वश्वेष्वग्नयः ॥

19. Fire is present in the earth, in plants, the waters hold fire in them, there is fire in stones. Fire abideth in men, fires abide in cows and steeds. (3273)[3]

२०. अग्निर्दिव आ तपत्यग्नेर्देवस्योर्व१न्तरिक्षम् । अग्निं मर्तास इन्धते हव्यवाहं घृतप्रियम् ॥

20. Fire gives shine and heat to the earth from the Sun, the spacious air is under the control of lustrous fire. Men enkindle fire, the lover of butter, and the bearer of oblation. (3274)

२१. अग्निवासाः पृथिव्यसितज्ञूस्त्विषीमन्तं संशितं मा कृणोतु ॥

21. O Motherland, thou art invested with a fiery mouth, thou art the displayer unto us of the unfettered God. Make me noble and energetic. (3275)

२२. भूम्यां देवेभ्यो ददति यज्ञं हव्यमरंकृतम् । भूम्यां मनुष्या जीवन्ति स्वधयान्नेन मर्त्याः ।
सा नो भूमिः प्राणमायुर्दधातु जरदष्टिं मा पृथिवी कृणोतु ॥

[1]Five human beings: Brahmanas, Kshatriyas, Vaishas, Shudras and Nishadas, or learned heroic persons, traders, artisans, and the illiterate.

[2]Indra may also mean, a just, truthful, brave king.

[3]There is fire in everything, whereby it preserves its existence. Fire adds to digestion and helps in the growth of plants.

22. On earth they offer sacrifice and dressed oblation to the learned. Mortal men live upon the earth by food and their inherent strength. May that Motherland grant us breath and vital power, O motherland, give me life of long duration! (3276)

२३. यस्ते गन्धः पृथिवि संबभूव यं बिभ्रत्योषधयो यमापः ।
यं गन्धर्वा अप्सरसश्च भेजिरे तेन मा सुरभिं कृणु मा नो द्विक्षत कश्चन ॥

23. Scent that hath risen from thee, O Earth! the fragrance which growing herbs and plants and waters carry, shared by men and women, therewith make thou me sweet: let no man hate me. (3277)[1]

२४. यस्ते गन्धः पुष्करमाविवेश यं संजभ्रुः सूर्याया विवाहे ।
अमर्त्याः पृथिवि गन्धमग्रे तेन मा सुरभिं कृणु मा नो द्विक्षत कश्चन ॥

24. Thy scent which entered and possessed the lotus, the scent which the immortal forces of nature like air assumed early in the morning, at the time of the rising of Dawn, O Earth! therewith make thou me sweet: let none hate me. (3278)[2]

२५. यस्ते गन्धः पुरुषेषु स्त्रीषु पुंसु भगो रुचिः । यो अश्वेषु वीरेषु यो मृगेषूत हस्तिषु ।
कन्यायां वर्चो यद् भूमे तेनास्माँ अपि सं सृज मा नो द्विक्षत कश्चन ॥

25. Thy scent in women and in men, the luck and light that is in males, the swiftness that is in heroes and in steeds, in sylvans beasts and elephants, the splendid energy of maids, therewith do thou unite us, O Motherland ! Let no man look on us with hate. (3279)

२६. शिला भूमिरश्मा पांसुः सा भूमिः संधृता धृता । तस्यै हिरण्यवक्षसे पृथिव्या अकरं नमः ॥

26. Rock, stone and dust constitute our Motherland, which being well-guarded by us, retains its independence. To this gold-breasted motherland, mine adoration do I pay. (3280)

२७. यस्यां वृक्षा वानस्पत्या ध्रुवास्तिष्ठन्ति विश्वहा ।
पृथिवीं विश्वधायसं धृतामच्छावदामसि ॥

27. On whom the trees, plants and herbs stand evermore immovable, we pay homage to that all-supporting motherland, whose independence we firmly protect. (3281)

२८. उदीराणा उतासीनास्तिष्ठन्तः प्रक्रामन्तः ।
पद्भ्यां दक्षिणसव्याभ्यां मा व्यथिष्महि भूम्याम् ॥

28. Sitting at ease or rising up, standing or going on our way, with our right foot and with our left we will not reel on the earth. (3282)

[1]Scent that hath risen: A philosophical definition of earth is gandhasvati, she who is endowed with fragrance or odour, which is regarded as its peculiar characteristic.

[2]Usha, Dawn, being the daughter of Sun is spoken of as सूर्या (विवाहे) प्रवाहे । प्रापणे.

२९. विमृग्वरीं पृथिवीमा वदामि क्षमां भूमिं ब्रह्मणा वावृधानाम् ।
ऊर्जं पुष्टं बिभ्रतीमन्नभागं घृतं त्वाभि नि षीदेम भूमे ॥

29. I speak to the vast Motherland, the purifier, patient, who groweth strong through the grace of God, O Earth ! may we recline on thee who bearest strength, increase, portioned share of food and butter. (3283)

३०. शुद्धा न आपस्तन्वे क्षरन्तु यो नः सेदुरप्रिये तं नि दध्मः ।
पवित्रेण पृथिवि मोत् पुनामि ॥

30. O Motherland ! let pure waters flow for our bodies. We treat him as our foe who would attack us. I cleanse myself through righteous conduct. (3284)

३१. यास्ते प्राचीः प्रदिशो या उदीचीर्यास्ते भूमे अधराद् याश्च पश्चात् ।
स्योनास्ता मह्यं चरते भवन्तु मा नि पप्तं भुवने शिश्रियाणः ॥

31. O Motherland! be thine eastern and thy northern regions, those lying southward and those lying eastward, propitious unto me in all my movements. Living in my country may I never suffer moral degradation. (3285)

३२. मा नः पश्चान्मा पुरस्तान्नुदिष्ठा मोत्तरादधरादुत ।
स्वस्ति भूमे नो भव मा विदन् परिपन्थिनो वरीयो यावया वधम् ॥

32. Drive us not from the west or east, drive us not from the north or south. Be gracious unto me, O Motherland! let not the robbers find us; keep death away from us. (3286)

३३. यावत् तेऽभि विपश्यामि भूमे सूर्येण मेदिना । तावन्मे चक्षुर्मा मेष्टोत्तरामुत्तरां समाम् ॥

33. Long as, O Motherland! on thee, I look around, with the help of kind Sun, so long, through each succeeding year, may not my power of vision fail. (3287)

३४. यच्छयानः पर्यावर्ते दक्षिणं सव्यमभि भूमे पार्श्वम् ।
उत्तानास्त्वा प्रतीचीं यत् पृष्टीभिरधिशेमहे ।
मा हिंसीस्तत्र नो भूमे सर्वस्य प्रतिशीवरि ॥

34. When, as I lie, O Earth, I turn upon my right side and my left, when stretched at all our length we lay our ribs on thee who liest beneath us, do us no injury there, O Earth who furnishest a bed for all. (3288)[1]

३५. यत् ते भूमे विखनामि क्षिप्रं तदपि रोहतु । मा ते मर्म विमृग्वरी मा ते हृदयमर्पिपम् ॥

35. Let what I dig from thee, O Earth! rapidly spring and grow again. O Purifier! let me not pierce through thy vitals or thy heart. (3289)[2]

[1] Let us enjoy undisturbed sleep in whatever posture we sleep.

[2] At the time of digging a plant or herb, one should be cautious not to injure the portion of the earth which possesses the juice and strength to help the growth of the plant.

३६. ग्रीष्मस्ते भूमे वर्षाणि शरद्धेमन्तः शिशिरो वसन्तः ।
ऋतवस्ते विहिता हायनीरहोरात्रे पृथिवि नो दुहाताम् ।।

36. O vast motherland, God hath created for thee, the summer, rainy, autumn, winter, dewy and spring seasons, years, day and night! may they all pour out abundance for us. (3290)

३७. याप सर्पं विजमाना विमृग्वरी यस्यामासन्नग्नयो ये अप्स्व१न्तः ।
परा दस्यून् ददती देवपीयूनिन्द्रं वृणाना पृथिवी न वृत्रम् । शक्राय दध्रे वृषभाय वृष्णे ।।

37. The purifying motherland is afraid of a person crooked like the serpent. In her reside highly learned persons found among the subjects. She shuns the god-blaspheming ignoble persons, accepts the prosperous king, and not a mean, low person, as her lord, and remains under the sway of the strong, mighty, powerful king. (3291)

३८. यस्यां सदोहविर्धाने यूपो यस्यां निमीयते । ब्रह्माणो यस्यामर्चन्त्यृग्भिः साम्ना यजुर्विदः ।
युज्यन्ते यस्यामृत्विजः सोममिन्द्राय पातवे ।।

38. On whom are erected Assembly halls and store-rooms for corn. On whom is hoisted the national flag of victory. On whom the Yaju-knowing Brahmanas worship God by reciting Rigvedic hymns and chanting the psalms of the Sāmaveda. On whom the Yogis, the worshippers of God in all seasons, resort to smadhi for the attainment of salvation for the soul. (3292)

३९. यस्यां पूर्वे भूतकृत ऋषयो गा उदानृचुः । सप्त सत्रेण वेधसो यज्ञेन तपसा सह ।।

39. On whom the ancient learned sages, who made the past of our country, sang forth Vedic verses, by controlling their seven organs, with their fervent zeal and sacrifice. (3293)

४०. सा नो भूमिरा दिशतु यद्धनं कामयामहे । भगो अनुप्रयुङ्क्तामिन्द्र एतु पुरोगवः ।।

40. May she, our Motherland, assign to us the opulence for which we yearn. May God aid us in every way, may He lead us on the right path. (3294)

४१. यस्यां गायन्ति नृत्यन्ति भूम्यां मर्त्या व्यै᳡लबाः ।
युध्यन्ते यस्यामाक्रन्दो यस्यां वदति दुन्दुभिः ।
सा नो भूमिः प्र णुदतां सपत्नानसपत्नं मा पृथिवी कृणोतु ।।

41. May she, our motherland, whereon men sing and dance, whereon warriors battle with varied shout and noise, and the war-cry and the drum resound, may she drive off our foemen, may Earth rid me of my foe. (3295)

४२. यस्यामन्नं व्रीहियवौ यस्यां इमाः पञ्च कृष्टयः । भूम्यै पर्जन्यपत्न्यै नमोऽस्तु वर्षमेदसे ।।

42. On whom grow wheat, rice and barley, on whom are born five races of mankind, homage to her, nourished by the cloud, and loved by the rain. (3296)[1]

४३. यस्याः पुरो देवकृताः क्षेत्रे यस्या विकुर्वते ।
प्रजापतिः पृथिवीं विश्वगर्भामाशामाशां रण्यां नः कृणोतु ॥

43. Whose castles and fortresses have been constructed by efficient engineers, in each province of whose men work hard for advancement, may God, the Lord of Life make our Motherland, who beareth all precious things in her womb, pleasant to us on every side! (3297)

४४. निधिं बिभ्रती बहुधा गुहा वसु मणिं हिरण्यं पृथिवी ददातु मे ।
वसूनि नो वसुदा रासमाना देवी दधातु सुमनस्यमाना ॥

44. May Earth, who bears her treasure stored up in many a place, grant me gold, gems and riches. May our Motherland the giver of opulence and the bestower of wealth nourish us with love and favour. (3298)

४५. जनं बिभ्रती बहुधा विवाचसं नानाधर्माणं पृथिवी यथौकसम् ।
सहस्रं धारा द्रविणस्य मे दुहां ध्रुवेव धेनुरनपस्फुरन्ती ॥

45. May my Motherland, bearing folk speaking different languages, holding different religious views, treating them all as residents of the same house, pour, like a constant cow that never fails, a thousand streams of treasure to enrich me. (3299)

४६. यस्ते सर्पो वृश्चिकस्तृष्टदंश्मा हेमन्तजब्धो भृमलो गुहा शये ।
क्रिमिर्जिन्वत् पृथिवि यद्यदेजति प्रावृषि तन्नः सर्पन्मोप सृपद् यच्छिवं तेन नो मृड ॥

46. Thy snake, thy sharply stinging scorpion, lying concealed, bewildered, chilled with cold of winter; the worm, O Motherland, each thing that in the rains revives and stirs, creeping, forbear to creep on us! With all things gracious bless thou us. (3300)

४७. ये ते पन्थानो बहवो जनायना रथस्य वर्त्मानसश्च यातवे ।
यैः संचरन्त्युभये भद्रपापास्तं पन्थानं जयेमानमित्रमतस्करं यच्छिवं तेन नो मृड ॥

47. Thy many paths on which the people travel, the road for car and wain to journey over, upon which walk both the virtuous and the sinners, that pathway may we attain without a foe or thief. With all things gracious bless thou us. (3301)

४८. मल्वं बिभ्रती गुरुभृद् भद्रपापस्य निधनं तितिक्षुः ।
वराहेण पृथिवी संविदाना सूकराय वि जिहीते मृगाय ॥

[1]Five races: The learned, the warriors, traders, artisans and labourers.

48. Earth, that supports all things light and heavy, that bears the corpses of the good and bad, that receives ample water from the rainy cloud, revolves round the Sun, that removes dirt and impurity with its rays. (3302)

४९. ये त आरण्याः पशवो मृगा वने हिताः सिंहा व्याघ्राः पुरुषादश्चरन्ति ।
उलं वृकं पृथिवि दुच्छुनामित ऋक्षीकां रक्षो अप बाधयास्मत् ॥

49. O Motherland, keep away at a distance from us, all sylvan beasts of thine, deer reared in the forest, man-eaters, like lions, tigers, hyena, wolf, annoying bear and violent persons! (3303)

५०. ये गन्धर्वा अप्सरसो ये चारायाः किमीदिनः ।
पिशाचान्त्सर्वा रक्षांसि तानस्मद् भूमे यावय ॥

50. O Motherland, keep far from us all libidinous men and women, misers, worthless persons who care not for the life and property of others, meat-eaters, and men of violent nature! (3304)

५१. यां द्विपादः पक्षिणः संपतन्ति हंसाः सुपर्णाः शकुना वयांसि ।
यस्यां वातो मातरिश्वेयते रजांसि कृण्वंश्च्यावयंश्च वृक्षान् ।
वातस्य प्रवामुपवामनु वात्यर्चिः ॥

51. On whom the winged bipeds, the swans, the eagles, and birds of various kinds fly together. On whom the Wind from heaven comes rushing, rousing the dust and uprooting trees. Fire kindles brighter by the blowing of air hither and thither. (3305)

५२. यस्यां कृष्णमरुणं च संहिते अहोरात्रे विहिते भूम्यामधि ।
वर्षेण भूमिः पृथिवी वृतावृता सा नो दधातु भद्रया प्रिये धामनिधामनि ॥

52. Earth, upon whom are settled, joined together, the night and day, the dusky and the ruddy, the vast motherland encompassed by the rain round her, happily may she establish us in each delightful dwelling place. (3306)

५३. द्यौश्च म इदं पृथिवी चान्तरिक्षं च मे व्यचः ।
अग्निः सूर्य आपो मेधां विश्वे देवाश्च सं ददुः ॥

53. Heaven, Earth, the realm of Middle Air, all these extended regions are meant for my advancement. May Fire, Sun, Waters, all the divine forces of nature grant me mental power to control them. (3307)[1]

५४. अहमस्मि सहमान उत्तरो नाम भूम्याम् । अभीषाडस्मि विश्वाषाडाशामाशां विषासहिः ॥

54. I am prepared to suffer for my country. I am called the lord superior on earth, triumphant, all-conquering, the conqueror on every side. (3308)

[1]Them: Heaven, Earth, Mid-Air realm.

५५. अदो यद् देवि प्रथमाना पुरस्ताद् देवैरुक्ता व्यसर्पो महित्वम् ।
आ त्वा सुभूतमविशत् तदानीमकल्पयथाः प्रदिशश्चतस्रः ॥

55. O beautiful Motherland, when in times immemorial the learned spoke of thee as vast and extended, and spread around that grandeur of thine; then into thee passed many a charm and glory; thou modest for thyself the world's four regions. (3309)

५६. ये ग्रामा यदरण्यं याः सभा अधि भूम्याम् । ये संग्रामाः समितयस्तेषु चारु वदेम ते ॥

56. In hamlets and in woodland, and in all Assemblys on earth, on battlefields and in conferences, we will sing thy glory, O motherland! (3310)[1]

५७. अश्व इव रजो दुधुवे वि तान् जनान् य आक्षियन् पृथिवीं यादजायत ।
मन्द्राग्रेत्वरी भुवनस्य गोपा वनस्पतीनां गृभिरोषधीनाम् ॥

57. Just as the horse scattereth the dust, so the motherland since its creation hath scattered all those persons who have tormented it. This motherland is full of delight, leader and head of all the world, the protector of the universe, the trees, protectoress and the plants' upholder. (3311)

५८. यद् वदामि मधुमत् तद् वदामि यदीक्षे तद् वनन्ति मा ।
त्विषीमानस्मि जूतिमानवान्यान् हन्मि दोधतः ॥

58. Whenever I speak of my country, I speak with honey-sweetness. Whenever I look upon my countrymen they love me in return, Dazzling, impetuous am I. I slay others who attack my country. (3312)

५९. शन्तिवा सुरभिः स्योना कीलालोध्नी पयस्वती ।
भूमिरधि ब्रवीतु मे पृथिवी पयसा सह ॥

59. May my vast motherland, mild, sweetly odorous, gracious, with food in her breast, full of milk and water, bestow her benison, with milk, on me. (3313)

६०. यामन्वैच्छद्धविषा विश्वकर्मान्तरर्णवे रजसि प्रविष्टाम् ।
भुजिष्यं१ पात्रं निहितं गुहा यदाविर्भोगे अभवन्मातृमद्भ्यः ॥

60. When God, the Doer of all deeds, desires to fill with corn, the Earth, set in the ocean of Mid air, all eatable objects hidden in the earth, appear for the devotees of their motherland. (3314)

६१. त्वमस्यावपनी जनानामदितिः कामदुघा पप्रथाना ।
यत् त ऊनं तत् त आ पूरयाति प्रजापतिः प्रथमजा ऋतस्य ॥

61. O Motherland, thou art the field, where men are born. Thou art undecaying, the fulfiller of our desires, and worthy of homage. God, Who existed before the creation of the universe, supplieth thee with whatever thou lackest! (3315)

[1]Assemblys: Rajya Sabha: Parliament; Vidya Sabha: Educational Conferences; Nyaya Sabha: Courts of Justice.

६२. उपस्थास्ते अनमीवा अयक्ष्मा अस्मभ्यं सन्तु पृथिवि प्रसूता: ।
दीर्घं न आयु: प्रतिबुध्यमाना वयं तुभ्यं बलिहृत: स्याम ॥

62. O Motherland, let our children reared in thy lap, be free from sickness and consumption. May we live long, Wakeful, watching, may we sacrifice our all for thee! (3316)

६३. भूमे मातर्नि धेहि मा भद्रया सुप्रतिष्ठितम् ।
संविदाना दिवा कवे श्रियां मा धेहि भूत्याम् ॥

63. O Motherland, set thou me happily in a position of honour. Of one accord with the Sun, O revolving Earth, set me in glory and in wealth. (3317)

Chapter (Anuvāka) 2

HYMN II

१. नडमा रोह न ते अत्र लोक इदं सीसं भागधेयं त एहि ।
यो गोषु यक्ष्म: पुरुषेषु यक्ष्मस्तेन त्वं साकमधराङ् परेहि ॥

1. O depraved person, be a prey to this sharp weapon. There is no place for thee in this world. Thou deservest to be shot with this lead bullet. Come hither to be slain. Thou art the giver of pain, like consumption to the kine and men, fall down with that, and run far away! (3318)[1]

२. अघशंसदु:शंसाभ्यां करेणानुकरेण च । यक्ष्मं च सर्वं तेनेतो मृत्युं च निरजामसि ।

2. Let us chase and banish from the State with a good device all consumptive malady and death, along with the chief agents and helpers of the sinners ann evil-doers. (3319)

३. निरितो मृत्युं निर्ऋतिं निररातिमजामसि ।
यो नो द्वेष्टि तमद्धयग्ने अक्रव्याद् यमु द्विष्मस्तमु ते प्र सुवामसि ॥

3. We expel from the state death and poverty. We drive away malignity. O King, thou who eatest not meat, punish him who hateth us: him whom we dislike we send to thee for justice. (3320)

४. यद्यग्नि: क्रव्याद् यदि वा व्याघ्र इमं गोष्ठं प्रविवेशान्योका: ।
तं माषाज्यं कृत्वा प्र हिणोमि दूरं स गच्छत्वप्सुषदोऽप्यग्नीन् ॥

4. If a meat-eater virulent like fire, or a person violent like a tiger, wandering, having no home, enters our Assembly-Hall, I turn him away with a deadly weapon. Let him appear before the strict officials of the King who rules over his subjects. (3321)[2]

[1]That: The low mentality of giving pain.
[2]अप्सु: प्रजासु ।

५. यत् त्वा क्रुद्धाः प्रचक्रुर्मन्युना पुरुषे मृते । सुकल्पमग्ने तत् त्वया पुनस्त्वोद्दीपयामसि ॥

5. O culprit, if angered persons full of righteous indignation, on the murder of a man, give thee condign punishment, thou shouldst tolerate it. We encourage thee again for noble conduct! (3322)[1]

६. पुनस्त्वादित्या रुद्रा वसवः पुनर्ब्रह्मा वसुनीतिरग्ने ।
पुनस्त्वा ब्रह्मणस्पतिराधाद् दीर्घायुत्वाय शतशारदाय ॥

6. O King, due to thy knowledge and valour, verily have the Aditya Brahmcharis, learned persons, noble men, the Vedic scholar, the bestower of good things, verily the lord of wealth, disposed thee for long life lasting through a hundred autumns. (3323)[2]

७. यो अग्निः क्रव्यात् प्रविवेश नो गृहमिमं पश्यन्नितरं जातवेदसम् ।
तं हरामि पितृयज्ञाय दूरं स घर्ममिन्धां परमे सधस्थे ॥

7. The meat-eating culprit, ferocious like fire, who enters our house, knowing the superior personality of the learned king, is taken away far by me to be punished by the state officials. May he be tried and sentenced in a supreme court of justice. (3324)[3]

८. क्रव्यादमग्निं प्र हिणोमि दूरं यमराज्ञो गच्छतु रिप्रवाहः ।
इहायमितरो जातवेदा देवो देवेभ्यो हव्यं वहतु प्रजानन् ॥

8. I take afar, the meat-eating culprit, May the sin-bearer appear before the state officials of the just King. In this world, the immaculate, virtuous king, the knower of the Vedas, anxious for conquest, full of knowledge, should bestow nice eatables on the learned. (3325)[4]

९. क्रव्यादमग्निमिषितो हरामि जनान् दृंहन्तं वज्रेण मृत्युम् ।
नि तं शास्मि गार्हपत्येन विद्वान् पितॄणां लोकेऽपि भागो अस्तु ॥

9. Deputed by the subjects, I destroy with weapon, the meat-eating culprit, ferocious like fire, who spreads Destruction amongst the people. To the virtuous, I, knowing well, always give instructions in the duties of domestic life, so that he may find a decent place in the society of the learned. (3326)[5]

१०. क्रव्यादमग्निं शशमानमुक्थ्यं१ प्र हिणोमि पथिभिः पितृयाणैः ।
मा देवयानैः पुनरा गा अत्रैवैधि पितृषु जागृहि त्वम् ॥

[1]If a culprit reforms himself by undergoing the punishment administered, he should be given every facility by the state officials to behave better and resort to noble conduct.

[2]Compare this verse with *Yajur*, 12-44.

[3]See *Rig*, 10-16-10. Me: An important public man.

[4]I: A responsible public-spirited person. See *Rig*, 10-16-9, *Yajur*, 35-19.

[5]I; The King.

10. Treading on the path of the learned, I keep far away from the virtuous, the meat-eating culprit, ferocious like fire. O sinner, don't come again on the path of the learned to disturb them! O virtuous, remain here, remain awake amongst learned Fathers! (3327)[1]

११. समिन्धते संकसुकं स्वस्तये शुद्धा भवन्तः शुचयः पावकाः ।
जहाति रिप्रमत्येन एति समिद्धो अग्निः सुपुना पुनाति ॥

11. Learned persons pure in mind, purifiers of others, clean in body, for the good of humanity, kindle a good ruler like fire. Under his sway, a sinner abandons his sin, and gives up his impurity. The refulgent ruler, an efficient purifier, purifies the sinner. (3328)

१२. देवो अग्निः संकसुको दिवस्पृष्ठान्यारुहत् । मुच्यमानो निरेणसोऽमोगस्माँ अशस्त्याः ॥

12. The Lustrous, Omniscient, God, the Chastiser of the wicked like fire, pervades all the worlds in space. Being Himself free from sin, He hath delivered us from guilt. (3329)

१३. अस्मिन् वयं संकसुके अग्नौ रिप्राणि मृज्महे ।
अभूम यज्ञियाः शुद्धाः प्र ण आयूंषि तारिषत् ॥

13. Under the guidance of this Omniscient God, we wipe our impurities away. In His Company we have become pure and fit to perform noble deeds. May He prolong our lives. (3330)

१४. संकसुको विकसुको निर्ऋथो यश्च निस्वरः । ते ते यक्ष्मं सवेदसो दूराद् दूरमनीनशन् ॥

14. A just ruler, an efficient administrator, a learned person, a constant preacher, all these benefactors of humanity, have expelled consumption far, far off from thee. (3331)[2]

१५. यो नो अश्वेषु वीरेषु यो नो गोष्वजाविषु । क्रव्यादं निर्णुदामसि यो अग्निर्जनयोपनः ॥

15. We expel the raw flesh-eating disease that troubles men, and is present in our horses, in our heroes, cows, goats and sheep. (3332)

१६. अन्येभ्यस्त्वा पुरुषेभ्यो गोभ्यो अश्वेभ्यस्त्वा ।
निः क्रव्यादं नुदामसि यो अग्निर्जीवितयोपनः ॥

16. O raw flesh-eating disease that destroys life, we expel thee from living men, cows and horses! (3333)

१७. यस्मिन् देवा अमृजत यस्मिन् मनुष्या उत ।
तस्मिन् घृतस्तावो मृष्ट्वा त्वमग्ने दिवं रुह ॥

17. O wise soul, under Whose shelter the sages and ordinary mortals have purified themselves, praising that Divine God, and releasing thyself from sins, mount up to the abode of salvation! (3334)

[1]I: The King.
[2]Thee: The subjects.

१८. समिद्धो अग्न आहुत स नो माभ्यपक्रमीः । अत्रैव दीदिहि द्यवि ज्योक् च सूर्यं दृशे ॥

18. O Adorable God, Resplendent art Thou, Desert us not. Remain here in our heart, so that we may see Thee for long, as we see the lustrous Sun in heaven! (3335)

१९. सीसे मृड्ढ्वं नडे मृड्ढ्वमग्नौ संकसुके च यत् । अथो अव्यां रामायां शीर्षक्तिमुपबर्हणे ॥

19. Just as lead removes the dross of a metal, so purify the soul through the Zeal of God's contemplation. Just as a sieve made of reed removes the chaff of flour, so purify thyself by passing thyself through austerity, the sieve of God. Just as dirt is burnt in an all-destroying fire, so purify thyself through the fervent devotion of God. Just as headache is removed by reclining on a pillow, so remove thy afflictions by resigning thyself to God, the Protector, and the Bestower of joy! (3336)

२०. सीसे मलं सादयित्वा शीर्षक्तिमुपबर्हणे । अव्यामसिक्न्यां मृष्ट्वा शुद्धा भवत यज्ञियाः ॥

20. O learned devotees of God, just as lead removes the dross of a mental, and headache is cured by reclining on a pillow, so abandoning all sins, purify yourselves by faith in God, the Protector, and free from fetters! (3337)

२१. परं मृत्यो अनु परेहि पन्थां यस्त एष इतरो देवयानात् ।
चक्षुष्मते शृण्वते ते ब्रवीमीहेमे वीरा बहवो भवन्तु ॥

21. Go onward, O Death, pursue thy special pathway apart from that which the emancipated souls are wont to tread. To thee I say who hast eyes and hearest: great grow the number of these stalwart persons around us! (3338)[1]

२२. इमे जीवा वि मृतैराववृत्रन्नभूद् भद्रा देवहूतिर्नो अद्य ।
प्राञ्चो अगाम नृतये हसाय सुवीरासो विदथमा वदेम ॥

22. All these souls are surrounded by different causes of death. Our prayer to God now is successful. Let us advance for dancing and for laughter. Being highly brave let us think of battle. (3339)

२३. इमं जीवेभ्यः परिधिं दधामि मैषां नु गादपरो अर्थमेतम् ।
शतं जीवन्तः शरदः पुरूचीस्तिरो मृत्युं दधतां पर्वतेन ॥

23. I lay this law for the living: let none of these transgress this law. May they survive a hundred lengthened years, and may they keep death away through the fulness of knowledge and Brahmcharya. (3340)[2]

[1]Spiritually-minded strong persons lead a long life. See *Rig*, 10-18-1; *Yajur*, 35-7.

[2]Pt. Khem Karan Das Trivedi has translated पर्वतेन as through the fulness of knowledge and Brahmcharya. See *Rig*, 10-18-4, and *Yajur*, 35-15. Maharshi Dayananda has commented upon this verse in the *Sanskār Vidhi* in Jāta Karma ceremony. I: God. God has fixed hundred years as the minimum age of man. Every one should try not to die before this age.

२४. आ रोहतायुर्जरसं वृणाना अनुपूर्वं यतमाना यदि स्थ ।
तान् वस्त्वष्टा सुजनिमा सजोषाः सर्वमायुर्नयतु जीवनाय ॥

24. O men, keeping old age far away, attain to full life. Striving regularly remain celibate in life. May God, your Friend, grant you a decent birth, and full age for existence! (3341)

२५. यथाहान्यनुपूर्वं भवन्ति यथर्तव ऋतुभिर्यन्ति साकम् ।
यथा न पूर्वमपरो जहात्येवा धातरायूंषि कल्पयैषाम् ॥

25. As the days follow days in close succession, and the seasons duly come with the seasons, as the son dies not before the father, so constitute the lives of these, O God! (3342)

२६. अश्मन्वती रीयते सं रभध्वं वीरयध्वं प्र तरता सखायः ।
अत्रा जहीत ये असन् दुरेवा अनमीवानुत्तरेमाभि वाजान् ॥

26. O friends, this world is a stream full of impediments and struggles, work in cooperation, have courage, cross it struggling hard. Throw in it the burden of your sins, and let us enjoy food free from disease! (3343)[1]

२७. उत्तिष्ठता प्र तरता सखायोऽश्मन्वती नदी स्यन्दत इयम् ।
अत्रा जहीत ये असन्नशिवाः शिवान्त्स्योनानुत्तरेमाभि वाजान् ॥

27. O friends, rise up erect, this stormy stream of the world is flowing fast before us. Abandon in it your malignant sins, let us obtain powers benign and friendly. (3344)

२८. वैश्वदेवीं वर्चस आ रभध्वं शुद्धा भवन्तः शुचयः पावकाः ।
अतिक्रामन्तो दुरिता पदानि शतं हिमाः सर्ववीरा मदेम ॥

28. Becoming pure and bright and purifying begin for splendour the study of the Vedas, the benefactors of all the learned. Overpowering troublous vices, may we rejoice with heroic sons for a hundred winters. (3345)

२९. उदीचीनैः पथिभिर्वायुमद्भिरतिक्रामन्तोऽवरान् परेभिः ।
त्रिः सप्त कृत्व ऋषयः परेता मृत्युं प्रत्यौहन् पदयोपनेन ॥

29. Highly advanced sages, through the exercises of breath-control, full of far-reaching consequences, leading to the Almighty God, overpowering the sufferings of life, have conquered death, by keeping its causes away, through righteous thought, word and deed, and correct use of the seven organs. (3346)[2]

[1]This verse preaches that life is a struggle. Success in it depends upon cooperation, courage, hard work, and nobility of character. Griffith interprets it, as if a corpse is being carried to the burial ground and a stony stream is to be crossed in the way. Sorry Griffith has not been able to understand the lofty significance of the verse. See *Rig* 10-53-8, *Yajur*, 35-10. This verse has been commented upon by Maharshi Dayananda in *Sanskāra Vidhi* in the chapter on marriage.

[2]Seven organs: Two eyes, two ears, two nostrils and mouth.

३०. मृत्योः पदं योपयन्त एत द्राघीय आयुः प्रतरं दधानाः ।
आसीना मृत्युं नुदता सधस्थेऽथ जीवासो विदथमा वदेम ॥

30. Avoiding the approach of death, prolonging this life, and making it fit to release us from all afflictions, exercising yogic practices, keep death at a distance. O mortals, sitting in an Assembly, let us exchange ideas on different topics of knowledge. (3347)

३१. इमा नारीरविधवाः सुपत्नीराञ्जनेन सर्पिषा सं स्पृशन्ताम् ।
अनश्रवो अनमीवाः सुरत्ना आ रोहन्तु जनयो योनिमग्रे ॥

31. Let these unwidowed dames with goodly husbands adorn themselves with fragrant balms and unguent. Decked with fair jewels, tearless, sound and healthy, let the dames occupy a foremost position in the house. (3348)

३२. व्याकरोमि हविषाहमेतौ ब्रह्मणा व्य१हं कल्पयामि ।
स्वधां पितृभ्यो अजरां कृणोमि दीर्घेणायुषा समिमान्त्सृजामि ॥

32. I endow both husband and wife with food, and equip them with Vedic knowledge. I grant immortal spiritual force to the learned sages, and to these men give life of long duration. (3349)[1]

३३. यो नो अग्निः पितरो हृत्स्व१न्तराविवेशामृतो मर्त्येषु ।
मय्यहं तं परि गृह्णामि देवं मा सो अस्मान् द्विक्षत मा वयं तम् ॥

33. O learned sages, that Immortal God hath entered and possessed our mortal bosoms. I grasp and hold Him within me. Let him not hate us, may we never hate Him. (3350)

३४. अपावृत्य गार्हपत्यात् क्रव्यादा प्रेत दक्षिणा ।
प्रियं पितृभ्य आत्मने ब्रह्मभ्यः कृणुता प्रियम् ॥

34. Go on treading the straight path of progress, abandoning that of ignorance, the enemy of knowledge. Do that which is delightful to the sages, Vedic scholars, and yourselves. (3351)

३५. द्विभागधनमादाय प्र क्षिणात्यवर्त्या । अग्निः पुत्रस्य ज्येष्ठस्य यः क्रव्यादनिराहितः ॥

35. A voracious vice, not banished, snatches double the wealth of a great reformer, and crushes him with poverty. (3352)[2]

३६. यत् कृषते यद् वनुते यच्च वस्नेन विन्दते । सर्वं मर्त्यस्य तन्नास्ति क्रव्याच्चेदनिराहितः ॥

36. What man acquires by plough, or inherits from ancestors, or earns through trade, he loses all if he does not give up the vice of meat-eating. (3353)

[1]I: God.

[2]Double wealth: The fruit of good acts performed in the past life and present one. Reformers should purge themselves of all vices. Even one vice unaverted is adequate to bring about his fall.

३७. अयज्ञियो हृतवर्चा भवति नैनेन हविरत्तवे । छिनत्ति कृष्या गोर्धनाद् यं क्रव्यादनुवर्त्तते ।।

37. A man addicted to the vice of meat-eating becomes unholy, splendour-rift. His sacrifice is unfit to eat. He is deprived of tilth, of cows, of riches. (3354)

३८. मुहुर्गृध्यैः प्र वदत्यार्ति मर्त्यो नित्य । क्रव्याद् यानग्निरन्तिकादनुविद्वान् वितावति ।।

38. The man, to whom the vice of meat-eating, troublesome like fire, sticks, knowing his nature, close at hand, is put to distress, and he cries again and again for objects he covets. (3355)

३९. ग्राह्याः गृहा सं सृज्यन्ते स्त्रिया यन्म्रियते पतिः ।
ब्रह्मैव विद्वानेष्योऽ यः क्रव्यादं निरादधत् ।।

39. When the husband of a woman loses spirits and becomes devoid of effort, the inmates of the house are plunged in distress. A learned Vedic scholar must be sought for to drive away the vice of meat-eating. (3356)[1]

४०. यद् रिप्रं शमलं चकृम यच्च दुष्कृतम् । आपो मा तस्माच्छुम्भन्त्वग्नेः संकसुकाच्च यत् ।।

40. Forsaking the company of a noble, just ruler, if we have committed any evil, act of impurity, or sin, let highly learned persons purge me from all that. (3357)[2]

४१. ता अधरादुदीचीराववृत्रन् प्रजानतीः पथिभिर्देवयानैः ।
पर्वतस्य वृषभस्याधि पृष्ठे नवाश्चरन्ति सरितः पुराणीः ।।

41. The highly learned sages, morally marching upward from a low position, equipped with lofty knowledge, behave like learned persons who resort to the means that lead to salvation. Just as on the summit of the raining mountain fresh streams are flowing from times immemorial, so on the support of the Benevolent God, the Rainer of all sorts of joys, roam about the aged and new young sages. (3358)

४२. अग्ने अक्रव्यान्निष्क्रव्यादं नुदा देवयजनं वह ।।

42. O God, Who behavest not like a flesh-eating animal or man, drive away the meat-eater, and bring unto us a noble person, the devotee of the learned. (3359)

४३. इमं क्रव्यादा विवेशायं क्रव्यादमन्वगात् । व्याघ्रौ कृत्वा नानानं तं हरामि शिवापरम् ।।

43. The vice of meat-eating hath caught hold of this man, who follows the vice of meat-eating, separating both these tigers one from the other, I bear away the ungracious vice. (3360)[3]

[1]An educated woman should not marry a man who is lacking in enterprise and has no guts. She should marry a learned person who can drive away all vices from the family.

[2]The word आपः has been translated by Maharshi Dayanand as highly learned persons. see *Yajur*, 6-27.

[3]Both the tigers: The vice of meat-eating, and the man addicted to it.

४४. अन्तर्धिर्देवानां परिधिर्मनुष्या॒णामग्निर्गार्हपत्य उभयानन्तरा श्रितः ॥

44. God, Who is worshipped by the house-holders, holds the sages within Himself, is the rampart and defence of men, stands between them both. (3361)

४५. जीवानामायुः प्र तिर त्वमग्ने पितॄणां लोकमपि गच्छन्तु ये मृताः ।
सुगार्हपत्यो वितपन्नरातिमुषामुषां श्रेयसीं धेह्यस्मै ॥

45. O God, prolong the lives of those who are energetic. Let the unenergetic even seek the company of the learned guardians. As a good king torments the foe, so give this devotee goodly wealth each morning! (3362)

४६. सर्वानग्ने सहमानः सपत्नानैषामूर्जं रयिमस्मासु धेहि ॥

46. Subduing all our adversaries, O King, give us their food, their strength and their possessions! (3363)

४७. इममिन्द्रं वह्निं पप्रिमन्वारभध्वं स वो निर्वक्षद् दुरितादवाद्यात् ।
तेनाप हत शरुमापतन्तं तेन रुद्रस्य परि पातास्ताम् ॥

47. Follow this king, the bearer of the burden of administration and the nourisher of his subjects. He will release you from trouble, and vice. With his help, O men, drive back the shaft that flies against you, with his aid, ward off the missile shot by a ferocious dacoit. (3364)

४८. अनड्वाहं प्लवमन्वारभध्वं स वो निर्वक्षद् दुरितादवद्यात् ।
आ रोहत सवितुर्नावमेतां षड्भिरुर्वीभिरमतिं तरेम ॥

48. O subjects, follow the king, who carries the ship of administration of the state, as an ox does the cart. He will release you from trouble and vice. Observe this state-policy of the King, which will enable you to overcome worldly afflictions and keep you in safe custody. Let us shun ignorance and unwisdom through six mighty forces! (3365)[1]

४९. अहोरात्रे अन्वेषि बिभ्रत् क्षेम्यस्तिष्ठन् प्रतरणः सुवीरः ।
अनातुरान्त्सुमनसस्तल्प बिभ्रज्ज्योगेव नः पुरुषगन्धिरेधि ॥

49. O God, the Giver of comfort to mankind like a couch, rearing and nourishing us day and night, the well-wisher of all, Mighty in power, steadfast, the Releaser of humanity from worldly griefs like a boat that makes the passengers cross the stream, Thou art ever active. Sustaining in Thyself the noble-minded and sinless persons, from times immemorial Thou art the Punisher of men for their ill deeds! (3366)

५०. ते देवेभ्य आ वृश्चन्ते पापं जीवन्ति सर्वदा ।
क्रव्याद् यानग्निरन्तिकादश्व इवानुवपते नडम् ॥

[1]Six mighty forces: Five organs of cognition and mind. This verse can be applied to God as well, Who carries the ship of the administration of the world.

50. They who sever themselves from the learned, always lead a life of sin, and misery. The vice of meat-eating, destructive like fire crushes them down from close at hand, as a horse tramples down the reeds. (3367)

५१. येऽश्रद्धा धनकाम्या क्रव्यादा समासते । ते वा अन्येषां कुम्भीं पर्यादधति सर्वदा ॥

51. The faithless, full of greed for wealth, who sit together to take meat, for ever set upon the fire the cauldron of others, not their own. (3368)[1]

५२. प्रेव पिपतिषति मनसा मुहुरा वर्तते पुनः । क्रव्याद् यानग्निरन्तिकादनु विद्वान् वितावति ॥

52. He whom the vice of meat-eating discovers from near and torments, though willing to go forward and make progress, is ever a prey to rebirth and degradation again and again. (3369)

५३. अविः कृष्णा भागधेयं पशूनां सीसं क्रव्यादपि चन्द्रं त आहुः ।
माषाः पिष्टा भागधेयं ते हव्यमरण्यान्या गह्वरं सचस्व ॥

53. O meat-eater, among tame beasts the black ewe is thy portion, thou deservest to be shot by the bright lead bullet, so do the learned say. Thou art fit to be crushed like mashed beans used for oblation. Go seek the dark wood and wildernesses. (3370)

५४. इषीकां जरतीमिष्ट्वा तिल्पिञ्जं दण्डनं नडम् ।
तमिन्द्र इध्मं कृत्वा यमस्याग्निं निरादधौ ॥

54. God, bestowing the laudable, attainable Vedic speech, revealing the mode of administration and punishment, entailing speedy action and exertion, has established the majesty of a just ruler. (3371)

५५. प्रत्यञ्चमर्कं प्रत्यर्पयित्वा प्रविद्वान् पन्थां वि ह्याविवेश ।
परामीषामसून् दिदेश दीर्घेणायुषा समिमान्त्सृजामि ॥

55. A highly learned person resigning himself to God, Who shines in the heart of each mortal, should attain to the path of salvation. I have controlled the subtle breaths of these seekers after salvation, and give them the boon of long existence. (3372)[2]

Chapter (Anuvāka) 3

HYMN III

१. पुमान् पुंसोऽधि तिष्ठ चर्मेहि तत्र ह्वयस्व यतमा प्रिया ते ।
यावन्तावग्रे प्रथमं समेयथुस्तद् वां वयो यमराज्ये समानम् ॥

[1]Faithless, greedy persons, having no resources of their own always depend upon the charity of others.

[2]I: God.

1. O man, lead other persons, Acquire knowledge. Therewith invoke the power thou lovest! Strong as ye were when first you met each other, still be your strength the same in household life. (3373)[1]

२. तावद् वां चक्षुस्तति वीर्याऽणि तावत् तेजस्ततिधा वाजिनानि ।
अग्निः शरीरं सचते यदैधोऽधा पक्वान्मिथुना सं भवाथः ॥

2. So strong your sight so may be your powers, so great your force, your energies so many. When the fire of Brahmcharya attends the body as its fuel, then may ye gain full strength of knowledge. (3374)

३. समस्मिँल्लोके समु देवयाने सं स्मा समेतं यमराज्येषु ।
पूतौ पवित्रैरुप तद्धवयेथां यद्यद् रेतो अधि वां संबभूव ॥

3. O husband and wife, remain together in this world, worship God together and exert together for the attainment of salvation. Purified by pure acts, invite the son born unto you! (3375)

४. आपस्पुत्रासो अभि सं विशध्वमिमं जीवं जीवधन्याः समेत्य ।
तासां भजध्वममृतं यमाहुर्यमोदनं पचति वां जनित्री ॥

4. O sons, praiseworthy among the mortals, associating yourselves with this soul, live in the company of the learned, mixing freely with them. In their midst serve the Immortal God, Whom the learned call the Rainer of joy, whom your Mother Nature pronounces as Firm and Established! (3376)

५. यं वां पिता पचति यं च माता रिप्रान्निर्मुक्त्यै शमलाच्च वाचः ।
स ओदनः शतधारः स्वर्ग उभे व्याऽप नभसी महित्वा ॥

5. O husband and wife, that God, Whom your mother and your sire, to banish sin and uncleanliness, remember fervently with their tongues, the Lord of myriad powers, the Bestower of joy, the Rainer of happiness, hath in His might pervaded earth and heaven! (3377)

६. उभे नभसी उभयांश्च लोकान् ये यज्वनामभिजिताः स्वर्गाः ।
तेषां ज्योतिष्मान् मधुमान् यो अग्रे तस्मिन् पुत्रैर्जरसि सं श्रयेथाम् ॥

6. O husband and wife, make earth, heaven your habitation. Live in the assembly of men and women. Live in comfortable positions secured by the sacrificers. Out of all these spheres, live in the foremost of them, full of light and knowledge, and remain there with your progeny till old age! (3378)

७. प्राचींप्राचीं प्रदिशमा रभेथामेतं लोकं श्रद्दधानाः सचन्ते ।
यद् वां पक्वं परिविष्टमग्नौ तस्य गुप्तये दम्पती सं श्रयेथाम् ॥

7. O husband and wife, advance to the East full of light. Such a brilliant position is acquired by the faithful alone. Stick together to domestic life to guard your mature knowledge you have dedicated to God! (3379)

[1]The power: God. You: Husband and wife. The pair should try to maintain during their domestic life the strength they possessed at the time of marriage, through observing the laws of Brahmcharya.

८. दक्षिणां दिशमभि नक्षमाणौ पर्यावर्तेथामभि पात्रमेतत् ।
तस्मिन् वां यमः पितृभिः संविदानः पक्वाय शर्म बहुलं नि यच्छात् ॥

8. O husband and wife, proceeding to the South, remember fully this God the Protector. Depending upon Him, acting upon the advice of the learned, your vow of Brahmcharya shall mightily protect your mature knowledge! (3380)

९. प्रतीची दिशामियमिद् वरं यस्यां सोमो अधिपा मृडिता च ।
तस्यां श्रयेथां सुकृतः सचेथामधा पक्वान्मिथुना सं भवाथः ॥

9. O husband and wife, best of the regions is indeed this western, where rules the Nourishing and Gracious God. Thither follow the pious, and resort to them for rest. Ye both with your mature knowledge should gain strength! (3381)

१०. उत्तरं राष्ट्रं प्रजयोत्तरावद् दिशामुदीची कृणवन्नो अग्रम् ।
पाङ्क्तं छन्दः पुरुषो बभूव विश्वैर्विश्वाङ्गैः सह सं भवेम ॥

10. Of all the regions, may the northern make our state victorious, first and foremost. Man has acquired independence through his vast dignity. May we gain strength with the help of all learned persons, possessing innumerable resources. (3382)[1]

११. ध्रुवेयं विराण्नमो अस्त्वस्यै शिवा पुत्रेभ्य उत मह्यमस्तु ।
सा नो देव्यदिते विश्ववार इर्य इव गोपा अभि रक्ष पक्वम् ॥

11. In the southern region reigns this Almighty God, Homage be to Him. May He be Gracious unto me and my sons. May the Divine, Unlimited, All-Bounteous God, like an expert herdsman protect our mature knowledge. (3383)

१२. पितेव पुत्रानभि सं स्वजस्व नः शिवा नो वाता इह वान्तु भूमौ ।
यमोदनं पचतो देवते इह तन्नस्तप उत सत्यं च वेत्तु ॥

12. O God, embrace us as a father clasps his children. Here on the earth let kindly breezes fan us. Let God, Whom these two devout souls worship fervently know our truthful behaviour and penance. (3384)

१३. यद्यत् कृष्णः शकुन एह गत्वा त्सरन् विषक्तं बिल आससाद ।
यद्वा दास्या३र्द्रहस्ता समङ्क्त उलूखलं मुसलं शुम्भतापः ॥

13. Whenever a degraded powerful thief comes and enters our house, and stealing different articles of food, settles in a hiding place, or if the slave girl, with wet hands touches the powerful king and renders him dirty and impure, cleanse them all, O learned persons. (3385)[2]

[1]Northern region is a symbol of height and loftiness. Just as the North is the highest of all regions, so should our state be first and foremost.

[2]Learned persons should save the king from moral degradation through low women, and protect the houses of the subjects against thieves.

१४. अयं ग्रावा पृथुबुध्नो वयोधाः पूतः पवित्रैरप हन्तु रक्षः ।
अा रोह चर्म महि शर्म यच्छ मा दम्पती पौत्रमघं नि गाताम् ॥

14. This preacher of religious lore, master of vast knowledge, full of vitality, purified by noble deeds, shall remove every sort of obstacle. O learned person, advance in knowledge, afford us great protection. Let not wife and husband find their sons in trouble. (3386)[1]

१५. वनस्पतिः सह देवैर्न अागन् रक्षः पिशाचाँ अपबाधमानः ।
स उच्छ्रयातै प्र वदाति वाचं तेन लोकाँ अभि सर्वाञ्जयेम ॥

15. The guardian of religious lore, overcoming all obstacles and ailments, hath come unto us with his excellent traits. May he progress, and preach the Vedic truths. May we win all the worlds with his help. (3387)[2]

१६. सप्त मेधान् पशवः पर्यगृह्णन् य एषां ज्योतिष्माँ उत यश्चकर्श ।
त्रयस्त्रिंशद् देवतास्तान्त्सचन्ते स नः स्वर्गमभि नेष लोकम् ॥

16. All souls have held the seven mutually united organs. The thirty three forces accompany them. Out of those souls, may one that is bright and master of subtle knowledge take us to the pleasant society of the learned. (3388)[3]

१७. स्वर्गं लोकमभि नो नयासि सं जायया सह पुत्रैः स्याम ।
गृह्णामि हस्तमनु मैत्वत्र मा नस्तारीन्निर्ऋतिर्मो अरातिः ॥

17. O God, Thou ever leadest us to a region full of joy. May we dwell in this world happily with our wife and children. May she, whose hand I grasp follow me as a devoted wife. Let not poverty, let not misfortune come hither and subdue us. (3389)

१८. ग्राहिं पाप्मानमति ताँ अयाम तमो व्यस्य प्र वदासि वल्गु ।
वानस्पत्य उद्यतो मा जिहिंसीर्मा तण्डुलं वि शरीर्देवयन्तम् ॥

18. Let us subdue the physical pain of gout, and mental anguish of untruth. O King speak sweetly having chased the darkness of our heart. O kingly punishment full of intensity like a wooden pestle, kill us not. Just as a pestle removes the husk, but breaks not the rice, so kingly punishment harm not a devotee! (3390)

१९. विश्वव्यचा घृतपृष्ठो भविष्यन्त्सयोनिर्लोकमुप याह्येतम् ।
वर्षवृद्धमुप यच्छ शूर्पं तुषं पलावानप तद् विनक्तु ॥

[1]The verse is applicable to a king as well, as has been interpreted by Pt. Jaidev Vidyalankara.

[2](वनस्पतिः) वनस्य संयजनीयस्य शास्त्रस्य पालको विद्वान—यथा दयानन्दभाष्ये यजु० 27-21.

[3]Seven organs: Skin, Eye, Ear, Nose, Tongue, Mind, Intellect. Thirty-three forces: Eight Vasus, Eleven Rudras, Twelve Adityas, Indra, Praja Pati.

19. O King, if thou likest to win world-renown, and shine like the Sun, enjoy this happy sovereignty along with thy subjects! Just as the winnowing-fan made of reeds that nourish in rains, separates the chaff and refuse, so shouldst thou, O King, utilise the services of an aged, experienced judge, and remove from thy state, despicable, violent persons! (3391)

२०. त्रयो लोकाः संमिता ब्राह्मणेन द्यौरेवासौ पृथिव्य१न्तरिक्षम् ।
अंशून् गृभीत्वान्वारभेथामा प्यायन्तां पुनरा यन्तु शूर्पम् ॥

20. A Vedic scholar hath full knowledge of the three worlds, yonder heaven, and the earth, and air's mid-region. O man and woman, just as you taking in hand the white grains of corn, sow them in the earth, which grow in abundance and come again on the winnowing-fan to be unhusked, so should the king and his subjects possess the knowledge of the three worlds, and separate the virtuous from the sinful! (3392)

२१. पृथग् रूपाणि बहुधा पशूनामेकरूपो भवसि सं समृद्ध्या ।
एतां त्वचं लोहिनीं तां नुदस्व ग्रावा शुम्भाति मलग इव वस्त्रा ॥

21. Manifold are the shapes of human beings. O King, thou by thy great splendour treats them all alike! Remove this iron covering of ignorance. Being wise purify thyself as a washerman cleanses the clothes. (3393)

२२. पृथिवीं त्वा पृथिव्यामा वेशयामि तनूः समानी विकृता त एषा ।
यद्यद् द्युत्तं लिखितमर्पणेन तेन मा सुस्रोर्ब्रह्मणापि तद् वपामि ॥

22. O Earth, I make thee of Matter. This visible shape of thine is deformed, but there is the other nascent state of Matter free from deformity. Whatever hath been worn off or scratched in fixing, I remove that through knowledge, destroy not thy true nature, O Earth! (3394)[1]

२३. जनित्रीव प्रति हर्यासि सूनुं सं त्वा दधामि पृथिवीं पृथिव्या ।
उखा कुम्भी वेद्यां मा व्यथिष्ठा यज्ञायुधैराज्येनातिषक्ता ॥

23. O subjects, just as mother lovingly takes the son in her lap, so do I unite thee, the renowned, with knowledge. Stagger not, stand firmly, just as pot and jar do on fire conjoined with sacrificial gear and butter. (3395)[2]

२४. अग्निः पचन् रक्षतु त्वा पुरस्तादिन्द्रो रक्षतु दक्षिणतो मरुत्वान् ।
वरुणस्त्वा दृंहाद्धरुणे प्रतीच्या उत्तरात् त्वा सोमः सं ददातै ॥

24. May the Omniscient God, strengthening thee preserve thee from the East. May the Opulent, Refulgent God guard thee from the South. May the Most Excellent God, with His strength, support thee from the West. May God, the Creator of the universe, hold thee together from the North. (3396)[3]

[1]I: God. God creates the universe from Matter, gives it visible shape, and resolves it again into its nascent state after dissolution.

[2]I: God.

[3]Thee: Man.

२५. पूताः पवित्रैः पवन्ते अभ्राद् दिवं च यन्ति पृथिवीं च लोकान् ।
ता जीवला जीवधन्याः प्रतिष्ठाः पात्र आसिक्ताः पर्यग्निरिन्धाम् ॥

25. Purified through virtuous deeds, they purify others through various devices. They acquire love for conquest, vast knowledge, and beautiful houses. Enjoying long life, being foremost among men, absorbed in God, they attain to fame. The Refulgent God, bestowing knowledge on them, makes them shine on every side. (3397)[1]

२६. आ यन्ति दिवः पृथिवीं सचन्ते भूम्याः सचन्ते अध्यन्तरिक्षम् ।
शुद्धाः सतीस्ता उ शुम्भन्त एव ता नः स्वर्गमभि लोकं नयन्तु ॥

26. They, full of love for conquest, acquire knowledge and enjoy it. With a pure heart they verily worship God. Purifying themselves they purify others. May they lead us to the pleasant assembly of the learned. (3398)

२७. उतेव प्रभ्वीरुत संमितास उत शुक्राः शुचयश्चामृतासः ।
ता ओदनं दम्पतिभ्यां प्रशिष्टा आपः शिक्षन्तीः पचता सुनाथाः ॥

27. They are full of strength, knowledge, lustre, pure in character, and enterprising. O learned people, full of faith in Vedic teachings, performing philanthropic deeds, austere in nature, establish God in the hearts of wife and husband! (3399)[2]

२८. संख्याता स्तोकाः पृथिवीं सचन्ते प्राणापानैः संमिता ओषधीभिः ।
असंख्याता ओप्यमानाः सुवर्णाः सर्वं व्यापुः शुचयः शुचित्वम् ॥

28. Highly learned persons, full of joy worship the Almighty Father. They are the support of mankind like life-breaths. They are known as the healers of mental anguish like medicines. Unnumbered, pure in character, free from deceipt, greed, desire, serving the populace, they spread freedom from moral pollution all round. (3400)

२९. उद्योधन्त्यभि वल्गन्ति तप्ताः फेनमस्यन्ति बहुलांश्च बिन्दून् ।
योषेव दृष्ट्वा पतिमृत्वियायैतैस्तण्डुलैर्भवता समापः ॥

29. Just as heated waters rage and boil in agitation, and cast about their foam and countless bubbles, so people fight together, attack each other, use sword, gun, and military arms, and fire bullets and gunpowder. But, O learned people, just as a woman seeing her husband unites with him for cohabitation, and just as boiling water mixes itself with rice to cook it, so should you live together in peace with those who tease and afflict you! (3401)

३०. उत्थापय सीदतो बुध्न एनानद्भिरात्मानमभि सं स्पृशन्ताम् ।
अमासि पात्रैरुदकं यदेतन्मितास्तण्डुलाः प्रदिशो यदीमाः ॥

[1]They: Noble persons, devotees of God.

[2]Learned persons should make the householders devoted to God.

30. O King, uplift these degraded, despicable persons, lying low like rice-grains at the bottom of the cauldron. Just as they are blent and mingled with waters, so let these depraved persons elevate their souls in the company of learned persons. Just as I measure this water in the cauldron with a spoon or ladle, and the rice-grains are also measured, so these people living in different regions, are known and controlled by their rulers! (3402)[1]

३१. प्र यच्छ पर्शुं त्वरया हरोषमहिंसन्त ओषधीर्दान्तु पर्वन् ।
यासां सोमः परि राज्यं बभूवामन्युता नो वीरुधो भवन्तु ॥

31. O agriculturist, take the sickle, use it quickly. Let peasants soon cut the ripe plants and joints without harming their roots. So may the plants be free from wrath against us, they o'er whose realm the Moon or water has won dominion! (3403)[2]

३२. नवं बर्हिरोदनाय स्तृणीत प्रियं हृदश्चक्षुषो वल्ग्वस्तु ।
तस्मिन् देवाः सह दैवीर्विशन्त्विमं प्राश्नन्त्वृतुभिर्निषद्य ॥

32. O men, spread the new mat for eating rice. It should look pleasant to the mind and beautiful to the eye. Let men and women sit on it, and sitting together let them take their food in different seasons! (3404)

३३. वनस्पते स्तीर्णमा सीद बर्हिरग्निष्टोमैः संमितो देवताभिः ।
त्वष्ट्रेव रूपं सुकृतं स्वधित्यैना एहाः परि पात्रे ददृश्राम् ॥

33. O King, thou keepest all under thy shelter like a big tree. Control thy subjects. Thou art extolled by learned persons and Vedic verses. Just as an expert carpenter with his hatchet makes a piece of wood beautiful and excellent to look at, so does God, with His divine power, lend beauty, brilliance and dignity to thee. Other minor rulers, working in collaboration with thee, and remaining under thy protection, remain present round thee! (3405)

३४. षष्ट्यां शरत्सु निधिपा अभीच्छात् स्वः पक्वेनाभ्यश्नवातै ।
उपैनं जीवान् पितरश्च पुत्रा एतं स्वर्गं गमयान्तमग्नेः ॥

34. A King, the guardian of Earth, should, with his mature strength, wish to enjoy his rule, a paradise on earth till his sixtieth year. On him may his parents and sons depend! O God, lead the king to the end of knowledge, and make his rule full of joy! (3406)[3]

३५. धर्ता ध्रियस्व धरुणे पृथिव्या अच्युतं त्वा देवताश्च्यावयन्तु ।
तं त्वा दम्पती जीवन्तौ जीवपुत्रावुद् वासयातः पर्यग्निधानात् ॥

[1]They: Rice-grains.

[2]Moon and water ripen the crop. Plants should not be uprooted. They will not feel angry if their roots are not cut. Just as wise peasants cut with the sickle the crop ripened by the Moon and water, and use the grain for their sustenance, so do people become happy by acquiring knowledge about God from the learned.

[3]पथिवी ह्येण निधिः । श० 6-5-2-3.

35. O King, thou art the supporter of the Earth. May thou be installed in an eminent position in the world. The learned tolerate thee, who never falters in his duty. May living man and wife with living children establish thee in their house in an exalted position in their worldly affairs! (3407)

३६. सर्वान्त्समागा अभिजित्य लोकान् यावन्तः कामाः समतीतृपस्तान् ।
वि गाहेथामायवनं च दर्विरेकस्मिन् पात्रे अध्युद्धरैनम् ॥

36. O King, meet all people, control them all, and fulfil all their desires. Just as both stirring-spoon and ladle are plunged in a cauldron, and rice is raised to be tested, so duly elevate the soul! (3408)

३७. उप स्तृणीहि प्रथय पुरस्ताद् घृतेन पात्रमभि धारयैतत् ।
वाश्रेवोस्रा तरुणं स्तनस्युमिमं देवासो अभिहिङ्कृणोत ॥

37. O learned preceptor, advance this deserving pupil, lead him forward to fame, let him duly shine with knowledge! O learned persons, elevate the soul, as a lowing cow welcomes the tender calf desirous to suck milk! (3409)

३८. उपास्तरीरकरो लोकमेतमुरुः प्रथतामसमः स्वर्गः ।
तस्मिञ्छ्रयातै महिषः सुपर्णो देवा एनं देवताभ्यः प्र यच्छान् ॥

38. O King, thou thyself buildest and advancest this state. May this state, a peerless paradise make full progress! The mighty king, equipped with knowledge rules over it. The learned place the state in the hands of able, efficient persons. (3410)

३९. यद्यज्जाया पचति त्वत् परःपरः पतिर्वा जाये त्वत् तिरः ।
सं तत् सृजेथां सह वां तदस्तु संपादयन्तौ सह लोकमेकम् ॥

39. O husband, whatever thy wife, away from thee, makes ready, or what, O wife, apart from thee, thy husband prepares, combine it all: let it be yours in common while you carry on your domestic life with joint endeavour. (3411)

४०. यावन्तो अस्याः पृथिवीं सचन्ते अस्मत् पुत्राः परि ये संबभूवुः ।
सर्वांस्तॉं उप पात्रे ह्वयेथां नाभिं जानानाः शिशवः समायान् ॥

40. Let all these sons of mine, whom this woman, my wife, hath borne me, be invited to the dining-table. They knowing their kinship should come there. (3412)[1]

४१. वसोर्या धारा मधुना प्रपीना घृतेन मिश्रा अमृतस्य नाभयः ।
सर्वास्ता अव रुन्धे स्वर्गः षष्ट्यां शरत्सु निधिपा अभीच्छात् ॥

[1]All the members of the family should dine together.

41. The soul forces, replete with joy, blent with knowledge, are the sources of full span of life for a hundred years. A happiness-bestowing person retains them all. A Brahmchari, the guardian of the treasure of semen, acquires them at the age of sixty. (3413)

४२. निधिं निधिपा अभ्येनमिच्छादनीश्वरा अभितः सन्तु येऽन्ये ।
अस्माभिर्दत्तो निहितः स्वर्गस्त्रिभिः काण्डैस्त्रीन्त्स्वर्गानरुक्षत् ।।

42. Let the king, the protector of Earth, attain to sovereignty over it. Let other powerless persons remain completely under his sway. We, the learned subjects build up the state and hand over this paradise to the king. May he attain to threefold pleasures through threefold acts. (3414)[1]

४३. अग्नी रक्षस्तपतु यद् विदेवं क्रव्यात् पिशाच इह मा प्र पास्त ।
नुदाम एनमप रुध्मो अस्मदादित्या एनमङ्गिरसः सचन्ताम् ।।

43. Let the fiery king punish the God-denying demon. Let no carnivorous, raw meat-eater get water to drink in the state. We drive him off. We keep him at a distance. Let learned persons and sages pursue him. (3415)

४४. आदित्येभ्यो अङ्गिरोभ्यो मध्विदं घृतेन मिश्रं प्रति वेदयामि ।
शुद्धहस्तौ ब्राह्मणस्यानिहत्यैतं स्वर्गं सुकृतावपीतम् ।।

44. I announce the Vedas full of knowledge, sweet like honey to the Brahmcharis and the sages. O pious couple, with pure hands never laid roughly on a Vedic scholar, go to the world of joy! (3416)[2]

४५. इदं प्रापमुत्तमं काण्डमस्य यस्माल्लोकात् परमेष्ठी समाप ।
आ सिञ्च सर्पिर्घृतवत् समङ्ग्ध्येष भागो अङ्गिरसो नो अत्र ।।

45. I have acquired the lofty Vedic knowledge, the light through which God, from His high pedestal, rules the universe. O Acharya, scatter beautiful knowledge all round, manifest it in fulness. May this useful act of the Acharya, be meant for us in this world. (3417)[3]

४६. सत्याय च तपसे देवताभ्यो निधिं शेवधिं परि दद्म एतम् ।
मा नो द्यूतेऽव गान्मा समित्यां मा स्मान्यस्मा उत्सृजता पुरा मत् ।।

46. We consign this rich store of knowledge to the enterprising Brahmcharis, for performing noble deeds, and acquiring prosperity. Let not this knowledge of ours be wasted in gambling or battle. O guardians of knowledge, don't impart this knowledge in my presence to an irreligious foe. (3418)[4]

[1]The verse preaches the doctrine of democracy. Learned subjects elect their ruler and hand over to him the administration of the state. He: King. Threefold acts: Mental, Vocal, Physical. Threefold pleasures: Spiritual, Elemental, Material.

[2]I: God. Couple: Husband and wife. Brahmcharis: Celibates, or who have got control over their passions in domestic life.

[3]Acharya: Guru, teacher, preceptor. I: A Brahmchari. Us: The Brahmcharis.

[4]We: Acharyas, teachers, gurus, preceptors.

४७. अहं पचाम्यहं ददामि ममेदु कर्मन् करुणेऽधि जाया ।
कौमारो लोको अजनिष्ट पुत्रो३न्वारभेथां वय उत्तरावत् ॥

47. I strengthen the store of knowledge, and impart it to the pupils. My wife also is engaged in charitable deeds. Our society is full of nice daughters and sons. O girls and boys, begin a higher moral life! (3419)

४८. न किल्विषमत्र नाधारो अस्ति न यन्मित्रैः सममान एति ।
अनूनं पात्रं निहितं न एतत् पक्तारं पक्वः पुनरा विशाति ॥

48. In this society of ours there is no sin, no degradation, no conduct, whereby friends are put to inconvenience. Our heart is entirely full of affection. Mature knowledge is acquired by him who strives hard for it. (3420)

४९. प्रियं प्रियाणां कृणवाम तमस्ते यन्तु यतमे द्विषन्ति ।
धेनुरनड्वान् वयोवय आयदेव पौरुषेयमप मृत्युं नुदन्तु ॥

49. To those we love may we do acts that please them. Away to darkness go all those who hate us! May cow, ox, corn and longevity approach us! Thus let them banish death of human beings. (3421)[1]

५०. समग्नयो विदुरन्यो अन्यं य ओषधीः सचते यश्च सिन्धून् ।
यावन्तो देवा दिव्या३तपन्ति हिरण्यं ज्योतिः पचतो बभूव ॥

50. Learned persons, glowing with knowledge like fire know each other. A physician who gathers medicinal plants, and a saint who contemplates on the banks of rivers also know each other. The lustre of Brahmcharis who preserve their semen through penance becomes glittering like gold, like all the luminous bodies that shine and glow in heaven. (3422)

५१. एषा त्वचां पुरुषे सं बभूवानग्नाः सर्वे पशवो ये अन्ये ।
क्षत्रेणात्मानं परि धापयाथोऽमोतं वासो मुखमोदनस्य ॥

51. Man hath received the skin without hair from nature. Of other animals not one is naked, all are full of hair on the skin. Ye man and woman clothe yourselves with raiment to protect your body, as an intelligently woven cloth covers the cooked food. (3423)

५२. यदक्षेषु वदा यत् समित्यां यद्वा वदा अनृतं वित्तकाम्या ।
समानं तन्तुमभि संवसानौ तस्मिन्त्सर्वं शमलं सादयाथः ॥

52. Whatever falsehood thou utterest in gambling, in the assembly, or through desire of riches, O man and woman, ye attribute that sin to the government machinery, as all impurity is deposited on the cloth one constantly wears. (3424)[2]

[1]Cow prolongs our life with her milk. Ox tills the land that grows corn, which sustains our life.

[2]It is the duty of the king to see that none of his subjects tells a lie, steals or commits a sin.

५३. वर्षं वनुष्वापि गच्छ देवांस्त्वचो धूमं पर्युत्पातयासि ।
विश्वव्यचा घृतपृष्ठो भविष्यन्त्सयोनिर्लोकमुप याह्येतम् ॥

53. O King, perform noble deeds, acquire laudable qualities, remove impurity from all sides of the body. Acquiring universal renown, longing for prosperity, assume the reins of this excellent state along with thy subjects. (3425)

५४. तन्वं१ स्वर्गो बहुधा वि चक्रे यथा विद आत्मन्नन्यवर्णाम् ।
अपाजैत् कृष्णां रुशतीं पुनानो या लोहिनी तां ते अग्नौ जुहोमि ॥

54. An aspirant after salvation brings about various changes in his body. When with his spiritual eye, he sees the body as different from his real self, he, purifying his bright intellect, suppresses his dark sinful behaviour. I, O soul, burn thy passionate nature with the fire of my knowledge! (3426)[1]

५५. प्राच्यै त्वा दिशेऽग्नयेऽधिपतयेऽसिताय रक्षित्र आदित्यायेषुमते ।
एतं परि दद्मस्तं नो गोपायतास्माकमैतोः ।
दिष्टं नो अत्र जरसे नि नेषज्जरा मृत्यवे परि णो ददात्वथ पक्वेन सह सं भवेम ॥

55. We present thee, O soul, to the eastern region, to God, the Father of the universe, to the Unfettered God, our Protector through the arrow-like efficacy of Vedic hymns! O learned persons, preserve this soul for us, for free actions! May God conduct us to noble deeds, to full old age. May full old age deliver us to death. May we then unite with the Unwavering God. (3427)

५६. दक्षिणायै त्वा दिश इन्द्रायाधिपतये तिरश्चिराजये रक्षित्रे यमायेषुमते ।
एतं परि दद्मस्तं नो गोपायतास्माकमैतोः ।
दिष्टं नो अत्र जरसे नि नेषज्जरा मृत्यवे परि णो ददात्वथ पक्वेन सह सं भवेम ॥

56. We present thee, O soul, to the southern region, to Refulgent God, the Father of the universe, to God, our protector from those who disobey the teachings of the Vedas, our saviour from the violent arrows of Death! O learned persons, preserve this soul for us, for free actions! May God conduct us to noble deeds, to full old age. May old age deliver us to death. May we then unite with the Unwavering God. (3428)

५७. प्रतीच्यै त्वा दिशे वरुणायाधिपतये पृदाकवे रक्षित्रेऽन्नायेषुमते ।
एतं परि दद्मस्तं नो गोपायतास्माकमैतोः ।
दिष्टं नो अत्र जरसे नि नेषज्जरा मृत्यवे परि णो ददात्वथ पक्वेन सह सं भवेम ॥

57. We present thee, O soul, to the western region, to Adorable God, our Protector from deadly violent persons, our Saviour through ignorance, dispelling impulses! O learned persons, preserve this soul for us, for free actions! May God conduct us to noble deeds, to full old age. May old age deliver us to death. May we then unite with the Unwavering God. (3429)

[1]I: God. Passionate: Rajsi.

५८. उदीच्यै त्वा दिशे सोमायाधिपतये स्वजाय रक्षित्रेऽशन्या इषुमत्यै ।
एतं परि दद्मस्तं नो गोपायतास्माकमैतोः ।
दिष्टं नो अत्र जरसे नि नेषज्जरा मृत्यवे परि णो ददात्वथ पक्वेन सह सं भवेम ॥

58. We present thee, O soul, to the northern region, to God, the Creator and Embodiment of peace, to the Unborn God, our Protector through His streams of unbounded knowledge! O learned persons, preserve the soul for us, for free actions! May God conduct us to noble deeds, to full old age. May old age deliver us to death. May we then unite with the Unwavering God. (3430)

५९. ध्रुवायै त्वा दिशे विष्णवेऽधिपतये कल्माषग्रीवाय रक्षित्र ओषधीभ्य इषुमतीभ्यः ।
एतं परि दद्मस्तं नो गोपायतास्माकमैतोः ।
दिष्टं नो अत्र जरसे नि नेषज्जरा मृत्यवे परि णो ददात्वथ पक्वेन सह सं भवेम ॥

59. We present thee, O soul, to the lower region, to the All-pervading God, to God, the Nourisher of the trees of different hues, to God, the Remover of all impediments like medicines of diseases! O learned persons, preserve the soul for us, for free actions! May God conduct us to noble deeds, to full old age. May old age deliver us to death. May we then unite with the Unwavering God. (3431)

६०. ऊर्ध्वायै त्वा दिशे बृहस्पतयेऽधिपतये श्वित्राय रक्षित्रे वर्षायेषुमते ।
एतं परि दद्मस्तं नो गोपायतास्माकमैतोः ।
दिष्टं नो अत्र जरसे नि नेषज्जरा मृत्यवे परि णो ददात्वथ पक्वेन सह सं भवेम ॥

60. We present thee, O soul, to the upper region, to God, the Lord of the Vedas and vast space, to God, the saviour of our souls from sinful acts, and our bodies from virile diseases like leprosy, through streams of knowledge! O learned persons, preserve the soul for us, for free actions! May God conduct us to noble deeds, to full old age. May old age deliver us to death. May we then unite with Unwavering God. (3432)[1]

Chapter (Anuvāka) 4
HYMN IV

१. ददामीत्येव ब्रूयादनु चैनामभुत्सत । वशां ब्रह्मभ्यो याचद्भ्यस्तत् प्रजावदपत्यवत् ॥

1. I give the beautiful Vedic speech to the learned Vedic scholars. Verily have the ancient sages known it through meditation. This gift of Vedic speech bringeth sons and progeny. So should the Acharya say to the pupils. (3433)[2]

[1]See *Atharvaveda*, Kāṇḍa 3, Suktā 27. Griffith considers this hymn to be obscure in parts and occasionally unintelligible to him. I find no obscurity in the hymn.

[2]वश-कमनीयानि-दयानन्दभाष्ये *Rigveda*, 2·24-13. कमनीयां प्रभ्वों वा वेदबाणीम् The Acharya (preceptor) should tell his pupils, that the knowledge of the Vedas elevates mankind, hence I teach them to you. See *Atharvaveda*, Kāṇḍa 10, Suktā 10.

२. प्रजया स ıव क्रीणीते पशुभिश्चोप दस्यति ।
य आर्षेयेभ्यो याचद्भ्यो देवानां गां न दित्सति ॥

2. He sells his sons, and is destroyed along with his cattle, who does not like to give Vedic speech to the Rishis' children, longing for success, when they ask for it. (3434)[1]

३. कूटयास्य सं शीर्यन्ते श्लोणया काटमर्दति । बण्डया दह्यन्ते गृहाः काणया दीयते स्वम् ॥

3. They perish who do not preach the Vedas. He who hoards the Vedic knowledge loses renown. Their houses are burnt who withhold the Vedic knowledge. He suffers utter destruction who preaches the Vedic without the support of Nirukta and Grammar. (3435)[2]

४. विलोहितो अधिष्ठानाच्छक्नो विन्दति गोपतिम् ।
तथा वशायाः संविद्यं दुरदभ्ना ह्यु१च्यसे ॥

4. A powerful person well-known through the lustre of celibacy, acquires Vedic knowledge, the sustainer of the world. Beautiful Vedic knowledge is termed 'worth knowing' for thou art called uncontrollable. (3436)[3]

५. पदोरस्या अधिष्ठानाद् विक्लिन्दुर्नाम विन्दति ।
अनामनात् सं शीर्यन्ते या मुखेनोपजिघ्रति ॥

5. Through the firm lustre of this Vedic knowledge, a man free from grief attains to fame. They perish who without going deep into its true significance, treat it lightly and recite it orally. (3437)

६. यो अस्याः कर्णावास्कुनोत्या स देवेषु वृश्चते ।
लक्ष्म कुर्व इति मन्यते कनीयः कृणुते स्वम् ॥

6. Whover hides the two sorts of knowledge of the Vedic speech, is separated from laudable qualities. If he deems, he is thereby doing a praiseworthy act, he lowers his dignity. (3438)[4]

७. यदस्याः कस्मै चिद् भोगाय बालान् कश्चित् प्रकृन्तति ।
ततः किशोरा म्रियन्ते वत्सांश्च घातुको वृकः ॥

[1](गाम्) वेदबाणीम् । गौर्वाङ्नाम—निघ० 1-11.

[2]The Vedas should be preached to all. None should be debarred from their benefit. This knowledge should not be kept in store or hoarded in the hearts of the learned. It should not be withheld from any body on score of caste, colour or creed. Vedic knowledge is blind without Nirukta and Vayakaran. It should always be preached, supported by Nirukta, Nighantu and Grammar.

[3]Thou: Vedic knowledge. Uncontrollable: The truths of the Vedas cannot be exploded. They are everlasting and universal.

[4]Two sorts: अभ्युदय and निः श्रेयम् i.e., temporal and spiritual Athiests and heretics who have no belief in the elevating worldly and spiritual knowledge of the Vedas, belittle and lower themselves.

7. If to his own selfish advantage one applies the elevating forces of this Vedic knowledge, his tiny children, in consequence thereof, die. Death destroys his progeny as a violent wolf destroys the calves. (3439)[1]

८. यदस्या गोपतौ सत्या लोम ध्वाङ्क्षो अजीहिडत् ।
ततः कुमारा म्रियन्ते यक्ष्मो विन्दत्यनामनात् ॥

8. If a depraved person crying like a crow, shows disrespect to the efficacy of Vedic knowledge possessed by a Brahmchari, its guardian, his young boys die thereof. Consumption overtakes them for not fully meditating over it. (3440)[2]

९. यदस्याः पल्पूलनं शकृद् दासी समस्यति । ततोऽपरूपं जायते तस्मादव्येष्यदेनसः ॥

9. If a violent man or woman disregards the wealthy store of knowledge of this Vedic speech, he or she gets the stain of inseparable infamy, due to that sin. (3441)

१०. जायमानाभि जायते देवान्त्सब्राह्मणान् वशा ।
तस्माद् ब्रह्मभ्यो देयैषा तदाहुः स्वस्य गोपनम् ॥

10. For the valorous and learned scholars is the Vedic knowledge produced when first it is revealed. Hence to the learned must it be given. Wise men call it as an act of preservation of mankind. (3442)[3]

११. य एनां वनिमायन्ति तेषां देवकृता वशा । ब्रह्मज्येयं तदब्रुवन् य एनां निप्रियायते ॥

11. The God-created Vedic knowledge belongs to those who come to ask for it. The learned call it an outrage on Vedic scholars when one retains Vedic knowledge as his own precious heritage. (3443)[4]

१२. य आर्षेयेभ्यो याचद्भ्यो देवानां गां न दित्सति ।
आ स देवेषु वृश्चते ब्राह्मणानां च मन्यवे ॥

12. He who withholds the Vedic knowledge acquired by the learned from Rishis' sons, his disciples, is deprived of all noble traits and deserves the righteous indignation of the learned. (3444)

१३. यो अस्य स्याद् वशाभोगो अन्यामिच्छेत तर्हि सः ।
हिंस्ते अदत्ता पुरुषं याचितां च न दित्सति ॥

[1]They who use the Vedic knowledge for immoral purposes, are put to grief.

[2]It: Vedic knowledge. When a depraved person disobeys the teachings of the Vedas, he and his family members suffer heavily.

[3]The learned preach the doctrines of the Vedas and preserve mankind from moral degradation.

[4]Vedas are meant for all. They are not the property of the selected. Everybody has the right to study them and acquire their knowledge.

13. He who wants to derive full advantage from this Vedic knowledge should aspire after this life-infusing knowledge. This knowledge, not given, harms a man, who does not impart it to others when they ask for it. (3445)

१४. यथा शेवधिर्निहितो ब्राह्मणानां तथा वशा । तामेतदच्छायन्ति यस्मिन् कस्मिंश्च जायते ॥

14. Like a rich treasure is this Vedic knowledge stored away in safety by the learned. Therefore men gladly come to him, whosoever possesses it. (3446)

१५. स्वमेतदच्छायन्ति यद् वशां ब्राह्मणा अभि ।
यथैनानन्यस्मिन् जिनीयादेवास्या निरोधनम् ॥

15. When Brahmcharis duly attain to Vedic knowledge, they acquire what is their own. He who withholds this knowledge from them, harms them through an act of irreligion. (3447)

१६. चरेदेवा त्रैहायणादविज्ञातगदा सती । वशां च विद्यान्नारद ब्राह्मणास्तर्ह्येष्याः ॥

16. May this flawless Vedic Knowledge, full of noble sentiments preach the three doctrines of Action, Contemplation and Knowledge. O learned person, when one has thoroughly understood it, he should seek for Brahmanas, to whom it may be imparted. (3448)[1]

१७. य एनामवशामाह देवानां निहितं निधिम् । उभौ तस्मै भवाशर्वौ परिक्रम्येषुमस्यतः ॥

17. Whoso calls the Vedic knowledge, the well preserved treasure of the learned, as worthless and undesirable, both ingoing and outgoing breaths put him to severe grief deadly like a shaft. (3449)[2]

१८. यो अस्या ऊधो न वेदाथो अस्या स्तनानुत । उभयेनैवास्मै दुहे दातुं चेदशकद् वशाम् ॥

18. The man who after study knows the beauties and lofty teachings of this Vedic knowledge, gets from it, happiness in this life and the next, if he is prepared to bestow it on others. (3450)[3]

१९. दुर दभ्नैनमा शये याचितां च न दित्सति ।
नास्मै कामाः समृध्यन्ते यामदत्वा चिकीर्षति ॥

19. Unavoidable adversity overtakes him, who does not like to part with Vedic knowledge even when it is asked for. His wishes and hopes are never fulfilled, which he would like to gain, withholding the Vedic knowledge. (3451)

[1]Brahmanas: Seekers after Vedic knowledge.
[2]Bhava: Prāna. Shavā: Apāna.
[3]It: Vedic knowledge.

२०. देवा वशामयाचन् मुखं कृत्वा ब्राह्मणम् । तेषां सर्वेषामददद्धेडं न्येॅति मानुषः ॥

20. The wise with a Vedic scholar as their mouth-piece ask for Vedic knowledge. The man who gives it not incurs the wrath of them all. (3452)[1]

२१. हेडं पशूनां न्येॅति ब्राह्मणेभ्योऽददद् वशाम् । देवानां निहितं भागं मर्त्यश्चेन्निप्रियायते ॥

21. When a man appropriates the beautiful Vedic knowledge, the well-preserved wealth of the learned, withholding her from the Brahmcharis, he incurs the anger of all persons. (3453)

२२. यदन्ये शतं याचेयुर्ब्राह्मणा गोपतिं वशाम् । अथैनां देवा अब्रुवन्नेवं ह विदुषो वशा ॥

22. If hundred weak, faithless persons beg of the Brahmcharis Vedic knowledge, the guardian of the universe, the sages say, it verily belongs to him who knows the truth. (3454)[2]

२३. य एवं विदुषेऽदत्त्वाथान्येभ्यो ददद् वशाम् । दुर्गा तस्मा अधिष्ठाने पृथिवी सहदेवता ॥

23. Whoso imparts this beautiful Vedic knowledge not to the learned but to the ignorant, Earth, with the sages, is hard for him to win and rest upon. (3455)[3]

२४. देवा वशामयाचन् यस्मिन्नग्रे अजायत । तामेतां विद्यान्नारदः सह देवैरुदाजत ॥

24. The learned begged the Vedic knowledge from God, in Whom it already existed. A man of learning should know that this Vedic knowledge has been revealed, full of lofty ideas. (3456)

२५. अनपत्यमल्पपशुं वशा कृणोति पूरुषम् । ब्राह्मणैश्च याचितामथैनां निप्रियायते ॥

25. Vedic knowledge deprives of progeny and makes him bereft of cattle, who retains it in his possession, even when the Brāhmans have asked for it. (3457)

२६. अग्नीषोमाभ्यां कामाय मित्राय वरुणाय च ।
तेभ्यो याचन्ति ब्राह्मणास्तेष्वा वृश्चतेऽददत् ॥

26. For the knowledge of electricity and water, for the attainment of desirable objects and for the control of Prāna and Apāna, for these the Brahmcharis ask for Vedic knowledge. He who giveth it not to them, shows disrespect unto them. (3458)

२७. यावदस्या गोपतिर्नोपशृणुयादृचः स्वयम् ।
चरेदस्य तावद् गोषु नास्य श्रुत्वा गृहे वसेत् ॥

[1]It: Vedic knowledge.

[2]A hundred ordinary ignorant persons can't propagate the Vedic teachings, so effectively as a learned man alone can do.

[3]He who gives Vedic knowledge not to the deserving, but to the undeserving, can occupy no position of influence in the world, nor can he command respect from the learned.

27. As long as a Brahmchari, the guardian of Vedic speech does not nicely master the laudable Vedic knowledge, till then let him exert in the Gurukula, to understand the words of God, and then return home to enter domestic life, when he has mastered the Vedic knowledge. (3459)[1]

२८. यो अस्या ऋच उपश्रुत्याथ गोष्वचीचरत् ।
आयुश्च तस्य भूतिं च देवा वृश्चन्ति हीडिताः ॥

28. He who hath studied the Vedas and still is a slave of passions, gets his life and his prosperity rent away by the learned in anger. (3460)

२९. वशा चरन्ती बहुधा देवानां निहितो निधिः ।
आविष्कृणुष्व रूपाणि यदा स्थाम जिघांसति ॥

29. Vedic knowledge appearing in its multifarious aspects is the well-preserved treasure of the learned. It reveals the essence of its knowledge, when a Brahmchari wants to reach his goal. (3461)[2]

३०. आविरात्मानं कृणुते यदा स्थाम जिघांसति ।
अथो ह ब्रह्मभ्यो वशा याञ्च्याय कृणुते मनः ॥

30. Vedic knowledge manifests its shape and form, when a Brahmchari wants to reach his goal. Then verily the Vedic knowledge to the Brahmcharis and their request. (3462)

३१. मनसा सं कल्पयति तद् देवाँ अपि गच्छति ।
ततो ह ब्रह्माणो वशामुपप्रयन्ति याचितुम् ॥

31. Vedic knowledge, through deep reflection by the Brahmcharis, strengthens them, and manifests itself unto them. Then verily the Brahmcharis approach the learned and ask for it. (3463)

३२. स्वधाकारेण पितृभ्यो यज्ञेन देवताभ्यः । दानेन राजन्योऽ वशाया मातुर्हेडं न गच्छति ॥

32. A King, who imparts the beautiful knowledge of the Vedas to the learned and the courageous, in a spirit of reverence and to the best of his capacity, does not incur the wrath of the mother. (3464)[3]

३३. वशा माता राजन्यऽस्य तथा संभूतमग्रशः । तस्या आहुरनर्पणं यद् ब्रह्मभ्यः प्रदीयते ॥

33. Beautiful Vedic knowledge is the mother of a prosperous king God hath so ordained from times immemorial. The learned say, it should never be forsaken, but constantly developed by being bestowed on the Brahmcharis. (3465)

[1]A Brahmchari should remain in the Gurukula and study the Vedas, and enter domestic life after finishing his Vedic studies and performing Samāvartan ceremony. नः मंत्रति । When he has finished his studies.

[2]Goal: The acquisition of Vedic knowledge.

[3]Mother: Vedic knowledge.

३४. यथाज्यं प्रगृहीतमालुम्पेत् स्रुचो अग्नये । एवा ह ब्रह्मभ्यो वशामग्नय आ वृश्चतेऽददत् ।।

34. As molten butter, held at length, drops down to fire from the spoon, so falls into suffering and is destroyed, he who imparts not Vedic knowledge to the Brahmcharis. (3466)

३५. पुरोडाशवत्सा सुदुघा लोकेऽस्मा उप तिष्ठति ।
सास्मै सर्वान् कामान् वशा प्रददुषे दुहे ।।

35. This Vedic knowledge the preacher of vast charity, the bearer of the fruits of actions, comes nigh to him in this world. To him who gives it as a gift, it grants every hope and wish. (3467)[1]

३६. सर्वान् कामान् यमराज्ये वशा प्रददुषे दुहे । अथाहुर्नारकं लोकं निरुन्धानस्य याचिताम् ।।

36. According to the law of God, the laudable Vedic knowledge fulfils all the wishes of its giver. The learned call the house of him a place of misery, who does not impart it, even when it is asked for. (3468)

३७. प्रवीयमाना चरति क्रुद्धा गोपतये वशा । वेहतं मा मन्यमानो मृत्योः पाशेषु बध्यताम् ।।

37. Vedic knowledge is full of anger for the king who restricts its propagation. Let the king who deems me barren and fruitless be bound in snares of Death. (3469)

३८. यो वेहतं मन्यमानोऽमा च पचते वशाम् । अप्यस्य पुत्रान् पौत्रांश्च याचयते बृहस्पतिः ।।

38. Whosoever looking on the Vedic knowledge as fruitless, defames it at home. God, the Lord of mighty worlds, reduces his sons and grandsons to extreme poverty. (3470)

३९. महदेषाव तपति चरन्ती गोषु गौरपि । अथो ह गोपतये वशाददुषे विषं दुहे ।।

39. Vedic knowledge preached in all parts of the world attains to fame and dignity. It brings misery and suffering on the king who restricts its spread. (3471)[2]

४०. प्रियं पशूनां भवति यद् ब्रह्मभ्यः प्रदीयते ।
अथो वशायास्तत् प्रियं यद् देवत्रा हविः स्यात् ।।

40. It conduces to the good of humanity, when Vedic knowledge is imparted to the Brahmcharis. It is for the good of Vedic knowledge, that it becomes acceptable to the learned. (3472)

४१. या वशा उदकल्पयन् देवा यज्ञादुदेत्य । तासां विलिप्त्यं भीमामुदाकुरुत नारदः ।।

[1]First him refers to the charitable person, who does not withhold the grant of Vedic knowledge.

[2]It is the duty of the king to propagate Vedic knowledge, otherwise his country can not progress, and he will suffer thereby.

41. Of all the beautiful forces, which the investigators after truth have accepted as excellent, elevating themselves through the contemplation of God, comradeship and charity, the sagacious learned person deems the Vedic knowledge to be most developed and majestic. (3473)[1]

४२. तां देवा अमीमांसन्त वशेया३मवशेति । तामब्रवीन्नारद एषा वशानां वशतमेति ॥

42. Scholars considered in doubt, whether Vedic knowledge was a desirable or undesirable object. The wise learned person declared it as the most desirable of desirable objects. (3474)

४३. कति नु वशा नारद यास्त्वं वेत्थ मनुष्यजाः ।
तास्त्वा पृच्छामि विद्वांसं कस्या नाश्नीयादब्राह्मणः ॥

43. O learned Acharya, how many beautiful forces knowest thou, born among mankind! I ask thee who dost know, which of them can a men devoid of Brahmcharya not enjoy! (3475)[2]

४४. विलिप्त्या बृहस्पते या च सूतवशा वशा ।
तस्या नाश्नीयादब्राह्मणो या आशंसेत भूत्याम् ॥

44. O research scholar, the guardian of Vedic knowledge, a man who is not a Brahmchari, and hopes for prosperity, cannot enjoy the beautiful knowledge of the Vedas, which is highly developed, and controls the created world! (3476)

४५. नमस्ते अस्तु नारदानुष्ठु विदुषे वशा । कतमासां भीमतमा यामदत्त्वा पराभवेत् ॥

45. Homage, O wise sage, to thee who knowest how to act quickly. Which of these beautiful forces is most majestic whose withholding brings defeat, humiliation! (3477)

४६. विलिप्ती या बृहस्पतेऽथो सूतवशा वशा ।
तस्या नाश्नीयादब्राह्मणो य आशंसेत भूत्याम् ॥

46. O learned person, the guardian of Vedic knowledge, a man who is not a Brahmchari, and longs for prosperity, cannot utilise the beautiful knowledge of the Vedas, which is highly developed, and controls the created world! (3478)[3]

४७. त्रीणि वै वशाजातानि विलिप्ती सूतवशा वशा ।
ताः प्र यच्छेद् ब्रह्मभ्यः सोऽनाव्रस्कः प्रजापतौ ॥

[1]Narada is not the name of any person. It means a wise learned man. (नारदः) नीतिप्रदो विद्वान् ।

[2]Answer to the question raised in this verse is given in the next verse.

[3]This verse is the answer to the question raised in the previous verse.

47. Three are the well-known teachings of the Vedic knowledge which is highly developed, the controller of the created world, and a beautiful force. He who bestows it on the Brahmcharis does not offend God. (3479)[1]

४८. एतद् वो ब्राह्मणा हविरिति मन्वीत याचितः । वशां चेदेनं याचेयुर्या भीमाददुषो गृहे ॥

48. Vedic knowledge in the house of its withholder is harmful. Hence when the Brahmcharis beg for it from him, he being asked for, should say 'O Brahmcharis, this is a thing worth being given unto you.' (3480)[2]

४९. देवा वशां पर्यवदन् न नोऽदादिति हीडिताः ।
एताभिर्ऋग्भिर्भेदं तस्माद् वै स पराभवत् ॥

49. Learned persons say, 'He who considers the laudable Vedic knowledge as causing disunion, and does not bestow it on us, suffers defeat and humiliation.' (3481)

५०. उतैनां भेदो नाददाद् वशामिन्द्रेण याचितः । तस्मात् तं देवा आगसोऽवृश्चन्नहमुत्तरे ॥

50. When an enemy of the Vedas, does not impart this knowledge to a Brahmchari when he asks for it; in strife for victory the learned destroy him for that sin of his. (3482)[3]

५१. ये वशाया अदानाय वदन्ति परिरापिणः । इन्द्रस्य मन्यवे जाल्मा आ वृश्चन्ते अचित्त्या ॥

51. The men of evil counsel who advise refusal of the grant of Vedic knowledge, miscreants, through their foolishness, are subjected to the wrath of a powerful person. (3483)

५२. ये गोपतिं पराणीयाथाहुर्मा ददा इति । रुद्रस्यास्तां ते हेतिं परि यन्त्यचित्त्या ॥

52. They who seduce the king and say, 'Propagate not Vedic knowledge,' encounter through their want of sense the missile shot by a powerful person. (3484)

५३. यदि हुतां यद्यहुताममा च पचते वशाम् ।
देवान्त्सब्राह्मणानृत्वा जिह्मो लोकान्निर्ऋच्छति ॥

53. If in his house alone one preserves the Vedic knowledge received from an Acharya or acquired otherwise, and imparts it not to others, the dishonest person, doing wrong to the learned and the Brahmcharis, departs from the world in a miserable plight. (3485)[4]

[1]Three teachings: Action (Karma) Contemplation (Upāsanā) Knowledge (Gyāna).

[2]A householder who withholds the knowledge of the Vedas does injustice to this knowledge and harms himself.

[3]Griffith considers Bheda to be the name of a person. The word means disunion.

[4]Achārya: Preceptor, Guru.

Chapter (Anuvāka) 5

HYMN V

Paryāya 1

१. श्रमेण तपसा सृष्टा ब्रह्मणा वित्तर्ते श्रिता ॥

1. Vedic knowledge is mastered through toil and holy fervour, and obtained by a devoted Brahmchari. It rests in God, the Embodiment of Truth. (3486)

२. सत्येनावृता श्रिया प्रावृता यशसा परीवृता ॥

2. It is invested with truth, surrounded with beauty and grandeur, encompassed about with glory. (3487)[1]

३. स्वधया परिहिता श्रद्धया पर्यूढा दीक्षया गुप्ता यज्ञे प्रतिष्ठिता लोको निधनम् ॥

3. It is girt round with inherent power, fortified with faith, protected by consecration, dependent upon God. The world is her resting place. (3488)

४. ब्रह्म पदवायं ब्राह्मणोऽधिपतिः ॥

4. Knowledge is its guide, God, its Lord. (3489)

५. तामाददानस्य ब्रह्मगवीं जिनतो ब्राह्मणं क्षत्रियस्य ॥

5. Of the Kshatriya who usurps this Vedic knowledge and oppresseth the Brahman. (3490)

६. अप क्रामति सूनृता वीर्यं१ पुण्या लक्ष्मीः ॥

6. The courteous language, the heroism, and the auspicious fortune depart. (3491)[2]

Paryāya 2

७. ओजश्च तेजश्च सहश्च बलं च वाक् चेन्द्रियं च श्रीश्च धर्मश्च ॥

7. The energy and vigour, the patience and might, the knowledge and mental strength, the glory and virtue. (3492)

८. ब्रह्म च क्षत्रं च राष्ट्रं च विशश्च त्विषिश्च यशश्च वर्चश्च द्रविणं च ॥

8. Devotion and princely sway, kingship and people, brilliance and honour, splendour and wealth. (3493)

[1]It means Vedic knowledge.

[2](1-6) The first three verses have been interpreted by Maharshi Dayananda in the *Rigveda adi-bhashya-bhumika*, pp. 101, 102, and the *Sanskārvidhi* in the chapter on Grihastha Ashram (Household life). In Hymn 4 the advantages of propagating Vedic knowledge are mentioned, and in Hymn are given the dangers of obstructing the dissemination of this knowledge.

९. आयुश्च रूपं च नाम च कीर्तिश्च प्राणश्चापानश्च चक्षुश्च श्रोत्रं च ॥

9. Long life and physical beauty, and name and fame, in-breathing and expiration, and sight, and hearing. (3494)

१०. पयश्च रसश्चान्नं चान्नाद्यं चर्तं च सत्यं चेष्टं च पूर्तं च प्रजा च पशवश्च ॥

10. Milk and butter, food and nourishing edibles, and right and truth, Vedic study, hospitality, and acts of public utility, and children and cattle. (3495)

११. तानि सर्वाण्यप क्रामन्ति ब्रह्मगवीमाददानस्य जिनतो ब्राह्मणं क्षत्रियस्य ॥

11. All these blessings of a Kshatriya depart from him when he oppresseth the Brahman and usurps the Vedic knowledge. (3496)

Paryāya 3

१२. सैषा भीमा ब्रह्मगव्य१घविषा साक्षात् कृत्या कूल्बजमावृता ॥

12. This Vedic knowledge is terrible for its reviler. When its spread is obstructed, it becomes fearfully venomous, visibly violent, and bringer of havoc on the earth. (3497)[1]

१३. सर्वाण्यस्यां घोराणि सर्वे च मृत्यवः ॥

13. Its opposition brings all horrors and all deaths. (3498)

१४. सर्वाण्यस्यां क्रूराणि सर्वे पुरुषवधाः ॥

14. Its obstruction creates all dreadful deeds, all slaughters of mankind. (3499)[2]

१५. सा ब्रह्मज्यं देवपीयुं ब्रह्मगव्या॒दीयमाना मृत्योः पड्बीश आ द्यति ॥

15. This Vedic knowledge, being snatched, holdeth bound in the fetter of Death, the oppressor of the Brahmcharis, the blasphemer of the sages. (3500)

१६. मेनिः शतवधा हि सा ब्रह्मज्यस्य क्षितिर्हि सा ॥

16. It is a hundred-killing bolt. It slays the injurer of Vedic preachers. (3501)

१७. तस्माद् वै ब्राह्मणानां गौर्दुराधर्षा विजानता ॥

17. Therefore, the Vedic knowledge is held inviolable by the wise. (3502)

[1]When the spread of Vedic knowledge is stopped, vice prevails in the world, which brings havoc and destruction in its train.

[2](13-14) With the disappearance of Vedic knowledge, sin spreads in the world, result ing in slaughter, and all sorts of horrible deeds.

१८. वज्रो वैश्वानर वैशानर उद्वीता ॥

18. Preached freely, it acts as a powerful force. Held in high esteem it acts as a benefactor of humanity like a leader. (3503)

१९. हेतिः शफानुत्खिदन्ती महादेवो३पेक्षमाणा ॥

19. It acts as a thunderbolt completely annihilating the usages and practices of a sinner. It acts as a conquest-loving hero throwing light on all topics. (3504)

२०. क्षुरपविरीक्षमाणा वाश्यमानाभि स्फूर्जति ॥

20. When it sees a man who stops its spread, it acts as a sharp razor. It thunders when it preaches its doctrines. (3505)

२१. मृत्युर्हिङ्कृण्वत्यु१ग्रो देवः पुच्छं पर्यस्यन्ती ॥

21. Contributing to the welfare and prosperity of a Brahmchari, it is Death unto him who opposes it. It removes carelessness and negligence, acting like a fierce conquest loving hero. (3506)

२२. सर्वज्यानिः कर्णौ वरीवर्जयन्ती राजयक्ष्मो मेहन्ती ॥

22. Infusing life in the learned, blocking the temporal and spiritual power of the opposer, it proves for him utterly destructive like consumption. (3507)

२३. मेनिर्दुह्यमाना शीर्षक्तिर्दुग्धा ॥

23. Vedic knowledge is a missile for the opposer, when studied by the learned, and headache for him, when it is preached and practised. (3508)

२४. सेदिरुपतिष्ठन्ती मिथोयोधः परामृष्टा ॥

24. Vedic knowledge brings sorrow to the opposer, when it befriends a scholar. It creates mutual fight amongst sinners, when it is pondered over by the learned. (3509)[1]

२५. शरव्या३ मुखेऽपिनह्यमान ऋतिर्हन्यमाना ॥

25. It wounds like an arrow, him who obstructs its free spread. It brings calamity on him who reviles and abuses it. (3510)

२६. अघविषा निपतन्ती तमो निपतिता ॥

26. It is fearfully venomous, when it is down-trodden by its foe. It brings death-like darkness on him who has degraded and dishonoured it. (3511)

२७. अनुगच्छन्ती प्राणानुप दासयति ब्रह्मगवी ब्रह्मज्यस्य ॥

27. Pursuing him, Vedic knowledge extinguisheth the vital breath of its injurer. (3512)

[1]Sinners fight amongst themselves blaming each other for their failure in its spread.

Paryāya 4

२८. वैरं विकृत्यमाना पौत्राद्यं विभाज्यमाना ॥

28. It is hostile to its desecrator, the bringer of woe to the children of its profaner and outrager. (3513)

२९. देवहेतिर्ह्रियमाणा व्यृऽद्धिर्हृता ॥

29. It weakens physically him who torments its preachers. It destroys the wealth of him who snatches it away from the learned. (3514)

३०. पाप्माधिधीयमाना पारुष्यमवधीयमाना ॥

30. It brings misery when it is suppressed, and contumely when it is shown disrespect. (3515)

३१. विषं प्रयस्यन्ती तक्मा प्रयस्ता ॥

31. It is deadly like poison to its foe, when it is opposed. It makes his life miserable when he torments it to the extreme. (3516)

३२. अघं पच्यमाना दुष्वप्न्यं पक्वा ॥

32. It is sinful to try to spoil it. Its destruction is distressing like an evil dream. (3517)

३३. मूलबर्हणी पर्याक्रियमाणा क्षितिः पर्याकृता ॥

33. It is uprooting when it is being disgraced, and destructive when it has been disgraced. (3518)

३४. असंज्ञा गन्धेन शुगुद्ध्रियमाणाशीविष उद्धृता ॥

34. It causes discord when it is suppressed, grief when it is being ousted. It acts as a serpent with poison in its fang when it has been ousted. (3519)

३५. अभूतिरुपह्रियमाणा पराभूतिरुपहृता ॥

35. It brings loss of power to its opponent who forcibly retards its progress, and humiliation when its spread has been retarded. (3520)

३६. शर्वः क्रुद्धः पिश्यमाना शिमिदा पिशिता ॥

36. Being anatomised it acts like a wrathful violent person. It destroys happiness when anatomised. (3521)[1]

३७. अवर्तिरश्यमाना निर्ऋतिरशिता ॥

[1]Griffith translates Simidā as a female demon, or a disease attributed to her influence. The word means, destroyer of noble acts and mental peace, vide *Niruktā* 5-12. Anatomised: Exploding of the doctrines of the Vedas.

37. It brings poverty when it is being outraged, and destruction, having been outraged. (3522)

३८. अशिता लोकाच्छिनत्ति ब्रह्मगवी ब्रह्मज्यमस्माच्चामुष्माच्च ।।

38. Vedic knowledge when desecrated cuts off the injurer of the learned from this world and the world yonder. (3523)

Paryāya 5

३९. तस्या आहननं कृत्या मेनिराशसनं वलग ऊबध्यम् ।।

39. Its censure is an act of violence. To injure its cause is dreadful like a thunderbolt. Its forcible limitation is highly painful. (3524)

४०. अस्वगता परिह्णुता ।।

40. He invites poverty who conceals and usurps it. (3525)

४१. अग्निः क्रव्याद् भूत्वा ब्रह्मगवी ब्रह्मज्यं प्रविश्यात्ति ।।

41. Having become the flesh-eating fire of the funeral pile, Vedic knowledge attacks and consumes the oppressor of the learned. (3526)

४२. सर्वास्याङ्गा पर्वा मूलानि वृश्चति ।।

42. It sunders all his organs and roots. (3527)

४३. छिनत्त्यस्य पितृबन्धु परा भावयति मातृबन्धु ।।

43. It cuts off his relationship on the father's side and destroys maternal kinship. (3528)

४४. विवाहां ज्ञातीन्त्सर्वानपि क्षापयति ब्रह्मगवी ब्रह्मज्यस्य क्षत्रियेणापुनर्दीयमाना ।।

44. Vedic knowledge, when its dissemination is restricted by a King, ruins the marital ties and all the kinsmen of the learned. (3529)

४५. अवास्तुमेनमस्वगमप्रजसं करोत्यपरापरणो भवति क्षीयते ।।

45. It makes him homeless, shelterless, childless: he is extinguished without any body to support him. (3530)[1]

४६. य एवं विदुषो ब्राह्मणस्य क्षत्रियो गामादत्ते ।।

46. So shall it be with the Kshatriya who takes to himself the Vedic knowledge of the learned Brahman. (3531)[2]

[1]It: Vedic knowledge. Him: The Kshatriya.

[2]A King who puts obstacles in the way of a Brahman for advancing his knowledge, and takes possession of his treasure of books, is reduced to this plight, for want of free flow of Vedic teachings.

Paryāya 6

४७. क्षिप्रं वै तस्याहनने गृध्राः कुर्वत ऐलबम् ।।

47. Quickly, when he is smitten down by death, the clamorous vultures cry. (3532)[1]

४८. क्षिप्रं वै तस्यादहनं परि नृत्यन्ति केशिनीराघ्नानाः पाणिनोरसि कुर्वाणाः पापमैलबम् ।।

48. Quickly, around his funeral fire hover women with dishevelled locks, striking the hand upon the breast and uttering their ominous shrieks. (3533)[2]

४९. क्षिप्रं वै तस्य वास्तुषु वृकाः कुर्वत ऐलबम् ।।

49. Quickly on his palaces the wolves howl. (3534)[3]

५०. क्षिप्रं वै तस्य पृच्छन्ति यत् तदासी३दिदं नु ता३दिति ।।

50. Quickly, the people ask about him, 'Is this the ruined palace which he occupied.' (3535)

५१. छिन्ध्या च्छिन्धि प्र च्छिन्ध्यपि क्षापय क्षापय ।।

51. Rend, rend to pieces, rend away, destroy, destroy him utterly. (3536)

५२. आददानमाङ्गिरसि ब्रह्मज्यमुप दासय ।।

52. Destroy, O Vedic knowledge, revealed by God! the wretch who robs and wrongs the learned. (3537)[4]

५३. वैश्वदेवी ह्यु१च्यसे कृत्या कूल्बजमावृता ।।

53. O Vedic knowledge, thou art called the mighty force of God. When obstructed, thou causest havoc on earth. (3538)

५४. ओषन्ती समोषन्ती ब्रह्मणो वज्रः ।।

54. Consuming, burning all things up, O Vedic knowledge! thou art the thunderbolt of God. (3539)

५५. क्षुरपविर्मृत्युर्भूत्वा वि धाव त्वम् ।।

55. Go thou, O Vedic knowledge! becoming Death sharp! as razor's edge, and attack thy reviler. (3540)

५६. आ दत्से जिनतां वर्च इष्टं पूर्तं चाशिषः ।।

[1]Him: The Kshatriya. Vultures making noise flock to eat his corpse.
[2]His: A reviler of the Vedas.
[3]The palaces are depopulated and dilapidated, where forest beasts roam and howl.
[4](आङ्गिरसि)—हे अङ्गिरसा महाविदुषा परमेश्वरेणोपदिष्टे । Griffith translates Angirasi as the cow belonging to Angiras and his representatives, the priests.

56. Thou snatchest the tyrants' strength, the fruit of their virtuous deeds and philanthropic acts, and their noble ambitions. (3541)

५७. आदाय जीतं जीताय लोके३ऽमुष्मिन् प्र यच्छसि ॥

57. O Vedic knowledge! catching hold the oppressor, thou sendest him to the next world to shorten his life. (3542)

५८. अघ्न्ये पदवीर्भव ब्राह्मणस्याभिशस्त्या ॥

58. O Deathless, Inviolable Vedic knowledge, become thou the path-finder, when a learned person is maliciously misrepresented! (3543)

५९. मेनिः शरव्या५ भवाघादघविषा भव ॥

59. O Vedic knowledge! become a bolt, an arrow, be terribly venomous on account of the sin of thy reviler. (3544)

६०. अघ्न्ये प्र शिरो जहि ब्रह्मज्यस्य कृतागसो देवपीयोरराधसः ॥

60. O Vedic knowledge! break thou the head of him who oppresses the learned, is criminal, blasphemer of the sages and niggard. (3545)

६१. त्वया प्रमूर्णं मृदितमग्निर्दहतु दुश्चितम् ॥

61. Let an awful King burn the spiteful wretch when crushed to death and slain by thee. (3546)[1]

Paryāya 7

६२. वृश्च प्र वृश्च सं वृश्च दह प्र दह सं दह ॥

62. Rend, rend to bits, rend through and through, scorch and consume and burn to dust. (3547)

६३. ब्रह्मज्यं देव्यघ्न्य आ मूलादनुसंदह ॥

63. Consume thou, even from the root, the sages' tyrant, O inviolable Vedic knowledge! (3548)

६४. यथायाद् यमसादनात् पापलोकान् परावतः ॥

64. That he may go punished by the court of justice to distant prisons, the homes of sinners. (3549)

६५. एवा त्वं देव्यघ्न्ये ब्रह्मज्यस्य कृतागसो देवपीयोरराधसः ॥

65. So, O inviolable Vedic knowledge, do thou from him, the sages' tyrant, criminal, blasphemer of the learned, niggard. (3550)

[1]Thee: Vedic knowledge.

६६. वज्रेण शतपर्वणा तीक्ष्णेन क्षुरभृष्टिना ॥

66. With hundred-knotted thunderbolt, sharpened and edged like razor-blades. (3551)

६७. प्र स्कन्धान् प्र शिरो जहि ॥

67. Strike off the shoulders and the head. (3552)

६८. लोमान्यस्य सं छिन्धि त्वचमस्य वि वेष्टय ॥

68. Snatch thou the hair from off his head, and from his body strip the skin. (3553)

६९. मांसान्यस्य शातय स्नावान्यस्य सं वृह ॥

69. Tear out his sinews, cause his flesh to fall in pieces from his frame. (3554)

७०. अस्थीन्यस्य पीडय मज्जानमस्य निर्जहि ॥

70. Crush thou his bones together, strike and beat the marrow out of him. (3555)

७१. सर्वास्याङ्गा पर्वाणि वि श्रथय ॥

71. Dislocate all his limbs and joints. (3556)

७२. अग्निरेनं क्रव्यात् पृथिव्या नुदतामुदोषतु वायुरन्तरिक्षान्महतो वरिम्णः ॥

72. From earth let the carnivorous fire of the funeral pile drive him, let air burn him from mid-air's broad region. (3557)

७३. सूर्य एनं दिवः प्र णुदतां न्योषतु ॥

73. Let the Sun drive him away from light and consume him. (3558)

BOOK (Kāṇḍa) XIII

Chapter (Anuvāka) 1

HYMN I

१. उदेहि वाजिन् यो अप्स्व१न्तरिदं राष्ट्रं प्र विश सूनृतावत् ।
यो रोहितो विश्वमिदं जजान स त्वा राष्ट्राय सुभृतं बिभर्तु ॥

1. Rise, O mighty King, who livest amongst his subjects, and enter this thy kingdom equipped with fine statesmanship. Let God Who created this all uphold thee carefully nurtured for supreme dominion. (3559)[1]

[1] (अप्सु) प्रजासु । आपः=आप्ताः प्रजाः दयानन्द भाष्ये यजु० ६-२७ ।

२. उद्वाज आ गन् यो अप्स्व१न्तर्विश आ रोह त्वद्योनयो याः ।
सोमं दधानोऽप ओषधीर्गाश्चतुष्पदो द्विपद आ वेशयेह ॥

2. O powerful King, thou risest in the midst of thy subjects through thy chivalry. Rule over the subjects who are thy creators. Possessing supremacy, let pure waters, plants, kine, bipeds and quadrupeds flourish in thy state! (3560)[1]

३. यूयमुग्रा मरुतः पृश्निमातर इन्द्रेण युजा प्र मृणीत शत्रून् ।
आ वो रोहितः शृणवत् सुदानवस्त्रिषप्तासो मरुतः स्वादुसंमुदः ॥

3. O strong and mighty soldiers, lovers of motherland, with king as ally crush down the foes. Ye bounteous givers, thrice-seven soldiers, who delight in dainty food, let God hear your prayer! (3561)[2]

४. रुहो रुरोह रोहित आ रुरोह गर्भो जनीनां जनुषामुपस्थम् ।
ताभिः संरब्धमन्वविन्दन् षडुर्वीर्गातुं प्रपश्यन्निह राष्ट्रमाहाः ॥

4. God rules over all progressive souls. Like the womb of mothers, He exists amongst all creatures. Known by all living beings, He seems pervading all the six wide regions. Revealing knowledge, He sheds His lustre in the universe. (3562)

५. आ ते राष्ट्रमिह रोहितोऽहार्षीद् व्यास्थन्मृधो अभयं ते अभूत् ।
तस्मै ते द्यावापृथिवी रेवतीभिः कामं दुहाथामिह शक्वरीभिः ॥

5. For thee hath God granted this dominion, scattered thine enemies, made thee free from fear. Let Heaven and Earth, with wealth and strength fulfil all thy wishes. (3563)[3]

६. रोहितो द्यावापृथिवी जजान तत्र तन्तुं परमेष्ठी ततान ।
तत्र शिश्रियेऽज एकपादोऽदृंहद् द्यावापृथिवी बलेन ॥

6. God gave the Earth and Heaven there being. There hath He extended Matter. Therein pervades the Eternal, One-footed God. He with His might hath established Earth and Heaven. (3564)[4]

७. रोहितो द्यावापृथिवी अदृंहत् तेन स्वः स्तभितं तेन नाकः ।
तेनान्तरिक्षं विमिता रजांसि तेन देवा अमृतमन्वविन्दन् ॥

[1]The subjects are the electors of the king, hence they are spoken of as creators.

[2]Thrice: Action (Karma) Contemplation (Upāsanā) Knowledge (Gyāna). Seven: Skin, Eye, Ear, Tongue, Nose, Mind, Intellect. Soldiers who acquire action, contemplation, knowledge through the help of seven organs.

[3]Thee: The King.

[4]One-footed: The sole shelter of the world.

7. God firmly established Earth and Heaven. He has granted us the worldly pleasure and the pleasure of salvation. He measured out mid-air and all the regions. Through His grace have the learned secured final beatitude. (3565)[1]

८. वि रोहितो अमृशद् विश्वरूपं समाकुर्वाणः प्ररुहो रुहश्च ।
दिवं रूढ्वा महता महिम्ना सं ते राष्ट्रमनक्तु पयसा घृतेन ॥

8. Arranging the materials and objects of the world God considered the universe in all its forms and phases. May He, higher than Heaven, with mighty glory, anoint thy sovereignity with milk and butter. (3566)[2]

९. यास्ते रुहः प्ररुहो यास्त आरुहो याभिरापृणासि दिवमन्तरिक्षम् ।
तासां ब्रह्मणा पयसा वावृधानो विशि राष्ट्रे जागृहि रोहितस्य ॥

9. O God, Thy creative powers, extraordinary forces, visible actions, wherewith Thou fillest heaven and air's mid-region—with the supreme force of these mighty powers, being Foremost of all, Thou grantest the fruit of actions in this world of the subjects created by Thee! (3567)

१०. यास्ते विशस्तपसः संबभूवुर्वत्सं गायत्रीमनु ता इहागुः ।
तास्त्वा विशन्तु मनसा शिवेन संमाता वत्सो अभ्येतु रोहितः ॥

10. O King, thy subjects have been created by God. They have come here in the wake of God, the Mighty Preacher, and Vedic knowledge ! With friendly heart let them approach to serve thee. May they visualise God, the Mother of all, the Mighty Preacher, the Creator of all ! (3568)

११. ऊर्ध्वो रोहितो अधि नाके अस्थाद् विश्वा रूपाणि जनयन् युवा कविः ।
तिग्मेनाग्निर्ज्योतिषा वि भाति तृतीये चक्रे रजसि प्रियाणि ॥

11. The Mighty, Wise God, creating all the objects of the world lives in extreme delight perceived in salvation. He is Refulgent in His heightened lustre. He has brought us joy and gladness in the third realm. (3569)[3]

१२. सहस्रशृङ्गो वृषभो जातवेदा घृताहुतः सोमपृष्ठः सुवीरः ।
मा मा हासीन्नाथितो नेत् त्वा जहानि गोपोषं च मे वीरपोषं च धेहि ॥

12. May the Refulgent, Mighty God, the Creator of the Vedas, the Giver of light, the Repository of joy, highly valiant, and supreme, ne'er quit me ; may I never forsake Thee. O God, give abundant knowledge and progeny. (3570)

[1]Final beatitude: Emancipation, Moksha.

[2]पयसा घृतेन may also mean corn and water.

[3]Third realm: The Sātwik (pure) stage, higher than the Tāmsik and Rājsik stages of ignorance and passion. Man enjoys happiness when his mind is pure, free from darkness and passion.

१३. रोहितो यज्ञस्य जनिता मुखं च रोहिताय वाचा श्रोत्रेण मनसा जुहोमि।
रोहितं देवा यन्ति सुमनस्यमाना स मा रोहैः सामित्यै रोहयतु ॥

13. God is the Father and Head of worship. Him do I adore with voice, ear, heart. Sages with joyful spirit go unto God. May He through different births raise me till I join Him. (3571)

१४. रोहितो यज्ञं व्य्दधाद् विश्वकर्मणे तस्मात् तेजांस्युप मेमान्यागुः।
वोचेयं ते नाभिं भुवनस्याधि मज्मनि ॥

14. God ordered sacrifice for a person wise in all deeds. From Him have I obtained this strength and energy. May I proclaim Thee as my kin over the greatness of the world. (3572)

१५. आ त्वा रुरोह बृहत्यु३त पङ्क्तिरा ककुब् वर्चसा जातवेदः।
आ त्वा रुरोहोष्णिहाक्षरो वषट्कार आ त्वा रुरोह रोहितो रेतसा सह ॥

15. O learned person, vast knowledge, fame, joy-bestowing grandeur have elevated thee on all sides, with great splendour. Loving, extensive charitable disposition has elevated thee. God has elevated thee in all respects with His might. (3573)

१६. अयं वस्ते गर्भं पृथिव्या दिवं वस्तेऽयमन्तरिक्षम्।
अयं ब्रध्नस्य विष्टपि स्व्र्लोकान् व्या्नशे ॥

16. God pervades the interior of the Earth, heaven and air's mid-region. He pervades the blazing part of the Sun, and all the worlds in space. (3574)

१७. वाचस्पते पृथिवी नः स्योना स्योना योनिस्तल्पा नः सुशेवा।
इहैव प्राणः सख्ये नो अस्तु तं त्वा परमेष्ठिन् पर्यग्निरायुषा वर्चसा दधातु ॥

17. O God, the Lord of Vedic speech, to us, may Earth be pleasant, pleasant our dwelling, pleasant be our conches. Even here may, life-breath be our friend. O God, Highest of all, may this learned person worship Thee with his long life and splendour! (3575)[1]

१८. वाचस्पत ऋतवः पञ्च ये नौ वैश्वकर्मणाः परि ये संबभूवुः।
इहैव प्राणः सख्ये नो अस्तु तं त्वा परमेष्ठिन् परि रोहित आयुषा वर्चसा दधातु ॥

18. O God, the Lord of Vedic speech, these our five seasons have been created for the performance of all deeds. Even here may life-breath be our friend. O God, Highest of all, may this learned person worship Thee with his long life and splendour! (3576)

१९. वाचस्पते सौमनसं मनश्च गोष्ठे नो गा जनय योनिषु प्रजाः।
इहैव प्राणः सख्ये नो अस्तु तं त्वा परमेष्ठिन् पर्यहमायुषा वर्चसा दधामि ॥

[1]Here; In this body. Friend; We may live long.

19. O God, the Lord of Vedic speech, let our mind be full of noble resolves; breed kine in our stall and children in our houses. Even here may life-breath be our friend. O God, Highest of all, I worship Thee with long life and splendour ! (3577)

२०. परि त्वा धात् सविता देवो अग्निर्वर्चसा मित्रावरुणावभि त्वा ।
सर्वा अरातीरवक्रामन्नेहीदं राष्ट्रमकरः सूनृतावत् ॥

20. May God protect thee from all sides. May a strong person full of zeal like fire protect thee. May Prāna and Apāna protect thee. O King, treading down all foes come hither. Make this kingdom pleasant and glorious. (3578)[1]

२१. यं त्वा पृषती रथे प्रष्टिर्वहति रोहित । शुभा यासि रिणन्नपः ॥

21. O God, Matter, worthy of close examination, is placed at thy disposal, in this beautiful world splendidly guiding human beings. Thou residest in the extreme joy of salvation! (3579)

२२. अनुव्रता रोहिणी रोहितस्य सूरिः सुवर्णा बृहती सुवर्चाः ।
तया वाजान् विश्वरूपां जयेम तया विश्वाः पृतना अभि ष्याम ॥

22. Goading, refulgent, golden, lofty Matter follows the command of God. Through Matter may we acquire food-grains, and be conquerors in every battle. (3580)

२३. इदं सदो रोहिणी रोहितस्यासौ पन्थाः पृषती येन याति ।
तां गन्धर्वाः कश्यपा उन्नयन्ति तां रक्षन्ति कवयोऽप्रमादम् ॥

23. Matter is the abode of God. That is the path the multi-hued Matter pursueth, Vedic scholars and learned persons lead it upwards and sages free from sloth ever guard it. (3581)[2]

२४. सूर्यस्याश्वा हरयः केतुमन्तः सदा वहन्त्यमृताः सुखं रथम् ।
घृतपावा रोहितो भ्राजमानो दिवं देवः पृषतीमा विवेश ॥

24. The All-pervading, Wise, Immortal attributes of God, draw on for ever the light-rolling beautiful chariot of the world. God, the Guardian of knowledge, Refulgent, hath entered into the serviceable multi-hued Matter. (3582)

२५. यो रोहितो वृषभस्तिग्मश्रृङ्गः पर्यग्निं परि सूर्यं बभूव ।
यो विष्टभ्नाति पृथिवीं दिवं च तस्माद् देवा अधि सृष्टीः सृजन्ते ॥

[1]Thee: The King.

[2]God pervades Matter, hence it is His dwelling-place. Griffith has interpreted Kasyapas; as a class of semi-divine genü or spirits who regulate the course of the Sun. The word means Vedic scholars. Gandharvas: has been interpreted by Griffith as celestial beings who dwell in the sky and govern the course of the heavenly bodies. The word means learned persons.

25. God, who is Almighty, and Chastiser of the sinners is higher than fire and Sun. He Who supports the sundered earth and heaven—through His grace the elements create different worlds. (3583)

२६. रोहितो दिवमारुहन्महतः पर्यर्णवात् । सर्वा रुरोह रोहितो रुहः ॥

26. God, the Creator, with His Vast fathomless power has established Law everywhere. He has created all the materials of the world. (3584)

२७. वि मिमीष्व पयस्वतीं धृताचीं देवानां धेनुरनपस्पृगेषा ।
इन्द्रः सोमं पिबतु क्षेमो अस्त्वग्निः प्र स्तौतु वि मृधो नुदस्व ॥

27. O learned person, achieve intellect full of truth and lustre. It is the inseparable companion of the learned like a milch-cow. May the exalted soul attain to the joy of salvation. Ours be peace and safety. Let the learned yogi praise God. Expel thy internal foes. (3585)[1]

२८. समिद्धो अग्निः समिधानो घृतवृद्धो घृताहुतः ।
अभीषाड् विश्वाषाडग्निः सपत्नान् हन्तु ये मम ॥

28. Just as kindling and inflamed fire adored with butter and enhanced thereby removes disease, so may this conquering hero, conqueror of all, destroy mine enemies. (3586)

२९. हन्त्वेनान् प्र दहत्वरिर्यो नः पृतन्यति । क्रव्यादाग्निना वयं सपत्नान् प्र दहामसि ॥

29. Let him smite down to death and burn the foeman who attacketh us with his army. May we consume our adversaries, just as the funeral fire does the corpse. (3587)

३०. अवाचीनानव जहीन्द्र वज्रेण बाहुमान् । अधा सपत्नान् मामकानग्नेस्तेजोऽभिरादिषि ॥

30. O mighty-armed king, beat down the sinners with thy bolt. I through the energy and force of God have subdued my internal foes! (3588)

३१. अग्ने सपत्नानधरान् पादयास्मद् व्यथया सजातमुत्पिपानं बृहस्पते ।
इन्द्राग्नी मित्रावरुणावधरे पद्यन्तामप्रतिमन्यूयमानाः ॥

31. O King, cast down our foes beneath our feet, O King, the master of various sciences, oppress our rebel kinsman. O King, mighty and active like the Sun and lightning, O King, comfort-giving and pain-alleviating like Prāna and Apāna, low let them fall, powerless to show their anger! (3589)

३२. उद्यंस्त्वं देव सूर्य सपत्नानव मे जहि । अवैनानश्मना जहि ते यन्त्वधमं तमः ॥

32. Being ever prosperous, O brilliant King, drive my foes away. Yea, beat them backward with the thunderbolt strong like stone: to deepest darkness let them go. (3590)

[1]Internal foes: Lust, anger, avarice, pride, infatuation,

३३. वत्सो विराजो वृषभो मतीनामा रुरोह शुक्रपृष्ठोऽन्तरिक्षम् ।
घृतेनार्कमभ्य॒र्चन्ति वत्सं ब्रह्म सन्तं ब्रह्मणा वर्धयन्ति ॥

33. God, the Engulfer of the universe, the Master of all eulogies and sciences, full of refulgence. pervades the atmosphere. The learned, through knowledge praise the Adorable God. Him, Who is God, they exalt through Vedic knowledge. (3591)

३४. दिवं च.रोह पृथिवीं च रोह राष्ट्रं च रोह द्रविणं च रोह ।
प्रजां च रोहामृतं च रोह रोहितेन तन्वं१ सं स्पृशस्व ॥

34. O man, rise up to salvation, control the Earth, rise up to kingship, rise up to opulence, attain to offspring, rise to a life of hundred years. Unite thy soul with God. (3592)

३५. ये देवा राष्ट्रभृतोऽभितो यन्ति सूर्यम् ।
तैष्टे रोहितः संविदानो राष्ट्रं दधातु सुमनस्यमानः ॥

35. With all the learned persons, who, upholding royal sway approach God from all sides, with all of these may God accordant, give sovereignty to thee with friendly spirit. (3593)[1]

३६. उत् त्वा यज्ञा ब्रह्मपूता वहन्त्यध्वगतो हरयस्त्वा वहन्ति ।
तिरः समुद्रमति रोचसेऽर्णवम् ॥

36. O God, sacrifices, purified through Vedic verses exalt Thee. Souls travelling on the path of salvation, instal Thee in their heart. Thy light shines over sea and billowy ocean. (3594)

३७. रोहिते द्यावापृथिवी अधि श्रिते वसुजिति गोजिति संधनाजिति ।
सहस्रं यस्य जनिमानि सप्त च वोचेयं ते नाभिं भुवनस्याधि मज्मनि ॥

37. God, the Conqueror of the worlds in which men inhabit, the Conqueror of luminary plants, the Conqueror of riches, is heaven's and earth's upholder. Whose countless acts of creation are connected with seven organs. O God, over earth's greatness would I tell my kinship with Thee ! (3595)

३८. यशा यासि प्रदिशो दिशश्च यशाः पशूनामुत चर्षणीनाम् ।
यशाः पृथिव्या अदित्या उपस्थेऽहं भूयासं सवितेव चारुः ॥

38. O God, Thou pervadest gloriously the regions and mid-regions. Thou art a glorious sight to beasts and men. On earths', ón Veda's bosom, bright with glory, fain would I equal the Sun in beauty! (3596)

३९. अमुत्र सन्निह वेत्थेतः संस्तानि पश्यसि । इतः पश्यन्ति रोचनं दिवि सूर्यं विपश्चितम् ॥

39. O God, Thou, yonder, knowest all things here, when here Thou knowest what is there. From here the learned see God, Resplendent like the Sun in heaven, and profoundly wise ! (3597)

[1]Thee: The King.

४०. देवो देवान् मर्चयस्यन्तश्चरस्यर्णवे । समानमग्निमिन्धते तं विदुः कवयः परे ।।

40. O God, Thou preachest noble virtues, and pervadest the universe. The higher sages only know Him, and thereby kindle themselves! (3598)

४१. अवः परेण पर एनावरेण पदा वत्सं बिभ्रती गौरुदस्थात् ।
सा कद्रीची कं स्विदर्धं परागात् क्वऽ स्वित् सूते नहि यूथे अस्मिन् ।।

41. This Vedic speech hath risen, preserving with its knowledge God, the Mighty Preacher, Who pervades from distance the near places, and from near the distant ones. What kind of speech is that? What Prosperous God does it resort to ? Wherefrom does it take its birth? Certainly not from this human agency. (3599)[1]

४२. एकपदी द्विपदी सा चतुष्पद्यष्टापदी नवपदी बभूवुषी ।
सहस्राक्षरा भुवनस्य पङ्क्तिस्तस्याः समुद्रा अधि वि क्षरन्ति ।।

42. This Vedic speech pervades the One solitary God. It deals with the animate and inanimate life. It expatiates on religion (Dharma), worldly prosperity (Artha), fulfilment of desire (Kāma), and salvation (Moksha). It gives us the instructions for guidance in four Ashramās and four Varnās. Its knowledge is acquired through nine organs. It grants us thousands of imperishable forces. It perfects the universe. Oceans of knowledge flow forth from her in all directions. (3600)[2]

४३. आरोहन् द्यामममृतः प्राव मे वचः ।
उत् त्वा यज्ञा ब्रह्मपूता वहन्त्यध्वगतो हरयस्त्वा वहन्ति ।।

43. O Immortal God, full of refulgence, listen to my supplication. The sacrifices sanctified by Vedic scholars exalt Thee. Followers of the teachings of the Vedas realise Thee ! (3601)

४४. वेद तत् ते अमर्त्य यत् त आक्रमणं दिवि । यत् ते सधस्थं परमे व्योऽमन् ।।

44. O Immortal soul, know thy progress towards salvation. Know God, thy constant companion, thy guardian in the state of emancipation ! (3602)

४५. सूर्यो द्यां सूर्यः पृथिवीं सूर्य आपोऽति पश्यति ।
सूर्यो भूतस्यैकं चक्षुरा रुरोह दिवं महीम् ।।

45. God pervades and knows fully, the Heaven, the Earth, and the subtle atoms of Matter. He is the single Seer of the universe. He pervades the Earth and Heaven. (3603)

[1]See *Rig*, 1-164-17, and *Atharva*, 9-9-17. The Vedas are revealed and not man-made.
[2]Four Ashramās: Brahmcharya, Grihastha, Ban Prastha, Sanyāsa. Four Varunās: Brahman, Kshatriya, Vaisha, Shudra. Nine Organs: Mind, intellect, two eyes, two ears, mouth, two nostrils. Through nostrils yogis perform Pranayam and Yoga, and thereby acquire Vedic knowledge. See *Atharva*, 9-10-21, *Rig*, 1-164-41, 42.

४६. उर्वीरासन् परिधयो वेदिर्भूमिरकल्पत् । तत्रैतावग्नी आधत्त हिमं घ्रंसं च रोहितः ।।

46. The earth was made the altar, and the wide directions were the fence. There God established both these fires, the fervent hot Sun and the cold Moon. (3604)[1]

४७. हिमं घ्रंसं चाधाय यूपान् कृत्वा पर्वतान् । वर्षाज्यावग्नी ईजाते रोहितस्य स्वर्विदः ।।

47. God established heat and cold. He made the mountains victory posts. Both the fires performed sacrifice with rain as butter, for God, the Giver of happiness and the Creator of all objects. (3605)

४८. स्वर्विदो रोहितस्य ब्रह्मणाग्निः समिध्यते ।
तस्माद् घ्रंसस्तस्माद्धिमस्तस्माद् यज्ञोऽजायत ।।

48. Through the Vedic knowledge of God, the Giver of happiness and the Creator of all objects, is kindled the light of heaven. From Him the heat, from Him the Cold, from Him the sacrifice (Yajna) was born. (3606)[2]

४९. ब्रह्मणाग्नी वावृधानौ ब्रह्मवृद्धौ ब्रह्माहुतौ । ब्रह्मेद्धावग्नी ईजाते रोहितस्य स्वर्विदः ।।

49. Both Agnis, made strong with Vedic knowledge, waxing by Vedic knowledge, adored by Vedic knowledge, enkindled by Vedic knowledge, perform sacrifice for God, the Giver of happiness. (3607)[3]

५०. सत्ये अन्यः समाहितोऽप्स्व१न्यः समिध्यते । ब्रह्मेद्धावग्नी ईजाते रोहितस्य स्वर्विदः ।।

50. Of the two, one helps in the acquisition of knowledge, the other is united with the organs of action. Both kindled by vedic knowledge perform sacrifice for the yogi aspiring for salvation. (3608)[4]

५१. यं वातः परि शुम्भति यं वेन्द्रो ब्रह्मणस्पतिः । ब्रह्मेद्धावग्नी ईजाते रोहितस्य स्वर्विदः ।।

51. Whom the Wind exalts, Whom the cloud, the lord of corn glorifies, for Him, the Giver of happiness both Sun and Moon, kindled by Vedic knowledge perform sacrifice. (3609)[5]

५२. वेदिं भूमिं कल्पयित्वा दिवं कृत्वा दक्षिणाम् ।
घ्रंसं तदग्निं कृत्वा चकार विश्वमात्मन्वद् वर्षेणाज्येन रोहितः ।।

52. God made the earth to be His altar, heaven His Dakshina. Then heat He took for Agni, and with rain for molten butter He created every living being. (3610)

[1]Some interpret the fires as Summer Sun and Winter Sun.
[2]Light of heaven, Sun.
[3]Agnis: Sun, Moon.
[4]Both: Prāna, Apāna.
[5]Whom, Him refer to God.

५३. वर्षमाज्यं घ्रंसो अग्निर्वेदिर्भूमिरकल्पत । तत्रैतान् पर्वतानग्निर्गीर्भिरूर्ध्वाँ अकल्पयत् ॥

53. In this Yajna of creation of the universe, the earth became an altar, heat became Agni, and the rain became butter. There God through His vast powers, made these mountains rise and stand erect. (3611)

५४. गीर्भिरूर्ध्वान् कल्पयित्वा रोहितो भूमिमब्रवीत् ।
त्वयीदं सर्वं जायतां यद् भूतं यच्च भाव्यम् ॥

54. Then having made the hills stand up, God spoke to Earth and said : In thee let every thing be born, what is and what is yet to be. (3612)[1]

५५. स यज्ञः प्रथमो भूतो भव्यो अजायत ।
तस्माद्ध जज्ञ इदं सर्वं यत् किं चेदं विरोचते रोहितेन ऋषिणाभृतम् ॥

55. God existed in the Past and shall exist in Future. From Him arose this universe full of brightness. He has sustained this world. (3613)[2]

५६. यश्च गां पदा स्फुरति प्रत्यङ् सूर्यं च मेहति ।
तस्य वृश्चामि ते मूलं न च्छायां करवोऽपरम् ॥

56. O disagreeable sinner, if thou showest disrespect to Vedic knowledge, or tormentest a learned person glittering like the Sun, thy root I sever : so that nevermore mayst thou perform such a disgraceful act ! (3614)[3]

५७. यो माभिच्छायमत्येषि मां चाग्निं चान्तरा ।
तस्य वृश्चामि ते मूलं न च्छायां करवोऽपरम् ॥

57. Thou who, casting his shadow on me the Guru, goest beyond me, or passest between me the pupil and the Guru refulgent like fire, thy root I sever : so that nevermore mayst thou perform such an act of ignorance. (3615)

५८. यो अद्य देव सूर्य त्वां च मां चान्तरायति । दुष्वप्न्यं तस्मिञ्छमलं दुरितानि च मृज्महे ॥

58. O learned Guru, whoever casts interruption between thee and me to-day, on him we wipe away ill-dream, troubles and impurity ! (3616)

५९. मा प्र गाम पथो वयं मा यज्ञादिन्द्र सोमिनः । मान्त स्थुर्नो अरातयः ॥

59. O God, let us never forsake the path of righteousness and Thy joy-bestowing contemplation. May our internal foes never have sway over us ! (3617)[4]

[1]The language is metaphorical. God spoke means God ordained.

[2]'I' may refer to the King. 'प्रत्यङ् सूर्यं च मेहति' may mean, if thou makest water before the Sun.

[3]To pass between the teacher and the pupil is a sign of disrespect. It is a mark of discourtesy to cast one's shadow on the Guru and go beyond him.

[4]Internal foes: Lust, anger, avarice, infatuation, and pride. See *Rig*, 10-57-1.

६०. यो यज्ञस्य प्रसाधनस्तन्तुर्देवेष्वाततः । तमाहुतमशीमहि ॥

60. May we obtain the Adorable God, Who perfecteth our sacrifice and pervades all the worlds through His subtlety. (3618)

Chapter (Anuvāka) 2

HYMN II

१. उदस्य केतवो दिवि शुक्रा भ्राजन्त ईरते । आदित्यस्य नृचक्षसो महिव्रतस्य मीढुषः ॥

1. The different sorts of knowledge, pure and radiant, of God, the Giver of happiness, the Mighty Creator, Sustainer and Dissolver of the universe, the Seer of the actions of men and their Rewarder, are visible in every affair. (3619)

२. दिशां प्रज्ञानां स्वरयन्तमर्चिषा सुपक्षमाशुं पतयन्तमर्णवे ।
स्तवाम सूर्यं भुवनस्य गोपां यो रश्मिभिर्दिश आभाति सर्वाः ॥

2. Let us laud God, who develops the intellects of the yogis with the light of His knowledge, as the Sun illumines all regions, Who pervading the Ocean of His knowledge granting wisdom to the yogis is the Protector of the universe, and the Illuminator of all regions with His powers. (3620)

३. यत् प्राङ् प्रत्यङ् स्वधया यासि शीभं नानारूपे अहनी कर्षि मायया ।
तदादित्य महि तत् ते महि श्रवो यदेको विश्वं परि भूम जायसे ॥

3. O God, Thou pervadest speedily the East and West like the Sun, Thou makest by Thy wonderful power the day and night of diverse colours. This is Thy highly transcendent glory, O God, that Thou alone are the Mightiest of all in the universe. (3621)

४. विपश्चितं तरणिं भ्राजमानं वहन्ति यं हरितः सप्त बह्वीः ।
स्रुताद् यमत्रिर्दिवमुन्निनाय तं त्वा पश्यन्ति परियान्तमाजिम् ॥

4. Just as seven different hued rays carry the Sun, so vital breaths support the soul. The Wise God lifts the soul from the earth to the state of emancipation. The learned behold thee. O soul, marching towards God, as an embodiment of knowledge and action, as emancipated and radiant! (3622)[1]

५. मा त्वा दभन् परियान्तमाजिं स्वस्ति दुर्गां अति याहि शीभम् ।
दिवं च सूर्य पृथिवीं च देवीमहोरात्रे विमिमानो यदेषि ॥

5. O soul, let not foes like lust and anger assail thee in thy journey towards salvation. Speedily overcome all temptations. May thou safely march on the path of salvation. O Yogi, lustrous like the Sun, passing thy days and nights justly, thou goest to God, Brilliant like the sky, and the Giver of shelter like the earth! (3623)

[1]Griffith translates Atri as a celebrated Rishi, said to have been thrown into a fiery pit by the Asuras. This explanation is unacceptable, as there is no history in the Vedas. The word means God. Seven rays: Violet, indigo, brown, green, yellow, orange, red.

६. स्वस्ति ते सूर्य चरसे रथाय येनोभावन्तौ परियासि सद्यः ।
यं ते वहन्ति हरितो वहिष्ठाः शतमश्वा यदि वा सप्त बह्वीः ॥

6. O soul, hail to thy excellent nature, wherewith thou circlest in a moment both the limits, which is supported by hundreds of attractive, active mental forces, arteries of the heart, and seven vital breaths! (3624)[1]

७. सुखं सूर्य रथमंशुमन्तं स्योनं सुवह्निमधि तिष्ठ वाजिनम् ।
यं ते वहन्ति हरितो वहिष्ठाः शतमश्वा यदि वा सप्त बह्वीः ॥

7. O soul, mount this body, coupled with the organs of cognition and action, which is beautiful, comfortable, which easily takes thee from one place to the other, and is full of strength. Thou art supported by hundreds of attractive, active mental forces, arteries of the heart, and seven vital breaths. (3625)

८. सप्त सूर्यो हरितो यातवे रथे हिरण्यत्वचसो बृहतीरयुक्त ।
अमोचि शुक्रो रजसः परस्ताद् विधूय देवस्तमो दिवमारुहत् ॥

8. The soul harnesses to the body, for the journey of life, seven attractive, brilliant, mighty forces of breath. It gets distant freedom from passion, emotion. Casting aside darkness, the soul attains to God. (3626)

९. उत् केतुना बृहता देव आगन्नपावृक् तमोऽभि ज्योतिरश्रैत् ।
दिव्यः सुपर्णः स वीरो व्यख्यददितेः पुत्रो भुवनानि विश्वा ॥

9. The brilliant soul advances with lofty intelligence. Freed from the coverings of ignorance, it obtains the light of God. The soul, the son of God, endowed through His kindness, with divine power, equipped with wisdom, heroic in nature, illumines all the worlds like the Sun. (3627)

१०. उद्यन् रश्मीना तनुषे विश्वा रूपाणि पुष्यसि ।
उभा समुद्रौ ऋतुना वि भासि सर्वांल्लोकान् परिभूर्भ्राजमानः ॥

10. O soul, rising, thou spreadest out thy grandeurs, thou nourishest all objects. Thou with thy knowledge and action illumest both the oceans, encompassing all spheres with thy refulgence! (3628)[2]

११. पर्वापरं चरतो माययैतौ शिशू क्रीडन्तौ परि यातोऽर्णवम् ।
विश्वान्यो भुवना विचष्टे हैरण्यैरन्यं हरितो वहन्ति ॥

11. Through supernatural power, both God and, acting as the leader and follower, sporting like two young creatures, work in the world. One of the pair beholds all living creatures: with beautiful organs the vital breaths bear the other. (3629)[3]

[1]'Which' refers to the nature of the soul. Both the limits: The eastern and western horizons.

[2]Both oceans: This world and the next, or the animate and inanimate world.

[3]God is the leader and soul the follower. 'One' refers to God, and 'other' to soul. See *Rigveda*, 10-85-18, *Atharva*, 7-81-1, and *Atharva*, 14-1-23.

१२. दिवि त्वात्रिरधारयत् सूर्या मासाय कर्तवे ।
स एषि सुधृतस्तपन् विश्वा भूतावचाकशत् ॥

12. O soul, God, free from three sorts of pains, has established thee in the region of salvation for the sake of penance. So on thou goest firmly held. Through thy refulgence thou bestowest knowledge on mankind. (3630)

१३. उभावन्तौ समर्षसि वत्सः संमातराविव । नन्वे३तदितः पुरा ब्रह्म देवा अमी विदुः ॥

13. Just as a child fondly goes to his father and mother, so dost thou, O emancipate soul, realise the true nature of God and soul. Surely, these learned persons know Him as God Immemorial! (3631)

१४. यत् समुद्रमनु श्रितं तत् सिषासति सूर्यः । अध्वास्य विततो महान् पूर्वश्चापरश्च यः ॥

14. The soul is willing to obtain God, Who lies in the ocean of joy. To reach Him, vast and mighty is the path laid down for the soul, for guidance in the past and future. (3632)

१५. तं समाप्नोति जूतिभिस्ततो नाप चिकित्सति । तेनामृतस्य भक्षं देवानां नाव रुन्धते ॥

15. A Yogi finishes his journey with the force of knowledge, and never turns his thought aside. Thereby he withholds not from the learned the enjoyment of food. (3633)[1]

१६. उदु त्यं जातवेदसं देवं वहन्ति केतवः । दृशे विश्वाय सूर्यम् ॥

16. The learned exalt the Omniscient God, and exert to visualise Him, the Urger of the whole universe. (3634)[2]

१७. अप त्ये तायवो यथा नक्षत्रा यन्त्यक्तुभिः । सूराय विश्वचक्षसे ॥

17. Just as Constellations with their gloom, disappear at dawn, due to the lustre of the Sun, the illuminator of the universe, so through the magnanimity of a yogi, do passions, lurking like thieves and bewitching the soul, depart. (3635)[3]

१८. अदृश्रन्नस्य केतवो वि रश्मयो जनाँ अनु । भ्राजन्तो अग्नयो यथा ॥

18. Learned persons, who impart the knowledge of this God to the world are seen working in various ways amongst ordinary mortals for their welfare. They pass a life of austerity and penance, like flames of fire that burn and blaze. (3636)

१९. तरणिर्विश्वदर्शतो ज्योतिष्कृदसि सूर्य । विश्वमा भासि रोचन ॥

[1]It is necessary for the learned to take nutritious food for preserving their physical, and mental vigour.

[2]See *Rig*, 1-50-1, *Yajur*, 7-4-1, *Atharva*, 20-47-13.

[3]See *Rig*, 1-50-2, *Atharva*, 20-47-14.

19. O Refulgent God, Thou art our Redeemer from ignorance, Thou art all-beautiful, Thou art Maker of the light, Thou illumest all the radiant realm! (3637)[1]

२०. प्रत्यङ् देवानां विशः प्रत्यङ्ङुदेषि मानुषीः । प्रत्यङ् विश्वं स्वर्दृशे ॥

20. O soul, thou risest high above the host of organs and life breaths. Thou comest hither to mankind. Thou risest high to behold the world with joy! (3638)[2]

२१. येना पावक चक्षसा भुरण्यन्तं जनाँ अनु । त्वं वरुण पश्यसि ॥

21. O Pure, Adorable God, behold us with the same eye of compassion, with which thou beholdest the benevolent one among mankind! (3639)[3]

२२. वि द्यामेषि रजस्पृथ्वहर्मिमानो अक्तुभिः । पश्यन् जन्मानि सूर्य ॥

22. O soul, just as the Sun measuring the day with his beams rises in the sky, so dost thou, with thy organs of cognition, acquiring the knowledge of vast worlds, and visualising thy innumerable births, rise to the refulgent realm of God. (3640)[4]

२३. सप्त त्वा हरितो रथे वहन्ति देव सूर्य । शोचिष्केशं विचक्षणम् ॥

23. O soul, shining like the Sun, radiant and wise, seven swift breaths support thee in the body. (3641)[5]

२४. अयुक्त सप्त शुन्ध्युवः सूरो रथस्य नप्त्यः । ताभिर्याति स्वयुक्तिभिः ॥

24. The wise soul hath yoked the seven pure, bright, unfailing breaths of the body. With their aid and with eight limbs of yoga, it travelleth to God, its goal. (3642)[6]

२५. रोहितो दिवमारुहत् तपसा तपस्वी ।
स योनिमैति स उ जायते पुनः स देवानामधिपतिर्बभूव ॥

25. The brilliant soul, devout, aflame through austerity marches on to salvation. It returns to its birth place. It is born again and again. It has become the ruler of vital breaths. (3643)

२६. यो विश्वचर्षणिरुत विश्वतोमुखो यो विश्वतस्पाणिरुत विश्वतस्पृथः ।
सं बाहुभ्यां भरति सं पतत्रैर्द्यावापृथिवी जनयन् देव एकः ॥

[1]See *Rig*, 1-50-4, *Yajur*, 33-36. [2]See *Rig*, 1-50-5. [3]See *Rig*, 1-50-6.
[4]See *Rig*, 1-50-7. [5]See *Rig*, 1-50-8.
[6]See *Rig*, 1-50-9. Eight limbs: Yama, Niyama, Āsana, Prānāyāma, Pratyahāra, Dhārnā, Dhyāna, Smādhi.

26. God keeps an eye on the whole world, preaches morality to humanity, is full of immense strength, is present everywhere. The Incomparable One Effulgent Lord, with mobile atoms, creating the Earth and Heaven, with His mighty power nourishes the universe. (3644)[1]

२७. एकपाद् द्विपदो भूयो वि चक्रमे द्विपात् त्रिपादमभ्येऽति पश्चात् ।
द्विपाद्ध षट्पदो भूयो वि चक्रमे त एकपदस्तन्वं१ समासते ॥

27. The sole God has surpassed the animate and inanimate worlds. God Who exists in the Past and Future is then realised everywhere in the world consisting of luminous, dark and mid-regions. God, Who pervades the animate and inanimate worlds, has certainly outstepped the world that consists of six directions. The Yogis enjoy the benevolence of the solitary God. (3645)[2]

२८. अतन्द्रो यास्यन् हरितो यदास्थाद् द्वे रूपे कृणुते रोचमानः ।
केतुमानुद्यन्त्सहमानो रजांसि विश्वा आदित्य प्रवतो वि भासि ॥

28. When the Unwearied God, through His impelling force pervades the beautiful directions, He, the Refulgent, creates the animate and inanimate worlds. O Indivisible God, full of Knowledge, Exalted, controlling all the worlds, Thou shinest from afar! (3646)

२९. बण्महाँ३असि सूर्य बडादित्य महाँ असि । महाँस्ते महतो महिमा त्वमादित्य महाँ असि ॥

29. O All-urging God, verily Thou art great. O Indestructible God, truly, Thou art great. Great is Thy grandeur, Mighty One. O Refulgent God, Thou art great! (3647)[3]

३०. रोचसे दिवि रोचसे अन्तरिक्षे पतङ्ग पृथिव्यां रोचसे रोचसे अप्स्व१न्तः ।
उभा समुद्रौ रुच्या व्याऽपिथ देवो देवासि महिषः स्वर्जित् ॥

30. In heaven, O God, and in mid-air Thou shinest, Thou shinest on the earth and in the waters. Thou hast pervaded with splendour both the animate and inanimate worlds. A God art Thou, O God, the Bestower of joy, and Mighty. (3648)

३१. अर्वाङ् परस्तात् प्रयतो व्यध्व आशुर्विपश्चित् पतयन् पतङ्गः ।
विष्णुर्विचित्तः शवसाधितिष्ठन् प्र केतुना सहते विश्वमेजत् ॥

31. God, Who pervades all places, distant and near, is Alert, Wise, Valorous, Dignified, Omnipresent, Realisable in various ways, and the Lord of all through His power, conquers through His knowledge, all that moves. (3649)

३२. चित्रश्चिकित्वान् महिषः सुपर्ण आरोचयन् रोदसी अन्तरिक्षम् ।
अहोरात्रे परि सूर्यं वसाने प्रास्य विश्वा तिरतो वीर्याऽणि ॥

[1]See *Rig*, 10-83-3, *Yajur*, 17-19.

[2]See *Rig*, 10-117-8, *Atharva*, 13-3-25. Luminous: The Heaven, the Sun. Dark: The Earth. Mid-region: The Atmosphere. Six directions: East, West, North, South, Nadir, Zenith.

[3]See *Rig*, 8-101-11, *Yajur*, 33-39, *Atharva*, 20-58-3.

32. Brilliant, Wise, Mighty God, the Nourisher, illumes both the spheres and air between them. Day and Night, sheltering on the Sun, spread forth more widely all His heroic powers. (3650)[1]

३३. तिग्मो विभ्राजन् तन्वं१ शिशानोऽरंगमासः प्रवतो रराणः ।
ज्योतिष्मान् पक्षी महिषो वयोधा विश्वा आस्थात् प्रदिशः कल्पमानः ॥

33. The strict, Refulgent God, the Augmentor of the spirit of service, most Active, the Bestower of the accomplishments of progress, lustrous, the Afforder of shelter, Mighty, Vigorous, and Resourceful, has pervaded all the big regions. (3651)

३४. चित्रं देवानां केतुरनीकं ज्योतिष्मान् प्रदिशः सूर्य उद्यन् ।
दिवाकरोऽति द्युम्नैस्तमांसि विश्वातारीद् दुरितानि शुक्रः ॥

34. The Marvellous, Life-infusing God, the Indicator of the moving planets, Refulgent, All-urging, rising high in all directions, the Maker of the day, the Powerful God, has transcended all forms of darkness and overcome all impediments. (3652)[2]

३५. चित्रं देवानामुदगादनीकं चक्षुर्मित्रस्य वरुणस्याग्नेः ।
आप्राद्द्यावापृथिवी अन्तरिक्षं सूर्य आत्मा जगतस्तस्थुषश्च ॥

35. God is wonderful, mightier than all the forces of nature and learned persons. He is the Displayer of air, water and fire. He is the Protector of the Sun, Earth and Atmosphere. He is Resplendent and soul of all that moves and all that moves not. (3653)[3]

३६. उच्चा पतन्तमरुणं सुपर्णं मध्ये दिवस्तरणिं भ्राजमानम् ।
पश्याम त्वा सवितारं यमाहुरजस्रं ज्योतिर्यदविन्ददत्रिः ॥

36. May we behold Thee O God, highly supreme, Omnipresent, Nourishing, Guide in all transactions, Refulgent, All-urging, Whom the learned call as Unwearied Light, Whom a yogi has visualised. (3654)[4]

३७. दिवस्पृष्ठे धावमानं सुपर्णमदित्याः पुत्रं नाथकाम उप यामि भीतः ।
स नः सूर्य प्र तिर दीर्घमायुर्मा रिषाम सुमतौ ते स्याम ॥

37. Longing for God, afraid of death, do I approach Him, the Controller of heaven, the Mighty Nourisher, the Devisor of the Vedas. O God, grant us long life. May we, unharmed, enjoy Thy gracious favour. (3655)

३८. सहस्राह्ण्यं वियतावस्य पक्षौ हरेर्हंसस्य पततः स्वर्गम् ।
स देवान्त्सर्वानुरस्युपदद्य संपश्यन् याति भुवनानि विश्वा ॥

[1]Both the spheres: The Sun and the Earth.
[2]See *Atharva*, 20-107-13.
[3]See *Yajur*, 7-42, 13-46, *Atharva*, 20-107-14, *Rig*, 1-115-1.
[4]Attri is not the name of a Rishi. A highly learned yogi is called Attri.

38. Both the wings of this Wise God, the Assuager of misery, the Possessor of the joy of salvation, are extended over unlimited time and place. Imbibing all divine virtues in Himself, He goes His way beholding every creature. (3656)[1]

३९. रोहितः कालो अभवद् रोहितोऽग्रे प्रजापतिः ।
रोहितो यज्ञानां मुखं रोहितः स्व१राभरत् ॥

39. Since the beginning of creation, God is the Lord of Time, the Fosterer of mankind, the head of all enterprises and the Bestower of divine light. (3657)[2]

४०. रोहितो लोको अभवद् रोहितोऽत्यतपद् दिवम् ।
रोहितो रश्मिभिर्भूमिं समुद्रमनु सं चरत् ॥

40. God is the Lord of all worlds. God gave the Sun its intense heat. God, through His manifold forces has set in motion the Earth, Moon, and Planets in space. (3658)

४१. सर्वा दिशः समचरद् रोहितोऽधिपतिर्दिवः । दिवं समुद्रमाद् भूमिं सर्वं भूतं वि रक्षति ॥

41. God, the imperial Lord of light pervades all the regions. He watches over heaven, ocean, and earth and all created beings. (3659)

४२. आरोहञ्छुक्रो बृहतीरतन्द्रो द्वे रूपे कृणुते रोचमानः ।
चित्रश्चिकित्वान् महिषो वातमाया यावतो लोकानभि यद् विभाति ॥

42. The Mighty, Unwearied, Resplendent God, reigning aloft in vast regions, creates the two worlds. The Marvellous, Wise, Powerful God, pervading the air, sends His light on all the worlds that exist. (3660)

४३. अभ्य१न्यदेति पर्यन्यदस्यतेऽहोरात्राभ्यां महिषः कल्पमानः ।
सूर्यं वयं रजसि क्षियन्तं गातुविदं हवामहे नाधमानाः ॥

43. Just as the Sun shines in day time, in one part of the world, and keeps the night afar in the other, so does God create the universe. Keeping afar its dissolution. So we, prey to passion, with humble prayer for aid call on God, who is our Path-shower. (3661)

४४. पृथिवीप्रो महिषो नाधमानस्य गातुरदब्धचक्षुः परि विश्वं बभूव ।
विश्वं संपश्यन्त्सुविदत्रो यजत्र इदं शृणोतु यदहं ब्रवीमि ॥

44. The Mighty God, the Filler of the Earth with all sorts of eatables, the Refuge of the distress, the Possessor of unfaltering vision, hath encompassed the whole world. May He, All-seeing, Wise, Charitable and Adorable, listen to the word I utter. (3662)

[1]Wings: Cause and Effect. Matter is the cause, and the created world the effect. God watches the conduct of every creature, and giving him reward or punishment continues to create, sustain and dissolve the universe.

[2]Time: Past, Present and Future.

४५. पर्यस्य महिमा पृथिवीं समुद्रं ज्योतिषा विभ्राजन् परि द्यामन्तरिक्षम् ।
सर्वं संपश्यन्त्सुविदत्रो यजत्र इदं शृणोतु यदहं ब्रवीमि ॥

45. Vast spread is the glory of God, Glowing with His Majesty, He hath compassed ocean, earth, heaven and air's mid-region. May He, All-seeing, Wise, Charitable and Adorable, listen to the word I utter. (3663)

४६. अबोध्यग्निः समिधा जनानां प्रति धेनुमिवायतीमुषासम् ।
यह्वा इव प्र वयामुज्जिहानाः प्र भानवः सिस्रते नाकमच्छ ॥

46. When the fiery soul of learned persons glitters with knowledge, then it advances towards refined intellect, just as a calf goes to the cow. Just as birds go to their nest on a tree, so do the emancipated yogis march on to the Joyful God and seek His refuge. (3664)[1]

Chapter (Anuvāka) 3

HYMN III

१. य इमे द्यावापृथिवी जजान यो द्रापिं कृत्वा भुवनानि वस्ते ।
यस्मिन् क्षियन्ति प्रदिशः षडुर्वीर्याः पतङ्गो अनु विचाकशीति ।
तस्य देवस्य क्रुद्धस्यैतदागो य एवं विद्वांसं ब्राह्मणं जिनाति ।
उद् वेपय रोहित प्र क्षिणीहि ब्रह्मज्यस्य प्रति मुञ्च पाशान् ॥

1. He Who engendered these, the earth and heaven, Who made the worlds the mantle that He weareth. In Whom abide the six wide-spreading regions through which God's light penetrateth. This God is wroth offended by the sinner who vexes the Brahman who hath gained this knowledge. Terrify him, O King, destroy him, entangle in thy snares the Brahman's tyrant! (3665)

२. यस्माद् वाता ऋतुथा पवन्ते यस्मात् समुद्रा अधि विक्षरन्ति ।
तस्य देवस्य क्रुद्धस्यैतदागो य एवं विद्वांसं ब्राह्मणं जिनाति ।
उद् वेपय रोहित प्र क्षिणीहि ब्रह्मज्यस्य प्रति मुञ्च पाशान् ॥

2. He from Whom winds blow pure in ordered season, from Whom the seas flow forth in all directions, this God is wroth offended by the sinner who vexes the Brahman who hath gained this knowledge. Terrify him, O King, destroy him ; entangle in thy snares the Brahman's tyrant! (3666)

३. यो मारयति प्राणयति यस्मात् प्राणन्ति भुवनानि विश्वा ।
तस्य देवस्य क्रुद्धस्यैतदागो य एवं विद्वांसं ब्राह्मणं जिनाति ।
उद् वेपय रोहित प्र क्षिणीहि ब्रह्मज्यस्य प्रति मुञ्च पाशान् ॥

3. He Who takes life away, He Who bestows it: from Whom cometh breath to every living creature, this God is wroth offended by the sinner who vexes the Brahman who hath gained this knowledge. Terrify him, O King, destroy him: entangle him in thy snares the Brahman's tyrant! (3667)

[1]See *Rig*, 5-2-1, *Yajur*, 15-24.

४. यः प्राणेन द्यावापृथिवी तर्पयत्यपानेन समुद्रस्य जठरं यः पिपर्ति ।
तस्य देवस्य क्रुद्धस्यैतदागो य एवं विद्वांसं ब्राह्मणं जिनाति ।
उद् वेपय रोहित प्र क्षिणीहि ब्रह्मज्यस्य प्रति मुञ्च पाशान् ॥

4. God fills the body from head to foot with Prāna, and with Apāna. He fills the interiors of excretory and urinary organs. This God is wroth offended by the sinner who vexes the Brahman who hath gained this knowledge. Terrify Him, O King, destroy him, entangle in thy snares the Brahman's tyrant! (3668)

५. यस्मिन् विराट् परमेष्ठी प्रजापतिरग्निर्वैश्वानरः सह पङ्क्त्या श्रितः ।
यः परस्य प्राणं परमस्य तेज आददे ।
तस्य देवस्य क्रुद्धस्यैतदागो य एवं विद्वांसं ब्राह्मणं जिनाति ।
उद् वेपय रोहित प्र क्षिणीहि ब्रह्मज्यस्य प्रति मुञ्च पाशान् ॥

5. In Whom the Earth, Water, Air, Fire, Atmosphere abide with the attributes of the organs of cognition. He Who hath taken under Him the breathing of distant humanity and the lustre of the Sun, this God is wroth offended by the sinner who vaxes the Brahman who hath gained this knowledge. Terrify him, O King, destroy him, entangle in thy snares the Brahman's tyrant. (3669)[1]

६. यस्मिन् षडुर्वीः पञ्च दिशो अधि श्रिताश्चतस्र आपो यज्ञस्य त्रयोऽक्षराः ।
यो अन्तरा रोदसी क्रुद्धश्चक्षुषैक्षत ।
तस्य देवस्य क्रुद्धस्यैतदागो य एवं विद्वांसं ब्राह्मणं जिनाति ।
उद् वेपय रोहित प्र क्षिणीहि ब्रह्मज्यस्य प्रति मुञ्च पाशान् ॥

6. On Whom rest six wide regions, five great primary elements, four subjects, three syllables of worship. He Who hath looked on the sinners between heaven and earth in anger, this God is wroth offended by the sinner who vexes the Brahman who hath gained this knowledge. Terrify him, O King, destroy him, entangle in thy snares the Brahman's tyrant. (3670)[2]

७. यो अन्नादो अन्नपतिर्बभूव ब्रह्मणस्पतिरुत यः । भूतो भविष्यद् भुवनस्य यस्पतिः ।
तस्य देवस्य क्रुद्धस्यैतदागो य एवं विद्वांसं ब्राह्मणं जिनाति ।
उद् वेपय रोहित प्र क्षिणीहि ब्रह्मज्यस्य प्रति मुञ्च पाशान् ॥

7. God is the Bestower and Master of food. He is the Guardian of Vedic knowledge. He was, is and shall be the Lord of the universe. This God is wroth offended by the sinner who vexes the Brahman who hath gained this knowledge. Terrify him, O King, destroy him, entangle him in thy snares the Brahman's tyrant. (3671)

[1]Organs of cognition: Ear, Nose, Eye, Tongue, Skin. Attributes: Hearing, Smell, Sight, Taste, Touch.

[2]Six regions: North, South, East, West, Nadir, Zenith. Five elements: Panch Bhutas, Earth, Water, Air, Fire, Atmosphere. Four subjects; Brahman, Kshatriya, Vaisha, Shudra, Three syllables, अ, उ, म्.

८. अहोरात्रैर्विमितं त्रिंशदङ्गं त्रयोदशं मासं यो निर्मिमीते ।
तस्य देवस्य क्रुद्धस्यैतदागो य एवं विद्वांसं ब्राह्मणं जिनाति ।
उद् वेपय रोहित प्र क्षिणीहि ब्रह्मज्यस्य प्रति मुञ्च पाशान् ॥

8. God creates the universe of thirty limbs, measured by day and night, the measurable universe of thirteen objects. This God is wroth offended by the sinner who vexes the Brahman who hath gained this knowledge. Terrify him, O King, destroy him, entangle in thy snares the Brahman's tyrant! (3672)[1]

९. कृष्णं नियानं हरयः सुपर्णा अपो वसाना दिवमुत् पतन्ति । त आववृत्रन्त्सदनादृतस्य ।
तस्य देवस्य क्रुद्धस्यैतदागो य एवं विद्वांसं ब्राह्मणं जिनाति ।
उद् वेपय रोहित प्र क्षिणीहि ब्रह्मज्यस्य प्रति मुञ्च पाशान् ॥

9. Highly talented souls aspiring after emancipation, enrobed in knowledge, move on to Pleasant God, and the glittering goal of salvation. After the expiry of the period of salvation, they return to Earth, through the force of their spiritual knowledge. This God is wroth offended by the sinner who vexes the Brahmin who hath gained this knowledge. Terrify him, O King, destroy him, entangle in thy snares the Brahman's tyrant! (3673)[2]

१०. यत् ते चन्द्रं कश्यप रोचनावद् यत् संहितं पुष्कलं चित्रभानु ।
यस्मिन्त्सूर्या आर्पिताः सप्त साकम् ।
तस्य देवस्य क्रुद्धस्यैतदागो य एवं विद्वांसं ब्राह्मणं जिनाति ।
उद् वेपय रोहित प्र क्षिणीहि ब्रह्मज्यस्य प्रति मुञ्च पाशान् ॥

10. O All-seeing God, Thy nature is Joyful, Refulgent, Strength-infusing, Constant, Lustrous. Under Thy Law, the seven rays of the Sun are gathered together. This God is wroth offended by the sinner who vexes the Brahman who hath gained this knowledge. Terrify him, O King, destroy him, entangle in thy snares the Brahman's tyrant! (3674)

११. बृहदेनमनु वस्ते पुरस्ताद् रथन्तरं प्रति गृह्णाति पश्चात् । ज्योतिर्वसाने सदमप्रमादम् ॥
तस्य देवस्य क्रुद्धस्यैतदागो य एवं विद्वांसं ब्राह्मणं जिनाति ।
उद् वेपय रोहित प्र क्षिणीहि ब्रह्मज्यस्य प्रति मुञ्च पाशान् ॥

11. In front the atmosphere holds God as its mouth and from behind the Earth embraces Him. Both these robe themselves in God with full care. This God is wroth offended by the sinner who vexes the Brahmin who hath gained this knowledge. Terrify him, O King, destroy him, entangle in thy snares the Brahman's tyrant! (3675)

[1]Thirty limbs: Four Vedas, Four Varnas, Four Ashramas, Eight Sidhis. (1) Fineness अणिमा (2) Lightness, लघिमा (3) Acquisition प्राप्ति (4) Irresistible Will प्राकाम्य (5) Glory महिमा (6) Superiority ईशित्वं (7) Control of passions वशित्वं (8) Stoicism कामावसायिता. Five primary elements, Throwing, Felling, Contraction, Expansion and Motion. Thirteen objects: Ear, Skin, Eye, Tongue, Nose i.e., five organs of cognition, Anus, organ of generation, hand, foot, mouth, i.e., five organs of action, Mind, Intellect, Soul.

[2]See *Rig*, 1-164-17, *Atharva*, 6-32-1 and 9-10-32. Period of salvation: 4320000000 years. Soul returns to the Earth. As its powers are finite, the result of their efforts cannot be infinite.

१२. बृहदन्यतः पक्ष आसीद् रथन्तरमन्यतः सबले सध्रीची । यद् रोहितमजनयन्त देवाः ।
तस्य देवस्य क्रुद्धस्यैतदागो य एवं विद्वांसं ब्राह्मणं जिनाति ।
उद् वेपय रोहित प्र क्षिणीहि ब्रह्मज्यस्य प्रति मुञ्च पाशान् ।।

12. When the fine qualities of God manifested Him, one of His wings was the Atmosphere, and the other the Earth, both being vigorous and working with one same purpose. This God is wroth offended by the sinner who vexes the Brahmin who hath gained this knowledge. Terrify him, O King, destroy him, entangle in thy snares the Brahman's tyrant ! (3676)

१३. स वरुणः सायमग्निर्भवति स मित्रो भवति प्रातरुद्यन् ।
स सविता भूत्वान्तरिक्षेण याति स इन्द्रो भूत्वा तपति मध्यतो दिवम् ।
तस्य देवस्य क्रुद्धस्यैतदागो य एवं विद्वांसं ब्राह्मणं जिनाति ।
उद् वेपय रोहित प्र क्षिणीहि ब्रह्मज्यस्य प्रति मुञ्च पाशान् ।।

13. That God shines like fire when darkness prevails. He is the Friend of all like the Sun rising in the morning. Just as the Sun moves through the atmosphere, so God, the Urger, pervades in the hearts of His devotees. The same God, being Indra, highly dignified shines like the Sun in the atmosphere. This God is wroth offended by the sinner who vexes the Brahmin who hath gained this knowledge. Terrify him, O King, destroy him, entangle in thy snares the Brahman's tyrant ! (3677)

१४. सहस्राह्ण्यं वियतावस्य पक्षौ हरेर्हंसस्य पततः स्वर्गम् ।
स देवान्त्सर्वानुरस्युपदद्य संपश्यन् याति भुवनानि विश्वा ।
तस्य देवस्य क्रुद्धस्यैतदागो य एवं विद्वांसं ब्राह्मणं जिनाति ।
उद् वेपय रोहित प्र क्षिणीहि ब्रह्मज्यस्य प्रति मुञ्च पाशान् ।।

14. Both the wings of this Omniscient God are specially defined, as is the path of the Sun who moves through the atmosphere in thousands of days and ages. Controlling all the forces of Nature, beholding the actions of all creatures, He goes on administering the universe. This God is wroth offended by the sinner who vexes the Brahman who hath gained this knowledge. Terrify him, O King, destroy him, entangle in thy snares the Brahman's tyrant! (3678)[1]

१५. अयं स देवो अप्स्व१न्तः सहस्रमूलः पुरुशाको अत्त्रिः । य इदं विश्वं भुवनं जजान ।।
तस्य देवस्य क्रुद्धस्यैतदागो य एवं विद्वांसं ब्राह्मणं जिनाति ।
उद् वेपय रोहित प्र क्षिणीहि ब्रह्मज्यस्य प्रति मुञ्च पाशान् ।।

15. He, Who brought all this world into existence, is the God Who dwells in the midst of His subjects, is the Most Efficient Cause of thousands of worlds, Master of power, and free from physical elemental and spiritual pangs. This God is wroth offended by the sinner who vexes the Brahman who hath gained this knowledge. Terrify him, O King, destroy him, entangle in thy snares the Brahman's tyrant! (3679)[2]

[1]See *Atharva*, 10-8, 18, 13-2-38. Two wings: Day and Night.

[2]Pt. Khem Karan Das Trivedi translates अत्त्रि as Wise, Intelligent God. Pt. Jaidev Vidyalankara translates the word as God Who devours us all at the time of dissolution, from the root अद to eat.

१६. शुक्रं वहन्ति हरयो रघुष्यदो देवं दिवि वर्चसा भ्राजमानम् ।
यस्योर्ध्वा दिवं तन्व१स्तपन्त्यर्वाङ् सुवर्णैः पटरैर्वि भाति ।
तस्य देवस्य क्रुद्धस्यैतदागो य एवं विद्वांसं ब्राह्मणं जिनाति ।
उद् वेपय रोहित प्र क्षिणीहि ब्रह्मज्यस्य प्रति मुञ्च पाशान् ।।

16. Highly active emancipated souls attain to the Refulgent God, aglow with splendour in the sky. Thousands of worlds high above created by Him illumine the heavens. He shines with innumerable Suns of fine colour in the lower part of the universe. This God is wroth offended by the sinner who vexes the Brahman who hath gained this knowledge. Terrify him, O King, destroy him, entangle in thy snares the Brahman's tyrant! (3680)

१७. येनादित्यान् हरितः संवहन्ति येन यज्ञेन बहवो यन्ति प्रजानन्तः ।
यदेकं ज्योतिर्बहुधा विभाति ।
तस्य देवस्य क्रुद्धस्यैतदागो य एवं विद्वांसं ब्राह्मणं जिनाति ।
उद् वेपय रोहित प्र क्षिणीहि ब्रह्मज्यस्य प्रति मुञ्च पाशान् ।।

17. Urged by God, the powerful forces of nature are setting the suns in motion. Through His company, various souls, equipping themselves with knowledge attain to salvation. God, the sole light, manifests Himself in various ways. This God is wroth offended by the sinner who vexes the Brahmin who hath gained this knowledge. Terrify him, O King, destroy him, entangle in thy snares the Brahman's tyrant! (3681)

१८. सप्त युञ्जन्ति रथमेकचक्रमेको अश्वो वहति सप्तनामा ।
त्रिनाभि चक्रमजरमनर्वं यत्रेमा विश्वा भुवनाधि तस्थुः ।
तस्य देवस्य क्रुद्धस्यैतदागो य एवं विद्वांसं ब्राह्मणं जिनाति ।
उद् वेपय रोहित प्र क्षिणीहि ब्रह्मज्यस्य प्रति मुञ्च पाशान् ।।

18. Seven organs unite the independent soul with the body. The undecaying, immortal, three-naved, solitary soul, the master of seven organs, takes itself to God, on Whom all these worlds of life are dependent. This God is wroth offended by the sinner who vexes the Brahman who hath gained this knowledge. Terrify him, O King, destroy him, entangle in thy snares the Brahman's tyrant! (3682)[1]

१९. अष्टधा युक्तो वहति वह्निरुग्रः पिता देवानां जनिता मतीनाम् ।
ऋतस्य तन्तुं मनसा मिमानः सर्वा दिशः पवते मातरिश्वा ।
तस्य देवस्य क्रुद्धस्यैतदागो य एवं विद्वांसं ब्राह्मणं जिनाति ।
उद् वेपय रोहित प्र क्षिणीहि ब्रह्मज्यस्य प्रति मुञ्च पाशान् ।।

[1]See *Atharva*, 9.9.2.

19. God, worshipped through eight limbs of Yoga, the Leader, Potent, the Father of the forces of Nature, the Creator of talented persons, upholds the universe. God, measuring in spirit the spread of knowledge, purifies all regions. This God is wroth offended by the sinner who vexes the Brahman who hath gained this knowledge. Terrify him, O King, destroy him, entangle in thy snares the Brahman's tyrant! (3683)[1]

२०. सम्यञ्चं तन्तुं प्रदिशोऽनु सर्वा अन्तर्गायत्र्याममृतस्य गर्भे ।
तस्य देवस्य क्रुद्धस्यैतदागो य एवं विद्वांसं ब्राह्मणं जिनाति ।
उद् वेपय रोहित प्र क्षिणीहि ब्रह्मज्यस्य प्रति मुञ्च पाशान् ॥

20. All regions rest on the All-pervading, Vast, Most Subtle God. They exist under the control of Immortal God, Who protects the life-breaths of all living beings. This God is wroth offended by the sinner who vexes the Brahman who hath gained this knowledge. Terrify him, O King, destroy him, entangle in thy snares the Brahman's tyrant! (3684)

२१. निम्रुचस्तिस्रो व्युषो ह तिस्रस्त्रीणि रजांसि दिवो अङ्ग तिस्रः ।
विद्मा ते अग्ने त्रेधा जनित्रं त्रेधा देवानां जनिमानि विद्म ।
तस्य देवस्य क्रुद्धस्यैतदागो य एवं विद्वांसं ब्राह्मणं जिनाति ।
उद् वेपय रोहित प्र क्षिणीहि ब्रह्मज्यस्य प्रति मुञ्च पाशान् ॥

21. There are three baser and three higher modes of conduct. There are three divisions of time. There are three usages. O God, we know thy three sources of realisation, and three manifestations of living beings. This God is wroth offended by the sinner who vexes the Brahman who hath gained this knowledge. Terrify him, O King, destroy him, entangle in thy snares the Brahman's tyrant! (3685)[2]

२२. वि य और्णोत् पृथिवीं जायमान आ समुद्रमदधादन्तरिक्षे ।
तस्य देवस्य क्रुद्धस्यैतदागो य एवं विद्वांसं ब्राह्मणं जिनाति ।
उद् वेपय रोहित प्र क्षिणीहि ब्रह्मज्यस्य प्रति मुञ्च पाशान् ॥

22. God, at the time of creation laid broad Earth open, and set the ocean of vapours in the air's mid-region. This God is wroth offended by the sinner who offends the Brahman who hath gained this knowledge. Terrify him, O King, destroy him, entangle in thy snares the Brahmin's tyrant! (3686)

[1]God decides how much of his infinite knowledge is to be revealed for the good and guidance of mankind. God is spoken of as Matrishwa as it pervades the atmosphere. (मातरिश्वा) मातरि आकाशे श्वयति गच्छति व्याप्नोति यः परमेश्वरः or Who pervades in Matter, the sustainer of all objects.

[2]Modes of conduct: Physical, Oral, Mental (Mānsik, Kāika, Vachika). Divisions of time: Past, Present, Future. Usages: Dharma, Artha and Kāma. Sources of realisation: Karma, Action, Upāsnā, Contemplation, Jnāna, Knowledge. Three manifestations: Satva, Rajas, Tamas.

२३. त्वमग्ने क्रतुभिः केतुभिर्हितोऽर्कः समिद्ध उदरोचथा दिवि ।
किमभ्यार्चन्मरुतः पृश्निमातरो यद् रोहितमजनयन्त देवाः ।
तस्य देवस्य क्रुद्धस्यैतदागो य एवं विद्वांसं ब्राह्मणं जिनाति ।
उद् वेपय रोहित प्र क्षिणीहि ब्रह्मज्यस्य प्रति मुञ्च पाशान् ॥

23. O God, with Thy marvellous deeds and intellectual powers, being highly benevolent, Thou hast shone in heaven like the enkindled Sun. Whom have the valiant, the respecters of the Vedas as their mother, worshipped, when the excellent qualities of God manifested Him. This God is wroth offended by the sinner who offends the Brahman who hath gained this knowledge. Terrify him, O God, destroy him, entangle in thy snare the Brahman's tyrant! (3687)[1]

२४. य आत्मदा बलदा यस्य विश्व उपासते प्रशिषं यस्य देवाः ।
योऽस्येशे द्विपदो यश्चतुष्पदः ।
तस्य देवस्य क्रुद्धस्यैतदागो य एवं विद्वांसं ब्राह्मणं जिनाति ।
उद् वेपय रोहित प्र क्षिणीहि ब्रह्मज्यस्य प्रति मुञ्च पाशान् ॥

24. God is the giver of spiritual force, and physical strength. His commandments all the learned persons acknowledge. He is the Lord of men and cattle. This God is wroth offended by the sinner who vexes the Brahman who hath gained this knowledge. Terrify him, O King, destroy him, entangle in thy snares the Brahman's tyrant! (3688)[2]

२५. एकपाद् द्विपदो भूयो वि चक्रमे द्विपात् त्रिपादमभ्येति पश्चात् ।
चतुष्पाच्चक्रे द्विपदामभिस्वरे संपश्यन् पङ्क्तिमुपतिष्ठमानः ।
तस्य देवस्य क्रुद्धस्यैतदागो य एवं विद्वांसं ब्राह्मणं जिनाति ।
उद् वेपय रोहित प्र क्षिणीहि ब्रह्मज्यस्य प्रति मुञ्च पाशान् ॥

25. The sole God has surpassed the animate and inanimate worlds. God Who exists in the Past and Future is then realised everywhere in the world, consisting of luminous, dark and mid-regions. God, Who pervades the four directions, being nearest in the hearts of men, performs His duty in beholding the fruit of their actions. This God is wroth offended by the sinner who vexes the Brahman who hath gained this knowledge. Terrify him, O King, destroy him, entangle in thy snares the Brahman's tyrant! (3689)[3]

२६. कृष्णायाः पुत्रो अर्जुनो रात्र्या वत्सोऽजायत ।
स ह द्यामधि रोहति रुहो रुरोह रोहितः ॥

26. After the dark Night of Dissolution, God creates the Sun, the Purifier, the Recipient of the essence of things, and the Afforder of shelter to mankind. The same God manifests Himself in the Sun. He has created all the materials of the world. (3690)

[1]The devotees of the Vedas worshipped none else but God.
[2]See *Atharva*, 4-2-1, *Rig*, 10-121, 2-3, *Yajur*, 25-13-11.
[3]See *Atharva*, 13-2-27, *Rigveda*, 10-117-8.

Chapter (Anuvāka) 4

HYMN IV

Paryāya 1

१. स एति सविता स्वऽर्दिवस्पृष्ठेऽवचाकशत् ॥

1. God, the Urger of all, is filled with joy, pervading the highest heaven, and watching the deeds of human beings. (3691)

२. रश्मिभिर्नभ आभृतं महेन्द्र एत्यावृतः ॥

2. Just as the entire atmosphere is filled with the rays of the Sun, so the entire inanimate world shines with the Lustre of God. Great God pervades all the worlds with His refulgence. (3692)

३. स धाता स विधर्ता स वायुर्नभ उच्छ्रितम् । रश्मिभिर्नभ आभृतं महेन्द्र एत्यावृतः ॥

3. God is the Creator and Sustainer. He is All-pervading and Powerful like air. He is the best Administrator and Most Exalted. Great God pervades all the worlds with His refulgence. (3693)

४. सोऽर्यमा स वरुणः स रुद्रः स महादेवः । रश्मिभिर्नभ आभृतं महेन्द्र एत्यावृतः ॥

4. God is Aryamā, the Lover of Justice. He is Varuna, Most Excellent. He is Rudra, the Chastiser of the sinners. He is Mahadev, the adorable God of gods. Great God pervades all the worlds with His refulgence. (3694)

५. सो अग्निः स उ सूर्यः स उ एव महायमः । रश्मिभिर्नभ आभृतं महेन्द्र एत्यावृतः ॥

5. He is Agni, Omniscient, He is Surya, the Urger. He is Mahāyama, the Great Leader. Great God pervades all the worlds with His refulgence. (3695)

६. तं वत्सा उप तिष्ठन्त्येकशीर्षाणोऽयुता दश । रश्मिभिर्नभ आभृतं महेन्द्र एत्यावृतः ॥

6. Ten dwelling places, in conjunction, serve God, their single leader. Great God pervades all the worlds with His refulgence. (3696)[1]

७. पश्चात् प्राञ्च आ तन्वन्ति यदुदेति वि भासति । रश्मिभिर्नभ आभृतं महेन्द्र एत्यावृतः ॥

7. The Prānās (vital breaths) go out from inside, when God manifests Himself and shines in various ways. Great God pervades all the worlds with His refulgence. (3697)

८. तस्यैष मारुतो गणः स एति शिक्याकृतः ॥

8. This multitude of human beings is God's creation. It is safe in the hands of God, like articles laid in a rope swing. (3698)

[1]Ten places: North, East, South, West, Nadir, Zenith, four sub-directions. Ten dwelling places may also mean ten prānās.

९. रश्मिभिर्नभ आभृतं महेन्द्र एत्यावृतः ।।

9. The Omnipresent Mighty God, hidden from all sides, pervades the clouds strengthened by rays. (3699)

१०. तस्येमे नव कोशा विष्टम्भा नवधा हिताः ।।

10. These nine coverings are laid by God in the body. They act differently as its nine supports. (3700)[1]

११. स प्रजाभ्यो वि पश्यति यच्च प्राणति यच्च न ।।

11. God keepeth watch over all created objects, that breathe and breathe not. (3701)

१२. तमिदं निगतं सहः स एष एक एकवृदेक एव ।।

12. God possesses this conquering might. He is the sole, the solitary one, the One alone. (3702)

१३. एते अस्मिन् देवा एकवृतो भवन्ति ।।

13. These luminous planets and learned persons reside and take shelter in this One God. (3703)

HYMN V

Paryāya 2

१४. कीर्तिश्च यशश्चाम्भश्च नभश्च ब्राह्मणवर्चसं चान्नं चान्नाद्यं च ।।

14. Renown and glory, force, and administrative capacity, the splendour of the knowledge of God and food, and nourishment are acquired by him. (3704)

१५. य एतं देवमेकवृतं वेद ।।

15. Who knoweth this God as One. (3705)

१६. न द्वितीयो न तृतीयश्चतुर्थो नाप्युच्यते । य एतं देवमेकवृतं वेद ।।

16. Neither second nor third, nor yet fourth is He called. (3706)[2]

१७. न पञ्चमो न षष्ठः सप्तमो नाप्युच्यते । य एतं देवमेकवृतं वेद ।।

[1]Nine coverings: Two eyes, two ears, two nostrils, mouth, anus, penis. These organs work differently with their inherent powers of seeing, hearing, smelling, tasting, etc.

[2](16, 17, 18) These three verses proclaim the Oneness of God. The science of Arithmetic depends on the ten digits which result from one by Arithmetical progression. All other numbers are the result of permutation and combination of these digits. When the existence of God is denied for all these digits except the one, it means, God cannot be spoken of by any arithmetical number except the one. These verses clearly establish the unity of God, a special characteristic of the Vedic religion. The Vedas preach monotheism. These are no traces of polytheism or henotheism in them as some scholars in vain try to find out.

17. He is called neither fifth, nor sixth, nor yet seventh. (3707)

१८. नाष्टमो न नवमो दशमो नाप्युच्यते । य एतं देवमेकवृतं वेद ।।

18. He is called neither eighth, nor ninth, nor yet tenth. (3708)

१९. स सर्वस्मै वि पश्यति यच्च प्राणति यच्च न । य एतं देवमेकवृतं वेद ।।

19. He watcheth over all objects that breathe and breathe not. (3709)

२०. तमिदं निगतं सहः स एष एक एकवृदेक एव । य एतं देवमेकवृतं वेद ।।

20. God possesses this conquering might. He is the sole, the solitary one, the One alone. (3710)

२१. सर्वे अस्मिन् देवा एकवृतो भवन्ति । य एतं देवमेकवृतं वेद ।।

21. These luminous planets and learned persons reside and take shelter in this One God. (3711)

HYMN VI

Paryāya 3

२२. ब्रह्म च तपश्च कीर्तिश्च यशश्चाम्भश्च नभश्च ब्राह्मणवर्चसं चान्नं चान्नाद्यं च ।
य एतं देवमेकवृतं वेद ।।

22. Knowledge, and religious fervour, and renown and glory, force and administrative capacity, splendour of the knowledge of God, and food and nourishment. (3712)

२३. भूतं च भव्यं च श्रद्धा च रुचिश्च स्वर्गश्च स्वधा च ।।

23. And past and future, and faith and lustre, and joy and spiritual power are acquired by him. (3713)

२४. य एतं देवमेकवृतं वेद ।।

24. Who knoweth this God as One. (3714)

२५. स एव मृत्युः सोऽमृतं सोऽभ्वं१ स रक्षः ।।

25. He is the Bringer of death, and the Bestower of salvation. He is unborn, and highly adorable. He is the Protector of all. (3715)[1]

२६. स रुद्रो वसुवनिर्वसुदेये नमोवाके वषट्कारोऽनु संहितः ।।

26. He is the chastiser of the sinners, the Ameliorator of the virtuous. In offering oblations in a Yajna, in uttering homage unto God, He is continually remembered as Benefactor. (3716)

[1]Griffith erroneously translates अभ्वम् as monster and रक्षः as fiend.

२७. तस्येमे सर्वे यातव उप प्रशिषमासते ॥

27. All revolving planets and moving creatures obey with reverence His behest. (3717)

२८. तस्यामू सर्वा नक्षत्रा वशे चन्द्रमसा सह ॥

28. All constellations yonder, with the Moon, are subject to His will. (3718)

HYMN VII

Paryāya 4

२९. स वा अह्नोऽजायत तस्मादहरजायत ॥

29. Just as the Sun was brought forth from Day and Day, derives its origin from him, so the existence of God is perceived by beholding the universe, which in reality is created by Him. (3719)

३०. स वै रात्र्या अजायत तस्माद् रात्रिरजायत ॥

30. Just as the Sun appears to be born of Night, as it appears after its expiry, and Night is born of the Sun as it sets in the evening, so the existence of God is perceived by beholding the Great Night of Dissolution, which in reality is created by Him. (3720)[1]

३१. स वा अन्तरिक्षादजायत तस्मादन्तरिक्षमजायत ॥

31. The Sun comes into existence after the atmosphere, as if he is produced from it, and the existence of atmosphere is realised by beholding the Sun. So the existence of God is perceived by beholding the Atmosphere which in reality is created by Him. (3721)

३२. स वै वायोरजायत तस्माद् वायुरजायत ॥

32. The existence of God is perceived by beholding Air, which in reality is created by Him. (3722)

३३. स वै दिवोऽजायत तस्माद् द्यौरध्यजायत ॥

33. The existence of God is perceived by beholding the Heaven, which in reality is created by Him. (3723)

३४. स वै दिग्भ्योऽजायत तस्माद् दिशोऽजायन्त ॥

34. The existence of God is perceived by beholding the regions, which in reality are created by Him. (3724)

३५. स वै भूमेरजायत तस्माद् भूमिरजायत ॥

[1]God creates the universe which last 4320000000 years which is called Brahma Day. He dissolves the universe. Matter goes into its atomic state, and thus lasts for the same period. It is called Brahma Night. This process is beginningless and endless.

35. The existence of God is perceived by beholding the Earth, which in reality is created by Him. (3725)

३६. स वा अग्नेरजायत तस्मादग्निरजायत ॥

36. The existence of God is perceived by beholding fire, which in reality is created by Him. (3726)

३७. स वा अद्भ्योऽजायत तस्मादापोऽजायन्त ॥

37. The existence of God is perceived by beholding the waters, which in reality are created by Him. (3727)

३८. स वा ऋग्भ्योऽजायत तस्मादृचोऽजायन्त ॥

38. The existence of God is perceived by studying the holy Vedic verses, which in reality are revealed by Him. (3728)

३९. स वै यज्ञादजायत तस्माद् यज्ञोऽजायत ॥

39. The existence of God is perceived by performing sacrifice (Yajna,) which in reality is ordained by Him. (3729)

४०. स यज्ञस्तस्य यज्ञः स यज्ञस्य शिरस्कृतम् ॥

40. God is the embodiment of sacrifice. His very nature betokens sacrifice. He, as Om, is the head of sacrifice. (3730)

४१. स स्तनयति स वि द्योतते स उ अश्मानमस्यति ॥

४२. पापाय वा भद्राय वा पुरुषायासुराय वा ॥

41-42. God shines in various ways for the virtuous, thunders for the sinners, and hurls stones on the enemies of the learned. (3731-2)[1]

४३. यद्वा कृणोष्योषधीर्यद्वा वर्षसि भद्रया यद्वा जन्यमवीवृधः ॥

43. O God, as Thou certainly formest growing plants, and sendest rain for happiness, and hast increased the race of man! (3733)

४४. तावांस्ते मघवन् महिमोपो ते तन्वः शतम् ॥

44. Such is Thy greatness, O liberal Lord. Infinite are thy favours. (3734)

४५. उपो ते बध्वे बद्धानि यदि वासि न्यर्बुदम् ॥

45. All beings are bound by Thy law, as Thou art All-pervading. (3735)

[1](41,42) Hurls stones: Gives heavy punishment.

HYMN VIII

Paryaya 5

४६. भूयानिन्द्रो नमुराद् भूयानिन्द्रासि मृत्युभ्यः ॥

46. O God, Thou art stronger than the Eternal Matter in its atomic shape, Thou are stronger than the created world which lasts not for ever. (3736)

४७. भूयानरात्याः शच्याः पतिस्त्वमिन्द्रासि विभूः प्रभूरिति त्वोपास्महे वयम् ॥

47. Yea, stronger than parsimony art Thou, O God, Lord of Might Calling Thee Omnipresent, Sovran Chief, we pay our reverence to Thee. (3737)

४८. नमस्ते अस्तु पश्यत पश्य मा पश्यत ॥

48. Worship to Thee, O Beautiful God. Have pity on me, Thy devotee, O All-seeing God! (3738)

४९. अन्नाद्येन यशसा तेजसा ब्राह्मणवर्चसेन ॥

49. Equip me, O God, with food and fame, with vigour, and with the splendour of a Vedic scholar! (3739)

५०. अम्भो अमो महः सह इति त्वोपास्महे वयम् । नमस्ते अस्तु पश्यत पश्य मा पश्यत ।
अन्नाद्येन यशसा तेजसा ब्राह्मणवर्चसेन ॥

50. O God, we pay Thee reverence calling Thee Omnipresent, Wise, Adorable and Patient! (3740)

५१. अम्भो अरुणं रजतं रजः सह इति त्वोपास्महे वयम् ।
नमस्ते अस्तु पश्यत पश्य मा पश्यत । अन्नाद्येन यशसा तेजसा ब्राह्मणवर्चसेन ॥

51. O God, we pay Thee reverence calling Thee Omnipresent, Omniscient, joyful, Refulgent and Patient! (3741)

HYMN IX

Paryāya 6

५२. उरुः पृथुः सुभूर्भुव इति त्वोपास्महे वयम् । नमस्ते अस्तु पश्यत पश्य मा पश्यत ।
अन्नाद्येन यशसा तेजसा ब्राह्मणवर्चसेन ॥

52. O God, we pay Thee reverence calling Thee Omnipotent, Omnipresent, the Good, and the Creator! (3742)

५३. प्रथो वरो व्यचो लोक इति त्वोपास्महे वयम् । नमस्ते अस्तु पश्यत पश्य मा पश्यत ।
अन्नाद्येन यशसा तेजसा ब्राह्मणवर्चसेन ॥

53. O God, we pay Thee reverence calling Thee Renowned, Adorable, Almighty, and Beautiful! (3743)

५४. भवद्वसुरिदद्वसुः संयद्वसुरायद्वसुरिति त्वोपास्महे वयम् ॥

54. O God, we pay Thee reverence calling Thee, the Bestower of opulence, the Ameliorator of the virtuous, the Controller of planets, and the Diffuser of the resources of habitation! (3744)

५५. नमस्ते अस्तु पश्यत पश्य मा पश्यत ॥

55. Worship to Thee, O Beautiful God. Have pity on me, Thy devotee, O All-seeing God! (3745)

५६. अन्नाद्येन यशसा तेजसा ब्राह्मणवर्चसेन ॥

56. Equip me, O God, with food and fame, with vigour, and with the splendour of a Vedic scholar! (3746)

BOOK (Kāṇḍa) XIV

Chapter (Anuvāka) 1

HYMN I

१. सत्येनोत्तभिता भूमिः सूर्येणोत्तभिता द्यौः ।
ऋतेनादित्यास्तिष्ठन्ति दिवि सोमो अधि श्रितः ॥

1. God upholds the Earth. The Sun upholds the heaven. By Law the luminous planets stand secure, and the Moon holds her place in heaven. (3747)[1]

२. सोमेनादित्या बलिनः सोमेन पृथिवी मही । अथो नक्षत्राणामेषामुपस्थे सोम आहितः ॥

2. By Soma the Āditya Brahmcharis are strong. By Soma the woman like the earth is mighty. Soma rests in steadfast ascetics like Moon in the midst of these constellations. (3748)[2]

३. सोमं मन्यते पपिवान्यत्संपिषन्त्योषधिम् ।
सोमं यं ब्रह्माणो विदुर्न तस्याश्नाति पार्थिवः ॥

3. A drinker of Soma thinks the plant to be Soma, which men bray as medicine but really God is Soma, Whom the learned know, and ordinary mortals do not realise. (3749)

४. यत्त्वा सोम प्रपिबन्ति तत आ प्यायसे पुनः ।
वायुः सोमस्य रक्षिता समानां मास आकृतिः ॥

4. O Moon, thou wanest when the Sun's rays drink thy juice, but thou waxest again. Air is the Moon's sentinel, just as the month is the shaper of years ! (3750)[3]

[1]The last part of the verse has been translated by Pt. Jaidev Vidyalankar as: Like the lustrous Sun, semen resides in an energetic person.

[2]Soma means semen.

[3]When the Sun's rays draw the Moon's juice, it comes down to the earth and strengthens vegetables and crops. The same juice is taken by the rays to the Moon again. Month shapes the years, so the rays of the Sun make the Moon wane and wax.

५. श्राच्छद्विधानैर्गुपितो बार्हतैः सोम रक्षितः ।
ग्राव्णामिच्छृण्वन् तिष्ठसि न ते अश्नाति पार्थिवः ।।

5. O God, preserved by Thy covering rules, guarded by the laws expounded in the Vedas, Thou standest listening certainly to the prayer of the learned. An ordinary mortal engrossed in worldly affairs does not realise Thee. (3751)[1]

६. चित्तिरा उपबर्हणं चक्षुरा अभ्यञ्जनम् । द्यौर्भूमिः कोश आसीद्यदयात् सूर्या पतिम् ।।

6. When a girl charming, and beautiful like the Sun, goes to her husband, her mental resolve is comfortable to her like the pillow, love in her eyes is solacing to her like the unguent, and heaven and earth are her treasure chest. (3752)[2]

७. रैभ्यासीदनुदेयी नाराशंसी न्योचनी । सूर्याया भद्रमिद्वासो गाथयैति परिष्कृता ।।

7. At the time of departure from the parental home, Vedic speech is the dowry of the beautiful girl. At the time of entering her husband's house, her renown is her ornament. Her noble acts are her garment. She marches embellished with Vedic knowledge worthy of being sung. (3753)[3]

८. स्तोमा आसन्प्रतिधयः कुरीरं छन्द ओपशः । सूर्याया अश्विना वराग्निरासीत्पुरोगवः ।।

8. May the Vedic verses be her guardians. May the performance of duty, and knowledge of the Vedas be the ornament of the head for the girl. May both husband and wife love each other. May the Ācharya brilliant with knowledge like fire be her precursor. (3754)[4]

९. सोमो वधूयुरभवदश्विनास्तामुभा वरा । सूर्यां यत्पत्ये शंसन्तीं मनसा सविताददात् ।।

9. May the highly qualified Brahmchari long for the bride. May both—learned husband and wife be full of affection, when the father bestows on her lord his daughter praising her husband willingly. (3755)[5]

१०. मनो अस्या अन आसीद् द्यौरासीदुत च्छदिः ।
शुक्रावनड्वाहावास्तां यदयात्सूर्या पतिम् ।।

10. Her spirit was the bridal car, the canopy thereof was heaven: Two stout oxen to draw the chariot of domestic life were husband and wife, when the girl came unto her lord. (3756)[6]

११. ऋक्सामाभ्यामभिहितौ गावौ ते सामनावैताम् ।
श्रोत्रे ते चक्रे आस्तां दिवि पन्थाश्चराचरः ।।

[1]See *Rig*, 10-84-5. [2]See *Rig*, 10-84-7. [3]See *Rig*, 10-84-6.

[4]Ācharya: Guru, preceptor. See *Rig*, 10-85-8.

[5]See *Rig*, 10-85-9. The verse has been explained by Maharshi Dayananda in the *Sanskār Vidhi* in the chapter on marriage.

[6]See *Rig*, 10-85-10.

11. May both husband and wife, the drivers of the chariot of domestic life go hand in hand, following the injunctions of the Rig and Sāma Vedas. O girl may both thy listening ears serve as chariot wheels. The whole world, animate or inanimate, is the path of thy car of domestic life ! (3757)[1]

१२. शुची ते चक्रे यात्या व्यानो अक्ष आहतः । अनो मनस्मयं सूर्यारोहत् प्रयती पतिम् ।।

12. O girl, pure as thou wentest were thy ears serving as chariot wheels. Life-infusing breath was the axle piercing them! The girl advancing to her lord rode on the chariot of her heart. (3758)[2]

१३. सूर्याया वहतुः प्रागात्सविता यमवासृजत् । मघासु हन्यन्ते गावः फल्गुनीषु व्यु॒ह्यते ।।

13. The dowry given by the father to the girl should go ahead. Words of praise should be uttered to pay her respects. She should be carried in the accompaniment of successful ritual observances. (3759)[3]

१४. यदश्विना पृच्छमानावयातं त्रिचक्रेण वहतुं सूर्यायाः ।
क्वैकं चक्रं वामासीत् क्व॒ देष्ट्राय तस्थथुः ।।

14. O husband and wife, when you go with the girl's dowry on your three-wheeled chariot, enquiring about your path, where was one chariot wheel of yours. Where did you stay to listen to the sermon of the preacher! (3760)[4]

१५. यदयातं शुभस्पती वरेयं सूर्यामुप ।
विश्वे देवा अनु तद्वामजानन् पुत्रः पितरमवृणीत पूषा ।।

15. Ye twin lords of lustre, at the time when you sit for the girl's marriage, let all learned persons agree to your proposal, may you as father and mother beget a stout son ! (3761)[5]

१६. द्वे ते चक्रे सूर्ये ब्रह्माण ऋतुथा विदुः । अथैकं चक्रं यत् गुहा तदद्धातय इद् विदुः ।।

16. O bride, two wheels of thy mental chariot the learned know at all seasons. The one wheel which is hidden is known only to those who possess the highest truths. (3762)[6]

[1]See *Rig*, 10-85-11. Just as both the wheels of a chariot work in unison, so should the ears of the bride do.

[2]See *Rig*, 10-85-12. The verse inculcates that the girl should be chaste, pure, self-controlled and full of mental vigour.

[3]See *Rig*, 10-85-13.

[4]See *Rig*, 10-85-14.

Three wheeled chariot: Karma (Action), Upāsnā (contemplation) Jnāna (Knowledge). One wheel: Self-knowledge. Husband and wife should possess Karma, Upāsnā, Jnāna, and have knowledge of self.

[5]Twin lords of lustre: Beautiful husband and wife. See *Rig*. 10-85-15.

[6]Two wheels: Karma (Action), Upāsnā (contemplation). One wheel: Jnāna (Knowledge) See *Rig*, 10-85-16.

१७. अर्यमणं यजामहे सुबन्धुं पतिवेदनम् । उर्वारुकमिव बन्धनात्प्रेतो मुञ्चामि नामुतः ।।

17. Worship we pay to God, the Finder of husbands, kindly Friend. As a cucumber is loosened from its stalk, so I release thee from here, not from there. (3763)[1]

१८. प्रेतो मुञ्चामि नामुतः सुबद्धाममुतस्करम् । यथेयमिन्द्र मीढ्वः सुपुत्रा सुभगासति ।।

18. I set her free from her parental home, but not from that of her husband. I nicely connect her with her husband's family. O Bounteous God, may she live blest in her fortune and sons ! (3764)[2]

१९. प्र त्वा मुञ्चामि वरुणस्य पाशाद् येन त्वाऽबध्नात् सविता सुशेवाः ।
ऋतस्य योनौ सुकृतस्य लोके स्योनं ते अस्तु सहसंभलायै ।।

19. Now I free thee from the restrictions of thy parents, wherewith thy blessed father hath bound thee. Talking sweetly with thy husband, may thou enjoy bliss in the house of thy noble, learned husband, and in his family of virtuous people. (3765)[3]

२०. भगस्त्वेतो नयतु हस्तगृह्याश्विना त्वा प्र वहतां रथेन ।
गृहान् गच्छ गृहपत्नी यथाऽसो वशिनी त्वं विदथमा वदासि ।।

20. Let the prosperous bridegroom take thy hand and hence conduct thee. Let thy husband and his brother on their car transport thee. Go to the house of thy husband to be the household's mistress. Controlling all members of the family, utter words full of knowledge. (3766)[4]

२१. इह प्रियं प्रजायै ते समृध्यतामस्मिन् गृहे गार्हपत्याय जागृहि ।
एना पत्या तन्वं१ सं स्पृशस्वाथ जिर्विर्विदथमा वदासि ।।

21. Happy be thou and prosper with thy children here: be vigilant to rule thy household in this home. Dedicate thyself to this man thy lord. So shalt thou till the end of your life spread knowledge. (3767)[5]

२२. इहैव स्तं मा वि यौष्टं विश्वमायुर्व्यश्नुतम् । क्रीडन्तौ पुत्रैर्नप्तृभिर्मोदमानौ स्वस्तकौ ।।

22. Be not divided; dwell ye here: reach the full time of human life. With sons and grandsons sport and play, rejoicing in your happy home. (3768)[6]

[1]We: The family members of the girl. Thee: The bride. From here: from thy father's house. From there: from thy new home where thy whole life is to be spent. See *Rig*, 7-59-12.

[2]I: The priest who afficiates at the marriage ceremony. See *Ri*, 10-85-25. Both verses 18th and 19th have been quoted and explained by Maharshi Dayananda in the *Sanskār Vidhi*.

[3]See *Rig*, 10-85-24. 'I' refers to husband.

[4]See *Rig*, 10-85-26.

[5]See *Rig*, 10-85-27. Here: In the house of thy husband.

[6]See *Rig*, 10-85-42.

२३. पूर्वापरं चरतो माययैतौ शिशू क्रीडन्तौ परि यातोऽर्णवम् ।
विश्वान्यो भुवना विचष्ट ऋतूँरन्यो विदधज्जायसे नवः ॥

23. Moving by magic power from east to westward, these two (Sun and Moon) revolve in the atmosphere sporting like two children. The one illumines all parts of the world. Thou, the other, art born anew, duly arranging seasons. (3769)[1]

२४. नवोनवो भवसि जायमानोऽह्नां केतुरुषसामेष्यग्रम् ।
भागं देवेभ्यो वि दधास्यायन् प्र चन्द्रमस्तिरसे दीर्घमायुः ॥

24. Thou, born afresh, art new and new for ever: ensign of days, before the Dawns thou goest. Coming, thou suppliest nourishment to vegetables, crops and trees. Thou lengthenest, Moon, the days of our existence. (3770)

२५. परा देहि शामुल्यं ब्रह्मभ्यो वि भजा वसु । कृत्यैषा पद्वती भूत्वा जाया विशते पतिम् ॥

25. O newly married person, eradicate the impurity of your heart, give money to the Vedic scholars. This wife cognizant of her duty, being prosperous enters the house of her lord. (3771)[2]

२६. नीललोहितं भवति कृत्यासक्तिर्व्यज्यते । एधन्ते अस्या ज्ञातयः पतिर्बन्धेषु बध्यते ॥

26. Wealth manifests itself, when the love of the dutiful wife towards her husband is firmly established. Then the relatives of the bride flourish, and the husband is bound fast in the bonds of love with his wife. (3772)[3]

२७. अश्लीला तनूर्भवति रुशती पापयामुया । पतिर्यद् वध्वो३ वाससः स्वमङ्गमभ्यूर्णुते ॥

27. When the husband wraps about his limbs the garment of his wife, his beautiful body becomes graceless due to this vicious deed. (3773)[4]

२८. आशसनं विशसनमथो अधिविकर्तनम् । सूर्यायाः पश्य रूपाणि तानि ब्रह्मोत शुम्भति ॥

28. O husband, watch the cutting, bursting, and severing of limbs and joints of your wife at the time of her menstruation. A learned person alone can rid her of these pains. (3774)[5]

२९. तृष्टमेतत् कटुकमपाष्ठवद्विषवन्नैतदत्तवे । सूर्यां यो ब्रह्मा वेद स इद् वाधूयमर्हति ॥

[1]See 10-85-18. See *Atharva*, 7-81-1, and 13-2-11. Just as the Sun and Moon do good to humanity observing the rule of God, so should husband and wife together serve mankind.

[2]Just as the Moon contributes to the growth of crops, vegetables and trees, so should husband and wife pass their life in the service of humanity.

[3]See *Rig*, 10-85-28.

[4]See *Rig*, 10-85-30. A husband should never wear the clothes used by his wife. It is an ungraceful and ugly act.

[5]See *Rig*, 10-85-35.

29. At the time of menstruation the woman feels the pangs of thirst, perceives irritating pimples on the body like a despicable thing. The fluid she emits is empoisoned. In that condition she is not fit for cohabitation. A Vedic scholar who knows these signs of the woman, is fit for marriage. (3775)

३०. स इत् तत् स्योनं हरति ब्रह्मा वासः सुमङ्गलम् ।
प्रायश्चित्तिं यो अध्येति येन जाया न रिष्यति ॥

30. The learned husband brings home the beautiful and serviceable cloth. He knows how to keep his mind pure, whereby the wife is kept unharmed. (3776)

३१. युवं भगं सं भरतं समृद्धमृतं वदन्तावृतोद्येषु ।
ब्रह्मणस्पते पतिमस्यै रोचय चारु संभलो वदतु वाचमेताम् ॥

31. Acquire, ye twain, happy and prosperous fortune, speaking the truth in faithful utterances. O God, the Guardian of the Vedas, dear unto her, make the husband. Pleasant be these words the wooer speaketh unto her! (3777)

३२. इहेदसाथ न परो गमाथेमं गावः प्रजया वर्धयाथ ।
शुभं यतीरुस्रियाः सोमवर्चसो विश्वे देवाः क्रन्निह वो मनांसि ॥

32. O enterprising women, remain ye even here, go not far away: strengthen this man with plenteous offspring! O noble women, be ye the harbingers of weal and lustrous like the moon. May all learned persons fix your minds here in domestic life! (3778)

३३. इमं गावः प्रजया सं विशाथायं देवानां न मिनाति भागम् ।
अस्मै वः पूषा मरुतश्च सर्वे अस्मै वो धाता सविता सुवाति ॥

33. O enterprising women, bless this newly married man with offspring. He never diminishes the respect due to the learned guests! May God, all learned persons, your father, your teacher hand ye over to this man. (3779)

३४. अनृक्षरा ऋजवः सन्तु पन्थानो येभिः सखायो यन्ति नो वरेयम् ।
सं भगेन समर्यम्णा सं धाता सृजतु वर्चसा ॥

34. Thornless and straight be the paths, whereby our fellows travel to the house of the bride. May God endue us with prosperity, respect for the learned and majesty. (3780)

३५. यच्च वर्चो अक्षेषु सुरायां च यदाहितम् । यद् गोष्वश्विना वर्चस्तेनेमां वर्चसाऽवतम् ॥

35. Whatever lustre is in the eyes of lovers, whatever lustre is in wealth, whatever lustre is in energetic persons, O men and women endue this dame therewith. (3781)

३६. येन महानघ्न्या जघनमश्विना येन वा सुरा । येनाक्षा अभ्यषिच्यन्त तेनेमां वर्चसाऽवतम् ॥

36. With all the lustre that accompanies the valour of an immaculate woman, with all the lustre of pelf, with all the lustre that lurks in the eyes of lovers, O ladies and gentlemen, adorn this dame therewith. (3782)

३७. यो अनिध्मो दीदयदप्स्व१न्तर्यं विप्रास ईडते अध्वरेषु ।
अपां नपान्मधुमतीरपो दा याभिरिन्द्रो वावृधे वीर्या॒वान् ॥

37. He, Who shines unseen amongst His subjects, Whom sages worship in their sacrifices (Yajnās). May He, the Guardian of humanity, grant us learned offspring, that enhances the power of a mighty man. (3783)[1]

३८. इदमहं रुशन्तं ग्राभं तनूदूषिमपोहामि । यो भद्रो रोचनस्तमुदचामि ॥

38. On entering domestic life I give up guilty conduct, harmful, and injurious to health, and follow that which is auspicious, and agreeable. (3784)

३९. आस्यै ब्राह्मणाः स्नपनीर्हरन्त्ववीरघ्नीरुदजन्त्वापः ।
अर्यम्णो अग्निं पर्येतु पूषन् प्रतीक्षन्ते श्वशुरो देवरश्च ॥

39. Hitherto let learned persons bring her bathing water: let them fetch such as guards the lives of heroes. Let her encircle the fire of the Yajna dedicated to God. Let her husband, her father-in-law and her husband's brothers look upon her fondly. (3785)[2]

४०. शं ते हिरण्यं शमु सन्त्वापः शं मेथिर्भवतु शं युगस्य तर्द्म ।
शं त आपः शतपवित्रा भवन्तु शमु पत्या तन्वं१ सं स्पृशस्व ॥

40. Blest be the gold ornaments to thee, and blest the offspring, blest be the mutual exchange of ideas, blest be thy seat made of straw. Blest be the waters, the purifiers of hundreds blest be thy devotion and loyalty to the husband. (3786)[3]

४१. खे रथस्य खेऽनसः खे युगस्य शतक्रतो । अपालामिन्द्र त्रिष्पूत्वाकृणोः सूर्यत्वचम् ।।

41. O multi-talented husband, purifying thy highly qualified wife through three devices, make her lustrous like the Sun, for realising the emotions of her body, for successfully passing her life and for deep absorption in contemplation. (3787)[4]

४२. आशासाना सौमनसं प्रजां सौभाग्यं रयिम् । पत्युरनुव्रता भूत्वा सं नह्यस्वामृताय कम् ॥

[1]Apsu: आपाः प्रजा Dayanand a commentary, *Yajur*, 6-27.

[2]After she has reached her husband's house, she should bother and perform Yajna.

[3]Seat: Āsana used for sitting upon in a Yajna.

[4]Three devices: (i) Karma (Deed); (ii) Upāsana (Contemplation); (iii) Jñāna (Knowledge). Griffith, following Sāyana considers Apālā, a woman afflicted with some cutaneous disease. He has fabricated a legend about her on the basis of Sāyāna, which cannot be relied upon, as there is no history in the Vedas.

42. O woman, longing for cheerfulness, children, prosperity, and wealth, devoted to thy husband, gird thyself for securing the full span of life for a hundred years with ease! (3788)

४३. यथा सिन्धुर्नदीनां साम्राज्यं सुषुवे वृषा । एवा त्वं सम्राज्ञ्येधि पत्युरस्तं परेत्य ॥

43. As mighty ocean won himself imperial lordship of the streams, so be imperial queen when thou hast come within thy husband's home. (3789)

४४. सम्राज्ञ्येधि श्वशुरेषु सम्राज्ञ्युत देवृषु । ननान्दुः सम्राज्ञ्येधि सम्राज्ञ्युत श्वश्र्वाः ॥

44. Over thy husband's father and his brothers be imperial queen. Over thy husband's sister and his mother bear supreme control. (3790)[1]

४५. या अकृन्तन्नवयन् याश्च तत्निरे या देवीरन्ताँ अभितोऽददन्त ।
तास्त्वा जरसे सं व्ययन्त्वायुष्मतीदं परि धत्स्व वासः ॥

45. Ladies who have spun, and woven and extended this garment, who have drawn its ends together, may they invest thee full long existence. Heiress of lengthened life, put on this garment. (3791)

४६. जीवं रुदन्ति वि नयन्त्यध्वरं दीर्घामनु प्रसितिं दीध्युर्नरः ।
वामं पितृभ्यो य इदं समीरिरे मयः पतिभ्यो जनये परिष्वजे ॥

46. At the time of the departure of the bride people weep for their beloved soul. They thereby destroy the grace and beauty of the sacred rite of marriage. Wise persons think of the distant future of marital tie. In fact those who arrange this beautiful marriage ceremony for the happiness of the parents, provide the lords, the joy of embracing their wives. (3792)[2]

४७. स्योनं ध्रुवं प्रजायै धारयामि तेऽश्मानं देव्याः पृथिव्या उपस्थे ।
तमा तिष्ठानुमाद्या सुवर्चा दीर्घं त आयुः सविता कृणोतु ॥

47. I place on the lap of Earth, O bride, a firm auspicious stone to bring thee children. Stand on it, thou, greeted with joy, resplendent: a long long life may God vouchsafe thee! (3793)[3]

४८. येनाग्निरस्या भूम्या हस्तं जग्राह दक्षिणम् ।
तेन गृह्णामि ते हस्तं मा व्यथिष्ठा मया सह प्रजया च धनेन च ॥

48. The purpose for which the king takes the powerful hand of this our Earth, even so I take and hold thy hand be not disquieted, remain with me, with children and with store of wealth. (3794)[4]

[1]Fathers: Father, uncles, grandfather. See *Rig*, 10-85-46. Maharshi Dayananda has commented upon the verse in the *Sanskār Vidhi* in the chapter on marriage.

[2]See *Rig*, 10-40-10. Maharshi Dayananda has explained this verse in the *Sanskār Vidhi* in the chapter on marriage. Relatives should not weep when the bride departs.

[3]I: The bridegroom. Just as the stone is firm, so should the bride remain steadfast and devoted to her husband, bear children and enjoy a long life.

[4]A King takes possession of the earth, so that it may grow more food, so the bridegroom marries a girl, that she may bear children and remain free from grief.

४९. देवस्ते सविता हस्तं गृह्णातु सोमो राजा सुप्रजसं कृणोतु ।
अग्निः सुभगां जातवेदाः पत्ये पत्नीं जरदष्टिं कृणोतु ॥

49. The Wise God shall take thy hand. The Dignified God, the Creator of all, shall make thee rich in goodly offspring. Let the Omnipresent God, the Bestower of riches, make thee prosperous, till old old age a wife unto thy husband. (3795)[1]

५०. गृह्णामि ते सौभगत्वाय हस्तं मया पत्या जरदष्टिर्यथासः ।
भगो अर्यमा सविता पुरन्धिर्मह्यं त्वादुर्गार्हपत्याय देवाः ॥

50. I take thy hand in mine for happy fortune that thou mayst reach old age with me thy consort. God, the Prosperous, the Respecter of the noble, the Urger of all, the Sustainer of the universe, and all learned persons, have given thee to be my household's mistress. (3796)

५१. भगस्ते हस्तमग्रहीत् सविता हस्तमग्रहीत् । पत्नी त्वमसि धर्मणाऽहं गृहपतिस्तव ॥

51. The Prosperous God has clasped thy hand. The All-creating God has taken thy hand. By rule and law thou art my wife: the master of thy house am I. (3797)

५२. ममेयमस्तु पोष्या मह्यं त्वादाद् बृहस्पतिः । मया पत्या प्रजावति सं जीव शरदः शतम् ॥

52. May it be my care to foster her: God hath made thee mine. A hundred autumns live with me thy husband, mother of my sons. (3798)

५३. त्वष्टा वासो व्यदधाच्छुभे कं बृहस्पतेः प्रशिषा कवीनाम् ।
तेनेमां नारीं सविता भगश्च सूर्यामिव परि धत्तां प्रजया ॥

53. The artisan, by order of God and the holy sages, hath prepared for glory this comfortable robe. Hence may the All-creating and Prosperous God bless with children this dame, glittering like the Sun. (3799)

५४. इन्द्राग्नी द्यावापृथिवी मातरिश्वा मित्रावरुणा भगो अश्विनोभा ।
बृहस्पतिर्मरुतो ब्रह्म सोम इमां नारीं प्रजया वर्धयन्तु ॥

54. May cloud and electricity, Heaven and Earth, subtle air in the atmosphere. Prāna and Apāna, the Sun, both Day and Night, God, the Lord of the Vedas, learned persons, Vedic knowledge, the husband, magnify this dame with offspring. (3800)

५५. बृहस्पतिः प्रथमः सूर्यायाः शीर्षे केशाँ अकल्पयत् ।
तेनेमामश्विना नारीं पत्ये सं शोभयामसि ॥

55. God first arranged the hair on the bride's head. Therefore, O ladies and gentlemen we adorn this woman for her lord. (3801)

[1]Shall take thy hand: shall help thee.

५६. इदं तद्रूपं यदवस्त योषा जायां जिज्ञासे मनसा चरन्तीम् ।
तामन्वर्तिष्ये सखिभिर्नवग्वैः क इमान् विद्वान् वि चचर्त पाशान् ॥

56. This is the external beauty of the bride she assumes herself. I want to know in spirit the real character of my wife. I will follow her with my companions who acquire and impart new and fresh knowledge. The Wise God has cut asunder the bonds of ignorance. (3802)

५७. अहं वि ष्यामि मयि रूपमस्या वेददित् पश्यन् मनसः कुलायम् ।
न स्तेयमद्मि मनसोदमुच्ये स्वयं श्रथ्नानो वरुणस्य पाशान् ॥

57. Knowing the nature of her mind and looking at her beauty, I fasten her in my love. I eat no stolen food: through self exertion untying the nooses of obstacles I am freed in spirit. (3803)

५८. प्र त्वा मुञ्चामि वरुणस्य पाशाद् येन त्वाऽबध्नात् सविता सुशेवाः ।
उरुं लोकं सुगमत्र पन्थां कृणोमि तुभ्यं सहपत्न्यै वधु ॥

58. O bride, I free thee from the restrictions of thy parents, wherewith thy blessed father hath bound thee. I give thee here beside thy husband an extensive house and nice resources to make the journey of life successful! (3804)[1]

५९. उद्यच्छध्वमप रक्षो हनाथेमां नारीं सुकृते दधात ।
धाता विपश्चित् पतिमस्यै विवेद भगो राजा पुर एतु प्रजानन् ॥

59. O heroes, lift up your weapons. Drive away the demons. Transport this woman to the world of virtue. The Most Wise God hath found for her a husband. Let the Refulgent, Prosperous, Omniscient God, give her right lead! (3805)[2]

६०. भगस्ततक्ष चतुरः पादान् भगस्ततक्ष चत्वार्युष्पलानि ।
त्वष्टा पिपेश मध्यतोऽनु वर्ध्रान्त्सा नो अस्तु सुमङ्गली ॥

60. God hath fashioned four desirable objects. God hath formed four Ashramās for saving us from violence. God hath shaped mutual relations between husband and wife for their favourable acts of progress and development. May the bride be a source of happiness for us. (3806)

६१. सुकिंशुकं वहतुं विश्वरूपं हिरण्यवर्णं सुवृतं सुचक्रम् ।
आ रोह सूर्ये अमृतस्य लोकं स्योनं पतिभ्यो वहतुं कृणु त्वम् ॥

61. O bride, glittering like the Sun, mount this, all hued, gold-tinted, strong-wheeled highly, brilliant, chariot lightly rolling, bound for the world of life immortal. Make for the relatives of thy husband a happy bride's procession. (3807)[3]

[1]I: The husband. Here: In domestic life.

[2]Drive away the demons: Remove the obstacles in the way of marriage.

[3]Chariot: Domestic life, Grihastha Ashrama. See *Rig*, 10-85-20, and *Nirukta*, 12-8. This verse has been commented upon by Maharshi Dayananda in the *Sanskār Vidhi* in the chapter on marriage.

६२. अभ्रातृघ्नीं वरुणापशुघ्नीं बृहस्पते । इन्द्रापतिघ्नीं पुत्रिणीमास्मभ्यं सवितर्वह ॥

62. To us, O God, bring her, kind to brothers; bring her, O Lord of the universe, gentle to the cattle. Bring her, O God, gentle to her husband: bring her to us, O Creator of the world, the bearer of children ! (3808)

६३. मा हिंसिष्टं कुमार्यं१ स्थूणे देवकृते पथि । शालाया देव्या द्वारं स्योनं कृण्मो वधूपथम् ॥

63. Harm not the girl, ye men and women, who travels upon the path designed by God. We make auspicious the portal of the heavenly home, and the road on which the bride travels to the house of her husband. (3809)

६४. ब्रह्मापरं युज्यतां ब्रह्म पूर्वं ब्रह्मान्ततो मध्यतो ब्रह्म सर्वतः ।
अनाव्याधां देवपुरां प्रपद्य शिवा स्योना पतिलोके वि राज ॥

64. Let Vedic verses be recited before and after, in the middle, at the end, all around her. Reaching the husband's house free from disease, being gentle and auspicious shine in thy lord's family. (3810)

HYMN II

१. तुभ्यमग्रे पर्यवहन्त्सूर्यां वहतुना सह । स नः पतिभ्यो जायां दा अग्ने प्रजया सह ॥

1. O Primordial God, in obedience to your command, we have brought the girl after marriage with her dowry; give us the relatives of the husband the wife with future children! (3811)[1]

२. पुनः पत्नीमग्निरदादायुषा सह वर्चसा । दीर्घायुरस्या यः पतिर्जीवाति शरदः शतम् ॥

2. God hath verily given the bride with splendour and a lengthened life. Long-lived be he who is her husband: a hundred autumns let him live. (3812)[2]

३. सोमस्य जाया प्रथमं गन्धर्वस्तेऽपरः पतिः । तृतीयो अग्निष्टे पतिस्तुरीयस्ते मनुष्यजाः ॥

3. O woman, mental peace or equilibrium is thy first guardian, observance of Vedic law is thy second guardian, knowledge and strength of character are thy third guardians. One born of woman is thy fourth guardian. (3813)[3]

४. सोमो ददद् गन्धर्वाय गन्धर्वो दददग्नये । रयिं च पुत्रांश्चादादग्निर्मह्यमथो इमाम् ॥

4. Tranquillity develops in the girl the sentiment of following the Vedic law, which in turn brings her knowledge and strength of character, which bestows on me riches and sons and this my bride. (3814)[4]

[1]See *Rig*, 10-85-38. Maharshi Dayananda has explained this verse in the *Sanskār Vidhi* in the chapter on marriage.

[2]See *Rig*, 10-85-39.

[3]See *Rig*, 10-85-40. Pt. Jaidev Vidyalankar interprets Soma as water, Gandharva as air, and Agni as fire.

[4]See *Rig*, 10-85-41.

५. आ वामगन्त्सुमतिर्वाजिनीवसू न्यश्विना हृत्सु कामा अरंसत ।
अभूतं गोपा मिथुना शुभस्पती प्रिया अर्यम्णो दुर्यां अशीमहि ॥

5. O husband and wife, may ye be blessed with nice determination may ye be the masters of strength and riches. Preserving your physical beauty and controlling your organs, with mutual cooperation perform the duties of domestic life. May we, the friends of God enjoy home comforts! (3815)[1]

६. सा मन्दसाना मनसा शिवेन रयिं धेहि सर्ववीरं वचस्यम् ।
सुगं तीर्थं सुप्रपाणं शुभस्पती स्थाणुं पथिष्ठामप दुर्मतिं हतम् ॥

6. Thou, Dame, rejoicing with blissful mind take laudable wealth, with all thy children! O husband and wife, lords of nice beautiful objects, construct a fair ford, good to drink at; plant trees on the pathway, and remove all mental agony! (3816)[2]

७. या ओषधयो या नद्यो३ यानि क्षेत्राणि या वना ।
तास्त्वा वधु प्रजावतीं पत्ये रक्षन्तु रक्षसः ॥

7. May all the plants, all the rivers, may all the fields, all the forests, O bride, protect thee from every sort of obstacle, guard thee, the mother of children, for thy lord! (3817)

८. एमं पन्थामरुक्षाम सुगं स्वस्तिवाहनम् । यस्मिन् वीरो न रिष्यत्यन्येषां विन्दते वसु ॥

8. Let us follow the convenient, blissful Vedic path, whereon no hero suffers harm, which gives us more wealth than all other paths. (3818)

९. इदं सु मे नरः श्रृणुत ययाऽऽशिषा दम्पती वाममश्नुतः ।
ये गन्धर्वा अप्सरसश्च देवीरेषु वानस्पत्येषु येऽधि तस्थुः ।
स्योनास्ते अस्यै वध्वै भवन्तु मा हिंसिषुर्वहतुमुह्यमानम् ॥

9. Hear these my words, ye men, the benediction through which the wedded pair have found high fortune. May the Vedic scholars and noble women, who reside in forests full of hermits, regard this bride with their auspicious favour, nor harm the nuptial dowry as it is being conveyed. (3819)

१०. ये वध्वश्चन्द्रं वहतुं यक्ष्मा यन्ति जनाँ अनु ।
पुनस्तान् यज्ञिया देवा नयन्तु यत आगताः ॥

10. Venerable guests who come along with other ordinary persons to see the bride's beautiful dowry, should be taken back to the place whence they came, by the learned relatives of the bridegroom. (3820)[3]

११. मा विदन् परिपन्थिनो य आसीदन्ति दम्पती । सुगेन दुर्गमतीतामप द्रान्त्वरातयः ॥

[1]See *Rig*, 10-40-12. [2]See *Rig*, 10-40-13. [3]See *Rig*, 10-85-31.

11. Let not the highway freebooters who lie in ambush find the wedded pair. Let husband and wife easily cross the dangerous Zone. Let their enemies run away in fear. (3821)[1]

१२. सं काशयामि वहतुं ब्रह्मणा गृहैरघोरेण चक्षुषा मित्रियेण ।
पर्याणद्धं विश्वरूपं यदस्ति स्योनं पतिभ्यः सविता तत् कृणोतु ॥

12. I show the bride's dowry with prayer and the gentle eye of friendship. All that is covered there in perfect beauty, may God make pleasant to the husband's family members. (3822)[2]

१३. शिवा नारीयमस्तमागन्निमं धाता लोकमस्यै दिदेश ।
तामर्यमा भगो अश्विनोभा प्रजापतिः प्रजया वर्धयन्तु ॥

13. This blessed dame has come to her husband's house. God hath given her this new society. May the King, dignified preceptor, learned men and women, and God, make her thrive with offspring. (3823)

१४. आत्मन्वत्युर्वरा नारीयमागन् तस्यां नरो वपत बीजमस्याम् ।
सा वः प्रजां जनयद् वक्षणाभ्यो बिभ्रती दुग्धमृषभस्य रेतः ॥

14. This spiritually advanced dame, fit for begetting children has come, sow, thou man, the seed in this physically fit woman. She from her teeming sides shall bear thee children, preserving in her womb the valuable semen of her strong husband. (3824)

१५. प्रति तिष्ठ विराडसि विष्णुरिवेह सरस्वति । सिनीवालि प्र जायतां भगस्य सुमतावसत् ॥

15. O learned women, remain firm like the Sun, here in domestic life, thou art the queen of the house. O lady, the master of provisions bear good offsprings, obedient to the command of God. (3825)

१६. उद् व ऊर्मिः शम्या हन्त्वापो योक्त्राणि मुञ्चत ।
मादुष्कृतौ व्येनसावघ्न्यावशुनमारताम् ॥

16. Ye, tranquil learned persons, may your perseverance advance. May you renounce ignoble deeds. Never may the holy pair, sinless, and innocent suffer harm. (3826)[3]

१७. अघोरचक्षुरपतिघ्नी स्योना शग्मा सुशेवा सुयमा गृहेभ्यः ।
वीरसूर्देवृकामा सं त्वयैधिषीमहि सुमनस्यमाना ॥

[1]See *Rig*, 10-85-32. Maharshi Dayananda has commented upon this verse in *Sanskâr Vidhi* in the chapter on marriage.

[2]i: The father of the bridegroom. All that is: The ornaments, clothes, utensils and household nice objects which constitute the dowry.

[3]See *Rig*, 3-33-13. Pair: Husband and wife.

17. Not evil-eyed, no slayer of thy husband, be consoling, kind, serviceable and law-abiding to thy household. Mother of heroes, wish for the welfare of thy husband's brother; be happy, and through thee may we too prosper. (3827)

१८. अदेवृघ्न्यपतिघ्नीहैधि शिवा पशुभ्यः सुयमा सुवर्चाः ।
प्रजावती वीरसूर्देवृकामा स्योनेममग्निं गार्हपत्यं सपर्य ॥

18. No slayer of thy husband or his brother, be benevolent to the cattle, law-abiding and prosperous. Longing for the welfare of thy husband's brother, employing servants, give birth to heroes. Tend well the household fire: be soft and pleasant. (3828)[1]

१९. उत्तिष्ठेतः किमिच्छन्तीदमागा अहं त्वेडे अभिभूः स्वाद् गृहात् ।
शून्यैषी निरृते याजगन्धोत्तिष्ठाराते प्र पत मेह रंस्थाः ॥

19. O poverty, begone from this house. What wish hath brought thee hither. I mightier than thee expel thee from my house. O poverty, willing to destroy my house, thou hast come here in vain. Get up, Malignity, fly off, stay here no longer! (3829)

२०. यदा गार्हपत्यमसपर्यैत् पूर्वमग्निं वधूरियम् । अधा सरस्वत्यै नारि पितृभ्यश्च नमस्कुरु ॥

20. When this woman hath first of all adored the sacred household fire, O Dame, then study the Vedas, and pay homage to the elders of the family. (3830)

२१. शर्म वर्मैतदा हरास्यै नार्या उपस्तरे । सिनीवालि प्र जायतां भगस्य सुमतावसत् ॥

21. O bridegroom, bring for this woman all comfortable and painless cloths to be spread on her bed. O lady, the controller of provisions, bear children, and live in God's grace! (3831)

२२. यं बल्बजं न्यस्यथ चर्म चोपस्तृणीथन । तदा रोहतु सुप्रजा या कन्याऽ विन्दते पतिम् ॥

22. Let her who shall be blest with sons, the maid who finds a husband, step upon the rough grass seat (Āsana) that ye spread and beneath which ye lay the deer-skin. (3832)

२३. उप स्तृणीहि बल्बजमधि चर्मणि रोहिते । तत्रोपविश्य सुप्रजा इममग्निं सपर्यतु ॥

23. Over the ruddy-coloured skin strew thou the grass seat. Let her, the mother of good sons, sit there, perform Havan and pray to God. (3833)[2]

२४. आरोह चर्मोप सीदाग्निमेष देवो हन्ति रक्षांसि सर्वा ।
इह प्रजां जनय पत्ये अस्मै सुज्यैष्ठ्यो भवत् पुत्रस्त एषः ॥

[1]Tend—fire: Perform Agni Hotra (Havan) daily.

[2]Thou: The husband.

24. Step on the deer-skin, and worship God, Who removes all obstacles, Here bear thou children to this man thy husband: let this thy son be endowed with noble traits. (3834)[1]

२५. वि तिष्ठन्तां मातुरस्या उपस्थान्नानारूपाः पशवो जायमानाः ।
सुमङ्गल्युप सीदेममग्निं संपत्नी प्रति भूषेह देवान् ॥

25. Let many babes of varied form and nature spring in succession from this fruitful mother. Worship God, thou bringer of good fortune. Here, acting as a good household-lady serve the learned guests. (3835)

२६. सुमङ्गली प्रतरणी गृहाणां सुशेवा पत्ये श्वशुराय शंभूः ।
स्योना श्वश्र्वै प्र गृहान् विशेमान् ॥

26. Bliss-bringer, furthering the welfare of thy householders, serving thy husband, gladdening thy father-in-law, and comforting thy mother-in-law, assume thou the domestic duties. (3836)

२७. स्योना भव श्वशुरेभ्यः स्योना पत्ये गृहेभ्यः ।
स्योनास्यै सर्वस्यै विशे स्योना पुष्टायैषां भव ॥

27. Be pleasant to thy fathers-in-law, sweet to thy householders and thy lord. To all this clan be gentle, and favour these men's prosperity. (3837)[2]

२८. सुमङ्गलीरियं वधूरिमां समेत पश्यत । सौभाग्यमस्यै दत्त्वा दौर्भाग्यैर्विपरेतन ॥

28. Ye learned persons, this bride is highly fortunate. Come all of you and look at her. Wish her prosperity. Keep evil luck away from her! (3838)[3]

२९. या दुर्हार्दो युवतयो याश्चेह जरतीरपि । वर्चो न्व१स्यै सं दत्ताथास्तं विपरेतन ॥

29. Ye youthful maidens, ill disposed, and all ye aged women here, give all your brilliance to the bride, then to your several houses depart! (3839)[4]

३०. रुक्मप्रस्तरणं वह्यं विश्वा रूपाणि बिभ्रतम् ।
आरोहत् सूर्या सावित्री बृहते सौभगाय कम् ॥

30. May this bride, fit to bear children, lustrous like the Sun, for high felicity alone, mount this litter of domestic life, wearing all sorts of loveliness and full of priceless beddings. (3840)

३१. आ रोह तल्पं सुमनस्यमानेह प्रजां जनय पत्ये अस्मै ।
इन्द्राणीव सुबुधा बुध्यमाना ज्योतिरग्रा उषसः प्रति जागरासि ॥

[1]Here: In domestic life.

[2](26, 27) Both these verses have been explained by Maharshi Dayananda in *Sanskār Vidhi* in the chapter on Grihastha Āshrama (Domestic life).

[3]See *Rig*, 10-85-33. Swami Dayananda has commented on this verse in the *Sanskār Vidhi* in the chapter on marriage.

[4]See *Rig*, 10-85-33. This verse has been explained by Swami Dayananda in the *Sanskār Vidhi* in the chapter on Grihastha Ashrama.

31. O bride, mount the bridal bed with cheerful spirit, here bring forth children to this man thy husband watchful and talented like a queen, wake thou before the earliest light of Morning. (3841)[1]

३२. देवा अग्रे न्यपद्यन्त पत्नीः समस्पृशन्त तन्वस्तनूभिः ।
सूर्येव नारि विश्वरूपा महित्वा प्रजावती पत्या सं भवेह ॥

32. Learned persons in ancient times lay down beside their consorts. O Dame, lustrous like the Sun, exquisite in her beauty, here rich in future children, meet thy husband ! (3842)

३३. उत्तिष्ठेतो विश्वावसो नमसेडामहे त्वा ।
जामिमिच्छ पितृषदं न्यक्तां स ते भागो जनुषा तस्य विद्धि ॥

33. O opulent bridegroom, rise from this place, with reverence we worship thee. Long for the highly decorated bride living in her father's house. She is meant for thee. Know her life-sketch from her birth. (3843)[2]

३४. अप्सरसः सधमादं मदन्ति हविर्धानमन्तरा सूर्यं च ।
तास्ते जनित्रमभि ताः परेहि नमस्ते गन्धर्वर्तुना कृणोमि ॥

34. Ladies rejoice and feast together between the Sun and earth, the place of offering oblations. These are thy kith and kin, go thou and join them. I at the time of menstruation, respect thee, O strong young bridegroom! (3844)[3]

३५. नमो गन्धर्वस्य नमसे नमो भामाय चक्षुषे च कृण्मः ।
विश्वावसो ब्रह्मणा ते नमोऽभि जाया अप्सरसः परेहि ॥

35. Homage we pay to the youngman's strength, obeisance to his eye and fiery anger. O opulent husband, we revere thee with Vedic verses. Go thou to thy wife fit to bear children. (3845)[4]

३६. राया वयं सुमनसः स्यामोदितो गन्धर्वमावीवृताम ।
अगन्त्स देवः परमं सधस्थमगन्म यत्र प्रतिरन्त आयुः ॥

36. May we be happy with abundant riches. May this learned bridegroom attain to an exalted position in the society. God occupies the loftiest position, we reach unto Him by prolonging our life. (3846)

३७. सं पितरावृत्विये सृजेथां माता पिता च रेतसो भवाथः ।
मर्य इव योषामधि रोहयैनां प्रजां कृण्वाथामिह पुष्यतं रयिम् ॥

[1]Verses 31-40 contain the epithalamium.
[2]See *Rig*, 10-85-21, 22.
[3]See *Atharva*, 7-109-3.
[4]Plural number has been used, whereas it conveys the sense of singular number.

37. In your due season, parents! come together. Mother and sire be ye of future children. Embrace this woman like a happy lover. Raise ye up offspring. Increase your riches here. (3847)[1]

३८. तां पूषञ्छिवतमामेरयस्व यस्यां बीजं मनुष्या३ वपन्ति ।
या न ऊरू उशती विश्रयाति यस्यामुशन्तः प्रहरेम शेपः ।।

38. O powerful husband, secure this bride, who shall be the sharer of thy pleasures; who shall twine her eager arms about her husband, and welcome all his love and soft embraces. (3848)[2]

३९. आ रोहोरुमुप धत्स्व हस्तं परि ष्वजस्व जायां सुमनस्यमानः ।
प्रजां कृण्वाथामिह मोदमानौ दीर्घं वामायुः सविता कृणोतु ।।

39. Up, happy bridegroom! with a joyous spirit caress thy wife and throw thine arm around her. O husband and wife, here, with pleasure procreate your offspring. May God bestow long life upon you both. (3849)

४०. आ वां प्रजां जनयतु प्रजापतिरहोरात्राभ्यां समनक्त्वर्यमा ।
अदुर्मङ्गली पतिलोकमा विशेमं शं नो भव द्विपदे शं चतुष्पदे ।।

40. May God, the Lord of life, vouchsafe you children. May God bind you, day and night together. Enter thy husband's house thou bride, free from ill fortune. Bring blessing to our bipeds and quadrupeds. (3850)

४१. देवैर्दत्तं मनुना साकमेतद् वाधूयं वासो वध्वश्च वस्त्रम् ।
यो ब्रह्मणे चिकितुषे ददाति स इद् रक्षांसि तल्पानि हन्ति ।।

41. The father, who gives to the learned bridegroom and the bride, the nuptial garment, fit to be worn as a mark of learning and presented by the learned and the King, also removes the obstacles in the way of their fame and dignity. (3851)

४२. यं मे दत्तो ब्रह्मभागं वधूयोर्वाधूयं वासो वध्वश्च वस्त्रम् ।
युवं ब्रह्मणेऽनुमन्यमानौ बृहस्पते साकमिन्द्रश्च दत्तम् ।।

42. The nuptial garment, fit to be worn as a mark of learning, which the twain have presented to me, longing for the bride, and my wife as award for scholarship,—this do ye both, learned Acharya and king bestow with loving kindness on me a Vedic scholar. (3852)[3]

४३. स्योनाद्योनेरधि बुध्यमानौ हसामुदौ महसा मोदमानौ ।
सुगू सुपुत्रौ सुगृहौ तराथो जीवावुषसो विभातीः ।।

[1]Here: In domestic life, or in this world. Verses 37, 38 have been explained by Swami Dayananda in the *Sanskār Vidhi* in the chapter on Grihastha Āshrama.

[2]See *Rig*, 10-85-37.

[3]Twain: The parents of the bride and bridegroom.

43. In your comfortable house awaking both together, revelling heartily with joy and laughter, rich with good cattle, brave sons, goodly homestead, live long to look on many radiant mornings. (3853)[1]

४४. नवं वसानः सुरभिः सुवासा उदागां जीव उषसो विभातीः ।
आण्डात् पतत्रीवामुक्षि विश्वस्मादेनसस्परि ॥

44. Clad in new garments, flagrant, well-apparelled, to meet effulgent Dawns do I rise, passing life happily. I, like a bird that quits the egg, am freed from sin and purified. (3854)[2]

४५. शुम्भनी द्यावापृथिवी अन्तिसुम्ने महिव्रते । आपः सप्त सुस्रुवुर्देवीस्ता नो मुञ्चन्त्वंहसः ॥

45. Father and mother, like the Sun and Earth are our well-wishers, revelling near us they afford us joy, and are the performers of mighty deeds. We have been equipped with seven divine organs. May they free us from sin. (3855)[3]

४६. सूर्यायै देवेभ्यो मित्राय वरुणाय च । ये भूतस्य प्रचेतसस्तेभ्य इदमकरं नमः ॥

46. I pay adoration to God, the Creator of the universe, to fire, water, air, serviceable forces of nature, to the Almighty Father, the Friend of all, the Most Exalted and to the Guru, the imparter of knowledge. (3856)[4]

४७. य ऋते चिदभिश्रिषः पुरा जत्रुभ्य आतृदः ।
संधाता संधिं मघवा पुरूवसुर्निष्कर्ता विह्रुतं पुनः ॥

47. He, Who without ligature, without incision in the neck, unites the joints in the beginning, Who healeth the dissevered parts, is the Most Wealthy Bounteous God. (3857)[5]

४८. अपास्मत् तम उच्छतु नीलं पिशङ्गमुत लोहितं यत् ।
निर्दहनी या पृषातक्य१स्मिन् तां स्थाणावध्या सजामि ॥

48. May the blue, the yellow, and the red dirt of sin remain away from us. May I remove with the help of God, the burning, painful ignorance that exists in the world. (3858)[6]

४९. यावतीः कृत्याः उपवासने यावन्तो राज्ञो वरुणस्य पाशाः ।
व्यृद्धयो या असमृद्धयो या अस्मिन् ता स्थाणावधि सादयामि ॥

[1]This verse has been explained by Maharshi Dayananda in the *Sanskār Vidhi* in the chapter on Grihastha Āshrama.

[2]I: Husband.

[3]See *Atharva*, 7-112-1. Seven organs. Two eyes, two ears, two nostrils, and mouth.

[4]I: Husband. See *Rig*. 10-85-17.

[5]See *Rig*, 8-1-12.

[6]I: Husband.

49. All acts of violence in my birth-place, all injunctions of the mighty king, all sorts of poverty and all misfortunes in the world, I leave to God for disposal. (3859)[1]

५०. या मे प्रियतमा तनूः सा मे बिभाय वाससः ।
तस्याग्रे त्वं वनस्पते नीविं कृणुष्व मा वयं रिषाम ॥

50. My body that I hold most dear is afraid of violence. O guardian of noble conduct, put a ban on violence in the very beginning! Let no misfortune fall on us. (3860)[2]

५१. ये अन्ता यावतीः सिचो य ओतवो ये च तन्तवः ।
वासो यत् पत्नीभिरुतं तन्नः स्योनमुप स्पृशात् ॥

51. May all the hems and borders, all the threads that form the web and woof, the garment woven by the ladies, be soft and pleasant to our touch. (3861)

५२. उशतीः कन्यला इमाः पितृलोकात् पतिं यतीः । अव दीक्षामसृक्षत स्वाहा ॥

52. These maids who from their father's house have come with longing to their lord have taken the strict vow of domestic life. This is an excellent teaching. (3862)[3]

५३. बृहस्पतिनावसृष्टां विश्वे देवा अधारयन् । वर्चो गोषु प्रविष्टं यत् तेनेमां सं सृजामसि ॥

53. The domestic law ordained by God is observed by all learned persons. With all the splendour—that exists in men of learning do we enrich this girl. (3863)

५४. बृहस्पतिनावसृष्टां विश्वे देवा अधारयन् । तेजो गोषु प्रविष्टं यत् तेनेमां सं सृजामसि ॥

54. The domestic law ordained by God is observed by all learned persons. With all the vigour that exists in men of learning do we enrich this girl. (3864)

५५. बृहस्पतिनावसृष्टां विश्वे देवा अधारयन् । भगो गोषु प्रविष्टो यस्तेनेमां सं सृजामसि ॥

55. The domestic law ordained by God is observed by all learned persons. With all good fortune that exists in men of learning do we enrich this girl. (3865)

५६. बृहस्पतिनावसृष्टां विश्वे देवा अधारयन् । यशो गोषु प्रविष्टं यत् तेनेमां सं सृजामसि ॥

[1]I: Husband.

[2]My refers to the bride. Guardian—conduct: Husband.

[3]Griffith remarks: "The meaning and the application of the stanza are obscure." I see no obscurity in it. The significance is quite clear. A maiden after marriage goes to the house of her husband, and takes the strict vow of leading the chaste and pure domestic life and perform all its duties faithfully and diligently.

56. The domestic law ordained by God is observed by all learned persons. With all the glory that exists in men of learning do we enrich this girl. (3866)

५७. बृहस्पतिनावसृष्टां विश्वे देवा अधारयन् । पयो गोषु प्रविष्टं यत् तेनेमां सं सृजामसि ॥

57. The domestic law ordained by God is observed by all learned persons. With all the knowledge that exists in men of learning do we enrich this girl. (3867)

५८. बृहस्पतिनावसृष्टां विश्वे देवा अधारयन् । रसो गोषु प्रविष्टो यस्तेनेमां सं सृजामसि ॥

58. The domestic law ordained by God is observed by all learned persons. With all the valour that exists in men of learning do we enrich this girl. (3868)

५९. यदीमे केशिनो जना गृहे ते समनर्तिषू रोदेन कृण्वन्तोऽघम् ।
अग्निष्ट्वा तस्मादेनसः सविता च प्र मुञ्चताम् ॥

59. If these distressed persons move about hither and thither in thy house, feeling misery, bewailing and crying, causing distress, may the learned Acharya free thee from that suffering, may God deliver thee from that. (3869)[1]

६०. यदीयं दुहिता तव विकेश्यरुदद् गृहे रोदेन कृण्वत्यघम् ।
अग्निष्ट्वा तस्मादेनसः सविता च प्र मुञ्चताम् ॥

60. If in thy house thy daughter weeps, with wild dishevelled locks, causing distress with her lament, may the learned Acharya free thee from that suffering, may God deliver thee from that. (3870)[2]

६१. यज्जामयो यद्युवतयो गृहे ते समनर्तिषू रोदेन कृण्वतीरघम् ।
अग्निष्ट्वा तस्मादेनसः सविता च प्र मुञ्चताम् ॥

61. If the bride's sisters, if young maids move about hither and thither in the house, bewailing and crying, causing distress, may the learned Āchārya free thee from that suffering, may God deliver thee from that. (3871)

६२. यत् ते प्रजायां पशुषु यद्वा गृहेषु निष्ठितमघकृद्भिरघं कृतम् ।
अग्निष्ट्वा तस्मादेनसः सविता च प्र मुञ्चताम् ॥

62. If any evil has been wrought by mischief-makers that affects thy progeny, cattle or house, may the learned Āchārya free thee from that woe, may God deliver thee from that. (3872)

[1]Thy: The father of the bride. After the departure of the bride, none should indulge in riotous, foolish or inauspicious doings.

[2]Savitā means God or father.

६३. इयं नार्युप ब्रूते पूल्यान्यावपन्तिका । दीर्घायुरस्तु मे पतिर्जीवाति शरदः शतम् ॥

63. This woman thus prays to God, as she offers husks of corn as an oblation: long live my husband! yea, a hundred autumns let him live! (3873)

६४. इहेमाविन्द्र सं नुद चक्रवाकेव दम्पती । प्रजयैनौ स्वस्तकौ विश्वमायुर्व्यऽश्नुताम् ॥

64. Persuade thou this couple, O God, like the Chakravāka and his mate: may they attain to full old age with children in their happy home. (3874)[1]

६५. यदासन्द्यामुपधाने यद् वोपवासने कृतम् । विवाहे कृत्यां यां चक्रुरास्नाने तां नि दध्मसि ॥

65. Whatever mischief hath been wrought on couch, cushion or canopy, every sort of disturbance created by mischief mongers to mar the wedding rites, all this we remove through our spiritual force. (3875)

६६. यद् दुष्कृतं यच्छमलं विवाहे वहतौ च यत् । तत् संभलस्य कम्बले मृज्महे दुरितं वयम् ॥

66. Whatever fault or error was in marriage or dowry, for that woe we hold responsible the lovely act of the sweet tongued match-maker. (3876)[2]

६७. संभले मलं सादयित्वा कम्बले दुरितं वयम् ।
अभूम यज्ञियाः शुद्धाः प्र ण आयूंषि तारिषत् ॥

67. We, having laid the stain and fault in marriage upon the match-maker's lovely act, are pure and meet for sacrifice. May he prolong our lives for us. (3877)[3]

६८. कृत्रिमः कण्टकः शतदन् य एषः । अपास्याः केश्यं मलमप शीर्षण्यंऽ लिखात् ॥

68. Let this artificial comb, wrought with a hundred teeth, remove all impurity from the hair and head of this woman. (3878)

६९. अङ्गादङ्गाद् वयमस्या अप यक्ष्मं नि दध्मसि ।
तन्मा प्रापत् पृथिवीं मोत देवान् दिवं मा प्रापदुर्व१न्तरिक्षम् ।
अपो मा प्रापन्मलमेतदग्ने यमं मा प्रापत् पितॄंश्च सर्वान् ॥

69. We take away disease from each and every limb of this bride. Let not this reach Earth, nor our organs like eye, ear, etc. Let it not reach the sky or air's wide region. Let not this dirty disease reach the Waters, O learned person!, nor air, nor all the seasons. (3879)[4]

[1]Chakravāka (Anas Casarca, commonly called the Brahmany duck). Chakwa and Chakwi are regarded as emblems of conjugal love and constancy. This verse has been explained by Maharshi Dayananda in the *Sanskār Vidhi* in the chapter on Domestic life.

[2]We: The members of the marriage procession.

[3]The interceder is responsible for any error in the marriage proceedings. He is responsible also to look after the comforts and health of the marriage party.

[4]पितॄन्=Seasons, vide Dayananda commentary on *Yajur*, 8-60.

७०. सं त्वा नह्यामि पयसा पृथिव्याः सं त्वा नह्यामि पयसौषधीनाम् ।
सं त्वा नह्यामि प्रजया धनेन सा संनद्धा सनुहि वाजमेमम् ॥

70. I gird thee with all the nourishing products of the Earth, with all the juice the plants contain I provide thee. I bless thee with children and riches. Do thou, thus girt, receive the offered wealth. (3880)

७१. अमोऽहमस्मि सा त्वं सामाहमस्म्यृक्त्वं द्यौरहं पृथिवी त्वम् ।
ताविह सं भवाव प्रजामा जनयावहै ॥

71. O bride, I am full of knowledge, so art thou. I am charming like the knowledge of salvation preached by the Sāmaveda, thou art pleasure-giving like the Rigveda that expounds the importance and utility of all objects. I am philanthropic like the Sun, thou art productive of progeny like the Earth of corn. Let us both dwell together here, parents of future children. (3881)[1]

७२. जनियन्ति नावग्रवः पुत्रियन्ति सुदानवः । अरिष्टासू सचेवहि बृहते वाजसातये ॥

72. Unmarried men like us desire to wed, wealthy giver wish for sons. Together may we dwell for high prosperity duly preserving our vital breaths. (3882)[2]

७३. ये पितरो वधूदर्शा इमं वहतुमागमन् । ते अस्यै वध्वै३ संपत्न्यै प्रजावच्छर्म यच्छन्तु ॥

73. May they, the elders, who, to view this bride, have joined this marriage party, pray for this lady and her lord, for children and peaceful happiness. (3883)

७४. येदं पूर्वागन् रशनायमाना प्रजामस्यै द्रविणं चेह दत्त्वा ।
तां वहन्त्वगतस्यानु पन्थां विराडियं सुप्रजा अत्यजैषीत् ॥

74. This vigilant and enterprising bride, who has for the first time come here, should be blessed with offspring and riches, and instructed to tread the untrodden future path of domestic life by the elders. May she in this Grihastha Ashrama excel all others, full of prosperity and blessed with progeny. (3884)

७५. प्र बुध्यस्व सुबुधा बुध्यमाना दीर्घायुत्वाय शतशारदाय ।
गृहान् गच्छ गृहपत्नी यथाऽसो दीर्घं त आयुः सविता कृणोतु ॥

75. Equipped with fine intellect and understanding, remain watchful throughout your long life of a hundred autumns. Acquire control over all articles of the house, and thereby become the household's mistress. May God vouchsafe thee a long life. (3885)[3]

[1]Maharshi Dayananda has explained this verse in the *Sanskār Vidhi* in the chapter on marriage. Here: In this world, or in this domestic life.

[2]See *Rig*, 7-96-4. This verse has been explained by Maharshi Dayananda in the *Sanskār Vidhi* in the chapter on Grihastha Ashrama.

[3]This verse has been explained by Maharshi Dayananda in the *Sanskār Vidhi* in the chapter on domestic life.

BOOK (Kāṇḍa) XV

Chapter (Anuvāka) 1

HYMN I

१. व्रात्य आसीदीयमान एव स प्रजापतिं समैरयत् ॥

1. The Adorable God is ever active. He manifests Himself in the form of material objects and living beings. (3886)[1]

२. स प्रजापतिः सुवर्णमात्मन्नपश्यत् तत् प्राजनयत् ॥

2. God perceives His refulgent nature. He creates the universe again and again. (3887)

३. तदेकमभवत् तल्ललाममभवत् तन्महदभवत् तज्ज्येष्ठमभवत् तद् ब्रह्माभवत् तत् ।
तपोऽभवत् तत् सत्यमभवत् तेन प्राजायत ॥

3. That became unique, that became distinguished, that became great, that became excellent, that became Devotion, that became holy Fervour, that became Truth, through that power of God, was this universe created. (3888)[2]

४. सोऽवर्धत स महानभवत्स महादेवोऽभवत् ॥

4. He manifested His strength. He became Adorable. He became the Great God. (3889)

५. स देवानामीशां पर्यैत्स ईशानोऽभवत् ॥

5. He gained the lordship of the forces of Nature. He became Lord. (3890)

६. स एकव्रात्योऽभवत्स धनुरादत्त तदेवेन्द्रधनुः ॥

6. He is the sole Lord of all animate and inanimate objects. He is the Master of the power of creation, which clothes souls with bodies. (3891)

७. नीलमस्योदरं लोहितं पृष्ठम् ॥

7. The positive knowledge of God is like the belly, His power of creation is like the back. (3892)[3]

८. नीलेनैवाप्रियं भ्रातृव्यं प्रोर्णोति लोहितेन द्विषन्तं विध्यतीति ब्रह्मवादिनो वदन्ति ॥

8. With His positive knowledge. God envelops a detested rival, with His power of creation. He pierces the man who hates his fellows. So do the theologians say. (3893)

[1]Pt. Jaidev Vidyalankara and Pt. Khem Karan Das Trivedi have translated the word Vrātya as God, the Controller of innumerable souls.

[2]That: The refulgent power of God.

[3]Knowledge and power of creation are innate in God, just as belly and back are the definite parts of the body.

HYMN II

१. स उदतिष्ठत्स प्राचीं दिशमनु व्यचलत् ॥

1. God appeared, and manifested Himself in the eastern region. (3894)

२. तं बृहच्च रथन्तरं चादित्याश्च विश्वे च देवा अनुव्यचलन् ॥

2. The vast atmosphere, the Earth, the lustrous suns, and all revolving worlds obey His command. (3895)

३. बृहते च वै स रथन्तराय चादित्येभ्यश्च विश्वेभ्यश्च देवेभ्य आ वृश्चते य एवं विद्वांसं व्रात्यमुपवदति ॥

3. He commits an offence against the atmosphere, the Earth, the Sun and the revolving worlds, who reviles God, the Possessor of knowledge. (3896)[1]

४. बृहतश्च वै स रथन्तरस्य चादित्यानां च विश्वेषां च देवानां प्रियं धाम भवति तस्य प्राच्यां दिशि ॥

4. He who hath the knowledge of God becomes the beloved home of the atmosphere, the Earth, the lustrous Suns and revolving worlds, and for such a learned person, in the eastern region. (3897)

५. श्रद्धा पुंश्चली मित्रो मागधो विज्ञानं वासोऽहरुष्णीषं रात्री केशा हरितौ प्रवर्तौ कल्मलिर्मणिः ॥

5. Faith is his leman, the Sun his panegyrist, knowledge his vesture, day his turban, night his hair, the Sun and Moon his ear-ornaments, the splendour of the stars his jewel. (3898)[2]

६. भूतं च भविष्यच्च परिष्कन्दौ मनो विपथम् ॥

6. Past and Future are his running footmen, mind is his war chariot. (3899)[3]

७. मातरिश्वा च पवमानश्च विपथवाहौ वातः सारथी रेष्मा प्रतोदः ॥

7. In-breath and out-breath are the horses of his chariot, air is his charioteer, storm his goad. (3900)

८. कीर्तिश्च यशश्च पुरःसरावैनं कीर्तिर्गच्छत्या यशो गच्छति य एवं वेद ॥

8. Fame and glory are his harbingers. Fame and glory come to him who hath this knowledge of god. (3901)[4]

[1]Commits an offence: Cannot derive full advantage from.

[2]Leman: Lover, sweetheart.

[3]Past and Future are the sentinels which guard him from behind and front.

[4]The learned visualise God in the northern and southern regions, in fact in all the four directions, East, South, West, North.

९. स उदतिष्ठत् स दक्षिणां दिशमनु व्यचलत् ॥

9. God appeared and manifested Himself in the southern region. (3902)[1]

१०. तं यज्ञायज्ञियं च वामदेव्यं च यज्ञश्च यजमानश्च पशवश्चानुव्यचलन् ॥

10. The Vedic knowledge, the five elements created by god (vāmdeva), noble conduct, the performer of noble deeds, all living beings work under His control. (3903)[1]

११. यज्ञायज्ञियाय च वै स वामदेव्याय च यज्ञाय च यजमानाय च पशुभ्यश्चा वृश्चते य एवं विद्वांसं व्रात्यमुपवदति ॥

11. He offends against Vedic knowledge, elements of Nature, noble conduct, the performer of noble deeds, and all living beings, who reviles God, the Possessor of Knowledge. (3904)

१२. यज्ञायज्ञियस्य च वै स वामदेव्यस्य च यज्ञस्य च यजमानस्य च पशूनां च प्रियं धाम भवति तस्य दक्षिणायां दिशि ॥

12. He who hath the Knowledge of God becomes the beloved home of the Vedic knowledge, the five elements, noble conduct, the performer of noble deeds, and all living beings. In the southern region, for such a learned person. (3905)

१३. उषाः पुंश्चली मन्त्रो मागधो विज्ञानं वासोऽहरुष्णीषं रात्री केशा हरितौ प्रवर्तौ कल्मलिर्मणिः ॥

13. Dawn is his leman, Vedic hymns his panegyrist, knowledge his vesture, day his turban, night his hair, the Sun and Moon his ear-ornaments, the splendour of the stars his jewel. (3906)

१४. अमावास्या च पौर्णमासी च परिष्कन्दौ मनो विपथम् ।
मातरिश्वा च पवमानश्च विपथवाहौ वातः सारथी रेष्मा प्रतोदः ।
कीर्तिश्च यशश्च पुरःसरावैनं कीर्तिर्गच्छत्या यशो गच्छति य एवं वेद ॥

14. New Moon Night and Full Moon Night are his running attendants, Mind is his war-chariot, In-breath and out-breath are the horses of his chariot, air is his charioteer, storm his goad. Fame and glory are his harbingers. Fame and glory come to him who hath this knowledge of God. (3907)[2]

१५. स उदतिष्ठत् स प्रतीचीं दिशमनु व्यचलत् ॥

15. God appeared and manifested Himself in the western region. (3908)

१६. तं वैरूपं च वैराजं चापश्च वरुणश्च राजानुव्यचलन् ॥

[1]Five elements: Earth, Air, Water, Fire, Atmosphere.
[2]Both these nights guard him.

16. The Vedic knowledge, the knowledge of salvation, material objects, all dignified noble persons, work under His control. (3909)

१७. वैरूपाय च वै स वैराजाय चाद्भ्यश्च वरुणाय च राज्ञ आ वृश्चते य एवं विद्वांसं व्रात्यमुपवदति ॥

17. He offends against Vedic knowledge, the knowledge of salvation, material objects, and all dignified noble persons, who reviles God the Master of knowledge. (3910)

१८. वैरूपस्य च वै स वैराजस्य चापां च वरुणस्य च राज्ञः प्रियं धाम भवति तस्य प्रतीच्यां दिशि ॥

18. He who hath the knowledge of god verily becomes the beloved home of Vedic knowledge, the expositor of different sciences, the knowledge of salvation, whereby God is visualised, material objects, all dignified influential persons. In the western region for such a learned person. (3911)

१९. इरा पुंश्चली हसो मागधो विज्ञानं वासोऽहरुष्णीषं रात्री केशा हरितौ प्रवर्तौ कल्मलिर्मणिः ॥

19. The earth is his leman, laughter his panegyrist, Knowledge his vesture, day his turban, night his hair, the Sun and Moon his ear-rings, the splendour of the stars his jewel. (3912)

२०. अहश्च रात्री च परिष्कन्दौ मनो विपथम् ।
मातरिश्वा च पवमानश्च विपथवाहौ वातः सारथी रेष्मा प्रतोदः ।
कीर्तिश्च यशश्च पुरः सरावैनं कीर्तिर्गच्छत्या यशो गच्छति य एवं वेद ॥

20. Day and Night are his running footmen, mind is his war chariot. In-breath and out-breath are the horses of his chariot, air is his charioteer, storm his goad. Fame and glory are his harbingers. Fame and glory come to him who hath this knowledge of God. (3913)

२१. स उदतिष्ठत् स उदीचीं दिशमनु व्यचलत् ॥

21. God appeared and manifested Himself in the northern region. (3914)

२२. तं श्यैतं च नौधसं च सप्तर्षयश्च सोमश्च राजानुव्यचलन् ॥

22. Vedic knowledge, the exhibition of the right path, the knowledge of salvation, the well-wisher of the sages, the seven Rishis, the dignified influential persons, all work under the control of God. (3915)

२३. श्यैताय च वै स नौधसाय च सप्तर्षिभ्यश्च सोमाय च राज्ञ आ वृश्चते य एवं विद्वांसं व्रात्यमुपवदति ॥

23. He offends against Vedic knowledge, knowledge of salvation, the seven Rishis, and dignified noble persons, who reviles God, the Master of knowledge. (3916)[1]

२४. श्यैतस्य च वै स नौधसस्य च सप्तर्षीणां च सोमस्य च राज्ञः प्रियं धाम
भवति तस्योदीच्यां दिशि ।।

24. He who hath the knowledge of God, verily becomes the beloved home of Vedic knowledge, knowledge of salvation, the seven Rishis, the dignified influential persons. In the northern region for such a learned person. (3917)

२५. विद्युत् पुंश्चली स्तनयित्नुर्मागधो विज्ञानं वासोऽहरुष्णीषं रात्री केशा हरितौ
प्रवर्तौ कल्मलिर्मणिः ।।

25. Lightning is his leman, thunder his panegyrist, Knowledge his vesture, day his turban, might his hair, the Sun and Moon his ear-rings, the splendour of the stars his jewel. (3918)

२६. श्रुतं च विश्रुतं च परिष्कन्दौ मनो विपथम् ।।

26. Fame and Celebrity are his running footmen, mind is his chariot. (3919)

२७. मातरिश्वा च पवमानश्च विपथवाहौ वातः सारथी रेष्मा प्रतोदः ।।

27. In-breath and out-breath are the horses of his chariot, air is his charioteer, storm his goad. (3920)

२८. कीर्तिश्च यशश्च पुरःसरावैनं कीर्तिर्गच्छत्या यशो गच्छति य एवं वेद ।।

28. Fame and glory are his harbingers. Fame and glory come to him who hath this knowledge of God. (3921)

HYMN III

१. स संवत्सरमूर्ध्वोऽतिष्ठत् तं देवा अब्रुवन् व्रात्य किं नु तिष्ठसीति ।।

1. For a whole year he stood erect, practising penance. The sages said unto him 'Why standest thou' O Brahmchari, 'Why don't you sit!' (3922)[2]

२. सोऽब्रवीदासन्दीं मे सं भरन्त्विति ।।

2. He answered and said, 'Bring an arm-chair or couch for me.' (3923)

३. तस्मै व्रात्यायासन्दीं समभरन् ।।

3. They brought an arm-chair or couch for that Brahmchari. (3924)

[1]Seven Rishis: Eye, Ear, Nostril, Tongue, Skin, Mind, Intellect सप्त ऋषयः प्रतिहिताः शरीरे । यजु० 34-55.

[2]In this hymn Vrātya means the Brahmchari, who fulfils his vow, who undertakes penance and welcomes suffering to achieve his pledge of celibacy.

४. तस्या ग्रीष्मश्च वसन्तश्च द्वौ पादावास्तां शरच्च वर्षाश्च द्वौ ॥

4. Two of its feet were Summer and Spring, and two were Autumn and Rains. (3925)[1]

५. बृहच्च रथन्तरं चानूच्ये३ आस्तां यज्ञायज्ञियं च वामदेव्यं च तिरश्च्येऽ ॥

5. Atmosphere, and the world conquerable through noble traits, were the two long planks, Vedic knowledge, the welfarer of sacrifices (Yajnas) and the five elements created by God the two cross planks. (3926)[2]

६. ऋचः प्राञ्चस्तन्तवो यजूंषि तिर्यञ्चः ॥

6. The verses of the Rigveda were its warp, and the verses of the Yajurveda its woof. (3927)[3]

७. वेद आस्तरणं ब्रह्मोपबर्हणम् ॥

7. Vedic lore was its blanket, and the knowledge of god its coverlet. (3928)[4]

८. सामासाद उद्गीथोऽपश्रयः ॥

8. The Sāmaveda was the cushion, and Om the pillow. (3929)

९. तामासन्दीं व्रात्य आरोहत् ॥

9. The Brahmchari ascended that couch. (3930)

१०. तस्य देवजनाः परिष्कन्दा आसन्त्संकल्पाः प्रहाय्या३ विश्वानि भूतान्युपसदः ॥

10. The hosts of learned persons were his attendants, solemn vows his messengers and all creatures his courtiers. (3931)[5]

११. विश्वान्येवास्य भूतान्युपसदो भवन्ति य एवं वेद ॥

11. All men become the admirers of him who possesses this knowledge. (3932)

HYMN IV

१. तस्मै प्राच्या दिशः ॥

1. For him from the eastern region. (3933)[6]

२. वासन्तौ मासौ गोप्तारावकुर्वन् बृहच्च रथन्तरं चानुष्ठातारौ ॥

[1]The chair of the celibate is not the ordinary chair on which people generally sit and take rest. His is the chair of knowledge, whose four feet are the four seasons.

[2](5-8) How beautiful is the description of the couch of knowledge on which the Brahmcharir ests.

[3]Its: Of the couch of knowledge of the Brahmchari.

[4]Coverlet: Quilt.

[5]Courtiers: Worshippers.

[6]Him: The learned Brahmchari. They: The sages. Made: Imagined. Two spring months: Chaitra, Vaisākha, mid-March to mid-May.

2. They made the two spring months his protectors, atmosphere, and the world conquerable through noble traits his attendants. (3934)

३. वासन्तावेनं मासौ प्राच्या दिशो गोपायतो बृहच्च रथन्तरं चानु तिष्ठतो य एवं वेद ॥

3. The two spring months protect from the eastern region, and atmosphere and the world conquerable through noble traits serve the man who possesses this knowledge of God. (3935)

४. तस्मै दक्षिणाया दिशः ॥

4. For him from the southern region. (3936)

५. ग्रैष्मौ मासौ गोप्तारावकुर्वन् यज्ञायज्ञियं च वामदेव्यं चानुष्ठातारौ ॥

5. They made the two summer months his protectors, Vedic knowledge. the well-farerer of sacrifices (Yajnas), and the five elements created by God, his attendants. (3937)[1]

६. ग्रैष्मावेनं मासौ दक्षिणाया दिशो गोपायतो यज्ञायज्ञियं च वामदेव्यं चानु
तिष्ठतो य एवं वेद ॥

6. The two summer months protect him from the southern region, Vedic knowledge, the well-farerer of sacrifices, and the five elements created by God, serve the man who possesses this knowledge of God. (3938)

७. तस्मै प्रतीच्या दिशः ॥

7. For him from the western region. (3939)

८. वार्षिकौ मासौ गोप्तारावकुर्वन् वैरूपं च वैराजं चानुष्ठातारौ ॥

8. They made the two Rain months his protectors, Vedic knowledge, the expositor of different sciences, and the knowledge of salvation, that leads to the attainment of God, his attendants. (3940)[2]

९. वार्षिकावेनं मासौ प्रतीच्या दिशो गोपायतो वैरूपं च वैराजं चानु तिष्ठतो य एवं वेद ॥

9. The two Rain months protect him from the western region, Vedic knowledge and the knowledge of salvation serve the man who possesses this knowledge of God. (3941)

१०. तस्मा उदीच्या दिशः ॥

10. For him from the northern region. (3942)

११. शारदौ मासौ गोप्तारावकुर्वञ्छ्यैतं च नौधसं चानुष्ठातारौ ॥

[1]Summer months: Jyeshtha and Āshādha; mid-May to mid-July.
[2]Rain months: Srāvana and Bhādra, mid-July to mid-September.

11. They made the two Autumn months his protectors, Vedic knowledge, the exhibitor of the right path, and the knowledge of salvation, the well-wisher of the Rishis, his attendants. (3943)[1]

१२. शारदावेनं मासावुदीच्या दिशो गोपायतः श्यैतं च नौधसं चानु तिष्ठतो य एवं वेद ॥

12. The two Autumn months protect him from the northern, Vedic knowledge and the knowledge of salvation serve the man who possesses this knowledge of God. (3944)

१३. तस्मै ध्रुवाया दिशः ॥

13. For him from the region of the nadir. (3945)

१४. हैमनौ मासौ गोप्तारावकुर्वन् भूमिं चाग्निं चानुष्ठातारौ ॥

14. They made the two Winter months his protectors, and earth and fire his attendants. (3946)[2]

१५. हैमनावेनं मासौ ध्रुवाया दिशो गोपायतो भूमिश्चाग्निश्चानु तिष्ठतो य एवं वेद ॥

15. The two winter months protect him from the region of the nadir, and earth and fire serve the man who possesses this knowledge of God. (3947)

१६. तस्मा ऊर्ध्वाया दिशः ॥

16. For him from the region of the Zenith. (3948)

१७. शैशिरौ मासौ गोप्तारावकुर्वन् दिवं चादित्यं चानुष्ठातारौ ॥

17. They made the two Dewy months his protectors, and Atmosphere and the Sun his attendants. (3949)

१८. शैशिरावेनं मासावूर्ध्वाया दिशो गोपायतो द्यौश्चादित्यश्चानु तिष्ठतो य एवं वेद ॥

18. The two dewy months protect him from the region of the Zenith, and atmosphere and Sun serve the man who possesses this knowledge of God. (3950)

HYMN V

१. तस्मै प्राच्या दिशो अन्तर्देशाद् भवमिष्वासमनुष्ठातारमकुर्वन् ॥

1. For him they made God, the foe of violence, his Guardian, from the intermediate space of the eastern region. (3951)[3]

२. भव एनमिष्वासः प्राच्या दिशो अन्तर्देशादनुष्ठातानु तिष्ठति नैनं शर्वो न भवो नेशानः ॥

[1]Autumn months: Āsvina, and Kārtika, mid-September to mid-November.

[2]Winter months: Agrahāyana and Pausha, mid-November to mid-January.

[3](1,2,3) Him: The learned Brahmchari. Bhava, Sarva, Īsāna are the names of God, denoting His different attributes. Made: Imagined. In this hymn seven different names according to His attributes have been mentioned, i.e., Bhava, Sarva, Īṣāna, Pashupati, Ugra, Rudra, and Mahādeva. God is Omnipresent. He pervades all regions and sub-regions and guards mankind. They: The sages, Rishis, learned persons.

2. God, the foe of violence, a Guardian, guards him from the intermediate space of the eastern region. Him, neither God, the Averter of suffering, nor the All-pervading God, the foe of violence, nor the Almighty God. (3952)

३. नास्य पशून् न समानान् हिनस्ति य एवं वेद ।।

3. Slays him who possesses this knowledge of God, or his cattle or his kinsmen. (3953)

४. तस्मै दक्षिणाया दिशो अन्तर्देशाच्छर्वमिष्वासमनुष्ठातारमकुर्वन् ।।

4. For him they made God, the Averter of suffering, the foe of violence, his Guardian from the intermediate space of the southern region. (3954)

५. शर्व एनमिष्वासो दक्षिणाया दिशो अन्तर्देशादनुष्ठातानु तिष्ठति नैनं शर्वो न भवो नेशानः ।
नास्य पशून् न समानान् हिनस्ति य एवं वेद ।।

5. God, the Averter of suffering, the foe of violence, a Guardian, guards him from the intermediate space of the southern region: Him, neither God, the Averter of suffering, nor God, the foe of violence, nor the Almighty God, slays, who possesses this knowledge of God, or his cattle or his kinsmen. (3955)

६. तस्मै प्रतीच्या दिशो अन्तर्देशात् पशुपतिमिष्वासमनुष्ठातारमकुर्वन् ।।

6. For him they made God, the Ruler of mankind, the foe of violence, his Guardian from the intermediate space of the western region. (3956)

७. पशुपतिरेनमिष्वासः प्रतीच्या दिशो अन्तर्देशादनुष्ठातानु तिष्ठति नैनं शर्वो न भवो नेशानः ।
नास्य पशून् न समानान् हिनस्ति य एवं वेद ।।

7. God, the Ruler of mankind, the foe of violence, a Guardian, guards him from the intermediate space of the western region. His, neither God, the Averter of suffering, nor God, the foe of voilence, nor the Almighty God, slays, who possesses this knowledge of God, or his cattle or his kinsmen. (3957)

८. तस्मा उदीच्या दिशो अन्तर्देशादुग्रं देवमिष्वासमनुष्ठातारमकुर्वन् ।।

8. For him they made the Awful God, the Foe of violence, his Guardian from the intermediate space of the northern region. (3958)

९. उग्र एनं देव इष्वास उदीच्या दिशो अन्तर्देशादनुष्ठातानु तिष्ठति नैनं शर्वो न भवो नेशानः ।
नास्य पशून् न समानान् हिनस्ति य एवं वेद ।।

9. The Awful God, the Foe of violence, a Guardian, guards him from the intermediate space of the northern region. Him, neither God, the Averter of suffering, nor God, the Foe of violence, nor the Almighty God slays, who possesses this knowledge of God, or his cattle or his kinsmen. (3959)

१०. तस्मै ध्रुवाया दिशो अन्तर्देशाद् रुद्रमिष्वासमनुष्ठातारमकुर्वन् ॥

10. For him they made God, the Eliminator of moral foes, the Foe of violence, his Guardian, from the intermediate space of the region of the nadir. (3960)

११. रुद्र एनमिष्वासो ध्रुवाया दिशो अन्तर्देशादनुष्ठातानु तिष्ठति नैनं शर्वो न भवो नेशानः ।
नास्य पशून् न समानान् हिनस्ति य एवं वेद ॥

11. God, the Eliminator of moral foes, the Foe of violence, a Guardian, guards him from the intermediate space of the region of the nadir. Him, neither God, the Averter of suffering, nor God, the Foe of violence, nor the Almighty God slays, who possesses this knowledge of God, or his cattle or his kinsmen. (3961)

१२. तस्मा ऊर्ध्वाया दिशो अन्तर्देशान्महादेवमिष्वासमनुष्ठातारमकुर्वन् ॥

12. For him they made the Refulgent God, the Foe of violence, his Guardian from the intermediate space of the region of the Zenith. (3962)

१३. महादेव एनमिष्वास ऊर्ध्वाया दिशो अन्तर्देशादनुष्ठातानु तिष्ठति नैनं शर्वो न भवो नेशानः ।
नास्य पशून् न समानान् हिनस्ति य एवं वेद ॥

13. The Refulgent God, the Foe of violence, a Guardian, guards him from the intermediate space of the region of the Zenith. Him, neither God, the Averter of suffering, nor God, the Foe of violence, nor the Almighty God slays him who possesses this knowledge of God, or his cattle or his kinsmen. (3963)

१४. तस्मै सर्वेभ्यो अन्तर्देशेभ्य ईशानमिष्वासमनुष्ठातारमकुर्वन् ॥

14. They made the Almighty God, the Foe of violence, his Guardian from all the intermediate regions. (3964)

१५. ईशान एनमिष्वासः सर्वेभ्यो अन्तर्देशेभ्योऽनुष्ठातानु तिष्ठति नैनं शर्वो न भवो नेशानः ॥

15. The Awful God, the Foe of violence, a Guardian, guards him from all the intermediate regions. Neither God, the Averter of suffering, nor God, the Foe of violence, nor the Almighty God. (3965)

१६. नास्य पशून् न समानान् हिनस्ति य एवं वेद ॥

16. Slays him who possesses this knowledge of God, or his cattle or his kinsmen. (3966)

HYMN VI

१. स ध्रुवां दिशमनु व्यचलत् ॥

1. God manifested Himself in the region of the nadir. (3967)

२. तं भूमिश्चाग्निश्चौषधयश्च वनस्पतयश्च वानस्पत्याश्च वीरुधश्चानुव्य॒ऽऽचलन् ॥

2. Earth, fire, cereals, trees, flowers, fruits, and shrubs and plants work under His control. (3968)

३. भूमेश्च वै सोऽग्नेश्चौषधीनां च वनस्पतीनां च वानस्पत्यानां च वीरुधां च
प्रियं धाम भवति य एवं वेद ॥

3. He who possesses this knowledge of God, becomes the dear home of earth, and fire and cereals, and trees, and fruits and shrubs. (3969)

४. स ऊर्ध्वां दिशमनु व्य॒चलत् ॥

4. God manifested Himself in the region of the Zenith. (3970)

५. तमृतं च सत्यं च सूर्यश्च चन्द्रश्च नक्षत्राणि चानुव्य॒चलन् ॥

5. True knowledge, and Indestructible Matter, and Sun and Moon and stars work under His control. (3971)

६. ऋतस्य च वै स सत्यस्य च सूर्यस्य च चन्द्रस्य च नक्षत्राणां च प्रियं धाम
भवति य एवं वेद ॥

6. He who possesses this knowledge of God, becomes the dear home of true knowledge, and Indestructible Matter, and Sun, and Moon and stars. (3972)

७. स उत्तमां दिशमनु व्य॒चलत् ॥

7. God manifested, Himself in the highest region. (3973)

८. तमृचश्च सामानि च यजूंषि च ब्रह्म चानुव्य॒चलन् ॥

8. Rigveda, and Sāmaveda, and Yajurveda, and Atharvaveda remain under His control. (3974)[1]

९. ऋचां च वै स साम्नां च यजुषां च ब्रह्मणश्च प्रियं धाम भवति य एवं वेद ॥

9. He who possesses this knowledge of God becomes the dear home of Rigveda, and Sāmaveda, and Yajurveda, and Atharvaveda. (3975)

१०. स बृहतीं दिशमनु व्य॒चलत् ॥

10. God manifested Himself in the great region. (3976)[2]

११. तमितिहासश्च पुराणं च गाथाश्च नाराशंसीश्चानुव्य॒चलन् ॥

11. The story of great men, and the history of ancient people, and the versified Vedic texts, and the eulogistic legends of heroes, remain under His control. (3977)

[1]Brahma is interpreted by Pt. Jaidev, Vidyalankar Pt. Khem Karan Das Trivedi and Pt. Damodra Satyavalekar as *Atharvaveda*, as it deals with the knowledge of God.

[2](10-12) Verses have been explained by Maharshi Dayanand in the *Rigveda ādi-bhashya-bhumika*.

१२. इतिहासस्य च वै स पुराणस्य च गाथानां च नाराशंसीनां च प्रियं धाम
भवति य एवं वेद ॥

12. He who possesses this Knowledge of God, becomes the dear home of the story of great men, and the history of ancient people, and the versified Vedic texts, and the eulogistic legends of heroes. (3978)[1]

१३. स परमां दिशमनु व्यऽचलत् ॥

13. God manifested Himself in the supreme. (3979)

१४. तमाहवनीयश्च गार्हपत्यश्च दक्षिणाग्निश्च यज्ञश्च यजमानश्च पशवश्चानुव्यऽचलन् ॥

14. The Āhavaniya, Gārhpatya, and Dakshina fires, and sacrifice and sacrificer, and all human beings remain under His control. (3980)[2]

१५. आहवनीयस्य च वै स गार्हपत्यस्य च दक्षिणाग्नेश्च यज्ञस्य च यजमानस्य
च पशूनां च प्रियं धाम भवति य एवं वेद ॥

15. He who possesses this knowledge of God, becomes the dear home of Āhavaniya, and Gārhpatya and Dakshina fires, and sacrifice, and sacrificer and all human beings. (3981)

१६ सोऽनादिष्टां दिशमनु व्यऽचलत् ॥

16. God manifested Himself in the unindicated region. (3982)

१७. तमृतवश्चार्तवाश्च लोकाश्च लौक्याश्च मासाश्चार्धमासाश्चाहोरात्रे चानुव्यऽचलन् ॥

17. The seasons, products of seasons, the worlds and their inhabitants, the months and half-months, the Day and Night remain under His control. (3983)

१८. ऋतूनां च वै स आर्तवानां च लोकानां च लौक्यानां च मासानां
चार्धमासानां चाहोरात्रयोश्च प्रियं धाम भवति य एवं वेद ॥

18. He who possesses this knowledge of God, verily becomes the dear home of seasons, and the products of seasons, and the worlds and their inhabitants, and the months and half-months, and the Day and Night. (3984)

१९. सोऽनावृत्तां दिशमनु व्यऽचलत् ततो नावर्त्स्यन्नमन्यत ॥

19. God manifested Himself in an unfrequented region. The learned Brahmchari thought, he would not return there. (3985)

[1]Becomes the dear home: Studies them and derives full benefit from them to multiply his store of knowledge.

[2]Āhavaniya: A consecrated fire taken from the householder's perpetual fire. Gārhpatya: One of the three sacred fires perpetually maintained by a householder, which he receives from his father and transmits to his descendants, and from which fires for sacrificial purposes are lighted. Dakshina: The sacred fire placed southwards.

२०. तं दितिश्चादितिश्चेडा चेन्द्राणी चानुव्यऽचलन् ॥

20. The destructible world, and the indestructible Matter, and Vedic speech, and soul-force, remain under His control. (3986)

२१. दितेश्च वै सोऽदितेश्चेडायाश्चेन्द्राण्याश्च प्रियं धाम भवति य एवं वेद ॥

21. He who possesses this knowledge of God, verily becomes the dear home of the destructible world, and the indestructible Matter, and Vedic speech, and soul force. (3987)

२२. स दिशोऽनु व्यऽचलत् तं विराडनु व्यऽचलत् सर्वे च देवाः सर्वाश्च देवताः ॥

22. God manifested Himself in all the regions. The resplendent world, divine objects and divine forces remain under His control. (3988)

२३. विराजश्च वै स सर्वेषां च देवानां सर्वासां च देवतानां प्रियं धाम भवति य एवं वेद ॥

23. He who possesses this knowledge of God, verily becomes the dear home of the resplendent world, and divine objects, and divine forces. (3989)

२४. स सर्वानन्तर्देशाननु व्यऽचलत् ॥

24. God manifested Himself in all the intermediate regions. (3990)

२५. तं प्रजापतिश्च परमेष्ठी च पिता च पितामहश्चानुव्यऽचलन् ॥

25. The King, the Acharya, the father and grandfather remain under His control. (3991)[1]

२६. प्रजापतेश्च वै स परमेष्ठिनश्च पितुश्च पितामहस्य च प्रियं धाम भवति य एवं वेद ॥

26. He who possesses this knowledge of God, becomes the dear home of the King, and Acharya, and father and grandfather. (3992)

HYMN VII

१. स महिमा सद्रुर्भूत्वान्तं पृथिव्या अगच्छत् स समुद्रोऽभवत् ॥

1. The Majestic and Powerful God pervaded the entire earth, and became beginningless and endless like space. (3993)

२. तं प्रजापतिश्च परमेष्ठी च पिता च पितामहश्चापश्च श्रद्धा च वर्षं भूत्वानुव्यऽवर्तयन्त ॥

2. The King, and the Āchārya or Sanyasi, the Father, and the Grandfather, and the noble deeds and religious faith in their excellence remain under His control. (3994)

३. ऐनमापो गच्छत्यैनं श्रद्धा गच्छत्यैनं वर्षं गच्छति य एवं वेद ॥

[1]Parmeshthin may also mean Sanyasi.

3. Noble deeds, religious faith approach him who possesses this knowledge of God. (3995)

४. तं श्रद्धा च यज्ञश्च लोकश्चान्नं चान्नाद्यं च भूत्वाभिपर्यावर्तन्त ॥

4. Faith and noble deeds, and the society, cereals, and nourishing meals in their excellence remain under His control. (3996)

५. ऐनं श्रद्धा गच्छत्यैनं यज्ञो गच्छत्यैनं लोको गच्छत्यैनमन्नं गच्छत्यैनमन्नाद्यं गच्छति य एवं वेद ॥

5. He who possesses this knowledge of God, is endowed with religious devotion, noble deeds, good society, cereals and nourishing meals. (3997)

Chapter (Anuvāka) 2

HYMN VIII

१. सोऽरज्यत ततो राजन्योऽजायत ॥

1. God was filled with love, hence he became the Ruler. (3998)

२. स विशः सबन्धूनन्नमन्नाद्यमभ्युदतिष्ठत् ॥

2. He became the Lord of men with their kinsmen, of cereals and nourishing meals. (3999)

३. विशां च वै स सबन्धूनां चान्नस्य चान्नाद्यस्य च प्रियं धाम भवति य एवं वेद ॥

3. He who possesses this knowledge of God becomes the dear of all men with their kinsmen of cereals and nourishing meals. (4000)

HYMN IX

१. स विशोऽनु व्यचलत् ॥

1. God revealed His law to the people. (4001)

२. तं सभा च समितिश्च सेना च सुरा चानुव्यचलन् ॥

2. Assembly, and Association, Army and Treasury remain under His control. (4002)

३. सभायाश्च वै स समितेश्च सेनायाश्च सुरायाश्च प्रियं धाम भवति य एवं वेद ॥

3. He who possesses this knowledge of God becomes the dear home of Assembly, and Association, Army and Treasury. (4003)

HYMN X

१. तद् यस्यैवं विद्वान् व्रात्यो राज्ञोऽतिथिर्गृहानागच्छेत् ॥

1. So let the king, to whose house, the Āchārya who possesses this knowledge of God, comes as a guest. (4004)

२. श्रेयांसमेनमात्मनो मानयेत तथा क्षत्राय ना वृश्चते तथा राष्ट्राय ना वृश्चते ॥

2. Honour him as superior to himself. Thus he does not act against the interests of his princely rank or his kingdom. (4005)[1]

३. अतो वै ब्रह्म च क्षत्रं चोदतिष्ठतां ते अब्रूतां कं प्र विशावेति ॥

3. May this system of honouring the guest uplift both the spiritual-minded, and martial families. They both should ask, what characteristic should they imbibe. (4006)

४. अतो वै बृहस्पतिमेव ब्रह्म प्र विशत्विन्द्रं क्षत्रं तथा वा इति ॥

4. Let spiritual-minded family learn the art of moral protection of mankind, and martial family of Royalty, was the answer. (4007)[2]

५. अतो वै बृहस्पतिमेव ब्रह्म प्राविशदिन्द्रं क्षत्रम् ॥

5. Hence, spiritual-minded people learnt the Vedas for moral protection of mankind and warlike people learnt the art of administration. (4008)

६. इयं वा उ पृथिवी बृहस्पतिर्द्यौरेवेन्द्रः ॥

6. This rule over Earth conduces to moral uplift of mankind and statesmanship to efficient administration. (4009)

७. अयं वा उ अग्निर्ब्रह्मासावादित्यः क्षत्रम् ॥

7. Verily this spiritual knowledge is resplendent like fire and martial spirit Is glittering like the Sun. (4010)

८. ऐनं ब्रह्म गच्छति ब्रह्मवर्चसी भवति ॥

8. He acquires spiritual knowledge and becomes spiritually pre-eminent. (4011)

९. यः पृथिवीं बृहस्पतिमग्निं ब्रह्म वेद ॥

9. Who considers the rule over Earth as conducive to moral uplift of mankind, and spiritual knowledge as shining like fire. (4012)

१०. ऐनमिन्द्रियं गच्छतीन्द्रियवान् भवति ॥

10. Great power comes to him and he becomes endowed with great power. (4013)

[1]If a king honours a learned guest and considers him to be his well-wisher, he profits by his advice and improves the administration of his country thereby.

[2]The Āchārya replies.

११. य आदित्यं क्षत्रं दिवमिन्द्रं वेद ॥

11. Who knows that physical force is lustrous like the Sun, and statesmanship is sovereignty. (4014)

HYMN XI

१. तद् यस्यैवं विद्वान् व्रात्योऽतिथिर्गृहानागच्छेत् ॥

1. Let him to whose house the Āchārya who possesses this knowledge of God, comes as a guest. (4015)

२. स्वयमेनमभ्युदेत्य ब्रूयाद् व्रात्य क्वाऽवात्सीर्व्रात्योदकं व्रात्य तर्पयन्तु व्रात्य यथा
ते प्रियं तथास्तु व्रात्य यथा ते वशस्तथास्तु व्रात्य यथा ते निकामस्तथास्त्विति ॥

2. Rise up of his own accord to meet him, and say, Āchārya, where dost thou live? Āchārya, here is water. Let my family members satisfy thee with meals. Āchārya, let it be as thou pleasest. Āchārya, as thy wish is so let it be. Āchārya, as thy desire is so let it be. (4016)

३. यदेनमाह व्रात्य क्वाऽवात्सीरिति पथ एव तेन देवयानानव रुन्द्धे ॥

3. When he says to his guest, where dost thou live? he reserves for himself the paths on which the sages tread. (4017)[1]

४. यदेनमाह व्रात्योदकमित्यप एव तेनाव रुन्द्धे ॥

4. When he says to him, Āchārya. Here is water for you, he secures thereby for himself, intellect, knowledge, and noble deeds. (4018)[2]

५. यदेनमाह व्रात्यं तर्पयन्त्विति प्राणमेव तेन वर्षीयांसं कुरुते ॥

5. When he says to him, Āchārya, let my family members satisfy thee with meals, he thereby prolongs his life. (4019)

६. यदेनमाह व्रात्य यथा ते प्रियं तथास्त्विति प्रियमेव तेनाव रुन्द्धे ॥

6. When he says to him, Āchārya, let it be as thou pleasest, he secures to himself what is pleasant. (4020)[3]

७. ऐनं प्रियं गच्छति प्रियः प्रियस्य भवति य एवं वेद ॥

7. He acquires what is pleasant, and he is the beloved of the beloved, who possesses this knowledge. (4021)

[1]He: The householder. A householder through conversation with a learned guest, derives spiritual knowledge which adds to his mental peace.

[2]See *Nighantu*, 2-1, where अपः is translated as deed.

[3]What is pleasant: Knowledge. The householder acquires knowledge from the learned guest,

८. यदेनमाह व्रात्य यथा ते वशस्तथास्त्विति वशमेव तेनाव रुन्द्धे ॥

8. When he says to him, Āchārya, as thy will is so let it be, he secures to himself thereby the fulfilment of his will. (4022)

९. ऐनं वशो गच्छति वशी वशिनां भवति य एवं वेद ॥

9. Authority comes to him who possesses this knowledge, and he becomes the controller of the powerful. (4023)

१०. यदेनमाह व्रात्य यथा ते निकामस्तथास्त्विति निकाममेव तेनाव रुन्द्धे ॥

10. When he says to him, Āchārya, as thy desire is so let it be, he secures to himself thereby the attainment of his desire. (4024)

११. ऐनं निकामो गच्छति निकामे निकामस्य भवति य एवं वेद ॥

11. His desire comes [to]him who possesses this knowledge, and he gains the complete satisfaction of his wish. (4025)

HYMN XII

१. तद् यस्यैवं विद्वान् व्रात्य उद्धृतेष्वग्निष्वधिश्रितेऽग्निहोत्रेऽतिथिर्गृहानागच्छेत् ॥

1. The man, to whose house, when the fires have been kindled, and Home (Yajna) has commenced, the Āchārya, possessing this knowledge of God, comes as a guest. (4026)

२. स्वयमेनमभ्युदेत्य ब्रूयाद् व्रात्यातिसृज होष्यामीति ॥

2. Should of his own accord rise to meet him and say, Āchārya, give me permission, I will perform sacrifice (Homa). (4027)

३. स चातिसृजेज्जुहुयान्न चातिसृजेन्न जुहुयात् ॥

3. And if he gives permission he should sacrifice, if he does not permit him he should not sacrifice. (4028)[1]

४. स य एवं विदुषा व्रात्येनातिसृष्टो जुहोति ॥

4. He, who sacrifices when permitted by the Āchārya who possesses this knowledge of God. (4029)

५. प्र पितृयाणं पन्थां जानाति प्र देवयानम् ॥

5. Well knows the path of the elders and that of the sages. (4030)

६. न देवेष्वा वृश्चते हुतमस्य भवति ॥

6. He does not act in opposition to the learned. His sacrifice becomes successful. (4031)

[1]The learned guest's permission is sought to perform the Yajna. He gives permission to the deserving and not to the undeserving.

७. पर्यस्यास्मिल्लोक आयतनं शिष्यते य एवं विदुषा व्रात्येनातिसृष्टो जुहोति ।।

7. The fame of the man who sacrifices when permitted by the Āchārya who possesses this knowledge of God, is long left remaining in this world. (4032)

८. अथ य एवं विदुषा व्रात्येनानतिसृष्टो जुहोति ।।

8. But he who sacrifices without the permission of the Āchārya who possesses this knowledge of God. (4033)

९. न पितृयाणं पन्थां जानाति न देवयानम् ।।

9. Knows not the path of the elders and that of the sages. (4034)

१०. आ देवेषु वृश्चते अहुतमस्य भवति ।।

10. He offends against the learned. His sacrifice does not achieve fulfilment. (4035)

११. नास्यास्मिल्लोक आयतनं शिष्यते य एवं विदुषा व्रात्येनानतिसृष्टो जुहोति ।।

11. The fame of the man who sacrifices without the permission of the Āchārya who possesses this knowledge of God is not left remaining in this world. (4036)

HYMN XIII

१. तद् यस्यैवं विद्वान् व्रात्य एकां रात्रिमतिथिर्गृहे वसति ।।

1. He, in whose house the Āchārya who possesses this knowledge of God stays as a guest for one night. (4037)

२. ये पृथिव्यां पुण्या लोकास्तानेव तेनाव रुन्द्धे ।।

2. Secures for himself thereby the company of holy persons who know the science of agriculture. (4038)[1]

३. तद् यस्यैवं विद्वान् व्रात्यो द्वितीयां रात्रिमतिथिर्गृहे वसति ।।

3. He, in whose house the Āchārya who possesses this knowledge of God stays as a guest for a second night. (4039)

४. येऽन्तरिक्षे पुण्या लोकास्तानेव तेनाव रुन्द्धे ।।

4. Secures for himself thereby the company of holy persons who know the science of aviation. (4040)[2]

[1]The learned Āchārya teaches the householder how to cultivate land and grow more food. Lokā means: Persons (लोकाः) लोकन्ते पश्यन्ति तेजनाः vide Maharshi Dayananda's commentary *Yajur*, 40-3. Plural number denotes the sense of singular. The Āchārya possesses the knowledge of Earth equal to the combined knowledge of many agricultural experts.

[2]The Āchārya instructs the householder in aviation, if he stays for one night more.

५. तद् यस्यैवं विद्वान् व्रात्यस्तृतीयां रात्रिमतिथिर्गृहे वसति ॥

5. He, in whose house the Āchārya who possesses this knowledge of God, stays as a guest for a third night. (4041)

६. ये दिवि पुण्या लोकास्तानेव तेनाव रुन्द्धे ॥

6. Secures for himself thereby the company of holy persons who know the Astrology. (4042)[1]

७. तद् यस्यैवं विद्वान् व्रात्यश्चतुर्थीं रात्रिमतिथिर्गृहे वसति ॥

7. He, in whose house the Āchārya who possesses this knowledge of God, stays as a guest for a fourth night. (4043)

८. ये पुण्यानां पुण्या लोकास्तानेव तेनाव रुन्द्धे ॥

8. Secures for himself thereby the company of the holier persons amongst the holy. (4044)

९. तद् यस्यैवं विद्वान् व्रात्योऽपरिमिता रात्रीरतिथिर्गृहे वसति ॥

9. He, in whose house the Āchārya who possesses this knowledge of God stays as a guest for unlimited nights. (4045)

१०. य एवापरिमिताः पुण्या लोकास्तानेव तेनाव रुन्द्धे ॥

10. Secures for himself thereby the company of unlimited holy persons. (4046)[2]

११. अथ यस्याव्रात्यो व्रात्यब्रुवो नामबिभ्रत्यतिथिर्गृहानागच्छेत् ॥

11. Now he, to whose house an ignorant person, calling himself a scholar, and one in name only, comes as a guest. (4047)

१२. कर्षेदेनं न चैनं कर्षेत् ॥

12. Should ignore him, and now verily discard such a counterfeit scholar. (4048)

१३. अस्यै देवताया उदकं याचमीमां देवतां वासय इमामिमां देवतां परि वेवेष्मीत्येनं परि वेविष्यात् ॥

13. He should serve the genuine scholar, saying to himself. To this scholar I offer water; I make him stay in my house, to such a scholar alone I serve with food such a scholar should be served with food. (4049)

[1]Astrology: The science of heavens. The Āchārya instructs the householder in Astrology, when he stays for the third night.

[2]The Āchārya possesses the knowledge of manifold sciences, and instructs the householder in them.

१४. तस्यामेवास्य तद् देवतायां हुतं भवति य एवं वेद ।।

14. The sacrifice (Yajna) of the man who serves a learned guest, who possesses this knowledge of God, achieves success. (4050)

HYMN XIV

१. स यत् प्राचीं दिशमनु व्यचलन्मारुतं शर्धो भूत्वानुव्य्‌चलन्मनोऽन्नादं कृत्वा ।।

1. He, when he went away to the eastern region, went away having acquired the strength of enemy-killing heroes, and having made Mind a preserver of life. (4051)[1]

२. मनसान्नादेनान्नमत्ति य एवं वेद ।।

2. He, who hath this knowledge of the Omnipresent God preserves life with Mind as life-preserver. (4052)

३. स यद् दक्षिणां दिशमनु व्यचलदिन्द्रो भूत्वानुव्य्‌चलद् बलमन्नादं कृत्वा ।।

3. He, when he went away to the southern region, went away having become Lord, and having made strength a preserver of life. (4053)

४. बलेनान्नादेनान्नमत्ति य एवं वेद ।।

4. He who hath this knowledge of the Omnipresent God preserves life with strength as life-preserver. (4054)

५. स यत् प्रतीचीं दिशमनु व्यचलद् वरुणो राजा भूत्वानुव्य्‌चलदपोऽन्नादीः कृत्वा ।।

5. He, when he went away to the western region, went away having become exalted like a king, and having made the organs, the preservers of life. (4055)

६. अद्भिरन्नादीभिरन्नमत्ति य एवं वेद ।।

6. He who hath this knowledge of the Omnipresent God preserves life with organs as life-preservers. (4056)

७. स यदुदीचीं दिशमनु व्यचलत् सोमो राजा भूत्वानुव्य्‌चलत् सप्तर्षिभिर्हुत
आहुतिमन्नादीं कृत्वा ।।

7. He, when he went away to the northern region, went away having become energetic like a king, and having made the seven Rishis' oblation a preserver of life. (4057)[2]

८. आहुत्यान्नाद्यान्नमत्ति य एवं वेद ।।

[1]He: The learned guest, Vrātya.

[2]Seven Rishis: Two eyes, two ears, two nostrils and mouth.

8. He, who hath this knowledge of the Omnipresent God preserves life with oblation as life-preserver. (4058)

९. स यद् ध्रुवां दिशमनु व्यचलद् विष्णुर्भूत्वानुव्य॒चलद् विराजमन्नादीं कृत्वा ॥

9. He, when he went away to the nadir region, went away having become a learned doer of deeds, and having made Earth a preserver of life. (4059)[1]

१०. विराजान्नाद्यान्नमत्ति य एवं वेद ॥

10. He who hath this knowledge of the Omnipresent God preserves life with Earth as life-preserver. (4060)

११. स यत् पशूननु व्यचलद् रुद्रो भूत्वानुव्य॒चलदोषधीरन्नादीः कृत्वा ॥

11. He, when he went away to animals, went away having become Rudra and having made herbs preservers of life. (4061)

१२. ओषधीभिरन्नादीभिरन्नमत्ति य एवं वेद ॥

12. He who hath this knowledge of the Omnipresent God preserves life with herbs as life-preservers. (4062)

१३. स यत् पितॄननु व्यचलद् यमो राजा भूत्वानुव्य॒चलत् स्वधाकारमन्नादं कृत्वा ॥

13. He, when he went away to the Fathers, went away having become justice-loving like a king and having made his innate strength a preserver of life. (4063)

१४. स्वधाकारेणान्नादेनान्नमत्ति य एवं वेद ॥

14. He who hath this knowledge of the Omnipresent God preserves life with his innate strength as life-preserver. (4064)

१५. स यन्मनुष्या३ननु व्यचलदग्निर्भूत्वानुव्य॒चलत् स्वाहाकारमन्नादं कृत्वा ॥

15. He, when he went away to contemplative persons, went away having become lustrous like fire and having made the propagation of Vedic doctrines a preserver of life. (4065)[2]

१६. स्वाहाकारेणान्नादेनान्नमत्ति य एवं वेद ॥

16. He who hath this knowledge of the Omnipresent God preserves life with the propagation of Vedic doctrines as life-preserver. (4066)

१७. स यदूर्ध्वां दिशमनु व्यचलद् बृहस्पतिर्भूत्वानुव्य॒चलद् वषट्कारमन्नादं कृत्वा ॥

[1]Pt. Khem Karan Das Trivedi translates Virajam as royal wealth. Pt. Jaidev Vidyalankar and Pt. Damodar Satavalekar translate the word as Earth.

[2]Fathers: Greatmen who protect humanity.

17. He, when he went away to the upper region, went away having become the protector of great sciences and having made the practice of charity a preserver of life. (4067)[1]

१८. वषट्कारेणान्नादेनान्नमत्ति य एवं वेद ।।

18. He who hath this knowledge of the Omnipresent God, preserves life, with the practice of charity as life-preserver. (4068)

१९. स यद् देवाननु व्यचलदीशानो भूत्वानुव्य्ऽचलन्मन्युमन्नादं कृत्वा ।।

19. He, when he went away to the learned, went away having become power and having made knowledge a preserver of life. (4069)

२०. मन्युनान्नादेनान्नमत्ति य एवं वेद ।।

20. He who hath this knowledge of the Omnipresent God, preserves life with knowledge as life-preserver. (4070)

२१. स यत् प्रजा अनु व्यचलत् प्रजापतिर्भूत्वानुव्य्ऽचलत् प्राणमन्नादं कृत्वा ।।

21. He, when he went away to living beings, went away having become protector of humanity and having made spiritual force a preserver of life. (4071)

२२. प्राणेनान्नादेनान्नमत्ति य एवं वेद ।।

22. He who hath this knowledge of the Omnipresent God, preserves life with spiritual force as life-preserver. (4072)

२३. स यत् सर्वानन्तर्देशाननु व्यचलत् परमेष्ठी भूत्वानुव्य्ऽचलद् ब्रह्मान्नादं कृत्वा ।।

23. He, when he went away to all the intermediate regions, went away having become the lord of all and having made God the Preserver of life. (4073)

२४. ब्रह्मणान्नादेनान्नमत्ति य एवं वेद ।।

24. He, who hath this knowledge of the Omnipresent God, preserves life with God as Life-preserver. (4074)

HYMN XV

१. तस्य व्रात्यस्य ।।

1. Of that learned guest wedded to the fulfilment of his vow. (4075)

२. सप्त प्राणाः सप्तापानाः सप्त व्यानाः ।।

2. There are seven vital airs (Prānās inhaled) seven Apānās (breaths exhaled) seven diffused breaths (Vyānās). (4076)

[1]Upper region: Zenith.

३. तस्य व्रात्यस्य । योऽस्य प्रथमः प्राण ऊर्ध्वो नामायं सो अग्निः ॥

3. His first vital breath, called Upward, is this Agni. (4077)[1]

४. तस्य व्रात्यस्य । योऽस्य द्वितीयः प्राणः प्रौढो नामासौ स आदित्यः ॥

4. His second vital breath, called Mature, is that Sun. (4078)[2]

५. तस्य व्रात्यस्य । योऽस्य तृतीयः प्राणो३भ्यूऽढो नामासौ स चन्द्रमाः ॥

5. His third vital breath, called Approached, is that Moon. (4079)[3]

६. तस्य व्रात्यस्य । योऽस्य चतुर्थः प्राणो विभूर्नामायं स पवमानः ॥

6. His fourth vital breath, called Pervading is this purifying air. (4080)[4]

७. तस्य व्रात्यस्य । योऽस्य पञ्चमः प्राणो योनिर्नाम ता इमा आपः ॥

7. His fifth vital breath, called source, are these Waters. (4081)[5]

८. तस्य व्रात्यस्य । योऽस्य षष्ठः प्राणः प्रियो नाम त इमे पशवः ॥

8. His sixth vital breath, called Dear, are these domestic animals. (4082)[6]

९. तस्य व्रात्यस्य । योऽस्य सप्तमः प्राणोऽपरिमितो नाम ता इमाः प्रजाः ॥

9. His seventh vital breath, called Unlimited, are these creatures. (4083)[7]

HYMN XVI

१. तस्य व्रात्यस्य । योऽस्य प्रथमोऽपानः सा पौर्णमासी ॥

1. His first outgoing breath is the time of Full Moon. (4084)

२. तस्य व्रात्यस्य । योऽस्य द्वितीयोऽपानः साष्टका ॥

2. His second outgoing breath is the eighth day after Full Moon. (4085)

३. तस्य व्रात्यस्य । योऽस्य तृतीयोऽपानः सामावास्याऽ ॥

3. His third outgoing breath is the night of New Moon. (4086)

[1]This breath signifies electricity, physical fire, earthly fire, and is the manifestor of the science of fire.

[2]It is the manifestor of the science of the Sun.

[3]It is the manifestor of the science of Moon.

[4]It is the manifestor of the science of air.

[5]It is the manifestor of the science of water.

[6]This breath is the manifestor of the science of cattle. It signifies how useful kine, horses, sheep, deer, camel, elephant etc., are to men in the world.

[7]It signifies how men living on Earth, Sun and Moon etc. should behave towards one another. The vital breaths of a yogi who comes as a guest signify the knowledge of different sciences.

४. तस्य व्रात्यस्य । योऽस्य चतुर्थोऽपानः सा श्रद्धा ॥

4. His fourth outgoing breath is Faith. (4087)

५. तस्य व्रात्यस्य । योऽस्य पञ्चमोऽपानः सा दीक्षा ॥

5. His fifth outgoing breath is Consecration. (4088)

६. तस्य व्रात्यस्य । योऽस्य षष्ठोऽपानः स यज्ञः ॥

6. His sixth outgoing breath is sacrifice. (4089)

७. तस्य व्रात्यस्य । योऽस्य सप्तमोऽपानस्ता इमा दक्षिणाः ॥

7. His seventh outgoing breath are these sacrificial fees. (4090)[1]

HYMN XVII

१. तस्य व्रात्यस्य । योऽस्य प्रथमो व्यानः सेयं भूमिः ॥

1. His first diffused breath is this Earth. (4091)[2]

२. तस्य व्रात्यस्य । योऽस्य द्वितीयो व्यानस्तदन्तरिक्षम् ॥

2. His second diffused breath is that Firmament. (4092)[3]

३. तस्य व्रात्यस्य । योऽस्य तृतीयो व्यानः सा द्यौः ॥

3. His third diffused breath is that Heaven. (4093)[4]

४. तस्य व्रात्यस्य । योऽस्य चतुर्थो व्यानस्तानि नक्षत्राणि ॥

4. His fourth diffused breath are those constellations. (4094)[5]

५. तस्य व्रात्यस्य । योऽस्य पञ्चमो व्यानस्त ऋतवः ॥

5. His fifth diffused breath are the Seasons. (4095)[6]

६. तस्य व्रात्यस्य । योऽस्य षष्ठो व्यानस्त आर्तवाः ॥

6. His sixth diffused breath are the products of seasons. (4096)[7]

[1](1-7) 'His' refers to the learned guest. Griffith remarks, 'I find this verse and the following absolutely unintelligible.' Apâna is the force that removes all sorrows and griefs (सर्वं दुःख अपानयति इति अपानः). Pauranmasi, Ashtakā, Amavasyā, Faith, Consecration, sacrifice (Yajna) charity remove the sorrows, griefs and agonies of a man. These seven forces are the seven outgoing breaths of a yogi.

[2]The learned yogi who comes as a guest preaches the science of geology and the art of administration.

[3]He preaches the science of air and clouds.

[4]He preaches the science of the Sun and vast Space.

[5]He preaches the science of stars, their movements, revolution, and mutual attraction.

[6]He preaches the science of seasons.

[7]He preaches how flowers, fruits, cereals and vegetables are grown in different seasons.

७. तस्य व्रात्यस्य । योऽस्य सप्तमो व्यानः स संवत्सरः ॥

7. His seventh diffused breath is the year. (4097)[1]

८. तस्य व्रात्यस्य । समानमर्थं परि यन्ति देवाः संवत्सरं वा एतदृतवोऽनुपरियन्ति व्रात्यं च ॥

8. The learned acquire the religious views of the philanthropic guest, and verily follow him as seasons do the year. (4098)

९. तस्य व्रात्यस्य । यदादित्यमभिसंविशन्त्यमावास्यां चैव तत्पौर्णमासीं च ॥

9. When they follow the renowned virtues of the learned guest, they learn the art of cooperation and analysing and examining things. (4099)[2]

१०. तस्य व्रात्यस्य । एकं तदेषाममृतत्वमित्याहुतिरेव ॥

10. The charitable act of the learned guest is verily their life. (4100)[3]

HYMN XVIII

१. तस्य व्रात्यस्य ॥

1. Of that learned guest. (4101)

२. यदस्य दक्षिणमक्ष्यसौ स आदित्यो यदस्य सव्यमक्ष्यसौ स चन्द्रमाः ॥

2. The right eye is the lustrous Sun and the left eye is the pleasant Moon. (4102)[4]

३. योऽस्य दक्षिणः कर्णोऽयं सो अग्निर्योऽस्य सव्यः कर्णोऽयं स पवमानः ॥

3. His right ear is fire and his left ear is purifying air. (4103)[5]

४. अहोरात्रे नासिके दितिश्चादितिश्च शीर्षकपाले संवत्सरः शिरः ॥

4. Day and Night are his nostrils. Evanescent created world, and eternal Matter are his skulls. The knowledge of time is his head. (4104)[6]

५. अह्ना प्रत्यङ् व्रात्यो रात्र्या प्राङ् नमो व्रात्याय ॥

[1] He preaches how months and seasons constitute the year, how the year is divided in days, weeks, and fortnights.

[2] They: The learned persons.

[3] Their: Of scholarly persons.

[4] The learned Sanyasi who comes as a guest, examining all things in their true aspect serves mankind like the Sun and Moon.

[5] He listens to noble teachings of the sages, and benefits humanity thereby like fire and air.

[6] The learned philanthropic guest prolongs the breaths in his nostril like day and night through Prānayāma, realises in his head the attributes of indestructible Matter and impermanent world and knowledge of time. In fact through his organs he masters the knowledge of the whole world.

5. The learned self-abnegating guest is worthy of adoration by every one in the days, and of special homage at night. Worship to such a guest. (4105)[1]

BOOK (Kāṇḍa) XVI

HYMN I

१. अतिसृष्टो अपां वृषभोऽतिसृष्टा अग्नयो दिव्याः ॥

1. God, the Lord of all creatures is free like the Sun, Lightning and fire. (4106)[2]

२. रुजन् परिरुजन् मृणन् प्रमृणन् ॥

2. A malady, that is breaking, breaking down, crushing, crushing to pieces. (4107)

३. म्रोको मनोहा खनो निर्दाह आत्मदूषिस्तनूदूषिः ॥

3. Vexations, mind-destroying, uprooting, consuming, ruiner of the soul, ruiner of the body. (4108)

४. इदं तमति सृजामि तं माभ्यवनिक्षि ॥

4. Now I destroy, and never let it develop. (4109)[3]

५. तेन तमभ्यतिसृजामो यो३स्मान् द्वेष्टि यं वयं द्विष्मः ॥

5. So we remove him who hates us and whom we dislike. (4110)

६. अपामग्रमसि समुद्रं वोऽभ्यवसृजामि ॥

6. O men, God is the resort of mankind. I consign ye to Him, the Elevator of humanity. (4111)[4]

७. यो३प्स्व१ग्निरति तं सृजामि म्रोकं खनिं तनूदूषिम् ॥

7. I remove the ailment, that in men is troublesome like fire, vexations, uprooting and ruiner of the body. (4112)[5]

८. यो व आपोऽग्निराविवेश स एष यद् वो घोरं तदेतत् ॥

[1] A learned sacrificing guest works for the good of humanity and at night is absorbed in the contemplation. Such a guest should be adored and worshipped by all.

[2] Apāna (अपाम्) आप:=आप्त: प्रजा: vide Dayananda commentary *Yajur*, 6-27.

[3] I: A lerned person.

[4] समुद्र: भूतानां समुदयकारकं परमात्मानम् । समुद्र: समुद्रवन्ति भूतानि यस्मात्स: vide Dayananda *Yajur*, 5-331. सर्वे देवा: सम्यगुत्कर्षेण द्रवन्ति यत्रेति समुद्र: vide Mahidhar commentary *Yajur*, 5-331.

[5] I: A learned person.

8. O learned persons knowing different sciences, the All-Pervading God, Who has pervaded you, pervades everything. Your mighty power has emanated from Him. (4113)[1]

९. इन्द्रस्य व इन्द्रियेणाभि षिञ्चेत् ॥

9. May He anoint you with the mighty power of a ruler. (4114)

१०. अरिप्रा आपो अप रिप्रमस्मत् ॥

10. May sinless learned persons cleanse us from sin. (4115)

११. प्रास्मदेनो वहन्तु प्र दुष्वप्न्यं वहन्तु ॥

11. May they carry sin away from us, may they carry away from us the ignoble thoughts arising out of the evil dream. (4116)[2]

१२. शिवेन मा चक्षुषा पश्यतापः शिवया तन्वोप स्पृशत त्वचं मे ॥

12. Look on me with a friendly eye, O learned persons, and touch my skin with your auspicious body. (4117)

१३. शिवानग्नीनप्सुषदो हवामहे मयि क्षत्रं वर्च आ धत्त देवीः ॥

13. We call the gracious learned persons who sit in our society. O godly subjects grant me princely power and splendour. (4118)

HYMN II

१. निर्दुरर्मण्य ऊर्जा मधुमती वाक् ॥

1. Let misfortune be away. Let my speech be forceful and sweet. (4119)

२. मधुमती स्थ मधुमतीं वाचमुदेयम् ॥

2. O learned persons, ye are full of knowledge! Let my speech be full of knowledge. (4120)

३. उपहूतो मे गोपा उपहूतो गोपीथः ॥

3. Reverently have I invoked my preceptor (Āchārya) the guardian of speech. Reverently have I invoked the king, the Lord of Earth. (4121)[3]

४. सुश्रुतौ कर्णौ भद्रश्रुतौ कर्णौ भद्रं श्लोकं श्रूयासम् ॥

4. Let my ears hear words of knowledge. Let my ears hear what is good. Fain would I hear auspicious words. (4122)

[1](आपः) हे विद्याव्यापिनो विपश्चितः vide Maharshi Dayananda's commentary *Yajur*, 6-27.

[2]They: Learned persons.

[3]I: A learned person.

५. सुश्रुतिश्च मोपश्रुतिश्च मा हासिष्टां सौपर्णं चक्षुरजस्रं ज्योतिः ।।

5. Let not my power of quick hearing and hearing from a distance. Let my vision be keen like that of an eagle. Let not its light ever fade. (4123)

६. ऋषीणां प्रस्तरोऽसि नमोऽस्तु दैवाय प्रस्तराय ।।

6. O God, Thou art the Expander of the learned seers (Rishis). Let homage be paid to the Divine Expander of the universe. (4124)

HYMN III

१. मूर्धाहं रयीणां मूर्धा समानानां भूयासम् ।।

1. May I be the lord of riches, and the leader of my equals. (4125)

२. रुजश्च मा वेनश्च मा हासिष्टां मूर्धा च मा विधर्मा च मा हासिष्टाम् ।।

2. Let not dignity and loveliness desert me. Let not the intellectual power and spiritual power forsake me. (4126)

३. उर्वश्च मा चमसश्च मा हासिष्टां धर्ता च मा धरुणश्च मा हासिष्टाम् ।।

3. Let not heroism and physical strength desert me. Let not the supporter and the sustainer forsake me. (4127)

४. विमोकश्च मार्द्रपविश्च मा हासिष्टामार्द्रदानुश्च मा मातरिश्वा च मा हासिष्टाम् ।।

4. Let not the raining cloud and the thundering lightning desert. Let not charity to the suppliant and ever growing prosperity forsake me. (4128)

५. बृहस्पतिर्म आत्मा नृमणा नाम हृद्यः ।।

5. My soul is full of knowledge and noble qualities, it is the friend of man and dear to my heart. (4129)

६. असंतापं मे हृदयमुर्वी गव्यूतिः समुद्रो अस्मि विधर्मणा ।।

6. May my heart be tranquil, free from sorrow. Vast may be my knowledge I am fathomless like an ocean in spiritual force. (4130)

HYMN IV

१. नाभिरहं रयीणां नाभिः समानानां भूयासम् ।।

1. May I be the centre of knowledge and riches, and the central figure amongst my equals. (4131)

२. स्वासदसि सूषा अमृतो मर्त्येष्वा ।।

2. O soul, thou possessest exquisite goodness; thou art beautiful like the Dawn. Thou art immortal amongst the mortals. (4132)

३. मा मां प्राणो हासीन्मो अपानोऽवहाय परा गात् ॥

3. Let not inward breath desert me; let not outward breath depart and leave me. (4133)[1]

४. सूर्यो माह्नः पात्वग्निः पृथिव्या वायुरन्तरिक्षाद् यमो मनुष्येभ्यः सरस्वती पार्थिवेभ्यः ॥

4. May God, the Urger of all, protect me from the fear of Day. May the Wise God, protect me from the fear of Earth. May the All-pervading God protect me from the fear of Firmament. May the Justice-loving God protect me from the fear of men. May the knowledgeful God protect me from the fear of dwellers on the earth. (4134)

५. प्राणापानौ मा मा हासिष्टं मा जने प्र मेषि ॥

5. Let not inward and outward breath fail me. May I not be destroyed among the men. (4135)

६. स्वस्त्य१द्योषसो दोषसश्च सर्व आपः सर्वगणो अशीय ॥

6. Propitious today be dawns and evenings. May I remain happy with all my people safe around me, O learned persons! (4136)

७. शक्वरी स्थ पशवो मोप स्थेषुर्मित्रावरुणौ मे प्राणापानावग्निर्मे दक्षं दधातु ॥

7. O learned persons, may ye be endowed with power! May all creatures stand beside me. May Mitra and Varuna strengthen my inward breath and outward breath. May God grant me practical wisdom. (4137)[2]

HYMN V

१. विद्म ते स्वप्न जनित्रं ग्राह्याः पुत्रोऽसि यमस्य करणः ॥

1. We know thine origin, O Idleness! Thou art the son of gout, the bringer of Death. (4138)[3]

२. अन्तकोऽसि मृत्युरसि ॥

2. Thou art the Ender of consciousness. Thou art Death. (4139)[4]

३. तं त्वा स्वप्न तथा सं विद्म स नः स्वप्न दुष्वप्न्यात् पाहि ॥

3. As such, O Idleness, we know thee well! As such preserve us from the ignoble thoughts arising out of an evil dream. (4140)

४. विद्म ते स्वप्न जनित्रं निर्ऋत्याः पुत्रोऽसि यमस्य करणः । अन्तकोऽसि मृत्युरसि ।
तं त्वा स्वप्न तथा सं विद्म स नः स्वप्न दुष्वप्न्यात् पाहि ॥

[1]I must enjoy the full span of life, and die not at an early age.

[2]Mitra and Varuna: Two learned friends.

[3]Tennyson describes sleep in Inmemoriam as 'twin sister of death.' Rabindra Nath Tagore condemns idleness as a traitor that betrays the soul. Sleep is equivalent to idleness.

[4]Thou: Idleness.

4. We know thine origin, O idleness! Thou art the son of Adversity, the bringer of Death. Thou art the Ender of consciousness. Thou art Death. As such, O Idleness, we know thee well! As such preserve us from the ignoble thoughts arising out of an evil dream. (4141)

५. विद्म ते स्वप्न जनित्रमभूत्याः पुत्रोऽसि यमस्य करणः । अन्तकोऽसि मृत्युरसि ।
तं त्वा स्वप्न तथा सं विद्म स नः स्वप्न दुष्वप्न्यात् पाहि ॥

5. We know thine origin, O idleness! Thou art the son of Poverty, the bringer of Death. Thou art the Ender of consciousness. Thou art Death. As such, O idleness, we know thee well! As such preserve us from the ignoble thoughts arising out of an evil dream. (4142)

६. विद्म ते स्वप्न जनित्रं निर्भूत्याः पुत्रोऽसि यमस्य करणः । अन्तकोऽसि मृत्युरसि ।
तं त्वा स्वप्न तथा सं विद्म स नः स्वप्न दुष्वप्न्यात् पाहि ॥

6. We know thine origin, O idleness! Thou art the son of Destruction, the bringer of Death. Thou art the Ender of consciousness. Thou art Death. As such, O idleness, we know thee well! As such preserve us from the ignoble thoughts arising out of an evil dream. (4143)

७. विद्म ते स्वप्न जनित्रं पराभूत्याः पुत्रोऽसि यमस्य करणः । अन्तकोऽसि मृत्युरसि ।
तं त्वा स्वप्न तथा सं विद्म स नः स्वप्न दुष्वप्न्यात् पाहि ॥

7. We know thine origin, O idleness! Thou art the son of Defeat, the bringer of Death. Thou art the Ender of Consciousness. Thou art Death. As such, O idleness, we know thee well! As such preserve us from the ignoble thoughts of an evil dream. (4144)

८. विद्म ते स्वप्न जनित्रं देवजामीनां पुत्रोऽसि यमस्य करणः ॥

8. We know thine origin, O idleness! Thou art the son of the disease of organs, the bringer of Death. (4145)

९. अन्तकोऽसि मृत्युरसि ॥

9. Thou art the Ender of consciousness. Thou are an embodiment of Death. (4146)

१०. तं त्वा स्वप्न तथा सं विद्म स नः स्वप्न दुष्वप्न्यात् पाहि ॥

10. As such, O idleness we know thee well! As such preserve us from the ignoble thoughts of an evil dream. (4147)[1]

HYMN VI

१. अजैष्माद्यासनामाद्याभूमानागसो वयम् ॥

[1]Swapna: Sleep, idleness. In this hymn idleness has beautifully been condemned as the root cause of man's degradation. One should always shun idleness.

1. Now have we subdued evil tendencies and obtained the desired aim we have been freed from sin today. (4148)

२. उषो यस्माद् दुष्वप्न्यादभैष्माप तदुच्छतु ॥

2. O Morning, dispel with thy light that evil dream that frightened us. (4149)

३. द्विषते तत् परा वह शपते तत् परा वह ॥

3. Bear that away to him who hates, away to him who curses us. (4150)[1]

४. यं द्विष्मो यश्च नो द्वेष्टि तस्मा एनद् गमयामः ॥

4. To the intemperate whom we abhor, to him who hates us do we send it hence. (4151)[2]

५. उषा देवी वाचा संविदाना वाग् देव्यु१षसा संविदाना ॥

5. May the Goddess Dawn be in accord with Vedic speech, and Vedic speech in accord with Dawn. (4152)[3]

६. उषस्पतिर्वाचस्पतिना संविदानो वाचस्पतिरुषस्पतिना संविदानः ॥

6. May an early riser be in accord with a learned person, and a learned person in accord with an early riser. (4153)[4]

७. तेऽमुष्मै परा वहन्त्वरायान् दुर्णम्नः सदान्वाः ॥

7. May they carry away to an intemperate person, poverty, abominable ills, and other calamities. (4154)[5]

८. कुम्भीका दूषीकाः पीयकान् ॥

8. Dropsy, poisonous, and deadly diseases. (4155)

९. जाग्रद्दुष्वप्न्यं स्वप्नेदुष्वप्न्यम् ॥

9. Evil day-dream, evil dream in sleep. (4156)

१०. अनागमिष्यतो वरानवित्तेः संकल्पानमुच्या द्रुहः पाशान् ॥

10. Wishes for boons that will not come, thoughts of indigence, the snares of malice which never releases. (4157)

[1]That: Fear.

[2]We, us: The physicians. It: Fear.

[3]Dawn and the recitation of Vedic verses should synchronise. Every one should recite Vedic Mantras early in the morning.

[4]He who is fond of knowledge should rise early for study. He who rises early can study and acquire knowledge better than a late riser. All scholars of the world were early risers.

[5]They: Laws of sanitation.

(7-11) In these verses it is mentioned an intemperate person is liable to become a prey to misery, poverty and fell diseases.

११. तदमुष्मा अग्ने देवाः परा वहन्तु वध्रिर्यथासद् विथुरो न साधुः ॥

11. O God, may the laws of sanitation take all these distressing ailments to an intemperate person, so that impious fellow may become emasculated and miserable. (4158)

HYMN VII

१. तेनैनं विध्याम्यभूत्यैनं विध्यामि निर्भूत्यैनं विध्यामि पराभूत्यैनं विध्यामि ग्राह्यैनं विध्यामि तमसैनं विध्यामि ॥

1. I torment this sinner with this weapon. With poverty I torment him. With destruction I torment him. With defeat I torment him. With gout I torment him. With death I torment him. (4159)[1]

२. देवानामेनं घोरैः क्रूरैः प्रैषैरभिप्रेष्यामि ॥

2. I torment him with the awful, cruel instruments of the learned. (4160)

३. वैश्वानरस्यैनं दंष्ट्रयोरपि दधामि ॥

3. I place him between the Jaws of Law. (4161)[2]

४. एवानेवाव सा गरत् ॥

4. Thus or otherwise let Law give him condign punishment. (4162)

५. योऽस्मान् द्वेष्टि तमात्मा द्वेष्टु यं वयं द्विष्मः स आत्मानं द्वेष्टु ॥

5. Him who hates us may his soul hate, and may he whom we hate, hate himself. (4163)[3]

६. निर्द्विषन्तं दिवो निः पृथिव्या निरन्तरिक्षाद् भजाम ॥

6. We deprive the man who hates us from enjoying the heaven and earth and firmament. (4164)

७. सुयामंश्चाक्षुष ॥

7. O efficient and far-sighted ruler. (4165)

८. इदमहमामुष्यायणेऽमुष्याः पुत्रे दुष्वप्न्यं मृजे ॥

8. I punish the offender for idleness, the descendant of such a family, son of such a woman. (4166)[4]

[1]I: A King.

[2]Law is Vaishwānara, as it treats all alike, and is not the respecter of persons.

[3]Him: The offender, culprit. Us: Virtuous people. An offender should be rebuked by his soul for hating good people. He should be ashamed and curse himself on seeing that he incurs the displeasure of godly persons.

[4]I: The Lord of justice.

९. यददोग्रदो ग्रभ्यगच्छन् यद् दोषा यत् पूर्वां रात्रिम् ॥

9. Whatever fault I find with the culprit, whether at dusk or during night. (4167)

१०. यज्जाग्रद् यत् सुप्तो यद् दिवा यन्नक्तम् ॥

10. Whether waking or sleeping, whether by day or by night. (4168)

११. यदहरहरभिगच्छामि तस्मादेनमव दये ॥

11. Whether I find it day by day or by night, for that I punish him. (4169)

१२. तं जहि तेन मन्दस्व तस्य पृष्टीरपि शृणीहि ॥

12. Slay O King the offender, behave heroically towards him, crush his ribs. (4170)

१३. स मा जीवीत् तं प्राणो जहातु ॥

13. Let him not live. Let the breath of life forsake him. (4171)

HYMN VIII

१. जितमस्माकमुद्भिन्नमस्माकमृतमस्माकं तेजोऽस्माकं ब्रह्मास्माकं स्वऽरस्माकं
यज्ञो३ऽस्माकं पशवोऽस्माकं प्रजा ग्रस्माकं वीरा ग्रस्माकम् ॥

1. Let us be victorious. Let us be prosperous. Let us be truthful. Let us be energetic. Let us be learned. Let our soul shine. Let our sacrifice (Yajna) be fruitful. Let us own cattle. Let our progeny progress. Let us have brave soldiers. (4172)

२. तस्मादमुं निर्भजामोऽमुमामुष्यायणममुष्याः पुत्रमसौ यः ॥

2. We banish him from the country for his aggression, who belongs to such a family, is the son of such a woman, and is the enemy of the country. (4173)

३. स ग्राह्याः पाशान्मा मोचि ॥

3. Let him not be freed from the punishment of the Executive power. (4174)

४. तस्येदं वर्चस्तेजः प्राणमायुर्नि वेष्टयामीदमेनमधराञ्चं पादयामि ॥

4. I bind up his splendour, his energy, his vital breath, his life, and cast him down beneath me. (4175)[1]

[1]I: A king.

५. जितमस्माकमुद्भिन्नमस्माकमृतमस्माकं तेजोऽस्माकं ब्रह्मास्माकं स्वऽरस्माकं
यज्ञो३ऽस्माकं पशवोऽस्माकं प्रजा अस्माकं वीरा अस्माकम् ।
तस्मादमुं निर्भजामोऽमुमामुष्यायणममुष्याः पुत्रमसौ यः । स निर्ऋत्याः पाशान्मा मोचि ।
तस्येदं वर्चस्तेजः प्राणमायुर्नि वेष्टयामीदमेनमधराञ्चं पादयामि ॥

5. Let us be victorious. Let us be prosperous. Let us be truthful. Let us be energetic. Let us be learned. Let our soul advance. Let our sacrifice be fruitful. Let us own cattle. Let our progeny progress. Let us have brave soldiers. We banish him from the country for his aggression, who belongs to such a family, is the son of such a woman, and is the enemy of the country. Let him not be freed from the noose of misfortune. I bind up his splendour, his energy, his vital breath, his life, and cast him down beneath me. (4176)[1]

६. जितमस्माकमुद्भिन्नमस्माकमृतमस्माकं तेजोऽस्माकं ब्रह्मास्माकं स्वऽरस्माकं
यज्ञो३ऽस्माकं पशवोऽस्माकं प्रजा अस्माकं वीरा अस्माकम् ।
तस्मादमुं निर्भजामोऽमुमामुष्यायणममुष्याः पुत्रमसौ यः । सोऽभूत्याः पाशान्मा मोचि ।
तस्येदं वर्चस्तेजः प्राणमायुर्नि वेष्टयामीदमेनमधराञ्चं पादयामि ॥

6. Let us be victorious. Let us be prosperous. Let us be truthful. Let us be energetic. Let us be learned. Let our soul advance. Let our sacrifice be fruitful. Let us own cattle. Let our progeny progress. Let us have brave soldiers. We banish him from the country for his aggression, who belongs to such a family, is the son of such a woman, and is the enemy of the country. Let him not be freed from the noose of poverty. I bind up his splendour, his energy, his vital breath, his life, and cast him down beneath me. (4177)

७. जितमस्माकमुद्भिन्नमस्माकमृतमस्माकं तेजोऽस्माकं ब्रह्मास्माकं स्वऽरस्माकं
यज्ञो३ऽस्माकं पशवोऽस्माकं प्रजा अस्माकं वीरा अस्माकम् ।
तस्मादमुं निर्भजामोऽमुमामुष्यायणममुष्याः पुत्रमसौ यः । स निर्भूत्याः पाशान्मा मोचि ।
तस्येदं वर्चस्तेजः प्राणमायुर्नि वेष्टयामीदमेनमधराञ्चं पादयामि ॥

7. Let us be victorious. Let us be prosperous. Let us be truthful. Let us be energetic. Let us be learned. Let our soul advance. Let our sacrifice be fruitful. Let us own cattle. Let our progeny progress. Let us have brave soldiers. We banish him from the country for his aggression, who belongs to such a family, is the son of such a woman, and is the enemy of the country. Let him not be freed from the noose of misery. I bind up his splendour, his energy, his vital breath, his life, and cast him down beneath me. (4178)

८. जितमस्माकमुद्भिन्नमस्माकमृतमस्माकं तेजोऽस्माकं ब्रह्मास्माकं स्वऽरस्माकं
यज्ञो३ऽस्माकं पशवोऽस्माकं प्रजा अस्माकं वीरा अस्माकम् ।
तस्मादमुं निर्भजामोऽमुमामुष्यायणममुष्याः पुत्रमसौ यः । स पराभूत्याः पाशान्मा मोचि ।
तस्येदं वर्चस्तेजः प्राणमायुर्नि वेष्टयामीदमेनमधराञ्चं पादयामि ॥

[1]Him: The sinner, the culprit.

8. Let us be victorious. Let us be prosperous. Let us be truthful. Let us be energetic. Let us be learned. Let our soul advance. Let our sacrifice be fruitful. Let us own cattle. Let our progeny progress. Let us have brave soldiers. We banish him from the country, for his aggression, who belongs to such a family, is the son of such a woman, and is the enemy of the country. Let him not be freed from the noose of defeat. I bind up his splendour, his energy, his vital breath, his life, and cast him down beneath me. (4179)

९. जितमस्माकमुद्भिन्नमस्माकमृतमस्माकं तेजोऽस्माकं ब्रह्मास्माकं स्व꣡रस्माकं
यज्ञो३ऽस्माकं पशवोऽस्माकं प्रजा अस्माकं वीरा अस्माकम् ।
तस्मादमुं निर्भजामोऽमुमामुष्यायणममुष्याः पुत्रमसौ यः । स देवजामीनां पाशान्मा मोचि ।
तस्येदं वर्चस्तेजः प्राणमायुर्नि वेष्टयामीदमेनमधराञ्चं पादयामि ॥

9. Let us be victorious. Let us be prosperous. Let us be truthful. Let us be energetic. Let us be learned. Let our soul advance. Let our sacrifice be fruitful. Let us own cattle. Let our progeny progress. Let us have brave soldiers. We banish him from the country, for his aggression, who belongs to such a family, is the son of such a woman, and is the enemy of the country. Let him not be freed from the noose of physical disorders. I bind up his splendour, his energy, his vital breath, his life, and cast him down beneath me. (4180)

१०. जितमस्माकमुद्भिन्नमस्माकमृतमस्माकं तेजोऽस्माकं ब्रह्मास्माकं स्व꣡रस्माकं
यज्ञो३ऽस्माकं पशवोऽस्माकं प्रजा अस्माकं वीरा अस्माकम् ।
तस्मादमुं निर्भजामोऽमुमामुष्यायणममुष्याः पुत्रमसौ यः । स बृहस्पतेः पाशान्मा मोचि ।
तस्येदं वर्चस्तेजः प्राणमायुर्नि वेष्टयामीदमेनमधराञ्चं पादयामि ॥

10. Let us be victorious. Let us be prosperous. Let us be truthful. Let us be energetic. Let us be learned. Let our soul advance. Let our sacrifice be fruitful. Let us own cattle. Let our progeny progress. Let us have brave soldiers. We banish him from the country, for his aggression, who belongs to such a family, is the son of such a woman, and is the enemy of the country. Let him not be freed from the noose of the Commander of the army. I bind up his splendour, his energy, his vital breath, his life, and cast him down beneath me. (4181)

११. जितमस्माकमुद्भिन्नमस्माकमृतमस्माकं तेजोऽस्माकं ब्रह्मास्माकं स्व꣡रस्माकं
यज्ञो३ऽस्माकं पशवोऽस्माकं प्रजा अस्माकं वीरा अस्माकम् ।
तस्मादमुं निर्भजामोऽमुमामुष्यायणममुष्याः पुत्रमसौ यः । स प्रजापतेः पाशान्मा मोचि ।
तस्येदं वर्चस्तेजः प्राणमायुर्नि वेष्टयामीदमेनमधराञ्चं पादयामि ।

11. Let us be victorious. Let us be prosperous. Let us be truthful. Let us be energetic. Let us be learned. Let our soul advance. Let our sacrifice be fruitful. Let us own cattle. Let our progeny progress. Let us have brave soldiers. We banish him from the country, for his aggression, who belongs to

such a family, is the son of such a woman, and is the enemy of the country. Let him not be freed from the noose of the king, the rearer of his subjects. I bind up his splendour, his energy, his vital breath, his life, and cast him down beneath me. (4182)

१२. जितमस्माकमुद्भिन्नमस्माकमृतमस्माकं तेजोऽस्माकं ब्रह्मास्माकं स्व᳡रस्माकं
यज्ञो३ऽस्माकं पशवोऽस्माकं प्रजा अस्माकं वीरा अस्माकम् ।
तस्मादमुं निर्भजामोऽमुमामुष्यायणममुष्याः पुत्रमसौ यः । स ऋषीणां पाशान्मा मोचि ।
तस्येदं वर्चस्तेजः प्राणमायुर्नि वेष्टयामीदमेनमधराञ्चं पादयामि ॥

12. Let us be victorious. Let us be prosperous. Let us be truthful. Let us be energetic. Let us be learned. Let our soul advance. Let our sacrifice be fruitful. Let us own cattle. Let our progeny progress. Let us have brave soldiers. We banish him from the country, for his aggression, who belongs to such a family, is the son of such a woman, and is the enemy of the country. Let him not be freed from the noose of the sages, the exhibitors of the path of rectitude. I bind up his splendour, his energy, his vital breath, his life, and cast him down beneath me. (4183)

१३. जितमस्माकमुद्भिन्नमस्माकमृतमस्माकं तेजोऽस्माकं ब्रह्मास्माकं स्व᳡रस्माकं
यज्ञो३ऽस्माकं पशवोऽस्माकं प्रजा अस्माकं वीरा अस्माकम् ।
तस्मादमुं निर्भजामोऽमुमामुष्यायणममुष्याः पुत्रमसौ यः । स आर्षेयाणां पाशान्मा मोचि ।
तस्येदं वर्चस्तेजः प्राणमायुर्नि वेष्टयामीदमेनमधराञ्चं पादयामि ॥

13. Let us be victorious. Let us be prosperous. Let us be truthful. Let us be energetic. Let us be learned. Let our soul advance. Let our sacrifice be fruitful. Let us own cattle. Let our progeny progress. Let us have brave soldiers. We banish him from the country, for his aggression, who belongs to such a family, is the son of such a woman, and is the enemy of the country. Let him not be freed from the injunctions of the religious doctrines formulated by the sages. I bind up his splendour, his energy, his vital breath, his life, and cast him down beneath me. (4184)

१४. जितमस्माकमुद्भिन्नमस्माकमृतमस्माकं तेजोऽस्माकं ब्रह्मास्माकं स्व᳡रस्माकं
यज्ञो३ऽस्माकं पशवोऽस्माकं प्रजा अस्माकं वीरा अस्माकम् ।
तस्मादमुं निर्भजामोऽमुमामुष्यायणममुष्याः पुत्रमसौ यः । सोऽङ्गिरसां पाशान्मा मोचि ।
तस्येदं वर्चस्तेजः प्राणमायुर्नि वेष्टयामीदमेनमधराञ्चं पादयामि ॥

14. Let us be victorious. Let us be prosperous. Let us be truthful. Let us be energetic. Let us be learned. Let our soul advance. Let our sacrifice be fruitful. Let us own cattle. Let our progeny progress. Let us have brave soldiers. We banish him from the country, for his aggression, who belongs to such a family, is the son of such a woman, and is the enemy of the country. Let him not be freed from the noose of the Vedic scholars. I bind up his splendour, his energy, his vital breath, his life, and cast him down beneath me. (4185)

१५. जितमस्माकमुद्भिन्नमस्माकमृतमस्माकं तेजोऽस्माकं ब्रह्मास्माकं स्वऽरस्माकं
यज्ञो३ऽस्माकं पशवोऽस्माकं प्रजा अस्माकं वीरा अस्माकम् ।
तस्मादमुं निर्भजामोऽमुमामुष्यायणममुष्याः पुत्रमसौ यः ।
स आङ्गिरसानां पाशान्मा मोचि ।
तस्येदं वर्चस्तेजः प्राणमायुर्नि वेष्टयामीदमेनमधराञ्चं पादयामि ॥

15. Let us be victorious. Let us be prosperous. Let us be truthful. Let us be energetic. Let us be learned. Let our soul advance. Let our sacrifice be fruitful. Let us own cattle. Let our progeny progress. Let us have brave soldiers. We banish him from the country, for his aggression, who belongs to such a family, is the son of such a woman, and is the enemy of the country. Let him not be freed from the grip of the warriors taught by the learned. I bind up his splendour, his vital breath, his life and cast him down beneath me. (4186)

१६. जितमस्माकमुद्भिन्नमस्माकमृतमस्माकं तेजोऽस्माकं ब्रह्मास्माकं स्वऽरस्माकं
यज्ञो३ऽस्माकं पशवोऽस्माकं प्रजा अस्माकं वीरा अस्माकम् ।
तस्मादमुं निर्भजामोऽमुमामुष्यायणममुष्याः पुत्रमसौ यः । सोऽथर्वणां पाशान्मा मोचि ।
तस्येदं वर्चस्तेजः प्राणमायुर्नि वेष्टयामीदमेनमधराञ्चं पादयामि ॥

16. Let us be victorious. Let us be prosperous. Let us be truthful. Let us be energetic. Let us be learned. Let our soul advance. Let our sacrifice be fruitful. Let us own cattle. Let our progeny progress. Let us have brave soldiers. We banish him from the country, for his aggression, who belongs to such a family, is the son of such a woman, and is the enemy of the country. Let him not be freed from the grasp of military commanders of determined mind. I bind up his splendour, his energy, his vital breath, his life, and cast him down beneath me. (4187)

१७. जितमस्माकमुद्भिन्नमस्माकमृतमस्माकं तेजोऽस्माकं ब्रह्मास्माकं स्वऽरस्माकं
यज्ञो३ऽस्माकं पशवोऽस्माकं प्रजा अस्माकं वीरा अस्माकम् ।
तस्मादमुं निर्भजामोऽमुमामुष्यायणममुष्याः पुत्रमसौ यः । स आथर्वणानां पाशान्मा मोचि ।
तस्येदं वर्चस्तेजः प्राणमायुर्नि वेष्टयामीदमेनमधराञ्चं पादयामि ॥

17. Let us be victorious. Let us be prosperous. Let us be truthful. Let us be energetic. Let us be learned. Let our soul advance. Let our sacrifice be fruitful. Let us own cattle. Let our progeny progress. Let us have brave soldiers. We banish him from the country, for his aggression, who belongs to such a family, is the son of such a woman and is the enemy of the country. Let him not be freed from the hold of the armies of determined military commanders. I bind up his splendour, his energy, his vital breath, his life, and cast him down beneath me. (4188)

१८. जितमस्माकमुद्भिन्नमस्माकमृतमस्माकं तेजोऽस्माकं ब्रह्मास्माकं स्व꣡रस्माकं
यज्ञो३ऽस्माकं पशवोऽस्माकं प्रजा अस्माकं वीरा अस्माकम् ।
तस्मादमुं निर्भजामोऽमुमामुष्यायणममुष्याः पुत्रमसौ यः ।
स वनस्पतीनां पाशान्मा मोचि ।
तस्येदं वर्चस्तेजः प्राणमायुर्नि वेष्टयामीदमेनमधराञ्चं पादयामि ॥

18. Let us be victorious. Let us be prosperous. Let us be truthful. Let us be energetic. Let us be learned. Let our soul advance. Let our sacrifice be fruitful. Let us own cattle. Let our progeny progress. Let us have brave soldiers. We banish him from the country, for his aggression, who belongs to such a family, is the son of such a woman, and is the enemy of the country. Let him not be freed from the hold of the administrators, the guardians of the subjects. I bind up his splendour, his energy, his vital breath, his life, and cast him down beneath me. (4189)

१९. जितमस्माकमुद्भिन्नमस्माकमृतमस्माकं तेजोऽस्माकं ब्रह्मास्माकं स्व꣡रस्माकं
यज्ञो३ऽस्माकं पशवोऽस्माकं प्रजा अस्माकं वीरा अस्माकम् ।
तस्मादमुं निर्भजामोऽमुमामुष्यायणममुष्याः पुत्रमसौ यः ।
स वानस्पत्यानां पाशान्मा मोचि ।
तस्येदं वर्चस्तेजः प्राणमायुर्नि वेष्टयामीदमेनमधराञ्चं पादयामि ॥

19. Let us be victorous. Let us be prosperous. Let us be truthful. Let us be energetic. Let us be learned. Let our soul advance. Let our sacrifice be fruitful. Let us own cattle. Let our progeny progress. Let us have brave soldiers. We banish him from the country, for his aggression, who belongs to such a family, is the son of such a mother, and is the enemy of the country. Let him not be freed from the fetter of the assistants of Government administrators. I bind up his splendour, his energy, his vital breath, his life, and cast him down beneath me. (4190)

२०. जितमस्माकमुद्भिन्नमस्माकमृतमस्माकं तेजोऽस्माकं ब्रह्मास्माकं स्व꣡रस्माकं
यज्ञो३ऽस्माकं पशवोऽस्माकं प्रजा अस्माकं वीरा अस्माकम् ।
तस्मादमुं निर्भजामोऽमुमामुष्यायणममुष्याः पुत्रमसौ यः । स ऋतूनां पाशान्मा मोचि ।
तस्येदं वर्चस्तेजः प्राणमायुर्नि वेष्टयामीदमेनमधराञ्चं पादयामि ॥

20. Let us be victorious. Let us be prosperous. Let us be truthful. Let us be energetic. Let us be learned. Let our soul advance. Let our sacrifice be fruitful. Let us own cattle. Let our progeny progress. Let us have brave soldiers. We banish him from the country, for his aggression, who belongs to such a family, is the son of such a woman, and is the enemy of the country. Let him not be freed from the restraint of the seasons. I bind up his splendour, his energy, his vital breath, his life, and cast him down beneath me. (4191)

२१. जितमस्माकमुद्भिन्नमस्माकमृतमस्माकं तेजोऽस्माकं ब्रह्मास्माकं स्वऽरस्माकं
यज्ञो३ऽस्माकं पशवोऽस्माकं प्रजा अस्माकं वीरा अस्माकम् ।
तस्मादमुं निर्भजामोऽमुमामुष्यायणममुष्याः पुत्रमसौ यः । स आर्तवानां पाशान्मा मोचि ।
तस्येदं वर्चस्तेजः प्राणमायुर्नि वेष्टयामीदमेनमधराञ्चं पादयामि ॥

21. Let us be victorious. Let us be prosperous. Let us be truthful. Let us be energetic. Let us be learned. Let our soul advance. Let our sacrifice be fruitful. Let us own cattle. Let our progeny progress. Let us have brave soldiers. We banish him from the country, for his aggression, who belongs to such a family, is the son of such a woman, and is the enemy of the country. Let him not be freed from the bonds of the products of seasons. I bind up his splendour, his energy, his vital breath, his life, and cast him down beneath me. (4192)[1]

२२. जितमस्माकमुद्भिन्नमस्माकमृतमस्माकं तेजोऽस्माकं ब्रह्मास्माकं स्वऽरस्माकं
यज्ञो३ऽस्माकं पशवोऽस्माकं प्रजा अस्माकं वीरा अस्माकम् ।
तस्मादमुं निर्भजामोऽमुमामुष्यायणममुष्याः पुत्रमसौ यः । स मासानां पाशान्मा मोचि ।
तस्येदं वर्चस्तेजः प्राणमायुर्नि वेष्टयामीदमेनमधराञ्चं पादयामि ॥

22. Let us be victorious. Let us be prosperous. Let us be truthful. Let us be energetic. Let us be learned. Let our soul advance. Let our sacrifice be fruitful. Let us own cattle. Let our progeny progress. Let us have brave soldiers. Let us banish him from the country, for his agression, who belongs to such a family, is the son of such a woman, and is the enemy of the country. Let him not be freed from the shackle of months. I bind up his splendour, his energy, his vital breath, his life, and cast him down beneath me. (4193)

२३. जितमस्माकमुद्भिन्नमस्माकमृतमस्माकं तेजोऽस्माकं ब्रह्मास्माकं स्वऽरस्माकं
यज्ञो३ऽस्माकं पशवोऽस्माकं प्रजा अस्माकं वीरा अस्माकम् ।
तस्मादमुं निर्भजामोऽमुमामुष्यायणममुष्याः पुत्रमसौ यः ।
सोऽर्धमासानां पाशान्मा मोचि ।
तस्येदं वर्चस्तेजः प्राणमायुर्नि वेष्टयामीदमेनमधराञ्चं पादयामि ॥

23. Let us be victorious. Let us be prosperous. Let us be truthful. Let us be energetic. Let us be learned. Let our soul advance. Let our sacrifice be fruitful. Let us own cattle. Let our progeny progress. Let us have brave soldiers. We banish him from the country, for his aggression, who belongs to such a family, is the son of such a woman, and is the enemy of the country. Let him not be freed from the check of the Half-months. I bind up his splendour, his energy, his vital breath, his life, and cast him down beneath me. (4194)

[1]Products of seasons: Heat, cold, rain etc.

२४. जितमस्माकमुद्भिन्नमस्माकमृतमस्माकं तेजोऽस्माकं ब्रह्मास्माकं स्वऽरस्माकं
यज्ञो३ऽस्माकं पशवोऽस्माकं प्रजा अस्माकं वीरा अस्माकम् ।
तस्मादमुं निर्भजामोऽमुमामुष्यायणममुष्याः पुत्रमसौ यः ।
सोऽहोरात्रयोः पाशान्मा मोचि ।
तस्येदं वर्चस्तेजः प्राणमायुर्नि वेष्टयामीदमेनमधराञ्चं पादयामि ॥

24. Let us be victorious. Let us be prosperous. Let us be truthful. Let us be energetic. Let us be learned. Let our soul advance. Let our sacrifice be fruitful. Let us own cattle. Let our progeny progress. Let us have brave soldiers. We banish him from the country, for his aggression, who belongs to such a family, is the son of such a woman, and is the enemy of the country. Let him not be freed from the restriction of Day and Night. I bind up his splendour, his energy, his vital breath, his life and cast him down beneath me. (4195)

२५. जितमस्माकमुद्भिन्नमस्माकमृतमस्माकं तेजोऽस्माकं ब्रह्मास्माकं स्वऽरस्माकं
यज्ञो३ऽस्माकं पशवोऽस्माकं प्रजा अस्माकं वीरा अस्माकम् ।
तस्मादमुं निर्भजामोऽमुमामुष्यायणममुष्याः पुत्रमसौ यः ।
सोऽह्नोः संयतोः पाशान्मा मोचि ।
तस्येदं वर्चस्तेजः प्राणमायुर्नि वेष्टयामीदमेनमधराञ्चं पादयामि ॥

25. Let us be victorious. Let us be prosperous. Let us be truthful. Let us be energetic. Let us be learned. Let our soul advance. Let our sacrifice be fruitful. Let us own cattle. Let our progeny progress. Let us have brave soldiers. We banish him from the country for his aggression, who belongs to such a family, is the son of such a woman, and is the enemy of the country. Let him not be freed from the grip of those who have control over day and night. I bind up his splendour, his energy, his vital breath, his life, and cast him down beneath me. (4196)[1]

२६. जितमस्माकमुद्भिन्नमस्माकमृतमस्माकं तेजोऽस्माकं ब्रह्मास्माकं स्वऽरस्माकं
यज्ञो३ऽस्माकं पशवोऽस्माकं प्रजा अस्माकं वीरा अस्माकम् ।
तस्मादमुं निर्भजामोऽमुमामुष्यायणममुष्याः पुत्रमसौ यः ।
स द्यावापृथिव्योः पाशान्मा मोचि ।
तस्येदं वर्चस्तेजः प्राणमायुर्नि वेष्टयामीदमेनमधराञ्चं पादयामि ॥

26. Let us be victorious, Let us be prosperous. Let us be truthful. Let us be energetic. Let us be learned. Let our soul advance. Let our sacrifice be fruitful. Let us own cattle. Let our progeny progress. Let us have brave soldiers. We banish him from the country, for his aggression, who belongs to such a family, is the son of such a woman, and is the enemy of the country. Let him not be freed from the grip of the Heaven and Earth. I bind up his splendour, his energy, his vital breath, his life, and cast him down beneath me. (4197)

[1]Control over: The Govt. authorities, the Police and C.I.D. officials who secretly watch the actions of the culprits day and night.

२७. जितमस्माकमुद्भिन्नमस्माकमृतमस्माकं तेजोऽस्माकं ब्रह्मास्माकं स्व꣡रस्माकं
यज्ञो३ऽस्माकं पशवोऽस्माकं प्रजा अस्माकं वीरा अस्माकम् ।
तस्मादमुं निर्भजामोऽमुमामुष्यायणममुष्याः पुत्रमसौ यः । स इन्द्राग्न्योः पाशान्मा मोचि ।
तस्येदं वर्चस्तेजः प्राणमायुर्नि वेष्टयामीदमेनमधराञ्चं पादयामि ॥

27. Let us be victorious. Let us be prosperous. Let us be truthful. Let us be energetic. Let us be learned. Let our soul advance. Let our sacrifice be fruitful. Let us own cattle. Let our progeny progress. Let us have brave soldiers. We banish him from the country, for his aggression, who belongs to such a family, is the son of such a woman and is the enemy of the country. Let him not be freed from the hold of lightning and Fire. I bind up his splendour, his energy, his vital breath, his life, and cast him down beneath me. (4198)

२८. जितमस्माकमुद्भिन्नमस्माकमृतमस्माकं तेजोऽस्माकं ब्रह्मास्माकं स्व꣡रस्माकं
यज्ञो३ऽस्माकं पशवोऽस्माकं प्रजा अस्माकं वीरा अस्माकम् ।
तस्मादमुं निर्भजामोऽमुमामुष्यायणममुष्याः पुत्रमसौ यः ।
स मित्रावरुणयोः पाशान्मा मोचि ।
तस्येदं वर्चस्तेजः प्राणमायुर्नि वेष्टयामीदमेनमधराञ्चं पादयामि ॥

28. Let us be victorious. Let us be prosperous. Let us be truthful. Let us be energetic. Let us be learned. Let our soul advance. Let our sacrifice be fruitful. Let us own cattle. Let our progeny progress. Let us have brave soldiers. We banish him from the country, for his aggression, who belongs to such a family, is the son of such a woman, and is the enemy of the country. Let him not be freed from the agony of in-going, out-going breaths. I bind up his splendour, his energy, his vital breath, his life, and cast him down beneath me. (4199)

२९. जितमस्माकमुद्भिन्नमस्माकमृतमस्माकं तेजोऽस्माकं ब्रह्मास्माकं स्व꣡रस्माकं
यज्ञो३ऽस्माकं पशवोऽस्माकं प्रजा अस्माकं वीरा अस्माकम् ।
तस्मादमुं निर्भजामोऽमुमामुष्यायणममुष्याः पुत्रमसौ यः ।
स राज्ञो वरुणस्य पाशान्मा मोचि ।
तस्येदं वर्चस्तेजः प्राणमायुर्नि वेष्टयामीदमेनमधराञ्चं पादयामि ॥

29. Let us be victorious. Let us be prosperous. Let us be truthful. Let us be energetic. Let us be learned. Let our soul advance. Let our sacrifice be fruitful. Let us own cattle. Let our progeny progress. Let us have brave soldiers. We banish him from the country, for his aggression, who belongs to such a family, is the son of such a woman, and is the enemy of the country. Let him not be freed from the control of the excellent King. I bind up his splendour, his energy, his vital breath, his life, and cast him down beneath me. (4200)

३०. जितमस्माकमुद्भिन्नमस्माकमृतमस्माकं तेजोऽस्माकं ब्रह्मास्माकं स्वऽरस्माकं
यज्ञो३ऽस्माकं पशवोऽस्माकं प्रजा अस्माकं वीरा अस्माकम् ॥

30. Let us be victorious. Let us be prosperous. Let us be truthful. Let us be energetic. Let us be learned. Let our soul advance. Let our sacrifice be fruitful. Let us own cattle. Let us progeny progress. Let us have brave soldiers. (4201)

३१. तस्मादमुं निर्भजामोऽमुमामुष्यायणममुष्याः पुत्रमसौ यः ॥

31. We banish him from the country, for his aggression, who belongs to such a family, is the son of such a woman, and is the enemy of the country. (4202)

३२. स मृत्योः षड्वीशात् पाशान्मा मोचि ॥

32. Let him not be freed from the fetter of Death. (4203)

३३. तस्येदं वर्चस्तेजः प्राणमायुर्नि वेष्टयामीदमेनमधराञ्चं पादयामि ॥

33. I bind up his splendour, his energy, his vital breath, his life, and cast him down beneath me. (4204)

HYMN IX

१. जितमस्माकमुद्भिन्नमस्माकमभ्यऽष्ठां विश्वाः पृतना अरातीः ॥

1. Let us be victorious. Let us be prosperous. I have conquered all the hostile forces. (4205)

२. तदग्निराह तदु सोम आह पूषा मा धात् सुकृतस्य लोके ॥

2. Thus does the Wise God preach. Thus does the All-creating God ordain. May the All-sustaining God keep me in the society of the virtuous. (4206)

३. अगन्म स्व१: स्वऽरगन्म सं सूर्यस्य ज्योतिषागन्म ॥

3. May we enjoy the pleasure of knowledge. May we feel the delight of salvation. May we be united with the light of Surya. (4207)

४. वस्योभूयाय वसुमान् यज्ञो वसु वंशिषीय वसुमान् भूयासं वसु मयि धेहि ॥

4. For the increase of prosperity, fain would I be wealthy. Sacrifice (Yajna) is synonymous with prosperity. I would win riches. Do Thou bestow, O God, wealth upon me. (4208)

BOOK (Kāṇḍa) XVII

HYMN I

१. विषासहिं सहमानं सासहानं सहीयांसम् । सहमानं सहोजितं स्वर्जितं गोजितं संधनाजितम् ।
ईड्यं नाम ह्व इन्द्रमायुष्मान् भूयासम् ॥

1. I praise the Adorable God, Indra by name, Vanquishing, Overpowering, the Conqueror, the Subduer of foes. Victorious, the Controller of the mighty the Embodiment of pleasure, the Lord of land and cattle and the Owner of riches. May I enjoy a long life. (4209)

२. विषासहिं सहमानं सासहानं सहीयांसम् । सहमानं सहोजितं स्वर्जितं गोजितं संधनाजितम् ।
ईड्यं नाम ह्व इन्द्रं प्रियो देवानां भूयासम् ॥

2. I praise the Adorable God, Indra by name, Vanquishing, Overpowering, the Conqueror, the Subduer of foes, Victorious, the Controller of the mighty, the Embodiment of pleasure, the Lord of land and cattle, the Owner of riches. May I be dear to the learned. (4210)

३. विषासहिं सहमानं सासहानं सहीयांसम् । सहमानं सहोजितं स्वर्जितं गोजितं संधनाजितम् ।
ईड्यं नाम ह्व इन्द्रं प्रियः प्रजानां भूयासम् ॥

3. I praise the Adorable God, Indra by name, Vanquishing, Overpowering, the Conqueror, the Subduer of foes, Victorious, the Controller of the mighty, the Embodiment of pleasure, the Lord of land and cattle, and the owner of riches. May my countrymen love me well. (4211)

४. विषासहिं सहमानं सासहानं सहीयांसम् । सहमानं सहोजितं स्वर्जितं गोजितं संधनाजितम् ।
ईड्यं नाम ह्व इन्द्रं प्रियः पशूनां भूयासम् ॥

4. I praise the Adorable God, Indra by name, and Vanquishing, Overpowering, the Conqueror, the Subduer of foes, Victorious, the Controller of the mighty, the Embodiment of pleasure, the Lord of land and cattle, and the Owner of riches. May mankind love me. (4212)

५. विषासहिं सहमानं सासहानं सहीयांसम् । सहमानं सहोजितं स्वर्जितं गोजितं संधनाजितम् ।
ईड्यं नाम ह्व इन्द्रं प्रियः समानानां भूयासम् ॥

5. I praise the Adorable God, Indra by name, Vanquishing. Overpowering, the Conqueror, the Subduer of foes, Victorious, the Controller of the mighty, the Embodiment of pleasure, the Lord of land and cattle, and the Owner of riches, May equals love me well. (4213)

६. उदिह्युदिहि सूर्य वर्चसा माभ्युदिहि ।
द्विषंश्च मह्यं रध्यतु मा चाहं द्विषते रधं तवेद् विष्णो बहुधा वीर्या॒णि ।
त्वं नः पृणीहि पशुभिर्विश्वरूपैः सुधायां मा धेहि परमे व्यो॒मन् ॥

6. Rise up, O All-pervading God, rise Thou up; with strength and splendour rise on me. Let him who hates me be my thrall; let me not be a thrall to him. Manifold are Thy great deeds. Thine, O God! Sate us with creatures of all forms and colours: set me in happiness, in the loftiest position! (4214)[1]

७. उदिह्युदिहि सूर्य वर्चसा माभ्युदिहि ।
यांश्च पश्यामि यांश्च न तेषु मा सुमतिं कृधि तवेद् विष्णो बहुधा वीर्याऽणि ।
त्वं नः पृणीहि पशुभिर्विश्वरूपैः सुधायां मा धेहि परमे व्योऽमन् ॥

7. Rise up, O All-pervading God, rise up; with strength and splendour rise on me. Make me the favourite of all, of those I see and do not see. Manifold are Thy great deeds, Thine, O God! Sate us with creatures of all forms and colours: set me in happiness in the loftiest position. (4215)

८. मा त्वा दभन्त्सलिले अप्स्व१न्तर्ये पाशिन उपतिष्ठन्त्यत्र ।
हित्वाशस्ति दिवमारुक्ष एतां स नो मृड सुमतौ ते स्याम तवेद् विष्णो बहुधा वीर्याऽणि ।
त्वं नः पृणीहि पशुभिर्विश्वरूपैः सुधायां मा धेहि परमे व्योऽमन् ॥

8. O God, the violent physical disturbances, wrought by Matter in this world, in the atmosphere and primary subtle elements, subdue. Thee not. Caring not for infamy, Thou art exalted in Thy behaviour. Grant us happiness. Let Thy gracious love attend us. Manifold are Thy great deeds, Thine, O God! Sate us with creatures of all forms and colours: set me in happiness in the loftiest position. (4216)[2]

९. त्वं न इन्द्र महते सौभगायादब्धेभिः परि पाह्यक्तुभिस्तवेद् विष्णो बहुधा वीर्याऽणि ।
त्वं नः पृणीहि पशुभिर्विश्वरूपैः सुधायां मा धेहि परमे व्योऽमन् ॥

9. Do Thou, O God, for our great good fortune, with thine inviolable lights of knowledge protect us! Manifold are Thy great deeds, Thine, O God! Sate us with creatures of all forms and colours: set me in happiness in the loftiest position. (4217)

१०. त्वं न इन्द्रोतिभिः शिवाभिः शंतमो भव ।
आरोहंस्त्रिदिवं दिवो गृणानः सोमपीतये प्रियधामा स्वस्तये तवेद् विष्णो बहुधा वीर्याऽणि ।
त्वं नः पृणीहि पशुभिर्विश्वरूपैः सुधायां मा धेहि परमे व्योऽमन् ॥

10. O God, with Thy favourable aids, rising high in the award of three boons, preaching just dealings unto us, a Friend of humanity, for the safety of our prosperity, and for our welfare, he most gracious unto us! Manifold are Thy great deeds, Thine, O God! Sate us with creatures of all forms and colours: set me in happiness in the loftiest position. (4218)[3]

[1]Rise on me: Show thy splendour and might to me.
[2]Disturbances: Rain, storm, thunder of lightning, inundation, earthquake etc. (अप्सु) आपो व्यापिकास्तनमात्राः दयानन्द भाष्ये—यजु० 27-25.
[3]Three boons: Income, Expenditure, Increase.

११. त्वमिन्द्रासि विश्वजित् सर्ववित् पुरुहूतस्त्वमिन्द्र ।
त्वमिन्द्रेमं सुहवं स्तोममेरयस्व स नो मृड सुमतौ ते स्याम तवेद् विष्णो बहुधा वीर्याऽणि ।
त्वं नः पृणीहि पशुभिर्विश्वरूपैः सुधायां मा धेहि परमे व्योऽमन् ।।

11. Thou art the Vanquisher of all, O God! Thou art Omniscient, and invoked by the sages. O God! accept this hymn that fitly lauds Thee. Favour us: let Thy gracious love attend us. Manifold are Thy great deeds, Thine, O God! Sate us with creatures of all forms and colours: set me in happiness in the loftiest position. (4219)

१२. अदब्धो दिवि पृथिव्यामुतासि न त आपुर्महिमानमन्तरिक्षे ।
अदब्धेन ब्रह्मणा वावृधानः स त्वं न इन्द्र दिवि षंच्छर्म यच्छ तवेद् विष्णो बहुधा वीर्याऽणि ।
त्वं नः पृणीहि पशुभिर्विश्वरूपैः सुधायां मा धेहि परमे व्योऽमन् ।।

12. O God, Thou art eternal in the region of emancipation and on earth. No soul can reach Thy greatness in the air's mid-region. Exalted by inviolate Vedic knowledge, as such, grant us happiness in salvation! Manifold are Thy great deeds, Thine, O God! Sate us with creatures of all forms and colours: set me in happiness in the loftiest position. (4220)

१३. या त इन्द्र तनूरप्सु या पृथिव्यां यान्तरग्नौ या त इन्द्र पवमाने स्वर्विदि ।
ययेन्द्र तन्वा३न्तरिक्षं व्यापिथ तया न इन्द्र तन्वा३ शर्म यच्छ तवेद् विष्णो
बहुधा वीर्याऽणि ।
त्वं नः पृणीहि पशुभिर्विश्वरूपैः सुधायां मा धेहि परमे व्योऽमन् ।।

13. O God, grant us happiness, with that power of creation of thine that is on earth, in fire, in waters, in purifying, ease-bestowing air, wherewith Thou hast pervaded in air's mid-region. Manifold are Thy great deeds, Thine O God! Sate us with creatures of all forms and colours : set me in happiness in the loftiest position. (4221)

१४. त्वामिन्द्र ब्रह्मणा वर्धयन्तः सत्रं नि षेदुर्ऋषयो नाधमानास्तवेद् विष्णो बहुधा वीर्याऽणि ।
त्वं नः पृणीहि-पशुभिर्विश्वरूपैः सुधायां मा धेहि परमे व्योऽमन् ।।

14. O God, extolling Thee with Vedic verses, imploring for salvation, the sages are absorbed in the sacrifice (Yajna) of knowledge. Manifold are Thy great deeds, Thine, O God! Sate us with creatures of all forms and colours: set me in happiness in the loftiest position. (4222)

१५. त्वं तृतं त्वं पर्येष्युत्सं सहस्रधारं विदथं स्वर्विदं तवेद् विष्णो बहुधा वीर्याऽणि ।
त्वं नः पृणीहि पशुभिर्विश्वरूपैः सुधायां मा धेहि परमे व्योऽमन् ।।

15. O God, Thou pervadest the vast atmosphere, and the excellent knowledge, that sustains the universe and gives us the joy of salvation! Manifold are Thy great deeds, Thine! O God! Sate us with creatures of all forms and colours: set me in happiness in the loftiest position. (4223)

१६. त्वं रक्षसे प्रदिशश्चतस्रस्त्वं शोचिषा नभसी वि भासि ।
त्वमिमा विश्वा भुवनानु तिष्ठस ऋतस्य पन्थामन्वेषि विद्वांस्तवेद् विष्णो
बहुधा वीर्याऽणि ।
त्वं नः पृणीहि पशुभिर्विश्वरूपैः सुधायां मा धेहि परमे व्योऽमन् ॥

16. O God, Thou guardest well the denizens of the four celestial regions. With Thy light and splendour Thou illuminest the heaven and earth. Thou givest help to all these living creatures. Being Omniscient Thou followest the path of truth. Manifold are Thy great deeds, Thine, O God. Sate us with creatures of all forms and colours: set me in happiness in the loftiest position. (4224)[1]

१७. पञ्चभिः पराङ् तपस्येकयार्वाङशस्तिमेषि सुदिने बाधमानस्तवेद् विष्णो बहुधा वीर्याऽणि ।
त्वं नः पृणीहि पशुभिर्विश्वरूपैः सुधायां मा धेहि परमे व्योऽमन् ॥

17. O God, Thou shinest afar from five! Thou shinest near one! Removing the curse of ignorance, Thou comest hither unto us in full lustre. Manifold are Thy great deeds, Thine, O God! Sate us with creatures of all forms and colours: set me in happiness in the loftiest position. (4225)[2]

१८. त्वमिन्द्रस्त्वं महेन्द्रस्त्वं लोकस्त्वं प्रजापतिः ।
तुभ्यं यज्ञो वि तायते तुभ्यं जुह्वति जुह्वतस्तवेद् विष्णो बहुधा वीर्याऽणि ।
त्वं नः पृणीहि पशुभिर्विश्वरूपैः सुधायां मा धेहि परमे व्योऽमन् ॥

18. O God, Thou art Mighty. Thou art Mightier than the mighty. Thou art the seer of all. Thou art the Nourisher of mankind. All acts of charity, worship, sacrifice are performed in obedience to Thy behest. Worshippers offer worship unto Thee. Manifold are Thy great deeds, Thine, O God! Sate us with creatures of all forms and colours: set me in happiness in the loftiest position. (4226)

१९. असति सत् प्रतिष्ठितं सति भूतं प्रतिष्ठितम् ।
भूतं ह भव्य आहितं भव्यं भूते प्रतिष्ठितं तवेद् विष्णो बहुधा वीर्याऽणि ।
त्वं नः पृणीहि पशुभिर्विश्वरूपैः सुधायां मा धेहि परमे व्योऽमन् ॥

19. In the impermanent world exists the Permanent God. On Immortal God depends this transitory world. Past is imposed on future, future is based on the past. Manifold are Thy great deeds, Thine, O God! Sate us with creatures off all forms and colours, set me in happiness in the loftiest position. (4227)[3]

[1]Four regions: East, South, West, North.

[2]Five: Five breaths or five elements. One: Mind or Matter.

[3]Past and Future are interlinked. The future of a nation depends upon the inspiration it derives from its glorious past. The examples of virtue, valour and nobility of character set by the ancients serves as land-marks for future posterity. The past of a country has a hand in shaping its future.

२०. शुक्रोऽसि भ्राजोऽसि । स यथा त्वं भ्राजता भ्राजोऽस्येवाहं भ्राजता भ्राज्यासम् ॥

20. O God, Pure art Thou, and Refulgent as Thou shinest with splendour, so I fain would shine with splendour! (4228)[1]

२१. रुचिरसि रोचोऽसि । स यथा त्वं रुच्या रोचोऽस्येवाहं पशुभिश्च
ब्राह्मणवर्चसेन च रुचिषीय ॥

21. O God, Thou art the Embodiment of Beauty. Highly Beautiful art Thou! As thou glowest with beauty so I too would shine with cattle and the lustre of learning. (4229)

२२. उद्यते नम उदायते नम उदिताय नमः । विराजे नमः स्वराजे नमः सम्राजे नमः ॥

22. Obeisance to God between the time of Dissolution and Creation. Obeisance to God at the time of Creation. Obeisance to God at the time of Dissolution of the universe. To Him Far-shining, the Self-Refulgent, to Him the Supreme Ruler be obeisance. (4230)[2]

२३. अस्तंयते नमोऽस्तमेष्यते नमोऽस्तमिताय नमः । विराजे नमः स्वराजे नमः सम्राजे नमः ॥

23. Obeisance to God between the time of Creation and Dissolution, Obeisance to God at the time of Dissolution, Obeisance to God at the time of creation of the universe. To Him Far-shining, the Self-Refulgent, to Him the Supreme Ruler be obeisance. (4231)

२४. उदगादयमादित्यो विश्वेन तपसा सह ।
सपत्नान् मह्यं रन्धयन् मा चाहं द्विषते रधं तवेद् विष्णो बहुधा वीर्याणि ।
त्वं नः पृणीहि पशुभिर्विश्वरूपैः सुधायां मा धेहि परमे व्योमन् ॥

24. With all His lustre this God hath manifested Himself in full glory, giving my foes into my hand. Let me not be my foeman's prey. Manifold are Thy great deeds, Thine, O God. Sate us with creatures of all forms and colours: set me in happiness in the loftiest position. (4232)

२५. आदित्य नावमारुक्षः शतारित्रां स्वस्तये । अहर्मात्यपीपरो रात्रिं सत्राति पारय ॥

25. O God, the Goader of the universe, Thou possessest for the good of humanity, the power of controlling the world, and sheltering innumerable beings. Thou hast made me perform my duty during the day, let me also perform me my duty during the night. (4233)

२६. सूर्य नावमारुक्षः शतारित्रां स्वस्तये । रात्रिं मात्यपीपरोऽहः सत्राति पारय ॥

26. O God, the Master of all, for the good of humanity, Thou possessest the power of urging the world, and making us tide over untold sufferings. Thou hast made me perform my duty during the night, let me also perform my duty during the day. (4234)

[1] I: The devotee. [2] Obeisance: Worship, salutation.

२७. प्रजापतेरावृतो ब्रह्मणा वर्मणाहं कश्यपस्य ज्योतिषा वर्चसा च ।
जरदष्टिः कृतवीर्यो विहायाः सहस्रायुः सुकृतश्चरेयम् ॥

27. Encompassed by God's Vedic knowledge as shield, with the bright light and splendour of God, the seer, reaching old age, may I, made strong and learned, live through a thousand years doing noble deeds. (4235)[1]

२८. परीवृतो ब्रह्मणा वर्मणाहं कश्यपस्य ज्योतिषा वर्चसा च ।
मा मा प्रापन्निषवो दैव्या या मा मानुषीरवसृष्टा वधाय ॥

28. Protected am I by Vedic knowledge, my shield and armour, protected by the bright light and splendour of God, the Seer, let not the calamities sent forth by natural forces reach me, nor those sent forth by men for my destruction. (4236)

२९. ऋतेन गुप्त ऋतुभिश्च सर्वैर्भूतेन गुप्तो भव्येन चाहम् ।
मा मा प्रापत् पाप्मा मोत मृत्युरन्तर्दधेऽहं सलिलेन वाचः ॥

29. Guarded am I by Truth and all the learned lovers of truth, protected by the past and by the future. Let not sin, yea, let not the fear of Death come nigh me : I defend myself with the force of Vedic knowledge. (4237)

३०. अग्निर्मा गोप्ता परि पातु विश्वत उद्यन्त्सूर्यो नुदतां मृत्युपाशान् ।
व्युच्छन्तीरुषसः पर्वता ध्रुवाः सहस्रं प्राणा मय्या यतन्ताम् ॥

30. On every side let Protecting God guard and save me; may the exalted God drive off the snares of Death. Let brightly flushing Dawns, firm-set mountains and manifold spiritual and physical forces be united with me. (4238)

BOOK (Kāṇḍa) XVIII

HYMN I

१. ओ चित् सखायं सख्या ववृत्यां तिरः पुरू चिदर्णवं जगन्वान् ।
पितुर्नपातमा दधीत वेधा अधि क्षमि प्रतरं दीध्यानः ॥

1. Fain would I win my friend to kindly friendship. O master of religious lore, highly brilliant and wise as thou art, let us obtain on the earth, through wedlock, the grandson of thy father. (4239)[2]

[1]God is spoken of as Prajāpati, as he protects and nourishes his subjects, i.e., all creatures. He is Kashayapa as He sees every thing.

[2]The first sixteen verses of this hymn are a dialogue between Yama and Yami, brother and sister, whereby marriage between real brother and sister is condemned. The description is superbly beautiful and instructive. In the first verse the sister asks the brother to marry her and produce a son. See *Rig*, 10-10-1· (अर्णवम्) अर्णवम् विज्ञानम्—Dayananda commentary *Yajur*, 12-49.

२. न ते सखा सख्यं वष्टयेतत् सलक्ष्मा यद् विषुरूपा भवाति ।
महस्पुत्रासो असुरस्य वीरा दिवो धर्तार उर्विया परि ख्यन् ।।

2. Thy friend loves not the friendship which considers her who is near in relation as a stranger. The brave sons. behaving like a wise person, have condemned such an alliance on the earth. (4240)[1]

३. उशन्ति घा ते अमृतास एतदेकस्य चित् त्यजसं मर्त्यस्य ।
नि ते मनो मनसि धाय्यस्मे जन्युः पतिस्तन्व१मा विविश्याः ।।

3. It is a well known fact, even the pure emancipated souls long for a scion of a unique person. Then let thy soul and mine be knit together. Embrace thy consort as her loving husband. (4241)[2]

४. न यत् पुरा चकृमा कद्ध नूनमृतं वदन्तो अनृतं रपेम ।
गन्धर्वो अप्स्वप्या च योषा सा नौ नाभिः परमं जामि तन्नौ ।।

4. Shall we do now what we never did before? Should we who spoke righteously talk impurely now. Man is born of semen and so is woman born of the same semen, such is our Kinship. Our mutual blood relation stands in the way of our wedlock. (4242)[3]

५. गर्भे नु नौ जनिता दम्पती कर्देवस्त्वष्टा सविता विश्वरूपः ।
नकिरस्य प्र मिनन्ति व्रतानि वेद नावस्य पृथिवी उत द्यौः ।।

5. Even in the womb God, the Creator, Vivifier, the Shaper of all forms, made us consorts. Ne'er are His holy laws transgressed : our father and mother know this act of God. (4243)[4]

६. को अद्य युङ्क्ते धुरि गा ऋतस्य शिमीवतो भामिनो दुर्हृणायून् ।
आसन्निषून् हृत्स्वसो मयोभून् य एषां भृत्यामृणधत् स जीवात् ।।

6. God ever yokes to the burden of heavy responsibility, the eulogisers of truth, the doers of noble deeds, the heroic, the indignant despisers of foes, the dischargers of arrows on the target, the piercers of the hearts of enemies, the bestowers of joy on the virtuous. Long shall he live who duly pays them homage. (4244)[5]

[1]Yama replies, I cannot marry you, you belong to the same family, to which I belong. Marriage can take place between man and woman belonging to different gotras i.e., families. All learned persons in the world condemn the marriage of brother and sister. See *Rig*, 10-10-2.

[2]Yami speaks. Don't say that wise persons have condemned such an alliance. Even emancipated souls long to see the son of a matchless man. See *Rig*, 10-10-13.

[3]Yama speaks. Spoke: Behaved. Same semen: The same source of parentage, the same father. As our father is the same, we are hence brother and sister, and cannot marry each other. See *Rig*, 10-10-4.

[4]See *Rig*, 10-10-5. Yami speaks; and argues that by making them of different sexes the Creator manifestly intended them to behave like husband and wife.

[5]See *Rig*, 1-84-16. This verse has been interpreted by Maharshi Dayananda in the *Rigvedā* in a different manner, as dilating upon the duties of a general Yama says to

७. को अस्य वेद प्रथमस्याह्नः क ईं ददर्श क इह प्र वोचत् ।
बृहन्मित्रस्य वरुणस्य धाम कदु ब्रव आहनो वीच्या नॄन् ॥

7. Who knows that earliest day whereof thou speakest? Who hath beheld it? Who can here declare it? Great is the law of God, the Urger and Excellent. What, wanton, wilt thou say to men to tempt them? (4245)[1]

८. यमस्य मा यम्यं१ काम आगन्त्समाने योनौ सहशेय्याय ।
जायेव पत्ये तन्वं१ रिरिच्यां वि चिद् वृहेव रथ्येव चक्रा ॥

8. I Yami am possessed by love of Yama, that I may rest on the same couch beside him. I as a wife would yield myself to my husband. Let us be united together in wedlock like the wheels of a car. (4246)[2]

९. न तिष्ठन्ति न नि मिषन्त्येते देवानां स्पश इह ये चरन्ति ।
अन्येन मदाहनो याहि तूयं तेन वि वृह रथ्येव चक्रा ॥

9. The moral laws of the learned never stop in their application, nor do they ever slacken. Ye wanton, go quickly with another besides me, and be united with him in wedlock like the two wheels of a car. (4247)[3]

१०. रात्रीभिरस्मा अहभिर्दशस्येत् सूर्यस्य चक्षुर्मुहुरुन्मिमीयात् ।
दिवा पृथिव्या मिथुना सबन्धू यमीर्यमस्य विवृहादजामि ॥

10. Let nights and days teach wisdom to this Yama, let the light of the Sun fall on him again and again to open his eyes. If both the Sun and Earth can live together, why cannot I live with Yama discarding our relation of a brother and sister. (4248)[4]

११. आ घा ता गच्छानुत्तरा युगानि यत्र जामयः कृणवन्नजामि ।
उप बर्बृहि वृषभाय बाहुमन्यमिच्छस्व सुभगे पतिं मत् ॥

11. Sure there will come future times when brothers and sisters will do acts unfit for kinsfolk. O fair one, seek another husband besides me, and extend thine arm for thy consort! (4249)[5]

Yami, you should behave like truthful and noble people, and utter not the false and immoral words that brother and sister are made husband and wife by God in the womb of the mother.

[1]Yama speaks. Thy argument of our being destined as husband and wife in the womb, is absolutely wrong. None knows that earliest day of conception, none has seen it. None can speak of it. Don't tempt men thou licentious woman by such false arguments. See *Rig*, 10-10-6.

[2]See *Rig*, 10-10-7.

[3]Yama replies, the moral laws of the learned are inviolable, hence I cannot my sister. See *Rig*, 10-10-8.

[4]Yami speaks. If days and nights being brother and sister can live as husband and wife, and the Sun and Earth mutually related can live as husband and wife, then why can't I, his sister live with him as wife, casting aside our near relation. He should open his eyes and learn wisdom from these material objects. See *Rig*, 10-10-9.

[5]See *Rig*, 10-10-10. A time may come when brothers and sisters will be united in wedlock, but I am not prepared to commit this immoral act.

१२. किं भ्रातासद् यदनाथं भवाति किमु स्वसा यन्निर्ऋतिर्निगच्छात् ।
कामभूता बह्व् ३तद् रपामि तन्वा॒ मे तन्वं१ सं पिपृग्धि ॥

12. Is he a brother, who leaves the sister helpless? Is she a sister who saves not his brother from destruction? Impelled by lust I utter these many words. Come near, and hold me in thy close embrace. (4250)[1]

१३. न ते नाथं यम्यत्राहमस्मि न ते तनूं तन्वा३ सं पपृच्याम् ।
अन्येन मत् प्रमुदः कल्पयस्व न ते भ्राता सुभगे वष्टचेतत् ॥

13. O Yami, I am not thy lord, hence I will not clasp and press thee to my bosom. Search for another person, besides me for enjoyment! I your brother do not like to become your husband. (4251)[2]

१४. न वा उ ते तनूं तन्वा३ सं पपृच्यां पापमाहुर्यः स्वसारं निगच्छात् ।
असंयदेतन्मनसो हृदो मे भ्राता स्वसुः शयने यच्छयीय ॥

14. O Yami, I will not fold my arms about thy body: the sages call it sin that a brother should cohabit his sister! This is abhorrent to my mind and spirit, that a brother should sleep on the same couch beside his sister. (4252)[3]

१५. बतो बतासि यम नैव ते मनो हृदयं चाविदाम ।
अन्या किल त्वां कक्ष्ये॒व युक्तं परि ष्वजातै लिबुजेव वृक्षम् ॥

15. Alas! thou art indeed a weakling, Yama. I have not been able to understand thy mind or spirit. Another woman will cling about thee, as the woodbine clings round a tree or a girdle about a yoked horse. (4253)[4]

१६. अन्यमू षु यम्यन्य उ त्वां परि ष्वजातै लिबुजेव वृक्षम् ।
तस्य वा त्वं मन इच्छा स वा तवाधा कृणुष्व संविदं सुभद्राम् ॥

16. O Yami, embrace another person. Let some one else embrace thee, as the woodbine clings round a tree! Win thou his heart and let him win thy fancy; so make with him a bond of blest alliance. (4254)

१७. त्रीणि च्छन्दांसि कवयो वि येतिरे पुरुरूपं दर्शतं विश्वचक्षणम् ।
आपो वाता ओषधयस्तान्येकस्मिन् भुवन आर्पितानि ॥

17. Learned persons have utilised in different projects, the three objects, which pervade the universe and are obtainable everywhere. They are multiformed, fair, all-beholding. These in one single world are placed and settled —the waters, the breezes, the growing plants. (4255)

[1]See *Rig*, 10-10-11. Destruction: Utter extinction of the family for refusal to marry.
[2]See *Rig*, 10-10-12. [3]See *Rig*, 10-10-12. [4]See *Rig*, 10-10-13.

१८. वृषा वृष्णे दुदुहे दोहसा दिवः पयांसि यह्वो अदितेरदाभ्यः ।
विश्वं स वेद वरुणो यथा धिया स यज्ञियो यजति यज्ञियाँ ऋतून् ॥

18. The Mighty, Immortal, Resplendent God, has provided innumerable delights for an enterprising person, through the wholeness of pleasure-giving Vedic speech. Just as the Almighty God knows the whole universe through His strength, so does a noble sacrificer values all precious seasons. (4256)[1]

१९. रपद् गन्धर्वीरप्या च योषणा नदस्य नादे परि पातु नो मनः ।
इष्टस्य मध्ये अदितिर्नि धातु नो भ्राता नो ज्येष्ठः प्रथमो वि वोचति ॥

19. Vedic speech, the preserver of the learned, the teacher of knowledge and action, worthy of adoration, clearly sings the glory of God. May He protect from all sides our knowledge for honouring His eulogiser. May the Vedic speech ever fulfil our desires. God, the Sustainer, Most Gracious, Foremost, instructs us first of all. (4257)[2]

२०. सो चिन्नु भद्रा क्षुमती यशस्वत्युषा उवास मनवे स्वर्वती ।
यदीमुशन्तमुशतामनु क्रतुमग्निं होतारं विदथाय जीजनन् ॥

20. Verily the Vedic speech, the well-wisher of mankind, replete with ennobling Vedic verses, full of moral vigour, the exhibitor of all objects like the Dawn, the imparter of knowledge, has been revealed for man. Out of those aspiring after various aims, the learned, for the acquisition of Vedic knowledge, bring forth him who is energetic, wise, magnanimous, and hankers after nothing but Vedic wisdom. (4258)[3]

२१. अध त्यं द्रप्सं विभ्वं विचक्षणं विराभरदिषिरः श्येनो अध्वरे ।
यदी विशो वृणते दस्ममार्या अग्निं होतारमध धीरजायत ॥

21. A determined, wise, soul attains to that gladdening, All-pervading and Learned God. When noble energetic seekers after truth, attain to that Beautiful, Merciful, Self-Refulgent God, then true knowledge dawns upon them. (4259)[4]

२२. सदासि रण्वो यवसेव पुष्यते होत्राभिरग्ने मनुषः स्वध्वरः ।
विप्रस्य वा यच्छशमान उक्थ्यो३ वाजं ससवाँ उपयासि भूरिभिः ॥

22. Just as a cattle fed on grass appears strong and beautiful to the owner, so dost Thou O God, being Immortal, always look elegant through the praises of man. When Thou art constantly admired and rightly interpreted, Thou, bestowing knowledge and power, are visualised in various ways. (4260)[5]

[1]Values: Makes the best use of. See *Rig*, 10-11-1.

[2]See *Rig*, 10-11-2. Griffith interprets Gandharvi to be the daughter of Surabbi, one of the daughters of Dakshan and the mother of the race of horses. This interpretation is unacceptable as there is no history in the Vedas. The word means, the Vedic speech that preserves the learned.

[3]See *Rig*, 10-11-3. [4]See *Rig*, 10-11-4. [5]See *Rig*, 10-11-5.

२३. उदीरय पितरा जार आ भगमियक्षति हर्यतो हृत्त इष्यति ।
विवक्ति वह्निः स्वपस्यते मखस्तविष्यते असुरो वेपते मती ॥

23. Just as the Sun spreads his lustre to all places, so shouldst thou, O man! extend thy wealth to thy parents. He who wants to worship them, being full of love for them, likes them from the bottom of his heart. God, the Lord of knowledge, instructs us in diverse ways. The Adorable God impels us to noble deeds. The Bestower of vital breaths makes us grow, and the sinners tremble with His might. (4261)[1]

२४. यस्ते अग्ने सुमतिं मर्तो अख्यत् सहसः सूनो अति स प्र शृण्वे ।
इषं दधानो वहमानो अश्वैरा स द्युमाँ अमवान् भूषति द्यून् ॥

24. Far-famed is he, the mortal man, O God! the Originator of power, who preaches Thy knowledge to others. He, gathering power, borne onward by his horses, in his splendour and might lives long for many days. (4262)[2]

२५. श्रुधी नो अग्ने सदने सधस्थे युक्ष्वा रथममृतस्य द्रवित्नुम् ।
आ नो वह रोदसी देवपुत्रे माकिर्देवानामप भूरिह स्याः ॥

25. O soul, listen to our prayer in the Assembly Hall. Harness thy rapid divine felicity. Equip thyself with Prāna and Apāna, vast like the Sun and Earth, the guardians of the learned. Be never afar from the organs. Always remain happy in their midst. (4263)[3]

२६. यदग्न एषा समितिर्भवाति देवी देवेषु यजता यजत्र ।
रत्ना च यद् विभजासि स्वधावो भागं नो अत्र वसुमन्तं वीतात् ॥

26. O Wise, Adorable God, when this laudable, brilliant concentration is focussed in the vital breaths, and when thou, Almighty God, dealest forth treasures, vouchsafe us too our portion of the riches. (4264)[4]

२७. अन्वग्निरुषसामग्रमख्यदन्वहानि प्रथमो जातवेदाः ।
अनु सूर्य उषसो अनु रश्मीननु द्यावापृथिवी आ विवेश ॥

27. The All-Pervading God hath incessantly created the vast Dawns. The Primordial, Knowledge-bestowing God hath uninterruptedly brought the days into existence. The same All-Impelling God, hath pervaded the earth and heaven, after the Dawns, after their rays of brightness. (4265)[5]

२८. प्रत्यग्निरुषसामग्रमख्यत् प्रत्यहानि प्रथमो जातवेदाः ।
प्रति सूर्यस्य पुरुधा च रश्मीन् प्रति द्यावापृथिवी आ ततान ॥

[1]Them: The parents. See *Rig*, 10-11-6.
[2]See *Rig*, 10-11-7. [3]See *Rig*, 10-11-9. [4]See *Rig*, 10-11-8.
[5]See *Atharva*, 7-82-4. See *Rig*, 4-13-1.

28. The All-pervading God hath explicitly created the vast Dawns. The Primordial, knowledge-bestowing God hath explicitly brought the days into existence. He hath extended explicitly in diverse forms the rays of the Sun; Heaven and Earth hath He extended. (4266)[1]

२९. द्यावा ह क्षामा प्रथमे ऋतेनाभिश्रावे भवतः सत्यवाचा ।
देवो यन्मर्तान् यजथाय कृण्वन्त्सीदद्धोता प्रत्यङ् स्वमसुं यन् ॥

29. Father and mother, first of all verily attain to fame, through truthful speech and Vedic knowledge. When God urges men to worship, He shines invisibly, controlling mankind, and pervading all like the subtle breath. (4267)[2]

३०. देवो देवान् परिभूर्ऋतेन वहा नो हव्यं प्रथमश्चिकित्वान् ।
धूमकेतुः समिधा भाऋजीको मन्द्रो होता नित्यो वाचा यजीयान् ॥

30. God controls all beneficial objects. O God, Thou art Omniscient, Immemorial ! Let us visualise Thy laudable nature through true knowledge. Thou art lustrous like fire, equipped with knowledge that cuts short all shackles, Beautiful, joyous, Most Charitable, Immortal and Worthy of worship through Vedic verses. (4268)[3]

३१. अर्चामि वां वर्धायापो घृतस्नू द्यावाभूमी शृणुतं रोदसी मे ।
अहा यद् देवा असुनीतिमायन् मध्वा नो अत्र पितरा शिशीताम् ॥

31. O father and mother, the purifiers of soul with knowledge, the controllers of vital breaths, listen to my praise. I admire ye both for the advancement of knowledge and noble acts. While days and revolving worlds go to God, the Bestower of breath, let ye, the parents sharpen us with knowledge. (4269)[4]

३२. स्वावृग् देवस्यामृतं यदी गोरतो जातासो धारयन्त उर्वी ।
विश्वे देवा अनु तत् ते यजुर्गुर्दुहे यदेनी दिव्यं घृतं वाः ॥

32. As the life-infusing power of God is easily available to the Earth; hence through it, the created beings sustain themselves on the Earth. O God, all learned persons follow that venerable act of Thine, as the revolving earth yields beautiful, invigorating, and excellent substances. (4270)[5]

३३. किं स्विन्नो राजा जगृहे कदस्याति व्रतं चकृमा को वि वेद ।
मित्रश्चिद्धि ष्मा जुहुराणो देवाञ्छ्लोको न यातामपि वाजो अस्ति ॥

[1]See *Atharva*, 7-82-5. [2]See *Rig*, 10-12-1.
[3]See *Rig*, 10-12-2. [4]See *Rig*, 10-12-4.
[5]It: Life-infusing power. See *Rig*, 10-12-3.

33. Why does God punish us? What law of His have we violated? This He alone knows. Even punishing the crooked, voluptuous souls, He is still their Friend. Is He, worthy of adoration by all, not the sole shelter of those who leave this world for the other. (4271)[1]

३४. दुर्मन्त्वत्रामृतस्य नाम सलक्ष्मा यद् विषुरूपा भवाति ।
यमस्य यो मनवते सुमन्त्वग्ने तमृष्व पाह्यप्रयुच्छन् ॥

34. In this world it is hard to understand the nature of soul, as the same uniform soul assumes different forms. O Great God, guard ceaselessly, him who ponders over Thy attributes easy to be comprehended. (4272)[2]

३५. यस्मिन् देवा विदथे मादयन्ते विवस्वतः सदने धारयन्ते ।
सूर्ये ज्योतिरदधुर्मास्य१क्तून् परि द्योतनिं चरतो अजस्रा ॥

35. Divine laws rejoice in the midst of knowledge, in God, where they operate in God's abode. They have given the Moon her beams, the Sun his splendour: the two unweariedly revolve round their orbit. (4273)[3]

३६. यस्मिन् देवा मन्मनि संचरन्त्यपीच्ये३ न वयमस्य विद्म ।
मित्रो नो अत्रादितिरनागान्त्सविता देवो वरुणाय वोचत् ॥

36. We do not know the Inscrutable God, Who is worthy of meditation. May God, the Friend, Immortal, the Creator, preach unto us the sinless and His devotee. (4274)[4]

३७. सखाय आ शिषामहे ब्रह्मेन्द्राय वज्रिणे । स्तुष ऊ षु नृतमाय धृष्णवे ॥

37. O Companions, we long for Vedic knowledge for worshipping the Almighty, Dignified God! I praise God alone, Who is the Foremost Leader, and the subduer of all. (4275)[5]

३८. शवसा ह्यसि श्रुतो वृत्रहत्येन वृत्रहा । मघैर्मघोनो अति शूर दाशसि ॥

38. O God, Thou art famed for might. Thou art known as the Destroyer of the demon of ignorance, as Thou removest nescience! O Hero, Thou surpassest wealthy persons in rich gifts! (4276)[6]

३९. स्तेगो न क्षामत्येषि पृथिवीं मही नो वाता इह वान्तु भूमौ ।
मित्रो नो अत्र वरुणो युज्यमानो अग्निर्वने न व्यसृष्ट शोकम् ॥

[1]को विवेद: may also mean who knows that? None knows except God. See *Rig*, 10-12-5.
[2]See *Rig*, 10-12-6.
[3]God's abode: Universe. They: The laws of God. Two: The Sun and Moon. See *Rig*, 10-12-7.
[4]See *Rig*, 10-12-8. [5]See *Rig*, 8-24-1. [6]See *Rig*, 8-24-2.

39. O God, just as a swift deer runs trespassing the great earth, so dost Thou surpass this universe the abode of innumerable souls! Here on vast earth let breeze blow upon us. Thou, our Friend, the Extirpator of afflictions, obtainable through deep concentration (smadhi) spreadest Thy lustre in the universe in diverse ways, like fire in the forest. (4277)[1]

४०. स्तुहि श्रुतं गर्तसदं जनानां राजानं भीममुपहत्नुमुग्रम् ।
मृडा जरित्रे रुद्र स्तवानो अन्यमस्मत् ते नि वपन्तु सेन्यम् ॥

40. O man, sing praise to God, Extolled in the Vedas, seated in the innermost recesses of the heart, Lord of men, Awe-inspiring, Chastiser of all for sinful acts, Almighty, O Maker of sinners weep, praised, be gracious to the learned eulogiser: let Thy forces of destruction spare us and smite down another. (4278)[2]

४१. सरस्वतीं देवयन्तो हवन्ते सरस्वतीमध्वरे तायमाने ।
सरस्वतीं सुकृतो हवन्ते सरस्वती दाशुषे वार्यं दात् ॥

41. The pious recite the Vedas, the word of God. They worship God, while sacrifice (Yajna) proceedeth. The virtuous invoke God. May the Almighty God send bliss to him who giveth. (4279)[3]

४२. सरस्वतीं पितरो हवन्ते दक्षिणा यज्ञमभिनक्षमाणाः ।
आसद्यास्मिन् बर्हिषि मादयध्वमनमीवा इष आ धेह्यस्मे ॥

42. Seated in the south of the Yajna, the learned recite the Vedas. Seated in this sacred Yajna, rejoice you worshippers. O Vedic knowledge, give thou us strengthening food that brings no disease! (4280)[4]

४३. सरस्वति या सरथं ययाथोक्थैः स्वधाभिर्देवि पितृभिर्मदन्ती ।
सहस्रार्घमिडो अत्र भागं रायस्पोषं यजमानाय धेहि ॥

43. O excellent Vedic knowledge, full of hymns noble teachings, and spiritual forces, hast thou come unto us, replete with merriment with the learned! Give in this world to the sacrificer plenteous wealth of thousand branches of valuable knowledge. (4281)[5]

४४. उदीरतामवर उत्परास उन्मध्यमाः पितरः सोम्यासः ।
असुं य ईयुरवृका ऋतज्ञास्ते नोऽवन्तु पितरो हवेषु ॥

[1]See *Rig*, 10-31-9. Steya has been interpreted as deer by Pt. Jaidev Vidyalankara, frog by Sāyana, as gatherer of Yajna's materials by Pt. Khem Karan Das Trivedi and Pt. Dāmodar Satvalekar. Griffith interprets it as a certain biting or stinging insect.

[2]Another: An immoral person, who reviles God. See *Rig*, 2-33-11.

[3]See *Rig*, 10-17-7. [4]See *Rig*, 10-17-8. [5]See *Rig*, 10-17-9.

44. May our parents, who are non-violent, know the truth, gain strength of battle, through control of breath, and protect us well. May the lowest, highest, midmost elders calm and peaceful in nature, urge us on to battle. (4282)[1]

४५. आहं पितॄन्त्सुविदत्राँ अवित्सि नपातं च विक्रमणं च विष्णोः ।
बर्हिषदो ये स्वधया सुतस्य भजन्त पित्वस्त इहागमिष्ठाः ॥

45. I know the elders, who impart sound knowledge. I know the eternal strength of God and His Creation of the universe. May those visit our houses, who solely devoted to God, with their soul-force and self-realisation, worship the Blissful Creator. (4283)[2]

४६. इदं पितृभ्यो नमो अस्त्वद्य ये पूर्वासो ये अपरास ईयुः ।
ये पार्थिवे रजस्या निषत्ता ये वा नूनं सुवृजनासु दिक्षु ॥

46. Now let us offer homage to the learned who are more advanced than us in age and knowledge, who have taken to Banprastha and Sanyās Ashramās, who are experts in statesmanship, and who work amongst the people of high character. (4284)[3]

४७. मातली कव्यैर्यमो अङ्गिरोभिर्बृहस्पतिर्ऋक्वभिर्वावृधानः ।
यांश्च देवा वावृधुर्ये च देवांस्ते नोऽवन्तु पितरो हवेषु ॥

47. An aspirant after knowledge prospers through learned teachers, an ascetic prospers through learned sages a guardian of Vedic knowledge prospers through Vedic scholars. Those whom the learned exalt, they who exalt the learned, may such elders aid us in battles and sacrifices (Yajnas). (4285)[4]

४८. स्वादुष्किलायं मधुमाँ उतायं तीव्रः किलायं रसवाँ उतायम् ।
उतो न्व१स्य पपिवांसमिन्द्रं न कश्चन सहत आहवेषु ॥

48. Yea, knowledge is good to taste and full of sweetness, verily it is invigorating and rich in flavour. No one can conquer the soul in the battles when he hath acquired it! (4286)[5]

[1]See *Rig*, 10-15-1, *Yajur*, 19-49. Highest: Learned teachers and gurus. Midmost: Father, grandfather. Lowest: Pupils, sons, grandsons. They are also called Pitars as they protect their parents and preceptors.

[2]See *Rig*, 10-15-3. *Yajur*, 19-56.

[3]See *Rig*, 10-15-2. See *Yajur*, 19-68.

[4]See *Rig*, 10-14-3. Griffith translates Mâtalī: a divine being identified with Indra whose charioteer was Mātalī. Kavyas: he translates as a class of Manes, the spirits of a pious race of ancient time. He translates Angirases as the typical first charioteers. He translates Rikvans as a class of spirits or deities who attend Brihaspati, and sing his praises. These explanations are unacceptable as they refer to history, but the Vedas are free from history.

[5]See *Rig*, 6-47-1.

४९. परेयिवांसं प्रवतो महीरिति बहुभ्यः पन्थामनुपस्पशानम् ।
वैवस्वतं संगमनं जनानां यमं राजानं हविषा सपर्यत ॥

49. O men, worship God with devotion, Who pervades the distant parts of the Earth, preaches the right path to innumerable souls, is highly Dignified, Controller and Lord of all! (4287)[1]

५०. यमो नो गातुं प्रथमो विवेद नैषा गव्यूतिरपभर्तवा उ ।
यत्रा नः पूर्वे पितरः परेता एना जज्ञानाः पथ्या३ अनु स्वाः ॥

50. The Just God knew in the beginning our path. None can avoid it. Our ancestors have gloriously travelled it, and all created beings will travel it according to their Karmas (deeds). (4288)[2]

५१. बर्हिषदः पितर ऊत्य१र्वागिमा वो हव्या चकृमा जुषध्वम् ।
त आ गतावसा शंतमेनाथा नः शं योररपो दधात ॥

51. O justice loving fathers, who sit in an exalted assembly, come, help us. Accept these eatables we have prepared for ye. Come to us with most auspicious favour, grant us happiness and purity of character, and keep miseries away from us! (4289)[3]

५२. आच्या जानु दक्षिणतो निषद्येदं नो हविरभि गृणन्तु विश्वे ।
मा हिंसिष्ट पितरः केन चिन्नो यद्व आगः पुरुषता कराम ॥

52. O ye all learned people, injure us not for any sin which we through human frailty have committed unto ye! Bowing with the bent knees and seated on the right we pay ye homage. Pray accept this food we offer ye. (4290)

५३. त्वष्टा दुहित्रे वहतुं कृणोति तेनेदं विश्वं भुवनं समेति ।
यमस्य माता पर्युह्यमाना महो जाया विवस्वतो ननाश ॥

53. God creates this vast universe out of Matter, hence this whole world remains in tact. The world producing Matter, a mighty creative force, regularly controlled by God, assumes different forms out of the power of God, the Lord of infinite worlds. (4291)

५४. प्रेहि प्रेहि पथिभिः पूर्याणैर्येना ते पूर्वे पितरः परेताः ।
उभा राजानौ स्वधया मदन्तौ यमं पश्यासि वरुणं च देवम् ॥

[1]See *Rig*, 10-14-1.

[2]God knows from the beginning that every body has to die. None can escape Death, Our ancestors have died. All created beings will die and be reborn according to their good or bad. deeds. See *Rig*, 10-14-2.

[3]See *Rig*, 10-15-4. *Yajur*, 19-55. Fathers: Learned guardians.

54. O man, go forth, go forth upon the pathways that lead to God, whither our sires of old have gone before us. Then shalt thou look on both the Refulgent God, and noble soul both enjoying in their lustrous, mature strength ! (4292)[1]

५५. अपेत वीत वि च सर्पतातोऽस्मा एतं पितरो लोकमक्रन् ।
अहोभिरद्भिरक्तुभिर्व्यक्तं यमो ददात्यवसानमस्मै ॥

55. O soul, thou goest far from this world after death. Thou goest in different directions. Thou finishest thy journey in diverse ways! Our learned ancestors have provided this world for enjoyment for the soul. God bestows for the souls to dwell in, this world adorned with days, waters, nights and beams of light. (4293)[2]

५६. उशन्तस्त्वेधीमह्युशन्तः समिधीमहि । उशन्नुशत आ वह पितॄन् हविषे अत्तवे ॥

56. O God, right gladly do we remember Thee. Right gladly do we nicely enkindle Thee in the heart. O Beautiful God, bring longing, learned persons to the Earth to reap the fruit of their acts! (4294)[3]

५७. द्युमन्तस्त्वेधीमहि द्युमन्तः समिधीमहि । द्युमान् द्युमत आ वह पितॄन् हविषे अत्तवे ॥

57. O God, we, splendid men, deposit Thee, we, splendid men enkindle Thee in the heart! O splendid God, bring splendid learned persons to the Earth to reap the fruit of their acts! (4295)

५८. अङ्गिरसो नः पितरो नवग्वा अथर्वाणो भृगवः सोम्यासः ।
तेषां वयं सुमतौ यज्ञियानामपि भद्रे सौमनसे स्याम ॥

58. Our elders are masters of different principles of knowledge, teachers of new expositions on problems of learning, devotees of non-violence, highly learned and deserving of supremacy. May we follow the sound advice of these adorable elders, and enjoy their gracious loving kindness. (4296)[4]

५९. अङ्गिरोभिर्यज्ञियैरा गहीह यम वैरूपैरिह मादयस्व ।
विवस्वन्तं हुवे यः पिता तेऽस्मिन् बर्हिष्या निषद्य ॥

59. O self-controlled person, come here in our Assembly with adorable highly learned persons, and satisfy us with Vedic knowledge, the expositor of various sciences. Nicely occupying an exalted position, I invoke God, thy Father. (4297)[5]

६०. इमं यम प्रस्तरमा हि रोहाङ्गिरोभिः पितृभिः संविदानः ।
आ त्वा मन्त्राः कविशस्ता वहन्त्वेना राजन्हविषो मादयस्व ॥

[1]See *Rig*, 10-14-7.
[2]See *Rig*, 10-14-9. *Yajur*, 12-45.
[3]See *Rig*, 10-16-12. *Yajur*, 19-70.
[4]See *Rig*, 10-14-6. *Yajur*, 19-50.
[5]See *Rig*, 10-14-5.

60. O King, come, discussing with venerable, elderly Vedic scholars, the art of administration, and seat thyself on this expanded seat (Āsana). May the sermons on statesmanship by the farsighted, wise persons, lead thee on the right path. O King, satisfy these persons with honourable gifts and presents. (4298)[1]

६१. इत एत उदारुहन् दिवस्पृष्ठान्यारुहन् । प्र भूर्जयो यथा पथा द्यामङ्गिरसो ययुः ॥

61. They who are reborn in these beautiful worlds for the enjoyment of the fruit of their actions, go from here, by the same path, by which went up the learned, who cut asunder the shackles of mundane existence and attained to salvation. (4299)

Chapter (Anuvâka) 2

HYMN II

१. यमाय सोमः पवते यमाय क्रियते हविः । यमं ह यज्ञो गच्छत्यग्निदूतो अरंकृतः ॥

1. Soul purifies itself for the attainment of God. To God is homage paid. To God sacrifice adorned with Vedic verses and heralded by fire goes. (4300)[2]

२. यमाय मधुमत्तमं जुहोता प्र च तिष्ठत । इदं नम ऋषिभ्यः पूर्वजेभ्यः पूर्वेभ्यः पथिकृद्भ्यः ॥

2. Use the sweetest, most respectful language for God, and attain to eminence and longevity. Bow down before the Rishis of the olden time, the ancient ones who showed us the path of rectitude. (4301)[3]

३. यमाय घृतवत् पयो राज्ञे हविर्जुहोतन । स नो जीवेष्वा यमेद् दीर्घमायुः प्र जीवसे ॥

3. Dedicate to God, the Just Ruler, resplendent knowledge, and devotion. So may He grant that we may live long days of life mid-living men. (4302)[4]

४. मैनमग्ने वि दहो माभि शूशुचो मास्य त्वचं चिक्षिपो मा शरीरम् ।
शृतं यदा करसि जातवेदोऽथेममेनं प्र हिणुतात् पितॄँरुप ॥

4. O learned preceptor, don't trouble this celibate disciple, don't put him to grief. Let not his skin and body decay. O learned teacher, having made him well-versed in knowledge, send him back to his parents. (4303)[5]

५. यदा शृतं कृणवो जातवेदोऽथेममेनं परि दत्तात् पितृभ्यः ।
यदो गच्छात्यसुनीतिमेतामथ देवानां वशनीर्भवाति ॥

[1]See *Rig*, 10-14-4. [2]See *Rig*, 10-14-13. [3]See *Rig*, 10-14-15.
[4]See *Rig*, 10-14-14. [5]See *Rig*, 10-16-1.

5. O renowned, learned preceptor, when thou hast made thy celibate disciple fully equipped with knowledge, send him back to his parents. When he will yoke wisdom with statesmanship, he will be able to control his organs throughout his life. (4304)[1]

६. त्रिकद्रुकेभिः पवते षडुर्वीरेकमिद् बृहत्। त्रिष्टुब् गायत्री छन्दांसि सर्वा ता यम आर्पिता ॥

6. The One Almighty God, pervades the six wide regions, with his triple power. The Gayatri, the Trishtup, all Vedic metres are contained in God. (4305)[2]

७. सूर्यं चक्षुषा गच्छ वातमात्मना दिवं च गच्छ पृथिवीं च धर्मभिः ।
अपो वा गच्छ यदि तत्र ते हितमोषधीषु प्रति तिष्ठा शरीरैः ॥

7. O man, receive the light of the Sun through thine eye, the wind through breath. Master heaven and earth realising their attributes. Understand the efficacy of waters! If you find any efficacy in plants, utilize it to your advantage with all their limbs and parts. (4306)[3]

८. अजो भागस्तपसस्तं तपस्व तं ते शोचिस्तपतु तं ते अर्चिः ।
यास्ते शिवास्तन्वो॒ जातवेदस्ताभिर्वहैनं सुकृतामु लोकम् ॥

8. O God, the unborn soul feels pain and pleasure in the body. Strengthen it through Brahmcharya and Vedic study. May the flame of Thy knowledge, and Thy lustre elevate it. With Thine auspicious powers bear this soul to the assembly of the pious. (4307)[4]

९. यास्ते शोचयो रंहयो जातवेदो याभिरापृणासि दिवमन्तरिक्षम् ।
अजं यन्तमनु ताः समृण्वतामथेतराभिः शिवतमाभिः शृतं कृधि ॥

9. O Omniscient God, let the flames of Thy knowledge and Thy kinetic forces, wherewith Thou pervadest heaven and earth's mid-region be easily procurable to the unborn soul, that works in obedience to them! Make the soul devout, patient, and perfect, through Thy other annoying but auspicious forces. (4308)[5]

१०. अव सृज पुनरग्ने पितृभ्यो यस्त आहुतश्चरति स्वधावान् ।
आयुर्वसान उप यातु शेषः सं गच्छतां तन्वा॒ सुवर्चाः ॥

[1]See *Rig*, 10-16-2.

[2]See *Rig*, 10-14-16. All Vedic verses in different metres are revealed by God. Triple force: Creation sustenance and Dissolution of the universe. Six wide regions: North, East, South, West, Nadir, Zenith, Sāyana mentions them to be the sun, earth, day and night, water and plants.

[3]See *Rig*, 10-16-3.

[4]See *Rig*, 10-16-4. Sāyana translates अज as a goat to be killed and offered in oblations in the Yajna. Vedas condemn human sacrifice, hence this explanation is irrational.

[5]Them: Knowledge and forces of God.

10. O learned Ācharya, prepare for serving his parents on return, the disciple, who equipped with semen, devoting himself to thee, leads the life of celibacy! Thy disciple in obedience to thy behest, remaining in thy company, should visit houses, and enjoy the company of householders with his splendid body. (4309)[1]

११. अति द्रव श्वानौ सारमेयौ चतुरक्षौ शबलौ साधुना पथा ।
अधा पितॄन्त्सुविदत्राँ अपीहि यमेन ये सधमादं मदन्ति ॥

11. O man, pass with devotion, ever fleeting day and night, born of Dawn, pervading all the four directions, bright and dark in appearance! Go near the learned gurus, who remain in pleasure in the company of God. (4310)[2]

१२. यौ ते श्वानौ यम रक्षितारौ चतुरक्षौ पथिषदी नृचक्षसा ।
ताभ्यां राजन् परि धेह्येनं स्वस्त्यस्मा अनमीवं च धेहि ॥

12. O God, ever fleeting are thy day and nigh, they watch living beings, pervade all the four directions, guard our pathway, keep an eye on men! O God, protect this soul, with both of them on all sides, and endow it with prosperity and health. (4311)[3]

१३. उरुणसावसुतृपावुदुम्बलौ यमस्य दूतौ चरतो जनाँ अनु ।
तावस्मभ्यं दृशये सूर्याय पुनर्दातामसुमद्येह भद्रम् ॥

13. Ever-fleeting, developers of intellect, highly powerful, God's two envoys roam among the people. May they restore to us again and again a fair existence here in this world, so that we may realise God. (4312)[4]

१४. सोम एकेभ्यः पवते घृतमेक उपासते । येभ्यो मधु प्रधावति तांश्चिदेवापि गच्छतात् ॥

14. Few learned persons attain to prosperity, few realise the real essence of things. There are others who speedily imbibe the knowledge of God. O man, approach all these learned persons, and derive knowledge from them. (4313)[5]

१५. ये चित्पूर्व ऋतसाता ऋतजाता ऋतावृधः ।
ऋषीन्तपस्वतो यम तपोजाँ अपि गच्छतात् ॥

15. O disciple, follower of the laws of celibacy, go to those sages, who are austere, penitent, full followers of Truth, lovers of Truth, and preachers of Truth! (4314)[6]

[1]See *Rig*, 10-16-5. Ācharya: Teacher, guru, preceptor.
[2]See *Rig*, 10-14-10. [3]See *Rig*, 10-14-11.
[4]See *Rig*, 10-14-12. Two envoys: Day and Night असुतृपौ: may also mean that feed on the breath of man, and daily diminish the duration of his existence. They are insatiate. असु means प्रज्ञा, intellect as well. They are the developers of intellect.
[5]See *Rig*, 10-154-1. [6]See *Rig*, 10-154-4.

१६. तपसा ये अनाधृष्यास्तपसा ये स्वर्ययुः । तपो ये चक्रिरे महस्तांश्चिदेवापि गच्छतात् ॥

16. O man, go to those persons who are invincible through fervour, who through penance have attained to God, and who have practised great austerity and learn austerity from them! (4315)[1]

१७. ये युध्यन्ते प्रधनेषु शूरासो ये तनूत्यजः । ये वा सहस्रदक्षिणास्तांश्चिदेवापि गच्छतात् ॥

17. O man, go to those heroes who fight in battles, and sacrifice their lives for their country, and who give away thousands in charity! and receive instruction from them. (4316)[2]

१८. सहस्रणीथाः कवयो ये गोपायन्ति सूर्यम् । ऋषीन् तपस्वतो यम तपोजाँ अपि गच्छतात् ॥

18. O Brahmchari, go to the sages, who are skilled in a thousand branches of knowledge, and study the Vedas, the repository of God's knowledge ; Rishis who practice austerity and are renowned for penance, and derive knowledge from them! (4317)[3]

१९. स्योनास्मै भव पृथिव्यनृक्षरा निवेशनी । यच्छास्मै शर्म सप्रथाः ॥

19. O Earth, be pleasant, thornless and habitable for this man. Vouchsafe him shelter, broad us thou art! (4318)[4]

२०. असंबाधे पृथिव्या उरौ लोके नि धीयस्व । स्वधा याश्चकृषे जीवन् तास्ते सन्तु मधुश्चुतः ॥

20. O man, reside on the vast space of Earth, free from pain and fear. Whatever measures thou adopted in thy life-time, for thy sustenance, development and protection, may they all bring thee joy. (4319)

२१. ह्वयामि ते मनसा मन इहेमान् गृहाँ उप जुजुषाण एहि ।
सं गच्छस्व पितृभिः सं यमेन स्योनास्त्वा वाता उप वान्तु शग्माः ॥

21. Hither I call thy mind with my mind. Come thou, delighting the inmates of these dwelling-places. Visit thy elders. Unite thyself with God. Strong and sweet be the winds that fan thee. (4320)[5]

२२. उत् त्वा वहन्तु मरुत उदवाहा उदप्रुतः । अजेन कृण्वन्तः शीतं वर्षेणोक्षन्तु बालिति ॥

22. O man, let learned persons quick like the wind, who dig streams for water, and float in water, uplift thee. May they with the help of the unborn God, advance thy mental peace, as clouds cool the earth with their falling rain! (4321)

[1]See *Rig*, 10-154-2. [2]See *Rig*, 10-154-3. [3]See *Rig*, 10-154-5.
[4]See *Rig*, 1-22-15. *Yajur*, 35-21.
[5]Men should invite learned persons with respect and receive good instruction and the knowledge of God from them, and thereby attain to happiness.

२३. उदह्वमायुरायुषे क्रत्वे दक्षाय जीवसे । स्वान् गच्छतु ते मनो अधा पितॄँरुप द्रव ॥

23. O man, I instruct thee to utilise life, for longevity, performance of noble deeds, acquisition of power, and leading a healthy life. Let thy mind go to the relatives. Go to the elders and receive knowledge and understanding from them! (4322)

२४. मा ते मनो मासोर्माङ्गानां मा रसस्य ते । मा ते हास्त तन्व१: किं चनेह ॥

24. O man, let not thy mind forsake thee. Let not thy breath leave thee. Let no organ of thine decay before time, Let not thy blood cease flowing. Let no part of thy body cease functioning early in thy life-time! (4323)[1]

२५. मा त्वा वृक्षः सं बाधिष्ट मा देवी पृथिवी मही । लोकं पितृषु वित्त्वैधस्व यमराजसु ॥

25. O man, let not this enjoyable world oppress thee. Let not this vast revolving earth weigh thee down. Find thy place among the saviours of the country, and thrive mid those whom God rules! (4324)

२६. यत्ते अङ्गमतिहितं पराचैरपानः प्राणो य उ वा ते परेतः ।
तत्ते संगत्य पितरः सनीडा घासाद् घासं पुनरा वेशयन्तु ॥

26. O man, if any organ of thy body has been dislocated, or vital breaths displaced, thy learned elders who dwell together shall meet, and reunite thee with all of these, piece after piece. (4325)

२७. अपेमं जीवा अरुधन् गृहेभ्यस्तं निर्वहत परि ग्रामादितः ।
मृत्युर्यमस्यासीद् दूतः प्रचेता असून् पितृभ्यो गमयां चकार ॥

27. Sentient preceptors made the Brahmchari refrain from enjoyment for the good of his householders. You can take him out of his seminary in all directions for service. Self-abnegation is the goader and educator of an ascetic. This imparts spiritual life to the sages. (4326)[2]

२८. ये दस्यवः पितृषु प्रविष्टा ज्ञातिमुखा अहुतादश्चरन्ति ।
परापुरो निपुरो ये भरन्त्यग्निष्टानस्मात् प्र धमाति यज्ञात् ॥

28. Those fiends who eat our oblations snatching them forcibly, and come in the garb of friends and relatives, mingled fraudulently with our elders, those who abduct our sons and grandsons should be exiled from the country by a strict ruler. (4327)

[1] All organs of a man should continue working in a healthy state till he reaches the age of one hundred years.

[2] A pupil, during the period of education should abstain from worldly pleasures. After finishing his education, he should go out of his place of education and serve humanity. Self-abnegation is the best inciter and educator of a self-restrained person. Self-abnegation alone gives spiritual life to the learned sages.

२९. सं विशन्त्विह पितरः स्वा नः स्योनं कृण्वन्तः प्रतिरन्त आयुः ।
तेभ्यः शकेम हविषा नक्षमाणा ज्योग् जीवन्तः शरदः पुरूचीः ॥

29. Bringing us delight, prolonging our existence, let our own elders dwell here together. Serving them with full devotion, let us live long lives for many years. (4328)[1]

३०. यां ते धेनुं निपृणामि यमु ते क्षीर ओदनम् । तेना जनस्यासो भर्ता योऽत्रासदजीवनः ॥

30. O noble person, be the supporter of the folk left in this world without a livelihood, by the cow I give thee, by the boiled rice set in milk I offer thee! (4329)[2]

३१. अश्वावतीं प्र तर या सुशेवार्क्षाकं वा प्रतरं नवीयः ।
यस्त्वा जघान वध्यः सो अस्तु मा सो अन्यद् विदत भागधेयम् ॥

31. O man, control thy organs of action, and thy organs of cognition, that lead thee to a new, dignified path. Thus pass thy life in happiness. He who slays thee deserves to be put to death. He is fit for no other punishment but death! (4330)

३२. यमः परोऽवरो विवस्वान् ततः परं नाति पश्यामि किं चन ।
यमे अध्वरो अधि मे निविष्टो भुवो विवस्वानन्वाततान ॥

32. The Refulgent God is distant and near. I see none higher than God. My non-violent life rests on Him. He has spread around different worlds. (4331)

३३. अपागूहन्नमृतां मर्त्येभ्यः कृत्वा सवर्णामदधुर्विवस्वते ।
उताश्विनावभरद् यत् तदासीदजहादु द्वा मिथुना सरण्यूः ॥

33. The laws of God, kept the Immortal Matter hidden after dissolution. At the time of creation, they made it firm, acceptable for the good of mortals, to carry out the behest of God. The universe was then imbued with vital breaths, and pairs were evolved out of Matter. (4332)[3]

३४. ये निखाता ये परोप्ता ये दग्धा ये चोद्धिताः । सर्वांस्तानग्न आ वह पितॄन् हविषे अत्तवे ॥

[1]Elders: Father, grandfather, mother, grandmother. Here: In this world.

[2]A noble man must support the weak, lame, blind persons and children who are unfit to earn their livelihood. A good man should be charitable towards disabled persons.

[3]Matter is resolved into its nascent atomic state by God at the time of dissolution. It is converted into a gross, visible shape at the time of creation of the universe, for the good of mankind, in obedience to the laws of God. 'They' refers to the laws of God and 'it' to Matter. Vital breaths: Prāna and Apāna. Pairs: Male and female. See *Rig*, 10-17-2. Griffith considers Saranyū, to be the daughter of Tavashtar and wife of Vivasvān, mother of Yama and Yami, and the twin Aswins. There is no history in the Vedas, hence this explanation is irrational. The word means Matter.

34. O householder, bring thou all learned persons to eat the food offered by thee. Those who are deep-rooted in celibacy, those who rear after their children, those who have eliminated their mental, physical and oral sins, those who occupy exalted positions. (4333)

३५. ये अग्निदग्धा ये अनग्निदग्धा मध्ये दिवः स्वधया मादयन्ते ।
त्वं तान् वेत्थ यदि ते जातवेदः स्वधया यज्ञं स्वधितिं जुषन्ताम् ॥

35. The Brahmcharis and householders who burn fire to perform Homa, and the Sanyāsis who have renounced the performance of Homa, and kindle only the fire of knowledge, O Omniscient God, Thou verily knowest them. They through their inherent mental strength, attain to Self-Existent God! (4334)

३६. शं तप माति तपो अग्ने मा तन्वं१ तपः । वनेषु शुष्मो अस्तु ते पृथिव्यामस्तु यद्धरः ॥

36. O Achārya, punish us for welfare. Don't punish us too heavily. Don't torment our body! Let thy force appear in thy disciples as that of fire in woods. May thy lustre spread on earth! (4335)[1]

३७. ददाम्यस्मा अवसानमेतद्य एष आगन् मम चेदभूदिह ।
यमश्चिकित्वान् प्रत्येतदाह ममैष राय उप तिष्ठतामिह ॥

37. I give this shelter to him who hath come hither and is my devotee in this world. The Omniscient God explicitly says unto him, "May thou my votary serve in this world to acquire the wealth of salvation." (4336)[2]

३८. इमां मात्रां मिमीमहे यथापरं न मासातै । शते शरत्सु नो पुरा ॥

38. This Vedic limit for life we settle once for all, that can't be fixt in another way. A hundred autumns; not before. (4337)[3]

३९. प्रेमां मात्रां मिमीमहे यथापरं न मासातै । शते शरत्सु नो पुरा ॥

39. This Vedic limit for life we decide once for all, that can't be decided in another way. A hundred autumns; not before. (4338)

४०. अपेमां मात्रां मिमीमहे यथापरं न मासातै । शते शरत्सु नो पुरा ॥

40. This Vedic limit for life we gladly measure once for all, that can't be measured in another way. A hundred autumns; not before. (4339)

४१. वीमां मात्रां मिमीमहे यथापरं न मासातै । शते शरत्सु नो पुरा ॥

41. This Vedic limit for life we distinctively define, that can't be defined in another way. A hundred autumns, not before. (4340)

४२. निरिमां मात्रां मिमीमहे यथापरं न मासातै । शते शरत्सु नो पुरा ॥

[1]Force: Intellectual and spiritual strength.
[2]I refers to God.
[3]The Vedas require that a man should live for at least a hundred years and not die earlier. This is the minimum age prescribed by the Vedas.

42. This Vedic limit for life we definitely mete out once for all, that can't be meted out in another way. A hundred autumns, not before. (4341)

४३. उदिमां मात्रां मिमीमहे यथापरं न मासातै । शते शरत्सु नो पुरा ॥

43. This Vedic limit for life we beautifully establish once for all, that can't be established in another way. A hundred autumns, not before. (4342)

४४. समिमां मात्रां मिमीमहे यथापरं न मासातै । शते शरत्सु नो पुरा ॥

44. This Vedic limit for life we fully measure out once for all, that can't be measured out in another way. A hundred autumns; not before. (4343)

४५. अमासि मात्रां स्व१रगामायुष्मान् भूयासम् । यथापरं न मासातै शते शरत्सु नो पुरा ॥

45. May I pass excellently the Vedic limit of life. May I attain to salvation, and live long. This limit cannot be defined except by the Vedas. A hundred autumns; not before. (4344)

४६. प्राणो अपानो व्यान आयुश्चक्षुर्दृशये सूर्याय । अपरिपरेण पथा यमराज्ञः पितॄन् गच्छ ॥

46. O man, thy in-breath, out-breath, breath diffused life, sight are meant for the realisation of God. Seek by a straight path free from disease and malice, the elders, whose Ruler is God! (4345)

४७. ये अग्रवः शशमानाः परेयुर्हित्वा द्वेषांस्यनपत्यवन्तः ।
ते द्यामुदित्याविदन्त लोकं नाकस्य पृष्ठे अधि दीध्यानाः ॥

47. The enterprising, laborious people, free from poverty, renouncing hatred have advanced in life. Such illustrious persons, acquiring knowledge, have rightly secured a place in final beatitude. (4346)[1]

४८. उदन्वती द्यौरवमा पीलुमतीति मध्यमा । तृतीया ह प्रद्यौरिति यस्यां पितर आसते ॥

48. Little knowledge is like a shallow stream. Medium knowledge is like a flowery plant, attractive only in appearance. Advanced knowledge is the third stage in which the learned sages dwell. (4347)[2]

४९. ये नः पितुः पितरो ये पितामहा य आविविशुरुर्व१न्तरिक्षम् ।
य आक्षियन्ति पृथिवीमुत द्यां तेभ्यः पितृभ्यो नमसा विधेम ॥

49. They, who are like our father's fathers, or like grandfathers, who fly in planes in the atmosphere, who rule over earth and space, deserve to be worshipped by us with reverence. (4348)

५०. इदमिद् वा उ नापरं दिवि पश्यसि सूर्यम् । माता पुत्रं यथा सिचाभ्ये१नं भूम ऊर्णुहि ॥

[1]Final beatitude: Salvation, Moksha.

[2](द्यौः) प्रकाशकर्मविद्या—दयानन्द भाष्ये, यजु० 18-8.

50. O soul, this alone is verily the All-pervading God, and none else. Thou canst visualise Him through the lustre of knowledge! O God, protect this soul, as a mother draws her skirt about her son! (4349)[1]

५१. इदमिद् वा उ नापरं जरस्यन्यदितोऽपरम् । जाया पतिमिव वाससाभ्ये̐नं भूम ऊर्णुहि ॥

51. O soul, this alone is verily the All-pervading God. For worship none else is deserving but Him. O God protect this soul, as a wife covers her husband with her robe. (4350)

५२. अभि त्वोर्णोमि पृथिव्या मातुर्वस्त्रेण भद्रया । जीवेषु भद्रं तन्मयि स्वधा पितृषु सा त्वयि ॥

52. O man, I cover thee with the bliss of God, the Diffuser of the world, as a child is wrapped with the mother's vesture. Whatever goodness there is in souls, may that reside in me. May the spiritual force of the sages reside in thee. (4351)

५३. अग्नीषोमा पथिकृता स्योनं देवेभ्यो रत्नं दधथुर्वि लोकम् ।
उप प्रेष्यन्तं पूषणं यो वहात्यञ्जोयानैः पथिभिस्तत्र गच्छतम् ॥

53. O learned and prosperous man and woman, makers of the path of virtue, give amply to the learned, pleasure, riches and rank. Realising the All-seeing God, Who leads us all on the straight paths, tread ye both on those paths! (4352)

५४. पूषा त्वेतश्च्यावयतु प्र विद्वाननष्टपशुर्भुवनस्य गोपाः ।
स त्वैतेभ्यः परि ददत् पितृभ्योऽग्निर्देवेभ्यः सुविदत्रियेभ्यः ॥

54. O soul, may the Omniscient God, the Non-destroyer of soul, the Guardian of the world, uplift thee. May the Wise God, consign thee to these learned wealthy parents and teachers! (4353)[2]

५५. आयुर्विश्वायुः परि पातु त्वा पूषा त्वा पातु प्रपथे पुरस्तात् ।
यत्रासते सुकृतो यत्र त ईयुस्तत्र त्वा देवः सविता दधातु ॥

55. O soul, may God, the Bestower of food to all, guard thee on all sides. May God, convey thee forward on the right path. May the All-creating God conduct thee thither where dwell the pious, and put you on the virtuous path trodden by them. (4354)[3]

५६. इमौ युनज्मि ते वह्नी असुनीताय वोढवे । ताभ्यां यमस्य सादनं समितीश्चाव गच्छतात् ॥

56. O man, I yoke thy soul that goes to the next world through breath, with two carriers the Prāna and the Apāna. Through their control through Yoga, seek shelter under God and communion with Him! (4355)

[1]See *Rig*, 10-18-11 and *Atharva*, 18-3-50. I: A learned person. Thee: Man. An aspirant after truth. Me: Learned person.
[2]See *Rig*, 10-17-3. [3]See *Rig*, 10-17-4.

५७. एतत् त्वा वासः प्रथमं न्वागन्नपैतदूह यदिहाबिभः पुरा ।
इष्टापूर्तमनुसंक्राम विद्वान् यत्र ते दत्तं बहुधा विबन्धुषु ॥

57. O soul, thou hast been equipped with a fine body, renounce the one possessed before! O wise soul, earn the reward of thy virtuous deeds and thy many gifts bestowed upon the friendless! (4356)[1]

५८. अग्नेर्वर्म परि गोभिर्व्ययस्व सं प्रोर्णुष्व मेदसा पीवसा च ।
नेत्त्वा धृष्णुर्हरसा जर्हृषाणो दधृग् विधक्षन् परीङ्खयातै ॥

58. O man, wear the shelter of God as thy armour with the help of Vedic verses. Encompass thyself all round with knowledge and physical strength, otherwise, the Powerful, Highly Joyful, Fearless God, punishing thee in diverse ways, will completely consume thee! (4357)[2]

५९. दण्डं हस्तादाददानो गतासोः सह श्रोत्रेण वर्चसा बलेन ।
अत्रैव त्वमिह वयं सुवीरा विश्वा मृधो अभिमातीर्जयेम ॥

59. Snatch government from the hand of a lifeless ruler, with the power of your knowledge, dignity and strength. Remaining in this world, let thou and us with brave soldiers win all battles and overcome enemies. (4358)[3]

६०. धनुर्हस्तादाददानो मृतस्य सह क्षत्रेण वर्चसा बलेन ।
समागृभाय वसु भूरि पुष्टमर्वाङ् त्वमेह्युप जीवलोकम् ॥

60. Snatch government from the hand of a lifeless ruler, with your martial spirit, dignity and strength. Having collected wealth and ample treasure, come hither to the assembly of enterprising persons. (4359)

Chapter (Anuvāka) 3

HYMN III

१. इयं नारी पतिलोकं वृणाना नि पद्यत उप त्वा मर्त्य प्रेतम् ।
धर्मं पुराणमनुपालयन्ती तस्यै प्रजां द्रविणं चेह धेहि ॥

1. O mortal man, this woman preserving faithfully the ancient custom, longing for the happiness of household life, approaches thee her dead husband! Bestow upon her both wealth and offspring. (4360)[4]

[1]Friendless: The poor, indigent persons. इष्टातम्: Performance of Yajnas, study of the Vedas, and charity. All these are virtuous deeds.

[2]See *Rig*, 10-16-7.

[3]Thou: A brave general. Government should always remain in the hands of strong persons. The weak are not fit to rule.

[4]After the death of her husband, wife is the owner of her husband's property and children. Sāyana's interpretation that a woman after the death of her husband should lay herself on the pyre along with her husband, and burn herself. This is inhuman and unacceptable.

२. उदीर्ष्व नार्यभि जीवलोकं गतासुमेतमुप शेष एहि ।
हस्तग्राभस्य दिधिषोस्तवेदं पत्युर्जनित्वमभि सं बभूथ ॥

2. Rise, come unto the world of living, O woman, come, he is lifeless by whose side thou art sitting. Accept the offspring of thy dead husband, who took thy hand in marriage, and supported and protected thee. (4361)[1]

३. अपश्यं युवतिं नीयमानां जीवां मृतेभ्यः परिणीयमानाम् ।
अन्धेन यत् तमसा प्रावृतासीत् प्राक्तो अपाचीमनयं तदेनाम् ॥

3. I saw the youthful living dame being escorted and carried far to the dead. When she with blinding darkness of grief was enveloped, then did I turn her back and lead her homeward. (4362)[2]

४. प्रजानत्यघ्न्ये जीवलोकं देवानां पन्थामनुसंचरन्ती ।
अयं ते गोपतिस्तं जुषस्व स्वर्गं लोकमधि रोहयैनम् ॥

4. Knowing the world fully well, O sinless woman, treading the path of the sages, joyfully serve this husband of thine, who is the guardian of thy vow of married life and give him intense joy. (4363)

५. उप द्यामुप वेतसमवत्तरो नदीनाम् । अग्ने पित्तमपामसि ॥

5. O learned person, acquiring the lustre of knowledge, and reverentially fully guarding the vastness of praises, thou art the splendour of the essence of life! (4364)[3]

६. यं त्वमग्ने समदहस्तमु निर्वापया पुनः । क्याम्बूरत्र रोहतु शाण्डदूर्वा व्यल्कशा ॥

6. O learned person, let the Brahmchari grow like the seed, whom thou hast made go through the penance of celibacy. Let him cultivate the power of spreading, Knowledge, alleviating misery, and replete with diverse grandeur! (4365)

७. इदं त एकं पर ऊ त एकं तृतीयेन ज्योतिषा सं विशस्व ।
संवेशने तन्वा३ चारुरेधि प्रियो देवानां परमे सधस्थे ॥

7. O learned person, here is one light for thee, another yonder, enter the third and be therewith united. Uniting thyself with the spirit of service be thou lovely, and dear to the learned in their sublimest position. (4366)[4]

[1]Accept: Look after, nourish, rear.

[2]I refers to the head of the family. If a widow is misguided by ignorant persons to immolate herself on the funeral pyre of her husband, the head of the family should dissuade her from doing this unvedic act.

[3]Essence of life: Prānas. Life depends upon the control of breath.

[4]One light: The gross material word, which is the Effect कार्य. Yonder light: The suble Matter in its atomic state, which is the physical cause of the universe. Third light: Refulgent God.

८. उत्तिष्ठ प्रेहि प्र द्रवौकः कृणुष्व सलिले सधस्थे ।
तत्र त्वं पितृभिः संविदानः सं सोमेन मदस्व सं स्वधाभिः ॥

8. O man, rise up, advance, go forward hastily, make thy dwelling in God cool like water! There dwelling in accordance with the Fathers, delight thyself with prosperity and spiritual forces. (4367)[1]

९. प्र च्यवस्व तन्वं१ सं भरस्व मा ते गात्रा वि हायि मो शरीरम् ।
मनो निविष्टमनुसंविशस्व यत्र भूमेर्जुषसे तत्र गच्छ ॥

9. O soul, gladly accept thy body, strengthen it well, so that thy limbs, thy frame may not leave thee earlier. Follow thy firm steadfast mind, go to whatever spot of earth thou lovest. (4368)

१०. वर्चसा मां पितरः सोम्यासो अञ्जन्तु देवा मधुना घृतेन ।
चक्षुषे मा प्रतरं तारयन्तो जरसे मा जरदष्टिं वर्धन्तु ॥

10. With splendour may the elders, the worshippers of God, with sweet knowledge and light may the sages anoint me. May they lead me on farther to minute vision and prosper me through life of long duration. (4369)

११. वर्चसा मां समनक्त्वग्निर्मेधां मे विष्णुर्न्यनक्त्वासन् ।
रयिं मे विश्वे नि यच्छन्तु देवाः स्योना मापः पवनैः पुनन्तु ॥

11. May Āchārya balm me thoroughly with splendour; may God fill my lips with understanding. May all the learned persons vouchsafe me riches, and pleasant self-abnegating scholars purify me with their elevating sermons. (4370)

१२. मित्रावरुणा परि मामधातामादित्या मा स्वरवो वर्धयन्तु ।
वर्चो म इन्द्रो न्यनक्तु हस्तयोर्जरदष्टिं मा सविता कृणोतु ॥

12. May mother and father nourish me in every way. May preceptors, splendid like the Sun exalt me with their knowledge. May the king fill my hands with strength. A long, long life may God vouchsafe me. (4371)[2]

१३. यो ममार प्रथमो मर्त्यानां यः प्रेयाय प्रथमो लोकमेतम् ।
वैवस्वतं संगमनं जनानां यमं राजानं हविषा सपर्यत ॥

13. O men, worship with devotion the justice-loving King, who is the well-wisher of human beings, and promoter of unity amongst them, who left this world as a great man, and who flourished in this world as a great man! (4372)

१४. परा यात पितर आ च यातायं वो यज्ञो मधुना समक्तः ।
दत्तो अस्मभ्यं द्रविणेह भद्रं रयिं च नः सर्ववीरं दधात ॥

[1]Fathers: Mother, Father, Āchārya.
[2]Me: A student. See *Rig*, 10-14-1.

14. O elders, your soul is full of knowledge. Go to distant places, and spread it, come hither from afar! Enrich us here with gifts of great possessions; grant us blessed wealth with ample store of heroes. (4373)

१५. कण्वः कक्षीवान् पुरुमीढो अगस्त्यः श्यावाश्वः सोभर्यर्चनानाः ।
विश्वामित्रोऽयं जमदग्निरत्रिरवन्तु नः कश्यपो वामदेवः ।।

15. May the wise, self-controlled, wealthy, sinless, intellectual, prosperous, pious, loving, energetic, ever-accessible, intuitive, God-fearing elders protect us. (4374)[1]

१६. विश्वामित्र जमदग्ने वसिष्ठ भरद्वाज गोतम वामदेव ।
शर्दिर्नो अत्रिरग्रभीन्नमोभिः सुसंशासः पितरो मृडता नः ।।

16. O loving, lustrous, dignified, learned, praiseworthy, God-fearing, strong, virtuous elders, be ye gracious unto us! May they, nice administrators favour us with strength to quell the foes. (4375)

१७. कस्ये मृजाना अति यन्ति रिप्रमायुर्दधानाः प्रतरं नवीयः ।
आप्यायमानाः प्रजया धनेनाध स्याम सुरभयो गृहेषु ।।

17. Purifying ourselves through knowledge, acquiring a prolonged, fresh life, we shun sin. Increasing in our children and our riches, may we nobly pass our time in our houses. (4376)

१८. अञ्जते व्यञ्जते समञ्जते क्रतुं रिहन्ति मधुनाभ्यञ्जते ।
सिन्धोरुच्छ्वासे पतयन्तमुक्षणं हिरण्यपावाः पशुमासु गृह्णते ।।

18. The worshippers of God, purify, develop, visualise, expand and extol the intellect. The yogis, who purify through penance (like gold with fire) their soul, the seer of God, and the diffuser of religious happiness, controlling their breath a gift from God, realise the soul in these internal arteries. (4377)

१९. यद् वो मुद्रं पितरः सोम्यं च तेनो सचध्वं स्वयशसो हि भूत ।
ते अर्वाणः कवय आ शृणोत सुविदत्रा विदथे हूयमानाः ।।

19. O elders, whatever act of yours is pleasant and noble, let us advance following in its wake, and be verily gracious in yourselves! Give ear and listen to our prayer, ye energetic sages, intellectual, wealthy, invoked in our learned assembly. (4378)[2]

२०. ये अत्रयो अङ्गिरसो नवग्वा इष्टावन्तो रातिषाची दधानाः ।
दक्षिणावन्तः सुकृतो य उ स्थासद्यास्मिन् बर्हिषि मादयध्वम् ।।

[1]The twelve words in the verse are not the names of Rishis as Sāyana and Griffith interpret. They denote our learned elders and sages possessing different qualities and virtues. As there is no history in the Vedas, the explanation of Griffith is unacceptable.

[2]Teachers, father, mother.

20. Ye elders, ever accessible, learned, praiseworthy, continual sacrificers, givers of liberal gifts, nourishers, guerdon grantors, devout and pious, sit in this Yajna (sacrifice) and be ye joyful! (4379)

२१. अधा यथा नः पितरः परासः प्रत्नासो अग्न ऋतमाशशानाः ।
शुचीदयन् दीध्यत उक्थशासः क्षामा भिन्दन्तो अरुणीरप व्रन् ॥

21. O learned person, just as our noble ancient elders, were the expounders of truth, pure in character, self-refulgent, preachers of truths, dispelling ignorance and darkness, spread Vedic teachings, so should we. (4380)[1]

२२. सुकर्माणः सुरुचो देवयन्तो अयो न देवा जनिमा धमन्तः ।
शुचन्तो अग्निं वावृधन्त इन्द्रमुर्वीं गव्यां परिषदं नो अक्रन् ॥

22. Learned persons, doing holy acts, beautiful, worshipping God, purify their human generation, as a blacksmith smelts iron. Enkindling the soul, exalting God, may they organise our assembly for learned discussions. (4381)[2]

२३. आ यूथेव क्षुमति पश्वो अख्यद् देवानां जनिमान्त्युग्रः ।
मर्तासश्चिदुर्वशीरकृप्रन् वृधे चिदर्य उपरस्यायोः ॥

23. Just as a wise shepherd watches the birth of herds of cattle in a foodful pasture, so does the Mighty God watch and guard from near the birth of the learned. Mortals only revel in women, but God, the Lord of all, develops the child in the womb. (4382)[3]

२४. अकर्म ते स्वपसो अभूम ऋतमवस्रन्नुषसो विभातीः ।
विश्वं तद् भद्रं यदवन्ति देवा बृहद् वदेम विदथे सुवीराः ॥

24. O God, we perform acts dedicating them to Thee, and thus acquire knowledge. May bright Dawns ever shine on our Yajna (sacrifice)! The learned safeguard all that is blissful. May we, full of-strength sing the praise of the Almighty Father in an assembly of the learned. (4383)[4]

२५. इन्द्रो मा मरुत्वान् प्राच्या दिशः पातु बाहुच्युता पृथिवी द्यामिवोपरि ।
लोककृतः पथिकृतो यजामहे ये देवानां हुतभागा इह स्थ ॥

25. May God, the Lord of heroes guard me from the calamities coming from eastward just as the Earth, controlled by the force of arms guards the king who rules over it. We worship those who are the benefactors of the world, show us the path of rectitude and who amongst the learned share the gifts we offer. (4384)

[1]See *Rig*, 4-2-16, *Yajur*, 19-69.
[2]See *Rig*, 4-2-17. [3]See *Rig*, 4-2-18. [4]See *Rig*, 4-2-19.

२६. धाता मा निर्ऋत्या दक्षिणाया दिशः पातु बाहुच्युता पृथिवी द्यामिवोपरि ।
लोककृतः पथिकृतो यजामहे ये देवानां हुतभागा इह स्थ ॥

26. May God, the nourisher of all, guard me from the calamities coming from southward, just as the Earth, controlled by the force of arms guards the king who rules over it. We worship those who are the benefactors of the world, show us the path of rectitude, and who amongst the learned share the gifts we offer. (4385)

२७. अदितिर्मादित्यैः प्रतीच्या दिशः पातु बाहुच्युता पृथिवी द्यामिवोपरि ।
लोककृतः पथिकृतो यजामहे ये देवानां हुतभागा इह स्थ ॥

27. May the Everlasting God, through his first created objects, guard me from the calamities coming from the westward just as the Earth, controlled by the force of arms, guards the king who rules over it. We worship those who are the benefactors of the world, show us the path of rectitude, and who amongst the learned share the gifts we offer. (4386)

२८. सोमो मा विश्वैर्देवैरुदीच्या दिशः पातु बाहुच्युता पृथिवी द्यामिवोपरि ।
लोककृतः पथिकृतो यजामहे ये देवानां हुतभागा इह स्थ ॥

28. May the All-creating God, through all the forces of nature, guard me from the calamities coming from the northward, just as the Earth, controlled by the force of arms, guards the king who rules over it. We worship those who are the benefactors of the world, show us the path of rectitude, and who amongst the learned share the gifts we offer. (4387)

२९. धर्ता ह त्वा धरुणो धारयाता ऊर्ध्वं भानुं सविता द्यामिवोपरि ।
लोककृतः पथिकृतो यजामहे ये देवानां हुतभागा इह स्थ ॥

29. May God, the strong, Firm sustainer bear thee in an exalted position, as the Sun bears aloft the shining heaven. We worship those who are the benefactors of the world, show us the path of rectitude, and who amongst the learned share the gifts we offer. (4388)[1]

३०. प्राच्यां त्वा दिशि पुरा संवृतः स्वधायामा दधामि बाहुच्युता पृथिवी द्यामिवोपरि ।
लोककृतः पथिकृतो यजामहे ये देवानां हुतभागा इह स्थ ॥

30. O God, I, full of resources, establish Thee in my soul-force in the eastern region, just as the Earth, controlled by the force of arms, establishes the king who rules over it! We worship those who are the benefactors of the world, show us the path of rectitude, and who amongst the learned share the gifts we offer. (4389)

३१. दक्षिणायां त्वा दिशि पुरा संवृतः स्वधायामा दधामि बाहुच्युता पृथिवी द्यामिवोपरि ।
लोककृतः पथिकृतो यजामहे ये देवानां हुतभागा इह स्थ ॥

[1]Thee: An enterprising person.

31. O God, I, full of resources, establish Thee in my soul-force in the southern region, just as the Earth, controlled by the force of arms establishes the king who rules over it! We worship those who are the benefactors of the world, show us the path of rectitude, and who amongst the learned share the gifts we offer. (4390)

३२. प्रतीच्यां त्वा दिशि पुरा संवृतः स्वधायामा दधामि बाहुच्युता पृथिवी द्यामिवोपरि ।
लोककृतः पथिकृतो यजामहे ये देवानां हुतभागा इह स्थ ।।

32. O God, I, full of resources, establish Thee in my soul-force in the western region, just as the Earth, controlled by the force of arms establishes the king who rules over it! We worship those who are the benefactors of the world, show us the path of rectitude, and who amongst the learned share the gifts we offer. (4391)

३३. उदीच्यां त्वा दिशि पुरा संवृतः स्वधायामा दधामि बाहुच्युता पृथिवी द्यामिवोपरि ।
लोककृतः पथिकृतो यजामहे ये देवानां हुतभागा इह स्थ ।।

33. O God, I, full of resources, establish Thee in my soul-force in the northern region, just as the Earth, controlled by the force of arms, establishes the king who rules over it! We worship those who are the benefactors of the world, show us the path of rectitude, and who amongst the learned share the gifts we offer. (4392)

३४. ध्रुवायां त्वा दिशि पुरा संवृतः स्वधायामा दधामि बाहुच्युता पृथिवी द्यामिवोपरि ।
लोककृतः पथिकृतो यजामहे ये देवानां हुतभागा इह स्थ ।।

34. O God, I, full of resources, establish Thee in my soul-force in the steadfast region, just as the Earth, controlled by the force of arms, establishes the king who rules over it! We worship those who are the benefactors of the world, show us the path of rectitude, and who amongst the learned share the gifts we offer. (4393)[1]

३५. ऊर्ध्वायां त्वा दिशि पुरा संवृतः स्वधायामा दधामि बाहुच्युता पृथिवी द्यामिवोपरि ।
लोककृतः पथिकृतो यजामहे ये देवानां हुतभागा इह स्थ ।।

35. O God, I, full of resources, establish Thee in my soul-force in the topmost region, just as the Earth, controlled by the force of arms, establishes the king who rules over it! We worship those who are the benefactors of the world, show us the path of rectitude, and who amongst the learned share the gifts we offer. (4394)[2]

३६. धर्तासि धरुणोऽसि वंसगोऽसि ।।

[1]Steadfast region: Nadir.

[2]Topmost: Zenith.

36. O God, Thou art the sustainer, the Upholder, and the Bestower of all desirable objects! (4395)

३७. उदपुरसि मधुपुरसि वातपुरसि ॥

37. O God, Thou art the Nourisher of the people through water, the Rearer of the people through cereals, the Guardian of the people through air! (4396)

३८. इतश्च मामुतश्चावतां यमे इव यतमाने यदैतम् ।
प्र वां भरन् मानुषा देवयन्तो आ सीदतां स्वमु लोकं विदाने ॥

38. O father and mother, behaving like twins working for the good of the world, let ye both protect me from near and far! May virtuous, learned persons protect ye. Knowing your distinct places be ye seated. (4397)

३९. स्वासस्थे भवतमिन्दवे नो युजे वां ब्रह्म पूर्व्यं नमोभिः ।
वि श्लोक एति पथ्येव सूरिः शृण्वन्तु विश्वे अमृतास एतत् ॥

39. For our welfare, let both of you sit on a good seat. For the sake of you both, with homage do I worship God, realised by the ancient yogis. A man well-versed in Vedic lore treads in various ways on the right path. Let all aged persons listen to this Vedic lore. (4398)[1]

४०. त्रीणि पदानि रूपो अन्वरोहच्चतुष्पदीमन्वैतद् व्रतेन ।
अक्षरेण प्रति मिमीते अर्कमृतस्य नाभावभि सं पुनाति ॥

40. The soul masters the three-fold knowledge of the Vedas. Through the vow of celibacy it studies the four Vedas. With the help of the Immortal Om it visualises the Adorable God in each object. It purifies itself realising through engrossment, God, the Refuge of the world. (4399)[2]

४१. देवेभ्यः कमवृणीत मृत्युं प्रजायै किममृतं नावृणीत ।
बृहस्पतिर्यज्ञमतनुत ऋषिः प्रियां यमस्तन्व१मा रिरेच ॥

41. God chose physical death only for the sages. He chose no immortality for ordinary men. God, the nourisher of vast worlds, All-seeing, spreads the Yajna of Creation, the same All-controlling God consumes the lovely body in the fire of death. (4400)[3]

[1]You: Father, mother. See *Rig*, 10-13-1, 2, *Yajur*, 11-5.

[2]Threefold: Knowledge (Jnānā) Action (Karma) Contemplation (Upāsanā). Four Vedas: *Rig*, *Yajur*, *Sāma*, *Atharva*. See *Rig*, 10-13-3. Griffith remarks this verse is unintelligible. He has failed to understand its significance.

[3]Sages die like ordinary mortals. Both die, with the only difference, that the sages immortalise their name through their noble, philanthropic deeds, posterity remembers them through ages; but ordinary mortals die unwept, unhonoured, and unsung: None remembers them after death. God creates and dissolves the universe. This is His Law. See *Rig*, 10-13-4.

४२. त्वमग्न ईडितो जातवेदोऽवाड्ढव्यानि सुरभीणि कृत्वा ।
प्रादाः पितृभ्यः स्वधया ते अक्षन्नद्धि त्वं देव प्रयता हवींषि ॥

42. O Omniscient God, Worthy of adoration, Thou givest us fragrant and nutritious cereals. Thou gives them to our parents, who utilise them to the best of their power! O God, Thou acceptest the gifts we offer Thee! (4401)[1]

४३. आसीनासो अरुणीनामुपस्थे रयिं धत्त दाशुषे मर्त्याय ।
पुत्रेभ्यः पितरस्तस्य वस्वः प्रयच्छत त इहोर्जं दधात ॥

43. O elders, lapped in the bosom of acquirable branches of knowledge, give riches to a charitable person. Grant to your sons a portion of that treasure. May you acquire energy in this world. (4402)[2]

४४. अग्निष्वात्ताः पितर एह गच्छत सदःसदः सदत सुप्रणीतयः ।
अत्तो हवींषि प्रयतानि बर्हिषि रयिं च नः सर्ववीरं दधात ॥

44. Sagacious elders, full of physical and spiritual glow, come to this Yajna (sacrifice) take ye each your proper seat. Eat the food offered in the Yajna: grant riches with a multitude of brave sons. (4403)[3]

४५. उपहूता नः पितरः सोम्यासो बर्हिष्येऽषु निधिषु प्रियेषु ।
त आ गमन्तु त इह श्रुवन्त्वधि ब्रुवन्तु तेऽवन्त्वस्मान् ॥

45. May they, the Fathers, who worship God, invited to favourite, precious oblations in the Yajna, come nigh unto us, listen to our prayer, preach unto us, and bless us. (4404)[4]

४६. ये नः पितुः पितरो ये पितामहा अनूजहिरे सोमपीथं वसिष्ठाः ।
तेभिर्यमः संरराणो हवींष्युशन्नुशद्भिः प्रतिकाममत्तु ॥

46. Our father's fathers and their sires, most noble, who administer the state one after the other, with these let the king yearning with the yearning, rejoicing eat our offerings at his pleasure. (4405)[5]

४७. ये तातृषुर्देवत्रा जेहमाना होत्राविदः स्तोमतष्टासो अर्कैः ।
आग्ने याहि सहस्रं देववन्दैः सत्यैः कविभिर्ऋषिभिर्घर्मसद्भिः ॥

47. Come, Āchārya, come with countless worshippers of God, with truthful sages who are full of knowledge, who are highly sagacious, who sit in the Yajna, who are ever exerting for the attainment of God, who are Vedic scholars, singers of praises with eulogistic words, and are thirsty for God's love! (4406)[6]

[1]See *Rig*, 10-15-12, *Yajur*, 19-66.
[2]See *Rig*, 10-15-7, *Yajur*, 19-63.
[3]See *Rig*, 10-15-11, *Yajur*, 19-59.
[4]See *Rig*, 10-15-5, *Yajur*, 19-57. Fathers: Elderly learned persons.
[5]See *Rig*, 10-15-8 and *Yajur*, 19-51.
[6]See *Rig*, 10-15-9.

४८. ये सत्यासो हविरदो हविष्पा इन्द्रेण देवैः सरथं तुरेण ।
आग्ने याहि सुविदत्रेभिरर्वाङ् परैः पूर्वैर्ऋषिभिर्घर्मसद्भिः ॥

48. Come Āchārya, with highly learned persons, with excellent artists, with sages glittering like the Sun, who are truthful, eat nice, pure food, protect estables, and travel with the rulers and a strong-foe-killing warrior! (4407)[1]

४९. उप सर्प मातरं भूमिमेतामुरुव्यचसं पृथिवीं सुशेवाम् ।
ऊर्णम्रदाः पृथिवी दक्षिणावत एषा त्वा पातु प्रपथे पुरस्तात् ॥

49. O king, study and utilise fully this Earth, our mother, far-spreading, vast in extent, very kind and gracious. May she, wool-soft unto a powerful man like thee, guard thee in front in thy journey in this mighty world. (4408)[2]

५०. उच्छ्वञ्चस्व पृथिवि मा नि बाधथाः सूपायनास्मै भव सूपसर्पणा ।
माता पुत्रं यथा सिचाभ्ये॒नं भूम ऊर्णुहि ॥

50. O Earth, may thou prosper. Torment not the king and the people who dwell upon thee. Afford easy access to the king, be pleasant for his travels! Just as a mother wraps her skirt about her child, so do thou protect the king with all thy food-products. (4409)[3]

५१. उच्छ्वञ्चमाना पृथिवी सु तिष्ठतु सहस्रं मित उप हि श्रयन्ताम् ।
ते गृहासो घृतश्चुतः स्योना विश्वाहास्मै शरणाः सन्त्वत्र ॥

51. May the Earth prosper through cultivation. May thousands of persons dwell together on it. May these houses, the suppliers of nutritious diet and comfort, afford refuge for ever in this world to their lord. (4410)[4]

५२. उत्ते स्तभ्नामि पृथिवीं त्वत् परीमं लोगं निदधन्मो अहं रिषम् ।
एतां स्थूणां पितरो धारयन्ति ते तत्र यमः सादना ते कृणोतु ॥

52. O King, I develop this Earth for thee. Building this house under thy protection, may I be free from injury. Learned persons lay for thee, the foundation-stone of this house. May a skilled architect construct houses for thee on their foundations. (4411)[5]

५३. इममग्ने चमसं मा वि जिह्वरः प्रियो देवानामुत सोम्यानाम् ।
अयं यश्चमसो देवपानस्तस्मिन् देवा अमृता मादयन्ताम् ॥

[1]See *Rig*, 10-15-10. [2]See *Rig*, 10-18-10. [3]See *Rig*, 10-18-11. [4]See *Rig*, 10-18-12.
[5]See *Rig*, 10-18-13. I: A skilled geologist and engineer.

53. O learned person, don't spoil and destroy this eatable food. The learned and greatmen love it. This food is the nourisher of our organs. Aged, learned persons derive pleasure through it. (4412)[1]

५४. अथर्वा पूर्णं चमसं यमिन्द्रायाबिभर्वाजिनीवते ।
तस्मिन् कृणोति सुकृतस्य भक्षं तस्मिन्निन्दुः पवते विश्वदानीम् ॥

54. The Firm God hath bestowed ample food on a majestic learned person. Through that a mighty man performs noble deeds, and ever keeps himself pure. (4413)

५५. यत्ते कृष्णः शकुन आतुतोद पिपीलः सर्प उत वा श्वापदः ।
अग्निष्टद्विश्वादगदं कृणोतु सोमश्च यो ब्राह्मणाँ आविवेश ॥

55. What wound soe'er the dark crow, the ant, or the serpent, or the wolf, hath inflicted, let fire that devoureth all things, or a physician living amongst the learned heal it. (4414)[2]

५६. पयस्वतीरोषधयः पयस्वन्मामकं पयः । अपां पयसो यत् पयस्तेन मा सह शुम्भतु ॥

56. The plants of earth are rich in sap, and rich in vital power is my knowledge. With the essence of the essence of waters may God adorn me. (4415)[3]

५७. इमा नारीरविधवाः सुपत्नीराञ्जनेन सर्पिषा सं स्पृशन्ताम् ।
अनश्रवो अनमीवाः सुरत्ना आ रोहन्तु जनयो योनिमग्रे ॥

57. Let these unwidowed dames with goodly husbands adorn themselves with fragrant balm and unguent. Decked with fair jewels, free from grief, free from ailment, bearing children, should first enter the Assembly. (4416)[4]

५८. सं गच्छस्व पितृभिः सं यमेनेष्टापूर्तेन परमे व्योमन् ।
हित्वावद्यं पुनरस्तमेहि सं गच्छतां तन्वा सुवर्चाः ॥

58. O man, enjoy the company of aged persons. Live in the company of Brahmcharies, taking shelter under the Mighty God, perform noble deeds of sacrifice, Vedic study and charity. Abandoning sin and evil, come back to thy house. Equipped with excellent glory work in the world with thy body. (4417)[5]

५९. ये नः पितुः पितरो ये पितामहा य आविविशुरुर्व१न्तरिक्षम् ।
तेभ्यः स्वराडसुनीतिर्नो अद्य यथावशं तन्वः कल्पयाति ॥

[1]See *Rig*, 10-16-8. [2]See *Rig*, 10-16-6.

[3]See *Rig*, 10-17-14. Essence of the essence: Semen.

[4]If ladies and gentlemen are to enter an Assembly hall, according to Vedic decorum, the ladies should enter first and men should follow them.

[5]See *Rig*, 10-14-8.

59. Our father's fathers and their sires, they who have entered into air's wide region in aeroplanes, to carry out their ideals shall the Self-Resplendent God, the Giver of vital breaths, strengthen our bodies according to our desire. (4418)[1]

६०. शं ते नीहारो भवतु शं ते प्रुष्वाव शीयताम् । शीतिके शीतिकावति ह्लादिके ह्लादिकावति ।
मण्डूक्य१प्सु शं भुव इमं स्व१ग्नि शमय ॥

60. Let the hoar-frost be sweet to thee, sweetly on thee the rain descend! O calm, cool subjects, tranquil in nature, thou pleasure-giving subjects, full of joyous acts, allay obstacles, just as water keeps the female frog cool. (4419)[2]

६१. विवस्वान् नो अभयं कृणोतु यः सुत्रामा जीरदानुः सुदानुः ।
इहेमे वीरा बहवो भवन्तु गोमदश्ववन्मय्यस्तु पुष्टम ॥

61. May the Resplendent God, good Rescuer, life Bestower, bounteous Giver, make us free from fear! Many in number be these heroic children of ours! Increase of wealth be mine in kine and horses! (4420)

६२. विवस्वान् नो अमृतत्वे दधातु परैतु मृत्युरमृतं न ऐतु ।
इमान् रक्षतु पुरुषाना जरिम्णो मो ष्वे्षामसवो यमं गुः ॥

62. May the Resplendent God grant us longevity! Go far from us O Death, let prolonged life come to us! To good old age may He protect these sons and grandsons of ours: let not their breaths pass away to Death in infancy. (4421)

६३. यो दध्रे अन्तरिक्षे न मह्ना पितॄणां कविः प्रमतिर्मतीनाम् ।
तमर्चत विश्वमित्रा हविर्भिः स नो यमः प्रतरं जीवसे धात् ॥

63. God, who is the Sage of Fathers, Wisest among the wise, verily holds all worlds with His might in air's mid-region. Praise Him ye lovers of mankind with devotion. To lengthened life shall He, the Just God, lead us. (4422)[3]

६४. आ रोहत दिवमुत्तमामृषयो मा बिभीतन ।
सोमपाः सोमपायिन इदं वः क्रियते हविरगन्म ज्योतिरुत्तमम् ॥

64. Attain to salvation, the highest stage of spiritual development, O Vedic seers, be not afraid! O yogis, the lovers of God, and preachers to humanity of the love of God, here is this store of knowledge reserved for ye, wherewith we attain to the loftiest light of God! (4423)

[1]See *Rig*, 10-15-14, *Yajur*, 19-60.
[2]See *Rig*, 10-16-14.
[3]See *Atharva*, 18-4-54.

६५. प्र केतुना बृहता भात्यग्निरा रोदसी वृषभो रोरवीति ।
दिवश्चिदन्तादुपमामुदानडपामुपस्थे महिषो ववर्ध ॥

65. A King glowing like fire shines through his superb intellect, just as the heat of the Sun roars between the Earth and Sky in the form of lightning and cloud, and approaches us from the sky's farthest limit. So the adorable king advances in the lap of his subjects. (4424)

६६. नाके सुपर्णमुप यत्पतन्तं हृदा वेनन्तो अभ्यचक्षत त्वा ।
हिरण्यपक्षं वरुणस्य दूतं यमस्य योनौ शकुनं भुरण्युम् ॥

66. O King, just as people with a delightful heart gaze on an eagle that is mounting skyward, so do they gaze with longing in their spirit, on thee, full of dignity, the bestower of noble virtues, powerful in the seat of justice, and rearer of thy subjects! (4425)[1]

६७. इन्द्र क्रतुं न आ भर पिता पुत्रेभ्यो यथा ।
शिक्षा णो अस्मिन् पुरुहूत यामनि जीवा ज्योतिरशीमहि ॥

67. O God, grant us wisdom as a father gives wisdom to his sons! Guide us, O much invoked God in this our journey of life: may we living long receive the light of knowledge! (4426)[2]

६८. अपूपापिहितान् कुम्भान् यांस्ते देवा अधारयन् ।
ते ते सन्तु स्वधावन्तो मधुमन्तो घृतश्चुतः ॥

68. O man, let these utensils filled with cakes, which the learned have given thee, be full of nice food for thee, sweet like honey, invigorating like clarified butter! (4427)

६९. यास्ते धाना अनुकिरामि तिलमिश्राः स्वधावतीः ।
तास्ते सन्तु विभ्वीः प्रभ्वीस्तास्ते यमो राजानु मन्यताम् ॥

69. O man, may all ennobling acts, acquirable through exertion, soul-uplifting, that I assign thee, be excellent and potent for thee. May thy self-controlled soul, a king, utilise them to the best advantage! (4428)[3]

७०. पुनर्देहि वनस्पते य एष निहितस्त्वयि । यथा यमस्य सादन आसातै विदथा वदन् ॥

70. O God, send back on Earth, this emancipated soul dwelling in Thee, so that it may remain in this world, preaching knowledge to ordinary mortals, remaining under Thy shelter! (4429)[4]

[1]See *Rig*, 10-123-5.

[2]See *Rig*, 7-32-26.

[3]See *Atharva*, 18-4-26. I: God.

[4]This verse preaches the return of soul to the Earth. The period of salvation cannot be unlimited, as the fruit of the efforts of a soul with limited powers cannot be unlimited. If there be no return from salvation, a time may come when all souls would be emancipated, and the world come to a standstill. Maharshi Dayanand has fully dilated upon this subject in the Satyarth Prakash. Whitney interprets the verse as putting the corpse in the hollow of a tree and Sayāna as burying the bones of a dead man beneath a tree. Both the explanations are irrational and unacceptable.

७१. आ रभस्व जातवेदस्तेजस्वद्धरो अस्तु ते । शरीरमस्य सं दहाथैनं धेहि सुकृतामु लोके ॥

71. O God, the knower of all created objects, take this man under Thy shelter, let his body glow through the penance of celibacy, and place him in the assembly of the virtuous. (4430)

७२. ये ते पूर्वे परागता अपरे पितरश्च ये । तेभ्यो घृतस्य कुल्यै्तु शतधारा व्युन्दती ॥

72. To these, thy Fathers who have passed away, or are living at present, let the full stream of joy run afresh, overflowing with a hundred waves. (4431)

७३. एतदा रोह वय उन्मृजानः स्वा इह बृहदु दीदयन्ते ।
अभि प्रेहि मध्यतो माप हास्थाः पितॄणां लोकं प्रथमो यो अत्र ॥

73. O man, go forward, purifying thy life, here thy kindred shine with lofty splendour. Live in their midst. Forsake not this world of thy fathers, which is highly excellent. (4432)[1]

Chapter (Anuvāka) 4

HYMN IV

१. आ रोहत जनित्रीं जातवेदसः पितृयाणैः सं व आ रोहयामि ।
अवाड्ढव्येषितो हव्यवाह ईजानं युक्ताः सुकृतां धत्त लोके ॥

1. O learned persons, following in the wake of sages, realise the power of God for creating the universe. I expound that to you! O recipients of knowledge, the soul offers eulogies to God. With mental concentration place the devout soul in the society of virtuous people. (4433)[2]

२. देवा यज्ञमृतवः कल्पयन्ति हविः पुरोडाशं स्रुचो यज्ञायुधानि ।
तेभिर्याहि पथिभिर्देवयानैर्यैरीजानाः स्वर्गं यन्ति लोकम् ॥

2. The learned and the Hotas arrange for the Yajna, butter, cake, ladles, sacrificial utensils. Tread thou the paths travelled by the sages, whereby the righteous performers of sacrifices attain to happiness. (4434)[3]

३. ऋतस्य पन्थामनु पश्य साध्वङ्गिरसः सुकृतो येन यन्ति ।
तेभिर्याहि पथिभिः स्वर्गं यत्रादित्या मधु भक्षयन्ति तृतीये नाके अधि वि श्रयस्व ॥

3. O man, carefully observe the path of truth whereon the righteous, learned persons travel. By those same pathways go thou up to final beatitude where the yogis, the true sons of God, enjoy the sweet company of God. There make thy home in the third Highest God! (4435)[4]

[1]Forsake not: Don't die early. Enjoy a long life.

[2]I: A learned person.

[3]Hotas: Those who watch the correct performance of a Yajna. Thou: A pious performer of the Yajna.

[4]Third: God, who is higher than and different from **Matter and Soul.**

४. त्रयः सुपर्णा उपरस्य मायू नाकस्य पृष्ठे अधि विष्टपि श्रिताः ।
स्वर्गा लोका अमृतेन विष्ठा इषमूर्जं यजमानाय दुह्राम् ॥

4. God, Soul, Matter, three nourishing forces are present in the thunder of the cloud, in the high region of the Sun, and in the atmosphere, by virtue of their inherent power. May all places, filled full of joy, yield knowledge and power to him who performs noble deeds. (4436)[1]

५. जुहूर्दाधार द्यामुपभृदन्तरिक्षं ध्रुवा दाधार पृथिवीं प्रतिष्ठाम् ।
प्रतीमां-लोका घृतपृष्ठाः स्वर्गाः कामंकामं यजमानाय दुह्राम् ॥

5. God has supported the lustrous Sun. He has supported the atmosphere. He has supported Earth, that affords shelter to all. Depending upon the same God, may all beautiful, comfortable places fulfil all the wishes of a man who performs noble deeds. (4437)[2]

६. ध्रुव आ रोह पृथिवीं विश्वभोजसमन्तरिक्षमुपभृदा क्रमस्व ।
जुहु द्यां गच्छ यजमानेन साकं स्रुवेण वत्सेन दिशः प्रपीनाः सर्वा धुक्ष्वाहृणीयमानः ॥

6. O God, control the All-sustaining Earth, O God, remain ever present in the atmosphere, O God, with Thy worshipper, pervade the Sun! O worshipper, without reluctance, fill all the vast quarters with knowledge as thy calf! (4438)[3]

७. तीर्थैस्तरन्ति प्रवतो महीरिति यज्ञकृतः सुकृतो येन यन्ति ।
अत्रादधुर्यजमानाय लोकं दिशो भूतानि यदकल्पयन्त ॥

7. Men can overcome mighty obstacles through religious lore, treading on the path on which the worshippers of God and the virtuous travel. When regions and creatures were created in the beginning they afforded shelter to a worshipper of God. (4439)[4]

८. अङ्गिरसामयनं पूर्वो अग्निरादित्यानामयनं गार्हपत्यो दक्षिणानामयनं दक्षिणाग्निः ।
महिमानमग्नेर्विहितस्य ब्रह्मणा समङ्गः सर्व उप याहि शग्मः ॥

8. God is the refuge of the sages. God is the refuge of the Āditya Brahmcharies. God is the refuge of the powerful. Realise thou the greatness of God as described in the Vedas, being full of knowledge, mentally alert, and powerful. (4440)[5]

[1]Compare *Rig*, 9-9-20, and 1-164-20.

[2]Juhu is the name of God, as He controls all objects animate or inanimate. Upbhrit is the name of God, as He rears and nourishes all. **Dhruva** is the name of God, as He is Firm, Constant and Unchangeable.

[3]Just as calf is used to make the cow yield milk, so should the worshipper spread knowledge in all directions. A worshipper of God, by daily performing Havan should send up to heaven fragrant fumes.

[4]A worshipper of God can feel no suffering. Human beings and nature's forces give him shelter.

[5]Purva Agni is the name of God, as He is Primordial, Most Efficient cause, Foremost Leader of all, and Lustrous like the Sun in the East. Garhpatya Agni is the name of God, as He is the Ruler of the universe as a householder is of his family. Dakshina Agni is the name of God, as he is the Bestower of power and kinetic energy.

९. पूर्वो अग्निष्ट्वा तपतु शं पुरस्ताच्छं पश्चात् तपतु गार्हपत्यः ।
दक्षिणाग्निष्टे तपतु शर्म वर्मोत्तरतो मध्यतो अन्तरिक्षाद् दिशोदिशो अग्ने परि
पाहि घोरात् ॥

9. O man, may God shine for thy welfare and peace in the East; may God shine for thy welfare in the West. May God shine as thy Well-wisher, and Protector! O God, guard me from dire calamity, from the North and Centre, from air's mid-region, on all sides! (4441)

१०. यूयमग्ने शंतमाभिस्तनूभिरीजानमभि लोकं स्वर्गम् ।
अश्वा भूत्वा पृष्टिवाहो वहाथ यत्र देवैः सधमादं मदन्ति ॥

10. O God and His manifold forces, ye all, with your most kindly aspects, being All-pervading, take the charitable, learned worshipper of God, to a place of intense joy, as a horse carries the load on his back, where the emancipated souls, in the company of the sages, enjoy pleasure. (4442)

११. शमग्ने पश्चात् तप शं पुरस्ताच्छमुत्तराच्छमधरात् तपैनम् ।
एकस्त्रेधा विहितो जातवेदः सम्यगेनं धेहि सुकृतामु लोके ॥

11. O God, strengthen this soul from the rear, from before, above, and under, as its well-wisher! O God, the Knower of all created objects, Thou art One, but triply known, place this soul in the world that holds the righteous. (4443)[1]

१२. शमग्नयः समिद्धा आ रभन्तां प्राजापत्यं मेध्यं जातवेदसः ।
शृतं कृण्वन्त इह माव चिक्षिपन् ॥

12. Let the lustrous, learned persons, highly advanced in knowledge, merrily commence this holy Yajna, in the name of God. Strengthening the soul, let them not allow it fall down in this world. (4444)

१३. यज्ञ एति विततः कल्पमान ईजानमभि लोकं स्वर्गम् ।
तमग्नयः सर्वहुतं जुषन्तां प्राजापत्यं मेध्यं जातवेदसः । शृतं कृण्वन्त इह माव चिक्षिपन् ॥

13. The Omnipotent and All-pervading God is realised by a devotee of the Vedas, who keeps the world of the righteous as his ideal. Illuminating learned persons approach such a holy worshipper of God. May they, strengthening him in his penance, let him not fall down in this world. (4445)

१४. ईजानश्चितमारुक्षदग्निं नाकस्य पृष्ठाद् दिवमुत्पतिष्यन् ।
तस्मै प्र भाति नभसो ज्योतिषीमान्त्स्वर्गः पन्थाः सुकृते देवयानः ॥

14. A worshipper of God, longing to acquire God in this comfortable world, takes shelter under the Conscious, Wise God. For him, God, lustrous like the Sun in heaven, shines, in the midst of darkness. This is the path obtainable with glee by a virtuous person, and called the path on which the sages tread. (4446)[2]

[1]Triply known: Known as Ahvaniya, Gārhpatya and Dakshin Agni. World: State of salvation.

[2]Sages tread: Devyāna path.

१५. अग्निर्होताध्वर्युष्टे बृहस्पतिरिन्द्रो ब्रह्मा दक्षिणतस्ते अस्तु ।
हुतोऽयं संस्थितो यज्ञ एति यत्र पूर्वमयनं हुतानाम् ।।

15. O man, let God, the Hota of thy Yajna, God, the Adhwaryu of thy Yajna, God, the Brahmā of thy Yajna of life, be always present on thy right hand! On the completion of life, this body is offered to fire, and the sacrificing soul goes to a place where the consecrated souls have gone before. (4447)[1]

१६. अपूपवान् क्षीरवांश्चरुरेह सीदतु ।
लोककृतः पथिकृतो यजामहे ये देवानां हुतभागा इह स्थ ।।

16. Enriched with cake and milk let abundant food be stored in this world. We worship the benefactors of humanity, and the exhibitors of the path of righteousness, who amongst the sages deserve to partake of these meals. (4448)

१७. अपूपवान् दधिवांश्चरुरेह सीदतु ।
लोककृतः पथिकृतो यजामहे ये देवानां हुतभागा इह स्थ ।।

17. Enriched with cake and curds let abundant food be stored in this world. We worship the benefactors of humanity, and the exhibitors of the path of righteousness, who amongst the sages deserve to partake of these meals. (4449)

१८. अपूपवान् द्रप्सवांश्चरुरेह सीदतु ।
लोककृतः पथिकृतो यजामहे ये देवानां हुतभागा इह स्थ ।।

18. Enriched with cake and diluted sour milk let abundant food be stored in this world. We worship the benefactors of humanity and the exhibitors of the path of righteousness, who amongst the sages deserve to partake of these meals. (4450)

१९. अपूपवान् घृतवांश्चरुरेह सीदतु ।
लोककृतः पथिकृतो यजामहे ये देवानां हुतभागा इह स्थ ।।

19. Enriched with cake and butter let abundant food be stored in this world. We worship the benefactors of humanity, and the exhibitors of the path of righteousness, who amongst the sages deserve to partake of these meals. (4451)

२०. अपूपवान् मांसवांश्चरुरेह सीदतु ।
लोककृतः पथिकृतो यजामहे ये देवानां हुतभागा इह स्थ ।।

[1]Hota, Adhvaryu, Brahma are the priests who watch, supervise and rightly conduct a Yajna. Agni, Brihaspati, Indra are the names of God.

20. Enriched with cake and articles developing intellect, let abundant food be stored in this world. We worship the benefactors of humanity, and the exhibitors of the path of righteousness, who amongst the sages deserve to partake of these meals. (4452)

२१. अपूपवानन्नवांश्चरुरेह सीदतु । लोककृतः पथिकृतो यजामहे ये देवानां हुतभागा इह स्थ ।।

21. Enriched with cake and cereals, let abundant food be stored in this world. We worship the benefactors of humanity, and the exhibitors of the path of righteousness, who amongst the sages deserve to partake of these meals. (4453)[1]

२२. अपूपवान् मधुमांश्चरुरेह सीदतु ।
लोककृतः पथिकृतो यजामहे ये देवानां हुतभागा इह स्थ ।।

22. Enriched with cake and mead let abundant food be stored in this world. We worship the benefactors of humanity, and the exhibitors of the path of righteousness, who amongst the sages deserve to partake of these meals. (4454)

२३. अपूपवान् रसवांश्चरुरेह सीदतु ।
लोककृतः पथिकृतो यजामहे ये देवानां हुतभागा इह स्थ ।।

23. Enriched with cake and juicy substances let abundant food be stored in this world. We worship the benefactors of humanity, and the exhibitors of the path of righteousness, who amongst the sages deserve to partake of these meals. (4455)

२४. अपूपवानपवांश्चरुरेह सीदतु । लोककृतः पथिकृतो यजामहे ये देवानां हुतभागा इह स्थ ।।

24. Enriched with cake and pure water let abundant food be stored in this world. We worship the benefactors of humanity and the exhibitors of the path of righteousness, who amongst the sages deserve to partake of these meals. (4456)

२५. अपूपापिहितान् कुम्भान् यांस्ते देवा अधारयन् ।
ते ते सन्तु स्वधावन्तो मधुमन्तो घृतश्चुतः ।।

25. O man, let the pots, covered with cakes and sustained by gods for thee, be rich with nectar, honey and dripping ghee for thy well-being. (4457)

२६. यास्ते धाना अनुकिरामि तिलमिश्राः स्वधावतीः ।
तास्ते सन्तूद्भ्वीः प्रभ्वीस्तास्ते यमो राजानु मन्यताम् ।।

26. Let the nectarine grains mixed with sesame that I properly scatter for thee enhance your prosperity and power. Let the king Yama approve them for thee. (4458)

[1]मांसं माननं वा मानसं वा मनोऽस्मिन्त्सदितोति वा, निरु० ४-३१ मननसाधकेन बुद्धिवर्धकवस्तुना युक्तः । 1. The word Mānsa does not here mean flesh, but sweet, juicy fruits, almonds, walnuts. The Vedas denounce the eating of flesh.

२७. अक्षितिं भूयसीम् ॥

27. A greater, more abundant inexhaustibleness. (4459)

२८. द्रप्सश्चस्कन्द पृथिवीमनु द्यामिमं च योनिमनु यश्च पूर्वः ।
समानं योनिमनु संचरन्तं द्रप्सं जुहोम्यनु सप्त होत्राः ॥

28. The pleasant already existent Sun is pervading the earth and the heavens, the source of animate and inanimate creation. I, along with seven hotas offer oblations to the pleasant Sun, moving among the equal source of creation of animate and inanimate world. (4460)[1]

२९. शतधारं वायुमर्कं स्वर्विदं नृचक्षसस्ते अभि चक्षते रयिम् ।
ये पृणन्ति प्र च यच्छन्ति सर्वदा ते दुह्रते दक्षिणां सप्तमातरम् ॥

29. The seers of God, who consider the pleasure-giving, Radiant, strong and Bounteous God with His manifold blessings, the source of all riches and strength and life, always nourish and cherish all the creatures. They derive all the desired objects from the mother-earth, the source of seven kinds of corns and metals. (4461)[2]

३०. कोशं दुहन्ति कलशं चतुर्बिलमिडां धेनुं मधुमतीं स्वस्तये ।
ऊर्जं मदन्तीमदितिं जनेष्वग्ने मा हिंसीः परमे व्योमन् ॥

30. Just as people draw water from a vesse with four taps, similarly people derive fourfold benefits from the cow-like earth, producing sweet articles on all the four quarters of it for the good of humanity. O King, don't ruin this imperishable earth, the source of food and strength, satisfying the populace, keeping under your vast regime. (4462)[3]

३१. एतत् ते देवः सविता वासो ददाति भर्तवे । तत्त्वं यमस्य राज्ये वसानस्तार्प्यं चर ॥

31. O man, the charitable Creator has given thee the clothing (i.e., body) for protection. Living in the kingdom of the Controller of all, enjoy thyself to thy satisfaction. (4463)

३२. धाना धेनुरभवद् वत्सो अस्यास्तिलोऽभवत् । तां वै यमस्य राज्ये अक्षितामुप जीवति ॥

[1]According to Pt. Jaidev Vidyalankar, the verse may mean: The semen of man, that was present before in man and then came into the womb of woman, pervades through both the splendour of man and the uterus of woman. I, the man offers it as oblations to Yosha-agni through seven Prānas (vital breaths) similarly the Divine semen is installed in the primodial cause of the universe in the very beginning of the creation.

[2]Pt. Damodar Satvalekar translates the verse as: Those who make the right use of money after earning it, get honour and glory in this world and happiness in the world hereafter. The verse also occurs as *Rig*, 10-107-4.

[3]The verse may also be translated, taking the 'cow' 'Vedic Lore' for the 'earth.' It occurs as *Yajur*, 13-47.

32. The parched rice (i.e., khilān) is cow and sesame is her calf. In the kingdom of the Controller of all, people subsist on her with imperishable sources of nourishment. (4464)[1]

३३. एतास्ते असौ धेनवः कामदुघा भवन्तु ।
एनीः श्येनीः सरूपा विरूपास्तिलवत्सा उप तिष्ठन्तु त्वात्र ॥

33. These cows may fulfil all thy desires. Mayst thou the wheatish, white khilān of the same colour or different colour with sesame as their calf. (4465)[2]

३४. एनीर्धाना हरिणीः श्येनीरस्य कृष्णा धाना रोहिणीर्धेनवस्ते ।
तिलवत्सा ऊर्जमस्मै दुहाना विश्वाहा सन्त्वनपस्फुरन्तीः ॥

34. The wheatish, bluish, white, dark and red parched rice, having the qualities of sustaining this world, serves as milch cows, giving invigorating vitamins to the body of the man. May they ever be free from danger and trouble of any sort. (4466)

३५. वैश्वानरे हविरिदं जुहोमि साहस्रं शतधारमुत्सम् ।
स बिभर्ति पितरं पितामहान् प्रपितामहान् बिभर्ति पिन्वमानः ॥

35. I (man) offer this oblation to the Benefactor of all, the fountain-head of hundreds and thousands of streams of material objects and spiritual benefits. He (God), being thus pleased, nourishes the fathers, grandfathers and great-grandfathers. (4467)

३६. सहस्रधारं शतधारमुत्समक्षितं व्यच्यमानं सलिलस्य पृष्ठे ।
ऊर्जं दुहानमनपस्फुरन्तमुपासते पितरः स्वधाभिः ॥

36. The guardians of the people worship, with their sustained efforts, the Indestructible fountain-head of hundreds and thousands of streams of material objects, appearing in manifold forms, giving strength and energy without any break or stoppage, all through the heavens or firmament. (4468)[3]

३७. इदं कसाम्बु चयनेन चितं तत् सजाता अव पश्यतेत ।
मर्त्योऽयममृतत्वमेति तस्मै गृहान् कृणुत यावत्सबन्धु ॥

[1]Parched rice (khilān), having the same qualities of nourishment as cow, is named cow here. Sesame with oily qualities of attachment is termed calf. Both provide means of subsistence to the populace. Thus they provide inexhaustible source of nourishment to them.

[2](33-34) In Indian life, a great significance is given to parched rice and sesame on all ceremonial occasions, due to their great qualities of nourishments. Thy: man's: Thou: man. The verse 34 may equally be applied to the cows of various colours. In their case, 'Tilwatsa' would mean with calves, with qualities of attachment like sesame.

[3]See *Yajur*, 13-49 also.

37. This semen, having been collected in the organs of man is born. O similarly-born relatives, come and see him. This mortal (embodied soul) becomes immortal. Ye, whoever are his relatives, erect buildings for him. (4469)

३८. इहैवैधि धनसनिरिहचित्त इहक्रतुः । इहैधि वीर्यवत्तरो वयोधा अपराहतः ॥

38. O man, thou dost prosper here in this very world, distributing wealth to others after having got knowledge and having done good deeds in this world. Being stronger than others and thus not being subdued by others, dost prosper here, having enough food and old age. (4470)[1]

३९. पुत्रं पौत्रमभितर्पयन्तीरापो मधुमतीरिमाः ।
स्वधां पितृभ्यो अमृतं दुहाना आपो देवीरुभयांस्तर्पयन्तु ॥

39. These people, with divine qualities, like pure waters, fully satisfying their sons and grandsons with sweet provisions and providing rich food and pure drinks like nectar to their elders may fully satisfy both the youngers and the elders. (4471)[2]

४०. आपो अग्निं प्र हिणुत पितॄँरुपेमं यज्ञं पितरो मे जुषन्ताम् ।
आसीनामूर्जमुप ये सचन्ते ते नो रयिं सर्ववीरं नि यच्छान् ॥

40. O waters, generate electricity with currents that produce and protect so many things. Let these productive currents serve my manufacturing concern. Let them provide stationary energy for it and thus give us wealth and riches with valorous army. (4472)[3]

४१. समिन्धते अमर्त्यं हव्यवाहं घृतप्रियम् । स वेद निहितान् निधीन् पितॄन् परावतो गतान् ॥

41. They (i.e., engineers) enkindle (set in motion) the imperishable, load-carrying water-loving electricity. He (an engineer) knows the storehouse of the secret currents of electricity that have gone far and wide over the country and even in the outer space. (4473)[4]

४२. यं ते मन्थं यमोदनं यन्मांसं निपृणामि ते । ते ते सन्तु स्वधावन्तो मधुमन्तो घृतश्चुतः ॥

[1]The soul in the form of a drop is spoken of as having undergone the ordeal of five 'agnis' is born after the 5th 'Yoshā-agni.'

[2]The verse ordains that it is the duty of the noble persons to upbring their progeny and properly look after their elders.

[3]In my opinion, the verse indicates how hydrogical power units can provide energy to the factories and the armies and thus enhance the prosperity and military strength of a nation. (my: a mill-owner's). Pt. Jaidev Vidyalankar applies it to noble men serving the nation and producing wealth for it. See Mansa-Parikram Mantra, 2 in *Vedic Sandhya*.

[4]The indestructiveness, the capacity for carrying heavy loads and affinity for water of electric currents is well-known. 'The engineers should provide secret store-house for the generated energy' is indicated by the latter half of the verse.

42. O man, whatever churned curd, cooked rice and wholesome pitty articles of food I (God) provide to satisfy thy hunger, may they be invigorating, sweet and energising to thee. (4474)

४३. यास्ते धाना अनुकिरामि तिलमिश्राः स्वधावतीः ।
तास्ते सन्तूद्भ्वीः प्रभ्वीस्तास्ते यमो राजानु मन्यताम् ।।

43. O man, the nourishing paddy along with sesame that I (a cultivator) sow for thee, may grow in abundance and provide vitality and strength to thee. May the controller, the king ordain its free use by thee. (4475)[1]

४४. इदं पूर्वमपरं नियानं येना ते पूर्वे पितरः परेताः ।
पुरोगवा ये अभिशाचो अस्य ते त्वा वहन्ति सुकृतामु लोकम् ।।

44. O man, this body is the chariot that was before and shall be provided even hereafter and by which thy fore-fathers have gone to the other world. These all-powerful bullocks, that yolked in front of this chariot are carrying thee to the world of the virtuous people. (4476)[2]

४५. सरस्वतीं देवयन्तो हवन्ते सरस्वतीमध्वरे तायमाने ।
सरस्वतीं सुकृतो हवन्ते सरस्वती दाशुषे वार्यं दात् ।।

45. The seekers of noble qualities worship God the source of all sweetness like a stream or Vedic lore. The sacrificers invoke the source of sweet blessings in the performance of the non-violent sacrifice. The virtuous call the same Saraswati. The fountain of all streams of blessings gives away the best gifts to the devotee. (4477)[3]

४६. सरस्वतीं पितरो हवन्ते दक्षिणा यज्ञमभिनक्षमाणाः ।
आसद्यास्मिन् बर्हिषि मादयध्वमनमीवा इष आ धेह्यस्मे ।।

46. The elders and the guardians of the land, sitting on the southern side of the sacrificial place call forth the Vedic lore and the lady of the house. O men, sitting in this great sacrificial place be happy and cheerful. O lady, give us food free from all disease and illness. (4478)[4]

४७. सरस्वति या सरथं ययाथोक्थैः स्वधाभिर्देवि पितृभिर्मदन्ती ।
सहस्रार्घमिडो अत्र भागं रायस्पोषं यजमानाय धेहि ।।

[1]cf. *Atharva*, 18-3-69 and 8-4-26.

[2]The five senses of knowledge and five organs of action are spoken of as bullocks carrying the body-chariot to the destination of the soul.

[3]The occidental and the oriental scholars who conceive Saraswati, as a certain goddess or a special river of that name, don't realise the real significance of the Vedic Text. It was given to Maharshi to unfold their real import by his rendite scholarship and learning. According to him Saraswati is a qualifying name of God, Wherefrom flow the manifold streams of knowledge, blessings and sweet things of this world and the other world.

[4]See 18.1.42 (श० 2.5.2.22)

47. O Divine Saraswati, ye who go along with the praise-songs, being pleased with self-sustaining elders, endow the sacrificer, here in this world with thousand-fold riches and prosperity of a part of food-grains. (4479)[1]

४८. पृथिवीं त्वा पृथिव्यामा वेशयामि देवो नो धाता प्र तिरात्यायुः ।
परापरैता वसुविद् वो अस्त्वधा मृताः पितृषु सं भवन्तु ॥

48. O lady, I (the householder) settle you on this earth. May the Creator prolong our lives. O people, may those amongst you, who go far and distant as traders, be able to acquire abundant wealth; and those, who die, be reborn to the elders amongst you. (4480)[2]

४९. आ प्र च्यवेथामप तन्मृजेथां यद् वामभिभा अत्रोचुः ।
अस्मादेतमघ्न्यौ तद् वशीयो दातुः पितृष्विहभोजनौ मम ॥

49. O husband and wife, whenever you transgress the right path, both of you seek light from the enlightened persons. Whatever they say in this matter, you should purify yourselves thereby. Ye, indestructible souls, come back from this path of evil. That would control all your evil propensities. Please stay here as protectors and guardians of me (the son) the giver of all comforts to you (my parents). (4481)[3]

५०. एयमगन् दक्षिणा भद्रतो नो अनेन दत्ता सुदुघा वयोधाः ।
यौवने जीवानुपपृञ्चती जरा पितृभ्य उपसंपराणयादिमान् ॥

50. This strong and energising cow has come to us from a noble person as a gift. Being given by him, she is easy to milk and prolongs our lives and nourishes the people in youth as well in old age. He continues feeding them through the elders for long long years. (4482)[4]

५१. इदं पितृभ्यः प्र भरामि बर्हिर्जीवं देवेभ्य उत्तरं स्तृणामि ।
तदा रोह पुरुष मेध्यो भवन् प्रति त्वा जानन्तु पितरः परेतम् ॥

51. I (the sacrificer) spread this seat of Kusha-grass for the elders and being alive, spread a higher seat for the teachers of divine qualities. O man, attaining purity and superiority, sit on this seat of honour, so that the elders may remember thee even when thou hast gone to a distant place or even to the other world. (4483)

[1]Here in Saraswati means both the Vedic lore and lady of the house as in 46 above. See 18.1.43.

[2]Pt. Damodar Satvalekar refers to the burying of the dead in the first half of the verse. But Pt. Jaidev Vidyalankar takes it as setting of a lady in the household by a household (Prithvi—woman) which is, to me, a better rendering as the very next clause prays for the long life of both. The verse refers to transmigration of soul.

[3]In the last part, the son, reborn as referred to in 48, invokes the protection of his parents.

[4]The verse emphasises the importance of cow as the nourisher of the people at large and hence 'Aghanya'—not to be killed by man.

५२. एदं बर्हिरसदो मेध्योऽभूः प्रति त्वा जानन्तु पितरः परेतम् ।
यथापरु तन्वं१ सं भरस्व गात्राणि ते ब्रह्मणा कल्पयामि ।।

52. O man, sit on this seat of Kusha-grass and be pure and worthy to perform the sacrifice. The elders may remember thee even when thou hast gone to distant lands. Strengthen thy body taking care of every organ of it. I (the learned preceptor) invigorate all thy organs of thy body with rich food. (4484)[1]

५३. पर्णो राजापिधानं चरूणामूर्जो बलं सह ओजो न आगन् ।
आयुर्जीवेभ्यो विदधद् दीर्घायुत्वाय शतशारदाय ।।

53. Just the cooked rice has a covering of leaf and gives us vigour, valour and splendour, so does a king provide a protective cover for his mobile populace with vigour, courage and glory. He gives a long lease of life to his subjects for hundred long, long years. (4485)[2]

५४. ऊर्जो भागो य इमं जजानाश्मान्नानामाधिपत्यं जगाम ।
तमर्चत विश्वामित्रा हविर्भिः स नो यमः प्रतरं जीवसे धात् ।।

54. The agriculturist produces a part (i.e., sixth) of food-grains for this king, who thus attains the lordship of the people, like a grinding stone of the food-grains. O benefactors of the populace, honour him (the king) thus by offering food-grains (as revenue in kind). The very same controller (of grains etc.) may give us nourishment to enable us to lead a long life. (4486)[3]

५५. यथा यमाय हर्म्यमवपन् पञ्च मानवाः । एवा वपामि हर्म्यं यथा मे भूरयोऽसत ।।

55. Just as five kinds of people erect a palace for the controller of the people (i.e., king), similarly do I build a mansion for myself so that many members of my family may live therein. (4487)[4]

५६. इदं हिरण्यं बिभृहि यत्ते पिताबिभः पुरा । स्वर्गं यतः पितुर्हस्तं निर्मृड्ढि दक्षिणम् ।।

56. O man wearest this gold ornament that thy father wore before. Purifiest thou the right hand of thy father, who is passing away to the yonder world of bliss. (4488)[5]

[1]Brahma: food, wealth, Vedic lore and God.

[2]In the regime of a good administrator, people enjoy long life hundred years.

[3]The king gets one-sixth of the food-grains and utilises it for the benefit of the people for enabling them to attain long life.

[4]Five: Brahman, Kshatriya, Vaishya, Shudra and Nishad. I: a householder. The verse gives equal right to an ordinary person to have as stately a house as a king may possess. There is no invidious distinction between the high and the low in the eyes of God.

[5]The verse ordains a person to undertake the duties of his father and be as rich as the deceased.

५७. ये च जीवा ये च मृता ये जाता ये च यज्ञियाः ।
तेभ्यो घृतस्य कुल्यैऽतु मधुधारा व्युन्दती ॥

57. May the sweet streams of clarified butter and other invigorating and energising provisions flow out to those, whoever are living, whoever are dead, whoever are born and whoever are sacrifice-minded. (4489)[1]

५८. वृषा मतीनां पवते विचक्षणः सूरो अह्नां प्रतरीतोषसां दिवः ।
प्राणः सिन्धूनां कलशाँ अचिक्रददिन्द्रस्य हार्दिमाविशन्मनीषया ॥

58. The soul, the showerer of various mental powers and seer of manifold learning, the mover of days, light and dawns, the very breath of the sense-organs, that ever flow like streams towards their objects of perception, setting in motion these bodies, enters the heart by the mental energy. (4490)[2]

५९. त्वेषस्ते धूम ऊर्णोतु दिवि षञ्छुक्र आततः । सूरो न हि द्युता त्वं कृपा पावक रोचसे ॥

59. O soul, thy grey-coloured light may spread afar and in the state of salvation, thy pure-white beauty may pervade all through and thou shinest with splendour like the Sun purifying all with thy spiritual powers. (4491)[3]

६०. प्र वा एतीन्दुरिन्द्रस्य निष्कृतिं सखा सख्युर्न प्र मिनाति संगिरः ।
मर्यं इव योषाः समर्षसे सोमः कलशे शतयामना पथा ॥

60. The emancipated soul, with charming qualities like the moon, attain to the actionless state of the Glorious God (in salvation). Then the friend (soul), holds mutual conversations with his Friend (God). Just as a powerful man affords happiness to many women by looking after them, so does the pleasure-giving God instills bliss in the heart of the countless emancipated souls. (4492)[4]

६१. अक्षन्नमीमदन्त ह्यव प्रियाँ अधूषत । अस्तोषत स्वभानवो विप्रा यविष्ठा ईमहे ॥

61. The self-enlightened, spiritually sublime souls taste and perpetually revel in the highest bliss of God. They shed off the worldly pleasures and become sinless. They praise the all-Blissful God. We, the men of lower attainments desire their guidance for spiritual knowledge. (4493)[5]

[1]All the four kinds of people, i.e., the living, the dead, the born and the sacrificers need the abundance of clarified butter and other provisions. The dead for the cremation of their bodies according to Vedic rites. The verse refers to a life of prosperity and abundance and not of penury and shortages also see 18.3.72.

[2]The verse enumerates the manifold powers of the mind of man, by cultivating which he can attain to sublime heights also see *Rig*, 9.86.1.

[3]Pt. Satvalekar applies this verse to ordinary fire only, which lowers the sublimity of the Vedic Text. The verse refers to the divine powers of a Yogi also see *Rig*, 6.26, and *Sama*, 1.83.

[4]The verse shows how the soul attains to the culmination of his object of life, i.e., salvation also see *Rig*, 9.86.10.

[5]The verse describes the state of emancipation and the aspirants are asked to look for guidance to the Jiwan-muktas also see *Rig*, 1.12.2 and *Yajur*, 3,51. Pt. Damodar Satva lekar applies to an ordinary sacrifice only.

६२. आ यात पितरः सोम्यासो गम्भीरैः पथिभिः पितृयाणैः ।
आयुरस्मभ्यं दधतः प्रजां च रायश्च पोषैरभि नः सचध्वम् ।।

62. O fore-fathers, who are acting according to your vow and being celebate, are in search of Divine bliss go forth on your difficult paths of spiritual attainments, worthy to be followed by the elderly people. Giving us long life and offspring, shower on us riches and vitalising means of subsistence. (4494)[1]

६३. परा यात पितरः सोम्यासो गम्भीरैः पथिभिः पूर्याणैः ।
अधा मासि पुनरा यात नो गृहान् हविरत्तुं सुप्रजसः सुवीराः ।।

63. O elders, who have taken the vow of celibacy for seeking the company of the pleasure-giving God, attain salvation by treading the difficult paths, leading to the final-abode of the Blissful Father. And on the completion of a month, come back to our homes, along with noble and brave disciples to partake of our sacrificial oblations. (4495)[2]

६४. यद् वो अग्निरजहादेकमङ्गं पितृलोकं गमयञ्जातवेदाः ।
तद् व एतत् पुनरा प्याययामि साङ्गाः स्वर्गे पितरो मादयध्वम् ।।

64. O elders, the well-enlightened king forces you to leave behind a partner of yours, while you are going to the abode of the elders (the forest for Banprasthies) I restore the same to you, so that you live in happiness there. (4496)[3]

६५. अभूद् दूतः प्रहितो जातवेदाः सायं न्यह्न उपवन्द्यो नृभिः ।
प्रादाः पितृभ्यः स्वधया ते अक्षन्नद्धि त्वं देव प्रयता हवींषि ।।

65. The learned person, well-versed in Vedic lore, sent as preachers should be respected morning and evening by men. O learned person of divine qualities, regularly take food, offered to thee and safely carry the vitalising food to the elders so that they may eat it. (4497)[4]

६६. असौ हा इह ते मनः ककुत्सलमिव जामयः । अभ्येनं भूम ऊर्णुहि ।।

66. O departed soul, thy mind is still set here in this world. O earth, cover him up, just women cover their shoulders. (4498)[5]

[1]A 'grihasthi': a householder wishes his fore-fathers to follow the difficult path of spiritual attainment and invoked their blessings for his own people.

[2]The same householder requests his Banprasthi, practising Yoga to come monthly to his home to share his offerings of a sacrifice.

[3]It is meaningless to think that a part of the body of the dead is left behind and is later on supplied to them by the surviving offspring by Pind-dān. The verse conveys that the son enables the mother, too, to join the father in the Ban-Prasth-Ashram, if she was prevented by some order of the king before.

[4]The verse refers to the regular contact between the Banprasthi elders and the Grihasthi progeny, through a learned person, who might be one of their disciples. cf. *Rig*, 4.54.1.

[5]This verse appears to be the origin of the burying of the dead by Christians and Muhammadans.

६७. शुम्भन्तां लोकाः पितृषदनाः पितृषदने त्वा लोक आ सादयामि ॥

67. The residential places of the elders may be well-decorated. I respectfully seat thee (an honoured guest) in the abode, fit for the elders' residence. (4499)[1]

६८. येऽस्माकं पितरस्तेषां बर्हिरसि ॥

68. Thou art the honoured seat for those who are our respectable elders or preceptors. (4500)[2]

६९. उदुत्तमं वरुण पाशमस्मदवाधमं वि मध्यमं श्रथाय ।
अधा वयमादित्य व्रते तवानागसो अदितये स्याम ॥

69. O God, Worthy of respect and choice by all, untie our bonds, the highest, the middle one, and the lowest and thus, O splendorous God, we may be sinless, under thy control, for the attainment of salvation. (4501)[3]

७०. प्रास्मत् पाशान् वरुण मुञ्च सर्वान् यैः समामे बध्यते यैर्व्यामे ।
अधा जीवेम शरदं शतानि त्वया राजन् गुपिता रक्षमाणाः ॥

70. O All-cherishable and Worthy God, set us free from all those bonds wherewith a man is bound in general and in particular. Thus, O Radiant God, being protected and guarded by thee, we may live hundreds of years. (4502)[4]

७१. अग्नये कव्यवाहनाय स्वधा नमः ॥

71. Respect and vitalising food to the leader, who provides proper provisions to the learned and the intelligent people. (4503)[5]

७२. सोमाय पितृमते स्वधा नमः ॥

72. Honour and energising provisions to the pleasure-giving king, along with elders. (4504)

७३. पितृभ्यः सोमवद्भ्यः स्वधा नमः ॥

73. Homage and strength-giving food to the respectable people, coming along with peace-giving king. (4505)

७४. यमाय पितृमते स्वधा नमः ॥

[1]The verse ordains that progeny should look to the needs of the elders for comfortable and beautiful houses for their elders and guests.

[2]It is the duty of a householder to provide a seat of honour for the elders and guests.

[3]The highest—'Pitra-yoni,' the middle one—Manushya-yoni,' the lowest 'Pashuyoni,' 'aditi'—'Deva-yoni' i.e., of emancipated souls.

[4]शतानि: means countless in the state of salvation.

[5](71-74) These verses lay down the duty of the general people to honour their king and the learned and the elders with rich food and respectful homage also see *Yajur*, 2.29.

74. Offerings of respect and rich food to the controller of men, coming with the elders. (4506)

७५. एतत् ते प्रततामह स्वधा ये च त्वामनु ॥

75. O Great-grandfather, here is this nourishing food for thee and those who follow thee. (4507)[1]

७६. एतत् ते ततामह स्वधा ये च त्वामनु ॥

76. O grandfather, here is this rich food for thee and those who follow thee. (4508)

७७. एतत् ते तत स्वधा ॥

77. O father, here is this vitalising food for thee. (4509)

७८. स्वधा पितृभ्यः पृथिविषद्भ्यः ॥

78. Nourishing food to the elders, who inhabit the earth. (4510)[2]

७९. स्वधा पितृभ्यो अन्तरिक्षसद्भ्यः ॥

79. Energising food to the elders, who have their abode in the firmament. (4511)

८०. स्वधा पितृभ्यो दिविषद्भ्यः ॥

80. Vitalising food to the elders, who have settled higher up in the celestial regions. (4512)

८१. नमो वः पितर ऊर्जे नमो वः पितरो रसाय ॥

81. O fathers, all honour to you for the nourishing food. O fathers, all respect to you for the medicinal juices or extracts. (4513)[3]

८२. नमो वः पितरो भामाय नमो वः पितरो मन्यवे ॥

82. O elders, all respect for your righteous indignation. O elders, all honour to your hatred of the evil forces. (4514)

८३. नमो वः पितरो यद् घोरं तस्मै नमो वः पितरो यत् क्रूरं तस्मै ॥

[1](75-77) These verses ordain the Pitri-yajna of the living elders and not the dead.

[2](78-80) These three verses clearly show that Vedic Rishis not only made this earth their place of residence, but were able to fly higher up in space and create places of living in outer space and even in heavens beyond that. Their offspring was able to keep in contact with them, which is still a dream for the modern scientists and technicians of the Rocket age also see *Yajur*, 2.32.

[3](81-85) The verses teach the young ones how they should be respectful to their elders and tolerate all their frownings and terrible moods. There goes the proverb—'Mother is cruel to be kind'.

83. O elders, we (the youngers) bow to whatever is terrible in you. O elders, we (the youngers) bow to whatever is cruel in you. (4515)

८४. नमो वः पितरो यच्छिवं तस्मै नमो वः पितरो यत् स्योनं तस्मै ।।

84. O fathers, we (the youth) respect whatever is peace-giving in you. O fathers, we honour whatever is ease-giving in you. (4516)

८५. नमो वः पितरः स्वधा वः पितरः ।।

85. O elders, all respect to you. O elders, we offer the energising food or libation to you. (4517)

८६. येऽत्र पितरः पितरो येऽत्र यूयं स्थ युष्माँस्तेऽनु यूयं तेषां श्रेष्ठा भूयास्थ ।।

86. O elders who are here. Other elders are also there. You stay here. The others may be lower thou ye. You may be the most excellent of these. (4518)[1]

८७. य इह पितरो जीवा इह वयं स्मः । अस्माँस्तेऽनु वयं तेषां श्रेष्ठा भूयास्म ।।

87. O fathers, here are (other) men. We are also here in this world. They may be lower than we. We may be the most excellent of them all. (4519)[2]

८८. आ त्वाग्न इधीमहि द्युमन्तं देवाजरम् ।
यद् घ सा ते पनीयसी समिद् दीदयति द्यवि । इषं स्तोतृभ्य आ भर ।।

88. O Radiant and Omniscient God, we worship Thee, the Effulgent, Imperishable one, as verily Thy Praiseworthy, Glorious Power shines forth in the heavens. Mayst Thou infuse the desired emotion and vigour in thy worshippers. (4520)[3]

८९. चन्द्रमा अप्स्व१न्तरा सुपर्णो धावते दिवि ।
न वो हिरण्यनेमयः पदं विन्दन्ति विद्युतो वित्तं मे अस्य रोदसी ।।

89. Just as the moon, with her beautiful rays speedily moves amidst the waters in the heavens, similarly, the soul, with charming radiances provided by God, freely moves through peace-infusing bliss of God in the state of emancipation. O self-luminous yogis, the general people bent upon the worldly possessions like gold, can't realise the importance of your state of beatitude. O teachers and preachers, do understand my (the divine-seeker's) needs. (4521)[4]

[1]A son wishes his own fore-fathers to the most superior to all others, this is not out of jealousy, but of envy.

[2]The offspring also wishes to be the most superior to all others in the same envious spirit, which is the right course for progress in life.

[3]cf. *Rig*, 5.6.4.

[4]The final emancipation of the soul is the culmination of his activities in the world. So it should be the ideal of every man on earth.

BOOK (Kāṇḍa) XIX

Chapter (Anuvāka) 1

HYMN I

१. सं सं स्रवन्तु नद्य१: सं वाताः सं पतत्रिणः ।
यज्ञमिमं वर्धयता गिरः संस्राव्येऽण हविषा जुहोमि ॥

1. Let the streams of prosperity flow perpetually like, ordinary stream. Let winds flow at the proper time (to bring in rains). Let boats with sails move on or airships fly continually. O reciters of Vedic hymns, strengthen my sacrifice. I offer oblations that may be the means of the flow of prosperity and well-being. (4522)[1]

२. इमं होमा यज्ञमवतेमं संस्रावणा उत । यज्ञमिमं वर्धयता गिरः संस्राव्येऽण हविषा जुहोमि ॥

2. O burnt oblations, protect this sacrifice of mine, O mixed offerings do ye also protect it. O reciters, strengthen my sacrifice. I offer my oblations of mixed materials. (4523)

३. रूपंरूपं वयोवयः संरभ्यैनं परि ष्वजे ।
यज्ञमिमं चतस्रः प्रदिशो वर्धयन्तु संस्राव्येऽण हविषा जुहोमि ॥

3. Having collected all kinds of cattle, food and means of power, I protect this king. May the men of all the four quarters enhance this sacrifice of mine. I offer my oblations for the progress and betterment of my nation. (4524)

HYMN II

१. शं त आपो हैमवतीः शमु ते सन्तूत्स्याऽः । शं ते सनिष्यदा आपः शमु ते सन्तु वर्ष्याऽः ॥

1. O man, may the waters from the snowy hills be peace-giving the thee. May the spring waters bring calmness to thee. May the swift-flowing waters be pleasant for thee. So may the rainy waters be a source of tranquility to thee. (4525)[2]

२. शं त आपो धन्वन्या३: शं ते सन्त्वनूप्याऽः ।
शं ते खनित्रिमा आपः शं याः कुम्भेभिराभृताः ॥

2. O man, sweet be the waters of the desert unto thee and so may be the waters of the pool. May the waters dug from the earth (i.e. of wells) be sweet as well as those stored in tanks. (4526)

३. अनभ्रयः खनमाना विप्रा गम्भीरे अपसः । भिषग्भ्यो भिषक्तरा आपो अच्छा वदामसि ॥

3. Just as super-intellectual persons are engrossed in deep meditation about God, similarly the learned persons, digging waters very deep without the tool to dig, find such waters better healers than the healing herbs even. We (the learned people) thoroughly explain their qualities (to the general public). (4527)

[1](1-3) The whole hymn describes the sacrifice of a patriotic citizen for the prosperity and well-being of his country.

[2](1-5) The whole hymn instructs man about various kinds of waters and the right use of their healing powers.

४. अपामह दिव्याऽनामपां स्रोतस्याऽनाम् । अपामह प्रणेजनेऽश्वा भवथ वाजिनः ॥

4. O man, who are fleet and strong like horses, be active, powerful and learned under the purifying influence of the waters from heavens, springs and other sources. (4528)

५. ता अपः शिवा अपोऽयक्ष्मंकरणीरपः । यथैव तृप्यते मयस्तास्त आ दत्त भेषजीः ॥

5. O learned persons, get hold of the waters of various qualities, soothing consumption-healing and possessing other healing powers, so that happiness and well-being of the people may be provided. (4529)

HYMN III

१. दिवस्पृथिव्याः पर्यन्तरिक्षाद्वनस्पतिभ्यो अध्योषधीभ्यः ।
यत्रयत्र विभृतो जातवेदास्तत स्तुतो जुषमाणो न एहि ॥

1. O electricity, the self-illumined and the illuminating of other, wheresoever you are borne, contained, being fit to be used by us come to us thence, from the heavens, from earth, from the atmosphere, from trees and from herbs. (4530)[1]

२. यस्ते अप्सु महिमा यो वनेषु य ओषधीषु पशुष्वप्स्व१न्तः ।
अग्ने सर्वास्तन्व१: सं रभस्व ताभिर्न एहि द्रविणोदा अजस्रः ॥

2. O electricity, whatever thy grandeur there is in floods, in forests, in medicinal herbs, in cattle and in waters, expose all thy forms well and come to us, giving continuous flow of wealth thereby. (4531)

३. यस्ते देवेषु महिमा स्वर्गो या ते तनूः पितृष्वाविवेश ।
पुष्टिर्या ते मनुष्येऽषु पप्रथेऽग्ने तया रयिमस्मासु धेहि ॥

3. O Effulgent God, whatever thy glory and bliss there are in the divine beings, whatever thy beautiful form has entered the life of the learned elders, whatever Thy vigour has pervaded the ordinary men, shower on us riches thereby. (4532)[2]

४. श्रुत्कर्णाय कवये वेद्याय वचोभिर्वाकैरुप यामि रातिम् ।
यतो भयमभयं तन्नो अस्त्वव देवानां यज हेडो अग्ने ॥

4. I (the devotee) approach Him, who is swift to listen, Wise and Worthy to be known, with suitable words of praise (i.e., with-mantras) for bounty. May be free from fear wherefrom there is danger. O all-leading God, keep away the wrath of the Devas from us. (4533)

[1](1-2) The verse instructs man to make use of electric power from all sources enumerated herein. When we compare modern developments, they would appear but a drop before the vast ocean thrown open to man by this verse.

[2](3-4) The protection and prosperity are prayed for from the Almighty Father.

HYMN IV

१. यामाहुतिं प्रथमामथर्वा या जाता या हव्यमकृणोज्जातवेदाः ।
तां त एतां प्रथमो जोहवीमि ताभिष्टुप्तो वहतु हव्यमग्निरग्नये स्वाहा ॥

1. The very first Instructive Voice, that was manifested by the Revealer of Vedas, the Protector of the people or which revealed itself and by which the creator made this comprehensible universe known to men. I offer this very Vedic Lore to thee. Being praised by those Vedic hymns, may the Illuminating God sustain this world worthy to be known and made the right use of. Our hearty prayers are to the same Effulgent God. (4534)[1]

२. आकूतिं देवीं सुभगां पुरो दधे चित्तस्य माता सुहवा नो अस्तु ।
यामाशामेमि केवली सा मे अस्तु विदेयमेनां मनसि प्रविष्टाम् ॥

2. I keep, in the fore-front, the secret-revealing will-power, blessed with fortune, the mother of all knowledge. May it be at our beck and call. Whatever intent I set before me, may it be my sole target, so that I may gain it that has taken possession of my mind. (4535)[2]

३. आकूत्या नो बृहस्पत आकूत्या न उपा गहि । अथो भगस्य नो धेह्यथो नः सुहवो भव ॥

3. O Lord of Vedic learning, come to us with the set purpose and strong will-power. Then shower on us the fortune of knowledge and be prompt to hear our call. (4536)

४. बृहस्पतिर्म आकूतिमाङ्गिरसः प्रति जानातु वाचमेताम् ।
यस्य देवा देवताः संबभूवुः स सुप्रणीताः कामो अन्वेत्वस्मान् ॥

4. May the All-penetrating Lord of the vast Vedic Lore invest me with deep thinking power and this befitting power of speech, so that well-regulated sense-organs of mine (whose) may become divine. Thus may the Fulfiller of the desires of all come to us. (4537)

HYMN V

१. इन्द्रो राजा जगतश्चर्षणीनामधि क्षमि विषुरूपं यदस्ति ।
ततो ददाति दाशुषे वसूनि चोदद्राध उपस्तुतश्चिदर्वाक् ॥

1. On this earth, the Glorious God is the Radiant master of all the people of the world and whatever there is of various kinds. Being prayed with devotion, He grants riches to the devotee and always bestows wealth, health and knowledge on him. (4538)

[1]The verse is very clear about the Vedas being the first revelation by God in the very beginning of the creation.

[2]It is the strong will-power that enables a person to achieve his set purpose.

HYMN VI*

१. सहस्रबाहुः पुरुषः सहस्राक्षः सहस्रपात् । स भूमिं विश्वतो वृत्वात्यतिष्ठद् दशाङ्गुलम् ।।

1. The All-pervading God has the power of a thousand arms, a thousand eyes, a thousand feet, penetrating the earth from all sides, he extends even beyond the ten quarters or the universe consisting of ten elements. (4539)[1]

२. त्रिभिः पद्भिर्द्यामरोहत्पादस्येहाभवत्पुनः । तथा व्यक्रामद्विष्वङशनानशने अनु ।।

2. God, the Emancipator rises far above in the well-lit state of emancipation beyond this creation, by three quarters. By one quarter he creates this universe again and again. Thus pervading the animate and inanimate world He stays there. (4540)[2]

३. तावन्तो अस्य महिमानस्ततो ज्यायांश्च पूरुषः ।
पादोऽस्य विश्वा भूतानि त्रिपादस्यामृतं दिवि ।।

3. So mighty is His grandeur, but far greater than this is the All-pervading God. All the worlds are but a part of Him. Three-fourths of Him exist as Immortal Resplendent Glory beyond the universe. (4541)[3]

४. पुरुष एवेदं सर्वं यद् भूतं यच्च भाव्यम् । उतामृतत्वस्येश्वरो यदन्येनाभवत्सह ।।

4. The Omnipresent Creator is manifest in this all, what has been created and what is to be created in future. He is also the Lord of Immortal and whatever has been created with the other (i.e. Prime cause) Prakriti of the universe. (4542)[4]

५. यत्पुरुषं व्यदधुः कतिधा व्यकल्पयन् । मुखं किमस्य किं बाहू किमूरू पादा उच्येते ।।

5. When the learned persons make expositions about the All-pervading God, in how many forms have they thought of Him. What has been described by them as His mouth, what, His arms, and what, His thighs and feet? (4543)[5]

*This hymn is called Purusha-sukta, because it describes the Omnipresent God, Who pervades this Puri in the shape of the Universe. cf. *Rig*, 10.90, *Yajur*, 31.

[1]Thousand: innumerable Deshangulum—the world, made up of 10 parts, 5 gross, sky (आकाश), air (वायु), fire (अग्नि), water (जल), earth (पृथिवी); 5 subtle elements, speech (शब्द), touch (स्पर्श), sight (रूप), taste (रस), smell (गंध). It may also mean 10 quarters 4 main, 4 intervening, above and below. It may mean heart, the souls, abode in the body. Griffith translates it as a space of ten fingers, which is inappropriate in view of the infinite immensity of God.

[2]The 'Akhand Brahma' has no parts. The verse describes His immensity in a figurative language. In the case of the soul, the 'sthul-sharira' is one part, whereas *sukhsham sharira* is three-fourth of it in importance.

[3]cf. *Rig*, 10.90.3, *Yajur*, 31.3.

[4]cf. *Rig*, 10.90.2, *Yajur*, 31.2.

[5]The Omnipresent and Omniscient Creator has no body and hence no limbs. In the figurative language here in the verse, He is imagined to be embodied in all humanity, whose limbs are being questioned to be described later on in the next verse. cf. *Rig*, 10.90.11, *Yajur*, 31.10.

६. ब्राह्मणोऽस्य मुखमासीद्बाहू राजन्योऽभवत् ।
मध्यं तदस्य यद्वैश्यः पद्भ्यां शूद्रो अजायत ॥

6. In the body-politic of human society pervaded through by God, Brahman is the head; Kshatriya, designated as arms, the Vaishya, its thighs; the Shudra, shown as feet. (4544)[1]

७. चन्द्रमा मनसो जातश्चक्षोः सूर्यो अजायत । मुखादिन्द्रश्चाग्निश्च प्राणाद्वायुरजायत ॥

7. The moon was created from His mental power. The Sun was born from His power of perception. The fire and electricity are brought to light from His all-consuming power. The air was His vitalising and life-infusing power. (4545)[2]

८. नाभ्या आसीदन्तरिक्षं शीर्ष्णो द्यौः समवर्तत ।
पद्भ्यां भूमिर्दिशः श्रोत्रात्तथा लोकाँ अकल्पयन् ॥

8. The mid-regions of the universe are nothing but central power of the Creator. The heavens are made by His topmost power. The earth came into existence from Primordial power and the quarters from power of space. Similarly were created the other worlds. (4546)[3]

९. विराडग्रे समभवद्विराजो अधि पूरुषः । स जातो अत्यरिच्यत पश्चाद् भूमिमथो पुरः ॥

9. In the very beginning of the creation was born All-luminous nebula (Brahmānd). The All-pervading Lord reigned supreme over it. The very created nebula was split into various forms of the universe. Last of all came the earth and then came the formation of bodies of different creatures on the earth. (4547)[4]

१०. यत्पुरुषेण हविषा देवा यज्ञमतन्वत । वसन्तो अस्यासीदाज्यं ग्रीष्म इध्मः शरद्धविः ॥

10. (*Adhyatmik*) When the learned persons perform the sacrifice of mental worship by meditating upon the Adorable God, morning is its butter, mid-day its fuel and mid-night its oblation. (*Adhi Devak*) The great sacrifice, which the forces of nature (like the Sun, etc.), spread far and wide, has Spring for its butter, Summer, its fuel and Autumn, its oblation. (4548)[5]

[1]cf. *Rig*, 10.90.12, *Yajur*, 31.11. The four castes of the human society are enumerated here as parts of the body, according to the functions and duties they have to perform in the body-politic. They are not based on birth nor do they spring from the different parts of God, Who is Formless and hence has no organs at all.

[2]cf. *Rig*, 10.90.13, *Yajur*, 31.12. The various powers of the All-Pervading Creator are supposed to create various objects of nature, having similar qualities.

[3]cf. *Rig*, 10.90.7, *Yajur*, 31.13. The other powers of God creating other regions and worlds.

[4]cf. *Rig*, 10.90.7, *Yajur*, 31.5. In *Yajur*, 31.5 ततः From Primordial Cause (i.e., प्रकृति) *Virad*: The matter shining brightly. It is the very first state of creation, when Prakriti is set into motion by the Creator. The verse clearly lays down the sequence of Creation.

[5]cf. *Rig*, 10.90.6, *Yajur*, 31.14. Butter: the igniting force; fuel—consuming force; Oblation—material provided for consumption and to be given away.

११. तं यज्ञं प्रावृषा प्रौक्षन्पुरुषं जातमग्रशः । तेन देवा अयजन्त साध्या वसवश्च ये ।।

11. The devotees instal, in the very recesses of their hearts through peace-showering meditation, the Adorable and Perfect God, Who is existent even before the creation of the universe. The learned persons, the yogis with special spiritual powers, and the self-controllers get united with Him in deep meditation. (4549)[1]

१२. तस्मादश्वा अजायन्त ये च के चोभयादतः ।
गावो ह जज्ञिरे तस्मात्तस्माज्जाता अजावयः ।।

12. From the great sacrifice initiated by God, the Creator, were born the horses and all cattle with two rows of teeth. Verily the cows were generated from Him. From Him were born the goats and the sheep. (4550)[2]

१३. तस्माद्यज्ञात्सर्वहुत ऋचः सामानि जज्ञिरे ।
छन्दो ह जज्ञिरे तस्माद्यजुस्तस्मादजायत ।।

13. From that Adorable God, whom all people pay their homage or Who consumes all (at the time of Pralaya) were revealed the Rigveda, the Sāmaveda. Chhandas i.e., Atharvaveda appeared from Him. Yajurveda came to light from Him. (4551)[3]

१४. तस्माद्यज्ञात्सर्वहुतः संभृतं पृषदाज्य॒म् ।
पशूँस्तांश्चक्रे वायव्या॒न्नारण्या ग्राम्याश्च ये ।।

14. Curd and clarified butter have been well-provided by the Adorable God, Who is respected by all. He created all those animals, that live in air, forests and in the villages. (4552)

१५. सप्तास्यासन्परिधयस्त्रिः सप्त समिधः कृताः ।
देवा यद्यज्ञं तन्वाना अबध्नन्पुरुषं पशुम् ।।

15. There are seven circumscribing limits and twenty-one kinds of fuel of the great sacrifice, in the vast performance whereof, the learned persons devoutly concentrate upon the Omniscient and the Knowable God. (4553)[4]

[1]cf. *Rig*, 10.90.7, *Yajur*, 31.9. The first half of the verse may also refer to the great sacrifice, by the forces of nature in the vast universe.

[2]cf. *Rig*, 10.90.10, *Yajur*, 31.8.

[3]cf. *Rig*, 10.90.9, *Yajur*, 31.7. The verse is quite clear about the revealing of all the four Vedas at the time of the creation of the universe. It is a pity that the Western scholars and their coup-followers, eastern scholars ignore such forceful evidence provided internally by the Vedas themselves and bases their various theories about the age of the Vedas on mere conjectures and prjudicial whims.

[4]cf. *Rig*, 10.90.15, *Yajur*, 31.65 *Seven limits*—seven chhandas (metres): or seven Dhatus in the body i.e., Ras, Rakta, mansa, meda, asthi, majja, virya; or five elements, mana and buddhi. *21 fuels*: प्रकृति, महतत्त्व, अहंकार, 5 महाभूत, 5 सूक्ष्मभूत, 5 ज्ञानेन्द्रिय, 3 'गुण' or अध्यात्म: 5 तन्मात्र, 5 महाभूत, 5 ज्ञानेन्द्रिय, 5 कर्मेन्द्रिय, मन । or 12 मास, 5 ऋतु, 3 लोक और आदित्य ।

१६. मूर्ध्नो देवस्य बृहतो अंशवः सप्त सप्ततीः । राज्ञः सोमस्याजायन्त जातस्य पुरुषादधि ॥

16. Seven fold seventy i.e., four hundred and ninety subtle elements were produced from the great, shining, topmost and radiant Soma, the source of all energy and motion, created by the All-pervading God. (4554)[1]

HYMN VII

१. चित्राणि साकं दिवि रोचनानि सरीसृपाणि भुवने जवानि ।
तुर्मिशं सुमतिमिच्छमानो अहानि गीर्भिः सपर्यामि नाकम् ॥

1. In the universe, the shining heavenly spheres of various colours are together moving on, some with slow speed and some, with rapid speed, in the heavens above. I, a learned person (an astronomer) desirous of evil-removing intelligence, try to discover the secrets of these indestructible heavenly spheres and peace-showering heavens. (4555)[2]

२. सुहवमग्ने कृत्तिका रोहिणी चास्तु भद्रं मृगशिरः शमार्द्रा ।
पुनर्वसू सूनृता चारु पुष्यो भानुराश्लेषा अयनं मघा मे ॥

2. O learned person, may Krittika and Rohini be at my beck and call (i.e. easily communicated to) may Mrigshiraḥ be a source of happiness and Ardra be peace-giving to me. May Punarvasu be a source of true knowledge, Pushyaḥ of beauty; Ashlesha, of brilliance like the Sun; Magha, a place for shelter for me. (4556)[3]

३. पुण्यं पूर्वा फल्गुन्यौ चात्र हस्तश्चित्रा शिवा स्वाति सुखो मे अस्तु ।
राधे विशाखे सुहवानुराधा ज्येष्ठा सुनक्षत्रमरिष्ट मूलम् ॥

3. In this world, two groups of Purva-Phalguni may bring good to me, and Hasta and Chitra may bring peace and Swāti happiness to me. Both the Vishakha may give me success. May Anuradha be easy to communicate to me. May Jyeshtha be a good constellation for me. May Mula keep me free from evils and disease. (4557)[4]

[1]The creation of 490 subtle elements from Soma is worth thorough research by the scientists of the modern age even.

[2]Work is worship. So 'सपर्यामि' here means devotedly work for discovering the secrets of the heavenly bodies and making the right use of the discoveries.

[3]The verse indicates the uses, to which a thorough knowledge of the various heavenly bodies can lead to.

[4](3-5) According to Maharshi Dayanand mere prayers don't bring in anything, it is by active pursuits thereof that a man achieve his object. So these verses indicate the path by which men can obtain various things, while these constellations shine above them. It is not the heavenly bodies that shower gifts from above, but it is the serious efforts by men that may win them riches and prosperity. It is for the scientists and technicians to investigate the truths; revealed by the bombardment of cosmoramic rays or waves from the various constellations, e.g., the easy communications under the influence of cosmic rays from Krittika, Rohini and Anuradha. This clue may help safe sending of space-ships or radio messages. The increased production of food and energising articles may be facilitated by the cosmic influence of the radiation from Purva Ashadha and Uttara Ashadha, if agricultural engineers care to take up such researches. In fine, there is ample scope to carry on researches in many fields of science, taking clues from this sukta.

४. अन्नं पूर्वा रासतां मे अषाढा ऊर्जं देव्युत्तरा आ वहन्तु ।
अभिजिन्मे रासतां पुण्यमेव श्रवणः श्रविष्ठाः कुर्वतां सुपुष्टिम् ॥

4. May Purva Ashādha give me food. May brilliant Uttra Ashādha bring me energy and vigour. Let Abhijit give me purity and Shravana and Shravishtha (Dhanushtha) give me good nourishment. (4558)

५. आ मे महच्छतभिषग्वरीय आ मे द्वया प्रोष्ठपदा सुशर्म ।
आ रेवती चाश्वयुजौ भगं म आ मे रयिं भरण्य आ वहन्तु ॥

5. Let the big Shat-bhishag bring me profuse riches. May both the Proshthpadas (i.e., Bhadrapadas, Purva and Uttara) provide me good shelter. May Revati and both the Ashvayuja bring me fortune. Let Bharni provide me with ample riches. (4559)

HYMN VIII

१. यानि नक्षत्राणि दिव्य१न्तरिक्षे अप्सु भूमौ यानि नगेषु दिक्षु ।
प्रकल्पयंश्चन्द्रमा यान्येति सर्वाणि ममैतानि शिवानि सन्तु ॥

1. Whatsoever constellations there are in the heavens, the mid-regions, observed through waters and on the earth, on the mountains and in all quarters, and the moon passes by them, revealing them, may they all be peaceful to me. (4560)

२. अष्टाविंशानि शिवानि शग्मानि सह योगं भजन्तु मे ।
योगं प्र पद्ये क्षेमं च क्षेमं प्र पद्ये योगं च नमोऽहोरात्राभ्यामस्तु ॥

2. The aforesaid twenty-eight constellations along with the moon may provide peace and happiness to me, so that I may acquire the desired object and be able to keep it intact and I may make the right use of my time all through day and night. (4561)[1]

३. स्वस्तितं मे सुप्रातः सुसायं सुदिवं सुमृगं सुशकुनं मे अस्तु ।
सुहवमग्ने स्वस्त्य१मर्त्यं गत्वा पुनरायाभिनन्दन् ॥

3. May the pleasant morning, the fair evening, the happy day, the beautiful animals roaming in the forest and cheering birds all be most peace-giving to me. O learned person, my good performance of sacrifice may bless me and you may come back here on earth, after attaining salvation and pleasing all. (4562)[2]

४. अनुहवं परिहवं परिवादं परिक्षवम् । सर्वैर्मे रिक्तकुम्भान्परा तान्त्सवितः सुव ॥

[1]Repetition of Yoga and Kshema twice is for the sake of emphasis. नम : right use.

[2]It may also refer to the sacrificial fire carrying the oblations to heaven and coming back with blessings to the sacrificer.

4. O God, throw away from me all envy, jealousy, fault-finding, hatred or impure food and empty vessels, the symbol of penury. (4563)[1]

५. अपपापं परिक्षवं पुण्यं भक्षीमहि क्षवम् । शिवा ते पाप नासिकां पुण्यगश्चाभि मेहताम् ॥

5. Keep away the food, unfit for consumption. Let us take the wholesome food. O evil-doer, let the peace-loving and righteous people spurn you in disgust (literally-make water on very nose). (4564)[2]

६. इमा या ब्रह्मणस्पते विषूचीर्वात ईरते । सध्रीचीरिन्द्र ताः कृत्वा मह्यं शिवतमास्कृधि ॥

6. O Lord of the Vedic learning and the Glorious God, setting these quarters, which the strong wind agitates, make them all most peaceful for me. (4565)

७. स्वस्ति नो अस्त्वभयं नो अस्तु नमोऽहोरात्राभ्यामस्तु ॥

7. Let there be all peace and happiness for us. Let us be free from fear. Let there be our full control over day and night. (4566)

HYMN IX

१. शान्ता द्यौः शान्ता पृथिवी शान्तमिदमुर्व१न्तरिक्षम् ।
शान्ता उदन्वतीरापः शान्ता नः सन्त्वोषधीः ॥

1. May the shining firmament be peace-showering to us. May the earth be peace-giving and the vast mid-regions be blissful, may the waters of the ocean with high tides peaceful and the herbs may also a source of calmness for us. (4567)[3]

२. शान्तानि पूर्वरूपाणि शान्तं नो अस्तु कृताकृतम् ।
शान्तं भूतं च भव्यं च सर्वमेव शमस्तु नः ॥

2. May the fore-casting signs of the coming events be peaceful and so may be our acts of omission and commission—may the past and the future bring peace and all may be blissful for us. (4568)

३. इयं या परमेष्ठिनी वाग्देवी ब्रह्मसंशिता । ययैव ससृजे घोरं तयैव शान्तिरस्तु नः ॥

3. May this divine speech, which is devoted to God and strengthened by Vedic lore by which are created all terrific situations, be source of peace and well-being for us. (4569)

[1]A prayer for righteous and rich living. The reading of omens by Sayāna and Griffith is to lower the grandeur of the Vedic Text.

[2]क्षु—इत्यन्ननाम निघं० 7.9. Pari Kshava—adulterated or impure food and not sneeze, as interpreted by Sayāna and Griffith. It is a mistake to interpret Vedic words in the light of ordinary Sanskrit words.

[3](1-5) Mere prayers won't effect anything. It is our acts executed in all serious steadfastness, that may enable us to achieve our object.

४. इदं यत्परमेष्ठिनं मनो वां ब्रह्मसंशितम् । येनैव ससृजे घोरं तेनैव शान्तिरस्तु नः ॥

4. O couple, here is this mind of yours, intent on the highest object, sharpened by Vedic lore and celibacy, May by this very mind, by which are perpetuated all deeds of cruelty, peace and calmness be brought to us. (4570)

५. इमानि यानि पञ्चेन्द्रियाणि मनःषष्ठानि मे हृदि ब्रह्मणा संशितानि ।
यैरेव ससृजे घोरं तैरेव शान्तिरस्तु नः ॥

5. Here, in my heart, are these five sense-organs with mind, as the sixth ones, which are strengthened and sharpened by Vedic lore and celibacy. By these very organs, by which are created terrific situations, may peace and happiness be brought for us. (4571)

६. शं नो मित्रः शं वरुणः शं विष्णुः शं प्रजापतिः । शं न इन्द्रो बृहस्पतिः शं नो भवत्वर्यमा ॥

6. May God, friendly like the breath be gracious to us. May God, tranquilliser like water be soothing to us. May All-pervading God be comfortable to us. May God, the Protector of all the people be peaceful to us. May God, the Lord of all riches and Vedic learning be kind to us. May God, the Just be pleasant to us. (4572)[1]

७. शं नो मित्रः शं वरुणः शं विवस्वाञ्छमन्तकः ।
उत्पाताः पार्थिवान्तरिक्षाः शं नो दिविचरा ग्रहाः ॥

7. May oxygen, with a great affinity to combine with other elements like a friend be peaceful to us. May hydrogen, the source of water, be comfortable to us. May the Sun, making the living of all creatures possible, be pleasant to us. May death be peaceful. All up-heavals of the earth or the atmosphere be peaceful. May all the planets, moving in the heavens shower peace and tranquillity on us. (4573)[2]

८. शं नो भूमिर्वेप्यमाना शमुल्का निर्हतं च यत् । शं गावो लोहितक्षीराः शं भूमिरव तीर्यतीः ॥

8. May the trembling earth (due to earth-quake) be gracious to us. May the flaming meteor, striking the earth with a force, be peaceful to us. May the cows, with red milk (due to some disease) be comfortable to us. May the sinking earth be peaceful to us. (4574)[3]

९. नक्षत्रमुल्काभिहतं शमस्तु नः शं नोऽभिचाराः शमु सन्तु कृत्याः ।
शं नो निखाता वल्गाः शमुल्का देशोपसर्गाः शमु नो भवन्तु ॥

[1]cf. *Rig*, 1.90.9, *Yajur*, 36.9. Herein the various powers of God are invoked to shower peace and tranquility on the devotees.

[2]cf. *Rig*, 1.90.9, *Yajur*, 36.9. Mitra and Varun in this verse are meant to convey the forces of nature, as the subsequent enumeration thereof shows.

[3]All prayers in this verse can be fulfilled only when we know fully well how to ward off these natural calamities.

9. Gracious be the meteor-struck constellation for us. The secret attacks and the missiles, thrown by the enemies be harmless to us. The mines and other deceitful means of destruction may bring no harm to us. May the meteors and uprisings in the country be harmless to us. (4575)[1]

१०. शं नो ग्रहाश्चान्द्रमसाः शमादित्यश्च राहुणा । शं नो मृत्युर्धूमकेतुः शं रुद्रास्तिग्मतेजसः ॥

10. May the lunar eclipses be peaceful to us. May the solar eclipse caused by 'Rahu' be gracious to us. May the comet, bringing in death and destruction (in its trail) be harmless for us. May Rudras with sharp, penetrating brilliance be comfortable to us. (4576)[2]

११. शं रुद्राः शं वसवः शमादित्याः शमग्नयः । शं नो महर्षयो देवाः शं देवाः शं बृहस्पतिः ॥

11. May the forty-four years old celibates bring peace to us. May the people, who observe celibacy up to twenty-four years be peaceful to us. May the celibates of forty-eight years bring tranquillity to us. May the learned people, the king and military chiefs be all sources of peace to us. May great seers, who shed light of knowledge all-round be gracious to us. May the brilliant scholars and the Lord of Vedic lore be kind to us. (4577)[3]

१२. ब्रह्म प्रजापतिर्धाता लोका वेदाः सप्तऋषयोऽग्नयः ।
तैर्मे कृतं स्वस्त्ययनमिन्द्रो मे शर्म यच्छतु ब्रह्मा मे शर्म यच्छतु ।
विश्वे मे देवाः शर्म यच्छन्तु सर्वे मे देवाः शर्म यच्छन्तु ॥

12. May God, the great, the Revealer of Vedic lore, the Protector of all His subjects, the Creator of the universe, all the worlds, the four Vedas, the seven sages or sense-organs, the three or five agnis, all provide a peaceful shelter for me. May the Lord of riches and prosperity grant me blissful refuge. May the Great Lord of the Vedas shower peace on me. May all learned people give peace and happiness. May all things of divine qualities be a source of peace for me. (4578)

[1]To read 'charms' and 'witch-craft' in अभिचाराः and कृत्याः is due to the ignorance of scientific warfare, which the modern science is bringing to light.

[2]Rahu and Ketu are not demons, as interpreted by Griffith and Sayāna. It is due to the ignorance of Astronomy. Rahu is the point, through which the moon passes and intercepts rays of light coming from the sun and prevents them from coming to the earth, therefore, causing solar eclipse. Similarly Ketu is the point through which the earth passes and cuts off the Sun-rays from falling on the moon and thus causing the lunar eclipse. Rudras: eleven kinds of gases, with sharp and penetrating powers of consuming brilliance. There are active, when it is raining, thundering and lightening. Their prototypes are in the bodies of creatures, performing various functions to maintain them.

[3]Rudras also mean: Ten vital breaths, Prāna, Apāna, Vyān, Samān, Udān, Nāga, Kurma, Devadatta, Dhananjaya and the soul. Vasavas—Agni, Vayu, Prithivi, Antariksh, Surya, Chandra, Dyaus, Nakshatra. Adityas—12 months of the year. Agnaya—5 Agnis (वेतो निकादि) or fire, electricity and the Sun.

१३. यानि कानि चिच्छान्तानि लोके सप्तऋषयो विदुः ।
सर्वाणि शं भवन्तु मे शं मे अस्त्वभयं मे अस्तु ॥

13. Whatsoever things, the seven sages or sense-organs know to be the sources of peace and comfort, may these be peaceful to me. Let there be all peace and calmness for me. May there be fearlessness for me. (4579)

१४. पृथिवी शान्तिरन्तरिक्षं शान्तिर्द्यौः शान्तिरापः शान्तिरोषधयः शान्तिर्वनस्पतयः
शान्तिर्विश्वे मे देवाः शान्तिः सर्वे मे देवाः शान्तिः शान्तिः शान्तिः शान्तिभिः ।
ताभिः शान्तिभिः सर्वशान्तिभिः शमयामोऽहं यदिह घोरं यदिह क्रूरं
यदिह पापं तच्छान्तं तच्छिवं सर्वमेव शमस्तु नः ॥

14. Let the earth, the atmosphere, the heavens, the waters, the herbs, the plants and trees, all the radiant things be each a source of peace and comfort for me. May all the learned people bless me with peace, comfort and happiness, through all means of pacification. May I attain perfect state of calmness by all and sundry means of peace. Whatever there is in this world, terrific, whatever there is cruel in this world, whatsoever there is evil in this world; let all that be peace-giving, let all that be gracious, let all that be harmless for us. (4580)[1]

Chapter (Anuvāka) 2

HYMN X

१. शं न इन्द्राग्नी भवतामवोभिः शं न इन्द्रावरुणा रातहव्या ।
शमिन्द्रासोमा सुविताय शं योः शं न इन्द्रापूषणा वाजसातौ ॥

1. May electricity and fire be peaceful to us by their means of protection. May electricity and water, the giving of articles worth having, bring us comfort and happiness. May electricity and extracts of medicines bring peace and remove disease for our comfortable living. May electricity and air (or earth) be gracious to us in attaining strength and victory in war. (4581)[2]

२. शं नो भगः शमु नः शंसो अस्तु शं नः पुरंधिः शमु सन्तु रायः ।
शं नः सत्यस्य सुयमस्य शंसः शं नो अर्यमा पुरुजातो अस्तु ॥

2. May fortune be auspicious to us. May our prayers be blessed for us. May our wisdom be agreeable to us. May our wealth of all kinds be peace-showering to us. May our exposition true rules of life be peaceful. May the Well-known, Just God shower bliss on us. (4582)[3]

[1]cf. *Yajur*, 36-17.

[2]cf. *Rig*, 7.35.1, *Yajur*, 36.11 (a) The use of electricity, combining it with various elements is emphasised here to get protection, desired articles of use, freedom from disease and valour and victory in war. It is for the scientists and the learned to do research work for the right use of these forces of nature. (b) In addition to the above (i) इन्द्र-अग्नी—air, and fire, king and chief of the army; Prān and Udān. (ii) इन्द्रा-वरुणा—air and cloud, king and chief of police; Prān and Vyān. (iii) इन्द्रा-सोमा—air and Surya; king and chief justice; Prān and Samān. (iv) इन्द्रा-पूषणा—Electricity and Vitamins; air and food, Prān and Apān.

[3]cf. *Rig*, 7.35.2.

३. शं नो धाता शमु धर्ता नो अस्तु शं न उरूची भवतु स्वधाभिः ।
शं रोदसी बृहती शं नो अद्रिः शं नो देवानां सुहवानि सन्तु ॥

3. May the Creator and nourishing father be pleasant to us. May the sustainer and the guardian be peaceful to us. May the vast earth or nature with rich means of subsistence bring happiness to us. May the extensive heavens and mid-regions shower peace on us. May the mountains and clouds be pleasant to us. May the preachings of the learned be tranquillising to us. (4583)

४. शं नो अग्निर्ज्योतिरनीको अस्तु शं नो मित्रावरुणावश्विना शम् ।
शं नः सुकृतां सुकृतानि सन्तु शं न इषिरो अभि वातु वातः ॥

4. May the flame-faced fire, the learned person who is torch-bearer of knowledge the king or chief of the fiery army, the Sun, with the shining beams as its army, and the Effulgent God, with the huge shining spheres to show His might, be all peaceful to us. May the positive and negative electricities be comfortable to us. May good deeds of the righteous or fine works of art of the good artists be pleasant to us. May the perpetually moving wind be propitious to us. (4584)

५. शं नो द्यावापृथिवी पूर्वहूतौ शमन्तरिक्षं दृशये नो अस्तु ।
शं न ओषधीर्वनिनो भवन्तु शं नो रजसस्पतिरस्तु जिष्णुः ॥

5. May the constellations and the earth, the first to shelter blessings on the people, both be auspicious to us. May the atmosphere be agreeable to us for seeing things clearly. May the herbs of the forest be comfort-giving to us. May the victorious lord of the worlds, the Sun be peaceful for us. (4585)

६. शं न इन्द्रो वसुभिर्देवो अस्तु शमादित्येभिर्वरुणः सुशंसः ।
शं नो रुद्रो रुद्रेभिर्जलाषः शं नस्त्वष्टा ग्नाभिरिह शृणोतु ॥

6. May the radiant Sun along with other Vasus be peaceful to us. May the well-praised water along with the rays of the Sun throughout the year be tranquillising to us. May the soul, the fulfiller of all desires with other Rudras, vital breaths be peaceful to us. May the engineer hear us calmly with electric waves of high frequency, here at our residence. (4586)[1]

७. शं नः सोमो भवतु ब्रह्म शं नः शं नो ग्रावाणः शमु सन्तु यज्ञाः ।
शं नः स्वरूणां मितयो भवन्तु शं नः प्रस्वः शम्वस्तु वेदिः ॥

7. May the medicinal extracts be peaceful to us. May Vedic lore, food and riches be all comfortable to us. May the preachers, the high-sounding mills and soldiers with loud war cries, all bring happiness to us. May sacri-

[1]The last portion of the verse gives clear indication of the telephone or the radio-broadcasts etc.

fices or industrial concerns be comfortable to us. May the various kinds of knowledge, explained by the learned preachers, be peaceful to us. May all sorts of production, from the herbs, cows, soil or females be source of happiness to us. May the sacrificial place and the earth be pleasant to us. (4587)[1]

८. शं नः सूर्य उरुचक्षा उदेतु शं नो भवन्तु प्रदिशश्चतस्रः ।
शं नः पर्वता ध्रुवयो भवन्तु शं नः सिन्धवः शमु सन्त्वापः ॥

8. May the Sun, with its far-flung, innumerable rays be peaceful to us. May all the four main quarters be pleasant for us. May the firm mountains be comfortable to us. May the speedy rivers and streams and other sources of water be agreeable to us. (4588)

९. शं नो अदितिर्भवतु व्रतेभिः शं नो भवन्तु मरुतः स्वर्काः ।
शं नो विष्णुः शमु पूषा नो अस्तु शं नो भवित्रं शम्वस्तु वायुः ॥

9. May the mother earth, with her fixed behaviours of evolutions be peaceful to us. May the winds, moving in the atmosphere be comforting to us. May the All-pervading God, the sacrifice and the Sun be all peaceful. May the nourishing food be pleasant for us. May water, the source of production be soothing to us. May air be comfortable to us. (4589)

१०. शं नो देवः सविता त्रायमाणः शं नो भवन्तूषसो विभातीः ।
शं नः पर्जन्यो भवतु प्रजाभ्यः शं नः क्षेत्रस्य पतिरस्तु शंभुः ॥

10. May the radiant Sun, which generates, protects and sets all in motion, be a source of comfort to us. May the specially brilliant dawn, be pleasant to us. May the clouds shower happiness and well-being on us, the people at large. May the comforting lord of the field, the farmer, the soul and God Himself be all peaceful. (4590)

HYMN XI

१. शं नः सत्यस्य पतयो भवन्तु शं नो अर्वन्तः शमु सन्तु गावः ।
शं न ऋभवः सुकृतः सुहस्ताः शं नो भवन्तु पितरो हवेषु ॥

1. May the protectors of truth and justice, like the religious leaders, judges and administrators be peace-giving to us. Let the horses and cows be sources of comforts to us. Let the expert technicians, well-versed in production of fine articles, be a source of well-being for us. Let the elders, vested with the authority to look after the welfare of the people bring us peace and tranquility. (4591)[2]

२. शं नो देवा विश्वदेवा भवन्तु शं सरस्वती सह धीभिरस्तु ।
शमभिषाचः शमु रातिषाचः शं नो दिव्याः पार्थिवाः शं नो अप्याः ॥

2. Let the good people, the best players of various games, the victorious soldiers, the prominent merchants, the brilliant scholars and scientists and the best artists be all peaceful to us. Let our speech along with high intelli-

[1]स्वरूणां मितयो does not mean the measuring of the typing posts, as interpreted by Sayāna or Griffith, but the preachings of knowledge of various kinds by the learned people.

[2]cf. *Rig*, 7.35.12.

gence be comforting to us. Let all the delegates, come together from all sides bring peace to us. Let assemblage of the donors and the donee be peaceful. Let all the celestial, the terrestrial and the acustic bodies be blissful for us. (4592)[1]

३. शं नो अज एकपाद् देवो अस्तु शमहिर्बुध्न्य१: शं समुद्रः ।
शं नो अपां नपात्पेरूरस्तु शं नः पृश्निर्भवतु देवगोपा ॥

3. Let the Glorious and Birthless God, who sustains all the creation by one-fourth of His being, be gracious to us. May the Indestructible, All-sustainer God be peace-showering. May God, Who engulfs all at the time of annihilation of the universe be blissful. May the Life-supporter and Evil-Destroyer God be peaceful to us. May God, Who maintains and protects all the divine beings shower peace and calmness on us. (4593)[2]

४. आदित्या रुद्रा वसवो जुषन्तामिदं ब्रह्म क्रियमाणं नवीयः ।
शृण्वन्तु नो दिव्याः पार्थिवासो गोजाता उत ये यज्ञियासः ॥

4. Let all the learned persons, observing celibacy for 48 years, 44 years and 24 years, respectively partake of this food or wealth which has newly been prepared or earned. Let the noble and respectable guardians of the land, born on the earth, listen to us. (4594)[3]

५. ये देवानामृत्विजो यज्ञियासो मनोर्यजत्रा अमृता ऋतज्ञाः ।
ते नो रासन्तामुरुगायमद्य यूयं पात स्वस्तिभिः सदा नः ॥

5. Whosoever there are among the learned, the performers of seasonal sacrifices, the respectable at sacrifices, the performers of mental sacrifice in the form of yoga, the immortal, the expert in Vedic learning, may they all deliver us a vast sermon about Vedic lore today. O the learned people, may you ever protect us with peace-giving means. (4595)[4]

६. तदस्तु मित्रावरुणा तदग्ने शं योरस्मभ्यमिदमस्तु शस्तम् ।
अशीमहि गाधमुत प्रतिष्ठां नमो दिवे बृहते सादनाय ॥

6. O God, Who are Friendly and Just and Radiant all these things be peaceful and evil-removing for us. May all this be most gracious for us. We may enjoy fortune and glory. May we have full control over vast earth and heavens for our residence. (4596)[5]

[1]cf. *Rig*, 7.35.12. cf. *Rig*. 7-35. 11.

[2]cf. *Rig*, 7.35.13. The verse may also mean एकपाद् अज=सूर्य (the Sun); अहिर्बुध्न्यः (the cloud in the atmosphere)समुद्र (sea) अपां नपात् (fire or electricity); पृश्नि (the earth).

[3]cf. *Rig*, 7.35.14. गोजाता well-known speakers or orators यज्ञियासः worthy to sit in sacrificial ceremonies.

[4]cf. *Rig*, 7.35.15. Griffith interprets उरुगायं 'broad path to travel,' which seems unsuitable here.

[5]cf. *Rig*, 5.47.7. This is a prayer for the highest prosperity and well-being on earth.

HYMN XII

१. उषा अप स्वसुस्तमः सं वर्तयति वर्तनिं सुजातता ।
अया वाजं देवहितं सनेम मदेम शतहिमाः सुवीराः ॥

1. The dawn, driving away the darkness of the self-slipping away night, and thus being born well, sets the world on its path of duty. Let us get strength and vigour by her and thus being strong and brave, enjoy life of hundred years. (4597)[1]

HYMN XIII

१. इन्द्रस्य बाहू स्थविरौ वृषाणौ चित्रा इमा वृषभौ पारयिष्णू ।
तौ योक्षे प्रथमो योग आगते याभ्यां जितमसुराणां स्व१र्यत् ॥

1. These wonderful arms of the Commander are stout like two bulls and are able to hurl missiles on the enemy and thus cross all hurdles in his way laid by his foe. I the foremost among the people, (the king) utilise them, by which the abode of the wicked enemies where they revel, is conquered, in getting hold of what is to be attained and protecting what has already been achieved. (4598)[2]

२. आशुः शिशानो वृषभो न भीमो घनाघनः क्षोभणश्चर्षणीनाम् ।
संक्रन्दनोऽनिमिष एकवीरः शतं सेना अजयत्साकमिन्द्रः ॥

2. The ideal commander is he, who is swift in action, keeps all his arms sharpened, can strike terror in the hearts of his foes like a bull, is well-versed in crushing the enemy, is able to make the people tremble with awe, (if ever they mean mischief), can cause the enemies weep, by challenging them fiercely, is constantly vigilant and alert; and can, single-handed conquer hundreds of armies together. (4599)[3]

३. संक्रन्दनेनानिमिषेण जिष्णुनाऽयोध्येन दुश्चयवनेन धृष्णुना ।
तदिन्द्रेण जयत तत्सहध्वं युधो नर इषुहस्तेन वृष्णा ॥

3. O people, conquer and subdue the fighting enemies with the help of such a commander of the armies, who is ever-vigilant and alert, can challenge the enemies ferociously and make them weep, is ready to fight and become victorious, is himself difficult to be subdued by his enemies, is forceful and pushing, can rain terror in the ranks of the enemy, being ever equipped with arms in his hands. (4600)[4]

४. स इषुहस्तैः स निषङ्गिभिर्वशी संस्रष्टा स युध इन्द्रो गणेन ।
संसृष्टजित्सोमपा बाहुशर्ध्यु१ग्रधन्वा प्रतिहिताभिरस्ता ॥

[1]cf. *Rig*, 6.17.15 and *Rig*, 10.172.4. To attain longevity of life, one should be up and doing at dawn and bathe in its life prolonging and invigorating rays.

[2]cf. *Sama*, 3.9.3.7.3.

[3]cf. *Rig*, 10.103.2, *Yajur*, 17.33. The king should put such a man, as has the qualities enumerated herein, at the head of his armies.

[4]cf. *Rig*, 10.103.2, *Yajur*, 17.34. Only a fearless and courageous commander can win battles for the nation.

4. He alone is the fit commander of the armies, who can fully control himself and the nation, with soldiers bearing armours and carrying missiles in their hands, can wage wars with the help of the swarms of his armies, is the subduer of the well-trained armies, drinks the juice of the herbs to enervate himself, defeats the enemy with the strength of arms, has terrific fire-power, and is the feller of the enemy in battle by directing the same terrific fire-power against him. (4601)[1]

५. बलविज्ञायः स्थविरः प्रवीरः सहस्वान्वाजी सहमान उग्रः ।
अभिवीरो अभिषत्वा सहोजिज्जैत्रमिन्द्र रथमा तिष्ठ गोविदन् ॥

5. The worthy commander is he, who knows well his own might as well as the striking potentialities of his adversary, is steadfast and unmoved even in reverses, is uncommonly brave, is courageous, powerful and equipped with ample supplies of provisions, arms and military strategy, able to subdue and strike terror among the enemy forces, surrounded by the brave warriors on all sides, bravely facing the enemy on all fronts, the conqueror, who can subdue the powers of all. O Controller of the earth, enthral yourself in this chariot or plane. (4602)[2]

६. इमं वीरमनु हर्षध्वमुग्रमिन्द्रं सखायो अनु सं रभध्वम् ।
ग्रामजितं गोजितं वज्रबाहुं जयन्तमज्म प्रमृणन्तमोजसा ॥

6. O friends, be happy in the company of this fierce brave commander or leader. Get you all ready in right earnest, to follow him, who is the vanquisher of the swarms of the enemy, the conqueror of the earth, whose arms have the striking power of the thunderbolt, the winner of war, and is a thorough smasher of the enemy with his striking valour. (4603)[3]

७. अभि गोत्राणि सहसा गाहमानोऽदाय उग्रः शतमन्युरिन्द्रः ।
दुश्च्यवनः पृतनाषाडयोध्योऽस्माकं सेना अवतु प्र युत्सु ॥

7. May the commander of the army, who is cruel and ferocious, the embodiment of hundred-fold anger, crushing under feet all the nations of the world on all sides, himself difficult to be subdued, can defeat the fighting forces of the foe, is too terrible to fight with, protect our army in wars. (4604)[4]

८. बृहस्पते परि दीया रथेन रक्षोहामित्राँ अपबाधमानः ।
प्रभञ्जञ्छत्रून्प्रमृणन्नमित्रानस्माकमेध्यविता तनूनाम् ॥

8. O the chief commander of the army, invade the enemy from all sides, killing the wicked and effacing the enemies, crushing the foes, and annihilating the adversaries, be the protector of our bodies on all sides. (4605)[5]

[1]cf. *Rig*, 10.103.3 'Ishu'—does not simply mean 'arrow.' It means any means of destruction capable of killing the enemy. Grenades, bombs and missiles, are all *Ishva* in the Vedic terminology and the mechanisms by which they are hurled at the enemy are Dhanus which does not simply mean a 'bow'.

[2]cf. *Rig*, 10.103.4.

[3]cf. *Rig*, 10.103.9 and *Atharva*, 6.97.3.

[4]cf. *Rig*, 10.103.7 [5]cf. *Rig*, 10.103.4.

९. इन्द्र एषां नेता बृहस्पतिर्दक्षिणा यज्ञः पुर एतु सोमः ।
देवसेनानामभिभञ्जतीनां जयन्तीनां मरुतो यन्तु मध्ये ॥

9. The king be the leader of these armies. The chief commander should be on the right side and the director of the movements of the various regiments in the military formation may move in front of all. Just in the middle of these fine armies, that are crushing the enemy forces on all sides and winning victories, the fast-moving warriors, raining death on the opposing forces, should rush on. (4606)[1]

१०. इन्द्रस्य वृष्णो वरुणस्य राज्ञ आदित्यानां मरुतां शर्ध उग्रम् ।
महामनसां भुवनच्यवानां घोषो देवानां जयतामुदस्थात् ॥

10. Fierce and terrible is the murderous onslaught of the killing and the engulfing forces of the king, who is the lord of fortunes, showerer of death on his enemies and of blessings on his subjects and is chosen by them and removes their difficulties and troubles. Thus goes up the cheering cry of the winning, noble warriors, who are stout-hearted and can destroy all worlds of big mansions of the enemy. (4607)

११. अस्माकमिन्द्रः समृतेषु ध्वजेष्वस्माकं या इषवस्ता जयन्तु ।
अस्माकं वीरा उत्तरे भवन्त्वस्मान्देवासोऽवता हवेषु ॥

11. May the commander of the army protect us when the flags are coming together (on the coming of the armies) close to each other. Let our missiles be victorious. Let our brave warriors overpower the enemy. Let all the warriors and the noble king, commander and other officers protect us in battles. (4608)[2]

HYMN XIV

१. इदमुच्छ्रेयोऽवसानमागां शिवे मे द्यावापृथिवी अभूताम् ।
असपत्नाः प्रदिशो मे भवन्तु न वै त्वा द्विष्मो अभयं नो अस्तु ॥

1. O king, I have got a splendid place of shelter. May the heavens and the earth be peaceful to me. May all the main quarters be free from enemies for me. We don't have any feeling of enmity for you; hence we may be free from fear. (4609)

HYMN XV

१. यत इन्द्र भयामहे ततो नो अभयं कृधि ।
मघवञ्छग्धि तव त्वं न ऊतिभिर्वि द्विषो वि मृधो जहि ॥

1. O God, make us free from fear, from whatever quarter we are afraid. O Lord of all riches, thou has the capacity to do so. Mayst thou completely destroy the violent enemies of ours. (4610)[3]

२. इन्द्रं वयमनूराधं हवामहेऽनु राध्यास्म द्विपदा चतुष्पदा ।
मा नः सेना अररुषीरुप गुर्विषूचीरिन्द्र द्रुहो वि नाशय ॥

[1]cf. *Rig*, 10.103.8. [2]cf. *Rig*, 10, 103.9 and *Yajur*, 17.43.
[3]cf. *Rig*, 8.61.13.

2. Let us pray to the Adorable Evil-Destroyer God, so that we may prosper with bipeds i.e., wives, sons and servants and quadrupeds, like cows, goats and horses. Let not the hosts of greedy people approach us. O king, put down all sorts of rebellions. (4611)

३. इन्द्रस्त्रातोत वृत्रहा परस्फानो वरेण्यः ।
स रक्षिता चरमतः स मध्यतः स पश्चात्स पुरस्तान्नो अस्तु ॥

3. The Mighty God is the Protector, Evil-Destroyer, the shielder from adverse forces of wickedness, and Worthy of respect by all. May He be our Protector from the extremes, in the middle, from behind and in front. (4612)

४. उरुं नो लोकमनु नेषि विद्वान्त्स्व१र्यज्ज्योतिरभयं स्वस्ति ।
उग्रा त इन्द्र स्थविरस्य बाहू उप क्षयेम शरणा बृहन्ता ॥

4. O Glorious God, Thou leadest us to the vast state of prosperity and well-being knowing full well that there is all bliss, light of knowledge, freedom from fear and perfect peace. Strong and stout are the arms of Thee, Who is Steadfast and Firm. May we find ample refuge there. (4613)[1]

५. अभयं नः करत्यन्तरिक्षमभयं द्यावापृथिवी उभे इमे ।
अभयं पश्चादभयं पुरस्तादुत्तरादधरादभयं नो अस्तु ॥

5. May the atmosphere be free from fear for us. May both these firmament and the earth be free from danger for us. Let there be freedom from all fear and danger for us, from behind, in front, from above and from below. (4614)

६. अभयं मित्रादभयममित्रादभयं ज्ञातादभयं पुरो यः ।
अभयं नक्तमभयं दिवा नः सर्वा आशा मम मित्रं भवन्तु ॥

6. Let there be fearlessness for us, from the friend, from the enemy, from the known, from the unknown, during the day and the night. Let all quarters (i.e., the people from all quarters) be my friends. (4615)

HYMN XVI

१. असपत्नं पुरस्तात्पश्चान्नो अभयं कृतम् । सविता मा दक्षिणत उत्तरान्मा शचीपतिः ॥

1. May king, the prime-mover of all things in the land and the wielder of power, the army-chief may provide us freedom from enemies, in the front and from fear from behind. May they make fearless from the right side (or south) as well as from the left (or north). (4616)

२. दिवो मादित्या रक्षन्तु भूम्या रक्षन्त्वग्नयः ।
इन्द्राग्नी रक्षतां मा पुरस्तादश्विनावभितः शर्म यच्छताम् ।
तिरश्चीनघ्न्या रक्षतु जातवेदा भूतकृतो मे सर्वतः सन्तु वर्म ॥

2. May, the twelve months of the year or the rays of the Sun, or cosmic rays protect me from heavens. May the leaders guard me from the earth. May air and fire protect me from the front. Let day and night, or the Sun

[1]cf. *Rig*, 4.47.8. This sukta may also be applied to seek protection and help from the king, as has been interpreted by Pt. Khem Karan Das Trivedi and Pt. Jaidev Vidyalankar.

and the moon, the army and the commander grant me shelter on both sides. May the learned person, who knows full well all the created things, protect the cattle, unworthy of destruction. May the invitors of various things provide armour for me, on all sides. (4617)

HYMN XVII

१. अग्निर्मा पातु वसुभिः पुरस्तात्तस्मिन्क्रमे तस्मिञ्छ्रये तां पुरं प्रैमि ।
स मा रक्षतु स मा गोपायतु तस्मा आत्मानं परि ददे स्वाहा ॥

1. May Radiant and All-Leading God protect me through Vasus, from the east or front side. I (a devotee) just step unto Him and take refuge under Him. I approach Him as a well-protected residential town. May He protect me. May He guard me I entrust myself completely to Him as an humble offering. (4618)[1]

२. वायुर्मान्तरिक्षेणैतस्या दिशः पातु तस्मिन्क्रमे तस्मिञ्छ्रये तां पुरं प्रैमि ।
स मा रक्षतु स मा गोपायतु तस्मा आत्मानं परि ददे स्वाहा ॥

2. May the Almighty protect me from this mid-quarter i.e., south-eastern direction through the atmosphere. I (the devotee) just step unto Him . . . so on like the above. (4619)[2]

३. सोमो मा रुद्रैर्दक्षिणाया दिशः पातु तस्मिन्क्रमे तस्मिञ्छ्रये तां पुरं प्रैमि ।
स मा रक्षतु स मा गोपायतु तस्मा आत्मानं परि ददे स्वाहा ॥

3. May the Creator protect me through Rudras, from the south or right side. I . . . . so on. (4620)[3]

४. वरुणो मादित्यैरेतस्या दिशः पातु तस्मिन्क्रमे तस्मिञ्छ्रये तां पुरं प्रैमि ।
स मा रक्षतु स मा गोपायतु तस्मा आत्मानं परि ददे स्वाहा ॥

4. May the most Adorable God protect me, through Adityas, from this mid-quarter i.e., south-west. I . . . . so on. (4621)[4]

५. सूर्यो मा द्यावापृथिवीभ्यां प्रतीच्या दिशः पातु तस्मिन्क्रमे तस्मिञ्छ्रये तां पुरं प्रैमि ।
स मा रक्षतु स मा गोपायतु तस्मा आत्मानं परि ददे स्वाहा ॥

5. May the All-shining God protect me, through the heavens and the earth from the west or the back side. I . . . . so on. (4622)[5]

६. आपो मौषधीमतीरेतस्या दिशः पान्तु तासु क्रमे तासु श्रये तां पुरं प्रैमि ।
ता मा रक्षन्तु ता मा गोपायन्तु ताभ्य आत्मानं परि ददे स्वाहा ॥

6. May the tranquilising God protect me with herbs-producing waters from this mid-quarter i.e., north-west. I . . . . so on (4623)

[1]The whole of this sukta can be applied to various forces of nature as well as various officers entrusted with different kinds of duties by the king.

[2]Vasus: Ether, air, fire, water, earth, Sun, constellations and electricity. 24 years old celibates, too.

[3]Rudra: Ten vital breaths and the soul; also 44 years old celibates.

[4]Adityas: Twelve months of the year; also 48 years old celibates.

[5]Marutas: strong winds, vital breaths as well brave persons. cf. *Atharva*, 3.27. 1-6, and 12.3.24.

७. विश्वकर्मा मा सप्तऋषिभिरुदीच्या दिशः पातु तस्मिन्क्रमे तस्मिञ्छ्रये तां पुरं प्रैमि ।
स मा रक्षतु स मा गोपायतु तस्मा आत्मानं परि ददे स्वाहा ॥

7. May God, the Architect of all protect me through seven seers, (i.e., seven sense-organs) from the north or the left side. I . . . . so on. (4624)

८. इन्द्रो मा मरुत्वानेतस्या दिशः पातु तस्मिन्क्रमे तस्मिञ्छ्रये तां पुरं प्रैमि ।
स मा रक्षतु स मा गोपायतु तस्मा आत्मानं परि ददे स्वाहा ॥

8. May the All-powerful God, with the brave persons, protect me from this mid-quarter i.e., north-east. I . . . . so on. (4625)

९. प्रजापतिर्मा प्रजननवान्त्सह प्रतिष्ठाया ध्रुवाया दिशः पातु तस्मिन्क्रमे
तस्मिञ्छ्रये तां पुरं प्रैमि ।
स मा रक्षतु स मा गोपायतु तस्मा आत्मानं परि ददे स्वाहा ॥

9. May the Protector of all, with His Creative powers, protect me from the stable quarter below. I . . . . so on. (4626)

१०. बृहस्पतिर्मा विश्वैर्देवैरूर्ध्वाया दिशः पातु तस्मिन्क्रमे तस्मिञ्छ्रये तां पुरं प्रैमि ।
स मा रक्षतु स मा गोपायतु तस्मा आत्मानं परि ददे स्वाहा ॥

10. May the Great Lord of Vedic learning and all divine beings protect me the quarter of the zenith, through all divine beings. I . . . . so on. (4627)

HYMN XVIII

१. अग्निं ते वसुवन्तमृच्छन्तु । ये माघायवः प्राच्या दिशोऽभिदासात् ॥

1. May the violent enemies, who come from the eastern or front quarter, with evil intention of killing us, come to our leading commander, surrounded by youthful warriors, to meet their death. (4628)[1]

२. वायुं तेऽन्तरिक्षवन्तमृच्छन्तु । ये माघायव एतस्या दिशोऽभिदासात् ॥

2. Let the evil-intentioned enemies, assaulting us with the murderous attack from the mid-quarter i.e., south-east approach our powerful commander, who has full control over the atmosphere with his speedy striking are power, to meet their end. (4629)[2]

३. सोमं ते रुद्रवन्तमृच्छन्तु । ये माघायवो दक्षिणाया दिशोऽभिदासात् ॥

3. The evil-international foes, who may dare to attack us from the south or the right side to subdue us, shall meet their fatal end, when they come near our commander, who is well-versed in mobilising his terrible forces, capable of making their enemies weep bitterly. (4630)

४. वरुणं त आदित्यवन्तमृच्छन्तु । ये माघायव एतस्या दिशोऽभिदासात् ।

4. The mischief-monger adversaries, coming from this mid-quarter, i.e., south-west, to vanquish us, may find their end, if they come face to face with

[1]The whole of the sukta deals with the mighty, crushing power of the army to deal a death-blow to all evil-designs of the enemy.

[2]It can also refer to the various powers of God, protecting us from the wicked enemies, like the previous sukta.

our commander, capable of warding off all attacks of the enemy, with the huge energy, stored from the rays of the Sun. (4631)

५. सूर्यं ते द्यावापृथिवीवन्तमृच्छन्तु । ये माघायवः प्रतीच्या दिशोऽभिदासात् ॥

5. Let the wicked enemies, who dare attack us from the west to enslave us, meet their doom at the very approach of our commander capable of burning all his foes, like the Sun with the energy from the earth and the cosmos. (4632)

६. अपस्त ओषधीमतीर्ऋच्छन्तु । ये माघायव एतस्या दिशोऽभिदासात् ॥

6. Let those, who come with the evil-desire to kill us from this mid-quarter i.e., north-west, find their instantaneous grave by drinking waters, mixed with fatal herbs, or smelling such gases. (4633)

७. विश्वकर्माणं ते सप्तऋषिवन्तमृच्छन्तु । ये माघायव उदीच्या दिशोऽभिदासात् ॥

7. May those, mischievous enemies, who dash against us to murder us from the north or left side, meet their death-blow from our Engineers, equipped with all the means and contrivances to detect their movements from afar. (4634)

८. इन्द्रं ते मरुत्वन्तमृच्छन्तु । ये माघायव एतस्या दिशोऽभिदासात् ॥

8. Let those wicked foes, who come with the murderous assault against us, meet their death by approach of our mighty commander, with warriors, possessing the striking power of the furious winds. (4635)

९. प्रजापतिं ते प्रजननवन्तमृच्छन्तु । ये माघायवो ध्रुवाया दिशोऽभिदासात् ॥

9. Let the enemies, with evil designs, coming from the lower regions (i.e., from underground hide-outs) to subdue us, meet their end as soon as, they approach our protector of the people, capable of producing ample means of destruction of the enemy. (4636)

१०. बृहस्पतिं ते विश्वदेववन्तमृच्छन्तु । ये माघायव ऊर्ध्वाया दिशोऽभिदासात् ॥

10. Let all the mischievous machinations of the enemies to suppress us on the high levels of political diplomacy, be set at naught by coming to the knowledge of the chief councilor, accompanied by all the learned persons. (4637)

HYMN XIX

१. मित्रः पृथिव्योदक्रामत्तां पुरं प्र णयामि वः ।
तामा विशत तां प्र विशत सा वः शर्म च वर्म च यच्छतु ॥

1. The fire gets enhanced by the help of the earth (in the form of fuel, wood, coal and oil, etc.). I lead you specially to that place of shelter, well-provided with it. Be ready to enter it and do enter it. May it grant you security and protection. (4638)[1]

[1]I: God or king. The connection between fire and earth is well-known. You: man, with his family.

२. वायुरन्तरिक्षेणोदक्रामत्तां पुरं प्र णयामि वः ।
तामा विशत तां प्र विशत सा वः शर्म च वर्म च यच्छतु ॥

2. The air gets advanced by the help of the atmosphere. I take you to that town in particular, which has ample breathing spaces in between. Be ready to enter it. Do enter it. May it grant you peace and security. (4639)[1]

३. सूर्यो दिवोदक्रामत्तां पुरं प्र णयामि वः ।
तामा विशत तां प्र विशत सा वः शर्म च वर्म च यच्छतु ॥

3. The Sun has its powers of nourishing the life all around by the help of other heavenly spheres. I lead you specially to the town or place of residence where there is ample Sun-light and Sun-shine. Be prepared to go there and do so. May it be for your well-being and protection. (4640)

४. चन्द्रमा नक्षत्रैरुदक्रामत्तां पुरं प्र णयामि वः ।
तामा विशत तां प्र विशत सा वः शर्म च वर्म च यच्छतु ॥

4. The moon, her powers of soothing through the constellations. I lead you to the city, which provides ample space for the moonlight. Prepare yourself to enter it. Do enter it. May it give you calmness and protection. (4641)

५. सोम ओषधीभिरुदक्रामत्तां पुरं प्र णयामि वः ।
तामा विशत तां प्र विशत सा वः शर्म च वर्म च यच्छतु ॥

5. The essence of medicines gets increased by herbs. I . . . . so on. (4642)

६. यज्ञो दक्षिणाभिरुदक्रामत्तां पुरं प्र णयामि वः ।
तामा विशत तां प्र विशत सा वः शर्म च वर्म च यच्छतु ॥

6. The value of the sacrifice is enhanced by the Dakshana, the reward given to its performers. I lead you to that town, where such sacrifices are the order of the day. Be prepared to go there and do so. May it bring peace and security for you. (4643)

७. समुद्रो नदीभिरुदक्रामत्तां पुरं प्र णयामि वः ।
तामा विशत तां प्र विशत सा वः शर्म च वर्म च यच्छतु ॥

7. The sea is expanded by the rivers falling into it. I lead you to the town by the sea-side to enjoy its celebrating climate. Get ready to go there. Do enter it. Let it be a source of peace and safety for you. (4644)

८. ब्रह्म ब्रह्मचारिभिरुदक्रामत्तां पुरं प्र णयामि वः ।
तामा विशत तां प्र विशत सा वः शर्म च वर्म च यच्छतु ॥

8. The significance of the Vedas along with their 'angas' and upangas is enhanced by those who study them for 24, 44 or 48 years with the vow of celibacy. I lead you (the young ones) to that town of leading which provides

[1](1-4) The people are instructed by God to have vast cities and towns, which are airy, sunlit, moonlit and ample fuels etc., provided with all means of peaceful living and protection.

this facility. Be prepared to cater it. Do enter it. May it grant you peace and security. (4645)

९. इन्द्रो वीर्ये३णोदक्रामत्तां पुरं प्र णयामि वः ।
तामा विशत तां प्र विशत सा वः शर्म च वर्म च यच्छतु ॥

9. The commander of the army or the king progresses by his prowess or valour. I lead you specially to the cantonment or the capital of his residence. Be ready to enter it, and do enter it. May it provide you with peace and protection. (4646)

१०. देवा अमृतेनोदक्रामंस्तां पुरं प्र णयामि वः ।
तामा विशत तां प्र विशत सा वः शर्म च वर्म च यच्छतु ॥

10. The yogis are enhanced by immortality. I lead you specially to their yog-ashrama. Be ready to enter it, if you are so inclined. Do enter it. Let it rain peace and security on you. (4647)

११. प्रजापतिः प्रजाभिरुदक्रामत्तां पुरं प्र णयामि वः ।
तामा विशत तां प्र विशत सा वः शर्म च वर्म च यच्छतु ॥

11. The Lord of the people, i.e., king has his worth expanded by the help of his subjects. I lead you to his capital specially. Prepare to enter it. Do enter it. May it be for security and safety for you. (4648)

HYMN XX

१. अप न्यधुः पौरुषेयं वधं यमिन्द्राग्नी धाता सविता बृहस्पतिः ।
सोमो राजा वरुणो अश्विना यमः पूषास्मान्परि पातु मृत्योः ॥

1. Let electricity and fire, air, the stirring sun, the essence of medicines the bright pure water, the physician and the druggist the celibate living, the nourishing mother earth, all guard us against death, which has been deadly hidden for taking away the life of men. (4649)[1]

२. यानि चकार भुवनस्य यस्पतिः प्रजापतिर्मातरिश्वा प्रजाभ्यः ।
प्रदिशो यानि वसते दिशश्च तानि मे वर्माणि बहुलानि सन्तु ॥

2. Whatever means of protection, the All-pervading Lord of the Universe and of the people living therein, created for His subjects, and whatever all the main quarters and those intervening are covering, may all they be profuse armour for me. (4650)

३. यत्ते तनूष्वनह्यन्त देवा द्युराजयो देहिनः । इन्द्रो यच्चक्रे वर्म तदस्मान्पातु विश्वतः ॥

3. The armour that the brave warriors, looking bright like the radiant heavens, fasten to their bodies and that which the king or the commander gets ready for himself, may protect us from all sides. (4651)

[1]The verse enumerates the forces of nature and other means to keep away death. It may also refer to the protection of the people by the various officers of the state entrusted with duties of looking after the welfare and security of the people to protect them from death, which may be caused by the means of destruction like mines deeply hidden by the enemies. The whole sukta shows the means for protection and security of man on earth.

४. वर्म मे द्यावापृथिवी वर्माहर्वर्म सूर्यः । वर्म मे विश्वे देवाः क्रन्मा मा प्रापत्प्रतीचिका ॥

4. Let the energy derived from the earth as well as from the cosmos, the day and the Sun, be all a shield for me. Let all the divine things and beings protect me, so that no evil or misfortune befall me (or let not the army of the enemy come near me). (4652)

Chapter (Anuvāka) 3

HYMN XXI

१. गायत्र्युश्णिगनुष्टुब्बृहती पङ्क्तिस्त्रिष्टुब्जगत्यै ॥

1. Gayatri (of 24 syllables); Ushnig (of 28 syllables); Anushttup (of 32 syllables); Brihti (of 36 syllables); Pankti (of 40 syllables), Trishttup (of 44 syllables); Jagati (of 48 syllables); are the seven meters which must be well-known to a student of the Vedas. (4653)[1]

HYMN XXII

१. आङ्गिरसानामाद्यैः पञ्चनुवाकैः स्वाहा ॥

1. O people, have a thorough knowledge of the 1st five Anuvākas i.e., Kāṇḍa suktas 1-28 of the Atharvaveda. (4654)

२. षष्ठाय स्वाहा ॥

2. Derive good lessons from the sixth Anuvāka, Kāṇḍa 1, suktas 29-35. (4655)

३. सप्तमाष्टमाभ्यां स्वाहा ॥

3. Learn lessons from the seventh and eighth anuvākas i.e., Kāṇḍa 2, suktas 1-5 and 6-10. (4656)

४. नीलनखेभ्यः स्वाहा ॥

4. Study thoroughly the nilnakha-named suktas, teaching how to quell the wicked with good armaments. (4657)

५. हरितेभ्यः स्वाहा ॥

5. Completely study the Harita suktas, giving ample knowledge of the plants and herbs. (4658)

६. क्षुद्रेभ्यः स्वाहा ॥

6. Have a thorough knowledge of the Kṣhudra sukta i.e., Skambha sukta giving complete version of the invisible God. (4659)

७. पर्यायिकेभ्यः स्वाहा ॥

[1]Enumerates the Vedic meters in a single line. But it has a great significance. It indicates that man should study the Vedas, taking the vow of celibacy for 24, 28, 32, 36, 40, 44, or 48 years according to his will-power. Seven meters are also related to seven elements in nature—Mahat, Shankar, and ether, air, fire, water and earth; also seven vital breaths or seven sense-organs or seven Dhatus in the body. Pt. Khem Karan Das Trivedi interprets it as: The Vedic lore is worth singing, lovable, vast, of great, significance instructing action, knowledge and prayer, ever-adorable and of great service to the ever-moving world.

7. Learn well the Paryayaka suktas. (4660)

८. प्रथमेभ्यः शङ्खेभ्यः स्वाहा ॥

९. द्वितीयेभ्यः शङ्खेभ्यः स्वाहा ॥

१०. तृतीयेभ्यः शङ्खेभ्यः स्वाहा ॥

8-10. The thorough knowledge of the 1st, 2nd and 3rd Shankla suktas be mastered. (4661-63)

११. उपोत्तमेभ्यः स्वाहा ॥

१२. उत्तमेभ्यः स्वाहा ॥

१३. उत्तरेभ्यः स्वाहा ॥

11-13. The suktas that are better, the near best and the best should be completely studied. (4664-66)[1]

१४. ऋषिभ्यः स्वाहा ॥

14. Know well the seers of the Vedas. (4667)

१५. शिखिभ्यः स्वाहा ॥

15. Know well the celibates who are studying the Vedas. They should have proper guidance. (4668)

१६. गणेभ्यः स्वाहा ॥

16. A thorough knowledge of suktas read in groups, like those of water, peace and security, etc., should be acquired. (4669)

१७. महागणेभ्यः स्वाहा ॥

17. Have a complete mastery of the suktas, read in large groups like that of Prithivi sukta. (4670)

१८. सर्वेभ्योऽङ्गिरोभ्यो विदगणेभ्यः स्वाहा ॥

18. Learn well all the suktas of Atharvaveda, seen by the seers of the Angiras or Atharvaveda. (4671)

१९. पृथक्सहस्राभ्यां स्वाहा ॥

19. Study well the Prithakah Sukta, i.e., eighteenth Kāṇḍa and the Pursha sukta, also called Sahasara sukta. (4672)

२०. ब्रह्मणे स्वाहा ॥

20. Have a thorough grounding in the sukta concerning Brahma the mighty Lord of the Vedas and the universe. (4673)

२१. ब्रह्मज्येष्ठा संभृता वीर्याणि ब्रह्माग्रे ज्येष्ठं दिवमा ततान ।
भूतानां ब्रह्मा प्रथमोत जज्ञे तेनार्हति ब्रह्मणा स्पर्धितुं कः ॥

[1](11-13) 'The better': concerning sacrifice or action. 'The near best'—concerning preparation for salvation by yogic exercises. 'The best'—concerning the state of bliss. Pt. Khem Karan Das Trivedi has given a different rendering to this as well as to the next hymn. But it seems to far-fetch the meanings of the numbers, given herein and the next hymn, too.

21. Brahma, the Almighty is the foremost amongst the powers that are borne in this world. He extended the huge constellations in the very beginning of the creation. He is the 1st among the created things. What is worthy to compete with that very Brahma, the mighty one? (4674)

HYMN XXIII

१. आथर्वणानां चतुर्ऋचेभ्यः स्वाहा ॥

1. Have good knowledge of the suktas of the Atharvaveda, which have four mantras. (4675)[1]

२. पञ्चर्चेभ्यः स्वाहा ॥

2. Learn well the suktas of five mantras. (4676)

३. षडृचेभ्यः स्वाहा ॥

3. Study well the suktas of six mantras. (4677)

४. सप्तर्चेभ्यः स्वाहा ॥

4. Completely learn the suktas with seven Richas. (4678)

५. अष्टर्चेभ्यः स्वाहा ॥

5. Thoroughly study the suktas, with eight Richas. (4679)

६. नवर्चेभ्यः स्वाहा ॥

6. Have full knowledge of the suktas with nine mantras. (4680)

७. दशर्चेभ्यः स्वाहा ॥

7. Know well the suktas of ten mantras. (4681)

८. एकादशर्चेभ्यः स्वाहा ॥

8. Learn thoroughly the suktas with eleven Richas. (4682)

९. द्वादशर्चेभ्यः स्वाहा ॥

9. Study completely the suktas of twelve mantras. (4683)

१०. त्रयोदशर्चेभ्यः स्वाहा ॥

10. Have full mastery over the suktas with thirteen Richas. (4684)

११. चतुर्दशर्चेभ्यः स्वाहा ॥

11. Acquire complete knowledge of the suktas of fourteen Richas. (4685)

१२. पञ्चदशर्चेभ्यः स्वाहा ॥

12. Have good knowledge of the suktas of fifteen mantras. (4686)

१३. षोडशर्चेभ्यः स्वाहा ॥

13. Study well the suktas of sixteen mantras. (4687)

[1]Pt. Khem Karan Das Trivedi has given different rendering of this sukta as well as of the previous. But to me it appears to be far-fetched. It is too difficult to give appropriate meanings to all the numbers given here. One can't maintain its appropriateness throughout. Both of these suktas are called. Smasa suktas, bringing together the whole of the *Atharva* to emphasise its thorough study.

१४. सप्तदशर्चेभ्यः स्वाहा ॥

14. Learn thoroughly the suktas of seventeen Richas. (4688)

१५. अष्टादशर्चेभ्यः स्वाहा ॥

15. Completely know the suktas of eighteen Richas. (4689)

१६. एकोनविंशतिः स्वाहा ॥

16. Thoroughly study the suktas, with nineteen mantras. (4690)

१७. विंशतिः स्वाहा ॥

17. Have a complete mastery of the suktas, with twenty mantras. (4691)

१८. महत्काण्डाय स्वाहा ॥

18. Learn the great Kāṇḍa (i.e., 12th or 20th) thoroughly well. (4692)

१९. तृचेभ्यः स्वाहा ॥

19. Study well the suktas with three Richas. (4693)

२०. एकर्चेभ्यः स्वाहा ॥

20. Learn completely the suktas with one mantra. (4694)

२१. क्षुद्रेभ्यः स्वाहा ॥

21. Thoroughly study the Kshudra sukta i.e., 10.10 Shamkha sukta. (4695)

२२. एकानृचेभ्यः स्वाहा ॥

22. Learn well the suktas, with one-fourth of the verse only i.e., Vratya sukta. (4696)

२३. रोहितेभ्यः स्वाहा ॥

23. Study well the Rohita sukta i.e., 13 Kāṇḍa. (4697)

२४. सूर्याभ्यां स्वाहा ॥

24. Have a thorough knowledge of two anuvākas of Surya i.e., 14 Kāṇḍa. (4698)

२५. व्रात्याभ्यां स्वाहा ॥

25. Completely study the two sukta of Vratya (i.e., 15 Kāṇḍa). (4699)

२६. प्राजापत्याभ्यां स्वाहा ॥

26. Learn well the two anuvākaṣ of Prajapati (i.e., 16 Kāṇḍa). (4700)

२७. विषासह्यै स्वाहा ॥

27. Study the 17th Kāṇḍa, with one Richa only (i.e., Vishasahi sukta). (4701)

२८. मङ्गलिकेभ्यः स्वाहा ॥

28. Thoroughly study the suktas, praying peace, happiness and well-being (19th Kāṇḍa). (4702)

२९. ब्रह्मणे स्वाहा ॥

29. Have a thorough grasp of the Brahma Kāṇḍa i.e., the 20th Kāṇḍa. (4703)

३०. ब्रह्मज्येष्ठा संभृता वीयाणि ब्रह्माग्रे ज्येष्ठं दिवमा ततान ।
भूतानां ब्रह्मा प्रथमोत जज्ञे तेनार्हति ब्रह्मणा स्पर्धितुं कः ॥

30. Brahma, the Almighty is the topmost power amongst the powers that are borne here in this universe. In the very beginning of the creation. He, the mighty Lord spread the heavens far and wide. He revealed Himself to be the foremost among all the created things. Who else can compete with Him, the mighty one? (4704)

HYMN XXIV

१. येन देवं सवितारं परि देवा अधारयन् । तेनेमं ब्रह्मणस्पते परि राष्ट्राय धत्तन ॥

1. O the learned person, well-versed in Vedic lore, invest this pushing king of noble qualities with royal robes as well authority for the very reason for which the nobility and intelligentsia of the land have upheld. (4705)

२. परीममिन्द्रमायुषे महे क्षत्राय धत्तन । यथैनं जरसे नयां ज्योक्क्षत्रेऽधि जागरत् ॥

2. Strengthen this glorious king for long life and great protection; so that we may lead him to advanced old age and he, being wide-awake may constantly protect us. (4706)

३. परीमं सोममायुषे महे श्रोत्राय धत्तन । यथैनं जरसे नयां ज्योक्श्रोत्रेऽधि जागरत् ॥

3. Cover him with this essence of medicines for long life and strong hearing power; so that we may lead him to far advance, old age, and he, being ever-vigilant, may protect us constantly. (4707)

४. परि धत्त धत्त नो वर्चसेमं जरामृत्युं कृणुत दीर्घमायुः ।
बृहस्पतिः प्रायच्छद्वास एतत्सोमाय राज्ञे परिधातवा उ ॥

4. O leaders of the nation, protect the land and clothe him with splendour through our aid. Prolong his life to enable him not to meet his death before advanced age. Let the Vedic scholar offer this royal robe to the peace-showering king to wear. (4708)

५. जरां सु गच्छ परि धत्स्व वासो भवा गृष्टीनामभिशस्तिपा उ ।
शतं च जीव शरदः पुरूची रायश्च पोषमुपसंव्ययस्व ॥

5. O king, do reach old age easily; put on this royal robe and be the guardian of the subjects all around; live upto hundred years and amass ample riches and prosperity, the source of all pleasures and joys. (4709)

६. परीदं वासो अधिथाः स्वस्तयेऽभूर्वापीनामभिशस्तिपा उ ।
शतं च जीव शरदः पुरूचीर्वसूनि चारुर्वि भजासि जीवन् ॥

6. O king, put on this royal robe and work as a guard against all the violent attacks on the farmers and the subjects of yours by the wicked people, for their welfare and happiness. Live for hundred years, while living, and enjoying all worldly pleasures, distribute profuse riches amongst your people. (4710)[1]

[1](1-6) Harmony among the king and his subjects is the key-note of a prosperous and peaceful life.

७. योगेयोगे तवस्तरं वाजेवाजे हवामहे । सखाय इन्द्रमूतये ॥

7. O friends, we seek the help of the mighty king, for whenever we wish to achieve new desired objects, at all occasions of wars or for protection. (4711)

८. हिरण्यवर्णो अजरः सुवीरो जरामृत्युः प्रजया सं विशस्व ।
तदग्निराह तदु सोम आह बृहस्पतिः सविता तदिन्द्रः ॥

8. O king, being charming and radiant like gold and keeping away old age, through well regulated life, and accompanied by brave warriors, get well enthralled along with your subjects till far advanced old age. This is what has been ordained by God, the Effulgent, the Peace-showering, the Lord of the Vedas, the Prime-mover of all creation and the Lord of fortunes. (4712)

HYMN XXV

१. अश्रान्तस्य त्वा मनसा युनज्मि प्रथमस्य च । उत्कूलमुद्वहो भवोदुह्य प्रति धावतात् ॥

1. O man, I (God) unite you with the mind of an untiring person, fit to be the foremost among all. Successfully carrying the burden of all your duties against odds, rush forward, on this race-course of life, excelling all by the successful performance of your responsibilities. (4713)[1]

HYMN XXVI

१. अग्नेः प्रजातं परि यद्धिरण्यममृतं दध्रे अधि मर्त्येषु ।
य एनद्वेद स इदेनमर्हति जरामृत्युर्भवति यो बिभर्ति ॥

1. The life-prolonging semen, which is produced by 'jathragni' bodily temperature, is maintained in the mortal bodies through-and-through. He, who knows the importance of it, does deserve it and who keeps it intact, attains to long, long old age before he dies. (4714)[2]

२. यद्धिरण्यं सूर्येण सुवर्णं प्रजावन्तो मनवः पूर्व ईषिरे ।
तत्त्वा चन्द्रं वर्चसा सं सृजत्यायुष्मान्भवति यो बिभर्ति ॥

2. O soul, the semen produces the radiance and splendour, (due to well-protected semen) having the beauty and glow like the Sun, which the men, who have gone before you, were able to attain. That very semen will produce in you the pleasant glory. He who bears it, attains to long life. (4715)

३. आयुषे त्वा वर्चसे त्वौजसे च बलाय च । यथा हिरण्यतेजसा विभासासि जनाँ अनु ॥

3. O man, this has been given to you for long life, for glory, for splendour and for strength and prowess, so that you may shine, with the radiance of Gold after the offspring even. (4716)[3]

[1]This verse is very instructive, teaching man how to overcome all difficulties and troubles with a determined mind and doggest persistence. That is the only way to excel others in life-struggle.

[2]The importance of not wasting one's semen for the longevity of life is emphasised here.

[3]The man, who does not waste his semen uselessly, is able to retain the glow and radiance even after giving birth to his progeny.

४. यद्वेद राजा वरुणो वेद देवो बृहस्पतिः ।
इन्द्रो यद् वृत्रहा वेद तत्त आयुष्यं भुवत्ते वर्चस्यं भुवत् ।।

4. Whatever knowledge about this vitalising thing (semen) the bright king has, whatever the noble Vedic scholar know about it and whatever the enemy-destroyer commander knows about it, may that all be life-prolonging to you. May it add to your splendour. (4717)

Chapter (Anuvāka) 4

HYMN XXVII

१. गोभिष्ट्वा पात्वृषभो वृषा त्वा पातु वाजिभिः ।
वायुष्ट्वा ब्रह्मणा पात्विन्द्रस्त्वा पात्विन्द्रियैः ।।

1. O man, let the powerful ox nourish you through cows by supplying milk. Let the strong horse serve you with fast horses. Let the wind protect you with food. Let electricity be of a great service to you, through electric machines or contrivances. (4718)

२. सोमस्त्वा पात्वोषधीभिर्नक्षत्रैः पातु सूर्यः । माद्भ्यस्त्वा चन्द्रो वृत्रहा वातः प्राणेन रक्षतु ।।

2. Let the essence of medicines protect you with the help of herbs. Let the Sun protect you along with the constellations. Let the cloud-smasher moon protect you through waters. Let the wind protect you through vital breaths. (4719)

३. तिस्रो दिवस्तिस्रः पृथिवीस्त्रीण्यन्तरिक्षाणि चतुरः समुद्रान् ।
त्रिवृतं स्तोमं त्रिवृत आप आहुस्तास्त्वा रक्षन्तु त्रिवृता त्रिवृद्भिः ।।

3. There are three kinds of celestial spheres, three kinds of terrestrial bodies, three kinds of mid-regions, four kinds of oceans, three kinds of element-groups, thrice-bound waters, they call. Let these thrice-bound protect thee three-fold. (4720)[1]

४. त्रीन्नाकांस्त्रीन्त्समुद्रांस्त्रीन्ब्रध्नांस्त्रीन्वैष्टपान् ।
त्रीन्मातरिश्वनस्त्रीन्त्सूर्यान्गोप्तॄन्कल्पयामि ते ।।

4. O soul, I (the Creator) create three states of perfect bliss, three oceans, three states of bondage, three stationary ones, three atmospheres, three Suns as thy protectors. (4721)[2]

[1]Three celestial spheres—the Sun, the planets, the stellites. Three terrestrial—The earth, the meteorites, the fine dust particles. Three mid-regions—the atmosphere, the stratosphere and outersphere. Four oceans—the vast expanse of water underground, the ocean on the surface of the earth, the watery expanse in the atmosphere, the rarified regions beyond. Three elements groups—(i) Group of 15 elements, (ii) Group of 17 elements, (iii) Group of 21 elements, (i) comprises Sattva, Raja, Tama, Mahat, Ahankar, 5 Tanmatra, 5 Sthulbhutas. (ii) Mahat, Ahankar, 5 tanmatras, 5 sense-organs, 5 vital breaths. (iii) Satva, Raja, Tama, Mahat, Ahankar, 5 Tanmatra, 5 vital breaths, 5 Sthulbhutas, and the soul.

[2]Three nakas: three states of bliss—सुषुप्ति—sound sleep; समाधि—deep meditation; मुक्ति—salvation. Three oceans, on earth, atmospheric, heavenly one (nebulea.) Three states of bondage (i) भोगयोनि—पशुयोनि (ii) कर्मयोनि—मनुष्ययोनि (iii) देवयोनि—

५. घृतेन त्वा समुक्षाम्यग्न आज्येन वर्धयन् । अग्नेश्चन्द्रस्य सूर्यस्य मा प्राणं मायिनो दभन् ॥

5. O king or leader, brilliant like fire, I (God) nurture you well with clarified butter, just as fire is increased by clarified butter. Let not the cheats destroy the life of the leader, who is charming and splendorous like the moon and the Sun. (4722)

६. मा वः प्राणं मा वोऽपानं मा हरो मायिनो दभन् ।
भ्राजन्तो विश्ववेदसो देवा दैव्येन धावत ॥

6. O learned people, let not the cheats end your incoming and outgoing breaths, nor your evil-destroying prowess. Let you be running far and wide, being glorious and possessing ample fortunes, by high quality means of transport, cars, trains, ships and aeroplanes. (4723)

७. प्राणेनाग्निं सं सृजति वातः प्राणेन संहितः । प्राणेन विश्वतोमुखं सूर्यं देवा अजनयन् ॥

7. As the outer air is well connected with the vital breath (inside), so does the man produce bodily temperature with the help of the vital breaths. The natural forces produced the Sun, which sheds its rays all around and thus faces all quarters, by the help of this very vital breath. (4724)

८. आयुषायुष्कृतां जीवायुष्मान्जीव मा मृथाः । प्राणेनात्मन्वतां जीव मा मृत्योरुदगा वशम् ॥

8. O man, live the life-span, attained by long-lived persons through regular and celibate living. Be long-lived. Don't die. Lead the life with the vital breaths of those, who attained mastery over themselves. Don't fall into the clutches of death. (4725)

९. देवानां निहितं निधिं यमिन्द्रोऽन्वविन्दत्पथिभिर्देवयानैः ।
आपो हिरण्यं जुगुपुस्त्रिवृद्भिस्तास्त्वा रक्षन्तु त्रिवृता त्रिवृद्भिः ॥

9. There is a hidden treasure (i.e., of semen) of good things or well-controlled sense-organs which the soul attained by the paths trodden by the divine beings i.e., salvation-seekers. These high-souled persons kept this brilliant object (i.e., semen) by three-fold vital breaths i.e., Pranayama. Let these three-fold vital breaths protect thee thrice-fold. (4726)[1]

१०. त्रयस्त्रिंशद् देवतास्त्रीणि च वीर्याणि प्रियायमाणा जुगुपुरप्स्वन्तः ।
अस्मिंश्चन्द्रे अधि यद्धिरण्यं तेनायं कृणवद्वीर्याणि ॥

10. There are thirty-three things of divine qualities and three kinds of sources of power, pleasant to man and kept concealed amongst vital breaths. Whatever there is splendour or glory in the moon, let him, the soul, produce the powers by its help. (4727)[2]

मुमु: Three stationary ones—Trees, herbs and grass. Three atmospheres—The narrowest one of mother's womb, the atmosphere and outer-space. Three Suns: The common sun in the solar system, the light of knowledge. The spiritual Sun, seen by the yogis in deep meditation.

[1]Three-fold vital breaths—Prān, Apān, Udān; Thrice-fold: Rechaka, Kumbhaka and Stambhaka. It is through Pranayama that the vitalising semen is kept intact, which is the cause of the splendorous aura of the sages.

[2]Trinshad Devatas—12 Months, 11 Vital breaths, 8 Vasus, Indra and Prajapati. Three powers: Physical, mental and spiritual. शारीरिक, मानसिक, आत्मिक ।

११. ये देवा दिव्येकादश स्थ ते देवासो हविरिदं जुषध्वम् ।।

11. Let the eleven devas, which stay in heavens, partake of this oblation of mine. (4728)[1]

१२. ये देवा अन्तरिक्ष एकादश स्थ ते देवासो हविरिदं जुषध्वम् ।।

12. Let those eleven devas, which reside in the atmosphere, partake of this oblation of mine. (4729)

१३. ये देवा पृथिव्यामेकादश स्थ ते देवासो हविरिदं जुषध्वम् ।।

13. Let the eleven devas, that are on the earth, share this oblation of mine. (4730)

१४. असपत्नं पुरस्तात्पश्चान्नो अभयं कृतम् । सविता मा दक्षिणत उत्तरान्मा शचीपतिः ।।

14. Let there be freedom from enemies for us from the front side, and freedom from fear from behind. Let the creative and stirring king protect me from the south or the right side. Let the commander of the powerful army guard me from the north or the left side. (4731)

१५. दिवो मादित्या रक्षन्तु भूम्या रक्षन्त्वग्नयः ।
इन्द्राग्नी रक्षतां मा पुरस्तादश्विनावभितः शर्म यच्छताम् ।
तिरश्चीनघ्न्या रक्षतु जातवेदा भूतकृतो मे सर्वतः सन्तु वर्म ।।

15. See 19.16.2 (4732)

HYMN XXVIII

१. इमं बध्नामि ते मणिं दीर्घायुत्वाय तेजसे । दर्भं सपत्नदम्भनं द्विषतस्तपनं हृदः ।।

1. O king or commander, I (the prohita) this radiating contrivance, made of Durbha-grass, vested with special qualities of radiation, for your long life and energy. It is capable of subduing the enemies by roasting their hearts. (4733)[2]

२. द्विषतस्तापयन्हृदः शत्रूणां तापयन्मनः । दुर्हार्दः सर्वांस्त्वं दर्भ घर्म इवाभिसंतापयन् ।।

2. O darbha, let thee roast the hearts of those who hate us. Let thee pierce the minds of the enemies. Let thee thoroughly burn all the wicked-hearted people like the cauldron. (4734)

३. घर्म इवाभितपन्दर्भ द्विषतो नितपन्मणे । हृदः सपत्नानां भिन्द्धीन्द्र इव विरुजं बलम् ।।

[1](11-13) According to Maharshi Dayanand in *Yajur*, 7.17 and In Dyu 11 Devasprān, Upāṅ, Udān, Smān, Vyān, Nāg, Kurm, Krikal, Devadatta, Dhananjaya and Jīva. In Antriksh, 11 devas—shrotra, twak, chakshu, rasna, ghrana, vak, vani, pada, Vayu, upastha and mana. On earth, 11 devas—Prithvi, Āp, Teja, Vayu, Akasha, Aditya, Chandra, Nakshatra, Ahankar, mahat-tatva, and Prakriti. cf. also *Rig*, 1.139.11, *Yajur*, 7.19.

[2]To me it appears that 'Darbha mani' is not a charm of Amulet as interpreted by Griffith or a fierce commander of the army, as interpreted by Pt. Jaidev Vidyalankar and Pt. Khem Karan Das Trivedi but some small radiating instrument or contrivance formed by the expert technicians from the 'Durbha grass', which is supposed to have certain special powers of radiation, due to which it finds extensive usage among the Hindus. Its special use as an instrument of destruction and protection against the enemies is worth exploring by the scientists,

3. O darbha-mani, completely burning like the cauldron, reduce the enemy to ashes; pierce the hearts of the foes, and smash their forces like electricity. (4735)

४. भिन्द्धि दर्भ सपत्नानां हृदयं द्विषतां मणे । उद्यन्त्वचमिव भूम्याः शिर एषां वि पातय ॥

4. O darbha mani, pierce the heart of the hating enemies. Just as the rising sun fells the cloud, that covers the earth like the skin, completely fallest thou off the heads of these enemies. (4736)

५. भिन्द्धि दर्भ सपत्नान्मे भिन्द्धि मे पृतनायतः ।
भिन्द्धि मे सर्वान्दुर्हार्दो भिन्द्धि मे द्विषतो मणे ॥

5. O Darbha, penetrate these enemies of mine. Crush those who come to fight with me. O radiating Mane, smash all these evil-hearted people. Crush all these haters of mine. (4737)

६. छिन्द्धि दर्भ सपत्नान्मे छिन्द्धि मे पृतनायतः ।
छिन्द्धि मे सर्वान्दुर्हार्दान् छिन्द्धि मे द्विषतो मणे ॥

6. O darbha, cut off the enemies of mine. Slay those who attack me with armies. O apane, slash off all these evil-designing foes of mine. Cut off all those who hate me. (4738)

७. वृश्च दर्भ सपत्नान्मे वृश्च मे पृतनायतः । वृश्च मे सर्वान्दुर्हार्दो वृश्च मे द्विषतो मणे ॥

7. Let darbha-mani tear my adversaries and the foes who come to fight against me. Let it tear all the wicked-hearted people who hate me. (4739)

८. कृन्त दर्भ सपत्नान्मे कृन्त मे पृतनायतः । कृन्त मे सर्वान्दुर्हार्दो कृन्त मे द्विषतो मणे ॥

8. Let the darbha-mani cleave my rivals and those who attack me with forces. Let it cleave the evil-natured haters of mine. (4740)

९. पिंश दर्भ सपत्नान्मे पिंश मे पृतनायतः । पिंश मे सर्वान्दुर्हार्दः पिंश मे द्विषतो मणे ॥

9. Let the darbha mani grind down the foes of mine and also those who come with the intention to fight. Let it also grind those who wish me evil and who hate me. (4741)

१०. विध्य दर्भ सपत्नान्मे विध्य मे पृतनायतः ।
विध्य मे सर्वान्दुर्हार्दो विध्य मे द्विषतो मणे ॥

10. Let the darbha-mani pierce my enemies and those who come to fight with me. Let it also pierce those who wish me evil and those who hate me. (4742)

HYMN XXIX

१. निक्ष दर्भ सपत्नान्मे निक्ष मे पृतनायतः । निक्ष मे सर्वान्दुर्हार्दो निक्ष मे द्विषतो मणे ॥

1. O darbha-mani, sting my adversaries like a serpent. Sting those who come with armies to battle with me. Sting all those who wish me ill, as well as those who hate me. (4743)[1]

[1]Fully describe what the 'Darbha-mani' can do for the protection of a king. From all these verses it is clear that it cannot but be a military weapon of defence with a forceful

२. तृन्द्धि दर्भ सपत्नान्मे तृन्द्धि मे पृतनायतः । तृन्द्धि मे सर्वान्दुर्हार्दस्तृन्द्धि मे द्विषतो मणे ॥

2. O darbha-mani, destroy my foes and those who send their forces to fight with me. Destroy all those who have evil designs against me and those who hate me. (4744)

३. रुन्द्धि दर्भ सपत्नान् मे रुन्द्धि मे पृतनायतः । रुन्द्धि मे सर्वान्दुर्हार्दो रुन्द्धि मे द्विषतो मणे ॥

3. Let the darbha-mani obstruct my rivals as well those who intend to fight with me. Let it obstruct all the wicked-hearted people and those who are full of hatred for me. (4745)

४. मृण दर्भ सपत्नान्मे मृण मे पृतनायतः । मृण मे सर्वान्दुर्हार्दो मृण मे द्विषतो मणे ॥

4. O darbha-mani, murder the foes of mine and those who rush their armies against me. Kill those who wish me evil and those who hate me. (4746)

५. मन्थ दर्भ सपत्नान्मे मन्थ मे पृतनायतः । मन्थ मे सर्वान्दुर्हार्दो मन्थ मे द्विषतो मणे ॥

5. O darbha-mani, churn (i.e., give a good shaking to) my enemies and those who with forces to fight against me. Churn those who have wicked-designs against me and those who hate me. (4747)

६. पिण्ड्ढि दर्भ सपत्नान्मे पिण्ड्ढि मे पृतनायतः ।
पिण्ड्ढि मे सर्वान्दुर्हार्दः पिण्ड्ढि मे द्विषतो मणे ॥

6. O darbha-mani, thoroughly crush my rivals and those who to fight with me with armies. Completely crush those who wish me ill and those who hate me. (4748)

७. ओष दर्भ सपत्नान्मे ओष मे पृतनायतः । ओष मे सर्वान्दुर्हार्द ओष मे द्विषतो मणे ॥

7. O darbha-mani, boil up my foes and those who lead their armies against me to fight. Boil up those who have evil designs against me as well those who are full of hatred towards me. (4749)

८. दह दर्भ सपत्नान्मे दह मे पृतनायतः । दह मे सर्वान्दुर्हार्दो दह मे द्विषतो मणे ॥

8. O darbha-mani, burn up my adversaries and those who approach me with armies to battle with me. Burn up the people who wish me evil and those who hate me. (4750)

९. जहि दर्भ सपत्नान्मे जहि मे पृतनायतः । जहि मे सर्वान्दुर्हार्दो जहि मे द्विषतो मणे ॥

9. O darbha-mani, put my foes to death and finish those who come with armies to fight with me. Leave no trace of those, who are evil-designed towards me and those who are full of hatred towards me. (4751)

HYMN XXX

१. यत्ते दर्भ जरामृत्युः शतं वर्मसु वर्म ते । तेनेमं वर्मिणं कृत्वा सपत्नाञ्जहि वीर्यैः ॥

1. O darbha-mani, thine is the capacity to ward off death till long, long age. Thine is the best armour of all the armours in the world. Shielding him

radiating energy to do all the havoc it is required to do. If a rod of graphite can set in motion the terrible energy to fission the atom, is it not worth trying to see if a small thread of 'Durbha-grass' can also do such wonders?

(the king) with the self-same armour, kill the enemies with thy strong powers. (4752)

२. शतं ते दर्भ वर्माणि सहस्रं वीर्या॒॑णि ते । तमस्मै विश्वे त्वां देवा जरसे भर्तवा अदुः ॥

2. O darbha, hundreds are thy shields and thousands are thy means of strength and power. All the learned scholars or the forces of nature have granted thee to him for protection till old age or for long life. (4753)

३. त्वामाहुर्देववर्म त्वां दर्भ ब्रह्मणस्पतिम् । त्वामिन्द्रस्याहुर्वर्म त्वं राष्ट्राणि रक्षसि ॥

3. They (people) call thee, O darbha, the divine shield and they call thee the lord of wealth, food and learning. They call the armour of the king or the commander of the armies. Thou protectest the nations. (4754)

४. सपत्नक्षयणं दर्भ द्विषतस्तपनं हृदः । मणिं क्षत्रस्य वर्धनं तनूपानं कृणोमि ते ॥

4. I (the engineer) make thee, O darbha, the means of destruction of the enemies, the boiler of the hearts of the foes, the radiating contrivance, the means of increasing the striking power of the Kshatriya, and protecting his body. (4755)[1]

५. यत्समुद्रो अभ्यक्रन्दत्पर्जन्यो विद्युता सह । ततो हिरण्ययो बिन्दुस्ततो दर्भो अजायत ॥

5. The brilliant drop of water falls from the very cloud, which rushes forth very high in the sky and which thunders with lightning. From that very drop is born the darbha-grass. (4756)[2]

HYMN XXXI

१. औदुम्बरेण मणिना पुष्टिकामाय वेधसा । पशूनां सर्वेषां स्फातिं गोष्ठे मे सविता करत् ॥

1. The learned officer, in charge of production of all kinds, may bring about the increase and betterment of all kinds of cattle in the dairies of mine, who am progress-minded, by the help of Audumber-mani. (4757)[3]

२. यो नो अग्निर्गार्हपत्यः पशूनामधिपा असत् । औदुम्बरो वृषा मणिः संमा सृजतु पुष्ट्या ॥

2. Let that fire, which we enkindle in our domestic sacrifice, be the nourisher of our cattle. May the generative Audumber-mani produce prosperity and welfare for me. (4758)

३. करीषिणीं फलवतीं स्वधामिरां च नो गृहे । औदुम्बरस्य तेजसा धाता पुष्टिं दधातु मे ॥

[1](1-4) The capacity of the radio-powered darbha-mani for protection and destruction is indicated here.

[2]The very root of the birth of darbha from the natural electric power from the clouds must have some aura bearing with its powers of radiation, which can usefully be employed in a weapon of protection as well as destruction. Let us make serious efforts to investigate it.

[3]Audumber-mani is not an amulet of Griffith, or Sayāna's description. To me it also appears to be a mechanical contrivance, emitting magnetic or electric currents through the wood of the fig-type tree, which is prepared for ladles in the sacrificial ceremonies of the Hindu for such powers of radiation. These radiations help the growth and breeding powers of the cattle and even grains. In my opinion, it is the peaceful use of radio energy of the suitable trees and grasses that is emphasised here and the previous and coming suktas.

3. Let the production-minded officer bring about fruitful grains and drinks, accompanied by profuse riches. May he create prosperity and well-being through the energy of the Audumber-mani. (4759)

४. यद् द्विपाच्च चतुष्पाच्च यान्यन्नानि ये रसाः । गृह्णेऽहं त्वेषां भूमानं बिभ्रदौदुम्बरं मणिम् ॥

4. Whatever there are bipeds, quadrupeds and whatever there are food-grains and whatever juices, I (a householder) get plenty of these, as I possess the Audumber-mani (the nourisher of all these). (4760)

५. पुष्टिं पशूनां परि जग्रभाहं चतुष्पदां द्विपदां यच्च धान्यम् ।
पयः पशूनां रसमोषधीनां बृहस्पतिः सविता मे नि यच्छात् ॥

5. I (a householder) have got abundance of cattle, quadrupeds, bipeds and food-grains in plenty. May the master-in-chief and the production-in-charge grant me the milk of cattle and the pleasant juices of herbs in abundance. (4761)

६. अहं पशूनामधिपा असानि मयि पुष्टं पुष्टपतिर्दधातु ।
मह्यमौदुम्बरो मणिर्द्रविणानि नि यच्छतु ॥

6. May I (the same householder) be the lord of cattle. May the chief nourisher give me enough nourishment and vigour. Let the Audumber-mani invest me with riches of all kinds. (4762)

७. उप मौदुम्बरो मणिः प्रजया च धनेन च । इन्द्रेण जिन्वितो मणिरा मागन्त्सह वर्चसा ॥

7. Let the Audumber-mani approach me with progeny and wealth, also produce glory, energy and splendour. (4763)

८. देवो मणिः सपत्नहा धनसा धनसातये । पशोरन्नस्य भूमानं गवां स्फातिं नि यच्छतु ॥

8. May the same mani, the giver of various things of daily usage, the destroyer of enemies, be the showerer of riches in the distribution thereof. May it grant us plenty of cattle and food-grains along with big herds of cows. (4764)

९. यथाग्रे त्वं वनस्पते पुष्टचा सह जज्ञिषे । एवा धनस्य मे स्फातिमा दधातु सरस्वती ॥

9. O Audumber-mani, the lord of heat and energy, just as thou revealest thyself with plenty and prosperity before so does this stream of sweet water provide me with abundance of riches from all sides. (4765)

१०. आ मे धनं सरस्वती पयस्फातिं च धान्यम् । सिनीवाल्युपा वहादयं चौदुम्बरो मणिः ॥

10. May the river, wife, and this Audumber-mani all help flow the stream of wealth, plenteous milk and sweet juices of herbs and food-grains from all sides for me. (4766)[1]

[1]Three things are essential for the plenteous inflow of the necessities of life for a householder i.e., a river of sweet water nearby, the wife and the Audumber-mani. Both Pt. Khem Karan Das Trivedi and Pt. Jaidev Vidyalankar have interpreted Audumber-mani, as the chief-officer in charge of looking after the nourishment of the people. But I have given a different direction to interpret these manis to open the field for research into the scientific truths, lying hidden in the Vedic texts. Let some scientists take up the clue.

११. त्वं मणीनामधिपा वृषासि त्वयि पुष्टं पुष्टपतिर्जजान ।
त्वयीमे वाजा द्रविणानि सर्वौदुम्बरः स त्वमस्मत्सहस्वारादरातिममतिं क्षुधं च ॥

11. O Audumber-mani, thou art the lord of all manis. Thou art the showerer of energy and fortunes. The nourisher-in-chief produced in thee a great store of energy and nourishment. In thee are stored all these sources of energy, food and riches. The self-same thou mayst keep away the enemy, the evil thinking and hunger from us. (4767)

१२. ग्रामणीरसि ग्रामणीरुत्थायाभिषिक्तोऽभि मा सिञ्च वर्चसा ।
तेजोऽसि तेजो मयि धारयाधि रयिरसि रयिं मे धेहि ॥

12. Thou art a sort of the leading instrument to decide the fate of the village. Being well-established therein, letst thou engulf me with glory and energy. Thou art the root-cause of all splendour, letst thou store all splendour in me. Thou art the lord of all wealth, letst thou store all wealth in me. (4768)

१३. पुष्टिरसि पुष्ट्या मा समङ्ग्धि गृहमेधी गृहपतिं मा कृणु ।
औदुम्बरः स त्वमस्मासु धेहि रयिं च नः सर्ववीरं नि यच्छ रायस्पोषाय प्रति
मुञ्चे अहं त्वाम् ॥

13. Thou art the embodiment of nourishment, cover me up with nourishment. Thou art enhancer of the peace of domestic life, mayst thou make me the lord of the household. O Audumber, letst the self-same thou invest with riches and completely surround us brave people. I instal thee for riches and prosperity. (4769)

१४. अयमौदुम्बरो मणिर्वीरो वीराय बध्यते ।
स नः सनिं मधुमतीं कृणोतु रयिं च नः सर्ववीरं नि यच्छात् ॥

14. Here is the Audumber-mani, the source of all energy and valour. It is installed for the brave and the courageous. Let it grant us sweet gifts, riches, brave offspring and warriors. (4770)

HYMN XXXII

१. शतकाण्डो दुश्च्यवनः सहस्रपर्ण उत्तिरः । दर्भो य उग्र ओषधिस्तं ते बध्नाम्यायुषे ॥

1. O man, I (a physician) tie this kusha-grass, which is a forceful, energising herb, with hundreds of reeds, infallible, with thousands of leaves and far efficacious than other herbs, for lengthening your life-span. (4771)[1]

२. नास्य केशान्प्र वपन्ति नोरसि ताडमा घ्नते । यस्मा अच्छिन्नपर्णेन दर्भेण शर्म यच्छति ॥

2. The various kinds of germs don't shear off the hair, nor do they dare attack his breast (i.e., the lungs and the heart) of him whom protection is

[1]I am at a loss to understand why should the specific properties of kusha-grass, mentioned herein and other suktas be ignored, as has been done by Griffith, who simply takes it as an Amulet only and Pt. Jaidev Vidyalankar, who interprets it as Commander of the army and Pt. Khem Karan Das Trivedi who refers to God sometimes and to the herb at other times.

granted by the kusha-grass, with its leaves, unshorn. (4772)[1]

३. दिवि ते तूलमोषधे पृथिव्यामसि निष्ठितः । त्वया सहस्रकाण्डेनायुः प्र वर्धयामहे ॥

3. O herb, (i.e., kusha-grass) thy main root is in the heavens but are firmly established on the earth. We prolong our lives through thee of thousands of reeds. (4773)[2]

४. तिस्रो दिवो अत्यतृणत्तिस्र इमाः पृथिवीरुत । त्वयाहं दुर्हार्दो जिह्वां नि तृणद्मि वचांसि ॥

4. O darbha, thy penetrating radiation through the three spectra, the ultra-violet, the common and the infra-red and also the three earths, i.e., the well-known earth, the dust particles and the meteorites. By thy help I may pierce the very tongue and voice of the evil-minded enemies (i.e., I am able to jam their broadcasts). (4774)

५. त्वमसि सहमानोऽहमस्मि सहस्वान् । उभौ सहस्वन्तौ भूत्वा सपत्नान्त्सहिषीवहि ॥

5. Thou art powerful enough to subdue the enemies. I am also strong enough to crush them. Both of us being strong and valorous, may suppress the foes. (4775)

६. सहस्व नो अभिमातिं सहस्व पृतनायतः । सहस्व सर्वान्दुर्हार्दः सुहार्दो मे बहून्कृधि ॥

6. O darbha, defeatest thou the proud foe of ours. Letest thou crush the attacking forces of the enemies. Conquer all the wicked-hearted people and make many people friends of mine. (4776)

७. दर्भेण देवजातेन दिवि ष्टम्भेन शश्वदित् । तेनाहं शश्वतो जनाँ असनं सनवानि च ॥

7. As there is perpetual growth attained by darbha born of natural forces, firmly established in heavens, so may I create, by its help, the perpetual attainment of people, as progeny and brave warriors. (4777)

८. प्रियं मा दर्भ कृणु ब्रह्मराजन्याभ्यां शूद्राय चार्याय च ।
यस्मै च कामयामहे सर्वस्मै च विपश्यते ॥

8. O kusha-grass, by your energising qualities, endear me to the Brahmans, Kshatriya, Shudras and the Vaishya. Make us lovable to him, whom we desire and all those who even look down upon us, or who specially look to us for help and guidance. (4778)

९. यो जायमानः पृथिवीमदृंहद्यो अस्तभ्नादन्तरिक्षं दिवं च ।
यं बिभ्रतं ननु पाप्मा विवेद स नोऽयं दर्भो वरुणो दिवा कः ॥

9. The self-same kusha-grass, which, when born, conserves the soil, makes the atmosphere and the heavens firm by its radiations, and the bearer whereof knows no evil, may be the warder-off of all troubles, the shedder of light

[1] The specific use of it in falling off hair and diseases of the respirating system are worth noting.

[2] The main root being in heavens is due to its being born from the brilliant drops from the thundering clouds accompanied by lightning. Wherever it grows, it covers up the earth fully and consolidates it against erosion by water. Its use for longevity of life is worth research.

like the day and a source of happiness and peace, due to its wonderful qualities. (4779)

१०. सपत्नहा शतकाण्डः सहस्वानोषधीनां प्रथमः सं बभूव ।
स नोऽयं दर्भः परि पातु विश्वतस्तेन साक्षीय पृतनाः पृतन्यतः ॥

10. This kusha-grass has been born the foremost of all the herbs, the enemy-destroyer, with hundreds of reeds, and capable of killing those whoever are inimical towards us. The self-same kusha-grass may protect us from all sides. By its help I may be able to subdue all the fighting forces of the enemies. (4780)[1]

HYMN XXXIII

१. सहस्रार्घः शतकाण्डः पयस्वानपामग्निर्वीरुधां राजसूयम् ।
स नोऽयं दर्भः परि पातु विश्वतो देवो मणिरायुषा सं सृजाति नः ॥

1. The same darbha-mani, which has thousands of energies, hundreds of reeds, nourishing juice, a fire among the water and a king among the plants and herbs, may protect us from all sides. This divine mani invest us with long life. (4781)[2]

२. घृतादुल्लुप्तो मधुमान्पयस्वान्भूमिदृंहोऽच्युतश्च्यावयिष्णुः ।
नुदन्त्सपत्नानधरांश्च कृण्वन्दर्भा रोह महतामिन्द्रियेण ॥

2. O darbha, besmeared with clarified butter, sweet, juicy, conserving the soil, unvenerable, capable of subduing others, pushing back and felling the enemies below, attain the high place through the valour and bravery of the great persons. (4782)

३. त्वं भूमिमत्येष्योजसा त्वं वेद्यां सीदसि चारुरध्वरे ।
त्वां पवित्रमृषयोऽभरन्त त्वं पुनीहि दुरितान्यस्मत् ॥

3. Thou penetratest the earth with strong energy and power. Thou sitest charming and beautiful at the altar in the non-violent sacrifice. The sages bear thee, the purifier. Thou purifiest all evils from us. (4783)

४. तीक्ष्णो राजा विषासही रक्षोहा विश्वचर्षणिः ।
ओजो देवानां बलमुग्रमेतत्तं ते बध्नामि जरसे स्वस्तये ॥

4. Thou art sharp, bright, possessed of various powers to subdue the enemies, germicide, invested with powers of revealing all things, the fierce power and energy of the natural forces (like electricity and water). I bind thee, such as mentioned above, for peace and well-being to attain longevity of life. (4784)

५. दर्भेण त्वं कृणवद्वीर्याणि दर्भं बिभ्रदात्मना मा व्यथिष्ठाः ।
अतिष्ठाया वर्चसाधान्यान्त्सूर्य इवा भाहि प्रदिशश्चतस्रः ॥

[1]The energy and power, derived from Kusha-grass for fighting against the fighting force is worth discovering. It appears to a mine of radiating energy. Let us find it out.

[2]Pt. Jaidev Vidyalankar has applied this sukta to the Army Commander. But I do feel strongly for making a thorough search into the high qualities of durbha and other herbs, mentioned herein and hereafter. Hence my different rendering all through.

5. O king, or man, achieving various powers with the help of darbha and bearing thyself, dost not thou worry at all. Overpowering all others with thy glory and splendour, shine like the Sun in all quarters of the world. (4785)

Chapter (Anuvāka) 5

HYMN XXXIV

१. जङ्गिडोऽसि जङ्गिडो रक्षितासि जङ्गिडः । द्विपाच्चतुष्पादस्माकं सर्वं रक्षतु जङ्गिडः ॥

1. O Jangida herb, thou art the consumer of all destructive forces in the form of germs, the secret weapons like mines etc., employed by the enemies. O jangida, thou art the protector. Let jangida guard all our men and cattle. (4786)[1]

२. या गृत्स्यस्त्रिपञ्चाशीः शतं कृत्याकृतश्च ये । सर्वान्विनक्तु तेजसोऽरसाञ्जङ्गिडस्करत् ॥

2. Let this potent herb destroy the women of ill repute, the large group of gamblers and hundreds of secret means of destruction like mines and dynamites employed by the enemy to harm us. Let it set all these at naught by its powerful energy and radiation. (4787)

३. अरसं कृत्रिमं नादमरसाः सप्त विस्रसः । अपेतो जङ्गिडामतिमिषुमस्तेव शातय ॥

3. Enfeeble the artificial high resoundings of the enemy. Make null and void all his evil efforts from all the seven directions. O Jangida, slash off the invincible foe from here, like an archer. (4788)

४. कृत्यादूषण एवायमथो अरातिदूषणः । अथो सहस्वाञ्जङ्गिडः प्र ण आयूंषि तारिषत् ॥

4. This Jangida is the destroyer of the secret weapons of destruction like mines etc., he is the killer of the enemy and hence capable of subduing the foe. Let it guard our lives well. (4789)

५. स जङ्गिडस्य महिमा परि णः पातु विश्वतः । विष्कन्धं येन सासह संस्कन्धमोज ओजसा ॥

5. That is the great importance of Jangida, that it may protect us from all sides. It is its efficacious power, by which it is able to suppress fatal diseases like acute rheumatism in the neck and the shoulder. (4790)

६. त्रिष्ट्वा देवा अजनयन्निष्ठितं भूम्यामधि । तमु त्वाङ्गिरा इति ब्राह्मणाः पूर्व्या विदुः ॥

6. The learned physicians grow thee well by transplanting thee thrice in the well-prepared soil. The learned Vedic scholars of yore, well-versed in biological science knew thee. (4791)

७. न त्वा पूर्वा ओषधयो न त्वा तरन्ति या नवाः ।
विबाध उग्रो जङ्गिडः परिपाणः सुमङ्गलः ॥

7. Neither the herbs that have grown before thee, nor those that are new ones, can surpass thee in efficacy. Thou art, O Jangida, the tormentor of the evil forces, germs etc., fierce, consumer of all inimical elements, all-round protector, and showerer of fortune and happiness in a pleasant manner. (4792)

[1]The superfine properties of Jangida are also worth research. They are mentioned to be so potent in removing so many fatal diseases.

८. अथोपदान भगवो जङ्गिडामितवीर्य । पुरा त उग्रा ग्रसत उपेन्द्रो वीर्यं ददौ ॥

8. O Jangida, protector of those who approach thee, the lord of fortunes the source of limitless valour, the terrible Indra has already showered on thee, the consumer of all great energy and power. (4793)

९. उग्र इत्ते वनस्पत इन्द्र ओज्मानमा दधौ । अमीवाः सर्वाश्चातयञ्जहि रक्षांस्योषधे ॥

9. O furious lord of heat and energy, the Almighty Lord has placed a great force in thee. O heat-storing herb, all the disease-breeding germs and microbes, tearing them off by your force. (4794)

१०. आशरीकं विशरीकं बलासं पृष्ट्यामयम् । तक्मानं विश्वशारदमरसां जङ्गिडस्करत् ॥

10. Let the Jangida herb, drive away the onslaught the following fatal diseases Asharika, Vishrika, the asthma, the cancer of the back-bone, the consumption, which consume all the energy of the body. (4795)

HYMN XXXV

१. इन्द्रस्य नाम गृह्णन्त ऋषयो जङ्गिडं ददुः । देवा यं चक्रुर्भेषजमग्रे विष्कन्धदूषणम् ॥

1. The seers, taking the name of the Enemy-Destroyer, Indra as the ideal, named the special tree, 'Arjuna' as 'Jangida', the consumer of the enemies, whom the learned scholars made the curer of the acute rheumatism of the neck. (4796)[1]

२. स नो रक्षतु जङ्गिडो धनपालो धनेव । देवा यं चक्रुर्ब्राह्मणाः परिपाणमरातिहम् ॥

2. The same Jangida, whom the learned people, versed in Vedic lore, made an all-round protector and enemy-destroyer may protect us just as the guardian of the wealth i.e., king protects the riches of a nation. (4797)

३. दुर्हार्दः संघोरं चक्षुः पापकृत्वानमागमम् ।
तांस्त्वं सहस्रचक्षो प्रतीबोधेन नाशय परिपाणोऽसि जङ्गिडः ॥

3. O Jangida, if I ever come across the furious-eyed wicked-hearted mischief-monger, destroy all of them, O wide-awake one, by your constant vigilance. You are the all-round guardian of the people. (4798)[1]

४. परि मा दिवः परि मा पृथिव्याः पर्यन्तरिक्षात्परि मा वीरुद्भ्यः ।
परि मा भूतात्परि मोत भव्याद् दिशोदिशो जङ्गिडः पात्वस्मान् ॥

4. Let Jangida completely protect me from all evils from heavens, from the atmosphere, from the earth and from the creepers. Let it thoroughly protect from the past, from the future and from every quarter. (4799)

५. य ऋष्णवो देवकृता य उतो ववृतेऽन्यः । सर्वांस्तान्विश्वभेषजोऽरसां जङ्गिडस्करत् ॥

5. Whatever troubles are man-made, brought by natural forces and created by the enemy, may all these be set at naught by the potent Jangida, which is the all-round physician or curer. (4800)

[1]This sukta may also be aptly applied Jangida, the Arjun tree which is called 'Indra' and 'Sahasra-Chakshu' in books of Ayurveda. It is not a charm or an amulet that is meant by 'Jangida,'

HYMN XXXVII

१. शतवारो अनीनशद्यक्ष्मान् रक्षांसि तेजसा । आरोहन्वर्चसा सह मणिर्दुर्णामचातनः ॥

1. The Shatavar (a medicinal root well-known in Ayurveda and Unani) can destroy the germs of consumption and fatal microbes by its heat and energy. The best of the herbs, growing with splendour and efficacious energy is the killer of the malignant diseases of the skin like ulcer, Eczema etc. (4801)[1]

२. शृङ्गाभ्यां रक्षो नुदते मूलेन यातुधान्यः । मध्येन यक्ष्मं बाधते नैनं पाप्माति तत्रति ॥

2. The above-mentioned herb (i.e., shatavar) drives off the atmospheric germs by its thorns, the contagious viruses of the earth by its root, and keeps in check the consumption by its middle part. No evil force can subdue its efficacy. (4802)

३. ये यक्ष्मासो अर्भका महान्तो ये च शब्दिनः । सर्वान् दुर्णामहा मणिः शतवारो अनीनशत् ॥

3. Whatever the stages of phthisis, the lowest ones, the enhanced ones, and the last ones, with high-sounding coughs, the Shatavar, the best of the herbs, thoroughly destroys all these malignant skin-diseases and ailments. (4803)

४. शतं वीरानजनयच्छतं यक्ष्मानपावपत् । दुर्णाम्नः सर्वान्हत्वाव रक्षांसि धूनुते ॥

4. This wonderful herb, creating hundreds of cells of energy and vigour, roots out the germs of consumption. Killing all the malignant viruses, causing skin diseases it smashes all the atmospheric germs or microbes of the fell diseases. (4804)

५. हिरण्यशृङ्ग ऋषभः शातवारो अयं मणिः । दुर्णाम्नः सर्वांस्तृड्ढ्वाव रक्षांस्यक्रमीत् ॥

5. This topmost medicinal herb has thorns of superfine qualities, is showerer of blessings on the patients, wards off various ailments. It puts down all the germs, after effacing all the persistent skin diseases. (4805)

६. शतमहं दुर्णाम्नीनां गन्धर्वाप्सरसां शतम् । शतं शश्वतीनां शतवारेण वारये ॥

6. I (a physician) keep off numerous malignant skin diseases, numerous fatal microbes carried by scents, and those moving freely in waters and hundreds of such, carried by dogs, by the use of Shatavar, capable of warding off various diseases. (4806)

HYMN XXXVII

१. इदं वर्चो अग्निना दत्तमागन्भर्गो यशः सह ओजो वयो बलम् ।
त्रयस्त्रिंशद्यानि च वीर्याणि तान्यग्निः प्र ददातु मे ॥

1. May this glory, splendour, fame, courage, brilliance, long life and

[1] I see no reason why 'Shatavara' may not be taken as a potent medicine, so useful for its healing power of all stages of consumptive diseases. Griffith has described all these useful herbs as charms or amulets, which is wrong. It is this wrong interpretation of the Vedic texts by him and of other Vedic scholars of his way of thinking, whether they be occidental or oriental, that has created a wrong impression amongst the English-educated people that the Vedas are especially *Atharvaveda* is full of charms and magic. It must be removed by the right interpretation being given to the Vedic words and texts. Pt. Jaidev Vidyalankar has taken it to mean an Army Commander, too.

strength, granted by God, the Effulgent, the learned person, the chief leader of the nation, or jathragni come to us. Whatever thirty-three kinds of means of strength and valour there are, let God, the learned teacher or preacher or the chief leader or commander or bodily temperature fully invest me with all these forces of action. (4807)[1]

२. वर्च आ धेहि मे तन्वां३ सह ओजो वयो बलम् ।
इन्द्रियाय त्वा कर्मणे वीर्या॒ाय प्रति गृह्णामि शतशारदाय ॥

2. O Agni of the above-mentioned descriptions, introduce into my body glory along with splendour or energy, long life and vigour for all activities of life. I imbibe thee for empowering and activising sense-organs, for all sorts of activities, for sources of energy and vigour, and for hundred years life. (4808)

३. ऊर्जे त्वा बलाय त्वौजसे सहसे त्वा । अभिभूयाय त्वा राष्ट्रभृत्याय पर्यूहामि शतशारदाय ॥

3. I accept thee for food, for vigour, for energy and for courage for dominance, for service of the nation and for long life of hundred years. (4809)

४. ऋतुभ्यष्ट्वार्तवेभ्यो माद्भ्यः संवत्सरेभ्यः । धात्रे विधात्रे समृधे भूतस्य पतये यजे ॥

4. I seek union with thee for peacefully enjoying the main seasons i.e., hot, rainy and the cold ones; and similarly passing the intervening season i.e. the autumn, the mild winter and the spring; for months; for years, for production; for administration; for progress and prosperity; and for the Lord of all creatures or the king, the master of all his subjects. (4810)

HYMN XXXVIII

१. न तं यक्ष्मा अरुन्धते नैनं शपथो अश्नुते । यं भेषजस्य गुल्गुलोः सुरभिर्गन्धो अश्नुते ॥

1. The fell disease, consumption does not pain him, nor does the evil-thinking of the enemy have any ill effect on him, whom the wholesome scent of the gugglu, having curing effect pervades. (4811)[2]

२. विष्वञ्चस्तस्माद्यक्ष्मा मृगा अश्वा इवेरते । यद् गुल्गुलु सैन्धवं यद्वाप्यासि समुद्रियम् ॥

2. All kinds of consumptive disease run away like the fast-running deer, from this medicine, which is called gugglu, from the trees grown by the river-side or even by the sea-coast. (4812)

३. उभयोरग्रभं नामास्मा अरिष्टतातये ॥

3. I (a physician) make use of both of these for the removal of the ailment of this patient. (4813)

HYMN XXXIX

१. ऐतु देवस्त्रायमाणः कुष्ठो हिमवतस्परि । तक्मानं सर्वं नाशय सर्वाश्च यातुधान्यः ॥

[1](1-4) It is through Agni, i.e., physical, spiritual and natural that a person can attain the benefits mentioned here.

[2]This sukta of three verses describes the superfine properties of the common medicine, Gugglu.

1. Let the herb, kushtha by name, possessed of superfine qualities come to us protecting from the snow-covered mountain (its birth-place). Let it destroy all kinds of fevers and all sorts of pain-giving diseases. (4814)[1]

२. त्रीणि ते कुष्ठ नामानि नद्यमारो नद्यारिषः ।
नद्यायं पुरुषो रिषत् । यस्मै परिब्रवीमि त्वा सायंप्रातरथो दिवा ॥

2. O Kushtha, three are thy names, naghmar or nadyamar (remover of all diseases caused by impure water from the rivers (like cholera, goitre, etc.). Naghavisha or nadyavisha (having the same meaning), or nagha or nadya (of the same import). This man (the patient), whom I (a physician) prescribe thee to be used thrice, in the morning, in the evening and once during the day (i.e., at noon) may shed off the disease. (4815)

३. जीवला नाम ते माता जीवन्तो नाम ते पिता ।
नद्यायं पुरुषो रिषत् । यस्मै परिब्रवीमि त्वा सायंप्रातरथो दिवा ॥

3. The life-infusing power is thy mother and the vital breath energising force is thy father. Let not this patient, whom I prescribe thee to be used in the morning and evening and at noon, be troubled by any ailment. (4816)

४. उत्तमो अस्योषधीनामनड्वान् जगतामिव व्याघ्रः श्वपदामिव ।
नद्यायं पुरुषो रिषत् यस्मै परिब्रवीमि त्वा सायंप्रातरथो दिवा ॥

4. O kushtha, thou art the best among the herbs, most powerful like the high-humped bull, among the cattle, most furious like the tiger among clawed-beasts. Let not this man, whom I . . . . by ailment. (4817)

५. त्रिः शाम्बुभ्यो अङ्गिरेभ्यस्त्रिरादित्येभ्यस्परि । त्रिर्जातो विश्वदेवेभ्यः ।
स कुष्ठो विश्वभेषजः । साकं सोमेन तिष्ठति । तक्मानं सर्वं नाशय सर्वाश्च यातुधान्यः ॥

5. This kushtha is of three kinds due to its being born from three kinds of waters, of rain, of rivers and of sea; also due to three kinds of juices, forming its parts, and also three kinds of months, hot, rainy or cold ones. It is thrice born from all natural forces. Hence this Kushtha is curer of all diseases. It stays along with Soma, the very essence of all medicines. Let it destroy all kinds of fevers and all kinds of pains of the body. (4818)

६. अश्वत्थो देवसदनस्तृतीयस्यामितो दिवि । तत्रामृतस्य चक्षणं ततः कुष्ठो अजायत ।
स कुष्ठो विश्वभेषजः साकं सोमेन तिष्ठति । तक्मानं सर्वं नाशय सर्वाश्च यातुधान्यः ॥

6. In third shining heaven from here, is the Sun, the source of all energy and power and the store-house of all super-fine attributes. There is the fountain-head of the life prolonging juices, whence is born this kushtha, the curer of all diseases. It stays . . . . body. (4819)

७. हिरण्ययी नौरचरद्धिरण्यबन्धना दिवि । तत्रामृतस्य चक्षणं ततः कुष्ठो अजायत ।
स कुष्ठो विश्वभेषजः साकं सोमेन तिष्ठति । तक्मानं सर्वं नाशय सर्वाश्च यातुधान्यः ॥

7. There is the bright boat of the light sailing in the heavens with the

[1]This sukta describes the useful properties the well known medicinal herb, known as Kushtha or simply kutha in general. They are worth research.

bright tices in the form of spectra of light. There is the fountain-head of all juices, whence is born .... body. (·820)

८. यत्र नावप्रभ्रंशनं यत्र हिमवतः शिरः । तत्रामृतस्य चक्षणं ततः कुष्ठो अजायत ।
स कुष्ठो विश्वभेषजः साकं सोमेन तिष्ठति । तक्मानं सर्वं नाशय सर्वाश्च यातुधान्यः ।,

8. Where the bright boat of light gets wrecked, due to high peaks, where lies the top of the snowy mountain, there is the fountain-head of all juices, whence .... body. (4821)

९. यं त्वा वेद पूर्व इक्ष्वाको यं वा त्वा कुष्ठ काम्यः ।
यं वा वसो यमात्स्यस्तेनासि विश्वभेषजः ।।

9. O kushtha, thou art the all-round physician, whom already know the Ikshwaka, a bird of high speed, the crows, the matsya-named bird, desirous of making use of thee. (4822)

१०. शीर्षलोकं तृतीयकं सदन्दिर्यश्च हायनः । तक्मानं विश्वधाषीर्याधराञ्चं परा सुव ।।

10. O kushtha, drive away all the diseases, of the head, the fever, attacking every third day, the constant fever, or the year-long disease, or malignant fevers, by bringing them low by thy various kinds of efficacious powers. (4823)

HYMN XL

१. यन्मे छिद्रं मनसो यच्च वाचः सरस्वती मन्युमन्तं जगाम ।
विश्वैस्तद् देवैः सह संविदानः सं दधातु बृहस्पतिः ।।

1. Whatever drawback there is of my mind and whatever failing there is of my speech, which my tongue underwent during the state of my being angry, may the learned person of Vedic lore remove it after full consultation with all other learned persons, or fully ascertaining them through all other sense organs. (4824)[1]

२. मा न आपो मेधां मा ब्रह्म प्र प्रथिष्टन । सुष्यदा यूयं स्यन्दध्वमुपहूतोऽहं सुमेधा वर्चस्वी ।।

2. O truthful learned persons of high-integrity and character, please don't let my intellect and Vedic knowledge get destroyed. Please cause this drying up source to have an easy flow again. Being favoured by you, I may be intellectual and glorious. (4825)

३. मा नो मेधां मा नो दीक्षां मा नो हिंसिष्टं यत्तपः ।
शिवा नः शं सन्त्वायुषे शिवा भवन्तु मातरः ।।

3. Let not our parents suppress our intelligence, nor our initiative, nor what has been achieved by our austerity. Let them be peaceful to as. May they bring peace for life. May our mothers be sources of happiness and well-being for us. (4826)

४. या नः पीपरदश्विना ज्योतिष्मती तमस्तिरः । तामस्मे रासतामिषम् ।।

[1]The weakness of the mind, the harshness of speech can easily be adjudged from the lustful eyes, and the reddened face of the man. My: man's. cf. *Yajur*, 36.2.

4. O parents, (or teachers and preachers) grant us that food and intellect which is full of light and brilliance and which may lead us across the deep darkness of ignorance. (4827)[1]

HYMN XLI

१. भद्रमिच्छन्त ऋषयः स्वर्विदस्तपो दीक्षामुपनिषेदुरग्रे ।
ततो राष्ट्रं बलमोजश्च जातं तदस्मै देवा उपसंनमन्तु ॥

1. In the very beginning of the creation, the well-enlightened sages, wishing well of the world, worship the Almighty Father with austerity and initiation. From thence is born the nation, with vigour and energy. Then all the learned people bow to it, i.e., such a powerful and vigorous nation. (4828)

HYMN XLII

१. ब्रह्म होता ब्रह्म यज्ञा ब्रह्मणा स्वरवो मिताः । अध्वर्युर्ब्रह्मणो जातो ब्रह्मणोऽन्तर्हितं हविः ॥

1. The mighty Revealer of the Vedas is Himself the hota-sacrificer. The same Lord of the Vedas is the source of all sacrifices, going on in the universe. He, Himself has created all these shining Suns. From Him was born the performer of all non-violent sacrifices. All materials of the sacrifices, like churning product and grains etc., are contained in the self-same Brahm. (4829)[2]

२. ब्रह्म स्रुचो घृतवतीर्ब्रह्मणा वेदिरुद्धिता ।
ब्रह्म यज्ञस्य तत्त्वं च ऋत्विजो ये हविष्कृतः । शमिताय स्वाहा ॥

2. It is the mighty Lord, who is the ladle, dripping clarified butter, in the form of rain drops. It is by Brahma that this vast altar i.e., the earth, is sustained. The sum and substance of the sacrifice is Brahma and all these forces of nature, like air, clouds, the sun, the sources of all seasons and materials are nothing but the Divine powers of the Brahma. Let they all be for peace and happiness. It is well-said of Him. (4830)

३. अंहोमुचे प्र भरे मनीषामा सुत्राव्णे सुमतिमावृणानः ।
इममिन्द्र प्रति हव्यं गृभाय सत्याः सन्तु यजमानस्य कामाः ॥

3. Seeking noble and pure thoughts, I make a clean breast of my deep-laid, keen desire at the feet of the guardian-Angel, who frees man from all sins. O Evil-Destroyer, accept this offering of mine. Let the desires of the sacrificer be true i.e., fulfilled completely. (4831)

४. अंहोमुचं वृषभं यज्ञियानां विराजन्तं प्रथममध्वराणाम् ।
अपां नपातमश्विना हुवे धिय इन्द्रियेण त इन्द्रियं दत्तमोजः ॥

4. I (a devotee) pray to God, the Freer of man from sins, the most Adorable of all those who are worthy of our respect (i.e., father, mother, teachers and others) the first and the most Brilliant of all the non-violent sacrificers, the Protector of the people, for wisdom and good actions. O parents, or

[1]cf. *Rig*, 1.46.6.

[2]In the vast sacrifice, going on in the universe, it is Brahma and Brahma, who is all in all, hota, Yajna, Adhvaryu and Havi even, He supplies everything for this great sacrifice.

teachers and preachers, imbibe the spiritual splendour through the splendour of the Evil-Destroyer of Indra and pass it on to others, too. (4832)

HYMN XLIII

१. यत्र ब्रह्मविदो यान्ति दीक्षया तपसा सह ।
अग्निर्मा तत्र नयत्वग्निर्मेधां दधातु मे । अग्नये स्वाहा ॥

1. May the Effulgent God or the learned person lead me to that high state, which the Vedic scholars attain, fully knowing God with their solemn vows and austerity. Let God or the learned person invest me with wisdom. My prayers to God or the learned person. (4833)[1]

२. यत्र ब्रह्मविदो यान्ति दीक्षया तपसा सह ।
वायुर्मा तत्र नयतु वायुः प्राणान्दधातु मे । वायवे स्वाहा ॥

2. May the Powerful God or strong man like air, lead me to . . . . austerity. May God or the powerful person invest me with vital breaths. I pray to God or the powerful man for it. (4834)

३. यत्र ब्रह्मविदो यान्ति दीक्षया तपसा सह ।
सूर्यो मा तत्र नयतु चक्षुः सूर्यो दधातु मे । सूर्याय स्वाहा ॥

3. May the Brilliant God or the teacher lead . . . . austerity. Let God or the teacher grant me sight to see afar. I pray to them for it. (4835)

४. यत्र ब्रह्मविदो यान्ति दीक्षया तपसा सह ।
चन्द्रो मा तत्र नयतु मनश्चन्द्रो दधातु मे । चन्द्राय स्वाहा ॥

4. May the All-pleasing God or the moon lead . . . austerity. Let God or the moon endow me with mental powers. That is my prayer to them. (4836)

५. यत्र ब्रह्मविदो यान्ति दीक्षया तपसा सह ।
सोमो मा तत्र नयतु पयः सोमो दधातु मे । सोमाय स्वाहा ॥

5. May the nourishing God or the essence of medicines lead . . . . austerity. Let God or Soma grant me sweet drinks. I pray to them for it. (4837)

६. यत्र ब्रह्मविदो यान्ति दीक्षया तपसा सह ।
इन्द्रो मा तत्र नयतु बलमिन्द्रो दधातु मे । इन्द्राय स्वाहा ॥

6. Let the mighty God or electricity lead . . . . austerity. May God or electricity bestow me with strength and vigour. That is my prayer to Indra. (4838)

७. यत्र ब्रह्मविदो यान्ति दीक्षया तपसा सह ।
आपो मा तत्र नयन्त्वमृतं मोप तिष्ठतु । अद्भ्यः स्वाहा ॥

7. Let the Peace-showering God or soothing waters lead . . . . austerity. May God or the waters shower nector on me. That is my prayer to God or waters. (4839)

[1](1-8) A devotee invokes God, with various powers, revealed through various forces of nature to lead him to the high state of bliss, attained by the learned yogis.

८. यत्र ब्रह्मविदो यान्ति दीक्षया तपसा सह ।
ब्रह्मा मा तत्र नयतु ब्रह्मा ब्रह्म दधातु मे । ब्रह्मणे स्वाहा ॥

8. Let the Vedic scholar, well versed in all the four Vedas lead me to that high state, where the Vedic scholars, fully conversant with God, revel through their solemn vows and austerity. Let the same Vedic scholar infuse complete knowledge of God into me. My prayers to God and the Vedic scholar. (4840)

HYMN XLIV

१. आयुषोऽसि प्रतरणं विप्रं भेषजमुच्यसे । तदाञ्जन त्वं शंताते शमापो अभयं कृतम् ॥

1. O Anjana, thou art the prolonger of life. Thou art called a wise physician, capable of removing various diseases. Letest such Thou be for peace and happiness. Let waters be peaceful and free from danger of all sorts. (4841)[1]

२. यो हरिमा जायान्योऽङ्गभेदो विसल्पकः । सर्वं ते यक्ष्ममङ्गेभ्यो बहिर्निर्हन्त्वाञ्जनम् ॥

2. Whatever there is the jaundice, the diseases, caused by the contact with women, aching of body, the Eczema, the consumption, let the Anjana drive out all these diseases from thy organs. (4842)

३. आञ्जनं पृथिव्यां जातं भद्रं पुरुषजीवनम् । कृणोत्वप्रमायुकं रथजूतिमनागसम् ॥

3. Let the Anjana, born of the earth, make the life of man happy and comfortable, free from the fear of premature death, full of bodily activity and free from all troubles and defects. (4843)

४. प्राण प्राणं त्रायस्वासो असवे मृड । निर्ऋते निर्ऋत्या नः पाशेभ्यो मुञ्च ॥

4. O Anjana, the very vital breath of life, guard our vital breath. O thrower-off of all troubles, bring happiness to the living creature. O Remover of all pains and diseases, free us from the snares of all ailments and mishaps. (4844)

५. सिन्धोर्गर्भोऽसि विद्युतां पुष्पम् । वातः प्राणः सूर्यश्चक्षुर्दिवस्पयः ॥

5. O Anjana, thou art the very essence of the waters of the rivers, the flower of electric powers, the vital breath of the air, the eye (the means of seeing) of the sun, and the sweet juice of the bright heavens, i.e., vested with the good qualities of all these natural forces. (4845)

६. देवाञ्जन त्रैककुदं परि मा पाहि विश्वतः । न त्वा तरन्त्योषधयो बाह्याः पर्वतीया उत ॥

6. O Anjana of divine qualities, thou art the best of all in three worlds. Letest thou protect me from all sides. None of the medicines, acquired from the mountains or from other parts in the plains, can surpass thee in efficacy. (4846)

७. वीइदं मध्यमवासृपद्रक्षोहामीवचातनः । अमीवाः सर्वाश्चातयन्नाशयदभिभा इतः ॥

[1]Anjana: the antimony or any ointment for the eyes, the body as well, having various properties to remove other fell diseases like jaundice, consumption, Eczema and aches, etc. It is for the physicians to discover it.

7. This very Anjana, the killer of germs, the remover of diseases has filtered into the middle of diseased part. Effacing all the ailments, let it put an end to all feelings of depression from me (i.e. the patient). (4847)

८. बह्वी३दं राजन्वरुणानृतमाह पूरुषः । तस्मात्सहस्रवीर्य मुञ्च नः पर्यंहसः ॥

8. O God, the Brilliant, the Adorable of all, this man on earth speaks all sorts of lies. O Possesser of thousands of powers, letest Thou free us completely from this sin of lying. (4848)[1]

९. यदापो अघ्न्या इति वरुणेति यदूचिम । तस्मात्सहस्रवीर्य मुञ्च नः पर्यंहसः ॥

9. O most Adorable God, whoever there are noble persons of unimpeachable character and who are unworthy to be harmed, and whatever we say and admit our failings; letest Thou, the Omnipotent God, free us for all that sin. (4849)

१०. मित्रश्च त्वा वरुणश्चानुप्रेयतुराञ्जन । तौ त्वानुगत्य दूरं भोगाय पुनरोहतुः ॥

10. O Anjana, let oxygen and hydrogen follow thee faithfully and chasing thee for long, let them once again carry on their burden of usefulness for the welfare of the people at large. (4850)[2]

HYMN XLV

१. ऋणादृणमिव संनयन्कृत्यां कृत्याकृतो गृहम् । चक्षुर्मन्त्रस्य दुर्हार्दः पृष्टीरपि शृणाञ्जन ॥

1. O Anjana, just as the debt is fully paid back to the creditor and the secret missible is repulsed to the house of the sender thereof, similarly dost thou break the back-bones of the wicked-hearted person, who, by sheer pointing of his eyes, orders us to be assailed by missiles. (4851)[3]

२. यदस्मासु दुष्वप्न्यं यद् गोषु यच्च नो गृहे । अनामगस्तं च दुर्हार्दः प्रियः प्रति मुञ्चताम् ॥

2. Whatever unconsciousness or fainting there is among our men, among our cattle or in our house, and the loss of memory of names even, let all these grip the person, who is dear to the wicked enemy. (4852)

३. अपामूर्जं ओजसो वावृधानमग्नेर्जातमधि जातवेदसः ।
चतुर्वीरं पर्वतीयं यदाञ्जनं दिशः प्रदिशः करदिच्छिवास्ते ॥

3. Let this Anjana, which is got from the mountains, which creates fourfold energy i.e., hydraulic power, enhancement of splendour, born of heat, predominating light, like the search-light, make all the quarters and the midquarters peaceful for thee (man or king). (4853)

[1](8-9) These verses have 'Varuna' as Devata.

[2](a) This verse appears to refer to some chemical process, where antimony or graphite may be utilised along with oxygen and hydrogen for some useful purpose. Let the scientists make a thorough research into it. (b) Mitra—the affinity for mixing with other things in nature is a well-known property of oxygen. Varun—the selective affinity of hydrogen is also apparent.

[3]Herein by Anjana, it is not any ointment or salve that is meant, but it seems to me some secret weapon of dark rays, emitted from some chemicals referred to in the last verse of the previous sukta, having the effect of cracking the body of the enemy as well as causing unconsciousness, spoken of in the second verse.

४. चतुर्वीरं बध्यत आञ्जनं ते सर्वा दिशो अभयास्ते भवन्तु ।
ध्रुवस्तिष्ठासि सवितेव चार्य इमा विशो अभि हरन्तु ते बलिम् ।।

4. O King, this Anjana, emitting forceful energy in all the four quarters has been firmly set up for thee. Let all the directions be free from danger for thee. Enthrall thyself firmly on thy throne like the Sun or the noblest person i.e., 'Arya'. Let these subjects bring their reverence to thee from all sides. (4854)

५. आक्ष्वैकं मणिमेकं कृणुष्व स्नाह्येकेना पिबैकमेषाम् ।
चतुर्वीरं नैर्ऋतेभ्यश्चतुर्भ्यो ग्राह्या बन्धेभ्यः परि पात्वस्मान् ।।

5. O man, put one of these best of preparations in thy eye i.e., to remove the defects therefore, make one of these the instrument of radiation and light, bathe by one, and d ink one of these. Thus this source of four-fold energy may guard us from all the four snares of diseases and ailments that get hold of us. (4855)[1]

६. अग्निर्माग्निनावतु प्राणायापानायायुषे वर्चस ओजसे तेजसे स्वस्तये सुभतये स्वाहा ।।

6. May God, the learned person, the king, commander or the natural fire, protect me with heat, light and energy for incoming vital breath, for outgoing vital breath, for long life, for glory, for splendour and for energy, for welfare and prosperous living. This is well said. (4856)

७. इन्द्रो मेन्द्रियेणावतु प्राणायापानायायुषे वर्चस ओजसे तेजसे स्वस्तये सुभूतये स्वाहा ।।

7. Let the mighty God, the soul, the Sun, the king, the commander or electricity protect . . . . said. (4857)

८. सोमो मा सौम्येनावतु प्राणायापानायायुषे वर्चस ओजसे तेजसे स्वस्तये सुभूतये स्वाहा ।।

8. Let the All-pleasant God, the moon, the physician or the essence of medicines protect . . . . said. (4858)

९. भगो मा भगेनावतु प्राणायापानायायुषे वर्चस ओजसे तेजसे स्वस्तये सुभूतये स्वाहा ।।

9. May the Fortune Distributer God, a wealthy king or person protect . . . . said. (4859)

१०. मरुतो मा गणैरवन्तु प्राणायापानायायुषे वर्चस ओजसे तेजसे स्वस्तये सुभूतये स्वाहा ।।

10. May the Almighty Father or the powerful air or commander protect me with numerous powers for . . . . said. (4860)

Chapter (Anuvāka) 6

HYMN XLVI

१. प्रजापतिष्ट्वा बध्नात्प्रथममस्तृतं वीर्याय कम् ।
तत्ते बध्नाम्यायुषे वर्चस ओजसे च बलाय चास्तृतस्त्वाभि रक्षतु ।।

1. The protector of the subjects appoints thee alone, the invincible for brave acts. So, O king, I (i.e., Prohita) employ him under you for long life,

[1]The four-fold use of Anjana, has one as '*mani*' which cannot but be an instrument of radiation, light and attraction, etc.

glory, energy and power. Let the invincible person protect thee in every way. (4861)

२. ऊर्ध्वस्तिष्ठतु रक्षन्नप्रमादमस्तृतेमं मा त्वा दभन्पणयो यातुधानाः ।
इन्द्र इव दस्यूनव धूनुष्व पृतन्यतः सर्वाञ्छत्रून्वि षहस्वास्तृतस्त्वाभि रक्षतु ॥

2. O Invincible person, letest thou, being constantly vigilant protect this king and thus stand above all (i.e., in his eyes). Let not the deceitful mischief-mongers suppress thee. Letest thou crush the usurpers of other's rights like Indra, the evil-destroyer. Letest thou thoroughly smash all the fighting forces of the enemy come against thee. May the unconquerable commander guard thee on all sides. (4862)

३. शतं च न प्रहरन्तो निघ्नन्तो न तस्तिरे ।
तस्मिन्निन्द्रः पर्यदत्त चक्षुः प्राणमथो बलमस्तृतस्त्वाभि रक्षतु ॥

3. The Lord of fortunes, the king fully entrusts the authority of vigilance, protection of life and property, sources of strength and energy to the man, whom hundreds of armies, attacking spilling blood-shed in their wake, can not subdue. (4863)

४. इन्द्रस्य त्वा वर्मणा परि धापयामो यो देवानामधिराजो बभूव ।
पुनस्त्वा देवाः प्र णयन्तु सर्वेऽस्तृतस्त्वाभि रक्षतु ॥

4. We (the general people), cover thee up with the armour of the king who is the lord of all riches and the chief of all the winning warriors. Let all the winning kings or warriors or the learned people again make thee their leader. May the unconquerable commander protect thee from all sides. (4864)

५. अस्मिन्मणावेकशतं वीर्याणि सहस्रं प्राणा अस्मिन्नस्तृते ।
व्याघ्रः शत्रूनभि तिष्ठ सर्वान्यस्त्वा पृतन्यादधरः सो अस्त्वस्तृतस्त्वाभि रक्षतु ॥

5. Hundred and one are the powers in this brave person, who is the best of all warriors. Thousand-fold is the force of vital breaths in this invincible person. He stands like a tiger amongst the force subduing them all. May he, whoever comes with armies to attack thee, be laid low. Let the unconquerable commander fully protect thee. (4865)

६. घृतादुल्लुप्तो मधुमान्पयस्वान्त्सहस्रप्राणः शतयोनिर्वयोधाः ।
शंभूश्च मयोभूश्चोर्जस्वांश्च पयस्वांश्चास्तृतस्त्वाभि रक्षतु ॥

6. O king, let the brave person, who knows no defeat, possessed of heat and energy, sweet-tongued, having plenty of energising juices, possessing the strength of thousands of vital breaths, having hundreds of places for shelter and protection, having strong vigour of life, capable of showering peace all around and making others happy and cheerful, energetic, provided with wholesome drinks, protect thee well. (4866)

७. यथा त्वमुत्तरोऽसो असपत्नः सपत्नहा ।
सजातानामसद्वशी तथा त्वा सविता करदस्तृतस्त्वाभि रक्षतु ॥

7. May the all-mover God make thee such as thou mayst be foeless, the

killer of enemies and far superior to others, and the controller of your equals. Let the invincible commander protect thee from all sides. (4867)[1]

HYMN XLVII

१. आ रात्रि पार्थिवं रजः पितुरप्रायि धामभिः ।
दिवः सदांसि बृहती वि तिष्ठस आ त्वेषं वर्तते तमः ॥

1. O night, terrestrial places along with places of the firmament have been with darkness of thine, that art well established in the vast regions of the heavens. The darkness, shining with light from stars, has engulfed everything. (4868)[2]

२. न यस्याः पारं ददृशे न योयुवद्विश्वमस्यां नि विशते यदेजति ।
अरिष्टासस्त उर्वि तमस्वति रात्रि पारमशीमहि भद्रे पारमशीमहि ॥

2. All things that are in motion are engulfed by the night, whose yonder boundary is never seen, nor does it ever get separated from the world. O great, dark night, may we find thy end uninjured, quite safe and sound. O gracious one, let us pass on to your end safely. (4869)

३. ये ते रात्रि नृचक्षसो द्रष्टारो नवतिर्नव । अशीतिः सन्त्यष्टा उतो ते सप्त सप्ततिः ॥

3. O night, whatever the number of watchers of humanity, looking after them during thy interval, whether it be ninety-nine or eighty-eight or seventy-seven. (4870)[3]

४. षष्टिश्च षट् च रेवति पञ्चाशत्पञ्च सुम्नयि ।
चत्वारश्चत्वारिंशच्च त्रयस्त्रिंशच्च वाजिनि ॥

4. O night, beautiful to look at, moving fast, whether it be sixty-six, or fifty-five, or forty-four, or thirty-three. (4871)

५. द्वौ च ते विंशतिश्च ते रात्र्येकादशावमाः । तेभिर्नो अद्य पायुभिर्नु पाहि दुहितर्दिवः ॥

5. Whether it be twenty-two or eleven at the least, letest thou, O daughter of heavens, protect us today by those protectors. (4872)

[1](1-7) Pt. Khem Karan Das Trivedi has interpreted अस्तृत: as unbreakable law fixed by God. Sayāna and Griffith as charm and amulet, which is meaningless.

[2]cf. *Nirukta*, 9.29.

[3](3-5) The number of watchers of humanity at night has been variously interpreted by different scholars. Griffith sees no sense in the numbers. Pt. Khem Karan Das Trivedi assigns the number of watchmen to be kept as guards at night, according to the convenience of the locality. Pt. Jaidev Vidyalankar takes it to be the number of the assemblies of the king to advise him, taking Ratri as the Parliament. (i) But to me, it appears that the numbers are very significant. There are 11 marutas in the atmosphere, surrounding the earth, which is one of the planets, moving round the Sun, which is the cause of day and night. There are nine such Planets, that are supposed to have the same number of marutas surrounding them. So the number is ninety-nine, when all of them are in motion, separately in the sky. When the axis of any two of them, chance to be collinear, the number becomes-eighty-eight, and so on, till all of them are co-eval, the number, of course, is eleven only. (ii) Else, it may refer to various justa-positions of the constellations during the course of the earth's movement round the Sun. Thus the numbers are meaningless due to our ignorance of Astronomical facts and laws. (iii) In addition to it, they teach arithmetical tables to man.

६. रक्षा माकिर्नो अघशंस ईशत मा नो दुःशंस ईशत ।
मा नो अद्य गवां स्तेनो मावीनां वृक ईशत ॥

6. O night, protect, so that no wicked person may rule us, nor may any evil-seeker hold sway over us. Let not any thief of cows, nor any killer of sheep like a wolf overpower us. (4873)

७. माश्वानां भद्रे तस्करो मा नृणां यातुधान्यः ।
परमेभिः पथिभि स्तेनो धावतु तस्करः । परेण दत्वती रज्जुः परेणाघायुरर्षतु ॥

7. O blessed one, let not the robber seize our horses nor the troublesome females harass our men. Let the thief as well as the robber run away by the paths far distant from us. Let the snake and the mischief-monger take to the far-off route. (4874)

८. अध रात्रि तृष्टधूममशीर्षाणमहिं कृणु । हनू वृकस्य जम्भयास्तेन तं द्रुपदे जहि ॥

8. O night, crush, the head of the serpant, emitting poisonous smoke through forceful hissing. Break into pieces of the jaws of the wolf. Letest thou kill him in the trap laid for him. (4875)

९. त्वयि रात्रि वसामसि स्वपिष्यामसि जागृहि । गोभ्यो नः शर्म यच्छाश्वेभ्यः पुरुषेभ्यः ॥

9. O comfort-giving night, we reside in thee and we shall sleep while thou keepest awake. Mayst thou give shelter to our cows, horses and men. (4876)

HYMN XLVIII

१. अथो यानि च यस्मा ह यानि चान्तः परीणहि । तानि ते परि दद्मसि ॥

1. O night, whatever we try to accumulate, and we lay hidden into the treasure-safe, we entrust all these to thee. (4877)

२. रात्रि मातरुषसे नः परि देहि । उषा नो अह्ने परि ददात्वहस्तुभ्यं विभावरि ॥

2. O bright, comfortable mother, night entrust us to the dawn. Let the dawn entrust us to the day and the day again to thee. (4878)

३. यत्किं चेदं पतयति यत्किं चेदं सरीसृपम् ।
यत्किं च पर्वतायासत्वं तस्मात्त्वं रात्रि पाहि नः ॥

3. Whatever there is that falls. (like the meteorites), whatever there is that crawls and creeps, (like serpents). Whatever there is evil in the mountains, (like the beasts of prey) mayst thou protect us from all these. (4879)

४. सा पश्चात्पाहि सा पुरः सोत्तरादधरादुत । गोपाय नो विभावरि स्तोतारस्त इह स्मसि ॥

4. Mayst thou, O bright night, guard us from behind, from the front side, from above and from below. Here we are the singers of thy praises. (4880)

५. ये रात्रिमनुतिष्ठन्ति ये च भूतेषु जाग्रति ।
पशून्ये सर्वान् रक्षन्ति ते न आत्मसु जाग्रति ते नः पशुषु जाग्रति ॥

5. The sentinels, who keep vigilance all the night long and keep watch and ward over the living beings and who protect all the cattle, are also watchful over bodies and our cattle as well. (4881)

६. वेद वै रात्रि ते नाम घृताची नाम वा असि ।
तां त्वां भरद्वाजो वेद सा नो वित्तेऽधि जाग्रति ।।

6. O night, verily do I know thy name to be Ghritachi, showerer of comforts, lustre and the enervating freshness of body. Thou bearest that name. The mind, full of energy and power is quite familiar with thee (as it is at night that it has its fee play of activities during the hours of sleep) such as thou art, keepest watch over our wealth. (4882)[1]

HYMN XLIX

१. इषिरा योषा युवतिर्दमूना रात्री देवस्य सवितुर्भगस्य ।
अश्वक्षभा सुहवा संभृतश्रीरा पप्रौ द्यावापृथिवी महित्वा ।।

1. Just as a young lady, desirous of seeking pleasure from her husband, who is possessed of fine qualities, capable of producing children and is fortunate, similarly the primordial cause of the universe i.e., Prakriti, lying latent in utter darkness in the state of annihilation, ever young, under the control of its Lord, seeks the touch of the Divine Creator, the Distributor of all fortunes to be set in motion to produce this universe. It (i.e., Prakriti) is capable of coming into brilliance at once, easy to handle and bearer of all forms of riches, completely fills the earth and the heavens with its grandeur. (4883)[2]

२. अति विश्वान्यरुहद् गम्भीरो वर्षिष्ठमरुहन्त श्रविष्ठाः ।
उशती रात्र्यनु सा भद्राभि तिष्ठते मित्र इव स्वधाभिः ।।

2. The Omnipresent God, Who lies hidden in the universe, surpasses all the created things. The Vedic scholars, possessing yogic powers reach Him, Who is the Best showerer of all blessings. The self-same Prakriti, desirous of His company, and peaceful stays all-around like a friend, with her sustaining powers. (4884)

३. वर्ये वन्दे सुभगे सुजात आजगन् रात्रि सुमना इह स्याम् ।
अस्मांस्त्रायस्व नर्याणि जाता अथो यानि गव्यानि पुष्ट्या ।।

3. O above-mentioned Ratri, worthy to be chosen, fortunate, well-born, thou ever comest in this form. Let me stay here in thee with a happy mind. Protect us all by nourishing and energising all created things, useful for men as well as for cattle. (4885)

४. सिंहस्य रात्र्युशती पींषस्य व्याघ्रस्य द्वीपिनो वर्च आ ददे ।
अश्वस्य ब्रध्नं पुरुषस्य मायुं पुरु रूपाणि कृणुषे विभाती ।।

4. O Ratri, thou covetous of various powers has taken up the strength of the lion, the mighty power of the elephant, the ferocity of the tiger and the daring of the leopard, the speed of the horse, the powerful speech of the

[1] भरद्वाज—mind and not any sage of that name.

[2] Here Ratri means the Prakriti, lying in state of utter darkness during प्रलय । Pt. Jaidev Vidyalankar has also referred to the Royal power, capable of producing peace and prosperity by its dominating influence. Ratri has been variously interpreted as Prakriti, Royal power or night according to the content of each verse.

man. In fine thou shinest with splendour, assuming various forms in this world. (4886)

५. शिवां रात्रिमनुसूर्यं च हिमस्य माता सुहवा नो अस्तु ।
अस्य स्तोमस्य सुभगे नि बोध येन त्वा वन्दे विश्वासु दिक्षु ॥

5. O fortunate one, knowest thou full well this praise, with which I bow to thee, the blissful like the effulgent God in all directions. Letest thou, the mother of coolness of snow, be easy to be called in for help. (4887)

६. स्तोमस्य नो विभावरि रात्रि राजेव जोषसे ।
असाम सर्ववीरा भवाम सर्ववेदसो व्युच्छन्तीरनूषसः ॥

6. O bright Ratri, peace-giving (Prakriti) thou appreciatest our praises like the king. Let us be brave in every respect, and possessed of all sorts of fortunes and knowledge, after the dawns, revealing them every morning. (4888)

७. शम्या ह नाम दधिषे मम दिप्सन्ति ये धना ।
रात्रीहि तानसुतपा य स्तेनो न विद्यते यत्पुनर्न विद्यते ॥

7. O Royal power, the peace-showerer is the name that thou bearest. Let those, who want to snatch away my wealth, find the end of their lives at thy hands, so that no thief may exist, nor again come into existence. (4889)

८. भद्रासि रात्रि चमसो न विष्टो विष्वङ् गोरूपं युवतिर्बिभर्षि ।
चक्षुष्मती मे उशती वपूंषि प्रति त्वं दिव्या न क्षाममुक्थाः ॥

8. O Ratri, thou art benign and youthful. Thou fillest the world in the form of the earth like a ladle that is full of clarified butter. Ever vigilant and possessed of divine qualities, wishing well of all the persons related to me, never forsake this earth. (4890)

९. यो अद्य स्तेन आयत्यघायुर्मर्त्यो रिपुः । रात्री तस्य प्रतीत्य प्र ग्रीवाः प्र शिरो हनत् ॥

9. O night, whatever thief, the murderer and the inimical person comes, fully recognizing him, or approaching him, let his neck or head be shattered into pieces. (4891)

१०. प्र पादौ न यथायति प्र हस्तौ न यथाशिषत् ।
यो मलिम्लुरुपायति स संपिष्टो अपायति । अपायति स्वपायति शुष्के स्थाणावपायति ॥

10. Let the feet be shorn, so that he may not come. Let his hands be cut off so that he may not be able to take his meals. Whatsoever robber or marauder comes near, may go off quite ground to dust. Let him be driven off. Let him be pushed off completely. Let him be reduced to the state of a dry stump of a tree. (4892)

HYMN L

१. अध रात्रि तृष्टधूममशीर्षाणमहिं कृणु । अक्षौ वृकस्य निर्जह्यास्तेन तं द्रुपदे जहि ॥

1. O the punishing authority, throw the thirst creating smoke on or cut off the head of him, who stings the interest of the nation like a serpent,

(like a fifth columnist). Drive out the eye-sockets of the highway-robber. Let him be killed by tying him to a post. (4893)[1]

२. ये ते रात्र्यनड्वाहस्तीक्ष्णशृङ्गाः स्वाशवः । तेभिर्नो अद्य पारयाति दुर्गाणि विश्वहा ॥

2. O royal majesty, whoever there are powerful persons, capable of bearing the burden of administration, equipped with very sharp weapons of defence, capable of mobilising their forces speedily, let them always be helpful to us in overcoming all difficult situations and even today. (4894)

३. रात्रिरात्रिमरिष्यन्तस्तरेम तन्वाऽ वयम् । गम्भीरमप्लवा इव न तरेयुररातयः ॥

3. Making use of this authority of defence and protection, let us bodily overcome all difficulties and troubles with our strength. Let not our enemies do so, as men without a boat cannot cross deep waters. (4895)

४. यथा शाम्याकः प्रपतन्नपवान्नानुविद्यते । एवा रात्रि प्र पातय यो अस्माँ अभ्यघायति ॥

4. Just the tiny millet, having fallen or flown away (by the gust of wind) cannot be traced, similarly, O Ratri, fell him to nullity, who comes with the intention of killing us. (4896)

५. अप स्तेन वासो गोअजमुत तस्करम् । अथो यो अर्वतः शिरोऽभिधाय निनीषति ॥

5. Totally efface the thief, who wants to steal our clothes, cows and goats, the robber, who wants to take our horses by tying their heads (i.e., to prevent them from coming back to us, as horses are well-known not to forget the path once seen by them). (4897)

६. यदद्या रात्रि सुभगे विभजन्त्ययो वसु । यदेतदस्मान्भोजय यथेदन्यानानुपायसि ॥

6. O fortune distributing authority, whatever gold or wealth thou grantest to us. Let it be enjoyed by us, so that it may not fall into the hands of others i.e., robbers or enemies. (4898)

७. उषसेनः परि देहि सर्वान् रात्र्यनागसः । उषा नो अह्ने आ भजादहस्तुभ्यं विभावरि ॥

7. O protecting authority, hand us, being sinless over to the dawn. Let the dawn hand us over to the day. Let the day once again entrust us to thee, the bright one at night. (4899)

HYMN LI

१. अयुतोऽहमयुतो म आत्मायुतं मे चक्षुरयुतं मे श्रोत्रमयुतो मे प्राणोऽयुतो
मेऽपानोऽयुतो मे व्यानोऽयुतोऽहं सर्वः ॥

1. I (a devotee) am fully engrossed (in the meditation of God) (literally not separated from Him) my soul is united with Him, my eye is fixed on Him, my ear is all-attention to Him, my ingoing breath is not separated from Him, my out-going breath is related to Him, my vital breath running through all my veins, is wrapt in Him, in short, the whole of myself is totally absorbed in Him. This is the state attained in Samādhi. (4900)[2]

[1]Here also Ratri means kingly power of protection and well-being, looking after the welfare of the people.

[2]It describes the state of smādhi, the means whereby it is attained.

२. देवस्य त्वा सवितुः प्रसवेऽश्विनोर्बाहुभ्यां पूष्णो हस्ताभ्यां प्रसूत आ रभे ॥

2. O meditation, I (the devotee), being moved by the strong hands oi ıne nourishing Father, the arms of the powerful forces of the Almighty, like electricity and air, father and mother, teacher and preacher, commence thee in the creation of the Divine Creator. (4901)

HYMN LII

१. कामस्तदग्रे समवर्तत मनसो रेतः प्रथमं यदासीत् ।
स काम कामेन बृहता सयोनी रायस्पोषं यजमानाय धेहि ॥

1. In the beginning of the creation, it was God, the Desire-Incarnate, imbued with the desire to create the universe. His desire was the first creative power of the Omniscient. The self same Desire-Incarnate and His great desire for creation were centred at the same place i.e., the whole expanse of space. O Kama, shower riches and prosperity on the sacrificer. (4902)[1]

२. त्वं काम सहसासि प्रतिष्ठितो विभुर्विभावा सख आ सखीयते ।
त्वमुग्रः पृतनासु सासहिः सह ओजो यजमानाय धेहि ॥

2. O Desirable God, Thou being Omnipresent, lord Thyself over all. O Friend, Thou shinest with full splendour for Thy friend, the soul. Thou, being Terrible overpowerest the fighting people. O the Valorous One, instill energy and power in the sacrificer. (4903)

३. दूराच्चकमानाय प्रतिपाणायाक्षये । आस्मा अशृण्वन्नाशाः कामेनाजनयन्त्स्वः ॥

3. All the quarters (i.e., the people thereof) Him, the Desire-Incarnate, the Protector, the Indestructible even from afar. It is with His help and grace that they produce happiness and well-being. (4904)

४. कामेन मा काम आगन्हृदयाद्धृदयं परि । यदमीषामदो मनस्तदैतूप मामिह ॥

4. The desire has come to me from the Desire-Incarnate ; the heart being attracted by the heart. Let the mind o fthese, (my relatives) that has gone astray, approach me again, or (let my enemies too be reconciled to me). (4905)

५. यत्काम कामयमाना इदं कृण्मसि ते हविः ।
तन्नः सर्वं समृध्यतामथैतस्य हविषो वीहि स्वाहा ॥

5. O Desirable One, whatever desiring, we make this offering to Thee, let all that grow in plenty for us. Let thee accept this offering. Let our desire be granted. (4906)

HYMN LIII

१. कालो अश्वो वहति सप्तरश्मिः सहस्राक्षो अजरो भूरिरेताः ।
तमा रोहन्ति कवयो विपश्चितस्तस्य चक्रा भुवनानि विश्वा ॥

1. Just as a fast horse, with seven-roped reins carries a chariot, similarly the All-stirring, Omnipresent, Omniscient, All-potent God, Who is possessed

[1] cf. *Rig*, 10. 129.

of thousand-fold powers of vigilance, Indestructible, the Almighty carries on this universe under His sway. The seers, possessing all kinds of knowledge and powers of action reach up to Him. All the worlds are sheer wheels of His machine of creation. (4907)[1]

२. सप्त चक्रान्वहति काल एष सप्तास्य नाभीरमृतं न्वक्षः ।
स इमा विश्वा भुवनान्यञ्जत्कालः स ईयते प्रथमो नु देवः ॥

2. The Kala carries along seven wheels. Seven are its naves and immortality is its axle. The self-same Kala, revealing all these worlds, is truly known to be the Primeval Lord. (4908)[2]

३. पूर्णः कुम्भोऽधि काल आहितस्तं वै पश्यामो बहुधा नु सन्तः ।
स इमा विश्वा भुवनानि प्रत्यङ्कालं तमाहुः परमे व्योमन् ॥

3. The whole of this universe is stationed in the Omnipresent and the Omnipotent God. We, the good ones on the earth, see Him in various ways. He brings to light all these worlds. Him they call the Kala, pervading through all the vast sky. (4909)

४. स एव सं भुवनान्याभरत्स एव सं भुवनानि पर्यैत् ।
पिता सन्नभवत्पुत्र एषां तस्माद्वै नान्यत्परमस्ति तेजः ॥

4. He alone pervades all the spheres. He also thoroughly surrounds them all. Being Father, the Creator, becomes their son, the Protector. No other energy is greater than He. (4910)[3]

५. कालोऽमूं दिवमजनयत्काल इमाः पृथिवीरुत । काले ह भूतं भव्यं चेषितं ह वि तिष्ठते ॥

5. The Kala created these heavenly spheres. Kala also made these terrestrial spheres. In the Kala is verily stationed, in various forms, all what was created before, and all what shall be created in future, and all that is moving on. (4911)

६. कालो भूतिमसृजत काले तपति सूर्यः । काले ह विश्वा भूतानि काले चक्षुर्वि पश्यति ॥

6. The Kala produced the very existence of the creation and the wealth thereof. The sun shines in the Kala. Verily in the Kala alone all the creatures find their existence. The organs like the eyes have their powers of perception due to Him. (4912)

[1]Kala is the All-pervading God with all the powers of sustaining, protecting and even destroying the universe.

[2]Seven wheels: Six pairs of months and the Malmas i.e., intercalary month. Seven naves: seven seasons of the year or seven chhandas or Vedic metres, it may also refer to seven parts of time: क्षण, पल, हीरा, महूर्त्त, प्रहर, दिन, रात्रि or अहोरात्र, सप्ताह, पक्ष, मास, ऋतु, आयण, सम्वतसर ।

[3]In this verse, the Father becoming the Son seems to be an enigma. But God, being the Creator is naturally the Father. The son's duty is to look after and remove all difficulties and troubles of his parents, so in this restricted sense of taking care of His own creation, He is called the son. Or it may point to the days, nights, weeks, fortnights, months, years, parts of the time, i.e., Kala from the earth, the moon, and the sun, created by God, the Kala.

७. काले मनः काले प्राणः काले नाम समाहितम् । कालेन सर्वा नन्दन्त्यागतेन प्रजा इमाः ॥

7. In the very Kala, are well placed, the mind, the vital breath and the name. All these subjects enjoy themselves at His very approach. (4913)

८. काले तपः काले ज्येष्ठं काले ब्रह्म समाहितम् ।
कालो ह सर्वस्येश्वरो यः पितासीत्प्रजापतेः ॥

8. In the self-same Kala are fully established, the austerity, the grandeur and the vast universe and the Vedic lore. He is the Lord of all; He is the Father or the Protector of the king or the Sun etc. (4914)

९. तेनेषितं तेन जातं तदु तस्मिन्प्रतिष्ठितम् । कालो ह ब्रह्म भूत्वा बिभर्ति परमेष्ठिनम् ॥

9. Stirred by Him, created by Him, this universe is firmly stationed in Him alone. The very Kala, being Brahma, the Mighty One, sustains the vast universe, the greatest sacrifice of His. (4915)

१०. कालः प्रजा असृजत कालो अग्रे प्रजापतिम् ।
स्वयम्भूः कश्यपः कालात्तपः कालादजायत ॥

10. The Kala created all the creatures. In the beginning, He created the Hiraṇyagarbha, the source of all-creation. The Self-existent, the Self-effulgent and the Heating-energy was simply His own-self, revealed to us. (4916)

HYMN LIV

१. कालादापः समभवन्कालाद् ब्रह्म तपो दिशः । कालेनोदेति सूर्यः काले नि विशते पुनः ॥

1. From the Mighty Creator were born the waters or atoms. From Him came the Vedic lore or Brahmaṇḍ, the heating fire, and the quarters. The Sun rises because of His Power, and in Him does it set again. (4917)

२. कालेन वातः पवते कालेन पृथिवी मही । द्यौर्मही काल आहिता ॥

2. The wind blows by His force. The great earth rotates and revolves through His energy. The vast heavens rest in Him. (4918)

३. कालो ह भूतं भव्यं च पुत्रो अजनयत्पुरा । कालादृचः समभवन्यजुः कालादजायत ॥

3. The so-called (mentioned in the 4th mantra of the previous sukta) Son, the Kala, produces the past and the future. From Him were born the Richas. Yajurveda was born of Him. (4919)

४. कालो यज्ञं समैरयद्देवेभ्यो भागमक्षितम् । काले गन्धर्वाप्सरसः काले लोकाः प्रतिष्ठिताः ॥

4. The mighty Father mobilised this huge sacrifice, providing ever-lasting share to the divine beings or natural forces well-stationed are in the Kala, all the creatures on earth or moving in the atmosphere. (4920)

५. कालेऽयमङ्गिरा देवोऽथर्वा चाधि तिष्ठतः ।
इमं च लोकं परमं च लोकं पुण्यांश्च लोकान्विधृतीश्च पुण्याः ।
सर्वाँल्लोकानभिजित्य ब्रह्मणा कालः स ईयते परमो नु देवः ॥

5. In the Omnipresent, rest this shining sun and the air. The Omnipotent is known to be the most potent of all; as He stays, conquering, by His Great

might, this world, the other world on high, the righteous states and regulations and all the worlds or situations. (4921)

Chapter (Anuvāka) 7

HYMN LV*

१. रात्रिरात्रिमप्रयातं भरन्तोऽश्वायेव तिष्ठते घासमस्मै ।
रायस्पोषेण समिषा मदन्तो मा ते अग्ने प्रतिवेशा रिषाम ।।

1. Just as fresh fodder is given every night to the horse, standing in the stable, so, O God, the learned person or the sacrificial fire, may we, your neighbours, not feel troubled, enjoying ourselves through increase of wealth and rich food. (4922)[1]

२. या ते वसोर्वात इषुः सा त एषा तया नो मृड ।
रायस्पोषेण समिषा मदन्तो मा ते अग्ने प्रतिवेशा रिषाम ।।

2. O Powerful God or wind, whatever means of providing wealth or living there are yours, here they are. Let you make us happy with these. O God, the king, the learned person or the sacrificial fire, let us be free from all troubles and difficulties, enjoying ourselves with the abundance of riches and plenty of provisions. (4923)

३. सायंसायं गृहपतिर्नो अग्निः प्रातःप्रातः सौमनसस्य दाता ।
वसोर्वसोर्वसुदान एधि वयं त्वेन्धानास्तन्वं पुषेम ।।

3. God, the learned man, or the sacrificial fire is the protector of our homes every evening. He is the giver of peace of mind and feeling of harmony every morning. O the Giver of wealth and riches of all sorts, may you shower all these on us. Worshipping, serving or enkindling thee, we may keep our bodies well-nourished and well-fed. (4924)

४. प्रातःप्रातर्गृहपतिर्नो अग्निः सायंसायं सौमनसस्य दाता ।
वसोवसोर्वसुदान एधीन्धानास्त्वा शतंहिमा ऋधेम ।।

4. Every morning, Agni is the Lord of our household. May He shower on us, harmony and peace, every evening. O Showerer of wealth, grant us wealth and riches of every kind. Worshipping, serving or enkindling thee, may we live for hundred years. (4825)

५. अपश्चा दग्धान्नस्य भूयासम् । अन्नादायान्नपतये रुद्राय नमो अग्नये ।।
सभ्यः सभां मे पाहि ये च सभ्याः सभासदः ।

5. O Agni, may I be one, whose power of digestion has not failed him. Obeisance to the king, who accepts grains, as revenue, is the lord of grains makes the wicked weep and consumes the evil doers by his burning powers of destruction. O king, worthy of presiding over the cabinet, protect this parliament of mine and whoever its worthy members. (4926)

६. त्वमिन्द्रा पुरुहूत विश्वमायुर्व्यश्नवत् ।
अहरहर्बलिमित्ते हरन्तोऽश्वायेव तिष्ठते घासमग्ने ।।

*This sukta prescribes Brahma-Yajña, Dev-Yajña, Atithi-yajña and even Pitri-Yajña to be performed daily both in the morning and the evening for the attainment of happiness and prosperity in life.

[1]cf. *Yajur*, 11.75; *Atharva*, 3.15.8.

6. O the mighty monarch, respected by many other kings and called in for help and protection by all the people fully enjoy the full span of your life i.e., hundred years. O Fiery Commander, here are the people bringing their tributes to thee every day just as the fodder is fed to the horse, stationed in the stable. (4927)

७. अहरहर्बलिमित्ते हरन्तोऽश्वायेव तिष्ठते घासमग्ने ।
रायस्पोषेण समिषा मदन्तो मा ते अग्ने प्रतिवेशा रिषाम ।।

7. Just as fresh grass is given each day to the horse, standing in the stable, so. O God, the learned person or the sacrificial fire, may we, your neighbours, not feel troubled, enjoying ourselves. (4928)

HYMN LVI

१. यमस्य लोकादध्या बभूविथ प्रमदा मर्त्यान्प्र युनक्षि धीरः ।
एकाकिना सरथं यासि विद्वान्त्स्वप्नं मिमानो असुरस्य योनौ ।।

1. O man, you are fully capable of controlling your vital breaths from the very central place, governing all the sense-organs in brain, self-controlled, thou setest the people on the right path, with joy and pleasure. Fully knowing and measuring the harmful state of laziness and sleepiness, used in the shattered place of the indulgent persons, thou passes on, along with your body, all alone. (4929)

२. बन्धस्त्वाग्रे विश्वचया अपश्यत्पुरा रात्र्या जनितोरेके अह्नि ।
ततः स्वप्नेदमध्या बभूविथ भिषग्भ्यो रूपमपगूहमानः ।।

2. O sleep or laziness, thou art a sort of knot of all sorts of ailments. If some experience thee even before nightfall or some, during the day-time, thou, therefore, concealing thy identity even from the physicians, becomest too powerful to be cured. (4930)

३. बृहद्गावासुरेभ्योऽधि देवानुपावर्तत महिमानमिच्छन् ।
तस्मै स्वप्नाय दधुराधिपत्यं त्रयस्त्रिंशासः स्वरानशानाः ।।

3. The state of unconsciousness, wherein the patient speaks aloud, has come to the self-controlled persons from those who revel in pleasures of life, wishing to attain its grandeur. The thirty-three divinities, enjoying happiness and calmness, have given predominence to this state of laziness or lassitude. (4931)[1]

४. नैतां विदुः पितरो नोत देवा येषां जल्पिश्चरत्यन्तरेदम् ।
त्रिते स्वप्नमदधुराप्त्ये नर आदित्यासो वरुणेनानुशिष्टाः ।।

4. Neither the elders nor the learned, in whose secret recesses of the heart this talk goes on, know the secret thereof. The solar nerves i.e., on the right side of the body, directed by the lunar ones i.e., on the left side of the body, have installed sleep in the threefold Aptya. (4932)[2]

[1]Even the good become vitiated in the company of the wicked. Or All the divine powers, working in the body, get tired and weary and fall a prey to sleep and dreaminess to get relief from tension. Even the good and the noble souls loose all their control over their sub-conscious mind in that state.

[2](a) The second line of this verse gives some definite clue to the coming on of sleep in the body. It is some physiological truth that is revealed here. It requires a thorough

५. यस्य क्रूरमभजन्त दुष्कृतोऽस्वप्नेन सुकृतः पुण्यमायुः ।
स्वर्मदसि परमेण बन्धुना तप्यमानस्य मनसोऽधि जज्ञिषे ॥

5. The evil-doers reap the cruel effect of this laziness. The virtuous attain long, virtuous life by alertness. O Idleness, thou shedest into oblivion, the happiness of the mind, undergoing all austerities, by thy great bondage, and thus overpowerest him. (4933)

६. विद्म ते सर्वाः परिजाः पुरस्ताद् विद्म स्वप्न यो अधिपा इहा ते ।
यशस्विनो न यशसेह पाह्यारादु द्विषेभिरप याहि दूरम् ॥

6. O sleepiness, we already know the evils, born of thee and also him who is your controller here. Letest thee protect us, the meritorious with renown in this world, even from a distance. Go away to a great distance along with thy evil effects. (4934)

HYMN LVII

१. यथा कलां यथा शफं यथर्णं संनयन्ति । एवा दुष्वप्न्यं सर्वमप्रिये सं नयामसि ॥

1. Just as the moon losing one Kala i.e., one sixteenth each day is reduced to a non-entity on the Amavas day, just as the path is fully covered step by step; and just debt is fully paid up by instalment. Similarly do we totally entrust all the bad dreams by slow degrees to the enemy or to 'Trita Aptya.' (4935)

२. सं राजानो अगुः समृणान्यगुः सं कुष्ठा अगुः सं कला अगुः ।
समस्मासु यद् दुष्वप्न्यं निर्द्विषते दुष्वप्न्यं सुवाम ॥

2. Just as the kings assemble in a war, just debts accumulate just as various kinds of leprosy gather together, just Kalas i.e., 16th part pile up to make the full moon; similarly the bad dreams that accumulate in us, may we drive them off to our foes in toto. (4936)

३. देवानां पत्नीनां गर्भ यमस्य कर यो भद्रः स्वप्न । स मम यः पापस्तद् द्विषते प्र हिण्मः ।
मा तृष्टानामसि कृष्णशकुनेर्मुखम् ॥

3. O sleep, thou art born of the protective powers of the sense-organs and art the inducer of the controlling energy. Whatever is peaceful and pleasant

research by our doctors, Vaids and scientists. Vedic science is definite that nerves on the right side of the body have solar energy, while those on the left side have lunar one. It is by their combined force, that the Trita Apt ya is generated inducing state of sleepiness in the brains. Even yogis are enabled to attain their smādhi by making these two forces combine in their Brahmrandhar. (b) By 'Trita Aptya', I think some combination of hydrogen atoms is meant. It has the effect of coolness, which in its turn is the inducer of sleep. Even the modern scientists have faced some sort of difficulty in the process of fusion of the hydrogen bomb. It requires very very high temperature to fuse two atoms of hydrogen into one, but as soon as the 3rd atom is combined and the 4th one is coming, the temperature falls down all of a sudden and the fusion process is retarded. So I think 'Tritya Aptya' may be some physical process of that sort, which may be an instrument of inducing the state of sleepiness. Let us search for it. Pt. Jaidev Vidyalankar and Pt. Khem Karan's renderings have not appealed to me. Hence the above rendering. I would like to have some guidance from some scientists, vaid or doctor in the matter.

in thee, let it be mine; whatever is evil or bad in thee, let us kick it off to the enemy. Let not thee be like the mouth of the crow, among the thirsty birds. (i.e., just as a thirsty crow caws and caws, so let us not be muttering aloud in our sleep like the thirsty crow). (4937)

४. तं त्वा स्वप्न तथा सं विद्म स त्वं स्वप्नाश्व इव कायमश्व इव नीनाहम् ।
अनास्माकं देवपीयुं पियारुं वप यदस्मासु दुष्वप्न्यं यद् गोषु यच्च नो गृहे ॥

4. O sleep or drowsiness, we know thee as such. The self-same thou mayst give a thorough shaking to the evil-doer, the hater of the noble persons, other than ourselves, just as horse shakes off the dust from his body and the saddle, etc., from his back. (4938)

५. अनास्माकस्तद् देवपीयुः पियारुर्निष्कमिव प्रति मुञ्चताम् ।
नवारत्नीनपमया अस्माकं ततः परि । दुष्वप्न्यं सर्वं द्विषते निर्दयामसि ॥

5. Whatever evil effects of the drowsiness there are in us, in our cattle or our homes, let all those be borne like an ornament, by the mischief-monger who hates the noble persons, other than ourselves. O bad dream, get thee off nine cubits away from us all around. We totally expell all this laziness towards the enemy. (4939)

HYMN LVIII

१. घृतस्य जूतिः समना सदेवा संवत्सरं हविषा वर्धयन्ती ।
श्रोत्रं चक्षुः प्राणोऽच्छिन्नो नो अस्त्वच्छिन्ना वयमायुषो वर्चसः ॥

1. Let the continuous flow of clarified butter, along with the learned or the natural forces, of the same accord, enhance the utility of the year, with the oblations all the year round. Let our hearing, sight and vital breath be uninjured. Let us be not separated from our life and vigour. (4940)

२. उपास्मान्प्राणो ह्वयतामुप वयं प्राणं हवामहे ।
वर्चो जग्राह पृथिव्य१न्तरिक्षं वर्चः सोमो बृहस्पतिर्विधत्ता ॥

2. Let the vital breath sustain us, let us keep intact our vital breath. Vigour has gripped the earth and mid-regions. The moon and the sun are the bearers of energy and force. (4941)

३. वर्चसो द्यावापृथिवी संग्रहणी बभूवथुर्वर्चो गृहीत्वा पृथिवीमनु सं चरेम ।
यशसं गावो गोपतिमुप तिष्ठन्त्यायतीर्यशो गृहीत्वा पृथिवीमनु सं चरेम ॥

3. The heavens and the earth have become the gatherers of energy and vigour. Having attained vigour and strength, let us follow the earth. Just as the cows, the rays, and the sense-organs approach the glorious cowherd, the Sun and the soul respectively, so should we, getting hold of, or making the right use of these coming cows, rays or organs, pass our life on the earth in glory. (4942)

४. व्रजं कृणुध्वं स हि वो नृपाणो वर्म सीव्यध्वं बहुला पृथूनि ।
पुरः कृणुध्वमायसीरधृष्टा मा वः सुस्रोच्चमसो दृंहता तम् ॥

4. Make big cow-sheds. These would truly be a great source of the nourish-

ment of the people. Prepare many, vast armours for protection of the body. Erect unvulnerable cities of iron for safety against the enemies' attack. Let not the water-tanks and the granaries of yours be leaky. Make them strong enough to keep all your supplies intact. (4943)[1]

५. यज्ञस्य चक्षुः प्रभृतिर्मुखं च वाचा श्रोत्रेण मनसा जुहोमि ।
इमं यज्ञं विततं विश्वकर्मणा देवा यन्तु सुमनस्यमानाः ।।

5. The eyes and the mouth of this sacrificing soul are nourishing well. And I offer my oblations with my voice, hearing and mind. The Creator of the universe has spread this sacrifice. Let the learned persons attain it with good mind. (4944)

६. ये देवानामृत्विजो ये च यज्ञिया येभ्यो हव्यं क्रियते भागधेयम् ।
इमं यज्ञं सह पत्नीभिरेत्य यावन्तो देवास्तविषा मादयन्ताम् ।।

6. Whoever there are the performers of the sacrifice among the learned persons, whoever there are worthy of respect and to whomsoever this oblation is offered as a special share, let all those great learned people come, along with wives, to this sacrifice and enjoy themselves. (4945)

HYMN LIX

१. त्वमग्ने व्रतपा असि देव आ मर्त्येष्वा । त्वं यज्ञेष्वीड्यः ।।

1. Oh! God or the learned scholar, you are the keeper of vows and are worthy of respect among the people. Your worshippers are respected in the sacrifices. (4946)

२. यद्वो वयं प्रमिनाम व्रतानि विदुषां देवा अविदुष्टरासः ।
अग्निष्टद्विश्वादा पृणातु विद्वान्त्सोमस्य यो ब्राह्मणाँ आविवेश ।।

2. Oh! learned people, whatever rules and regulations of yours, we, the ignorant people, have broken, may God or the scholar make good the deficiency of all that. He, who, knowing the All-moving God, is present among the Brahmans. (4947)

३. आ देवानामपि पन्थामगन्म यच्छक्नवाम तदनुप्रवोढुम् ।
अग्निर्विद्वान्त्स यजात्स इद्धोता सोऽध्वरान्त्स ऋतून्कल्पयाति ।।

3. Let us also follow the path of the learned people. May he follow it as far as we can. God knows it. He enables us to stick to it. He is the giver of all comforts. He produces all the non-violent sacrifices and seasons. (4948)

HYMN LX

१. वाङ्म आसन्नसोः प्राणश्चक्षुरक्ष्णोः श्रोत्रं कर्णयोः ।
अपलिताः केशा अशोणा दन्ता बहु बाह्वोर्बलम् ।।

1. May the power of speech remain intact in my mouth; the vital breath in my nostrils; the sight in my eyes; the hearing in my ears. Let my hair never

[1]This verse must be an eye-opener to those, who think the Vedas to be mere songs of the cowherds and shepherds.

grow white and teeth, redden. Let there be great strength in my arms. (4949)

२. ऊर्वोरोजो जङ्घयोर्जवः पादयोः । प्रतिष्ठा अरिष्टानि मे सर्वात्मानिभृष्टः ।।

2. Let there be vigour in my thighs; speed in my legs and stability in my feet. Let all the organs of my body be free from diseases and the soul be not down-cast. (4950)

HYMN LXI

१. तनूस्तन्वा ऽ मे सहे दतः सर्वमायुरशीय । स्योनं मे सीद पुरुः पृणस्व पवमानः स्वर्गे ।।

1. May my body remain along with bodily strength and energy. I may, therefore, complete full span of life. Oh ! God, Nourisher of all, keep me happy and cheerful and purify me and enthrall me in the blissful state. (4951)

HYMN LXII

१. प्रियं मा कृणु देवेषु प्रियं राजसु मा कृणु । प्रियं सर्वस्य पश्यत उत शूद्र उतार्ये ।।

1. Oh! God, make me the beloved of the learned people and also make me lovable among the ruling classes. Make me beloved of all the creatures (i.e. those who see), among the Shudra and the Vaishya. (4952)

HYMN LXIII

१. उत्तिष्ठ ब्रह्मणस्पते देवान्यज्ञेन बोधय ।
आयुः प्राणं प्रजां पशून्कीर्ति यजमानं च वर्धय ।।

1. Oh! Lord of the universe, the Vedas, the riches and of foodgrains, or the Vedic scholar, be ready and enlighten all the learned people or the natural forces, by the sacrifice and enhance the life, the vital breath, the off-spring, the cattle, the renown of the sacrificer. (4953)

HYMN LXIV

१. अग्ने समिधमाहार्षं बृहते जातवेदसे । स मे श्रद्धां च मेधां च जातवेदाः प्र यच्छतु ।।

1. Oh! God, the Omniscient, the master of learning, I have brought for the great store-house of knowledge and brilliance, this soul of mine as a fuel. Let both of you conversant with the Vedas and givers of knowledge of all things to the people, grant me faith and sharp intellect. (4954)

२. इध्मेन त्वा जातवेदः समिधा वर्धयामसि । तथा त्वमस्मान्वर्धय प्रजया च धनेन च ।।

2. Oh! Lord of learning, or the preceptor, just as the fire is enkindled by the fuel, so do I increase your grandeur by my enlightened soul. Similarly may Thou make us prosperous with progeny and wealth. (4955)

३. यदग्ने यानि कानि चिदा ते दारूणि दध्मसि । सर्वं तदस्तु मे शिवं तज्जुषस्व यविष्ठ्य ।।

3. Oh! All-knowing God, or the teacher, whatever kinds of praises I offer thee, like the wooden fuel to the fire, may all that be peaceful to me. Oh! Most-Potent, accept all that. (4956)

४. एतास्ते अग्ने समिधस्त्वमिद्धः समिद्भव । आयुरस्मासु धेह्यमृतत्वमाचार्या ऽ य ।।

4. Oh! Effulgent God, these are Thy powers of brilliance. Being well-lit, shine in the heart and grant us long life and immortality to our preceptor. (4957)

HYMN LXV

१. हरिः सुपर्णो दिवमारुहोऽर्चिषा ये त्वा दिप्सन्ति दिवमुत्पतन्तम् ।
अव तां जहि हरसा जातवेदोऽबिभ्यदुग्रोऽर्चिषा दिवमा रोह सूर्य ॥

1. Oh! Yogin, shedding off all ignorance, shining like the Sun, fully equipped with all powers, rise to the highest state of bliss by your glory and grandeur. Whoever want to suppress you from flying to the highest state of beatitude, crush them by your force of destroying evil. Being fearless and terrible by your grandeur, let you rise to the most shining state of bliss. (4958)[1]

HYMN LXVI

१. अयोजाला असुरा मायिनोऽयस्मयैः पाशैरङ्किनो ये चरन्ति ।
तांस्ते रन्धयामि हरसा जातवेदः सहस्रऋष्टिः सपत्नान्प्रमृणन्याहि वज्रः ॥

1. Whoever the powerful, the deceitful enemies, with iron nets and bearing numbers of these regiments, move about with iron snares, crush them all. Oh! fiery king, with thy force of destruction. Let thou, who possessest thousands of arms and is like a thunder-bolt, protect us by thoroughly killing thy enemies. (4959)

HYMN LXVII

१. पश्येम शरदः शतम् ॥

1. May we see for hundred years. (4960)

२. जीवेम शरदः शतम् ॥

2. May we live for hundred years. (4961)

३. बुध्येम शरदः शतम् ॥

3. May we acquire knowledge for hundred years. (4962)

४. रोहेम शरदः शतम् ॥

4. May we go on prospering and progressing for hundred years. (4963)

५. पूषेम शरदः शतम् ॥

5. May we go on being nourished for hundred years. (4964)

६. भवेम शरदः शतम् ॥

6. May we remain strong and sturdy for hundred years. (4965)

७. भूयेम शरदः शतम् ॥

7. May we retain our prestige and influence for hundred years. (4966)

८. भूयसीः शरदः शतात् ॥

[1]Similarly a king by overcoming all opposing forces of the enemies may reach the highest throne of monarch.

8. May we retain all these powers of sight etc., for for greater number of years than hundred. (4967)

HYMN LXVIII

१. अव्यसश्च व्यचसश्च बिलं वि ष्यामि मायया । ताभ्यामुद्धृत्य वेदमथ कर्माणि कृण्महे ॥

1. Thoroughly pondering over the finite and the infinite with the help of my intellect. I realise the secret thereof. Deriving knowledge of both of these, we perform our actions accordingly. (4968)

HYMN LXIX

१. जीवा स्थ जीव्यासं सर्वमायुर्जीव्यासम् ॥

२. उपजीवा स्थोप जीव्यासं सर्वमायुर्जीव्यासम् ॥

३. संजीवा स्थ सं जीव्यासं सर्वमायुर्जीव्यासम् ॥

४. जीवला स्थ जीव्यासं सर्वमायुर्जीव्यासम् ॥

1-4. Oh! men of noblest character, peaceful like waters, you are capable of leading a long life. May I also live long. May I complete the full span of life. Oh! noble persons, you are capable of increasing your life. May I also do so: (1) May I live for the full span of life (2) Oh! noble souls, you lead a good life. (3) May I also do so. May I live for the full span of life. (4) Oh! noble souls, you are able to instill life into others. May I live long. May I complete the full span of life. (4969-72)

HYMN LXX

१. इन्द्र जीव सूर्य जीव देवा जीवा जीव्यासमहम् । सर्वमायुर्जीव्यासम् ॥

1. Let the Glorious God infuse life into me. Let the shining Sun infuse life into me. Let the learned people and the national forces infuse life into me. May I live long. May I complete the full span of life. (4973)

HYMN LXXI

१. स्तुता मया वरदा वेदमाता प्र चोदयन्तां पावमानी द्विजानाम् ।
आयुः प्राणं प्रजां पशुं कीर्तिं द्रविणं ब्रह्मवर्चसम् । मह्यं दत्त्वा व्रजत ब्रह्मलोकम् ॥

1. I have sung the praises of the Veda-revealing power of God, which showers its blessings and purifies the Brahmans, Kshatriyas, Vaishyas. Oh! learned persons you should also preach it well. Let you attain Brahm Loka, the state of salvation, after giving me life, vital breath, off-spring, the cattle, fame, the riches and godly splendour. (4974)

HYMN LXXII

१. यस्मात्कोशादुदभराम वेदं तस्मिन्नन्तरव दध्म एनम् ।
कृतमिष्टं ब्रह्मणो वीर्येण तेन मा देवास्तपसावतेह ॥

1. From whichever treasure-house, i.e., God, we pick up the Vedas (Vedic knowledge), we entrust it into that very store-house. O learned persons, by whatever power of God or Vedic learning, this sacrifice is performed, let you protect us in this world by the same austerity. (4975)

BOOK (Kāṇḍa) XX

Chapter (Anuvāka) 1

HYMN I

१. इन्द्र त्वा वृषभं वयं सुते सोमे हवामहे । स पाहि मध्वो अन्धसः ॥

1. O adorable God, just as in a sacrifice when Soma juice is produced the powerful king is called to drink it, so do we call You at the Subar of grass at the attainment of Dharm-Megh Smādhi Let thou protect us with life prolonging sweet nectar, (4976)[1]

२. मरुतो यस्य हि क्षये पाथा दिवो विमहसः । स सुगोपातमो जनः ॥

2. O brave warriors moving fast like the winds, the best protector is the man under whose shining and specially glorious shelter you guard the nation or in the case of God. O Vital breaths, Well-protector and the Creator is God under Whose glorious and splendorous shelter you protect all the creatures and the worlds. (4977)[2]

३. उक्षान्नाय वशान्नाय सोमपृष्ठाय वेधसे । स्तोमैर्विधेमाग्नये ॥

3. With these songs of praises we worship the Effulgent God, the Creator, whom the Sun is a source of food, the earth is a source of food and Soma essence of herbs as the back-bone. (4978)[3]

HYMN II

१. मरुतः पोत्रात्सुष्टुभः स्वर्कादृतुना सोमं पिबतु ॥

1. Let the learned persons or vital breaths drink the life-invigorating juice, suitable to the seasons, from the Purifying, Praiseworthy God, Who is worthy of our worship. (4979)[4]

२. अग्निराग्नीध्रात्सुष्टुभः स्वर्कादृतुना सोमं पिबतु ॥

2. Let the brilliant scholar drink the essence of medicines, suitable to the seasons from the Praiseworthy and the Worshipful God, Who is the Bearer of all heat and energy. (4980)

३. इन्द्रो ब्रह्मा ब्राह्मणात्सुष्टुभः स्वर्कादृतुना सोमं पिबतु ॥

3. Let the fortunate Vedic scholar, well-versed in all the four Vedas drink the medicinal juice, according to the requirement of the season from the praiseworthy and respectable Brahman, who is fully conversant with Vedic sciences. (4981)[5]

४. देवो द्रविणोदाः पोत्रात्सुष्टुभः स्वर्कादृतुना सोमं पिबतु ॥

4. Let the learned donor of riches drink the essence of herbs suitable to the season from the purifying, praiseworthy and respectable physician, possessing knowledge of Ayurveda. (4982)[6]

[1]cf. *Rig*, 3.40.1, *Atharva*, 20.6.1
[2]*Rig*, 1.86.1. [3]*Rig*, 8.43.1.
[4]cf. *Rig*, 1.15.2 and 2.36.2.
[5]*Rig*, 1.15.5. [6]*Rig*, 1.15. (8, 9, 10).

HYMN III

१. आ याहि सुषुमा हि त इन्द्र सोमं पिबा इमम् । एदं बर्हिः सदो मम ॥

1. O mighty king, come here. Verily have we prepared this essence of herbs for thee. Please drink it. Here is this seat of mine, please be seated on it. (4983)

२. आ त्वा ब्रह्मयुजा हरी वहतामिन्द्र केशिना । उप ब्रह्माणि नः शृणु ॥

2. O glorious God, let these two (i.e., intellect and soul) destroying evil united in deep meditation, with Thee, the Brahma and lit with the rays of spiritual light, carry Thee along. Letest Thou listen to our Vedic prayers. (4984)

३. ब्रह्माणस्त्वा वयं युजा सोमपामिन्द्र सोमिनः । सुतावन्तो हवामहे ।

3. O splendorous God, we, immersed in deep meditation, conversant with Vedic lore, and tasting Thy Bliss, thus producing the Brahmanas, call Thee for help and guidance. (4985)[1]

HYMN IV

१. आ नो याहि सुतावतोऽस्माकं सुष्टुतिरुप । पिबा सु शिप्रिन्नन्धसः ॥

1. O God, come to us, who have been able to produce spiritual knowledge in deep meditation and listen to our praises. O Beautiful One, make us drink deep of Thy Bliss. (4986)

२. आ ते सिञ्चामि कुक्ष्योरनु गात्रा वि धावतु । गृभाय जिह्वया मधु ॥

2. O man, I pour out this Soma into both sides of thy belly. Let it then run through all thy organs. Taste this sweet juice with thy tongue. (4987)

३. स्वादुष्टे अस्तु संसुदे मधुमान्तन्वे३ तव । सोमः शमस्तु ते हृदे ॥

3. O noble donor, let this sweet Soma be tasteful to thee. Let it be peaceful to thy body and wholesome to thy heart. (4988)[2]

HYMN V

१. अयमु त्वा विचर्षणे जनीरिवाभि संवृतः । प्र सोम इन्द्र सर्पतु ॥

1. O Powerful guardian of the people, let this creative power come to Thee, just as the bride-groom protected and surrounded by brave persons approaches the bride. (4989)[3]

२. तुविग्रीवो वपोदरः सुबाहुरन्धसो मदे । इन्द्रो वृत्राणि जिघ्नते ॥

2. The Almighty Father, with His multifarious powers, the Creative Energy and Powerful gripping arms destroys all evils in the very rupture of the Soma. (4990)

३. इन्द्र प्रेहि पुरस्त्वं विश्वस्येशान ओजसा । वृत्राणि वृत्रहं जहि ॥

3. O Lord of splendour, the Destroyer of all the handicaps, ruling over

[1](1-3) cf. *Rig*, 8.17. (1-3). [2](1-3) cf. *Rig*, 8.17 (4-6).
[3](1-7) (a) cf. *Rig*, 8.17. (6-13). (b) The whole of this sukta may also be referred to the king as Indra.

the whole universe by Thy Valour and Prowess, Thou movest in front of all and effaces all the impediments. (4991)

४. दीर्घस्ते अस्त्वङ्कुशो येना वसु प्रयच्छसि । यजमानाय सुन्वते ॥

4. Long be Thy goading power, by which Thou grantest riches and wealth to the creative sacrificer. (4992)

५. अयं त इन्द्र सोमो निपूतो अधि बर्हिषि । एहीमस्य द्रवा पिब ॥

5. O glorious God, here is all-creative Energy of Thine well-purified and crystallised in this vast sky. Pervade it through and through. Let it flow on and on and keep it intact for protection of the universe. (4993)

६. शाचिगो शाचिपूजनायं रणाय ते सुतः । आखण्डल प्र हूयसे ॥

6. O the Almighty God, the Lord of all moving spheres, the source of most powerful rays of light, worthy of worship even by the mightiest of the mighty, here is this universe for Thy revelling. O the Omnipresent, the Pervader of all parts of the creation, it is Thou, Who is called most of all for help and protection. (4994)

७. यस्ते शृङ्गवृषो नपात्प्रणपात्कुण्डपाय्यः । न्य॒स्मिन्दध्र आ मनः ॥

7. O All-powerful God, whatever Destructive or Peace-showering Force, the Up-holding Power, the special Energy of sustenance, the great forces of Annihilation and Protection are Thine, Thou art fully engrossed in the working thereof. (4995)

HYMN VI

१. इन्द्र त्वा वृषभं वयं सुते सोमे हवामहे । स पाहि मध्वो अन्धसः ॥

1. O Mighty God, in this created world, we call Thee, the showerer of blessings. Letest Thee protect us with delicious food and drinks. (4996)[1]

२. इन्द्र क्रतुविदं सुतं सोमं हर्य पुरुष्टुत । पिबा वृषस्व तातृपिम् ॥

2. O most Praiseworthy God, the Distributer of fortunes, desirest Thou the produced Soma, the source of actions and knowledge and satisfaction for all. Guard it and shower it on all the people. (4997)

३. इन्द्र प्र णो धितावानं यज्ञं विश्वेभिर्देवेभिः । तिर स्तवान विश्पते ॥

3. O Lord of all fortunes, praises and subjects, enhance our sacrifice, showering riches and wealth, with the help of all the forces of nature. (4998)

४. इन्द्र सोमाः सुता इमे तव प्र यन्ति सत्पते । क्षयं चन्द्रास इन्दवः ॥

4. O adorable Lord of the noble people, these fortunate, pleasant (like the moon) and learned persons, fully equipped with spiritual powers in deep meditation, specially seek Thy shelter. (4999)

५. दधिष्वा जठरे सुतं सोममिन्द्र वरेण्यम् । तव द्युक्षास इन्दवः ॥

5. O glorious God, in the act of the creation of the universe, Thou bearest this spiritual sun, worthy to be attained in deep meditation. All these

[1](1-7) (a) cf. *Rig*, 3.40. (b) This sukta may also be applied to the king or the preceptor.

yogis, shining with the brilliance of yog-smādhi are Thine. (5000)

६. गिर्वणः पाहि नः सुतं मधोर्धाराभिरज्यसे । इन्द्र त्वादातमिद्यशः ॥

6. O God, worthy to be praised by our speech, protect this product of ours. Thou art revealed by the currents of sweet bliss. O Glorious God, all this fame and renown is given by Thee. (5001)

७. अभि द्युम्नानि वनिन इन्द्रं सचन्ते अक्षिता । पीत्वी सोमस्य वावृधे ॥

7. All the indestructible riches, renown, fame etc., of the devotees are fully entrusted to the Lord of all fortunes. He enhances His Glory by protecting this creation. (5002)

८. अर्वावतो न आ गहि परावतश्च वृत्रहन् । इमा जुषस्व नो गिरः ॥

8. O Lord of all the forces of destruction of ignorance and darkness from the nearest places as well as from afar. Please accept these praise-songs of ours. (5003)

९. यदन्तरा परावतमर्वावतं च हूयसे । इन्द्रेह तत आ गहि ॥

9. Whatever the place, whether distant, intervening or nearest, whence Thou art called, O Radiant God, comest Thou here to us from thence. (5004)

HYMN VII

१. उद्धेदमि श्रुतामघं वृषभं नर्यापसम् । अस्तारमेषि सूर्य ॥

1. O brilliant yogin, shining like the Sun, thou risest up by the spiritual attainment to the All-stirring God, Well-known Lord of fortunes, the Powerful Showerer of blessings and well-being, the Doer of deeds, beneficial to men. (5005)

२. नव यो नवतिं पुरो बिभेद बाह्वोजसा । अहिं च वृत्रहावधीत् ॥

2. Electricity, which breaks, by the energy of its arms (i.e., positive and negative currents) the ninety-nine cities (i.e., the so-called elements, known to the modern scientists, but called Bhogas in the Vedic terminology), destroys the cloud, which covers the rays of the sun, the source of all energy and power. (5006)

३. स न इन्द्रः शिवः सखाश्वावद् गोमद्यवमत् । उरुधारेव दोहते ॥

3. That very electric power may be our peaceful friend, providing us with the horse-power to drive our machines, light to lighten our houses, and power to produce grains in the fields. Let it bring on prosperity and well-being for us by flowing into numerous currents. (5007)

४. इन्द्र क्रतुविदं सुतं सोमं हर्य पुरुष्टुत । पिबा वृषस्व तातृपिम् ॥

4. Let electricity, so highly spoken of by many learned people, help extract the essence of medicines, thus produced by those, who are well-versed in manufacturing things. Let it keep it safe and shower, on us the juice, satisfying all. (5008)[1]

[1](1-4) (a) cf. *Rig*, 8.93 (1-3), and 3.40.2, and *Atharva.*, 20.6.2. (b) I have interpreted (2-4) verses taking Indra to mean electricity. Pt. Jaidev Vidyalankar has referred to God, king and teacher as well.

HYMN VIII

१. एवा पाहि प्रत्नथा मन्दतु त्वा श्रुधि ब्रह्म वावृधस्वोत गीर्भिः ।
आविः सूर्यं कृणुहि पीपिहीषो जहि शत्रूँरभि गा इन्द्र तृन्धि ।।

1. O the Almighty, Thou alone maintainest this universe as of old (i.e., in the previous creation). Let it be a source of pleasure to Thee. Hear the Ved-mantras (recited by us, Thy devotees) and thus Thy Greatness be enhanced by our speeches. You bring the sun to light. You fulfil the desires of your subjects and nourish them with food, etc. Let all our enemies be destroyed, with all their organs cut-off. (5009)

२. अर्वाङेहि सोमकामं त्वाहुरयं सुतस्तस्य पिबा मदाय ।
उरुव्यचा जठर आ वृषस्व पितेव नः शृणुहि हूयमानः ।।

2. O Adorable God, reveal Thyself to all of us. They call Thee 'Desirous of Creation.' Here is this created universe. Let Thee drink deep of it for the sake of pleasure Pervading it through and through saturate it with peace and grace. Being called, listen to us like a father. (5010)

३. आपूर्णो अस्य कलशः स्वाहा सेक्तेव कोशं सिसिचे पिबध्यै ।
समु प्रिया आववृत्रन्मदाय प्रदक्षिणिदभि सोमास इन्द्रम् ।।

3. This universe of His is fully complete in every way and well-spoken of in the Vedas. Like an irrigator, He irrigates this reservoir of all choicest blessings for the satisfaction of His people. All the loving devotees, surrounding Him from all sides, sit well around Him. (5011)[1]

HYMN IX

१. तं वो दस्ममृतीषहं वसोर्मन्दानमन्धसः । अभि वत्सं न स्वसरेषु धेनव इन्द्रं गीर्भिर्नवामहे ।।

1. Just as the cows rush towards their calves at the night-fall so do we worship with our songs of praises the Adorable God, Who is so charming to look at by you (i.e., the people in general) the Destroyer of all evils, the showerer of all joys from wealth and foodgrains, etc. (5012)[2]

२. द्युक्षं सुदानुं तविषीभिरावृतं गिरिं न पुरुभोजसम् ।
क्षुमन्तं वाजं शतिनं सहस्रिणं मक्षू गोमन्तमीमहे ।।

2. We always pray to God, the Radiant, the Good Donor, Equipped with all sort of powers, the Giver of many eatables like a mountain to grant us wealth of foodgrains, cattle, with hundreds and thousands of riches of all kinds. (5013)[3]

३. तत्त्वा यामि सुवीर्यं तद् ब्रह्म पूर्वचित्तये ।
येना यतिभ्यो भृगवे धने हिते येन प्रस्कण्वमाविथ ।।

[1]God, being Omnipresent, cannot be surrounded by His devotee. It is in the recesses of their hearts in deep meditation, that they a feeling of engulfing Him in high rapture, although He is All-pervading. It is a figurative language to describe the highest bliss of the yogis.

[2]cf. *Rig*, 8.78.1. [3]cf. *Rig*, 8.88.2.

3. O God, I (Thy devotee) approach Thee, for acquiring complete knowledge to give me that noble energy and that Vedic lore, by which Thou protectest the self-controlled, the learned people, capable of shunning off all the evil-propensities and the highly intellectual person, with appropriate money for their well-being and livelihood. (5014)[1]

४. येना समुद्रमसृजो महीरपस्तदिन्द्र वृष्णि ते शवः ।
सद्यः सो अस्य महिमा न संनशे यं क्षोणीरनुचक्रदे ॥

4. O the Almighty, that is Thy peace-showering might, by which Thou createst the sea and the mighty waters thereof. O people, that Grandeur of His cannot be surpassed at once. All the creatures of the world constantly speak of it. (5015)[2]

HYMN X

१. उदु त्ये मधुमत्तमा गिर स्तोमास ईरते ।
सत्राजितो धनसा अक्षितोतयो वाजयन्तो रथा इव ॥

1. Just as the warriors in strong and stout military vehicles or aeroplanes, equipped with invincible means of defence, distributing money all along and conquering all together in a single attack, rush headlong on their assault against the foe, so do these sweetest songs of praises, gush out of our hearts. (5016)

२. कण्वा इव भृगवः सूर्या इव विश्वमिद्धीतमानशुः ।
इन्द्रं स्तोमेभिर्महयन्त आयवः प्रियमेधासो अस्वरन् ॥

2. Just as the wise people, like evil-smashing pious persons, equipped with brilliant knowledge like the Sun, acquire the knowledge of the whole of the universe in deep contemplation so do those persons, to whom intellect is very dear, and who worship the Adorable God with songs of praises, do preach the same to others. (5017)[3]

HYMN XI

१. इन्द्रः पूर्भिदातिरद्दासमर्कैर्विदद्वसुर्दयमानो वि शत्रून् ।
ब्रह्मजूतस्तन्वा॒ वावृधानो भूरिदात्र आपृणद्रोदसी उभे ॥

1. The Glorious God, the Smasher of the heavenly spheres at the time of the total annihilation of the universe, empowers His subject, the soul, by the rays of light of the Vedas, dispells all his (soul's) foes in the form of drawbacks and foibles, impelled by Vedic prayers and thus enhanced in grandeur and vast glory, distribute His bounties in plenty, and pervades both the heavens and the earth. (5018)[4]

२. मखस्य ते तविषस्य प्र जूतिमियर्मि वाचममृताय भूषन् ।
इन्द्र क्षितीनामसि मानुषीणां विशां दैवीनामुत पूर्वयावा ॥

[1]cf. *Rig*, 8.3.9. [2]cf. *Rig*, 8.3.10. Pt. Jai Dev Vidyalankar has referred it to the king also. Griffith's talking of special Rishis by Bhrigu, Kanva and Praskanva is due to ignorance of the etymology of the Vedic words.

[3](1-2) cf. *Rig*, 8.3. (15-16). This sukta can also be applied to infallible weapons of destruction like the Brahmastra in the Mahābharata. But that requires thorough research.

[4](1-11) cf. *Rig*, 3.34. The sukta may be applied to the king also.

2. O mighty God, Thou art the Primal refuge of Thy subjects, the men and the natural forces like the Sun, the moon etc., well stationed in Thee. Desirous of being capable of attaining salvation I approach the fast energy and the vast Vedic speech of Thee, the Omnipotent and the Adorable. (5019)

३. इन्द्रो वृत्रमवृणोच्छर्धनीतिः प्र मायिनाममिनाद्वर्पणीतिः ।
अहन्व्यंऽसमुशधग्वनेष्वाविर्धेना अकृणोद्राम्याणाम् ॥

3. God, the Evil-Destroyer, utilising His mighty power, effaces all traces of ignorance and darkness, and revealing His deftness in various forms, completely puts an end to all the machinations of the deceitful persons. He shatters all evil to pieces, just as the fire in the jungle reduces everything to ashes. It is He, Who reveals the Vedic Richas through the sages, who revel in Him in the beginning of the creation. (5020)

४. इन्द्रः स्वर्षा जनयन्नहानि जिगायोशिग्भिः पृतना अभिष्टिः ।
प्रारोचयन्मनवे केतुमह्नामविन्दज्ज्योतिर्बृहते रणाय ॥

4. The Splendorous and Peace-showering God, the Fulfiller of all desires, creating the shining spheres, overpowers all the subjects with His overwhelming glory. He makes the sun shine for man to dispel darkness. He displays the highest lustre for the yogis to revel in the highest bliss. (5021)

५. इन्द्रस्तुजो बर्हणा आ विवेश नृवद्दधानो नर्या पुरूणि ।
अचेतयद्धिय इमा जरित्रे प्रेमं वर्णमतिरच्छुक्रमासाम् ॥

5. Just as the chief commander of the army provides numerous things for the comfort and protection of his men, so does the Almighty God, by His All-moving Powers, maintains many spheres, fit for the abode of men, and pervades them all. He inspires all these thinking powers and actions of the worshipper and enhances the pure form thereof. (5022)

६. महो महानि पनयन्त्यस्येन्द्रस्य कर्म सुकृता पुरूणि ।
वृजनेन वृजिनान्त्सं पिपेष मायाभिर्दस्यूँरभिभूत्योजाः ॥

6. The learned persons praise the great, good deeds of this Almighty Creator, Who possessing overpowering valour grinds to dust all the wicked people by His evil-destroying powers and thoroughly crushes the mischief-mongers by His dextrous acts. (5023)

७. युधेन्द्रो मह्ना वरिवश्चकार देवेभ्यः सत्पतिश्चर्षणिप्राः ।
विवस्वतः सदने अस्य तानि विप्रा उक्थेभिः कवयो गृणन्ति ॥

7. The Mighty God, Who is the Lord of the virtuous and the Fulfiller of the desires of men, creates many good things and qualities for the divine beings and forces by His evil-quelling might. Under the shelter of this Radiant God shining like the sun, the wise sages preach those divine qualities through the Ved-mantras. (5024)

८. सत्रासाहं वरेण्यं सहोदां ससवांसं स्वऽरपश्च देवीः ।
ससान यः पृथिवीं द्यामुतेमामिन्द्रं मदन्त्यनु धीरणासः ॥

8. The yogis, who revel in deep meditation, enjoy the bliss after the peace-showering God, Who sustains this vast earth and the heavens, overpowers all with His lonely might, is worthy of choice by all, the Giver of all powers, and is the maintainer of the celestial bodies and the divine actions and laws for regulating them. (5025)

९. ससानात्याँ उत सूर्यं ससानेन्द्रः ससान पुरुभोजसं गाम् ।
हिरण्ययमुतभोगं ससान हत्वी दस्यून्प्रार्यं वर्णमावत् ॥

9. The Fortune-showering God grants us (the souls) the fast-moving organs of the body, as well as the light of knowledge like the Sun. He gives us power of speech, the cow and the earth the sources of enjoyable objects. He showers on us wealth, and all means of enjoyment of life. Destroying the wicked, He protects the good and the virtuous people, like Brahmans, Kshatriya, Vaishya and Shudras and others. (5026)[1]

१०. इन्द्र ओषधीरसनोदहानि वनस्पतीँरसनोदन्तरिक्षम् ।
बिभेद वलं नुनुदे विवाचोऽथाभवद्दमिताभिक्रतूनाम् ॥

10. The Bounteous God gives us (the souls) the energising herbs and plants. He provides us days for working, the big trees for comfort and shelter as well as the atmosphere to breathe in and move freely about. He dispels the darkness or ignorance and revolves all those who speak ill of or anything against us (the devotees). Then He becomes the controller or pacificer of those, who perform good deeds or acquire good knowledge. (5027)

११. शुनं हुवेम मघवानमिन्द्रमस्मिन्भरे नृतमं वाजसातौ ।
शृण्वन्तमुग्रमूतये समत्सु घ्नन्तं वृत्राणि संजितं धनानाम् ॥

11. In this great sacrifice for acquiring knowledge, power, and wealth, we (the devotees) call for help the Adorable God, the most Virtuous, the most Bountiful, the Best of all leaders, the Listener of the people's prayers for help and protection, the most Terrible for the wicked, the Destroyer of all impediments in the path of deep contemplation of the yogis and the conqueror of all riches and fortunes. (5028)

HYMN XII

१. उदु ब्रह्माण्यैरत श्रवस्येन्द्रं समर्ये महया वसिष्ठ ।
आ यो विश्वानि शवसा ततानोपश्रोता म ईवतो वचांसि ॥

1. O learned people, chant aloud the Ved-mantras, full of true knowledge, revealed to the Rishis in the beginning of the universe. Well-disciplined scholar, sing, amongst the assembled people, the glory of the Almighty God, Who has spread all the worlds by His might and pervades them all and Who listens to the prayers of the worshipper like me. (5029)[2]

[1](a) (9) Others: nishad, as five kinds of people are sometimes mentioned. (b) The whole of this sukta can be applied in the case of a king too. (c) cf. *Rig.*, 3.34. (1-11).

[2](1-6) cf. *Rig*, 7.23. (1-6), and (7) cf. *Rig*, 5.40.4.

२. अयामि घोष इन्द्र देवजामिरिरज्यन्त यच्छुरुधो विवाचि ।
नहि स्वमायुश्चिकिते जनेषु तानीदंहांस्यति पर्ष्यस्मान् ॥

2. O mighty Lord, this loud cry, friendly to the brave warriors, or the learned people, is raised and highly enhanced by those who speedily check the onslaught of the enemy in the battlefield, wherein all sorts of voices are heard. None among the people knows the duration of his life. It is Thou, Who enables us to overcome all evils, to avoid cutting short of our life. (5030)[1]

३. युजे रथं गवेषणं हरिभ्यामुप ब्रह्माणि जुजुषाणमस्थुः ।
वि बाधिष्ट स्य रोदसी महित्वेन्द्रो वृत्राण्यप्रती जघन्वान् ॥

3. I (a devotee) unite my soul in deep meditation, with all the sense-organs fully engrossed, being impelled by Prān and Apān, the two powerful horses. All the people worship the most Powerful Lord of the Vedas. The self-same mighty God, dispelling all forces of ignorance and darkness, upholds the earth and the heavens in a befitting manner. (5031)

४. आपश्चित्पिप्यु स्तर्यो३ न गावो नक्षन्नृतं जरितारस्त इन्द्र ।
याहि वायुर्न नियुतो नो अच्छा त्वं हि धीभिर्दयसे वि वाजान् ॥

4. Just as the vast earths, the cows and the rays prosper and progress by coming in contact with waters, so do the Ved-mantras and worshippers' prosper. O mighty God, approaching Thee, the Peace-showerer and Thy true knowledge. Just air attains all sorts of speed and power, so dost Thou move with all forces of action and movement. Truly dost Thou invest us with all kinds of food, power, knowledge and wealth by Thy wisdom and power of action. (5032)

५. ते त्वा मदा इन्द्र मादयन्तु शुष्मिणं तुविराधसं जरित्रे ।
एको देवत्रा दयसे हि मर्तानस्मिञ्छूर सवने मादयस्व ॥

5. O the Radiant God, all those various kinds of joys and pleasures gush out of Thee, the Almighty and Lord of innumerable riches and fortunes, for the sake of the worshipper. O Omnipotent, Thou alone of all the divine forces, protectest the mortals and rejoicest in this creation of Thine. (5033)

६. एवेदिन्द्रं वृषणं वज्रबाहुं वसिष्ठासो अभ्यर्चन्त्यर्कैः ।
स न स्तुतो वीरवद्धातु गोमद्यूयं पात स्वस्तिभिः सदा नः ॥

6. The well-poised learned devotees worship, with various praise-songs, the Mighty Lord, with Thunderbolt-like power of gripping, the Showerer of comforts and blessings, in this way alone. Thus praised, may He grant us wealth of brave offspring and cattle. O people, let you all ever guard us with means of peace and happiness (5034)

[1]The verse may be interpreted as below: O Electricity, this high sound accompanied by friendly natural forces, is raised. The aerials speedily checking it, amplify it in the sets, producing sounds of various sorts. None among the people know the duration of the sound-wave. It is thou (i.e., electricity) which enablest the sound-waves to cross all hurdles in the way.

७. ऋजीषी वज्री वृषभस्तुराषाट्छुष्मी राजा वृत्रहा सोमपावा ।
युक्त्वा हरिभ्यामुप यासदर्वाङ् माध्यंदिने सवने मत्सदिन्द्रः ॥

7. Let the Glorious God, the Lord of all fortunes, the Emblem of destruction of evil and ignorance, the showerer of all comforts, the conqueror of the fast-moving foes of humanity, the Powerful, the Radiant, the Dispeller of darkness of ignorance, the Generator of the essence of medicines, and of bliss in salvation, united with His forces of attraction and sustenance. He reveals Himself to the yogis in deep contemplation and shines like the mid-day sun in their hearts. (5035)

HYMN XIII

१. इन्द्रश्च सोमं पिबतं बृहस्पतेऽस्मिन्यज्ञे मन्दसाना वृषण्वसू ।
आ वां विशन्त्विन्दवः स्वाभुवोऽस्मे रयिं सर्ववीरं नि यच्छतम् ॥

1. O King or commander and the Vedic scholar, both of you are the givers of riches and place of shelter to the people. Enjoy the pleasure of governing and guiding the nation, rejoicing in this act of sacrifice and service to it. The fame and glory, automatically coming out of this act, may engulf you. Let you grant us wealth of the brave and valorous persons. (5036)[1]

२. आ वो वहन्तु सप्तयो रघुष्यदो रघुपत्वानः प्र जिगात बाहुभिः ।
सीदता बर्हिरुरु वः सदस्कृतं मादयध्वं मरुतो मध्वो अन्धसः ॥

2. O brave and the learned persons, moving fast like the wind, let the fast-moving horses, the automobiles or the gliders carry you in all directions. Rushing speedily on your feet or wheels, thoroughly conquer the foes with strong arms or missiles. Be seated on the throne. Here is a grand palace built for you. Enjoy yourselves with sweet dishes of rich food. (5037)[2]

३. इमं स्तोममर्हते जातवेदसे रथमिव सं महेमा मनीषया ।
भद्रा हि नः प्रमतिरस्य संसद्यग्ने सख्ये मा रिषामा वयं तव ॥

3. We eulogise this praise-song for the Praiseworthy Lord of the Vedas or the Vedic scholar, with our well-disciplined intellect, just as a chariot or car or vehicle or plane is well-equipped before the ride. In the assembly or the company of this king or the scholar, let our power of thinking be gracious. O King, commander, or the learned person, let us not feel troubled in your company. (5038)[3]

४. ऐभिरग्ने सरथं याह्यर्वाङ् नानारथं वा विभवो ह्यश्वाः ।
पत्नीवतस्त्रिंशतं त्रींश्च देवाननुष्वधमा वह मादयस्व ॥

4. O King, commander or the learned scholar, come, along with these brave persons, in your chariot, car or plane, accompanied by numerous cars or planes of others in the vanguard. May your fast cavalcade or squadron have a special striking power. Let all the thirty-three divine powers, along with

[1]cf. *Rig*, 4.50.10. [2]cf. *Rig*, 1.85.6. [3]cf. *Rig*, 1.94.1.

subsidiary energies, enhanced by suitable processes be carried along with you and be a source of pleasure and joy for you. (5039)[1]

Chapter (Anuvāka) 2

HYMN XIV

१. वयमु त्वामपूर्व्य स्थूरं न कच्चिद्भरन्तोऽवस्यवः । वाजे चित्रं हवामहे ॥

1. O Peeless one, we (the people) desirous of protection, cherishing Thee with our homage, like some strong and steady person, call Thee, the Wonderful, for help in war. (5040)[2]

२. उप त्वा कर्मन्नूतये स नो युवोग्रश्चक्राम यो धृषत् ।
त्वामिद्धयवितारं ववृमहे सखाय इन्द्र सानसिम् ॥

2. O mighty king, we, the people, approach thee in all acts and for protection. Thou art the most youthful and terrible amongst us. We make thee, the commander who can subdue the enemy. We, thy friends choose thee alone as our protector and distributor of riches and wealth. (5041)

३. यो न इदमिदं पुरा प्र वस्य आनिनाय तमु व स्तुषे । सखाय इन्द्रमूतये ।

3. O friends, I sing praises and seek the protection of the king, who brought us all sorts of comforts and riches before. (5042)

४. हर्यश्वं सत्पतिं चर्षणीसहं स हि ष्मा यो अमन्दत ।
आ तु नः स वयति गव्यमश्व्यं स्तोतृभ्यो मघवा शतम् ॥

4. I sing the praises of the king, who is equipped with fast-moving vehicles, is the guardian of the virtuous people, and can keep the people well under control. It is he who is ever cheerful and keeps others happy and joyful. Such a fortunate personality bestows on us, his faithful subjects, hundreds of riches and wealth of cattle i.e., milch cows and fast horses. (5043)

HYMN XV*

१. प्र मंहिष्ठाय बृहते बृहद्रये सत्यशुष्माय तवसे मतिं भरे ।
अपामिव प्रवणे यस्य दुर्धरं राधो विश्वायु शवसे अपावृतम् ॥

1. I (a Vedic scholar) preach the knowledge of the most Adorable, the Omnipotent, of Invincible Power of Truth, the most Powerful the source of the Highest motion, Whose uncontrollable Prowess is revealed in all directions and at all times, for deeds of valour and energy, just as waters flow with the highest speed from upper regions to the lower ones. (5044)

[1]cf. *Rig*, 3.6.9. Thirty-three: 12 Adityas, 11 Rudras, 8 Vasus, Indra and Prajapati, i.e., all these natural forces must be utilised for making useful means of conveyance and defence by a king, commander or a learned person.

[2](1-4) cf. *Rig*, 8.21. (1, 2, 9, 10).

*(1-6) (a) cf. *Rig*, 1.57. (1-6). (b) It can be interpreted in the case of a king and electricity as well. (c) (i) Electricity also runs speedily from higher potentiality to lower one. (ii) The verse refers to the powerful source of energy of waters and electricity for production of all sorts. (iii) Telephone, radio, electric motors or engines, television and radar, etc. are meant.

२. अध ते विश्वमनु हासदिष्टय आपो निम्नेव सवना हविष्मतः ।
यत्पर्वते न समशीत हर्यत इन्द्रस्य वज्रः श्नथिता हिरण्ययः ॥

2. Just as all productive works of the manufacturer depend upon waters flowing downward with speed, so do all the desired objects of him depend upon thee, i.e., electricity, king or God, as its powerful striking force cannot be obstructed by any cloud, or mountain in the way, It smashes all impediments, with its radiant energy. (5045)

३. अस्मै भीमाय नमसा समध्वर उषो न शुभ्र आ भरा पनीयसे ।
यस्य धाम श्रवसे नामेन्द्रियं ज्योतिरकारि हरितो नायसे ॥

3. O well-versed engineer make use of this terrible electric power fit to be utilised for useful purposes by controlling it, for non-violent, brilliant light like the dawn. It has the potentiality to help hearing, control, energy and spread light in all quarters. (5046)

४. इमे त इन्द्र ते वयं पुरुष्टुत ये त्वारभ्य चरामसि प्रभूवसो ।
नहि त्वदन्यो गिर्वणो गिरः सघत्क्षोणीरिव प्रति नो हर्य तद्वचः ॥

4. O Lord of Fortunes, the most Adorable, we, the devotees, who do all our works, placing Thee in the fore-front, are all Thine alone, none else than Thee deserves our praises. Listen to our prayers like the all-tolerant earth. (5047)

५. भूरि त इन्द्र वीर्यं१ तव स्मस्यस्य स्तोतुर्मघवन्काममा पृण ।
अनु ते द्यौर्बृहती वीर्यं मम इयं च ते पृथिवी नेम ओजसे ॥

5. Far Great is Thy Prowess, O mighty Lord, we are Thine. O Lord of Riches, fulfil the desire of this devotee of Thine. These vast heavens are mere creations of Thy Energy. This earth also bows to Thy splendour. (5048)

६. त्वं तमिन्द्र पर्वतं महामुरुं वज्रेण वज्रिन्पर्वशश्चकर्तिथ ।
अवासृजो निवृताः सर्तवा अपः सत्रा विश्वं दधिषे केवलं सहः ॥

6. Just as thundering-electricity reduces the vast cloud to nothing by its thunderbolt, so dost thou, O king, equipped with piercing weapons like the thunderbolt, smash into pieces the vast armies of the enemy, consisting of various units, by your striking power like the thunderbolt. Just as the waters of the cloud released by the electricity, fall down and flow over the earth, similarly the well-equipped armies of the enemy; being subdued by the might of the king, are duly regulated by him. Truly dost thou alone, O king, hold all the power to subdue the foes. (5049)

HYMN XVI*

१. उदप्रुतो न वयो रक्षमाणा वावदतो अभ्रियस्येव घोषाः ।
गिरिभ्रजो नोर्मयो मदन्तो बृहस्पतिमभ्य१र्का अनावन् ॥

1. Just as the birds, flying up from the surface of water, for the protection of their lives, and just as the continually thundering clouds produce sounds, just as the water currents flowing rapidly down the slopes of the mountains,

*(1-12) cf. *Rig*, 10.68. (1-12).

produce sounds, so do the worshippers, reciting the Ved-mantras and revelling in His Bliss, sing the praises of the mighty Lord of the Vedic Lore. (5050)[1]

२. सं गोभिराङ्गिरसो नक्षमाणो भग इवेदर्यमणं निनाय ।
जने मित्रो न दम्पती ग्रनक्ति बृहस्पते वाजयाशूँरिवाजौ ।।

2. Just as the Vedic scholar, with his learned talks, and the distributor of wealth, enlarging the prestige of the nation, keep the just king on the right path, just as a friendly person enlightens the couple with the right guidance, amongst the populace, so mayst thou, O Vedic scholar, enhance the courage and valour of the fast-moving warrior, horses vehicles, etc., in a war. (5051)

३. साध्वर्या ग्रतिथिनीरिषिरा स्पार्हाः सुवर्णा ग्रनवद्यरूपाः ।
बृहस्पतिः पर्वतेभ्यो वितूर्या निर्गा ऊपे यवमिव स्थिविभ्यः ।।

3. Just as a farmer separates pure barley from the husks from the winnowing baskets, so does the Sun release from the clouds its straight, pure, useful (hence worthy of respect) the fast-moving, charming, beautiful rays of blameless form; and so does a Vedic scholar separate from the nourishing parents their daughters, the would-be good house-wives, respectable like a guest, moved by desire for domestic life, lovable, good-looking and of blemishless form, and offers them in marriage to the well-disciplined persons for procreation like the meteor from the sky. (5052)

४. ग्राप्रुषायन्मधुन ऋतस्य योनिमवक्षिपन्नर्क उल्कामिव द्योः ।
बृहस्पतिरुद्धरन्नश्मनो गा भूम्या उद्नेव वि त्वचं बिभेद ।।

4. Just as the Sun, felling down the cloud (i.e., the store-house of water, completely irrigates the earth with water, so does a Vedic scholar, picking up Vedic speeches from the Omnipresent God, dispels the darkness of ignorance from his disciple's heart, as the crust of the earth is corroded away by water. (5053)

५. अप ज्योतिषा तमो ग्रन्तरिक्षादुद्नः शीपालमिव वात ग्राजत् ।
बृहस्पतिरनुमृश्या वलस्याभ्रमिव वात ग्रा चक्र ग्रा गाः ।।

5. Just as the fast wind removes the moss from the surface of water, similarly does the Sun efface darkness from the atmosphere by its light. Just as the strong wind, dispersing the darkening cloud, reveals the rays of the Sun, so does a Vedic scholar dispelling the forces of darkness and ignorance, spreads the light of knowledge all around. (5054)

६. यदा वलस्य पीयतो जसुं भेद् बृहस्पतिरग्नितपोभिरर्कैः ।
दद्भिर्न जिह्वा परिविष्टमाददाविर्निधीँरकृणोदुस्रियाणाम् ।।

6. When the Sun breaks away the force of the engulfing cloud by its heating rays, just as the tongue gulfs the morsel, chewn by the teeth, it breaks open the treasures of its rays, similarly, the Vedic scholar effacing the forces of the darkness of ignorance by his energising forces of knowledge, like the

tongue taking in the morsel, well-chewn by the teeth, he lays bear the storehouse of beams of knowledge. (5055)

७. बृहस्पतिरमत हि त्यदासां नाम स्वरीणां सदने गुहा यत् ।
आण्डेव भित्वा शकुनस्य गर्भमुदुस्रियाः पर्वतस्य त्मनाजत् ॥

7. When the Vedic scholar realises the full import of these enlightening Ved-mantras, hidden deep in the Invisible source of theirs (i.e., God), he reveals them with his own power of knowledge, as the rays of light from the Almighty Father, just like the mother-bird, taking out its young one by breaking open the egg. (5056)

८. अश्नापिनद्धं मधु पर्यपश्यन्मत्स्यं न दीन उदनि क्षियन्तम् ।
निष्टज्जभार चमसं न वृक्षाद् बृहस्पतिर्विरवेणा विकृत्य ॥

8. Just as the people can easily see the fish, living in a shallow water, similarly does the great Vedic scholar perceive the sweet knowledge of the Vedas, lying hidden in the All-pervading God. He extracts it by explaining the Vedic words with special exposition, just as a carpenter carves out a ladle from the tree (i.e., wood). (5057)

९. सोषामविन्दत्स स्वः सो अग्निं सो अर्केण वि बबाधे तमांसि ।
बृहस्पतिर्गोवपुषो वलस्य निर्मज्जानं न पर्वणो जभार ॥

9. He (the learned Vedic scholar) attains the splendour of the dawn. He attains the bliss of God. He gets united with God, the source of all knowledge and Energy. He removes all traces of darkness and ignorance by the sun-like light of learning. He brings out self-knowledge from the darkening ignorance which shuts out all forms of literature from the masses like the marrow, brought out of bone-joints. (5058)

१०. हिमेव पर्णा मुषिता वनानि बृहस्पतिनाकृपयद्वलो गाः ।
अनानुकृत्यमपुनश्चकार यात्सूर्यामासा मिथ उच्चरातः ॥

10. Just as the leaves of the trees of the jungles are withered away by frost or snow, similarly the Vedic Richas are imbibed and their vocal form strengthened and energised by the great Vedic seer. This act of revelation is done by none else and not repeated again (i.e., It is done once only in the very beginning of the creation only). From thence the teacher and the disciple, like the sun and the moon, together repeat the same Vedic Lore between themselves (i.e., The Vedic lore, once revealed in the beginning of the universe, is transferred from the teacher to the disciple from generation to generation till its end). (5059)

११. अभि श्यावं न कृशनेभिरश्वं नक्षत्रेभिः पितरो द्यामपिंशन् ।
रात्र्यां तमो अदधुर्ज्योतिरहन्बृहस्पतिर्भिनदद्रिं विदद्गाः ॥

11. Just as the people decorate the black steed with ornaments like the pearl-necklaces, etc., similarly do the protecting forces of nature decorate the heavens with numerous constellations. These forces allot darkness to the night and light to the day. The Sun shatters the cloud of darkness and reveals the rays. (5060)

१२. इदमकर्म नमो अभ्रियाय यः पूर्वीरन्वानोनवीति ।
बृहस्पतिः स हि गोभिः सो अश्वैः स वीरेभिः स नृभिर्नो वयो धात् ॥

12. We pay this homage to the learned person, who rains down the previously revealed Vedic teachings. May he invest us with food, power, knowledge, action and life, with the help of cows, horses, brave sons and other leading men. (5061)

HYMN XVII*

१. अच्छा म इन्द्रं मतयः स्वर्विदः सध्रीचीर्विश्वा उशतीरनूषत ।
परि ष्वजन्ते जनयो यथा पतिं मर्यं न शुन्ध्युं मघवानमूतये ॥

1. Just as the women, overwhelmed with desire, embrace the beautiful person, as their husband, so do all my yearning devotional praise-songs, full of the light of knowledge, expressive of all desires in perfect unison serve the Adorable God, the Lord of all fortunes. (5062)

२. न घा त्वद्रिगप वेति मे मनस्त्वे इत्कामं पुरुहूत शिश्रय ।
राजेव दस्म नि षदोऽधि बर्हिष्यस्मिन्त्सु सोमेऽवपानमस्तु ते ॥

2. O much-invoked God, my mind has fully set all its desires on Thee. It does not go astray from Thee. O Beautiful One, Thou art well-installed in this vast universe like a king on his throne. Let Thy satisfying sweet juice of spiritual knowledge be installed in this soul (i.e., of devotee). (5063)

३. विषूवृदिन्द्रो अमतेरुत क्षुधः स इद्रायो मघवा वस्व ईशते ।
तस्येदिमे प्रवणे सप्त सिन्धवो वयो वर्धन्ति वृषभस्य शुष्मिणः ॥

3. The Lord of all fortunes removes poverty and hunger. He alone, the master of fortunes, the settler of all the people, rules over all riches. These seven rivers flowing down the current of creation enhance the power of the Almighty God, the showerer of all blessings, alone. (5064)[1]

४. वयो न वृक्षं सुपलाशमासदन्त्सोमास इन्द्रं मन्दिनश्चमूषदः ।
प्रैषामनीकं शवसा दविद्युतद्विदत्स्व१र्मनवे ज्योतिरार्यम् ॥

4. Just as the birds sit on a tree, with good foliage, similarly do the happy military officers and the leaders thereof take shelter under the king. Their armies shine with the splendour of power and daring and shed pure light of peace and plenty on the common masses.

Or

In case of soul and God :

Just as the birds perch on a tree, with large foliage, similarly do the revelling yogis, immersed in the bliss of God, take refuge under the Blissful God. Their face shines with the Glory of God and shed an aura of pure spiritual light all around on the people in general. (5065)

*cf. *Rig*, 10.43. (1-11), and 7.97.10.

[1]Seven rivers: Mahat, Ahankar and five Bhutas, the source of all creation; seven dhatus in the body of man to maintain it.

५. कृतं न श्वघ्नी वि चिनोति देवने संवर्गं यन्मघवा सूर्यं जयत् ।
न तत्ते अन्यो अनु वीर्यं शकन्न पुराणो मघवन्नोत नूतनः ॥

5. As the self-ruining gambler piles up his winnings, so does the darkness-effacing Sun is won by the Lord of Fortunes. O Glorious God, none else, neither the old one, nor the new one, can subdue that Power of Thine. (5066)

६. विशंविशं मघवा पर्यशायत जनानां धेना अवचाकशद् वृषा ।
यस्याह शक्रः सवनेषु रण्यति स तीव्रैः सोमैः सहते पृतन्यतः ॥

6. All sorts of people have an easy access to the Lord of Fortunes. The Showerer of Blessings keeps in view all the calls of the people. The devotee, in whose mental sacrifices or spiritual struggles, the Almighty Father revels (i.e., is pleased to help), puts down all the opposing forces of evil by strong, calming forces of the spirit. (5067)

७. आपो न सिन्धुमभि यत्समक्षरन्त्सोमास इन्द्रं कुल्या इव ह्रदम् ।
वर्धन्ति विप्रा महो अस्य सादने यवं न वृष्टिर्दिव्येन दानुना ॥

7. As the waters flow down to the sea and small streams to a reservoir of water, so do the salvation-seekers approach the most Adorable God and being specially filled with His Bliss, enhance His Glory, under His shelter, just as the rain enhance barley by rain-drops from heaven. (5068)

८. वृषा न क्रुद्धः पतयद्रजःस्वा यो अर्यपत्नीरकृणोदिमा अपः ।
स सुन्वते मघवा जीरदानवेऽविन्दज्ज्योतिर्मनवे हविष्मते ॥

8. He, who makes these natural forces, the controlled protective powers of the master, Himself, pervades all the regions like a furious bull. He, the Lord of Riches, displays His Brilliance to the living person, who offers his oblations, with devotion and prayers. (5069)

९. उज्जायतां परशुर्ज्योतिषा सह भूया ऋतस्य सुदुघा पुराणवत् ।
वि रोचतामरुषो भानुना शुचिः स्व१र्ण शुक्रं शुशुचीत सत्पतिः ॥

9. Let the axe, cutting asunder the forces of evil, rise along with the light of knowledge. Let the truth-bearing sharp intellect easily milking the nector, be in perfect unison with the Primal Lord. Let the refulgent soul specially shine with the brilliance of the spiritual Sun. May the Lord of the virtuous shed His splendour, pure and serene like the Sun. (5070)

१०. गोभिष्टरेमामतिं दुरेवां यवेन क्षुधं पुरुहूत विश्वाम् ।
वयं राजभिः प्रथमा धनान्यस्माकेन वृजनेना जयेम ॥

10. O much-invoked God, may be put down painful poverty by the help of our cattle and lands and remove all kinds of hunger by food-grains. We, the first in rank, allied with kings, may win riches and wealth by our power of repulsing the foes. (5071)

११. बृहस्पतिर्नः परि पातु पश्चादुतोत्तरस्मादधरादघायोः ।
इन्द्रः पुरस्तादुत मध्यतो नः सखा सखिभ्यो वरिवः कृणोतु ॥

11. May the Mighty Lord of the universe, the king or the Vedic scholar

protect us from the attacking foe from behind, above or below. May the Evil-Destroyer God, king or learned person, from the front-side or the middle. Being our friend, may He grant us, His friends riches and glory (5072)

१२. बृहस्पते युवमिन्द्रश्च वस्वो दिव्यस्येशाथे उत पार्थिवस्य ।
धत्तं रयिं स्तुवते कीरये चिद्यूयं पात स्वस्तिभिः सदा नः ॥

12. O Vedic scholar and the powerful king both of you contain the celestial and the terrestrial riches of all sorts. Invest the devoted, learned person with wealth and well-being. O learned persons, let you protect us, the people in general, by peaceful means. (5073)

Chapter (Anuvāka) 3

HYMN XVIII

१. वयमु त्वा तदिदर्था इन्द्र त्वायन्तः सखायः । कण्वा उक्थेभिर्जरन्ते ॥

1. O mighty God, we, the learned people. Thy friends, desirous of having communion with Thee, in this world as well as in the other world, sing Thy praises with Ved-mantras. (5074)[1]

२. न घेमन्यदा पपन वज्रिन्नपसो नविष्टौ । तवेदु स्तोमं चिकेत ॥

2. O Evil-Destroyer, I praise none else in the beginning of all actions of mine. I know only Thy praise-songs. (5075)

३. इच्छन्ति देवाः सुन्वन्तं न स्वप्नाय स्पृहयन्ति । यन्ति प्रमादमतन्द्राः ॥

3. The persons of divine qualities like the ever active people. They don't like the lazy and the idle ones. The ever-vigilant persons control their slothful nature. (5076)

४. वयमिन्द्र त्वायवोऽभि प्र णोनुमो वृषन् । विद्धी त्व१स्य नो वसो ॥

4. O Adorable God, the showerer of peace and blessings we, the devotees, desirous of attaining Thee, bow to Thee alone. O Settlers of all, Thou knowest this action of devotion of ours. (5077)[2]

५. मा नो निदे च वक्तवेऽर्यो रन्धीरराव्णे । त्वे अपि क्रतुर्मम ॥

5. O Lord of ours, let us not be put under the control of a reviler, the harsh-tongued one, or the miserly person. All thoughts, knowledge or actions of mine are set on Thee alone. (5078)

६. त्वं वर्मासि सप्रथः पुरोयोधश्च वृत्रहन् । त्वया प्रति ब्रुवे युजा ॥

6. O Destroyer of all forces of darkness and ignorance, Thou art the armour, being All-pervading and in the vanguard. Being united with Thee, I am capable of retaliating against my opponents. (5079)

HYMN XIX

१. वार्त्रहत्याय शवसे पृतनाषाह्याय च । इन्द्र त्वा वर्तयामसि ॥

[1](1-3) cf. *Rig*, 8.2. (16-18).
[2](4-6) cf. *Rig*, 7.31. (4-6).

1. O mighty God, king, commander or electricity, we turn to Thee for acquiring power and daring to destroy the mischief-monger and conquer the fighting forces of the foes. (5080)[1]

२. अर्वाचीनं सु ते मन उत चक्षुः शतक्रतो । इन्द्र कृण्वन्तु वाघतः ॥

2. O mighty God, king, commander or electricity, the Performer of hundred sacrifices we draw thy mind and eyes towards us by our praise-songs. (5081)

३. नामानि ते शतक्रतो विश्वाभिर्गीर्भिरीमहे । इन्द्राभिमातिषाह्ये ॥

3. O Indra, the Performer of numerous acts of daring and knowledge we invoke Thee in various forms through all our prayer-songs for subduing the proud enemy. (5082)

४. पुरुष्टुतस्य धामभिः शतेन महयामसि । इन्द्रस्य चर्षणीधृतः ॥

4. We, the devotees, enhance the glory of the most Adorable God, Who nourishes and supports all the people by His hundreds of sustaining powers and shelters. (5083)

५. इन्द्रं वृत्राय हन्तवे पुरुहूतमुप ब्रुवे । भरेषु वाजसातये ॥

5. We pray to the much-invoked Indra for destroying the evil-doer, and for distribution of wealth, food, power and knowledge at the time of wars. (5084)

६. वाजेषु सासहिर्भव त्वामीमहे शतक्रतो । इन्द्र वृत्राय हन्तवे ॥

6. O Indra of Diversified Powers, be the queller of foes in the wars. We cherish Thee for crushing the wicked enemy. (5085)

७. द्युम्नेषु पृतनाज्ये पृत्सुतूर्षु श्रवःसु च । इन्द्र साक्ष्वाभिमातिषु ॥

7. O mighty Lord, letest Thee be capable of acquiring wealth and riches, conquering the fighting forces of the foes in wars, destroying the enemy's armies in the war, acquisition of food-grains or performance of acts of valour and glory, and overpowering the proud adversary. (5086)

HYMN XX

१. शुष्मिन्तमं न ऊतये द्युम्निनं पाहि जागृविम् । इन्द्र सोमं शतक्रतो ॥

1. O mighty God, king, commander or electricity, the master of numerous of powers, protect the smart, ever vigilant, the wealthy and the most powerful person for our protection and safety. (5087)[2]

२. इन्द्रियाणि शतक्रतो या ते जनेषु पञ्चसु । इन्द्र तानि त आ वृणे ॥

2. O mighty Lord of various powers, whatever powers of vigilance and perception of Thine there are amongst the five kinds of people. I accept all these. (5088)[3]

३. अगन्निन्द्र श्रवो बृहद् द्युम्नं दधिष्व दुष्टरम् । उत्ते शुष्मं तिरामसि ॥

[1]cf. *Rig*, 3.37. (1-7)

[2](1-4) cf. *Rig*, 3.37. (8-11), (5-7) cf. *Rig*, 2.41. (10-12). [3]Five: Brahmaṇ, Kshatrya, Vaishaya, Shudra, Nishad.

3. O mighty Lord, you possess great Glory, and bear unlimited wealth and riches, and we enhance Thy might and power (i.e., by our praises). (5089)

४. अर्वावतो न आ गह्यथो शक्र परावतः । उ लोको यस्ते अद्रिव इन्द्रेह तत आ गहि ॥

4. O Almighty God, come to us from near as well as from afar. O mighty Lord of Invincible Prowess, come to us from whatever place of Thine is. (5090)[1]

५. इन्द्रो अङ्ग महद्भयमभी षदप चुच्यवत् । स हि स्थिरो विचर्षणिः ॥

5. Verily the mighty Lord, conquering all, drives away the mighty fear. He is firm and specially guards all the people against the evil. (5091)

६. इन्द्रश्च मृलयाति नो न नः पश्चादघं नशत् । भद्रं भवाति नः पुरः ॥

6. The Adorable God blesses us with peace and happiness. Let no evil and trouble assail us from behind. Let there be peace and well-being in our front. (5092)

७. इन्द्र आशाभ्यस्परि सर्वाभ्यो अभयं करत् । जेता शत्रून्विचर्षणिः ॥

7. Let Evil-Destroyer God, king, commander or electricity the conqueror of foes and the special guardian of the people, create fearlessness from all quarters. (5093)

HYMN XXI

१. न्यू३षु वाचं प्र महे भरामहे गिर इन्द्राय सदने विवस्वतः ।
नू चिद्धि रत्नं ससतामिवाविदन्न दुष्टुतिर्द्रविणोदेषु शस्यते ॥

1. We respectfully offer good praises for the mighty God. In the house of a devotee prayers go forth to thy Adorable Lord. Just as the precious wealth of the sleeping persons is stolen away by the thieves, so are the means of comforts and pleasures taken away from those, who slacken in their devotion to God. Hence any aversion to prayers does not behave the donors of wealth. (i.e., Those who want to be donors of riches to others, must realise the importance of daily prayers to the mighty God. (5094)[2]

२. दुरो अश्वस्य दुर इन्द्र गोरसि दुरो यवस्य वसुन इनस्पतिः ।
शिक्षानरः प्रदिवो अकामकर्शनः सखा सखिभ्यस्तमिदं गृणीमसि ॥

2. O mighty God, Thou art the Giver of the horse, or fast moving vehicles; of the cow, land, power of speech; of food-grains like barley etc. Thou art the Master and Ruler of all wealth and riches. Thou art the Educator of the people, and the Regulator of all behaviour not Impelled by any desire Thyself, Thou art the friend for the friends. We praise Thee such, as above. (5095)

३. शचीव इन्द्र पुरुकृद्द्युमत्तम तवेदिदमभितश्चेकिते वसु ।
अतः संगृभ्याभिभूत आ भर मा त्वायतो जरितुः काममूनयीः ॥

[1]God, being Omnipresent does not come from far and near. It is the realisation of God by the soul, that is meant for the devotee. He is near at hand, for the non-believers. He is far distant or rather, nowhere. But the time come when even the well-known atheists are flushed with the Refulgence of the Lord.

[2]cf. *Rig*, 1.53. (1-11)

3. O God, the Most-Powerful, the Creator of numerous worlds and the people, the most splendid, this vast wealth spread all around, is known to be Thine alone O Lord of fortunes of all quarters, gathering therefrom, invest us with it in full. Let not the desire of his who likes Thee and sings Thy praises, remain unfulfilled. (5096)

४. एभिर्द्युभिः सुमना एभिरिन्दुभिर्निरुन्धानो अमतिं गोभिरश्विना ।
इन्द्रेण दस्युं दरयन्त इन्दुभिर्युतद्वेषसः समिषा रभेमहि ॥

4. Well-pleased with these bright flames and sweet juices, Thou removest our poverty with the help of cows, lands, rays and power of speech, and horses and fast-moving vehicles. Crushing the usurping enemy with the help of the king, commander or the electric force and speedy mobile forces being freed from hatred, let us be equipped with power, knowledge and food. (5097)

५. समिन्द्र राया समिषा रभेमहि सं वाजेभिः पुरुश्चन्द्रैरभिद्युभिः ।
सं देव्या प्रमत्या वीरशुष्मया गोअग्रयाश्वावत्या रभेमहि ॥

5. O mighty Lord, let us be fully provided with plenteous wealth, food, powers and riches, with numerous means of pleasures and glory. Let us be united with the victorious army of brave warriors, equipped with speedy means of conveyance and transport and suitable instruments of rays like radar etc. (5098)

६. ते त्वा मदा अमदन्तानि वृष्ण्या ते सोमासो वृत्रहत्येषु सत्पते ।
यत्कारवे दश वृत्राण्यप्रति बर्हिष्मते नि सहस्राणि बर्हयः ॥

6. O Protector of the virtuous, may these cheering, powerful pleasure-giving brave warriors encourage thee in the destruction of the wicked, so that thou mayst completely inihilate tens of thousands of them at one stroke for the active, prosperous king. (5099)

७. युधा युधमुप घेदेषि धृष्णुया पुरा पुरं समिदं हंस्योजसा ।
नम्या यदिन्द्र सख्या परावति निबर्हयो नमुचिं नाम मायिनम् ॥

7. O Adorable God, Thou verily approachest the Yogi, seeking union with Thee by Thy evil-destroying and uniting power. By thy splendorous Prowess, Thou completely smashes the fortress of evil from Thy vast fortress of the universe. In the highest place of shelter, along with Thy humble friend, the yogi, mayst Thou fully set at liberty the person, who is too engrossed in the worldly affairs to be liberated with ease.

Or

O mighty king, thou can easily get at the striking power of the enemy by thy overwhelming striking force. Being well-entrenched in thy sheltered place of defence, thou canst thoroughly break the defences of the enemy to smithers. Completely crush the deceitful enemy, unfit to be left alive, through thy faithful ally, although stationed at a distance. (5100)[1]

[1]Griffith's refers to demons like Namuchi, etc., quite in disregard of etymological meanings of the words.

८. त्वं करञ्जमुत पर्णयं वधीस्तेजिष्ठयातिथिग्वस्य वर्तनी ।
त्वं शता वङ्गृदस्याभिनत्पुरोऽनानुदः परिषूता ऋजिश्वना ।।

8. O mighty king or electricity, thou killest the violent enemy, equipped with speedy means of communication like cars or airships, a hindrance in the way of the persons who are worthy of respect, cows or land by thy consuming and splendorous power. Thou shatterest hundred forts of the adversary who obstructs thy communications or breaks thy regulations and does not pay tributes to thee established by straightforward negotiations. (5101)[1]

९. त्वमेतां जनराज्ञो द्विर्दशाबन्धुना सुश्रवसोपजग्मुषः ।
षष्टिं सहस्रा नवतिं नव श्रुतो नि चक्रेण रथ्या दुष्पदावृणक् ।।

9. O king or commander, by means of thy encircling formation of the army units, which is too strong to be broken through by the enemy, thou art capable of checking the onslaught of even twenty kings or commanders and sixty thousand and ninety-nine warriors through the help of a single commander of well-known fame or renown, with none else to help him. This is ordained by the Vedas.

Or

O electricity, thou canst, by thy circular motion like the wheel of a chariot, which is too powerful to be checked, well keep under control all these twenty basic elements, sixty thousand and ninety-nine organic and inorganic bodies, by a single transmitter of high quality, with no other force to help it. (5102)[2]

१०. त्वमाविथ सुश्रवसं तवोतिभिस्तव त्रामभिरिन्द्र तूर्वयाणम् ।
त्वमस्मै कुत्समतिथिग्वमायुं महे राज्ञे यूने अरन्धनायः ।।

10. O mighty king, thou protectest this person of high refute, plenteous food-grains and knowledge by thy protecting means, as well as the commender, with speedy means of striking the enemy, with thy forces of protection and safety. Thou keepest in control the wicked as well as the respectable persons for the sake of this youthful, great prince.

Or

O electricity, thou keepest in safety this good listening set by thy means of safety and protectest the commander, with speedy mobile forces by thy strong means of defence. Thou controllest the sharp weapons, equipped with striking powers of limitless time and speed for this great, youthful king. (5103)[3]

११. य उदृचीन्द्र देवगोपाः सखायस्ते शिवतमा असाम ।
त्वां स्तोषाम त्वया सुवीरा द्राघीय आयुः प्रतरं दधानाः ।।

[1]In case of electricity—hundred forts—hundred elements. It breaks all these its power of fission, overcoming all resistances and obstructions in the way. Griffith's talk of demons like Kranga, Parnaya, Vangrida, Rijishvana is due to his aversion to interpret the Vedic words according to Nirukta and Nighantu.

[2]The verse refers to the military strategy of encircling the enemy forces to check their onward march by a single unit an expert military chief of an outstanding repute. or A single transmitter of high voltage can control all around.

[3]It is not the demons, as referred by Griffith, but the fatal weapons of high striking power of limitless time and speed that are meant here.

11. O mighty God, king, commander, or electricity, attaining the highest bliss, position or post, and being protected by divine forces, learned persons or pure organs, we may be Thy peaceful friends. Well-enervated by Thee, leading a very long and noble life we sing Thy praise-songs. (5104)

HYMN XXII

१. अभि त्वा वृषभा सुते सुतं सृजामि पीतये । तृम्पा व्यश्नुही मदम् ॥

1. O king, the showerer of peace and happiness among the people, I produce this rational wealth of production for the satisfaction of thee, who art well-installed in the country. Enjoy thyself to thy fill with all the means of pleasure and enjoyment. (5105)[1]

२. मा त्वा मूरा अविष्यवो मोपहस्वान आ दभन् । माकीं ब्रह्मद्विषो वनः ॥

2. O king, let not the foolish people, seeking thy protection or those who mock at thee overwhelm thee. Also love not those, who hate God, Vedas and the Vedic scholars. (5106)

३. इह त्वा गोपरीणसा महे मन्दन्तु राधसे । सरो गौरो यथा पिब ॥

3. Let the people please and satisfy thee with large means of pleasure and satisfaction, like the sweet juices with cow's milk and other products of the land, for great fortunes. Let thee enjoy thyself to thy fill, like the deer at the tank of water. (5107)

४. अभि प्र गोपतिं गिरेन्द्रमर्च यथा विदे । सूनुं सत्यस्य सत्पतिम् ॥

4. O man, worship well the Adorable God, or the king, the Protector of the earth, speech or sense-organs, the Lord of the virtuous and the Generator of truth or true behaviour, by thy speech or praises. (5108)

५. आ हरयः ससृज्रिरेऽरुषीरधि बर्हिषि । यत्राभि संनवामहे ॥

5. Just as the red rays of the sun instal it well on its axis, similarly, the glorious, learned persons enthral the king well on the high throne, where we, the common people bow to him from all around. (5109)

६. इन्द्राय गाव आशिरं दुदुह्रे वज्रिणे मधु । यत्सीमुपह्वरे विदत् ॥

6. Just as cows give milk to the cowherd, similarly the lands produce food-grains to the powerful king, the Ved-mantras generate sweet nectar of spiritual knowledge to the evil-destroying soul, who attains to the Almighty Father in his heart's cave. (5110)[2]

HYMN XXIII

१. आ तू न इन्द्र मद्र्यग्घुवानः सोमपीतये । हरिभ्यां याह्यद्रिवः ॥

1. O king or commander, equipped with sharp weapons like the thunderbolt, letest thou come to us with the two fast horses, yolked to thy chariot, for enjoying the fortunes of the nation, just in front of me (the chief-minister). (5111)[3]

[1](1-3) *Rig*, 8.45 (22-24); (4-6) *Rig*, 8.58. (4-6) I: an officer, working under him.
[2]उपह्वरे—in the cavity of the heart, appears to me to be a suitable rendering.
[3]cf. *Rig*, 3.41. (1-9)

२. सत्तो होता न ऋत्वियस्तिस्तिरे बर्हिरानुषक् । अयुज्रन्प्रातरद्रयः ॥

2. O king, just as the sacrificer, performing the sacrifices according to the seasons, is seated on his seat, ever spread in the altar, accompanied by grinding stones in the morning, similarly mayst thou be ever seated on thy throne, accompanied by the invincible brave warriors. (5112)

३. इमा ब्रह्म ब्रह्मवाहः क्रियन्त आ बर्हिः सीद । वीहि शूर पुरोलाशम् ॥

3. O king, worthy to be maintained by the learned Vedic scholars, these deeds of all sorts, are performed according to Vedic instructions. Mayst thou be well enthralled on thy throne. O brave king, accept the national wealth, respectfully offered to thee for the well-being of the nation. (5113)

४. रारन्धि सवनेषु ण एषु स्तोमेषु वृत्रहन् । उक्थेष्विन्द्र गिर्वणः ॥

4. O most Adorable God, king, commander or Vedic scholar worthy of being respected through Ved-mantra, Evil-Destroyer be pleased amongst these deeds of production, Vedic knowledge and praise-songs of ours. (5114)

५. मतयः सोमपामुरुं रिहन्ति शवसस्पतिम् । इन्द्रं वत्सं न मातरः ॥

5. The wise persons cherish the Vast, Almighty Father, the Protector of the Universe, the Evil-Destroyer, just as the mother-cows lick their calves, similarly the wise cherish or espouse the mighty king, capable of protecting his vast kingdom and destroying the wicked enemies, like the cows licking the calf. (5115)

६. स मन्दस्वा ह्यन्धसो राधसे तन्वा महे । न स्तोतारं निदे करः ॥

6. O God or king, mayst Thou be pleased or satisfied with offering us food and the great wealth, acquired through body. Letest not Thy devotee be exposed to reproach by others. (5116)

७. वयमिन्द्र त्वायवो हविष्मन्तो जरामहे । उत त्वमस्मयुर्वसो ॥

7. O Adorable God or king, we, wishing to approach Thee, and being equipped with means of subsistence and knowledge, sing Thy praises. O Settler of all, Thou likest to have us as Thy devotees. (5117)

८. मारे अस्मद्वि मुमुचो हरिप्रियार्वाङ् याहि । इन्द्र स्वधावो मत्स्वेह ॥

8. O Lover of the Learned persons, letest thee not be separated far from us, but be pleased to reveal Thyself to us. O mighty Lord, the Sustainer of all, be pleased to shower happiness and peace in this world or country. (5118)

९. अर्वाञ्चं त्वा सुखे रथे वहतामिन्द्र केशिना । घृतस्नू बर्हिरासदे ॥

9. O Radiant God, the refulgent Prān and Udān, reposed in peaceful state of the soul, may bring Thee to the fore-front vision of the soul, in the very core of his heart, where Thou art well-seated.

Or

O Glorious king, the two horses, with their long manes, shedding their valour and energy, yolked to thy comfortable chariot, may bring thee, well-seated in thy large seat to our fore-front. (5119)[1]

HYMN XXIV

१ उप नः सुतमा गहि सोममिन्द्र गवाशिरम् । हरिभ्यां यस्ते अस्मयुः ॥

1. O king, get firm hold of the wealth and fortune of the land, produced by us with the help of cattle and knowledge fit to be achieved by us, through thy power and valour of subduing thy enemies. (5120)[2]

२. तमिन्द्र मदमा गहि बर्हिष्ठां ग्रावभिः सुतम् । कुविन्न्वऽस्य तृष्णवः ॥

2. O mighty king, achieve that vast paraphernalia of enjoyment and pleasure, which is produced by the learned people and sharp-weaponed warriors. Verily a large number of people shall be satisfied thereby. (5121)

३. इन्द्रमित्था गिरो ममाच्छागुरिषिता इतः । आवृते सोमपीतये ॥

3. My speeches, thus moved by the impulses of the people, are well presented to the mighty king for the protection and satisfaction of the people, well-guarded on all sides, or covering all spheres of activities. (5122)

४. इन्द्रं सोमस्य पीतये स्तोमैरिह हवामहे । उक्थेभिः कुविदागमत् ॥

4. We (the populace) invite the king here at our place, with respectful prayers to enjoy himself with the means of enjoyment and pleasure we can offer. May he come often at our respectful invitations. (5123)

५. इन्द्र सोमाः सुता इमे तान्दधिष्व शतक्रतो । जठरे वाजिनीवसो ॥

5. O king or soul, performer of hundred sacrifices or deeds, or equipped with hundreds of powers, here are produced these means of pleasure and enjoyment. Take them in to thy fill, O settlers of brave warriors. (5124)

६. विद्मा हि त्वा धनंजयं वाजेषु दधृषं कवे । अधा ते सुम्नमीमहे ॥

6. O wise king, truly we know thee to be the conqueror of the wealth of thy enemies and subduer of thy foes. We wish thee all peace and plenty. (5125)

७. इममिन्द्र गवाशिरं यवाशिरं च नः पिब । आगत्या वृषभिः सुतम् ॥

7. O Mighty king, coming along with powerful warriors, protect and enjoy this national fortune, produced from the land by cattle and scientific knowledge and based on food-grains and the enemy-destroying soldiers. (5126)

८. तुभ्येदिन्द्र स्व ओक्ये३ सोमं चोदामि पीतये । एष रारन्तु ते हृदि ॥

8. O king or soul, I mobilise all the means of enjoyment and pleasure at thy residence alone for thy satisfaction. Let it fill thy heart with pleasure and joy. (5127)

९. त्वां सुतस्य पीतये प्रत्नमिन्द्र हवामहे । कुशिकासो अवस्यवः ॥

9. O king or soul, we, the enlightened persons, well-versed in speech or

[1]The full vision of God is revealed to a Yogi in deep meditation, after the full control of Prān and Udān.

[2]cf. *Rig*, 3.42. (1-9)

learning, seeking self-protection, ever call thee, the old respectable one, for guarding as well as enjoying the generated wealth and fortune. (5128)[1]

HYMN XXV

१. अश्वावति प्रथमो गोषु गच्छति सुप्रावीरिन्द्र मर्त्यस्तवोतिभिः ।
तमित्पृणक्षि वसुना भवीयसा सिन्धुमापो यथाभितो विचेतसः ।।

1. O All-Protector God or king, the man, who is well-protected by Thy means of safety, moves as the first in war, where horses or speedy means of communication are used, and as master of the cattle and sense-organs. Thou fillest him alone with large fortune. Just as the waters from all sides run into the ocean, similarly the persons, with multifarious forms of learning approach Thee from all quarters. (5129)[2]

२. आपो न देवीरुप यन्ति होत्रियमवः पश्यन्ति विततं यथा रजः ।
प्राचैर्देवासः प्र णयन्ति देवयुं ब्रह्मप्रियं जोषयन्ते वरा इव ।।

2. O God or king, just as heavenly waters flow down, similarly the virtuous people with divine qualities, approach Thee, Who is able to protect and offer comforts and well-being to them. Just as the people see the dust or sunlight spread all around in the sky, similarly they see Thy vast means of protection and safety, throughout the universe. The divine-natured persons attain Thee by their highest endeavours. The noble people love Thee who likes the Vedas and the Vedic scholars, just as the relatives of the bridegroom love him. (5130)

३. अधि द्वयोरदधा उक्थ्यं१ वचो यतस्रुचा मिथुना या सपर्यतः ।
असंयत्तो व्रते ते क्षेति पुष्यति भद्रा शक्तिर्यजमानाय सुन्वते ।।

3. O God or king, Thou offerest good counsel, worthy to be preached, to the couple, who, controlling their semen and vital breaths worship Thee with devotion. The one, who does not follow Thy rules and regulations of life, is ruined. The peaceful power of the generating sacrificer, acting according to Thy instructions, is enhanced all the more. (5131)

४. आदङ्गिराः प्रथमं दधिरे वय इद्धाग्नयः शम्या ये सुकृत्यया ।
सर्वं पणेः समविन्दन्त भोजनमश्वावन्तं गोमन्तमा पशुं नरः ।।

4. The learned persons, who kindle the sacrificial fires and impell their leaders to shed the light of knowledge and prosperity by their noble actions, just as the people light their fires with the wood of the shami-tree, obtain food, knowledge and power of the best quality. They fully get all sorts of means of subsistences fit for the people of good behaviour. Such people get plenteous wealth of cattle in the form of horses and milch cows, etc. (5132)[3]

[1] 'Kushitas' does not refer to the members of the family of Kuṣhika, but the learned persons, well-versed in speech, etc. Vedas contain no history of any king or individual.

[2] (1-6) cf. *Rig*, 1.83. (1-6); 7 cf. *Rig*, 10.104.3.

[3] Pani—is no demon, but a person, well-versed in good behaviour of the world.

५. यज्ञैरथर्वा प्रथमः पथस्तते ततः सूर्यो व्रतपा वेन आजनि ।
आ गा आजदुशना काव्यः सचा यमस्य जातममृतं यजामहे ॥

5. The non-violent Lord, who was present even before the creation of the universe, spread far and wide, the various courses for innumerable spheres to run, by His powers of synthesis and analysis. Thence came to light the refulgent sun, working according to the set laws by the Ordainer. The same radiant sun, the store-house of transmission of light all around, sets in motion all the planets, like the earth, all around itself. Then we, the people of the world, all together, get the everlasting creation of the Controller of the universe for our working here. (5134)[1]

६. बर्हिर्वा यत्स्वपत्याय वृज्यतेऽर्को वा श्लोकमाघोषते दिवि ।
ग्रावा यत्र वदति कारुरुक्थ्य१स्तस्येदिन्द्रो अभिपित्वेषु रण्यति ॥

6. God, king or a learned person is well-pleased in the efforts to get hold of the country or kingdom, where food or provisions are offered to the good progeny and where the enlightened scholar, worthy of respect by the people explains aloud the Veda-mantras for the enlightenment of the public, and where the Vedic preacher versatile in the performance of good deeds, fully equipped with Vedic knowledge preaches the Dharma, the path of virtue. (5135)

७. प्रोग्रां पीतिं वृष्ण इयर्मि सत्यां प्रयै सुतस्य हर्यश्व तुभ्यम् ।
इन्द्र धेनाभिरिह मादयस्व धीभिर्विश्वाभिः शच्या गृणानः ॥

7. O Powerful God, king or learned person, equipped with Evil-destroying powers, I implore or impell Thee for the unfailing terrible means of protection and safety, for achieving the statehood, well-furnished with all the means of prosperity and well-being. O Mighty Lord, king or learned person, be well-pleased here, instructing all by Thy might, all the Veda-mantras, cows, good deeds and wisdom. (5136)

Chapter (Anuvāka) 3

HYMN XXVI

१. योगेयोगे तवस्तरं वाजेवाजे हवामहे । सखाय इन्द्रमूतये ॥

1. In every act of meditation and in every act of acquiring knowledge, we, the friends, we call the Almighty for our help and guidance.

Or

In every war or in every act of valour and prowess we, the friends, seek the help of the very powerful king for our safety and protection. (5137)[2]

२. आ घा गमद्यदि श्रवत्सहस्रिणीभिरूतिभिः । वाजेभिरुप नो हवम् ॥

2. Let the king or commander, if he hears our call, truly come to us, with thousands of means of protection and sources of power and energy. (5138)

३. अनु प्रत्नस्यौकसो हुवे तुविप्रतिं नरम् । यं ते पूर्वं पिता हुवे ॥

[1]अमृतं—Everlasting—lasting for a very, very long period till प्रलय. Ushna Kanya is no Rishi as Sayāna or Griffith says.

[2](1-3) cf. *Rig*, 1-30 (7-9), (4-6) cf. *Rig*, 1.6. (1-3).

3. I call the leader of the old country, capable of facing the enemy, just as my father has been calling him before this. (5139)

४. युञ्जन्ति ब्रध्नमरुषं चरन्तं परि तस्थुषः । रोचन्ते रोचना दिवि ॥

4. They (the divine forces) unite the moving, refulgent assemblage of beams of light all round the core, which is comparatively stationary, (in the formation of the Sun). Thus formed, the constellations shine in the heavens. (5140)[1]

५. युञ्जन्त्यस्य काम्या हरी विपक्षसा रथे । शोणा धृष्णू नृवाहसा ॥

5. The same divine forces unite in its chariot, two kinds of radiant, magnetic energies of topmost speed, working all around it, capable of overcoming all resistance and carrying the leading planets along with it in their orbits. (5141)[2]

६. केतुं कृण्वन्नकेतवे पेशो मर्या अपेशसे । समुषद्भिरजायथाः ॥

6. O men, look at him (the Sun), born along with the dawns, giving intelligence to the sleeping men, who had lost all sense of perception during sleep, and giving form and shape to things, which had lost all their identity in the darkness of the night. (5142)

HYMN XXVII

१. यदिन्द्राहं यथा त्वमीशीय वस्व एक इत् । स्तोता मे गोषखा स्यात् ॥

1. O Lord of fortunes, if I (Thy Devotee) become the sole master of all riches, like Thee, my admirer may become the friend of all land, learning and wealth of cattle like cows etc. (5143)[3]

२. शिक्षेयमस्मै दित्सेयं शचीपते मनीषिणे । यदहं गोपतिः स्याम् ॥

2. O Lord of power and learning, I (Thy devotee) may instruct and wish to give this learned person of high thinking powers, land, wealth and cows, if I become the lord of land, learning, cows and riches. (5144)

३. धेनुष्ट इन्द्र सूनृता यजमानाय सुन्वते । गामश्वं पिप्युषी दुहे ॥

3. O Adorable Lord, Thy cow, the Vedic Lore, full of truth and fulfiller of all desires of man, nourishes him with all sorts of riches in the form of land, wealth, cows and horses. (5145)

४. न ते वर्तास्ति राधस इन्द्र देवो न मर्त्यः । यद्दित्ससि स्तुतो मघम् ॥

4. O Lord of fortunes, there is no divine power or human being, who can ward Thee off from giving riches and wealth, when Thou, being worshipped and praised, want to shower fortunes on Thy devotees. (5146)

५. यज्ञ इन्द्रमवर्धयद्यद् भूमिं व्यवर्तयत् । चक्राण ओपशं दिवि ॥

5. The sacrifice enhances the atmospheric electric energy, causing clouds in the sky, and then returning it to the earth, in the form of rain. (5147)

[1]The verse refers to the formation of the sun and constellations, shining in the heavens above.

[2]It is the forces of attraction of the sun that are described in the verse.

[3]cf. *Rig*, 8.14. (1-6).

६. वावृधानस्य ते वयं विश्वा धनानि जिग्युषः । ऊतिमिन्द्रा वृणीमहे ॥

6. O Mighty God, king or electricity, we pray for the protection and safety, from Thee, the Enhancer and conqueror of all the riches of the world. (5148)

HYMN XXVIII

१. व्य१न्तरिक्षमतिरन्मदे सोमस्य रोचना । इन्द्रो यदभिनद्वलम् ॥

1. When the Almighty God shatters the darkening cloud of the Primal matter (प्रकृति) in the very exhilaration of the creation of the universe, spreads the mid-regions with constellations. (5149)[1]

२. उद्गा आजदङ्गिरोभ्य आविष्कृण्वन्गुहा सतीः । अर्वाञ्चं नुनुदे वलम् ॥

2. Felling down the cloud of darkness of ignorance, He reveals the hidden Vedic Richas and offers them to the radiant sages (i.e., Agni, Vayu, Aditya and Angira) for the benefit of humanity. (5150)

३. इन्द्रेण रोचना दिवो दृढानि दृंहितानि च । स्थिराणि न पराणुदे ॥

3. The shining constellations have been well established and secured in the heavens, by the Almighty God. They are so firm and immovable that they defy destruction or ruination. (5151)

४. अपामूर्मिर्मदन्निव स्तोम इन्द्राजिरायते । वि ते मदा अराजिषुः ॥

4. O All-powerful God, Thy laud gushes forth like the joyous waves of waters and Thy pleasant deeds shine forth in various forms. (5152)

HYMN XXIX

१. त्वं हि स्तोमवर्धन इन्द्रास्युक्थवर्धनः । स्तोतॄणामुत भद्रकृत् ॥

1. O Adorable God, Thou art the nourisher of the created world as well the enhancer of the importance of the Vedic lore. Thou art the Well-wisher of Thy devotees. (5153)[2]

२. इन्द्रमित्केशिना हरी सोमपेयाय वक्षतः । उप यज्ञं सुराधसम् ॥

2. The two refulgent horses carry Indra to the sacrifice, full of good fortunes, for enjoying Soma-ras. (5154)[3]

३. अपां फेनेन नमुचेः शिर इन्द्रोदवर्तयः । विश्वा यदजय स्पृधः ॥

3. The Sun, overcoming all contending forces of nature, shatters down the head of the cloud, which resists letting down water in the form of rain, by the mere force of the foam of waters, struggling against one another.

Or

The king, overcoming all contending forces of the enemy, cuts off the head

[1]cf. *Rig*, 8.14 (7-10).

[2]cf. *Rig*, 8.14 (11-15).

[3]अध्यात्म—Pran and Apān—(horses); Indra—soul; sacrifice—deep meditation; Soma—bliss. In case of the Sun or electricity—Positive and negative electricity—horses ; Indra—the Sun or electricity; sacrifice the solar-system or the factory; Soma—the well-being of humanity.

In case of God—सजीव—निर्जीव समाधि—horses, Indra—God, sacrifice—spiritual meditation. Soma—beatitude.

of the foe, unfit to be left alive by the concentration of all his forces at one point. (5155)

४. मायाभिरुत्सिसृप्सत इन्द्र द्यामारुरुक्षतः । अव दस्यूँरधूनुथाः ॥

4. O mighty king or soul, crush down the violent foes or the evils, desirous of rising above and even flying to the heavens by various means of intelligent constructions and designs, like aeroplanes or space-ships. (5156)[1]

५. असुन्वामिन्द्र संसदं विषूचीं व्यनाशयः । सोमपा उत्तरो भवन् ॥

5. O mighty king or soul, tearing off all the organisation of those, who refuse to pay revenues or taxes to thee, overpowering them, be the protector of the nation and destroy them all. (The soul must be powerful enough to curb all his sense-organs going astray from its control and thus protect its body.) (5157)

HYMN XXX

१. प्र ते महे विदथे शंसिषं हरी प्र ते वन्वे वनुषो हर्यतं मदम् ।
घृतं न यो हरिभिश्चारु सेचत आ त्वा विशन्तु हरिवर्पसं गिरः ॥

1. O God, king, learned person or electricity, I (a devotee) fully praise Thy two forces of protection and destruction in this great universe, which is a great sacrificial place or battlefield of life. I highly cherish Thy beautiful exhilaration, destroying the evil forces of the enemy. Thou showerest various forms of fortunes through Thy blessing powers of speedy action, like waters from the clouds. Let all praises find their abode in Thee of charming splendour. (5158)[2]

२. हरिं हि योनिमभि ये समस्वरन्हिन्वन्तो हरी दिव्यं यथा सदः ।
आ यं पृणन्ति हरिभिर्न धेनव इन्द्राय शूषं हरिवन्तमर्चत ॥

2. O men, worship the might, fully equipped with the powers of protection and destruction, of the Almighty God, king, the learned person or electricity, whom their devotees fully satisfy by various sorts of offerings, just as the cows satisfy their owners by milk. The learned persons, reposing as if in the divine shelter, and enhancing His glorious powers, well sing the praises of Him, Who is the source of all creation, and Who is the Evil-Destroyer as well as the showerer of blessing. (5159)

३. सो अस्य वज्रो हरितो य आयसो हरिर्निकामो हरिरा गभस्त्योः ।
द्युम्नी सुशिप्रो हरिमन्युसायक इन्द्रे नि रूपा हरिता मिमिक्षिरे ॥

3. Here is the blue or green coloured thunderbolt of iron of the King. There is also the beautiful horse of iron of high speed. Here is also the horse-power of the rays of the Sun or electricity. There is also shining arrow, capable of destroying the pride of the enemy and having a very high speed. In

[1]The soul should be powerful enough to shed off all evil forces, that may try to gain ascending over it by deceitful means or by lures of the world,

[2]cf. *Rig*, 10.96. (1-5).

short, many kinds of weapons have been made through electric power for the king. (5160)[1]

४. दिवि न केतुरधि धायि हर्यतो विव्यचद्वज्रो हरितो न रंह्या ।
तुददहिं हरिशिप्रो य आयसः सहस्रशोका अभवद्धरिंभरः ॥

4. Like a radiant spot, it is well placed in the heavens, then with a high speed, the terribly destructive missile spreads in all quarters like the Sun. The destructive missile, made of iron, possessing speed of electric power, crushing the serpent-natured enemy, becomes lit up with thousands of lights and loaded with destructive rays of various kinds. (5161)[2]

५. त्वंत्वमहर्यथा उपस्तुतः पूर्वेभिरिन्द्र हरिकेश यज्वभिः ।
त्वं हर्यसि तव विश्वमुक्थ्य१मसामि राधो हरिजात हर्यतम् ॥

5. O Radiant God, king, learned person or electricity, well-known amongst the shining or speedy things, Thou and Thou alone art seen all around. Thou art praised by the sacrificers of yore. Thou likest all. Thou alone deservest all praise. The whole of the beautiful fortune belongs to Thee alone. (5162)

HYMN XXXI

१. ता वज्रिणं मन्दिनं स्तोम्यं मद इन्द्रं रथे वहतो हर्यता हरी ।
पुरूण्यस्मै सवनानि हर्यत इन्द्राय सोमा हरयो दधन्विरे ॥

1. Those two speedily-moving forces of attraction and repulsion propel the electric current, powerful like the thunderbolt, pleasant and praiseworthy, in this pleasant plane or car. Manifold are the generating powers for the refulgent electricity borne by the speedy-moving Somas—various kinds of liquid fuels. (5163)[3]

२. अरं कामाय हरयो दधन्विरे स्थिराय हिन्वन्हरयो हरी तुरा ।
अर्वद्भिर्यो हरिभिर्जोषमीयते सो अस्य कामं हरिवन्तमानशे ॥

2. The above-mentioned speedy forces of two kinds set in motion strong currents, capable of maintaining steady progress in the attainment of one's objective in plenty. Whatever complex is attained by these fast-moving horsepowers, is enough to achieve the beautiful objective of his, the manufacturer. (5164)

३. हरिश्मशारुर्हरिकेश आयसस्तुरस्पेये यो हरिपा अवर्धत ।
अर्वद्भिर्यो हरिभिर्वाजिनीवसुरति विश्वा दुरिता पारिषद्धरी ॥

3. The protector of the brave warriors, who being equipped with some strong weapons of iron, like flame-throwers (with powerful flames serving as moustaches and hair for them) enhances his striking power in the fast mobilisation of forces of protection and defence. He overcomes all the difficult

[1]To me it appears that the verse enumerates various forms of destructive weapons, which can be made by the use of electric power.

[2]Some highly destructive missile is meant.

[3](1-2) To me it appears that the sukta depicts the uses of the two forces of attraction and repulsion, so powerful in nature as well as in the manufacturing processes of man.

situations, having the wealth of energetic armies of fast-moving horse-powers. (5165)

४. स्रुवेव यस्य हरिणी विपेततुः शिप्रे वाजाय हरिणी दविध्वतः ।
प्र यत्कृते चमसे मर्मृजद्धरी पीत्वा मदस्य हर्यतस्यान्धसः ।।

4. The king or commander, whose two wings of the army fall speedily on his enemy, like the ladle in the sacrifice, and whose fast-moving forces dash against the foe in the war, enhances his power and valour after enjoying the satisfying, charming fortunes of the nation, just as a man comfortably rubs his eyes with his hands, after enjoying the charming sweet dish well-served on the plate. (5166)

५. उत स्म सद्म हर्यतस्य पस्त्योऽरत्यो न वाजं हरिवाँ अचिक्रदत् ।
मही चिद्धि धिषणाहर्यदोजसा बृहद्वयो दधिषे हर्यतश्चिदा ।।

5. The man, equipped with the two forces of attraction and repulsion gains speed like that of a horse and makes his abode on the beautiful earth and heavens alike. The vast earth likes to be owned by the high energy of such a person and bears plenteous food-grains for such an energetic person. (5167)

HYMN XXXII

१. आ रोदसी हर्यमाणो महित्वा नव्यंनव्यं हर्यसि मन्म नु प्रियम् ।
प्र पस्त्यमसुर हर्यतं गोराविष्कृधि हरये सूर्याय ।।

1. O Mighty Lord, Thou, thoroughly supporting the heavens and the earth by Thy might and grandeur, truly revealest new, new pleasant things for deep thinking and brooding over. O Controller of vital breaths, Thou bringest to light the beautiful source of Vedic lore for the brilliant learned scholar. (5168)[1]

२. आ त्वा हर्यन्तं प्रयुजो जनानां रथे वहन्तु हरिशिप्रमिन्द्र ।
पिबा यथा प्रतिभृतस्य मध्वो हर्यन्यज्ञं सधमादे दशोणिम् ।।

2. O Adorable God, out of the general people, those yogis, who are immersed in deep meditation, may have a clear vision of Thee, Who art so Beautiful, Evil-Smasher and Speedy-Mobiliser into highest bliss. Letst Thee engulf the sacrificing soul, with all its ten sense-organs or ten vital breaths, all at once into Thy blissful fold, just as a guest takes in the sweet dish offered to him. (5169)

३. अपाः पूर्वेषां हरिवः सुतानामथो इदं सवनं केवलं ते ।
ममद्धि सोमं मधुमन्तमिन्द्र सत्रा वृषञ्जठर आ वृषस्व ।।

3. O Almighty Lord, fully equipped with powers of destruction, thou hast already taken into Thy shelter the previous creations. This created universe is also Thine alone. Letst Thee cherish this immortal soul, engulfed in Thy

[1]cf. *Rig*, 10.96. (11-13).

bliss. Letst Thee pour this Dharm-medh yogi into Thy belly of beatitude. (5170)[1]

HYMN XXXIII

१. अप्सु धूतस्य हरिवः पिबेह नृभिः सुतस्य जठरं पृणस्व ।
मिमिक्षुर्यमद्रय इन्द्र तुभ्यं तेभिर्वर्धस्व मदमुक्थवाहः ॥

1. O Mighty God, king, commander, soul or electricity, possessed of powers of evil or trouble-removing and peace-showering protect whatever has been generated amongst the subjects, waters or vital breaths and cherish and enjoy the fortunes produced by the people. Whatever wealth has been showered down by the clouds or mountains, may enhance Thy pleasure-giving blessings, according to the Vedic instructions. (5171)[2]

२. प्रोग्रां पीतिं वृष्ण इयर्मि सत्यां प्रयै सुतस्य हर्यश्व तुभ्यम् ।
इन्द्र धेनाभिरिह मादयस्व धीभिर्विश्वाभिः शच्या गृणानः ॥

2. O All-powerful God, king, commander, soul, or electricity, showerer of blessings, possessed of speedy mobilising forces, I (a devotee) fully attain Thy strong infallible protection for going on the right course in this world to attain Thee. Letst Thou be fully satisfied and satisfy others in this world by being praised by all the praise-songs, intelligence, deeds and powers. (5172)

३. ऊती शचीवस्तव वीर्येण वयो दधाना उशिज ऋतज्ञाः ।
प्रजावदिन्द्र मनुषो दुरोणे तस्थुर्गृणन्तः सधमाद्यासः ॥

3. O Lord of All-Fortunes, and All-Powers, through Thy protection and energy, the self-controlled truth-seers, leading long life blessed with off-spring, enjoying all together at one place and preaching Vedic learning to others, stay in the mortal bodies. (5173)

Chapter (Anuvāka) 4

HYMN XXXIV

१. यो जात एव प्रथमो मनस्वान्देवो देवान्क्रतुना पर्यभूषत् ।
यस्य शुष्माद्रोदसी अभ्यसेतां नृम्णस्य मह्ना स जनास इन्द्रः ॥

1. O men, He is the Mighty Lord, Who alone is Well-known to be the Foremost of all, full of thinking powers, the Radiant, Bestower of all powers and the Guardian of all, Who controls all the divine forces by His might and adds to their lustre and beauty, and from Whose might, the heavens and the earth tremble with awe, due to the high prowess, pervading through men, with leading energies. (5174)[3]

२. यः पृथिवीं व्यथमानामदृंहद्यः पर्वतान्प्रकुपिताँ अरम्णात् ।
यो अन्तरिक्षं विममे वरीयो यो द्यामस्तभ्नात्स जनास इन्द्रः ॥

[1] God being formless has no belly or other organs. It is a figurative language to describe the enruptured state of a mukta yogi.

[2] cf. *Rig*, 10. 104. (2-4).

[3] (1-18) cf. *Rig*, 2.12. (1-15) (12, 16, 17) are not from *Rigveda*.

2. O people of the world, He is the Omnipotent Lord, Who makes the earth moving with such a high speed, firm in its orbit, Who calms the furious mountains (giving out red-hot lava), who measures and spreads out the vast mid-regions and Who supports the heavens. (5175)

३. यो हत्वाहिमरिणात्सप्त सिन्धून्यो गा उदाजदपधा वलस्य ।
यो अश्मनोरन्तरग्निं जजान संवृक्समत्सु स जनास इन्द्रः ॥

3. O men, He is the Almighty God, Who pervading the everlasting primal matter, sets in motion the seven rivers, Who, removing the darkness of ignorance, reveals the rays of light of Vedic lore in the hearts of the primal sages, Who generates the Sun between the heavens and the earth, like the fire generated by the friction of two stones or aims; and Who removes all handicaps in the general behaviours of the people of the world. (5176)[1]

४. येनेमा विश्वा च्यवना कृतानि यो दासं वर्णमधरं गुहाकः ।
श्वघ्नीव यो जिगीवाँल्लक्षमाददर्यः पुष्टानि स जनास इन्द्रः ॥

4. O people, He is the All-Powerful Lord, by Whom all these worlds have been set in motion in their respective orbits, Who enthralls in the sky all this perishable universe; Who controls all the apparent creation, just as a gambler grapple all the money won by him or a hunter catches hold of the kill secured by him; Who showers all the nourishing things on the people. (5177)

५. यं स्मा पृच्छन्ति कुह सेति घोरमुतेमाहुर्नैषो अस्तीत्येनम् ।
सो अर्यः पुष्टीर्विज इवा मिनाति श्रदस्मै धत्त स जनास इन्द्रः ॥

5. O men, He is the Almighty God, the Terrible one, about Whom the people ask, "Where is He?" And many say about Him, "He is not there (in the world)." O men, have faith in Him, Who destroys even the able-bodied wicked person like the lion, killing its prey. (5178)

६. यो रध्रस्य चोदिता यः कृशस्य यो ब्रह्मणो नाधमानस्य कीरेः ।
युक्तग्राव्णो योऽविता सुशिप्रः सुतसोमस्य स जनास इन्द्रः ॥

6. O people, He is the Almighty Lord, Who showers fortunes on the rich as well as the poor; who gives to the beseeching Brahman and any other supplicant of disturbed mind; Who is the protector of an energetic yogi, given to deep meditation through Pranayam, and immersed in deep bliss. (5179)

७. यस्याश्वासः प्रदिशि यस्य गावो यस्य ग्रामा यस्य विश्वे रथासः ।
यः सूर्यं य उषसं जजान यो अपां नेता स जनास इन्द्रः ॥

7. O men, He is the Omnipotent God, under Whose control and discipline are the powerful spheres like the Sun and the fast-moving earths, the groups of sense-organs and all these means of pleasure like the bodies, etc. Who generates the Sun, the dawn, Who directs the working waters, oceans, the learned persons and intelligence. (5180)

[1]Seven rivers: Mahatattva, Ahankar, and five Tanmatras or seven smashthi vital breaths.

८. यं क्रन्दसी संयती विह्वयेते परेऽवर उभया अमित्राः।
समानं चिद्रथमातस्थिवांसा नाना हवेते स जनास इन्द्रः ॥

8. O people, He is the All-Powerful God, Whom the well-disciplined heavens and the earth and the people thereof, the couple or the teacher and the taught call for help in their praise-songs; Whom the high and the low and both the adversaries call for help in many ways; Whom the passengers, sitting in the same means of transport remember in various ways. (5181)

९. यस्मान्न ऋते विजयन्ते जनासो यं युध्यमाना अवसे हवन्ते ।
यो विश्वस्य प्रतिमानं बभूव यो अच्युतच्युत्स जनास इन्द्रः ॥

9. O men, He is the Almighty Lord, without Whom people cannot win, Whom the fighting people call for protection and safety, Who, being the Creator of the world has become its model or idol, Who is the Smasher of the imperishable even. (5182)

१०. यः शश्वतो मह्येनो दधानानमन्यमानाञ्छर्वा जघान ।
यः शर्धते नानुददाति शृध्यां यो दस्योर्हन्ता स जनास इन्द्रः ॥

10. O people, He is the mighty God, Who, by His power of destruction punishes those, who are constant bearers of great sins, and yet refuse to give them up and even to admit them, Who does not bless the wicked fault-finder, with any power of control, and Who destroys the violent person. (5183)

११. यः शम्बरं पर्वतेषु क्षियन्तं चत्वारिंश्यां शरद्यन्वविन्दत् ।
ओजायमानं यो अहिं जघान दानुं शयानं स जनास इन्द्रः ॥

11. O men, He is the All-powerful Lord, Who re-sets the moon at the same spot in the sky in the 40th year of her motion through months of two parvas each. Who destroys the passion of lust, lying hidden crooked in the heart like a serpent and affecting the vital parts. (5184)[1]

१२. यः शम्बरं पर्यतरत्कसीभिर्योऽचारुकास्नापिबत्सुतस्य ।
अन्तर्गिरौ यजमानं बहुं जनं यस्मिन्नामूर्छत्स जनास इन्द्रः ॥

12. O men, He is the Almighty God, Who suppresses the darkness of ignorance by His light of knowledge; Who saps up this creation by His terrible mouth of destruction, and under Whom many sacrificing people are elevated to the highest position of mukti, just as a person rises to the highest level among the mountains. (5185)[2]

१३. यः सप्तरश्मिर्वृषभस्तुविष्मानवासृजत्सर्तवे सप्त सिन्धून् ।
यो रौहिणमस्फुरद्वज्रबाहुर्द्यामारोहन्तं स जनास इन्द्रः ॥

13. O people, He is the All-powerful Lord, Who, being equipped with seven fold powers of control, like the seven-beams of light of the Sun showerer of

[1]The verse may be applied to the Aditya Brahmchari who attains complete grasp of the Vedic lore in 40 years of celibacy, suppressing all passions of lust, distracting him from the right path.

[2]The verse is not found in *Rig*, V. God being formless, has no organ like the mouth. It is a figurative language here. This sukta can be applied to the king as 'Indra'.

fortunes and All-powerful, Who with thunderbolt in kind, cuts off the Banyan tree in the form of the universe, rising to the heavens. (5186)

१४. द्यावा चिदस्मै पृथिवी नमेते शुष्माच्चिदस्य पर्वता भयन्ते ।
यः सोमपा निचितो वज्रबाहुर्यो वज्रहस्तः स जनास इन्द्रः ॥

14. The heavens and the earth bow to Him. From His power alone, the mountains and the clouds tremble with awe. O men, verily He is the Almighty Lord, Who is the Protector of the created world, is All-pervading, Smasher of all evils and Terrible Punisher of the wicked. (5187)

१५. यः सुन्वन्तमवति यः पचन्तं यः शंसन्तं यः शशमानमूती ।
यस्य ब्रह्म वर्धनं यस्य सोमो यस्येदं राधः स जनास इन्द्रः ॥

15. O men, He is the Mighty God, Who protects the sacrificer, the maturer of his power, knowledge and semen, and the singer of praise-songs, and the self-elevator by His means of safety; Whose glory is enhanced by the Vedic Lore, Whose creation is the universe, and Whose is all this wealth and fortune. (5188)

१६. जातो व्य१ख्यत्पित्रोरुपस्थे भुवो न वेद जनितुः परस्य ।
स्तविष्यमाणो नो यो अस्मद् व्रता देवानां स जनास इन्द्रः ॥

16. Just as the newly born baby gives expression to its various feelings in the lap of its parents, but does not know its mother nor its father; similarly being praised, God reveals to us the various laws, duties and powers of ours and the divine forces of nature (unknown to us). O men, He is the Almighty Father. (5189)

१७. यः सोमकामो हर्यश्वः सूरिर्यस्माद्रेजन्ते भुवनानि विश्वा ।
यो जघान शम्बरं यश्च शुष्णं य एकवीरः स जनास इन्द्रः ॥

17. O men, He is the All-powerful God, Who is the Beloved of the Yogis, immersed in deep-meditation, is Refulgent and Fast-moving, stirrer of all, getting energy from Whom, all the spheres of the universe are in constant motion. It is He, Who destroys the forces of darkness, and removes the drying up forces of hunger, thirst and other handicaps. He is the sole source of bravery and courage. (5190)

१८. यः सुन्वते दुध्र आ चिद्वाजं दर्दर्षि स किलासि सत्यः ।
वयं त इन्द्र विश्वह प्रियासः सुवीरासो विदथमा वदेम ॥

18. O Almighty God, surely True art Thee, Who, being Invincible, showers all power and food-grains, knowledge and wealth on the sacrificing and hospitable person. May we ever be loved by Thee and being brave and courageous, ever sing Thy praise. (5191)

HYMN XXXV

१. अस्मा इदु प्र तवसे तुराय प्रयो न हर्मि स्तोमं माहिनाय ।
ऋचीषमायाध्रिगव ओहमिन्द्राय ब्रह्माणि राततमा ॥

1. I (a devotee) offer my well-thought-out praises and Vedic Richas, most

worthy to be offered, to the Powerful, Fast-moving, Great, All-pervading, Mighty Lord, of the form mentioned in the Richas, like food to the honoured guest. (5192)[1]

२. अस्मा इदु प्रय इव प्र यंसि भराम्याङ्गूषं बाधे सुवृक्ति ।
इन्द्राय हृदा मनसा मनीषा प्रत्नाय पत्ये धियो मर्जयन्त ॥

2. I (a devotee) offer my devout praises to the Adorable Lord, like food to an honoured guest. I pour forth my devotional songs for driving away my difficulties and troubles. People purify their intellects by controlling their mental energy, through the disciplined mind and heart, for the mighty Lord, Who is the Ruler of their hearts, from times of yore. (5193)

३. अस्मा इदु त्यमुपमं स्वर्षां भराम्याङ्गूषमास्ये॒न ।
मंहिष्ठमच्छोक्तिभिर्मतीनां सुवृक्तिभिः सूरिं वावृधध्यै ॥

3. For this Mighty God alone, I offer the happy, pleasant praise-songs by my mouth, for the enhancement of the glory of the Wisest and the most Refulgent God, Who is the most Adorable among the thoughtful people, well-spoken words, capable of removing all troubles and vexations. (5194)

४. अस्मा इदु स्तोमं स हिनोमि रथं न तष्टेव तत्सिनाय ।
गिरश्च गिर्वाहसे सुवृक्तीन्द्राय विश्वमिन्वं मेधिराय ॥

4. Just as a mechanic mobilises a vehicle, so do I, well-mobilise all my praise-songs, capable of achieving all objects for this Blissful Lover, Who is worthy of all adorable speech, Remover of all troubles and handicaps, and is the Purest of all. (5195)

५. अस्मा इदु सप्तिमिव श्रवस्येन्द्रायार्कं जुह्वा३ समञ्जे ।
वीरं दानौकसं वन्दध्यै पुरां गूर्तश्रवसं दर्माणम् ॥

5. Just as a fast horse is yolked to a chariot; so do I unite my devotional and worshipful song to this Lord of all fortunes for food-grains, fame, glory and knowledge, and offering my prayers to the Brave, the source of bounties, the All-Glorious and the Breakers of all bondages of the soul like the smashers of the castles of the enemy. (5196)

६. अस्मा इदु त्वष्टा तक्षद्वज्रं स्वपस्तमं स्वर्यं१ रणाय ।
वृत्रस्य चिद्विदद्येन मर्म तुजन्नीशानस्तुजता कियेधाः ॥

6. Just as a mechanic manufactures a missile, with the deadly smashing power, and of a good craftmanship, capable of flying through the sky in a war, for this king, who, striking at the vital points of the enemy and crushing him in various ways and thus over-powering him, attains glory, so does a yogi develops such a spiritual force for the attainment of the Almighty by his virtuous deeds, as enables him to revel in His Bliss, after crushing the evil forces of sin and ignorance in various ways and thus gaining, self-control attains the highest state of salvation. (5197)

[1] cf. *Rig*. 1-61. (1-16).

७. अस्येदु मातुः सवनेषु सद्यो महः पितुं पपिवां चार्वन्ना ।
मुषायद्विष्णुः पचतं सहीयान्विध्यद्वराहं तिरो अद्रिमस्ता ॥

7. Verily mighty is the performance of the Creator of the Universe in all the states of creation, sustenance and annihilation in that He constantly continues consuming the nourishing and charming means of subsistence. The All-powerful and All-pervading God suddenly annihilates the fully created universe at the time of the deluge, just the breaker of the clouds, the Sun, dispels the cloud by its piercing rays. (5198)[1]

८. अस्मा इदु ग्नाश्चिद्देवपत्नीरिन्द्रायार्कमहिहत्य ऊवुः ।
परि द्यावापृथिवी जभ्र उर्वी नास्य ते महिमानं परिष्टः ॥

8. For this Glorious Lord alone do the Vedic praise-songs and the Divine powers of protection uphold the moral standards for dispelling the clouds of ignorance. He pervades the vast heavens and the earth. But they don't limit His Grandeur by themselves (i.e., it extends far, far beyond them.) (5199)

९. अस्येदेव प्र रिरिचे महित्वं दिवस्पृथिव्याः पर्यन्तरिक्षात् ।
स्वरालिन्द्रो दम आ विश्वगूर्तः स्वरिरमत्रो ववक्षे रणाय ॥

9. The Mighty Power of This God far excells that of the heavens, the earth and of the mid-regions. The self-Effulgent, All-Adorable, Self-reliant Lord of Glory overpowers and sustains all in the universe, like a powerful king, capable of speedily dashing against his foe, subduing him and carrying everything before him in the war. (5200)

१०. अस्येदेव शवसा शुषन्तं वि वृश्चद्वज्रेण वृत्रमिन्द्रः ।
गा न व्राणा अवनीरमुञ्चदभि श्रवो दावने सचेताः ॥

10. The Mighty Lord of Glory and fortunes smashes the drying-up clouds of ignorance and evil in various ways, by His strength and valour. The Loving God showers food-grains, fame, knowledge on the charitable person like the rays of the Sun, releasing the pent-up waters of a cloud on the earth, which is worthy of protection. (5201)

११. अस्येदु त्वेषसा रन्त सिन्धवः परि यद्वज्रेण सीमयच्छत् ।
ईशानकृद्दाशुषे दशस्यन्तुर्वीतये गाधं तुर्वणिः कः ॥

11. It is through His resplendent Glory alone that the rivers revel all over the earth. It is He Who controls them in every respect by His mighty Power. Just as speedily moving electricity endows its full energy and glory to the fast-moving person, similarly does, the All-Glorious God, instantly pervading the universe and controlling it showers His fortunes and knowledge on the devotee, quickly desirous of attainment of salvation. (5202)[2]

[1]Griffith and other western scholars find it hard to interpret this verse, because they see the Vedic words as ordinary Sanskrit words, as वराह—boar अद्रि—mountain while Nighantu gives वराह+अद्रि in the list of मेघ—names. The verse describes the working of the universe i.e., all the three processes of creation, maintenance, and destruction all along and even the final annihilation like the creation and sustaining and dispersal of the clouds by the rays of the Sun. पचतं—Well-cooked, completely created creation.

[2]The verse can apply to the king and an engineer, too.

१२. अस्मा इदु प्र भरा तूतुजानो वृत्राय वज्रमीशानः कियेधाः ।
गोर्न पर्व वि रदा तिरश्चेष्यन्नर्णांस्यपां चरध्यै ॥

12. O Mighty Lord, giving the highest speed to the universe and controlling it in numerous ways of substance and modes of valour, Thou usest Thy mighty striking power like the thunderbolt for darkening clouds of the Primordeal matter to set in motion the Primeval Waters for the creation of the universe, just as electricity splits asunder the various parts of the rays of light to let fall the waters of the clouds on the earth.

Or

O mighty king, speedily setting in motion the machinery of the administration, controlling your state, in various ways of power-control or checks and curbs on the unruly elements, desirous of the prosperity and well-being of the state, you strike with the speed of lightning, this overpowering enemy and split asunder the various parts of the earth (in the forms of canals) for the free flow of waters to irrigate the land. (5203)[1]

१३. अस्येदु प्र ब्रूहि पूर्व्याणि तुरस्य कर्माणि नव्य उक्थैः ।
युधे यदिष्णान आयुधान्यृघायमाणो निरिणाति शत्रून् ॥

13. O learned person, when this king speedily goes forth to wage war, using deadly weapon and crushing the enemy, progresses further, thoroughly expose the valorous deeds of his forefathers, as he is worthy of such praise.

Or

In the case of waging war with internal enemies of man, i.e., lust, anger, greed, indulgence and vanity, when a person earnestly sets forth on this path of conquest, using various means of overpowering these internal enemies and vanquishes them and moves on further, on the path of virtue let the learned person thoroughly lay the exposition of the previous deeds of the creation of the universe by God, for it is He, Who alone is worthy to be praised. (5204)

१४. अस्येदु भिया गिरयश्च दृढा द्यावा च भूमा जनुषस्तुजेते ।
उपो वेनस्य जोगुवान ओणिं सद्यो भुवद्वीर्याय नोधाः ॥

14. Through fear of This Creator, the mountains are firm, the heavens and the earth are in motion. The suppliant devotee, desirous of seeking protection of the All-Intelligent and Refulgent God, quickly becomes a powerful and valorous. (5205)

१५. अस्मा इदु त्यदनु दाय्येषामेको यद्वव्ने भूरेरीशानः ।
प्रैतशं सूर्ये पस्पृधानं सौवश्व्ये सुष्विमावदिन्द्रः ॥

[1](i) Griffith and Sayāna have done the greatest disservice to the Vedic lore and humanity at large by interpreting 'गो' as cow or ox. (ii) cf. Pt. Bhagvaddatta, detailed commentary of this verse in his Nirukta Shastra wherein he has interpreted 'गो' as ray of light, giving ample proof in support of his interpretation from the Vedas, Brahmanas and Nirukta. In addition to the above (iii) in my view 'गो' can also be interpreted as 'earth.' See the 2nd version of the verse above. (iv) I am surprised to find why the western scholars have rushed to interpret 'गो' as cow and ox. Why could not they see 'इन्द्र धनुष' as splitting of the various parts of the ray of light, accompanied by rain, as the right interpretation of 'गोर्न पर्व वि रदा । (v) Jaidev has interpreted 'गो' as Ved-vani also.

15. To Him alone is offered the best of all these worldly objects (i.e., Soma) which is accepted by the Lord of all prosperity and fortunes. The self-same Lord of fortunes well protects the fully devoted transmigrating soul, struggling hard for the attainment of the most glorious state of salvation, with all the organs at his command.

Or

The wind thoroughly protects the raining cloud, struggling hard in the powerful light of the Sun, equipped with the most beautiful horses, in the form of its rays. (5206)[1]

१६. एवा ते हारियोजना सुवृक्तीन्द्र ब्रह्माणि गोतमासो अक्रन् ।
ऐषु विश्वपेशसं धियं धाः प्रातर्मक्षू धियावसुर्जगम्यात् ॥

16. O Mighty Lord, Whom the learned persons, well-versed in the Vedic lore, perceive through Yog i.e., concentration of all senses in deep meditation and sing the (charming) attractive Vedic verses. Thou showerest on these (devotees) all sorts of retentive intelligence and ability to do good deeds. Mayst Thou quickly come to us early in the morning, showering all fortunes and shelter. (5207)[2]

HYMN XXXVI

१. य एक इद्धव्यश्चर्षणीनामिन्द्रं तं गीर्भिरभ्यर्चं आभिः ।
यः पत्यते वृषभो वृष्ण्यावान्त्सत्यः सत्वा पुरुमायः सहस्वान् ॥

1. With these hymns, I worship that Mighty Lord, Who alone is to be invoked by men, Who is known to be the Showerer of all blessings, All-powerful, True, Lord of all existence, Victorious, Full of Wisdom and Wonderful powers of creation. (5208)[3]

२. तमु नः पूर्वे पितरो नवग्वाः सप्त विप्रासो अभि वाजयन्तः ।
नक्षद्दाभं ततुरिं पर्वतेष्ठामद्रोघवाचं मतिभिः शविष्ठम् ॥

2. Our fore-fathers as well as the new-singers of praise-songs, the most intelligent ones like the seven vital breaths serving the soul, extol him alone through thoughtful praises; deriving knowledge, power and wealth from Him, Who is the Destroyer of all evils and enemies, Remover of all difficulties and troubles, the Topmost and the most stable (e.g., sitting on the top of a mountain) the Invincible Ordainer, and the Almighty One. (5209)[4]

३. तमीमह इन्द्रमस्य रायः पुरुवीरस्य नृवतः पुरुक्षोः ।
यो अस्कृधोयुरजरः स्वर्वान्तमा भर हरिवो मादयध्यै ॥

3. We seek that Lord of Fortune to get His riches, equipped with numerous brave persons, servants and ample food-grains. O Lord of speedy forceful

[1] Sayāna and Griffith read history in the verse, whereas there is no trace of it herein.

[2] Gautamas are not the clan of Rishis of specific name, as interpreted by Griffith and Sayāna but the general learned persons, well-versed in the Vedic Lore.

[3] (1-11) cf. *Rig*, 6.22.1-11.

[4] The navgavas are not the clan of Rishis of specific name, as Sayana and Griffith would have it, but simply new singers of praises.

powers, invest us with that strange fortune for enjoyment and pleasure, who art Everlasting, Indestructible, undecaying and Lord of celestial wealth. (5210)

४. तन्नो वि वोचो यदि ते पुरा चिज्जरितार आनशुः सुम्नमिन्द्र ।
कस्ते भागः किं वयो दुध्र खिद्वः पुरुहूत पुरूवसोऽसुरघ्नः ॥

4. O Unconquerable and much-invoked Subduer of the enemies and Destroyer of evils, Lord of all fortunes and Settlers of many and Slayer of Demons, tell us the same blissful fortune, which the previous worshippers of Thine got from Thee and also what Thy share and portion is. (5211)

५. तं पृच्छन्ती वज्रहस्तं रथेष्ठामिन्द्रं वेपी वक्वरी यस्य नू गीः ।
तुविग्राभं तुविकूर्मिं रभोदां गातुमिषे नक्षते तुम्रमच्छ ॥

5. The self-same devotee, whose inquisitive, active and fluent faculty of speech wishes to sing the praises of that Mighty Lord, with the thunderbolt in His Hand, well-entrenched in the hearts of the blissful souls, Sustainer of innumerable worlds, and Doer of numerous deeds, attains well the Remover of all obstructions and handicaps. (5212)

६. अया ह त्यं मायया वावृधानं मनोजुवा स्वतवः पर्वतेन ।
अच्युता चिद् वीलिता स्वोजो रुजो वि दृढा धृषता विरप्शिन् ॥

6. O mighty king, relying on your own power and valour completely crush the progressing foe with deadly weapons, moving swiftly with the speed of mind and with such dexterity, as shatters the unshakable and firm forces and fortifications of the enemy to smithereens with overwhelming power. (5213)

७. तं वो धिया नव्यस्या शविष्ठं प्रत्नं प्रत्नवत्परितंसयध्यै ।
स नो वक्षदनिमानः सुवह्मेन्द्रो विश्वान्यति दुर्गहाणि ॥

7. O people of the world, you should glorify the most mighty and Ancient God with fresh devotion, like the ancient people. That Mighty Lord and Good Leader of Boundless Prowess can lead us across all difficult situations. (5214)

८. आ जनाय द्रुह्वणे पार्थिवानि दिव्यानि दीपयोऽन्तरिक्षा ।
तपा वृषन्विश्वतः शोचिषा तान्ब्रह्मद्विषे शोचय क्षामपश्च ॥

8. O powerful king (capable of raining death on the foes) set aflame all the earthly, atmospheric and heavenly things for the oppressing persons full of hatred and animosity. Consume them with blazing heat on every side. Heat earth and waters for him, who hates God and Vedic lore. (5215)

९. भुवो जनस्य दिव्यस्य राजा पार्थिवस्य जगतस्त्वेषसंदृक् ।
धिष्व वज्रं दक्षिण इन्द्र हस्ते विश्वा अजुर्य दयसे वि मायाः ॥

9. O invunerable, mighty king of splendid appearance, thou art the king of heavenly folk and of earthly creatures. Grasp the deadly weapon like the thunderbolt in your right hand. Thou crushest all deceitful attempts (to overpower thee). (5216)

१०. आ संयतमिन्द्र णः स्वस्ति शत्रुतूर्याय बृहतीममृध्राम् ।
यया दासान्यार्याणि वृत्रा करो वज्रिन्त्सुतुका नाहुषाणि ॥

10. O Lord of destruction or fortunes, equipped with lethal weapons, supply us the huge, indestructible, well-controlled gun, capable of hurling big shots to destroy the foes. By such means thou turnest the wicked enemies into noble persons and ordinary people into those of good offspring. (5217)

११. स नो नियुद्भिः पुरुहूत वेधो विश्ववाराभिरा गहि प्रयज्यो ।
न या अदेवो वरते न देव आभिर्याहि तूयमा मद्र्यद्रिक् ॥

11. O much-invoked, highly honoured and wise administrator come to us with well-controlled fighting forces, capable of warding off all the foes as well as all the handicaps. Come swiftly towards me with these forces, whom neither the inglorious nor the glorious can obstruct or ward off. (5218)

HYMN XXXVII

१. यस्तिग्मश्रृङ्गो वृषभो न भीम एकः कृष्टीश्च्यावयति प्र विश्वाः ।
यः शश्वतो अदाशुषो गयस्य प्रयन्तासि सुष्वितराय वेदः ॥

1. The king who is terrific like the rain-pouring Sun with sharp rays like the horns, and who alone subdues all the subjects and ever givers of the wealth of the niggard to the liberal-minded person, offering oblation generously. (5219)[1]

२. त्वं ह त्यदिन्द्र कुत्समावः शुश्रूषमाणस्तन्वा॒ समर्ये ।
दासं यच्छुष्णं कुयवं न्य॒स्मा अरन्धय आर्जुनेयाय शिक्षन् ॥

2. O Lord of destruction and fortunes, thou usest the proper deadly weapon for protection in large wars, bodily rendering your services therein, when thou subduest the oppressor, the blood-sucker and the adulterator for the sake of this civilised and educated person. (5220)[2]

३. त्वं धृष्णो धृषता वीतहव्यं प्रावो विश्वाभिरूतिभिः सुदासम् ।
प्र पौरुकुत्सिं त्रसदस्युमावः क्षेत्रसाता वृत्रहत्येषु पूरुम् ॥

3. O Smasher of foes, thou protectest the good doner, capable of acquiring good provisions, by all means of protection with thy smashing force. In case of winning land and destruction of obstructing enemies, you provide a complete protection to the defender of the subjects equipped with various weapons of destruction, striking terror in the minds of wicked mischief-mongers. (5221)[3]

४. त्वं नृभिर्नृमणो देववीतौ भूरीणि वृत्रा हर्यश्व हंसि ।
त्वं नि दस्युं चुमुरिं धुनिं चास्वापयो दभीतये सुहन्तु ॥

[1](1-11) cf. *Rig*, 7, 19, 1-11.

[2]Rendering of Kutsa, Dasa, Sushrushma and Kuyava, by Sayāna and Griffith as proper historic persons is wrong on the very face of it.

[3]Similarly as above, Sayāna and Griffith are wrong in speaking of Sudasa, Paurukutsa, Trasdasyu, Pūru as persons of history.

4. O mighty Lord of swift-moving forces, well-disposed towards leaders, you destroy lot of inimical forces and evils in the war or the sacrifice, performed by divine forces or men. Well-equipped with proper means of destruction you completely annihilate the wicked person, who robs and harasses the people for the maintenance of well-controlled administration.

Or

O current electricity of high voltage, safely carried by electric wires, you kill many enemies in the war, waged by learned persons or through the help of natural forces. To keep all the evil forces under control, you, being well-equipped with good means of destruction completely lay down to lasting sleep the evil forces that rob and harass the general public. (5222)[1]

५. तव च्यौत्नानि वज्रहस्त तानि नव यत्पुरो नवतिं च सद्यः ।
निवेशने शततमाविवेषीरहं च वृत्रं नमुचिमुताहन् ॥

5. O mighty king, with thunderbolt in hand, those are thy enemy-crushing powers, which swiftly ruin numerous (i.e., 99) fortresses and drive him out of them. Thou gettest well-entrenched in the 100th feet. Thou killest the over powering foe and destroyest him, who is not to be spared at any cost.

Or

O Atomic energy, with deadly force in hand, thou at once smashest all the 99 (so-called elements, such are thy powers of fission. Thou art well-entrenched in the 100th place of shelter (in the very core of the matter). Thou consumest all covering material and even the substance, which resists all forces to fission it. (5223)[2]

६. सना ता त इन्द्र भोजनानि रातहव्याय दाशुषे सुदासे ।
वृष्णे ते हरी वृषणा युनज्मि व्यन्तु ब्रह्माणि पुरुशाक वाजम् ॥

6. O Lord of fortunes, ancient are those means of enjoyment and pleasure, which you give to the generous-minded, good donor, who freely gives away what is worth giving. O Lord of many powers and energies, I, the devotee, unite the two powerful horses, in the form of Prān and Apān to attain to Thee, the Mighty One. Let our Vedic prayers and wealth be devoted to Thee, the Powerful One. (5224)[3]

७. मा ते अस्यां सहसावन्परिष्टावघाय भूम हरिवः परादै ।
त्रायस्व नोऽवृकेभिर्वरूथैस्तव प्रियासः सूरिषु स्याम ॥

7. O Mighty Lord of all powerful and swift-moving natural forces, let us not go in for sin, which is to be shun with care, in this sacrificial act to serve

[1]The verse can apply equally to the king as well as to current electricity (ii) Rendering of 'Chumuri,' 'Dhuni' and 'Dabhiti' as persons by Sayāna and Griffith is wrong.

[2]The number 99 is significant. To me it appears, it refers to the number of so-called elements, known to the scientists. These are called भोग in the Vedic verses. The verse explains the working of the atomic energy quite well. (ii) 'Namuchi and Vritra' are not demons, as interpreted by Sayāna and Griffith. They simply refer to non-conductors or substance difficult to fission.

[3]The verse can be applied to the king also.

Thee. Protect us through honest and non-violent forces. May be dear to Thee among the learned and the wise. (5225)

८. प्रियास इत्ते मघवन्नभिष्टौ नरो मदेम शरणे सखायः ।
नि तुर्वशं नि याद्वं शिशीह्यतिथिग्वाय शंस्यं करिष्यन् ॥

8. O Lord of fortunes, may we live in joy and pleasure under Thy protection, acting according to Thy will, thus enduring to Thee alone as Thy friends. Letest Thee fully energise the person, who is keen to control the violent pushing and respectful towards the guests, thus wishing to do a noble deed. (5226)[1]

९. सद्यश्चिन्नु ते मघवन्नभिष्टौ नरः शंसन्त्युक्थशास उक्था ।
ये ते हवेभिर्वि पणी रदाशन्नस्मान्वृणीष्व युज्याय तस्मै ॥

9. O Bounteous Lord, the leading persons, skilled in preaching Vedic knowledge, ever preach the Vedic truths under your guidance and direction. They set at naught the efforts of the niggardly covetous people at Thy calls. Please accept us too for the same good sacrificial act. (5227)

१०. एते स्तोमा नरां नृतम तुभ्यमस्मद्रयञ्चो ददतो मघानि ।
तेषामिन्द्र वृत्रहत्ये शिवो भूः सखा च शूरोऽविता च नृणाम् ॥

10. O chief among the leaders, these are praises for thee. They present all sorts of riches to thee in our presence. In the very act of destruction of the enemy, be a source of comfort and ease to them. Be a brave friend and protector of the people and leaders. (5228)

११. नू इन्द्र शूर स्तवमान ऊती ब्रह्मजूतस्तन्वा वावृधस्व ।
उप नो वाजान्मिमीह्युप स्तीन्यूयं पात स्वस्तिभिः सदा नः ॥

11. O brave and bounteous king, being praised and respected by us for protection, develop your bodily power with rich food and wealth. Shower on us fortunes, provisions and strength, shelter and offspring. O divine persons or forces, ever protect us with all comforts and blessings. (5229)

HYMN XXXVIII

१. आ याहि सुषुमा हि त इन्द्र सोमं पिबा इमम् । एदं बर्हिः सदो मम ॥

1. O Lord of fortunes, come, here is this essence of medicinal herbs, drink it and sit on this seat of respect of mine. (5230)

२. आ त्वा ब्रह्मयुजा हरी वहतामिन्द्र केशिना । उप ब्रह्माणि नः शृणु ॥

2. O Mighty Lord, let these brilliant horses in the form of Prāna and Apāna, yoked in deep Vedic meditation approach Thee. Please listen to our Vedic prayers. (5231)

३. ब्रह्माणस्त्वा वयं युजा सोमपामिन्द्र सोमिनः । सुतावन्तो हवामहे ॥

[1]Turvasha, Yadu, stithigana are not the persons as declared by Sayāna and Griffith. They have lowered the dignity of the Vedic teachings of high order by reading history here and there.

3. O Mighty God, we, the well-versed in Vedic lore, immersed in deep meditation, desirous of drinking the nectar of salvation, having cultivated complete concentration call Thee, the Protector of Perfect Bliss. (5232)

४. इन्द्रमिद् गाथिनो बृहदिन्द्रमर्केभिरर्किणः । इन्द्रं वाणीरनूषत ॥

4. The singers and the reciters of praise songs extol the mighty Lord alone. Even the Vedic verses praise Indra. (5233)

५. इन्द्र इद्धर्योः सचा संमिश्ल आ वचोयुजा । इन्द्रो वज्री हिरण्ययः ॥

5. Electricity is well-mixed up with Prāna and Apāna, the two horse powers, yoked to power of speech. Electric power has the striking power of a deadly weapon and full of brilliance. (5234)

६. इन्द्रो दीर्घाय चक्षस आ सूर्यं रोहयद्दिवि । वि गोभिरद्रिमैरयत् ॥

6. The Mighty Lord has raised the Sun aloft in the heavens for long vision. He disperses the cloud with the rays of light. (5235)[1]

HYMN XXXIX

१. इन्द्रं वो विश्वतस्परि हवामहे जनेभ्यः । अस्माकमस्तु केवलः ॥

1. We pray to the Lord of fortunes from all sides for you; the general people. May He be our lonely shelter! (5236)[2]

२. व्यन्तरिक्षमतिरन्मदे सोमस्य रोचना । इन्द्रो यदभिनद्वलम् ॥

2. When the wind disperses the darkening cloud, the brilliant rays of light pervade the atmosphere in the very ecstacy of Soma. (5237)[3]

३. उद् गा आजदङ्गिरोभ्य आविष्कृण्वन्गुहा सतीः । अर्वाञ्चं नुनुदे बलम् ॥

3. The Omniscient God, revealing the Vedic knowledge, present in the innermost recesses of mind, to the seers, shatters down the darkening ignorance. (5238)[4]

४. इन्द्रेण रोचना दिवो दृळ्हानि दृंहितानि च । स्थिराणि न पराणुदे ॥

4. The shining stars of heaven have been established firm and secure by the Mighty God, so stable that they do not go astray from their respective orbits. (5239)

५. अपामूर्मिर्मदन्निव स्तोम इन्द्राजिरायते । वि ते मदा अराजिषुः ॥

5. O Mighty Lord, Thy energy and glory go on joyously forward like the wave of waters. They shine in various forms in the world. (5240)

HYMN XL*

१. इन्द्रेण सं हि दृक्षसे संजग्मानो अबिभ्युषा । मन्दू समानवर्चसा ॥

[1]cf. *Rig*, 8.17.1-3, and 1.7. 1-3. The verse can be applied to the king and soul even.

[2]cf. *Rig*, 1.7. 10, and 8. 14. 7-10.

[3]'Bala' is a cloud and not a 'demon' of that name as interpreted by Griffith.

[4]'Angiras' are not a special tribe of sages, but it is a general term for the seers of truths of Vedic learning.

*cf. *Rig*. 1.6. 7-8, 1.6.4.

1. O brave person, verily you look excellent in the company of the fearless king or commander of the army. Equally glorious both of you are a source of joy and pleasure to the people. (5241)

२. अनवद्यैरभिद्युभिर्मखः सहस्वदर्चति । गणैरिन्द्रस्य काम्यैः ॥

2. The very sacrificial act of subduing the enemy by the faultless, splendorous units of the army, so beloved of the king or army-chief, enhances the glory of him. (5242)

३. आदह स्वधामनु पुनर्गर्भत्वमेरिरे । दधाना नाम यज्ञियम् ॥

3. The souls, even after shaking off this body, take rebirth according to their potential worths and capabilities, worked up by the good deeds or otherwise performed during the life. (5243)

HYMN XLI*

१. इन्द्रो दधीचो अस्थभिर्वृत्राण्यप्रतिष्कुतः । जघान नवतीर्नव ॥

1. The Atomic Energy fissions the ninety-nine elements, covering its path by the bombardments of neutrons without let or hindrance. (5244)

२. इच्छन्नश्वस्य यच्छिरः पर्वतेष्वपश्रितम् । तद्विदच्छर्यणावति ॥

2. Desirous of striking the head i.e., the chief part of the swift power, hidden in the mass of molecular adjustments of the elements, this atomic energy approaches it in the very act of fissioning it by the above-noted bombardments. (5245)

३. अत्राह गोरमन्यत नाम त्वष्टुरपीच्यम् । इत्था चन्द्रमसो गृहे ॥

3. Herein verily the scientist know the similar hidden striking force of the rays of the Sun working in the orbit of the moon. (5246)

HYMN XLII**

१. वाचमष्टापदीमहं नवस्रक्तिमृतस्पृशम् । इन्द्रात्परि तन्वं ममे ॥

1. I, the devotee, fully understand the vast Vedic lore, having eight parts, nine kinds of composition, full of truth, from the Greatest Guru, the God. (5247)[1]

२. अनु त्वा रोदसी उभे क्रक्षमाणमकृपेताम् । इन्द्र यद्दस्युहाभवः ॥

2. O the mighty Lord of Destruction, when Thou actest as the Destroyer of Evil forces, let both the worlds (i.e., the earth and the heavens) be in accordance with Thee, crushing the wicked and the mischievous. (5248)

३. उत्तिष्ठन्नोजसा सह पीत्वी शिप्रे अवेपयः । सोममिन्द्र चमू सुतम् ॥

*cf. *Rig*, 1.84. 13-15. 'Dadhichi' is not a Rishi of that name, but the central core of the atom, i.e., neutron. 'Indra' means the master of Destruction, i.e., the fissioning force in the form of Atomic energy. (ii) To me, the whole stanza appears to describe the clear working of the atomic energy rather than anything else.

**cf. *Rig*, 8.76. 12, 11, 10.

[1] 8 padas 4 Vedas and 4 up-Vedas; 9 sraktis: Shiksha, Kalpa, Vigyana, Nighantu, Nirukta, Jyotish, Chhandas, Dharmashastra and Mimansa (Pt. Jaidev).

3. O mighty king, having acquired the state of plenty and prosperity through the struggle between thy armies and those of the foe, mobilise the forces with your prowess and valour.

Or

O soul, having drunk deep the divine nectar through deep meditation by the help of Prāna and Apāna, the vital breaths, rising higher and higher on the path of salvation, through Power of knowledge shake off the internal and external fies of actions. (5249)

HYMN XLIII*

१. भिन्धि विश्वा अप द्विषः परि बाधो जहि मृधः । वसु स्पार्हं तदा भर ।।

1. O king, shatter away all the enemies, crush the fighting forces and acquire the desirable riches. (5250)

२. यद्वीलाविन्द्र यत्स्थिरे यत्पर्शाने पराभृतम् । वसु स्पार्हं तदा भर ।।

2. O Mighty Lord, bless us with all the desirable fortunes and wealth that is stored in high energy, strong rocks and sources of water like clouds. (5251)

३. यस्य ते विश्वमानुषो भूरेर्दत्तस्य वेदति । वसु स्पार्हं तदा भर ।।

3. O Lord of Fortunes, shower on us the desirable riches, which all the people of the world get from thee, the Great Donor. (5252)

HYMN XLIV**

१. प्र सम्राजं चर्षणीनामिन्द्रं स्तोता नव्यं गीर्भिः । नरं नृषाहं मंहिष्ठम् ।।

1. O people, praise the Mighty Lord, the monarch of all the people, the praise-worthy leader, the controller of the people, the great donor, with your speeches. (5253)[2]

२. यस्मिन्नुक्थानि रण्यन्ति विश्वानि च श्रवस्या । अपामवो न समुद्रे ।।

2. In whom all the glorifying praise-songs look befitting and appropriate, just as the flow of waters fits into the sea. (5254)

३. तं सुष्टुत्या विवासे ज्येष्ठराजं भरे कृत्नुम् । महो वाजिनं सनिभ्यः ।।

3. I praise him, the greatest king, the destroyer of the foes in the war, the most powerful person, for his munificence with good praises. (5255)

HYMN XLV***

१. अयमु ते समतसि कपोत इव गर्भधिम् । वचस्तच्चिन्न ओहसे ।।

1. O king or commander, this national estate is thine. Thou approachest it just as the male pigeon does the female one. Similarly dost thou lovingly listen to our words. (5256)

२. स्तोत्रं राधानां पते गिर्वाहो वीर यस्य ते । विभूतिरस्तु सूनृता ।।

*cf. *Rig*, 8. 45, 40-42. **cf. *Rig*, 8. 16. 1-3.
***cf. *Rig*, 1.30. 4-6.

2. O Brave Lord of fortunes or riches, Worthy of respectful praise, Whose alone is this praise-song. May Thy manifold bounties be true and everlasting. (5257)

३. ऊर्ध्वस्तिष्ठा न ऊतयेऽस्मिन्वाजे शतक्रतो । समन्येषु ब्रवावहै ॥

3. O Lord of hundreds acts and sacrifices, letst Thou stand far above all for our protection and shelter in this great struggle of life. Let us both counsel together in other things, too. (5258)

HYMN XLVI*

१. प्रणेतारं वस्यो अच्छा कर्त्तारं ज्योतिः समत्सु । सासह्वांसं युधामित्रान् ॥

1. May he approach well the good leader of the fortunes, showing an enlightened lead and glory in the wars or great festive occasions, and subduing the foes through war and valour. (5259)[1]

२. स नः पप्रिः पारयाति स्वस्ति नावा पुरुहूतः । इन्द्रो विश्वा अति द्विषः ॥

2. That Lord of Destruction, fulfiller of all objects or Pervader of the universe, much-invoked leads us across all inimical forces with ease and comfort, like a boatman with a boat. (5260)

३. स त्वं न इन्द्र वाजेभिर्दशस्या च गातुया च । अच्छा च नः सुम्नं नेषि ॥

3. O Mighty Lord, Thou protectest us through Thy prowess and fortunes, and well leadest us through the right path to prosperity and plenty. (5261)

HYMN XLVII**

१. तमिन्द्रं वाजयामसि महे वृत्राय हन्तवे । स वृषा वृषभो भुवत् ॥

1. Let us enhance the glory of the Mighty Lord of Destruction for the destruction of the great obscuring demon of ignorance. Let the most Powerful God shown His blessings on us. (5262)

२. इन्द्रः स दामने कृत ओजिष्ठः स मदे हितः । द्युम्नी श्लोकी स सोम्यः ॥

2. That Donor is made for giving the various gifts. The most Mighty One is engrossed in providing the best joys and pleasures to His subjects. He is Glorious, Praiseworthy and Pleasure-giving. (5263)

३. गिरा वज्रो न संभृतः सबलो अनपच्युतः । ववक्ष ऋष्वो अस्तृतः ॥

3. He is equipped with energy and glory like the thunderbolt through the Vedic verses. He is the Almighty, Invincible, Indestructible, the smasher of evil forces and bears the universe. (5264)

४. इन्द्रमिद् गाथिनो बृहदिन्द्रमर्केभिरर्किणः । इन्द्रं वाणीरनूषत ॥

५. इन्द्र इद्धर्योः सचा संमिश्ल आ वचोयुजा । इन्द्रो वज्री हिरण्ययः ॥

६. इन्द्रो दीर्घाय चक्षस आ सूर्यं रोहयद्दिवि । वि गोभिरद्रिमैरयत् ॥

4-6. See 20. 38. (4-6). (5265-67)

*cf. *Rig*, 8. 16. 10-12.

**cf. *Rig*, 8. 93. 7-9, I.7. 1-3; VIII. 17. 1-3; I.6. 1-3; I. 50. 1-9.

७. आ याहि सुषुमा हि त इन्द्र सोमं पिबा इमम् । एदं बर्हिः सदो मम ।।

८. आ त्वा ब्रह्मयुजा हरी वहतामिन्द्र केशिना । उप ब्रह्माणि नः शृणु ।।

९. ब्रह्माणस्त्वा वयं युजा सोमपामिन्द्र सोमिनः । सुतावन्तो हवामहे ।।

7-9. See 20. 3. (1-3) and 20.38. (1-3). (5268-70)

१०. युञ्जन्ति ब्रध्नमरुषं चरन्तं परि तस्थुषः । रोचन्ते रोचना दिवि ।।

११. युञ्जन्त्यस्य काम्या हरी विपक्षसा रथे । शोणा धृष्णू नृवाहसा ।।

१२. केतुं कृण्वन्नकेतवे पेशो मर्या अपेशसे । समुषद्भिरजायथाः ।।

10-12. See 20. 26. (4-6). (5271-73)

१३. उदु त्ये जातवेदसं देवं वहन्ति केतवः । दृशे विश्वाय सूर्यम् ।।

१४. अप त्ये तायवो यथा नक्षत्रा यन्त्यक्तुभिः । सूराय विश्वचक्षसे ।।

१५. अदृश्रन्नस्य केतवो वि रश्मयो जनाँ अनु । भ्राजन्तो अग्नयो यथा ।।

१६. तरणिर्विश्वदर्शतो ज्योतिष्कृदसि सूर्य । विश्वमा भासि रोचन ।।

१७. प्रत्यङ् देवानां विशः प्रत्यङ्ङुदेषि मानुषीः । प्रत्यङ् विश्वं स्वर्दृशे ।।

१८. येना पावक चक्षसा भुरण्यन्तं जनाँ अनु । त्वं वरुण पश्यसि ।।

१९. वि द्यामेषि रजस्पृथ्वहर्मिमानो अक्तुभिः । पश्यञ्जन्मानि सूर्य ।।

२०. सप्त त्वा हरितो रथे वहन्ति देव सूर्य । शोचिष्केशं विचक्षणम् ।।

२१. अयुक्त सप्त शुन्ध्युवः सूरो रथस्य नप्त्यः । ताभिर्याति स्वयुक्तिभिः ।।

13-21. See 13. 2. (16-24). (5274-82)

HYMN XLVIII*

१. अभि त्वा वर्चसा गिरः सिञ्चन्तीराचरण्यवः । अभि वत्सं न धेनवः ।।

1. O God, the Vedic verses, moving in all directions, approach Thee with glory from all sides, just as the cow does her calf. (5283)

२. ता अर्षन्ति शुभ्रियः पृञ्चन्तीर्वर्चसा प्रियः । जातं जात्रीर्यथा हृदा ।।

2. These pure and loving Vedic songs, touching Thee with splendour come to Thee like the mother, hugging her newly born baby to her heart. (5284)

३. वज्रापवसाध्यः कीर्तिर्म्रियमाणमावहन् । मह्यमायुर्घृतं पयः ।।

3. The vital breaths, Prāna and Apāna produced through electrolysis and glorious energy revitalise the dying person even. Let them provide me too, with long life, clarified butter and milk (nourishing drinks).

Or

The vitalising deeds and intelligence invest a powerful and daring person with glory and fortune. Let them provide me also with long life, nourishing food and drink like butter and milk. (5285)

४. आयं गौः पृश्निरक्रमीदसदन्मातरं पुरः । पितरं च प्रयन्त्स्वः ।।

५. अन्तश्चरति रोचना अस्य प्राणादपानतः । व्यख्यन्महिषः स्वः ।।

६. त्रिंशद्धामा वि राजति वाक्पतङ्गो अशिश्रियत् । प्रति वस्तोरहर्द्युभिः ।।

*Verses 1-3 are not from *Rigveda* or any other Veda.

4-6. See A.V.6.31. (1-3). (5286-88)[1]

HYMN XLIX

१. यच्छक्रा वाचमारुहन्नन्तरिक्षं सिषासथः । सं देवा अमदन्वृषा ॥

1. When the energetic devotees, carried by the Vedic praise-songs in ecstasy, reach the innermost recesses of the mind in deep meditation, they revel in the highest bliss, along with the showerer of all blessings.

Or

When the Vedic prayers, raising aloft the pure energetic soul, touch the innermost recesses of the mind, the enlightened soul revels in the highest state of beatitude along with the showerer of all blessings. (5289)[2]

२. शक्रो वाचमधृष्टायोरुवाचो अधृष्णुहि । मंहिष्ठ आ मर्दादिवि ॥

2. O devoted soul, purifying and energising yourself, cultivate the Vast Vedic learning for the invincible state of salvation. Attaining the highest position, revel in the state of bliss in all respects.

Or

O devotee, fully praise the Almighty with the Vedic verses; sing the praises of the most Terrible with Vedic songs. The most Liberal God revels in the brilliant state of salvation, attained by thee. (5290)

३. शक्रो वाचमधृष्णुहि धामधर्मन्विराजति । विमदन्बर्हिरासरन् ॥

3. O devoted soul, being pure and powerful, be the torch-bearer of the Vedic lore, for it is the energetic who shines full in all places and duties and attains the highest seat of salvation in perfect bliss.

Or

O devotee, praise the Almighty with Vedic prayers. He is shining everywhere. Revelling there, He pervades the whole universe. (5291)

४. तं वो दस्ममृतीषहं वसोर्मन्दानमन्धसः । अभि वत्सं न स्वसरेषु धेनव इन्द्रं गीर्भिर्नवामहे ॥

५. द्युक्षं सुदानुं तविषीभिरावृतं गिरिं न पुरुभोजसम् ।
क्षुमन्तं वाजं शतिनं सहस्रिणं मक्षू गोमन्तमीमहे ॥

६. तत्त्वा यामि सुवीर्यं तद् ब्रह्म पूर्वचित्तये ।
येना यतिभ्यो भृगवे धने हिते येन प्रस्कण्वमाविथ ॥

७. येना समुद्रमसृजो महीरपस्तदिन्द्र वृष्णि ते शवः ।
सद्यः सो अस्य महिमा न संनशे यं क्षोणीरनुचक्रदे ॥

4-7. See A.V. 20. 9. (1-4). (5292-95)

HYMN L

१. कन्नव्यो अतसीनां तुरो गृणीत मर्त्यः । नही न्वस्य महिमानमिन्द्रियं स्वर्गृणन्त आनशुः ॥

[1](4-6) cf. *Rig*, 10.184 or A.V. 6.31. Verse 3 has two readings, (ii) is according to Krishna Lal edited Samhitā.

[2]Verses 1-3 have two readings each. Second readings are according to the versions, edited by Sevak Lal and Griffith.

1. How should the new person sing the praises of the Powerful mover of the swift-moving forces? Have not the sages, praising the greatness and fortunes of Him attained to state of highest bliss? (i.e., verily they have). (5296)[1]

२. कदु स्तुवन्त ऋतयन्त देवत ऋषिः को विप्र ओहते ।
कदा हवं मघवन्निन्द्र सुन्वतः कदु स्तुवत आ गमः ॥

2. O God, how do the truth-seekers praise Thee? Who is the wise person, capable of realising the real import of the Vedic verses, that discusses about Thee. When dost Thou, the Lord of all fortunes, hear the call of Thy devotee? When dost Thou come to him who sings Thy praises? (5297)

HYMN LI*

१. अभि प्र वः सुराधसमिन्द्रमर्च यथा विदे ।
यो जरितृभ्यो मघवा पुरूवसुः सहस्रेणेव शिक्षति ॥

1. O learned person, in order that you may know Him, fully espouse Him and worship Him, the Lord of Fortunes, Who is Bounteous Lord of all riches and wealth and gives the devotees in a thousand ways. (5298)

२. शतानीकेव प्र जिगाति धृष्णुया हन्ति वृत्राणि दाशुषे ।
गिरेरिव प्र रसा अस्य पिन्विरे दत्राणि पुरुभोजसः ॥

2. As if with a hundred armies, He subdues and destroys the evil forces with the crushing blow, for him who pays his homage to Him. Like the waters from the mountains flow and nourish the people, the various gifts of Him, Who is gifted with numerous means of enjoyment and well-being. (5299)

३. प्र सु श्रुतं सुराधसमर्चा शक्रमभिष्टये । यः सुन्वते स्तुवते काम्यं वसु सहस्रेणेव मंहते ॥

3. O devotee, thoroughly worship Him, Who is well-known, through the Vedic verses, Worthy to be worshipped through deep meditation, and All-powerful, in order to attain your desired object, and Who showers the desired fortunes on the devoted praise-singer in a thousand ways. (5300)

४. शतानीका हेतयो अस्य दुष्टरा इन्द्रस्य समिषो महीः ।
गिरिर्न भुज्मा मघवत्सु पिन्वते यदीं सुता अमन्दिषुः ॥

4. Many-faced are the invincible weapons of destruction and great are the forces of mobilisation of This Lord of Destruction. He satisfies the fortunate ones to their fill, like the mountain or the cloud, pouring the blessed showers of water to the needy, when the medicinal juices, produced by the devotees, gladden Him. (5301)

HYMN LII**

१. वयं घ त्वा सुतावन्त आपो न वृक्तबर्हिषः ।
पवित्रस्य प्रस्रवणेषु वृत्रहन्परि स्तोतार आसते ॥

[1]cf. *Rig*, 8.3. (13-14) (i) The example of the old sages sets the pace for the new. (ii) The answers to all these questions are self-evident.

*cf. (1-2) *Rig*, 8.49. 1-2, (3-4) *Rig*, 8.50.1-2 (Also *Rig*, Valakhilya 1.1-2; 2. 1-2).

**cf. *Rig*, 8.33. 1-3; *Ath*, 20.57.14-16; *Sam*, (Pu) 3/7/9; II. 2/2/तृच 12.

1. O Destroyer of forces of evil and ignorance, we, the devotee having shed off feelings of hatred and attachment, and gained some inkling of realisation of Thy knowledge, have now fully entrusted ourselves to Thee, just as waters, felling off the growing paddy, find their permanent abode in springs of pure water. (5302)

२. स्वरन्ति त्वा सुते नरो वसो निरेक उक्थिनः ।
कदा सुतं तृषाण ओक आ गम इन्द्र स्वब्दीव वंसगः ॥

2. O Shelterer of the world, certain learned persons specially sing Thy praises in this world, created by Thee. Just as a thirsty person approaches a source of water, when wilt Thou, O mighty Lord, bless us with Thy blessings like the cloud, pouring down pure water on the thirsty earth? (5303)

३. कण्वेभिर्धृष्णवा धृषद्वाजं दर्षि सहस्त्रिणम् ।
पिशङ्गरूपं मघवन्विचर्षणे मक्षू गोमन्तमीमहे ॥

3. O Lord of conquest and sustenance, Thou honourest the wise persons with thousand-fold prowess and wealth, capable of subduing others. O Lord of Fortunes and seers of all, we ever pray for the splendorous and brilliant state of beatitude. (5304)

HYMN LIII*

१. क ईं वेद सुते सचा पिबन्तं कद्वयो दधे ।
अयं यः पुरो विभिनत्त्योजसा मन्दानः शिप्रचन्धसः ॥

1. In this created world, who knows Him, Who takes in all this universe at one draught (at the time of the deluge) and how much life-giving energy He bears? The self-same One Who shatters the whole universe to smithreens. by His Prowess, just as the commander of an army, being energised by rich food and vital power, mobilises his jaws of destruction and annihilates the towns and fortresses of the foe. (5305)

२. दाना मृगो न वारणः पुरुत्रा चरथं दधे ।
नकिष्ट्वा नि यमदा सुते गमो महांश्चरस्योजसा ॥

2. O Commander of the armies, or soul, you roam about in many places, like the wild elephant incited by the vital force. There is none to obstruct thy movements. You vehemently move on to excellence and get the medicinal juice, prepared for thee, or (the nectar of salvation for the soul). (5306)

३. य उग्रः सन्ननिष्टृत स्थिरो रणाय संस्कृतः ।
यदि स्तोतुर्मघवा शृणवद्धवं नेन्द्रो योषत्या गमत् ॥

3. The same commander or the soul, who is fortunate, terrible, energetic, unconquerable, steadfast in resolve, ever ready for the fight with the forces of evil or ignorance, never falters but does come at the beck and call of the praise-singer if and when he hears his call. (5307)

*cf. *Rig*, 8.33. 7-9; *Ath*, 20.57 11-13; (1) *Sam*, (Pu) 4/1/5; U., 8/2/तृच 15.

HYMN LIV*

१. विश्वाः पृतना अभिभूतरं नरं सजूस्ततक्षुरिन्द्रं जजनुश्च राजसे ।
क्रत्वा वरिष्ठं वर आमुरिमुतोग्रमोजिष्ठं तवसं तरस्विनम् ॥

1. With one accord, the people made and proclaimed for ruling over them the mighty king, the person, who can vanquish the enemies in the wars, is most eminent in actions and intelligence, the destroyer of the foes, fierce, most valorous stalwart and very quick in action. (5308)

२. समीं रेभासो अस्वरन्निन्द्रं सोमस्य पीतये ।
स्वर्पतिं यदीं वृधे धृतव्रतो ह्योजसा समूतिभिः ॥

2. Whenever the devotee jointly call the mighty Lord of all Bliss and pleasures for drinking deep the nectar of Beatitude, He, the sustainer of All laws comes with force and all means of protection and safety.

Or

In the case of a king, whenever the people unanimously call for their aid and enhancement of their well-being, the great king, the source of all happiness, readily comes to their rescue, with valour and means of shelter and safety. (5309)

३. नेमिं नमन्ति चक्षसा मेषं विप्रा अभिस्वरा ।
सुदीतयो वो अद्रुहोऽपि कर्णे तरस्विनः समृक्वभिः ॥

3. The learned persons, singing together with vision of knowledge and realisation, bow to Him, Who is worthy to be bowed to and is the Prime-mover, like the Sun. Similarly, O people, you, shunning malice in hearing good teaching and being thus enlighted and energised to activity, should pay your homage to Him with Vedic verses. (5310)[1]

HYMN LV**

१. तमिन्द्रं जोहवीमि मघवानमुग्रं सत्रा दधानमप्रतिष्कुतं शवांसि ।
मंहिष्ठो गीर्भिरा च यज्ञियो ववर्तद्राये नो विश्वा सुपथा कृणोतु वज्री ॥

1. I, the devotee often remember and call that Lord of fortunes equipped with all wealth and riches, Terrible, Unbearable and Bearer of all powers, altogether. He pervades all space, worthy to be worshipped and revered. May He, the Remover of all evils and difficulties make all our paths good for attaining fortunes and riches. (5311)

२. या इन्द्र भुज आभरः स्वर्वाँ असुरेभ्यः ।
स्तोतारमिन्मघवन्नस्य वर्धय ये च त्वे वृक्तबर्हिषः ॥

2. O Lord of Fortunes, equipped with all means of happiness and enjoyment, whatever means of subsistence Thou showerest on the living-beings,

*cf. *Rig*, (सायणभा.) 8.86 (10-12) (Max Müller, *Rig*, 8.97. 10-12); साम. 3.3/1 तृच 14.

[1]Sayāna's interpretation of Medhātithi's story is baseless and conjectured. मेष refers to the Sun commencing the year from the constellation of that name.

**cf. *Rig*, 8.86 (13, 1.2) (Max Müller 8.97. (13, 1, 2) (1) साम. पू० 5/8/4; (2) पू० 3/7/2.

mayst Thou, Lord of riches and wealth, supply them in plenty to Thy devotees, who have given themselves up to Thee. (5312)

३. यमिन्द्र दधिषे त्वमश्वं गां भागमव्ययम् ।
यजमाने सुन्वति दक्षिणावति तस्मिन्तं धेहि मा पणौ ॥

3. Whatever limitless, enjoyable wealth, in the form of cows and horses. Thou bearest, O Lord of Fortunes, invest the same on the donating sacrificer, who offers oblations, and not on the niggard. (5313)

HYMN LVI*

१. इन्द्रो मदाय वावृधे शवसे वृत्रहा नृभिः ।
तमिन्महत्स्वाजिषूतेमर्भे हवामहे स वाजेषु प्र नोऽविषत् ॥

1. The mighty king or commander, the destroyer of foes has been installed to power and joy by the leaders of the people. We call him for and in great wars as well as in small battles. May he protect us in great acts of valour and wars. (5314)[1]

२. असि हि वीर सेन्योऽसि भूरि परादददिः ।
असि दभ्रस्य चिद् वृधो यजमानाय शिक्षसि सुन्वते भूरि ते वसु ॥

2. O brave king or commander, thou art a worthy warrior and hast vanquished thy foes many a time. Thou art an uplifter of the lowly even. Thou givest thy great wealth to the sacrificing worshipper. (5315)

३. यदुदीरत आजयो धृष्णवे धीयते धना ।
युक्ष्वा मदच्युता हरी कं हनः कं वसौ दधोऽस्माँ इन्द्र वसौ दधः ॥

3. When wars spring up, all sorts of riches are offered to the brave person, who crushes the enemy. Letst thou, lord of destruction and fortunes, yoke the two horses of strength and valour shedding joy and pleasure all around. Whom wilt thou kill? Whom wilt thou submerge in wealth? Letst thou immerse us in riches and wealth. (5316)

४. मदेमदे हि नो ददिर्यूथा गवामृजुक्रतुः ।
सं गृभाय पुरू शतोभयाहस्त्या वसु शिशीहि राय आ भर ॥

4. O mighty Lord or king, on every occasion of joy and pleasure, being equipped with highly simple and straight act of knowledge, valour or sacrifice, Thou offerest us herds of cows. Dole us out hundred sorts of riches by getting hold of them with both the hands and invest us with wealth. (5317)

५. मादयस्व सुते सचा शवसे शूर राधसे ।
विद्मा हि त्वा पुरूवसुमुप कामान्त्ससृज्महेऽथा नोऽविता भव ॥

5. O Great Destroyer of evil forces or brave king or commander, refresh Thou in this world for bounty and strength. Verily we know Thee as Lord of great fortunes. We leave our desires for Thee to be fulfilled. Letst Thou be our Protector. (5318)

*cf. *Rig*, 1.81. (1-3) *Sam.* उ० 3/2/तृच. 14. मन्त्र । पू० 5/3/3.

६. एते त इन्द्र जन्तवो विश्वं पुष्यन्ति वार्यम् ।
अन्तर्हि ख्यो जनानामर्यो वेदो अदाशुषां तेषां नो वेद आ भर ॥

6. O Lord of fortunes, these creatures of Thine nourish all sorts of attainable objects. Thou hast certainly the inner vision of all people, being the Lord of all. Thou seest the wealth of the miserly people, too. Bring us this wealth of theirs. (5319)

HYMN LVII*

१. सुरूपकृत्नुमूतये सुदुघामिव गोदुहे । जुहूमसि द्यविद्यवि ॥

1. Day by day, we invoke for protection the Creator, Who gives shape to so many beautiful things, just as an easily milked cow is called for milking. (5320)

२. उप नः सवना गहि सोमस्य सोमपाः पिब । गोदा इद्रेवतो मदः ॥

2. O Lord of bounties, come to us in our sacrificial ceremonies. Letst Thee, the Protector of all creation, protect this essence of herbs produced by us. Verily Thou art the Giver of all articles of enjoyment and means thereof like cow, vigour of all sense-organs and Vedic lore and land to the fortunate devotee (soul). (5321)[1]

३. अथा ते अन्तमानां विद्याम सुमतीनाम् । मा नो अति ख्य आ गहि ॥

3. O Lord, let us realise Thy real form from the wise persons given to deep meditation and who have attained Thy company and nearness. Reveal Thyself to us, but don't neglect us. (5322)

४. शुष्मिन्तमं न ऊतये द्युम्निनं पाहि जागृविम् । इन्द्र सोमं शतक्रतो ॥

५. इन्द्रियाणि शतक्रतो या ते जनेषु पञ्चसु । इन्द्र तानि त आ वृणे ॥

६. अगन्निन्द्र श्रवो बृहद् द्युम्नं दधिष्व दुष्टरम् । उत्ते शुष्मं तिरामसि ॥

७. अर्वावतो न आ गह्यथो शक्र परावतः । उ लोको यस्ते अद्रिव इन्द्रेह तत आ गहि ॥

८. इन्द्रो अङ्ग महद्भयमभी षदप चुच्यवत् । स हि स्थिरो विचर्षणिः ॥

९. इन्द्रश्च मृलयाति नो न नः पश्चादघं नशत् । भद्रं भवाति नः पुरः ॥

१०. इन्द्र आशाभ्यस्परि सर्वाभ्यो अभयं करत् । जेता शत्रून्विचर्षणिः ॥

4-10. See Ath. 20.20 (1-7). (5323-29)

११. क ईं वेद सुते सचा पिबन्तं कद्वयो दधे ।
अयं यः पुरो विभिनत्त्योजसा मन्दानः शिप्रचन्धसः ॥

१२. दाना मृगो न वारणः पुरुत्रा चरथं दधे ।
नकिष्ट्वा नि यमदा सुते गमो महांश्चरस्योजसा ॥

१३. य उग्रः सन्ननिष्टृत स्थिरो रणाय संस्कृतः ।
यदि स्तोतुर्मघवा शृणवद्धवं नेन्द्रो योषत्या गमत् ॥

*cf. *Rig*, 1.4. (1-3); 3-37. (8-11); 2.41. (10-12); 8.33 (7-9), (1-3).

[1](1-2) Coming of God to the devotees means being realized by them els He is present everywhere, even in their innermost recesses of their hearts.

11-13. See Ath. 20.53 (1.31). (5330-32)

१४. वयं घ त्वा सुतावन्त आपो न वृक्तबर्हिषः ।
पवित्रस्य प्रस्रवणेषु वृत्रहन्परि स्तोतार आसते ॥

१५. स्वरन्ति त्वा सुते नरो वसो निरेक उक्थिनः ।
कदा सुतं तृषाण ओक आ गम इन्द्र स्वब्दीव वंसगः ॥

१६. कण्वेभिर्धृष्णवा धृषद्वाजं दर्षि सहस्रिणम् ।
पिशङ्गरूपं मघवन्विचर्षणे मक्षू गोमन्तमीमहे ॥

14-16 See Ath. 20.52 (1-3). (5333-35)

HYMN LVIII*

१. श्रायन्त इव सूर्यं विश्वेदिन्द्रस्य भक्षत ।
वसूनि जाते जनमान ओजसा प्रति भागं न दीधिम ॥

1. O people of the world, partake of all the riches of the world relying on the Lord of fortunes alone, just as all the planets and stellites depend upon the Sun for the light. In this created and the would-be created world, let us get hold of our share of the riches and fortune with our own strenuous efforts and hard labour. (5336)

२. अनर्शराति वसुदामुप स्तुहि भद्रा इन्द्रस्य रातयः ।
सो अस्य कामं विधतो न रोषति मनो दानाय चोदयन् ॥

2. O man, worship Him, Whose gifts are flawless and Who is the Giver of riches and wealth. Auspicious and propitious, are the bounties of the Lord of fortunes. He does not turn down the desire of this devotee of His in anger, but He is bent upon granting boons. (5337)

३. वण्महाँ असि सूर्य बडादित्य महाँ असि । महस्ते सतो महिमा पनस्यतेऽद्धा देव महाँ असि ॥

3. O All-Impeller and All-Creator, Thou art truly Great. O God, the Annihilator and Controller of all Creation, Thou art truly Great. O Lord of Everlasting Existence, Thy renown is verily sung to be highly grand. O source of all fine qualities and lights, Thou art really great and mighty. (5338)

४. बट् सूर्य श्रवसा महाँ असि सत्रा देव महाँ असि ।
मह्ना देवानामसुर्यः पुरोहितो विभु ज्योतिरदाभ्यम् ॥

4. O Refulgent and Life-sustainer, Thou art verily Great through Thy Splendour, Valour, Fame and Knowledge. O Resplendent God, Thou art Great indeed. Thou art the Infuser of life amongst all divine powers, their foremost leader, Omnipresent and Invincible source of light and splendour. (5339)

*cf. *Rig*, (N.M.) 8.99. (3-4); 8-101. (11-12) (सायण भाष्य) 8.88. (3-4), 8-90) (11-12).

HYMN LIX*

१. उदु त्ये मधुमत्तमा गिर स्तोमास ईरते ।
सत्राजितो धनसा अक्षितोतयो वाजयन्तो रथा इव ॥

२. कण्वा इव भृगवः सूर्या इव विश्वमिद्धीतमानशुः ।
इन्द्रं स्तोमेभिर्महयन्त आयवः प्रियमेधासो अस्वरन् ॥

1-2. See 10. (1-2). (5340-41)

३. उदिन्न्वस्य रिच्यतेऽशो धनं न जिग्युषः ।
य इन्द्रो हरिवान्न दभन्ति तं रिपो दक्षं दधाति सोमिनि ॥

3. His All-pervading Prowess and Glory goes on excelling like the spoils of the victorious. No foibles and drawbacks overpower that mighty Lord, Who is the master of mobile forces. He invests the sacrificer with all strength and dexterity. (5342)

४. मन्त्रमखर्वं सुधितं सुपेशसं दधात यज्ञियेष्वा ।
पूर्वीश्चन प्रसितयस्तरन्ति तं य इन्द्रे कर्मणा भुवत् ॥

4. O people, in all sorts of sacrificial acts state-affairs or assemblies or conferences, make use of mutual consultation or Vedic text in a well-thought, beautifully arranged and humbly-put manner. All the traditions and antici-dents previously set up, lead him, easily across all difficulties and troubles, who ever remains under the shelter of the mighty Lord or king, with full activity. (5343)

HYMN LX**

१. एवा ह्यसि वीरयुरेवा शूर उत स्थिरः । एवा ते राध्यं मनः ॥

1. O Mighty Lord or king, Thou art truly the accomplice of the brave. Thou art chivalrous and steady indeed. Verily Thy Real Self is worthy to be worshipped. (5344)

२. एवा रातिस्तुवीमघ विश्वेभिर्धायि धातृभिः । अधा चिदिन्द्र मे सचा ॥

2. O Lord of vast fortunes and wealth, all the sustainer and nourishers of the world have rightly availed themselves of Thy gifts. In the same manner, letst Thou, O Lord of fortunes, be with me, (Thy devotee). (5345)

३. मो षु ब्रह्मेव तन्द्रयुर्भुवो वाजानां पते । मत्स्वा सुतस्य गोमतः ॥

3. O Lord of wealth, power and grains, don't be like a slothful priest. Rejoice in the acquired fortunes, full of wealth of cattle, etc. (5346)

४. एवा ह्यस्य सूनृता विरप्शी गोमती मही । पक्वा शाखा न दाशुषे ॥

4. So is truly fruitful His Vedic lore, full of true knowledge and the earth, equipped with wealth of cows, etc., grains and source of all articles of use like a ripe branch, to the generous-minded worshipper. (5347)

*cf. *Rig*, 8.3 (15-16); 7.32. (12-13); (1-2) *Ath*, K. 20. S. 10. (1-2).
**cf. *Rig*, 8.81. (28-30); 1.8. (8-10).

५. एवा हि ते विभूतय ऊतय इन्द्र मावते । सद्यश्चित्सन्ति दाशुषे ।।

5. O Mighty Lord of all fortunes, all Thy mighty powers and riches verily become means of protection, at once, for a devotee like myself. (5348)

६. एवा ह्यस्य काम्या स्तोम उक्थं च शंस्या । इन्द्राय सोमपीतये ।।

6. Truly His Vedic verses and Vedic lore is worth acquiring and praiseworthy. He is for the full satisfaction of the soul, desirous of drinking deep the nectar of salvation. (5349)

HYMN LXI*

१. तं ते मदं गृणीमसि वृषणं पृत्सु सासहिम् । उ लोककृत्नुमद्रिवो हरिश्रियम् ।।

1. O Showerer of All-blessings, we sing the praises of That Pleasure-giving Energy of Thine, which showers all well-being and prosperity, infuses courage and valour in all fighting forces, creates the worlds, and maintains all mobiles forces in the universe. (5350)

२. येन ज्योतींष्यायवे मनवे च विवेदिथ । मन्दानो अस्य बर्हिषो वि राजसि ।।

2. By which (i.e., above-mentioned Energy) Thou revealeth all sources of light (i.e., the Sun, the moon, electricity, etc., to the living beings and the learned persons. Revelling Thyself Thou shinest forth in this vast universe. (5351)[1]

३. तदद्या चित्त उक्थिनोऽनु ष्टुवन्ति पूर्वथा । वृषपत्नीरपो जया दिवेदिवे ।।

3. Even up-to-date, the devotees sing Thy praises as here-to-fore. Daily Thou keepest under Thy control all the pious persons like the Sun controlling the raining and nourishing powers of the clouds. (5352)

४. तम्वभि प्र गायत पुरुहूतं पुरुष्टुतम् । इन्द्रं गीर्भिस्तविषमा विवासत ।।

4. O learned persons, fully and thoroughly sing the praises of Him, Whom many invoke and worship. Engulf the Powerful Lord of fortunes with the Vedic songs. (5353)

५. यस्य द्विबर्हसो बृहत्सहो दाधार रोदसी । गिरीँरज्राँ अपः स्वर्वृषत्वना ।।

5. Whose (i.e., Indra, spoken of above) Great might, having Two strong energies, upholds the heavens and the earth, fast-moving clouds, mountains, waters and the sky by His Powers of showering or attraction. (5354)

६. स राजसि पुरुष्टुतँ एको वृत्राणि जिघ्नसे । इन्द्र जैत्रा श्रवस्या च यन्तवे ।।

6. O Mighty Lord, much invoked, Thou, all alone shinest forth over all the creation and destroyest all the forces of evil and ignorancc and controllest all fortunes of victory and high renown. (5355)

HYMN LXII**

१. वयमु त्वामपूर्व्य स्थूरं न कच्चिद्भरन्तोऽवस्यवः । वाजे चित्रं हवामहे ।।

*cf. *Rig*, 8.15. (4-6), (1-3).

[1]Griffith's reference to special personalities by Ayu and Manu is incorrect.

**(1-4) *Atharv*, 20.14. (1-4); (5-7) *Rig*, 8.98. (सायण 87) (1-3); (8-10). *Atharva*, 20.61. (4-6).

२. उप त्वा कर्मन्नूतये स नो युवोग्रश्चक्राम यो धृषत् ।
त्वामिद्ध्यवितारं ववृमहे सखाय इन्द्र सानसिम् ॥

३. यो न इदमिदं पुरा प्र वस्य आनिनाय तमु व स्तुषे । सखाय इन्द्रमूतये ॥

४. हर्यश्वं सत्पतिं चर्षणीसहं स हि ष्मा यो अमन्दत ।
आ तु नः स वयति गव्यमश्व्यं स्तोतृभ्यो मघवा शतम् ॥

1-4. See 20. 14. (1-4). (5356-58)

५. इन्द्राय साम गायत विप्राय बृहते बृहत् । धर्मकृते विपश्चिते पनस्यवे ॥

5. O persons, sing the great song (in the form of Bihati verses of Sam Ved), for the Mighty God, Who is All-wise, the Sustainer, Ordainer, the Omniscient, Praiseworthy, and Bestower of all blessing and fortunes. (5359)

६. त्वमिन्द्राभिभूरसि त्वं सूर्यमरोचयः । विश्वकर्मा विश्वदेवो महाँ असि ॥

6. O Mighty Lord, Thou art Omnipresent and Almighty. Thou enlightenest the Sun. Thou art the Great Creator of the universe and the Bestower of all the divine forces and Worthy to be worshipped by the learned persons. (5360)

७. विभ्राजं ज्योतिषा स्व१रगच्छो रोचनं दिवः । देवास्त इन्द्र सख्याय येमिरे ॥

7. O Lord of riches and fortunes, Radiant with splendour and Illuminator of the heavens, Thou pervadest the sky. All the learned persons and the divine forces ever try to seek Thy friendship. (5361)

८. तम्वभि प्र गायत पुरुहूतं पुरुष्टुतम् । इन्द्रं गीर्भिस्तविषमा विवासत ॥

९. यस्य द्विबर्हसो बृहत्सहो दाधार रोदसी । गिरीँरज्राँ अपः स्वर्वृषत्वना ॥

१०. स राजसि पुरुष्टुतँ एको वृत्राणि जिघ्नसे । इन्द्र जैत्रा श्रवस्या च यन्तवे ॥

8-10. See 20.61. (4-6). (5362-64)

HYMN LXIII*

१. इमा नु कं भुवना सीषधामेन्द्रश्च विश्वे च देवाः ।
यज्ञं च नस्तन्वं च प्रजां चादित्यैरिन्द्रः सह चीक्लृपाति ॥

1. Let us all the learned persons and brave warriors keenly desirous of victory along with the commander of the army bring under our sway all these worlds. The Mighty Lord or king energises our acts of sacrifice, bodies and offspring through the help of the rays of the Sun and the learned persons of highest calibre. (5365)

२. आदित्यैरिन्द्रः सगणो मरुद्भिरस्माकं भूत्वविता तनूनाम् ।
हत्वाय देवा असुरान्यदायन्देवा देवत्वमभिरक्षमाणाः ॥

2. When the victorious, brave persons come back, after killing the wicked persons and maintaining their tradition of being victorious and glorious, let

*(1-2) cf. *Rig*, 10.157. (1-2); (3) *Rig*, 6.17.15; (4-6) *Rig*, 1.84. (7-9); (7-9) *Rig*, 8.12 (1-3).

the powerful king along with the highly learned persons and swarms of swift moving forces be the protector of our bodies and properties. (5366)

३. प्रत्यञ्चमर्कमनयञ्छचीभिरादित्स्वधामिषिरां पर्यपश्यन् ।
अया वाजं देवहितं सनेम मदेम शतहिमाः सुवीराः ।।

3. Bringing, down to a focus the mobile, sustaining energy of the rising Sun, through the rays, catching them from all around, let us gain strength, speed, grains and wealth thereby and rejoice for hundred years, along with brave offspring. (5367)

४. य एक इद्विदयते वसु मर्ताय दाशुषे । ईशानो अप्रतिष्कुत इन्द्रो अङ्ग ।।

4. O learned person, He alone is the Mighty Lord, All-ruling and Invincible, Who gives the riches and wealth to the liberal-minded person. (5368)

५. कदा मर्तमराधसं पदा क्षुम्पमिव स्फुरत् । कदा नः शुश्रवद् गिर इन्द्रो अङ्ग ।।

5. O learned person, (none knows) when He will trample under feet the niggardly like the mushroom, and when We will hear our call. (5369)

६. यश्चिद्धि त्वा बहुभ्य आ सुतावाँ आविवासति । उग्रं तत्पत्यते शव इन्द्रो अङ्ग ।।

6. O learned person, he, who, being equipped with earned wealth and fortune, spends it all around for the sake of many in His cause, the Mighty Lord of fortune invests him with irresistible power and might. (5370)

७. य इन्द्र सोमपातमो मदः शविष्ठ चेतति । येना हंसि न्य१त्रिणं तमीमहे ।।

7. O Lord of destruction, the mightiest of the mighty, we pray for that power and valour, with which Thou killest the wicked blood-suckers of the people and that exhililating spirit, which most highly nourishes all means of enjoyment and well-being and energises the people. (5371)

८. येना दशग्वमध्रिगुं वेपयन्तं स्वर्णरम् । येना समुद्रमाविथा तमीमहे ।।

8. O Mighty Lord, we seek the same might and strength with which, Thou protectest the Sun, perpetually moving all the heavenly bodies without any obstruction in all the ten directions, all the intervening space and the oceans on the planets. (5372)

९. येन सिन्धुं महीरपो रथाँ इव प्रचोदयः । पन्थामृतस्य यातवे तमीमहे ।।

9. O Mighty God, we request Thee to grant us the same prowess and energy, with which Thou so efficiently directest and mobilisest the big channels of waters towards the oceans (both the terrestrial and interspatial) just as the driver directs the vehicles or other means of transport like the train or aeroplane; with which Thou moves the universe on the right path, according to Thy set laws of nature. (5373)[1]

HYMN LXIV*

१. एन्द्र नो गधि प्रियः सत्राजिदगोह्यः । गिरिर्न विश्वतस्पृथुः पतिर्दिवः ।।

[1](7-9) (i) These verses can be interpreted in case of king or commander, as well. (ii) Griffith's reading of Adhrigu, Dashgava as persons is wrong.

*cf. (1-3) *Rig*, 8 98 (87, सायण) (4-6); (4-6) *Rig*, 8.24. (16-18). (1) 'coming to us,' means 'being realised by us,' as He is present everywhere

1. O Mighty God, come to us, Dear One, ever Victorious, Uncealable, Vast and Great on all sides like a mountain and the Lord of Heavens. (5374)

२. अभि हि सत्य सोमपा उभे बभूथ रोदसी । इन्द्रासि सुन्वतो वृधः पतिर्दिवः ॥

2. O Truth-incarnate, Protector of the Universe and Sustainer of all means of joy and happiness, Thou fully controllest both the worlds indeed. O Lord of fortunes, Thou art the nourisher of Thy devotee and the master of heavens. (5375)

३. त्वं हि शश्वतीनामिन्द्र दर्ता पुरामसि । हन्ता दस्योर्मनोर्वृधः पतिर्दिवः ॥

3. O Mighty Lord of Destruction, king or commander, Thou art the smasher of the constant heavenly bodies at the time of deluge (or forts of the foe) the Destroyer of the wicked forces of ignorance and darkness, the Impeller of the thoughtful and Protector of the forces of light and knowledge. (5376)

४. एदु मध्वो मदिन्तरं सिञ्च वाध्वर्यो अन्धसः । एवा हि वीर स्तवते सदावृधः ॥

4. O Sacrificer, pour down the sweet essence of herbs and foodgrains, capable of affording excellent joy and pleasure. For it is thus alone that the ever-progressive, brave person is praised and honoured. (5377)

५. इन्द्र स्थातर्हरीणां नकिष्टे पूर्व्यस्तुतिम् । उदानंश शवसा न भन्दना ॥

5. O Mighty God or king, the Sustainer of moving forces of the universe, or ᐟ ɔres, none else has achieved or excelled Thy full praise of qualities by his power or beneficial acts. (5378)

६. तं वो वाजानां पतिमहूमहि श्रवस्यवः । अप्रायुभिर्यज्ञेभिर्वावृधेन्यम् ॥

6. O people, we, the learned persons, desirous of getting foodgrains, strength, knowledge, riches and fame, invoke Him, Who is your Defender of all these things, i.e., food, energy, knowledge and wealth and renown, and Who is the Progresser of His devotees, by our constant acts of sacrifice and devotion. (5379)

HYMN LXV*

१. एतो न्विन्द्रं स्तवाम सखाय स्तोम्यं नरम् । कृष्टीर्यो विश्वा अभ्यस्त्येक इत् ॥

1. O friends, come, let us praise the Mighty God or king Who, all alone, controls all the spheres, held in the sky by mutual attraction or the subjects and Who is the mover or leader, Worthy to be lauded. (5380)

२. अगोरुधाय गविषे द्युक्षाय दस्म्यं वचः । घृतात्स्वादीयो मधुनश्च वोचत ॥

2. Friends, for the praises of the Refulgent God, Who does not keep back His rays of Light and Learning, but spreads the Vedic lore, speak beautiful words, far sweeter than butter and honey even. (5381)

Note:—The verse can also apply to the king.

३. यस्यामितानि वीर्या३ न राधः पर्येतवे । ज्योतिर्न विश्वमभ्यस्ति दक्षिणा ॥

*cf. *Rig*, 8.24. (19-21).

3. (Sing His praises, as shown above), Whose acts of prowess and valour are limitless, Whose wealth cannot be surpassed, Whose Generosity overwhelms all in the universe like light. (5382)

HYMN LXVI*

१. स्तुहीन्द्रं व्यश्ववदनूर्भि वाजिनं यमम् । अर्यो गयं मंहमानं वि दाशुषे ॥

1. O man, like a self-controlled person, worship the Mighty God, Who is ever calm and Unperturbed, source of all strength, wealth, energy, knowledge and fame, Controller of all and Who invests the devotee with offspring and wealth. (5383)

२. एवा नूनमुप स्तुहि वैयश्व दशमं नवम् । सुविद्वांसं चर्कृत्यं चरणीनाम् ॥

2. O man, who has all sense-organs under full control, verily do praise Him, Who is the Tenth One above all the nine directions and Who is ever the New One and knows all full well and Who is ever Worthy to be worshipped by the devotees, practising deep meditation. (5384)

३. वेत्था हि निर्ऋतीनां वज्रहस्त परिवृजम् । अहरहः शुन्ध्युः परिपदामिव ॥

3. O self-possessed devotee, armed with full energy of warding off evil propensities, thou truly knowest the means of keeping off wicked tendencies and art the daily effacer of all troubles and difficulties, (in thy path of spiritual progress). (5385)

HYMN LXVII**

१. वनोति हि सुन्वन्क्षयं परीणसः सुन्वानो हि ष्मा यजत्यव द्विषो देवानामव द्विषः ।
सुन्वान इत्सिषासति सहस्रा वाज्यवृतः । सुन्वानायेन्द्रो ददात्याभुवं रयिं ददात्याभुवम् ॥

1. O Mighty Lord or king, Thy devotee, sacrificing and thus propitiating Thee, gets a suitable shelter for him. Thus striving and being vigilant from sides, he destroys the foes as well as the enemies of the learned and holy persons. The devoted alone, being powerful and learned and uninterupted by handicaps, achieves thousands of fortunes and riches. The Lord of Fortunes or king invests the faithful devotee with wealth giving all sorts of joys and pleasures, power and glory. (5386)

२. मो षु वो अस्मदभि तानि पौंस्या सना भूवन्द्युम्नानि मोत जारिषुरस्मत्पुरोत जारिषुः ।
यद्वश्चित्रं युगेयुगे नव्यं घोषादमर्त्यम् ।
अस्मासु तन्मरुतो यच्च दुष्टरं दिधृता यच्च दुष्टरम् ॥

2. O brave persons, let not those acts or means of valour of yours which have ever been done by you for our sake, forsake us. Let not the constant glory and fortune fade away. Let not our forts and towns be perished. Whatever is declared wonderful new and everlasting glory and riches, whatever is difficult to achieve and whatever is unsurmountable, let that be ours, O brave persons. (5387)

*cf. *Rig*, 8.24. (22-24).
**cf. *Rig*, (1) 1.133.7; (2) 1.139.8; (3) 1.127.1; (4-6) 2.36 (2, 4, 5) (7) 2.37.2,

३. अग्निं होतारं मन्ये दास्वन्तं वसुं सूनुं सहसो जातवेदसं विप्रं न जातवेदसम् ।
य ऊर्ध्वया स्वध्वरो देवो देवाच्या कृपा ।
घृतस्य विभ्राष्टिमनु वष्टि शोचिषाजुह्वानस्य सर्पिषः ॥

3. I (a devotee) regard the Refulgent God, the Benefactor, the All-pervader and All-settler, Revealing Himself through His Almighty power and energy, the Omniscient, the Exposer of all things and Vedic learning like a wise and learned person. He is the One, Who is Self-effulgent as well as Enlightener of all, the non-violent sacrificer and nourisher of the universe, through His Supreme might and splendorous energy. He shines forth through manifold lights by His own splendour and glory like the clarified butter, liquified and offered in a sacrifice. (5388)

४. यज्ञैः संमिश्लाः पृषतीभिर्ऋष्टिभिर्यामञ्छुभ्रासो अञ्जिषु प्रिया उत ।
आसद्या बर्हिर्भरतस्य सूनवः पोत्रादा सोमं पिबता दिवो नरः ॥

4. O vital breaths, the energisers of the nourished body or the universe united with sacrificing souls or the sacrifices, and equipped with means of sustenance and breeding, brightly shining in the receptacle in the form of body or vast firmament, quite lovely in various forms of sense-organs; sitting in the seat of highly powerful soul or God, being the leaders of divine powers, achieve the vital energy from the purifying soul or Lord.

Or

O pious persons, immersed in deep meditation like the sons of the All-nourishing God, in unison with acts of devotion and worship, equipped with all powers of pushing up the soul, purified by the contact with the Mighty Lord, turned attractive or charming by acts of knowledge or enlightenment, being reposed in the lap of Great Brahm, drink deep the sweet nectar of bliss from the Divine Purifier.

Or

O brave leaders of the king's assembly of the learned persons, the creation and the movers of the all-sustaining king, who nourishes all his subjects, embellished by honours and titles of respect, boarding the vehicles, equipped with strong horses and deadly weapons, shining and charming through the display of high powers of heart and head, occupying the high positions, enjoy yourselves the full fortunes of the nation, by pure acts of duty, performed through glorious qualities. (5389)

५. आ वक्षि देवाँ इह विप्र यक्षि चोशन्होतर्नि षदा योनिषु त्रिषु ।
प्रति वीहि प्रस्थितं सोम्यं मधु पिबाग्नीध्रात्तव भागस्य तृप्णुहि ॥

5. O All-Intelligent God, Thou sustains all the divine powers, persons or bodies in this universe and wishing them well, knits them into harmonious working of it. O the Great Sacrificer, Thou, pervadest through all the three worlds. Letest Thou protect the sweet, beneficial and well-established means of joy and pleasure, surcharging each article through Thy presence. Letest Thou satisfy and cherish that the world with Thy share of glory or splendour

through the fire-bearing spheres like the sun, etc.

Or

O learned person, letest thee acquire all good qualities, and desirous of doing, good make use of these for the benefit of others. O sacrifices, stay steadfast throughout the performance of all the three sacrificial fires, i.e., Āhavanyia Gārhapatya, Dakshinia i.e., Brahmcharya, Grahastha and Vana prastha. Desireto have the sweet essence of herbs, brought or presented to thee. Drink the remaining share of the Anidhra sacrifice and be content with thy share of it. (5390)

६. एष स्य ते तन्वो॑ नृम्णवर्धनः सह ओजः प्रदिवि बाह्वोर्हितः ।
तुभ्यं सुतो मघवन्तुभ्यमाभृतस्त्वमस्य ब्राह्मणादा तृपत्पिब ॥

6. O king, this right of thy kingship of the nation, increasing the national wealth like your body, has been invested in the assembly or legislatures of the learned persons, just as power and valour are placed in the arms of a person. O fortunate one, this (right) has now been invested in you and offered to you at the coronation ceremony. You should have it from the priest, well-versed in the Vedic lore, be satisfied enjoy yourself and guard it thoroughly. (5391)

७. यमु पूर्वमहुवे तमिदं हुवे सेदु हव्यो ददिर्यो नाम पत्यते ।
अध्वर्युभिः प्रस्थितं सोम्यं मधु पोत्रात्सोमं द्रविणोदः पिब ऋतुभिः ॥

7. Whomever I (i.e., the priest) call first of all, I offer him (this right of kingship mentioned above) and instruct him accordingly. Whoever has been made the king of the nation, he alone is worthy of honour and able to give aid and protection to the nation. O King, the giver of fortune, just as the sun draws water through its rays all through the seasons, so should you enjoy the sweet fruit of national fortune by your pure and protective acts, performed through the learned administrators of the kingdom. (5392)[1]

HYMN LXVIII*

१. सुरूपकृत्नुमूतये सुदुघामिव गोदुहे । जुहूमसि द्यविद्यवि ॥
२. उप नः सवना गहि सोमस्य सोमपाः पिब । गोदा इद्रेवतो मदः ॥
३. अथा ते अन्तमानां विद्याम सुमतीनाम् । मा नो अति ख्य आ गहि ॥

1-3. See 20.57. (1-3). (5393-95)

४. परेहि विग्रमस्तृतमिन्द्रं पृच्छा विपश्चितम् । यस्ते सखिभ्य आ वरम् ॥

4. O learned person, keep away from evils and wicked persons, seek knowledge and good counsel from the Infallible, Lord of Wealth and Learning the master of all sorts of sciences, Who gives to thy friends all what is good and excellent, (or is far better than thy friends). (5396)

५. उत ब्रुवन्तु नो निदो निरन्यतश्चिदारत । दधाना इन्द्र इद्दुवः ॥

5. Let the learned persons, taking the vow of service to the mighty God alone, preach to us. Let the revilers go away from here and even from other places, too. (5397)

[1]I: the priest investing the king, with powers of Royalty.

*cf. (1-10) *Rig*, 1.4. (1-10), (11-12) *Rig*, 1.5. (1-2).

६. उत नः सुभगाँ अरिर्वोचेयुर्दस्म कृष्टयः । स्यामेदिन्द्रस्य शर्मणि ।।

6. O Beautiful God or Lord of Destruction, let the enemies and even the ordinary people say good things to us. Let us be ever under the shelter of the protecting king, capable of warding off the foes. (5398)

७. एमाशुमाशवे भर यज्ञश्रियं नृमादनम् । पतयन्मन्दयत्सखम् ।।

7. O God or priest, shower on this quick-witted disciple the energising glory of sacrifice, exhilarating the people, acting like a friend lifting the spirits and cheering his companion. (5399)

८. अस्य पीत्वा शतक्रतो घनो वृत्राणामभवः । प्रावो वाजेषु वाजिनम् ।।

8. O the hero of hundreds of acts of valour and sacrifice, be the destroyer of evil forces by drinking it, and fully protect the powerful, speedily-moving, with all supplies, the army in wars. (5400)

९. तं त्वा वाजेषु वाजिनं वाजयामः शतक्रतो । धनानामिन्द्र सातये ।।

9. O mighty king or commander, the hero of various expeditions of courage and bravery, we enhance your striking power in times of war and on the occasions of the acquisition and distribution of wealth and riches. (5401)

१०. यो रायो३वनिर्महान्त्सुपारः सुन्वतः सखा । तस्मा इन्द्राय गायत ।।

10. O people, sing the praises of That Mighty Lord of Fortunes, or king, Who is the Protector and Shelterer of all riches and Great and Perfect Nourisher and Friend of the devotee. (5402)

११. आ त्वेता नि षीदतेन्द्रमभि प्र गायत । सखाय स्तोमवाहसः ।।

11. O friends, the reciters of the Vedic verses, come from all sides and sit all around and sing well the songs, aiming at the Mighty Lord for Fortunes or king. (5403)

१२. पुरूतमं पुरूणामीशानं वार्याणाम् । इन्द्रं सोमे सचा सुते ।।

12. O people unanimously enthral the powerful king, the best protector and defender of the various subjects and the master of all desirable fortunes at the head of the well-established empire. (5404)

HYMN LXIX*

१. स घा नो योग आ भुवत्स राये स पुरंध्याम् । गमद्वाजेभिरा स नः ।।

1. May He (i.e. God) or king or commander help us acquire the unattained objects or in deep meditation! May He or he help us get riches or attain high proficiency in intelligence and maintenance of towns or fortresses! May He or he stand by us with food, riches, power and knowledge and renown. (5405)

२. यस्य संस्थे न वृण्वते हरी समत्सु शत्रवः । तस्मा इन्द्राय गायत ।।

2. O devotees, sing the praises of the Destroyer of forces of evil ignorance at Whose well-establishment in the innermost recesses of the heart in the

*cf. **(1-8)** *Rig*, 1.5. (3-10); **(9-12)** 1.6. (1-4), also **(9-11)** *Atharva*, 20.26. (4-6).

states of perfectly deep meditation (i.e., Samādhi) or perfect bliss (i.e., salvation) no wicked enemies (like Kama, Krodha, etc.) engulf the soul.

Or

O people, extol the high qualities of the mighty king at whose being well-established in his empire, no enemies can overpower his mobile forces of offence and defence at the time of wars or on the occasions of festive occasions. (5406)

३. सुतपाव्ने सुता इमे शुचयो यन्ति वीतये । सोमासो दध्याशिरः ॥

3. These pure, unblemished, sweet-natured souls, initiated into deep devotion like sons to their fathers, quite lost in deep meditation are well set on their path to attain to the Protector, Who shelters His devotees like sons. (5407)

४. त्वं सुतस्य पीतये सद्यो वृद्धो अजायथाः । इन्द्र ज्यैष्ठचाय सुक्रतो ॥

4. O Mighty Lord, king or soul, Performer of noble deeds, Thou, at once, appeareth Great and Extolled for the satisfaction and protection of this created world and for the establishment of Thy Highest Grandeur. (5408)

५. आ त्वा विशन्त्वाशवः सोमास इन्द्र गिर्वणः । शं ते सन्तु प्रचेतसे ॥

5. O Worship-worthy Lord of Learning and Light, king or soul, let the swift-moving forces of nature and sweet-natured, bliss-seeking, learned persons, find their abode in Thee. Let them be all peace and tranquility for attaining Thee, the sources of all knowledge and light. (5409)

६. त्वां स्तोमा अवीवृधन्त्वामुक्था शतक्रतो । त्वां वर्धन्तु नो गिरः ॥

6. O Performer of hundreds of acts of munificence, let our singing the collection of Vedic verses enhance Thy Glory. The Vedic songs also extol Thee. Let our speeches also enhance Thee, by preaching Thy good qualities to the people. (5410)

७. अक्षितोतिः सनेदिमं वाजमिन्द्रः सहस्रिणम् । यस्मिन्विश्वानि पौंस्या ॥

7. Let the Mighty Lord or king of Indestructible power of protection and defence, in Whom there are all powers and energies shower this wealth of thousands of kinds in the form of food, power, knowledge and renown. (5411)

८. मा नो मर्ता अभि द्रुहन्तनूनामिन्द्र गिर्वणः । ईशानो यवया वधम् ॥

8. O Great Lord of Destruction, Worthy of our praise-songs, let not men injure our bodies, but being the Ruler of all, keep away any murderous attack on us. (5412)

९. युञ्जन्ति ब्रध्नमरुषं चरन्तं परि तस्थुषः । रोचन्ते रोचना दिवि ॥

१०. युञ्जन्त्यस्य काम्या हरी विपक्षसा रथे । शोणा धृष्णू नृवाहसा ॥

११. केतुं कृण्वन्नकेतवे पेशो मर्या अपेशसे । समुषद्भिरजायथाः ॥

9-11. See 20.24. (4-6). (5413-15)

१२. आदह स्वधामनु पुनर्गर्भत्वमेरिरे । दधाना नाम यज्ञियम् ॥

12. See 20.40.3. (5416)

HYMN LXX*

१. वीलु चिदारुजत्नुभिर्गुहा चिदिन्द्र वह्निभिः । अविन्द उस्रिया अनु ॥

1. O soul, thou mayst speedily visualise rays of spiritual light through the sustaining capacity of the vital breaths, tamed through hard process of Pranayam.

Or

O mighty king, thou canst capture the most fertile lands, after speedily destroying the secret forts of the enemies with thy forces of smashing fire-power. (5417)[1]

२. देवयन्तो यथा मतिमच्छा विदद्वसुं गिरः । महामनूषत श्रुतम् ॥

2. Just as the learned persons or the enemy-slayer brave persons desirous of seeking the shelter of the Glorious God or king know Him or him to be Thoughtful, capable of giving shelter to all, the Great and the Most-Renowned in the world, so do they sing His or his praises. (5418)[2]

३. इन्द्रेण सं हि दृक्षसे संजग्मानो अबिभ्युषा । मन्दू समानवर्चसा ॥

3. The soul (i.e., Jivatma) fearlessly well-united with the mighty Lord, verily looks charming. Both, having the same Glory and splendour, rejoice together. (5419)

४. अनवद्यैरभिद्युभिर्मखः सहस्वदर्चति । गणैरिन्द्रस्य काम्यैः ॥

4. The powerful sacrifice (i.e., the creation of the universe) of the mighty Lord is highly praised by the brilliant blameless and lovable learned persons. (5420)

५. अतः परिज्मन्ना गहि दिवो वा रोचनादधि । समस्मिन्नृञ्जते गिरः ॥

5. O Omnipresent Lord, setting in motion all the spheres of the universe, come (to us, the devotees) from this brilliant and shining heavens (i.e., be realised by us). All of our Vedic praises do unite well in Thee. (5421)

६. इतो वा सातिमीमहे दिवो वा पार्थिवादधि । इन्द्रं महो वा रजसः ॥

6. We, the devotees, pray the mighty Lord of fortune for the munificence of riches and wealth from the heaven from the earth and from the great firmament. (5422)

७. इन्द्रमिद् गाथिनो बृहदिन्द्रमर्केभिरर्किणः । इन्द्रं वाणीरनूषत ॥

८. इन्द्र इद्धर्योः सचा संमिश्ल आ वचोयुजा । इन्द्रो वज्री हिरण्ययः ॥

९. इन्द्रो दीर्घाय चक्षस आ सूर्यं रोहयद्दिवि । वि गोभिरद्रिमैरयत् ॥

7-9. See 20.38 (4-6) or 47. (4-6). (5423-25)

*cf. (1-6) *Rig*, 1.6. 15-10; (7-16) *Rig*, 1.7. (1-10); (17-20); *Rig*, 1.8, (1-4).

१०. इन्द्र वाजेषु नोऽव सहस्रप्रधनेषु च । उग्र उग्राभिरूतिभिः ॥

10. O Mighty Lord of Destruction and Protection or powerful king, being Terrible, protect us in thousands of great wars or acts of valour and daring by Thy Terrific means of defence and offence. (5426)

११. इन्द्रं वयं महाधन इन्द्रमर्भे हवामहे । युजं वृत्रेषु वज्रिणम् ॥

11. We invoke the Powerful Destroyer or commander in great wars, as well as in small battles. We call Him, our Helper, equipped with deadly weapons like the thunderbolt in all acts of smashing the wicked and evil forces. (5427)

१२. स नो वृषन्नमुं चरुं सत्रादावन्नपा वृधि । अस्मभ्यमप्रतिष्कुतः ॥

12. O showerer of blessings and gifts, Lord of All Beneficence or Constant Distributor of the fruit of acts of the souls, under that share of fruit of our actions, which is ours. Thou turnest away none unrewarded from Thy door. (5428)

१३. तुञ्जेतुञ्जे य उत्तरे स्तोमा इन्द्रस्य वज्रिणः । न विन्धे अस्य सुष्टुतिम् ॥

13. I find no adequate praise-words for This mighty Lord of fortunes. Whatever highest words of praise there are at the time of each gift, are for the Powerful God, the Evil-Destroyer. (5429)

१४. वृषा यूथेव वंसगः कृष्टीरियर्त्योजसा । ईशानो अप्रतिष्कुतः ॥

14. Just as the strong-bodied bull adds to the stature of the herd of cattle and energises the process of agriculture by his vital energy, similarly the Mighty God, showerer of all blessings and well-being, Pervading all created things, the Irresistible Ruler of all energises all the spheres of the universe, held in space by mutual attraction, by His strong energy and power. (5430)

१५. य एकश्चर्षणीनां वसूनामिरज्यति । इन्द्रः पञ्च क्षितीनाम् ॥

15. He is the Mighty God, Who all alone controls all the worlds, giving place of shelter to all the creatures, all the subjects, consisting of five sorts of classes of people, i.e., Brahman, Kshatrya, Vaishya, Shudra and Nishad. (5431)

१६. इन्द्रं वो विश्वतस्परि हवामहे जनेभ्यः । अस्माकमस्तु केवलः ॥

16. See 20.31.1. (5432)

१७. एन्द्र सानसिं रयिं सजित्वानं सदासहम् । वर्षिष्ठमूतये भर ॥

17. O Great God or king, for our protection and safety amass the huge wealth and fortunes, capable of giving us all comforts and joys, enabling us to conquer and subdue our rival forces of evil and darkness. (5433)

१८. नि येन मुष्टिहत्यया नि वृत्रा रुणधामहै । त्वोतासो न्यर्वता ॥

18. By which (i.e., the above-mentioned wealth) being protected by Thee (God or king) we may completely ward off all forces of wickedness or ignorance, by killing evil propensities to lead astray the soul from the right path and by strong force of light and knowledge. (5434)

१९. इन्द्र त्वोतास आ वयं वज्रं घना ददीमहि । जयेम सं युधि स्पृधः ॥

19. O Mighty Lord of Destruction or king, being protected by Thee or thee, being enabled to smash the evil forces of ignorance or the foe give a thoroughly deadly blow like a thunderbolt to them (these forces) and completely vanquish these warring elements. (5435)

२०. वयं शूरेभिरस्तृभिरिन्द्र त्वया युजा वयम् । सासह्याम पृतन्यतः ॥

20. O Great Destroyer of forces of evil and darkness, being united with Thee, we may bring under control the fighting forces of evil or the foe by the help of the brave warriors, having all sorts of missiles. (5436)[1]

HYMN LXXI*

१. महाँ इन्द्रः परश्च नु महित्वमस्तु वज्रिणे । द्यौर्न प्रथिना शवः ॥

1. Just as the heavens are great due to their vastness and just as the sun is great due to its vast light, similarly the Might Lord is Great due to His Immensity, pervading the universe and even beyond that is the grandeur and huge power in the Almighty, with the thunderbolt. (5437)

२. समोहे वा य आशत नरस्तोकस्य सनितौ । विप्रासो वा धियायवः ॥

2. All the persons, who are engaged in war, or busy generating offspring, or the learned and the wise bent upon achieving pursuits of intelligence and action, (do sing Thy praises). (5438)

३. यः कुक्षिः सोमपातमः समुद्र इव पिन्वते । उर्वीरापो न काकुदः ॥

3. He is the Mighty God, holding all energy in His lap, the Best Protector of the Creation, Deep like the ocean, nourishes all the creatures and the worlds, like the waters of the cloud irrigating the vast lands. (5439)[2]

४. एवा ह्यस्य सूनृता विरप्शी गोमती मही । पक्वा शाखा न दाशुषे ॥

५. एवा हि ते विभूतय ऊतय इन्द्र मावते । सद्यश्चित्सन्ति दाशुषे ॥

६. एवा ह्यस्य काम्या स्तोम उक्थं च शंस्या । इन्द्राय सोमपीतये ॥

4-6. See 20.60. (4-6). (5440-42)

७. इन्द्रेहि मत्स्यन्धसो विश्वेभिः सोमपर्वभिः । महाँ अभिष्टिरोजसा ॥

7. O Powerful God or king, come (i.e., enable us to realise Thou) Thou gladdenest (the devotees) by all means and resources full of pleasure-giving essence of food-grains etc. By virtue of Thy Energy and Valour, Thou art a Great Object worth achieving. (5443)

८. एमेनं सृजता सुते मन्दिमिन्द्राय मन्दिने । चक्रिं विश्वानि चक्रये ॥

8. O learned persons, let this active and cheering soul be wholly entrusted to the Beneficent God, the source of all bliss and happiness and Creator of all the Worlds. (5444)

[1]The verse can apply to the king as well.

*cf. (1-6) *Rig*. 1.8. (5-10) also (4-6) *Atharva*, 20. 60 (4-6); (7-16) *Rig*, 1.9. (1-10).

[2]The verse can apply to the king even.

९. मत्स्वा सुशिप्र मन्दिभि स्तोमेभिर्विश्वचर्षणे । सचैषु सवनेष्वा ॥

9. O Graceful Lord of Omniscience, be pleased with these gladdening songs of praises and also gladden us who are busy in these sacrificial acts of devotion. (5445)

१०. असृग्रमिन्द्र ते गिरः प्रतित्वामुदहासत । अजोषा वृषभं पतिम् ॥

10. O Showerer of Blessings, I (the devotee) pour out the Vedic songs for Thee, the Protector of all, the Benefactor and the Almighty Lord. They aim at Thee alone and express their ideas, (like the females doing so towards their husband, the source of happiness and joy to them). (5446)

११. सं चोदय चित्रमर्वाग्राध इन्द्र वरेण्यम् । असदित्ते विभु प्रभु ॥

11. O Mighty Lord of all fortunes, fully mobilise towards us, the wonderful glorious bounties of Thine, which are worth achieving, all-pervading and all-powerful. (5447)

१२. अस्मान्त्सु तत्र चोदयेन्द्र राये रभस्वतः । तुविद्युम्न यशस्वतः ॥

12. O Most Glorious and Bounteous God, thoroughly stimulate us, the active and worthy aspirants to the proper destination, for acquiring wealth and riches. (5448)

१३. सं गोमदिन्द्र वाजवदस्मे पृथु श्रवो बृहत् । विश्वायुर्धेह्यक्षितम् ॥

13. O Showerer of Gifts, completely invest us with the vast, great life-prolonging and imperishable wealth and glory of cows, horses, etc. (5449)

१४. अस्मे धेहि श्रवो बृहद्द्युम्नं सहस्रसातमम् । इन्द्र ता रथिनीरिषः ॥

14. O Mighty Lord of all bounties, shower on us the immense glory, food-grains, knowledge and strength and wealth, capable of affording thousands of comforts and joys. Also give us these armies, which are fully equipped with all means of transport, or those keen inner impulses which may be full of Divine Bliss. (5450)

१५. वसोरिन्द्रं वसुपतिं गीर्भिर्गृणन्त ऋग्मियम् । होम गन्तारमूतये ॥

15. O learned persons, we invoke the Mighty God, the Protector of all the worlds and the people living therein, the source of the Vedic verses, the Omnipresent and the Omniscient, for the protection of the people. (5451)

१६. सुतेसुते न्योऽकसे बृहद्बृहत एदरिः । इन्द्राय शूषमर्चति ॥

16. Even the owner of the greatest wealth and riches seeks and prays for the powerful helping hand of Mighty Lord of fortunes, secretly residing in each and every article of creation. (5452)

HYMN LXXII*

१. विश्वेषु हि त्वा सवनेषु तुञ्जते समानमेकं वृषमण्यवः पृथक्स्वऽः सनिष्यवः पृथक् ।
तं त्वा नावं न पर्षणिं शूषस्य धुरि धीमहि ।
इन्द्रं न यज्ञैश्चितयन्त आयव स्तोमेभिरिन्द्रमायवः ॥

*cf. *Rig*, 1.131 (2.3.6).

1. O Adorable God, in all acts of sacrifice or worship, all the people, desirous of attaining happiness and well-being, severally worship or sing praises of Thee alone Who are Universal and Well-known to be the Showerer of all blessings and bounties. We remember the self-same Thee as the boat for crossing all streams of hurdles and difficulties and the centre of all strength and prowess, just as the people think of the Mighty Lord through sacrificial acts and they (i.e., people) praise Him through Vedic songs. (5453)

(note: 'This verse can be applied to king even)

२. वि त्वा ततस्रे मिथुना अवस्यवो व्रजस्य साता गव्यस्य निःसृजः सक्षन्त इन्द्र निःसृजः ।
यद् गव्यन्ता द्वा जना स्व१र्यन्ता समूहसि ।
आविष्करिक्रद्वृषणं सचाभुवं वज्रमिन्द्र सचाभुवम् ॥

2. O Great Lord of Protection and Beneficence, the couples, (i.e., husband and wife; the disciple and the preceptor; the king and the subjects, the mind and the soul, etc.,) desirous of their protection and satisfaction, wholly dash towards Thee and completely entrust themselves to Thee and fully revel in Thee in the very act of acquisition of the Vedic lore or light of knowledge and herds of cows or mastery of sense-organs. When Thou takes under Thy shelter, these groups of two, achieving perfect happiness and Vedic learning, cows and control of senses, Thou revealest Thy Terrible Might of warding off evil and darkness, together with Thy kind nature of showering gifts and blessings, along with inner feeling of bliss and joy. (5454)

३. उतो नो अस्या उषसो जुषेत ह्य१र्कस्य बोधि हविषो हवीमभिः स्वर्षाता हवीमभिः ।
यदिन्द्र हन्तवे मृधो वृषा वज्रिञ्चिकेतसि ।
आ मे अस्य वेधसो नवीयसो मन्म श्रुधि नवीयसः ॥

3. Let the Worship-Worthy God accept our prayers, at this time of dawn, and know of our faithful devotion along with the praises. He is the Showerer of Bliss though our offerings. O Mighty God of Destruction of forces of evil and ignorance, when Thou, the Most-Powerful. One energises us to smash our enemies, like Kama, Krodha, etc., with the great spiritual force, deadly like the thunderbolt, letst Thou listen to the well-meditated prayer of me, this newly enlightened devotee of Thine. (5455)[1]

HYMN LXXIII*

१. तुभ्येदिमा सवना शूर विश्वा तुभ्यं ब्रह्माणि वर्धना कृणोमि । त्वं नृभिर्हव्यो विश्वधासि ॥

1. O Evil-Destroyer, all these sacrificial acts are for Thee alone, I (the devotee) recite the Vedic verses of enhance Thy Glory. Thou, the Sustainer of the universe art worthy of praise by the people. (5456)

२. नू चिन्नु ते मन्यमानस्य दस्मोदश्नुवन्ति महिमानमुग्र । न वीर्य१मिन्द्र ते न राधः ॥

2. O Graceful and Highly Powerful Lord, is there any one who can ever surpass Thy Greatness, worthy of respect and honour by all? O Mighty God,

[1]The verse also applies to the yogis.
*cf. (1-2) *Rig*, 7.22. (7-8); (3) 7.31.10; (4-0) *Rig*, 10.23. (3-5).

there is none who can excell Thy Power or Glory and Wealth. (5457)

३. प्र वो महे महिवृधे भरध्वं प्रचेतसे प्र सुमतिं कृणुध्वम् । विशः पूर्वीः प्र चरा चर्षणिप्राः ।।

3. O learned persons, fully entertain and cherish good thoughts and praise-words for the Almighty, the source of all Prosperity and Progress, the Perfect Enlightener. O Fulfiller of the aspirations of the people, fulfill the desires of the people of their hearts' content. (5458)

४. यदा वज्रं हिरण्यमिदथा रथं हरी यमस्य वहतो वि सूरिभिः ।
आ तिष्ठति मघवा सनश्रुत इन्द्रो वाजस्य दीर्घश्रवसस्पतिः ।।

4. When the two horses in the form of acts and knowledge enable the state of perfect Bliss His (i.e., God) to be attained by the learned devotees and He reveals His Brilliant Thunderbolt (to destroy all evil propensities of the soul), the Mighty Lord of Fortunes, the master of High Glory and Grandeur, of knowledge, power and riches, of ancient Renown and Fame, the Fortunate One, installs Himself fully in the hearts of the devotees (5459)

५. सो चिन्नु वृष्टिर्यूथ्या३ स्वा सचाँ इन्द्रः श्मश्रूणि हरिताभि प्रुष्णुते ।
अव वेति सुक्षयं सुते मधूदिद्धूनोति वातो यथा वनम् ।।

5. Just as rain irrigates the green vegetation all around, so does a learned person or a king saturates all those dependent hordes of people with favours and fortunes, like his moustaches. He obtains a good shelter, sweet fruit of his labours and throws off all forces of evil or wickedness, like the strong wind felling the jungle trees. (5460)

६. यो वाचा विवाचो मृध्रवाचः पुरू सहस्राशिवा जघान ।
तत्तदिदस्य पौंस्यं गृणीमसि पितेव यस्तविषीं वावृधे शवः ।।

6. We sing the praises of those various powers of the Almighty, the highly learned or the great preceptor, Who by His or his powerful preachings smashes the persons of inimical and violent speech and many, thousands of evil forces, and enhances the power and strength of the virtuous. (5461)

HYMN LXXIV*

१. यच्चिद्धि सत्य सोमपा अनाशस्ता इव स्मसि ।
आ तू न इन्द्र शंसय गोष्वश्वेषु शुभ्रिषु सहस्रेषु तुवीमघ ।।

1. O Truthful and Constant Protector of the created universe, and Lord of Immense fortunes, make us fully instructed and well-disciplined in whatever acts and on whatever occasions, we may be found lacking in discipline and good behaviour and invest us with wealth of cows, horses, knowledge and bodily activity and thousand acts of glory and brilliance. (5462)[1]

*The verses of sukta 73 can also apply to the king. cf. *Rig*, 1.29. (1-7).

[1](1-7) 2nd part is repeated in each verse to impress upon the king his duty towards the welfare of his subjects.

२. शिप्रिन्वाजानां पते शचीवस्तव दंसना ।
आ तू न इन्द्र शंसय गोष्वश्वेषु शुभ्रिषु सहस्रेषु तुवीमघ ॥

2. O Powerful Lord of all fortunes, foodgrains, power, knowledge and fame, equipped with all means of strength and energy, Glorious are Thy ways of doing things, make us fully renowned in thousands of glorious fortunes, comprising of cows, horses, knowledge and power of body and mind. (5463)

३. नि ष्वापया मिथूदृशा सस्तामबुध्यमाने ।
आ तू न इन्द्र शंसय गोष्वश्वेषु शुभ्रिषु सहस्रेषु तुवीमघ ॥

3. Let the couple, looking at each other (with love and affection) enjoy sound sleep and remain there unconscious of any danger or dread (under Thy peaceful regime) (i.e., the householders may enjoy perfect peace and tranquility at night). (2nd part is the same as above).

Or

O king or commander, let the rival persons, looking at you with jealousy be thrown into the state of swooning, bordering on perfect sleep and let them remain quite unconscious. 2nd part, the same as above. (5464)

४. ससन्तु त्या अरातयो बोधन्तु शूर रातयः ।
आ तू न इन्द्र शंसय गोष्वश्वेषु शुभ्रिषु सहस्रेषु तुवीमघ ॥

4. O king or commander, let those enemies be induced into sleep and let the brave warriors, rendering help to you, keep alert and awake. 2nd part the same as before. (5465)

५. समिन्द्र गर्दभं मृण नुवन्तं पापयामुया ।
आ तू न इन्द्र शंसय गोष्वश्वेषु शुभ्रिषु सहस्रेषु तुवीमघ ॥

5. O Lord of justice, thoroughly destroy the person, who kills others by poison, and who speaks ill, wicked or deceitful words in this sinful manner. 2nd part, the same. (5466)

६. पताति कुण्डृणाच्या दूरं वातो वनादधि ।
आ तू न इन्द्र शंसय गोष्वश्वेषु शुभ्रिषु सहस्रेषु तुवीमघ ॥

6. Better it is, if the fire-enkindling wind keeps away from the forest, similarly it is better that the strong and powerful agitator, enkindling the fire of enmity and hatred by crooked means is kept away from the people. 2nd part, the same. (5467)

७. सर्वं परिक्रोशं जहि जम्भया कृकदाश्वम् ।
आ तू न इन्द्र शंसय गोष्वश्वेषु शुभ्रिषु सहस्रेषु तुवीमघ ॥

7. O king or commander, smash all those who revile and destroy those, who secretly arrange murderous attack against you. 2nd part as before. (5468)

HYMN LXXV*

१. वि त्वा ततस्रे मिथुना अवस्यवो व्रजस्य साता गव्यस्य निःसृजः सक्षन्त इन्द्र निःसृजः।
यद् गव्यन्ता द्वा जना स्व१र्यन्ता समूहसि।
आविष्करिक्रद्वृषणं सचाभुवं वज्रमिन्द्र सचाभुवम्॥

1. See 20.72.2. (5469)

२. विदुष्टे अस्य वीर्य१स्य पूरवः पुरो यदिन्द्र शारदीरवातिरः सासहानो अवातिरः।
शासस्तमिन्द्र मर्त्यमयज्युं शवसस्पते।
महीममुष्णाः पृथिवीमिमा अपो मन्दसान इमा अपः॥

2. O fortunate soul, the breaker of the bondage of karmas, the power inspiring sense-organs of yours know your strength, by which overcoming all obstacles, you cross the fortresses in the form of years and break through the bodily forts. O powerful soul, destroyer of evil forces, you control that mortal body, having no permanent alliance with you; and capture that vast state of grand bliss, having cheerfully performed these various kinds of noble acts and acquired glorious knowledge. (5470)

३. आदित्ते अस्य वीर्य१स्य चर्किरन्मदेषु वृषन्नुशिजो यदाविथ सखीयतो यदाविथ।
चकर्थ कारमेभ्यः पृतनासु प्रवन्तवे। ते अन्यामन्यां नद्य१ं सनिष्णत श्रवस्यन्तः सनिष्णत॥

3. After this, they, the yogis (i.e., disciple) spread this power of thine (i.e., the perfect yogi) by extolling it, when thou, O inspirer of happiness and joy in the hearts of those, who desire your company and friendship and whom you get and protect in everyway. Then you induce in them the capability of enjoying more glorious fortunes in superior states of meditation full of bliss. Thereafter they, desirous of greater and greater glory attain to one stream after another of spiritual grandeur and dip deep into these. (5471)

HYMN LXXVI**

१. वने न वा यो न्यधायि चाकञ्छुचिर्वां स्तोमो भुरणावजीगः।
यस्येदिन्द्रः पुरुदिनेषु होता नृणां नर्यो नृतमः क्षपावान्॥

1. O vital breaths, prāna and apāna, nourishing like parents, that pure radiant energy and strength, which has been invested in the soul, worthy of service by all, really belongs to you, covering you as it were; whose (of energy) lonely bearer, the evil-destroyer soul, for many days, becomes the best among men and the most efficient leader of the people, shining like the moon. (5472)

२. प्र ते अस्या उषसः प्रापरस्या नृतौ स्याम नृतमस्य नृणाम्।
अनु त्रिशोकः शतमावहन्नॄन्कुत्सेन रथो यो असत्ससवान्॥

2. O pure soul, let us be highly raised spiritually at the attainment of this enlightened state of spiritual advancement like the day-dawn and the next one of thee, the most leading one amongst spiritual leaders. After attaining the

*cf. *Rig*, 1.131. (3-5); also (1) *Atharva*, 20.72.

**All the three verses can apply to the king; cf. *Rig*, 10.29. (1-8).

effulgent state of three radiances of speech, mind and vital breaths, by your capacity to shear off ties of ignorance and evil, you become the mobile force of happiness and bliss and enjoy perfect beatitude, and enable to force hundreds of people to follow you by your spiritual power. (5473)

३. कस्ते मद इन्द्र रन्त्यो भूद्दरो गिरो अभ्युग्रो वि धाव ।
कद्वाहो अर्वागुप मा मनीषा आ त्वा शक्यामुपमं राधो अन्नैः ॥

3. O Mighty Lord of Bliss, what is this exhilarating spirit of Thine which is so charming and pleasure-giving. Letst Thee rush towards our praise-songs as people do towards the doors of their houses. When wilt Thou reveal Thy current of constant bliss to me; fully controlling my mind, so that I may enjoy all the wealth of glorious bliss, being near Thee, through all means of enjoyment. (5474)[1]

४. कदु द्युम्नमिन्द्र त्वावतो नॄन्कया धिया करसे कन्न आगन् ।
मित्रो न सत्य उरुगाय भृत्या अन्ने समस्य यदसन्मनीषाः ॥

4. O Adorable Lord of fortunes, when wilt Thou shower Thy riches? With what sort of intelligence or act or sustaining energy dost Thou turn people like Thyself (i.e., raise them to be Sachchidanand in the sate of salvation) when wilt Thou be achieved by us? Steadfast like a friend, Worthy of High-praise, the controlling powers of the self-same Thee rightly remain the nourishing and developing ones in the eatables of all animals. (5475)

५. प्रेरय सूरो अर्थं न पारं ये अस्य कामं जनिधा इव ग्मन् ।
गिरश्च ये ते तुविजात पूर्वीर्नर इन्द्र प्रतिशिक्षन्त्यन्नैः ॥

5. O Mighty Lord of High Renown and Glory, energise those, who enable this soul to attain his highest object and desire of salvation, like the husbands fulfilling the wishes of their wives and the Sun lights up mobiling all objects; and also those, who offer Thee their praise-songs, full of right knowledge and purpose, along with all means of sustenance. (5476)

६ मात्रे नु ते सुमिते इन्द्र पूर्वी द्यौर्मज्मना पृथिवी काव्येन ।
वराय ते घृतवन्तः सुतासः स्वाद्मन्भवन्तु पीतये मधूनि ॥

6. O Almighty Creator, verily well-measured and well-planned are the vast heavens by Thy great power and the earth by Thy high intelligence. All the articles, created by Thee, like butter, milk,'etc., are quite tasteful and of high-quality for eating and sweet for drinking. (5477)

७. आ मध्वो अस्मा असिचन्नमत्रमिन्द्राय पूर्णं स हि सत्यराधाः ।
स वावृधे वरिमन्ना पृथिव्या अभि क्रत्वा नर्यः पौंस्यैश्च ॥

7. The devotees offer their oblations, full of sweet juices of herbs to the Mighty God. Verily He is Full and Constant Lord of Wealth master of Great Strength and Benefactor of the people. He spreads His Grandeur far and wide

[1]God's rushing towards devotees' songs means readily accepting them. Pt. Jaidev has applied all the verses of this Sukta to king also.

by fully completing the earth by His creative faculty and intelligence and vast powers. (5478)

८. व्यानलिन्द्रः पृतनाः स्वोजा श्रास्मै यतन्ते सख्याय पूर्वीः ।
श्रा स्मा रथं न पृतनासु तिष्ठ यं भद्रया सुमत्या चोदयासे ॥

8. The Mighty Lord of High Energy and Valour pervades all through men and opposing forces of nature. The noblest persons full of high qualities of head and heart have ever tried to win His friendship. O my soul, fully stay in this body, the source of all pleasures and joys, amongst men like the chariot amidst the fighting armies, which thou mobilises through peaceful and good intellect. (5479)

HYMN LXXVII*

१. आ सत्यो यातु मघवाँ ऋजीषी द्रवन्त्वस्य हरय उप नः ।
तस्मा इदन्धः सुषुमा सुदक्षमिहाभिपित्वं करते गृणानः ॥

1. May Truthful Lord of Wealth, the Straightforward, leading all on the right path, come and His evil-destroying forces of light and knowledge rush towards us (i.e., we may be able to realise Him quickly). We offer this well-prepared juice of food-grains as oblation for His sake alone. Thus praised with song, let Him invest us with our object. (5480)
(note: This verse may also be applied to the preceptor or the king).

२. अव स्य शूराध्वनो नान्तेऽस्मिन्नो अद्य सवने मन्दध्यै ।
शंसात्युक्थमुशनेव वेधाश्चिकितुषे असुर्या्य मन्म ॥

2. "O Destroyer of evil propensities and thus the Breaker of the ties of Bondage, just as at the end of the path, the horses are unyoked from the chariot, similarly set us free from the bondage of body-chariot at the end of this journey of life for enjoying the bliss of salvation." Thus prays the learned person, like a keenly desirous man, the praise-song, worthy of meditation, to the Evil-Destroyer God, Who revels in vital breaths and is the Benefactor of all creaters. (5481)[1]

३. कविर्न निण्यं विदथानि साधन्वृषा यत्सेकं विपिपानो अर्चात् ।
दिव इत्था जीजनत्सप्त कारूनह्ना चिच्चक्रुर्वयुना गृणन्तः ॥

3. When developing the various sorts of Yogic powers, a devoter saturated with Dharm-megh Smādhi, drinking deep the secret dripping of highest bliss, like a seer, who has crossed all hurdles of ignorance and darkness, worships God, he generates seven kinds of lights, like those of the sun from his head in such a way, as to turn out floods of light like the day, while describing or explaining various acts of spiritual learning. (5482)[2]

*cf. *Rig*, 4.16. (1-8).

[1]Griffith's interpretation of 'Ushana' as a special sage of that name is incorrect.

[2]'*Sapta Karu*'—seven-coloured lights, visualised by yogis internally on their way to salvation, when finally the flood-gates of perpetual Divine splendour are flung wide open, so much so that even the lights from crores of the suns of the universe are no match for it,

४. स्व१र्यद्वेदि सुदृशीकमर्कैर्महि ज्योती रुरुचुर्यद्ध वस्तोः ।
अन्धा तमांसि दुधिता विचक्षे नृभ्यश्चकार नृतमो अभिष्टौ ॥

4. When the noblest leader of men, (the Refulgent God), generates the great shining splendour, making the altar, in the innermost recesses of the heart of a Yogi, look so beautiful and bright, which all the divine beings so keenly desire to attain, He effaces all deep darkness of ignorance and evil and creates all facilities for men to see clearly their object of attainment. (5383)

५. ववक्ष इन्द्रो अमितमृजीष्यु१भे आ पप्रौ रोदसी महित्वा ।
अतश्चिदस्य महिमा वि रेच्यभि यो विश्वा भुवना बभूव ॥

5. The Mighty Creator, the Regulator of the universe on right lines, bears an Immeasurable Power and Energy. He fully fills-up both the heavens and the earth by His Grandeur. His Majesty, Who rules over all the worlds, is far greater than this. (5484)

६. विश्वानि शक्रो नर्याणि विद्वानपो रिरेच सखिभिर्निकामैः ।
अश्मानं चिद्ये बिभिदुर्वचोभिर्व्रजं गोमन्तमुशिजो वि वव्रुः ॥

6. Just as the cloud releases its waters through the help of winds, similarly does a selfless, powerful learned person fully devotes all his knowledge and actions for the benefit of the people. Those who are desirous of attaining the highest state of beatitude, shatter the cloud of darkness and ignorance and throw open the flood-gates of the fold of light and Vedic learning and ultimately the radiant state of salvation. (5485)

७. अपो वृत्रं वव्रिवांसं पराहन्प्रावत्ते वज्रं पृथिवी सचेताः ।
प्रार्णांसि समुद्रियाण्यैनोः पतिर्भवञ्छवसा शूर धृष्णो ॥

7. O brave and daring person, capable of smashing the forces of the enemy or evil, thou shatterest the overwhelming foe or the darkening forces of ignorance and thy deadly weapon of high power and knowledge attains thee the vast lands pulsating with life and energy. Being the master by thy power, thou completely regulated the waters of the oceans, both terrestrial and atmospheric. (5486)[1]

८. अपो यदद्रिं पुरुहूत दर्दराविर्भुवत्सरमा पूर्व्यं ते ।
स नो नेता वाजमा दर्षि भूरिं गोत्रा रुजन्नङ्गिरोभिर्गृणानः ॥

8. O much-invoked God or soul, just as the atmospheric electricity shatters the cloud to release its waters, so do you tear off the covering of ignorance of the soul to release the drops of bliss when Thy Primordeal constant current of nectar reveals itself. The self-same Begetter of ours to attain immense power, wealth and knowledge, Thou, effacing the hurdles from the rays of light and learnings, and being praised by the learned devotees, revealest Thyself. (5487)

[1]Sarma and Angiras are not special personages, as noted by Sayāna and Griffith.

HYMN LXXVIII*

१. तद्वो गाय सुते सचा पुरुहूताय सत्वने । शं यद् गवे न शाकिने ॥

1. O learned persons, you all together sing the praises of that much-invoked, the Powerful and Energising God, Who may be all peace and tranquility for our sense-organs and cattle even. (5488)

२. न घा वसुर्नि यमते दानं वाजस्य गोमतः । यत्सीमुप श्रवद् गिरः ॥

2. Whenever He hears our prayers, surely He, the Omnipresent Creator never keeps back His gift of wealth, power and knowledge in the form of land, food, cattle and Vedic lore, just as the Sun, the source of life on the earth, never keeps off its energy and light. (5489)

३. कुवित्सस्य प्र हि व्रजं गोमन्तं दस्युहा गमत् । शचीभिरप नो वरत् ॥

3. The Destroyer of the wicked and evil forces, enables the soul, who is enjoyer of various joys, to achieve the highest state of spiritual enlightenment i.e., salvation and throws open its gates by His radiant Energy. (5490)

HYMN LXXIX**

१. इन्द्र क्रतुं न आ भर पिता पुत्रेभ्यो यथा ।
शिक्षा णो अस्मिन्पुरुहूत यामनि जीवा ज्योतिरशीमहि ॥

1. See Ath. 18.3.67. (5491)

२. मा नो अज्ञाता वृजना दुराध्यो३ माशिवासो अव क्रमुः ।
त्वया वयं प्रवतः शश्वतीरपोऽति शूर तरामसि ॥

2. O Mighty Lord or king, the Destroyer of the wicked forces of evil and ignorance, let not the unknown, the violent irresistible and the wicked forces of the foes or evil, overpower us. We, the devotees, being prospered by Thee, may cross all hurdles of actions bringing us for so long, like the waters of the perpetual streams. (5492)

HYMN LXXX***

१. इन्द्र ज्येष्ठं न आ भरँ ओजिष्ठं पपुरि श्रवः ।
येनेमे चित्र वज्रहस्त रोदसी ओभे सुशिप्र प्राः ॥

1. O Mighty Lord of fortunes, fill us with the most powerful and best fortune of food and learning, which may be capable of nourishing and pushing us to completion, and by which, O Wonderful, Beautiful and Thunderbolt-armed one, Thou art filling both the earth and the heavens. (5493)

२. त्वामुग्रमवसे चर्षणीसहं राजन्देवेषु हूमहे ।
विश्वा सु नो विथुरा पिब्दना वसोऽमित्रान्सुषहान्कृधि ॥

2. O Effulgent Ruler of the World, we call Thee for our protection as the most Terrible amongst the divine forces and the Controller of all the worlds and the people. O Settlers of all, let all the trouble-creators be silenced and all enemies be easily conquered by us. (5494)

*cf. *Rig*, 6.45. (22-24). **cf. *Rig*, 7.32. (26-27). ***cf. *Rig*, 6.46 (5-6).

HYMN LXXXI*

१. यद् द्याव इन्द्र ते शतं शतं भूमीरुत स्युः ।
न त्वा वज्रिन्त्सहस्रं सूर्या अनु न जातमष्ट रोदसी ॥

1. O Almighty Creator, the hundreds of celestial bodies and hundreds of earths, which are Thine, O Lord of Deadly Weapons like the thunderbolt the thousands of Suns, the universe and the galaxies cannot match Thee. (5495)[1]

२. आ पप्राथ महिना वृष्ण्या वृषन्विश्वा शविष्ठ शवसा ।
अस्माँ अव मघवन्गोमति व्रजे वज्रिञ्चित्राभिरूतिभिः ॥

2. O Almighty God, the Showerer of all blessings and joys, Thou art spreading all around Thy Powerful Forces by Thy Great Might. Letst Thee, O Lord of Riches and Wealth and Deadly Weapons, protect us in this fold of sense-organs i.e., body. (5496)

HYMN LXXXII**

१. यदिन्द्र यावतस्त्वमेतावदहमीशीय । स्तोतारमिद्दिधिषेय रदावसो न पापत्वाय रासीय ॥

1. O Mighty Lord of fortunes, if I become the master of as much wealth as Thou hast, I would maintain and nourish the praise-singer alone and would not, O Scatterer of Wealth, give it away for sin and evil. (5497)

२. शिक्षेयमिन्महयते दिवेदिवे राय आ कुहचिद्विदे ।
नहि त्वदन्यन्मघवन्न आप्यं वस्यो अस्ति पिता चन ॥

2. Every day do I (i.e., God) immensely give away wealth and riches to the devoted person, wherever he may be. O Lord of Wealth and riches, none else except Thee is our kinsman nor is there a better Father to us than Thou art. (5498)

HYMN LXXXIII***

१. इन्द्र त्रिधातु शरणं त्रिवरूथं स्वस्तिमत् ।
छर्दिर्यच्छ मघवद्भ्यश्च मह्यं च यावया दिद्युमेभ्यः ॥

1. O Mighty Protector, grant a peaceful and comfortable shelter, made of three sustaining forces and capable of warding off three kinds of evils or difficulties, to the rich people and myself, and keep away the burning missile or anger from these. (5499)[2]

*cf. *Rig*, 8.70 (5-6).

[1] 'यद्' has been translated by 'if' by Pt. Jaidev and Griffith. I don't see any sense in doubting the ownership of the Creator. It is already His, hence 'यद्' by 'which.'

**cf. *Rig*, 7.32. (18-19).

[2] cf. *Rig*, 6.46. (9-10). (i) त्रिधातु—consisting of gold, silver and iron, three-storied; Bāt, Pit and Kuf or Prān, Apān and Udān. (ii) त्रिवस्थाम्—capable of warding off Ādhyātmik, Ādhibhautik and Ādhidaivik calamities; or mental, vocal and bodily pains or drawbacks; or cold, heat and rain.

२. ये गव्यता मनसा शत्रुमादभुरभिप्रघ्नन्ति धृष्णुया ।
अध स्मा नो मघवन्निन्द्र गिर्वणस्तनूपा अन्तमो भव ॥

2. O Adorable, Mighty Lord of Destruction and Fortunes, there being people, who completely annihilate their enemy by their overpowering force, with a mind to grab the lands and cattle of their enemy, letest Thee be the closest Protector of our bodies. (5500)

HYMN LXXXIV*

१. इन्द्रा याहि चित्रभानो सुता इमे त्वायवः । अण्वीभिस्तना पूतासः ॥

1. O Almighty God, of Wonderful Radiance thoroughly reveal Thyself, here are these purified, devoted souls desirous of attaining Thee, ever glorified and sanctified by subtle yog-practices and spiritual lights. (5501)

२. इन्द्रा याहि धियेषितो विप्रजूतः सुतावतः । उप ब्रह्माणि वाघतः ॥

2. O most Adorable Lord, fully reveal Thy Identity, being desired and prayed by the wise and the learned people, who are offering sacrifices and preaching the Vedic teachings to the people. (5502)

३. इन्द्रा याहि तूतुजान उप ब्रह्माणि हरिवः । सुते दधिष्व नश्चनः ॥

3. O Mighty Lord of mobile forces, like the sun and the energetic learned persons, being most energetic Thyself, accept our Vedic songs and invest us with food and fortunes in this created world. (5503)

HYMN LXXXV**

१. मा चिदन्यद्वि शंसत सखायो मा रिषण्यत ।
इन्द्रमित्स्तोता वृषणं सचा सुते मुहुरुक्था च शंसत ॥

1. O learned friends never sing the praises of anyone else and thus never fall in trouble, combining together in this world, worship the most Adorable Lord alone, Who is showerer of all gifts and blessings; and sing His praises only again and again. (5504)

२. अवक्रक्षिणं वृषभं यथाजुरं गां न चर्षणीसहम् ।
विद्वेषणं संवननोभयंकरं मंहिष्ठमुभयाविनम् ॥

2. (Again and again sing the praises of) from above and God, Who Attracts and Controls all, showers joys and blessings, is Ageless, overpowers all like the sun, hates the wicked and evil persons, is worthy to be worshipped by the virtuous, capable of doing both—punishment and award; suppressing the evil and encouraging the good, the most Bounteous, and protects both the animate and the inanimate creation. (5505)

३. यच्चिद्धि त्वा जना इमे नाना हवन्त ऊतये ।
अस्माकं ब्रह्मेदमिन्द्र भूतु तेहा विश्वा च वर्धनम् ॥

*cf. *Rig*, 1.3. (4-6). **cf. *Rig*, 8.1. (1-4).

3. O Most Adorable Lord, although these people of the world invoke Thee for their protection, in various ways, yet these Vedic verses praise-songs of ours may for all days, be propagating Thy qualities. (5506)

४. वि तर्तूर्यन्ते मघवन्विपश्चितोऽर्यो विपो जनानाम् ।
उप क्रमस्व पुरुरूपमा भर वाजं नेदिष्ठमूतये ॥

4. O Mighty Lord of Fortunes, the progressive, the wise and the learned persons of creative genius amongst the general people of the world, specially surpass others. Letest Thee be near us for our protection and completely fill us with food, power, wealth and learning. (5507)

HYMN LXXXVI*

१. ब्रह्मणा ते ब्रह्मयुजा युनज्मि हरी सखाया सधमाद आशू ।
स्थिरं रथं सुखमिन्द्राधितिष्ठन्प्रजानन्विद्वाँ उप याहि सोमम् ॥

1. This verse appears to be addressed from a perfect yogi to his disciple-yogi:

O soul, desirous of effacing all evil and wicked propensities of the spirit, I (i.e., the preceptor Yogi) tie in unison with the mighty Brahm, thy swift, friendly horses in the form of the vital breaths, Prān and Apān, fit to be united with Brahm in the blissful state of perfect smādhi. Keeping thy body steady, in a comfortable posture (Āsan) and having developed special spiritual light and knowledge, finally approach the highest state of perfect beatitude. (5508)

HYMN LXXXVII**

१. अध्वर्यवोऽरुणं दुग्धमंशुं जुहोतन वृषभाय क्षितीनाम् ।
गौराद्वेदीयाँ अवपानमिन्द्रो विश्वाहेद्याति सुतसोममिच्छन् ॥

1. O learned persons of non-violent sacrifices, offer libations, consisting of radiant essence of herbs to the life-infusing soul, amongst the body-sustaining vital breaths. The soul, more powerful than the vital breaths revelling amidst the sense-organs, desirous of drinking deep the divine Bliss, constantly moves on to the final destination. (5509)

२. यद्दधिषे प्रदिवि चार्वन्नं दिवेदिवे पीतिमिदस्य वक्षि ।
उत हृदोत मनसा जुषाण उशन्निन्द्र प्रस्थितान्पाहि सोमान् ॥

2. O soul, thou desirest to have the satisfaction of daily enjoying the pleasant and exhilarating nectar, which thou bearest in the highest state of spiritual elevation. Let thee, O keen soul, drink deep these essences of bliss, set forth before thee, fully gratified in heart and spirit. (5510)

३. जज्ञानः सोमं सहसे पपाथ प्र ते माता महिमानमुवाच ।
एन्द्र पप्राथोर्व१न्तरिक्षं युधा देवेभ्यो वरिवश्चकर्थ ॥

*cf. *Rig*, 3.35. 4. **cf. *Rig*, 7.98. (1-7).

3. O Mighty Creator, generating the universe through Thy Power, Thou protectest and maintainest it. The primordial matter bespeaks Thy Grandeur. Thou fully pervadest the vast interspaces. Thou investest the heavenly bodies with splendour and glory by forces of friction. (5511)

४. यद्योधया महतो मन्यमानान्साक्षाम तान्बाहुभिः शाशदानान् ।
यद्वा नृभिवृ॑त इन्द्राभियुध्यास्तं त्वयाजिं सौश्रवसं जयेम ॥

4. O Mighty Lord of Destruction, king or commander, whenever Thou presentest an occasion to fight the tearing forces of the enemies, priding themselves to be superior, we may be able to vanquish them by force of our arm. And whenever being surrounded by efficient leaders, Thou Thyself smashest them, we may win that war, full of glory and fortunes. (5512)

५. प्रेन्द्रस्य वोचं प्रथमा कृतानि प्र नूतना मघवा या चकार ।
यदेददेवीरसहिष्ट माया अथाभवत्केवलः सोमो अस्य ॥

5. Let me thoroughly explain the deeds of the mighty Creator done in the previous creations. Let me also do so the new ones; which the Lord of Fortunes did in this creation. When He surely overpowers all the non-luminous bodies of the matter, then the whole universe becomes His alone. (5513)

६. तवेदं विश्वमभितः पशव्यं१ यत्पश्यसि चक्षसा सूर्यस्य ।
गवामसि गोपतिरेक इन्द्र भक्षीमहि ते प्रयतस्य वस्वः ॥

6. O Mighty Lord or king, all this animate creation all around is Thine, the one that Thou sees or revealest by the light of the Sun. Thou art the Sole master or Protector of all cattle or lands. We enjoy the riches and wealth of Thee, the Noblest Controller. (5514)

७. बृहस्पते युवमिन्द्रश्च वस्वो दिव्यस्येशाथे उत पार्थिवस्य ।
धत्तं रयिं स्तुवते कीरये चिद्यूयं पात स्वस्तिभिः सदा नः ॥

7. See Ath. 20.17.12. (5415)

HYMN LXXXVIII*

१. यस्तस्तम्भ सहसा वि ज्मो अन्तान्बृहस्पतिस्त्रिषधस्थो रवेण ।
तं प्रत्नास ऋषयो दीध्यानाः पुरो विप्रा दधिरे मन्द्रजिह्वम् ।

1. The ancient, wise seers, engrossed in deep meditation, set before themselves the Blissful God, shedding Radiance and Glory all around, the self-same Lord of the Great Vedic lore, and the vast universe present in all three places, heavens, interspace and the earth, Who completely upholds the extremes of the earth by His Power and mobile force and energy. (5516)

२. धुनेतयः सुप्रकेतं मदन्तो बृहस्पते अभि ये नस्ततस्रे ।
पृषन्तं सृप्रमदब्धमूर्वं बृहस्पते रक्षतादस्य योनिम् ॥

*cf. *Rig*, 4.50. (1-6).

2. O Mighty Lord of the vast universe, the Vedic Lore, and the great nation, (king, commander or the learned person) whoever amongst us, capable of making the rival forces tremble and cheering up the friendly ones, spread all around the glory of Thee of supreme knowledge and splendour. O Mighty Protector, (king, commander or the learned person) letest Thee protect the shelter or Vedic lore of this group of ours, full of bounties, vast, invincible, and great. (5517)

३. बृहस्पते या परमा परावदत ग्रा त ऋतस्पृशो नि षेदुः ।
तुभ्यं खाता अवता ग्रद्रिदुग्धा मध्व श्चोतन्त्यभितो विरप्शम ॥

3. O Mighty Lord of Vedic learning, getting inspired from that sublimest source of the highest knowledge, i.e., Vedic lore, the truth-seeking, learned persons sit all-absorbed in Thee. Just as the deep-dug wells, the fountains, filled with sweet waters from the clouds or mountains, trickle out plenteous sweet streams of water, similarly the devoted yogis, digging deep in meditation, nourishing spiritual glory, capable of shedding Dharm-megh Blissful rain of perfect serenity all around, trickle out plenty of sweet waters of nectar on all sides. (5518)

४. बृहस्पतिः प्रथमं जायमानो महो ज्योतिषः परमे व्योऽमन् ।
सप्तास्यस्तुविजातो रवेण वि सप्तरश्मिरधमत्तमांसि ॥

4. The Almighty God, generating the very creation in the great and highest space of light and splendour thoroughly effaces all forces of darkness and evil by His forceful instruction and preachings, Himself being the master of seven meters of the Vedic verses, revealing Himself in various ways, like the Sun of seven-coloured rays. (5519)

५. स सुष्टुभा स ऋक्वता गणेन वलं रुरोज फलिगं रवेण ।
बृहस्पतिरुस्रिया हव्यसूदः कनिक्रदद्वावशतीरुदाजत् ॥

5. Just as a great commander of the army shatters with the thundering clatter of arms, the malignant besieging foe, equipped with all sorts of deadly weapons, by force of his intelligent hordes of armies, capable of smashing, the onslaught of the enemy, similarly does the highly learned person, well-versed in Vedic learning, tears off the forces of evil and darkness, besetting the general people, by his swarms of wise and intelligent, learned persons, capable of checking the mischievous forces, through forceful preachings. He, preaching loudly, well explains the well-sung Vedic verses, showering knowledge, worth grasping, just as the lowing cows, shower milk and butter, worth having. (5520)[1]

६. एवा पित्रे विश्वदेवाय वृष्णे यज्ञैर्विधेम नमसा हविर्भिः ।
बृहस्पते सुप्रजा वीरवन्तो वयं स्याम पतयो रयीणाम् ॥

6. Let us thus pay our homage to the Great Protector, the Nourisher, the

[1]'Vala' is not a special demon of that name but it refers to any wicked for or force of evil nature.

Radiant Lord of all people, the Benefactor of all, the All-powerful and the Showerer of all bliesings, by our sacrificial acts and bowings and oblations. O Mighty Lord of fortunes, king, commander or learned person, may be the masters of good progeny, heroic persons, and the riches of all sorts. (5521)

HYMN LXXXIX*

१. अस्तेव सु प्रतरं लायमस्यन्भूषन्निव प्र भरा स्तोममस्मै ।
वाचा विप्रास्तरत वाचमर्यो नि रामय जरितः सोम इन्द्रम् ॥

1. O soul, just as the archer continues hurling afar swift-moving arrows and the decorator goes on ornamenting, similarly shouldst thou go on offering the song-verses profusely to Him, This Lord of thine. O Wise persons, just as the warriors overwhelm the voice of the enemy by their own vehement voice, similarly should you cross the Divine Lore by your fervent prayers. O devout soul, completely cheer up thy soul in the Blissful God. (5522)

२. दोहेन गामुप शिक्षा सखायं प्र बोधय जरितर्जारमिन्द्रम् ।
कोशं न पूर्णं वसुना न्यृष्टमा च्यावय मघदेयाय शूरम् ॥

2. O devoted, learned person, just as the cow is secured for the purpose of milching, similarly attain to the Radiant and the Omnipresent One to drink deep the spiritual bliss, and fully bestir thyself to the realisation of the Glorious Lord, thy Friend and Destroyer of all traces of evil and ignorance, and be in complete unison with the Giver of fortunes, the Refuge of all and the Remover of all difficulties, just as the treasury, filled with all sorts of riches is sought after for fame and fortune. (5523)

३. किमङ्ग त्वा मघवन्भोजमाहुः शिशीहि मा शिशयं त्वा शृणोमि ।
अप्नस्वती मम धीरस्तु शक्र वसुविदं भगमिन्द्रा भरा नः ॥

3. O Dear Lord of fortunes, why do the people call Thee the Bounteous nourisher or Protector? (because Thou feedest all and protectest all) I (Thy devotee) hear Thee as the Latent Inspirer of all, pleasest Thou to sharpen my intellect. Let my intelligence be active and smart. O Powerful Lord of fortunes, fully invest us with fortunes, full of all sorts of riches and wealth. (5524)

४. त्वां जना ममसत्येष्विन्द्र संतस्थाना वि ह्वयन्ते समीके ।
अत्रा युजं कृणुते यो हविष्मान्नासुन्वता सख्यं वष्टि शूरः ॥

4. O Mighty Lord of destruction and protection, the people invoke Thee for their aid, in their disputes to establish their own rights as just and proper, or while fighting pitched battles and sacrificing their lives in wars. But Thou, O Brave and Courageous Lord, likest to befriend only him, who is ready to make sacrifices and has creative genius in this world. (5525)

*cf. *Rig*, 10.42. (1-11).

५. धनं न स्पन्द्रं बहुलं यो अस्मै तीव्रान्त्सोमाँ आसुनोति प्रयस्वान् ।
तस्मै शत्रून्त्सुतुकान्प्रातरह्नो नि स्वष्ट्रान्युवति हन्ति वृत्रम् ॥

5. The big landlord, with plenty of food-grains, who offers to this king, the energetic, brave youngmen like the mobile wealth of cattle, horses etc., in ample quantity, drives away the violent foes, equipped with deadly weapons, from him and completely destroys the besieging enemy, like the day's dawn effacing the darkness of the night. (5526)

६. यस्मिन्वयं दधिमा शंसमिन्द्रे यः शिश्राय मघवा काममस्मे ।
आराच्चित्सन्भयतामस्य शत्रुर्न्यस्मै द्युम्ना जन्या नमन्ताम् ॥

6. Let the foe tremble with fear even at a distance from Him, and let all human glories bow to Him, the Mighty Lord of Adoration, fortunes and destruction and protection, in Whom we uphold all our praise-songs and Who, the master of riches, sustains our aspiration and desires. (5527)

७. आराच्छत्रुमप बाधस्व दूरमुग्रो यः शम्बः पुरुहूत तेन ।
अस्मे धेहि यवमद् गोमदिन्द्र कृधी धियं जरित्रे वाजरत्नाम् ॥

7. O Much-invoked Lord of destruction and fortunes, drive away the enemy to a distance from afar with that weapon, which is fierce and capable of calming down the foe; invest us with wealth of corn and cattles, and make the intellect and the actions of Thy devotee radiant with energy and knowledge. (5528)

८. प्र यमन्तर्वृषसवासो अग्मन्तीव्राः सोमा बहुलान्तास इन्द्रम् ।
नाह दामानं मघवा नि यंसन्नि सुन्वते वहति भूरि वामम् ॥

8. Does the Glorious Lord of Fortunes, Whom the energetic, bliss-blessed devotees, with powerful, internal means of attaining Dharm-megha, having cut off all ties of darkening attachment, attain in perfect meditation (i.e., smādhi) give nothing to the perfect devotee? Surely He infests the creative devotee with profuse wealth of glory and riches. (5529)[1]

९. उत प्रहामतिदीवा जयति कृतमिव श्वघ्नी वि चिनोति काले ।
यो देवकामो न धनं रुणद्धि समित्तं रायः सृजति स्वधाभिः ॥

9. See Ath. K.7.50.6. (5530)

१०. गोभिष्टरेमामतिं दुरेवां यवेन वा क्षुधं पुरुहूत विश्वे ।
वयं राजसु प्रथमा धनान्यरिष्टासो वृजनीभिर्जयेम ॥

११. बृहस्पतिर्नः परि पातु पश्चादुतोत्तरस्मादधरादघायोः ।
इन्द्रः पुरस्तादुत मध्यतो नः सखा सखिभ्यो वरीयः कृणोतु ॥

10-11. See Ath. K.20.17. (10-11). (5531-32)

HYMN XC*

१. यो अद्रिभित्प्रथमजा ऋतावा बृहस्पतिराङ्गिरसो हविष्मान् ।
द्विबर्हज्मा प्राघर्मसत्पिता न आ रोदसी वृषभो रोरवीति ॥

[1]Pt. Jaidev has applied the verse to the king, too.
*cf. *Rig*, 6.73. (1-3).

1. The Great Protector of the vast universe, the master of the Vedic knowledge, Who is the Breaker of the darkening clouds of ignorance and evil, the First Revealer, the Regulator of the natural laws, the Refulgent Pervador of the creation, the Supplier of provisions to all the creatures, firmly stationed in both the earth and the heavens in friend and foe and in knowledge and action, Dweller in burning heat like the sun, the Protector and Nourisher like a father, the Showerer of Blessings, loudly proclaims His instructions all around the earth and heavens. (5533)

२. जनाय चिद्य ईवत उ लोकं बृहस्पतिर्देवहूतौ चकार ।
घ्नन्वृत्राणि वि पुरो दर्दरीति जयञ्छत्रूंरमित्रान्पृत्सु साहन् ॥

2. The Mighty Lord of Protection, king or the learned person, Who creates a place of honour and glory for the coming generation, in the acts of sacrifice and worship, smashing the forces of ignorance and evil, completely tears off the bonds of bodies of the souls or the forts of the enemy, conquering the inimical forces of evil or the foe, subdues the various other unfriendly elements in wars of spiritual supremacy or earthly dominance. (5534)

३. बृहस्पतिः समजयद्वसूनि महो व्रजान्गोमतो देव एषः ।
अपः सिषासन्त्स्व१रप्रतीतो बृहस्पतिर्हन्त्यमित्रमर्कैः ॥

3. The king of the vast kingdom or the master of the vast spiritual light has won fortunes or glories. This victorious king or yogi has well achieved large herds of cows or huge storage of impounded rays of light, earthly or divine. He unimpeded by any one, desirous of allotting the peaceful duties of administration or attaining the various stages of spiritual enlightenment, kills the enemy or evil by rays of light, mundane or divine. (5535)

HYMN XCI*

१. इमां धियं सप्तशीर्ष्णीं पिता न ऋतप्रजातां बृहतीमविन्दत् ।
तुरीयं स्विज्जनयद्विश्वजन्योऽयास्य उक्थमिन्द्राय शंसन् ॥

1. The chief, Tranquil and Untiring Protector and Nourisher invests us with this great, seven-headed, truth-generating intelligence and energy of actions, generates the fourth stage of salvation, beneficial to all and instructs the soul with Vedic teachings. (5536)

२. ऋतं शंसन्त ऋजु दीध्याना दिवस्पुत्रासो असुरस्य वीराः ।
विप्रं पदमङ्गिरसो दधाना यज्ञस्य धाम प्रथमं मनन्त ॥

2. The brave learned persons, glowing with spiritual splendour, sons of the Radiant, All-pervading God, preaching the true laws of nature, and deeply immersed in meditation of straightforward Godhead, upholding the highest state of spiritual knowledge and vision, are engrossed in perpetual meditation

*cf. *Rig*, 10.67 (1-12) (1) 'seven-headed!: consisting of seven metres cultivated by seven vital breaths or seven sense-organs. *Āyāsya* is not a special personage of that name It means 'Untiring,' 'Tranquil', and 'Chief' qualifying God, the Protector. 'Angiras' are of the highest splendour of the Adorable God. (5537)

३. हंसैरिव सखिभिर्वावदद्भिरश्मन्मयानि नहना व्यस्यन् ।
बृहस्पतिरभिकनिक्रदद् गा उत प्रास्तौदुच्च विद्वाँ अगायत् ॥

3. The Mighty God or the yogi of high spiritual power, tearing off the bonds of stony walls of black actions, as if through the friendly and the spiritual-knowledge-preaching, perfect yogis, throws open the flood gates of spiritual light. Thereafter the learned person heartily praises Him and loudly sings the praises. (5538)

४. अवो द्वाभ्यां पर एकया गा गुहा तिष्ठन्तीरनृतस्य सेतौ ।
बृहस्पतिस्तमसि ज्योतिरिच्छन्नुदुस्रा आकर्वि हि तिस्र आवः ॥

4. The Mighty Lord of the vast universe or the Vedic lore or the great yogi, wishing to diffuse or attain spiritual enlightenment, amidst the binding darkness of the inert matter, of Vedic knowledge or spiritual light, lying deep in the secret recesses of the soul, just beneath the power of mental concentration and far above the organs of sense and actions, realises the three lights of Rig, Yajur and Sāma or knowledge, action and devotion and reveals all the three of them. (5539)

५. विभिद्या पुरं शयथेमपाचीं निस्त्रीणि साकमुदधेरकृन्तत् ।
बृहस्पतिरुषसं सूर्यं गामर्कं विवेद स्तनयन्निव द्यौः ॥

5. Thus the Yogi of vast spiritual power, through the cultivation of deep meditation, i.e., smādhi, thoroughly shatter the down-faced fort of conscience, completely cuts off simultaneously all the three circles of spiritual impediments through 'Dharm-megha' state and finally realises his real-self attaining 'Vishoka-Prajya' i.e., state of supreme splendour and glory, Vedic light, and perfectly luminous state of the Sun, worth adoration, just as thundering lightning reveals and illumines the heavens. (5540)[1]

६. इन्द्रो वलं रक्षितारं दुघानां करेणेव वि चकर्ता रवेण ।
स्वेदाञ्जिभिराशिरमिच्छमानोऽरोदयत्पणिमा गा अमुष्णात् ॥

6. The Yogi, equipped with special glories of yoga, thoroughly cuts asunder, through the internal unbeaten sound, the darkening cover, of evil and ignorance checking the free flow of streams of spiritual light and splendour, like the enemy being torn by hand-weapon, i.e., sabre. Again he subdues the vital breath of various activities in the body through sweat-bearing exercises of the vital breaths, desirous of attaining Divine Bliss, and finally steals away the rays of spiritual radiance. (5541)[2]

not a special tribe of sages, but the general term for learned persons, endowed with the highest glow of spiritual splendour and glory.

[1]Three impediments, of ignorance, sin and mental agitation 'Apachim Puram'—is not 'Western Castle' but refers to the downward propensities of nature of the soul, forming a prison-house for him.

[2]'Vala' is not a special demon, but general term for a dark cloud of water or ignorance. 'Pani' also refers to a tight-fisted businessman.

७. स ईं सत्येभिः सखिभिः शुचद्भिर्गोधायसं वि धनसैरददः ।
ब्रह्मणस्पतिर्वृषभिर्वराहैर्घर्मस्वेदेभिर्द्रविणं व्यानट् ।।

7. Just as the learned yogi specially destroys ignorance covering the rays of light of knowledge and learning through the truthful, friendly, pure and brilliant preceptors, showering wealth of knowledge and spiritual light, similarly the learned person, well-versed in the Vedic lore, thoroughly brings under control the swift-moving mind by the well-controlled heat, sweat-generating and bliss-showering powerful vital breaths. (5542)

८. ते सत्येन मनसा गोपतिं गा इयानास इषणयन्त धीभिः ।
बृहस्पतिर्मिथोअवद्यपेभिरुदुस्रिया असृजत स्वयुग्भिः ।।

8. They, (the vital breaths) being controlled by truthful mind, energise and reveal the rays of spiritual light and the master thereof, through intelligence and actions. The great yogi of high spiritual power generates streams of highest bliss through learned persons, immersed in deep concentration of self and mutually protecting one another from blemishing behaviour. (5543)

९. तं वर्धयन्तो मतिभिः शिवाभिः सिंहमिव नानदतं सधस्थे ।
बृहस्पतिं वृषणं शूरसातौ भरेभरे अनु मदेम जिष्णुम् ।।

9. Exalting, by peaceful praises, Him, the Lord of the Vast Universe or the Yogi of high spiritual glory, roaring like a lion, in His universe or body, Powerful showerer of blessings and Victorious like a commander in every war and the display of spirit of daring and adventure, let us rejoice after Him or him. (5544)

१०. यदा वाजमसनद्विश्वरूपमा द्यामरुक्षदुत्तराणि सद्म ।
बृहस्पतिं वृषणं वर्धयन्तो नाना सन्तो बिभ्रतो ज्योतिरासा ।।

10. When the yogi of supreme spiritual power attains the energy of variegated forms and rises up to the radiant stages and lofty mansions of salvation, the pious persons, lit with splendour, extol the powerful yogi, in various ways by word of mouth. (5545)

११. सत्यामाशिषं कृणुता वयोधै कीरिं चिद्ध्यवथ स्वेभिरेवैः ।
पश्चा मृधो अप भवन्तु विश्वास्तद्रोदसी शृणुतं विश्वमिन्वे ।।

11. O learned persons, shower your true blessings for the longevity of life and ever protect your praise-singer with your knowledge. Let the violent foe or calamity be kept off. Let the teacher and the taught, the father and the mother, and the male and the female, satisfying the world with knowledge and food, listen to that Vedic teaching of ours. (5546)

१२. इन्द्रो मह्ना महतो अर्णवस्य वि मूर्धानमभिनदर्बुदस्य ।
अहन्नहिमरिणात्सप्त सिन्धून्देवैर्द्यावापृथिवी प्रावतं नः ।।

12. Just as strong wind or electricity completely shatters the head of the cloud of the vast ocean (i.e., atmosphere by its great energy and causes the flowing waters to rain down, while destroying the cloud, similarly does the

Great Lord, the Destroyer of Ignorance and evil, the preceptor or the learned person, thoroughly breaks open the secrets of vast ocean of knowledge, the source of all joys, and destroying the dark clouds of ignorance and evil, sets in motion the seven vital breaths to spiritual light. O teacher and disciple, father and mother, male or female, thoroughly protect us through divine qualities. (5547)[1]

HYMN XCII*

१. अभि प्र गोपतिं गिरेन्द्रमर्च यथा विदे । सूनुं सत्यस्य सत्पतिम् ॥

२. आ हरयः ससृज्रिरेऽरुषीरधि बर्हिषि । यत्राभि संनवामहे ॥

३. इन्द्राय गाव आशिरं दुदुह्रे वज्रिणे मधु । यत्सीमुपह्वरे विदत् ॥

1-3. See Ath. 20. 22. (4-6). (5548-50)

४. उद्यद् ब्रध्नस्य विष्टपं गृहमिन्द्रश्च गन्वहि । मध्वः पीत्वा सचेवहि त्रिः सप्त सख्युः पदे ॥

4. When I (a devotee) and the Mighty Lord of Destruction of evil and ignorance together climb-up to the shelter, free from all the three kinds of misteries and troubles, (i.e., Adhyatmic, Adhibhautic and Adhidaivic) of the shelterer of all, we, drinking deep the sweet nectar, contact the highest state of the Friend, Radiant with 21 times splendour and glory. (5551)

५. अर्चत प्रार्चत प्रियमेधासो अर्चत । अर्चन्तु पुत्रका उत पुरं न धृष्ण्वर्चत ॥

5. O learned seers of lovely intelligence, worship Him, the suppressor of all evil forces. Thoroughly sing His praises. Do pray to Him. Let the sons pay their homage to Him and pay your obeisance to Him, Who subdues all evils like a fort. (5552)

६. अव स्वराति गर्गरो गोधा परि सनिष्वणत् । पिङ्गा परि चनिष्कददिन्द्राय ब्रह्मोद्यतम् ॥

6. Let the sound-producing 'Gargara' (a mechanism like the mike) generate the tunes of the loftiest Vedic songs, and 'Godha' (i.e., the broadcasting station) spread these all around and the 'Pinga' (i.e , the receiving string or set) pick it up from all around and reproduce it for the king or the soul. (5553)[2]

७. आ यत्पतन्त्येन्यः सुदुघा अनपस्फुरः । अपस्फुरं गृभायत सोममिन्द्राय पातवे ॥

7. O learned persons, immersed in deep meditation catch hold of the opportunity to drink the undisturbed and constant bliss, when the calm and tranquil streams of nectar flow internally like the milk-streams of white-coloured cows that are easy to milch, free from any obstruction on their part. (5554)

[1](i) 'Arbuda' is not a demon but a 'cloud.' (ii) Similarly 'Ahi' is not a serpent but a 'cloud.' (iii) 'Sapta'—'सर्पण करने वाले' flowing.

*cf. *Rig*, 8.58 (M. Muller 69) 4-18, 59. (M. Muller 70) 1-6. (i) It is the soul that climbs up to this highest state of beatitude, while the Omnipresent God is present everywhere throughout. It is He, Who lifts His friend, the devotee to the highest state of refulgence.

[2]To me it appears, the verse gives the perfect mechanism of the broadcasting system.

८. अपादिन्द्रो अपादग्निर्विश्वे देवा अमत्सत ।
वरुण इदिह क्षयत्तमापो अभ्यनूषत वत्सं संशिश्वरीरिव ।।

8. Just as the cows low, while looking at the calf, similarly do the learned persons, well-versed in Vedic lore and engrossed in deep meditation, sing His praises in every way. The soul drinks this nectar. The chief, learned person drinks it. All the learned persons or all sense-organs revel in it. The pious and the holy person certainly stays steady herein. (5555)

९. सुदेवो असि वरुण यस्य ते सप्त सिन्धवः । अनुक्षरन्ति काकुदं सूर्म्यं सुषिरामिव ।।

9. O the noblest soul (i e., Yogin) thou art a divine personality, whose seven vital breaths combined into one well-formed stream flow towards the palate. (5556)

Note: The seven vital breaths of a practising yogi trickle as nectar from the palate, as if flowing into one stream.

१०. यो व्यतीँरफाणयत्सुयुक्ताँ उप दाशुषे । तक्वो नेता तदिद्वपुरुपमा यो अमुच्यत ।।

10. The well-versed yogi, who, controlling the vital breaths of the sense-organs, fully concentrates them on the devotee's self-sacrifice, abnegation and brings them in unison with it, being an austere leader, attains Him and finally leaves off his body-shackles and revels in salvation. (5557)

११. अतीदु शक्र ओहत इन्द्रो विश्वा अति द्विषः । भिनत्कनीन ओदनं पच्यमानं परो गिरा ।।

11. The powerful yogi surely surpasses all impediments of inimical forces of evil and ignorance, and attaining a very charming form beyond the sense-organs and mind even, by his devotional praise-singing, succeeds in breaking open the gate, the highest post of salvation, the ripe fruit of his life-long efforts. (5558)

१२. अर्भको न कुमारकोऽधि तिष्ठन्नवं रथम् । स पक्षन्महिषं मृगं पित्रे मात्रे विभुक्रतुम् ।।

12. Just as a small child, riding a new chariot, goes out to control a mighty lion and thus pleases his father and mother, similarly the well-versed yogi, assuming a subtle state and adopting a new body, accepts the Mighty God of Vast Repository of knowledge and actions, Worthy of Acquisition and being sought after, as his father and mother. (5559)

१३. आ तू सुशिप्र दंपते रथं तिष्ठा हिरण्ययम् ।
अध द्युक्षं सचेवहि सहस्रपादमरुषं स्वस्तिगामनेहसम् ।।

13. O powerful controller of mental power, be fully stationed in your state of radiant spirituality. Then we shall both (i.e., husband and wife, preceptor and disciple) together attain the heavenly highest state of bliss of thousand powers of stable tranquility and calmness, effulgent, peaceful and serene, free from all sin and evil. (5560)

१४. तं घेमित्था नमस्विन उप स्वराजमासते । अर्थं चिदस्य सुधितं यदेतव आवर्तयन्ति दावने ।।

14. In this way, the reverent devotees come to Him alone, Who is self-radiant, when they, to achieve the highest object of His (i.e., salvation) well-

placed and protected, revert to Him again and again for self-devotion and self-abnegation. (5560)

१५. अनु प्रत्नस्यौकसः प्रियमेधास एषाम् । पूर्वामनु प्रयतिं वृक्तबर्हिषो हितप्रयस आशत ॥

15. Out of all these (i.e., human beings) the wise persons, lovers of Vedic lore, performers of non-violent sacrifices, taking congenial food or doing suitable acts, attain to the ancient and constant place of shelter of the Almighty Father in accordance with their good efforts of the previous births. (5561)

१६. यो राजा चर्षणीनां याता रथेभिरध्रिगुः ।
विश्वासां तरुता पृतनानां ज्येष्ठो यो वृत्रहा गृणे ॥

16. I (i.e., devotee) praise the qualities of Him, Who shines like a king amongst the people (or who is the enlightener of all the sense-organs), who moves unrestrained amongst the moving spheres, who is the subduer of all forces of evil and darkness, the mightiest of all and is the Dispeller of Ignorance. (5562)[1]

१७ इन्द्रं तं शुम्भ पुरुहन्मन्नवसे यस्य द्विता विधर्तरि ।
हस्ताय वज्रः प्रति धायि दर्शतो महो दिवे न सूर्यः ॥

17. O learned person of great knowledge, dilate upon the qualities of the Mighty Lord of Destruction and protection, Whose twofold qualities, Kindness and Control are held in His form of a Sustainer for the protection of the creation. For the annihilation of the wicked, the deadly weapon of the thunderbolt is kept and there is the Sun in heavens, for the great sight and guidance. (5563)

१८. नकिष्टं कर्मणा नशद्यश्चकार सदावृधम् ।
इन्द्रं न यज्ञैर्विश्वगूर्तमृभ्वसमधृष्टं धृष्णवोजसम् ॥

18. Either by deeds or by sacrifices, none can attain the position of the Great God, Who has produced the ever-increasing universe, Who is praised by all people, Beloved of the Intelligent, Invincible, Full of Overwhelming Energy and Splendour. (5564)

१९. अषाल्हमुग्रं पृतनासु सासहिं यस्मिन्महीरुरुज्रयः ।
सं धेनवो जायमाने अनोनवुर्द्यावः क्षामो अनोनवुः ॥

19. (In continuation of the above verse) On Whose revelation, (i.e., When His Great power is revealed to all by His creation) the great heavens and the earths (i.e., the people residing therein) with great praise-songs, sing His praises and pay their homage to Him, Who is Resistless, Fierce conqueror amongst the fighting Forces. (5565)

२०. यद् द्याव इन्द्र ते शतं शतं भूमीरुत स्युः ।
न त्वा वज्रिन्त्सहस्रं सूर्या अनु न जातमष्ट रोदसी ॥

[1](16-18) Pt. Jaidev has applied these verses to the well-versed yogi.

२१. आ पप्राथ महिना वृष्ण्या वृषन्विश्वा शविष्ठ शवसा ।
अस्माँ अव मघवन्गोमति व्रजे वज्रिञ्चित्राभिरूतिभि: ।।

20-21. See Ath. 20.81 (1-2). (5566-67)

HYMN XCIII*

१. उत्त्वा मन्दन्तु स्तोमा: कृणुष्व राधो अद्रिव: । अव ब्रह्मद्विषो जहि ।।

1. O Mighty Lord of Destruction, may our praise-songs please Thee. Let Thee invest us with wealth of food, knowledge and devotion and destroy those who hate God, Veda and Vedic learned persons. (5568)

२. पदा पणीँ रराधसो नि बाधस्व महाँ असि । नहि त्वा कश्चन प्रति ।।

2. Crush under feet the niggardly people, offering nothing to the poor and the deserving. Mighty art Thou, none is equal to Thee. (5569)

३. त्वमीशिषे सुतानामिन्द्र त्वमसुतानाम् । त्वं राजा जनानाम् ।।

3. Thou art the Lord of the created world as well as of the uncreated matter. Thou art the Radiant King of all people. (5570)

४. ईङ्खयन्तीरपस्युव इन्द्रं जातमुपासते । भेजानास: सुवीर्यम् ।।

4. Taking shelter under Him, putting forth their best efforts, and singing the praises of the Most Powerful Lord of fortunes, the people attain to Him, Revealed in their hearts. (5571)

५. त्वमिन्द्र बलादधि सहसो जात ओजस: । त्वं वृषन्वृषेदसि ।।

5. O Mighty God, Thou art well-renowned from Thy strength, vanquishing power and energy. O Showerer of peace and blessings, Thou art truly a sprinkler of comforts and well-being. (5572)

६. त्वमिन्द्रासि वृत्रहा व्य१न्तरिक्षमतिर: । उद् द्यामस्तभ्ना ओजसा ।।

6. O Adorable Lord, Thou art a Dispeller of clouds of ignorance and darkness, a Pervader of all interspace and the Upholder of the heavens through Thy valour and energy. (5573)

७. त्वमिन्द्र सजोषसमर्कं बिभर्षि बाह्वो: । वज्रं शिशान ओजसा ।।

7. O Mighty Lord, whetting the thunderbolt with Thy Great Might and Splendour, Thou upholds the Sun through Thy arms, acting together (in forms of the north and south poles). (5574)

८. त्वमिन्द्राभिभूरसि विश्वा जातान्योजसा । स विश्वा भुव आभव: ।।

8. O Mighty God, Thou art the Overpowerer of all the created things through Thy Power and Energy. He pervades all the places. (5575)

HYMN XCIV**

१. आ यात्विन्द्र: स्वपतिर्मदाय यो धर्मणा तूतुजानस्तुविष्मान् ।
प्रत्वक्षाणो अति विश्वा सहांस्यपारेण महता वृष्ण्येन ।।

*cf. *Rig*, 8.53. (1-3); 10.153. (1-5).
**cf. *Rig*, 10.44. (1-11).

1. Let the Adorable Lord, king or soul, Who is the master of wealth, swiftly moving by His self-bearing laws or powers, Strong and Overwhelming all the daring forces of the foe or evil by His limitless, Great strength of raining down destruction and protection, come to our rejoicings. (5576)

२. सुष्ठामा रथः सुयमा हरी ते मिम्यक्ष वज्रो नृपते गभस्तौ ।
शीभं राजन्त्सुपथा याह्यर्वाङ् वर्धाम ते पपुषो वृष्ण्यानि ॥

2. O king or soul, let thy vehicle be of firm durability (in times of war) and thy horses well-controlled, let there be the deadly weapons in thy hands. Let thee come quickly in the forefront by a good path. Let us add to the striking powers of thee, the protector of the nature. (5577)

३. एन्द्रवाहो नृपतिं वज्रबाहुमुग्रमुग्रासस्तविषास एनम् ।
प्रत्वक्षसं वृषभं सत्यशुष्ममेमस्मत्रा सधमादो वहन्तु ॥

3 Let those amongst us, who are capable of carrying on the state-affairs of the king, who are fierce, strong and pleased to work together, support this king, who has deadly weapons in his hands, is capable of destroying his enemies, powerful, and is of infallible energy and strength. (5578)

४. एवा पतिं द्रोणसाचं सचेतसमूर्ज स्कम्भं धरुण आ वृषायसे ।
ओजः कृष्व सं गृभाय त्वे अप्यसो यथा केनिपानामिनो वृधे ॥

4. O king or soul, thus thou fosters under thy administration the person, who is the protector, domicile of the state, ever vigilant pillar of energy and valour, muster up courage and daring, completely take up reins of the administration in thy own hands and be thyself the lord for the prosperity and progress of the wise. (5579)

५. गमन्नस्मे वसून्या हि शंसिषं स्वाशिषं भरमा याहि सोमिनः ।
त्वमीशिषे सास्मिन्ना सत्सि बर्हिष्यनाधृष्या तव पात्राणि धर्मणा ॥

5. May all sorts of riches come to us. I (a devotee) praise Thee alone. Come to the sacrifice of the votary, full of blessings. Thou art the Lord of all. Let Thee grace this seat of the great sacrifice (by Thy Beneficent Presence). Inviolable are Thy Protecting and Nourishing Powers through Thy sustaining laws. (5580)

६. पृथक्प्रायन्प्रथमा देवहूतयोऽकृण्वत श्रवस्यानि दुष्टरा ।
न ये शेकुर्यज्ञियां नावमारुहमीर्मैव ते न्यविशन्त केपयः ॥

6. The foremost pious persons, the divine worshippers, who cultivate the glorious acts, difficult to achieve, go on the best path of virtue separately, while the treaders on the wrong path, who cannot get into the boat of sacrificial spirituality go down and down in this world of indebtedness. (5581)[1]

७. एवैवापागपरे सन्तु दूढ्योऽश्वा येषां दुर्युज आयुयुज्रे ।
इत्था ये प्रागुपरे सन्ति दावने पुरूणि यत्र वयुनानि भोजना ॥

[1]In this world, a man owes three debts पितृ ऋण, देव ऋण, ऋषि-ऋण.

7. Thus the other persons, whose uncontrolled sense-organs are absorbed in frittering objects of the world, become men of wicked nature, going down and down in level of spirituality. In this way, those, who adopt the upward and higher path of piety, finally rest in God, the Showerer of bliss and the Destroyer of evil, where there are many kinds of means of knowledge, action, and fruition. (5582)

८. गिरीँरज्रान्रेजमानाँ अधारयद् द्यौः क्रन्ददन्तरिक्षाणि कोपयत् ।
समीचीने धिषणे वि ष्कभायति वृष्णः पीत्वा मद उक्थानि शंसति ॥

8. The Splendorous God firmly holds the constantly moving and trembling clouds and mountains, thunders and bestirs the interspacial things. He specially upholds the heavens and the earth, the supporters of all and interlinked by force of attraction. Protecting and nourishing all means of showering joy and bliss, inspires the Vedic songs in the very act of reveling and rejoicing at the creation. (5583)

९. इमं बिभर्मि सुकृतं ते अङ्कुशं येनारुजासि मघवं छफारुजः ।
अस्मिन्त्सु ते सवने अस्त्वोक्यं सुत इष्टौ मघवन्बोध्याभगः ॥

9. O Lord of fortunes, I (the devotee) undertake upon myself Thy well-ordained restraint (in the form of Vedic lores) by which Thou treadest under foot the wicked persons, who tread the innocent under feet. Let there a good shelter for us in this creation of Thine. O All-round Distributor of bounties, letst Thou enlighten us in this great sacrifices performed by Thee (i.e., creation of universe). (5584)

१०. गोभिष्टरेमामतिं दुरेवां यवेन क्षुधं पुरुहूत विश्वाम् ।
वयं राजभिः प्रथमा धनान्यस्माकेन वृजनेना जयेम ॥

११. बृहस्पतिर्नः परि पातु पश्चादुतोत्तरस्मादधरादघायोः ।
इन्द्रः पुरस्तादुत मध्यतो नः सखा सखिभ्यो वरिवः कृणोतु ॥

10-11. See Atha. 89. (10-11) and 17. (10-11). (5585-86)

HYMN XCV*

१. त्रिकद्रुकेषु महिषो यवाशिरं तुविशुष्मस्तृपत्सोममपिबद्विष्णुना सुतं यथावशत् ।
साईं ममाद महि कर्म कर्तवे महामुरुं सैनं सश्चद्देवो देवं सत्यमिन्द्रं सत्य इन्दुः ॥

1. In all the three worlds, i.e., heaven, atmosphere and the earth, the Almighty God, the Lord of Great Energy and Strength, infuses the energising force, capable of both analysis and synthesis and maintains it with His All-pervading power, by which He keeps the creation under control. He exhilirates this great yogi of vast spiritual light to do great deeds of knowledge and piety. That brilliant, truthful and glorious devotee attains to This Radiant, Constant Lord of Fortunes and Adoration. (5587)

According to *Anūkramni* the following two verses (*Rig*. 2.22. (2-3) are also included in, this suktas although they are not found in any 'Saṃhitā', available at present.

*çf. *Rig*, 2.22.1; 10.133. (1-3).

Then the Refulgent God thoroughly overpowers the forces of evil and ignorance by His splendour and Energy, completely fills the heaven and the earth and fully reveals His superiority by its great strength and power. He keeps the one under His Control, while endows the other for the benefit of the people. That brilliant, truthful and glorious devotee attains to This Effulgent, Constant Lord of Bounties.

Or

The Mighty God becomes well-known by His Great sacrifice of knowledge and actions (i.e., revelation of the Vedas and the creation of the universe) altogether. He upholds the universe by His energy and strength at the same time. His Greatness is enhanced by the various powers of His, revealed at the same time. He crushes the violent and evil forces and supervises all the worlds. He is the Giver of Wealth and desirable riches to the praise-singers. That . . . . . (Bounties) as above.

२. प्रो ष्वस्मै पुरोरथमिन्द्राय शूषमर्चत । अभीके चिदु लोककृत्संगे समत्सु वृत्रहास्माकं बोधि
चोदिता नभन्तामन्यकेषां ज्याका अधि धन्वसु ॥

2. Fully sing the praises of the strength of the foremost chariot of this great king. He, being the benefactor of the people in the fearless assemblage of the people, the destroyer of the enemies in wars and energiser of us all, knows our interests quite well. Let bow-strings upon the bows of the wicked enemies break down. (5588)

३. त्वं सिन्धूँरवासृजोऽधराचो अहन्नहिम् । अशत्रुरिन्द्र जज्ञिषे विश्वं पुष्यसि वार्यं
तं त्वा परि ष्वजामहे नभन्तामन्यकेषां ज्याका अधि धन्वसु ॥

3. O Mighty king, thou channelisest the waters of the great rivers to flow down into canals (to irrigate the landside). Killing the enemy, just as the Sun shatters the cloud, thou art known to be foe-less. Thou pushest up all objects worth achieving. We, therefore, embrace and endear the self-same thee. Let the bow-strings......enemies, break down. (5589)

४. वि षु विश्वा अरातयोऽर्यो नशन्त नो धियः । अस्तासि शत्रवे वधं यो न इन्द्र
जिघांसति या ते रातिर्ददिर्वसु नभन्तामन्यकेषां ज्याका अधि धन्वसु ॥

4. Let all the fighting foes be thoroughly destroyed, and our prayers be with you. O Lord of destruction, thou throwest murderous missile on him, who wants to kill us. Whatever thy bounty, it gives us wealth and fortune. Let the bow-strings......break down. (5590)

HYMN XCVI*

१. तीव्रस्याभिवयसो अस्य पाहि सर्वरथा वि हरी इह मुञ्च ।
इन्द्र मा त्वा यजमानासो अन्ये नि रीरमन्तुभ्यमिमे सुतासः ॥

1. O king or soul, destroyer of evil foes or forces, drink deep this bliss, strong and fully equipped with fruition of noble acts, and let loose the horses

*cf. *Rig*, X, 160. (1-5); 161. (1-5); 162. (1-6); 163. (1-7); 164.1.

in the form of Prāna and Apāna, reveling in various bodies. Let not the other objects of senses leading thee on the wrong path, entangle thee into evil. Here are these internal sources of bliss created for thee. (5591)

२. तुभ्यं सुतास्तुभ्यमु सोत्वासस्त्वां गिरः श्वात्र्या आ ह्वयन्ति ।
इन्द्रेदमद्य सवनं जुषाणो विश्वस्य विद्वाँ इह पाहि सोमम् ॥

2. O soul, all these created things are for thee alone. The would-be created things are also for thee. The clear and swift-moving Vedic verses call thy attention. Today, partaking of this sacrifice, and realising the secrets of the universe, drink deep the internal bliss in this world. (5592)

३. य उशता मनसा सोममस्मै सर्वहृदा देवकामः सुनोति ।
न गा इन्द्रस्तस्य परा ददाति प्रशस्तमिच्चारुमस्मै कृणोति ॥

3. The Mighty Lord of Bounties does not allow the fading away of the powers of sense-organs or speech of him who, with keenly desirous mind and whole heart, highly wishing to attain to the Adorable God, generates the spiritual state of bliss, but makes everything charming and of the highest quality for him. (5593)

४. अनुस्पष्टो भवत्येषो अस्य यो अस्मै रेवान्न सुनोति सोमम् ।
निररत्नौ मघवा तं दधाति ब्रह्मद्विषो हन्त्यनानुदिष्टः ॥

4. This Lord of Wealth and riches fully reveals Himself to him, who cultivates spiritual tranquility and calmness like a wealthy person in His devotion, and keeps him in His joy-giving hands and destroys, unasked, all the tendencies of mind inimical to God and the Vedic lore. (5594)

५. अश्वायन्तो गव्यन्तो वाजयन्तो हवामहे त्वोपगन्तवा उ ।
आभूषन्तस्ते सुमतौ नवायां वयमिन्द्र त्वा शुनं हुवेम ॥

5. O Mighty Lord of fortunes, we (the devotees) desirous of horses or action-organs' agility, cows or sense-organs' perception, and food or power, knowledge and wealth, wanting to approach Thee, invoke Thee, Enhancing Thy Glory and being in Thy new Good Will, we call Thy Peaceful and Bounteous-self. (5595)

६. मुञ्चामि त्वा हविषा जीवनाय कमज्ञातयक्ष्मादुत राजयक्ष्मात् ।
ग्राहिर्जग्राह यद्येतदेनं तस्या इन्द्राग्नी प्र मुमुक्तमेनम् ॥

७. यदि क्षितायुर्यदि वा परेतो यदि मृत्योरन्तिकं नीत एव ।
तमा हरामि निर्ऋतेरुपस्थादस्पार्शमेनं शतशारदाय ॥

८. सहस्राक्षेण शतवीर्येण शतायुषा हविषाहार्षमेनम् ।
इन्द्रो यथैनं शरदो नयात्यति विश्वस्य दुरितस्य पारम् ॥

९. शतं जीव शरदो वर्धमानः शतं हेमन्तान्छतमु वसन्तान् ।
शतं त इन्द्रो अग्निः सविता बृहस्पतिः शतायुषा हविषाहार्षमेनम् ॥

6-9. See Ath. 3.11. (1-4). (5596-99)

१०. आहार्षमविदं त्वा पुनरागाः पुनर्णवः । सर्वाङ्ग सर्वं ते चक्षुः सर्वमायुश्च तेऽविदम् ।।

10. See Atharva, 8.1.20. (5600)

११. ब्रह्मणाग्निः संविदानो रक्षोहा बाधतामितः । अमीवा यस्ते गर्भं दुर्णामा योनिमाशये ।।

11. O lady, let the learned physician, well-versed in the science of killing germs of all diseases, in consultation with a Vedic scholar, efface from here the malignant disease, which has taken hold of thy uterus. (5601)

१२. यस्ते गर्भममीवा दुर्णामा योनिमाशये । अग्निष्टं ब्रह्मणा सह निष्क्रव्यादमनीनशत् ।।

12. O lady, let the expert physician, with his Vedic knowledge and learning, thoroughly destroy the malicious disease, which is lying latent in thy organs of generation. (5602)

१३. यस्ते हन्ति पतयन्तं निषत्स्नुं यः सरीसृपम् । जातं यस्ते जिघांसति तमितो नाशयामसि ।।

13. O female, we shall destroy altogether from this world, the person or the disease-germ which kills the sperm in the very act of falling in thy organ of generation, which kills it in the iambic stage which kills it when it has begun its movements in the womb, which wishes to kill it when it is born. (5603)[1]

१४. यस्त ऊरू विहरत्यन्तरा दम्पती शये । योनिं यो अन्तरारेल्हि तमितो नाशयामसि ।।

14. O woman, we will altogether efface from this world, the person or the disease-germ, that sets thy thighs apart, or rests between thee and thy husband or hurts thy vagina from inside. (5604)

१५. यस्त्वा भ्राता पतिर्भूत्वा जारो भूत्वा निपद्यते ।
प्रजां यस्ते जिघांसति तमितो नाशयामसि ।।

15. O woman, we will altogether exterminate, from this world, the wicked person, who enjoys thee in the assumed garb of a brother, husband or the lover, and kills thy progeny. (5605)

१६. यस्त्वा स्वप्नेन तमसा मोहयित्वा निपद्यते । प्रजां यस्ते जिघांसति तमितो नाशयामसि ।।

16. O lady, we will exterminate from this world, the wicked person, who enjoys thee, making thee unconscious or enticing awav through sleep or darkness, and kills thy progeny. (5606)

१७. अक्षीभ्यां ते नासिकाभ्यां कर्णाभ्यां छुबुकादधि ।
यक्ष्मं शीर्षण्यं मस्तिष्काज्जिह्वाया वि वृहामि ते ।।

१८. ग्रीवाभ्यस्त उष्णिहाभ्यः कीकसाभ्यो अनूक्यात् ।
यक्ष्मं दोषण्य१मंसाभ्यां बाहूभ्यां वि वृहामि ते ।।

१९. हृदयात्ते परि क्लोम्नो हलीक्ष्णात्पार्श्वाभ्याम् ।
यक्ष्मं मतस्नाभ्यां प्लीह्नो यक्नस्ते वि वृहामसि ।।

२०. आन्त्रेभ्यस्ते गुदाभ्यो वनिष्ठोरुदरादधि । यक्ष्मं कुक्षिभ्यां प्लाशेर्नाभ्या वि वृहामि ते ।।

२१. उरुभ्यां ते अष्ठीवद्भ्यां पार्ष्णिभ्यां प्रपदाभ्याम् ।
यक्ष्मं भसद्यं१ श्रोणिभ्यां भासदं भंससो वि वृहामि ते ।।

[1](13-16) We: the physician and the king.

२२. अस्थिभ्यस्ते मज्जभ्यः स्नावभ्यो धमनिभ्यः ।
यक्ष्मं पाणिभ्यामङ्गुलिभ्यो नखेभ्यो वि वृहामि ते ॥

२३. अङ्गेअङ्गे लोम्निलोम्नि यस्ते पर्वणिपर्वणि ।
यक्ष्मं त्वचस्यं ते वयं कश्यपस्य वीबर्हेण विष्वञ्चं वि वृहामसि ॥

17-23. See Atha, 2.33. (1-7). (5607-13)

२४. अपेहि मनसस्पतेऽप क्राम परश्चर । परो निर्ऋत्या आ चक्ष्व बहुधा जीवतो मनः ॥

24. O the depressor of the mind, evil though or bad dream, get away; depart and vanish far away. Order the evil tendency to be away. Manifold is the working of mind of the living soul. (5614)

HYMN XCVII**

१. वयमेनमिदा ह्योपीपेमेह वज्रिणम् । तस्मा उ अद्य समना सुतं भरा नूनं भूषत श्रुते ॥

1. In this world, we (the devotee) enhanced the glory of this Lord of Destruction and Fortune yesterday (i.e., in the past) let us even today (i.e., at the present time) with one mind, offer our devotional activity for Him alone. Certainly you shall grace yourself in Vedic learning. (5615)

२. वृकश्चिदस्य वारण उरामथिरा वयुनेषु भूषति ।
सेमं नः स्तोमं जुजुषाण आ गहीन्द्र प्र चित्रया धिया ॥

2. Even a wicked person trampling others under his heels like a wolf, marauding sheep and moving intoxicated like the mad elephant, becomes graceful and adorned with good nature under the knowledge and instructions of Him. O Evil-Destroyer Lord, the self-same Thou, listen to this praise-song of our, come to us (i.e., be realised by us) with wonderful intelligence and action. (5616)

३. कदू न्व१स्याकृतमिन्द्रस्यास्ति पौंस्यम् । केनो नु कं श्रोमतेन न शुश्रुवे जनुषः परि वृत्रहा ॥

3. What act of daring and vigour there is that has not been done by the Mighty Lord or the king? Who has not heard His fame or glory through wonderful acts worth hearing. He is the Destroyer of the evil forces of Ignorance and darkness all over the Creation. (5617)

HYMN XCVIII**

१. त्वामिद्धि हवामहे साता वाजस्य कारवः । त्वां वृत्रेष्विन्द्र सत्पतिं नरस्त्वां काष्ठास्वर्वतः ॥

1. O Mighty Lord of fortunes and riches, or king, we, the skilled mechanics or engineers, invoke Thee alone for the distribution of power, knowledge, food, wealth and speed. The leaders of the people, being attacked by overpowering wicked enemies, call Thee, the Protector of the good and the pious. They seek Thee in various directions to be reached on horses or other means of speedy transport. (5618)

*cf. *Rig*, 8.66. (7-9).
**cf. *Rig*, 6.46 (1-2).

२. स त्वं नश्चित्र वज्रहस्त धृष्णुया मह स्तवानो अद्रिवः ।
गामश्वं रथ्यमिन्द्र सं किर सत्रा वाजं न जिग्युषे ॥

2. O Wonderful Lord of Destruction and Protection, equipped with deadly weapons like the thunderbolt, Highly Praised through Thy Vanquishing power, Invincible, the self-same Thou shower on us wealth of cows, Vedic lore, horses, swift-moving means of transport, plenty of food, knowledge, power and riches, for being victorious. (5619)

HYMN XCIX*

१. अभि त्वा पूर्वपीतय इन्द्र स्तोमेभिरायवः ।
समीचीनास ऋभवः समस्वरन्रुद्रा गृणन्त पूर्व्यम् ॥

1. O Adorable God, in order to fully attain Thee, the ordinary persons, the learned persons of deep insight and the thoroughly praising the truth-preachers sing Thy praises all together through the Vedic praise-songs. (5620)

२. अस्येदिन्द्रो वावृधे वृष्ण्यं शवो मदे सुतस्य विष्णवि ।
अद्या तमस्य महिमानमायवोऽनु ष्टुवन्ति पूर्वथा ॥

2. The Mighty Lord enhances the peace-showering power in the All-pervading bliss of this created spiritual enlightenment. Even today the common people praise His Greatness and sublimity as before. (5621)

HYMN C**

१. अधा हीन्द्र गिर्वण उप त्वा कामान्महः ससृज्महे । उदेव यन्त उदभिः ॥

1. O Adorable Lord, Worthy of Worship, now we may get fulfilled our great wishes through Thee, just the people get many benefits from the running waters, (like hydraulic electricity, irrigation, bathing, etc). (5622)

२. वार्ण त्वा यव्याभिर्वर्धन्ति शूर ब्रह्माणि । वावृध्वांसं चिदद्रिवो दिवेदिवे ॥

2. O Invincible Lord of Courage and Daring, just as waters of the ocean are increased by the waters of the rivers, similarly do the Vedic songs add to Thy Glory, which is ever on the increase itself. (5623)

३. युञ्जन्ति हरी इषिरस्य गाथयोरौ रथ उरुयुगे । इन्द्रवाहा वचोयुजा ॥

3. Just as two horses are yoked to the swift-moving king's chariot, having a heavy yoke, similarly are yoked the unmoving vital breaths, Prāna and Apāna, ever uniting with the speech and carrying the soul along with them, to the great chariot of rejoicing, highly connected with yogic powers of ever progressive soul in spiritual enlightenment, through praise-songs or worshipful devotion. (5624)

HYMN CI***

१. अग्नि दूतं वृणीमहे होतारं विश्ववेदसम् । अस्य यज्ञस्य सुक्रतुम् ॥

*cf. *Rig*, 8.3 (7-8).
**cf. *Rig*, 8.98. (7-9).
***cf. *Rig*, 1.12 (1-3).

1. We (the devotees) espouse the Refulgent God, leader or the learned person or fire (light) as our messenger, who is the showerer of all joys and fortunes, master of all fortunes and sciences and expert performer of this great sacrifice of the creation or the nation. (5625)

२. अग्निमग्निं हवीमभिः सदा हवन्त विश्पतिम् । हव्यवाहं पुरुप्रियम् ॥

2. O people, let you ever, through praise-songs and good means invoke the Radiant God, king, leader or fire (light), the Protector of the people, the Enabler of attaining the desired object, and the Beloved of all. (5626)

३. अग्ने देवाँ इहा वह जज्ञानो वृक्तबर्हिषे । असि होता न ईड्यः ॥

3. O Splendorous Lord, king, leader, learned person or fire (light) letest Thee provide the divine powers or forces, revealing Thyself in this vast universe or nation. Thou art the worship-worthy Benefactor of us all. (5627)

HYMN CII*

१. ईडेन्यो नमस्यऽस्तिरस्तमांसि दर्शतः । समग्निरिध्यते वृषा ॥

1. The Effulgent God, king, the learned person, leader or fire (light) the Showerer of peace and blessings, Beautiful to look at, Praise-worthy, Deserving our obeisance, Dispelling the darkness of ignorance, fully shines forth. (5628)

२. वृषो अग्निः समिध्यतेऽश्वो न देववाहनः । तं हविष्मन्त ईडते ॥

2. The Brilliant God, king, commander, leader or the learned person, or light, showering peace and blessings like a cloud, carrying the divine forces, like a horse, carrying the victorious king, thoroughly sheds His splendour all around. The devoted persons, equipped with all means of worship and sacrifice praise Him. (5629)

३. वृषणं त्वा वयं वृषन्वृषणः समिधीमहि । अग्ने दीद्यतं बृहत् ॥

3. O Peace-showering Refulgent God, king, commander, leader, learned person or light, we, ourselves being powerful, well enhance the glory of Thee, who is All-Powerful and highly splendorous. (5630)

HYMN CIII**

१. अग्निमीडिष्वावसे गाथाभिः शीरशोचिषम् ।
अग्निं राये पुरुमीलह श्रुतं नरोऽग्निं सुदीतये छर्दिः ॥

1. O highly munificent learned person, sing the praises of the shining God, Who is All-glorious by nature, through the Vedic verses, for thy protection and safety. O learned person of great beneficence, all the people worship the Renowned Effulgent God for wealth and fortune, so you should sing, through speeches, the praises of the sheltering Radiant God for good

*cf. *Rig*, 3.27. (13-15).

**cf. *Rig*, 8.71. (Sayâna 66) 14; 49. (1-2). 'Purumilha' and Angiras are not special personages as interpreted by Griffith and others, but merely qualifying epithets.

glory and fame. (5631)

२. अग्न आ याह्यग्निभिर्होतारं त्वा वृणीमहे ।
आ त्वामनक्तु प्रयता हविष्मती यजिष्ठं बर्हिरासदे ॥

2. O Splendorous God, king, commander, leader, learned person, or light, come to us with various lights spiritual or material. We accept Thee as our benefactor. Let the well-spread (vast heaven and earth, full of all means of sacrifice and offerings, be a fit seat for Thee, the Greatest synthesizer or Analyser. (5632)

३. अच्छा हि त्वा सहसः सूनो अङ्गिरः स्रुचश्चरन्त्यध्वरे ।
ऊर्जो नपातं घृतकेशमीमहेऽग्निं यज्ञेषु पूर्व्यम् ॥

3. O Energiser of all powers and strength, shining like the Sun, all ladles move well in the non-violent sacrifice for Thy sake. We pray Thee, the Infallible source of power, Full of rays of brilliant light, foremost of all, Source of all knowledge and light. (5633)

HYMN CIV*

१. इमा उ त्वा पुरूवसो गिरो वर्धन्तु या मम ।
पावकवर्णाः शुचयो विपश्चितोऽभि स्तोमैरनूषत ॥

1. O Lord of Plenteous wealth, may these Vedic songs of mine extoll Thee! Let the brilliant, pious and wise persons; well-versed in the Vedic lore, thoroughly applaud Thee with Vedic verses. (5634)

२. अयं सहस्रमृषिभिः सहस्कृतः समुद्र इव पप्रथे ।
सत्यः सो अस्य महिमा गृणे शवो यज्ञेषु विप्रराज्ये ॥

2. This Creator of Energy and Strength, Vast and Limitless source of all fortunes and well-being is glorified thousand-fold by the seers. True is His Grandeur and His Power is praised in the sacrifices and in the glowing hearts of the learned persons. (5635)

३. आ नो विश्वासु हव्य इन्द्रः समत्सु भूषतु ।
उप ब्रह्माणि सवनानि वृत्रहा परमज्या ऋचीषमः ॥

3. May the Worship-Worthy, Mighty Lord or king grace us in all the states of rejoicings or Wars! May the Destroyer of evil forces or foes, conqueror of main difficulties or obstacles, Pervading all the Vedic verses, grace the occasions of our singing of Vedic songs and praises and the sacrificial acts. (5636)

४. त्वं दाता प्रथमो राधसामस्यसि सत्य ईशानकृत् ।
तुविद्युम्नस्य युज्या वृणीमहे पुत्रस्य शवसो महः ॥

4. O God or king, Thou art the foremost Giver of all riches; Thou art the True Investor of Ruling Powers. We (the devotees) espouse alliance

*cf. *Rig*, 8.3. (3-4); 90. (1-2).

with the Highly Glorious One, Protector of great strength and power. (5637)

HYMN CV*

१. त्वमिन्द्र प्रतूर्तिष्वभि विश्वा असि स्पृधः ।
अशस्तिहा जनिता विश्वतूरसि त्वं तूर्य तरुष्यतः ॥

1. O Mighty Lord of Destruction, king, commander or soul, Thou art the vanquisher of all fighting forces of evil or foe. Being a Generator of good plans, Thou art the Destroyer of wicked designs of the evil or foe, the thorough smasher of the violent forces of evil or the wicked enemy. Letest Thou tear off the violent and the wicked. (5638)

२. अनु ते शुष्मं तुरयन्तमीयतुः क्षोणी शिशुं न मातरा ।
विश्वास्ते स्पृधः श्नथयन्त मन्यवे वृत्रं यदिन्द्र तूर्वसि ॥

2. O Great Lord of Destruction, king, commander or soul, the rulers and the ruled like the earth and heaven, high and low both follow Thy might, just as father and mother follow their baby, when Thou destroyest the overwhelming evil or the foe, all the rival forces get slackened before Thy Wrath. (5639)

३. इत ऊती वो अजरं प्रहेतारमप्रहितम् । आशुं जेतारं हेतारं रथीतममतूर्तं तुग्र्यावृधम् ॥

3. O people, for your protection and safety, approach the Ageless, Expert in striking others, but never being struck by others, the swift-mover, the Victorious, the Destroyer of the wicked, the best of charioteers, the Enhancer of the strength of the brave, foe-killing forces. (5640)

४. यो राजा चर्षणीनां याता रथेभिरध्रिगुः ।
विश्वासां तरुता पृतनानां ज्येष्ठो यो वृत्रहा गृणे ॥

५. इन्द्रं तं शुम्भ पुरुहन्मन्नवसे यस्य द्विता विधर्तरि ।
हस्ताय वज्रः प्रति धायि दर्शतो महो दिवे न सूर्यः ॥

4-5. See Atharva, 20.92. (16-17). (5641-42)

HYMN CVI**

१. तव त्यदिन्द्रियं बृहत्तव शुष्ममुत क्रतुम् । वज्रं शिशाति धिषणा वरेण्यम् ॥

1. The Intelligence and devotion sharpen (i.e., increase the influence of) Thy that Great Glory, high Energy, supreme knowledge activation and terrible might, which is so acceptable and worthy of choice. (5643)

२. तव द्यौरिन्द्र पौंस्यं पृथिवी वर्धति श्रवः । त्वामापः पर्वतासश्च हिन्विरे ॥

2. O Mighty Lord, the heavens and the earth enhance (i.e., show the grandeur of) Thy Might and Glory. The waters of the oceans and rivers etc., and the mountains also hint at Thee (i.e., be speak highly of Thy Greatness). (5644)

३. त्वां विष्णुर्बृहन्क्षयो मित्रो गृणाति वरुणः । त्वां शर्धो मदत्यनु मारुतम् ॥

3. The big sun, the earth, the fire, the water and the high power of the

*cf. *Rig*, 8.99 (सायण 88) (5-7), (सायण 59) (1-2); also *Atharva*, 20-92. (16-17).
**cf. *Rig*, 8-15. (7-9).

wind all revel after Thee. (5645)[1]

HYMN CVII

१. समस्य मन्यवे विशो विश्वा नमन्त कृष्टयः । समुद्रायेव सिन्धवः ॥

1. All the people of the world bow down to His (God's) Wrath, as do the subjects to the king and the rivers to the sea. (5646)[2]

२. ओजस्तदस्य तित्विष उभे यत्समवर्तयत् । इन्द्रश्चर्मेव रोदसी ॥

2. Just as the skin of the dear is spread and rolled together (at the will of the user) similarly when the mighty Lord sets in motion and again rolls up both the earth and the heavens (at His Will). His Energy and Power shines forth just then. (5647)

३. वि चिद्वृत्रस्य दोधतो वज्रेण शतपर्वणा । शिरो बिभेद वृष्णिना ॥

3. Just as a king breaks the head of the wicked person, who strikes terror in the hearts of the general people, with his deadly weapon of hundred parts, similarly does the Mighty God shatters forces of evil and ignorance, agitating the world with His strong and deadly means of destruction, working in hundreds of ways. (5648)

४. तदिदास भुवनेषु ज्येष्ठं यतो जज्ञ उग्रस्त्वेषनृम्णः ।
सद्यो जज्ञानो नि रिणाति शत्रूननु यदेनं मदन्ति विश्व ऊमाः ॥

५. वावृधानः शवसा भूर्योजाः शत्रुर्दासाय भियसं दधाति ।
अव्यनच्च व्यनच्च सस्नि सं ते नवन्त प्रभृता मदेषु ॥

६. त्वे क्रतुमपि पृञ्चन्ति भूरि द्विर्यदेते त्रिर्भवन्त्यूमाः ।
स्वादोः स्वादीयः स्वादुना सृजा समदः सु मधु मधुनाभि योधीः ॥

७. यदि चिन्नु त्वा धना जयन्तं रणेरणे अनुमदन्ति विप्राः ।
ओजीयः शुष्मिन्त्स्थिरमा तनुष्व मा त्वा दभन्दुरेवासः कशोकाः ॥

८. त्वया वयं शाशद्महे रणेषु प्रपश्यन्तो युधेन्यानि भूरि ।
चोदयामि त आयुधा वचोभिः सं ते शिशामि ब्रह्मणा वयांसि ॥

९. नि तद्दधिषेऽवरे परे च यस्मिन्नाविथावसा दुरोणे ।
आ स्थापयत मातरं जिगत्नुमत इन्वत कर्वराणि भूरि ॥

१०. स्तुष्व वर्ष्मन्पुरुवर्त्मानं समृभ्वाणमिनतममाप्तमाप्त्यानाम् ।
आ दर्शति शवसा भूर्योजाः प्र सक्षति प्रतिमानं पृथिव्याः ॥

११. इमा ब्रह्म बृहद्दिवः कृणवदिन्द्राय शूषमग्रियः स्वर्षाः ।
महो गोत्रस्य क्षयति स्वराजा तुरश्चिद्विश्वमर्णवत्तपस्वान् ॥

१२. एवा महान्बृहद्दिवो अथर्वावोचत्स्वां तन्व१मिन्द्रमेव ।
स्वसारौ मातरिभ्वरी अरिप्रे हिन्वन्ति चैने शवसा वर्धयन्ति च ॥

[1]'Vishnu'—the Sun, क्षय—the earth, the abode of all creatures, मित्रः—fire, having synthetic power' वरुण—water, having selective quality.

[2]cf. (1-3) *Rig*, 8.6. (4-6); **(4-12)** *Rig*, 10.120. also *Atharva*, 5.2. (1-9); **(13-14)** *Atharva*, 13 2. (34-35) **(15)** *Rig*, 1.115. (2).

4-12. See Atharva, 5.2. (1-9). (5649-57)

१३. चित्रं देवानां केतुरनीकं ज्योतिष्मान्प्रदिशः सूर्य उद्यन् ।
दिवाकरोऽति द्युम्नैस्तमांसि विश्वातारीद्दुरितानि शुक्रः ॥

१४. चित्रं देवानामुदगादनीकं चक्षुर्मित्रस्य वरुणस्याग्नेः ।
आप्राद् द्यावापृथिवी अन्तरिक्षं सूर्य आत्मा जगतस्तस्थुषश्च ॥

13-14. See Atharva, 13.2. (34-35). (5658-59)

१५. सूर्यो देवीमुषसं रोचमानां मर्यो न योषामभ्येऽति पश्चात् ।
यत्रा नरो देवयन्तो युगानि वितन्वते प्रति भद्राय भद्रम् ॥

15. Just as a man goes round and round after a beautiful female of good qualities (at the time of marriage ceremony) so does the Sun revolves after the radiant and charming dawn. There the people, desirous of attaining divine qualities, manage to interrelate good couples for the well-being of the good and the noble. (5660)

HYMN CVIII*

१. त्वं न इन्द्रा भरँ ओजो नृम्णं शतक्रतो विचर्षणे । आ वीरं पृतनाषहम् ॥

1. O Adorable Lord, Master of manifold Intelligence, Supervisor of all, letest, Thee fully invest us with valour and energy, wealth, vigour and daring, capable of subduing the enemy. (5661)

२. त्वं हि नः पिता वसो त्वं माता शतक्रतो बभूविथ । अधा ते सुम्नमीमहे ॥

2. O Shelterer of hundred-fold Intelligence, Thou art our Father and mother. That is why we pray for peace and prosperity from Thee. (5662)

३. त्वां शुष्मिन्पुरुहूत वाजयन्तमुप ब्रुवे शतक्रतो । स नो रास्व सुवीर्यम् ॥

3. O Powerful and much invoked God of manifold Intelligence and activity we sing the praise of Thee, the giver of wealth, grains, power, knowledge and agility. The self-same Thou givest us high energy and valour. (5663)

HYMN CIX**

१. स्वादोरित्था विषूवतो मध्वः पिबन्ति गौर्यऽः ।
या इन्द्रेण सयावरीर्वृष्णा मदन्ति शोभसे वस्वीरनु स्वराज्यम् ॥

1. Just as white rays of the penetrating Sun drink the sweet waters, similarly do the people of the earth enjoy the sweet fortunes of the vast kingdom of the ruler. The subjects, who always move with, i. e., co-operate with the powerful and wealthy king, under his permanent domicile and patronage, revel in pleasures, in accordance with their self-rule, for great fame and glory. (5664)

२. ता अस्य पृशनायुवः सोमं श्रीणन्ति पृश्नयः ।
प्रिया इन्द्रस्य धेनवो वज्रं हिन्वन्ति सायकं वस्वीरनु स्वराज्यम् ॥

2. Those well-knit or organised people of various colours (i.e., variegated

*cf. *Rig*, 8.99 (88 S.) (10-12).

**cf. *Rig*, 1.84. (10-12) (1) स्वादः मध्वः: the sweet waters, i.e., bereft of any trace of salt of the saline waters of the sea.

interests) foster the development of this state of the mighty king, whom they love like the milchcows, and being fully settled and wealthy, according to self-rule, hurl the deadly weapon capable of destroying the enemy of their king. (5665)

३. ता अस्य नमसा सहः सपर्यन्ति प्रचेतसः ।
व्रतान्यस्य सश्चिरे पुरूणि पूर्वचित्तये वस्वीरनु स्वराज्यम् ॥

3. Those subjects, being wide-awake and vigilant, respect the vanquishing power of this king with obeisance and revenue, etc. Being well-settled and prosperous according to self-rule, they whole-heartedly observe the manifold rules and regulation of his (i.e., king's) for attaining full consciousness of their national interests or responsibility. (5666)

HYMN CX*

१. इन्द्राय मद्वने सुतं परि ष्टोभन्तु नो गिरः । अर्कमर्चन्तु कारवः ॥

1. Our speeches may sing the praises of the Created Universe, regimes or sacrifice, for the Exhilirating Mighty God, king or soul. Let the learned persons or mechanics worship the splendorous God, king or soul. (5667)

२. यस्मिन्विश्वा अधि श्रियो रणन्ति सप्त संसदः । इन्द्रं सुते हवामहे ॥

2. In this world, regime or sacrifice, we (the devotees) invoke the Adorable Lord, king or soul, under whom, all the seven kinds of fortunes and worlds, departments of administration or sense-organs, grace us. (5668)

३. त्रिकद्रुकेषु चेतनं देवासो यज्ञमत्नत । तमिद्वर्धन्तु नो गिरः ॥

3. In the three worlds, or assemblies or states (Jagrit, swapna and smādhi the divine forces, persons or sense-organs, extend or reveal the glory of the All-knowing, All-combining God, king or soul. Let our speeches extoll Him, or him alone. (5669)

HYMN CXI**

१. यत्सोममिन्द्र विष्णवि यद्वा घ त्रित आप्त्ये । यद्वा मरुत्सु मन्दसे समिन्दुभिः ॥

1. O electricity (i.e., positive one) when thou settest the negative electricity (i. e., Soma) in the Sun or in the atmospheric waters (where helium gets converted) and amidst 'marutas' or noble gases, flow in currents, thou thyself gets exhilarated (i e., begin to run in currents). (5670)

२. यद्वा शक्र परावति समुद्रे अधि मन्दसे । अस्माकमित्सुते रणा समिन्दुभिः ॥

2. O powerful electric power, thou revelest over the distant sea or the high up atmospheric ocean. Even in the projects, built by us, thou shouldst freely run into currents. (5671)

*cf. *Rig*, 8.92 (81.S.) (19-21) 'सप्त संसद' (i) Seven worlds' in case of God (ii) Seven Departments or assemblies in case of king (iii) Seven sense-organs or vital breaths or Dhatus in case of souls.

**cf. *Rig*,8. 12. (16-18). I have applied this sukta to electricity, while Pt. Jaidev applies to the spiritual powers of the soul.

३. यद्वासि सुन्वतो वृधो यजमानस्य सत्पते । उक्थे वा यस्य रण्यसि समिन्दुभिः ॥

3. O Protector of the good people, when thou art enhanced in power and energy by the creative sacrificer, under whose broadcast, thou flowest out in waves. (5672)

HYMN CXII*

१. यदद्य कच्च वृत्रहन्नुदगा अभि सूर्य । सर्वं तदिन्द्र ते वशे ॥

1. O Mighty Lord, king or soul or electric power, the Destroyer of the overwhelming forces, splendorous like the Sun, whatever Thou or thou aimest at today, all that is under Thy control. (5673)

२. यद्वा प्रवृद्ध सत्पते न मरा इति मन्यसे । उतो तत्सत्यमित्तव ॥

2. O Most-Powerful Lord of the Good, when Thou thinkest that Thou art Deathless (Immortal) certainly that is true of Thine. (5674)

३. ये सोमासः परावति ये अर्वावति सुन्विरे । सर्वांस्ताँ इन्द्र गच्छसि ॥

3. O Mighty Lord, king or soul, whatever means of joy and happiness are created in the highest state of bliss or near at hand in this world, Thou hast access to all these. (5675)

HYMN CXIII**

१. उभयं शृणवच्च न इन्द्रो अर्वागिदं वचः ।
सत्राच्या मघवा सोमपीतये धिया शविष्ठ आ गमत् ॥

1. May the Mighty God, king, soul or electricity hear this speech of both kinds (Vedic or Laukik, worldly or other-worldly) of ours. Let Him, the Master of Wealth and Riches and All-powerful come to protect the universe, the nation or the sacrificial project with a truthful and determined mind and activity. (5676)

२. तं हि स्वराजं वृषभं तमोजसे धिषणे निष्टतक्षतुः ।
उतोपमानां प्रथमो नि षीदसि सोमकामं हि ते मनः ॥

2. Just as the heavens and the earth clearly carve out Him alone, the Self-Luminous, the Mighty One for energy and valour, similarly do the supporting subjects and the ruling classes specially select him alone, the self-brilliant highly powerful one, as their king for glory and strength, (O Mighty Lord or king,) letest Thee (thee) stay as the Foremost one amongst all near Thee. Thy mind is really desirous of the creation or the kingdom under Thee. (5677)

HYMN CXIV***

१. अभ्रातृव्यो अना त्वमनापिरिन्द्र जनुषा सनादसि । युधेदापित्वमिच्छसे ॥

1. O Great God, king or soul, Thou (thou) art by nature Foeless, Leaderless and companionless from ancient times (for ever). Thou seekest comradeship through yog or war (in case of king only). (5678)

*cf. *Rig*, 8.93 (82 S.) (4-6). **cf. *Rig*, 8.61 (S.50) (1-2). ***cf. *Rig*, 8.21. (13-14).

२. नकी रेवन्तं सख्याय विन्दसे पीयन्ति ते सुराश्वः ।
यदा कृणोषि नदनुं समूहस्यादित्पितेव हूयसे ।।

2. Thou never befriendest the niggardly wealthy persons, who, being intoxicated with wine, such the blood of the poor and the needy. When Thou Thunderest and gatherest up peace-showering power, Thou art called like a father. (5679)

HYMN CXV*

१. अहमिद्धि पितुष्परि मेधामृतस्य जग्रभ । अहं सूर्य इवाजनि ।।

1. Surely I (i.e., God) alone fully conceive the penetrating intelligence of the natural laws of the protector and creator of the universe. I reveal myself as the Sun, lighting the whole creation. (5680)

२. अहं प्रत्नेन मन्मना गिरः शुम्भामि कण्ववत् । येनेन्द्रः शुष्ममिद्दधे ।।

2. I reveal the Vedic verses, like the wise learned seer through the ancient Vedic knowledge, by which the soul or king may attain power and strength (to lead his life aright on the earth). (5681)

३. ये त्वामिन्द्र न तुष्टुवुर्ऋषयो ये च तुष्टुवुः । ममेद्वर्धस्व सुष्टुतः ।।

3. O king or soul, the wise seers, who don't satisfy you, or who satisfy you (leave them alone). Let you prosper being well-directed by Me alone, (through Vedic teachings spoken of above). (5682)

HYMN CXVI**

१. मा भूम निष्टचा इवेन्द्र त्वदरणा इव । वनानि न प्रजहितान्यद्रिवो दुरोषासो अमन्महि ।।

1. O Mighty Lord of Unconquerable Power, we may never be, through Thy kindness, like the helpless and downtrodden, the powerless and the unhappy nor like the totally rejected trees, quite unfit for burning even. (5683)

२. अमन्महीदनाशवोऽनुग्रासश्च वृत्रहन् । सुकृत्सु ते महता शूर राधसानु स्तोमं मुदीमहि ।।

2. O Brave Destroyer of the forces of evil and ignorance or the enemy, we (the ordinary persons) think ourselves not so swift-moving, nor so terrible (as fighting warriors). Yet once we may rejoice in praise of Thy great Bounties and fortunes. (5684)

HYMN CXVII***

१. पिबा सोममिन्द्र मन्दतु त्वा यं ते सुषाव हर्यश्वाद्रिः । सोतुर्बाहुभ्यां सुयतो नार्वा ।।

1. O powerful king, soul, master of swift-moving-forces,enjoy the national fortune that thy unvulnerable regime has produced. It may be a source of pleasure for thee. Let it take the right course, through strong arms, i.e., the army and the police of the energising and creative group of ministers like the well-trained horses. (5685)

२. यस्ते मदो युज्यश्चारुरस्ति येन वृत्राणि हर्यश्व हंसि । स त्वामिन्द्र प्रभूवसो ममत्तु ।।

*cf. *Rig*, 8.6 (10-12) I: God, Himself, throughout the sukta.

**cf. *Rig*, 8.1. (13-14).

***cf. *Rig*, 7.22. (1-3).

2. O Mighty Lord of Profuse Wealth and riches, Master of swift-moving forces whatever pleasant, unifying and charming strength Thou (thou) hast, by which Thou killest the forces of evil or foe, let it please Thee well. (5686)

३. बोधा सु मे मघवन्वाचमेमां यां ते वसिष्ठो अर्चति प्रशस्तिम् ।
इमा ब्रह्म सधमादे जुषस्व ॥

3. O fortunate king, thoroughly understand this good instruction of mine (God's) which the best priest preaches to thee in the form of a good sermon. Even in the assembly-hall faithfully follow these Vedic instructions. (5687)

HYMN CXVIII*

१. शग्ध्यू३षु शचीपत इन्द्र विश्वाभिरूतिभिः ।
भगं न हि त्वा यशसं वसुविदमनु शूर चरामसि ॥

1. O Brave, Mighty Lord of Protection and Destruction, Master of All Power and Energy, invest us with all means of peaceful existence through all Thy means of protection and safety. We certainly follow Thee, the Glorious One, capable of giving wealth and riches, like a distributor of fortunes. (5688)

२. पौरो अश्वस्य पुरुकृद् गवामस्युत्सो देव हिरण्ययः ।
नकिर्हि दानं परिमर्धिषत्त्वे यद्यद्यामि तदा भर ॥

2. O Bounteous Lord, Thou art the Increaser of horses, the multiplier of cows and the repository of gold. Surely none can destroy the gift made by Thee, whatever things I request for, let these be provided to me by Thee. (5689)

३. इन्द्रमिद्देवतातय इन्द्रं प्रयत्यऽध्वरे । इन्द्रं समीके वनिनो हवामह इन्द्रं धनस्य सातये ॥

3. In order to achieve divine qualities or honour the learned persons, we invoke the Adorable God, king or soul. In the very beginning of a non-violent sacrifice we call Him (or him). Worshipping the Adorable Lord or king or soul, we invoke Him (him) at the time of a war. Even to achieve wealth and riches, we seek His aid. (5690)

४. इन्द्रो मह्ना रोदसी पप्रथच्छव इन्द्रः सूर्यमरोचयत् ।
इन्द्रे ह विश्वा भुवनानि येमिर इन्द्रे सुवानास इन्दवः ॥

4. The Mighty Lord of Creation, by His Great strength, extends the heavens and the earth. The self-same Lord lights the sun. Certainly all the worlds are well-regulated under the rules and regulations of Mighty Lord. All the fluids, capable of producing things of creation animal or vegetation are under Him. (5691)

HYMN CXIX**

१. अस्तावि मन्म पूर्व्यं ब्रह्मेन्द्राय वोचत । पूर्वीर्ऋतस्य बृहतीरनूषत स्तोतुर्मेधा असृक्षत ॥

1. O learned persons, the ancient Vedic lore is praised to be worthy of meditating upon; make its thorough exposition to reveal the qualities of the

*cf. *Rig*, (1-2) 8.61 (50 सायण) (5-6); (3-4) 8.3. (5-6).

**cf. *Rig*, 8.52. (9); 8.57. (10). Also 'Vālakhilya' 4.9. and 3.10,

Adorable Lord to the general people and sing the vast Vedic verses, full of natural laws and truths. The sharp intelligence of the praise-singer of verses is generated of itself. (5692)

२. तुरण्यवो मधुमन्तं घृतश्चुतं विप्रासो अर्कमानृचुः ।
अस्मे रयिः पप्रथे वृष्ण्यं शवोऽस्मे सुवानास इन्दवः ॥

2. The swiftly-acting, wise people worship the Adorable God, Full of knowledge and sweet bounties, splendorous Himself and shedding splendour all around. He spreads all sorts of riches and fortunes amongst us and invests us with gift-showering power, and instills in us the generative fluids, like semen etc. (5693)

HYMN CXX*

१. यदिन्द्र प्रागपागुदङ्न्यग्वा हूयसे नृभिः । सिमा पुरू नृषूतो अस्यानवेऽसि प्रशर्ध तुर्वशे ॥

1. O Mighty Lord of High Destructive Power, Most Honourable One, as Thou art called by the people from the front, behind, above and below, Thou art highly worshipped by the people amongst the learned and desirous ones, aiming at fourfold ideals of life (i.e., Dharma, Artha, Kama and Moksha). (5694)

२. यद्वा रुमे रुशमे श्यावके कृप इन्द्र मादयसे सचा ।
कण्वासस्त्वा ब्रह्मभि स्तोमवाहस इन्द्रा यच्छन्त्या गहि ॥

2. O Almighty God, when Thou dispassionately fills the preaching person (i.e., Brahman) the protecting one (i.e., Kshatriya) the businessman (i.e., Vaishya) and the physical labourer (i.e., Shudra) with pleasure, one and all together, the wise and learned persons, singing Vedic verses, approach Thee with Vedic songs and praises. Completely reveal Thyself to them. (5695)

HYMN CXXI**

१. अभि त्वा शूर नोनुमोऽदुग्धा इव धेनवः । ईशानमस्य जगतः स्वर्दृशमीशानमिन्द्र तस्थुषः ॥

1. O Brave, Adorable God, we, like the unmilked milch cows to the milkman, bow to Thee, Who art the Ruler, Brilliant like the sun, of this world, moving and immobile, or animate and inanimate. (5696)

२. न त्वावाँ अन्यो दिव्यो न पार्थिवो न जातो न जनिष्यते ।
अश्वायन्तो मघवन्निन्द्र वाजिनो गव्यन्तस्त्वा हवामहे ॥

2. There is none like Thee, Mighty Lord, of fortunes divine or terrestrial neither born nor to be born. We, desirous of wealth of horses and cows, and being master of foodgrains, power, knowledge, wealth and agility, invoke Thee. (5697)

HYMN CXXII***

१. रेवतीर्नः सधमाद इन्द्रे सन्तु तुविवाजाः । क्षुमन्तो याभिर्मदेम ॥

*cf. *Rig*, 8.4. (1-2); (1) 'Anus' and 'Turuvasha' are not special tribes of these names but qualifying epithets.

**cf. *Rig*, 7.32. (22-23).

***cf. *Rig*, 1.30. (13-15).

1. Let those females or the subjects, with whom we, being well-provided with foodgrains, riches etc., enjoy ourselves, being fortunate, possessing strength and wealth in plenty, revel themselves along with us in this fortunate household or nation. (5698)

२. आ घ त्वावान्त्मनाप्त स्तोतृभ्यो धृष्णवियानः । ऋणोरक्षं न चक्र्योः ॥

2. O Mighty God or king, capable of subduing the forces of evil or the enemy, Thou, Master of Thyself (i.e., having full control of thyself) firmly established by Thy own might like the axle of the wheels of the car, being requested by the worshippers or praise-singers, Thou certainly showerest Thy blessings on them. (5699)

३. आ यद्दुवः शतक्रतवा कामं जरितॄणाम् । ऋणोरक्षं न शचीभिः ॥

3. O Powerful Lord or king of hundreds of sacrifices or actions motivating all, like the axle of a car by propelling forces, Thou fully grantest the desired objects of the worshippers after accepting their homage. (5700)

HYMN CXXIII*

१. तत्सूर्यस्य देवत्वं तन्महित्वं मध्या कर्तोर्विततं सं जभार ।
यदेदयुक्त हरितः सधस्थादाद्रात्री वासस्तनुते सिमस्मै ॥

1. It is surely the divine quality and grandeur of the Sun that it takes back the light, which it had spread throughout the interspace of the created world and when it loosens the rays from the high pedestal where they had collected, thereby weaves out night and day like a cloth for the whole creation in a uniform manner. (5701)

२. तन्मित्रस्य वरुणस्याभिचक्षे सूर्यो रूपं कृणुते द्योरुपस्थे ।
अनन्तमन्यद्रुशदस्य पाजः कृष्णमन्यद्धरितः सं भरन्ति ॥

2. That is the shape or form that the Sun gives to Mitra i.e., lit-up Prāna-light (day time) and Varuna—Water (night time) in the vicinity of the heavens. His rays well maintain his limitless might, bright at one time, (during the day) and dark at another (i.e., during the night). (5702)

HYMN CXXIV**

१. कया नश्चित्र आ भुवदूती सदावृधः सखा । कया शचिष्ठया वृता ॥

1. We (the devotees) don't know by what means of protection or through what sort of powerful behaviour, That Wonderful Friend, Who ever pushes up our well-being and prosperity, may reveal Himself to us. (5703)

२. कस्त्वा सत्यो मदानां मंहिष्ठो मत्सदन्धसः । दृह्ळा चिदारुजे वसु ॥

2. O Adorable Lord or king, what genuine and most liberal means of enjoyment, amongst all joys of fortunes will exhilarate Thee, so that Thou may throw open the strongest treasures of wealth to Thy devotees? (5704)

*cf. *Rig*, 1. 115. (4-5).

**cf. *Rig*, 4.31 (1-3); (4-6) *Atharva*, 20.63. (1-3). (10.157; 6.17.15).

३. अभी षु णः सखीनामविता जरितॄणाम् । शतं भवास्यूतिभिः ॥

3. O Lord of Protection or king, Thou art an allround Defender and Protector of our friends and worshippers with hundreds of means of protection and defence. (5705)

४. इमा नु कं भुवना सीषधामेन्द्रश्च विश्वे च देवाः ।
यज्ञं च नस्तन्वं च प्रजां चादित्यैरिन्द्रः सह चीक्लृपाति ॥

५ आदित्यैरिन्द्रः सगणो मरुद्भिरस्माकं भूत्वविता तनूनाम् ।
हत्वाय देवा असुरान्यदायन्देवा देवत्वमभिरक्षमाणाः ॥

६. प्रत्यञ्चमर्कमनयञ्छचीभिरादित्स्वधामिषिरां पर्यपश्यन् ।
अया वाजं देवहितं सनेम मदेम शतहिमाः सुवीराः ॥

4-6. See Atharva, 20.63 (1-3). (5706-8)

HYMN CXXV*

१. अपेन्द्र प्राचो मघवन्नमित्रानपापाचो अभिभूते नुदस्व ।
अपोदीचो अप शूराधराच उरौ यथा तव शर्मन्मदेम ॥

1. O Brave and Mighty God of Protection and Destruction and Fortunes, or king, capable of warding off all forces of evil and ignorance or the enemy, drive away the enemies from the east, the west, from the north and from below, i.e., the south, so that we may be happy and pleasant under Thy vast shelter. (5709)

२. कुविदङ्ग यवमन्तो यवं चिद्यथा दान्त्यनुपूर्वं वियूय ।
इहेहैषां कृणुहि भोजनानि ये बर्हिषो नमोवृक्ति न जग्मुः ॥

2. O Dear Lord or king, just as the agriculturists with barley-fields, reap the barley, separating the stalks one after the other, similarly in various parts of the land make arrangements for the meals of those who have not gone astray from the path of sacrifice and worship. (5710)

३. नहि स्थूर्यृतुथा यातमस्ति नोत श्रवो विविदे संगमेषु ।
गव्यन्त इन्द्र सख्याय विप्रा अश्वायन्तो वृषणं वाजयन्तः ॥

3. As the destination cannot be reached in time by going on a one-horsed vehicle, nor can glory be achieved by going, by the same transport, to wars or assemblies. The learned and the wise persons, desirous of the wealth of cows, horses, foodgrains, power, knowledge and riches, choose the Fortune-showering Lord as their friend. (5711)

४. युवं सुराममश्विना नमुचावासुरे सचा । विपिपाना शुभस्पती इन्द्रं कर्मस्वावतम् ॥

4. O strong and active officers of both the departments, civil and military, unanimously acting in the annihilation of the wicked person or the enemy, who is not fit to be forsaken or forgiven, being the defender of good actions and protecting the nation, well-equipped with fortunes in various ways and actions, both of you should protect this great king in all affairs. (5712)

*cf. *Rig*, 10. 131. (1-7).

५. पुत्रमिव पितरावश्विनोभेन्द्रावथु: काव्यैर्दंसनाभि: ।
यत्सुरामं व्यपिब: शचीभि: सरस्वती त्वा मघवन्नभिष्णक् ॥

5. O Mighty king, let both the officers of the civil and the military departments, strong and quick in taking decisions, protect thee by their wise and thoughtful counsels and determined enemy-crushing actions, like the parents protecting their son. O king of fortunes, when thou enjoyest the national fortunes and well-being, the assembly of the learned persons makes thee free from all troubles and difficulties. (5613)

६. इन्द्र: सुत्रामा स्ववाँ अवोभि: सुमृडीको भवतु विश्ववेदा: ।
बाधतां द्वेषो अभयं न: कृणोतु सुवीर्यस्य पतय: स्याम ॥

७. स सुत्रामा स्ववाँ इन्द्रो अस्मदाराच्चिद् द्वेष: सनुतर्युयोतु ।
तस्य वयं सुमतौ यज्ञियस्यापि भद्रे सौमनसे स्याम ॥

6-7. See Atharva, 7.91.92. (5714-15)

HYMN CXXVI*

१. वि हि सोतोरसृक्षत नेन्द्रं देवममंसत ।
यत्रामदद्वृषाकपिरर्य: पुष्टेषु मत्सखा विश्वस्मादिन्द्र उत्तर: ॥

1. The various sense-organs certainly try to secure peace and happiness in various ways, but they don't know the splendorous God or the soul, Who is the Giver of all these things and powers. My friend, the Mighty Lord is there in the inner recesses of the heart, where the soul, stirring all his sense-organs to activation revels in joys, like the master having the sense of pleasure amongst his well-fed servants or relations. The Adorable Lord is far superior to all the world. (5716)

२. परा हीन्द्र धावसि वृषाकपेरति व्यथि: ।
नो अह प्र विन्दस्यन्यत्र सोमपीतये विश्वस्मादिन्द्र उत्तर: ॥

2. O Adorable Lord, when Thou runs away from the soul, trembling at the sight of troubles and miseries, (due to his ignorance). Thou becomest a source of great pain and agony to him. And Thou art not, found even after a great search, for the protection of the soul or blessing him with peace and tranquility at other places even. The Great God is far greater than all others. (5717)

३. किमयं त्वां वृषाकपिश्चकार हरितो मृग: ।
यस्मा इरस्यसीदु न्व१र्यो वा पुष्टिमद्वसु विश्वस्मादिन्द्र उत्तर: ॥

3. O Almighty God, what has this soul, brilliant like the Sun, peace-showering in Dharm-Megh Smādhi, like a raining cloud, attracted by Thy magnetic Power and keenly searching Thee, like a deer (in search of water in the desert), done for Thee that Thou goest on showering wealth and fortune to feed and nourish him, like the master showering these things on his servants etc? (5718)

*cf. *Rig.* 10.86. (1-23) 'Indra': God; 'Indrani': Prakriti (matter) Vrishakapi-Jivatma (soul); *Vrishakaper*-soul's force.

४. यमिमं त्वं वृषाकपिं प्रियमिन्द्राभिरक्षसि ।
श्वा न्वस्य जम्भिषदपि कर्णे वराहयुर्विश्वस्मादिन्द्र उत्तरः ॥

4. O Mighty Lord of Protection, the body, sensual like a dog desirous of vital breaths for energising it, ensures, for fruit of action, even this lovely powerful and brilliant soul, whom Thou protectest in every way. (5719)

५. प्रिया तष्टानि मे कपिर्व्यक्ता व्यदूदुषत् ।
शिरो न्वस्य राविषं न सुगं दुष्कृते भुवं विश्वस्मादिन्द्र उत्तरः ॥

5. The soul, agitated and fickle like a monkey, (under the spell of his passions) enjoys, in various ways, all the sweet-looking objects, clearly cut and created out of me, (the primeval matter). Surely I (i.e., the same matter) destroy his head (i.e., all the thinking faculties, so that he becomes, forgetful of his own real identity). I (the matter) don't become a source of pleasure and happiness to the evil-doer. The Mighty Lord is far Glorious than all others. (5720)

६. न मत्स्त्री सुभसत्तरा न सुयाशुतरा भुवत् ।
न मत्प्रतिच्यवीयसी न सक्थ्युद्यमीयसी विश्वस्मादिन्द्र उत्तरः ॥

6. No female is more charming and attractive than myself (i.e., matter) nor more comfortable a companion to her husband than I. No female is more amenable to her husband's approaches than I, nor is she ready to bear the burden of her husband upon herself so readily, as do I, the huge splendour of God, my husband. He is far greater than all. (5721)[1]

७. उवे अम्ब सुलाभिके यथेवाङ्ग भविष्यति ।
भसन्मे अम्ब सक्थि मे शिरो मे वीव हृष्यति विश्वस्मादिन्द्र उत्तरः ॥

7. O powerful, comfort-affording and dear mother (i.e., primeval matter) as you had been before, so shall you remain in future. O mother, let thy splendour, the synthetic energy and power of perception of all the sense-organs in the head, be all a source of joy and happiness to me. The Mighty Lord is the Mightiest of all. (5722)[2]

८. किं सुबाहो स्वङ्गुरे पृथुष्टो पृथुजाघने ।
किं शूरपत्नि नस्त्वमभ्यमीषि वृषाकपिं विश्वस्मादिन्द्र उत्तरः ॥

8. O Primeval matter, capable of ensnaring the souls in thy beautiful arms of attractive charms, possessed of brilliance in every parts of thine, spreading thy long tantacles, like the hair-knots of a woman, having vast and pervading energy, with this Brave Lord as thy master, why art thou angry with this powerful and energetic soul of ours? The Almighty God is the supremest of all. (5723)

९. अवीरामिव मामयं शरारुरभि मन्यते ।
उताहमस्मि वीरिणीन्द्रपत्नी मरुत्सखा विश्वस्मादिन्द्र उत्तरः ॥

9. This violently malignant one, (i.e.,) soul completely considers me bereft

[1](5-6) Verses relate the relation of the soul and matter and matter and God respectively.
[2]The soul addresses the matter.

of a heroic supporter or helper. I (i.e., the mother) am, on the other hand, the mother of the brave offspring in the form of vital breaths and a thing well-protected by the Almighty God, the friend of Marutas, the noble gases in the atmosphere. The Almighty God is Supreme over all. (5724)

१०. संहोत्रं स्म पुरा नारी समनं वाव गच्छति ।
वेधा ऋतस्य वीरिणीन्द्रपत्नी महीयते विश्वस्मादिन्द्र उत्तरः ॥

10. Just as a female goes to a sacrifice or war and is respected as the ordainer of the true knowledge, mother of brave sons and wife of a powerful and fortunate husband, similarly in the very beginning of the creation, the primeval matter, the constant companion of the Leader of all, assumes the collective sustaining power in greatest sacrifice of the creation of the universe and gets extolled as the sustainer of the laws of nature, the source of all powers and energies and well-protected and nourished by the Mighty Lord. The Mighty Lord is the greatest of all. (5725)

११. इन्द्राणीमासु नारिषु सुभगामहमश्रवम् ।
नह्यऽस्या अपरं चन जरसा मरते पतिर्विश्वस्मादिन्द्र उत्तरः ॥

11. Amongst all the females, I (the devotee) hear the primeval matter the constant companion of the Mighty Lord of fortunes, the most fortunate one, as her Lord never dies of old age, like those of others. The Great God is Supreme over all. (5726)

१२. नाहमिन्द्राणि रारण सख्युर्वृषाकपेर्ऋते ।
यस्येदमप्यं हविः प्रियं देवेषु गच्छति विश्वस्मादिन्द्र उत्तरः ॥

12. O Indrani, the primordial matter, I (God) don't rejoice or have any fun in the form of the creation of the world, without my friend, the powerful and energetic Jivatma (the soul), whose favourite means of subsistence based on water or vital breaths go to breathe life into his organs of sense or action. The Mighty God reigns supreme over all. (5727)[1]

१३. वृषाकपायि रेवति सुपुत्र आदु सुस्नुषे ।
घसत्त इन्द्र उक्षणः प्रियं काचित्करं हविर्विश्वस्मादिन्द्र उत्तरः ॥

13. O Primeval matter, the mother of bliss-showering or thrilling devotees, the fortunate one, producer of good off-spring and the generator of comforts and well-being, thy Lord (Indra) takes in all the means of bliss-showering and the sweet material, productive of happiness and ease (at the time of deluge). The Adorable Lord is the mightiest of all. (5728)

१४. उक्ष्णो हि मे पञ्चदश साकं पचन्ति विंशतिम् ।
उताहमद्मि पीव इदुभा कुक्षी पृणन्ति मे विश्वस्मादिन्द्र उत्तरः ॥

14. The fifteen objects, endowed with the capacity to instil power and energy, unanimously ripen or mature twenty things for me (the soul). Then I enjoy them grow strong and powerful. They fully develop my both the sides. Supreme is the Lord over all. (5729)[2]

[1]God addressing matter on the importance of the soul, His constant friend, for whose sake He creates the universe.

[2](14) '*Fifteen*'- *five* subtle elements, *five* 'sthūl' elements and *five* vital breaths. '*Twenty*':

१५. वृषभो न तिग्मश्रृङ्गोऽन्तर्यूथेषु रोरुवत् ।
मन्थस्त इन्द्र शं हृदे यं ते सुनोति भावयुर्विश्वस्मादिन्द्र उत्तरः ॥

15. Just as a bull, with sharp horns, bellows loudly amidst the herds of cattle, so dost Thou, O Mighty Lord, Blessing-showerer, with sharp rays of light of knowledge to dispel darkness of ignorance and evil, resound Thy Inner Voice of warning amongst the assemblage of persons. The devotional spirit, capable of subduing all evil propensities, that a devotee cultivates for Thee instills all peace and calmness in the heart. The Mighty God is Grander than all. (5730)

१६. न सेशे यस्य रम्बतेऽन्तरा सक्थ्या३ कपृत् ।
सेदीशे यस्य रोमशं निषेदुषो विजृम्भते विश्वस्मादिन्द्र उत्तरः ॥

16. He, whose head hangs in shame or difference between his thighs (in the face of his rival), he is not fit to rule. Only he, whose mouth, decorated with moustaches, widely opens to give various orders at the very sitting of his on the throne, rules the nation. Mighty God is the greatest of all.

Or

The soul, whose easily-satisfied mind hangs between the ensnaring objects of the world, cannot be the ruler of the world. Only he, whose face, lit up with the rays of spiritual light, specially opens to pour out good sermons, sitting well at the dais, is able to rule the world. The Mighty God is the greatest of all. (5731)[1]

१७. न सेशे यस्य रोमशं निषेदुषो विजृम्भते ।
सेदीशे यस्य रम्बतेऽन्तरा सक्थ्या३ कपृद्विश्वस्मादिन्द्र उत्तरः ॥

17. He, whose moustached mouth simply yawns, while sitting cannot rule others. Only he, whose capacity to create happiness and well-being spreads far between the earth and the heavens, rules the world. The mighty God is the Supremest of all. (5732)

१८. अयमिन्द्र वृषाकपिः परस्वन्तं हतं विदत् ।
असिं सूनां नवं चरुमादेधस्यान आचितं विश्वस्मादिन्द्र उत्तरः ॥

18. O Mighty God, let this soul, capable of cultivating the blissful state of mind by shaking off the evil propensities the source of all trouble and unhappiness, know it for certain that the feeling 'that he is away from God' is dead and gone and that he has achieved the sharp weapon of spiritual grandeur with which he can cut asunder the binding knot of troubles and miseries, the sharp intellect generating divine qualities, new devotional be-

five sense-organs, *five* action-organs, *five* vital breaths, *four* Antakarn i.e., मन, बुद्धि, चित्त, अहंकार and *20th* body.

Note: Sayāna and Griffith are quite wrong in ascribing the verses (12) and (14) to slaughtering of bulls due to their wrong interpretation of the word (उक्षण), which being taken as adjective instead of as noun, gives a different scientific and noble version of the Vedic text.

[1](16,17) Griffith has passed over these verses thinking them as indecent, probably due to Sayāna's indecent rendering; while there is none.

haviour, and life, fully saturated with high splendour and glory. The Almighty God is Supreme over all. (5733)[1]

१६. अयमेमि विचाकशद्विचिन्वन्दासमार्यम् ।
पिबामि पाकसुत्वनोऽभि धीरमचाकशं विश्वस्मादिन्द्र उत्तरः ॥

19. Here am I, the God, Who go about supervising and distinguishing between the Arya (i.e., the good and noble person) and Dasa (i.e., the wicked and evil-natured). I accept and protect him, who cultivates self-knowledge and blissful state of mind by deep-meditation, see the intelligent person, engrossed in deep devotion and meditation and show his worth to the world. The same God is greater than the whole world. (5734)

२०. धन्व च यत्कृन्तत्रं च कति स्वित्ता वि योजना ।
नेदीयसो वृषाकपेऽस्तमेहि गृहाँ उप विश्वस्मादिन्द्र उत्तरः ॥

20. O bliss-generating and evil-shaking soul, how many yojanas (i.e., 4 miles each) far away are those deserts and jungles, full of thorns? Surely come to thy own house, nearest to other houses (i.e., There is no use flying away from one's own house into the jungles) Mighty Lord is Supreme over all. (5735)

२१. पुनरेहि वृषाकपे सुविता कल्पयावहै ।
य एष स्वप्ननंशनोऽस्तमेषि पथा पुनर्विश्वस्मादिन्द्र उत्तरः ॥

21. O bliss-creating and ignorance-dispelling soul, (i.e., Vimukta Atman) come again into the world, we both (i.e., Primeval Matter and God) shall generate happiness and all means of well-being for thee, who, again destroying or shaking off death by the same path as before, goest to his own shelter (i.e., the God) in the state of salvation. Great God is the Supremest of all. (5736)[2]

२२. यदुदञ्चो वृषाकपे गृहमिन्द्राजगन्तन ।
क्व१स्य पुल्वघो मृगः कमगं जनयोपनो विश्वस्मादिन्द्र उत्तरः ॥

22. O Powerful and energetic soul, blessed with fortunes of bliss, when the up-rising souls, finally reach their home (i.e., the God) in the state of salvation, where is that soul of manifold sins and seeker of the various objects of senses gone? (i.e., he is no more there). He has gone to the Blissful God. Greatest of all is the Mighty Lord. (5737)

२३. पर्शुर्ह नाम मानवी साकं ससूव विंशतिम् ।
भद्रं भल त्यस्या अभूद्यस्या उदरमामयद्विश्वस्मादिन्द्र उत्तरः ॥

23. Surely that is genetic energy of human beings, which together creates twenty organs i.e., *five* sense-organs, *five* action-organs, four Antashkaraṇ मन, बुद्धि, चित्त, अहंकार and 20th body. O soul, that has been for the good

[1]The western scholars have read animal slaughter in this verse, due to their ascribing meanings of laukik Sanskrit to the Vedic text, thereby bringing the Vedas into contempt.

[2]The cycle of going into the state of salvation and returning to life and death on the earth, goes on turn by turn.

and well-being of her, whose belly thou hast been paining. Mighty Lord is far supreme to all. (5738)[1]

HYMN CXXVII

(Kuntap Suktas)

१. इदं जना उप श्रुत नराशंस स्तविष्यते । षष्टिं सहस्रा नवतिं च कौरम आ रुशमेषु दद्महे ॥

1. O persons, listen attentively. The qualities of the leader of the people is being described here. O king or commander, revelling on the earth, or in the war, we appoint 6090 warriors in the enemy-destroying battallions of the army. (5739)[2]

२. उष्ट्रा यस्य प्रवाहणो वधूमन्तो द्विर्दश । वर्ष्मा रथस्य नि जिहीडते दिव ईषमाणा उपस्पृशः ॥

2. (The above-mentioned leader is one), whose vanguard of twenty vehicles or aeroplanes or ships is fire-thrower and death-raining on the enemy; whose squadron of 20 airships or missiles, touching the heavens and getting the mastery thereof, raining death over the enemy thoroughly raises him to the ground. (5740)

३. एष ऋषय मामहे शतं निष्कान्दश स्रजः । त्रीणि शतान्यर्वतां सहस्रा दश गोनाम् ॥

3. To set all the above-mentioned mechanism of destruction, this leader employs the hundred units of energy, ten wreaths of coil, 300 horse-power and ten thousand rays of light. (5741)

४. वच्यस्व रेभ वच्यस्व वृक्षे न पक्वे शकुनः । ओष्टे जिह्वा चर्चरीति क्षुरो न भुरिजोरिव ॥

4. O broadcaster, go on broadcasting thy speech, like parrots on a tree, laden with ripe fruits. The tongue goes on uttering words between the lips, just as the cutting line goes on moving between the blades of a scissors. (The verse indicates the way how the voice of the broadcaster goes on moving in a wave-line, like the one made of the cutting of a scissors). (5742)[3]

५. प्र रेभासो मनीषा वृषा गाव इवेरते । अमोतपुत्रका एषाममोत गा इवासते ॥

5. The intelligent broadcasters propagate the speeches like the bulls stimulating the cows, some of these speech-waves, produced by them stay there at the station (i.e., are lost there and then) while others go to the earth and rest there. (The verse describes the well-known truth in radio transmission). (5743)[4]

६. प्र रेभ धीं भरस्व गोविदं वसुविदम् । देवत्रेमां वाचं श्रीणीहीषुर्नावीरस्तारम् ॥

6. O broadcasting engineer, set up such an intelligent mechanism, which may be capable of giving shelter as well as expression to the speech-waves (i.e., in the form of transmission and receiving sets). Let you make this voice pervade through other divine forces like ether, air, light, water and the

[1]This verse is inexplicable to the western scholars because they want to read history therein, whereas it simply explains a biological truth.

[2]6090 is probably the strength of a battallion inclusive of officers and servants.

[3]'Rebha': One who makes use of 'ribhus' i.e., magnetic or electric waves.

[4]गाः speech-waves, light, rays as well as earth.

earth, just as an archer hurls off his arrow. (That is the broadcaster hurls the voice into the space like an arrow). (5744)[1]

७. राज्ञो विश्वजनीनस्य यो देवोऽमर्त्यां॑ अति । वैश्वानरस्य सुष्टुतिमा सुनोता परिक्षितः ॥

7. O persons, listen well to the thorough description of the king who is the protector and settler of all people, the chief leader of all the prominent persons, the well-wishers of all the subjects and who, being victorious and donor of gifts, excells all the persons. (5745)

८. परिच्छिन्नः क्षेममकरोत्तम आसनमाचरन् । कुलायन्कृण्वन्कौरव्यः पतिर्वदति जायया ॥

8. The same king, settling all under his protection, thoroughly dispelling darkness of ignorance and evil, establishes our well-being and prosperity. The same king, dextrous in the management of state-affairs, forming a sort of family ties with his subjects, speaks lovingly with them like a husband, speaking to his wife. (5746)

९. कतरत्त आ हराणि दधि मन्थां परि श्रुतम् ।
जायाः पतिं वि पृच्छति राष्ट्रे राज्ञः परिक्षितः ॥

9. Under the regime of the all-protecting king, the people are so well-off that the wife asks her husband, as to what she should bring for him, the yoghurt or the churned butter-milk (i.e., mathā or lassī) or barley preparation (i.e., There is no dearth of milk and its products as well foodgrains in the state). (5747)

१०. अभीवस्वः प्र जिहीते यवः पक्वः पथो बिलम् । जनः स भद्रमेधति राष्ट्रे राज्ञः परिक्षितः ॥

10. Just as the ripe barley stalk stands erect on the cleft under the sunshine, similarly the subject people enjoy all the well-being and prosperity under regime of the all-defending and the well-settling king. (5748)

११. इन्द्रः कारुमबूबुधदुत्तिष्ठ वि चरा जनम् । ममेदुग्रस्य चर्कृधि सर्व इत्ते पृणादरिः ॥

11. The powerful and wealthy king alerts the energetic man of actions, "stand to, roam about instructing all people, Go on working under me alone, who am strong and terrible. Let even the enemy, too, nourish and protect thee". (5749)

१२. इह गावः प्रजायध्वमिहाश्वा इह पूरुषाः । इहो सहस्रदक्षिणोऽपि पूषा नि षीदति ॥

12. Let the cows breed here in my regime, let the horses and the brave men also grow in plenty. Herein resides the king, the giver of thousands of gifts and the protector and nourisher of his people. (5750)

१३. नेमा इन्द्र गावो रिषन्मो आसां गोप रीरिषत् । मासाममित्रयुर्जन इन्द्र मा स्तेन ईशत ॥

13. O Mighty king, let not these cows be injured, let their master be not hurt. Let no inimical hearted person rule over them. O king of protection and defence, let no robber be their master. (5751)

१४. उप नरं नोनुमसि सूक्तेन वचसा वयं भद्रेण वचसा वयम् ।
वनादधिध्वनो गिरो न रिष्येम कदा चन ॥

[1]Shows the manner in which voice-waves are hurled into space by the transmission apparatus.

14. We bow to and worship the leader of the people with well-sung Vedic verses and praise him with good voice. He may accept our praise-songs, uttered in high pitch. Let us never be injured or hurt under him. (5752)

HYMN CXXVIII

१. यः सभेयो विदथ्युः सुत्वा यज्वाथ पूरुषः । सूर्यं चामु रिशादसंतद्देवाः प्रागकल्पयन् ॥

1. The learned persons make him their foremost leader, who is fit to carry out the affairs of the assembly, expert in war and councils, creative administrator, good organiser, brave and courageous, brilliant like the sun and destroyer of the wicked and violent enemy. (5753)

२. यो जाम्या अमेथयस्तद्यत्सखायं दुधूर्षति । ज्येष्ठो यदप्रचेतास्तदाहुरधरागिति ॥

2. The person, who defiles his sister, who intends to kill his friend and who is disrespectful towards his elder, is declared to be an outcaste (thrown down by the society). (5754)

३. यद्भद्रस्य पुरुषस्य पुत्रो भवति दाधृषिः । तद्विप्रो अब्रवीदुदग् तद् गन्धर्वः काम्यं वचः ॥

3. When the son of a good person becomes daring enough to subdue the forces of evil and ignorance, the learned person addresses sweet and pleasant words to him and thus he goes high up in the estimation of the society. (5755)

४. यश्च पणि रभुजिष्ठचो यश्च देवाँ अदाशुरिः । धीराणां शश्वतामहं तदपागिति शुश्रुम ॥

4. We hear that the successful businessman, who does not make good use of his wealth nor does he help the poor and the needy with it, and the non-donating wealthy person are certainly looked down upon amongst the wise and honourable persons. (5756)

५. ये च देवा अयजन्ताथो ये च परादविः । सूर्यो दिवमिव गत्वाय मघवानो वि रप्शते ॥

5. The persons, who honour and respect the learned persons and make right uses of the divine forces of nature and give profusely to the poor and the needly, reaching the highest state of spiritual brilliance, i.e., salvation, like the Sun reaching the heavens and becoming fortunate and glorious, shine forth with a special splendour and lustre. (5757)

६. योऽनाक्ताक्षो अनभ्यक्तो अमणिवो अहिरण्यवः । अब्रह्मा ब्रह्मणः पुत्रस्तोता कल्पेषु संमिता ॥

6. The person, who lacks vision of discrimination like the unointed eye, who is not charming and healthy, like the unointed body, who is virtueless like the unornamented who is poor and lustreless, like the goldless, who is ignorant of the Vedic lore and devotion to God in spite of his being the son or disciple of a Brahman, all these persons are regarded as of the same category in the procedures of actions. (5758)[1]

७. य आक्ताक्षः सुभ्यक्तः सुमणिः सुहिरण्यवः । सुब्रह्मा ब्रह्मणः पुत्रस्तोता कल्पेषु संमिता ॥

[1]Here in this sukta the use of various directions is made to show the level of a person with certain qualities or drawbacks, in the society. Griffith's translation of "तोता कल्पेषु संमिता" by "these things are ordered in the rules" has no relevancy here.

7. All the following persons are considered equal in the capacity of their work and actions. The son or disciple of a Brahman, becoming well-versed in Vedic lore and devotion to God, the person, equipped with the vision of discrimination, like the ointed eye, the person looking beautiful and healthy like the ointed body, the person, full of virtue and piety, like the one ornamented with precious stones, the person, lustrous with fine qualities, like the one, rich with gold and other precious metals. (5759)[1]

८. अप्रपाणा च वेशन्ता रेवाँ अप्रतिदिश्ययः । अयभ्या कन्याऽ कल्याणी तोता कल्पेषु संमिता ॥

8. All the following are considered of the same category in their capacities or qualities. The artisan wells or pools, whose water is unfit for drinking or have no ghats to enable persons to drink the water thereof, the wealthy person, who is not a donor; the girl, who is graceful, yet difficult to approach, or who is both unpleasant to look at as well as hard to be won over. (5760)

९. सुप्रपाणा च वेशन्ता रेवान्त्सुप्रतिदिश्ययः । सुयभ्या कन्याऽ कल्याणी तोता कल्पेषु संमिता ॥

9. The water tanks or pools, whose water is fit for drinking and have good ghats; the rich person, who gives profusely; the pretty girl, who is easy of approach. All of these are considered equal in their use. (5761)

१०. परिवृक्ता च महिषी स्वस्त्याऽ च युधिंगमः । अनाशुरश्चायामी तोता कल्पेषु संमिता ॥

10. The deserted wife or queen, the person, who safely avoids going to war, the horse that is not fleet, the man, who obeys no rules and regulations; all of these are regarded equal in their uselessness. (5762)

११. वावाता च महिषी स्वस्त्याऽ च युधिंगमः । श्वाशुरश्चायामी तोता कल्पेषु संमिता ॥

11. The following are all considered equally useful. The wife or the queen, beloved and obedient; the soldier who readily goes to the war, the horse that is fleet-footed and the person, strictly observing all rules and regulations. (5763)

१२. यदिन्द्रादो दाशराज्ञे मानुषं वि गाहथाः । विरूपः सर्वस्मा आसीत्सह यक्षाय कल्पते ॥

12. When the Mighty king fearlessly treads through the kingdoms of all the ten directions, like a super human being, and becomes the refuge of all people against all miseries and trouble and against the incursions of the enemies, certainly he alone becomes fit for the great sacrifice, in the form of the organisation of the state-affairs. (5764)

१३. त्वं वृषाक्षुं मघवन्नम्रं मर्याकरो रविजम् । त्वं रौहिणं व्याऽस्यो वि वृत्रस्याभिनच्छिरः ॥

13. O fortunate, powerful and chief leader, thou bendest low the jealous enemy, who has spread his tantacles far and wide like a tree. Thou completely rootest out the deep-root foe and thoroughly shatterest the head of thy adversary who tries to overwhelm thee like a cloud. (5765)

१४. यः पर्वतान्व्यदधाद्यो अपो व्यगाहथाः । इन्द्रो यो वृत्रहा महान्तस्मादिन्द्र नमोऽस्तु ते ॥

14. O powerful king, thou, who fully smashes the foes, firm and strong like the mountains, and who penetrates the enemy's forces streaming like

[1]Griffith and other western scholars' reading of history in these verses is merely conjectural and inappropriate.

currents of water, the mighty lord, who is a great destroyer of the foes, let our respectful obeisance be to thee. (5766)

१५. प्रष्टिं धावन्तं हर्योरौच्चैः श्रवसमब्रुवन् । स्वस्त्यश्व जैत्रायेन्द्रमा वह सुस्रजम् ॥

15. The radio-operators direct the swiftly running vehicle, tank or aeroplane, equipped with the loud-speaking mechanism of both the positive and negative electricity to carry the great commander in a good formation of the vehicles like a wrath for victory and success. (5767)

१६. युक्त्वा श्वेता श्रोच्चैः श्रवसं हर्यो र्युञ्जन्ति दक्षिणम् ।
पूर्वतमं स देवानां बिभ्रदिन्द्रं महीयते ॥

16. After applying white-coloured rays of electric power, they fix the loud-speaking or transmitter on the right side. Conveying the foremost mighty commander amongst the learned persons, it glorifies and adds to the glorification of the commander. (5768)[1]

HYMN CXXIX*

(Aiṭash Suktas)

१. एता अश्वा आ प्लवन्ते ॥

1. These passions of the senses are running on all sides. (5769)

२. प्रतीपं प्रातिसुत्वनम् ॥

2. They are going contrary to their instigator i.e., soul. (5770)

३. तासामेका हरिक्निका ॥

3. One of them is the volition, that carries everything with it. (5771)

४. हरिक्निके किमिच्छसि ॥

4. O Volition, what dost thou desire? (5772)

५. साधुं पुत्रं हिरण्ययम् ॥

5. I want the soul, the subduer of all passions, the protector against evil and misery, and lustrous with spiritual splendour and glory. (5773)

६. क्वाह तं परास्यः ॥

6. Who would speak of it to thee? He is far distant, inexplicable and imperceptible by the senses. (5774)

७. यत्रामूस्तिस्रः शिंशपाः ॥

7. He is there, where three external entities (i.e., Brahm, Jiva and Prakriti) stand guard over the latent identity. (5775)

८. परित्रयः ॥

8. Those three are also very far (i.e., two difficult to realise). (5776)

९. पृदाकवः ॥

[1](15-16) I have not translated 'Uchchaishrava' as an ordinary or special horse of that name. I have sensed higher knowledge of science to be conveyed by these verses.

*Pt. Jaidev has applied these suktas to the army and the female also. But I think their application to spirituality would give better sense.

9. All the three are full powerful. (5777)

१०. शृङ्गं धमन्त आसते ॥

10. All the three sit, lighting up the root cause (i.e., the creation of the universe or birth of a newly born). (5778)

११. अयमिहागतो अर्वा ॥

11. Here is this soul united with the body, like a horse yolked to a chariot. (5779)

१२. स इच्छकना संज्ञायते ॥

12. He can well be known here in the body, by his powers of seeing, hearing and talking etc. (5780)

१३. गोमयाद् गोगतिरिव ॥

13. Just as the direction of the movement of the cows is traced from the cow-dung littered on the path, similarly the existence of the master of the sense-organs can be established from the working of the sense-organs. (5781)

१४. पुसां कुले किमिच्छसि ॥

14. O soul, what do you want amongst the groups of vital breaths? (5782)

१५. पक्वौ व्रीहियवा इति ॥

15. I want means of progress and prosperity and capacity to put an end to misery and trouble as the ripe fruit of my actions, just as a farmer desires paddy and barley, as ripe harvest of his labours. (5783)

१६. व्रीहियवा अद्या इति ॥

16. O soul, thou enjoyest 'paddy' or prosperity and well-being as well as barley, i.e., uniting with and separation from thy body (at the time of births and deaths, (as the fruit of thy actions). (5784)

१७. अजगर इवाविका: ॥

17. I like that I should be able to move freely from one body to another without reaping the fruit of actions, just as a snail gets sleep etc., without any effort on its part. (5785)

१८. अश्वस्य वारो गोशफश्च ते ॥

18. O soul, the good and desirable things, achieved by the help of organs of actions, and the knowledge, secured through the organs of speech or other senses are all for thee. (5786)

१९. श्येनपर्णी सा ॥

19. Thou requirest that state of spirituality which protects the learned persons. (5787)

२०. अनामयोपजिह्विका ॥

20. That state, which is free from all disease, sorrow, fear, pain or trouble and which is sweet and pleasant like the sweet things tasted by the tongue. (5788)

HYMN CXXX

१. को अर्यं बहुलिमा इषूनि ॥

1. Who enjoys these juices? (5789)[1]

२. को असिद्याः पयः ॥

३. को अर्जुन्याः पयः ॥

४. कः कार्ष्ण्याः पयः ॥

2-4. Who enjoys the juices of the Prakriti, deep-red, white and black? (i.e., rajas, satva, and tama Gunas). (5790-92)

५ एतं पृच्छ कुहं पृच्छ ॥

5. Ask this learned person? Where should I ask? (5793)

६. कुहाकं पक्वकं पृच्छ ॥

6. Where? Which learned person of ripe and mature knowledge should I ask this question? (i.e., it is not an easy thing to find out such a person, hence the repetition of the question). (5794)

७. यवानो यतिस्वभिः कुभिः ॥

7. The means of ending the cycle of births and deaths cannot be attained by a man of evil nature. (5795)

८. अकुप्यन्तः कुपायकुः ॥

8. Even those who are not amenable to anger, become angry. (i.e., lose control over themselves). (5796)

९. आमणको मणत्सकः ॥

9. Even those, with wealth of precious stones, get bereft of these, (and thus become penniless). (5797)

१०. देव त्वप्रतिसूर्य ॥

10. O God, may I attain Thee, the Resplendent One. (5798)

११. एनश्चिपङ्क्तिका हविः ॥

11. O Lord, that White Lustre, effacer of all troubles and miseries is Thine. Thou art the Destroyer of all unhappiness and pain. (5799)

१२. प्रदुद्रुदो मघाप्रति ॥

12. All people of the world run after fortunes. (5800)

१३. शृङ्ग उत्पन्न ॥

१४. मा त्वाभि सखा नो विदन् ॥

13-14. On attaining topmost spiritual light, our friend may know me and Thee, too. (i.e., Realisation of the soul and God is achieved only at the highest stage of spiritual attainment). (5801-2)

१५. वशायाः पुत्रमा यन्ति ॥

[1]This sukta explains that the souls enjoy the benefits of Prakriti under the guidance of God, the Lord of all.

15. All persons seek refuge under the devotee, the off-spring of the controlling Power of God. He is then capable of leading others across all miseries and troubles. (5803)

१६. इरावेदुमयं दत्त ॥

16. Just as the earth is a source of joy and satisfaction to the king or water to the thirsty, so does God, the fountain-head of knowledge and light exhilarate the learned person. (5804)

१७. अथो इयन्नियन्निति ॥

17. Then he realises, "It is He, It is He" Truly does he come face to face with Him. (5805)

१८. अथो इयन्निति ॥

18. Then again it is He. Certainly it is He. (i.e., At the full realisation, God, the devotee's ecstasy knows no bounds. He goes on exclaiming. (5806)

१९. अथो श्वा अस्थिरो भवन् ॥

19. Let not the souls, the active enjoyers of this all, be destroyed. (5807)

२०. उयं यकांशलोकका ॥

20. Of this great measure is the Prakriti. (5808)

HYMN CXXXI

१. आमिनोनिति भद्यते ॥

1. The evil that pains the soul is destroyed. (5809)

२. तस्य अनु निभञ्जनम् ॥

2. Shear it off. Completely shatter it (i.e., the evil). (5810)

३. वरुणो याति वस्वभिः ॥

3. The soul, warding off evil or inimical forces, goes along with the vital breaths, the mainstay of life. (5811)

४. शतं वा भारती शवः ॥

4. There are hundreds of controlling means with the chief soul. (5812)

५. शतमाश्वा हिरण्ययाः । शतं रथ्या हिरण्ययाः ।
शतं कुथा हिरण्ययाः । शतं निष्का हिरण्ययाः ॥

5. There are hundreds of splendorous powers, like the horses. (5813)

६. अहल कुश वर्त्तक ॥

6. There are hundreds of means of enjoyment and revelling like the chariots or ships. (5814)

७. शफेनइव ओहते ॥

7. There are hundreds of treasures of glorious virtues like those of gold. (5815)

८. आय वनेनती जनी ॥

8. There are hundreds of decorative qualities like the ornaments. (5816)

९. वनिष्ठा नाव गृह्यन्ति ।।

9. Thou art everlasting, like the kusha-grass, difficult to be uprooted. (5817)

१०. इदं मह्यं मदूरिति ।।

10. Just as the whole body is borne on the hoof, similarly is borne the whole of the universe on a single part of the Almighty. (5818)

११. ते वृक्षाः सह तिष्ठति ।।

11. Thou (God) actest like an igniting force in setting the universe into motion. (5819)

१२. पाक बलिः ।।

12. Nothing lies hidden even in the innermost recesses of the universe. (5820)

१३. शक बलिः ।।

13. O happiness-generating force, let this clear-cut knowledge be mine. (5821)

१४. अश्वत्थ खदिरो धवः ।।

14. Those yogis, who are deeply immersed in meditation, sit firm like the trees. (5822)

१५. अरदुपरम ।।

15. The soul becomes powerful and strong with the ripening of knowledge and experience of the world. (5823)

१६. शयो हतइव ।।

16. The soul gets energised by his union with the Almighty. (5824)

१७. व्याप पूरुषः ।।

17. He (i.e., God), is *everlasting* and *all-pervading*, like 'Ashvatha tree, *firm* and *steady* like 'Khadira' tree, *pure* and *spotless* like a 'Dhava' tree. (5825)

१८. अदूहमित्यां पूषकम् ।।

18. He (God) is Free from attachment of all sorts, like the leaves of an Artoo tree. (5826)

१९. अत्यर्धर्चं परस्वतः ।।

19. He (the soul or God) lies (latent) unknown, like a dead person. (5827)

२०. दौव हस्तिनो दृती ।।

20. The Almighty God is omnipresent. (5828)

२१. अदुहन्नित् पीयूषम् ।।

21. Just as the milk is milked, from the cow similarly is the nectar is got from Him. (5829)

२२. अध्यर्धश्च परस्वतः ।।

22. He (God) is far more powerful than the other strong soul or Prakṛti. (5830)

२३. द्वौ च हस्तिनो दृती ॥

23. Both the knowledge and action of the soul are the means of cutting off the knot of bondage of births and deaths for him. (5831)

HYMN CXXXII

१. आदलाबुकमेककम् ॥

1. Then the soul alone crosses the sea of life like the gourd and does not sink in it. (5832)[1]

२. अलाबुकं निखातकम् ॥

2. Just as the gourd is made hollow and lighter by taking out inner matter from it, so is the soul made pure and lighter by driving out the inner impurities of its nature, which make it heavy and burdensome. (5833)

३. कर्करिको निखातकः ॥

3. The soul is freed of inner impurities, like the karkari fruit, freed of its inner material. (5834)

४. तद् वातः उन्मथायति ॥

4. He is propelled by the vital breaths. (5835)

५. कुलायं कृणवादिति ॥

5. He (soul) creates a place of refuge for himself under Him (God). (5836)

६. उग्रं वनिषदाततम् ॥

6. He then enjoys a vast and huge fortune. (5837)

७. न वनिषदनाततम् ॥

7. He is not content with limited fortune. (5838)

८. क एषां कर्करी लिखत् ॥

8. Which amongst the vital breaths, creates a (Karkari) vacuum for him to rise higher up in spiritual elevation. (5839)

९. क एषां दुन्दुभिं हनत् ॥

9. Which of these vital breath strikes internal chord? (5840)

१०. यदीयं हनत् कथं हनत् ॥

10. Whichever strikes it, how does it do so? (5841)

११. देवी हनत् कुहनत् ॥

11. The inner voice of the soul strikes it. Where does it do so? (5842)

१२. पर्यागारं पुनःपुनः ॥

12. The self-same soul comes back again and again to his place of shelter, the body. (i.e., the cycle of births, deaths and rebirths of the soul goes on uninterrupted). (5843)

१३. त्रीण्युष्ट्रस्य नामानि ॥

[1]The pithy verses of suktas 129 to 132 can be variously interpreted as they are full of mysterious import. I have simply given their Adhyatmik version only.

13. There are three names given to the destroyer of the forces of oppression and aggression. (5844)

१४. हिरण्य इत्येके अब्रवीत् ।।

14. "One is the splendorous soul", so says the learned person. (5845)

१५. द्वौ वा ये शिशवः ।।

15. Two are glory and energy (i.e., men of glory and energy). (5846)

१६. नीलशिखण्डवाहनः ।।

16. The vital breath in the Brahmrandhra strikes the inner chord of the soul. (5847)

HYMN CXXXIII

१. विततौ किरणौ द्वौ तावा पिनष्टि पूरुषः । न वै कुमारि तत् तथा यथा कुमारि मन्यसे ।।

1. The heavens and the earth or man and woman or Prakriti and Jivatma are like two stones of the grinding mill and the All-Pervading God alone grinds them both. O virgin, (female, earth or Prakṛti) that secret of the Godhead is not so simple, as the short-sighted virgin like thee understands it. (5848)[1]

२. मातुष्टे किरणौ द्वौ निवृत्तः पुरुषानृते । न वै कुमारि तत् तथा यथा कुमारि मन्यसे ।।

2. All the above pairs;—the heaven and the earth, husband and wife, the matter and the soul, are moved into action by the ordaining and All-powerful God, but they are quite different from Him. O virgin, ... it." (as above). (5849)

३. निगृह्य कर्णकौ द्वौ निरायच्छसि मध्यमे । न वै कुमारि तत् तथा यथा कुमारि मन्यसे ।।

3. O Intervening Power of God, All-pervading, controlling both the creative parts of the above-mentioned pairs, Thou completely binds them together by forces of attraction and affection. O virgin,. . . . . it. (as above). (5850)

४. उत्तानायै शयानायै तिष्ठन्ती वाव गूहसि । न वै कुमारि तत् तथा यथा कुमारि मन्यसे ।।

4. O Almighty God, Thou embraces (i.e., pervades) the Prakriti lying flat, upward, while standing erect Thyself (i.e., God even in His stationary (unmoved) state is the pervader of the matter lying low at His feet. O virgin, . . . it. (as above). (5851)

५. श्लक्ष्णायां श्लक्ष्णिकायां श्लक्ष्णमेवाव गूहसि । न वै कुमारि तत् तथा यथा कुमारि मन्यसे ।।

5. Just as a loving husband embraces his charming and beloved wife, similarly does the almighty God, desirous of creation of the universe, embraces the Prakriti, which is also impelled by forces of cohesion and attraction, inherent in it. O virgin, ... it. (as above). (5852)

६. अवश्लक्ष्णमिव भ्रंशदन्तर्लोममति ह्रदे । न वै कुमारि तत् तथा यथा कुमारि मन्यसे ।।

6. Just as a greasy article easily slips into the tank, covered with moss,

[1]Although Griffith has left this sukta as indecent yet, it conveys the scientific knowledge of the process of the procreation of humanity, which is very essential for its good.

similarly does the synthesising force of the creator works through the whole moss of the matter. O virgin, ... it. (as above). (5853)

HYMN CXXXIV

१. इहेत्थ प्रागपागुदगधराग्—अरालागुदभर्त्सथ ॥

1. In this world, all the four quarters, the front, the hind one, the above and the below, are full of waters as well souls, just as pots are filled with waters. (5854)

२. इहेत्थ प्रागपागुदगधराग्—वत्साः पुरुषन्त आसते ॥

2. In this world, ... below the worlds, serving as abode for the souls, stay in the Omnipresent God, like drops of clarified butter in water. (5855)

३. इहेत्थ प्रागपागुदगधराग्—स्थालीपाको वि लीयते ॥

3. In this world, ... below, and material objects get ripened and thereafter annihilated or disintegrated, like the leaves of the pipal tree, falling off, when dry. (5856)

४. इहेत्थ प्रागपागुदगधराग्—स वै पृथु लीयते ॥

4. I this world, ... below, ignorance gets dispelled at the very touch of the Omniscient God, like a drop of water, touched by hand losing its identity. (5857)

५. इहेत्थ प्रागपागुदगधराग्—आष्टे लाहणि लीशाथी ॥

5. In this world, ...below, don't be greedy of having birth in this world, which is a source of pain and trouble like the hot iron (i.e., any thing placed on a hot spoon and put into mouth cannot but burn the mouth). (5858)

६. इहेत्थ प्रागपागुदगधराग्—अक्ष्लिली पुच्छिलीयते ॥

6. In this world, . . . below, this Prakriti full of attachment embroils the Almighty Who is free from attachment of any sort and succeeds in getting the universe created by Him, like an ant carrying the seed of the banyan tree and having it grown. (5859)

HYMN CXXXV

१. भुगित्यभिगतः शलित्यपक्रान्तः फलित्यभिष्ठितः । दुन्दुभिमाहननाभ्यां जरितरोऽथामो दैव ॥ (5860)

२. कोशबिले रजनि ग्रन्थेर्धानमुपानहि पादम् । उत्तमां जनिमां जन्यानुत्तमां जनीन् वर्त्मन्यात् ॥ (5861)

३. अलाबूनि पृषातकान्यश्वत्थपलाशम् ।
पिपीलिकावटश्वसो विद्युत्स्वापर्णशफो गोशफो जरितरोऽथामो दैव ॥ (5862)

४. वीमे देवा अक्रंसताध्वर्यो क्षिप्रं प्रचर । सुसत्यमिद् गवामस्यसि प्रखुदसि ॥ (5863)

५. पत्नी यदृश्यते पत्नी यक्ष्यमाणा जरितरोऽथामो दैव । होता विष्टीमेन जरितरोऽथामो दैव ॥ (5864)

६. आदित्या ह जरितरङ्गिरोभ्यो दक्षिणामनयन् ।
तां ह जरितः प्रत्यायंस्तामु ह जरितः प्रत्यायन् ॥ (5865)

७. तां ह जरितर्नः प्रत्यगृभ्णांस्तामु ह जरितर्नः प्रत्यगृभ्णः ।
अहानेतरसं न वि चेतनानि यज्ञानेतरसं न पुरोगवामः ।। (5866)

८. उत श्वेत आशुपत्वा उतो पद्याभिर्यविष्ठः । उतेमाशु मानं पिपर्ति ।। (5867)

९. आदित्या रुद्रा वसवस्त्वेनु त इदं राधः प्रति गृभ्णीह्यङ्गिरः ।
इदं राधो विभु प्रभु इदं राधो बृहत् पृथु ।। (5868)

१०. देवा ददत्वासुरं तद् वो अस्तु सुचेतनम् । युष्माँ अस्तु दिवेदिवे प्रत्येव गृभायत ।।
(5869)

११. त्वमिन्द्र शर्मरिणा हव्यं पारावतेभ्यः । विप्राय स्तुवते वसुवनि दुरश्रवसे वह ।। (5870)

१२. त्वमिन्द्र कपोताय च्छिन्नपक्षाय वञ्चते । श्यामाकं पक्वं पीलु च वारस्मा अकृणोर्बहुः ।।
(5871)

१३. अरंगरो वावदीति त्रेधा बद्धो वरत्रया । इरामह प्रशंसत्यनिरामप सेधति ।। (5872)

(3 Pratirādha)

1. The soul is the enjoyer of things. That is why he has come into the body, (just a dog comes near at the sight of a piece of bread).[1]

2. When the body gets worn out, he goes out of it, like a bird flying out of its nest.

3. It (the creation) breaks into two i.e., males and females, like a cow's hoof breaking into two.

(6 Pravadas)

1. O learned person, devoted to praise-singing of God, we explain the secret of the saying that the same person grinds the two means of grinding: Just as the same person beats the drum with two striking rods at one and the same time, similarly the soul moves the body by Prāna and Apāna and God regulates the heavens and the earth at one and the same time.

2. Just as there may be two holes or hollow-spaces in the same treasure-box or scabbard, similarly the pairs mentioned before stay in the All-pervading God.

3. Just as knot is secured in a rope, similarly the above pairs are held secure by the Almighty.

4. Just as the foot is enveloped in the shoes, similarly does the Almighty Father stands engulfed by the lowlying matter although partially.

5. Just as the antimony-ointmenting rod is kept into the bottle thereof, so does He penetrate the matter, full of attachment and cohesion.[2]

6. The greasy article slips into the pool, covered with moss or algae, like the antimony rod, slipping under the hairy eye-lid.

6 (Ajiñāsenya)

1. How should the learned remain unattached, although surrounded by all odds and ends? Ans. Like gourd in waters.

[1]The verses in this sukta are a sort of answer to the riddles mentioned in Sukta 133.
[2](5) The text of this verse is not clear. It is missing in some compilations.

2. How do all the worlds in the universe resemble drops? Ans: Like drops of clarified butter in water.

3. How do the souls, attaining maturity of knowledge and spiritual grandeur, submerge their identity in the Blissful God? Ans: Like the leaves of the pipal tree falling off, when dry and withered.

4. How does ignorance disappear at the very touch of divine knowledge and light? Ans: Like a drop of water touching the hand.

5. How does the matter involve the unattached God into the very act of generating the universe? Ans: Like the ant carrying the seed of the banyan tree.

6. Why should not one covet births and rebirths? Ans: Because this cycle of birth and deaths is like the hot spoon burning the mouth of the user thereof.

(Three Pratiradhas)

1. How does the soul, desirous of enjoyment of the world enter it? Ans: Like a dog, seeing a piece of bread.

2. How does the soul go out of the body? Ans: Like a bird fiying out of its nests.

3. How does the creation stand after breaking into two i.e., male and female? Ans: Like the cow's hoof split into two. Thus do we explain thy sayings, O praise-singer.

(Atívada)

4. These sense-organs run after various objects of their own liking. O imperishable soul, thou thyself shouldst move quickly as their leader. Thou art an easy shelter for all the sense-organs. Thou art an enjoyer of peace and bliss thyself.

5. O praise-singing learned persons, the Prakriti, the nourisher of the world, being attached to the Almighty appears as it were the supporting wife of Him i.e., protecting and feeding His creatures. He Himself, pervading in it, is the Great Giver and Upholder. Thus we know and proclaim it to all.

(17 Devmithakhya)

6. O Preacher of Vedic lore, the persons-in-charge of collection of the revenue under a king bring gifts to the learned persons. They may not accept them or they may accept them, as they like.

7. O learned preacher of Vedic lore, if they don't accept it, you should also not accept it. O persons, when this learned person is there, don't lead a life of ignorance and illiteracy. O learned persons, when this highly learned person is there, don't move about as a leaderless group (i.e., choose him your leader and then proceed).

8. And this upright, brilliant learned person is expert in going about his business quickly, speedy in his movements, and is readily satisfied by honour and respect, shown to him.

9. O learned person, the highly learned persons, the brave and the common people all praise thee. Kindly accept this bounty of theirs. This wealth is excellent and supreme. It is great and vast.

10. Let the generous-minded persons give away gifts, worthy of acceptance by the learned people. That wealth may enhance your learning and knowledge. Let it be so daily. Let you accept it, O learned persons.

(Three Bhūtechhed)

11. O fortunate man of wealth and riches, thou shouldst afford shelter, food and money to the persons, who are given to deep meditation of and devotion to God in an advanced stage. Thou shouldst also give shelter and wealth to the praise-singing, wise and learned person who is well-known far and wide and recites the Vedic verses in high tones.

12. O man of fortune and wealth, thou shouldst provide the cooked food like black rice and fruit, shelter and plenty of water to the shelterless person, well-versed in various sciences and roaming about like a featherless pigeon.

13. Even the best preacher, when obliged by gifts worthy of acceptance as if tied down with a rope, goes on preaching and sings the praises of the donor of food etc., and leaves alone the non-giver.

HYMN CXXXVI*

16 (Ahansya)

१. यदस्या अंहुभेद्याः कृधु स्थूलमुपातसत् । मुष्काविदस्या एजतो गोशफे शकुलाविव ॥

1. When the small or great portion of the land or the subjects, worth freeing from evil or sin, is destroyed, then the thief-like sinful men and women tremble like fish, entangled in the hoof of an animal. (5873)

२. यदा स्थूलेन पससाणौ मुष्का उपावधीत् । विष्वञ्चा वस्या वर्धतः सिकतास्वेव गर्दभौ ॥

2. When the king punishes the thief-like guilty men and women for a small crime even, by his highly efficient administration, the people with high aspirations, spread far and wide in every nook and corner of the land, feel highly elated like the donkeys revelling in the sandy places, where they lie flat quite gleefully. (5874)

३. यदल्पिकास्वऽल्पिका कर्कन्धूकेव पद्यते । वासन्तिकमिव तेजनं यन्त्यवाताय वित्पति ॥

3. When the populace is small, or rather very small in number it is considered like the fruit of tiny shrub. But it gradually spreads its lustre far and wide, like the reed of the sun of the spring season. (5875)

*This sukta describes the intercourse of the husband and wife according to Sayāna. Griffith has left it untranslated as indecent. Pt. Khemkaran Dass Trivedi and Pt. Jaidev have interpreted it as relating to a king and his subjects and king and his assembly respectively. I think there is no point in considering it indecent and thus shunning it altogether or giving it other interpretation. After all the intercourse between the husband and the wife is such an important event in their lives as it deserves to be given a place of sanctity as in Gurbhadhān Sanskar of the Vedic Shastras. It is not the intercourse between the husband and wife that is indecent, rather it is the immoral meeting of a person with another's wife that is so. Although I have given the interpretation of these verses like Pt. Jaidev and Pt. Khemkaran Dass Trivedi yet I do believe that this sukta gives the right type of knowledge of science of procreation.

४. यद् देवासो ललामगुं प्रविष्टीमिनमाविषुः । सकुला देदिश्यते नारी सत्यस्याक्षिभुवो यथा ॥

4. When the victory-seeking people secure as head of the nation, the services of a person who is learned and sweet-tongued, the leading assembly under him unanimously directs the affairs of the state and its directions are as authentic as the true facts, seen by the eye. (5876)

५. महानग्न्यृतृप्नद्वि मोक्रददस्थानासरन् । शक्तिकानना स्वचमशकं सक्तु पद्यम ॥

5. The assembly, like a beautiful lady, takes pride in its achievement. The learned head goes about addressing the general public loudly like the free horse moving about neighing loudly. The lustrous assembly gets its authority enhanced by the ready consensus amongst its members. (5877)

६. महानग्न्युलूखलमतिक्रामन्त्यब्रवीत् । यथा तव वनस्पते निरघ्नन्ति तथैवेति ॥

6. The assembly, like a beautiful lady, presenting the precedent of pestle and mortar says, "O king, the master of great actions, we, the members of the assembly thoroughly discuss the matt ers and arrive at certain decisions and then act accordingly, just as paddy is completely thrashed before the rice is separated from the chaff and then made use of." (5878)

७. महानग्न्युप ब्रूते भ्रष्टोऽथाप्यभूभुवः । यथैव ते वनस्पते पिप्पति तथैवेति ॥

7. The great assembly says, "O king, the protector of the subjects, even if you get astray from your right path, we, the members of the assembly completely thrash out and ponder over your doings and chalk out the right course, like the paddy being thrashed and the chaff removed from rice." (5879)

८. महानग्न्युप ब्रूते भ्रष्टोऽथाप्यभूभुवः । यथा वयो विदाह्य स्वर्गे नमवदह्यते ॥

8. The great assembly says, "O king, when you fall down from the right course of action, all my organs ache and burn with wrath, just the fire burns and damages the jungle." (5880)

९. महानग्न्युप ब्रूते स्वसावेशितं पसः । इत्थं फलस्य वृक्षस्य शूर्पे शूर्पं भजेमहि ॥

9. The great council of state says, "Let all the people, coming together, live in peace and prosperity. Let us thus enjoy the shelter of the discriminating king, who should be able to efface the enemy, worthy of being cut asunder like a tree just as a sieve is used to remove the chaff from the husked, ripe paddy." (5881)

१०. महानग्नी कृकवाकं शम्यया परि धावति ।
अयं न विद्म यो मृगः शीर्ष्णा हरति धाणिकाम् ॥

10. The great council of state peacefully follows the sweet-tongued head of the state. They say, "We know not as to which lion-hearted person bears on his head all the burden of nourishing and feeding the populace (i.e., every thing goes on smoothly and imperceptibly). (5882)

११. महानग्नी महानग्नं धावन्तमनु धावति । इमास्तदस्य गा रक्ष यभ मामद्ध्यौदनम् ॥

11. The great parliament moves quickly after the swift-moving, charming and learned leader. O self-same leader thou shouldst protect these lands and

languages of this state. Let thee enjoy the power, wealth and fortune thereof along with me (i.e., the assembly), just as a husband enjoys his wife. (5883)

१२. सुदेवस्त्वा महानग्नीर्बबाधते महतः साधु खोदनम् । कुसं पीबरो नवत् ॥

12. O great parliament, the brilliant king of good qualities, churns thee thoroughly and gets ample fortune and happiness from the big state under him. The strong destroy the weak. The strong parliament removes the weak king. So thou should enjoy all the fortunes of the state in unison with me (i.e., parliament) like the husband, enjoying his wife. (5884)

१३. वशा दग्धामिमाङ्गुरि प्रसृजतोऽग्रतं परे । महान् वै भद्रो यभ मामद्धचोदनम् ॥

13. Just as the well-controlled earth or the subjects, like a milched cow, yields the revenue worth acquiring, without raising a finger even, (i.e., spontaneously). Mighty is the king, who is strong and thorny like the Bilva tree and peace-showering, at the same time. O king, enjoy the authority and fortunes of the state along with me, (the parliament) like a husband, enjoying his wife. (5885)

१४. विदेवस्त्वा महानग्नीर्विबाधते महतः साधु खोदनम् ।
कुमारिका पिङ्गलिका कार्द भस्मा कु धावति ॥

14. O great parliament, the victorious king of manifold fine qualities, exploits thee in various ways and extracts the best fortunes from the vast state under him. The glorious army, like a charming young girl, finishing its job, goes running forward to the higher ranks. (5886)

१५. महान् वै भद्रो बिल्वो महान् भद्र उदुम्बरः । महाँ अभिक्त बाधते महतः साधु खोदनम् ॥

15. The mighty king, capable of smashing the enemy, can bring peace and prosperity to the people. Only the highly powerful king is a surity for peace and happiness of the state. The great king alone is capable of securing the good persperity and well-being of the big state on all sides. (5887)

१६. यः कुमारी पिङ्गलिका वसन्तं पीबरी लभेत् । तैलकुण्डमिमाङ्गुष्ठं रोदन्तं शुदमुद्धरेत् ॥

16. Just as fat, young girl, getting a thin and lean person for her husband is not satisfied with him, similarly a strong parliament, finding a weakling as king, roots him out like the finger out of the hot oil in cauldron. (5888)

HYMN CXXXVII*

१. यद्ध प्राचीरजगन्तोरो मण्डूरधाणिकीः । हता इन्द्रस्य शत्रवः सर्वे बुद्बुदयाशवः ॥

1. When the big guns of steel, hurling big shots of steel, move forward as the vanguard, all the foes of the mighty king are shattered like bubbles of water. (5889)

२. कपृन्नरः कपृथमुद् दधातन चोदयत खुदत वाजसातये ।
निष्टिग्र्यः पुत्रमा च्यावयोतय इन्द्रं सबाध इह सोमपीतये ॥

2. O leaders of the people, the mighty king is quite capable of running the administration and looking after the welfare of the people. Enthral him

*cf. *Rig*, 10. 155.4; 101, 12; 4.39. 6; 9.101. 4-6; 8.85. 13-17; 82, 7-9.

on the high position of a protector and defender of the people's welfare and prosperity. Stimulate him to win war and attain fortunes and make him happy and well-pleased. O people, working all together in this state, assist the powerful king for the defence and attainment of national well-being and fortune, acting as a protector of the council secretly controlling all the affairs of the state. (5890)

३. दधिक्राव्णो अकारिषं जिष्णोरश्वस्य वाजिनः ।
सुरभि नो मुखा करत् प्र ण आयूंषि तारिषत् ॥

3. I (the priest) enthrone as the head of the state, the smart, learned person, powerful and swift like a horse, victorious and capable of nourishing and sustaining others, so that he may replenish the chief persons amongst us with grace and glory and enhance and prolong our lives by his good administration. (5891)

४. सुतासो मधुमत्तमाः सोमा इन्द्राय मन्दिनः । पवित्रवन्तो अक्षरन् देवान् गच्छन्तु वो मदाः ॥

4. The sweetest essences of herbs and other means of joys and happiness may exhilarate the king, the destroyer of the enemy. O people, let all your means of pleasures and rejoicing flow to the learned persons, acting as the purifying force. (5892)

५. इन्दुरिन्द्राय पवत इति देवासो अब्रुवन् । वाचस्पतिर्मखस्यते विश्वस्येशान ओजसा ॥

5. 'The learned and devoted person, moved by pity towards the poor and the needy, works for the mighty God', so say the learned persons. The master of the Vedic lore is honoured and respected. He is the Ruler of the universe by His glorious energy. (5893)

६. सहस्रधारः पवते समुद्रो वाचमीङ्खयः । सोमः पती रयीणां सखेन्द्रस्य दिवेदिवे ॥

6. The friend of the Powerful God or king, the master of riches the energiser of all, well-versed in speech and knowledge, the bearer of manifold branches of science, deep and solemn like the sea, full of all good qualities, stands as a great force by himself. (5894)

७. अव द्रप्सो अंशुमतीमतिष्ठदियानः कृष्णो दशभिः सहस्रैः ।
आवत् तमिन्द्रः शच्या धमन्तमपस्नेहितीर्नृमणा अधत्त ॥

7. The proud and crafty enemy, oppressing the people, invading the land with thousands of forces, occupies the partitioning boundary line or the river. Let the mighty king, winning the hearts of the people check the haughty foe with his full force and root out the violent army of the adversary. (5895)

८. द्रप्समपश्यं विषुणे चरन्तमुपह्वरे नद्यो अंशुमत्याः ।
नभो न कृष्णमवतस्थिवांसमिष्यामि वो वृषणो युध्यताजौ ॥

8. O brave warriors, capable of raining death into the lines of the enemy, I see the haughty foe, moving about stealthily and busy in inimical action, all along the bank of the partitioning river, coming down like a crow from the sky, I wish that you should give battle to him and crush him. (5896)

९. अध द्रप्सो अंशुमत्या उपस्थेऽधारयत् तन्वं᳡ तित्विषाणः ।
विशो अदेवीरभ्याऽचरन्तीर्बृहस्पतिना युजेन्द्रः ससाहे ॥

9. And the proud enemy, getting glorious and majestic expands his kingdom and holds it near the partitioning river or boundary line. The mighty and powerful king is able to subdue the subjects, acting like the revolting and non-paying persons, along with the help of the great commander of the armieș. (5897)[1]

१०. त्वं ह त्यत् सप्तभ्यो जायमानोऽशत्रुभ्यो अभवः शत्रुरिन्द्र ।
गूढे द्यावापृथिवी अन्वविन्दो विभुमद्भ्यो भुवनेभ्यो रणं धाः ॥

10. O mighty king or soul, letst thee, becoming well-known, be surely the destroyer of inimical forces of the enemy or evil, for seven kinds of friendly subjects or seven sense-organs, wage war for these seven kinds of men of good fortunes or great energy and strength and thus attain the well-being and prosperity of both the ruling and the ruled under thy good protection (5898)

११. त्वं ह त्यदप्रतिमानमोजो वज्रेण वज्रिन् धृषितो जघन्थ ।
त्वं शुष्णस्यावातिरो वधत्रैस्त्वं गा इन्द्र शच्येदविन्दः ॥

11. O powerful king, the wielder of deadly weapons, the self-same thou certainly attainest an immeasurable strength and power by being a smasher of the enemy, with thy fatal armaments. Thou art the destroyer of the blood-sucking enemy by thy death-raining means of destruction. Thou controls the lands by thy great might. (5899)

१२. तमिन्द्रं वाजयामसि महे वृत्राय हन्तवे । स वृषा वृषभो भुवत् ॥

१३. इन्द्रः स दामने कृत ओजिष्ठः स मदे हितः । द्युम्नी श्लोकी स सोम्यः ॥

१४. गिरा वज्रो न संभृतः सबलो अनपच्युतः । ववक्ष ऋष्वो अस्तृतः ॥

12-14. See Atharva 20.47. (1-3). (5900)

HYMN CXXXVIII

१. महाँ इन्द्रो य ओजसा पर्जन्यो वृष्टिमाँइव । स्तोमैर्वत्सस्य वावृधे ॥

1. The Mighty God, king or man of fortunes, Who showers bounties on the people like a raining cloud is highly extolled by the praises of the loving people who reside under his shelter. (5901)[2]

२. प्रजामृतस्य पिप्रतः प्र यद् भरन्त वह्नयः । विप्रा ऋतस्य वाहसा ॥

2. When the persons, responsible for carrying out the administration of state-affairs, fulfilling the laws of nature and the state, feed and nourish the subjects, like the husbands looking after the welfare of their wives, the learned and the intelligent people become the custodian of the rules and regulations of the state. (5902)

३. कण्वा इन्द्रं यदक्रत स्तोमैर्यज्ञस्य साधनम् । जामि ब्रुवत आयुधम् ॥

[1](7-9) 'Anshumati' is no legendry river of that name. It means simply the partitionary boundary line or river, between any two countries. It is wrong to read history into these verses.

[2]cf. *Rig*, 8.6. (1-3).

3. When the wise and the intelligent persons enable the powerful king to be a means of carrying out the state-affairs for the public good, there is hardly any necessity to keep or use weapons. (i.e., the administration becomes so efficient that all the people feel quite safe and well-protected and find arms unnecessary). (5903)

HYMN CXXXIX

१. श्रा नूनमश्विना युवं वत्सस्य गन्तमवसे । प्रास्मै यच्छतमवृकं पृथु च्छर्दिर्युयुतं या अरातय: ॥

1. O Parents; teacher and preacher; prāna and apāna; the king and commander; the sun and the moon; air and water; fire and water; electricity and air; electricity and water; etc., let all of you paired groups, come for the protection of the people, well-settled in the state and devoted to it and provide them with an ample shelter, free from violence and danger from thieves or dacoits, and drive away all those, who are troublesome agitators. (5904)[1]

२. यदन्तरिक्षे यद् दिवि यत् पञ्च मानुषाँ अनु । नृम्णं तद् धत्तमश्विना ॥

2. O paired groups, (mentioned above) uphold and give that wealth and fortune, which is in the atmosphere which in the heavens; and which is suitable for the five kinds of the people, i.e., Brahmana, Kshatriya, Vaishya, Shudra and Nishada. (5905)

३. ये वां दंसांस्यश्विना विप्रास: परिमामृशु: । एवेत् काण्वस्य बोधतम् ॥

3. O Aṣvint, in the same way, think of the interests and well-being of the wise and the learned persons, who thoroughly meditate on your acts of beneficence and munificence. (5906)

४. अयं वां घर्मो अश्विना स्तोमेन परि षिच्यते ।
अयं सोमो मधुमान् वाजिनीवसू येन वृत्रं चिकेतथ: ॥

4. O chemists, here is the high temperature produced by you, with the thorough interaction of various elements. O creators of strength and energy, here is this sweet essence of herbs, with which you cure the malignant disease, the deadly enemy of the patient. (5907)

५. यदप्सु यद् वनस्पतौ यदोषधीषु पुरुदंससा कृतम् । तेन माविष्टमश्विना ॥

5. O physician and druggists, expert in various acts operation and production, whatever you produce in waters, in herbs and in medicinal objects, protect me thereby. (5908)

HYMN CXL

१. यन्नासत्या भुरण्यथो यद् वा देव भिषज्यथ: ।
अयं वां वत्सो मतिभिर्न विन्धते हविष्मन्तं हि गच्छथ: ॥

1. O unfailing and energising 'Aṣvins', possessing divine qualities, beneficial to all, as you nourish like the vital breaths and cure and treat like the physicians, not only the person who loves you like a child, attains you

[1]cf. *Rig*, 8.9. (1-5). अश्विना two strong forces, working in pairs in the world at large:—father and mother; teacher and preacher; king and commander; the sun and the moon; air and water; air, fire; electricity and water; fire and water; physicians and druggist.

through thoughtful actions but you yourselves certainly approach the person, having all means and provisions. (5909)[1]

२. आ नूनमश्विनोॠ॑षि स्तोमं चिकेत वामया । आ सोमं मधुमत्तमं घर्मं सिञ्चादथर्वणि ।।

2. The deep-sighted scientists surely gets to know a thorough knowledge of the various attributes and properties of the 'Ashvis' by his sharp scientific insight, and saturates the non-violent devotee with the sweetest essence of medicinal herbs and strong energy and vigour. (5910)

३. आ नूनं रघुवर्तनिं रथं तिष्ठाथो अश्विना । आ वां स्तोमा इमे मम नभो न चुच्यवीरत ।।

3. O 'Aṣvins', let you station yourselves fully in the fast-moving vehicle (i.e., car or aeroplane) or in the body, so that all these useful properties of yours, utilised by me may trickle down like the rays of the sun in the sky. (5911)

४. यदद्य वां नासत्योक्थैराचुच्युवीमहि । यद्वा वाणीभिरश्विनेवेत् काण्वस्य बोधतम् ।।

4. O Aṣvins, who never fail in your actions or effects when we enhance your power and effect by these descriptions of your attributes today, you should, at the same time, enlighten the wise and the intelligent person by your speeches. (5912)

५. यद्वां कक्षीवाँ उत यद् व्यश्व ऋषिर्यद् वां दीर्घतमा जुहाव ।
पृथी यद्वां वैन्यः सादनेष्वेवेदतो अश्विना चेतयेथाम् ।।

5. O Aṣvins, whenever, the controller, the swift-powered, the seer, the destroyer of all forces of evil or wickedness, the splendorous one or the defender of vast land call you for help, you should energise them in their own places. (5913)[2]

HYMN CXLI

१. यातं छर्दिष्पा उत नः परस्पा भूतं जगत्पा उत नस्तनूपा । वर्तिस्तोकाय तनयाय यातम् ।।

1. O Aṣvins, let you come as protectors of our shelter as well as great defenders of ours. Let you be the protectors of the world as well as of our bodies. Please come to our houses for the sake of our sons and offspring. (5914)[3]

२. यदिन्द्रेण सरथं याथो अश्विना यद्वा वायुना भवथः समोकसा ।
यदादित्येभिॠ॑भुभिः सजोषसा यद्वा विष्णोर्विक्रमणेषु तिष्ठथः ।।

2. O Aṣvins, the two powerful forces, as you move along with the same vehicle as the sun, as you share the same space with the strong wind, as you pulsate and invigorate with the magnetic forces of cosmic rays during all the twelve months of the year, as you find a place in the circular motion of the all-pervading ether. (5915)

३. यदद्याश्विनावहं हुवेय वाजसातये । यत् पृत्सु तुर्वणे सहस्तच्छ्रेष्ठमश्विनोरवः ।।

3. (Continued from above) as I call you today for the distribution of power, energy, food, wealth and knowledge, the power and energy, which you dis-

[1]cf. *Rig*, 8.9. (6-10).
[2]No special personalities are referred herein.
[3]cf. *Rig*, 8.9. (11-15).

play in wars and the destruction of the enemy and evil forces, is the best protecting power of you, Ashvis. (5916)

४. आ नूनं यातमश्विनेमा हव्यानि वां हिता ।
इमे सोमासो अधि तुर्वशे यदाविमे कण्वेषु वामथ ॥

4. O Aṣvins, you must certainly come, here are these means of enjoyment, worthy of being taken by you. These sources of pleasures and joys, which are under the control of the persons, trying to achieve the fourfold aims of life and of the wise and intelligent people, are all for you. (5917)

५. यन्नासत्या पराके अर्वाके अस्ति भेषजम् । तेन नूनं विमदाय प्रचेतसा छर्दिर्वत्साय यच्छतम् ॥

5. O infallible Aṣvins, endowed with special intelligence, whatever there is capable of warding off diseases or other difficulties and troubles, at a distant place or near at hand, certainly give shelter to the well-settled person, specially enjoying peace and prosperity under you, with that. (5918)[1]

HYMN CXLII*

१. अभुत्स्यु प्र देव्या साकं वाचाहमश्विनोः । व्यावर्देव्या मति वि राति मर्त्येभ्यः ॥

1. I (a devotee) have got enlightened by the enlightened speech of the teacher and the preacher, just the people get awakened by the rays of the brilliant dawn. That enlightening speech or sermon clearly explains to the persons, enough material to ponder over and convey the same to others. (5919)

२. प्र बोधयोषो अश्विना प्र देवि सूनृते महि । प्र यज्ञहोतरानुषक् प्र मदाय श्रवो बृहत् ॥

2. O bright, respectable dawn, fully equipped with natural forces awaken the Aṣvins, the two powerful forces of nature. O performer of the sacrifice at dawn, continually go on energising these forces and offering profuse food-grains and material for attainment of happiness and joy. (5920)

३. यदुषो यासि भानुना सं सूर्येण रोचसे । आ हायमश्विनो रथो वर्तिर्याति नृपाय्यम् ॥

3. When the dawn moves on with splendour and glory and shines with the sun, surely this chariot of the Aṣvins, the two strong forces of nature, reaches the houses and bodies of the people protecting and invigorating them. (5921)

४. यदापीतासो अंशवो गावो न दुह्र ऊधभिः । यद्वा वाणीरनूषत प्र देवयन्तो अश्विना ॥

4. When the slightly yellowish rays are generated like streams of milk from the udders of the cows, and when the worshipping devotees pray through their praise-songs, let the Aṣvins, the two powerful forces of nature, awaken us to health and happiness. (5922)

५. प्र द्युम्नाय प्र शवसे प्र नृषाह्याय शर्मणे । प्र रक्षाय प्रचेतसा ॥

5. Let the above-mentioned, specially energising forces awaken us for fortune and glory, power and strength, courage and daring to subdue the enemy or forces of evil, ability to give shelter to the poor and the helpless, and skill and dexterity in the execution of our duties. (All these qualities are the products of early rising). (5923)

*(4-5) यदु, and तर्वश, विमद, and वत्स are not proper names but are qualifying words.
[1]cf. *Rig*, 8.9. (16-21).

६. यन्नूनं धीभिरश्विना पितुर्योना निषीदथः यद्वा सुम्नेभिरुक्थ्या ॥

6. O 'Aṣvins,' as you certainly occupy the position of the parents by your intelligence and actions and by your pleasure-giving means and knowledge, you are worthy of our respect and praise. (5924)

HYMN CXLIII

१. तं वां रथं वयमद्या हुवेम पृथुज्रयमश्विना संगतिं गोः ।
यः सूर्यां वहति वन्धुरायुर्गिर्वाहसं पुरुतमं वसूयुम् ॥

1. O Aṣvins, we invoke, today, that vehicle of transport of yours, which is of vast power and energy, wherein are focussed the rays of the Sun, which carries the dawn along with it, the mainstay of all, the conveyer of rays or voice, the vastest of all and the uniter of all sources of life on the earth or elsewhere. (5925)[1]

२. युवं श्रियमश्विना देवता तां दिवो नपाता वनथः शचीभिः ।
युवोर्वपुरभि पृक्षः सचन्ते वहन्ति यत् ककुहासो रथे वाम् ॥

2. O Aṣvins, the upholders of heavens, or born of heavens, you attain glory and splendour, loved by the divine beings or forces, by your energising power and intelligence. When the great heavens carry you along with their pleasure-giving vehicle, highly invigorating forces unite with your forms. (5926)

३. को वामद्या करते रातहव्य ऊतये वा सुतपेयाय वार्कैः ।
ऋतस्य वा वनुषे पूर्व्याय नमो येमानो अश्विना ववर्तत् ॥

3. O preceptor and preacher, who is the offerer of provisions etc., who makes arrangements, today, for sustenance of your living or for essence of herbs for your drinks, with honour and worship. Who is the disciple, who stays with you, paying homage to you for getting the true Vedic lore, current from the ancient times. (5927)

४. हिरण्ययेन पुरुभू रथेनेमं यज्ञं नासत्योप यातम् ।
पिबाथ इन्मधुनः सोम्यस्य दधथो रत्नं विधते जनाय ॥

4. O never-failing both units of energy and power, stepping up to high voltage, come to this factory or manufacturing unit through a conveyer of iron or gold. Make use of this suitable chemical preparation and provide precious wealth and means of pleasure and joy to the person, utilising your services. (5928)

५. आ नो यातं दिवो अच्छा पृथिव्या हिरण्ययेन सुवृता रथेन ।
मा वामन्ये नि यमन् देवयन्तः सं यद् ददे नाभिः पूर्व्या वाम् ॥

5. O king or commander, or both units of energy, come to us from the heavens as well as from the earth through an aeroplane of golden colour or of iron, which is well regulated and is of high speed. Let not those, who

[1]cf. *Rig*, 4.44. (1-7); 4.57.3; 8.57.3 (Valkhilya 9.3).

want to show respect to you impede you in the way or any other preplanned machinations of the enemy hinder your advance. (5929)[1]

६. नू नो रयिं पुरुवीरं बृहन्तं दस्रा मिमाथामुभयेष्वस्मे ।
नरो यद् वामश्विना स्तोममावन्त्सधस्तुतिमाजमीढासो अग्मन् ॥

6. O Aṣvins, beautiful to look at and capable of warding off difficulties and troubles, definitely generate amongst us both males and females, plenty of wealth and riches along with brave sons and offspring. When the general public offers its praises to you, the wealthy persons, endowed with ghee and wealth, also join them in your praises, at the same time. (5930)

७. इहेह यद् वां समना पपृक्षे सेयमस्मे सुमतिर्वाजरत्ना ।
उरुष्यतं जरितारं युवं ह श्रितः कामो नासत्या युवद्रिक् ॥

7. O Aṣvins, having precious wealth of food, knowledge, power and speed and never failing in your effect and strength, working in harmony, whatever there is sound and right sort of intelligence in you, let the same good intelligence be infused into us. Let you protect the person, who expatiates your attributes. My keen desire is certainly bent upon you. (5931)

८. मधुमतीरोषधीर्द्याव आपो मधुमन्नो भवत्वन्तरिक्षम् ।
क्षेत्रस्य पतिर्मधुमान्नो अस्त्वरिष्यन्तो अन्वेनं चरेम ॥

8. May the plants and herbs be sweet (i.e., efficacious for us! May the heavens, the waters and the mid-regions be all sweet (i.e., healthful and invigorating) for us! May the land-lord (i.e., the producer of grains and vegetables) be sweet (i e., friendly and helpful) for us. Let us follow him (act according to his wishes and convenience) being free from disease and trouble of any sort. (5932)

९. पनाय्यं तदश्विना कृतं वां वृषभो दिवो रजसः पृथिव्याः ।
सहस्रं शंसा उत ये गविष्टौ सर्वाँ इत् ताँ उप याता पिबध्यै ॥

9. O Aṣvins, that act of yours is praise-worthy, by which you act as a powerful ruler of the heavens, the atmosphere and of the earth and thousands of praise-worthy acts, which are performed through speech, sense-organs, the earth or rays. Let you approach all of these for the protection and satisfaction of all. (5933)

[1]'Agmilhasa' does not refer to a family of special name but it is an epithet for the rich possessing plenty of edibles like ghee (clarified butter) etc., and wealth of gold etc.

GLOSSARY AND INDEX